THE FRANCHISE PARADOX

New Directions, Different Strategies

The Franchise Paradox

New Directions, Different Strategies

Stuart Price

CASSELL

Cassell
Wellington House
125 Strand
London
WC2R 0BB

PO Box 605
Herndon, VA 20172

First published 1997

British Library Cataloguing-in-Publication Data
A catalogue record for this book is available from the British Library.

ISBN 0-304-33368-9

Designed and typeset by Kenneth Burnley in Irby, Wirral, Cheshire.
Printed and bound in Great Britain by Redwood Books, Trowbridge, Wiltshire.

Contents

Acknowledgements

It is often said that everybody has a book in them and a select few have several. No book, however, can be written without an initial spark and the assistance and advice of others, or a network of experienced and kindly disposed individuals. My efforts are no exception. The idea for this book came from Alan Felstead's *The Corporate Paradox: Power and Control in the Business Franchise*. For helping me to articulate and hone some of the ideas and arguments contained within this book, I am heavily indebted for the continued help, new insights, and encouragement from the following people:

Stephen Ball (University of Huddersfield), Peter Bassett (KPMG Management Consulting), Jane Borer (KPMG Information Services), Monica Briggs, Jaqui Clavey, Steve Dixon, Christopher Easingwood (Manchester Business School), Patrick Kaufmann (Georgia State University), Brian Kenny (University of Huddersfield), Simon Johnson (BZW Securities), Michael Jones (Brewery History Society), Jayne Little, Charles Moore (Taylor Nelson AGB), Andrew Nicholson (KPMG Tourism & Leisure), Howard Price (KPMG Management Consulting), Angela Roper (Oxford Brookes University), Andrew Sangster (*Caterer & Hotelkeeper*), Professor John Stanworth (University of Westminster), Jerry Thomas (RSL), Dominic Walsh (*The Guardian*), Emyr Williams (KPMG Management Consulting), Jim Winship (Pizza & Pasta Association), and Fiona Wood (Brewers and Licenced Retailers Association).

I am equally indebted to Naomi Roth and David Barker of Cassell and Ruth Taylor for their unflagging enthusiasm, and to the librarians at London Business School, Science Reference Library, the University of Huddersfield, and the University of Westminster for their admirable patience, persistence and professionalism in dealing with my more obscure requests for information. Most of all, however, I am grateful to my wife Fiona for her efforts, sacrifice and support. From now on, the weekends are yours . . . well, at least until the next project!

Every effort has been made to acknowledge sources, to locate and correct errors and to ensure that all material facts and the results of empirical work contained within this book are accurate. Any remaining deficiencies, inaccuracies in, or omissions from the text are mine.

STUART PRICE

List of tables

List of figures

Preface

The economic importance of franchising, both in the UK and internationally, has seldom been reflected in terms of the quality of research and scholarship it has promoted. A great deal of what has in fact been written on franchising can be subsumed under the 'How to . . .' heading. Such literature is largely prescriptive and heavily influenced by lawyers and management consultants, frequently with the intention of promoting their own services.

By way of contrast, the academic literature has tended to be very narrowly focused and has been overly influenced by writers from a marketing disciplinary background. Issues governing the initial decision to franchise, the balance of franchisee to franchisor-owned outlets, plus debates concerning outlet concentration, have tended to dictate the debate, to the almost total exclusion of any concepts or ideas from the social sciences or the field of organizational theory. It is against this background that we must begin to appreciate the quality and uniqueness of Stuart Price's book.

The author is a leading British authority in the field of franchising, having previously both earned a living as a consultant in the field of franchising and having also made a contribution to the serious academic literature on the subject, largely through his connections with the International Franchise Research Centre at the University of Westminster.

This book represents a major breakthrough in bringing together the disparate approaches used in various previous publications and, as such, must be welcomed by all concerned. This is a major work of unusually high quality and one which should catapult thinking in the field of franchising. It is difficult to imagine any subsequent publication this side of the year 2000 not referencing this book.

Though illustrative examples are usually drawn from the hotel and catering industrial sector, the book is in no way limited by the use of cases from this industry. The issues addressed would appear to apply more generally to most sectors. Indeed, some of the most interesting original data – that on franchise attrition rates for instance – covers a whole range of franchise industry sectors.

Here, for the first time, we see a major text which is genuinely multi-disciplinary. We see the world of franchising made up of individuals and organizations, cultures and markets, decisions and complexity. The often simplistic relationships posed in previous publications are here replaced by a detailed examination of sociological factors (age, gender, prior employment histories, local, national and international cultures). To these factors are added issues of organizational choice, organizational strategies and the challenges associated with organizational change. Issues of product and service, pricing and location, innovation and consistency, success and failure also feature strongly.

The sheer detail on individual companies and markets is quite stunning and the style of presentation is nothing if not open and accessible. Few writers in the field of franchising have drawn parallels between the world of franchising and the more conventional business area. But, in reality, many franchisors and most franchisees are, in essence, small businesses. In this instance, the author is well enough acquainted with both areas of knowledge and debate to compare and contrast the two.

The field of franchising (sometimes through no fault of its own) tends to attract a great deal of 'hype'. As such, it is often claimed to be largely immune to the pressures prevailing in other areas of economic activity and recession-proof. The current text uses both original and secondary data to demonstrate that franchising is, in fact, no panacea for new or distressed businesses wishing to escape normal economic realities. Rather, conditions prevailing in the wider economy, and differences in the fortunes of different industry sub-sectors, almost invariably have the effects that logic would suggest.

There is a sub-text to the entire book and that surrounds the issue of innovation – 'How can franchisors stress uniformity and conformity, rather than innovation, and also simultaneously expect fewer failures than independent businesses?', asks the author. This, for the author, is the essential 'franchise paradox' heralded in the book's title. Franchising, in itself, can indeed be regarded as an innovation, harnessed in order to overcome challenges and maximize opportunities. However, in a world of rapid change, the emphasis on standardization and conformity, which are key elements of any franchise formula, can stifle the processes of innovation and change so vital to future success. Again, the discussion is strong and informative.

A wealth of strong 'plus' points, not forgetting a massively detailed bibliography, make this book the best in its field. It justifies a place on every franchise and business bookshelf into the next millennium.

PROFESSOR JOHN STANWORTH

Foreword:
Nature of the paradox

*A trend is a trend / But the question is, will it bend? / Will it alter its course /
Through some unforeseen force / And come to a premature end?*

Alec Cairncross, Scottish economist, *Economic Journal*, 1969

*. . . propaganda, the uncertainty of corporate life and the American Dream of being
your own boss . . . is driving more and more baby boomers – the average age of new
franchisees is 40 – into the arms of franchisors. This year the International
Franchise Association expects 20,000 people to buy into franchising, almost
double the number ten years ago. That's one new franchisee every 26 minutes
sinking his or her savings into everything from the Body Shop to Swisher Hygiene,
a toilet cleaning outfit.*

Laura M. Holson, business writer, *SmartMoney* 1996

There have been more innovations and developments in technology this
century than at any other point in our history. Although not expressed in terms of being
an innovation, franchising is often claimed to be one such development because it offers
companies an alternative way to grow their business and offers individuals another career
path. The spread of franchising is such that it permeates most service industries –
everything from fast food outlets, drainage services, milk delivery, printing, estate
agencies, one-hour photography shops, to renting a car and filling it with petrol. It is also
international in scope and has been expanding at a rapid rate around the world, especially
within countries in the Pacific Rim and Middle East. What appears to be remarkable is that
franchising's spread has only really occurred since the early 1950s – it's a baby boomer in
its own right. Franchising has become an especially important method of expansion
within the international hotel, fast food, and restaurant industries. In Britain, for
example, the British Franchise Association suggests that about 17% of all franchisors and
about 12% of all franchised units are in the hotel and catering industry (see Table 1
below). Although franchising is one of the more noticeable features of the hotel and
catering and other retail markets, it is only one of an array of organizational development
strategies currently employed.

According to practitioners, academics, and the popular franchise press, a key
driver of the spread of franchising in the hospitality industries and elsewhere is that there
is a lower probability of failure than other routes to starting or growing a business. But,
while the belief in a low rate of failure in franchising may have had some effect on its rapid
rate of diffusion, there is still much which is unknown. For example:

1. Why did franchising evolve when it did?
2. Why do certain individuals and companies choose to franchise and others
   do not?
3. Given that research on the success rates of new products shows that about
   80% fail, are the low rates of failure a true reflection of the franchise market?

Sector	1993	1994	1995	1995 (%)
Dairy	8,000	7,000	6,000	23
Retail	3,385	4,515	4,355	17
Direct selling/distribution	2,030	2,910	3,315	13
Catering, hotels	3,380	3,095	3,070	12
Vehicle services	1,690	1,555	1,655	6
Cleaning services	1,520	1,510	1,625	6
Parcel and courier services	675	1,095	1,120	4
Commercial and industrial	845	1,085	1,105	4
Building services	1,015	925	1,000	4
Domestic and personal	675	1,110	880	3
Employment agencies	505	530	600	2
Quick printing, copying	675	635	570	2
Estate agents	505	435	405	2
Total	24,900	26,400	25,700	100

Source: NatWest/BFA Franchise Surveys (March 1993/1994/1995/1996).

Table 1: *Franchising activity in the UK – estimate of units*

This book seeks to provide an answer to each of these questions but, in doing, it is readily acknowledged that a variety of other potential answers could and undoubtedly do exist. Explaining these other perspectives, however, must be the subject of additional research.

In answering the first question, Chapter 1 explores the development of franchising as a form of innovation of feudal society. Franchising has been with us in various guises since medieval times, but has only been used within commercial settings since the late seventeenth century; and one particular form, business format, exploded into use in the 1950s and in the UK in the 1980s. Chapter 1 suggests that because of franchising's roots in medieval Europe, its diffusion today is the commercialization of feudalism and its spread has been helped by changes in society, such as the emergence of standardization and simplification of retail units among other factors. Possibly as a result of the varying influences of certain antecedent variables, the diffusion of franchising has occurred at differing rates throughout the different sub-sectors comprising the hospitality industry. The differing rates of penetration also reflect the decision to franchise by firms and individuals in order to further their respective careers.

By examining the rapid diffusion of franchising in terms of being an innovation, insights can be made to the motivations to franchise. In some instances these insights are complementary to existing research, in other cases the concepts may be newer to the franchise literature. For example, it is apparent that most attempts at explaining why some firms decide to franchise have predominantly relied on single-factor explanations. Although significant in their own right, these explanations are rarely sufficient to encompass the diversity of rationale prompting some companies to pursue franchise-based expansion, while others choose other routes. In answering the second question,

Chapters 2, 3 and 4 argue that in order to understand why the diffusion rates of franchising differ, we must look beyond macro-explanations (for example, culture, language, tax, etc.) and adopt a micro, or organizational-level, approach. Of particular importance are the influences affecting the array of choices to decision-makers in developing their businesses (franchising is only one option), such as the decision-making process itself, impediments to change, and whether the competition has adopted it.

Of course, franchising could not exist without another set of adopters, the franchisees. In order to explain why certain individuals become franchisees and others do not, the micro-level approach is maintained in Chapter 5 by arguing that the decision to become a franchisee reflects a career-orientation rather than being a decision to buy a product. While there has been a tendency by some of the franchise literature to treat the explanatory factors behind the decision to become a franchisee and franchisor as separate, arguably the two streams are related and intertwined: organizations and individuals both exhibit career histories. At the organizational level, careers reflect the process by which the firm renews itself and takes differing forms as it matures within varying organizational development stages; at the individual level, careers are a series of choices made by people between different opportunities presented to them (Gunz, 1989). In a few instances, the individual's career choice to be self-employed may, depending on a whole host of subsequent events and choices, lead them to become franchisors or to convert their businesses to being a franchisee. Such research may be of specific interest to both existing and budding franchisors as well as labour market modellers. Given the slow economic growth of the 1990s, the widening polarity between large and small franchisors, and a growing number of companies seeking franchise-based expansion, there is a fundamental need for such investigative effort. It could assist franchisors, for example, to improve the efficiency and effectiveness of their recruitment and selection procedures as well as, perhaps, reduce the potential for the disconfirmation of new franchisees' expectations.

To many franchisors, the act of franchising their business is, in itself, an innovative process requiring substantial changes to the existing organizational culture and structure. In order to realize some of the benefits of franchising, such as increased brand value, retail franchisors typically stress conformity to standards and try to suppress deviations from the business blueprint. Reflecting this behaviour, Rosenbloom (1995; p. 256) quotes the following piece from an article in the *Wall Street Journal* called 'Testing Psyches of Future Franchisees' (1988; 20 May, p. 27):

> IF YOU'RE NOT CREATIVE AND INDEPENDENT WE WANT YOU
> AS A CHANNEL MEMBER
> That's right – if you're not a creative or independent personality you are more likely to be selected as a channel member in many franchised channels.
>
> This is how it should be, according to Ken Franklin (president of Franklin Development Inc.) . . . He argues creativity and independence are the traits most heavily displayed by true entrepreneurs and therefore exactly the wrong traits needed in franchising. Why? – because he claims that creative and independent people will naturally want to do things their way rather than conform to rigid policies and operating procedures characteristic of most successful franchise systems.
>
> Thus, they will inevitably try to change the system based on their own ideas and initiative. But in a successful franchise these usually admirable qualities can

be disastrous, because the essence of so many franchised systems is standardization and identical formats among all franchisees. Franklin's firm sells its services to the franchisors who want to assure that the franchisees they select will not be so creative and independent that they would resist taking directions from the franchisor. Franklin's method relies on in-depth psychological tests to assess prospective franchisees' personalities. If the personality profile shows a prospective franchisee to have a creative and independent bent, Franklin recommends that person not to be selected as a franchisee. The 'hot prospects' – those who according to the psychological profile are not very creative and independent – are the 'winners' that Franklin recommends his clients select as franchisees.

Such a sentiment has been reproduced elsewhere. The usual views on franchising, therefore, appear to suggest that franchisees are simply 'shirk-proof' channel mechanisms which facilitate the realization of franchisor objectives rather than being more participative. Within this argument, franchises are perceived to entail the transfer of information, knowledge, technologies, skills or products (or 'technological transfers') from one party to another. Arguably, however, such a perspective means that the level of ongoing competitive advantages derived from franchising may be limited and raises a paradox which is fundamental to further research:

> *How can franchisors stress uniformity and conformity, rather than innovation, and also simultaneously expect fewer failures than independent businesses?*

Surely, in an environment where the pace of innovation and competition is increasing, either one or both of the observations in the question cannot be true. Either franchises are innovative and/or the rate of attrition is higher than practitioners, academics, and the popular franchise press tell us. Firms cannot maintain the *status quo* through dampening innovative efforts of franchisees – the people closest to customers and who possess knowledge of the system – without the loss of market share, competitive advantage, and profitability. The paradox appears to raise some important questions concerning possible biases in prior franchise research. For example, why should the rate of franchise attrition have remained static throughout the last few decades when:

1. most economies have experienced at least three recessions;
2. the USA, Australia, Canada and the UK have experienced maturing franchise markets; and
3. the failure rates amongst small businesses (of which franchises are a sub-set) have continued to climb and mirrored the prevalent economic and market climates?

A wealth of research (Kay, 1993; Hunt and Morgan, 1995; Porter, 1980) indicates that innovation can be a source of competitive and comparative advantage which, in turn, is instrumental in affecting the ability to sustain demand and business success. This rationale is one of the reasons why franchise companies such as Pizza Hut and KFC are increasingly dependent on new product development to maintain and grow market share:

> We've long known that great products build great brands. The challenge is to create exciting new products and to make our products more widely available, so hungry consumers can easily reach them anytime and anywhere . . . Brand leadership contemplates, in part, the need to be innovative by providing new products and programs to respond to consumer needs while maintaining a value orientation. (PepsiCo shareholder report, 1995: pp. 11 and 23)

But Pizza Hut and KFC are clearly not unique in this respect: the rate of new product innovation and new ways of reaching the consumer is ever increasing in all sectors of the economy, but has become particularly marked in the foodservice industry. For example, in an article analyzing the success of McDonald's, the *Economist* (1996) points to the presence of innovation in four main areas of the firm's strategy:

> Mr Quinlan [McDonald's chairman] dreams of an America in which nobody is more than four minutes away (by foot or car) from a Big Mac. In an attempt to fill every possible market niche, McDonald's is packing in high streets with tiny McDonald's Express 'storefront' restaurants, adding McDonald's to petrol stations and building outlets in Wal-Mart stores. 'Happy Meals' for children are even being served on United Airlines flights . . . One of the strengths of Oak Brook [the location of McDonald's headquarters] is that, although McDonald's fixation with burger domination often verges on the fanatical, the firm is swift to recognize its weaknesses. Mr Quinlan's white-shirted battalions have launched counter-attacks on Burger King on three fronts. The first is by cutting operating costs, which have been rising faster than revenues. By simplifying its restaurants, McDonald's has already reduced the average cost of a new one to $1.2m in America, down 25% on six years ago. It has also simplified the menu.
>
> Mr Quinlan's second tactic is to move upmarket. Last month, in its biggest product launch since the birth of the Big Mac in 1968, the firm unveiled the Arch Deluxe . . . Thirdly, McDonald's is redoubling its marketing offensive . . . It signed a ten-year alliance that will make McDonald's the primary global fast food marketing partner of Walt Disney . . .
>
> Outside the United States McDonald's faces no big organized competitors . . . McDonald's global distribution, purchasing, operational and marketing infrastructure is the most effective in the business, as even its rivals concede. The appetite of communist, ex-communist and developing countries for McAnything seems insatiable. McDonald's operating profits should grow by close to 20% a year.
>
> To achieve this, Mr Quinlan is pushing ahead with a salad of deals, alliances and joint ventures. (29 June; pp. 77–78)

Such activity suggests that innovation is a central pillar of competitive advantage and a sustainable business. It is necessary to observe, however, that the realization of competitive advantages based on innovation is often linked to how the firm is structured as well as the success of relationships between it and its suppliers and customers (or what Kay terms 'architecture'), as well as whether it is easily imitable, whether it is continuous and the reward systems employed to encourage suggestions. Potential sources of innovation are evident through the architecture between customers, suppliers, staff, franchisees, and if diversified, other divisions within the firm and may exist between large and small firms. For example, Shan *et al* (1994) and Kotabe and Swan (1995) indicate that, especially in emerging industries, there may be opportunities for co-operation between small start-ups and large established firms in order to exploit technological spill-overs, increase the rate of innovation and transfer resources for product commercialization.

Despite anecdotal evidence to the contrary, some researchers have assumed that the sources of innovation are asymmetric in franchises, deriving from the franchisor and their suppliers. In a review of innovation activity in franchises, however, Tannenbaum (1996) shows that this situation is simply not true. He argues that while the operating rules for franchisees often seem to leave little room for innovation, many of the better franchisors give franchisees the latitude to tinker with the format and develop new ideas. He also shows that many of the more successful innovations have derived from the franchisees because of their closeness to the consumer. In their time, franchisees have been responsible for:

- the 'Filet of Fish', 'Egg McMuffin', and the 'Big Mac' in the McDonald's system. The Egg McMuffin was an important development in allowing McDonald's realize its potential in the breakfast market and the Big Mac is synonymous with McDonald's. Its spread is such that the *Economist* magazine employs the price of Big Macs to measure the purchasing power of differing currencies around the world;
- the introduction of 'value meals' – or set meals at a discounted price – in the KFC and Burger King systems. Value meals have become an important competitive weapon in the fast food industry;
- the introduction of annual club memberships to customers in Moto Photo in order to generate repeat business;
- the introduction of T-bone steaks on the International House of Pancake's menu;
- within the printing services franchise, Kall Kwik, a franchisee was responsible for redesigning the work-flow process; and
- the first mixing of ingredients such as coconut, bananas and pecan nuts into a basic vanilla frozen dessert to create the 'Blizzards' product range in the International Dairy Queen chain. The 'Blizzards' range is the chain's signature product.

There have been, of course, numerous other innovations in these chains and others. Unfortunately, despite its presence, the underlying motivating factors influencing innovative activity in franchises are not understood. Yet there is a fundamental need for such research. For example, one current recommendation within the popular franchise press, particularly the 'How-to' literature, is that franchisees need to assess the viability of a franchise system before they join. As part of the assessment process, potential investors are asked to establish whether demand for the final products is sustainable. How can supplying that demand be sustainable if innovation does not occur?

It is apparent that a number of factors work in concert to engender innovation. A person's independence and creativity together cannot jointly determine innovative activity: there are many other stimuli and, arguably, creativity is of more importance than independence (otherwise franchisees would not have been responsible for the innovations listed above, among others). Contrary to the opinions of other researchers, franchisees are indeed a potential source of innovation. Accordingly, Chapter 6 devotes some effort to discussing some of the determinants and moderating factors affecting the process of innovation within franchise systems. The foundation for this focus is a review of whether franchising is a form of strategic alliance as McIntyre *et al* (1994) propose or not, as Yoshino and Rangan (1995) suggest. Under the former interpretation, franchising (itself an innovation) is viewed as an organizational form under which the franchisor and franchisee 'band together' over a given period of time to gain a competitive advantage over other firms in their respective markets. That competitive advantage has typically been viewed as deriving from increased numbers of outlets and market share, but it can also derive from innovation.

Franchises, like other organizations, have implicit innovative capability. It is embodied in the creative ability of their employees, suppliers, and franchisees; it also derives from the differing competitive environments in which franchisees operate and the diversity of career histories of the franchisees themselves. The possession of tacit knowledge and their operational skills, derived from practising the transfer of know-how from the franchisor, by franchisees suggests that the latter at least have some capacity for continuous innovation. The 'triggers' to deploy this capacity are manifold, but are dependent on the realization or recognition that some form of innovative behaviour is necessary. Such a process suggests that organizations are experiential learning systems which respond to opportunities and threats in the external environment; these responses are translated as changes to strategy and structure, and derive from the reading and interpretation of competitors' actions, intentions, or the firm's own internal situation. Once the need for innovation is recognized, as Chapter 7 shows, the extent to which individual innovative capacity is deployed to resolve certain operational problems and is shared is dependent on the nature of relations between the franchisee and franchisor.

Like strategic alliances, competitive advantages are founded on a reciprocal relationship between the franchisor and franchisee and include gaining market access, being a source of capital, reducing the effects of shirking, as well as product development and innovation. Some researchers (Justis and Judd, 1989) have indicated that collaboration between franchisor and franchisee reduces the costs and risks associated with a number of activities, including product testing and development. It is posited, therefore, that despite the significance of adaptation to exogenous variables for survival, social exchanges have primacy in affecting franchise system innovativeness. In order to compete effectively, maintain/increase franchisee satisfaction, and facilitate survival, the franchisor must harness franchisees' innovative capability in a positive way by, for example, employing methods similar to strategic alliances. If the franchisor seeks to maintain the *status quo* to the detriment of franchisee performance, dissatisfaction and conflict may result, which can be damaging to brand equity and affect the potential queue of investors.

Following this discussion, Chapters 8 and 9 seek to empirically establish the rate of franchisor and franchisee failure. Fast food franchises have been promoted by the popular and academic press alike as a relatively risk-free entry method to potential entrants to the hospitality industry. But most of these claims are founded on uncorroborated franchisor-reported sources emphatic of the norms of the franchise fraternity as a whole rather than being, perhaps, indicative of norms of specific industries in which franchises can be found. As such, when evaluating venture risk, potential investors, such as new franchisees and franchisors, are not measuring like with like.

Chapters 8 and 9 outline the different interpretations and measurements of failure and its magnitude in the UK hospitality industry and among franchisors (using three approaches in the latter instance). It also posits that, in order to reduce the incidences of franchisee failure, there is a need for franchisors to monitor franchisee performance to identify those experiencing decline and to assist floundering franchisees to engineer turnarounds in their fortunes. Realizing such performance improvements is a process of innovation which may serve either to lower the business's cost base or reposition the concept. It is also a process which requires some franchisors to be more responsible and ethical or, in the words of one commentator on franchising, these franchisors

> . . . need to grow up – morally and commercially . . . some franchisors make 'wildly inaccurate' claims about potential earnings, supply inadequate information about costs and operate poor recruitment standards. (Angus MacMillan, 1996)

Not all franchisors, however, can be tarnished with the same brush – there are those who actively seek to assist their franchisees. Although in the minority, such companies have possibly learnt that another source of competitive advantage is their reputation (Kay, 1993), and that the costs of litigation not only encompass financial payments. Ill-management of franchisees will also lead to the development of a bad reputation in the marketplace and, therefore, be potentially detrimental to developing and sustaining competitive advantage in the medium to long term. Franchisees are guilty too: some franchisees actively flaunt contractual rules and act in ways which could be detrimental to the development of brand equity. Nonetheless, these behaviours are often symptomatic of a need to alter the blueprint because of competitive pressure as well as the tone and nature of relations between the franchisor and franchisee. If franchisors had a better idea of the individuals they wanted as franchisees, employed other recruitment slogans than 'Low rates of failure' and 'Become your own boss', and attempted to harness their franchisees' implicit innovative capability, perhaps incidences of such behaviour could be lower. After all, if people come to the franchise relationship expecting the freedoms and latitude of behaviour associated with being your own boss, and subsequently have those expectations dampened by the franchisor, dissatisfaction will result.

Chapter 9 also empirically investigates, through a sample of fifty-nine limited liability/corporate franchisees operating over 250 stores between 1989 and 1993, the extent to which franchisee solvency scores and other performance measures alter under certain environmental conditions. Of course, one possible interpretation of extant efforts propounding low rates of innovation and failure may be that franchises inhabit stable environments where the need for ongoing adaptation is minimal. But, if anything, franchise firms are susceptible to the same market forces as their relevant industry and sub-sector peer group, and some franchisee-owned operations are exposed to greater environmental volatility than their franchisor-owned counterparts. As such, innovation, rather than conformity, may be a prerequisite to survival and superior performance (Banbury and Mitchell, 1995). The chapter also provides for tests on the null hypotheses that brand affiliation and involvement in interlocking directorates yields performance differences. Finally, the implications of the research for turnaround strategies within constrained business units are discussed.

The final chapter contends that the future of franchise research lies in exploring how networks, cultures and innovations within franchise systems interact to influence behaviour and performance. The chapter provides an overview of learning in intra-organizational networks, and argues that environmental uncertainty and increasingly sophisticated consumers means that the formation of cross-organizational teams – or inter-organizational networks – are important to the realization of competitive advantages based on innovation. Within both types of networks, the culture plays a facilitating role and there are distinct individual roles which act as information gatekeepers.

One caveat is important at this juncture. The book employs the context of the hotel and catering market to elucidate certain points, rather than exploring a variety of industry settings. While this may preclude generalizations to be made to all franchise contexts, franchising in the hospitality sector has one of the highest levels of penetration. This suggests that the findings may be of some interest to those outside the hospitality market. The illustrations used in the book take two forms: at the end of some chapters case studies are provided as appendices, while in others, the chapter embodies examples within the main text. The subjects of the specific case studies include:

1. The development of KFC in Britain.
2. The interwined histories of Burger King and Wimpy.
3. Trends in the organization of hotel food and beverage services.
4. The emergence of consortia in the pizza home delivery sector.
5. Efficiency in the bakery market.
6. Quests for competitive advantages in the UK sandwich sector.

Some people may question the inclusion of bakeries as part of the hotel and catering industry, but this really comes down to how one perceives the structure of the industry. So what is meant by 'hotel and catering', or its shorthand terminology of 'hospitality', and why has it been chosen? The term hospitality refers to the provision of accommodation, food and beverages to customers when away from home. Each service may be offered either singly or in combination and either for profit or not. Traditionally, the hospitality market is viewed to comprise hotels, motels, bed and breakfast establishments, restaurants, public houses, restaurants, fast food and staff canteens. It is used as a context because it is in this industry perhaps more lucidly than any other, that it is possible to see the diffusion of franchising to varying degrees and in differing guises. It is an industry from which it is also possible to suggest some of the future trajectories that franchising may take.

Partially as a response to the oligopolistic market conditions of the grocery retail sector, the targeting of the hospitality market by suppliers, and consumer's desire for value for money, quality and convenience, so other retailers have entered the hospitality market via product diversity. In mature economies, such as the USA, UK and Japan, the provision of hospitality products – especially food and beverages – has become diverse to the extent that the traditional delineators of industry boundaries, standard industrial classification codes, are no longer sufficient to encompass the range of firms involved in the activity and its economic contribution (Clarke, 1989). The effect of this product diversity has served to blur the boundaries of the industry such that the contemporary market incumbents who, traditionally, supplied substitute products. Specifically, the hospitality market also includes operations such as retail bakeries, leisure and entertainment facilities (such as bowling alleys), supermarkets, petrol forecourt stations and specialist meat retailers.

To some degree, the firms operating such establishments have been innovative and noted for their use of an array of differing organizational arrangements including concessions, management contracting, business format franchising, image menu franchising, joint ventures, tenancies and consortia. Whilst there may be a variety of reasons behind the dearth of specific literature on the topic in relation to the hospitality industry, it has almost become axiomatic that strategies of co-operation, rather than pure competition, will become increasingly commonplace in the next millennium. Clearly, therefore, the paucity of discourse devoted to the subject does not do justice to its increasing significance, relevance and complexity within the contemporary hospitality marketplace.

In researching this book, two main approaches were employed. First, at a general level, the trade press and financial press as well as franchisor-specific literature were monitored. In addition to monitoring the three main popular franchise magazines (*Franchise World*, *Business Franchise Magazine* and *Franchise Magazine*), segment-specific texts were also consulted. These ranged from UK publications such as *Pizza and Pasta News*, *Convenience Store*, *Forecourt News*, *Caterer & Hotelkeeper*, *Motor Trader*, *The Grocer*, *Supermarketing*, to US magazines such as *Restaurants & Institutions*, *Pizza Today*, *Hotels*, *Restaurant Business* and *Nation's Restaurant News*. These were supplemented by reviews of the franchise fraternity by the *Financial Times* and the *Wall Street Journal*.

Then, more specifically, academic articles, symposium papers and books on franchising were also monitored. Where possible, financial details of franchisees and franchisors were sought and acquired from Companies House. The details contained within their accounts permitted the testing of specific hypotheses. Other sources of information were borrowed from the International Franchise Research Council in order to help build the argument that potential franchisees employ a career decision-making process when contemplating whether to franchise or not. Additional sources of data used in compiling the book were: *Yellow Pages*, *United Kingdom Franchise Directory*, *Franchise World Directory* and the annual British Franchise Association (BFA) and National Westminster Bank ('NatWest') surveys.

On a stylistic note, the text often refers to the franchisess and franchisor as 'he'. This is because franchising is a male-dominated domain; for example, Dant *et al* (1996) indicate that, in the USA, only 10% of franchisees are women and also concludes that women business-owners tend not to employ franchising as a method of expansion for their companies. Whilst some franchisors and a number of researchers are investigating these phenomena, 'he' is employed for the sake of accuracy and grammar. Equally, as so much in franchising appears insufficiently explored, tested and corroborated (including why numerous businesses become franchises), terms such as 'maybe', 'perhaps', 'could be' and 'might' are frequently used rather than more positivistic terminology. Arguably, within the limited franchise research conducted thus far, there is too much of this latter type of language with an over-reliance on empiricism such that sometimes the reader is left wondering whether the researchers are attempting to develop a 'science of franchising'. Yet, there problems with this *modus operandi*, and it is not always appropriate.

Empirical work is essential to any successful science, and to organizational theory. Empiricism, which is to empirical work as arson is to central heating does more harm than good. The fundamental problem about empiricism is over-confidence in observation and a consequent impatience with the difficulties and uncertainties that theorists encounter when they go beyond observing and operationalizing to theorizing. That last activity usually involves postulating states and events that are not themselves observable but are causes of states and events that are . . . we cannot always evaluate competing ways of explaining organizational behaviour by reference to predictive ability. (Hartman, 1988; p. 21).

Given the theme of franchising as an innovation and the use of the hospitality industry as a context, this book is not a 'How-to' text, nor does it seek to contribute to that substantial body of work. If you want to learn the processes and requirements of how to become either a franchisee or franchisor, in all probability this book is not for you. If, however, you have specific queries then some of these may be answered within particular chapters. For example, if you want to examine and put a figure against the potential risk of becoming either a franchisor or franchisee, Chapters 8 and 9 will be of interest. Equally, Chapter 5 provides some insight to the process of becoming a franchisee. Nonetheless, the book is not prescriptive but descriptive: it does not seek to provide pre-specified solutions to problems experienced by either franchisors or franchisees, but provides additional data to help facilitate a particular answer. Given this focus, how would one describe this book? If it has to categorized, one description of the book – as good as any – is that it is a reply. It seeks to provide some answers to a fundamental paradox apparent in both the popular and academic franchise press alike. As the titles of numerous management books attest, there are undoubtedly other paradoxes in franchising and business life alike. Therefore, this book does not seek to be comprehensive, but if it acts as a spur to much-needed future research it will have achieved its objective. If nothing else, the bibliography should enable the researcher to reduce the time-costs typically associated with investigating the franchise fraternity.

Introduction:
Interpretations of franchising

Franchising is based on a relationship of mutual trust: The franchisor must be able to introduce structure and discipline, standardization of operating procedure, and sophisticated control techniques that ordinarily would be unavailable to the operator of a single unit. On the other hand, the franchisee must be able to introduce an entrepreneurial 'spirit' – a dedication and willingness to devote long hours and hard work to the enterprise – that would not be usually obtained by the franchisor from its employees.

David Seltz, President of Seltz Franchising Developments Inc., *The Complete Handbook of Franchising*

The key advantage to being part of a franchise organization is that the franchisor is striving for the very same goals on your behalf. A good franchisor will constantly be looking for ways in which to develop the franchise, not only to strengthen the existing network of franchise outlets but to encourage new franchisees into the business. Your success and development is of as much concern as it is to you.

Andrew Constandinos, UK franchisee, *Business Franchise*, September 1994

The schizophrenia of franchising

Almost Jekyll and Hyde-like, there are two faces of franchising. One face offers the promise of personal and financial success through a mutually beneficial partnership between the investor (the franchisee) and the franchisor. The dominant themes of this image are the messages of low rates of failure and the wealth creation by franchise companies, such as McDonald's and KFC among others. In this vein, some commentators (such as those quoted above) suggest that franchising represents a form of alliance between two parties with mutual interests. That is, the participants are independent organizations engaged in a co-operative agreement for the achievement of common goals. The mutuality of benefits does not imply equality of benefits, but means that all parties to the alliance will receive benefit in proportion to the contributions made. Thus, while there may be some disparity in the returns accruing to the participants, the extent of the variance is assumed to be relatively small. These are the positive images of franchising expounded by franchisors, franchise exhibition organizers, franchise magazines, and other popular investment texts as well as some commentators from the academic fraternity.

The other face of franchising is the dark side, where franchisees are portrayed to be victims of outrageous claims, spurious success stories and myths, and images of self-employment made by sometimes fraudulent franchisors (Baillieu, 1988; Holson, 1996). Some critics have sometimes gone as far as labelling franchising as a 'trap for the trusting' (Brown, 1969). In this image, the disparity of interests and goals between the franchisor and franchisee is extreme; franchises are not a form of alliance because the agreement is not mutually beneficial and the franchisee is not as independent as the other face of franchising would have people believe. But which image is the more accurate?

The dissemination of good practice suggests that it is essential to portray the reality of franchise relations, rather than this dichomic conception. An objective perspective of franchising may permit more fact-founded decision-making through providing a better understanding of what it entails. The realization of this situation requires interested parties to partake in greater disclosure of franchisors' activities and histories and, hardest of all, to put aside the vested interests and the emotion attached to these stakes. While the achievement of these requirements may be unattainable in the short term, advancing knowledge and comprehension about the activities and range of behaviours encompassed in franchises may be partially achieved through exploring the permeations of meaning contained within extant definitions of franchising. Unfortunately, despite the importance of the activity, even the definitional aspect of franchising illustrates little consensus among practioners. Yet the definition of franchising is important for a number of reasons.

It is essential in establishing which business a firm is in, its competitors, the available opportunities and threats as well as the necessary technologies and behaviours to be successful. A carefully constructed definition can permit the boundaries of the activities to be drawn, thereby enabling the importance of the franchising to the economy to be established and growth patterns recognized. It also provides a framework from which it is possible to evaluate the structure of the activity, as well as a benchmark to compare and contrast how franchises differ from one another. Such information has critical value to potential investors and entrants seeking to fill a market gap because it provides a suggestion of the degree of independence the incumbent parties may enjoy. The information is also of importance to government bodies wishing to monitor industrial activity.

Numerous authors have observed that no unequivocal definition of franchising exists. Whilst unfortunately true, it is not a fruitful perspective when so many fail to rectify the situation by entering into some form of debate, academic or otherwise. The lack of definitional consensus only serves to reinforce any misunderstanding that people may have concerning the range of behaviours encompassed, and variety of economic sectors, within the world of franchises. The resultant confusion surrounding franchises has been implicit not only in its definition, therefore, but has also affected calculations to establish the extent of its diffusion and performance. For example, according to the *United Kingdom Franchise Directory*, there were 615 franchisors (albeit of a wider array of franchise types than those covered by the BFA) in Britain in 1995. By contrast, the survey conducted by the Natwest/BFA (1995) indicates that there were 474 franchisors.

Unfortunately, trade and research bodies such as the BFA only examine one particular form of franchise rather than being perhaps more comprehensive. The fact that their statistics are based on sampling rather than by census suggests that the trade body's research does not cover all activity even in the types of franchises they do embrace. Nonetheless, their data is one of the only regularly-produced sources which places a market size value on franchising activity in Britain. Despite not covering all types of franchises their data is helpful in analyses of the trajectory of franchising's diffusion curve. But at the expense of being potentially confusing, in order to be comprehensive this book employs a variety of sources when illustrating the size of the franchise fraternity. In part, the abundance of interpretations can be blamed on the different contexts to which the term has been applied. In addition to confusion concerning the size of the franchise fraternity and the array of behaviours encompassed in franchising, the outcome of a lack of a consistent definition of franchising is cacophony rather than harmony. Eventually, someone may provide a synthesis that does justice to the increasing significance of the activity and sat-isfies many of the perspectives currently employed. In the meantime, however, the plethora of disagreements concerning the definition of franchising can be confusing to an outsider who looks to the experts for some consistency and unity of perspective con-cerning the scale of the franchise fraternity, its trends, structure, and intensity of competitive rivalry.

The 'jungle' of franchise definitions

Franchising means different things to different users. Despite its age, expansion and significance to the hospitality industry, especially its fast food and restaurant sub-sectors (Khan, 1992), there has been little in-depth research into franchising. This has resulted in low levels of understanding, confusion between other growth methods and, potentially, misrepresentation. Much of the lack of understanding of franchising as a dis-tribution strategy stems from its diverse, heterogeneous and hybrid forms (Hackett, 1977; Winsor and Quinones, 1994), which precludes consistency and agreement among the various sources of data examining the size and structure of the franchise fraternity. Con-sequently, numerous definitions and estimations of franchising's industrial size abound, which confuses attempts to estimate the value of the activity to wealth creation in economies, and complicates attempts to estimate the rate and extent franchising's diffu-sion. Such a plethora of translations has also resulted in a long-running definitional debate (Curran and Stanworth, 1983; Hunt, 1973; Konopa, 1963), with some researchers being of the view that definitions are simply adapted to the situation (Hough, 1986) and others to argue that the term is essentially meaningless. Part of this debate is caused, in part, by the disparate business activities it encompasses. The term has, for example, been employed to label business relationships as diverse as the right to:

1. broadcast television programmes within certain territories (Domberger and Middleton, 1985; Jaffe and Kanter, 1990; Prager 1990; Veljanovski, 1987; Zupan, 1989);
2. operate airline and railway routes;
3. be able to offer legal aid;
4. supply electrical services and other privatized utilities (Ridley, 1995; Vickers and Yarrow, 1988);
5. play American football, baseball and basketball in a particular city in the rel-evant American sports league (Shropshire, 1995);
6. use cartoon characters on products;
7. sell petrol (Izraeli, 1971; Shepard, 1993); and
8. make use of a complete training package (Feuer, 1989; Hall and Dixon, 1989; Shook and Shook, 1993).

Franchising has also been recommended as a method of growth and efficient local mar-ket servicing by charities (Houghton and Timperley, 1992) and by retail banks in order to reduce labour costs and improve operating efficiency. Franchising is also a term employed by brand managers to describe and summarize high levels of customer loyalty and recog-nition to their products (Tauber, 1981). Most recently, it has also been used as a vehicle for universities and colleges to lease their name to both under-graduate and post-graduate courses to other educational establishments. Mendelsohn (1992), however, suggests that much of the pervasiveness is not due to franchising existing in so many forms, but more due to the misuse and incorrect application of the term to express what was formerly described as a licensing arrangement. Given the breadth of applications, some researchers have sought clarity by categorizing the various types of franchise into sub-groups (Sanghavi, 1990). For example, basing his categorization on the differing components of the supply chain, Charles Vaughn (1979) suggests that there are four types of franchise:

1. *The Manufacturer-Retailer Franchise* – a manufacturer grants the right to a retailer to sell the product to the final consumer. The franchisee may operate the franchise as his sole business activity or, alternatively, as an activity within an existing business. Automobile dealerships, public houses and petrol service stations are examples.

2. *The Manufacturer-Wholesaler Franchise* – a manufacturer grants the right to a wholesaler to distribute a product. The main examples of this form of franchising is the soft drinks industry where companies such as Coca-Cola and PepsiCo, sell franchises to independent bottlers who, in turn, distribute to retailers.

3. *The Wholesaler-Retailer Franchise* – a wholesaler grants the right to a retailer to trade under a certain name. Perhaps the best-known examples here are the 'voluntary' groups in grocery retailing where the wholesaler (the franchisor) supplies products to the retailer (the franchisee) who is signed on a voluntary basis.

4. *The Retailer-Retailer Franchise* – a retailer grants the right to another retailer to trade under the same name. Usually called 'business format franchising', the franchisor has a product or service to be marketed under a common trade-name by, usually, standardized outlets. These types of franchises are based on the 'cloning' principle and include fast food outlets, car hire, and hotel franchising.

Possibly compounding the definitional issue, research has elucidated other interpretations of franchise systems. For example, Winsor and Quinones (1994) and Sherman (1993) quote from Pintel and Diamond (1991):

- *Territorial:* The franchise granted encompasses several counties or states. The holder of the franchise assumes the responsibility for setting up and training individual franchisees within his territory and obtains an 'override' on all sales in his territory.

- *Operating:* The individual independent franchisee who runs his own franchise. He deals either directly with the parent company or with the territorial franchise holder.

- *Mobile:* A franchise that dispenses its product from a moving vehicle, which is either owned by the franchisee or leased from the franchisor.

- *Distributorship:* The franchisee takes title to various goods and distributes them to sub-franchisees. The distributor has exclusive coverage of a wide geographical area and acts as a supply house for the franchisees who carry the product.

- *Co-ownership:* The franchisor and franchisee share in the investment and profits, for example, Denny's Restaurants.
- *Co-management:* The franchisor controls the major part of the investment. The partner-manager shares profits proportionately.
- *Leasing:* The franchisor leases the land, buildings and equipment to the franchisees. Leasing is used in conjunction with other provisions.
- *Licensing:* The franchisor licenses the franchisee to use his trademarks and business techniques. The franchisor either supplies the product or provides the franchisees with a list of approved suppliers.
- *Manufacturing:* The franchisor grants a franchisee to manufacture its product through the use of specified materials and techniques. The franchisee distributes the product, using the franchisor's techniques. This method enables a national manufacturer to distribute regionally when distribution costs from central manufacturing are prohibitive.
- *Service:* The franchisor describes patterns by which a franchisee supplies a professional service, as exemplified by employment agencies.

Less specific typology distinguishes between tradename/product franchises and business format franchises. 'Product' or 'tradename' franchises embrace the fields of car and petroleum distribution, the soft-drink bottlers and, in the UK, tenanted public houses and the mobile ice-cream franchises, such as Wall's Whippy (MMC, 1994), as well as voluntary chains. These examples are often categorized as 'first generation' franchises and, in spite of their importance, are almost totally side-lined from mainstream debates on modern franchising to the extent that they are omitted from statistical/market research studies. By contrast, business format franchises, which have accounted for a great deal of the growth in franchised-based expansion in recent years, involve a full business system, close ongoing franchisor-franchisee relationships and are more service-orientated, embracing such areas as fast food, fast printing, cleaning, hygiene, rental, employment and health services etc. Due to the broader array of operating standards and business areas, business format franchises have been alternatively labelled 'a system leasing arrangement' (Gerstenhaber, 1988) since the franchisee acquires from the franchisor the right to duplicate the franchisor's existing system of providing a product and/or service to the end user.

> An alternative name for franchising is system leasing. The franchisor is leasing to the franchisee the use of his systems for a definite period of time and within a specific market. The franchisor will expect ongoing payments for the use of the system and these payments will be determined by the success of the business to capture a large market share in the community where it operates. Therefore, the obligation of the franchisee is to use the system to the full. (Gerstenhaber, 1988; p. 14)

Throughout most of the literature the prevalence of business format franchises has been such that the term has been used almost interchangeably with franchising, whilst the discourse referring to product/tradename franchises has tended to be marginalized. Although Chapter 2 shows that, in the UK at least, this latter form of franchising is generally predominant, the focus of the book is the business format franchise because of its significance in the hospitality industry. Most of the definitions of business format franchises are emphatic of the franchisee's autonomy, conformance to standards and the contractual nature of the agreement, as the following sampled definitions attest.

Definition 1

Franchising is a system for the selective distribution of goods and/or services under a brand name through outlets owned by independent businessmen, called 'franchisees'. Although the franchisor supplies the franchisee with knowhow and brand identification on a continuing basis, the franchisee enjoys the right to profit and runs the risk of loss. The franchisor controls the distribution of his goods and/or services through a contract which regulates the activities of franchisee, in order to achieve standardization. (Rosenberg and Bedell, 1969; p. 41)

Definition 2

First and foremost, franchising is a marketing system, a method of distributing goods or services to the consumer. In simplest terms, franchising involves two levels of business people: the franchisor, who has developed the system and lends its name or trademark to it, and the franchisee, who buys the right to operate the business under the franchisor's name or trademark. (Raab and Matusky, 1987; p. 20)

Definition 3

An arrangement whereby the manufacturer or sole distributor of a trade-marked product or service gives exclusive rights of local distribution to independent retailers in return for their payment of royalties and conformance to standardized operating procedures. A party granting a right (or franchise) is known as the franchisor, while the recipient is called the franchisee. (Seltz, 1982; p. 1)

From these definitions, the recurring features of franchise contractual agreements are, in their simplest forms, the determination (to varying degrees) of where a franchisee may compete, whether the region is exclusive to the franchisee, the ownership of intellectual property, what a franchisee may supply, the payment of royalties or 'rent' for borrowing the business idea, the length of time of the agreement, the provision of know-how to the franchisee via an operating manual and training, provisions for the franchisor to police the franchisee's operation in order to ensure standardization. In short, the franchise relationship is founded on a contract which is written to benefit the franchisor (Hunt, 1972). This contract and the franchisor's behaviour determines the franchisee's degree of independence and, thus, the extent of franchisor power over its franchisees. In the limitation of autonomy, a paradox (albeit a literal one) is evident. According to Shook and Shook (1993), for example, the word 'franchising' literally means freedom to own, manage, and direct their own business – as any truly self-employed person would do. This theme of self-employment is also a recurrent message employed by franchisors, franchise advisers, and public relations officers in order to attract new franchisees. In one sense, franchisees are indeed self-employed. Franchisors do not pay their franchisees a salary or wage, and therefore are not required to pay the tax or social security costs associated with employees; in the UK, they are also not required to conform to labour law, or consumer law, but rather a patchwork of statutes.

When you buy a franchise, you may think that you're buying into a business partnership. You run the day-to-day operation and your franchisor trains you, drums up business through advertising and promotion, and makes experts available for trouble-shooting.

Think again. To most franchisors, you're just another customer. That's not just our opinion; that's the law. The Federal Trade Commission, which oversees the industry, looks upon buying a franchise as a consumer endeavor rather than a commercial one. Its concern is that you don't get ripped off when you make a purchase. As to problems that may develop later between you and the franchisor, you're on your own. (Holson, 1996; p. 118)

Although this quote may aptly summarize the situation in the USA, in other countries where there is no equivalent of a Federal Trade Commission or specific franchise legislation protecting franchisees, the franchisee is susceptible to abuse and the reputable franchisors' positions are undermined. Clearly, contractual obligations and restrictions concerning the latitude of franchisees' behaviour mean that there are limitations to that freedom: it is not necessary for individuals to have a contract of employment in order to be controlled and managed like an employee.

Among other co-ordinating and controlling functions, among some contract cleaning franchises it is the franchisor who contacts potential customers and then invoices them for work performed by the franchisee. The customer pays the franchisor who, after deducting the appropriate royalties and charges, sends the franchisee the remainder of the revenue. In such situations the franchisee could not be said to be an 'entrepreneur' (as many economists label franchisees) because they have not necessarily sought out their own customers via negotiation and certainly do not illustrate the independence of action typically associated with self-employed persons. Rather, they appear to be a form of casual labour who have bought their jobs through the payment of up-front fees and the payment of royalties. As a result of their payment for only the work they have conducted, franchisees, in this instance, are little more than 'jobbers' as opposed to being the self-employed capitalists that the populist franchise press, and others, portray them to be.

> The novel ingredient distinguishing franchising from most other forms of business activity is the symbiotic relationship between two legally distinct economic entities. The close ties existing between franchisor and franchisee (Spriggs and Nevin, 1994) have led to their relationship often being described as a partnership or strategic alliance (McIntyre, Young and Gilbert, 1994). (Stanworth and Kaufmann, 1996; p. 57)

Nor are they necessarily the alliance partners that some have suggested because of the overt power imbalance in the relationship, and nor is the franchisor seen (in general) to stand in a fiduciary relationship to the franchisee, unlike (for example) a solicitor and client. That is, he is not seen to have rights and powers which he is bound to exercise for the benefit of the franchisee. Rather, the franchisor is permitted (this is, however, a matter of degree and on local legislation) to derive profit and advantage from the relationship without the consent of the franchisee. Further differences are evident because of an apparent lack of reciprocal organizational learning and idea exchanges between the parties (see Chapters 6 and 7).

In one of the few academic texts exploring the inaccuracies in the pop''' sages of self-employment, Felstead (1993) researches the subject of freedo' within the franchise relationship in some depth. His approach differs from the traditional school of thought employed by franchise theorists, the New Institutional Approach (otherwise called 'agency theory') and begins with an assessment for the rationale behind businesses pursuing franchised expansion. Felstead's approach differs because it explicitly accounts for the dynamic role of power within franchise relationships. According to the traditional approach, firms decide to franchise their operations because it is a cheaper alternative to growth through opening company-owned units. As such, franchising permits the franchisor to increase revenues and efficiency through reducing the input costs associated with growth.

There are two components to the lower costs associated with franchising, both of which are referred to in the sampled definitions above. The first strand of the traditional approach is that franchising lowers the cost of monitoring geographically dispersed outlets as the franchisee is renumerated by his operation's residual profit, which means that they are prepared to work themselves and their employees harder to increase the value of the unit. Reflective of this situation, franchise businesses have been described in the popular press as anaemic or 'lean' organizations because of the high number of business-level employees and franchisees compared to the number of people at system headquarters (NatWest/BFA, 1995). By implication, those businesses which are not franchised are characterized by taller hierarchies to ensure conformance to organizational objectives.

The other reason for the lower monitoring costs is that franchisees, upon entering the system, are required to pay an initial payment which represents the present value of the expected profit stream from the outlet and the brand value inherent to the franchise (Rubin, 1978; Sen, 1993). According to some, this payment also represents a consideration of the value of the franchisor's know-how and ongoing assistance, which should lead to lower expectations of failure. This payment not only allows the franchisor to raise capital, but also affects franchisee innovative behaviour (see Chapter 6). As the costs of entry require the franchisee to risk his own capital (be that either redundancy payments or fixed assets such as his house), the propensity is to engage in behaviour, such as offering poor service quality and selling products outside of those contractually specified, that jeopardizes the realization of a return on this investment, is lowered. The franchisor is also tied to the fortunes of the franchisee through the payment of royalties, which serves to lower the cost of developing brand equity through advertising and contributes to the costs of managing the franchise. The potential for falling revenues, which are perceived to derive from lower levels of service quality and opportunistic behaviour rather than being symptomatic of lower competitiveness *vis-à-vis* similar businesses (franchised or not), mean that franchisors have a vested interest in monitoring the quality and quantity of goods/services supplied.

Although it is apparent that, even within the parameters of the New Institutionalist Approach, franchising is biased more in favour of the franchisor than the franchisee, the extent of this disparity is limited. As a result of the franchisor's dependence on the franchisee for revenue and efficiency gains deriving from low-cost growth, and the franchisee's reliance on the franchisor's know-how and brand name, the New Institutionalists' suppose that franchise relationships are characterized by mutual interest. By summarizing and applying a substantial body of social science research and other limited studies of power in the franchise relationship (Anand, 1987; Hough, 1986; Lewis and Lambert, 1991), Felstead (1993), however, contends otherwise.

Felstead's analysis of franchising

In analyzing the manner in which franchising works in favour of the franchisor, Felstead employs an essentially Marxist theoretical framework. Such an approach is implicitly different from previous analyses of the power differences in the franchise relationship. It differs because it relates the power stratification in franchises to those evident in societal contexts, rather than suggesting that franchises exist in a vacuum or that they are an egalitarian form of organization. Stratification is all-pervasive. It is not a sub-system of society in the same sense as, for example, the economy or education; rather it is a generalized aspect of the structure of all complex social systems and there is a reciprocal process between social stratification in the sphere of industry and in the wider community (Parker *et al*, 1972).

Within the confines of the Marxist analytic construct, the key to social stratification and power differences between different classes of people is the concentration of ownership, expressed in legal form, of factors of production – land, capital, labour, and entrepreneurship – and the process of the production process, or the labour-technology mix. The capitalist class includes those who own and control the means of production, while labour constitutes those who do not own or control such factors and who have to sell their willingness and ability to work to capitalists in order to make a living. The relationship between the ownership of factors of production and the energy, technology, and knowledge required to transform such ingredients into revenue producing end-product and services therefore forms the basis of society's class system. Such relations determine how individuals gain access to the productive forces and to the consumption of other products/services in society. For example, individuals in technology-intensive economies possessing appropriate knowledge will be able to command higher revenues than those who do not. Equally, an entrepreneur may have the access to raw materials, premises, skill, and technology to produce a particular service, whereas an employee may not own any of these factors other than his labour. The entrepreneur's income is the profit realized from selling the transformed raw materials and know-how to people with the capital to purchase the product of his efforts. An employee, on the other hand, gains a return on his labour through wage bargaining, but the latitude for such bargaining in both the employment and franchise contract is limited. All too often, potential employees and franchisees are offered contracts on a 'take it or leave it' basis (see Chapter 7).

The differences in ownership of factors of production between the wage-labourer and the entrepreneur means that the former is under an economic compulsion to work for the propertied class in order to purchase the necessities of life. The lack of ownership of factors of production means that the wage labourer occupies a weaker bargaining position relative to the capitalist prior to the formation of a contractual agreement between the two parties. In addition to being economically inferior to the franchisor, franchisees do not possess the same level of knowledge about the franchise or business. Thus, the parties of the franchise contract are not approximately equal when they enter into negotiations because of the franchisor's expert knowledge. This suggests that there exists a *de facto* situation in which the potential franchisee transfers power to the franchisor because of the inequality in experience, economic power, etc. Although the potential franchisee has the broad choice of whether or not to enter into a relationship with the franchisor, once having chosen to have such a relationship, the weaker party has

no choice with respect to his vulnerability within it. In turn, this means that the capitalist is able to differentiate his knowledge according to necessity and, thereby, affect
labour's perception of the business during the negotiation process. Indicative of the franchisor's ability to tailor the information and influence perceptions, Brian Smart, Director
of the BFA, indicates that:

> . . . all good franchisors . . . disclosed [information] and . . . they did it in a way
> that secured understanding. In order to do that, they managed the disclosure
> process according to the needs of the individual applicants. (*Franchise World*,
> July-August 1996, pp. 7–8)

With the exception of the USA and Canada, there is a lack of legal necessity for franchisors
to disclose a variety of potentially useful information in such a way that permits easy comparison. As such, potential franchisees are not free to compare and contrast competing
franchise offerings on a like-for-like basis; franchisors further control the information disclosure process by only permitting potential investors to talk to those existing franchisees
who can be trusted to portray the business in a positive light. One of the reasons for the
reluctance displayed by franchisors in disclosing information is the fear that they may be
informing a potential competitor, and thus be instrumental in their own loss of market
share. When one considers that potential franchisees have been shown to choose industrial sector (or type of business) over legal form (Kaufmann and Stanworth, 1995), there
may be some foundation to this fear.

Yet franchises are not unique in forming contractual relationships with rivals.
Another research vein (Hergert and Morris, 1988), discovered that most alliances occur
between rivals: over 71% of alliances on their INSEAD database were between companies
operating in the same market. It would seem, therefore, that as alliances contain a competitive element it is the post-contractual conditions which are of importance, rather
than the pre-contractual bargaining. Indeed, franchisees have been shown to be motivated by gaining access to an established business concept; it is the desire to gain access
to the franchisor's expert knowledge and the revenues accruing from well-known brands
that motivate them to become a franchisee, rather than the promise of being self-
employed. This is one of the reasons why franchising continues to flourish in countries
such as the USA and Canada, where franchisors are legally obliged to provide the potential franchisee with a detailed history of the company and its directors. Although most
franchise agreements contain clauses which prevent the franchisee from competing in a
direct way by operating a similar business in a similar location and during a specified time
period after the termination of the franchise contract, there are limits to these constraints.

> A restraint on the former franchisee soliciting customers and employees has a
> chance of success, if that is in fact what the franchisee is doing. No restraint can
> prevent a customer going where he freely chooses, however, nor . . . can a per-
> son be restrained from freely exercising his trade, except in so far as doing so
> interferes with the interests of the former employer which the law protects.
> (Adams and Pritchard-Jones, 1990; p. 99)

According to Marx, class relations are 'exploitative' because they involve the appropria-
tion by the propertied class of the 'surplus labour' created by another class. Because the

entrepreneur possesses the means of his own subsistence he is, therefore, under no economic compulsion to work for others. As a result, his 'surplus labour' (where the returns of an individual's labour accrues to some one else) can only be appropriated by 'extra-economic' compulsion, such as being dependent on another capitalist because of their legally enforceable economic monopolies. For example, a restaurant owner may be reliant on bank loans to finance the set-up costs of another unit. The interest payments on the loans represent 'surplus labour' because the owner has to work to meet these contractually binding instalments in the short term or else risk losing his outlet. As a consequence of the potential exploitation of non-propertied classes, relations between labour and capital are inherently interdependent but conflictual as labour seeks to minimize the degree of abuse and the propertied seek to maximize it. The aim of the capitalist is to make profits which can be used to accumulate more capital and yet more profits. The aim of the working classes is to earn higher wages to improve their standard of living. This conflict means that the capitalist is confronted with the problems of control and monitoring labour:

> Capitalism, being based upon the exploitation of those who sell their labour, necessarily sets the capitalist, or his agents, problems of control, direction and legitimacy. Employees cannot be 'trusted' to identify with the goals of management, or adhere to the spirit – or letter – of their work instructions, for the goals of the organization, and the procedures and specifications which follow from them, are quite antithetical to their interests. The structure of the organization, and everything within it, reflects the employer's pursuit of profit at the expense of his employees and the constant probability and occasional reality, of their apprehending this over-riding fact, either as a source of withdrawal, 'instrumentality' or bloody-mindedness or as a cause for group, organized resistance. (Salaman, 1981; p. 164)

The same is true in franchising. In addition to monitoring franchisees to establish whether they are conforming to standards and are operating within the constraints of the franchise contract, franchisors are motivated to control their franchisees because this process permits them to accrue wealth:

> The goodwill associated with the trade name and marks (registered and unregistered), etc is built up by the franchisor and the franchisees. If a licensor did not monitor quality, and a licensee built up a reputation in the [trade] mark by controlling quality, it would be unfair that the licensee who had built up the goodwill associated with the mark should see it transfer to the licensor at the end of the licence. The same thing would apply to other distinctive insignia which fulfil similar functions to trade marks and are protected by copyright, etc. In the case of franchising however where the franchisor fulfils a central role in building up the goodwill by controlling all his franchisees, there would not appear to be this objection. On the contrary, it seems reasonably clear that for this reason the goodwill accrues to the franchisor. (Adams and Pritchard-Jones, 1990; p. 28)

The control of work and workers is a central theme of scientific management practices. These managerial systems require the close specification of work roles, times and conditions to maximize output and employ close supervision to ensure diligence. Managerial control effort is reduced through the simplification and standardization of work activities into well-defined and simple-to-measure tasks in which labour has no discretion. The simplification and standardization of tasks and work practices permits not only better control and comparisons between outlets, but also allows the franchisor to recruit those people who do not necessarily possess high levels of technical skill. Although it may be tempting to suggest that capitalists devised scientific management to permit the further exploitation of labour, via the deskilling process, such an argument is not convincing. Robertson and Aston (1992), for example, conclude that while some technology is deskilling, much of it is not, and even when technology is deskilling this does not necessarily imply that the wages of workers are reduced. In some instances, depending upon whether the technology can be substituted for all the skills of a given group of workers, the new technology may actually enhance the power of the remaining workforce. Thus, they contend that whether technology enhances skills or deskills is frequently more a result of technological choice than a motivation for technological choice.

We can see this situation in the restaurant and fast food sectors, where deskilling and low wages have become a key feature of the *modus operandi*. According to Langdon (1986), the deskilling process was the result of a desire for greater speed, efficiency and productivity rather than a way of subjegating labour to the wishes of business owners *per se*. As a result of the lower level of skill and knowledge requirement, labour is in a comparatively weaker bargaining position than those workers who are able to exercise discretion and technical ability in their tasks. These aspects of managerial control serve to erode skills, worker independence, and reduce the significance of the worker's knowledge of their craft. Additionally, labour is excluded from decisions about methods and the pace of work through their lack of involvement in innovative behaviour.

Supplementing the capitalist control of labour through the routinization and simplification of tasks, Blau and Schoenherr (1971) argue that people who do not own the factors of production are also managed through insidious means. These insidious controls affect behaviour and attitudes in ways that do not necessarily involve the experience of being controlled or manipulated. That is, capitalists create the illusion of independence in order to achieve legitimacy for their controls by designing them in ways that make them unobstrusive. Insidious controls are necessary because managers rely on the acceptance of values associated with capitalism. The extent of compliance with managerial control is a measure of the social acceptance of those values, and ensures discipline and predictability in behaviour and decisions. The aspects of such insidious control include:

1. control through expert power where educated and qualified employees can be controlled by appealing to their professional commitment to their work rather than through more obvious methods such as threats and physical force;
2. control through selective recruitment: rather than recruiting whoever applies for work, capitalists hire only those with the technical competence or other desirable attributes and professional interest to perform on their own the necessary tasks to the required performance levels; and
3. control through allocation of resources: in some business units, administrators cannot significantly interfere with the operational management rather control is exercised by the determination of which units to support, which to milk for revenue, and which to divest.

How do each of these control mechanisms function within business format franchise operations? As reflected in the definitions above and as will be argued below, one of the foundations of the business format franchise is the standardization and simplification of tasks to permit ease of control and replication, and productive efficiency. The contractual requirement of franchisees to maintain the uniformity of their units means that deviances from the business blueprint may be spotted, and pressure brought to bear to retain the *status quo*. These deviations may be observed through the royalty mechanism and/or through the franchisor's supervisory functions, their area/territory managers and the employment of 'mystery shoppers' to report on standards of service and cleanliness, etc. In some franchise systems, franchisees are only permitted to acquire additional units depending on their adherence to franchisor-determined standards of behaviour. That is, they are rewarded for conforming to the franchisor's objectives rather than by financial performance alone.

Controls in the franchise relation are also insidious in nature, in addition to being more conspicuous. For example, within the confines of the New Institutionalist Approach, some people are motivated to become franchisees because they perceive that the franchisor's know-how and brand capital confers lower levels of risk of failure than if they were to operate independent businesses. Felstead (1993) concurs with this perspective; he contends that those people who opt to become franchisees do so on the basis of a set of perceived advantages: being provided with a ready-made business idea, a tried and tested format with which to operate, and the help and support of a large company readily at hand (p. 84). The fear of jeopardizing the loss of access to this expertise serves to control franchisee behaviour. Perhaps indicative of the importance of expert power in franchising, franchisee failure is often attributed to the lack of commitment to and understanding of their work (see Chapter 9). Another form of insidious control are the visits by the franchisor's representatives, such as area managers, to their franchisee's operations to see how they are doing; this is often little more than an opportunity to ensure conformance to the business blueprint.

Additional support for the insidous nature of controlling franchisees is provided by MacMillan (1995). He suggests that franchisors are biased away from recruiting those people with prior industry and self-employment experience because they fear that they may bring undesirable habits and malpractices to the relationship, which have the potential to disrupt other franchisor-franchisee relations. The franchisor is also able exercise control via the allocation of resources, such as the advertising levy. Although franchisees contribute to the advertising fund through the royalty process, it is the franchisor as the owner of the intellectual property who decides which media agency to use, the promotional message, and the promotional strategy. For example, the joint promotional campaign between McDonald's and Disney is controlled by the franchisor, not the franchisee. Furthermore, it is the franchisor who decides the regional mix of any advertising effort, which means that some franchisees receive less customer exposure than others. In short, therefore, the franchisee is open to exploitation in two ways and derives from the imbalance of power, differing objectives, and the possession of knowledge:

1. the contractual conditions of the franchise agreement which permits the opportunity for the franchisor to drive costs down whilst driving revenues up; and
2. the lack of support for the franchisee by the franchisor once the contract has been signed.

Clearly, franchisees are not free men as the popular press, among others, would have people believe. Importantly, the franchise relationship is also characterized by goal conflict: franchisees are motivated by profits and franchisors are orientated towards sales growth. Despite the arguments of the agency theorists, sales growth does not necessarily equate with profit growth. Indeed, reflective of this distinction, McKiernan (1992) depicts a portfolio matrix which differentiates those businesses pursuing sales growth from those which are more profit growth orientated, and suggests that different managerial capabilities are required to achieve each objective. This situation means that the franchisor is able to exploit the franchisee by pursuing strategies and offering promotions which maximize sales growth whilst having little effect on unit profitability.

Indicative of the conflict of interests in franchise relationships, Cohen (1971) indicates that among other common requirements (written or unwritten) in franchise arrangements which may maximize profits for the franchisor while minimizing them for the franchisee are:

1. *site location:* the franchisee must seek the franchisor's approval concerning the site location which means that the franchisee is not free to use a site which he believes to be to his best advantage;
2. *rental of signs from the franchisor:* in some cases identical signs meeting the franchisor's specifications could be purchased at a much lower cost from an independent source at a much lower cost;
3. *paying a percentage of gross sales for advertising:* in most instances the franchisee has little voice in how or where the advertising will be spent, which means that franchisors are appropriating the 'surplus labour' of their franchisees; and
4. *approval of the franchisor before the franchisee can sell any part of his business,* while the franchisee has no veto of a sale by the franchisor.

In order to ensure conformance to the business blueprint, franchisees are constrained by strict contractual controls, the lack of ownership of intangible assets (the intellectual property) which subjects the franchisee to limitations on establishing an independent business of a similar nature and in a comparable location as the franchised unit, and are typically subject to unilateral changes imposed by the franchisor, all of which distinguish them from being self-employed in a true sense and permits the franchisor to exploit their franchisees.

> In its more extreme form . . . the franchising system, with its present degree of strong market control over franchisees, provides for outright exploitation of the franchisees by the franchisor. This is accomplished through such methods as: forcing unprofitable volume on the franchisee in cases where the franchisor is paid a royalty related to gross volume; forcing franchisees to purchase over-priced equipment and supplies from the franchisor; disallowing the franchisee to sell profitable complementary or supplementary products of other firms; acquiring a site location for reasons other than profitable potential for the franchisee; exploiting the franchisee while being his landlord as well as the franchisor; taking over highly profitable franchisees as corporate stores; and so on. (Mallen, 1978; p. 198)

Franchisors also control their franchisees through contractually restricting the source of their purchases, which means that their costs of sales have the potential to be higher than, and their gross margins to be lower than, those generated by independent businesses. Franchisees are only able to purchase supplies from nominated suppliers and, in some instances, they are required to buy certain items from the franchisor (Lafontaine, 1992). While some concern has been expressed as to whether such practices constitute a restraint of trade, franchisors have defended their position by claiming that constraining franchisee discretion in this area serves to retain product quality and brand image (Adams and Pritchard-Jones, 1990).

These restrictions and the potential for exploitation does not mean, however, that franchisees could be construed to represent labour in the true sense of the Marxist meaning. Depending on the nature of the product/service basis of the franchise, franchisees employ their own labour and, in some instances, fixed assets such as machinery. This situation means that franchisees act as capitalists because they can exploit their work-force and assets in order to accumulate wealth (Krueger, 1991). Using the Marxist framework, therefore, it is also possible to suggest reasons why some franchisees are eager to acquire additional units from the franchisor: it permits them to accumulate wealth by exploiting their own labour forces while, at the same time, benefitting from the additional exposure of the brand within a given territory. As a result of the legally enforceable restrictions imposed by the franchisor and the ownership of labour-services, however, they cannot be construed to be capitalist in the true sense of Marxist meaning either. The franchisee is therefore a hybrid because he stands midway between labour and the capitalist. Unlike the employee, he enjoys possession of some means of production and control over his own labour. Unlike the capitalist, who enjoys outright ownership of the means of production (intellectual and physical), complete control over his own labour and full ownership of the product of his work, the franchisee has only conditional possession of the intellectual means of production (dependent upon the payment of initial payments, royalties and the purchase of certain contractually-specified products from the franchisor over the period of the contract). He also has partial control over his own labour (since he has to conform to the franchisor's brand specifications/marketing mix, but may have some leeway over opening hours) and partial ownership since the fruits of the franchisee's labour accrue to the franchisor via the royalty mechanism and through his contribution to building the brand equity of the system. Given these restrictions, the contention by Shook and Shook (1993), among others, that franchisees are self-employed is misleading because it suggests that franchisees are a propertied class: they are owners of land, labour, capital, and know-how. In fact, they are no such thing:

> . . . the appearance of franchisees investing large sums of money in the purchase of the *physical* means of production (raw materials, plant, equipment) and the hiring of their own workforce should not be taken automatically as evidence of their unambiguously capitalist credentials. To be sure, production cannot be set into motion without the physical means of production and labour power to be put to work; but the franchisor's organizing ability, the use of a well-known trademark, and access to a depth of experience and 'know-how' is also crucial to the success of the franchisee's business. It is through the provision of the so-called *mental* means of business that franchisors have a 'hold' on their franchisees' businesses and the grounds on which they are able to take a part of the value produced . . . (Felstead, 1993; p. 76 – emphasis in the original)

In sum, Felstead's (1993) consideration of the role of power, in both its insidious and conspicuous forms, within franchise relationships permits the researcher to understand the managerial and operational boundaries of franchising. As shall be argued in Chapter 7, power relations serve to act as either a facilitator or inhibitor to the flow of new ideas and concepts between the franchisor and franchisee, and are therefore instrumental in affecting the development of competitive advantages and, ultimately, survival. Unlike other behavioural studies (such as Hough, 1986) of the power disparity between franchisors and their franchisees, Felstead's application of the Marxist perspective also permits dynamic analysis of franchise relationships. Franchising is not an isolated context of life, producing various psychological and economic states for individuals, but derives from complex social relationships and interactions between the franchisee and franchisor as well as between the various social networks to which they belong.

The perspicuousness of Felstead's arguments also allows the researcher to position franchisee-franchisor relations within a broader societal framework via a consideration of the franchisee's ownership of factors of production. From this work, the observation can be made that franchisees are not self-employed in a pure sense because they are subject to controls other than those imposed by society and they pay the franchisor rent for the use of his intellectual capital and, in some instances, certain fixed assets. Nor are they necessarily labour in a pure sense because they employ and exploit their own workforces in order to get more profit out of less cost and, thereby, accumulate their own wealth. Despite the utility of his work, there are however limitations because his analysis requires additional insight into the following issues, among others.

Alternative explanations of the motivation to franchise

If franchises are an efficient organizational form because they permit the franchisor to accumulate capital through the surplus labour of franchisees, why is franchising activity more pronounced in some economic sectors, as Chapters 1 and 2 show, than others? One potential explanation for varying levels of diffusion among economic markets and sub-sectors suggested by both the New Institutionalists and by Felstead is that management does not behave in a totally rational manner. This is because people are perceived to have limited analytical and data processing powers compared to the economist's assumption of rational behaviour. Thus, the lack of adoption of franchising by some businesses is partially attributable to management's lack of realization that it is a more efficient method of capital accumulation than other organizational forms.

This said, however, the New Institutionalist's evidence for supporting the contention of franchising's efficiency *vis-à-vis* other structural types is somewhat spurious because of its narrow focus. When comparing the costs and speed of expansion, for example, between wholly-managed and franchised chains, agency theorists examine the associated costs with each type to illustrate how franchising is superior. Although of interest, such comparisons appear to made without consideration for why and how franchising emerged when it did, as well as without regard for other organizational forms operating within a particular economic setting. Arguably, franchisors are only one set of business types within a market (see Chapter 4). Furthermore, those presenting the positive face of franchising suggest that the activity is a form of alliance. Extant research concerning the motivations for alliance formation, however, indicates that there is a plethora of reasons for their existence (including gaining access to sources of continuous innovation), not all of which have been explored in the franchise literature.

Others may argue that the technological and human capital differences required to operate in different markets accounts for some of the variation in the penetration of the activity (Micheal, 1996). While both explanations are valid arguments, they are not complete. One additional reason for the variation is that the decision to franchise a business entails change and disruption to the existing power relations within an organization (see Chapter 3). Resistance to this change may derive from various levels and pockets of power within the organization and serve to dampen the potential impact an innovation may have. For example, a business owner made decide not to become a franchisor because he feels unabe to trust franchisees in spite of the presence of legal frameworks to reduce the incidences of opportunistic behaviour.

Resistance to change may also derive from labour. Although Marxist researchers could contend that this behaviour is an expression of the labour's conflict with capitalists, it is apparent that some groups are more resistant than others to changes and, in some firms, it is labour which initiates changes in working practices that impact the functioning and existence of other members of the workforce. The point is that labour does not act in a unified way to counterbalance the power of the capitalist and nor do the varying classes of labour have common values – or 'cultures' (Riley, 1984). Thus, whilst the working class is subordinate to capitalists because of their lack of possession of factors of production, some people within this class may perceive franchising in a negative way even though it could permit them to acquire more capital than their current position allows.

Small businesses

Felstead makes an important point about franchisors, but fails to develop it further when analyzing the motivation to franchise. He indicates that franchising has few natural barriers to potential entrants and the majority of franchisors are small businesses. As a consequence of this situation, owners of small businesses are motivated to franchise in order to overcome resource constraints, such as lack of access to capital, local market knowledge and a managerial infrastructure to establish, implement, monitor and control operating standards, via the franchisee's payments and motivation. In short, therefore, it could be argued that franchising permits the franchisor to avoid the issues usually associated with expansion and the achievement of market power:

> ... chains are like the Roman Empire: the lines of communication grow long, the attention that the owners can give becomes diluted, standards slip and, before you know it, you're in trouble. (Miller, 1996; p. 5)

In turn, such behaviour suggests that firms are engaged in bench-marking activities and that the decision to franchise is, for some businesses, indicative of a desire to negate or to realize the potential competitive advantages accruing from franchising. The view that franchising may permit the franchisor to surmount a plethora of limitations to realizing growth means that it has some innate attractions. The attractions possibly increase the likelihood of imitation within a specific economic setting. But, such reasoning by managers, academics, and the popular franchise press runs the risk of being tautological; it seems to postulate that firms involved in attractive activities, such as franchising, are successful. Unfortunately, however, it does not address why some incumbent businesses are in advantageous positions in the first instance, and why some firms are able to sustain these and others are not.

Other evidence shows that strategies based on the achievement of market power can be damaging to the firm, with financial performance showing a negative relationship to market power-based strategies (Black and Boal, 1994). Thus, despite the potential benefits accruing from franchise-based expansion, franchising cannot be seen as a panacea for all limitations to growth. Additionally, the size differences between franchisors suggests that the franchise fraternity can be structurally differentiated into core and periphery players, with the latter being most at risk from failure. In other words, some franchisors are not the large organizations they are thought to be, nor do they necessarily possess the culture, experience, resources, competences, or capabilities required to be involved in franchising.

Furthermore, the structural differentiation of franchisors means that the activity may not be the success that the positive face of franchising would have people believe (see Chapter 8), especially as competitive advantage depends on a business's underlying technical skills rather than on particular products or services (Hamel and Prahalad, 1990). In order to maintain and improve competitive position, therefore, the knowledge and skill base must be actively managed. After all, like labour, some capitalists have greater power than others because of their knowledge and skills, and such a condition may have implications for the way in which we conceptualize the structure of the franchise fraternity. Instead of thinking of capitalists as omnipotent, some franchisees in small systems may be in better bargaining positions relative to those in larger systems.

Labour market inequalities

Felstead explores the rationale why people want to become a franchisee by interviewing a number of existing franchisees. His summarized responses of a survey of about 200 franchisees indicate that people are driven to pursue this career option because of three main reasons:

1. they wanted to be self-employed but lacked a business idea to put into practice;
2. they wanted security against failure; or
3. they wanted to be associated with a company.

While these results are consistent with other research findings (Knight, 1984), there is also some suggestion that franchisees are purchasers of investment products:

> Since franchise opportunities are investment products, it is not unreasonable to expect potential entrepreneurs to be most concerned about risk and return . . . The franchisees do not prefer one industry or franchisor *per se*. Industry or 'brand' loyalty can be explained by the franchisee's education and managerial experience. If these skills match the requirements, it reduces the risk and raises the return from purchasing a franchised outlet in a specific industry or from a particular franchisor. (Martin, 1996; p. 102)

There are, however, several important failings in such an argument. Firstly, cross-cultural analyses of potential franchisees in Britain and the USA (Stanworth and Kaufmann, 1996) illustrate that differing franchisees prefer specific industries and franchisors. Franchisees have been shown to choose from a few options, typically up to five, and all seem to be within a particular economic setting (Hatcliffe *et al*, 1995). Furthermore, the decision to be a franchisee is often a secondary consideration to the type of business the person would like to operate. In addition, potential franchisees have shown a tendency to elect business sectors in which they have had no or little prior work experience. Secondly, education and managerial experience are but two of the variables influencing the decision to become a franchisee and the type of franchise purchased. For example, Fulop's (1996) survey of over 400 UK franchisees indicates that 44% quoted previous experience as a major factor in the decision to enter a particular franchise sector. A quarter of the sample mentioned that 'personal interest' was the most important reason for their decision.

Of particular significance is both Felstead's and Martin's omission to explore the broader implications of labour market inequalities, despite the former's mention of franchisor's recruitment biases, and their impact on the decision to become a franchisee. In any society, there exist non-class forms of inequality based on status, such as gender, race, and religion, which often cut across social divisions based on property. These non-property bases of social division also serve to prevent some people from gaining access to the factors of production and, consequently, are worthy of further exploration to elucidate

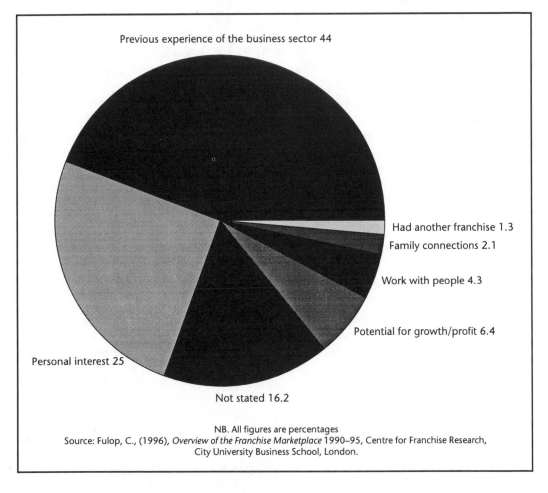

Previous experience of the business sector 44

Had another franchise 1.3

Family connections 2.1

Work with people 4.3

Potential for growth/profit 6.4

Personal interest 25

Not stated 16.2

NB. All figures are percentages
Source: Fulop, C., (1996), *Overview of the Franchise Marketplace* 1990–95, Centre for Franchise Research,
City University Business School, London.

Figure I: Reasons why franchisees select a particular franchise sector

their impact on the decision to become a franchisee. For example, the franchise fraternity is biased by gender – women represent only a minority of franchisees (Dant *et al*, 1996) – and there are also ethnic differences, among others. To be fair, however, this is often a criticism of the Marxist model of society *per se* rather than one which is necessarily unique to Felstead.

Furthermore, not all people want to become franchisees, even if they could afford to. In some instances, the financing issue plays only a minor role in affecting the decision to become a franchisee. Banks are often willing to lend finance to potential investors with collateral at low rates of interest because they perceive that franchising is low risk (Stern and Stanworth, 1988; 1994), which serves to reduce some of the financial barriers to entry. In addition, a small minority of franchisors provide part or all of the funding themselves to suitable applicants (the loan is repaid like other business loans). Other UK franchisors have used the Government Loan Guarantee Scheme, but this had the disadvantage that it excluded retailers. Such options mean that people have an array of options in financing a franchise, but there appears to be a shortfall of prospective franchisees nonetheless (MacMillan, 1995).

Arguably, there is an implicit issue of status, which is another form of social stratification and has some connections with power. According to Conway *et al* (1996), for example, higher occupational status is usually associated with greater power due to high-status individuals' social positions, control over punishment and rewards (via the ownership of factors of production), or knowledge. Thus, franchisors may be perceived as having greater status than franchises and some franchisors (and other capitalists) have more status and power than others. Equally, Conway *et al* argue that people with greater power are often attributed greater status. Status seems to result from the unequal rewards and power attached to different occupational positions, which are a cause of the mobility of individuals into certain positions. Hence, working in a fast food restaurant, for example, may be considered by some people as being low status because: it is in the service sector; it requires low levels of technical knowledge; it has low levels of discretion and authority; and it generates low levels of pay relative to other occupations.

This situation may also suggest that some people do not categorize franchising as a career alternative because they do not perceive that franchising confers the status and privileges they desire. In addition, some franchises have longer queues of potential investors because they are perceived to have better status – such as a longer track record in franchising – than other franchise enterprises, and are perceived to be better able to fulfil the investor's status ambitions. It is important to observe that these perceptions are coloured by people's network culture, or the common value system of prestige and status among a group of interacting and interlocking individuals rather than just economic criteria alone. In other words, people at differing levels of the social hierarchy may have different perceptions of what constitutes 'high status' not only by virtue of their relative occupational position but also because of the cultural milieu of their immediate network.

Culture does not only serve to colour perceptions but can also serve to hamper the realization of occupational status by certain groups, such as women, because of the actions (based on cognitive categorizations, beliefs, and values) of other groups. Howard (1994) – to name but one social scientist arguing in the same vein – contends that social cognition and culture concerns how people make sense of other people and of themselves. They determine the individual's status relative to others; some manual workers, for instance, may categorize their non-manual counterparts as being of lower status because they perceive them as having lower levels of utility to society (Parker *et al*, 1972). The terms refer to both the acquisition and the processing of social information, and to the social context in which and through which these activities occur.

Howard (1994) argues that social cognition articulates explicitly how social structures are carried in individuals' mental systems through the process of categorization, a process which shapes and is shaped by culture. The content of the group dimensions on which people are prone to categorize reveals the connections between social and cognitive structures; categorization, therefore, affects stereotyping, prejudice, and discrimination and leads to selective information gathering. For example, women are perceived as having lower status than men in many cultures. Conway *et al* (1996) suggest that some of the foundation of this situation derives from the perception by women themselves and characterization by men that they are more communal and nurturant and less agentic and assertive than men. Such perceptions may, in turn, affect both the type of jobs women apply for and the openings made available to them. In addition, franchisees may be less prone to collectivization because they categorize themselves as independent entrepreneurs (capitalists); collectivization may be construed as being a form of unionism, and thus more of an activity associated with labour.

Clearly, culture, status and economic position are potentially important explanatory factors concerning the diffusion of franchising and type of investor attracted to the activity. In this sense, Felstead's and others (for example, Peterson and Dant, 1990) analysis of the motivating factors influencing the decision to become a franchisee omits the effects of culture and social cognition on career choice. The omission of any consideration of the importance that culture and social cognition plays in affecting the diffusion of franchising as a career option and as a choice of organizational structure is therefore of particular significance not only in Felstead's work, but in franchise research at large.

Continuity and change

One of the key features of the Marxist perspective is social reproduction, which refers to the way in which the ideologies of the capitalist class (those who occupy positions of the greatest power and privilege), because of their access to legitimating bodies, are propagated through institutions such as schools, the law, and political interests. That is to say, the social and political definitions of those in dominant positions tend to become objectified and enshrined in major institutional orders, so providing the moral framework of the entire social system (Parkin, 1971). This is not to say, however, that this class shares common values *per se*, but the differences are not likely to be fundamental with regard to the values underlying class inequalities and its institutional supports. Equally, it is not to say that the differing strata of society necessarily illustrate a set of common values. Rather,

> ... it could ... be suggested that the subordinate value system represents what could be called a 'negotiated version' of the dominant value system. That is to say, dominant values are not so much rejected or opposed as modified by the subordinate class as a result of their social circumstances and restricted opportunities. Members of the underclass are continually exposed to the influence of the dominant values by way of the education system, newspapers, radio and

television, and the like. By virtue of the powerful institutional backing they receive these values are not readily negated by those lacking other sources of knowledge and information . . . The tendency among the under-priviliged is not to reject these values, and thus create an entirely different normative system, but to negotiate or modify them in light of their own existential conditions. (Parkin, 1971; p. 92)

As franchise contracts – like employment contracts – are inherently biased in favour of the franchisor and franchisees are only permitted to gain access to the franchisor's brand capital for a specific period of time, it may be argued that franchising serves is a form of social reproduction. Franchising, in embodying a form of capitalism, serves to accumulate wealth and knowledge for the capitalist without necessarily tranferring ownership to franchisees, but also offers the potential to accumulate their own wealth via the exploitation of their labour. It is this promise, as well as cultural issues and labour market inequalities, which permit the franchises to reproduce their particular form of capitalism via appealing to franchisees who, in turn, manipulate their own labour force as a way of accumulating their own capital. Furthermore, franchising may be chosen because it is seen as being a superior method of accumulating capital by both the franchisor and franchisee. But, there is also a capacity for opposition to the dominant ideology:

> Structuralist theories of reproduction present the dominant ideology . . . as impenetrable. Everything its too neatly. Ideology always pre-exists and pre-empts any authentic criticism. There are no cracks in the billiard ball smoothness of process. All specific contradictions and conflicts are smoothed away in the universal reproductive functions of ideology. [But] . . . social agents are not passive bearers of ideology, but active appropriators who reproduce existing structures only through struggle, contestation and a partial penetration of those structures. (Willis, 1977; p. 175)

Franchise systems are implicitly conflictful, which is evident from another manifestation of social reproduction. Franchises are based, ideally, on a proven and tried-and-tested recipe for business success. The importance of replication and standardization which this implies suggests that franchisee-originated innovation is seen as inherently illegitimate. Nonetheless, innovation occurs – albeit to varying degrees. One rationale for its occurrence among some franchisees is the implicit conflict between the franchisor and the franchisee deriving from the incongruity of their objectives, and between the franchisee and his labour-force. This variance points to a situation where some members of the subordinate class are willing to accept the *status quo*, but others do not necessarily perceive that such fatalism is the only response compatible with adaptation. Indeed, despite possible comparisons with unionism, some franchisees form buying groups in order to improve their bargaining position *vis-à-vis* their franchisor (Honig-Haftel and Jones, 1996) and, thus, their material situation; others engage in incremental innovations in order to improve their position. In as far as such actions are not fatalistic, they could be construed to reflect beliefs and values regarding the inequalities of distribution of rewards. But, despite the belief held by some franchisors that such actions are radical because they threaten the *status quo* of the franchise relationship, it is perhaps reasonable to regard such actions as an accommodative response to inequality; the responses do not call into question the values underlying the existing reward structure, nor do they pose any threat to the institutions which support this structure (Parkin, 1971) because conflict in franchise relations is often latent (not expressed overtly). The accommodative nature of these actions differentiates them from the behaviour advocated by the more radical Marxists, whose beliefs are fundamentally opposed to those underlying the institutions of capitalism. In the societal context franchises inhabit, therefore, is the theme of continuity and change arising out of the inevitable struggle between those who own and control the means of production and those who do not:

> This history of all hitherto society is the history of class struggles. Freeman and slave . . . oppressor and oppressed, stood in constant opposition to one another, carried on an uninterrupted, now hidden, now open fight, a fight that each time ended, either in a revolutionary reconstitution of society at large, or in a common ruin of contending parties. (Marx and Engels, 1967; p. 1)

This inevitable struggle for status and access to the factors of production suggests that there is an in-built tendency for the adoption of new practices and behaviours within franchises designed to increase wealth accumulation. Unfortunately, Felstead does not consider the practicalities nor the historical potential of such conflict within the franchise relationship but, given ever-shortening product life cycles and the intensification of competition, there is a fundamental need for innovation. It is also conceivable that franchising is, in itself, a form of innovation and has feudal society as its foundation stone.

Towards an alternative perspective

Felstead's industry represents a structural sociology of franchising because it analyzes the patterns of human behaviour and interactions among individuals and groups that enable franchises to function. But, while Felstead's work deserves applause because it represents one of the few applications of the structural sociology approach to examining franchise relationships, his efforts are a stepping block to other research efforts in this vein. The issues listed above suggest that the successful application of the Marxist conceptualization of society to the franchise context has its limitations and is, therefore, perhaps indicative of the need for additional work. Specifically, the inability of the framework to provide a comprehensive analysis of some of the more micro-issues in franchising possibly warrants a modified approach. After all, the Marxist perspective represents a macro-level theory because of its emphasis on production relations, class, and society. As a reflection of the varying levels of social organization, the complexity of social environments, and the relative nature of social structures, however, there exist other perspectives of behaviour. For example, Levi-Strauss and Howard (1994) are emphatic of the 'deep structure' of language and how people interpret the world around them, and Burt (1992) is concerned with the distribution and patterns of social positions within networks.

Continuing in the vein of structural sociology, one alternative to the pure Marxist approach is the social closure theory, which has applications to extant perspectives concerning the origin of competitive advantages as well as the stratification of society (Kay, 1993; Porter, 1985). Under this construct, for example, members of a group of strategically similar firms seek the monopolization of resources via collaboration between other members at the same level of production, or at other stages of the supply chain, in order to help guarantee themselves advantages and the exclusion of social and economic opportunities to outsiders. In industry, therefore, closure occurs through the presence of barriers to entry and mobility (see Chapter 4), such as high fixed costs, expert knowledge and exclusive contracts with buyers. For example, brewers have sought to exclude other such companies from market access in some regions through 'tying' the publican with sole supply agreements for their beer in exchange for loans and other financial incentives (see Chapter 1). Such behaviour has also been observed historically; Braudel (1982) shows that the medieval traders influenced the wealth accumulation of other members of their class:

> Solidarity between merchants was in some ways solidarity within a class, though it did not of course rule out business rivalries between individuals, cities and between 'nations' as a national group of merchants were called . . . Trade circuits and communications were regularly dominated by powerful groups who appropriated them and might forbid other groups to use them. (p. 153)

According to Parkin (1974), the social closure framework provides superior explanatory power with which to examine and analyze the social inequalities between and within social classes, and observe inequalities based on ethnicity, religion, and gender. It is superior to the pure Marxist approach because the framework suggests that conflict within and between status groups is not purely an economic phenomenon, nor governed solely by economic considerations. Distinctions are also observable by status, where the stress on status is on expressing esteem and prestige rather than on the equal rights of citizenship created by the modern legal order. Status differences cannot be fully understood, however, without accounting for some of the economic and cultural differences between them. Within the same profession, therefore, it is possible that incumbents belong to different status groups according to their social origin, education, and gender. For example, propertyless, contract employees are often internally differentiated according to attributes of their contract of employment, such as salary conditions, security of employment, pension entitlements, and career prospects. These are often the marginal forms of employment carried out by ethnic minorities and/or women because this is the only type of employment open to them.

At the other end of the social spectrum, there is some evidence to suggest that the retail sector is to some extent the Cinderella of the business elite, characterized by a relatively plebian leadership and a high degree of fragmentation because of little use of integrating mechanisms. Nonetheless, the directors of large retail organizations illustrate collectivist exclusion because of a tendency to recruit family members to the topmost positions; they have also attended the traditional elite schooling institutions, which possibly differentiates them from other leaders in the retail industry, but they are similar in that they illustrate limited levels of connectedness with other large retailers (Berkley-Thomas, 1978).

For Parkin (1974), groups seek the 'monopolization' of resources in order to increase their rewards and opportunities, which is achieved by the closure of social and economic openings, and leads to competition for resources and conflict. This closure exists in two main forms: exclusionary and usurpationary. Within instances of exclusionary closure, one group attempts to secure for itself a privileged position, at the expense of some other group, through a process of subordination and the downward exercise of power which leads to the creation of a group, class or stratum of inferiors (Stokowski, 1994). Unlike the Marxist analysis of exclusionary closure based on property, Parkin indicates that exclusion can be effected by a plethora of other criteria, including ethnicity, gender, age, etc. Thus, Parkin provides a richer framework than that encompassed by the Marxist approach. Indeed, most students of stratification would agree that social inequality is a multi-dimensional phenomenon and cannot be explained on any one single criteria.

Parkin (1974) also observes that there are two main types of exclusionary closure: collectivist and individualist. These two routes to social privilege form two ends of a continuum rather than being mutually exclusive variants. At the collectivist extreme, an individual possesses privileges as a member of a group deriving from their biological make-up and are based on inheritance, such as ethnicity and/or gender, which reduces social mobility and encourages class reproduction. For example, labour market inequalities based on race has had the effect of forcing ethnic minorities into alternative forms of employment, such as self-employment and franchising (see Chapter 5). At the other pole, the individualist end of the spectrum, exclusion is effected by criteria which are purely individual, such as the possession of academic qualifications or the ownership of experiences and/or skills which serve to differentiate an individual/business from another, and have limited transferability because of their tacitness. This is an acquired form of exclusion. As inferred above, it is this form of exclusionary closure which differentiates the more successful franchisors from the rest. Between the two poles are those forms of social privilege which can be both inherited and acquired, such as private property. In this sense, becoming a franchisee does not permit the individual to bequeath a business which, if the popular press is to be believed, has a higher chance of success to his heirs because of the limitations concerning ownership and the fixed time period of the majority of franchise contracts. What can be bequeathed, however, is the capital wealth and access to property ownership that being a franchisee supposedly brings [for legal interpretations see: Prontaprint Plc v. Landon Litho Ltd (1987); Herbert Morris Ltd v. Saxelby (1916); Bridge v. Deacons (1984); and Kall Kwik Printing (UK) Ltd v. Rush (1996)].

Parkin (1974) observes that exclusionary closure is the more prevalent form of closure in society, but such exclusion can provoke attempts at usurpationary closure, or the use of upward power. This is designed either to try and stem the degree of exploitation by capital, or to try and counteract it through collectivization, such as trade unions and franchisee buying groups. Usurpationary power may also be translated as resistance to change or the attempted implementation of innovations from above, and derive from people's low tolerance of ambiguity and uncertainty, as well as a lack of trust. The anxiety and apprehensiveness that they suffer may lead them to oppose changes that they consider to be beneficial. Such behaviour, for example, may hamper a business's conversion to being a franchise, as well as pursuing other developmental options such as joint ventures. Furthermore, some individuals may be unwilling to change their current occupational status even though they consider that franchising may permit them to accumulate greater levels of capital than they now generate.

In some cases, particular social groups can adopt the strategy of dual closure where a subordinated group is, itself, responsible for the exclusion of some other social group. For example, a worker – whose class is defined by the lack of ownership of the means of production – may be adverse to including women and ethnic minorities in their work setting. Such usurpationary struggle may occur for a number of reasons. One such reason is that the group incumbents feel that the inclusion of those people perceived to be of lower status may affect the way in which they feel about themselves, and the ability to monopolize certain resources and power positions. For instance, certain trades are marked by entry qualifications, such as having reached a certain level of training and competence; once passed, the individual is permitted to perform certain functions and thereby accumulate capital from those activities. Another reason may be that the incumbents would have to alter their beliefs, values, and behaviour (including their language) – that is, they feel that would have to change their culture. Thirdly, the incumbents feel that the inclusion of women and ethnic minorities, who are seen as part of the marginal workforce, may reduce their latitude to negotiate pay increases and, thereby, widen the gap between capital and labour.

The characteristic chosen as the pretext for exclusion is often that which is most easily seized upon, such as religion, gender, educational qualifications, and/or race. Not all attempts at exclusion, however, are successful. This is because the ability of one subordinated group to exclude some other subordinated group is a consequence of the latter being defined as legally or socially inferior by the dominant class and state. In other words, exclusionary closure is attainable if it is sanctioned – overtly or otherwise – by those who own the factors of production. From this situation, two observations are evident. Firstly, the latter group are already vulnerable to exclusion because the less-propertied class express a similar ideology as their more propertied peers; and secondly, class societies, via the propertied classes' control of the 'mental means of production', are reproduced by the normative integration of the mass of the population (Parkin, 1974).

Arguably, this suggested framework of analysis enriches the Marxist meta-theory by accounting for non-economic forms of inter-class differentiation. It also helps to account for intra-class differences through the issue of status. What are the implications of this suggested framework for interpreting the dynamics of franchising?

Implications for franchise research

Much of the popular press, and certainly members of the franchise fraternity itself, propound that franchises are a form of alliance or partnership. Under this guise, franchisees are typically described as being 'in business for themselves, but not by themselves', and there exists a commonality of interests and goals. This is the 'Jekyll' face of franchising, and one which has been repeatedly employed to recruit investors. Felstead (1993) has questioned both the level of independence of the franchisee as well as the degree to which the parties to the relationship illustrate common objectives. Using a Marxist paradigm, he suggests that the franchisee does not own the mental means of production nor some of the more physical methods so much as rent them. He indicates that the franchisor is able to control the franchisee through both insidious and overt methods. As insightful as his work is, there are, however, limitations. These limitations lie primarily in the lack of debate concerning several increasingly important topics in franchise research. These subjects include: explanations for the motivation to franchise; the role of small businesses in franchising; the role of labour market inequalities; and the issues surrounding continuity and change. Yet, arguably, these subjects are of central importance to understanding the diffusion of franchising as an innovation and how innovation arises from within franchises, as well as the organizational form's future progress.

While Felstead's (1993) application of the Marxist framework to describe the power differences in franchise relationships is undoubtedly an appropriate one, it does not go far enough. This framework only employs the individual's access to factors of production as the differentiating variable. Non-class forms of inequality are evident in society, however, and these differences are apparent within and between classes. Thus, at differing levels of social strata, some groups are perceived as having more status than others. These differences within and between classes are culturally embedded and are maintained through exclusionary closure and the attempted monopolization of resources. Such differences do not only pertain to social settings but also the business arena. Some franchisors, for example, are better able to attract suitable investors because of their reputation and status. This situation suggests that such firms are able to realize competitive advantages because of the resources that the investors bring to the relationship. By contrast, those firms unable to gain access to such resources are more likely to withdraw from franchising. Furthermore, the dynamics within a competitive group can influence the decision to pursue franchising as firms manoeuvre for the monopolization of resources and for competitive advantage (see Chapter 4). As the task environments, technologies, and cultures of different competitive groups vary, so they may use alternative methods to accumulate capital and, thereby, status.

By applying Parkin's (1974) social closure theory additional insight may be provided to the important areas not covered by Felstead. For example, arguably one of the reasons why franchising illustrates varying degrees of diffusion by economic sector is because it has differing levels of status; in some firms franchising may not be adopted because of usurpationary power issues. Status also plays an important role in the decision to become a franchisee. Firstly, the decision may be aspirational: some people may want to improve their status through access to capital that franchising is perceived to bring. Secondly, some people may be of the opinion that franchising imbues increased status on them within their peer group because of the association with a brand name and that they are 'self-employed'. Thirdly, some individuals may become franchisees because of their exclusion from other forms of employment, as well as from their belief that franchising provides them with a less risk-laden route to improved social standing and capital accumulation than their own business would realize. Franchising has proved a popular career option by some people who have been made redundant. To others, franchising has no such status because it is not perceived as meeting their needs.

One implication for franchise research deriving from the use of Parkin's (1974) approach, is that there needs to be more emphasis on the birth, diffusion, survival and death processes in franchising and especially the role that innovation plays in each. Arguably, extant franchise research, particularly that from the USA, has been overly reliant on empirical analysis in an attempt to generate general 'laws' of behaviour in franchising. Empirical analysis is not, itself, the issue because appropriate statistical techniques serve to add insight and test hypotheses, especially about the fundamentally important life and death issues in franchising. Extant franchise research is also characterized by over-emphasis on explaining the minutiae of franchise relations, rather than analyzing the broader issues at stake. Academics of the franchise fraternity have usually shied away from contentious debates and, instead, either concerned themselves with essentially micro issues, such as 'encroachment' and local pricing policies or, alternatively, more theoretical discourse on transaction cost analysis, agency theory, ownership redirection, hierarchies versus markets debates, etc. Within such efforts, there has been too much emphasis on developing franchising as a science, where the general 'laws' are usually explanatory and predictive, unlike some aspects of the social sciences. The result, however, seems to be disparate and often confusing points of view with many important topics left unexplored.

Unfortunately, it seems that by focusing on the science of franchising, researchers have almost omitted to observe that their focus of debate is people's decision-making processes. Many of these decisions will not be rational, but will be shaped by their beliefs, their social network, their access to the factors of production, to name but a few variables. These decisions may conform to some of the general 'laws' of franchising, but cannot necessarily be predicted or deduced from such laws. Rather, such events as the decision to enter or withdraw from franchising requires some *post factum* rationale. As stated above, for example, not all individuals want to become a franchisee even if they could afford to do so. Some researchers have attributed such behaviour to a lack of awareness about franchising, but there potentially exists a plethora of other explanations which stem from the franchisor's exclusionary power, the investor's belief that franchising is a low status option, and their ability to pursue other career paths in settings where dual closure is not sanctioned.

Some commentators may be tempted to object to the application of closure theory on two counts. Firstly, the more empirically orientated franchise researchers may wish to criticize the application because it represents an *a priori* schema to analyzing the diffusion of franchising and the success of some franchises. In other words, the successful application of closure theory requires the adjustment of the facts to fit its tenets. Others may dismiss it as pure tautology because the theory is fundamentally descriptive in nature rather than being explanatory and predictive. In one sense these claims are valid, but these objections may not prove sufficient in themselves to reject closure theory. The failings of much extant franchise research to provide a framework of analysis, and an underlying need for augmenting Felstead's Marxist meta-descriptive theory of franchising, means that a descriptive approach is urgently required. Although only one possibility, Parkin's theory may help to classify and to make sense of what is happening when firms decide to franchise or to leave the activity, as well as when individuals decide to become franchisees. In this respect, the following analysis of franchising will hopefully provide at least the basis of such a descriptive approach and, thereby, differ from the majority of extant research efforts exploring the world of franchises.

Issues concerning the birth and diffusion of franchising

1 | Franchising: the commercialization of 'bastard' feudalism?

Time and time again we find . . . that inventions and discoveries we have made, and regarded as interesting technical developments, require the stimulation of a perceived need before they are developed and exploited, so often in ways quite different from the original perception.

John Harvey-Jones, Chairman of ICI, *Making It Happen*

We've fabricated a society of wolves and coyotes. Why does anybody think that we are better than we were in robber baron days?

Louis Auchinloss, US novelist and lawyer, *Honorable Men*

Introduction

Diffusion is the process by which an innovation is disseminated among potential users. The diffusion and adoption of franchising is such that franchises punctuate most aspects of everyday commercial life. They are particularly prevalent in petrol retailing, fast food, restaurants, and other service sectors – anywhere, it seems, where there are customers to be served. Most of the popular household brand names operating in the foodservice market, such as McDonald's, KFC, and Burger King, are franchises. Of late, franchising has been associated with government privatization activities, such as the railway network, and is also a technique employed by manufacturers in order to help realize market share objectives. Soft drink companies, such as Coca-Cola and PepsiCo, have contracted other businesses to bottle and distribute their products throughout supply chains. The soft drink companies sell their syrups to bottlers, who 'finish' the products and then sell them on. In the USA, business format and product-name franchises are recorded as representing over 35% of total retail sales; in Britain, patchy data suggests that both forms of franchising account for about 10% of retail sales (Felstead, 1993; Trutko *et al*, 1993). There are estimated to be around 500,000 franchise outlets in the USA and approaching 70,000 in Britain if the same definition is applied. Business format franchises, however, represent only a minority of the total franchise market. In Britain, they account for about 3% of retail sales, compared to 8% in the USA.

Many researchers of franchises concur that the majority of the development of business format franchising has occurred since the 1950s, but have not sought to explore why franchising grew so spectacularly when it did or how its rate of diffusion differs by industrial setting. Although widely used, franchising is certainly not a new concept: there were incidences of such arrangements being employed in medieval Europe. What is new, however, is the extent and scale of its use, the nature of modifications to its original form, and application to different industrial settings. As a result, the contemporary form of franchising could be construed to be the commercialization of a particular form of feudalism and, therefore, an innovation. This chapter explores a fundamental and largely unresolved question in extant franchise research: what were the conditions that favoured the growth of franchising or, rather, the application of feudalism to commercial settings?

Franchising as an innovation

By contending that franchising could be construed to be the commercialization of 'bastard' feudalism (see below), there is an implicit assumption that franchising is an innovation (and one which reinforces the capitalist system). The popular conception of an innovation is that of a form of technology, such as a computer, automobile, or some other form of machinery. The interpretation of technology and innovation with machines, apparatus, and equipment is of some concern because it has too narrow a focus and is, consequently, of limited use. Exploring the connotations of technology from a broader perspective, Winner (1977) has observed that three uses of the term have been prevalent in the social sciences:

1. technology refers to equipment and machinery;
2. technology refers to knowledge and skills; and
3. technology refers to the locus of the worker and arrangement of materials.

Such an approach is of particular interest because, as will be argued below, the diffusion of franchising has been influenced by an underlying trend towards standardization and uniformity, which has been achieved through the adoption of certain types of equipment and machinery and via the specification of tasks, authority, and responsibility in the workplace. As seen from the definitions of franchising above, the description is also pertinent to the relative position of power which franchisees occupy, as well as to the issues concerning training and the dissemination of knowledge throughout a franchise system.

Reflecting the differing approaches to defining technology, there is a variety of definitions of innovation and the literature usually draws a distinction between 'innovation' and 'invention' (Clipson, 1991; Davis, 1991). Invention usually implies 'break-through' (often of a technical nature), whilst innovation implies successful commercial use of such an invention, or some novel administrative use of a previously established body of knowledge (Aiken and Hage, 1971). Scarborough and Lannon (1994), for example, suggest that innovation includes adapting both ideas and artefacts into workable, productive applications in the specific product markets or work processes of individual firms or profit centres. Kanter (1985) offers a slightly differing approach:

> Innovation refers to the process of bringing any new, problem-solving idea into use. Ideas for reorganizing, cutting costs, putting in new budgeting systems, improving communication or assembling products in teams, are also innovations. Innovation is the generation, acceptance and implementation of new ideas, processes, products or services. It can thus occur in any part of a corporation, and it can involve creative use as well as original invention. Application and implementation are central to this definition; it involves the capacity to change or adapt. And there can be many kinds of innovation, brought about by . . . different kinds of people; the corporate equivalent of entrepreneurs. (p. 20)

Whether invention is part of innovation is a debate in its own right which need not impede us here. The point is that these definitions are sufficiently broad to include differing types and magnitudes of innovation pertaining to all parts of organizations and all aspects of their operation. To many companies, franchising represents a form of innovation because becoming a franchisor entails changes to the management of the organization, its strategy, structure, culture, and allocation of resources. To some degree, the cultural aspects of managing franchisees are, in themselves, relevant to innovation. The franchise literature argues that effective management of franchisees requires a multitude of skill-sets and an organizational culture which is suited to franchising (Forward and Fulop, 1993a; 1993b). As such, franchisee management inevitably entails innovation since it requires different skills to those required to manage employees. For some type of franchisor, this change is a potential source of failure. The franchisor may be unable to develop a distinctive competence (Blois, 1983; Porter, 1980) to encompass the rigours of franchisee management and the changing nature of the franchisor-franchisee relationship over time. To some degree, these relational changes will not just occur because of the franchisee's increasing confidence and ability as he gains experience, but also because of the increasing illiberality of the franchisor's and/or franchisee's the product/service marketplace. Arguably, therefore, the franchisor must be open to ongoing modifications in order to maintain/increase competitive position along the product/service life-cycle and be aware of the nature of that trajectory.

Shapes of franchise life-cycles

It is axiomatic in marketing, biological and sociological texts that products and life-forms experience birth, mature and suffer death. Despite an increasingly acrimonious debate concerning the death-rates of in franchise systems (see Chapters 8 and 9), franchising is no exception. If franchising is a form of innovation, then it should illustrate a distinct diffusion pattern at a general level as well as within the various economic sectors in which franchising is used as a vehicle for growth. The shape of the diffusion distribution is not a matter of being merely pedantic. The shape of the diffusion curve is important because it suggests the position of a particular innovation and where significant barriers to adoption may occur. By indicating the approximate location of the diffusion stage, a variety of suggestions may be offered to prolong the distribution of the innovation. It may also provide some insight to the time taken to provide a certain level of penetration. Given the efforts of the popular franchise press, among others, to portray franchising in a positive light, one may be forgiven in believing that the diffusion pattern was in the shape of a hockey-stick.

> Franchisors and their trade organizations insist that things aren't all that bad in the business. They regard the critics as overzealous, often misinformed, and sometimes dated in their understanding of current franchise practices . . . Despite the problems and abuses, most people in the industry see a boundless future for franchising. The future is there, to be sure, if the system can cope successfully with some thorny problems . . . When companies reach the point of dealing candidly and openly with the issue of independence, they may still have dissatisfied franchisees. But they will avoid that special bitterness that comes

from having been led down the garden path by a mirage-like American dream. (Burck, 1970; p. 152)

Such a 'J-shaped' pattern, however, may not be a wholly accurate depiction of the diffusion of franchising. Among such reasons as the vested interests in portraying growth in this manner, it seems to suggest that franchising *per se* becomes increasingly commonplace as a result of a desire to pursue growth. Arguably, in order to have a 'boundless future' franchising must be boundaryless and, thus, be suitable for use in broad array of economic sectors. Yet, not only are there a variety of other vehicles for realizing this objective and different options appear to be favoured in different industries (see Chapter 2), but diffusion curves can take a plethora of shapes. Indeed, according to numerous researchers of consumer behaviour, the diffusion of innovations, strategies and organizational designs typically take an 's-shaped' pattern (Brown, 1991; Gatignon and Robertson, 1989; Gold, 1981; Kikulis *et al*, 1995). This pattern is based on the rate of adoption by both customers purchasing a particular innovation and the actions of suppliers, providers of substitute products, potential new entrants, and competitors. Affecting this rate of adoption are: the degree of perceived risk in becoming an adopter; the perceived comparative advantage of the new product relative to that which is currently in use; barriers such as the life-style attributes and cultures of certain sets of consumers; experience effects; the presence of exogenous factors such economic uncertainty; and the extent and means to which information about the innovation is transmitted within the social milieu (Day, 1984).

Reflecting these forces, Rogers (1995) shows that the adopters of innovations may be classified, depending on their position in a normal distribution curve, as:

1. *innovators,* who are venturesome and whose interest in new ideas distinguishes them from social groups marked by peer pressures;
2. *early adopters,* who occupy positions of respect and status within local networks, and who therefore decrease uncertainty about a new idea by adopting it;
3. *early majority,* whose adoption is more deliberate and takes longer than either the innovators or early majority, but whose position between the very early adopters and the relatively late to adopt makes them an important category of people to the further diffusion of a particular innovation;
4. *late majority,* who are typically sceptical and cautious about adopting an innovation but may do so out of economic necessity and/or peer pressure; and
5. *laggards,* who are the last in the social social system to adopt a particular innovation because of their relatively low status position in their networks, and because their traditional focus means that they are extremely cautious in their adoption behaviours.

These categories can be applied to franchisors and franchisees, and may provide some insight to the time differences between networks of competing firms and their decision to franchise (see Chapter 4), and the adoption patterns by franchisees (see Chapter 5). Depending upon their level of investment and innovation, researchers of competitive strategy and market entry indicate that it is the innovators and early adopters who are able to realize positions of leadership (Buzzell and Gale, 1987). Accordingly, the maintenance of market share/competitive position cannot be achieved by overt emphasis on retaining the *status quo*.

The presence of an 's-shaped' diffusion curve may be visualized by a brief comparison between the development of franchising in Britain and the USA. As a result of the differences in the quality and availability of data recording the development of franchising in the two countries, two sources of information were used. To depict the pattern of diffusion in the USA, information recording the number of business format franchises and the population of product/tradename forms was used. This data derives from the annually produced *Franchising in the Economy* surveys produced by the US Department of Commerce. The development of franchising in Britain has been recorded on a semi-annual basis since 1984 in the jointly produced NatWest/BFA reports. The first edition of these reports (Power, 1984) provides a useful survey of franchising activity in the country between 1963 and 1984. Using the results of this survey and their summary of franchising's development between 1984 and 1990, it is apparent that the activity's diffusion is marked by a long tail of evolution and development between 1963 and 1984 and then a period of explosive growth until 1990. Indeed, the NatWest/BFA's figure of 379 franchise systems operating in Britain in 1990 represented an absolute increase of 46% over the 203 systems entering the market between 1963 and 1984.

Within the confines of the diffusion-cycle, it is apparent that business format franchising, like other innovations, has undergone a period of evolution, followed by rapid growth as other firms enter the market and compete for share. Figure 1.1 shows that, in the USA, a 'typical' 's-shaped' adoption curve, or life-cycle effect has evolved, with a period of consolidation occurring the late 1980s. This latter situation suggests two issues may be apparent in the US franchise market: first, that there has been/will be some shake-out of the smaller and weaker players (see Chapter 8); and second, that some form of innovation to the concept itself and/or the way it is marketed is necessary to rejuvenate growth. The trend in the USA reflects the ready acknowledgement by many researchers that much of the real development in franchising has occurred since World War II, with the growth method being used by both old and new companies alike, as well as in emerging sub-sectors where incumbents were eager to gain market share and the benefits associated with leadership. As with other innovations concerning organizational developments, franchising's diffusion has been assisted by the impossibility of creating property rights in the structural form itself. Structures, like strategies, can be imitated without fear of infringing patents or paying licence fees (Teece, 1980). The spread of franchising has also been facilitated by management consultants, banks, solicitors and the press, all of whom view the spread of franchising as an opportunity to accumulate capital and status.

The long tail of evolution and development in Britain, however, presents something of a dilemma. According to Rogers (1995), 'innovators' and 'early adopters' have high levels of influence and peer status which encourages others to take on the innovation, which results in an 's-shaped' curve. The long tail of evolution in the British franchise market suggests that:

1. the innovators and early adopters did not have as much influence as the behavioural assumptions embedded within the traditional 's-shaped' diffusion suggest. In other words, environmental considerations, such as a

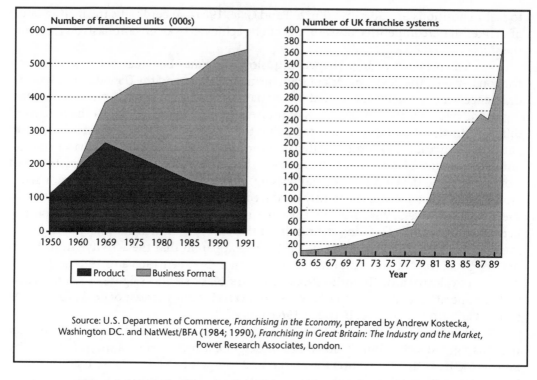

Source: U.S. Department of Commerce, *Franchising in the Economy*, prepared by Andrew Kostecka, Washington DC. and NatWest/BFA (1984; 1990), *Franchising in Great Britain: The Industry and the Market*, Power Research Associates, London.

Figure 1.1: *Growth of franchising in the USA, 1950–91 and the UK, 1963–90*

change in the availability of small-business finance, the rapid growth in the demand for services, or an increase in unemployment, may have had greater effect;

2. the time delay could be attributed to some firms waiting to see the successes of the early adopters before committing themselves. In turn, this may result in some firms illustrating a long time lag between inception and their decision to franchise but presents a number of other and additional questions, such as why would a competitor permit its rival to realize a potentially lower cost and faster rate of expansion and leave itself open to a lower rate of growth and sub-optimal performance?; and

3. the influence exerted by the early adopters to adopt franchising is felt, primarily, by the smaller and newer industry incumbents. These new entrants may have believed that franchising was a method of gaining market share rapidly and could, thereby, assist them to realize ambitions about corporate status and compete more effectively against their larger and earlier franchised counterparts. In this instance, there would be a comparatively short period of time between inception and embarking on franchised growth.

By examining one of the few sets of franchise directories covering the period 1984 to 1995, *The United Kingdom Franchise Directory* and reclassifying the 1,121 usable business format franchise entries (see Chapter 8 for further information) according to their Standard Industrial Classification codes (Table 1.1), it is evident that there appears to be substantial variation in the time differences between a firm's inception and embarking on franchising. This variability is evident from the coefficient of variation, which measures the relative magnitude of the standard deviation as compared with the average of the distribution of the time difference between inception and beginning to franchise. This measure suggests that, relative to the average time difference for each sub-sector, the average time difference for each hotel and catering franchise has been almost twice as variable as franchises in the accounting and advertising sub-sectors. In turn, these figures suggest that there are groups of firms within industries who possibly follow one another, but it is the newer businesses who appear to be more prone to franchising within a short period after inception. Although of interest, such figures do not necessarily show the shape of the

SIC sector description	Sub-sector	Inception versus franchising		
		Time difference in years		
		Average	Standard deviation	Coefficent of variation
Manufacture of pulp and paper products; publishing and printing	Print and publishing	2.9	5.2	1.79
Construction	Construction	4.2	8.9	2.12
Wholesale and retail trade; repair of motor vehicles, motorcycles and personal and household goods	Car maintenance	5.5	15.4	2.80
	Wholesale	5.4	17.6	3.26
	Retail	8.1	22.2	2.74
	Non-store retail	6.7	18.1	2.70
Hotels and restaurants	Hotel and catering	11.1	34	3.06
Transport, storage and communication	Taxi/cabs	6.6	4.8	0.73
	Travel agency	10.5	17.0	1.62
	Courier	3.5	5.4	1.54
Financial intermediation	Financial services	10.9	31.8	2.92
Real estate, renting and business activities	Real estate	5.2	8.2	1.58
	Rental	3.8	7.5	1.97
	Consultancy	10.5	31.9	3.04
	Accounting	3.7	5.5	1.49
	Employment agency	5.7	12.6	2.21
	Legal	1.1	0.8	0.73
	Advertising	2.1	3.3	1.57
	Commercial cleaning	3.4	5.5	1.62
	General business	2.9	5.6	1.93
Health and social work	Health care	2.2	2.3	1.05
Other community, social and personal service activities	Drainage	2.2	4.0	1.82
	Personal services	5.1	8.2	1.60
	Domestic services	1.8	1.6	0.89
	Driving school	15.4	28.8	1.87

Table 1.1: Time difference between inception and embarking on franchising

diffusion curve, but can be a step to assist in describing the skewness of the diffusion curves by industry sub-sector.

From both the analysis of the franchise directories and the surveys produced by the NatWest/BFA it is apparent that there appear to be differing levels of diffusion within different industries. Unfortunately, few analysts have explored either the pattern of development or the implications deriving from the shape of franchising's diffusion at a sectoral level. As such we do not know whether the aggregation of the sectoral effects could have resulted in the diffusion of franchising as a whole taking the form of an 's-shaped' curve. Equally, we do not possess insight concerning the speed with which markets reach saturation and when the probability of shake-out increases; and, importantly, because no account was taken of non-adopters we do not know if the 's-shaped' diffusion curve of franchising is, in fact, an accurate depiction of its spread. There is, therefore, a fundamental need to explore the diffusion patterns at both an aggregate and a sectoral level because:

1. the implications of the potential future of franchising as a strategy for expansion within those markets;
2. to indicate where possible barriers to adoption are present;
3. to provide some indication of the life-cycle stage of the franchise fraternity within a market under consideration. As strategies differ by life-cycle stage (Porter, 1980; Strebel, 1987), establishing the type of life-cycle and its present stage may be of use to incumbents to formulate appropriate strategic choices;
4. to suggest the potential attractiveness of franchising activity in a particular sector to those considering on pursuing this strategy for growth.

As many students will attest, the appearance of product life-cycles is usually shown as an 's-shape' form, with the varying number stages of development indicative of increasing levels of market illiberality. It would, however, be erroneous to suppose that the shape of such cycles is fixed. In fact, product life-cycles have highly variable shapes, such as style, fashion and fad life-cycles. The same is true for statistical distribution curves; in terms skewness, they can be: negatively skewed with the tail to the left; positively skewed with the tail to the right; or symmetrical. By establishing the median time difference between inception and becoming a franchisor for each of the sectors in Table 1.1, and the average and standard deviations of those values, an estimation of skewness is presented in Table 1.2. The table shows that the almost all of the various sub-sectors comprising the British franchise fraternity illustrate a positive skew on the time of between inception and franchising, which is in line with the shape of the sector illustrate above.

In addition to illustrating different degress of skewness, diffusion curves also differ by the degree of peakedness, or kurtosis. In terms of kurtosis, a distribution curve can be: platykurtic, flat with the observations distributes evenly across the classes; leptokurtic, peaked, with the observations concentrated within a narrow range of values; or mesokurtic, in which the distribution of values results in a line graph which is neither flat nor peaked. As such, any analysis of the diffusion of an innovation must be able to account for skewness and kurtosis. According to Easingwood (1987), the differing life-cycle shapes of adoption can be classified by using mathematical diffusion models in order to provide an underlying theoretical explanation of the behavioural rationales of the adoption of innovations. In order to model the array of other adoption curves, it is

		Inception versus franchising			
		Time difference in years			
		Average	Standard deviation	Pearson's coefficient of skewness	Bias
SIC sector description	Sub-sector				
Manufacture of pulp and paper products; publishing and printing	Print and publishing	2.9	5.2	1.10	+ve
Construction	Construction	4.2	8.9	1.08	+ve
Wholesale and retail trade; repair of motor vehicles, motorcycles and personal and household goods	Car maintenance	5.5	15.4	0.86	+ve
	Wholesale	5.4	17.6	0.83	+ve
	Retail	8.1	22.2	1.00	+ve
	Non-store retail	6.7	18.1	0.95	+ve
Hotels and restaurants	Hotel and catering	11.1	34	0.80	+ve
Transport, storage and communication	Taxi/cabs	6.6	4.8	2.06	+ve
	Travel agency	10.5	17.0	1.68	+ve
	Courier	3.5	5.4	1.39	+ve
Financial intermediation	Financial services	10.9	31.8	0.93	+ve
Real estate, renting and business activities	Real estate	5.2	8.2	1.17	+ve
	Rental	3.8	7.5	0.72	+ve
	Consultancy	10.5	31.9	0.75	+ve
	Accounting	3.7	5.5	1.47	+ve
	Employment agency	5.7	12.6	0.88	+ve
	Legal	1.1	0.8	0.38	+ve
	Advertising	2.1	3.3	0.00	symmetry
	Commercial cleaning	3.4	5.5	1.58	+ve
	General business	2.9	5.6	1.02	+ve
Health and social work	Health care	2.2	2.3	1.57	+ve
Other community, social and personal service activities	Drainage	2.2	4.0	1.65	+ve
	Personal services	5.1	8.2	1.13	+ve
	Domestic services	1.8	1.6	1.50	+ve
	Driving school	15.4	28.8	1.50	+ve

Table 1.2: Skewness of the time difference between inception and embarking on franchising

necessary to briefly describe the attributes comprising the typical 's-shaped' diffusion curve. One of the best-known differential equation models of this type is propounded by Bass (1969):

$$dN(t) / dt = a[\bar{N}-N(t)] + b/\bar{N} \cdot N(t) \cdot [\bar{N}-N(t)] \text{ or} \tag{1}$$

$$dF(t) / dt = [a + bF(t)][1 - F(t)] \tag{2}$$

where $N(t)$ is the cumulative number of adopters/market share of a product at time t, N is the upper limit of the market share, a is the coefficient of innovation, b is the mathematical shorthand for indicating the coefficient of imitation or internal influence relating word-of-mouth communication between adopters and potential adopters to the rate of adoption. The proportion of potential adopters, $F(t)$, who adopt the innovation by time t is derived by: $N(t) / \bar{N}$. The first term in (1) shows the adoptions by innovators and the second term, adoptions by imitators.

Easingwood *et al* (1981; 1983) contend that there are three main limitations to the 's-shaped' diffusion curve. All three limitations stem from the typical behavioural assumption behind the 's-shaped' product life-cycle that the innovation is adopted by a few adopters ('innovators') who, because of their influence and status over others, influence them to adopt it. But the presence of different shaped diffusion curves suggests that the word-of-mouth effect does not remain constant over the entire time frame of diffusion. Rather the effect can increase, decrease, or remain constant depending on the speed of adoption within particular sub-sets of the total diffusion time frame. As a consequence of these differing shapes, the assumptions concerning the influence of innovators and early adopters, behind the 's-shaped' diffusion curve do not necessarily hold. Secondly, as inferred in the classification of different adopters by Rogers (1995), later adopters, such as those in the late majority and laggard categories, may be in a better position to assess the relative merits of an innovation; they can see the impact it has had on earlier users as well as some of the errors made by the initial incumbents. For example, within a 'typical' product life-cycle effect, the costs associated with production are believed to decline over time as experience and knowledge is gained, and as the productive techniques become more systemetized. The rate of adoption, however, suggests that in some instances organizational learning must occur at a very rapid rate in order to maintain/increase one's competitive position.

Depending on how late they decide to adopt, the diffusion curve may take a number of trajectories and therefore illustrate different word-of-mouth effects. An important feature of Rogers' (1995) typology of innovation diffusion, indicates that influence – or peer pressure – exerted by the early, socially active adopters is perceived to be greater than for the later, less socially integrative adopters. The differing shapes of the adoption curves and large time differences between inception and pursuing franchised expansion in the tables above, however, suggests that the innovators and early adopters may not have as much influence on affecting the choices of the later adopters as Rogers and others contend. Thirdly, Easingwood *et al* (1983) argue that the 's-shaped' curve assumes that for any innovation, the diffusion curve is symmetric; the diffusion pattern before the stage of maximum adoption rate ('the point of inflection') is a mirror image of the stage before the period of inflection. There is, however, no reason why the two sets of adopters should behave in a similar manner. That is, b does not have to constant. Accordingly, this model may not be as insightful to the sectoral diffusion patterns in franchising in the USA and Britain as one which accounts for the differing substitution patterns, such as that propounded by Easingwood *et al*. For anyone who argues that a franchise is a form of investment product (Martin, 1988; 1996), the title of Easingwood's (1987) article,'Early Product Life Cycle Forms for Infrequently Purchased Major Products', possibly increases the aesthetic applicability of the model to the franchise context.

In order to overcome the inherent limitations of the 's-shaped' adoption pattern, Easingwood *et al* (1981; 1983) propose a model of diffusion in which the coefficient of imitation changes over time, and which allows the diffusion curve to be symmetrical as well as non-symmetrical with the point of inflection responding to the diffusion process.

They propose that the coefficient of imitation can be made a function of penetration, expressed by the following equation:

$$w(t) = b[N(t) / \bar{N}]^\alpha \qquad [3]$$

where α is a constant and $w(t)$ is the time-varying coefficient of imitation. Easingwood *et al* (1983) then substitute (3) into (2) to produce their 'non-uniform influence diffusion model':

$$dF(t) / dt = [a + bF(t)^\delta][1-F(t)] \qquad [4]$$

where a, b, δ are model parameters, and where $\delta = \alpha+1$. This equation includes a non-linear interaction term to represent the word-of-mouth communication between adopters and non-adopters. Thus if it is assumed that becoming a franchisor, for example, occurs without any influence $\delta = 0$; on the other hand, if diffusion occurs with uniform influence, $\delta = 1$ (this is the Bass model). Where $\delta > 0$ and less than unity, an acceleration of influence is seen to be evident, which causes an earlier and higher peak in the level of adoptions. Values of $\delta > 1$ suggest that influence increases over time and results in a later and lower peak (for a given beta and initial market share figure). The value of b, the coefficient of internal influence (or coefficient of imitation) controls the average rate at which the entire population adopts. Based on the actual values observed, the full range of values of b is divided into low ($0 < b < 0.4$), medium ($0.4 \leq b \leq 0.8$), and high ($b > 0.8$). Easingwood (1987) indicates that the value of δ, a non-uniform influence factor (that is, word-of-mouth communication) controls the shape of the coefficient of influence and can have three very different effects. It can produce values of the coefficient of influence that are:

1. decreasing ($0 < \delta < 0.8$);
2. approximately constant ($0.8 \leq \delta \leq 1.2$);
3. increasing ($\delta > 1.2$).

Hence, although combining any value of δ with any value of b generates an infinite number of diffusion curves, the broad array of possibilities can be defined into a particular range of the diffusion model parameters, b and δ, such that all diffusions in a particular class have a distinctively shaped coefficient of influence/imitation. The various coefficient bands yield nine classes of diffusion, which are defined and labelled in Easingwood's (1987) matrix below. Thus, for example, a b of 0.28 refers to the situation where the coefficient of internal influence is low, and depending on the value of δ will result in a diffusion trajectory being 'Plateau', 'Slow Uniform', or 'Low Uniform'. By comparing the classifications in Easingwood's matrix to the diffusion of franchising illustrated in Figure 1.1, and without the benefit of empirical analysis, it appears that the UK sector could be defined as a 'Late Rush'/'Delayed', whereas the US market is more 'Accelerated'/'Uniform'. In the depiction of the various diffusion curves, a is excluded because it has no effect on the coefficient of influence and has a negligible impact on the shape of the curve (when viewed from the product classification system standpoint).

In a refinement of Easingwood's model, Balasubramanian and Ghosh (1992) comment that an innovation's position on the diffusion map may be affected by the

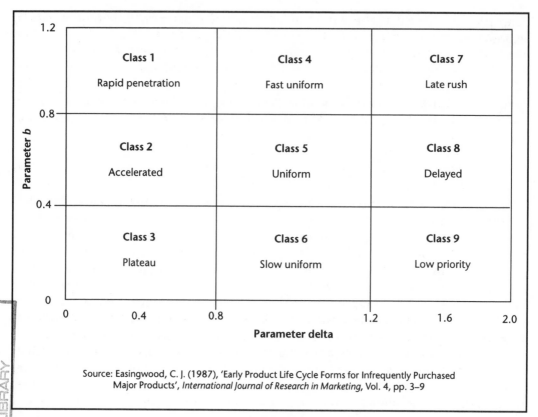

Source: Easingwood, C. J. (1987), 'Early Product Life Cycle Forms for Infrequently Purchased Major Products', *International Journal of Research in Marketing*, Vol. 4, pp. 3–9

Figure 1.2: Easingwood's (1987) diffusion map

instability of the parameters, rather than being a reflection of characteristics in its early history. Easingwood's life-cycle classifications of products are entirely based on point estimates of b and δ parameters. But, Balasubramanian and Ghosh argue, point parameter estimates are not necessarily reliable because assigning a product to a product class by merely plotting a point provides no assurance that this classification decision carries a high degree of confidence. By estimating the parameters by calculating a joint confidence region to take into account the inter-relationship between both parameters of interest, they find that the result classification is reliable by being consistent and is unique. That is, the joint confidence region method produces consistent classification classes for different time frames of the product under review. Furthermore, it results in a unique representation because the product is assigned to a particular diffusion map class out of the nine possible classes (Balasubramanian and Ghosh, 1992b). To do this, they conducted a nonlinear least-squares regression test on equation (4) separately for the different time frames for each of their sampled products and obtained approximate 95% contours by searching the b-δ parameter space. This permitted them to locate the set of all co-ordinates $[b', \delta']$ in order to satisfy the function:

$$S(b', \delta') = S(b, \delta)\{1 + [p/(n - p)]F\} \qquad [5]$$

where $S = dF(t) / dt$; $S(\cdot)$ is the residual sum square for equation (4) such that $S(b', \delta') = \Sigma_n\{S_t - S_t'\}$ and S_t' is obtained by entering in equation (4) the estimates of the product share values and a 'candidate' pair of b and δ values; n = the estimation sample size for equation (4); $p = 2$ (to compute the confidence region for the two parameters b and δ); and F denotes the $F(p, n-p, 0.95)$ statistic. As a result of its robustness, it is this modified approach which is employed in an application to the franchise sectors in the USA and Britain.

Application

To illustrate the application of the non-uniform diffusion model to the franchise fraternity, time series data for the UK and US franchise fraternities were examined. For parsimony, a holistic analysis covering each of the industries comprising the respective franchise fraternities was not conducted. Rather, estimations of the non-uniform influence model were conducted for the following data sets:

- the value (at non-inflation adjusted prices) of business format franchising activity as a proportion of total consumer expenditure in Britain;
- the value (at 1990 prices) of business format franchising activity in Britain as a proportion of total consumer spending;
- the value of business format franchising activity in the USA as a proportion of total franchising (business format franchising and product name);
- the value of business format franchising activity in the US foodservice market (comprising the following sectors: 1. hamburgers; 2. chicken restaurants; 3. pizza restaurants; 4. Mexican restaurants; and 5. seafood restaurants) as a proportion of total franchising activity (business format and product name);
- the share of business format franchising in the US Mexican restaurants as a share of total expenditure in foodservice franchising;
- the share of business format franchising in the US seafood restaurant market as a share of total expenditure in foodservice franchising; and
- the share of business format franchising in the US pizza restaurant market as a share of total expenditure in foodservice franchising.

The data was obtained from government statistics (such as *Business Monitor* and the HMSO's *Annual Abstract of Statistics*), the US Department of Commerce's franchise surveys and their annual statistical abstracts, the National Restaurant Association, the NatWest/BFA annual surveys covering the British market. As these latter studies do not analyze franchising activity in Britain effectively prior to 1980, the UK analysis is constrained[1] to its recent history. By comparison, the data for the USA is much richer and covers a longer period of time and so permitted a comparative analysis of franchising's development between 1973 and 1988 (the production of the Department of Commerce reports was cancelled by the US government, which means that evaluating the extent and growth of franchising post-1988 has become very difficult). Table 1.3 presents some of the descriptive statistics of each of the data sets.

Figure 1.3 presents the fitted data plotted against the actual time series as well as an indication of the beta and delta values, and a description of the diffusion curve type. As can be seen, the recent UK franchise market shows a 'Plateau' trajectory, like that of the

Measure	Business format as a share of total franchising	Food service as a share of total franchising	Pizza	Mexican	Seafood	UK franchising as a share of total expenditure	Inflation adjusted
Mean	32.17	8.20	13.18	4.6	3.31	1.10	1.09
Median	33.07	8.21	12.99	4.5	3.36	1.25	1.23
Standard error	1.09	0.405	0.915	1.43	0.19	0.101	0.098
Standard dev.	4.49	1.62	3.66	1.72	0.75	0.349	0.34
Variance	20.18	2.62	13.41	2.95	0.56	0.122	0.115
Kurtosis	−1.027	−0.988	−1.41	−1.39	2.26	−0.78	−0.68
Skewness	−0.13	−0.206	0.08	0.009	−1.43	−0.81	−0.788
Range	14.55	5.40	10.96	4.96	2.822	1.045	1.037
Minimum	24.91	5.15	7.48	2.05	1.41	0.451	0.459
Maximum	39.46	10.55	18.44	7.005	4.23	1.496	1.496

Table1.3: Descriptive statistics for sampled franchise sectors

USA. Research by Grant (1985) and Haverson (1991) has suggested that the explanation for this situation is the later entry of franchising to some economic sectors and the low penetration of franchising *per se* when compared to total consumer expenditure. While partly true, it is not the whole argument because franchising's diffusion in the UK has been affected by a number of macro-economic factors (see below). The sampled sectors of the US foodservice market tend to illustrate a 'Low Priority'/'Delayed' trajectory. The same is apparent for business format franchising in the USA as a proportion of total franchising activity. Although only a small number of examples have been used, it may be suggested that the diffusion of franchising follows different trajectories in differing industries, rather than simply being 's-shaped' or following the 'J-shaped' curve that some elements of the franchise press and others would have people to believe. It has been suggested that it is the combined later entry date and the diffusion trajectories of franchising at a sectoral level which, combined, shaped the overall diffusion curve of franchising. As the diffusion curves tend not to be 's-shaped', the examples also serve to provide some statements concerning the adoption behaviours of franchisors.

The effects of word-of-mouth communication are apparent through the values of δ, and can be confirmed through:

$$db(t)/dN = b(\delta-1)N^{\delta-2}$$ [6]

where $db/dN < 0$ for $0 < \delta < 1$; $db/dN = 0$ for $\delta = 1$; and $db/dN > 0$ for $\delta > 1$. Perhaps significantly, only one of the tests illustrates a delta value in excess of unity, which suggests that there is a general tendency within the sampled data of a high initial word-of-mouth influence which decreases with penetration. Where delta equates to zero, a constant coefficient of imitation is evident. The declining word-of-mouth communication situation seems to be apparent in spite of the success rhetoric associated with franchising, and the presence of benchmark organizations such as McDonald's, KFC, Burger King, etc., who have done much to establish standards of best practice (especially in Britain).

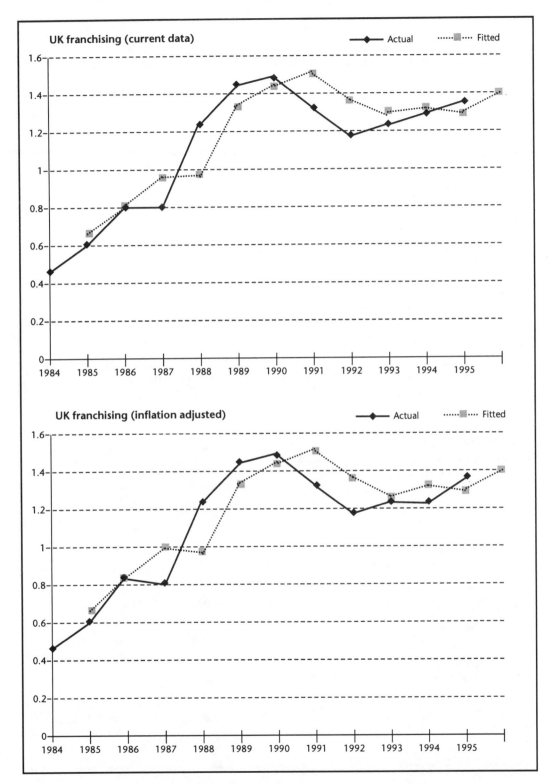

Figure 1.3: *An application of Easingwood's (1987) diffusion map to franchising in the USA and Britain*

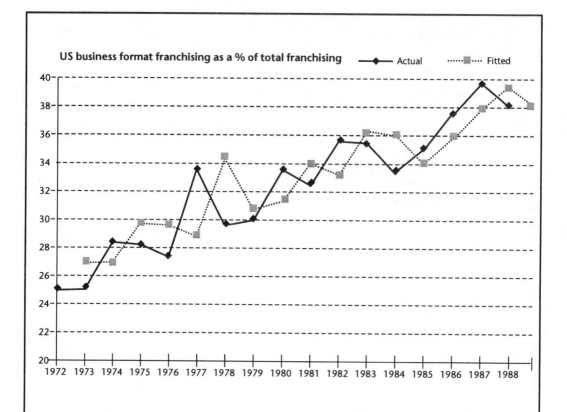

Test	Beta	Maximum	Delta	Description
Non-inflation adjusted UK franchising	0.360	1.496	0.555	'Plateau'
Inflation adjusted UK franchising	0.348	1.496	0.488	'Plateau'
Business format franchising as a % of total US franchising	0.161	39.46	0.000	'Plateau'
US foodservice franchising as a share of total franchising	0.139	10.56	0.000	'Plateau'
US Mexican restaurants as a % of total foodservice franchising	0.400	7.01	1.799	'Low priority'/'Delayed'
US Seafood restaurants as a % of total foodservice franchising	0.259	4.23	0.000	'Plateau'
US Pizza restaurants as a % of total foodservice franchising	0.413	18.44	2.213	'Low priority'/'Delayed'

Figure 1.3 (continued)

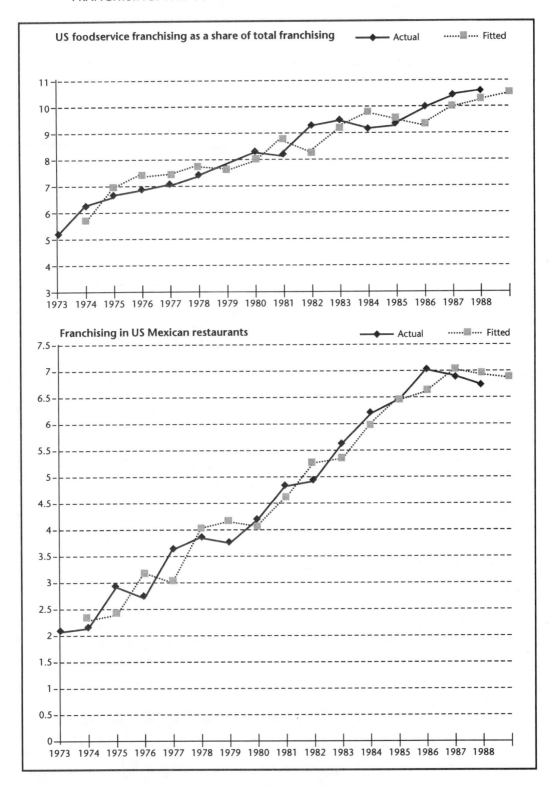

Figure 1.3 (continued)

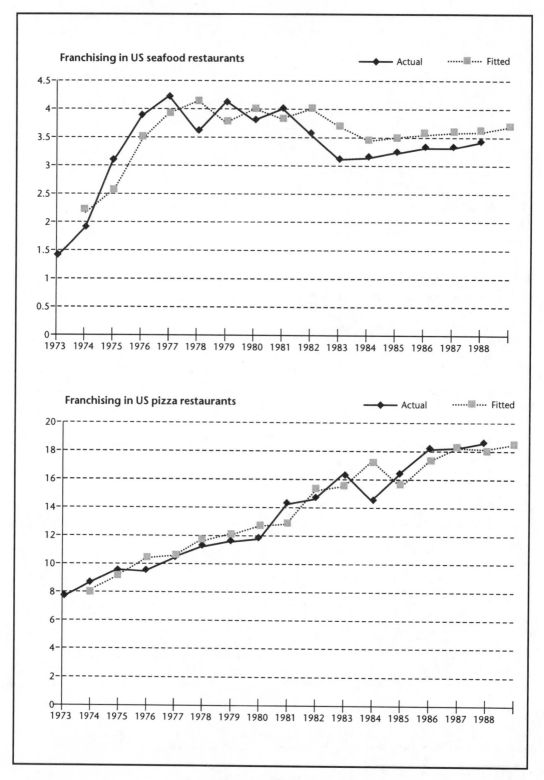

Figure 1.3 (continued)

Combined, b and δ give rise to a steep start to the diffusion curve, but this is short-lived and replaced by a number of years in which the adoption rate is low and somewhat constant (Easingwood, 1987). The slowest take-up of all in the series of tests are the US Mexican and Pizza restaurant franchises, which illustrate 'Low Priority'/'Delayed' diffusions. In such markets, the impact of word-of-mouth is low throughout but especially initially.

Looking at the coefficient of imitation alone, the non-uniform diffusion model application to the franchise market values shows all fall within the range $0 < b < 0.4$. For example, the coefficient of imitation (b) for UK business format franchising as a share of total consumer spending is about 0.29, which suggests that the average rate at which the entire population adopts is low, except for a brief initial period in which it is relatively high. Using function (7), which is a reformulation of (3), it is also possible to make some comparisons of the coefficients of imitation at initial stages of the diffusion trajectory with that at the final stages.

$$w(t) = bF(t)^{\delta-1} \qquad\qquad\qquad [7]$$

Using (7), and examining the 'Plateau' type trajectories in the first instance, the initial period estimate for the coefficient of imitation is 1.6 times the final period value for the market value of non-inflation adjusted UK franchising, 1.7 times final period estimate for inflation-adjusted UK franchising, 1.5 times final period estimate for US business format franchising as a share of total US franchising, 2.05 times final period estimate for US food-service franchising as a share of total franchising, 2.4 times final period estimate for US Seafood restaurant franchises as a share of total US foodservice franchises. For the 'Low Priority'/'Delayed' trajectories, in which the coefficient of imitation is increasing with penetration, the final period value is 2.6 times the initial period value estimate for US Mexican restaurants, and 3.1 times for US pizza restaurants.

While these tests illustrate some of the underlying characteristics affecting the diffusion of it should be observed that these results are strictly limited. Firstly, the diffusion curves are susceptible to yielding different results according to the nature of the data used. Secondly, the UK data derives from the non-census data generated by the BFA, a situation which may require a modified approach to that presented here and limited the value of conducting a sectoral analysis of the franchise fraternity in Britain by using, for example, the sample illustrated in Table 1.1 and 1.2. Thirdly, and arguably, if data restrictions could be overcome to permit a comparative analysis of the market value and volume of business format franchising since its emergence in the 1950s, different results may have ensued. Fourthly, some of the diffusion curves in this study have been calculated over long time-frames rather than only evaluating the earlier developmental years. If the earlier time periods were to be examined, different trajectories and classifications of those curves could emerge. In addition, the results do not illustrate some of the antecedent variables affecting the emergence of business format franchising in the first instance. For explanations of these factors, it is necessary to look elsewhere.

Why the different shapes?

From the above application, two questions arise: what are the behavioural patterns being described by the different diffusion trajectories of franchising?; and why did they emerge when they did? As indicated above, the coefficient of imitation shows that the effects of word-of-mouth communication diminishes with penetration. This situation possibly points to barriers to adoption, such as the degree of perceived risk in becoming an adopter. In addition, this position exists despite the presence of certain exogeneous macro-level factors that were conducive to the growth of franchising. Yet another reason may be that franchising has different levels of status, an observation which is reflected elsewhere. For example, in the status-capitalist model suggested in the Introduction, one reason an innovation is diffused is because it is sanctioned by the dominant class and by labour. Examining the dynamics of this sanctioning process through the life and death process of organizations, the Population Ecologists observe all populations of organizations undergo a process of legitimation. A population refers to the collection of organizations within a particular form (franchises, for example), and legitimation describes the 'taken-for-grantedness' of the organizational form within a particular industry setting. Legitimation does not signify the formal legality of a population of organization and, therefore, also applies to illegal activities. According to Hannan and Carroll (1992), an organizational form acquires legitimation when there is little question in the minds of actors that it serves as the natural way to effect some kind of collective action. In other words, the innovation attains a certain status among a certain social network that permits them to possibly accelerate their rate of capital accumulation. In turn, this rate and the lure of increased status can help to cause the mobility of certain individuals and firms to that status. The differing diffusion shapes of franchising shown above illustrate that the legitimation process occurs at different rates for different industries and, by implication, for possibly different reasons. As a result of the kurtosis in different curves, it is apparent that there are limits to this legitimation process, which is indicative of changing tastes, environments, and the emergence of alternative methods of attaining status and capital.

The issues of legitimation and capacity are central tenets of the Population Ecology model. It propounds that industries and their sub-sectors can only hold so much capacity of particular types of organizations, which may prompt the formation of an alternative organizational form and is indicative of the presence of dual closure. Within the constraints of this carrying-capacity model, legitimation dominates the early development of an organizational population (Carroll and Swathinathan, 1991; Carroll and Wade, 1991). The population acquires legitimacy through increased prevalence, which gives rise to the generation of messages such as those indicated in the positive (or 'Jekyll') face of franchising in order to attain further or maintain existing legitimation. As the number of organizations adopting the form increases, new investors and the capital markets see the form as viable and imitable, prompting additional increases in the number of adopters and a fall in the barriers to capital (recall, for instance, that the clearing banks are generally favourable towards franchise lending). In this sense, there are some parallels with Rogers' (1995) adopter categories of innovators and early adopters as well as the notion that the new organizational form is accommodative to the capitalist system (or it would not be sanctioned). As a result of their influence/status as well as the institutional support they marshal, others imitate the innovation. As shown in Chapter 2, however, different organizational forms have varying levels of density within different sub-sectors of the same industry, which suggests that the process of acquiring the status of legitimation occurs within relatively tightly defined spheres of activity. For example, consortia are an implicit feature of the hotel industry but have yet to emerge with any force in their bed and breakfast and budget hotel sub-sectors; nor are they readily apparent in the fast food market (see Case Study 3).

As part of the legitimation process, two kinds of activity are undertaken. One is collective action to define, explain and codify its organizational form and to defend itself from claims and attacks by rival forms. The second is collective learning by which 'effective routines become collectively fine-tuned, codified, and promulgated' (Hannan and Carroll, 1992; p. 41). Both of these aspects are more than evident in the franchising fraternity. On the one hand, there is (as shown in the Introduction to this book) an ongoing definitional debate about the differing types of franchising; there is also an increasingly vitriolic dispute concerning the survival and performance rates *vis-à-vis* non-franchised businesses (see Chapters 8 and 9). In this latter debate, franchisees are perceived to illustrate lower rates of failure and risk compared to other organizational forms, such as independent business start-ups, and franchisors generate levels of return on capital which exceed their industry peer group. In other words, franchising is defended on the grounds that it is a superior method of capital accumulation than others. On the other hand, are frequent claims that the illegitimate fringe in franchising is receding because of self-regulation by trade, and that franchising is a form of best practice because it sensitizes the organization to the conditions of certain task environments and is a way of reducing operating costs.

To some degree, the Population Ecology model itself provides some support for the low mortality rates propounded by the franchise fraternity. It suggests that when a small population grows in numbers, density should have a positive effect on the number of new entrants and a negative impact on the mortality rate. Given the rhetoric of many in the franchise fraternity that it has low rates of withdrawal/failure, it is possible that this is the situation that is being described. There are, however, limits to this tendency of increased legitimacy and low mortality rates. As a population grows further, legitimacy gains diminish and at this point competition within a particular industry increases with the growth in organizational population size. At this stage, for example, franchisors are competing with each other for franchisees and new entrants require substantial differentiation, access to resources and experience in order to compete and survive. When a population reaches its carrying capacity, competition intensifies further and density has a positive effect on mortality. Given the rapid development of franchising in some economic sectors, it is therefore apparent that for those sectors the 'Jekyll' face of franchising is possibly no longer appropriate to such populations because continuing legitimation serves to be counter-productive.

Given Norton's (1988) argument that franchises are an organizational form and the focus on the issues of life and death encompassed by the Population Ecology perspective, the theory is of particular use and power in helping franchise researchers to examine some of the more macro issues in their subject matter. Although it is possible to see a ready application of the model to franchising, there are, however, two points which require some further comment because they are of some importance to the understanding of the birth and diffusion processes of franchises: first, the measure of density; and second, the process of legitimation. For example, Hannan and Carroll (1992) indicate that a precondition to an organizational form's 'social-fact-like' status is widespread identification and recognition, which are more likely to occur when organizations are numerous. Therefore, one rationale for the dearth of franchised hotels in Europe compared to direct ownership and those affiliated to consortia, is the fact that there is a low presence of such organizations in the first instance. Endorsement by powerful actors and organizations (such as government representatives, trade bodies, and the clearing banks) also facilitates recognition and acceptance because it provides the form with a status which some people may wish to try to employ to accumulate capital. There are, however, limitations to these tendencies. For example, the application of Easingwood *et al's* (1983) non-uniform influence model to franchising above shows that the diffusion of fast food franchises is non-symmetrical. It is unclear whether the innovators influenced the later adopters because of the status and wealth that they managed to accumulate through franchised expansion, or whether there were environmental forces which contributed to the trajectory of the organizational form in the UK between 1950 and 1995.

The measure of density

According to Hannan and Carroll (1992), the density of organizational forms is measured as the number of organizations in the population within specified spatial and temporal boundaries. While instructive because it is possible to analyze both the effects of intra-population competition and legitimation on survival rates, as well as the shape of the diffusion curve of a specific organizational form, it does not necessarily provide insight to the effects of substitution (or inter-population competition). Yet, Hannan and Carroll (1992) indicate that the impact of the growth, or decline, of a particular population may have implications for the life chances of other organizational populations, via the following scenarios:

1. the growing density of one population may serve to legitimate another until its numbers become sufficiently large that competitive interactions come to dominate;
2. there is competition between the two organizational forms from the outset; and
3. the two organizational forms cohabit within a particular setting without competitive interaction.

In analyzing the birth and diffusion of franchising, it this latter form of competition which is perhaps of more pertinence than intra-population dynamics *per se*. As suggested by Easingwood *et al's* model (1983), inter-population dynamics are relevant because becoming a franchisor entails the business owner to have an existing business which is then converted to a franchise in order to pursue organizational development and capital accumulation. Additionally, Ozanne and Hunt (1971) observed that some franchisors would illustrate a tendency to buy back their franchised operations and revert to being a wholly-owned chain once some measure of critical mass had been achieved. Thus, it may be possible that some organizational innovations become popular in terms of the number of adopters but do not become institutionally legitimated such that other forms are not recognized. That is, organizational heterogeniety within certain industries is the norm because some legitimating forces do not recognize one form to the exclusion of others; this observation may help explain the tendency for ownership redirection in favour of the franchisor to vary by industry setting. Firms who decide to follow the technology, such as franchising, must be aware of the trajectory and decide whether to follow it. Firms that do not decide to franchise may possibly create a new trajectory; equally, adopters may elect some other technology if the existing one does not meet pre-set objectives.

The diffusion and density of franchising, it seems, is affected by the range of alternatives and the decision-maker's awareness of them, willingness to change, and overcoming any resistance to change within the organization (via usurpationary power). Hannan and Carroll (1992), however, also observe that important socio-political events, such as legal issues, have substantial effects on density levels. For example, the Prohibition era in the 1920s and 1930s served to reduce the density of brewers in the USA. For parsimony, they tend not to explore some of the historical socio-political forces affecting the density of the particular population under review. They argue that the forces affecting legitimation will affect the density of the organizational form and, as such, focus on the result of the causal factor rather than the factor itself. Unfortunately, in franchise research there has been little overt recognition or exploration of the effect certain socio-political factors have had on density. Whether this is because of parsimony is not clear. Instead, the focus of attention by researchers has been more orientated towards firm-specific issues, and it has been suggested that even this emphasis has been insufficient. For example, Kaufmann and Dant (1996) suggest that there has been little consideration of multi-unit/brand franchisees, which are now particularly commonplace with the fast food and retail sectors. Equally, there appears to be insufficient accent on developing a theoretical framework which goes some way to explaining why certain individuals decide to become franchisees and others do not. Arguably, it is here that the social closure theory may serve to complement the Population Ecology approach because it helps to focus on the underlying forces affecting continuity and change and, therefore, the resultant movements in density.

In focusing on the movements in density, of particular interest is the nature of relationship between two, or more, organizational forms such as the tendency and preference to pursue direct ownership compared to franchising (and vice versa). While calls for direct measurement of inter-population competition have become routine, such measures are beset by data collection problems. Accordingly, Population Ecology has been developed via a variety of measures to calculate the indirect effects of inter-population competition. Hannan and Carroll (1992), for example, test for competition by inferences from the effects of density on vital rates, but Hannan et al (1995) observe that density-dependence theory's empirical footing would be more sound if some tests took a different route. These measures differ from those employed in some strategic management texts. Arguably, as many proponents of business portfolios (such as McKiernan, 1992) may concur, relative market share information may be instructive for inter-population-level analysis, and is an easily calculable variable employed by some researchers to examine whether ownership redirection is occurring. The measure is, however, of limited utility to examine the effects of competition. Such a measure of market share permits the observer to gain some insight into the position of one organizational form within an industry relative to others in use in the same setting very quickly. Some sectors, for example, illustrate limited heterogeneity because there are only two organizational forms in use, such as franchises and direct company-ownership; others are more homogeneous because other variants are not seen as legitimate by the industry incumbents, which would be reflected in the lack of market share. Unfortunately, the relative market share measure does not tell us whether the organizational forms cohabit and mutually benefit each other or are in competition with each other.

An alternative approach to those illustrated above would be to calculate the substitution effect through a measure of cross elasticity in which complementary organizational forms have negative cross elasticities and substitutes have positive measures. Arguably, cross elasticity does not allow for a direct interaction between certain firms, which may serve to affect the adoption of certain organizational forms and the occupation of specific niches. Yet another approach would be through the use of differential equations, such as 'predator-prey', mutualism, or competition interaction.

The process of legitimation

In exploring some of the aspects concerning the birth and diffusion of franchising, of more immediate concern to this section of the book is Hannan and Carroll's (1992) observation about the legitimation process. In their analysis and application of the Population Ecology theory, they pose a pertinent point concerning the diffusion procedure: 'What are the underlying mechanisms which cause some organizational forms to become taken for granted?' They observe that institutional theory is essentially phenomenological and because little empirical evidence exists, the answer must be speculative. While the phenomenological aspect may be an accurate description of the legitimation process of franchises, this latter observation may not be accurate in a general sense but is particularly so in respect to franchising.

There is, possibly contrary to Hannan and Carroll's comment, an increasing amount of empirical research examining the diffusion of organizational innovations and the way in which they become the accepted norm. There is, for instance, abundant research on the conditions that lead to the creation and diffusion of strategic alliances (Hagedoorn, 1993). In addition, the different diffusion trajectories of a variety of telecommunication products has been explored by Easingwood and Lunn (1992), who indicate that there are five inter-related factors influencing adoption rates:

1. the environment, such as regulatory changes and macro factors;
2. the target user group, whether industrial or consumer and whether it is specific to niche or mass consumer groups;
3. company barriers, such as lack of resources and the degree of specialization;
4. innovation characteristics, such as its compatibility, complexity, trialability, observability/communicability, and the degree of relative advantage it accrues; and
5. the perceived risk of adoption, including the scale of the performance/financial risk and the professional/social risk.

If a new organizational form is viewed as an innovation, arguably similar processes are at play. Given that franchising is both an innovation and an organizational form, and given some of the limitations of extant approaches describing the process, there is a need for some additional effort to provide a fuller consideration of the legitimation process of franchising by exploring the predecessors to business format franchising.

In answering their own question, Hannan and Carroll (1992) suggest that the underlying mechanisms which cause some organizational forms to attain a status of being 'taken for granted' are: the density of the organizational form; the codification and dissemination of the organizational form among social networks; and the defence of that organizational form against competing alternatives. As insightful as these explanations are, there remains, however, the question of how franchising arose when it did. In this vein, some franchise researchers have suggested that the density levels of franchises are prone to variation by the actions of entrepreneurs and capitalists seeking to accumulate additional wealth and status, rather than necessarily also considering macro-factors such as technology and legal issues, etc. In such Schumpeterian terms, franchising as a new organizational form derived from a comparison of the differing costs of expansion, such as franchising versus company ownership, and the existing level of resources. This Schumpeterian position, therefore, starts with the role of business profits in the evolution of the capitalist system. Profits, beyond their normal function of ensuring a competitive return on the four factors of production (land, labour, capital, and entrepreneurship), acted as a motivation for innovation. Perhaps reflecting this position, Miles and Snow (1986) suggest that the evolutionary stages of an industry cycle are characterized by 'prospectors', or firms which are 'first to the market' with a new product or service and differentiate themselves by using their ability to be innovative. It also places them in a position of possible advantage to accumulate wealth and status. Franchising permitted the capitalist to accumulate additional capital through the realization of economies of scale and brand equity by using the franchisee's motivation and investment while, concurrently, lowering input costs, such as remuneration and associated benefits, via the legal independence of the franchisee. Others of the capitalist class in the same economic sector then mimicked the practice in order to try and realize the same benefits as their competitors, and help to negate first mover advantages and to prevent the monopolization of those resources.

While there has been some degree of anecdotal support for this 'technology-push' explanation of franchising, it cannot be the whole rationale because it ignores the effects of technology-pull. At this end of the technology push-pull continuum, Schmookler (1966) argued that innovations were created by a demand (and presumably, the existence of environmental variables and resources which permitted that demand to be satisfied) for new products and processes by the market that pulled them away from the firm. Under this explanation, the rise of franchising derived from usurpationary power expressed as the demand for a second career option which did not entail the risks of pure self-employment and also did not necessarily possess the status of labour (see Chapter 5). In this process, the legitimation of franchising occurred because supply filled the demand for them. Although not applied to the franchise context, where the legitimation process is indeed speculative, these opposing explanations of innovation diffusion have been subject to much empirical analysis. The findings of such effort have noted, firstly, that the primacy of market demand within the innovation process has little support and, secondly, that both supply and demand factors play an important role in the innovation diffusion process and the life-cycles of products and processes. In effect, therefore, Schumpeterian processes are possibly more important at the birth/evolutionary stages of a life cycle, but are moderated by Schmookler effects over time. Perhaps reflecting this situation, the growth in fast food franchising in the USA during the post-war period, labelled by Hackett (1977) as the 'acceptance and boom' period, has been attributed to social, financial and marketing explanations (Mockler and Easop, 1968; Vaughn, 1979), which encompass both technology-push and technology-pull factors.

Several social, or technology-pull, factors contributed to the expansion of business format franchising in the USA during the 1950s and 1960s. Some of these factors were also conducive to the development of fast food *per se* (Khan, 1992; Yavas, 1988):

- the urbanization of population;
- increased female participation in the workforce, and the rise of youth culture;
- the USA does not have a long-established food tradition to overcome;
- Americans have adopted a faster life-style, greater disposable income and greater car ownership (especially conducive to drive-in and drive-through concepts), giving less inclination to cook at home;
- the growth of inter-state highways (this, combined with car ownership, was particularly conducive to the growth of motels and auto-based franchises);
- an inclination by post-war GIs to want to operate their own business and use their military bonuses to purchase a franchise; and
- the recession of 1957 to 1958, prompting some of those made redundant to consider becoming a franchisee whilst also prompting some companies to consider franchising as a method of expansion.

Some of the marketing, or technology-push, reasons for the expansion of business format franchising at the time include:

- increased market competition amongst retailers and manufacturers leading some firms to attempt to secure market access points;
- the use of commission-based selling techniques by some companies to promote their franchise offerings;
- concurrent with fast food development in the 1920s, the retail stores were also moving to a self-service format; and
- a desire for greater control and opportunities for the monopolization of resources (such as market access) than was achievable through voluntary chains.

Also of significance to the growth of franchising in the USA was the expanding credit market of the 1950s, permitting potential franchisees with low-cost capital to invest in franchises. The Federal Government also facilitated the growth of franchising through the introduction of a franchise business opportunities programme under Title IV of the Economic Opportunities Act, 1964. This programme gave the Small Business Administration the authority to lend up to US$25,000 for up to fifteen years to persons with low incomes who wished to start their own business. In so doing, the expanding credit market and the programme were additional pull-factors since they essentially served to increase demand. By increasing demand, the supply of franchises expanded to meet it. A similar situation is apparent in Hungary, in an organization called the Hungarian American Enterprise Fund.

Although compelling, the polar arguments concerning the legitimation of franchises *per se*, and within specific economic sectors, are not persuasive. Figure 1.1 and case histories of companies such as Wimpy (see Case Study 2) suggest that business format franchises emerged in both the USA and Britain as a result of the Schumpeterian process. The development of franchising in both the UK and the USA, however, can be attributed more to the Schmooklerian position, which reflects the differing shaped diffusion curves in each country. For example, Fulop (1996) opines, that the development of business format franchising during the late 1970s and 1980s, rather than earlier, was the widespread prevalence of pyramid selling in the 1960s. Such pyramid selling resulted in highly publicized and substantial financial losses for many investors. Franchising was associated with pyramid selling because this was how such schemes were described in order to mislead potential investors, which meant that franchising gained a damaged reputation. These effects of pyramid selling on franchising were eventually addressed through the Fair Trading Act 1973, which regulated such schemes. From this situation, it would appear reasonable to expect that there was a low level of legitimation during franchising's developmental years, and low and possibly declining imitation and influence coefficients. This is not supported by Easingwood et al's (1981; 1983) model. Nonetheless, this situation illustrates that demand and socio-political forces affect the density of organizational forms, but that these effects are often endogeneous. The timing and form of legislation is affected by the dynamics of the organizational form.

From the Population Ecologist's framework, it appears that the diffusion of franchising is partially based on the awareness of franchising itself, the presence of antecedent conditions permitting that awareness, and the ability to adapt franchising to new uses (Nelson and Winter, 1983). After all, invention and innovation rarely happen just spontaneously and nor are they autonomous of the state of technological knowledge, social factors, or history. Figure 1.1 shows that the growth in business format franchises in the USA has exceeded that of their product/tradename counterparts which, in turn, suggests that it has become (in some industries) the preferred franchise option. This characteristic of succession is a feature of many industries. For example, Pinch and Bijker (1984), in their study of the development of the bicycle, show how the penny-farthing was rivalled by a range of possible variations but remained dominant until superceded by the safety bicycle. Thus, alternative organizational forms to those currently employed may gain currency because there exist historical precedents for their use, and they could be construed to be not that radically different from their predecessor and, therefore, less likely to question the legitimacy of the dominant ideology. They are only different in that they represent the adaptation of a particular form to a different technological operating environments and time. What are these antecedent variables? The remainder of this chapter contends that some of the conditions necessary for the emergence of business format franchising within a certain economic setting could be:

1. the pre-existence of franchising of some description in other economic sectors;
2. a trend towards standardization and efficiency;
3. the presence of legislative frameworks to help safeguard trademarks;
4. the presence of 'early pioneers' or individuals (franchisors and franchisees) capable of recognizing that an opportunity exists; and
5. factors conducive to the growth of small firms *per se.*

The pre-existence of franchising

Within the tenets of the Population Ecology model, prior models of franchising may have lost primacy as adopters prefer a new form because of technological developments, the need for adaptations to the original form in order to be applied to new economic and cultural settings, and the saturation of the existing form. Nonetheless, in being only a modification, the new model still maintains at least some of the characteristics of the original form. Business format franchises illustrate some of the features of product name franchises which, in turn, have some of the traits of feudalism, a contention which is explored further below. Modifications to the feudal form of organization and/or the application to new uses leads to new levels of development which has been, in turn, conducive to its further diffusion throughout society. This diffusion process has, however, entailed modifications to the context in which feudalism occurs, resulting in altering its manifestation from a product/tradename type to the emergence of the business format employed by companies such as McDonald's.

Perhaps one of the main similarities between product name franchises and their business format counterpart lies in the tie concerning products. Possibly reflecting some similarity with its counterpart, the business format franchisor typically receives some form of ongoing payments to be generated from the franchisees' activities. The franchisor may also, or alternatively, place a mark-up on goods supplied to franchisees. Some fast food franchisors use this as their main source of income and charge either a very low or non-existent management service fee. Others still take a commission on products sold by third parties to franchisees. Although such tie-ins can economize on policing franchisee units (Klein and Saft, 1985), there is an argument that such franchisors are behaving as a type of wholesaler. Most business format franchise organizations are not vertically integrated concerns. Instead, to help preserve brand and product standardization, they contract a manufacturer to produce own-label products which are then sold directly to franchisees. Some franchisors then take a percentage of the value of the purchases. This may then permit the franchisor to develop further their core competence. For example, Bennetton key competence is design because the manufacture of the clothes is subcontracted and the retail units are predominantly franchised. English (1993) argues that although the visibility of the franchise outlet causes the franchise to be classified as a retail phenomenon, the franchise company actually gets its direction and its identity from the franchisor, who is basically a wholesaler. Some business format franchise chains, therefore, are run by and for the wholesale link in the marketing channel, but to some anti-trust researchers, such arrangements constitute a form of 'exclusive dealing'. Exclusive dealing contracts constrain a seller to marketing the goods of only a single supplier (Marvel, 1982; Sass and Gisser, 1989), and therefore represents a form of exclusion

While there are similar ties regarding products in both types of franchise, there are also differences. Grant (1985) labels business format franchises as 'second generation' because they are perceived to be different from their predecessors since they refer to a distinct way of starting and operating a business as opposed to being only a way of distributing an existing product (Batchelor, 1991). By encompassing more than a licence to distribute a product, the business format franchise is where the franchisor allows franchisees to operate 'clones' of the business under the same name, system and operating procedures in return for an initial fee, which would be based on a percentage of total revenue. As a consequence of operating 'clones', business format franchise contracts are, usually, more encompassing and restrictive than product/tradename forms. In addition to these fees, a business format franchisor may also charge a franchisee a mark-up on the services and equipment that he contractually requires the franchisee to purchase (Luxenberg, 1985).

While these fees and restrictions may serve to differentiate business format franchises from their tradename counterparts, it has been cautioned that the initial fee should not be too high for a relatively newly established franchisor. High fees may serve to deter potential franchisees, especially as the demand for new franchises can be relatively price elastic (Weinrauch, 1986). When establishing initial fees, franchisors often take into account the fees that other franchisors are charging in the same business sectors and other related business sectors (an aspect which is explored further in Chapter 4). Other researchers have established that there is a positive relationship between the value of the franchise and the initial fee and ongoing royalties (Baucus *et al*, 1993; Sen, 1993). They argue that, in general, the better franchises are those with high initial fees, such as McDonald's.

Such modifications are not unique: most innovations, throughout the adoption process, undergo a change in accordance with the changing demands of the environment, suppliers, and customers. For example, in tourism, texts are replete with examples of how a particular destination is transformed by the number and type of adopters. Boorstin's (1964) main observation in his essay on the 'lost art of travel' is that the majority of modern tourists are simply passive onlookers who seek to enjoy the extravagantly strange from the security of the familiar. Unlike early adopters who seek to enjoy the 'reality' of a destination and stay in unsophisticated accommodation, the late adopters are isolated from the host environment and local people; they travel in guided groups enjoying 'pseudo-events', while disregarding the 'real' world surrounding them. The late adopters prefer to observe the strangeness of the host environment from the security of their immediate surroundings, such as international hotels. Tempting as it may be to explore only product name franchises as the predecessor of the business format version, to do so would be to present an incomplete analysis of franchising. Some research in the franchising field has pointed to the presence of franchising in the Middle Ages and, as such, a review of the legitimation of franchising necessitates this research to be accounted for. In addition to shedding some light on the diffusion process, reference to this period provides some indication of the extent of the underlying forces of continuity and change as well as to provide some insight to the workings of the franchise relationship.

Franchising: the social reproduction of 'bastard' feudalism?

It is important to observe that innovations, whilst new to the adapting organization or economic sector, are not necessarily new ideas *per se*. For example, supply chain texts are replete with the notion of partnerships. This is where a buyer and seller of services/products engage in collaborative behaviour for mutual medium- and long-term benefit, involving substantial contributions by partners of capital, technology, know-how and other assets (Mowery, 1983). Such an organizational form is often touted within the populist press as though partnerships, as well as flexible working, and out-sourcing, are the latest idea from management schools, management consultancies, and the like, to enable firms to improve efficiency, effectiveness, and their stock of knowledge.

Like franchising, however, these organizational forms have a long history. For example, flexible working practices were widely practised in the eighteenth and nineteenth centuries. At this time, there was a preference to do business with independent entrepreneurs, even within the same factory. As the product moved from process to process, it was not uncommon to find each department under the control of an independent sub-contractor who employed his own workers (MacMillan and Farmer, 1979). Similarly, Huberman (1995) provides evidence of work-sharing in the Lancastrian cotton textile industry prior to the 1850s; Thompson (1991) indicates that sub-contracting and out-sourcing was commonplace during the first half of the nineteenth century, in which there are some parallels with franchising and the presence of dual closure:

> The first half of the nineteenth century must be seen as a period of chronic under-employment, in which the skilled trades are like islands threatened on every side by technological innovation and by the inrush of unskilled or juvenile labour. Skilled wages themselves often conceal a number of enforced outpayments: rent of machinery, payment for the use of motive power, fines for faulty work or indiscipline, or compulsory decisions of other kinds. Subcontracting was predominant in mining, iron and pottery industries, and fairly widespread in building, whereby the 'butty' or 'ganger' would himself employ less skilled labourers [like franchisees do]; while children – pieceners in the mills or hurryers in the pits – were customarily employed by the spinner or the collier . . . In every industry . . . the wages quoted by workers reveal a different complexion from those quoted by employers. 'Truck', or payment in goods, and 'tommy shops' complicate the picture further; while seamen and waterside workers were subject to particular extortions, often at the hands of publicans – for example, the Thames coal-whippers who, until a protective Act in 1843, could only gain employment through the publicans who, in their turn, would only employ men who consumed up to 50% of their wages in the public house. (pp. 269–70)

Additionally, Mathers (1988) and Ellis (1996) argue that industry during the medieval period was marked by a variety of collaborative relationships, such as joint shipping ventures and joint stock companies, among others. Political and military history is also replete with the use of alliances and co-operative agreements between differing factions and nation-states to achieve expansionist or defensive objectives. Within legal practices, co-operative behaviour has a long history and is also widely apparent today: the majority of barristers are self-employed, but some share offices with each other and use pooled administrative resources (Morison and Leith, 1992).

As with the use of other co-operative behaviour, there is little doubt that business arrangements similar to franchising, as currently employed, have also been in existence – albeit in institutional organizations – since at least the Middle Ages. Grant (1985) and Smith (1990), for example, suggest that King John offered franchises to individuals to become tax collectors. The prospective tax collector, or franchisee, would pay a fee to King John for the privilege of collecting taxes in his name and passing them on to him. In exchange, the franchisee would retain a percentage of the collection for his efforts. Franchising activity was not, however, restricted to the collection of taxes: it was also evident in many local administrative and judicial functions. For example, as late as the fifteenth century manorial courts, operated by lords, exercised franchisal rights such as:

> ... supervision of the police arrangement within the allocated territory, inspection of weights and measures, and of the quality and measurement of essential victuals such as bread and ale; the presentment and punishment of petty crimes, especially assault; encroachments on common roads, and diversion of water courses. Very frequent were the presentment and punishment of failure to repair walls, ditches, roads, and bridges; of nuisances such as fouling of wells, of deceitful methods of trading, and of haunters of taverns. A lord might also have the right to hold a hundred court, still active for the collection of petty debts ... The countless manorial courts, often meeting every three weeks, and the kind of franchises just described, mattered more in the normal routine of great numbers of humble folk than the operations of royal justice in legislation or administration ... (Myers, 1971; pp. 146–47)

Arguably, however, the medieval lords cannot be construed to be franchisees in quite the same way as much of the popular franchise press seems to suggest. As a result of the tighter contractual obligations of the modern single unit franchisee, the medieval lords are more akin to master or territorial franchisees. These are individuals who have administrative roles via contracting with the franchisor to sell franchises in a specific geographic area or territory, and are primarily responsible for the recruitment and qualifying of franchisees within the given area (Justis and Judd, 1986). The 'owner'-operator franchisee is more akin to the peasant owing either labour-services or some form of rent to the lord. The peasant's position in differing classes of producers (determined in terms of their property rights) is similar to the 'owner'-operator franchisee in three respects:

1. access to the means of production (land) was conditional upon paying royalties and rent – just like the franchisee who pays for the right to access the franchisor's mental means of production (that is, the business blueprint);
2. they have only partial control of their own labour power because of the lack of ownership of the mental means of production; and
3. they have only partial possession of the product of their labour because they have to pay rent and royalties, among other payments.

While some of the activities performed by the medieval lords came to an end when the Council of Trent, in 1562, discouraged such activities, the organizational arrangements between medieval Cistercian monasteries and the Roman Catholic Church could be interpreted as a form of franchise arrangement (Davidson, 1995). The local monasteries possessed some degree of monopoly power in distributing salvation due to the assignment of exclusive territories and the lack of competing religious organizations. In exchange, the monasteries paid royalties of up to 5% of their gross annual income to a bishop on his annual visitation. Those monasteries that were not under a bishop's jurisdiction were required to pay for papal confirmation of all new abbots – or, in franchise terminology, an initial fee. Abell (1989) views the origin of franchising in commercial settings citing that, in China and 'Chinese Colonies', the *Mai Toi* (or table rent) agreement for operating restaurants has existed for centuries; he also notes that, in Japan, the

Norenkai system, by which a former employee opens an independent branch operation in return for a royalty, has operated since the Tokugawa era, which began in the early sixteenth century.

While such studies serve to deepen our understanding of the origins of franchising, the applications only cite examples of the context in which it was used. Franchising during the medieval era, and its use today, is not only the commercialization of what was an institutionalized approach to management, but indicative of a broader, societal, organizational form. Arguably, the examples of early franchising activity, cited above, are an application of the social structure of western Europe in the tenth, eleventh, and twelfth centuries: feudalism. Not only is feudalism like franchising, as we shall see, but franchising also existed at differing strata within this franchise-like society (such as within the administrative functions and the Cistercian Church).

Indicative of franchising's feudalistic origins is the word itself. Indeed, the derivative of the verb 'to franchise', *affranchir,* is the medieval French term for 'to set free', which referred to releasing someone from serfdom, and formed one of the central pillars of feudalism. There are other linguistic similarities: 'franc-archer' refers to a member of a body of archers established by Charles VII and exempted from taxes in consideration of their services; Poly and Bournazel (1991) the term 'franc' has a triple meaning: noble-free-Frankish and refers to the notion of the collective nobility of the Franks. But, the similarity goes beyond mere linguistics. There are direct parallels between franchising as it is employed today and its medieval connotations. Unlike the misinterpretation of the term by those seeking to promote franchises, enjoying freedom did not connotate the same associations as it does today. Freedom in the Middle Ages referred to the essential prerogative of being tried in the public courts, but also meant that he owed obedience to a higher authority:

> In the countries which made up the Frankish state, innumerable enfranchisements had taken place . . . sometimes the freedman was no longer subject to any private authority save that of those whose support he might seek of his own free will. Sometimes, on the contrary, he remained liable, in his new status, to certain duties of submission, either towards his former master or towards a new one – a church, for example – to whom that master agreed to surrender him. Since these obligations were generally regarded as transmissible from generation to generation, their effect was to create a true hereditary clientage. (Bloch, 1962; pp. 258–59)

By taking each of the characteristics of feudalism and comparing it with franchising, it is apparent that there are substantial similarities between the two. As is noted by Postan (1962; 1986), feudalism is commonly taken to refer to the legal or customary principles embodied by military organization in the Middle Ages, and the story of baronial and knightly contracts of service. According to this approach, feudalism embodied the following four attributes:

1. a development pushed to extremes of the element of personal dependence, with a specialized military class;
2. an extreme subdivision of the rights of real property;
3. a graded system of rights over land created by this subdivision and corre-

sponding in broad outline to the grades of personal dependence; and

4. a dispersal of political authority amongst a hierarchy of persons who exercise in their own interest powers normally attributed to the State.

A variety of historians appear to concur, however, that feudalism is more a type of society, which took differing manifestations ranging from forms such as the samurai type distinguishing Japanese feudalism from some western incarnations. Examples of feudalistic societies in Europe include France, Germany, and Britain. Indicative of the perception of feudalism as a form of society, Davis (1922) describes the medieval feudal state as encompassing the following characteristics:

> In this period the lawyers have arrived at the doctrine that all land is held from the King either mediately or directly. The King is himself a great landowner with demesnes scattered over the length and breadth of the realm; the revenues of these estates supply him with the larger part of his permanent income. The King is surrounded by a circle of tenants-in-chief, some of whom are bishops and abbots and ecclestiastical dignitaries of other kinds; the remainder are dukes, counts, barons, knights. All these, laymen and churchmen alike, are bound to perform more or less specific services in return for their lands; the most important is military service, with a definite quota of knights, which they usually render at their own charge; but they are also liable to pay aids (auxilla) of money in certain contingencies, to appear regularly at the King's council and to sit as assessors in his law court . . . These tenants-in-chief have on their estates a number of sub-tenants, who are bound to them by similar contracts and a similar personal relation. (pp. 88–89)

As a societal form, Bloch (1962) argues that feudalism can be regarded, to greater or lesser degrees according to the society under review, as a body of institutions creating and regulating the obligations of obedience and service. These services might be domestic, economic, or military in nature, on the part of a free man (the vassal) towards another free man (the lord), and the obligations of protection and maintenance on the part of the lord to his vassal of a unit of real estate known as a fief (Gansof, 1966).

Significant to the comparative process between franchising and feudalism is the role of the Carolingian vassalage. At the end of the seventh and early eighth centuries, the Frankish monarchy was involved in almost continuous warfare, some of which was civil as well as against foreign enemies such as the Saxons. The objectives of this warfare were threefold: the reconstitution of power of a central government (which had been destroyed); the re-establishment of order and Christian peace; and the continuation of a holy war against the infidel. As the incumbent institutions were inadequately resourced for realizing these goals, members of the Carolingian aristocracy decided to employ an existing and firmly established network of protective relationships. This entailed forming a contract between a lord and vassal, whereby the former undertook to protect the latter in exchange for obedience and loyalty (that is not exercising usurpationary power through raising forces against the lord). This loyalty often took the form of fighting in the lord's name and wearing the lord's heraldic colours, a practice which could be construed to be similar to the franchisee having the right to display the franchisor's corporate livery. These contracts also served to help the lord monopolize, via exclusionary closure, the resources embodied by the vassal such as their willingness to fight and the ability to raise forces. There are also parallels between the Carolingian vassalage and franchising in the reward structure.

As with franchises today, a lord's choice of rewarding a vassal for services rendered was twofold. Either he could keep the vassal in his own house and feed, clothe and equip him at his own expense (which is akin to the employment contract), or he could endow him with an estate or regular income derived from the land (a fief) and leave him to provide for his own maintenance. In other words, the lord had two options in managing with the costs of his workforce: he could either pay his vassal the equivalent of a salary, or he could make him 'self-employed' but still contractually beholden to the lord to raise forces in his name. For tax, social security and labour law reasons, a franchisee is a legally separate entity to the franchisor, a feature which has facilitated the perception that franchisees are self-employed. Despite legal independence, however, the franchisees (like their vassal counterparts) are performing the role of 'satellites' to lesser or greater degrees (Stanworth, 1995).

While in some situations the franchisee is dependent on the franchisor for the majority of its output, in others the franchisee may have more operational autonomy than may be apparent at first sight (Stanworth *et al*, 1984). Thus, some vassals and franchisees have greater bargaining power (determined by their ownership and use of the factors of production) and opportunity to accumulate capital than others. Furthermore, franchisee motivation not only derives from the opportunity to accumulate capital from the franchisor's brand capital and the surplus labour of his own labour force, but also derives from the potential of generating a further income stream (and potential social status) from new business units and the potential of contract renewal. The franchisee gets these opportunities in exchange for meeting franchisor-specified contractual performance objectives, such as meeting sales growth targets and conformance to the business blueprint (that is, for loyalty and obedience).

At this point, a caveat is necessary. It would be an error to suppose that all fiefs were in fact created by a grant made by the lord to the vassal. Many fiefs originated in a 'gift' by the vassal to the lord, suggesting that the man who sought a protector had to frequently pay for the privilege by surrendering his property as well as his labour (Bloch, 1962). The lord retained legal ownership of the land which he granted; once awarded a fief, the vassal would accumulate capital through the surplus labour of the workers on his property (they paid rent in services and monies). In exchange for the property, the lord undertook not to act in any way that would injure the life, honour, or property of the vassal (Milsom, 1976). He was equally bound to assist his vassal by his advice and to act fairly and justly by him. In franchising, some retail franchisors require that the franchisees find a suitable property from which to operate. Once approved by the franchisor, the 'ownership' of the site is passed from the franchisee to the franchisor, who retains the property freehold and/or lease. In this sense, the franchisor gains another site through the efforts of the potential investor as well as the opportunity to accumulate capital through the franchisee's surplus labour (via the royalty mechanism).

In the above paragraphs, the protective nature of the Carolingian vassalage network has been referred to twice. How is the protective feature of this form of feudalism evident in franchise relationships? Although extant research into the motivations to become a franchisee is limited, Felstead (1993) and Fulop (1996) opine that some individuals seek to become a franchisee because they perceive that the risk of failure is lower than being self-employed. In other words, they perceive that the franchisor's investment in brand capital, experience, and operating methods protects them from a higher risk failure, the loss of their initial and ongoing investments, as well as the stigma of being associated with failure. In exchange for this lower level of risk, the franchisee forgoes certain rights and gains access to sources of advice and expertise. As with the vassalage, however, the capability to function as a protective force is not only a function of the number of vassals (or franchisees) but also the quality of resources they embody.

Because of the perceived quality and knowledge power (expert, information, and tradition) of those franchises with superior brand capital, experience, resources and reputations (which tend to be held by the more mature franchisors), many well-qualified potential investors actively 'self-select' themselves into those franchises displaying such characteristics (Carney and Gedjalovic, 1991). In short, the potential franchisee targets only franchises which he believes to be of sufficient stature to help him accumulate capital and status via association by virtue of the franchisor's scale of operations and depth of experience. These actions suggest that some franchisors, like the Carolingian lords, are better able to afford security to their franchisees than others, and those with access to superior resources (and the contractual monopolization of those resources) are seen to possess competitive advantages over those of lesser status.

Like the resources embodied by vassals, the franchisees' are their skills, knowledge, and capital. Although some of these may derive from collectivist exclusionary criteria, such as the result of lineage, for some part they are individualist. This individualist theme is also reflected in another aspect of the Carolingian vassalage. As noted in the introduction to this book, individualist exclusion is effected by criteria which are purely individual, such as the possession of experiences and skills, and are tacit. Like franchising, vassalage was not transmitted by inheritance, ownership of the fief reverted to the lord as soon as services ceased to be rendered. Land was itself valued above all because it enabled a lord to provide himself with men by supplying remuneration for them, which was a source of capital, power and status. As in franchising, the lord was not responsible for the vassal's men which allowed him to reduce the costs of running his estates, but there was also some dependence on the vassal for finance. In its earliest form, financial payments (or 'taille') was an occasional gift from the vassal to the lord. During the eleventh and twelfth century in feudal France, however, the payment of taille became increasingly widespread as a result of the increasing circulation of money deriving from the increasing levels of population urbanization (Mayhew, 1995). Such tallage progressively became less arbitrary and its payment became fixed in terms of time and amount, like taxes and franchise royalties.

Within the trappings of feudalism, barons were awarded the right to collect taxes in specified territories (recall the master franchisee point above) and, as in the Cistercian church, the lords also exercised their rights of purveyance – they were paid a lump sum on the occasion of their visits. These payments benefitted only the lords and was conceived as the expression of their superior rights and status over the soil. In franchising, royalty payments represent the franchisor's superior rights over the trademarks and other intangible assets of the business (that is, the mental means of production). Thus, like feudalism, the franchisor may accumulate capital without the franchisee being able to reap the rewards of their own efforts which, in turn, means that the franchisor benefits from the surplus labour by its franchisees. In feudal societies, the lord was able to generate wealth, power and status as a result of the accumulation of land as well as some financial linkages. Arguably, the payment of land to the lord by the vassal could be taken to represent a non-refundable initial fee because the vassal bequeathed hereditary rights to it upon acceptance by the lord. In franchising, an initial and non-refundable fee is typically charged by the franchisor to cover (in theory at least) the costs of setting up the franchisee in business (Hall and Dixon, 1989).

While there appear to be a number of apparent similarities between feudalism and franchising, there is an additional point to be made. The traditional view of feudalism is that the lord gained the majority of his manpower resources from his estate: the parallel in franchising may be that the franchisor gains all of his resources from his franchisees. Yet, as with some businesses today, this was not the case and as such other contractual methods were used in tandem within the feudalistic societal form. These other methods have been described by historians as 'bastard feudalism'. According to Bellamy (1989), bastard feudalism is where the features of feudalism still subsist, though only superficially, and where the tenurial bond between lord and vassal has been superseded as the primary tie by the personal contract. As seen from the above description, feudalism was a social system based on the ownership of land; the occupiers did not own it absolutely but held it in tenancy for services (such as military services, the provision of certain numbers of knights, as well as wardship). While franchising is a somewhat shorter contract (often only five years duration) than the feudal commission, like its modern application the landlord was not only a farmer or renter of lands to tenants, but a master franchisee because of the additional jurisdiction over their labour. Bastard feudalism, by contrast, consisted of payments of cash for short-term services that were easily terminated: a form of part-time employment; but it also could be taken to be a full-time commission depending on the continuity of the engagement. Following Bellamy's definition, therefore, if franchising is a form of feudalism it exists in societies which are no longer feudal, but which are based on (for example) the employer-employee contract.

In his recent book, *Bastard Feudalism*, Hicks (1995) contends that this form of feudalism was an integral part of society rather than being parasitical, or an appendage to feudalism proper. He defines bastard feudalism as the set of relationships with their social inferiors that provided the English aristocracy with the manpower they required, and indicates that it existed in Britain as early as 1140 and that some vestiges were apparent post 1650. Power and influence in feudal societies ultimately derived from the manpower that lords could deploy; like franchises, however, it was power as a function of the quantity and quality of the resources available. Bastard feudalism permitted the lord to create the power which was deployed in many differing contexts, other than warfare, such for political influence. What is central and unique to feudalism, Hicks argues, is defined as the bond between lord and vassal based on the hereditary tenure of land and its use for military service. By contrast, what is unique and central to bastard feudalism is the periodic payment for service through monies and retainers. Thus, for example, enfranchised peasants were sometimes paid for their military services in order to enlarge the size of a lord's fighting forces; in a similar vein, the knight in Chaucer's *Canterbury Tales* has been described as being a mercenary rather than necessarily being the epitome of the feudal knight that many readers of that text may assume. Hicks emphasizes that both feudalism and bastard feudalism involved other types of service, in other venues, and from non-aristocrats and that these others were more numerous and more frequent than either payment with land or fees. He also observes that there was a long period of overlap in the two forms of feudalism, and that this is unsurprising since the functions of feudal tenure and bastard feudalism were very similar. The personal contract, however, enabled a lord to extend his effective authority beyond the bounds of his own land, and to enlist the influence of recipients in his own service, as well as to add their military sources to his own. As the contractee was able to accumulate capital through financial reward, the benefits were mutual but not equal.

What are the parallels with this form of feudalism and franchising? Although further comparative work is necessary to draw out the full extent of the similarities and differences, *primae facie*, there appear to be several likenesses. In one of the various examples Hicks (1995) cites that bastard feudalism, as short-term paid employment, was implicit in the professionalization process of noble bureaucracies. He observes that every major estate had a hierarchy of administrators paid with annuities and liveries: they had, for instance, estate officers who orchestrated the farming of the land, managed the parks and game, collected rents and other dues from the tenants. Some of these were employed via retainers and received expenses for time on the job. In franchising, as with the majority of other businesses since the eighteenth century at least, contract labour permeates most aspects of the manual and administrative functions (in some cases these are performed by franchisees of 'professional service' franchises). Secondly, not all franchisors are totally franchised (some have substantial portfolios of company-owned operations), and suggests that franchising does not necessarily provide the franchisor with all the manpower required to compete.[2] A similar situation exists among some franchisees who do not only operate the franchisor's concept but have also developed their own. Secondly, as will be shown in Chapter 6, some franchisee and franchisor firms are characterized by interlocking directorates, by which the director of one company will be a non-executive director on another. Another similar characteristic is that of the multi-brand franchisee which, although not numerous in the UK, are especially populous in the USA and Canada.

A key feature of the Carolingian version of feudalism was loyalty and this was expressed by a vow not to raise forces against the lord. Tenants were tied to particular estates by a plethora of inescapable obligations, such as to turn out for battle for their lord. As such, the highest standards of fidelity were always expected. A key element of bastard feudalism, however, is that some individuals could serve under other lords but for possibly different tasks and with permission. Some tenants did not turn out because military service was not specified as a contractual obligation, but others did so because of coercion and payment. Thus, some franchisees are able to become multi-brand operations because they are permitted to do so by the franchisors, as long as the additional operations are not direct competitors. Reflecting this situation, multi-brand franchisees in Britain operate units such as KFC, Wimpy, Burger King, and Spud-U-Like rather than being outlets from (for example) McDonald's and Burger King. While this situation may possibly serve to mitigate against the notion of exclusionary power and the monopolization of resources by the capitalist class, one reason why some are able to become multi-brand franchisees is because it is not in the interests to oppose rigorously such action. It may, in fact, be a source of innovation and competitive advantage (see Chapter 6).

The above paragraphs have suggested that franchising is a form of feudalism, and displays some attributes of bastard feudalism. It is apparent that there are several similarities, especially in terms of an initial fee, the contractual nature of the tie and some of the financial linkages. In this sense, business format franchising itself perhaps represents the bastardization of feudalism and suggests that, as an innovation, its development in contemporary society in the form of business format franchising is dependent on previous manifestations and adaptations to prevailing conditions. The following paragraphs outline some of the other antecedent variables which were significant to the emergence of business format franchising.

Product name franchises

The development of product name franchising and business format franchising is typically attributed to the USA and, in particular, to the efforts of the following companies: Singer Sewing Machine Company began franchising in 1863, McCormick reapers in the 1870s, General Motors in 1898, Coca-Cola in 1899, Rexall Drugs in 1902, and PepsiCo in 1905 (Ayling, 1988; Batchelor, 1991; Kursch, 1968; Tarbutton, 1986). In this vein, Dicke (1992), by adopting a case-study approach to examining the development of franchising in the USA since 1840, propounds that the use of franchising was initiated by Singer and McCormick reapers in order to surmount specific problems. Both companies produced complex durable goods requiring technical knowledge and skill among sellers and those providing after-sales care. High transportation costs precluded McCormick from centralizing production and shipping to widely scattered final points of sale, so reapers were produced by independent agents. Eventually, falling transportation costs and concerns over quality led to centralized production but, due to the seasonality of demand, the company developed a network of independent dealers rather than erode profitability by maintaining a network of company agents. Singer's decision to franchise was based on a shortage of working capital to develop its own system of dealers, so it used contracts to control independent dealers through establishing retail prices and helped its agents through national advertising and credit facilities.

Attributing the growth of franchising to these companies, however, cannot be strictly true if feudalism is seen as the precursor. While there appear to be some similarities between feudalism and franchising, there are also some differences which represent the latter's varying adaptations and commercialization since the medieval era. In franchising, as shown above, the components of feudalism still exist, but it has become more of a distributive mechanism permitting franchisors to increase market share rather than being a wholly institutional device. It would be a misconception, therefore, to suggest that the companies were responsible for the commercialization of feudalism. While they may be applauded for adopting product name franchising and for being instrumental in its diffusion, the commercialization process, however, began during the feudal era. For example, freemen or citizens of a city were given franchises to sell their produce on city land at markets and fairs in return for payment. As significant as these early practices are, they are not as important as those of British and some German brewers, who have been awarded the accolade for the widespread use of franchise-like arrangements through their use of the tied house system.

The term 'tied house' is used to describe the ownership of licensed houses by brewers, who lease the houses to tenants on the condition that only beers sold by the owners of the houses shall be sold in them. Traditionally, there was no requirement as to the brands of wines or spirits sold in these houses. The brewer owns either the freehold or leasehold of the premises and lets as a tenancy at will (Housden, 1984). The tied house estate slowly emerged in the latter half of the eighteenth century. Before this period,

Monckton (1966; 1969) observes that brewers did not wish, nor did they feel the need to have their own tied outlets, for two reasons: first, by custom and convenience, it was traditional for retailers to obtain all their beer from the same brewer; second, the brewers were unwilling to raise the capital to buy outlets, let alone the burden of administering them.

This situation changed when the sales of porter (an ale which, introduced c. 1720, combined the qualities of brown ale, old ale and pale ale) began to decline because of changing beer-drinking habits by the public. With the decline of porter, publicans turned to other suppliers of paler beers, which were replacing it. This change prompted some brewers to vertically integrate in order to exercise some control over the retailing of their beers, a process which became increasingly widespread during the 1780s. According to Vaizey (1960), the perishability of beer meant that public houses with small sales could not economically stock the supplies of more than one brewer if the beer was to be sold in good condition. Above all, he argues, because draught beer was an unbranded product it was highly susceptible to misrepresentation and adulteration through watering the beer.

Another reason for the emergence of tied estates was because of higher retail sales in public houses and a growing number of publicans owing quite large sums of money. Monckton (1966; 1969) shows that it was a simple matter for the brewer to convert the overdue portion of the account into a loan in return for a mortgage on the premises, or frequently a mortgage on the publican's lease from the freeholder, in which case the publican was tied by a loan. If the publican then failed to keep his business financially buoyant, the brewer was faced with the choice of forcing a sale or buying the premises himself. In order to preserve his beer outlets the brewer was more or less driven into the public house property market. The early development of the tied estate was such that by the time of the 1816 Select Committee on conditions of the beer trade, there were 14,200 tied houses out of a population of 48,000 licensed ale houses. The tied house system grew up, therefore, partly by necessity and partly by choice but was an *ad hoc* affair.

Up until 1869, not all brewers had tied estates, and the beer house itself had virtually no value because there were few refusals of licences to sell beer, which also facilitated the low barriers to entry as a beer producer (Donnachie, 1977). The permissive legislative framework and the rapid growth of demand for beer enabled numerous brewery concerns to expand their trade without becoming too actively involved in the retail market (Hawkins and Pass, 1979). The demand for beer was such that production rose from sixteen million barrels a year in the early 1850s to more than thirty million barrels in the 1890s. In 1869 licence restrictions were introduced via the Beer and Wine Act and, consequently, licensed property had a higher scarcity value. Many entrants found it difficult to raise the capital to surmount this entry barrier and turned to the brewers for loans, which were often granted in return for a tie on the supplies of beer. The brewers themselves, recognizing that outlets were dwindling, competed among themselves to secure as many licences as they could in order to safeguard their trade, but this occurred within the context of a cartel.

> The London System was a mechanism by which London beer outlets were loan tied to breweries, who felt secure from the need to add extra expense to their operations by agreeing not to poach each other's premises . . . The beauty of the London System was its self-regulating nature. Brewers all lent to landlords at a basic 5%. Few others would lend at that rate since the risk of losing the licence

was too great, so the brewers cornered the market of credit, though a small amount of public house finance was advanced by the distillers too. Any landlord could change his supplier should he so choose. There was no binding agreement with the brewer, though both parties understood that, if the publican did change, the brewer would call in the loan. While another brewer might advance the loan, the cash flow crisis the change in supplier would cause was sufficient to apply enough deterrence to enforce the working of the system. (Haydon, 1995; p. 257)

Such activity, however, did not occur in the same manner across the country. In London, for example, freeholds were rarely sold which meant that the freehold on public houses tended not to be held by brewers; instead most properties were held on long lease at low ground rents. Before 1890, nearly all London publicans owned the leases of their public houses; but because the price of the lease was high, they obtained a large proportion of the purchase price on a mortgage from a brewer, who in return obtained an exclusive sales agreement (Knox, 1958). In regions outside London, property freeholds were not only available for purchase but were so at prices within the financial capability of brewers. As such, brewers outside London tended to own their own estates. By 1900, the tied house system dominated the London public house market, but were less important in Wales, Scotland (where the licensing system was different) and almost unknown in Ireland. Although the London Loan System served to accelerate the process of forward vertical integration, the recessionary economic climate meant that it began to illustrate its defects.

There are a number of reasons for this situation. From the mid-1870s, London licensed property prices began to boom, meaning that publicans and brewers had higher costs of entry. These costs, combined with an increased level of tax on beer production, placed increased pressure on the price of beer in order to try to realize adequate return on capital. At the same time, because of the per capita demand of beer was falling (consumption during the 1880s was between twenty-seven and twenty-eight million barrels a year), publicans profit were under increased pressure. While some resorted to adulteration of the beer, others sought alternative and cheaper sources of capital. As the more willing providers of such cheap loans were the non-London based brewers, so these actions served to destabilize the London cartel. Confronted with a potentially reduced size of estate, a race for tied houses began which served to drive up the prices further and fuelled a frenzy of mergers and acquisitions. In order to help finance the purchase of tied estates and build and/or acquire production capacity, some 200 brewing companies were quoted on the stock exchange between 1870 and 1914 (Gourvish and Wilson, 1985). At the same time, however, the brewery industry was rapidly consolidating into an oligopolistic structure through a sequence of acquisitions of tied estates and shake-out of financially weak players (Watson, 1996) such that, by 1963, the top eight brewing companies controlled a combined tied estate of 33,900 public houses. In his examination of the brewing industry between 1886 and 1951, Vaizey (1960) indicates that by 1950 about 70% of all beer brewed was sold through the tied public house. While there has been some decline in the number of tied houses since the enforcement of the Monopolies and Merger Commission's 'Beer Orders' in 1992 (see Chapter 2), these first generation franchises continue to be an implicit and distinguishing feature of the British public house market. It is also one which is under threat from the use of business format franchises, a situation which is mirrored in the petrol retailing market.

In the USA, the growth of product name franchises was primarily conducted by the petrol companies (Dixon, 1967), who had profitability problems with their service stations (which were almost entirely company-owned at this time). These problems derived from the price wars with local competitors, who were more responsive to their local customer demands than their chain-owned counterparts. Vaughn (1979) indicates that the problems were exacerbated by the protectionist sentiments by states such as Iowa, who were increasingly antagonistic to non-home grown chains. In 1930, the 'Iowa plan' was instituted, when the Standard Oil of Indiana first leased a petrol station to the salaried manager for his independent operation. As this practice was adopted by other companies, so new costs were imposed on 'foreign chains', so much so that competitiveness was reduced. The result was a move toward franchising, which permitted the reduction of the oil companies' Social Security taxes and wage costs and resulted in greater flexibility to local conditions, improved service (thereby increasing petrol volumes), and rental income from leasing their sites to franchisees. During the same period, franchising was employed by automobile manufacturers (such as Ford), soft-drink bottling companies, and operators in the foodservice sector as a vehicle to expansion. For example, A&W Restaurants was established in 1919 and offered its franchises six years later; Howard Johnson began franchising their in-store ice-cream business in 1935 and, as a result, expanded to 107 restaurants in 1939. Since the oil crisis in 1974, there has been a decline in the number of product name franchised units in the USA. In 1974, there were about 231,000 such establishments; by 1984, there were 161,000; and in 1991 there were an estimated 134,000 (Horwath, 1991).

In Britain, the use of product name franchises in petrol retail did not emerge until the 1950s. Before World War II most selling points, or sites, for the retail of petrol were individually owned by the retailers who operated them. Some companies, for example Esso, had tried to open company-owned units but these were vigorously opposed (Dixon, 1963). Due to this situation, most of the petrol sites in the UK were multi-product, selling different brands of petrol. The trading relationship with the retailer and supplying company was typically informal (Dixon, 1962). Only during early 1950 did Esso begin to experiment with a new technique of petrol marketing which became known as the 'solus' system. By helping retailers who took their total requirement from Esso to rejuvenate their sites, which would also serve to attract additional custom, in exchange for a promise for them to maintain their existing arrangement, Esso was able to generate both brand and distribution economies. Being an oligopolistic supplier market, Esso's practice was quickly imitated and by early 1951 over half of all garages had a tie of some type; by 1956 the proportion had reached almost 89%, but most of these ties were exclusive supply agreements. It was not until 1954 that some petrol companies began to seek forward integration and acquire direct control of retail sites by purchase and long-term leases. Between 1964 and 1977, tenanted/licensed petrol stations grew from 5,435 (or about 14% of the total) to 7,326, which represented a quarter of stations in Britain. Although there were no company-owned garages in 1964, by 1977 there were 1,555 or 5% of the total market.

As important as the development and diffusion of product name franchising has been to the emergence of business format franchising, it was not the sole factor. The basis of a business format franchise is a business blueprint which permit the franchisor to replicate the original concept, and control franchisees through using the design as a benchmark. The essence of this blueprint is development in the standardization and systemization of operations, particularly in the USA, in order to help realize efficiency and marketing economies.

The role of standardization and systemization

Of significance to the emergence of business format franchising in the USA were three combined underlying trends: chain-ownership; the development of mass marketing; and restaurant design changes to permit productivity gains and appeal to a broad customer base. Chain-ownership among retailers had been facilitated by product name franchises and acquisition policies in the nineteenth century, but the emergence of standardized chains is a more recent development. Like product name franchising, the trend towards standardization and systemization can also be traced to the early hospitality industry.

Unfortunately, like franchising, there exists a lack of serious scholarship regarding the early development of the hospitality industry (Woods, 1991), and much ignorance. For example, the results of a survey asking participants how the hamburger was named reported the following: 14% believed that it was originally made from ham; another 14% believed it was named after the Earl of Burger, because it was his favourite meal; 27% had no idea as to its origins; and 11½% thought it was named because the beef steak was flattened into a patty with a hammer; the remaining third answered correctly (*Nation's Restaurant News*, 1995). The name derived from the Baltic provinces of Russia in the Middle Ages, where various tribes liked steak tartare. These Tartares introduced the delicacy to their German trading partners from the port city of Hamburg. They fried the meat and seasoned it with onions. When German immigrants arrived in the USA, they brought the steak with them.

What little accurate historical information exists is potentially illuminating when examining the antecedent variables affecting the growth of business format franchising. According to Bryson (1994), the consumption of fast food (a term which did not appear in popular vocabulary until 1954, followed by 'takeout food' in 1962) was apparent among the early pioneers of the USA. Eating out in taverns and restaurants was a popular activity in the late 1700s and early 1800s, but such establishments were primarily orientated towards feeding and accommodating travellers. It was not until the 1820s that restaurants dedicated to those wishing to dine out for pleasure began to emerge, and then rapidly to proliferate. In Boston, Ye Olde Union Oyster House opened in 1826, and Durgin Park followed in 1827; in New York, two Swiss brothers, Giovanni and Pietro DelMonico, opened a coffee and pastry shop in 1827. Inspired by these pioneers, others – especially Italian immigrants – quickly followed suit. The rate of expansion was such that, in New York alone, there were over 5,000 restaurants by the 1870s; by 1925, there were 17,000.

This same period saw the emergence of both retail bakery chains and multi-unit catering operations in Britain (Burnett, 1963). For example, in 1862 the Aerated Bread Company Ltd (A.B.C. Ltd) was founded; it moved from its emphasis on the production and sale of bread in the 1880s to the development of its catering side. By 1885, the firm had more than thirty outlets, and more than one hundred by the turn of the century. Similarly, J. Lyons & Company Ltd opened its first branch 1894 and by 1900 some forty outlets were in operation. In being vertically-integrated concerns, the wholesale baking business and retail sales of bread were of secondary importance to the provision of catering services (Jeffreys, 1952). The development of this type of chain-owned catering business was such that there were seven large multiple branch cafe and restaurant firms (such as J. Lyons, A.B.C. Ltd, Carricks (Caterers) Ltd, Cadena Cafes Ltd and Zeeta Company Ltd) operating 500 stores by 1950. It was also during the 1850s that the Khardoma restaurant chain operation began which, under the ownership of Forte, became a franchisor in the 1980s but withdrew shortly thereafter.

Fish and chips shops, the mainstay of the British fast food industry with over 20,000 outlets in the late 1950s, also had their origins in the nineteenth century. While their appears to be some debate concerning the origins of fish and chips, there is little argument that the majority of such shops were independently owned and operated, rather than chain-affiliated. Of course, there were exceptions to this rule, such as the presence of 150 fish and chips shops in Bristol, some of who were affiliated through a tied-house system (Walton, 1992). A person who appears central to the debate of the origins of the fish and chip shop chain is 'Granny' Duce, who came from Bradford and operated two or three greengrocery-plus-fish and chips shops between the 1860s and early 1880s. At some point thereafter, she moved to Watford, North London, and developed a chain of 'Duces Fish Cafes' between Aylesbury and Hazelmere. This situation was atypical, however, of other early fast food operations in Britain.

The fragmented nature of the market at this time is partially attributable to the comparatively low costs of entry to the activity and the activities of equipment manufacturers. Indeed, further fuelling the debate on the origins of fish and chips, a Rochdale-based company called Nuttalls argued that fish and chips were first combined by an Oldham tripe-dresser named Dryson in the 1860s, and have manufactured equipment for retailers since 1866 (Priestland, 1972). The low costs of entry provided an opportunity for some of the many poorer members of society to acculumate capital as city and town populations burgeoned during the industrialization era. In his social history of London in the mid-Victorian era of the late 1840s and early 1850s, Henry Mayhew (1861) records the presence of food for sale in public houses and over thirteen types of itinerant fast food vendors. Although Mayhew does not mention the sale of fish *and* chips (Barker *et al*, 1966), his work illustrates just how widespread the sale of fast food was at this time:

> Two of the condiments greatly relished by the chilled labourers and others who regale themselves on street luxuries are 'pea-soup' and 'hot-eels'. Of these tradesmen there may be 500 now in the streets on a Saturday . . . These dealers are stationary, having stalls or stands in the street, and the savoury odour from them attracts more hungry-looking gazers and longers than does a cook-shop window . . . Among the cooked food which has for many years formed a portion of the street trade is fried fish . . . The capital requirement to start properly in the business is: frying-pan 2s. (second-hand 9d.); tray 2s. 6d. (second-hand 8d.); salt-box 6d. (second-hand 1d.); and stock-money 5s. – in all 10s. A man has gone into trade, however, with 1s., which he expended in fish and oil, borrowed a frying pan, borrowed an old tea-board, and so started on his venture . . . The sale of sheep's trotters, as a regular street-trade, is confined to London, Liverpool, Newcastle-on-Tyne, and a few more of our greater towns. The 'trotter', as it is called, is the boiled foot of the sheep . . . From fifteen to twenty years ago glue and size, owing principally to improved modes of manufacture, became cheaper, so that

it paid the fellmonger better to dispose of the trotters as an article 'cooked' for the poor, than to the glue-boiler . . . The *baked potato trade*, in the way it is at present carried on, has not been known more than fifteen years in the streets. Before that, potatoes were sometimes roasted as chestnuts are now, but only on a small scale . . . The ham-sandwich-seller carries his sandwiches on a tray or flat basket, covered with a clean white cloth; he also wears a white apron, and white sleeves. His usual stand is at the doors of theatres . . . The trade was unknown until eleven years ago, when a man who had been unsuccessful in keeping a coffee-shop in Westminster, found it necessary to look out for some mode of living, and he hit upon the plan of vending sandwiches, precisely in the present style, at the theatre doors . . . To start in the ham-sandwich street-trade requires 2s. for a basket, 2s. for kettle to boil ham in, 6d. for knife and fork, 2d. for mustard-pot and spoon, 7d. for ½ cwt of coals, 5s. for ham, 1s. 3d. for bread, 4d. for mustard, 9d. for basket, cloth, and apron, 4d. for over-sleeves – or a capital of 12s. 11d. . . . The sale of hot green peas in the streets is of great antiquity, that is to say, if the cry of 'hot peas-cod' . . . may be taken as having intimated the sale of the same article. In many parts of the country it is, or was, customary to have '*scaldings* of peas', often held as a sort of rustic feast. The peas were not shelled, but boiled in the pod, and eaten by the pod dipped in melted butter, with a little pepper, salt, and vinegar, and then drawn through the teeth to extract the peas, the pod being thrown away . . . The vending of tea and coffee, in the streets, was little if at all known twenty years ago, saloop being the beverage supplied from stalls to the late and early wayfarers. Nor was it until after 1842 that the stalls approached to anything like their present number, which is said to be upwards of 300 – the majority of proprietors being women . . . The itinerant trade in pies is of the most ancient of the street callings of London. The meat pies are made of beef or mutton; the fish pies of eels; the fruit of apples, currants, gooseberries, plums, damsons, cherries, raspberries, or rhubarb, according to the season – and occasionally of mince-meat. A few years ago the street pie-trade was very profitable, but it has been almost destroyed by the 'pie-shops' . . . The sale of *boiled* puddings, meat and currant – which might perhaps be with greater correctness called dumplings – has not been known for twelve to fourteen years . . . (pp. 118–37; emphasis in the original)

By contrast, chain ownership in the UK hotel industry was pioneered by the London and Birmingham Railway Company, which opened the Euston and Victoria Hotels in London and Birmingham respectively in 1839. These initial moves were followed by further hotel openings both by that company and other railway businesses such that by the time of their forced disposal under the Transport Act of 1981, there were over 140 premises as well as a number of smaller inns and licensed premises (Carter, 1990; Taylor, 1977).

Although there were certainly small restaurant chains in the mid-nineteenth century, it was not until 1876 that the first standardized chain-owned concepts began to emerge in the USA. Frederick Harvey (an Englishman) is noted as the pioneer who created uniformity in signage, furnishings and service staff attire. His restaurants were located along the railways of the USA and, by the time of his death in 1901, there were forty-five restaurants operating in twelve states. In spite of his achievements, however, he was not the inventor of the standardized chain-owned restaurant concept, but more an innovator. As contractor for the large railroad companies, who sought efficiencies from uniformity, he was able to gain insight and knowledge concerning the benefits of standardization and how it could be implemented. Harvey's restaurants were also designed to appeal to travellers and, in this sense, their marketing orientation was perhaps more reflective of that of traditional inns and taverns.

The main feature of both Harvey's concept and the development of restaurants in major towns and cities at this time, was their focus on the higher social classes. The opportunity of feeding the working classes their lunch through chain-owned operations was realized by altering the way in which food was served and priced. Lunchrooms began appearing as early as 1869, serving simple food quickly and inexpensively (Pillsbury, 1990); in 1872 lunch wagons emerged when Walter Scott began selling fast food items, such as sandwiches, from a parked wagon outside the offices of the *Providence Journal*. These were followed by lunch counters in 1873, and self-service restaurants emerged when 'The Exchange Buffet' opened on 4 September 1885, in New York. Cafeterias began to proliferate after John Kruger, an entrepreneur who modified the Swedish smorgasbord idea to a self-service format, exhibited the concept at the World's Colombian Exposition in Chicago in 1893. Six years later, the self-service cafeteria concept was further modified when William and Samuel Childs introduced the tray to their restaurant, called '130 Broadway', and they also implemented a foodservice delivery system based on the tray.

These innovations reflected a concern with mass marketing and efficiency which mirrored many industries during the late nineteenth century, both within the USA and elsewhere. In 1911, the focus on efficiency and labour productivity was crystallized and summarized by Frederick Taylor in his book *The Principles of Scientific Management*. Although famed for its use in the automobile industry by Henry Ford, the essence of the approach involves the simplification of tasks, the divorce of management and task, strict adherence to job descriptions, resulting in low employee autonomy and a clearly delineated organizational structure. The application of these principles has been widely acknowledged as being a prominent feature of the contemporary hospitality industry, especially within the McDonald's chain (Jones, 1988). Clearly, however, these principles were not new when Taylor wrote his book but, like franchising, what is new is the degree and scale of the application of scientific management methods in society. Within the hospitality industry, Tayloristic features were most noted in the development of the cafeteria in the 1890s and, later, by the opening of Horn & Hardart's first automat restaurant at 818 Chesnut Street, Philadelphia, on 9 June 1902. These foodservice systems were designed to increase the speed of delivery, the volume of customers through low prices, and were emphatic of self-service to permit productivity and efficiency gains.

This emphasis was further developed in the 1920s, when the application of efficiency and standardized image was epitomized by the emergence of the White Castle chain in Columbus, Ohio. The founder, Walter Anderson, began business in 1916 when he opened a shop selling hamburgers. The quality of Anderson's hamburgers were superior to the typical offerings served at carnivals, fairs and amusement parks, such that he was able to open two additional stores. In order to continue growing, Anderson teamed up with Edgar Waldo Ingram who later, in 1933, bought Anderson's share of the business. They opened their first White Castle store with a US$700 loan and sold hamburgers at five cents each and encouraged their customers to 'buy 'em by the sack'. The hamburger permitted the owners to realize efficiencies and profit within the context of small stores. As the product required little space for preparation and cooking, it could be produced systematically (Langdon, 1986). This systemization and standardization was further facilitated by White Castle's use of frozen ground beef patties in 1931.

The use of ready-to-heat foods, the simplification of menu variety, and standardization were quickly replicated by other businessmen both within foodservice and elsewhere, who also adopted other systems and design features to improve efficiency and present a uniform image. For example, the diffusion of the automobile and the growing tendency for car travel in the USA prompted the emergence of motels, such that there were 2,000 by 1925 (Bryson, 1994). Their development posed a threat to the hotel trade of the day because motels were cheap and were not located near to train stations (reflecting some bias towards travellers by rail). E. M. Statler responded to this threat to the hotel industry by augmenting his hotels' services, through adding private baths and family dining areas. He also cut prices, moved away from luxury provision and instigated the use of service standards.

When the first branded and 'high' technology fast food outlet was introduced in the 1950s, this marked fundamental product and process innovation. The innovation entailed a move from cooking being a personalized art form towards the organization of factory-styled, 'Fordist', assembly-line workers operating like a 'crack drill team' (Carnes and Brand, 1977; Love, 1986; Nowlis, 1988; Palmer, 1983). In addition to fragmenting the tasks and employing closer supervision of staff, the attitudes and even the personality of the workers had to be influenced (Kottak, 1983; Leidener, 1993; Nichols, 1988) for the sake of standardization. Factory production techniques and principles, 'Fordism' and Taylorism, had been around for decades but their disciplined application to the restaurant industry was innovative because it initiated the industrialization, or 'technocratization', of service (Levitt, 1976; Reiter, 1991). From a Marxist perspective, Braverman (1974) argues that the process of Taylorization was not a result of technological change within the production process (the technology itself is seen as neutral) but more a form of implementation of technology to ensure capitalist control. It achieved this via dissociating the labour process from the skills of the workers; secondly to separate conception from execution; and thirdly, to use the resulting monopoly of knowledge to control each step of the labour process and its execution. Arguably, however, this was the result of the systemization process. The prime objective was the realization of efficient gains.

In marking the end of the dominance of non-branded/non-scientific approach to fast food, this product/process innovation was not revolutionary as some contest. The resultant new stores and new processes were the synthesis of trials in fast food companies in the 1920s and 1930s. In this development is the gentler, and more subtle, historical process of continuity and change rather than constituting a revolutionary approach to foodservice. Similarly, the growth and expansion of business format franchising is a product of the trend towards efficiency and application and modification of existing techniques, rather than being revolutionary. Although radical to some, these innovations were not necessarily discontinuous: they did not wholly break with past practices, but made them more efficient. These innovations, therefore, did not generate a 'new' industry so much as to rejuvenate an existing one by helping companies to realize higher levels of growth and brand dissemination. That legacy continues today as systemization has facilitated the decoupling of the production and service cores in foodservice operations. Such process innovations have permitted some foodservice operations to focus on realizing production economies, closer control of production factors and greater market presence as a result of being able to operate smaller, kiosk-type formats within a given location (Chase, 1978; Fitzsimmons, 1985; Jones, 1988; McMahon and Schmelzer, 1989). Whilst such process innovation may appear to be incremental, especially given McDonald's approach to the market, to others, such as traditional restaurants, the decoupling process may be more radical (Jones, 1988). Such innovation may otherwise be termed 'architectural innovation' (Henderson and Clark, 1989) as it reflects changes in which the components of the foodservice system are linked together.

Of course, these developments may have only facilitated chain ownership through company affiliation rather than franchising if it had not been for the other antecedent variables, such as product name franchises. Without these additional factors, business format franchising may have emerged at a later date. For example, in the UK, the growth of multiple retailing had become significant by the 1880s, and, like the USA, it was during the inter-war years that the multiples came to dominate Britain. According to Scott (1994), in 1920 the multiple chains accounted for between 7% and 10% of the value of retail sales and, by 1939, this market share increased to between 18 to 19½%. This growth was facilitated by a munificent property market, the availability of inexpensive finance, changing demand patterns, the rise of advertised products and the desire to realize purchasing and transport economies.

Contractual issues

The decision to franchise by some entrepreneurs in the 1950s, was partially assisted not only by the franchising activities occurring in other industries and the potential of their own concepts, but also the development of legal precedents and the use of trademarking to establish uniform standards for franchisors. The presence of a legal framework to protect brand image and violations of trademarks meant that business owners were able to lease their operating methods and concepts with reduced risk of loss of ownership, loss of power, or being copied directly. In other words, it served to realize dual closure: direct imitation by other capitalists and ownership of the mental means of production. In 1938, the US Department of Justice issued a consent decree involving the car manufacturer Ford and its tied sales finance companies; these dealers were allocated exclusive territories within which to work and in return they agreed to sell only those cars manufactured by the parent company. This decree may account for many of the changes in franchise agreements. In 1946 the passing of the Lanham Act paved the way for the development of business format franchising; it codified the concept that a trademark which was synonymous with quality could be used by its owner and those licensed by him, providing the owner controlled the quality of the goods sold under the trademark by the licensee. Prior to the Langham Act firms were protected to varying degrees by legislation regarding the direct imitation of concepts and designs. For example, in 1930 the hamburger chain White Castle won legal proceedings against White Tower, a company that copied its formula so completely that it was ordered to change its name, slogan, and style of architecture. They were also protected by contract law, as the first soft-drink bottling franchise agreement between two Tennessee lawyers and business partners, Benjamin Franklin Thomas and Joseph Brown Whitehead, and Asa Candler, the owner of the Coca-Cola trade mark attests:

On July 21, 1899, Asa Candler called the men back into his office to approve their plan. Casually, the partners handed him the 600-word contract they had prepared and signed. After carefully reading it over, Candler also signed the document. Clearly relieved, Thomas and Whitehead assured Candler that he would not regret it and turned to go before he changed his mind . . . [the contract] bound the bottlers to use only the Coca-Cola syrup, banning any substitutes, and it expressly excluded the soda fountain business, which would remain the sole province of the Coca-Cola Company . . . He agreed to sell them the syrup at $1 a gallon and to provide their advertising needs . . . [but] . . . Candler set no term on his contract. As long as Thomas and Whitehead fulfilled their end of the deal, it was permanent . . . in addition, the agreement did not include a provision for modifying the price of syrup, should the cost of ingredients increase. The two jokers in the contract would haunt The Coca-Cola Company in the next century, resulting in numerous lawsuits. (Pendergrast, 1993; pp. 74–75)

The contractual issue is also of some importance to the rise of business format franchising in Britain during the 1980s. Adams and Pritchard-Jones (1990) illustrate that the idea of trademarks emerged in the nineteenth century, and that this concept affected the later development of licensing in the UK. These developments permit the franchisees to operate under the tradename associated with the franchisor, and the franchisor's continuing control over the way in which the franchisee does business. The result is a uniformity between outlets designed to lead the public into believing that they are dealing with a single business. Of particular importance to British franchising was the Trade Marks (Amendment) Act 1984 because it introduced and distinguished between goods mark and service mark registration. So far as goods are concerned:

'Trade mark' means . . . a mark used or proposed to be used in relation to goods for the purpose of indicating, or so as to indicate, a connection in the course of trade between the goods and some person having the right either as proprietor or as registered user to use the mark, whether with or without indication of the identity of that person . . .

The definition of a service mark is slightly different, but meant that the franchisor had greater control of his intellectual property in service businesses:

'Service mark' means a mark . . . used or proposed to be used in relation to services for the purpose of indicating, or so as to indicate that a particular person is connected, in the course of business, with the provision of those services whether with or without indication of the identity of that person . . .

Such trademarks prevent franchisees and competitors from copying the concept and passing it off as their own.

Pioneers of business format franchising

It was not until the 1940s and 1950s that business format franchising, especially within the fast food market, began to be employed with increased vigour. Its emergence represented the combination of standardization, trademark protection and product name franchising. This post-World War II period saw the beginnings of many of the contemporary fast food chains and some hotel concerns. For example, Baskin-Robbins was established in 1940, Dunkin' Donuts in 1950, Burger King in 1954, Hilton Inns in 1947, Holiday Inn in 1952, and Pizza Hut in 1958. It was also during this period that some companies founded during the pre-World War II era began to seek franchised expansion. For example, the contemporary McDonald's concept was founded in 1948 and by 1954 (when Ray Kroc came along), there were a dozen franchises operating. The first McDonald's franchise opened in Phoenix, Arizona, in 1952. Others had started to employ business format franchising too, partially led by the actions of ice-cream concern Dairy Queen, which grew to about 2,500 outlets between 1944 and 1948 (Love, 1986), and competitors such as Carvel and Tastee Freez. Carvel was started in 1934 and, by 1952, had grown to 200 units; Tastee Freeze was founded in 1949 by Leo Maranz, and by 1953 operated 600 outlets throughout the USA. The other leading light at this time was the full-service chain, Big Boy. In 1937 the founder, Robert Wian, launched his chain of Bob's Big Boy (later called Big Boy) drive-ins that offered coffee-shop-style indoor seating in addition to kerb service (Langdon, 1986); by 1967, when Wian sold the worldwide rights to the Big Boy chain to Marriott, there were 600 units in operation. There are, of course, other examples of chain operated fast food companies in operation during this period, a few of which are shown in Table 1.4.

The extent of franchised growth during the immediate post-war period can be visualized by the fact that in 1945, there were only one hundred soft serve ice-cream stands in the USA, whereas by 1960 there were almost 18,000 (Mockler and Easop, 1968). Similarly, KFC had grown to 600 units and McDonald's to 228 by 1960; in 1961, Dairy Queen had 3,500 stores and Howard Johnson's, 727 units. The rapid economic expansion of the mid-1960s saw the continued rapid proliferation of franchised-based expansion, the initial forays by hoteliers and fast food companies into international territories, stock market listings and acquisitions in an attempt to realize both critical mass and new distribution routes by equipment and food manufacturers.

By 1964, the US Department of Commerce found franchising firms in ninety-eight standard industrial classification (SIC) codes, the largest proportion being in retail and service fields, especially fast food (Bernstein, 1969); between 1964 and 1969, an estimated 100,000 new franchise businesses were initiated and, in 1968, more fast food businesses were born than in all previous history (Ayling, 1988; Vaughn, 1979). By contrast, the development of business format franchising in Britain was much slower. Although manufacturer-retailer franchises had long been employed in the public house market, the first business format franchise was the Wimpy Hamburger chain in 1952 (an outline of this firm's development is provided as part of the Burger King case study at the end of this chapter). Like the use of voluntary chains in mainland Europe, this concept was imported from the USA. Servicemaster, a carpet and upholstery cleaning franchise was another import from the USA which came to Britain in 1958 after Raymond Church bought the rights to the brand for Europe. The ice-cream businesses, Lyons Maid and Mr

Fast food company	Founded	Sector	Franchise
Abbott's Frozen Custard	1903	Sweets	1954
Bain's Deli	1910	Sandwiches	1910
Brigham's Inc.	1914	Ice-cream	1977
Nathan's Famous	1916	Hot-dogs	1988
A&W Restaurants	1919	Hamburgers	1925
Maid-Rite	1926	Sandwiches	1926
Orange Julius	1926	Hot-dogs	1948
Bresler's	1930	Ice-cream	1963
KFC	1930	Chicken	1952
The Krystal Co.	1930	Hamburgers	1989
Carvel Corp.	1934	Ice-cream	1947
Big Boy	1937	Hamburgers	1952
Dairy Queen	1940	Ice-cream	1944

Table 1.4: Examples of pre-World War II fast food activities

Softee are also credited with offering franchises in the 1950s. As seen from Figure 1.1, franchising's cycle of growth only began to expand with any real momentum during the 1970s and 1980s, and was occurring at the same time as the growth of small firms generally and the internationalization of US-based franchisors.

The break-neck rate of expansion in the USA, however, could not be sustained indefinitely. The early 1970s, within the context of a wavering economy attempting to recover from the impact of OPEC's oil price increases, saw the beginnings of the first shake-out (Emerson, 1980; 1990) in the fast food market and the product name franchise sector (with its prevalence in the petrol retail and car dealing market). The main casualties of this process were those who had ill-founded concepts and lack of a managerial structure and culture to cope with franchises. Despite the shake-out (or perhaps because of it) and economic decline, business format franchises continued to expand during the 1970s (Marquardt and Murdock, 1986). By 1975 there were about 43,000 franchised restaurants generating US$12.3 billion, or a 24% share of the US$52 billion restaurant market; the hotel market, by contrast, generated some US$4.6 billion from 6,400 units.

In order to gauge the rate of diffusion of franchised expansion in the fast food industry, a survey of 400 US-based companies was conducted which compared the year in which the firm was founded (or incorporated) to when they started franchising. The companies advertised their offerings in the *Entrepreneur* (1990) magazine's annual survey of franchising and the IFA's *World Wide Franchising Directory* (1990). The data was plotted against the key franchise development dates, which are the pre-World War II period and each decade since 1950. The survey suggests that, despite the frantic development between 1950 and 1975, few operators appear to have survived the period. Indeed, about 58% of the sampled companies were established after 1975 which, in turn, suggests the newness of franchising in some product sub-sectors. Of the six product areas surveyed, more ethnic, sandwich and pizza and pasta companies were established in the 1975 to 1979 period than the 1980 to 1984 and 1985 to 1989 periods. Perhaps indicative of the early imitation of concepts such as KFC and McDonald's and others, the chicken and hamburger sectors show the opposite trend. These differences, therefore, reveal that the use of franchising illustrates sectoral differences as well as temporal ones. The diffusion of business format franchising, it appears, has varied according to the development of the industry, the emergence of new sub-sectors and chain growth activity within them. As the survey suggests that there have been numerous withdrawals from franchising over the period, there is also some question as to whether franchises are as safe as the popular press portray them to be (this contention is explored in further depth later).

Figure 1.4 shows that the late 1970s and 1980s (with a second shake-out occurring in the early 1980s) saw continued emphasis on franchised-based expansion. Indeed, the number of franchised restaurants increased to 102,200 generating sales of US$77 billion in 1990; the hotel sector saw the number of franchised units rise to 11,000 and sales to US$23.8 billion. The growth of hospitality franchises was such that they accounted for about 11½% of all franchised units in 1975, but 22% in 1990. In sales terms, they accounted for a tenth of all franchise turnover, but 14.2% in 1990.

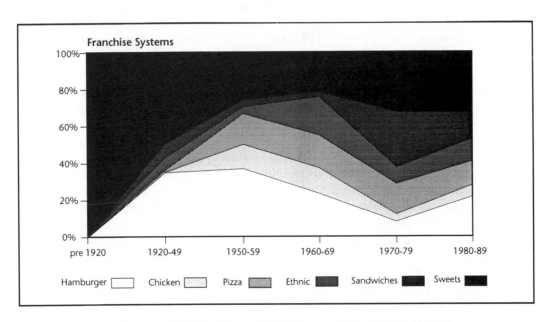

Figure 1.4: Sectoral and temporal differences in fast food franchising

Influences on small-firm growth and franchising in Britain

Prior to the 1970s and 1980s, the small firm had declined in significance in Britain since the early 1900s, with there being little specific government assistance to their growth. Indeed, before the influential Bolton Committee Report on small firms in 1971, government assistance to small firms was generally *ad hoc*, emerging more as a by-product of policies towards industrial efficiency, training, technology, organization or location. The prevailing emphasis at this time was one based on large organizational size and attempts to realize economies of scale especially within the context of the manufacturing industries. During the 1970s and particularly the 1980s, concurrent with the rise in services and an exacerbation of the decline in Britain's manufacturing base, there was a rapid increase in the population of small firms such that the number of self-employed persons increased from two million in 1979 to over three million in 1994. The prevalence of small businesses in Britain is such that, in 1993, enterprises with up to nine employees accounted for 94% of all UK firms. In the hospitality industry, such firms represent 90% of the market's total (see below).

Stanworth (1994) argues that franchises, especially within the hospitality market, are a sub-set of the small firm population in general and the diffusion of franchising is affected by the tendency towards self-employment in the labour market. Supporting this contention, he shows that the average size of franchisors is small: in Britain, the majority of franchisors have about six franchisees and have been operating less than five years. Perhaps reflecting their belief that being a franchisee means more than self-employment in a legal sense, franchisees are often seen as being as interested in self employment in general as they are in franchising *per se* and harbour the same motivations as other potentially self-employed workers when contemplating entering into business (Boe *et al*, 1987; Mendelsohn, 1992; Scase and Goffee, 1987; Stanworth and Smith, 1991; Stern and Stanworth, 1988).

Stanworth (1994) suggests that the conditions which were conducive to the emergence of small firms are also important explanatory factors affecting the rise of franchising in Britain. According to Storey (1994), small firms began to proliferate in the 1980s as a result of the combined effects of government assistance, the rise of services, the trend towards the decentralization of large firms, rising unemployment, and government assistance orientated towards small-business start-ups. Examining these effects in more detail, Keeble and Walker (1986) suggest that each of these variables alone is insufficient to help explain the rise of small firms (and, therefore, franchising) in Britain. For example, the increases in unemployment in the early 1980s may have been conducive to the rise of small firms because the profile of those made redundant, mainly skilled workers and middle managers, and the uncertainty of finding a new job meant that the attractiveness of self-employment increased.

There are, however, several modifying conditions to relying on 'unemployment-push' theories to explain the rise in the small-firm population. Firstly, not all individuals are motivated, whatever the circumstances, to become self-employed. Reflecting this situation, Meager (1992) argues that increased unemployment might be expected in an increased flow into self-employment among only some people. Other support is evident from a longitudinal study of entrepreneurship in Cleveland by Storey and Strange (1992), who show that the figure for those previously unemployed was lower than may have been expected; while a fifth of their 1990 sample of employed founders denoting motives classified as having been forced into proprietorship, about half of the unemployed founders fell into the same category. In 1987, Storey and Johnson discovered that the proportion of founders previously unemployed varied between a quarter and a half. Within franchising, some franchisors are loathe to contract the unemployed because they believe

Industry	All	Micro (0–9)	Small (10–99)	Medium (100–499)	Large (500+)
Agriculture and fishing	209,693	206,744	2,879	62	8
Mining and quarrying	7,709	7,156	431	87	35
Manufacturing	417,047	369,521	40,975	5,383	1,168
Energy and water	2,387	2,195	131	22	39
Construction	706,059	691,722	13,512	693	132
Wholesale, retail and repairs	620,200	574,508	43,003	2,175	514
Hotels and restaurants	160,919	143,800	16,369	618	132
Transport and communication	201,259	191,697	8,694	664	204
Financial intermediation	60,580	56,790	3,435	413	212
Business services	607,132	577,672	26,861	2,186	413
Education	101,798	99,027	2,398	345	28
Health and social work	191,897	173,407	17,730	528	232
Other	294,519	285,686	8,293	452	88
All industries	**3,581,469**	**3,379,925**	**184,711**	**13,628**	**3,205**

NB. Size determined by number of employees
Source: *DTI Statistical Bulletin*, June 1995

Table 1.5: Number of businesses in the UK by size of business and industry, 1993

them to be of lower quality than those moving from a position of full-time employment.

Secondly, there is some question as to the degree of commitment to being self-employed; certain individuals use self-employment as a 'stop-gap' between posts in full employment, while others will be unsuccessful and seek full-time employment. According to Evans and Leighton (1990), those in the latter category are likely to comprise mainly unemployed founders. They suggest that while self-employment provides an outlet for unemployed workers, they do not do very well at self-employment: they fail more often and earn less than entrants from waged work. As a result of the failure explanation and commitment issue, there is some suggestion that a component of the new firm foundations are cyclical. A third issue regarding 'employment-push' explanations is that there appears to be a regional bias in the formation of new firms which, in turn, suggests that when the level of unemployment surpasses some threshold within a locality, there is less incentive to for new start-ups to emerge. Indeed, the area of fastest small-business growth has been in regions less affected by high levels of unemployment. Bevan *et al* (1989), for example, show that self-employment generally shows a bias towards southern and away from northern England, a pattern which is also typical of franchising in Britain.

Perhaps an important antecedent variable to the development of franchising in the UK, is the fragmentation and decentralization of large firms. According to Fuller (1994), hierarchies which were once suitable to the management of stable organizations in stable environments have been considerably reduced. The result has been flatter organizations with fewer managerial layers between strategic decision-makers and those at the operational levels. Such moves have been facilitated by information technology and have been instigated to realize reductions in labour costs, but also as part of targeting different sets of customers. These trends have been especially prevalent in service organizations catering to a varied set of clients with diverse needs, a process which requires less communicative distance between the clients and the relevant portions of the system serving them (Kochen and Deutsch, 1980). The key values of decentralization are quick responsiveness, reliability, and the quality of service on offer. Recessionary pressures in the British economy may have renewed the trend towards devolution, but increasingly sophisticated customers and global competition has meant that the key values of decentralization have become significant to sustaining competitive advantages. Shutt and Whittington (1986) suggest that there are three ways by which such advantages have been sought:

1. decentralization of production in which large organizations are hived off into smaller plants, but are retained under the same ownership;
2. a detachment where firms cease the management of units, but retain revenue links with them (for example, franchising); and
3. disintegration of production and innovation by which large firms cease to own business units but retain control through market power or through the power to re-purchase the units.

The common denominator to each of these methods is the need for increased flexibility to cope with increasingly uncertain trading environments. Achieving this flexibility has entailed changes to managerial practices and beliefs. Some managers have traditionally argued for total integration because they believe that such an approach is conducive to realizing superior shareholder value, efficiency, assured supply routes, and raising barriers to entry (Stuckey and White, 1993). The decentralization trends identified by Shutt and Whittington (1986) suggest that companies have been retreating from total integration. Pressures, such as high labour costs and the need to access specialized skills, have forced managers to believe that flexibility is required in order to compete in an increasingly global market characterized by shortening life-cycles, the deregulation of markets, and continually fluctuating demand (Harrison and Kelly, 1988). Flexibility in employment allows firms to adjust and readjust their labour costs in line with fluctuations in the level of business activity (Beatson, 1995). For example, many small firms do not have accountants but rely on contracting in their services as and when required. This practice has been conducive to the emergence of franchised accountancy services to support the increased population of small firms. Such behaviour is not new, except perhaps to those employing the techniques to help them realize greater flexibility, as employer's have long employed techniques to exploit a cheap and variable labour force (Pollert, 1986).

Of significance to the emergence of franchising during the 1980s was the trend towards out-sourcing of non-core but labour-intensive functions, such as catering and cleaning facilities. Although the proportion of out-sourced functions has been rising, Bresnen and Fowler (1995) present evidence to suggest that out-sourcing has been adopted in an *ad hoc* manner as and when needed, rather than as part of an overall, coherent strategy. One, related rationale for the diffusion of franchising has been the desire by some medium-sized to large firms to reduce their risk within certain markets by transferring that risk to franchisees. For example, the 1980s witnessed a rapid expansion in the number of franchised milk delivery-rounds from about 200 in 1978 to 5,000 in 1992. Although the initial motivation may have been to lower the managerial costs associated with milk delivery, the continuing competition from supermarkets in terms of price, range, and availability means that the doorstep delivery share of milk by households is in decline (O'Connell-Davidson, 1991; Boyle, 1994). In 1990, the National Dairy Council estimated that about 72% of all household milk purchases were home delivered; in 1994, it was 49%. Meanwhile, the franchisees have assumed higher levels of risk.

While there has been a trend towards greater decentralization, this has not been matched by a similar movement in power and authority. For example, while many firms are out-sourcing their finance functions, British companies have tended to out-source their basic bookkeeping operations but kept in-house those areas of finance that are strategic or require commercial judgement. To some degree this retention of power combined with decentralization of operations by British companies is also evidenced by the rapid diffusion of the multi-divisional (M-) form of organization (Hill and Pickering, 1986) and has served to benefit the use of franchising by some firms. The M-form of organization is characterized by the decentralization of operational decision-making to profit accountable divisions, and the provision of appraisal, planning, and divisional monitoring systems at head office (Chandler, 1962). Corporations in the USA have used the M-form of organization since the 1920s, but its diffusion in the UK has only occurred since the 1960s.

In both instances, the adoption of the M-form was in response to administrative problems created by the incompatibility and ineffectiveness of existing organizational structures to cope with a strategy based on diversification into new markets and new products (Teece, 1980; Thompson, 1983). The incompatibility of strategy and structure resulted in cumulative control loss and the compounding of difficulties in making strategic and operational decision-making (Donaldson, 1987; Williamson, 1975). While research showing that improvements in financial performance have resulted from the adoption of the M-form is inconclusive (Armour and Teece, 1978; Karpik and Riahi-Belkaoui, 1994), there does appear to be some agreement that the structural type has facilitated greater operational control, accountability, and flexibility to divest underperforming businesses. Business format franchises seem to be structured in much the same way as the M-form, but within the context of a business focused on a particular product market. At the unit level, franchisees have limited autonomy to make strategic decisions but have more latitude on some operational issues (Stanworth, 1984), and the franchisor both monitors and appraises performance through the royalty process.

Of additional importance to the emergence of franchising in the 1980s was the creation of an enterprise economy by successive governments since 1979, in order to encourage entrepreneurship and investment in new businesses. Such industrial policy has included specific initiatives such as the Loan Guarantee Scheme, the Business Expansion Scheme, as well as the emergence of Training and Enterprise Councils designed to help small firms. At a more general level, Storey (1994) argues that the emergence of franchising in the 1980s has been the result of wider policies of deregulation, privatization, and tax regimes in favour of small firms, as well as a range of measures designed to stimulate more open competition and the emergence of new opportunities. Although some government policies may have been conducive to the resurgence of small firms in Britain, they do not represent a primary rationale. Keeble *et al* (1993), for example, indicate that there are three weakness in the policy explanations of small-business formation:

1. the resurgence of small firms generally predated the introduction of most government initiatives (but have since been accelerated);
2. many of the new businesses which benefitted under the schemes would have started up anyway, without government support; and
3. many of the direct schemes have only helped a minority of firms.

One of the factors which also served to assist the diffusion of business format franchising in the USA was the availability of capital for franchisees. Viewing franchising very much as an avenue into small business rather than as a big business activity, the main British clearing banks have been instrumental in the diffusion process. In 1981, the National Westminster and then Barclays appointed franchise managers to co-ordinate their activities in the franchise field; other banks followed suit thereafter. In general, these banks have been to lend up to two-thirds of the finance required to open a franchise. The importance of bank finance to franchisees is reflected by research conducted by Hatcliffe *et al* (1995), who indicate that between one-third and one-half of those buying franchises use banks for part of their financial requirements.

Internationalization of US franchisors

As noted above, the emergence of business franchising in Britain is due, in part, to the entry of US-based franchisors, such as Wimpy and Servicemaster. While instrumental at the early stages of growth, the continued expansion of business format franchising has also been facilitated by other market entries from the USA. Attracted by the cultural similarities, the successes of companies such as Wimpy and KFC, rising retail sales, ease of royalty repatriation, and the lack of franchise specific legislation, the influx of franchises from the USA has been such that they account for 17% of all franchises in Britain. Unlike their British counterparts, however, which are very small organizations with weak brand names and small market shares, the US franchises in the UK are generally household names and are large operations. Within the context of the UK foodservice sector, for example, it is clear that the major US brands have come to dominate. The tables show that, in 1974, the top four fast food companies, McDonald's, KFC, Burger King, and Pizza Hut, generated £4.3 million in revenue; in 1993 the combined sales of the four companies, excluding franchisees, reached almost £870 million – a phenomenal growth of 20,000%. When compared to consumer expenditure patterns, the combined sales growth of these four companies has increased from a share of 0.24% of total expenditure on meals consumed outside the home in 1973 to almost 7% in 1992. Together, the tables refer to the increasing demand for foodservice products which has had the effect of attracting new entrants to the sector and encouraged the development of chain-owned operations, including franchises.

Of the major foodservice operations in Britain, McDonald's has shown the greatest propensity for growth. By 1992, the company accounted for £0.45 out of every £10 spent on meals consumed outside the home (excluding contributions by franchisees – system wide sales in 1994 were an estimated £720 million or about 5.3% of total expenditure on meals consumed outside the home). In the USA, in 1992, McDonald's alone recorded system-wide sales greater than the top 100 chain restaurants in 1972. In some parts of the UK, McDonald's power is such that their market share is in excess of the 'technical monopoly' threshold of 25%, but this position has been primarily achieved through non-franchised expansion. In the UK, McDonald's began franchising in 1986 when it had 231 units, whereas KFC has been involved in the activity since 1965 and Burger King since 1980. Pizza Hut's position has been developed through a franchise agreement with Whitbread, a UK brewing company.

Despite some cultural similarities and historical ties between the USA and the UK, business format franchising has not illustrated the same impact as it has in the USA. The two case studies located at the end of this chapter, presenting the diffusion of the KFC and Burger King systems in Britain illustrate that these franchise chains have been assisted by the use of acquisitions and contracting of franchisees from the USA to operate in Britain, but have also been affected by the emergence of competitors from their own stock of franchisees. Nonetheless, franchising in the UK has at least some parallels with product/tradename franchises in the USA. For example, Hall (1964) observes that one of the explanations behind the growth of voluntary chains in the inter-war years was for agglomerate reasons (Astley and Fombrun, 1983), specifically as a response to heavy discounting by the major multiples, the growth of the large chain and exclusion of small independents from shopping centres. A similar process had begun in the 1930s in the USA, when wholesaler-retailer franchises, such as Walgreen, Super Valu Stores and the Independent Grocer's Alliance, among others, started. By combining, the independent and small retailers could strengthen their bargaining power with suppliers and improve marketing efforts. Unlike the USA, the emergence of franchising has occurred at a much slower pace but similar conditions have contributed to its diffusion in Britain. These are the pre-existence of chain-owned operations, rising demand for services, the use of manufacturer-retail and wholesaler-retail franchising, a pool of investors, and trademark laws. There is an important distinction to be made, however, since business format franchising was introduced from the USA and is not a home-grown business strategy.

YEAR	KFC[a] £ million	Pizza Hut £ million	Burger King[a] £ million	McDonald's £ million	TOTAL £ million
1974	4.3	n/a	n/a	0.03	4.33
1975	4.7	n/a	n/a	0.69	5.39
1976	4.6	0.27	n/a	3.3	8.17
1977	4.3	0.34	n/a	6.6	11.24
1978	5.8	0.53	n/a	13.8	20.13
1979	7.8	0.87	n/a	25.8	34.47
1980	11.3	1.6	1.7	39.9	54.50
1981	13.9	3.1	1.6	50.7	69.30
1982	14.6	4.7	2.6	67.1	89.00
1983	35.3	10.9	4.0	88.4	138.60
1984	25.1	19.6	5.0	112.4	162.10
1985	25.7	29.9	7.5	149.7	212.80
1986	12.1[b]	46.4	9.3	195.2	263.00
1987	34.0[c]	63.9	13.0	257.6	368.50
1988	33.7	82.5	n/a	314.8	431.00
1989	51.4	105.6	24.0[d]	373.2	554.20
1990	49.9	131.2	22.2	441.1	644.40
1991	50.9	142.2	38.3	480.0	711.40
1992	56.4	146.8	71.6	532.0	806.80
1993	51.0	158.6	74.5	585.7	869.70

Source: Company Data

[a]: KFC and Burger King sales figures do not include revenue from franchisees; that is, sales only refer to company-owned outlets. McDonald's revenue does not include franchisees' contributions as from 1986 (when the firm began franchising); [b]: 30 weeks only; [c]: 69 weeks; and [d]: 74 weeks.

Table 1.6: Growth in sales of major UK fast food brands (current prices), 1974–93

YEAR	Combined sales of the major US fast food brands £ million (actual)	Estimated grossed-up value of all meals £ million (actual)	Market share of major brands %
1974	4.33	1,786	0.24
1975	5.39	2,038	0.26
1976	8.17	2,503	0.33
1977	11.24	3,056	0.37
1978	20.13	3,630	0.55
1979	34.47	4,020	0.86
1980	54.50	4,880	1.12
1981	69.30	4,863	1.43
1982	89.00	5,211	1.71
1983	138.60	5,983	2.34
1984	162.10	6,510	2.49
1985	212.80	7,437	2.86
1986	263.00	8,320	3.16
1987	368.50	9,087	4.06
1988	431.00	10,065	4.28
1989	554.20	10,987	5.04
1990	644.40	12,684	5.08
1991	711.40	11,537	6.16
1992	806.80	11,831	6.82
1993	869.70	13,017	6.70

Source: company data/CSO statistics

Table 1.7: *Market shares of major fast food companies in Britain, 1974–93*

Summary and conclusion

Most current texts on franchising fall into one of two categories. At one extreme, typical marketing, retailing, and supply chain texts deal with franchising in an almost cursory manner. This form of discourse, at best, provides only a few pages defining the parameters of franchising and its relative merits as a form of organizational growth and distribution. At the other end of the spectrum are specialist books detailing a wealth of legal cases and precedents, as well as case studies of how a firm can become a franchisor, and details of processes of how to buy a franchise. There also exists a plethora of academic articles and symposium papers all examining the different operational aspects of franchising, but these do not necessarily lead to the establishment of research frameworks because the individual pieces lack academic cohesion (Littlejohn, 1993).

One implication from this chapter is that perhaps the greatest single lacuna is the corpus of scholarship concerned with the diffusion processes of franchising. Yet it is this approach which is potentially insightful to the birth, diffusion and death issues in franchising. By arguing that business format franchising is a form of innovation and through the application of Easingwood *et al*'s (1983) non-uniform diffusion model, the

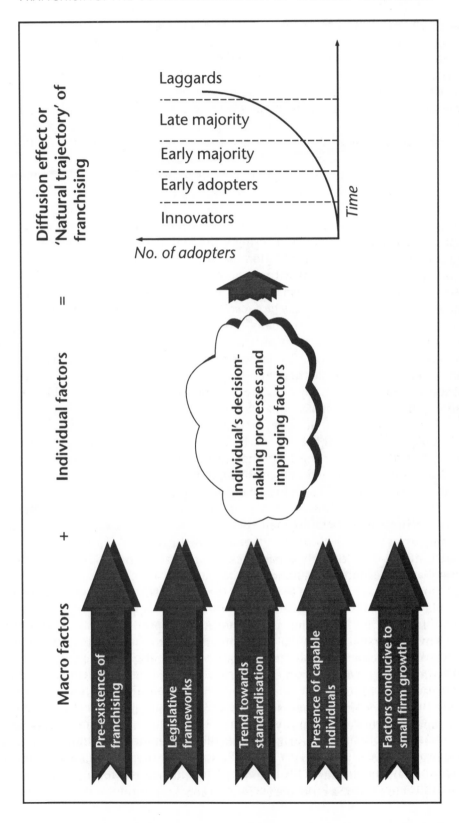

Figure 1.5: Some antecedent factors influencing the diffusion of franchising

trajectory of franchising in Britain and the USA was examined. The legitimation process of franchising has been influenced, among other factors, by at least four antecedent factors: the use of other forms of franchising, the underlying trend towards systemization and standardization, contract law, and the availability of a ready pool of investors (summarized in the schematic below). In Britain, even though it was introduced from the USA in the 1950s, the rapid diffusion of franchising occurred at a much later date. The growth of British franchising in the 1980s occurred when there was a greater emphasis on small firms, the rise of services, decentralization, and chain development by US companies in particular, in the hospitality industry.

This chapter has also sought to provide some background to the emergence of franchising in contemporary society. In so doing, we have argued that franchising, with its roots in feudal society, is also an innovation: it is the 'bastardization' of feudalism, a notion which permits a clearer picture to be painted to depict the franchise relationship. In this sense, perhaps, viewing franchising as the commercialization of feudalism permits us to add to Felstead's (1993) contention that the franchise relationship is a paradox: it is the decentralization of labour without autonomy. The modern-day vassals, the franchisees, are freemen but are constrained by the contract between them and their lord, the franchisor. While franchising may be construed to be, in itself, an innovation it is also an innovation in another sense. As many researchers examining the relational aspects of franchising will attest, the activity entails a different set of managerial skills from those required to direct employees. Franchisees are not employees in a true sense, and the changes required to manage them necessitate new sets of behaviours by managers and business owners. Put alternatively, the adoption of franchising for whatever reason requires innovation in organizational culture, structure, and processes.

The adoption and diffusion process of franchising by businesses has been a significant factor in attracting academic debate from a broader set of disciplines than social science. The growth of franchising in the USA and the UK since the 1950s has led to this organizational form assuming an increasing importance in a number of academic debates, including the fields of law, marketing, labour and organization theory, services growth and political economy paradigms. Some of the most interesting issues are the potential of franchising to provide self-employment opportunities, franchisor internationalization programmes, as well as decisions to adopt initially the franchise format. Other targets for research interest and scholarly debate include processes of franchisee recruitment, patterns of franchisee motivation, franchisor-franchisee locational issues, and the ownership redirection thesis, to name but a few. Each of these topics is touched upon elsewhere in this book, but only from the perceptive of franchising as an innovation.

Interpreting franchising as an innovation helps to answer, among other questions, why some franchise firms fail, while others go on to realize market share objectives. As there are numerous franchise texts which begin by emphasizing the importance of franchising, the style of this chapter does not differ from existing discourse. The majority of researchers within the field do not refer to franchising as a modification of feudalism directly, but the opening sentences of their articles, symposium papers, discussion documents, and books typically quantify the scale and rate of expansion of franchise activities. Such sentences are designed, usually, to underline the significance of franchising and its rather neglected state as a topic of serious academic debate. Nonetheless, by starting in this way, researchers are implicitly acknowledging that franchising is an innovation, but they have yet to provide a rationale for its diffusion.

Instead of seeking answers to questions regarding the diffusion process, researchers have concentrated their focus on issues other than franchising's permeation throughout the post-World War II society. As part of their work, many writers have readily acknowledged that franchising is an organizational form based on a legal agreement between a parent organization (the franchisor) and a local outlet (the franchisee) to sell a product, or service, developed by the franchisor. A few have explained how franchising has been used to diffuse, or distribute, a particular product throughout a particular market. Newby and Hardwick's (1979) description of how KFC was developed in Britain through the use of franchising, and Andrew Jack's (1957) work, *The Channels of Distribution for an Innovation: The Sewing Machine Industry in America 1860–1865*, are examples of such an approach. The notion and diffusion of franchising as an innovation in itself is, however, a *sine qua non* condition to this and other franchise research.

Although extant research is significant to the understanding of the dynamics of franchising, it is far from comprehensive; it has tended to reflect certain issues within franchising from legal, economic and sociological schools of thought rather than, perhaps, placing more emphasis on alternative explanations, such as those contained within strategic management texts and that propounded by Population Ecologists. The traditional schools of thought appear to concur that franchising is, indeed, an organizational form (Brickley and Dark, 1987), but have tended to side-step the notion that the realization of this form is the result of a chain of events. A franchise, as an organizational form, is the outcome of a strategy, which in turn is a pattern of actions based on decisions made by managers and entrepreneurs (Mintzberg *et al*, 1990; Shook and Shook, 1993). These decisions do not simply come out of the ether or occur within a vacuum: they are based, typically, on what already exists and applying those preconditions to the situation in hand. By understanding some of the antecedent factors affecting the emergence of franchising, other fruitful avenues may be explored. For example, it permits some analyses of some of the influencing factors affecting the choice to franchise which, in turn, yields greater insight which can be made to the understanding of another grossly underresearched but fundamental franchising issue (Dant, 1996): why do businesses choose to grow and expand through franchising compared to other competing alternatives?

Whilst the 'macro' explanatory factors explored in this chapter have, undoubtedly, at least some bearing on the rate and extent of adopters of franchising, the chapter has not sought to explain why some organizations are more prone to franchise-based expansion than others. Establishing an explanation for this phenomenon, however, may enrich our understanding for the diffusion of franchising across different economic sectors and economies. Nonetheless, despite some efforts (Kaufmann and Lafontaine, 1994; Martin, 1988), our understanding of the impediments and facilitating factors affecting the diffusion of franchising at an organizational level remains under-developed. Arguably, this dearth exists because researchers of franchising have not explicitly accounted for the role of strategic choice. This chapter briefly introduced the issue of choice: firms which might benefit from adopting franchising must be aware of its trajectory and decide whether to follow it; those who do not, may not be aware of other innovations which are perceived to permit the realization of their objectives more closely. This issue of choice, therefore, is of singular importance to completing our understanding of the diffusion of franchising and its future trajectories (Dant, 1996).

CASE STUDY 1:
The development of KFC (GB) Ltd

Ever since Colonel Sanders signed Pete Harman in Salt Lake City to become the first Kentucky Fried Chicken (KFC) franchisee in 1952 and subsequently (in 1954) charged some fast food operators 3% of gross sales for using his 'eleven secret herbs and spices', a plethora of case-study research detailing the growth of the KFC chain in the USA, Australia, South Africa, and Japan (for example, Angeline and Hale, 1970; Bartlett and Rangan, 1987; Khan, 1992; Klein, 1979; Tomlinson and Waters, 1988) and its quality management programme (Apte and Reynolds, 1995) has emerged. The same cannot be said of the brand in the UK, but like Wimpy and Burger King, KFC has had a varied and rich history here. The following paragraphs therefore provide a 'potted history' of the chain's fortunes in Britain to help redress this omission. KFC opened its first UK unit in 1965 under a master franchise agreement in Preston (by Ray Allen and Harry Latham) and by 1967 there were three other units in the north of England (specifically, Liverpool, Leeds and Blackpool). After this period, a more 'scatter-gun' approach was adopted with outlets opening in London and the south coast in 1968.

Arguably, it was the inability to control effectively the franchisees as well as the lack of profitability of the area franchisees that caused them to sell to Heublein in 1973. Heublein bought 50% of KFC (GB) Ltd in 1969 and agreed to buy the rest on a formula based on the number of outlets (Heublein purchased KFC worldwide in July, 1971, for about US$275 million). Thereafter, the master franchisee opened stores rapidly – indeed, there were over 250 in 1973. Most showed good profits and therefore increased the purchase price. Heublein's acquisition of the stores was adversely affected by the miners' strike and the three-day working week and was, in part, helped by its franchisees. Between 1973 and 1984, the KFC continued to open small takeaway units throughout the UK via a combination of franchises and company-operated stores such that, by 1983, there were 360 KFC stores operating – the majority by franchisees – throughout Britain.

In 1984, however, upon the imposition of value added tax on takeaway food products, KFC suffered a decline in turnover and profits. According to *Popular Food Service* magazine, turnover across the network of 373 stores (of which sixty-five were company-owned) fell by a fifth, but some franchisees saw sales fall by over 35%. A customer survey at this time also showed that KFC offered little value for money and this spurred the acquisition of several multi-unit franchisees, namely Albany Foods and Valleythorn Ltd, to improve quality control and revenue flows. Some have indicated that the buy-backs of these two multi-unit franchisees was not just a response to these aspects, but a reaction to the ongoing loss of market share. Allegedly, KFC held a 6% market share of the UK fast food sector in 1975 and, by 1982, this had gradually eroded to 4%.

The Birmingham-based Albany Foods was originally a subsidiary of the US food giant General Foods which took over the KFC franchise for the Midlands in 1971. It had plans to open one hundred stores, but by 1976 it only had fifteen units (KFC had 260 stores by then, seventy of which were company-owned). In this year, General Foods withdrew from the global fast food industry after losing a substantial sum (about US$75 million) with Burger Chef (the chain was once a market leader in the US fast food industry; it was acquired by General Foods in 1968 as a distribution route for its equipment division and later acquired by hamburger concern Hardee's and converted to that trading format). Consequently, Albany Foods was sold to entrepreneur Stanley Cohen for only £25,000 (or about £1,700 per store), who imme-diately sold one unit for £15,000 (in effect reducing the purchase price to about £715 per store!). By 1984, Albany Foods had thirteen stores, eight of which were in central Birming-ham and one in each of the following areas: Leicester, Nottingham, Oxford, Warley and Wolverhampton. The stores were purchased for £2.293 million (or the equivalent of about £176,400 per store).

By contrast, Valleythorn was purchased from the franchisee's parent company, Sumeray & Rogers, for a smaller consideration – about £1 million. Valleythorn was the first KFC franchisee in London when they opened a store in North Finchley in 1969. Although the com-pany's parent company (involved in wholesale poultry and provision) had to write off the initial £8,000 investment, the company reached profitability by persuading KFC to let them raise prices. Between 1969 and 1973, Valleythorn benefitted from Heublein's agreement with Allen and built thirty units. In 1973, eleven of these were sold off. At this time, KFC had 150 outlets, sixty company-owned and ninety franchised (in the hands of twenty franchisees).

Whilst both acquisitions are significant as they mark the start of the repositioning of the chain, they are perhaps not as important as the events in 1986 and 1987. The former year saw a change in ownership from RJR Nabisco (Nabisco became the owners of the KFC brand in 1982 when they purchased Heublein) to PepsiCo for US$841 million cash in 1986 and, later that year, the formation of a joint venture between Forte Plc (then Trusthouse Forte) and Pep-siCo to manage KFC (GB) Ltd. These moves signalled a more aggressive strategic turnaround of the company to retain existing and attract new custom by investing in smarter high street outlets and encouraging staff to monitor operating standards in franchised outlets. Those fran-chisees unwilling or unable to convert their outlets to the new style were refused a new contract once their franchise came up for renewal. Some were asked to close down their units even though investments had been made to reposition their stores. Many franchisees were unhap-py at the idea of their small but often profitable stores being closed. KFC came to an agreement with those franchisees who wished to remain in the fast food business that they could do so provided they removed the KFC logo from their outlets. An estimated eighty-six franchisees left the KFC system in 1986, reducing the number of stores from about 380 (of which sixty-six were company-owned) to less than 290.

It was this repositioning strategy which also, therefore, initially succeeded in increas-ing KFC's direct competition in the UK. Most of these rivals were born out of the decision to move away from predominantly small takeaways located in secondary sites, to counter service operations akin to those operated by McDonald's and Burger King. Spawning from the ranks of ex-franchisees are numerous chicken-menu chains, such as Miss Millies (operated by Latham, the accountant responsible for introducing KFC to the UK), Favorite Fried Chicken (operated by disenchanted franchisee, Frankirk Foods Ltd), Dixy Fried Chicken, and Tennessee Fried Chicken to name but a few. It has not stopped there either. In 1993, for example, Ray Allen's son launched a chicken-menu based business format franchise called Allen's Fried Chicken.

These divisions and changes have been widely acclaimed by some (for example, mar-ket researchers Mintel and Euromonitor) as being significant as they mark an increase in the number of KFC's direct competition in the UK in terms of product offering and chicken-based franchises. The lack of marketing power and geographic spread, however, has partially negat-ed their importance – indeed of more significance to both KFC and these smaller chains are the hamburger operators with their own chicken products (which also benefit from the perception by customers that they are healthier than those sold in specialist chicken operations). Perhaps of some significance to KFC was the temporary dilution of some of the company's intangible resources at two levels. Initially, there was some loss of intangible resources which were assets and which enjoyed legal protection (intellectual property rights and trade secrets), such as the company's operating procedures. KFC also suffered a dilution of skill-based intangible resources such as the distinctive competencies of the franchisees, and a potential source of new ideas to rebuild the business.

As the companies have gone their own ways, however, so their intangible resources have also changed and they have developed new ones. Whilst the chicken fast food segment saw increased fragmentation after 1987, KFC did not seek to reclaim its former strength simply through new unit openings. Between 1987 and 1994, there was little emphasis on expansion via franchising but, rather, carefully staged growth through company-owned units, tighter control of franchisees and greater stress on quality, service and cleanliness. Indeed, by 1989, KFC operated 273 stores in the UK of which sixty-nine were company-owned; in 1988, there were 268 units, 205 of which were franchised. The company also sought to modify the marketing mix through:

- the introduction of new products to stimulate customer interest and the offering of menu items designed to expand the times that customers visit the restaurants;
- increasing the distribution of products through distributive diversity (such as 'Express' units in 1993, drive-through – KFC opened Britain's first drive-through restaurants in 1983 in Bracknell, Milton Keynes and London's Old Kent Road – and home delivery in 1994);
- changing their name and brand livery from 'Kentucky Fried Chicken' to KFC in 1993 (one of the few complete modernization programmes carried out since 1978/79);
- improving the orientation towards children and families via 'Happy Meals' and toy offerings and increasing brand awareness through television and radio advertising (reflecting this, KFC's franchise fees increased from 7% to 10%); and
- introducing value-orientated menus, such as buffets, 'Mega-Meals' and £9.99 offers to increase volumes.

The introduction of new products has been both of a longer-term and short-term nature. Short-term items have been evident in the form of such snack items as 'Chicken Popcorn' – a promotion which ran for about two months in 1993. The introduction of these snack-type foods and, to a lesser extent, burgers has been designed to increase the menu variety of the KFC brand. Lack of menu variety affected the degree of customer appeal and visit frequency as well as attract new and retain old customers, who were perhaps beginning to tire of the 'old recipe'. To this end, the KFC menu was expanded to include a 'Hot 'N' Spicy' range. Further, the introduction of snack items, such as 'Dippers', 'Hotwings' and 'Popcorn' were designed to appeal to children and families, as well as to reinforce the image that KFC was different from most other fast food operations because they supplied:

- unique products, but they are easily imitated by competitors as well as the hamburger chains. For instance, McDonald's, Burger King, Wimpy and Wendy's all have their own version of chicken dippers;
- low-priced products in order to emphasize the perception of customer value.
- added menu variety;
- products designed to widen the customer's experience of chicken. However, this

may be too narrow since the product diversification moves of the main burger chains has been orientated toward non-hamburger products, such as fish, pizza, salad items and desserts;
- products that attracted children/teenagers and under-24-year-olds.
- products that proved successful in the USA and other test markets, such as Australia and Canada, in terms of increasing store volumes and add-on purchases. Since these snacks are often of small portion sizes, they are more likely to encourage add-on sales as opposed to the main hamburger chains, whose products tend to be more filling;
- products supported by strong advertising and merchandising support such as 'T'-shirts.

These modifications, such as increased advertising and promotional activity entailed, required financing, and the franchisor increased its fees from 7% to 10%. This served to create some dissent among KFC franchisees, but seems to have abated once the advertising campaign started (Reeve, 1995). In 1993, the joint venture between Forte and PepsiCo was dissolved and KFC was bought back for £40 million. Since regaining control, the company has begun to seek rapid expansion and has begun franchising with more vigour than perhaps was apparent under Forte. As part of the change in ownership, PepsiCo also purchased Europe's largest KFC franchisee, Roberts Restaurants, which had fifty-two units located in south east England. Roberts Restaurants was incorporated in 1984 after the acquisition of Southern Fast Foods and their fifty KFC stores from distributors H. A. Job Ltd. The acquisition/reorganization was achieved by a demerger of H. A. Job Ltd to permit it to concentrate on its core activities. Subsequently, in 1985, Roberts Restaurants purchased another franchisee operation, Jessup Foods Ltd (which had five KFC stores) for a consideration of about £0.5 million. Prior to its purchase by KFC, Roberts Restaurants generated annual average sales of £21 million.

KFC (GB) Ltd has also re-entered the Scottish market, opening Europe's largest KFC unit (with over 250 seats) in Glasgow in summer 1992 and five smaller satellite stores (all company-owned). The larger unit has taken over the role of being the business's UK flagship store from its Marble Arch outlet in London (with 230 seats and which is located on an old Julie's Pantry – a Forte fast food brand – and Wimpy site). Prior to 1992, KFC had a problematic history in Scotland. The biggest KFC franchisee in Scotland was the hotel and casino group Stakis, which had fourteen stores in 1979. When Stakis reorganized its business portfolio in the early 1980s, it sold its KFC units to Scotia Stores. This company left the KFC system with eight stores in 1987 and subsequently opened their own brand, Mississippi Fried Chicken (now dissolved).

The following graph (Figure 1.6) represents the sales of KFC (GB) Ltd between 1974 and 1994 expressed in current prices and deflated according to price indices for meals consumed outside the home (MCOH) since rather than the index for takeaway food since these latter indices are not available prior to 1980. It should be observed that MCOH indices are higher than the all-item retail price index, but on average are slightly lower than the takeaway food ones. Sales only refer to those revenues deriving from company-owned stores and from franchisee royalty payments; KFC's systemwide sales in the UK, including franchisees, is an estimated £180 million a year – of this total about two-thirds derives from franchisees. After 1984, all figures are presented net of VAT, which was imposed on take-out food in that year's government budget. From the graph, it is apparent that, in real terms, sales volumes have stagnated since 1988. The figures do not necessarily reflect the changes and buy-back policies in the early 1980s and in 1994 due to time lags in reported data and some alteration in reporting (there is some suggestion that, for example, the contribution from the Roberts Restaurants

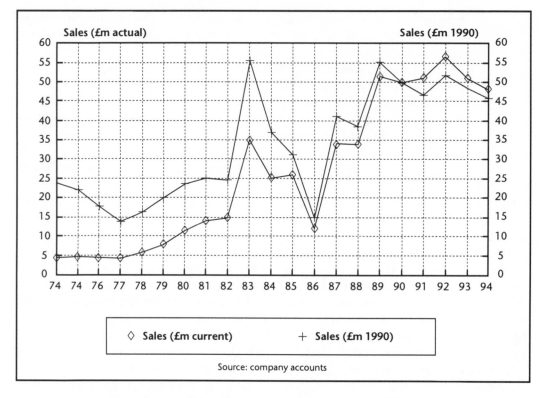

Figure 1.6: KFC (GB) Ltd's sales, 1974–94: current and 1990 prices

acquisition is incorporated under PepsiCo Restaurants Europe Ltd). Nevertheless, the down-turn in the company's fortunes during this period are apparent. Please note that 1986 figures are for thirty weeks only and 1987 are for sixty-nine weeks (due to acquisition by PepsiCo then).

To some extent, the brand's stagnating performance in the UK is reflected interna-tionally. According to PepsiCo's annual accounts, KFC's system-wide presence grew by an average annual rate of 3.4% between 1991 and 1994, and average sales increased by 1%. The brand has illustrated a lower operating margin than its sister brands, Taco Bell and Pizza Hut (see the table below). Some efforts have been made to rejuvenate the brand with product inno-vations such as 'Marinated Original' fried chicken and the launch of 'Colonel's Crispy Strips' and 'Chicken Pot Pie', as well as delivery services from its existing restaurant infrastructure (rather than necessarily building specialist stand-alone units).

KFC has some way to go in the UK in order to reach its target of 500 stores in the UK by the year 2000. Against a background of an increasingly competitive UK fast food indus-try, new product development and possibly a new offering may be required in the longer term. In the USA, KFC has introduced rotisserie chicken, dual concept branded units with KFC and Taco Bell and a cafe-type concept called 'Colonel's Kitchen'. Depending on their success in the USA, there is some suggestion that they may be applicable to the UK, meanwhile the UK mar-ket has seen the emergence of a dual brand-store featuring Pizza Hut and KFC.

Variable/brand	Pizza Hut	Taco Bell	KFC	McDonald's
Number of units	11,700	6,200	9,600	16,400
Total sales ($US billion)	7.4	4.8	7.5	30
Five-year average growth (%)	11	16	6	10
Contribution to PepsiCo's profits	16	12	9	n/a
% units company-owned	53	55	33	20
Average unit sales (US$000s)	670	950	730	1,800
Operating margin (%)	6.6	7.9	6.2	26.7
Return on assets	11.6	11.3	7.3	16.5

Table 1.8: Comparative position of KFC International

CASE STUDY 2:
The intertwined histories of Burger King and Wimpy

The histories of the second and third largest hamburger operations in the UK, Burger King and Wimpy, in the UK appear to be intertwined, and some strategic similarities are also evident. Starting with Burger King, the following case study outlines their respective histories. Burger King began business as InstaBurger King in Miami in 1954 and began franchising in 1959 when the chain had five stores. The subsequent owners of the concept, James W. McLamore (1926–96) and David R. Edgerton were originally franchisees of InstaBurger King, having obtained the franchise from two Jacksonville operators, Keith Kramer and Mattey Burns, who had bought the national franchising rights to an automatic broiler (Love, 1986). They became the only successful InstaBurger King franchisees by redesigning the broiler to rectify major flaws in the original system; they dropped 'Insta' from the name in 1957, the same year as the 'Whopper'™ was introduced, and revised the menu under the Burger King name. Importantly, they began franchising under their own name and gave away exclusive rights to large territories and allowed franchisees to buy land and build as many stores as they wished. By 1961, there were forty-five Burger King units in operation in the south west region of the USA. At that time, the Jacksonville operators were experiencing financial difficulties, so McLamore and Edgerton acquired the national and international rights to the company. A franchisee was free to sell sections of his territory to others if he wished and was also able to invest in other fast food concepts. The boom in franchising in the late 1950s and 1960s meant that there were 274 stores by 1967 when the two founders sold the chain to Pillsbury for US$18 million, they also meant that the new parent company had power differences when it tried to change some practices (Smith, 1980). Some of the difficulties in managing the chain were also apparent and possibly exacerbated in the firm's international operations.

Burger King first came to the UK in 1976 and between then and 1989 experienced numerous difficulties in achieving economies of scale. Part of this problem arose due to the over-reliance on franchising as a vehicle to growth, insufficient franchisee support, the general economic conditions between 1979 and 1984 and the cost of the franchise relative to others in the UK – about £375,000, and ongoing levies of 8%. For Burger King, the finance burden created friction with their first UK franchisees, entrepreneur Peter Gooch, M.A.M. Inns &

Restaurants Ltd and Sperrings Fast Food Restaurants Ltd. In 1982, for example, M.A.M. Inns & Restaurants reported in its end-of-year accounts that, due to the trading performance of its Burger King units (located in Reading and Hounslow, London), the expenditure incurred in acquiring the development and franchise rights and pre-operating costs had to be written-off. More publicly, the franchisee blamed its £170,000 loss on poor television advertising by Burger King. In 1983, the franchisee shelved plans to open a third unit in Aldershot. All of this was in contrast to the initial agreement with Burger King in 1980, which saw the franchisee sign a deal for £6 million to open sixteen units in the London area. Later in 1983, the Burger King units had still not produced the required return and were sold back to Burger King. The story was repeated with Sperrings Fast Food Restaurants (a subsidiary of Sperrings Convenience Stores which was acquired by Circle K in 1987 for £20 million in exchange for 184 stores – thirteen operated by franchisees) and with Peter Gooch (an ex-Wimpy and Golden Egg franchisee). Like the others, Peter Gooch was unhappy about the unit's performance, but, unlike the others, he sold his unit to a Wimpy franchisee.

The lack of initial success in establishing its formula in the UK forced Burger King, in 1984, to consolidate and improve its company base in order to provide a sound foundation for its subsequent expansion. Part of this retrenchment entailed the provision of seating facilities in its units and drawing 'new' UK franchisees from established franchisees in the USA. In order to gain familiarity with the UK business culture, these franchisees were encouraged to form joint ventures with existing businesses. For example, the first new UK franchisee, Gowrings Food Services, was the result of an agreement with Jim Crossen (who had eight Burger King units in the USA and a 50% share of the venture) and the Gowrings Motor Group. The second franchisee, Pickfords (since dissolved), was given technical expertise by the US-based Pickering Corp., which also had interests in hotels. In 1988, now under the guidance of Grand Metropolitan after acquiring the Burger King brand as part of the purchase of Pillsbury, the company's presence was significantly increased by the purchase of nine 'Quick' units from Whitbread. After this there was a slow, but steady, increase in the number of units to the extent that, prior to the acquisition of Wimpy in 1989, Burger King reported it had twenty-eight stores of which four were franchised (by Gowrings, Pickfoods, the US Army & Airforce Exchange and Shan Trading Ltd). Since 1989, Burger King has pursued a consistent policy of attaining critical mass through new store openings, signing multi-unit franchisees, pursuing distributive diversity, new product development, targeting children and increasing above-the-line advertising expenditures. The first of the following two graphs (Figure 1.7) shows Burger King's growth in sales (as a franchisor) since 1980 in both current terms and at 1990 prices. The second graph (Figure 1.8) illustrates Burger King's systemwide sales between 1992 and 1994, and shows that about a third of all sales derive from company-owned stores.

Wimpy is the original hamburger chain in the UK, but it is not of British origin. Wimpy was formed in Chicago, Illinios, in 1934. The name 'Wimpy' came from J. Wellington Wimpy, the archetypal hamburger-guzzling character in the Popeye cartoon strip. Eddie Gold, the concept's founder, wished to sell the worldwide rights (excluding North America) to J. Lyons & Co. in 1952. Although J. Lyons were originally reluctant, they tested the concept at the Ideal Home Exhibition in 1954 and found it to be a success. Due to a post-war currency shortage, J. Lyons could not afford to pay a large royalty and so a joint venture was formed whereby Gold owned a third. In the USA, only thirty-six stores opened and thus the chain has been perceived as British since the first Wimpy bar opened in 1955. The first franchised unit opened in May 1957 and then grew rapidly in the UK until the arrival of McDonald's and, to a lesser extent, Burger King in the 1970s. In 1958, Lyons formed a subsidiary, Pleasure Foods Ltd, to develop and man-

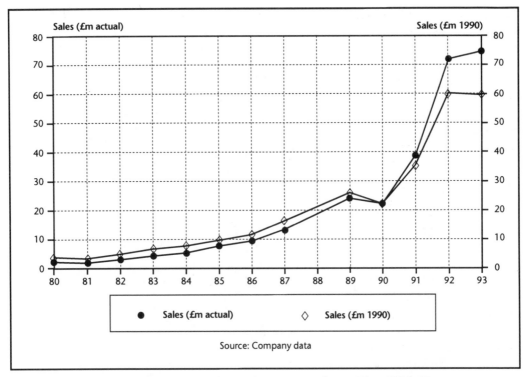

Figure 1.7: Burger King's UK company-owned store sales, 1980–93

age the franchise operation and its international arm (in 1957 Wimpy opened its first international unit in Portugal). The rate of expansion was facilitated by the low cost of the franchise –
typically between £15,000–£25,000 plus a one-time tradename royalty of £750 – and the lack
of competition. Indeed, by 1976, the chain had 815 stores in Europe (648 in the UK) and a further 685 units in twenty-three countries around the world. Due to adverse trading conditions
and high levels of debt from over-expansion, Lyons sold the Wimpy brand and its other catering interests to United Biscuits in 1976 for £7 million (possibly reflecting the value of the few
company-owned operations and some consideration for the brand value). After the acquisition, United Biscuits undertook to modernize the chain and make it a profit centre with its own
staff training, research and development, field supervision and marketing department. Franchisees not meeting standards were disenfranchised to the extent that, by 1984, its number of
table service outlets fell to 360 (only three of which were company-owned), but there were an
additional sixty-four counter-service (of which twenty-two were company-owned).

The investment required from a Wimpy franchisee for a counter service operation
ranged from £200,00 to £500,000, but typically cost between £320,000 and £390,000. Most
significant was the move from table-service facilities to counter-service operations in the UK,
as the following table attests. By 1987, the counter-service operations accounted for over half
(£67 million) of Wimpy's system-wide sales (£132 million). In 1988, system-wide sales amounted to £152 million generating profits of £9.3 million.

To some degree, the table depicting Wimpy's changing portfolio possibly disguises
the true extent of decline in the number of units operated in the UK. For example, the numbers have been buoyed to reflect the result of acquisitions, such as seventeen Huckleberry's
units in 1984 (for a consideration of between £7½ million and £8¼ million) and over forty

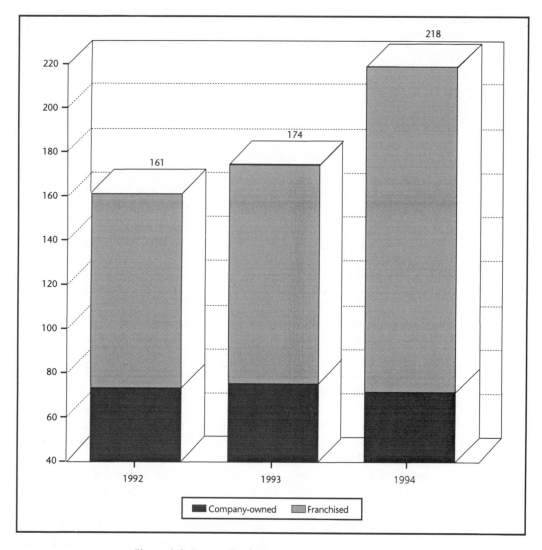

Figure 1.8: Burger King's UK systemwide sales, 1992–94

restaurants from its franchisee Empire International Restaurants Ltd for £4 million in 1979. The decline in numbers not only illustrates the refocusing of the chain, but also the fact that numerous franchisees left the Wimpy stable to form their own chains – which they then franchised. Hamburger operations deriving from Wimpy include Burgerland, Burger Park (now both dissolved, but was a franchise operation), Starburger (some of whose franchisees have begun to convert to the Burger King brand), Jenny's Burgers (a predominantly franchised operation), Casey Jones (recently converted to the Burger King brand after the parent company, Travellers Fare, was acquired by contract catering concern, Compass Plc in 1992), Great British Burger (now rejoined the Wimpy brand as a franchisee), Burger Delight and Mr Big (now dissolved) to name but a few.

Whilst Wimpy has had some history in counter-service outlets, its recent return to table service units is the result of a management buy-out from Grand Metropolitan. Wimpy, now the UK's third-largest hamburger brand after McDonald's and Burger King, was previously

YEAR	Number of table tervice stores	Number of counter service stores	TOTAL
1981	500	34	534
1986	330	94	426
1987	129	256	385
1988	148	239	387
1989/90	165	216	381

Source: Price, S., (1992), 'Fast food provision in the UK', Section 3, pp. 39–61, in Ball, S. (ed.), *Fast Food Operations and their Management*, Stanley Thornes (Publishers) Ltd, Cheltenham.

Table 1.9: Development of Wimpy counter service, 1981–90

owned by United Biscuits' Restaurant division and was part of a group of other restaurants including Pizzaland and Perfect Pizza. Perfect Pizza apart, these restaurant chains had an international presence, but Wimpy was the largest. Wimpy's international operations (comprising about 200 franchised units with an additional fifteen company-owned stores in 1995) are managed by a separate company, United Restaurants International Ltd (this company does not have the rights to the Wimpy brand in Europe, except Spain). In a separate company from Wimpy International and United Restaurants International, is the South African-based Pleasure Foods Pty Ltd which operates over 170 units under the Wimpy brand.

Grand Metropolitan, which had acquired the Pillsbury Group including Burger King in 1987, purchased the entire UB Restaurants division in 1989 for £180 million and subsequently sold off those parts which did not fit its emphasis on international food and drink brands. Perfect Pizza was sold to Scott's Hospitality, Pizzaland was sold to a management buy-out team called Brightreasons and the Wimpy table service units were sold to a management buy-out team headed by Max Woolfenden (funded by a syndicate of investment/venture capital groups 3i, County NatWest and Lloyds) for £20 million for less than £1 million of tangible assets. Under the terms of the sell-off, Wimpy had to remain out of counter service/takeaway provision for three years. Wimpy is now one of the largest independently held hamburger operations in Europe and largest hamburger table service operator in the UK. The counter-service units and some table service operations were converted to the Burger King brand. Since the acquisition, a number of Wimpy franchisees have converted to the Burger King brand, but a few have only converted some of their units. These latter franchisees have become multi-concept franchisees. Other closures, thirty-one of them since 1990, have occurred in order to maintain standards. Most of the franchisees which converted to Burger King have also become multi-unit franchisees, owning more than one Burger King unit as well as more than one Wimpy table service operation. Yet others have diversified further into other fast food brands, such as Häagen Dazs and KFC as well as developing their own concepts. Since 1989, Wimpy has sought further growth through franchising, has dabbled in distributive diversity (in addition to some kiosk units with bowling alley operator Allied Leisure – once one of the largest Wimpy franchisees in the UK with twenty-one units, but sold them in 1989/90; a drive-through operation has recently opened and the company has signed an agreement with a motorway services company – RoadChef – to develop the kiosk brand – Wimpy Express – in this market), and has been involved in promotional tie-ins with Disney characters and above-the-line advertising. In 1994, there were 270 Wimpy units in the UK, of which 262 were franchised. Since 1989, the franchisor company has generated, on average, sales of £19 million from its franchise and stores. System-wide sales, in 1994, have been estimated at about £75 million, compared to total system UK sales of £720 million by McDonald's and £220 million by Burger King, or about 6% of the British hamburger segment (McDonald's has an estimated 65% share and Burger King over a fifth). It is widely believed that Grand Metropolitan will sell the Burger King brand – possibly to PepsiCo in order to focus on its main business of branded food and drink manufacture and reduce its debt levels.

Notes

1. This need not represent too much of a constraint because it is possible to account for the impact of the height of start point. That is it is possible to consider the market size of the franchise industry in 1984, and then model it to its peak in 1990 and beyond. Figure 1.9 shows that by using a coupled differential equation, it may be possible to estimate franchisingís trajectory: The symbols are as follows: u = the initial growth rate; h = starting value of the franchise fraternity; v = growth trajectory after the peak, α = initial angle of growth trajectory; and θ = angle of trajectory post peak.

2. To some, this point may be a little 'chicken and egg'-like. As will be shown in later chapters, one of the motivating factors to franchise is lack of resources which constrains growth through company-owned methods. The argument here, however, is that franchises can be construed to be a form of feudalism; because of the use of paid employees (part-time and otherwise) and company-owned units, franchising is more akin to bastard feudalism than feudalism in its 'pure' form.

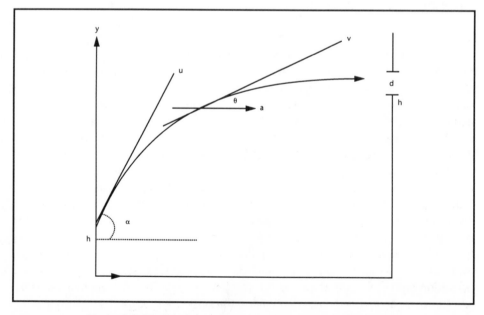

Figure 1.9: *Model to show hypothetical trajectory of franchising*

2 | To franchise or not to franchise? The role of strategic choice

Parkinson's Third Law: expansion means complexity, and complexity, decay. Or: the more complex the sooner dead.

C. Northcote Parkinson, US management consultant, *Liberation Management*

How does an industrial giant act as it grows? First, management concludes that a company cannot depend on individuals. After all, they have personalities and finite life spans. A corporation is supposed to be impersonal and external. Next thing you know, committees and working groups are spewing out procedures and regulations and stomping out individuality and spontaneity.

Ricardo Semler, CEO of Semco, *Maverick*

Introduction

Although the macro-level antecedent variables, such as culture, previous incarnations, and within and between class conflict, etc., affecting the growth of franchising have not been discussed by researchers, some of the more micro-level issues concerning the diffusion of franchising have been a semi-regular feature of the popular franchise literature. While some texts are devoted to selling the idea of franchising to both prospective franchisees and franchisors alike, others have concentrated their attention on the implications of pursuing the franchised route. Most of the latter discussion appears to be focused on answering requests for information on how either an individual or firm becomes a franchisee or franchisor. In all probability, such discourse, however, appeals to those people who may have already made the decision to pursue a certain course in franchising. Kaufmann (1991) suggests that people have a natural propensity to seek confirming evidence and to discard disconfirming evidence when it is present. In this sense such literature implicitly suggests that the decision to franchise is a discrete choice between two alternatives: whether or not to franchise? Much of the franchise literature does not tend to consider alternative forms of expansion. In other words, it does not address the process of legitimation. Yet, as shown in this chapter, business format franchising is not ubiquitous: it tends to be like other organizational development options – more prevalent in some industries and sub-sectors rather than others.

Much of the literature's foundation has derived largely from the economists' view of 'rational' decision-making, with its underlying rationale that these books will serve to enhance managerial discretion, improve analytical and rational capabilities and permit either the manager or potential franchisee to plan comprehensively. As most decisions are assumed to be rational, the diffusion of franchising within and among industries requires a focus on dispersing its benefits within the communication channels and the social system (Gatignon and Robertson, 1989; Mahajan *et al*, 1990; Rogers, 1983), as well as illustrating that franchising is a superior option to the one currently employed. Unfortunately, a key weakness of such texts is a general tone that is overly prescriptive, and a suggestion that franchising is an optimal choice. Like some strategic management discourse, it suggests that answers to such questions as the future strategic direction of the firm derives from the leadership, vision and objectives of management who behave in an optimizing and rational manner. The lists of the relative advantages of franchising to both sets of investors permit the decision-maker to identify and evaluate the economic opportunities and threats in the franchise environment, and assess the benefits and disadvantages of franchising against their perceptions of their current position. This literature is designed to permit strategic and business plans to be devised which, in turn, facilitate the realization of ambitions by marshalling and employing resources to exploit franchise opportunities. The future direction of the firm is seen, within these texts, to be the outcome of a situational analysis (establishing the relative strengths, weaknesses, opportunities and threats to the firm). For example, it has been inferred by one cohort of theorists (such as Brickley and Dark, 1987; Krueger, 1991) that franchising, in itself, is a form of innovation deriving from resource constraints (Caves and Murphy, 1976). Ideally, franchising permits the parent company to overcome problems of lazy employees and low levels of motivation. It has therefore been recommended as a method of reducing the costs associated with managing employees because franchising (above all other options it seems) provides them with less incentive to shirk. Others argue that of ultimate significance to the franchisor is that the strategy is, in essence, a hybrid capital market since it permits expansion via employing other people's money. Frequently, franchisors have been constrained by the non-availability of finance in the early stages of growth and have sold franchises to raise money to fund further expansion. Mature franchisors have, thus, been able to use the capital from franchisee royalties to fund international expansion and new product research.

Whilst promoting the benefits of franchising may serve to increase awareness of the strategy and the probability of raising the number of potential adopters, the failure to target differing sets of budding franchisees possibly limits its appeal. The prime criterion contained in much of the franchise literature is, typically, maximization of long-run profitability. Choice is essentially a matter of maximizing return on investment either through choosing the 'right' franchise or optimizing the existing business through franchising. But, decisions are more multi-faceted than economists' suggest. Chapter 1 posited, for example, that some freemen chose to become a vassal because of the benefits of protection that exercising such a choice entailed; a similar argument may also be extended to franchisees because, as Felstead (1993) observes, some people prefer the franchise option above self-employment as they want to be associated with an established company. Furthermore, within a body of literature focusing on the franchisor's activities, the issue of choice has only explored the operational alternatives available to individuals and companies that have already taken the decision to franchise. Baron and Schmidt (1991), for example, reported on the experiences of four and five franchisees and franchisors as regards the franchise agreement, selection of franchisees, finance and insurance, location of premises, shop-fitting, quality of products, advertising and point-of-sale promotions, initial franchise training, the specific skill requirements of franchisees, and the franchisor's ability to monitor the network and acquire feedback. Forward and Fulop (1993) extended this work, by studying thirteen well-established UK companies who had opted to grow through franchising, to elucidate operational choices regarding franchisee recruitment and selection, selection procedures and criteria, site selection procedures, fee setting policies, length of contractual tenure and aspects concerning ongoing support.

But, as with the solution to any problem, especially those associated with strategic direction issues, a variety of answers may exist. In spite of the promotional efforts devoted to expounding the advantages of franchising to both budding franchisees and franchisors, and the awareness by some companies that their competition is franchised, a question arises: if franchising construes such benefits and management are aware of them, why isn't the rate of diffusion higher and why does it illustrate different levels of diffusion within different economic settings? After all, given its potential benefits, all that remains is confirmation that franchising is preferable, in the case of the firm, to company-ownership and, at the individual level, self-employment. Clearly, firms and individuals are able to choose from a broad menu of possible development options and some have greater degrees of legitimation than others within a specific economic setting. This situation, in turn, suggests that extant franchise discourse is limited by its focus on the manner by which an ambition to be a franchisor or franchisee can be realized. Furthermore, problems have been frequently described as varying on a continuum from 'well-structured' to being 'ill-structured'. Mintzberg *et al* (1990) indicate that an ill-structured problem is a task which requires decision processes that have not been encountered in quite the same form for which no predetermined and explicit responses exist.

Developing from this definition, Kaufmann (1991) argues that it is important to distinguish between the different and independent determinants of ill-structuredness: novelty, complexity and ambiguity. Novelty refers to the unfamiliarity of the goal structure to be ascertained; complexity refers to the number of elements which have to be used and manipulated in order to realize the objective; and ambiguity is where more than one potential solution exists. Strategic direction issues tend to illustrate all of these attributes and that novelty, complexity, and ambiguity may call for different capacities and approaches by the problem-solver. Thus, the decision to franchise may not be, for some firms, the optimal or rational choice. Possibly supporting such a contention, there is a wealth of research which suggests that management does not behave in a rational or even optimizing manner. For example, Cyert and March (1963) have observed that managerial search for solutions to particular problems is 'simple-minded' and as over-emphasizing previous experience, by selectively searching in regions close to where previous solutions have been found (Kaufmann, 1991). That is, for some, the decision to franchise is possibly based on what other people have done within certain peer groups (see Chapter 4): in the process legitimation is gained because of increased density. Other constraints on the objectivity and rationality of decision-making and, thus, the decision to franchise exist. These are explored in Chapter 3.

While there is undoubtedly a market need for the extant literature concerning the decision to franchise, the arguments are incomplete and too narrow. Unfortunately, they ignore a number of personality, situational and economic correlates that are likely to affect the decision-maker's perceptions and decisions (Peterson and Dant, 1990), and they fail to consider why franchising and other relational forms tend to be clustered within certain economic sub-sectors. As the first part of a trilogy of chapters examining the decision to franchise, and thus the factors affecting legitimation, there is a need, therefore, to illustrate how certain strategies are grouped within differing economic settings.

Strategic choices and relational issues

All strategic choices entail issues concerned with relationships. Most strategic management texts concur that organizations have relationships with employees and other organizations, be they customers, suppliers, competitors, potential market entrants, and governmental or trade associations. In some cases, these relationships or 'architecture' will be no more than an acknowledgement that the other exists and, in others, could represent a deeper, mutually beneficial agreement (Kay, 1993). Some of the relationships are critical to the survival of the organization while others are perceived as trivial. Either way, these relationships do not just happen: they occur in an environment and situational context and for good reasons (Hall, 1987). By exercising choice and altering the course of a firm's trajectory, the nature of these relationships may change. For example, by seeking to introduce a new product, a firm may have to contract another supplier, take into account any potential retaliatory action by competitors, train staff to order the product and promote it, as well as consider the impact on the existing array of products. Equally, a firm may decide to form a joint venture to learn about a particular market and key skills possessed by its partner (Hamel, 1991).

Over recent years there has been a wealth of research examining a variety of inter-organizational relational forms employed within various markets, including those between tourism resorts and chambers of commerce and regional tourism associations (Selin and Beason, 1991) as well as between hotels and travel agents (Schulz, 1994). Reflecting the increasing diffusion of franchising and other such relational forms in the development of businesses, the last two decades have witnessed a metamorphosis in the scale and nature of research concerning organization design. Whatever the type of relationship, whether a joint venture or franchise, many of researchers have tended to analyze and describe the same phenomena: the causes of the restructuring, disintegration and blurring of organizational and market boundaries through various mechanisms. Within this literature, organizational development via the blurring of firm boundaries has been observed across a broad spectrum of industries including automobiles, airlines, biotechnology, electronic equipment, food manufacture, pharmaceuticals, robotics, steel, and telecommunications. Although some researchers have not generated models of the various network forms of relationship employed, other work has either developed a typology which is specific to that market or has only concentrated on one particular form, rather than developing a categorization of the differing hybrid forms employed within industry *per se*. Yet other research has generated typologies at such a broad level of abstraction that they may be of little interest or use to practioners.

Indicative of the latter approach, Lorange and Roos (1993) and Williamson (1975; 1991), among others, argue that relational choices essentially comprise three different, but generic types: hierarchy, markets, and hybrid forms. While markets and hierarchies may be self-explanatory, hybrid arrangements encompass a bewildering array of forms, including product name and business format franchises. A summary of the key differences between markets, networks and hierarchies as shown in Table 2.1.

Powell's (1990) matrix indicates that market transactions are characterized by clarity in the benefits to be exchanged, no trust is required, agreements are bolstered by the power of legal sanction, and price is the form of communication. Examples of such transactions permeate everyday life, and encompass activities such as buying groceries

Key features	Forms		
	Market	Hierarchy	Network
Normative basis	Contract – property rights	Employment relationship	Complementary strengths
Means of communication	Prices	Routines	Relational
Methods of conflict resolution	Haggling – resort to courts for enforcement	Administrative fiat – supervision	Norms of reciprocity – reputational concerns
Degree of flexibility	High	Low	Medium
Amount of commitment	Low	Medium to high	Medium to high
Tone or climate	Precision and/or suspicion	Formal, bureaucratic	Open-ended, mutual benefits
Actor preferences or choices	Independent	Dependent	Interdependent

Source: Powell, W. W., (1990),'Neither Market nor Hierarchy: Network Forms of Organization', *Research in Organizational Behaviour*, Vol. 12, pp. 295–356.

Table 2.1: Stylized comparison of forms of economic organization

from a supermarket, purchasing a newspaper, or sending a letter. Markets are characterized by simple buyer-seller relations (such as some of those evident in bastard feudalism) and, although potentially open to all, does not feature strong bonds between the two parties. This situation means that the participants to the relationship are free of any future commitments. By contrast, communication in hierarchies occurs in the context of the employment contract; as a result of the dependent nature of the agreement patterns of exchange matter, relationships are shaped by previous exchanges and by the position of authority. Hierarchies are conceptualized as bureaucracies since individual employees operate under a regime of administrative procedures, work roles are defined by higher-level supervisors and management, there are clear departmental boundaries, detailed reporting mechanisms, and formal decision-making procedures. In hybrid (or network) relational forms, individuals exist in relation to other units. These affiliations take considerable time and effort to establish and sustain and, as such, constrain both participants' latitude to behave individually; they are characterized by sequential transactions within a general pattern of interaction where the parties are perceived to be interdependent.

The use of networks has transcended all stages of industry life-cycles (Primeaux, 1985) and has had the effect of transforming fragmented industries into relatively consolidated ones (Dollinger, 1990), reducing industry variety (Miles *et al*, 1993) through increased brand dissemination and increasing the level of rivalry between firms pursuing similar strategies (Cool and Dierickx, 1993). It is evident, however, that the array and diffusion of network forms of organization differ by industry and sub-sector. Other differences are evident because some industries illustrate a tendency toward hybrid forms that are nearer to the market end of network continuum while others are closer to hierarchical mechanisms. As a result of the subtle differences employed within varying industries and sub-sectors, the term 'network form' is perhaps too encapsulating. After all, as suggested above, managers do not necessarily elect to choose the network form itself, but a specific type of hybrid arrangement such as franchising.

As a result of the differing interpretations of franchising and continuing debate concerning what franchising comprises, it is possible to generate a continuum of franchise types from this which organizational members may elect to develop their business in one or more forms. The presentation of the potential array of organizational development options available to the firm, requires the generation of a suggested taxonomy. According to Greenwood and Hinings (1988), constructs such as taxonomies are significant because they are ways of abstracting and directing key theoretical ideas, from which debate may ensue. The researchers argue that taxonomies are particularly important and central to organizational theory because of the general proposition that there are different types of organization. These differences have differences for performance, power, decision-making, conflict, morale, job satisfaction, communication, etc. The key point about taxonomic approaches is that they are multi-dimensional and more holistic in nature (Miller, 1981; Morrison and Roth, 1992); they emphasize a more encompassing array of relationships between a set of concepts, rather than limited aspects of organizational structures such as centralization, formalization, diversification, verticality, relatedness (Wrigley, 1970; Rumelt, 1974).

The other key notion behind taxonomies of organizational development is that they reflect strategic choice or an array of alternative strategies which are considered to best meet the enterprise's objectives (Child, 1972). Taxonomies show the approaches adopted by existing and/or previous incumbents in a market, but they also illustrate some alternatives which another firm could employ. Accordingly, some of the choices presented in some taxonomies could also be construed as innovations because they are new to the adopting organization. By formulating a taxonomy of relational choices, it is possible to see that firms have a broad array of choices from which to select their future trajectory. Selecting a particular course of action entails a process that involves focusing on a few alternatives, considering the selection factors, evaluating the options against these criteria, and making the actual choice (Marlin et al, 1994). This process may not be exhaustive or objective, but it occurs nonetheless.

Depending upon the intentions of management, the decision to franchise and the type of franchise chosen will either be intentional or emergent. The differences between the two approaches is probably best captured by Mintzberg and Waters (1985), who observe that intended strategies are carefully formulated, deliberately implemented and, by doing so, realized. Organizations that have intentionally pursued franchise-based expansion on the basis of an organized, purposeful and systematic process. Emergent strategies are apparent where an organization makes a series of important decisions which are woven into a meaningful pattern which can only be identified in retrospect. In other words, the organization may have developed into a franchise not because it intended to do so but, rather, because the firm's technology and trajectory suggested that franchising was an appropriate strategy to achieve additional growth in market share and possibly reduce the costs associated with acquisitions and green field developments. There are, of course, cases where the intended strategy is never executed, resulting in what Mintzberg calls 'unrealized strategy'. The issues of choice exist prior to the start-up of an organization as well as comprise a significant feature of its post-natal life, and are important to the stage at which the decision to franchise is taken (as shown in Chapter 3).

Unfortunately, in focusing on discrete choices between two options, many studies concerning organizational development have also illustrated a tendency to assume that each form is mutually exclusive rather than being, say, hierarchical. As noted above, however, these discrete choices are not an accurate representation of the dynamics of inter-organizational relations (IORs). While this point is explored further in a case study (located at the end of the chapter) of developments in the hotel restaurant segment, some franchisees form linkages between themselves to increase their buying power and some independent fast food companies have illustrated a tendency to become multi-unit franchisees. Examples of these 'convert' franchisees, are evident from France (Spizza '30 to Pizza Hut), Britain (Great British Burger to Wimpy and American Pizza to Domino's Pizza), and Australia (Sylvio's Pizza to Domino's Pizza). There has also been a continuing trend towards dual distribution systems as franchisors simultaneously use both company-owned and franchisees to realize market share objectives. For instance, for ten years, from 1956 to 1966, only franchisees sold Kentucky Fried Chicken: there were no restaurants opened by the parent organization; after that period there was increased company presence to increase control over the system. Nevertheless, despite a clear tendency toward increasing relational complexity, it is appropriate to begin to conceptualize the differing forms of hybrid organization and how they relate to each other.

Towards a taxonomy of hybrid forms

The few extant taxonomic approaches conceptualizing the array of hybrid arrangements employed within the retail and hospitality industries use uni-dimensional proxies. For example, Bailey *et al* (1995) suggest that the varying layers of their hierarchy of alliance types employed in retailing may be differentiated by the relative costs of exit. Accordingly, company ownership is associated with high costs of exit, whereas membership of a trade association is comparatively cheaper to leave. In their depiction of the array of relational techniques employed in the hotel sector, Harrison and Johnson (1992) differentiate between organizations which are asset-based versus those that are more cash-orientated. Their typology shows that those companies involved in management contracts are more cash-focused, while those involved in the day-to-day operation and control of hotels are more asset-orientated. Although instructive, these dimensions also have implications for other aspects of the business, such as risk, conformance to standards, and income flow. There is also an underlying issue of trust which links each relational choice. For example, some entrepreneurs will not enter into franchise agreements as they feel that they cannot trust the franchisee; they feel that they would incur lower rates of system growth rather than risk or jeopardize non-conformance to standards and perceived loss of control. Reflecting this situation, Ring and Van de Ven (1992) suggest that where the perceived level of risk is high and trust is low, then full-ownership is likely to be pursued and maintained; where there is high risk and high trust, relationships are governed by long-term contracts characterized by elaborate safeguards to reduce the possibility of conflict (for example, joint ventures and franchises). By contrast, where the perceived risk is low and trust is high, relationships are governed by recurrent contracts – a situation which has been explored in the book publishing sector by Stanworth and Stanworth (1995). They show that some publishers are in active contact with about twelve freelance workers, but only half that number are used on a regular basis and personal compatibility with freelancers is deemed important in their choice.

The diagram below (Figure 2.1) presents a suggested taxonomy of relational choices exercised with the hospitality industry, but it is acknowledged that it may have broader applications and that it is incomplete. The position of each relational form is substantiated by a broad array of literature on hybrid organizational forms (Bailey *et al*, 1995; Housden, 1984; Lorange and Roos, 1993; Wicking, 1995). While the definitions and descriptions of each form are developed in the narrative that follows, there are, however, two issues in need of clarification. Firstly, once a particular relational choice is pursued, it cannot be changed with ease. For example, it may be relatively difficult for a brewer to convert tenants into franchisees because they would have to relinquish some autonomy; it would also entail the development of a different set of skills and management information systems by the brewer in order to manage the franchisees effectively. Secondly, the overview of relational choices omits, for reasons of parsimony, territory franchises and concessions.

Empowerment

The quality of people-management in service organizations is crucial to determining the quality of customer experiences. In spite of this importance, much of the industrial relations research of managerial styles within hospitality firms, particularly at the operational level, concurs that it is highly authoritarian, paternalistic, and non-participative (Byrne, 1986; White, 1973). In short, people-management in the catering industry is marked by its lack of sophistication, and by its emphasis on deploying the cor-

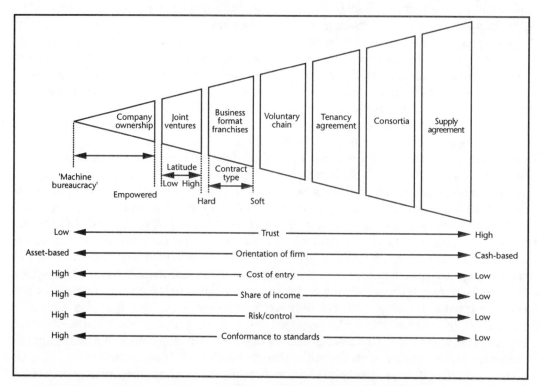

Figure 2.1: Toward a taxonomy of hybrid organizational forms

rect numbers and skills at the right (often the lowest) price. It is of little surprise that, as a consequence, the hospitality industry is marked by the widespread incidence of high labour turnover, persistent absenteeism, pilfering and poor employee performance. As the sector comprises mainly small- and medium-sized enterprises it is, perhaps, less surprising that these characteristics have also been witnessed in other organizations of a similar size. For example, a central concern of Scott *et al* (1989) and Rainnie (1989) was the identification of control methods used by employers in their conduct of day-to-day industrial relations; they found that the methods used were informal, and that there was widespread denial by owners that conflict existed. The small-business owners also perceived employee relations as non-problematic, and although they often spoke of a 'family atmosphere', this was often used to justify an authoritarian management style.

Of late, however, some companies have begun to adopt 'empowerment' as a route to reduce the costs associated with the traditional afflictions associated with the hospitality industry. Such moves may offer some light, albeit not that bright, within the otherwise dark world of small businesses and the hospitality industry's people-management records. A wealth of research has emerged concerning empowerment and some of it has made spectacular claims about the benefits of the approach. The key feature of the empowerment process is that employees have power to make decisions concerning how to perform their tasks, but it also necessitates sharing with employees information and knowledge that enables them to understand and contribute to organizational performance (Hitt and Tyler, 1991), and may be conducive to realizing small-scale innovations. The key benefits of empowerment, according to Bowen and Lawler (1992), include:

- quicker on-line responses to customer needs during service delivery;
- quicker on-line responses to dissatisfied customers during service recovery because employees are able to make the necessary amends;
- employees feel better about themselves and their jobs and this gives them a sense of worth and ownership;
- employees interact with customers with more warmth and enthusiasm, which may raise customer satisfaction levels;
- employees become a source of innovation and ideas about customer expectations; and
- the probability of word-of-mouth advertising and customer retention.

Unfortunately, like franchising, empowerment has been used to describe a wide variety of initiatives ranging from employee share ownership, suggestion schemes, quality-of-life programmes and quality circles, to delayering and autonomous and semi-autonomous work groups (Lashley, 1994). Clearly, the term 'empowerment' imbues different meanings and values to different managers, and the variety of differing mechanisms under the umbrella of empowerment reflects differing managerial motives. For example, the suggestion schemes in McDonald's and quality circles in the Accor Group reflect management's desire to learn from their employees and benefit from their ideas, experiences and involvement with customers. By contrast, the semi-autonomous work groups used in some restaurant chains are designed to relieve management from scheduling and could be construed as a tactic to delayer the organization.

Arguably, the type of empowerment policy chosen is dependent on establishing what employees want and systematic analysis of their need patterns. Often-cited motivational theories by Herzberg and Maslow, for example, suggest that employees want economic security, a sense of belonging, recognition and self-worth. Depending upon which one of these wants is dominant, then the appropriate policy is put in place (Alpander, 1991) and, as these wants change, there is a need to alter the empowerment policy accordingly. No one fixed programme works for ever; the better empowerment programmes are constantly up-dated, improved and revised. Employee wants are not the only contingency factor and these wants may become subordinate to issues concerning business strategy, the length of tenure with the customer, the sophistication of technology, the predictability of the environment and the learning capability of employees. For example, where the business strategy is orientated towards standardization and low price certain types of empowerment may not be suitable.

The differing types of empowerment also reflect the notion that empowerment is a matter of degree rather than absolute. Reflecting this situation, Ford and Fottler (1995) construct a taxonomy of empowerment types around two proxies, job content and job context (see Figure 2.2). Job content represents the tasks and procedures necessary for carrying out a particular job. Job context is a much broader concept; it refers to the rationale for why an organization requires a particular job to be done and includes both how it fits into the overall organizational mission, goals, and objectives and organizational setting within which that job is done. An individual's or team's decision-making authority over job content and job context rises in relationship to increasing involvement in the decision-making process.

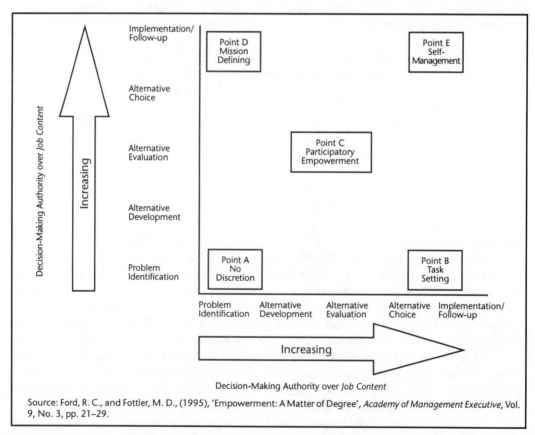

Source: Ford, R. C., and Fottler, M. D., (1995), 'Empowerment: A Matter of Degree', *Academy of Management Executive*, Vol. 9, No. 3, pp. 21–29.

Figure 2.2: Ford and Fottler's empowerment taxonomy

In the archetypal fast food store, employees are perceived to have little discretion since the job is designed by someone other than the worker and monitored by someone else. Ritzer (1983) concludes that the aims of such low discretion are identified as efficiency, predictability, calculability and control. To achieve these objectives, human participation and autonomy are reduced to a minimum; the results of such actions are dehumanization and other negative consequences, such as low work esteem and high labour turnover, but to some businesses this may permit them to compete on price:

> ... the fast food chains, by and large, actually count upon frequent turnover. Just about every job in the restaurant changes hands three or four times per year. In most businesses such turnover would be catastrophic. In the fast food business almost everyone is paid minimum wage and almost no-one ever gets a merit increase or joins a union. They are simply not around long enough. The whole system is designed to have labour turnover, thus averting pay increases. (Keegan, 1983)

> ... each store is a factory where workers' skills have been eliminated and labour costs kept to a bare minimum. No chefs, no apprentices wanted on this burger line: everyone has been levelled down to the uniform 'crew member' rushing between stations to perform tasks learnt in a day. (Lamb and Percy, 1987; p. 17)

As some hospitality firms have become more enlightened about the role of their employees, so they have given them greater responsibility for the job content but little over the context (Jones and Davies, 1991). In Ford and Fottler's (1995) view, the employee is empowered to make decisions about the best way to get the assigned task accomplished. In such cases, management defines the goals and tasks to be done, the employees are empowered to use their knowledge of their tasks to continuously improve what they do in their jobs. This form of empowerment is similar to quality circles, or 'work study' groups.

Ford and Fottler's (1995) third empowerment type is called 'participatory empowerment', where individuals are given some decision-making involvement in both job context and job content. They suggest that this form of empowerment is rare, but not perhaps as rare as their fourth category, 'mission defining'. This is where employees are empowered to decide only on job context dimensions. The authors cite one example of this form of empowerment as when employees are asked to decide whether an outside vendor could perform a particular task more effectively than existing employees.

Their final type of empowerment is called 'self-management', and to some within the franchise fraternity, it is this form which is encompassed by franchising. In this context, employees are given total decision-making authority for both job content and job context. Ford and Fottler (1995) argue that this situation requires considerable faith and trust in the abilities of the employees to use their new-found empowerment in ways that will contribute to the organization's effectiveness. Although the popular franchise press argues that franchisees are empowered such that they are 'self-employed', there appears to be little evidence to support this belief. As shown in Chapters 6 and 7, the latitude of franchisees is limited in order to maintain system standardization.

As with other strategic choice decisions, empowerment is a process requiring radical change. Organizations must change their policies, practices, and structures to create and sustain empowerment (Belasco and Stayer, 1994; Bowen and Lawler, 1995; Brown, 1992). It entails moving the basis of the organization from one based on simplified tasks, clear division of labour, reduced employee discretion and low trust to a system characterized by shared information about organizational performance, knowledge contributions and power to make decisions. In addition to the costs of change are those associated with the costs of sustaining empowerment. These include high costs of selection and training, a mismatch between customer demands for standardization and consistent use of procedures, as well as the costs of 'giving away' products and bad decisions. In spite of these costs, Jones and Davis (1991) suggest that there is evidence to suggest that empowerment will become a significant factor in affecting the manner by which hotel and foodservice firms are managed. Research in the United States by Heskett *et al* (1994) and in Europe by Vandermerwe *et al* (1994), has also indicated that 'service-breakthrough' firms have partly achieved their success by empowering their employees. One of these successes is the fast food chain Taco Bell.

Although the fast food industry is often noted for its use of Tayloristic management principles, some move towards empowerment has been witnessed. One example of its use is described in Schlesinger and Hallowell's (1991) analysis of Mexican-theme fast food chain, Taco Bell which was acquired by PepsiCo in 1978. During the period between acquisition until the mid-1980s, Taco Bell was structured much like any other fast food operation, emphatic of line management, standardization, suffered high labour turnover and located in high streets. During the 1980s, the US fast food market began to mature; labour costs increased at a faster rate than menu prices and property costs rose at a faster pace than inflation. As a response to this situation, Taco Bell sought alternative distribution routes and also undertook research concerning customer wants and to elucidate differences in store performance.

By examining employee turnover records for individual stores, Taco Bell discovered that a fifth of the stores with the lowest employee turnover rates enjoyed double the sales and 55% higher sales than the 20% with high employee turnover rates (Heskett *et al*, 1994). Not only did they seek to lower employee turnover but also sought to restructure their operation in order to deliver what customers said they wanted: 'FACT': fast food *Fast*; fast food orders *Accurate*; fast food served in a restaurant that was *Clean* and at the appropriate *Temperature* (Schlesinger and Hallowell, 1991). As both employee turnover and customer satisfaction were linked, setting about to solve the problems was achieved by changing the restaurant manager position through empowering them with decision-making authority, rewarding like franchisees (incentives linked to store performance) and helped them with training and methods to reduce labour turnover. Changes in the restaurant manager's job description were complemented by the alteration in the district manager's role. Rather than being responsible for between six to twelve stores, the 'market manager' (as they were retitled) now controlled twenty restaurants. The increased span of control did not just represent job enlargement; the market manager's typical day was spent reviewing the financial performance of restaurants within his territory and assisting those that were under-performing. Those that were maintaining or increasing performance were visited less frequently.

Joint ventures

Although joint ventures have a long history and were used in ancient Egypt and Syria (Harrigan, 1988) their use in the hospitality industry is sporadic and not as favoured as other network and hierarchical forms. A joint venture is like a partial merger consisting of a shared equity enterprise wherein the participants have committed less than all of their resources (Kent, 1991). Joint ventures occur both horizontally (that is, with companies at the same stage of production) or vertically (either with suppliers if a retailer, or with retailers if a supplier). They have a limited life-span, a limited scope of operations and tend to be employed in international markets. The main advantage of joint ventures comes from the synergistic combination of complementary assets of the parent company with those of the local partner, but the realization of this is dependent on the nature of the agreement. Unlike their name suggests, joint ventures are not necessarily operated mutually; some agreements are marked by a single dominant parent firm and others by a more independent local partner (Killing, 1982). Depending upon the type of joint venture, the parent company provides firm specific knowledge such as technology, management, access to finance, etc., whereas the local partner provides 'location-specific' knowledge such as market infrastructure, supplier networks, political trends, local legislation, etc. Reflecting this complementarity of knowledge, Teare and Olsen (1992) indicate that the usual joint venture strategy employed in the hotel industry is between a large real-estate developer/holder and a hospitality/travel-related firm. This combination of knowledge reduces the costs of collecting and assimilating information in foreign investments and, therefore, should offer lower long-term average costs when compared to the establishment of company-owned stores in a foreign country.

Table 2.2 provides information concerning the number and value of cross-border acquisitions and joint ventures in the international hotel and catering industry compared to the total number of deals. It shows that, in some years, the average value of cross-border joint ventures in hotel and catering exceeded the all industry values. It also shows that the popularity of acquisitions in the hotel and catering industry is such that they account for about two-thirds of all deals.

Industry	1991		1992		1993		1994		1995	
	No.	US$m	No.	US$m	No.	US$m	No.	US$m	No.	US$m
Hotel and catering										
Total	68	1223	75	2910	93	3008	126	3826	98	5062
Acquisitions	46	617	41	1195	59	959	73	2531	63	4349
Ave. value of JV		27.5		50.4		60.3		24.4		20.4
All industries										
Total	4165	86209	4036	127695	3811	152273	5312	196334	5952	229368
Acquisitions	1979	49730	2141	75382	1921	64242	2703	108732	3221	134629
Ave. value of JV		39.4		27.6		46.6		33.6		39.0

Source: KPMG Corporate Finance.

Table 2.2: Number and value of cross-border deals in the hotel and catering market, 1991–95

In some regions, market entry through company-ownership or through franchising is not possible due to political factors. The primary rationale for government's legislation in favour of joint ventures is the necessity to develop their country's infrastructure and industry. The factors concerning infrastructure development are clearly illustrated by McDonald's experience in the former Yugoslavia and Russia. The agreement between McDonald's and R.O. Prokupac (a Serbian food processing company) to develop the McDonald's concept in the former Yugoslavia had to win government approval. In an economy where only companies exporting to the West had the means to import from the West, the key factor was whether R.O. Prokupac could earn enough foreign currency to pay McDonald's for the franchise. This dilemma was partially solved by the terms of the agreement which allowed the Yugoslav company (which grew and canned tomatoes) to earn foreign currency by exporting tomato ketchup to McDonald's.

In addition to joint ventures being employed in the fast food market, they have been widely used in the brewing industry. For example, Bass formed a joint venture with Grolsch in order to distribute the product in Britain and, prior to its acquisition, Courage and Grand Metropolitan formed a venture called Intraprenneur Estates. Under the terms of the agreement, an annual property revaluation is necessary as is the maintenance of a specific loan-to-asset ratio. Both partners were required to inject funds to reduce the loans-to-asset ratio to an agreed level. Joint ventures have begun to emerge in the hotel industry and vary in scale. In 1993, two competing convention hotels in New York began marketing themselves jointly under the name 'NY-5000', reflecting that their combined capacity was 5,000 rooms (Koss-Feder, 1994). Additionally, Agip formed a fifty-fifty joint venture for selected hotels with Forte. In 1993, Choice Hotels International formed a joint venture with Journey's End Corp., whereby all Journey's End properties add a Choice brand name.

In an analysis of joint ventures, Harrigan (1988) suggests that they will tend to be formed when demand is growing rapidly and when demand uncertainty is high. There will be less of a tendency to form joint ventures when demand is growing slowly or declining and when demand uncertainty is low. The low level of joint venture activity in the industry suggests, within the confines of Harrigan's observation, that either demand uncertainty is low or demand is growing slowly. While there are variations on a country by country basis, in general tourism is one of the fastest-growing markets suggesting that demand uncertainty is of primary importance to joint venture activity in the hotel sector. Perhaps reflecting this situation, Dunning and Khandu's (1995) study of internationalization in the hotel sector indicates that the three main factors influencing foreign direct investment as opposed to equity involvement were:

1. knowledge of tastes and requirements of the home country clients;
2. trademark and brand image of the parent company; and
3.   investment in training.

However, there was also more of tendency to employ market entry methods other than joint ventures, which is consistent with other research. For example, using Dunning and McQueen's (1982) study as evidence Davé (1984) showed that one-third of multi-national (MNE) hotels in the 1970s were associated through equity participation, and the other two-thirds had some form of contractual arrangement, with management contracts accounting for at least two-thirds of such contractual involvement. These contractual arrangements were particularly prevalent within developing countries, with 63% of MNE hotels being associated through management contracts. Pannell Kerr Forster (1993) observes that US international hotel growth will be based, primarily, on franchising and management contracting with some asset-acquiring activity by non-publicly quoted concerns.

Business format franchises

Franchisors, through their contracts, specify what, when, how and where their products are to be sold and receive royalties on sales as well as, in some instances, payment from the franchisees for products which are then sold on to customers. This contractual form is the most popular in the hotel and catering industry, such that they represent about a fifth of all franchise systems in Britain. When the key definitional features of franchising are taken together and interpreted within the context of network analysis (Nohria and Eccles, 1992), franchisors appear to occupy a point of centrality – or, perhaps more specifically, a nexus of contracts – which is also reflective of their power. Barley *et al* (1992) observe that centrality can be measured in several ways, each of which is associated with differing substantive interpretation. For example, Freeman (1979) summarized three related measures of centrality (degree and betweenness) where a firm's degree of centrality is the number of other organizations to which the focal organization is tied. *Degree* is typically used as a measure of an actor's involvement in a network and is calculated by simply counting the number of adjacent links to or from an actor. By contrast, *betweenness* measures of centrality calculate the extent to which actors fall between other actors on the shortest path (the geodesic) and is usually interpreted as a measure of an actor's power (Brass and Burkhardt, 1992). An organization garners power over any two organizations when it lies on the shortest path between the two in a given network of relations. For example, in the franchise context, the franchisor garners a position of power over the franchisee and its suppliers since the franchisor contractually determines the majority of the franchisee's suppliers the franchisee should use and, in some systems, the suppliers are sub-contracted by the franchisor. Although instructive, such an example is inherently simplistic since, in reality, the franchise network is more complex. The following paragraphs outline the main network characteristics of franchising.

The initial premise of the diagram is that there is a variety of franchisee categories, rather than the myth propounded by some marketers that franchise systems comprise, predominantly, single-unit operators. In addition to these latter forms are multi-unit franchisees (those operating more than one unit of a particular brand) and multi-brand franchisees (those operating more than one brand) and corporate franchisees this is where an existing company becomes a franchisee to operate the brand through their own existing and new operations). In the multi-brand case, the franchisee may be a single-unit operator of one brand and a multi-unit operator of another or could be a single-unit operator of a plethora of brands. In some instances, especially in the fast food market, multi-brand franchisees have also developed their own brands which are, typically, operated as company-owned operations. In each case, the relationship between the franchisor and franchisee is potentially different. The single-unit franchisee (relationship E) is often depicted as being more dependent on the franchisor and having lower levels of bargaining power. But even this situation is not open to generalization since that

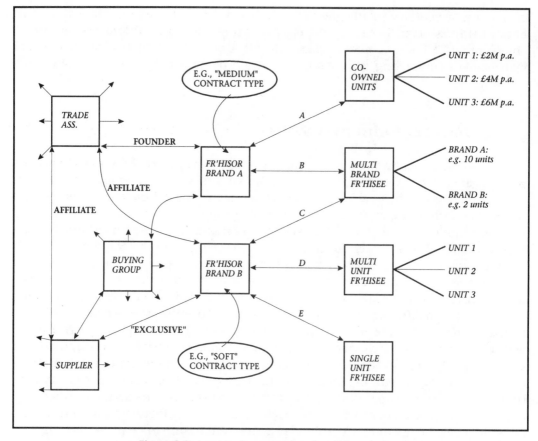

Figure 2.3: *A network approach to franchise relations*

franchisee may generate greater sales volumes than some multi-unit operators. Those with more than one unit and brand (relationships B to D) are seen as having greater bargaining power and lower levels of dependency (Bygrave, 1992). These features, in turn, suggest that there is structural differentiation between the franchisor and their differing franchisees. Such differentiation means that some franchisees may have more to contribute to the overall business in terms of potential innovation and mentor to other franchisees.

In addition to the presence of franchisee-operated units are company-owned units. These units may have a differing relationship (*A*) with the corporate headquarters than the franchisees. As with the franchisees, however, the relationship is not straightforward. For illustrative purposes, the company-owned units are depicted as generating differing levels of economic rents. Due to these differences, it may be that the manager of unit 3 has a different relationship and budget allocation than the others (which, perhaps, have different bargaining positions with headquarters). Of course, this situation may also be apparent within multi-unit and multi-brand franchisee operations.

Thirdly, the diagram suggests that, in addition to intra-franchise system differences is inter-franchise differentiation, where the point of variation is the degree of contractual control. Focusing on this issue specifically, Felstead (1993) formulates a continuum of 'hard' and 'soft' contractual types based on six key elements of the franchise contract. Each element was allotted a score of zero if absent, one if present and, where appropriate, two if present in a stronger form. The former contractual types are depicted as those whose lines of contractual control were tight; 'softer' forms were those where the franchisee enjoyed greater levels of autonomy. Hard contracts were those that:

1. permitted the franchisee qualified or non-exclusive territories;
2. set some commitment to franchisor-set performance targets (such as in-building some expectation of the franchisee becoming a multi-unit operator);
3. permitted the franchisor to have a 'stake' in the tangible business assets, such as telephone lines, sites and equipment;
4. permitted unilateral change by the franchisor to the operations manual;
5. set out post-contractual termination restrictions; and
6. give the franchisor the right to police franchisee operations either with reasonable or no prior notice.

Whether such contractual powers are used, however, is dependent upon, primarily, the nature of the market being served. For example, in the fast food market where the consumers tend to illustrate high expectations of uniformity, franchisors are, on the whole, less tolerant of variation. Equally, in those systems where high levels of brand equity exist, franchisors are more likely to engage in stringent policing activities. In the diagram, the franchisor of brand *A* controls its franchisees through a 'medium-type' contract. This means that whilst it may be stringent on some aspects, it is less so on others. For purposes of illustration, this assumption is, perhaps, a necessary one since if the contract was of a 'hard' nature, then arguably it may not permit its franchisees to become multi-branded operators. For example, PepsiCo was highly reluctant to permit one of its larger franchisees, National Pizza Co., to acquire a seafood fast food chain called Skipper's. Those with 'softer' contracts, such as brand *B*, may be more lenient in this respect.

Figures from the USA suggest that there has been greater emphasis on franchised growth than on company-owned expansion, but there are substantial variations concerning the reliance on franchising. For example, the majority of companies have a mix of franchised and non-franchised outlets, while others are almost totally reliant on their franchisees. Out of the top 100 firms, franchised operations represent about 60% of all units.

From Table 2.3, it is apparent that these franchise systems are large concerns, but it would be an error to suppose that this situation was also true of Britain. Purdy *et al* (1996) show that the franchise fraternity in Britain comprises a few large operators but is dominated by small operations. In fact, in 1995, 43% of franchisors had ten units or less, 59% had between eleven and twenty outlets. Of equal importance is the fact that few franchisors have a significant number of company-owned units themselves. This polarization suggests that franchisees may not be as safe as much of the popular literature portrays them to be. If the majority of franchisors do not have franchisees, how do they monitor movements in the marketplace? Those franchisors with only one company-owned outlet are not better placed to monitor the market: they can only do so in one location. This weakness and other deficiencies within franchising are explored in the remaining chapters of the book.

	1995			1994			1993		
Company	Total	Co	Fr'chise	Total	Co	Fr'chise	Total	Co	Fr'chise
McDonald's	11,368	1,839	9,529	10,238	1,645	8,593	9,397	1,456	7,941
Subway	10,093	0	10,093	8,970	1	8,969	7,815	2	7,813
Pizza Hut	8,883	5,201	3,682	8,618	5,249	3,369	8,428	5,055	3,373
Burger King	6,492	448	6,044	6,090	540	5,550	6,064	909	5,155
Taco Bell	6,490	3,133	3,357	5,684	3,232	2,452	4,809	3,006	1,803
Service America Corp	5,700	5,700	0	5,575	5,575	0	5,750	5,750	0
KFC	5,152	2,031	3,121	5,149	2,039	3,110	5,128	2,048	3,080
Dairy Queen	5,000	0	5,000	4,914	1	4,913	4,860	1	4,859
7-Eleven	4,973	2,077	2,896	5,102	2,167	2,935	5,258	2,287	2,971
Little Caesar's	4,720	1,620	3,100	4,610	1,610	3,000	4,500	1,600	2,900
Domino's Pizza	4,242	698	3,544	4,243	702	3,541	4,340	696	3,644
Wendy's	4,197	1,200	2,997	3,998	1,168	2,830	3,791	1,132	2,659
Hardee's	3,395	864	2,531	3,404	820	2,584	3,372	805	2,567
Marriott Management	3,100	3,100	0	3,071	3,071	0	2,921	2,921	0
Dunkin' Donuts	3,043	18	3,025	2,865	12	2,853	2,690	4	2,686
Arby's	2,798	366	2,432	2,656	289	2,367	2,550	261	2,289
TCBY	2,533	42	2,491	2,660	96	2,564	2,408	121	2,287
Baskin-Robbins	2,504	5	2,499	2,398	5	2,393	2,266	5	2,261
Aramark Global Food	2,400	2,400	0	2,242	2,242	0	2,211	2,211	0
Holiday Inns	1,697	70	1,627	1,630	210	1,420	1,660	200	1,460
Top 100 (000's)	138.7	54.3	84.4	132.0	53.8	78.3	124.8	51.7	73.2

Source: *Nation's Restaurant News*: 'Top 100 Chains Ranked by U.S. Systemwide foodservice sales', 7 August 1995.

Table 2.3: Company-owned and franchised units in the USA, 1993–95

Franchise outlets	No. of franchisors	%	Company owned outlets	No. of franchisors	%
1–5	171	30.2	None	129	22.8
6–10	75	13.3	One	204	36.0
11–20	86	15.2	Two	64	11.3
21–50	113	20.0	Three	25	4.4
51–100	58	10.2	Four	19	3.4
101–200	35	6.2	Five	11	1.9
201–500	19	3.4	Six to ten	39	6.9
501–1,000	4	0.7	More than eleven	75	13.3
1,001 +	5	0.9			
Total	566	100.0	Total	566	100.0

Source: Purdy, D., Stanworth, J., and Hatcliffe, M., (1996), *Franchising in Figures*, Lloyds Bank Plc/IFRC
Franchising in Britain, Vol. 1, No. 2. University of Westminster.

Table 2.4: Distribution of franchise and company outlets per franchise system in Britain, 1995

Voluntary chains

The main role for voluntary groups has been to provide marketing services, at a fee, to mostly single store independent retailers in order to give these operators some of the benefits enjoyed by multiple retailers. These benefits include a degree of central purchasing, a corporate fascia, marketing, merchandizing, product range advice, store refits, advertising, loyalty schemes and information technology. Such an organizational form is of direct interest to the hospitality industry since an increasing number of voluntary chain stores provide fast food products such as sandwiches, rolls, pies and pasties, and may provide a vehicle for some owner-operators to help counter the increasing polarity in the market. They may also represent a vehicle for some food and drink manuafacturers to build brand awareness among customers via offering café, coffee shop and restaurant owners to rebadge and redecorate their units according to the producer's specifications.

Voluntary chains – or symbol groups – did not emerge in Europe until 1932 after a Dutch wholesaler, Mr A. J. M. van Well, reacted to a decline in business by visiting the US-based Red and White voluntary chain in 1931 and formed the Spar organization. After an initial start with sixteen retailers around the Hague, the business expanded rapidly for the remainder of the decade. Between 1947 and 1955 the Spar organization diversified its operations to Belgium, Luxembourg, Germany, Denmark, Austria and France, but did not emerge in the UK until 1957. At this time there was a general trend towards the formation of voluntary chains by independent retailers with the emergence of such names as Vivo, Centra, Wavy Line and Maid Marian (all of which have failed), as well as those that have continued to survive. During the decade 1961 to 1971 voluntary chains in the grocery sector expanded rapidly. Quoting A. C. Neilsen data, Howe (1992) shows that while the share of the total grocery independents as a whole fell from 53% in 1961 to 42% in 1971, the voluntary chain affiliated stores raised their market share from 13% to 22%. By contrast, the market share held by the non-voluntary group affiliated stores fell from 40% to 20%.

The contemporary food retail sector consists of four main voluntary chains which have been in existence since the 1950s and 1960s, and two more recent additions. Although Spar boasted between5,000 to 6,000 members in the 1960s, it has refocused its emphasis on high volume stores meaning that there has been a decline in membership to 2,400. One the smaller voluntary chains, VG, was founded in 1954 and is based on a Dutch trading format. During the 1984 the traditional VG format began to be replaced with a convenience store format such that, in 1995, there were fewer than 100 VG-type stores. Spar's main competitor, Londis, was formed in 1959 by a group of independent retail grocers who were members of the London District Council of the National Grocers Federation (hence the name Londis) and had 1,400 members in 1995; Mace evolved in 1960 from the former buying group Distributive Marketing Services (established in 1953) and in 1995 reported over 1,200 members. In 1984, a new symbol group, Costcutter, emerged and has grown to 700 members and has been followed, in 1994, by the launch of Select & Save, which had 100 members in 1995. In addition to these voluntary groups are those operated by food and grocery wholesalers, with a combined membership of 5,000 members. The cumulative number of members within all of these operations suggests that grocery voluntary chains are approximately half the size of the UK franchise industry, with its 20,000 franchisees. When non-grocery voluntary chains are included, however, the total number of members rises to about 23,000.

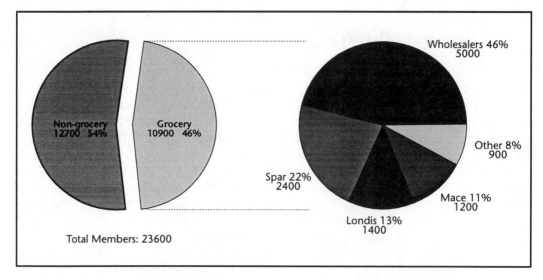

Non-grocery
12700   54%

Grocery
10900   46%

Total Members: 23600

Wholesalers 46%
5000

Other 8%
900

Mace 11%
1200

Londis 13%
1400

Spar 22%
2400

Figure 2.4: Segmentation of the voluntary chain fraternity, 1995

Two of the main reasons for the emergence of voluntary chains in the UK in the 1950s and 1960s was, according to Howe (1992), the emergence of price competition in many areas where prior to this time it was dormant or proscribed (due to resale price main-tenance), and the rise of multiple retailers. The pressure for collectivization via voluntary chains was exacerbated by the government's move against anti-competitive practices and the outlawing of resale price maintenance in the 1956 Restrictive Trade Practices Act and the 1964 Resale Prices Act. Additionally, between 1957 and 1961, the multiple retailers, especially the grocers, were extremely active increasing sales by about 30% compared with increases of 11% by independents (Boyd and Piercy, 1963).

Such laws essentially served to increase the bargaining power of the larger mul-tiples who could increase their margins and fund expansion to the detriment of independent retailers. Being placed in a position where price discrimination could occur, voluntary chains – such as Spar, VG, Londis and Mace – emerged in order to attempt to trade on the same terms as the multiples (Leal, 1974). This meant that, based on buying goods at a discount, the groups were able to obtain special terms from suppliers which could be passed on to the retailer and finally the customer in the form of lower prices. Fur-thermore, the chains could also obtain discounts on fixtures and fittings thereby allowing their members to improve the appearance and layout of their stores as well as reduce administrative costs and time through the provision of pre-printed order forms. They also assisted their members to compete through advertising campaigns conducted at both national and local levels. Such promotional expenditure – too high for the average inde-pendent – was realized through taking a small contribution from each member.

Tied houses and tenancies

As noted in Chapter 1, the tied house system is used to describe the ownership of licensed houses by brewers who lease the houses to tenants on condition that only beers supplied by the owners of the houses are sold in them (Knox, 1958). Tenancies have been categorized as a first generation franchise because they constitute a supply agreement between the brewer and retailer without specifying exact brand specifications. Tenancy agreements are also employed outside the brewing industry, but these are in the minority. As some public houses have moved into the renting of bedrooms in order to increase asset utility and sales, tenancy agreements have permeated the hotel sector but the idiosyncrasy of these operations precludes systematic analysis in the hotel sector (Johnson and Harrison, 1993).

By any normal criteria, the brewing industry experienced a dramatic change in its structure after the introduction of tenancy agreements in the last century. The number of brewers halved to 1,100 between 1881 and 1914. In 1930, there were 1,418 breweries and 559 (428 by 1940) brewing companies; by 1973, there were 162 and 88 respectively. Through the use of acquisitions and mergers, the rising concentration transformed the industry and gave rise to the emergence of national brewers in the 1960s. The most significant acquisitions during this period were:

- Scottish Brewers with Newcastle Breweries to form Scottish & Newcastle in 1960;
- Allied with Tetley Walker in 1959, Ind Coope and Friary Meaux in 1964 to form Allied Breweries;
- Bass, Mitchells and Butler with Charrington to form Bass Charrington in 1967;
- Courage with John Smith's Tadcaster Brewery in 1970; and
- Truman, Hanbury and Buxton with Watney Mann to form Watney Mann and Truman.

The contemporary market structure has also been realized through forward and vertical integration, again based primarily on acquisition. This strategy has been a consequence of severe restrictions on the number of licensed premises. For example, Bass and Allied Breweries originally had small tied estates, but pursued a series of takeovers to ensure market access through a concentration of outlets within specific regional markets. The pursuit of market access created a two-tiered oligopoly, and the tied public house system represented a barrier to entry into brewing and to expansion by existing brewers. Without the tie, there would be no guarantee that public houses within a particular portfolio would buy the brewer's products, or if they did so, would not show preference for house brands when conducting promotional campaigns. Thus, an alternative measure of the importance of the major companies is the number of outlets they control. It was this aspect which the Monopolies and Mergers Commission (MMC) sought to loosen and, thereby, increase consumer choice and competition in the market. Under the traditional system, the supply of beer was controlled through the following systems:

- managed public houses, in which the publican and staff are employees of the brewing company and the brewer sets the retail price of beer, etc.;
- tenanted public houses, where the publican is not an employee of the brewer-landlord, but pays the brewer a rent for the premises and earns his living from the retail profit made by the outlet. The majority of tenanted houses are brewery-owned although there has been a trend towards ownership by specialist public house retail companies and property companies. Non-brewers tend to have exclusive beer agreements for their estates;

- loan tie, in order to secure exclusivity for their own products in a free house (a retail unit not owned by a brewer), or a minimum throughput, a brewer offered a loan to the owner(s) of the house at interest rates below the market rates of interest. The MMC estimated that a quarter of free houses in Britain were tied to a brewer through the loan mechanism.

The brewing market has been subject to a number of investigations by the Monopolies and Mergers Commission, but only the 1989 report on the supply of beer concluded that the sector was a 'complex monopoly'. Accordingly, the brewers were compelled to adhere to the following conditions by November 1992:

1. brewers owning more than 2,000 public houses were to release half of those above that number from the tie, either by selling them or leasing them without a tie;
2. all publicans tied to national breweries were to be free to choose at least one cask-conditioned guest beer;
3. abolition of the tie on drinks other than beer; and
4. a requirement to supply beer to independent wholesalers on the basis of published maximum list prices; and loan ties to be more easily terminated.

The main structural change to the brewing industry has been the abandonment of the traditional public house tenancy in favour of managed houses or ordinary commercial leases. The table below shows that the number of tenant operated public houses within the national brewers' portfolio fell by 56%, whereas those under the regional brewers' increased by 11%. Since 1992, the structure of the public house market has changed such that over 55% of public houses are owned by the independents, a quarter held by the nationals and the remainder by the regional brewers. Among the national brewers, tenant operated public houses account for half of the 15,000 they control. In addition to changes in the structure of the market, were alterations in the function performed by tenants. Under the traditional agreement, the tenant had to fulfil a simple distributive function by selling the brewery's beer and managing its public house for a period, typically, of three years (Table 2.6). The tenant's autonomy was limited as were the expected business skills; the brewery charged him a low rent, maintained his building, whilst charging him a high price for the products he sold his customers. Given the uncertainty of the new market conditions, brewers have sought to alter the tenant's role and seek those with more experience and take a more holistic view of the market. The changes have also altered the tenant's role because the new leases can be for periods of up to twenty years and the breweries have increased rents and require lessees to maintain the property.

Part of this change has been necessary due to the emergence of specialist public house companies, who are developing expertise as retailers rather than product distribution mechanisms. Although some of these retail companies emerged as a result of the brewers reducing the size of their estate, the multiple retailers were in existence prior to the enforcement of the MMC report's findings. The rationale of their emergence in the 1980s, in particular, is attributable to four factors: buoyant consumer spending; a surplus of brewery-owned public houses; sell-offs of public houses by the largest brewers as part of their portfolio rationalization prior to the MMC investigation; and decisions of regional brewers to divest from brewing to focus on public house retailing. The retailers were

Type of brewer	Pre-MMC	Nov. 1992	% change
Independents			
Single	16,000	15,800	−1
Multiple	nil	8,000	n/a
Total	16,000	23,800	49
National			
Tenant	22,000	9,700	−56
Managed	10,000	9,500	−5
Total	32,000	19,200	−40
Regional			
Tenant	9,000	10,000	11
Managed	3,000	5,000	66
Total	12,000	15,000	25
Industy total	60,000	58,000	−30

Source: *The Publican*, January 1993.

Table 2.5: Changes in the structure of the UK public house market

Company	Sycamore Inns	Greene King	Mansfield	Marston's	Cafe Inns
Duration (years)	3	9	3	6	3
Must the tenant live on premises?	Yes	Yes	Yes	Yes	Yes
Does the brewer/pub firm have access to tenant's accounts?	No	By mutual consent	No	Some	Yes
Who is responsible for the internal decor?	Tenant	Tenant	Tenant	Tenant	Tenant
Who is responsible for the external decor?	Landlord	Landlord	Landlord	Landlord	Landlord
Must the outlet carry the brewer/pub firm's name?	No	Yes	Yes	Yes	No
How frequently is rent payable?	Monthly	Weekly	Weekly	Weekly	Monthly
Is the tenant tied to: a) lager; b) bitter; c) cider; d) wines & spirits; and e) soft drinks	a, b, c	a, b, c, d, e	a, b, c	depends	a, b, c, d, e

Source: *The Publican*, 12 August 1996.

Table 2.6: Examples of the legal conditions in tenancy agreements

able to develop further as multiple operators as a result of the depressed public house property market and brewers illustrating a strong preference by the breweries for the sale or leasing of whole sections of their estates to independent public house companies and the release of leased houses from the tie. The changes have brought publicans some discomfort too; they find themselves with new leases, new supply arrangements, increased rents, difficulties in gaining access to finance, and a Uniform Business Rate. All these factors increase the pressure on the retail price of beer from public houses, which has been rising at a faster rate than that sold from supermarkets and specialist off-licences.

Although the MMC has had the effect of increasing competition amongst beer retailers through placing a ceiling on the amount of public houses a brewer may own, in manufacturing terms the range of competitors has declined. The increasing concentration since the MMC indicates that the major operations have been increasing their market share at the expense of the smaller manufacturers. Since the major operations are the main owners and licensees of branded, heavily advertised beer products, the introduction of the 'guest beer' policy has opened the market and thereby the way for the national brands to overcome the smaller, regional concerns. This situation may prompt the formation of marketing consortia among the regional brewers. The ownership of key brands means that the publicans have low levels of bargaining market. The extent to which price discounts are offered in supply agreements is determined by individual negotiation and factors such as:

1. the volume of beer purchased;
2. the location of the public house and the intended method of delivery;
3. the level of promotional support;
4. the maintenance of dispensing equipment;
5. whether an opportunity for increased business with the customer exists; and
6. the strategic advantage of being presented in a particular unit or region.

In spite of the impact of the MMC on the structure of the public house sector, further changes are due to the tied house system in the UK since they contravene the European Commission's competition policy. For example, finance loans from brewers are increasingly accompanied by purchasing restrictions: about a third of brewery loans to publicans have a beer tie. A block exemption was granted in 1984 and is due to expire in 1997, with the larger brewers likely to have the most to lose. In 1992, the European Commission ruled that brewers with annual beer production of 200,000 hectolitres or less or where 'the total number of tied outlets is limited in relation to the total number of outlets on the market' would be free to retain their tied estates after 1997. For this reason, some operators are moving towards business franchise agreements.

Consortia

With tourism in Europe expected to grow rapidly, there is a greater need to raise customer awareness of the hotel brand through increased presence and marketing activity. Recent surveys of the European hotel industry show that the top ten chains operating in Europe provide as much capacity as the next forty chains combined. This situation suggests that the pressure for increased size, in order to gain marketing economies and offer a greater variety of hotels in major destinations, within both unaffiliated and small chains, is substantial (Slattery and Johnson, 1992). Unlike the USA and Canada, where there are in excess of 12,000 franchised and motel establishments and where chains account for over a quarter of roomstock, the affiliation practice of most European hotel chains has been independence and ownership. This practice has been forced to change. Due to changes in the attitude of many stock exchanges to asset-based businesses combined with a weak property market, and stagnating occupancy levels, the propensity for hotel companies to expand through ownership is low. Instead, growth has derived from the use of more cash-orientated forms of affiliation, such as consortia, rather than business format franchising. There are a number of reasons for the preference for consortia within the European hotel industry, and the following paragraphs suggest some reasons for the situation.

A consortium is an organization of firms, usually, but not necessarily, owned autonomously which combine resources in order to establish joint purchasing/trading arrangements and operate other management services such as marketing, public relations and personnel and training – a kind of mutual self-help organization (Johnsson and Harrison, 1993; Litteljohn, 1982). In the hospitality industry, consortia are typically found in the hotel sector but there is also some evidence of their activities in the pizza foodservice market (see the Case Study at the end of this chapter) as well as in the restaurant market through the services of credit card companies promoting certain restaurants. An example of an international restaurant consortia is a company called Transmedia. This organization, and others like it, operate on the basis of issuing and marketing a private restaurant card, called (for example), the 'Executive Savings Card', which entitles its holders to a 25% discount when dining at restaurants participating in its programme. The companies provide the restaurants that join their network with two essential needs: advance financing and additional diners. Membership of the network also precludes the restaurant from having dedicated sales and marketing staff. Also of significance to the restaurant trade has been the development of delivery services. These organizations operate on the basis of providing a dine-at-home or office service, delivering high quality food from renowned restaurants. Although numerous restaurants have been approached by such organizations, many have expressed doubts about how well they would be able to increase market share and about their pricing structure.

Hotel consortia are believed to have been introduced to the UK in 1966, with the formation of Prestige Hotels (Litteljohn, 1985) and have developed to over thirty different organizations representing about 1,500 hotels with a capacity of 57,000 rooms (Johnson and Harrison, 1993). Whilst the population of consortia has increased, there is little academic research investigating their strategic, structural and process characteristics (Roper, 1992; 1995). This situation has, in turn, served to limit our understanding of the diffusion process of both specific forms of consortia as well as more general types.

Although hotel consortia were originally developed to assist independent hoteliers to benefit from the advantages of economies of scale, during the 1980s a key development was the emergence of company hotels, either separately or collectively, in consortia membership (Byrne, 1993; Johnson and Harrison, 1993). This trend was particularly apparent between 1985 and 1988 when over a quarter of all consortia members were company hotels, but these levels have since subsided. Johnson and Harrison suggest that the main reason for the entry of company hotels into consortia was to weaken the competitive position that independents had established for themselves via their consortia affiliations.

Whilst such an explanation may be appropriate for the hotels within larger hotel company portfolios, two additional explanations are also apparent. Some of the company hotels within consortia belonged to the smaller groups and, given the polarized structure of the industry, were seeking to improve their competitive position *vis-à-vis* their larger competitors. Other hotel consortia members belonged to concerns whose main business activities and revenue streams were outside the hotel arena. Membership of a consortia could permit such hotels access to core competences and specialist managerial support other than those within their own parent organization – a form of surrogate parenthood. Another factor explaining the membership, as well as multiple consortia membership, is the geographic reach of the consortium. From these characteristics, it is apparent that there is substantial variance in organizational size, their country of origin, their geographic reach, and category of membership (whether single or multiple members and/or corporate or independently owned and operated). In these aspects, consortia appear similar to franchises but there are several distinguishing features.

Other than definition and penetration dissimilarities, there are three main differences between brand name franchising and business format franchising in the hotel industry:

1. the degree of managerial discretion; range of services;
2. the costs of development; and
3. the level of standardization. (Housden, 1984)

The main operational difference is that business format franchises do not have the discretion to reject reservations offered from the central reservations system. As the business format hotel franchise is often little more than the owner of a hotel brand, a central reservations system and other corporate services, the franchisee must use the corporate services such as central reservations, marketing, advertising, purchasing or training provided.

In a comprehensive review of the role of consortia and their development, Roper (1992) suggests that hotel consortia perform at least one common administrative function, such as marketing, purchasing, or recruitment. These functions permit consortia to be classified along two dimensions: the kind of services they provide and the extent of those services. She groups consortia into three types, those providing:

1. marketing-orientated services;
2. human resource services; and
3. production services.

Marketing services

The original concept of hotel consortia was that they should offer marketing and promotional services and from these two forms of organization have emerged: reservation systems and referral consortia. While the reservation system is self-explanatory, Slattery *et al* (1985) suggest that referral consortia were affiliations by hotels with airlines and their reservation systems. In these instances, it was often chains rather than independent hotels that affiliated with the airline. Consortia have adopted two broad approaches related to their orientation of their marketing services. Initially, certain consortia emphasize the geographic scope of their operations and this focus is sometimes reflected in their titles (for example, Thames Valley Hotels, Hospitality Hotels of Cornwall, and South Hampshire Tourism Group). As well as promoting certain regions and localities, the second focus is the hotel product itself. This second form of consortia specialize within a certain market niche, for example the two-star and four-star hotel segments. The kind of services that these consortia provide includes access to a centralized telephone system, production of hotel directories, the distribution of individual hotel brochures, the production of an in-house magazine, and promotional leaflets.

Human resource services

Within the UK hotel sector, there is only one consortium (Concord Hotels) which explicitly provides training services. Other consortia, however, offer in-house training programmes incorporating their entire hotel portfolio. The range of services encompassed by this form of consortia includes recruitment, formulation of job descriptions, industrial relations advice as well as specific training schemes.

Production services

A variety of consortia, both specific to the hotel trade and more generally, have emerged to provide bulk purchasing agreements that materially assist their membership. Roper (1992) indicates that production services explicitly include benefits which are cost-reducing and which entail the supply of more efficient distribution, cheaper cost and increased quality of raw materials. That is, they refer to input factors and have the potential to increase bargaining power over suppliers and efficiency. She observes that purchasing services may either be in-house to the consortia or contracted out to another organization and that the main purchasing device is the buying directory. The more items that are bought through this purchasing scheme, the greater the ability for the consortium to increase bargaining power. Some consortia also provide 'purchasing surveys' which provides consultancy services to members on how to maximize their purchasing requirements and how to select suppliers. Other consortia require their membership to use promotional items, such as consortium identity, which reflects an attempt to build greater marketing cohesiveness, and others are able to negotiate discounts on the use of credit cards by members.

When a hotel business is franchised, it is marketed to two distinct groups. The outlets will need to continue marketing to the consumer of the services, but it is also marketed to potential investors and franchisees. A clear identity and a distinctive name and image, which differentiates the hotel from the competition, must therefore exist in order not only to sell the franchise, but also the end-service to customers. A prerequisite for business format franchising therefore is that there is a hotel brand, such as Holiday Inn, Travelodge and Ramada, which acts as a blueprint for franchisees. Whilst the requirements of business format franchises are relatively stringent, consortia require that the independent hotel be of a certain standard and offer specified amenities.

Table 2.7 suggests that a further difference between consortia and franchises in the hotel industry lies in the comparison of fees. Some of the lowest total cost percentages (as a proportion of room revenue) belong to the brand name franchises, such as Best Western (with 1%) and Preferred Hotels (with 1.3%). This suggests that, since such organizations are more cost-orientated than profit-orientated, the average margin of profit realized by the business format franchise chains is in the range of 4% to 4.6%. The lower initial costs also suggest

Hotel type	Total initial fee (US$)[a]	Annual Royalty Fee (US$)	Annual Reservation Fee (US$)	Annual Advertising Fee (US$)	Total cost as % of total $100 revenue
Economy type (100 rooms)[b]	20,750	379,240	112,500	201,905	5.1
Mid-rate type (200 rooms)[c]	40,000	1,475,137	466,677	693,677	5.9
First-class (300 rooms)[d]	64,865	3,447,631	950,300	1,777,134	5.9

a: based on room count; b: average of 14 franchises; c: average of 14 franchises; d: average of 9 franchises.

Table 2.7: Differences between hotel franchises and market levels

that the brand name franchise would be preferable to many independent operators. These people do not necessarily have access to the required capital which would permit them to become business format franchisees and others do not wish to be as closely controlled as business format franchising requires. The table also shows that initial fees in the hotel industry vary by market level, with some of the cheapest being budget/economy types.

The main strategic difference is that business format franchises rely on a standard set of specifications, each being of a consistent standard and marketing mix in order to appeal to target markets. In the context of the fast food industry, franchise agreements require each unit to have set internal specifications (that is, a set quality of furnishings), external specifications (that is, architecture and design), same service offerings and products, as well as sharing the same brand name (Slattery, 1991). In Europe, for example, McDonald's has essentially seven building designs; some external and internal changes are made to suit a country's culture, but the buildings follow a standard blueprint thereby permitting savings in development costs.

By contrast, much of Europe's hotel stock is not of a consistent standard, with varying types of architecture being inherent to many hotel portfolios, and thus business format (as practised in the USA) has not proved feasible (Connell, 1992; Slattery and Litteljohn, 1991; Slattery and Johnson, 1992). For example, there are fewer than two hundred business format franchised hotels in Britain and fewer than 1,000 in Europe as a whole. This situation means that, as an organizational form within the European hotel industry, franchising has not gained legitimacy or currency. These features mean that, if hotel franchisors are to expand in Europe and reap the benefits of the single market, they will need to redefine their brand specifications and adapt to the European market in terms of investment requirement. By restricting themselves to new-build hotels, they will realize only slow growth. A softer approach to brand specification offers a faster route to business format franchise expansion. The main problem is that the major US hotel brands have fewer than one hundred units in mainland Europe between them. Due to this size constraint, they are less able to convince potential business format franchises of the possible competitive advantages and cost economies of belonging to a standardized network of units.

Unlike Europe, the USA is the home place of the hotel brand, being more developed there than other markets. This is because the main method of hotel stock expansion in the USA has been through new build, thereby permitting cloning, whereas in Europe (especially the UK and Germany), the primary method of growth has been via acquisitions, with many of the acquired properties showing various design styles. Moreover, the EC internal market is stimulating hotel expansion, but not in new investments. One area of possible expansion is budget/economy services due to their location in periphery sites, their simplistic utilitarian-orientated nature, and their price points. For example, prior to acquisition, budget hotel group Climat de France, part of the Elitair Group, had expanded to over 140 hotels in France, Germany, Spain and the UK, using business format franchising. The future route to franchising in Europe could be where an existing European hotel chain has franchised some of its hotels to one of the major brands. Queens Moat Houses, for example, has franchised most of its gateway city hotels to Holiday Inn and Movenpick Hotels in Switzerland has franchised its hotels to Radisson. Such a strategy may be expanded to non-affiliated hotels, as Choice International has done. Another alternative is the master franchise, whereby all European hotels are franchised.

Roper (1992) suggests that the rationale for the evolution and existence of consortia appears to be determined by the hotel's specific competitive contexts. In particular, the growth of consortia in the hotel industry has been attributed to the growth of hotel chains, the need for differentiation and economies of scale in communicating with fragmented customers. For the smaller independently run hotels, consortia permit revenue growth to accrue through collective advertising and promotion, central reservation systems and better representation. They also permit the hotelier to achieve lower operating costs by out-sourcing managerial functions such as marketing, purchasing and training. Although these benefits may be significant to the survival of small hotels, an important question remains. If the rationale for consortia has emerged from the increasing presence and strength of competition in the accommodation market, why has the bed and breakfast establishment market remained fragmented and remained predominantly characterized by owner-operators?

Consortia and franchising activity has been established in the US hotel industry since the early 1950s but its use in the US bed and breakfast sector is a recent phenomenon. It has only been apparent since Choice Hotels International began offering franchises to small, upscale boutique inns and hotels in 1989. In the UK, bed and breakfast establishments have long been advertised and included in books such as the various AA, Michelin and Egon Ronay guides, and so could already be seen to be part of consortia. Although established in this format, collectivization through a central reservations system is not developed. Such a state prevails despite a decline in the population of bed and breakfast establishments, ease of entry through the conversion of existing properties to bed and breakfast use, increasing competition from budget hotels, saturation in some regions and a decline in occupancies such that many are dependent on government payments to the unemployed and homeless to make a living. The table below, for example, indicates that the population of bed and breakfast establishments in England has seen increased penetration in some areas while others have declined. Bed and breakfast establishments in the USA confront similar issues, but research to elucidate the disposition of owners to consortia membership established that such collectivization was not viewed favourably. Such feelings were prevalent irrespective of the size of their property, previous employment in the lodging industry or geographic location (Poorani and Smith, 1994).

The research suggests that in order to help surmount the high levels of resistance to collectivization, consortia need to persuade bed and breakfast accommodation owners of the benefits and illustrate the potential of central reservation systems:

Region/year	1989	1990	1991	1992
Cumbria	450	551	593	584
East Anglia	1,103	1,211	1,310	1,454
East Midlands	625	713	814	853
Heart of England	1,249	1,261	1,248	1,193
London	949	737	766	761
Northumbria	452	499	456	477
North West England	456	610	636	619
South East England	1,296	1,386	1,427	1,268
South of England	1,388	1,480	1,525	2,378
Thames & Chilterns	873	974	990	*n/a*
West Country	1,525	1,587	1,711	1,582
Yorkshire & Humberside	488	850	922	911

Source: English Tourist Board Annual Survey (various years).

Table 2.8: Regional distribution of bed and breakfast establishments in Britain, 1989–92

1. to generate new business;
2. not to interfere with their ability to run their own business;
3. not to inhibit the close relationships that some owners form with their guests;
4. to be an efficient alternative to advertising in tourism brochures, travel guides, telephone directories and the local press.

This research serves to underline the difficulty of diffusing an innovation that has the potential to reduce the autonomy enjoyed by non-affiliated organizations. In this aspect, at least, some parallel may be drawn with the attempt by some brewers to alter their existing tenancies into fuller franchise agreements.

Management contracts

The management contract form of operating agreement was introduced into the hotel and accommodation industry in December 1949, when the 300-room Hilton, San Juan, Puerto Rico, opened. Such agreements increased the number of rooms managed with a minimum investment and encouraged investment by development-owners, who had no experience or expertise in the hotel sector, to take advantage of the potentially high returns from hotel and motor inn management (Eyster, 1977; Horwath International, 1992). Despite this potential advantage, the level of legitimation remained low between 1950–1970 because of a preference for alternative forms of affiliation. It emerged out of the recession of 1970–74 as real estate investment trusts rationalized. Under this type of affiliation, hotel organization can own a proportion of the equity in a hotel (for example) or, indeed, own none of the equity but be contracted by the owners of the property to manage it as a hotel. Within the confines of the contractual agreement, the owner of the property employs the operator as an agent to assume full responsibility for operating and managing the property in exchange for a management fee. All other revenues accrue to the property owner, who is required to supply the property, fixtures and fittings, and assumes full legal and financial responsibility for the operation. To date there has been some degree of specialization evident among contractors: some focus only on hotel and others (contract caterers) on the provision of food. Contract caterers are typically contracted by organizations such as local authorities and banks to operate staff canteens, and, since changes in legislation, school meals. This form of contract has illustrated substantial growth throughout the 1980s and 1990s as businesses and institutions sought to reduce their labour costs, focus on core activities, and improve efficiency. According to the 1993 Compass Lunchtime Report, there has also been increased concern with the welfare of their employees, with the majority of business directors indicating that the provision of a staff restaurant is an important factor in improving morale. The report also suggests that a staff restaurant can improve productivity. In Britain, the top ten (ranked by sites) contract catering organizations in 1994 were:

Company	Contracts	Sites	Employees
Gardner Merchant	4,800	5,400	46,219
Compass Group	n/a	3,000	25,000
Catering Direct	40	2,200	7,550
Sutcliffe Catering	1,980	2,100	20,050
BET Catering Services	1,838	1,838	6,809
Quadrant	348	1,000	2,500
CCG Catering	155	770	7,000
ARA Services	335	385	8,500
Forward Catering Services	150	300	n/a
Catering & Allied	219	219	2,078
Total	9,865	17,142	125,706

Source: Caterer & Hotelkeeper, 14 January 1995.

Table 2.9: Top ten contract catering concerns in Britain, 1994

According to Housden (1984), the most frequent reason given by client companies for employing contract caterers is that it releases the firm from the time-consuming activity of monitoring the catering function and to the resource required to recruit, interview and manage catering personnel. They also reduce the time costs associated with menu planning, budgeting, and new product introduction, etc. Furthermore, contract caterers are able to bulk-buy their food supplies (thereby generating economies of scale and stock control efficiency) and offer standardized catering services within geographically dispersed offices. During the 1990s, there has been an increasing shift away from the traditional core sector of business and industry. According to the British Hospitality Association, this segment has fallen in its share of contracts from 7,775 in 1991 to 7,132 in 1993. Whilst some of this was due to an increase in the number business failures, it is also due to a broader array of venues in the leisure, transport, and hospital sectors. A key development in the USA and Britain has been the move by contract catering concerns to become multi-unit and multi-brand franchisees for the major fast food brands. This trend has permitted fast food operations to reach new customer segments and extend their brand dissemination. As a result of the power of these corporate franchisees, the royalty rates are usually smaller than the typical franchise contract offered to individual franchisees.

Combining the approaches

The above discourse suggests that each organizational form is employed to varying degrees within the hospitality industry. It is also apparent that empowerment and becoming a voluntary chain or consortia member are primarily employed to build an existing business rather than building additional capacity. These forms are also used to increase penetration within an existing customer niche; franchising, joint ventures, tenancies and management contracts are methods of broadening the brand dissemination of an existing business through additional capacity. The two dimensions of existing/additional business and customer markets are used to generate a matrix, illustrated in Figure 2.5. The dimensions concerning new customer markets are described by employing a typology employed by Hamilton (1996), and represent the differing distribution methods – or channels – to distribute foodservice products. According to Hamilton, the channel choice is a function of consumer knowledge, access, convenience and the saturation of the traditional channels. It is also a function of customers' level of acceptability in using a particular technology. The chart below shows some of the new distribution and marketing channels that food and foodservice companies have both used and are considering.

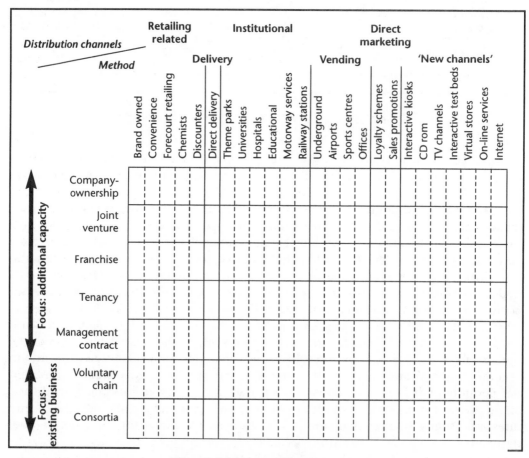

Figure 2.5: *Market and business mixes*

Perhaps reflecting its maturity, at least within the USA, business format franchises have continued to grow, but of late the rate of growth appears to have slowed (Trutko *et al*, 1993). This suggests that perhaps the future for franchising is not infinite as some (Justis *et al*, 1986) suggest, but requires those involved to seek new geographic territories and new formats, especially in their domestic markets, in order to realize growth. Indeed, the 1990s have seen increased internationalization activity, for example, by many of the larger franchise chains in response to market saturation and slow economic growth. It has also seen the reformulation of the marketing mix of many, especially foodservice concerns, to appeal both to new customer segments and investors, via both product and 'distributive' diversity. These features suggest that franchising is changing trajectory along different routes, and these trajectories are consistent with extant portfolio theory, which suggests that firms seek diversification to survive and maintain growth levels (McKiernan, 1992). There are two broad types of diversification, both of which summarize two of franchising's new trajectories: market penetration and geographic diversity.

Product diversity

This strategy has been evident for some time with the main hamburger chains selling pizza, chicken, fish, baked potatoes, sandwiches and salads. Their provision means that chains are able to offer existing customers a new experience (and thereby sustain interest) and appeal to a new customer base – with the net effect of raising market penetration levels. In so doing, they are also taking custom from more specialized units. In the USA, product diversity has taken a branded route with companies supplying complementary products forming alliances, such as that between sandwich concern Miami Subs and ice-cream vendor Baskin-Robbins, and McDonald's and Taco Bell, to cite but two examples.

Distributive diversity

Other than operations illustrating combined counter-service, table-service and take-away facilities, the breadth of distributive diversity options evident in the market is a relatively new characteristic of the UK fast food industry. It is essentially manifested in the changing size and format of the food delivery systems from being primarily high street counter-service units to kiosks, mobile carts, drive-through, home delivery, supermarket goods and vending. Such alterations have permitted the chains to enter non-traditional sites such as roadside catering, staff canteens, garage forecourts, universities, hospitals, book shops, transport termini as well as small towns and villages. The main issue arising from this diversity is that each form of distribution can be franchised in its own right and can exacerbate the demise of the independent operator. The emergence of large chains in non-traditional locations, therefore, means that chain restaurant food will become nearly ubiquitous.

In the USA, Taco Bell has dramatically increased its 'points of access' from 4,500 in 1992 to 25,000 at the end of 1994. By the end of the 1990s, it plans to have more than 200,000 units – with the majority being in non-traditional locations. Others involved in the same process include: Nathan's Famous which has signed up with Unocal petrol stations; California Pizza Kitchen has licensed Westin Hotels to sell its products as part of the hotels' room service; Subway sandwiches are now available on some Continental Airlines flights; McDonald's with Wal-Mart stores and Home Depot. In the UK, the move towards non-traditional sites has only just begun and already seems to be favouring the larger

Distribution type	Product-sector market					
	Pizza & pasta	Burgers	Chicken	Fish & chips	Ethnic & other	Bakery/ ice-cream
Table service eat-in	Pizza Hut; Bella Pasta; Deep Pan; Pizzaland; Pizza Express	Hard Rock; Wimpy	Reds		Chiquito's	Häagen Dazs
Counter service eat-in	McDonald's	Wimpy; Burger King; McDonald's; Wendy's; Jenny Burgers	KFC; TFC; Reds; Burger King; McDonald's; Wendy's; Perfect Pizza	Merryweathers; Harry Ramsden; McDonald's; Burger King; Hudson's	Taco Bell; Manchu Wok; Spud-U-Like; McDonald's	Greggs; Häagen Dazs; Aroma; Pret A Manger
Take away	Pizza Hut; Deep Pan; McDonald's; Domino's; Perfect Pizza	Wimpy; Burger King; McDonald's; Wendy's; Jenny Burgers	KFC; TFC; Reds; Burger King; McDonald's; Wendy's; Perfect Pizza	Merryweathers; Harry Ramsden; McDonald's; Burger King; Hudson's	Taco Bell; McDonald's; Spud-U-Like; Manchu Wok	Greggs; Häagen Dazs; Aroma; Pret A Manger
Home delivery	Pizza Hut; Deep Pan; McDonald's; Domino's Perfect Pizza	McDonald's	KFC; Perfect Pizza; McDonald's	McDonald's	Curry-in-a-Hurry	
Drive-thru	McDonald's	McDonald's; Wimpy; Burger King	KFC; Burger King; McDonald's	McDonald's; Burger King; Hudson's	McDonald's	
Snack/ Express	Pizza Hut; Perfect Pizza	Burger King	Burger King; KFC		Manchu Wok	
Mobile unit	Pizza Hut	McDonald's; Burger King	Burger King; McDonald's; KFC	McDonald's		Häagen Dazs; Mister Softee
Microwave/ chilled cabinet	McCain's					Häagen Dazs
Vending	American Pizza; Autosel; Micro Gourmet	Autosel; Micro Gourmet				

Table 2.10: Distribution and product configurations in the UK foodservice market

brands. Some of the main reasons for the dominance of the larger brands is that when the perceptions of store names are favourable, the buyer's perceptions of product quality are higher. In other words, by coming to an agreement with a well-known brand name, the host organization also benefits.

Table 2.10 uses the differing existing configurations in the foodservice sector by utilizing distributive variety and product sector orientation as proxies. All of the sampled companies operate in the UK. The diagram shows that Pizza Hut operates in almost all methods of distribution with the exception of counter-service eat-ins, drive-throughs, vending and micro-wave food. Pizza Hut (and its sister company, KFC) can be seen to be market specialists as they are using a variety of distributive techniques but remain within one product niche. Pizza Hut has attempted a pizza drive-through concept called 'Fastino's', which closed at the end of 1994. In contrast, McDonald's and Burger King are attempting to be category killers as they are utilizing a combination of both product and distributive diversity. In New York, for example, McDonald's has implemented its first comprehensive delivery test at about forty company-owned and franchised stores. The company also has a central telephone system. It would be erroneous to view each of these distribution/product configurations as being the expression of an intentional strategy. Reflecting Mintzberg and Water's (1985) argument that strategies may either be intentional or emergent, an interview with a key member of McDonald's UK management team suggested that accessing non-traditional sites has been conducted on an *ad hoc* basis:

> Accessing non-traditional sites is an important element of the strategy growth, but the main emphasis is on increasing total numbers of outlets . . . Non-traditional sites have tended to be evaluated on an opportunist basis. Each of these types of site tend to have some major limiting factor associated with them. For example, theme parks have attractive numbers of visitors, but the drawback is limited opening hours and limited open season . . . On the positive side, McDonald's has gained valuable experience from developing and running alternative formats. Key areas of value have been from an operational view – such as staffing levels, type of equipment, and which menu items are attractive propositions at such units versus others.

Summary and conclusion

The franchise literature has tended to assume that the decision to become a franchisor is a discrete one: whether or not to franchise? In such literature, the decision not to franchise is often translated as a preference for company ownership and is assumed to be a rational/intentional choice. It is evident that there is a widespread use of hybrid organizational forms in the hospitality industry and that particular forms have higher levels of density, and thus legitimation, in some sectors. This situation, in turn, suggests that the decision to pursue a particular path is affected by the norms of each sub-sector as well as the array of organizational forms known to the decision-maker. Each one of these forms represents a choice to the decision-makers of the selection of a particular type according to the resource constraints, level of trust, and objectives. If the decision-maker wishes to expand the existing business, the empowerment and/or consortia option may be adopted. On the other hand, if growth and brand dissemination is sought other contractual forms may be employed. This situation infers that the decision to franchise is not as discrete as is inferred within the franchise literature: franchising is only one option which could be used to facilitate growth. As such, a question remains: why should franchising be chosen over other organizational forms? There is also some question as to the rationality of these choices because, arguably, there are some companies who would benefit from franchising their business but do not do so. Equally, there are some franchisors who would realize greater returns from some other strategy. If true, what are the inhibitors to realizing franchising and/or other organizational forms? The following chapters present some possible answers to these queries, but entail a move away from the dominant economics paradigm employed by franchise researchers to those used by students of strategy and organization.

Case Study 3:
The new fasces[1] of the fast food market?
The emergence of consortia in pizza home delivery

The following Case Study provides an analysis of the UK pizza and pasta market and presents the findings of a survey of independent operators and their feelings of whether a consortium or consortia would be appropriate given increasingly illiberal market conditions. In other words, it tests whether consortia have gained a degree of legitimation given the dynamics of the pizza home delivery operating environment. The analysis of the market is a summary and adaptation of a discussion paper entitled *The UK Pizza Market: The Twilight of Adolescence?* (Price, 1995b) presented to attendees of a trade association (the Pizza & Pasta Association) Open Day on 29 June 1995.

Introduction
A recent article by Ball (1996) charted the decline of independent operators running small single unit establishments selling take-away food products. Summarizing reported trends elsewhere (Price, 1991; 1992; 1993a; 1993b), he contends that the decline in market share held by the independents has been a result of the following inter-related factors:

1. the development of chain-owned operations via franchising and piecemeal acquisitions;
2. variation in their product-service delivery configurations (Pickworth, 1988) to include drive-through and kiosk-type outlets (among others), which permit access to non-traditional sites;
3. menu extensions; and
4. the increasing significance of substitute products such as chilled and frozen foods.

While the effects of the chains' investments in brand capital via above-the-line and below-the-line advertising activities were omitted, Ball's analysis indicates that, by most measures of rivalry, competition in the fast food sector has become increasingly acute and characterized by a sharply dichotomous structure. Indeed, within the hamburger sector the concentration ratio of the top three players is in excess of 85% (Price, 1993a). In order to increase the propensity for survival of the independent (that is, non-chain affiliated) owner manager stores, he argues that 'the way forward' is to:

1. differentiate themselves on service, via increased emphasis on training and longer opening hours;
2. provide niche and value-added products;
3. seek to improve efficiency of production; and
4. become a member of a consortium for marketing, purchasing, and human resource development.

The first three of these options have also been recommendations for independent food retailers and hoteliers to help combat the incursion of the grocery multiples and hotel chains into their core consumer base (Howe, 1992; Koss-Feder, 1994; Marshall and Warren, 1987). In isolation, however, these suggestions have not necessarily proved sufficient to stem the loss of market share. For example, as a result of the grocery multiples' investments in product range, convenience, advertising, pricing activities, and an increasing propensity to change the format of their store designs to facilitate entry to non-traditional sites (Duke, 1991), they have been able to take market share away from the independently operated concerns such that the top four operators accounted for some 40% of Britain's £76 billion expenditure on groceries in 1995 (Anon, 1996). Arguably, of greater consequence to survival and market share in both the food retail and hotel industries has been the willingness of some owner-operators to collectivize via the formation of hybrid organizations, such as voluntary chains and consortia. Such flocking behaviour has permitted them to seek to leverage the buying power accruing from larger size as well as to realize increased marketing levels.

Collectivizing, however, has exacted a price. It has entailed some loss of independence, a price that some operators have been unwilling to pay and has reduced the level of legitimation, but has resulted in improved chances of sustaining revenue flows and survival. But, despite the broad strategic similarities between the multiple grocers and the chain-owned fast food operations and the strategic importance of hybrid organizational forms to permitting the collectivization of independents, there is little evidence of their presence in the fast food sector other than business format franchising. This Case Study will compare and contrast some of the factors impeding the diffusion of such organizational forms through presenting the results of a survey of independent pizza home delivery operators. In order to elucidate some of the challenges facing these operators, a model summarizing the key dimensions of competing in the fast food industry is presented. This is then applied to the pizza home delivery market.

Depicting competition in fast food

With a number of definitions propounding fast food as a form of technology and others arguing that it is a form of retail outlet, it has been observed that no unequivocal definition of the term exists (Jones, 1993; Sholl-Poensgen, 1983). In an attempt to move the definitional stalemate forward, Price (1991) suggests that it is necessary to focus on what is traded rather than how it is produced or sold. He argues that it is only defining fast food as an end or finished product that the competitive dynamics, the array of substitute products, barriers to entry, structure of the market, and the effects of recent food safety legislation can be observed effectively. Accordingly, he suggests that a fast food is differentiated from other types by four basic and generic components:

1.   low monetary price compared to other foodservice products;
2.   the end product is served quickly (for example, up to five minutes for take-away or eat-on-site products and approximately thirty minutes for home delivery);
3.   the product is suitable for eating with the fingers, has disposable packaging and, where applicable, disposable cutlery; and
4.   finished product durability (such as maintenance of heat, nutrition value, etc.) of minutes and hours, as opposed to longer periods of time for snack foods.

Typical products falling within this generic definition include hamburgers, fish and chips, scooped ice-cream, kebabs, fried and broiled chicken, French fries, pizza, Chinese and Indian take-away food, sandwiches, and other forms of similar ready-to-eat foods and ready-to-drink beverages. From this definition, Price (1991, 1993) develops two 'tools' to help analyze the dynamics of the fast food market:

1.   a fast food typology for retail outlets selling fast food products, which Ball (1996) adapts and presents in his analysis of take-away outlets; and
2.   a continuum of a sample of the differing food systems employed.

While there is little overt consideration of geographic diversity in a direct sense, used in tandem both of these typologies are pertinent to analyzing the competitive issues in the pizza home delivery market and other fast food segments. Along with the array of product diversification options presented in Chapter 2, all three typologies are presented as a cube in the diagram below (Figure 2.6). The figure summarizes three of the key trends evident within the fast food market: product diversity; distributive diversity; and incumbent diversity. While issues concerning product diversity and distributive diversity have been described in Chapter 2, incumbent diversity refers to the degree to which a retail outlet sells fast food products (calculable by a specialization ratio: total fast food sales/total unit sales *100). By summarizing the specialization ratio into three brands, a typology of fast food operations emerges. Thus, specialists are those stores which derive a high proportion of their sales from fast food, half-way houses have intermediate levels of sales deriving from fast food, and non-specialists derive comparatively the lowest levels of unit sales deriving from fast food product. Moving along any one proxy of the cube may either be achieved through two main methods, depending on the tolerance for risk, level of trust, and loss of control:

1.   company-owned diversification; or
2.   via the formation of an alliance to realize some of the mutual benefits deriving from the experiences and competencies necessary to operate in a different part of the strategic space.

Combined, the different trends encompassed by the cube point to competition moving from intertype to intratype (Ingene, 1983) and, thus, to the presence of low barriers of entry. The faster rates of market growth for value-added products such as convenience foods and fast foods, compared with the almost static demand for home food items (see the diagram below), has attracted the supermarkets and specialist food retailers, such as bakers and butchers, to the sectors. Such diversification by the more specialist food retailers has also occurred because of the incursions of the grocery multiples into their core product-customer segments. In addition, it has also arisen because of the emergence of manufacturers making value-added products

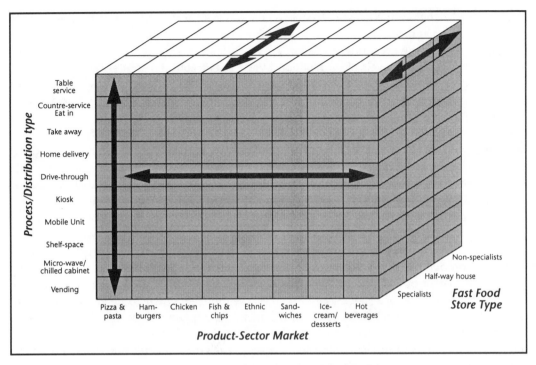

Figure 2.6: *Cube of strategic configurations within the UK fast food market*

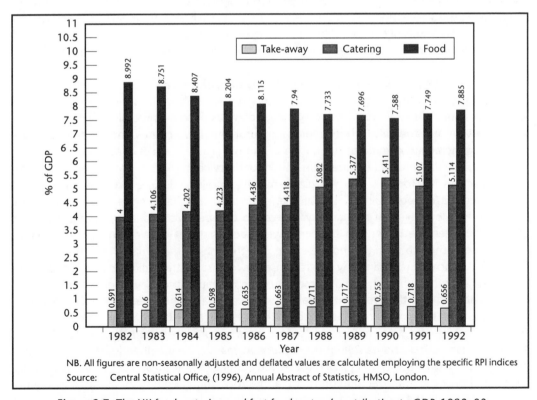

Figure 2.7: *The UK food, catering and fast food sectors' contribution to GDP, 1982–92*

such as sandwiches who then seek to derive economies of scale and competitive advantage through gaining as broad a supply base as possible (see the Case Study: 'Quests for Competitive Advantages in the UK Sandwich Sector', p. 233).

Although the levels of domination by the major companies alter by product type, service-delivery type, and type of fast food store, it is possible to suggest that some segments of the cube illustrate asymmetric permeability (Caves and Ghemawat, 1992; Hatten and Hatten, 1987). That is, the major operators can move to new positions within the strategic space encompassed by the cube without fear of retaliation from existing occupants of that space. For example, McDonald's can move into pizza home delivery, but few specialist pizza home delivery players necessarily have the human capital capability, resources, or will, to enter into counter-service and take-away hamburger provision. Equally, the supermarkets have moved into sandwich retailing without fear of reprisal from specialist operators' diversification into grocery retailing. Where retaliatory action is most likely to be centred will be around product mix issues because of the lower costs of entry and lower levels of risk associated with such diversification efforts. In order to raise the barriers to entry within a particular segment, therefore, not only is product differentiation necessary, but so too is continuous innovation and the development of market power through critical mass. Arguably, both of these are more realizable through the formation of alliances rather than via the more expensive route of company ownership. Yet, despite the potential for such benefits, there appears to be some reluctance for independent owner-operators to form hybrid organizations, such as consortia. They seem to prefer instead those options where they have greater levels of control (Osborne, 1991). It is this reluctance and lack of legitimation of alternative organizational forms among this group, perhaps more than any other reason, which is the true cause of the decline of the independents. By applying the above model to the context of the UK pizza home delivery market and reporting some of the results of a survey of independent owner-operators in that market, it is possible to see the reluctance to collectivize in the face of increasing competitive pressure in action.

Competitive dynamics of the UK pizza and pasta sector

Analysts of the pizza and pasta foodservice market (comprising mainly home delivery and restaurant operations) concur that the sector has become increasingly competitive in both the USA and the UK. In both regions, incumbents have been vying for market share against a general background of stagnating economic growth, lack of consumer confidence, growing direct and indirect competition within foodservice markets *per se*, the entry of companies such as McDonald's into the pizza market, an oligopolistic grocery sector and the emergence of a 'coupon-culture'. The UK market, in particular, has experienced a slowing rate of expansion, low levels of profitability, increasing competitive turbulence and a widening polarity between the larger and smaller players such that it is dominated by three chains. Although common to both the independents and the chains, this situation has been exacerbated by the increasing reliance by public houses on food sales, the rapid expansion of delivery services in the ethnic market, and the ease with which restaurants can augment their trade and productivity through the provision of delivery services. Many of the casualties of such conditions have been the smaller operators and franchisees (Price, 1995a).

In 1994, the £745 million foodservice pizza sector represented about 14% of the UK fast food market and about 72% of the total pizza market's value. In volume terms, Taylor-Nelson/AGB data suggests that pizza represented about 6% of all meals consumed outside the home and only a fifth of the total (in-home and out-of-home) volume of pizza consumed in Britain. Given that the foodservice market accounted for three-quarters of the market value in

1990, pizza operations have clearly come under increasing pressure from the grocers and food manufacturers. As a result of continuing investments in product quality, advertising, range development and the offering of perceived value for money by manufacturers, the competition between foodservice pizza and its retail counterpart has become increasingly acute. There has also been an escalating threat of substitution from the grocers; in 1994, supermarkets accounted for between 80% and 90% (it differs by type of pizza) of the retail pizza market and, reflective of oligopolistic rivalry, were also active in introducing new product variants, as well as the direct targeting of take-away/home delivery by the grocery multiples. For example, in 1994, the grocers were responsible for the introduction of over 160 new pizza products; most foodservice chains introduce, on average, between one and four new menu items a year. In 1995, the supermarkets accounted for 112 new pizza products. Of this total 109 were whole pizzas rather than pizza slices; sixty-nine were chilled and the remainder were frozen. Of the chilled 81% were own-label versus 42% for the frozen versions (Dixon *et al*, 1995). In Britain, the array of choice of pizza is such that a customer is able to choose from the following gamut of alternatives:

- making one's own pizza from home-made or bought-in ingredients;
- buying frozen whole pizzas or pizza slices to cook and eat at home;
- buying a ready-prepared whole pizza or pizza slices to cook and eat at home;
- having a pizza made to the personal requirements of the customer in a supermarket or delicatessen to cook and eat at home (that is, take and bake);
- having a pizza made to the customer's requirements and cooked at a take-away/home delivery unit or table-service restaurant;
- ordering a standardized pizza/pizza slice – that is, a pizza which is not prepared and cooked for any one particular customer – from a fast food store (specialist or otherwise), public house, take-away home delivery, kiosk, or mobile cart unit (not necessarily a specialist pizza business);
- selecting a ready-prepared pizza that can be cooked in a microwave located in a convenience store or garage forecourt to eat immediately; and
- selecting a ready-prepared pizza from a vending machine.

Such direct and indirect competing offerings and the increasing ubiquity of the product have affected the demand for pizza during the evenings, the peak demand period for home delivery services. Growth in the £280 million retail pizza market has been favourably affected by the expansion of chilled pizza (in 1994, representing almost 38% of the retail market value). This growth is of real threat to the pizza restaurant and home delivery trade – not only because of price (home delivery is more expensive), but also because about two-thirds of chilled pizza consumers purchase the product for same-day consumption. The customer emphasis on freshness, convenience and value within the in-home market is also borne out by data which indicates that the frozen and home-made pizza sector has suffered decline, whilst the chilled pizza market has grown continuously throughout the 1990s (Price, 1995a).

Pizza restaurants and home-delivery players have also come under competitive fire from other foodservice operators, in particular public houses and ethnic food operations. This competition was especially apparent from pizza's consumption patterns. In terms of market share by time and day of week, Taylor Nelson AGB data shows that the main periods for the consumption of pizza are evenings (despite the efforts by some to build a lunch-time trade through buffets), with weekend evenings, especially Sundays, being particularly buoyant. The market share for pizza, however, never exceeds 10%. By contrast, ethnic operators' (Chinese and Indian delivery) share exceeds 25% during the weekend evenings and is 24% (compared to 8% for pizza) during evenings between Monday and Thursday, but the competition from the ethnic operations lacks coherence because of their fragmentation and the dominance or owner-operator concerns.

As shown in the discourse concerning tenancies, the public house market is somewhat concentrated and, as such, has posed a more immediate threat to pizza chains. Both the brewers and public house companies have become increasingly reliant on food sales given the long-term decline in beer sales. Evidence of the significant threat that the public houses posed – but may be a source of opportunity to pizza suppliers – to the pizza foodservice market can also be seen from time and day of week data. During weekend evenings public houses represent between 11% to16% share of the volume of meals sold. On evenings between Monday and Thursday, public houses represent a 12% of the volume of meals consumed outside the home. Furthermore, whilst pizza's share of the lunch-time trade (all week) registers, on average, at about 3%, public houses have 23% and, on Sundays, 48%.

The public house food market has proved to be one of the fastest-growing sectors of Britain's eating out market – worth over £3.3 billion in 1994 – and over 90% of public houses sell food. Given a decline in the volume of beer consumed, food has become of strategic importance to public house revenues; food accounts for approximately 20% of the average public house revenues. One of its main threats is the perception that public house food represents value for money. Recent research has shown that over half of customers believe that public house food represents value for money compared to only 18% for pizza and pasta. Furthermore, public houses account for about a third of the volume of business meals consumed, whereas pizza establishments have only about 1% of that customer segment. The public houses also have an older age profile than pizza establishments: whereas pizza establishments represent 10% (9% for public houses) of the volume of all meals consumed by those aged between 16 and 24, pubs represent a quarter of all meals consumed by those aged between 45 and 64 (versus 3% for pizza).

The market has also illustrated a strong regional bias in the distribution of pizza restaurants and takeaways with almost half of all the UK's 5,560 outlets being located in South East England. Customer data also reflects this: Taylor Nelson AGB data shows that pizza accounts for 7% of all meals consumed in the South versus 6% in the North and 4% in the Midlands. All of these conditions combined infer that the sector has moved further along its life-cycle and is mature as well as being, perhaps, saturated within some geographic areas. The subject of 'saturation', especially within the context of the pizza market, has proved a particularly emotive one. Part of this is due to the ambiguous nature of the term. Saturation does not mean that no new stores can be opened or that new stores will cannibalize the sales of existing ones. Here, saturation means that new stores will operate at levels of sales below those operated by a given chain nationally or in a region against a background of relatively slow market expansion (Emerson, 1990).

Although saturation may be more pronounced in the pizza restaurant market (valued at £545 million), the home delivery sector has illustrated one of the fastest rates of expansion – more than quadrupling in value since 1989 to be worth about £200 million in 1994. This said, much of the growth has derived from new entrants (especially via restaurants adding new delivery systems) and additional units, rather than organically. Symptomatic of the low barriers to entry, many of the home delivery players remain strategically weak because of low profitability, low returns, over reliance on an evening trade, lack of investment in above-the-

line advertising, undifferentiated products, over-emphasis on price, and disgruntled franchisees. These effects, combined, have resulted in high levels of volatility. Home delivery has
also suffered from the development of discount-priced buffet lunches by the main pizza restaurant operators. After all, customers can only eat so much pizza per week! This situation
underlines the necessity for operators to convert non-users and low users (such as older customers), to differentiate their products, services and identity to compete on a different playing
field to chilled pizza operations.

Following initiatives in the USA, Canada, and Australia, some chain operations, such
as Perfect Pizza and Pizza Hut, have responded to this situation by developing their own central ordering systems, designed to improve the speed and efficiency of deliveries. The central
ordering systems also have their own customer record-keeping information system. Combined, the systems are designed to increase efficiency and marketing power for foodservice
operations in one geographical area. Cummings (1987) argues that the benefits of such systems typically include:

1. the promotional strength of using a single telephone number for all unit loca-
    tions;
2. call routeing of phone-in orders to the nearest foodservice unit;
3. on-screen history for repeat callers; and
4. well thought-out managerial reports, including uniquely accessible data on the
    location derivation of call-in orders.

Access to such remedies and benefits requires the ownership of both financial and managerial
resources, however, which many independents and small chains simply do not possess, or they
require the formation of alliances in order to gain access to such resources. Nevertheless, some
independent-owner operators believe otherwise. As such, and as Ball (1996) observes, it is
these operations which will continue to lose market share and realize lower levels of profitability compared to chain-owned concerns.

The financial performance of the independents and small chains has also been
adversely affected by inflationary pressure deriving from the food manufacturers. It is well
known that the food manufacturers have been under substantial pressure from the multiple
grocers and, in general, have low levels of bargaining power. The supermarkets determine not
only what is to be delivered, but also where, when and how, and the use of own-label
products has strengthened their position (Duke, 1991). By contrast, purchasing behaviour and
sophistication in the catering market, let alone the pizza sector, is not as developed as the grocers. The fragmented state of the catering market means that bargaining power is more in
favour of the supplier (Dixon, 1983). This situation means that manufacturers are better able
to pass on rising costs of raw materials, fuel, and wages among caterers. For example, between
1990 and 1995, the average input costs to bread and confectioners (which includes pizza base
manufacturers) rose at an average annual rate of 4% and their output costs (factory gate prices)
by over 5%, suggesting that the prices of bread-based products to supermarkets and caterers
have also increased. When the retail price of bread and takeaway foods are examined, however, it is apparent that (as retail bread prices have risen by about 3% since 1990) a greater
proportion of these costs have been passed on to the independent fast food operator. Of
course, some caterers only deal with local suppliers and this situation suggests a 'comfort zone'
position in which prices are mutually negotiable. In general, however, there is more than circumstantial evidence to observe the tendency by the manfacturers to pass on more of their

increased costs of production along those distribution channels in which bargaining power is balanced in their favour.

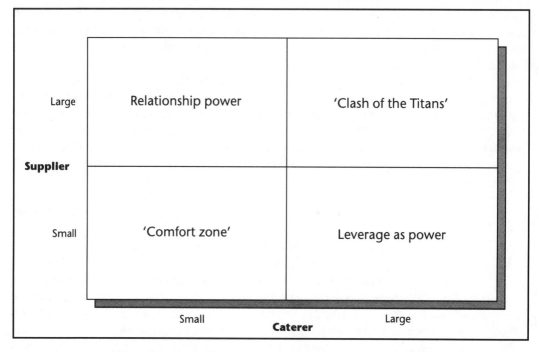

Figure 2.8: *Concentration of buying power in the catering sector*

One of the key features of the foodservice pizza market has been its continuing polarization. This is evident in both the home delivery and restaurant markets, despite chain owned stores representing only a quarter of the UK's population of pizza and pasta outlets. In Britain, the pizza restaurant market is dominated by four players generating, in 1994, about £285 million from 545 units. By comparison, the three main players in the home delivery market generate about 48% of the sub-sector's sales from 400 units. It is expected that this polarization will continue and give rise to oligopolistic competition, especially as the pizza restaurants have undergone some rejuvenation and are cash rich (thereby giving them funds to open new outlets and acquire smaller players). As a result, there may be less emphasis on price as a continuing strategy, but more on providing the customer with an 'experience', above-the-line advertising and the introduction of switching costs in order to attach a cost to customers who shop elsewhere – especially as slow market growth continues. In short, the restaurant market has become the pizza sector's cash cow.

As the impact of direct and indirect substitution has become increasingly acute, competition has also taken new forms which has served to exacerbate the degree of polarization. Moves into non-traditional sites, such as garage forecourts, railway termini, hospitals and universities as a result of franchise agreements between the major brands, such as Pizza Hut, and contract caterers has meant that chain food has almost become ubiquitous. It is also expected that the larger home delivery operators will increase investment in central telephone systems and complement this by use of the Internet system, to provide them some opportunities in targeted promotions, opportunities for up-selling activity, and productivity improvements through encouraging off-peak purchases. Given the current state of development in this area, there may also be an opportunity for someone to develop a marketing consortia – similar to those operated in the hotel industry – and help the smaller operators compete more efficiently and effectively against their larger counterparts. Reflecting this opportunity, the UK has witnessed the emergence of central telephone ordering companies targeting their marketing and reservations services to both small pizza chains and independent operators.

Study of independent pizza and pasta operations

As seen from the nature of competition within the pizza and pasta market, there may be some potential for consortia within the segment. But, the decision to become a member of a consortium also entails some degree of change in managerial practices and some loss of control. Not all people welcome and embrace change – despite a clear need for change and that change having the potential to alleviate particular issues. In order to help establish whether independent operators felt that there was a need for such organizational forms as consortia, a questionnaire was distributed among attendees to a seminar discussing industry issues (not a trade association convention) and placed in the UK's Pizza & Pasta Association's (PAPA) membership magazine, *Pizza & Pasta*. The questionnaire was modelled on that used by Poorani and Smith (1994) in their survey of the likelihood of independent owners of US-based bed and breakfast establishments becoming consortia members. The exercise yielded eighty-seven useable responses from operators with an average portfolio of two stores. Interestingly, some of the non-useable responses were from franchisees, who indicated a wilingness to become members of a consortium. This situation suggests that not all of their requirements are being met by their franchisors, and that there is some room for improvement.

For parsimony, only some of the results are presented and summarized in the three tables shown below. In the same edition of *Pizza & Pasta* (November, 1995) the trade association launched its 'PAPA Marketing Club' and another company, 'Pizza from Hell!', also formally launched as a marketing services consortium, suggesting an increasing interest by suppliers of marketing services (especially those with central ordering services) in the organizational form. The latter organization also has the facilities and materials to provide the operator with corporate livery and branded merchandizing equipment to advertise the 'Pizza from Hell!' logo, and expressed some interest in being able to negotiate with suppliers to the pizza trade. As such, this organization also had the flexibility to become a voluntary chain. Table 2.11 compares whether the operators perceived that the intensity of competition in their local market had increased or decreased over the short term against the likelihood of their joining a consortium. It shows that, in general, there was a perception that competition in the pizza and pasta market had increased; there was also a tendency amongst those who thought that the competition had intensified to be in favour of consortia. When probed further, the majority of respondents thought that the main source of competition derived from other pizza operations (chain-affiliated and otherwise), ethnic delivery operations, and the supermarkets. Only a very small minority thought that their local competition had increased through the activities of chain-operations such as McDonald's, Burger King, and KFC.

The second table (2.12) compares the likelihood of joining a consortium with the business's main source of business. It shows that those business owners whose main source of custom is via repeat patronage or word-of-mouth are less likely to join a consortium; instead they rely on customers' trust of their previous experience. For such operators, there is perhaps the fear that consortium membership would sacrifice their individuality and personalization of service. Those who rely on advertising and brochures/leaflets tend to be more in favour of

Nature of competition/ likelihood	Definitely	Probably	Maybe	Probably not	Definitely not
More intense	22	10	6	10	2
Slightly more intense	5	0	11	6	0
Not changed	0	0	10	1	4

Table 2.11: Perceptions of local competition versus likelihood of consortium membership

Source of business/ likelihood	Definitely	Probably	Maybe	Probably not	Definitely not
Repeat patronage/ word of mouth	8	0	12	12	6
Brochures/leaflets	15	7	1	3	0
Yellow Pages/ Thomson Directories	4	3	4	1	0
Advertising (e.g. local newspapers)	0	0	7	1	0
Walk-in	0	0	3	0	0

Table 2.12: Main sources of business versus likelihood of consortium membership

Occupational satisfaction/ likelihood	Definitely	Probably	Maybe	Probably not	Definitely not
Do it again	12	6	3	13	0
Not do it	15	4	14	2	6
Do it differently	0	0	10	2	0

Table 2.13: Occupational satisfaction versus likelihood of consortium membership

joining. For these latter businesses, the incentives to join a marketing consortium, in particular, are threefold:

1. the economic and time costs associated with the activity (on average, these operators spend over 6% of sales on advertising);
2. the effectiveness of such efforts in generating additional sales is typically low; and
3. the expertise required to design advertisements.

Similar findings are also evident within Poorani and Smith's (1994) study; they find that bed and breakfast operations in the USA generated very little business through their own marketing efforts.

Table 2.13 compares the occupational satisfaction to the likelihood of consortium membership. It shows that the majority of respondents appear to exhibit low levels of satisfaction and would not become a pizza-store owner if they could choose their career again. On the whole, those owners who indicated that they would not become a pizza store owner have also indicated that they would not become a consortium member. One possible rationale for this situation is that membership would increase their commitment to a sector in which they are, perhaps, reluctant incumbents. When their responses were cross-tabulated with why they chose to be an independent pizza-store owner and why they would not like to join a consortium, they suggested that they were either made redundant from their previous position and/or did not want to become a franchisee. The reason for not joining a consortium was, invariably, that such owners perceived that it was a high-risk option to growth, they would lose too much control, or more practical considerations such as they 'did not have a computer'. Of the owners who, if given the choice, would operate their pizza business differently, none indicated that they would join a consortium. The majority of this category entered the market because they wanted to be their own boss and did not want to become a franchisee; they also tended to fear the loss of control by becoming a consortium member. In other words, they did not tend to perceive consortia as a suitable alternative to help them run their business differently, or as a vehicle to help improve performance. Of those respondents who would do it again, the majority indicated that they were interested in consortium membership. Most of these operators entered the market with prior experience of working in the hospitality industry and wanted to become their own boss.

Summary

While there is some agreement about the decline of the independent take-away since the 1970s, the four potential options to help stem the domination of the chains suggested by Ball (1996) is a source of debate. Rather than there being individual options, a multi-dimensional approach is required in which the development of market power through collectivization is central. Combined efforts focused towards product and service differentiation and increased bargaining power results in raising barriers to entry, and thus to the opportunity to generate superior returns (Porter, 1980). From the depiction of the competition within the fast food market and the case study of the UK pizza and pasta market, it is evident that operating conditions are increasingly illiberal. This situation is unlikely to change for the better. The main source of the rivalry derives from the major pizza foodservice operations, supermarkets, public houses and ethnic home delivery operations. Despite such illiberality and the availability of suitable technology, consortia in the market are still at the embryonic stages and are yet to emerge with any force. They are at the early stages of legitimation and have low status. In turn, this situation suggests that the dominance of the chains has gone virtually unchallenged. The survey of independent operators suggests that the lack of development may be due to some reservations about membership. Such reservations are perhaps well founded – after all, consortium membership in itself is not a panacea. In order to diffuse consortia membership further in the market, owners' reservations must be overcome by consortia actively negating the disadvantages of collectivization. As in Poorani and Smith's (1994) study, the research suggests that consortia need to persuade owners of the benefits of membership and illustrate the benefits of central reservation systems, for example, to:

1. generate new business;
2. not to interfere with their ability to run their own business;
3. not to inhibit the close relationships that some owners form with their customers; and
4. to be an efficient alternative to advertising in brochures, telephone directories, and the local press.

From a theoretical perspective, this study suggests that the tendency towards hybrid organizational forms cannot be solely attributed to environmental factors such as increased rivalry, polarization and weakening competitive positions. In the final analysis, it is the owner's choice whether to join or not. Until such time that there is a consortium or other hybrid organization which is tailored to meeting the needs of the independent pizza home delivery operator and there is wider consensus on the need to collectivize, as well as institutional support for such an organizational form, the dominance of the chains will continue unchallenged and unabated.

Case Study 4:
The changing face of hotel restaurants

Reflecting eating out's increasingly significant position in British culture, the volume of meals consumed outside the home has, on ᵕverage, risen by about 4% a year since 1991. Against this general background of growth, the volume of meals consumed in hotel restaurants, according to market researchers Taylor Nelson/AGB, declined by 11% between 1991 and 1995 to represent only 3% market share of all meals eaten outside the home. A similar situation is apparent in Japan, Australia, USA and Canada. The decline in hotel restaurant volumes has exacerbated pressure on margins and been caused, in part, by the rapid development of specialist restaurant and fast food companies and the evolution of new menu and theme concepts (Langston and Price, 1994). The competitive dynamics of the foodservice market has meant that the management of restaurant brands has become increasingly sophisticated and proactive to influencing consumer tastes. Consequently, hoteliers have become concerned to try and improve the performance of their food and beverage operations – a process which has required them to change the importance attached to their restaurants and room service activities and the role that they serve. The restaurant and its auxiliary services (such as banqueting, bar and lounge, and room service) are often regarded as profitable facilities, but secondary in importance, of most hotels (Solomon and Katz, 1981; Carper, 1994).

As the main source of revenue in hotels derives from rooms, typically, restaurants have been treated more as amenities rather than profit centres in their own right. Arguably, therefore, some of the decline in volumes can be attributed to a possible lack of attention by hoteliers as well as the effects of competition and recession (Schneider-Wexler, 1992; 1994). Deriving from the need to generate contribution to the high fixed costs that the provision of accommodation entails, hoteliers are often focused on selling room space. Indeed, 1994 figures from BDO Hospitality Consulting show that, on average, UK hotels derived about 46% of their sales from food and beverages. Although significant contributors to total hotel sales, the operating profit margins realized by food and beverage departments ranged from 29% at lower market levels to 40% at the higher levels. By contrast, the average operating profit margins achieved within room divisions ranged between 66% and 75%, depending on market level.

Variable	1993	1992	Variable	1993	1992
Total food and beverage sales (% of total revenue)			*Total room sales (% of total turnover)*		
Lower quartile	42.3	41.9	Lower quartile	37.3	36.1
Median	48.9	48.8	Median	44.4	43.5
Upper quartile	55.2	56.0	Upper quartile	52.3	51.8
Departmental operating profit (% of F&B sales)			*Departmental operating profit (% of room sales)*		
Lower quartile	29.4	25.0	Lower quartile	64.3	62.5
Median	35.4	32.0	Median	69.2	68.2
Upper quartile	40.6	36.3	Upper quartile	73.3	72.5

Source: BDO Hospitality Consulting (1994), *United Kingdom Hotel Industry,* London.

Table 2.14: Performance of hotel food and beverage facilities

Such performance suggests that few hoteliers necessarily have the key skills and capabilities to manage their food and beverage divisions on the same basis as specialist restaurateurs. To some hoteliers, restaurants are little more than a necessary evil. Recently, however, North American hoteliers and, to a lesser extent, their UK counterparts have begun to focus on using branding and alliances to improve the revenue-generating propensities of their hotels' food and beverage facilities. These alliances are focused on capitalizing on restaurateurs' specialist skills, marketing effort, existing brand capital, and advertising. In leveraging the specialist skills the hotelier is able to learn and adopt appropriate practices to other food and beverage facilities; for the domestic customer there is perhaps less perceived risk, higher perceived quality and lower prices than non-affiliated hotel restaurants (Lichtenstein and Burton, 1989; Parasuraman *et al*, 1988; Wheatley *et al*, 1981; Zeithaml *et al*, 1988), and the restaurateur benefits from additional market share and exposure to international visitors. Some alliances also allow the hotelier to lower overheads by reducing food and beverage management costs and staffing levels. Such benefits accrue because the restaurants are usually stand-alone with separate kitchens and staff (costs which are not then attributable to the hotelier). To many commentators on the hotel industry, these efforts clearly mark a 'revolution' in the way hoteliers manage their restaurants and have been directed to take the following forms:

- Co-branding via franchise agreements with national chains. For example, Stakis Hotels with Henry J. Bean, Radisson with TGI Friday, McDonald's within some Hospitality Franchise System hotels (Super 8, Days Inn, Ramada, and Howard Johnson); Choice Hotel's partnership with Pizza Hut. Branding has also been extended to room service with some Holiday Inns serving pizza offerings from Pizza Hut and Little Caesar's. In some instances, where the hotel chain is franchised, the hotelier has joined with the restaurant franchisor in order to offer a combined franchise package to new investors and the opportunity for their franchisees to purchase the restaurant brand.

- Moving restaurants to street level and creating separate entrances from the hotel.
- Leasing space to restaurateur to via concession agreements.
- Attaching 'star' chefs to hotel restaurant concepts (for example, Chez Nico at Grosvenor House and Marco Pierre White at the Hyde Park) either through lease agreements, management or consulting contracts.
- Developing restaurant operations such that they are operated as independent business units where the chef 'owns' the concept and is responsible for creating a profit-orientated business.
- Reducing the size and changing the orientation of restaurants such that they are built for lunch and dinner rather than being devoted to serving breakfast traffic.
- Putting manufacturer brands onto menus, for example some Hilton properties serve low-calorie and low-fat 'Weight-Watcher' meals.
- Augmenting hotel food and beverage revenues by providing off-premise food-services, for example event catering and contract catering.

The suitability of each of these options to the hotelier is dependent on the extent to which management wishes to relinquish control and their reaction to changing to someone else's concept. Some US and UK hoteliers, for example, have expressed some reluctance to co-brand because of a 'not-made-here' tendency, even though there are instances where franchises have served to increase sales by substantial margins:

> . . . because our preference is to completely manage our own F&B services to provide food, service and quality consistency from property to property. (John Randall, senior director for F&B concepts for Marriott, quoted in Hensdill, 1996; p. 58)

To a large degree, however, the 'alliance option' is also governed by the market level of the hotel and by customers' expectations (Crawford-Welch, 1991). At the more luxurious market levels, individuality and quality of service are perceived as important by guests. This situation suggests that mid-spend provision and standardized own-brands may not be appropriate. Equally, the use of 'star' chefs may require some degree of modification too. For example, higher market-level hotel properties in regional locations may be better served by leveraging the local reputation of their chefs and empowering him/her along the lines of Ford and Fottler's (1995) self-management category (see the section on empowerment, in Chapter 2), by providing the opportunity to operate the restaurant as an independent concept. Operating margins may be improved by tying the chef's renumeration to profit performance and by the restaurant's membership of a consortia. The nationally and internationally famous 'star' chefs are, perhaps, more appropriate for 'flag-ship' properties. At the budget-end of the market, co-branding with fast food and cafe chains may be more suited to achieving improved performance because accommodation and food and beverage provision are aligned to customers' expectations and spending budgets.

Notes

1. Derived from Roman history, fasces were rods in a bundle with an axe, carried by lictors before the superior magistrates as an emblem of power. More recently, fasces were used as a symbol in Mussolini's Fascist Italian movement (1922–43) to depict power through unity.

3 | Evaluating the decision to franchise

Too many people rely too heavily upon theories and rigid formulas because they are looking for an easy, structured approach to business decisions.
Harold Geneen, Chairman of ITT, *Managing*

Business leaders often get credit for the successful decisions that were forced on them.
Oliver A. Fick, US environmental services manager, *Harvard Business Review* 1986

Introduction

Based on a strategy to realize brand dissemination, a franchise business is an organizational form which permits the franchisee to operate one or more business units under the franchisor's brand name and according to the latter's contractually specified standards and procedures. In addition to new entrants, many larger organizations such as Marks & Spencer, Kodak, and IBM have actively expressed interest in franchising but, as shown in the last chapter, there are varying degrees of density and (by implication) legitimation. Why should this be? In spite of its significance to some economies and individual firms operating in a variety of economic sectors and sub-sectors, however, there appears to be substantial uncertainty among researchers and practitioners concerning why some businesses franchise and others do not (Dant, 1996; Michael, 1996). This issue, however, is of fundamental importance to explaining the differing levels of penetration and diffusion trajectories of franchising. Perhaps one of the reasons for this uncertainty has been the tendency to explore the decision to franchise from three interrelated perspectives: resource scarcity, agency theory, and risk spreading (Mathewson and Winter, 1985; Williamson, 1991).

The first, resource scarcity, is founded on the logic from the product life-cycle which suggests that new, small franchisors use franchising to access resources, such as capital, limited managerial capabilities, and local market knowledge (Thompson, 1994). In maturity, the franchisor repurchases the franchisee operated units and fully owns a large network. According to the second approach, agency theory, businesses decide to franchise based on the costs of monitoring a unit operated by a franchisee compared to one operated by a hired manager. Finally, the risk spreading theory contends that franchisors, like international businesses, attempt to shed risk by licensing the riskier locations to franchisees. Safer sites are maintained by the franchisor (Dev *et al*, 1990). As will be shown below, these explanations are problematic because of their emphasis on resource constraints, such as the lack of capital, costs of monitoring and supervision, and management resources. Difficulties exist because these explanations have been treated in almost a separate manner from other theories of the motivations to form inter-organizational relationships *per se*, and because as explanations in themselves they exhibit a number of weaknesses. Perhaps most significantly, none of the theories have resulted in a model with strong explanatory power (Combs and Castrogiovanni, 1994) nor have they necessarily employed decision-making frameworks – despite talking of the very decision to franchise. This chapter explores existing approaches concerning the decision to franchise and proposes that a more eclectic framework is necessary which may also facilitate understanding why some companies choose not to franchise.

Whilst there are undoubtedly other weaknesses, the basis of the eclectic method derives from the contention that the main limitations of extant approaches derive from the lack of overt consideration of two significant additional explanations: contingency theory and managerial cognitive attributes. Each of these additional explanations of why firms differ have well-founded empirically-supported literatures (Tyler and Steensma, 1995). For example, with regard to cognitive issues, Prahalad and Bettis (1986) argue that a crucial determinant of diversification into new products and markets is the 'dominant logic' or 'mind set' of management; the conceptualization of the business by management affects the degree to which management is able to control, co-ordinate, and direct activities which, at face value, appear disparate:

> Strategically similar businesses can be managed using a single dominant general management logic. A dominant general management logic is defined as the way in which managers conceptualize the business and make critical resource allocation decisions – be it in technology, product development, distribution, advertising or in human resource management. (p. 490)

Accordingly, the dominant management logic could also affect the decision to franchise, but this variable also requires some consideration of other factors which have been shown to influence strategy and organizational structure. Found in every text book on organizational design, the contingency approach theory of organizations specifies that size, technology, and environment are the relevant conditional factors determining efficient organizational structure (Donaldson, 1987). Many of the franchise texts describing the influencing factors concerning the decision to franchise appear to ignore these variables, but they are significant in determining whether a business is suitable to be franchised. For example, in their book *How to Franchise Your Business*, Mendelsohn and Acheson (1989) indicate that an assessment of whether or not a business can be franchised should include the following considerations:

- the concept must be proved by operation to be demonstrably successful (that is, it must have reached a certain size);
- the distribution should be distinctive in its brand image and in its system and method (that is, its technology);
- the system and method must be capable of being passed on successfully to others within an economically sensible time frame (the technology must be transferable);
- the financial returns from the operation of the franchised business must be sufficient to enable:

   – the franchisee to obtain a reasonable return on the assets employed in his business,
   – the franchisee to earn a reasonable, if not good, reward for his labours, and

- the franchisee to make payment to the franchisor of a reasonable fee for the services which he will continue to supply to the franchisee;
- demand for the products must be sustainable and the business must be competitive with other similar offerings in the environment; and
- the franchisor must be able to make a sufficient ongoing profit from fees received from franchisees.

Motivations for franchising

The reasons purported to prompt business can be separated into four classifications:

1. resource scarcity;
2. agency theory;
3. risk spreading; and
4. the rationale for inter-organizational relationships in general.

Each of these reasons is considered in turn.

Resource constraints

According to this stream of research, the underlying rationale for the study of inter-organizational relations, such as franchises, derives from the open-systems premise that organizations are dependent on their task environments for inputs which are essential to their functioning, such as raw materials, information, customers, and legitimacy. Under this perspective, it is proposed that organizations enter into relationships with others in order to obtain required resources to enhance their power, extend the rate of capital accumulation, and via contracting the monopolization of those resources. As such resources are generally scarce, organizations tend to compete with one another, attempting to gain power and control over essential resources while trying to reduce dependencies threatening organizational autonomy. Many of the explanations for franchising have only sought to examine this argument from the franchisor's perspective, but it may also have some application to franchisees. For example, within Britain's retail bakery market, some companies have franchised their units, albeit only to a limited extent, because they have been persuaded by a local entrepreneur to do so. In addition, people who wish to become franchisees may do so in order to access the franchisors' know-how of operating a business rather than acquiring the perceived additional risk of running their own, independent concern.

According to the resource scarcity explanation of franchising, franchisors are beset with a variety of inhibitors which, individually or in tandem, preclude the realization of growth to generate economies of scale and to build brand name capital through wholly-controlled methods (Martin, 1988). These scarce resources include capital, managerial talent, motivated labour, and local knowledge. The initial motivation to franchise within these constraints derives from the belief that franchisee funds are an inexpensive source of capital and not only accrue through the payment of an initial fee, but also through ongoing contributions labelled 'management services fee'. Viewed from a Marxist perspective, the franchisee could be construed to be similar to an employee because they assist in the capitalist's (that is, the franchisor's) accumulation of wealth whilst, at the same time, not owning the assets (Felstead, 1991; 1993). The second motivation derives from the perspective that franchisees are a self-selected pool of qualified manage-rial talent, that is people who have chosen to invest their capital in a business which is seen as having a lower probability of failure than independently-owned concerns, and, therefore, more likely to help to accumulate them further capital and status. Finally, as gathering information concerning local market conditions such as sites, potential demand, culture, etc., is expensive, franchisees are viewed as a source of reliable and cheap knowledge. As the franchise business expands, the effects of the resource constraints diminish, and the franchisor may buy back franchisee-operated concerns in accordance with the lapsing of the contracts. Such repurchases provide the firm with additional con-trol and the revenues which would have otherwise been the property of the franchisee. Over time, the firm is transformed into a wholly-owned concern with any franchisees being in less profitable, outlying regions (Oxenfeldt and Kelly, 1969; Thompson, 1994; Caves and Murphy, 1976).

This life-cycle approach has witnessed varying levels of empirical support. Ever since Oxenfeldt and Kelly's (1969) provocative analysis of franchising in the USA, the sub-ject of ownership redirection in franchising has attracted some attention by franchise researchers. The essence of the ownership redirection thesis refers to the contention that franchising may only be a short-term development strategy, employed by the franchisor to realize market share objectives or to surmount temporary constraints on management resources, finances, or those pertaining to lack of local knowledge. In other words, fran-chise systems, like other organizations, have life-cycles that affect aspects of their strategy, structure and processes. Once these objectives have been attained and the constraints largely overcome, the franchisor reverts to company-ownership as the main strategic option to realize growth. Such a policy may be conducted in part or in whole which, in the latter case, has the effect of withdrawing from the franchise market. The franchisor may equally, however, revert to company ownership in order to balance its portfolio. A more equitable balance of company owned stores to franchised units is necessary to main-tain and monitor standards (thereby maintaining brand consistency) on a day-to-day basis, and to resolve any problems encountered by franchisees, a process which helps to facilitate greater motivation. Other reasons for such investment include:

- to facilitate more thorough testing of new products, services, and systems;
- the ability to monitor market trends more accurately;
- to increase the strength of the franchisor *vis-à-vis* the franchisees; and
- to give the franchise credibility to potential investors.

In a literature review of the ownership redirection thesis, Dant and Schul (1992) and Dant *et al* (1996) indicate that much of the research on this topic has yet to provide conclusive evidence that the penetration of franchising, by industry, is waning. Much of the incon-clusiveness, they argue, derives from several unresolved methodological issues. These issues revolve around the motives and intentions underlying the ownership redirection patterns, and the use of aggregated data to an industry or sectoral level as opposed to more micro-level approaches (such as the failure to employ the Population Ecology model and/or other techniques to depict diffusion shapes). Of those researchers who have focused their atten-tion at the individual firm, the freedom to make generalizations about the overall direction of the future of franchising has been precluded because of the use of small, non-represen-tative, sample sizes. Another is the failure to employ differential equation methods.

Given the prevalence of franchising in the fast food sector in the USA and its relatively mature nature in that country, it is perhaps unsurprising that the market has been regularly employed as a sample frame as part of both cross-sectional and sector-specific research designs. In one of the earliest tests of the thesis, Hunt's (1973) study of the fast food industry's franchise sector found that ownership redirection was occurring. Similar conclusions were also found by other researchers, such as Lillis *et al* (1976), Brickley and Dark (1987), and Manolis *et al* (1995), to name but a few. Others, however, have illustrated that the degree to which ownership redirection is occurring is dependent on the industry sector and sub-sector under review as well as the measure employed.

When franchising is considered as an innovation, with varying levels of diffusion and maturity within each industry segment, such mixed results are perhaps understandable. Of further note is the level of competitive rivalry within each segment *per se*. For example, in markets where there are high levels of risk, franchisors in the hotel industry have been shown to favour franchises but tend to locate company-owned units in regions where risk levels are lower (Dev and Brown, 1990). Although there is still some argument as to whether ownership redirection is occurring at a sectoral level, the issue of electing to franchise or withdraw from the activity is a strategic choice concern.

In spite of this support, the resource constraints approach has received severe criticism from some researchers, especially economists, who suggest that franchising is an inefficient method to raise capital when compared to traditional capital markets, such as banks. Rubin (1978), for example, advocates that the selling of shares within a diversified portfolio of company-owned outlets as a superior alternative to franchising. Furthermore, Lafontaine (1992) finds that some franchisor companies offer financing to their franchisees and that such businesses had a greater proportion of franchised outlets than others; these franchisors appear to find franchising appealing for reasons that have nothing to do with a need for capital. Norton (1988a), however, observes that franchising may still be an attractive option to those with resource constraints because franchises represent a bundle of resources, financial and information; the costs of acquiring these resources as a bundle, rather than individually, may be cheaper than procuring them separately. The main weakness behind the resource constraint perspective is the assumption that franchisors have a long-term perspective of their business; unfortunately there appears to be little evidence which finds support for such behaviour.

Agency theory

Whilst there is still some debate as to the appropriateness of the resource explanations of franchising, the agency theory of franchising is well established. Under this approach, individuals will misrepresent information concerning their skills and effort when they have an incentive to do so in order to gain access to capital and status (Kaufmann and Dant, 1996). The agency perspective relates to the perception that franchising is an effective method to problems of employee motivation and low levels of productivity without incurring the costs associated with monitoring and supervision (the franchisee's motivation partially precludes the need for direct monitoring). Those adopting the agency perspective argue that franchising is cost effective when the marginal costs of monitoring company-owned units are higher than those associated with franchise contracts. These costs are viewed to be lower because the franchisee is seen as illustrating a similar perspective to the franchisor: revenue growth. According to the theory (Brickley and Dark, 1987; Carney and Gedajlovic, 1991), the costs associated with supervising company-owned operations are affected by the:

1. availability of managerial talent;
2. importance of local knowledge;
3. geographic distance of units from headquarters;
4. local population density; and
5. the relative proximity of the brand's locations to one another.

Each of these factors affects the cost and efficiency of communications, travel and effective decision-making between unit managers and head office. Franchising can reduce many of these costs; this is because the franchisee is motivated to realize a return on the initial investment and, because of the franchisor's power to refuse to renew franchise contracts without cause (Klein, 1980), the franchisee is less likely to shirk. Against these incentives, however, is possible resistance by the franchisee to incur further investments, such as those associated with the costs of changing the corporate livery, because of uncertainty that the additional expenditure will result in increases in revenue. If increases in revenue are not accrued, then the rate of return will be lower. Another disincentive to franchising within the agency perspective is where the franchised units have a low proportion of repeat purchases. Minkler (1990) shows that, due to unit standardization, customers perceive that a local store is owned and operated by the same organization; a franchisee in a location with little repeat patronage has the incentive to lower service quality leading to lost customer confidence in the brand because they believe the characteristic to be implicit to all units within the system.

Although there is a wealth of supporting empirical evidence for the agency explanation of franchising (Brickley and Dark, 1987; Norton, 1988b; Caves and Murphy, 1976), there is also evidence to the contrary. One of the main weaknesses of agency theory is its suggestion that franchisors weigh the cost drivers associated with monitoring company-owned units against the supervisory issues inherent in franchising, such as lack of investment and behaviour which is damaging to brand equity (Combs and Castrogiovanni, 1994). According to this approach the firm will seek a balance according to its own cost configuration. There is, however, little evidence to support the notion that potential franchisors engage in such comparative behaviour and the theory seems to ignore the problem of the franchisor's entry costs. Although propounded to be a low-cost growth option, entry into franchising entails substantial investments (see Chapter 8), such as contractual fees, pilot units, and recruitment costs; as the majority of franchisors are small businesses, these entry costs could prove prohibitive and therefore unattractive – irrespective of the potential ongoing benefits. In addition, because a characteristic of agency theory is that retail outlets which are geographically dispersed are franchised, the approach does not wholly explain the tendency for the use of multi-unit franchisees (Kaufmann and Dant, 1996). As the costs of monitoring multi-unit franchisees should be cheaper, and the revenues accruing from them are higher, it is possible that franchisors are attempting to reconcile capital accumulation motives along with motivational ones rather than just one alone.

Risk spreading

The third perspective of franchising relates to the view that franchisors are risk averse and seek to retain control over more profitable units, while shedding more 'risk-laden locations'. Such a perspective is implicit to studies of internationalization. These studies suggest that market entry into locations with different cultures, consumer behaviour, political risk and legislative differences will be characterized by the use of third parties, such as joint ventures, franchising, and licences (Dunning, 1989). Within the confines of a local market, issues concerning risk may be less overt and be more related to issues concerning viability of units and their location, as detailed in the resource constrained approach. Martin (1988) has provided some empirical support for risk-spreading behaviours by showing how some franchisors tend to purchase and/or own units with the highest sales, and that unpredictability of unit sales relates to whether the units are franchised. Such behaviour has been observed in the hotel industry (Dev and Brown, 1990), as well as in the UK brewing and public house retailing sector where low-volume units tend to be the ones which are tenanted (Housden, 1984). To some degree, the risk-spreading behaviour associated with particular locations may, indeed, be attributed to franchisor actions, but in others it is less clear. While some franchisors find and specify suitable locations to be franchised, others are less sophisticated; they rely on the franchisee's search and selection of a site. Thus, in the first instance, risk spreading may be an intentional aspect of brand dissemination; in the second scenario the viability of the unit is only known once opened and, therefore, a franchisor's risk-spreading behaviour is emergent – rather post-rationalized by researchers.

Links with other explanations

Other explanations of the decision to franchise exist and these, like the others, are related to explanations for the formation of inter-organizational relationships *per se*. Much has been written on the motives for forming alliances and inter-organizational relationships (for example, Contractor and Lorange, 1988; Gomes-Casseres, 1996), with the recurring themes behind their formation being:

- gaining access to complementary skills by tapping into sources of knowledge possessed by individuals and firms outside the boundaries of the organization;
- sharing risks for activities which are beyond the capability of the organization, such as gaining rapid market entry and payback, in reducing fixed costs, and diversification;
- corporate ambition;
- fashion and fear. Arguably, the rapid growth of franchising in Britain during the 1980s and the consolidation experienced in the 1990s is indicative of a fashion life-cycle (that is, their popularity grew slowly, increased and remained fashionable for a while, and declined slowly);
- to reduce or spread the risk in turbulent and uncertain environments, such as those with low levels of demand, cultural, lingual, and political differences, and intense levels of competition;
- for defensive/offensive reasons such as reducing competition or increasing the costs and/or lower market share for a third company; and
- gaining market access to markets and territories.

Although some of these rationales are an implicit feature of much of the extant franchise research, some of these explanations have tended to play a secondary role in the literature. For example, fashion and defensive and offensive reasons have been insufficiently explored. Of particular importance in this lack of exploration of alternative rationales for embarking on franchising, but one which is contained within the mainstream alliance discourse, is that of learning objectives. Berg and Friedman (1980), for instance, conclud-ed from a study of over 300 alliances that they are more likely to be chosen to transfer organizational knowledge, as opposed to realizing market power. As capitalists, firms attempt to increase the accumulation of wealth through the possession of expert knowl-edge. The exchange of expertise or skills between partners, therefore, can be a major objective of an alliance.

At a broader level of abstraction, the differing reasons for the emergence of inter-organizational relationships (IORs) and formation of alliances, have emerged in two overlapping schools of thought: political and behavioural. Within each school of thought, it is possible to apply the rationale for IORs to both formation of franchises and collective strategies, such as buying groups, occurring within franchises and elsewhere. Within the political framework, Galaskiewicz (1979; 1985) identifies three basic explana-tions for the emergence of IORs: resource procurement (see the resource constraints theory) and allocation, political advocacy and organizational legitimation. Relatedly, Oliver (1990) suggests that the motivations for inter-organizational relations can be dis-tilled to six reasons: necessity, asymmetry, reciprocity, efficiency, stability (which refers to overcoming environmental uncertainty by accessing local knowledge) and legitimacy. The following paragraphs outline each reason and apply it to the franchise context.

Although termed 'necessity' by Oliver, political advocacy refers to linkages with other organizations in order to meet legal or regulatory requirements from authorities such as government agencies, industry or professional regulatory bodies. The extent to which political advocacy has an influence varies by industry and by economy. For exam-ple, in a comparative study examining the reasons behind formation of joint ventures in developed countries (DCs) and lesser developed countries (LDCs), Beamish (1985) showed that government suasion/legislation in LDCs played a significantly greater influ-ence on joint venture formation in LDCs. In franchising channels, this is not a usual reason for explaining their existence, with the exception, perhaps, in franchisor's inter-nationalization programmes (Shane, 1996), as described below.

Franchising is more prevalent in industrialized countries rather than lesser developed countries (LDCs). For example, the Economist Intelligence Unit (1995) shows that Spain has the highest average number of franchisees per franchisor, while France has the greatest number of franchisees and franchisors. Nonetheless, business format fran-chising focuses upon the transfer of know-how; it is most likely to have a direct effect on the economic progress of developing and post-command economies (Kaufmann and Leibenstein, 1988). Franchises do not only serve to transfer management know-how from developed economies, but also promote the development of locally-owned businesses, provide job opportunities, and serve to furnish customers with a wider choice (Tuncalp, 1991; Whitehead, 1991). In general, however, LDCs have illustrated a preference to import foreign technology via equity involvement. Some Pacific Rim countries have, however, built upon their early learning experiences resulting from the importation of US franchise operations. They have added to the stock of franchised businesses through the emergence of home-grown franchise chains.

In their study of Indonesia, Chan and Justis (1995) found that imported fran-chises were having a useful 'role model' effect in encouraging local entrepreneurs to establish their own franchises and even consider expanding these outside Indonesia. A similar situation is apparent in Brazil (Josias and McIntyre, 1995). Franchising, however, can often have a lower priority for LDCs who are keener on the importation of know-how

Country	Franchisors	Franchisees	Average number of franchisees/franchisor
Austria	170	2,700	16
Belgium	135	2,495	18
Denmark	42	500	12
France	500	30,000	60
Germany	420	18,000	43
UK	396	24,900	63
Italy	370	18,650	50
Netherlands	340	12,120	36
Portugal	70	800	11
Spain	250	20,000	80
Sweden	200	9,000	45
Total	*2,893*	*139,165*	*48*

Source: EIU (1995), 'Retail Franchising in Italy', *Marketing in Europe, Group 3: Chemists' Goods, Household Goods, Domestic Appliances,* September, pp. 87–98.

Table 3.1: The presence of franchising in Europe

from advanced technology firms, rather than franchise retailers. In this activity, franchising could be argued to be a form of innovation because it serves to introduce retail formats to new economic settings, and represents a flexible repertoire of skills and methods of attaining desired results and permits the franchisor to avoid failure under varying circumstances (Merrill, 1968).

One of the reasons for preferring industrialized economies is due to the small size and youth of many fast food franchisors. For such companies, the costs of technology transfer associated with movement into LDCs may be perceived as prohibitive whereas they are lower in industrialized countries. These lower costs may result from higher educational standards as well as higher savings ratios, indicating the potential presence of finance available for investment in franchising. It is, however, probable that individuals from industrialized countries are in more of a position to approach franchisors, which suggests that franchisor internationalization is essentially reactive to opportunities (McGee *et al*, 1995). Walker (1989), for example, examined reasons given by US companies in identifying a country to receive their first venture in international expansion. Perhaps surprisingly, the reasons given did not reflect the degree of proactive planning that might have been expected. For instance, 44% had simply responded to a first/only contact from a foreign 'prospect'. After that came 'proximity to the USA' (28%) and 'similarities to the US/English language' with 18% combined, possibly reflecting a bias toward lowering policing costs. A wealth of other research also empirically illustrates how market uncertainty, caused by deficient knowledge, can influence choice of entry mode. In markets illustrating cultural proximity (and thus markets about which US firms can be expected to be knowledgeable), firms may resort to equity involvement. Conversely, where firms are knowledge-deficient they may employ entry modes such as franchising and licensing. Given the relatively small size of many franchisors and the costs of accessing knowledge and subsidiary maintenance, size may act as a moderating factor to determining whether franchising is employed as a vehicle to entry. Equally, in some countries, there still may be a technological transfer cost associated with the concept of franchising itself.

In addition to employing franchising to realize growth objectives, there has been a tendency for franchisors to use it as a capital market; for smaller franchisors the issue of repatriation of profits may be of more importance than for larger franchisors. Although repatriation considerations may, in turn, be a reflection of the relative size of franchisors attracted to LDCs, some franchisors have sought to differentiate themselves according to the investment requirement of franchisees. This situation means that franchisees in LDCs may have higher economic costs of buying a franchise and thereby have implications for the calibre of franchises that gravitate towards LDCs versus those that gravitate towards industrialized nations. Such effects may be enhanced by the use of specific instruments by LDC governments to facilitate the entry of international franchisors. Beamish (1985) claims that government persuasion/legislation has a significant impact on entry to LDCs compared with developed countries. Within the context of franchising, Ashman (1987) identifies that governmental and legal restrictions were the main problems encountered by US firms establishing franchises in foreign countries.

Although significant in that it provides additional evidence for the varying rates and extent of diffusion of franchising, these studies concentrate on only explaining the differences across countries rather than industries or sub-sectors. Specifically, they suggest that the differing rates of diffusion of franchising are due to variances in legal, tax, cultural, ethical, trust, economic, language and market size. These environmental features affect the extent to which franchised-based expansion is employed within firms' internationalization strategies, but are possibly moderated by contextual factors. For example, within the context of fast food franchising in the Pacific Rim, Yavas and Vardiabasis (1987) establish that the environmental correlates prompting internationalization were market size of the satellite country, the level of urbanization of its population, the ratio of female workers to the total labour force, the proportion of people under 20 years old and growth in domestic competition. Reflecting the intensity of domestic competition within each sector, a large number of US-based franchisors have international presence or have plans to internationalize (Julian and Castrogiovanni, 1995; Shane, 1996), and, whilst the figures vary from sector to sector, the hospitality sector (especially fast food businesses) illustrates a greater propensity to seek internationalization (Hoffman and Preble, 1995).

In addition to environmental issues, other factors such as strategic and transaction-specific variables may interact to help a firm determine the appropriate mode for organizing its international business activities (Hill *et al*, 1990) and, in turn, affect the diffusion of franchising. For example, one of the reasons for US business format franchisors' gravitation to developed nations is that they can do so without substantial alteration to the concept. The extent to which standardization may be realized across marketing mix variables is partially determined by the cultural, socio-political and competitive proximity of the satellite country. Other reasons affecting the diffusion of foreign franchises within different macro-economic environments include franchisor-specific ones, such as: difficulties in selecting appropriate advertising media to promote franchises; costs of identifying, screening and selecting qualified franchisees; difficulty in policing quality standards; difficulties in servicing franchisees; fear of creating local competition as the franchise concept is mimicked (Storholm and Kavil, 1992). For companies seeking to maintain their domestic orientation, the issue of innovation will become increasingly significant.

According to Oliver (1990), the contingency of asymmetry refers to IORs prompted by the potential to exercise power or control over another organization or its resources. Referred to as 'agglomerate collectives' by Astley and Fombrun (1983), such IORs are clusters of organizations of the same species that compete for a limited supply of similar resources. These are found in populations with many small homogenous units: retail, farms, and small manufacturers. Resource scarcity prompts organizations to attempt to exert power, influence, or control over organizations that possess the required scarce resources. Oliver observes that inter-organizational power is a function of size, control over the rules governing exchange, the ability to choose a 'do without strategy', the effectiveness of coercive strategies, and the concentration of inputs. Such a rationale has been observed in a plethora of settings, but are most prevalent in hotels, independent grocers and food manufacturers as well as franchises, through the existence of consortia and symbol groups.

Resource constraints apart, Oliver (1990) suggests that the other main explanatory factor behind the formation of IORs is legitimation. This stems from an organizations' motives to demonstrate or improve its reputation, image, prestige, or congruence with prevailing norms in its institutional environment. For example, small businesses generally have problems in accessing additional capital to fund growth from banks and other institutional investors. As banks in Britain and the USA are generally better disposed to franchisors (Stern and Stanworth, 1994) it could prompt the decision to franchise. Furthermore, some organizations seek to place members of other firms on their board of directors and these can, in some instances, act as a catalyst to franchised expansion. This argument may have some application to understanding the motivation of some franchisees to join certain systems; they perceive that by joining McDonald's, for example, rather than establishing their own business, they will improve their prestige, image and local reputation.

Relationship formation can also be based on reciprocity, or rather for the purpose of pursuing mutually beneficial goals or interests. Reciprocity emphasizes co-operation and collaboration rather than domination, power and control. Potential partners to an exchange will perceive that the benefits of forming a linkage far exceed the disadvantages such as lack of autonomy (Gray, 1985). The reciprocity model of IORs is rooted within exchange theory and, accordingly, participants are seen to be involved in collaborative behaviour in return for meeting other objectives. For example, a firm may decide to franchise its business in order to raise capital and the franchisee offers his labour in exchange for knowledge of operating a business and the perceived security of being a member of an organizational form with a lower probability of failure. In this sense, reciprocity may also have its theoretical roots in resource constraints.

Drawing on Williamson's (1975) transaction cost economics theory, Oliver (1990) indicates that balancing efficiency and protection over their reputation, know-how, etc., leads firms to select a mix of hierarchies and markets to manage transactions. Within an efficiency conversation, Mahoney and Pandian (1992) posits that the choice of organizational form depends on the degree to which non-separable team effort is required, the ability to programme tasks, and the level of asset specificity. Analyzing the latter variable, Williamson (1985) suggests that asset specificity is the extent to which an asset can be redeployed to alternative uses and by alternative users without sacrifice of productive value. When assets are not tied to a specific strategy, hybrid organizational forms are preferable and that form may be determined by distinguishing between the following six attributes:

1. *Site-specificity:* Can the location be used for other uses? Are there alternative ways by which to distribute the product?
2. *Physical asset specificity:* Is there a need to have dedicated technologies for the production and distribution of products?
3. *Human asset specificity:* Is there a need to have highly trained individuals who possess propriety knowledge?
4. *Brand name capital:* How much investment is required to develop the brand? Can the costs of development be shared?
5. *General assets* dedicated to specific customer: and
6. *Temporal specificity:* Site specificity which requires on-site human assets.

Reflecting how some of these asset specificity issues affect sectoral differences of franchise diffusion, Michael (1996) shows that some firms elect to franchise because of the level of risk and importance of human capital (that is, the opportunity to deploy know-how to adapt to environmental conditions). Specifically, he finds first that franchising will be chosen less frequently relative to other organizational forms (full integration) the higher the proportion of failures in a given industry. Secondly, he shows that the higher the level of human capital required the less franchising will be used. Thus, according to Michael, one of the reasons that franchising is popular in fast food (for instance) is because the high level of mechanization and standardization means that the franchisor is better able to control franchisees. The other inference is that franchising is more popular in fast food compared to other sectors because it has lower levels of risk than in other sectors. Yet, if anything, the foodservice market is one of the most volatile markets in the USA and UK economies and human capital is actually enhanced by franchisor training. Furthermore, some companies offer their employees franchises to preclude the loss of human capital.

Efficiency arguments have also been employed by Felstead (1991), who suggests that franchising may be considered by large firms in order to reduce their labour costs, but simultaneously retain control of key assets, such as brand image. Although efficiency is desirable, it can take other forms than franchising, and its pursuit may be moderated by contextual issues, such as culture and extant technological development. Arguably, if it were, we would witness franchising activity in sectors such as retail bakeries, among others. So far, in the UK at least, franchise activity is not evident in the bakery market to any large degree despite separable team effort being feasible, tasks highly programmable, retail assets non-specific and the market in decline. Instead, despite selling and distributing between 50% and 75% of their sales mix as fast food products, full integration, acquisitions and company ownership is widespread and sub-optimal performance appears to be tolerated (see the Case Study at the end of the chapter). There also appears to be an issue of culture; although most managers of retail bakery operations readily acknowledge that they compete in the fast food sector, few are willing to make the transition to altering their stores' marketing mix such that they reflect the norms of the fast food industry. In short, despite being in the fast food market, retail bakery outlets do not necessarily exhibit fast food chain store characteristics. Instead, there is a variety of brand names (which typically reflect regional biases), negligible advertising and promotion, lack of electronic point-of-sale technology, wide product variety and limited opening hours.

From an alternative perspective, if efficiency was not moderated by such factors then there may have been greater diffusion of monocratic bureaucracy. A useful illustration to examine this contention is the following quote from Weber:

Experience tends universally to show that the purely bureaucratic type of administrative organization – that is, the monocratic variety of bureaucracy – is, from a purely technical point of view, capable of attaining the highest degree of efficiency and is in this sense formally the most rational means of carrying out imperative control over human beings. It is superior to any other form in precision, in stability, in the stringency of its discipline, and its reliability. It thus makes possible a particularly high degree of calculability of results of the heads of the organization and for those acting in relation to it. It is finally superior both in intensive efficiency and the scope of its operations, and is formally capable of application to all kinds of administrative tasks. (1947)

Within the context of the hospitality industry, the contention that Weber's ideal type of bureaucracy is the superior type of organization for attaining efficiency has been subject to some debate. Although Burns and Stalker's (1961) mechanistic organizational form, monocratic bureaucracy, is unlikely to exist in concrete reality (Mouzelis, 1975; Zanzi, 1987), it can be utilized as a yardstick to evaluate degrees of bureaucratization. In order to use the framework as a benchmark, its superiority requires qualification and contextualization – does it, for example, refer to efficiency because it enhances control and superiority for whom: customers? employees? managers? shareholders? Clearly, as organizations are bureaucratized to varying degrees there can be no one optimum form of organizational structure. Instead, according to contingency theorists, organizational designs vary according to a variety of often inter-related and multi-causal criteria. These include: environmental determinants (Burns and Stalker, 1961; Ranson *et al*, 1980), organizational size (Blau, 1973; Donaldson, 1985; Utterback and Abernathy, 1975; Walsh and Dewar, 1987); organizational strategy (Chandler, 1962; Rumelt, 1974, 1991; Mintzberg, 1979; Wrigley, 1970). Importantly, organizational structures alter according to national and business cultures as well as the operational norms, and histories of behaviours of the incumbents.

These differing determinants of organizational structure suggest that the superior or most efficient form of organization is dependent upon the situational context in which it is placed, and in part, dependent upon the predominant managerial world view (Prahalad and Bettis, 1986) of the governing bodies' and coalitions' ability and degree of latitude to react to changes. For example, within the context of the hospitality industry, Shamir (1978; 1981) shows that traditional UK hotels exhibit both mechanistic and organic practices and argues, consequently, that the mechanistic-organic continuum is not, in itself, a viable concept. He suggests that the hotel industry is characterized by a desire for rigidity in operations at corporate level and flexibility in the business units. According to Shamir (1978), traditional hotels exhibit tall hierarchical structures and high division of labour within clearly demarcated departments, both of which are reflective of mechanistic organizations (Slattery, 1976), typified by highly authoritarian leadership styles (Hornsey and Dann, 1984; White, 1973). It would, hence, be expected that sophisticated integrating mechanisms would exist in order to facilitate the 'resolution of conflicts and to co-ordinate the activities of various departments' (p. 294). As none were found, there is a suggestion that traditional hotels deviate from monocratic bureaucracies in spite of illustrating high hierarchies. Shamir (1978) establishes that traditional hotels also deviate from the mechanistic model in the following ways:

1. some departments have more autonomy than others;
2. communication flows verbally, directly and across departmental boundaries;
3. they preserve the ability to transfer resources from one department to another;
4. the inseparability of work and non-work activity (Shamir, 1981); and
5. the non-formalization of services and behaviour – operational manuals are not commonplace throughout all hotel departments.

In addition to these deviations from the monocratic form is the perspective that the employee does entirely work for the hotel, but is partially self-employed (Butler and Skipper, 1981; Mars and Mitchell, 1976; Mars and Nicod, 1984; Whyte, 1948). In traditional restaurants and hotels, triadic relationships are evident because waiting staff are dependent on both customers and employers for their earnings, rather than the traditional employee-employer dyad (Nailon, 1982). According to Suprenant and Soloman (1987), such behaviour involves foodservice personnel engaging in activities, called 'informal theatricality', likely to increase their earnings from tips and customers' experience of the restaurant. By being informal, such behaviour is not necessarily compliant to pre-set job descriptions and other bureaucratic mechanisms designed to delineate and define an individual's actions and interactions with customers. Rather, the individual is empowered to employ those tasks and activities which will serve to realize both the waiter's and employer's goals (that is, increased revenue) and customer satisfaction through product promotional activity, friendly rapport and exhibiting both technical skills and, in some instances, athletic forms of service. In deviating further from the norms of the ideal type of bureaucracy, there is little separation between work and non-work activities in hotels. For example, some employees 'live-in' and socialize in the hotel/bar facilities after their shifts (Shamir, 1981). Within the context of traditional hotels, therefore, some form of structural compromise is evident between the demands of the environmental and the desire for rigidity and control by the managing coalitions.

Inter-organizational collaborations are increasingly being recognized as offering a middle path between the markets and hierarchies alternatives of organizational design. Rationales for collaborative ventures include spreading risk, increasing market power, sharing resources and organizational learning (Hamel, 1991). The above discourse suggests that there is a degree of commonality in the reasons behind the variety of hybrid organizational forms. Accordingly, at this level of abstraction, knowing the motive behind IORs cannot help us in predicting or prescribing organizational form. Conversely, knowing the organizational form cannot help us to infer the motive: small firms, for example, have been shown to use collective strategies of all types and this usage is ubiquitous: it permeates all types of environmental conditions (Dollinger and Golden, 1992). The existence of commonality of rationale and diversity of relational form suggest that managers are able to illustrate some degree of choice. For instance, it is evident that not all firms within an economic sector are involved in similar hybrid organizational forms. Some public house companies are all company-owned, others have a mix of company-owned and tenancies, and some employ business format franchising. In spite of similar rationales for the formation of IORs, therefore, there is a tendency within different sub-sectors to gravitate more to one type than another. In the brewing market, for instance, tenancies prevail; in fast food, business format franchising is dominant as is consortia in hotels. Why should there be this difference?

Towards a broader perspective

Why do some firms franchise and why are some economic sectors marked by higher numbers of franchised businesses than others? The introduction to this book suggested that franchising has almost become ubiquitous – ranging from public services (Gretton and Harrison, 1983), charities, to retailing – but when examined further, its pervasiveness has more to do with a broad-based definition rather than all firms striving towards some form of strategic homogeniety. After all, the growth of franchising as a regular discussion feature within the popular press, the emergence of specialist magazines, and consultants within the field have done much to broaden awareness of the subject. While extant frameworks have proved instructive to analyzing the adoption of franchising, arguably they could be applicable to the formation of other hybrid organizations apart from franchises. The lack of adoption by certain firms is perhaps even more vexing because organizations frequently alter strategies and structures in response to a plethora of criteria; while some firms adopt similar approaches, the question of why others elect alternative structures takes on added interest. The remainder of this chapter provides some insight to this phenomenon by starting with a description of an organizational career.

An organizational career

As noted in Chapter 2, Mintzberg (1979) suggests that strategies can be intentional or emergent. In turn, this infers that the issue of strategic choice is pertinent to the decision to franchise and other aspects concerning organizational structure, especially in the period prior to launch. For example, an individual may decide to become self-employed because he wishes to, or is unable to find a full-time job offering the rewards to maintain at least a pre-determined standard of living (that is, they are reluctant entrepreneurs). Some of these individuals will readily adapt to the rigours of self-employment, others may choose to leave because they are coerced to do so as a result (for instance) of lack of adaptability or family concerns (Greenhaus and Bentall, 1985), or because they had no intention of staying self-employed in the first instance.

There are a number of antecedent variables influencing the career path (including self-employment) that a certain individual may pursue, and these are discussed in more depth in a consideration of franchisee adoption patterns. Nevertheless, once the decision to become self-employed has been made, choices are then made as to the business and product-market that the individual wishes to operate in. At this stage, self-efficacy expectations will, in part, affect the decision-making process. Self-efficacy expectations refer to an individual's beliefs in their abilities to perform particular behaviours successfully and are developed from their experiences of their own past behaviours (Waldinger et al, 1985). These expectations may be based on their closure from certain occupations and derive from prior educational, ethnicity, work and/or personal experiences and seem to be evident throughout all permeations of the career decision (Chapter 5). For example, some people have made decisions to enter the restaurant trade (in particular) based on their closure from other types of work. Equally, a survey of hotel general managers reported that over a third would like to be self-employed (Ashdown Group,

1994). Furthermore, prospective franchisees have been shown (Kaufmann and Stanworth, 1995) to choose the business category before the decision to operate as a franchisee. When deciding on such issues not only are there social considerations but also the individual's ability to overcome the financial and human capital barriers to entry to the market. According to Porter (1980), there are six elements entering into the potential entrant's decision:

1. the profits presently earned by the industry occupants;
2. the static or structural entry costs, such as knowledge, location costs, capital requirements etc.;
3. the existing player's expected reactions to entry;
4. other members of the queue of potential entrants, and their likely behaviour;
5. any relevant sources of advantage (for example, experience, brand identity, absolute cost advantages; supply agreements, trademarks) already in the hands of the entrant; and
6. the irreversible costs of gathering information and making the decision.

The degree of rigour employed in quantifying and codifying the above considerations in a written form is highly variable, but the decision of how to surmount these barriers will affect the entry mode, whether that be via adopting an incremental approach through (for example) product diversification, forming an alliance with an existing business, or through developing or acquiring a dedicated business unit. If a more developmental approach is adopted, the planning stage requires that the potential incumbent envisage what the organization is going to be and to make decisions specific to the structure of the organization; these are partially based on the customer need that the firm is seeking to satisfy, knowledge concerning existing technology, and perceptions of the environmental constraints that the firm will be operating in. Often, these decisions are codified in a business plan, but are not holistic because people are rational only to a limited degree.

Via codification, the entrepreneur's vision, choices and perceptions of the future business present a blueprint of the organizational strategy, structure and market as well as expected returns from this mix. As part of this vision, franchising may be suggested as a method of growing the business and, subsequent to formation, this intent may be implemented via the introduction of process and product structures that enable the business to be franchised. Indeed, an often-heard ambition by some new entrants to the foodservice industry is that they want their business to be the next McDonald's of their particular market niche; the entrepreneur begins business with an intent of transforming it into a franchised entity. Of course, the implicit assumptions behind the business plan are subject to review and modification with the acquisition of new knowledge and insight. Some of this newly acquired information will be taken into account and, in other instances, ignored and this suggests that the decision to franchise may also be unintentional as well as intentional. Once operating, a firm's trajectory is determined, in part, by choices concerning organizational development, which refers to the manner by which a firm (or other entity) evolves from one level of complexity and size to the next.

Most models of organizational development appear to assume a continuous progression from introduction, through growth, maturity and decline, or from stage to stage (Greiner, 1972) to reveal an 'S-shaped' curve. The initial stage is, typically, the owner-operator organization which comprises self-employed individuals who formally employ no labour. At this stage, the owner-operator is the value chain, but within Lowe's (1988) typology of small hotels, this stage is characterized by the use of immediate family members and other members of a close-knit social network. The majority of businesses will remain at this stage and not evolve beyond it because of resource constraints or out of personal preference: for example, the owner-operator may be satisfied with the level of performance, or only sees self-employment as a 'stop-gap' between full-time employment or may be unwilling to delegate (another form of the monopolization of work). Reflecting the lack of development, this first stage is typically the largest group of self-employed persons, accounting for about two-thirds of the self-employed in Britain (DTI, 1995; Hakim, 1987). The subsequent stages in organizational development are characterized by increasing levels of bureaucratization and the emergence of an organizational hierarchy with defined roles, authority and responsibilities.

The underlying rationale of these models is that each stage of organizational development requires different managerial demands and requirements resulting in distinct levels of complexity. It is during these transition stages that the relative merits of franchising and other organizational development methods may be considered in order to achieve a certain rate of expansion along a pre-specified strategic direction. Whilst each model propounds a varying number of developments, only a few deal with the discontinuities or radical innovations required to pass from one stage of organizational development to the next. Understanding these discontinuities and the moderating factors is fundamental to the understanding as to why some organizations adopt franchising and others either elect or are coerced into choosing alternative structural forms. One such moderating factor may be the type of innovation itself (Damanpour, 1991; Meyer and Goes, 1988; Moch and Morse, 1977). For example, franchising may not be adopted because it is perceived as too radical, too expensive and results in too much loss of power compared to company-ownership. Equally, strategic choice seems to infer that firms do not necessarily follow the 'S-shaped' curve hypothesis, and a recurrent theme throughout Business Policy texts is the issue of strategic direction – or rather questions of 'Where does the company go from here and how do we achieve it?' Luffman *et al* (1991) indicate that both product and process innovations are encompassed in the array of possible directions a firm may pursue:

- *no change:* manufacture or supply the same product or same service to the same customers;
- *backward vertical integration:* to manufacture or supply a product or service which is currently purchased from another company;
- *forward vertical integration:* to manufacture or supply a product which is currently produced by a customer;
- *product extension:* the development of the product offering from the existing product, through variants, to a completely new product offering;
- *market extension:* the development of the markets served from the existing markets through entry to new segments, to sales to a completely different market.

Of the few models that concern themselves with the transition stages, a recurrent theme is that the organizational development process entails protracted periods of incremental changes punctuated by short periods of discontinuity (Mount *et al*, 1993). The protracted periods will feature sporadic modifications to the existing value chain (such as altering product components, store fascia and the existing administrative procedures), but the organization will remain essentially embedded within a particular developmental stage and the framework of its existing strategy. The periods will also be characterized by stability where the main focus concerns day-to-day business activities. These can often be quite satisfying because organizational tasks are performed in the presence of a set of principles that are so well assimilated and practised they require little conscious thought (Johnson, 1992). These satisfaction levels and assimilation of tasks may serve to embed an organization within a particular stage because the perceived costs of changing (that is, conflict) the tasks and orientation of the firm will outweigh maintaining the *status quo*.

The periods of discontinuity are in response to, or in anticipation of, environmental changes or a managerial need to improve performance through altering the existing value chain to another configuration. Realizing these radical changes and choices necessitates shifts in organizational strategy, structure, culture, power, and control. Underlying these approaches to organizational development is the rationale that it is the coherence between structural design elements and institutional values that is the basis for understanding variety in organizational design and patterns of organizational change (Donaldson, 1987; Kikulis *et al*, 1995; Nelson, 1991). That is, like business formation, organizational structure is the manifestation of a set of ideas, beliefs and values that shape what the organization should be doing, of how it should be doing it and how it should be judged (Ranson *et al*, 1980). Of primary interest to understanding this contention is Greenwood and Hining's (1988a) diagram (Figure 3.1) illustrating the dynamics of organizational change.

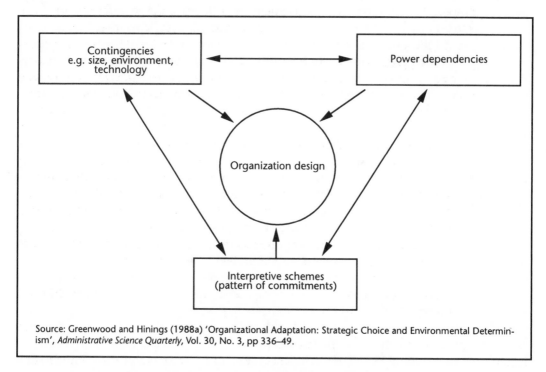

Source: Greenwood and Hinings (1988a) 'Organizational Adaptation: Strategic Choice and Environmental Determinism', *Administrative Science Quarterly*, Vol. 30, No. 3, pp 336–49.

Figure 3.1: *Strategic choice and environmental determinism*

At the centre of the diagram is a particular structural configuration (that is, the mix of job descriptions, information systems, manager selection systems, reward systems, etc.) connected to three potential dynamics of change. There is no assumption that the structure and processes are congruent with each or any of the three potential dynamics. In essence, the diagram summarizes a good deal of strategic management and structural contingency research which shows that strategic change is shaped by such things as environment, size, technology, the perceptions and biases of key decision-makers (Schwenk, 1985), and organizational and structural constraints (Hall and Saias, 1980). Each of these variables is now reviewed.

'Structural contingencies'

In studying the development of large organizations in the USA, Chandler (1962) observed that increases in unit volume, geographic dispersion, and horizontal and vertical integration were followed by changes in organizational structure. From this study, he observed that 'structure follows strategy'. Numerous subsequent studies have tested this tenet and found similar results, but within them strategy has tended to be associated with logical systems of analysis and planning. Such frameworks have, however, been based on what researchers and writers say that managers should do rather than observations about strategies come about (Johnson, 1992). Within much of the prescriptive literature concerning strategy formulation, there appears to be an implicit emphasis on the unitary perspective of industrial relations and that decision-makers are rational, that is electing strategy which maximizes return on investment and shareholder value. By emphasizing the unitary perspective, some strategic management theorists assume that the organization is a team, goals are common, resistance is irrational, and that consensus is often a matter of communication. As a result of this unitary orientation within organizations, management are able to adapt to the rigours of the environment with relative ease by altering their strategy and organizational structure and processes. Under this construct, the decision to franchise is the result of a rational decision-making process based on environmental dictates: either the firm franchises or suffers the pains of sub-optimal performance or eventual death (Donaldson, 1987). Unfortunately, this construct also reduces the role of management to being 'structural adjusters': they are there to ensure that the correct organizational structure is in place to facilitate survival growth. In this role, the 'structural contingency theory' assumes that management does not confront pockets of power within their organization, competing interests, and the effects of either potential or actual conflict. If opposition does occur, it is viewed as some form of aberration, instigated by troublemakers or misinformed individuals (Fox, 1973) and, once dealt with, management is able to implement the necessary adjustments in order to ensure that strategy and organizational structure is contingent with the environment. A plethora of research, however, illustrates that not all firms are able to adapt to environmental conditions in a similar manner (Hrebiniak and Joyce, 1985; Marlin *et al*, 1994) which, in turn, suggests that there are impediments to the ability to realize congruence or 'fit' with external constraints. The structural contingency approach is encapsulated in the following function: environment → strategy → structure.

According to this function, organizational dynamics involve the compatibility between, on the one hand, contingencies such as size, technology and environment, and on the other hand, organizational structure (Barley, 1990; Donaldson, 1982; Rumelt, 1974). Contingency theory infers that a linear relationship between technology, size, environment and structure is apparent and the 'goodness of fit' between the variable serves to influence performance levels (Schöonhoven, 1981). Despite some weaknesses, the contingency approach has provided a wealth of data on relationships between several contextual variables and organization design, competitive advantages and performance, and could be related to extant explanations of the decision to franchise.

For example, one contingency which has been shown to affect both organizational structures *per se* and the decision to franchise is the differing stages of the product life-cycle. At the evolutionary stage of the cycle, when the product is being created and offered to the market for the first time, the critical task is increment innovation which entails developing the product and achieving acceptable product characteristics (Donaldson, 1985; 1986). During this stage, the product will be differentiated permitting a premium price to be charged, thereby relieving the firm of pressure to minimize costs. As diffusion and imitation ensues, demand increases lead to incremental changes in the product (such as standardization) and alterations in productive capacity, equipment and organization. As noted by Oxenfeldt and Kelly (1969) one of these cost changes may be the need to lower the costs associated with expansion, possibly resulting in the adoption of franchising. With imitation, so comes increased pressure on prices and costs and stress on the organization to seek cost reduction change and standardization, meaning that the firm may become more bureaucratized. Such action could entail a buy-back policy of franchisee-operated units.

Another contingency is organizational size. Within the size structure contingency, bureaucracy theorists argue that larger size requires delegation down to an extended hierarchy (Child, 1972). Examining this argument, Donaldson (1982) indicates that this could be attained in several ways, including product divisionalization, but also through decentralization of decision-making. As the majority of franchisors operate within a single product-market, there may be less pressure for divisionalization according to product but as the number of business units increases so there is greater pressure on existing supervisory capacity (Thompson, 1994) and other organizational functions. Within the context of the hotel industry, Slattery and Clark (1988) illustrate that group head offices and the functional characteristics of such bodies are determined by the size of the portfolio (as measured by number of hotels, number of bedrooms, number of hotel employees and the revenue of hotels), and the portfolio technology. In short, they established that the larger the hotel portfolio and the more complex its technological mix, the greater the need for support services. Size appears to be an integral part of extant approaches to the decision to franchise because of references to the decision to franchise by a business which is held back by its smallness and from realizing greater size through direct ownership.

Another strand of the contingency approach has sought to formulate broad generalizations about the relationship with technology. The perspective originated from the work of Woodward (1965), who argued that technologies directly determine differences in aspects such as span of control, centralization of authority, and the formalization of rules and procedures. Unfortunately, the relationship between organizational structure and technology appears to be omitted from the majority of franchise texts, with the possible exception of Michael (1996) who shows that franchises appear to be prevalent in sectors with low levels of human capital (that is, among 'low technology' firms), but it is of singular importance in influencing the decision to franchise. Chapter 1 argued that the trend towards standardization, predictability, and deskilling played a significant role in the emergence of business format franchising and it also has relevance for determining a franchise-based strategy. The essence of business format franchising is uniformity, pre-dictability and routinization, which is achieved through deskilling and the transfer of know-how from the franchisor to the franchisee. The franchisor also employs monitor-ing mechanisms, such as visits from regional managers and 'mystery shoppers' in order to ensure conformance to standards. In the deskilling process, theorists argue that entrenched interests, established ideologies, cultures and institutions place a premium on managerial control and the progressive separation of manual and conceptual work. In franchising, the manual work is often performed by franchisees and the conceptual work is owned and controlled by the franchisor. As franchising is dependent on technologies which deskill labour and fragment work, they permit increased control and greater poten-tial diffusion among people from a variety of educational and employment backgrounds as well as increase the revenues to franchisors (who incur less risk). Franchises could there-fore be said to engender a labour process that gradually tightens the association between technology and bureaucracy (Barley, 1990).

An approach similar to the environment → structure explanations has been employed by a number of researchers to provide explanations for the decision to fran-chise. For example, through interviewing a small number of franchisors, Dant (1996) indicates that the motivation to franchise derived from market growth. Such an observa-tion is similar to that propounded by Hoffman and Preble (1991), who suggest that franchising is employed in environments characterized by buoyant customer demand and fragmented market conditions. Under this construct, environmental conditions (for example, rapid market growth, an illiberal capital market, high information costs, etc.) determine that franchising is employed by firms as a strategy in order to capitalize on this growth. Another environmental factor is the role of the competition and the degree to which they are franchised (see Chapter 4 for an explanation and a methodology). In order to optimize performance, the organizational structure must be able to support, co-ordi-nate, and control franchise-based expansion. It is inferred that those firms that do not adopt franchising and a suitable structure and culture to support franchisees from which to maintain brand value will under-perform. This contention is borne out by a deluge of research with similar empirical results, such that it is almost axiomatic within strategic management texts that (given certain environmental conditions) an appropriately designed structure (togther with a suitable culture) is required to facilitate the implemen-tation of a firm's strategy. Thus, the relationship between environment and organization structure is deterministic. The implications of such a deterministic approach suggest three attributes (Schreyögg, 1980) about organizational development and success:

1. there is only one best structural 'answer' to a specific contextual situation. This means that within situations there is no choice among structural arrangements. According to the logic of any of the contingency theories that relate structure to size, environment, competitive context (Porter, 1980), or technology, the structure of organizations should be similar for a given mar-ket. Their structures align because a common environmental field pressures them to prevailing norms. If isomorphism prevails, how then are we to explain the apparent variety of organizations that nonetheless exist within

industries, and intra-industry groups of companies exhibiting similar strategic configurations?

2. the environment is to be considered as given, which means that the organization has no possibility of influencing or controlling its environmental situation. Yet, some market leaders do, or at least attempt to do, exactly that by increasing their size and control over scarce resources (Porter, 1985);

3. the organization has to achieve a certain level of economic performance in order to survive; and

4. the criteria against which its performance is assessed are defined externally, which means that level and criteria are outside the control of the firm.

Where structure is congruent with the contingency variables, then the organization is perceived to be at equilibrium and superior performance should result. Where disequilibrium between the contingency variable and structure exists, pressure for reorientation exists. Such pressure may be manifest via a need for a company to alter its existing strategy because of an opportunity in the environment or as a result or sub- optimal performance. For example, a firm may decide to franchise because property developments and organizational resource constraints are such that they preclude the firm from benefiting from rapid market growth. Maintaining the existing strategy and structure results in mismatch and has a negative impact on performance. Depending on the competitiveness in the environment and the tolerance for sub-optimal performance, the firm may reconfigure structure to be congruent with the environment (Donaldson, 1987).

Primae facie, the contributions from the structural contingency theorists offer compelling reasons for the motivations to franchise, but they are not convincing. Importantly, the structural contingency theory has received severe criticism for ignoring the perceptive and cognitive differences of managers. Individuals in an organization, via the divergence of their interests, the consequent differences in their choices and how their conflict over organizational resources shape organizational structure and power differences. As noted by Marxian organizational theorists, the fact that members of an organization do not perceive its objectives, structure, and processes in a purely similar manner does not necessarily signify that the latter are absent (Braverman, 1974). The reality of organizational life is the existence of conflict, some decisions being political rather than rational and power differences. Clearly, there are constraints to the extent to which some firms are able to choose and implement franchised-based expansion.

Interpretive schemes

Alone, contingency theory is not a sufficient explanation for the variety of organizational forms evident within a particular industry or its sub-sectors. Nevertheless, contingency variables are important to creating pressure for organizational change. According to Huff *et al* (1992), the effect of contingency factors is gradually to build up stress within the organization that may remain by incremental innovations. They argue that stress reflects the dissatisfactions of individual actors and imperfections in the fit between the organization and its environment. The main characteristic of the accumulation of stress is that, once it has gone beyond a certain threshold, important actors within the organization are forced to resolve the issues responsible for the stress. The resolution process is then put into action by consideration of the advantages and disadvantages of the existing strategy and structural form versus those of one or more alternatives. The comparative process may take into account some of the relative merits of franchising, as set out below, but the current position of the decision-maker, in the 'how-to' franchising literature, is typically assumed to be company-ownership rather than being (for example) a tenancy. The comparative process may take into account some of the relative merits of franchising, as set out at the end of this chapter. Analyzing the pluses and minuses of the existing strategy will tend to be conducted in an abstract and, possibly, in a rational manner but will not be holistic.

Benefits of franchising

Some of the *benefits* of franchising accruing to the franchisor are as follows:

- Able to secure present and future market share due to buying restrictions within the agreement.
- Lower unit costs of materials due to increased bargaining power over suppliers.
- Wider brand awareness and dispersion permitting greater brand valuations.
- Increased direct control over promotional take-up and own-label marketing than is possible with voluntary symbol groups.
- Greater return on capital because the franchisee is required to invest in fixed assets.
- Ownership advantages without the associated problems of staff, payroll and day-to-day administration. The opportunity cost of this is lower return, but higher return on capital.
- Lower head office staff requirement (Churchill, 1991; Sanghavi, 1990).
- Franchisees could be a good source of innovation and, hence, competitive advantage (see Chapter 6).
- Franchisees will often shun unionism and have knowledge of local labour markets (Jordans, 1988). This said, union density within the catering market is the lowest in the UK economy.
- Increased flexibility in the management of labour through distancing.
- Motivated management since income is related to profit. Empirical literature has generally been supportive of the idea that incentive ideas are important issues in terms of the extent to which firms rely on franchising as opposed to company ownership and the extent to which they rely on royalties. However, a franchisee has the incentive to free ride on the franchisor's trademark if the outlet is frequented by non-repeat customers and cheats by substituting low quality for high quality in order to reduce costs (Klien, 1980; Minkler, 1990). Indeed, in some chicken menu franchises, franchisees have been observed purchasing raw material from specified suppliers (such as supermarkets).
- As franchisees pay a fee based on a percentage of their sales, franchisors should enjoy a positive cash flow (albeit possibly short-term) from the franchisees even if the franchisees are not making a profit.
- Lowers risk of testing particular markets/products. However, there has been

some suggestion that this option may be the preserve of large companies. For example, Marks & Spencer has seventy-four franchises in overseas markets but none in the UK. There is some suggestion that smaller companies tend to employ franchising as a vehicle to growth rather than market testing (Gourlay, 1994).

- Franchising should enable the franchisor (depending on the costs of entry, the height and nature of barriers to entry, and the 'saleability' of the franchise) to increase the number of distributive outlets, market coverage, market share and build brand equity with limited capital investment.
- Business units more likely to be accepted as local; however, given the level of uniformity inherent to franchises there may equally be a perception that it is in fact not franchised.

Disadavantages of franchising

The *disadvantages* of franchising to the franchisor are:

- May be difficult to exercise tight control over the franchisee because the lack of a traditional employer-employee relationship.
- Contrary to popular myth, the costs of entry and franchisee recruitment can be expensive (see Chapter 8).
- Franchising may be viewed as a form of business restructuring since it alters the franchisor's capital structure, asset mix and organization through the redeployment of assets (Rock and Rock, 1990). Whilst such restructuring potentially offers a rapid means of implementing a new product or concept (Housden, 1984), it results in a more difficult and slower process in subsequently altering the system, than may occur in a wholly-owned business. This is due, in part, to the need to sell the benefits to, and persuade the franchisee and overcoming the expression of usurpationary power, to make the alterations.
- Changes in corporate strategy may take longer to implement, perhaps allowing competitors to quickly negate or realize first mover advantages (Robinson *et al*, 1992; Kerin *et al*, 1992; Leiberman and Montgomery, 1988);
- There is a necessity to develop an organizational culture and structure geared toward the management of franchisees (Forward and Fulop, 1993).
- Franchisor cannot always be sure that the franchisee is declaring the true level of business activity.
- Activities of unscrupulous franchisors and franchisee demotivation can be damaging to brand equity.
- Communication and motivation highly dependent upon trust between the two parties (Lewis and Lambert, 1991; Lusch 1977; Meloan, 1988).
- Franchisee motivation changes over time (Hall and Dixon, 1989), with distinct periods of disconfirmation and demotivation being evident. Given that franchisees join a system at different times and illustrate differing rates of maturity, such sentiment could have a multiplier effect and 'colour' new franchisees' perception of the franchisor.
- Franchisor may experience difficulties in recruiting franchisees with the necessary investment capability and who are risk averse but want to be self-employed.

There appears to be an implicit assumption within the strategic management and franchise texts that the process of considering the firm's future direction will be conducted in a methodological and rational manner. Deriving from a landmark study by Mintzberg in 1973 of managerial activity, an increasing number of researchers have questioned whether, in fact, decision-makers follow the precepts of the more rational decision-making models. By understanding some of their concerns, some light may be shed on the sectoral differences in the application and use of franchising. Mintzberg showed that much managerial time is spent on day-to-day trouble-shooting and *ad hoc* problems of organization and regulation; he also showed that little time is spent on any one particular activity and, especially, on the conscious, systematic formulation of plans. Planning and decision-making tend to take place in the course of other activity. Furthermore, Isenberg (1987) indicates that senior management rend to rely on general thought processes such as using inituition, managing a network of inter-related problems, dealing with ambiguity, inconsistency, novelty and surprise when making routine tactical manoeuvres.

When issues of decision-making are examined under conditions of strategic choice, rationality does not tend to prevail. Although both Ellingham (1995) and Seltz (1982) employ financial models to illustrate the potential cash-flow implications of pursuing franchised expansion, empirical studies of strategic investment decisions confirm that financial techniques are much abused, even ignored, and sometimes not even used (Whittington, 1993). Others have recognized that the decision to franchise may derive from analyses based on employing techniques such as the Boston Consulting Group's market growth/relative market share matrix (Hoffman and Preble, 1991; McKiernan, 1992; McDonald, 1992). Within the confines of this contruct, the decision to franchise may be based on a need to increase market share and cash flows quickly while the market is expanding rapidly. The overly prescriptive managerial actions deriving from a firm's position in such matrices should, however, be treated with some caution. Under the recommendations of theory, companies with low market share operating in low growth markets should be disposed of. Yet, there are some such companies/business units which are profitable because they are focused concerns operating within particular product/geographic niches. Subsequent research from the original work conducted by Mintzberg (1973) concerning managerial decision-making suggests that the rationality and rigour with which decisions are made are limited. Strategies, including the decision to franchise, it seems, form out of a mixture of analysis and intuition, routine and spontaneity, top and down, and fortune and error (Whittington, 1993). Perhaps more specifically, strategic choice occurs within the context of a condition called 'bounded rationality', which serves to limit the legitimation process.

Under conditions of bounded rationality, individuals seek a solution which is 'good enough' and collect information which is pertinent to resolving a particular problem. Thus, the problem selects the first alternative which meets some minimum standard of satisfaction. As decision-makers are bound by their cognitive limitations and the resources of the organization, they may be unable to choose an optimal alternative. Instead, they choose from a limited number of alternatives rather than all of them, and 'muddle through'. As part of this process, the problem-solver may employ a strategy that initially functions well, but later on blocks the realization of new and simpler solutions to similar problems (Kaufmann, 1991). Although untested, such an observation may also be a rationale for the buy-back policy adopted by some franchisors. This satisficing behaviour within the strategic choice process has been supported elsewhere and is also an implicit part of contracts. Related to bounded rationality, Barr *et al* (1992) suggest that individuals have 'mental maps' of the world, which represent concepts and relationships an individual uses to understand various situations or environments. They posit that:

> . . . given human frailties as information processors, mental models allow individuals and organizations to make sense of their environment and act within it. The problem, of course, is that mental models may be, or become, inaccurate. Given cognitive limitations, mental maps will always be incomplete; inaccuracy may increase, however, as environments change.

Such a sentiment is echoed by MacCaskey (1991):

> When a terrain is poorly mapped, what can managers do? Researchers of business and public administration have made several suggestions. In such situations, managers often shift from optimizing to 'satisficing'. Instead of trying to perform a complete analysis that will identify the best course of action, they settle for taking the first satisfactory alternative that comes along. This represents an important shift in outlook and captures an attitude of mind more likely to be effective in moving through uncharted territory. (pp. 148–49)

Johnson (1992) indicates that differences between existing mental maps and the environment lead to strategic drift – or incongruence between structure, strategy and the environment. Barr *et al* (1992) also show that mental models can exacerbate a mismatch between data availability and information processing in three important ways. First, mental models determine what information will receive attention because status is applied to that information as well as to the manner in which it is delivered (Howard, 1994). Individuals recall the elements or features of a stimulus situation that are the most prominent in their mental models. Managers have a tendency to focus their attention on environmental changes that are most salient to, or offer support for, their current mental models, while other potentially important changes in the environment may not be recognized. Secondly, the stimuli gaining attention tend to be interpreted in relation to the individual's current mental model rather than being seen as a signal of needed change. Even if events growing out of a dynamic environment are noticed, then managers may not perceive a need for change because of their lack of experience and/or skill. According to Neisser (1976) experience and skill are important antecedent variables affecting the amount of information a decision-maker is able to extract from a particular situation.

> The difference between a skilled and unskilled perceiver is not that the former adds anything to the stimulus but that he is able to gain more information from it: he detects features and higher-order structure to which the naive viewer is not sensitive. (p. 20)

A third key finding from cognitive research is that mental maps direct action by limiting the range of alternative solutions to the issues that have been identified. Related to mental modes is Dutton's (1993) strategic issue diagnosis which describes the individual-level, cognitive process through which decision-makers form interpretations about organizational events, developments and trends. The diagnosis of strategic issues is consequential both for decision-makers who do it and for the organizations that employ them. The diagnosis will identify who will be involved in an issue, what role the individual is likely to play and the amount of resources allocated to an issue. A decision-maker may have one of two responses to a strategic issue: automatic or custom-made. A custom-made diagnosis is typically a long and considered process that requires the decision-maker to formulate differing scenarios and results from an array of possible choices. An automatic diagnosis involves the activation of ready-made issue categories in the mind of decision-makers that have been built from encounters with issues in the past. This classification of an issue into a ready-made category reduces the amount of thought applied to an issue and activates a set of scripted responses and, thus, the decision to franchise may not be a decision at all, but a routine. This cognitive category-setting may be an inappropriate way to interpret an issue because it might be out-dated. According to Dutton (1993), there are three sets of conditions which can be isolated to diagnosing an issue:

1. decision-maker's connection to the issue, which encompasses aspects concerning tenure, the frequency of dealing with strategic issues, and the functional training of the individual;
2. issue context factors, such as time pressure, specialization of the issue, and information load; and
3. organizational characteristics, encompassing past performance success, the norms for consistency, and management activities (for example, environmental scanning).

Most of the 'How to franchise' press seems to concern itself with organizational issues rather than the time frame or the decision-maker's connection to the issue, but illustrates some inconsistency. For example, some commentators refer to the point that an essential criterion for franchise success is proven prior success, but if the business is successful there may be less of a tendency to change. Performance levels, particularly if buoyant, serve to reinforce the *status quo* rather than create pressure to change the existing recipe. It is also equally apparent that the environmental scanning activities of small companies are limited: they tend not to purchase market research reports and rely on *ad hoc* means to learn about their environment, such as social network, for competition, and some newspapers. Although confident about their abilities to create and distribute questionnaires to an appropriate sample and integrate the results into their decision-making process, small-business owners do not possess all of the skills necessary to properly gather, analyze, and interpret research data (Callahan and Cassar, 1995; Lyles *et al*, 1993). This situation may not only limit the degree to which franchising may be elected as a strategy for growth, but also the extent of rigour with which the decision to franchise is implemented.

The franchise press also appears to assume that the decision to franchise is conducted from a rational perspective, with systematic planning, etc. Not only does this contradict the findings of Mintzberg (1973) and others examining managerial activities, but also studies of small-business owners. These two research strands suggest that small-business owners are constrained by time and their ability to cope with issues requiring substantial information processing. Both of these issues infer that, if anything, the decision to franchise is *ad hoc* rather than strategic. Given this situation, it is likely that the decision to franchise by some firms is inspired by the actions of the competition, rather than occurring within a vacuum. In this way, there may be a hidden assumption within the decision-making process: if firm x employed franchising to resolve a particular problem, then the management of firm y (who are confronting similar problems) may believe that it is a suitable option for them. As an increasing number of firms within a network of firms adopt the organizational form, so others may decide to adopt – including new entrants – until it becomes a 'legitimate' form of structuring within an industry sector.

The lack of analysis of new franchisors concerning their length of tenure, frequency of strategic decision-making, and functional training precludes the provision of examples pertinent to the franchise decision. Nonetheless, broad inferences can be made. With regard to functional training, for example, Miller (1977) and Argenti (1976) indicate that one of the key characteristics of failed firms is the pressure of an unbalanced board of directors, or the dominance of people on a decision-making committee with similar educations and functional training. Conflictual thinking, or opposing ideas, is a potentially powerful spur for new ideas. Thus, these firms fail because there is a tendency to interpret problems from a similar perspective and without anyone playing devil's advocate. That is, failure ensues because management suffer from 'functional fixedness' (Duncker, 1945): they have a block to using an object in an alternative way. Conversely, the manager who makes a decision using multiple perspectives has been shown to make better decisions (Nutt, 1993). To some degree, the functional training may also be indicative of the educational bias and level of education of the board. As an individual's education increases, and their training experiences become broader, their paradigmatic perspectives become more complete and rounded (Hitt and Tyler, 1991). The issue of functionality is aptly summarized by Lessard and Zaheer (1996):

> In reality, strategic decisions are often unstructured and emergent . . . evolving from complex interactions among individuals and groups in different divisions, functions and situations. They are often made in event time rather than calender time: in response to competitors' actions, to changes in the environment, or to internal innovations that cannot wait for the planning cycle . . .

> The way in which subunits 'frame' a particular strategic problem and see their own roles in relation to that problem will affect their reponses to it or the extent to which they co-operate with other subunits in dealing with it, thus affecting the quality of the response. (pp. 513 and 519)

With regard to tenure, research suggests that boards experiencing low turnover often tolerate top management inefficiency for the sake of cohesion and conformity to the existing organizational culture which, in turn, can lead to poor performance. The longer groups work together the greater the tendency for individuals to work to the group norms and act in ways which reinforce those norms and values. Thus, there may be less of an incentive to change the orientation and trajectory of the organization to a different track (Greenwood and Hinings, 1988). Conversely, new management teams may not have experience of making strategic decisions and, as such, be more orientated to those areas in which they feel comfortable.

Power dependencies

According to Greenwood and Hinings (1988b), organizational structures serve the interests of some groups rather than others and act as delineators of advantage, status, divisional cultures (departments develop shared languages reflecting similarities in members' responses and interpretation of information), and privilege. Structural change is affected by the extent to which groups are dissatisfied with the accommodation of their interests; *and*, by the ability of groups to express and protect those interests in structural and processural terms, in effect by using structures to obtain and utilize power. They argue that patterns of commitment to prevailing or alternative interpretative schemes have to be related to the power structure of an organization. Thus, innovation and change processes may be seen as outcomes of the competition for power and status between organizational stakeholders, who each interpret a strategy's meaning from a different perspective (Hutt *et al*, 1995). Furthermore, Stanislao and Stanislao (1983) suggest that, even with adequate planning, resistance to change, the expression of usurpationary and exclusive power, will be encountered. For example, within the UK public house market, there has been some resistance by tenants to the use of franchising; this resistance has resulted from a fear of a loss of independence by the tenants. Such resistance stems from fear and it is easier to prevent than it is to remove once it has developed. It is for this reason that the often *ad hoc* decisions to franchise may be supported by feasibility studies and other formal analysis techniques, but when done are conducted to varying levels of rigour and quality. Langley (1990) indicates that:

> Formal analysis is often initiated by people who are already convinced about what should be done and use analysis simply to bring other people over to their point of view (persuasion), or perhaps just to make their views known (positioning). Sometimes, the initiator of analysis will carry out a study him or herself. At other times, an attempt may be made to increase the credibility of the analysis by hiring an outside consultant or staff person to do the work.

In this confirmation bias situation, the amount of expertise called upon influences other aspects of the decision-making process by drawing interests into the decision arena whose contribution must be evaluated and integrated with that from other sources. If the formal study and/or the decision-maker is unable to convince other organizational members of the benefit of franchising for either enhancing or reinforcing their power positions, structural inertia is evident. For example, some firms may not elect to franchise because the management perceive that it would disrupt the existing power relations: they perceive that standardization, performance and control would be jeopardized by franchisees. Additionally, a firm may remain an owner-operator firm because the individual does not want to delegate authority and responsibility. Cuba and Milbourn (1982) cite that the lack of delegation of responsibility can be a cause of failure in small firms. In such scenarios, the business owner chooses not to devolve certain tasks because he only sees employment as a 'gap-stop' in full-time employment; by not employing additional people, it gives him additional flexibility to exit at will. Other reasons for the lack of delegation include:

- The belief that employees do not have the job skills or motivation to accomplish tasks as well as he can. As a result, he attempts to do everything himself believing that greater overall efficiency will result from his speed.
- Fear of losing control. This may result from the belief that the employees may take advantage of him or he may become vulnerable to employee demands or lose employee respect.
- Possible lack of skill. Setting objectives, planning, directing, and co-ordinating the work of others may be difficult things for the owner to do.
- Reluctance to abandon the enjoyable activities.
- The view that employees are often reluctant to accept new tasks. This resistance often manifests itself in poor task performance and general apathy, both of which may circumvent the owner's attempt to delegate but may also be reflective of the perception that the employees do not have the skills for the job.

The lack of diversity by small firms and the lack of development by some is also indicative of inertia. That is, the owner-operator's behaviours and ways of conducting business have become embedded along a certain trajectory out of choice and habit. Such organizations are the embodiment of organic structures and are marked by two key features: the ability to quickly respond to opportunities and the reliance on prior experience. To pursue organizational development through taking on additional staff or via diversifying will entail changing these behaviours and the business's resource mix. For example, they may have to learn how to trust, delegate, accept that employees may achieve better results by doing things differently, recruit, detail job descriptions, train staff and motivate them. Depending on the nature of the owner-operator, these are changes that could be inconsistent to the realization of his objectives and jeopardize his power base, beliefs and the accomplishment of certain tasks.

The configuration of power-dependence can also operate as a destabilizing dynamic for change if the dominant power coalition embraces an alternative interpretative scheme, or if it perceives its interest to be ill-served by existing structures. For example, some franchisors have decided to withdraw from the activity when a key sponsor of franchising has left the organization and has been replaced by another who is less committed to the activity. Such a situation is not unique to franchising: strategies often reflect the values of top managers and their conception of the organization and the external environment, substantive changes in strategic direction are often associated with changes in senior management because they bring different interpretations and values from those of the previous management.

Summary and conclusion

This chapter has shown that extant literature attributes the decision to franchise to three main frameworks: resource constraints, agency theory and risk-reduction. While these arguments have attracted increasing acceptance by researchers, they are not comprehensive rationales. Specifically, they are not comparative with companies which have decided not to franchise, and make assumptions about managerial decision-making which bears little relation to studies of management activities performed by Mintzberg (1973) and others. These latter studies infer that management does not have a long-term orientation and that managers are essentially reactive and pressed for time. In addition, strategies may be afforded differing status depending on their ability to further desires for organizational power and status. That status is not only dependent upon the acceptance by institutions, such as banks, but also the immediate industry peer group, and the perceptions of the decision-maker. Accordingly, this chapter has argued that the theories require augmentation by consideration of contributions from the structural contingency theorists and cognitive issues.

By employing the eclectic theoretical framework employed by Greenwood and Hinings (1988a), the chapter has suggested that the extant theories of franchising could be seen to be related to the structural contingency approach. Some of the tenets embodied within the life-cycle and size explanations of the decision to franchise are inherent to some of the structural contingency perspectives. The degree to which such contingencies have a deterministic effect on organizational structure may be mitigated by the mental modes of the incumbent management. These modes are affected by the length of tenure, their task environment, and prior experiences. Also pertinent to the decision to franchise are the existing power dependencies within the firm. This model places the decision to franchise within the context of organizational change *per se* and, accordingly, franchising is likely to be considered during periods of transition and be affected by core rigidities to change (Leonard-Barton, 1992). These rigidities or impediments to franchising occur because the innovation will disrupt existing processes, technologies, power structures, and embedded beliefs and values. In such instances, inertia may prevail or some other, less radical, organizational form may be adopted. Given that franchising is rarely, or should not be treated as an 'add-on' activity, Greenwood and Hining's framework also serves to provide some insight as to why some firms may decide not to franchise.

Case Study 5:
Efficiency in the UK bakery industry

Measures of efficiency

The transaction cost approach to organizational governance has received criticism along an array of fronts. Perhaps one of the more important dimensions of this criticism are issues concerning efficiency. Studying the effects of mergers and acquisitions specifically, Cowling *et al* (1980) posit that efficiency refers to the process of converting given inputs into given outputs. As a result of increased size, efficiency improvement is seen to accrue in two ways: economies of large-scale production, and the application of superior management skills to a larger organization. Their measure can also be used to evaluate efficiency levels generally, not just in relation to mergers and acquisitions. Although some (for example, Misterek *et al*, 1991) have argued that one method of analyzing efficiency is labour productivity or output per man, this measure is a particularly blunt tool. Labour is only one of many factors of production inputs, such as raw materials, machinery, fuel, and packaging. Factor substitution, or a change in the extent of vertical integration, would make output per man an unreliable evaluation of total factor productivity. Cowling *et al*'s (1980) method of evaluating efficiency is to think of the firm as part of a value chain, purchasing certain inputs and using them to produce certain outputs, which are then sold on. They define an increase in efficiency as a reduction in the ratio of inputs used to outputs produced, and quantify efficiency by the function: $k = P_0/P_i(1 - \Pi/R)$ where:

k = efficiency; P_O = revenue from unit price of output; P_i = unit price of all production factors; R = total revenue from output produced; Π = total profits from production. Although Cowling *et al* (1980) suggest that a common interpretation of value added may be the function: $P_O[1-(\Pi/R)]$, this is simply average unit cost. When this function is deflated by P_i, the average unit cost after allowing for a change in input prices is derived.

Table 3.2 illustrates the input-output prices for fifteen sub-sectors, including bakeries, of the UK food and drink manufacturing sector. These figures are derived from the Government's *Producer Price Indices*. The figures refer to the estimated prices of materials and fuel purchased by firms within each of the sub-sectors between 1988 and 1994. The table reveals that increases in input prices have been particularly acute within the margarine/cooking fats, dairy, fruit and vegetable processing and bakery sectors. These sectors have been adversely affected by shortages in key material areas, such as wheat, grains, and cherries, as well as suffer input price increases passed on from other supplier industries (such as packaging). Although input prices have begun to fall in some instances, the sharp increases experienced since 1990 served to adversely affect profit margins and efficiency. The impact on profitability and the efficiency of converting inputs into outputs was also affected by pressures on output prices and constraints on pushing increases in input prices through the supply chain. According to Messinger and Narasimhan (1995), these aspects are indicative of the increased power that the grocers hold *vis-à-vis* the food manufacturers, and derives from increased concentration among food retailers, as well as the the desire for more variety and 'one-stop shopping' by customers. The pressure on output prices was primarily caused by the substantial bargaining power held by UK supermarket multiples and continued intensity of price and value-for-money based competition amongst the grocery retailers and pressure on their profit margins.

Whilst manufacturers' output prices are under pressure, profit margins have been affected by rises in unit labour costs – despite a fall in the number of employees resulting from rationalization and decentralization programmes. Total employee numbers fell from 564,000 in 1989 to 425,000 in 1994. According to the *Labour Market Trends* publication, manual labour costs in the food and drink manufacturing industry increased by approximately 15% a year from £231 per week in 1988 to £320 in 1994; non-manual labour costs rose from £259 per week to £381. Although some effort has been made by manufacturers to reduce labour costs through redundancies, effort to control input prices through reviews of purchasing processes, product range analysis, the formation of a purchasing consortia, increased usage of hedging and dealing with commodity futures was less pervasive. Equally, alternative growth methods such as joint ventures, franchised distribution and other third-party/contractual-based routes were not widespread.

Industry characteristics
The bakery industry essentially comprises three sub-divisions:

1. specialist manufacturers;
2. vertically integrated concerns; and
3. retailers, including master craft bakers.

Over the last fifty years there has been a marked move away from master craft bakers. During the nineteenth century, bakers and bakers' shops were a staple feature of the UK economy: in 1862, for example, there were 50,360 bakers (Burnett, 1963). From an essentially craft-based

Sub-sector	Input prices		Output prices	
	1990–4	1990–3	1990–4	1990–3
Margarines/fats	9.0	5.6	2.5	2.8
Organic fats	5.1	3.9	12.0	7.6
Bacon curing	0.2	0.3	2.6	3.5
Poultry slaughter	1.5	2.2	1.0	3.5
Dairy	4.1	4.9	3.9	4.7
Fruit and vegetables	3.2	1.8	2.2	2.4
Fish processing	2.0	1.2	2.7	3.6
Grain milling	−0.3	4.1	5.0	5.9
Starch	−0.1	3.5	5.3	8.3
Bakery/cakes/pastries	3.9	4.6	5.2	6.2
Biscuits and crispbread	4.5	4.0	4.4	5.1
Chocolate and confectionary	4.2	3.9	3.0	4.5
Miscellaneous	6.0	3.1	4.2	4.9

Source: Adapted from CSO *Producer Price Indices*, HMSO, London.
NB: 1990 = 100.0; figures are average annual growth (%).

Table 3.2: Input and output figures for the food and drink manufacturing sector

approach to market, modifications to the preparation and mixing of bread and new insights into the chemistry of bread-making from Pasteur's discovery of the true nature of fermentation, paved the way to the adoption of mass production methods. Pasteur's findings also served to benefit the brewing industry (Sigsworth, 1965). Initially, the diffusion of these methods was slow because master bakers did not sell enough volume to warrant the expenditure on new equipment but, according to Burnett (1963), the diffusion and impact of the technologies were such that by 1914, most of the present-day characteristics of the baking sector were already discernible: declining emphasis on price competition, the growth of large-scale centralized production, and the increasing reliance on the services of science and technology.

The contemporary baking industry also developed as a result of increased automation during the 1950s and 1960s and the introduction of new forms of packaging. Large bakeries acquired many of the smaller concerns, whilst the growth of supermarkets helped to rationalize the number of retail bakeries. In the post-1945 era, the increasing efficiency of plant bakers' distributive networks caused many craft bakers to close. Plant bakeries increasingly became wholesale operations and by the mid-1970s, the top three producers accounted for 60% of the UK's £3.6 billion bread and fresh pastry goods market. At the retail end of the market, Government figures indicate that outlet and bakery business numbers have declined. Additionally, retail bakery sales have shown limited growth from £1.2 billion in 1988 to about £1.5 billion in 1992 (see Figure 3.2). Of all retail outlets, approximately a quarter are chain affiliated through vertical integration with plant manufacturers. The reliance on retailers by the bakery sector is such that 56% of their total output is directed to supermarkets, caterers and convenience stores to satisfy final demand. Against a general background of restructuring and rationalization within the market, there has been a decline in the consumption of bread, low retail prices, rising costs of raw materials, low levels of bargaining power with supermarket multiples, the rise of own-label bread (estimated to represent over 50% of bread volumes and values), the rise of in-store bakeries in supermarkets from about 600 in 1984 to 1,330 in 1995, over-capacity (estimated to be over 15%), and low levels of investment in advertising and marketing. Since the mid-1980s this situation has been exacerbated by increasing demand for convenience foods and value-added products, such as sandwiches, as well as the tendency by supermarket multiples to use bread as a weapon in their promotional and pricing battles. Additionally, labour costs have continued to rise, while sales growth has stagnated (see Table 3.3 below) In short, the market is in decline requiring incumbent firms to focus on both process and product innovations to increase revenues and reduce overcapacity.

Perhaps reflecting the declining market, the average sales per employee in baker's shops is low at about £18,000; within the restaurant and fast food market, the top 525 players record average sales per employee of £33,500 (with a standard deviation of £24,950). Applying Cowling *et al*'s (1980) efficiency calculation to the bakery manufacturing industry and comparing it to the average for thirteen other food manufacturing sectors, it is possible to see that the efficiency with which inputs are converted into outputs is in decline, despite obvious pressures to remedy the situation. The table below (Table 3.4) shows that input prices have, on average, risen by an average annual rate of 3.2% while factory gate prices have increased by 5.2%. According to Government figures, the retail price of bread has increased by a compound rate of 4.4%, which suggests that some increases in factory gate prices are being passed on to end-consumers but not necessarily all of them. The main reason for this situation is the oligopolistic structure of the UK grocery sector and the substantial bargaining powers they possess. Stigler (1964) argues that the fewer the number of firms within an industry, the easi-

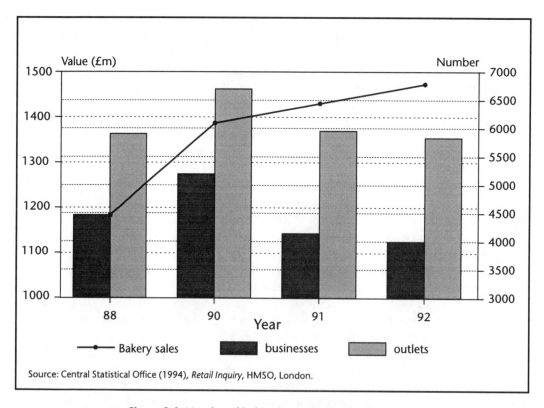

Source: Central Statistical Office (1994), *Retail Inquiry*, HMSO, London.

Figure 3.2: *Number of bakery businesses and retail outlets*

Employee type	1986	1987	1988	1989	1990	1991	1992	1993
Operatives	6.0	6.2	6.5	6.8	7.4	8.0	8.5	8.3
Admin, technical and clerical	8.4	8.7	10.0	10.9	12.0	13.9	14.7	13.9
Average	6.0	6.3	6.6	7.1	7.7	8.5	9.0	9.0

Source: Central Statistical Office (various years), *Census of Production*, HMSO, London.

Table 3.3: Wages and salaries per head (£000s) in the bread and fresh pastry goods sector

er it is for changes in the marketing mix to be detected. Dixon (1983) shows that prices lag behind costs and there may be a tendency for 'fewness', as far as price increases are concerned, to be associated with 'slowness of adjustment'. Supporting this contention, Scherer (1980) observes that there is a tendency for concentrated industries to pass on, in the time-frame they occurred, a smaller fraction of cost increases than atomistically structured industries. As a result of the growth in the sandwich manufacturing sector (see Case Study 6) and its fragmentation, as well as that experienced in some parts of the catering industry, it is probable that increased material and packaging costs have been passed on to these players in the form of higher prices. These operators, in turn, pass on their higher input costs to the consumer. Reflecting this situation, retail price inflation in the UK catering industry has been rising at a rate which is more than double that of food prices in supermarkets. The major multiple grocers, however, have substantial bargaining power and it is they who dictate price to the manufacturer. The table also shows that, in spite of rising factory gate prices, the efficiency with which input factors were converted into outputs by the bakery industry has continued to fall at a faster rate than the all-food manufacturing sector average.

One expectation from these calculations was that the larger industry incumbents should outperform their sector averages. This expectation arose from the fact that the larger firms, with their usual emphasis on branded, heavily advertised products, had relatively better bargaining positions with their customers relative to their smaller competitors. Such businesses may also be expected to illustrate lower input costs due to volume discounts and the advantages accruing from large size. Furthermore, cost saving policies employed during

Variable/year	1988	1989	1990	1991	1992	1993	1994
Bakery:							
Input costs	96.2	97.9	100.0	105.6	109.4	114.3	116.4
Output prices	90.5	94.4	100.0	107.8	112.8	119.7	122.7
Retail prices	89.2	94.1	100.0	109.7	112.4	116.7	115.5
Efficiency (*k%*)	68.4	71.4	78.0	84.4	90.3	94.8	97.1
Sector efficiency (*k%*)	72.0	75.8	80.0	86.8	89.9	94.5	96.6

Source: Central Statistical Office (various years), *Census of Production*, HMSO, London.

Table 3.4: Efficiency in the bakery market

the period may have had a magnified effect on the larger concerns. When the calculations were applied to the largest and smaller bakery manufacturing concerns, the results did not necessarily support these expectations; some smaller firms also illustrate efficiency levels higher than the industry benchmark, which suggests that size, in itself, may not be a suitable guide to generalizing about efficiency differences.

Unless the existing structural features of the baking industry remain unchecked, the forecast for the bread market and plant bakeries is less than buoyant: it is estimated that there will be minimal sales growth and that further rationalization through plant closures will ensue. There are, however, options available to incumbent firms to help rejuvenate their fortunes and efficiency. The extent to which they are implemented is dependent on whether management teams are able to surmount structural and power impediments to change. Some of these options are:

- Focusing more on supplying fragmented industries, such as the catering market and sandwich manufacturing sectors.
- Diversification into the manufacture of sandwiches and pizza bases.
- Restructuring/re-engineering their organizations and their manufacturing base in particular.
- Developing branded, well-merchandized sandwiches to jump over the shoulder of retailers. For plant bakers employing above-the-line advertising, this should be less risk-laden than for others. Rather than developing new capacity devoted to the production of such products, a more incremental market entry strategy could be pursued which:

  1. uses existing spare capacity;
  2. exploits periods of supplier overcapacity;
  3. charges higher prices thereby giving retailers the opportunity to realize higher margins; and
  4. exploits existing technology and know-how to enhance product quality.

- Demerge the production capability from the retail divisions to become less integrated. Such a move would permit the bakery firm to reduce the capital intensity of their businesses and, for, example, out-source their deliveries/logistics services. It would also permit the better use of transfer pricing.
- Divest the retail units or improve/standardize their livery and technology mix (for example, EPOS, deskilling). Part of this 'build' process may require the development of a specialist retail division as well as, perhaps, the need for the company to become a corporate franchisee as a learning vehicle. The retail units could then be franchised in their own right either to suitable existing management or potential franchisees generally.
- License the brand name of a particular loaf of bread to sandwich manufacturers; and
- Adopt a 'piggy-back' approach to distribution; although usually seen as a vehicle to internationalization, the strategy also has domestic applications. Piggy-backing entails (Terpstra and Yu, 1988) a non-equity agreement between two firms of differing sizes or resources to collaborate in market entry and penetration activity. The larger firm has usually achieved market entry and has

experienced personnel and procedures needed for the operation; the smaller firm, the 'rider', has a product range which is complementary to those of the carrier without competing with them or duplicating them. Within the bakery sector, operators could join forces with a pizza home delivery company, which would allow them a two-pronged approach to market:

1. establish the home delivery concept as a stand-alone only operation; or
2. put them in-store and develop a home delivery service for all their bakery products, as well as gain access to an evening trade.

4 | Strategic groups, multi-market contact, and the decision to franchise

Without competitors there would be no need for strategy.

Kenichi Ohmae, Business author, *Mind of the Strategist*

Imitation is not only more abundant than innovation, it is actually a much more prevalent road to business growth and profits . . . innovation is not the only choice of market entry, and in many instances may not even be the best choice.

Steven P. Schnaars, US academic, *Managing Imitation Strategies*

Introduction

As noted earlier, a franchise business is an organizational form which is based on a strategy to realize brand dissemination, that permits the franchisee to operate one or more business units under the franchisor's brand name, and according to the latter's contractually specified standards and procedures. While franchises have, in tandem with other hybrid organizational types, become increasingly populous, there appears to be substantial uncertainty among researchers and practioners alike concerning the motivation to franchise (Dant, 1996; Martin, 1996; Micheal, 1996). This issue, however, is of fundamental importance to explaining the differing levels of legitimation and diffusion trajectories of franchising throughout economic sectors and sub-sectors.

Extant explanations of the motivations to franchise are problematic because, as shown in Chapter 3, they are in themselves incomplete rationales. Indeed, the book has suggested that firms elect to franchise rather than being necessarily coerced by environmental forces, and that there are several decisional routes which firms go through in order to become a franchisor. In some instances, the decision to franchise will be intentional and deliberate, in others it will be non-intentional. In addition to the choice being influenced by the bounded rationality of the entrepreneur and the degree of usurpationary power within the organization, the diffusion rate is also partially impeded/determined by certain contingencies within a particular economic setting. Perhaps it is the incompleteness of previous explanations which has mitigated against the development of a general model with strong explanatory power (Combs and Castrogiovanni, 1994).

In addition to aspects of focus, the problems with prior efforts may be due to methodological issues, as there seems to have been a tendency for researchers to place emphasis on industry-level[1] and firm-level analysis. In one recent example, Lafontaine and Shaw (1996) explored the degree to which the variation in the terms of franchise contracts, namely royalty rates and franchise fees, was attributable to firm-level variables or sectoral ('industry') attributes. They found that sectoral differences accounted for very little of the variation, and that firm-level variables had significant effects especially on franchise fees but, on the whole, their model left much variance unexplained. There must, therefore, be other factors at play. Relatedly, numerous market research studies of the franchise fraternity usually refer to this collective as an 'industry'. Yet, how can the collective of franchises constitute an industry when many of the businesses with which franchisors directly compete are not franchised, but sell many of the same products and services as the franchised concerns? While it is true that franchise companies may be different from their non-franchised counterparts because they sell licences to investors, franchises *per se* do not necessarily compete with one another. Franchising brings those firms selling similar end products into closer competition, however, because it serves to increase the probability of two, or more, companies being in similar geographic locations and rivalry for resources such as those possessed by franchisees. Indicative of low levels of rivalry among franchises in different economic sectors, Kaufmann and Stanworth (1995) show that potential franchisees have been shown to consider sector issues ahead of legal form.

Other franchise researchers have focused more on the dyadic relations (Achrol, 1996), to investigate the power, influence, dynamics and the impact on satisfaction and performance.[2] For example, recently reported research by Spinelli (1996) suggests that franchisee satisfaction appears to be more closely linked to the manner in which the relationship is conducted rather than to issues involving finance. His research also found that most franchisees would like to see an improvement in the provision of some services provided by the franchisor, such as resolving disagreements fairly, national advertising, promoting new products and services, market information and analysis, and advice on financial management. In this vein of research, therefore, emphasis has been put on relational exchanges such as trust, commitment and the social norms of governance, which are indirectly concerned with the effects of competition and the generation of competitive advantages (but not overtly so).

Unfortunately it appears that both the firm-level and industry-level streams, almost without exception, have tended not to consider the impact of non-franchised concerns. Relatedly, and equally significantly, franchise researchers have tended not to consider group-level approaches by employing, for example, the increasingly rich vein of work by those propounding the strategic group framework. Yet, the most relevant 'peer population' of the franchisor is not other franchisors, but all contemporary product competitors and businesses selling potential substitutes (Miller and Ginter, 1979; Huszagh *et al*, 1992). Thus, the diffusion of franchising is not just a function of agency theory, resource constraints and risk aversion, etc., but also the dynamics of competition and learning among a firm's peer group or potential contemporaries. These dynamics help to provide legitimacy to certain organizational forms and suggest that while it is management who may choose to franchise their business, they do so with reference to a peer group. Within such groups, the influencers may not be the initial adopters of franchising, but the latter ones. This contention is partially borne out by the coefficient of imitation data shown in Chapter 1, whereby the statistic for UK franchising pointed to the situation whereby influence fell as penetration increased.

Using groups as the focal point for research may be instructive to elucidating some of the additional reasons for franchising. But, when the franchises alone are explored from a closer perspective, it is evident that there is substantial variation in the manifestation of that strategy (which also partly contributes to the definitional confusion inherent in franchising). For example, franchisors differ in the assistance they offer their franchisees, the amount of product they require their franchisees to purchase from them, the 'hardness' of 'softness' of the franchise agreement, and there are differences according to the level of their initial payments and royalty rates (Felstead, 1993; Lafontaine and Shaw, 1996). This chapter argues therefore that, in addition to some of these variations in the franchise form due to technological and human capital differences (Michael, 1996), the extent of similarity among franchises is limited not only according to particular sectors, but also to particular groups within each sector. For example, Case Studies 1 and 2 showed that, in Britain, during their histories KFC and Wimpy have both experienced the loss of a number of franchisees from their system who have subsequently gone on to establish their own fast food chains. It is, perhaps, no coincidence that these ex-franchisees have not only established businesses in the same format and in the same product market, but also offer franchises which are contractually similar to those of their ex-franchisors. Although such action may be reflective of the technologies and *modus operandi* of the particular concept (Lafontaine and Shaw, 1996; Martin, 1996), it cannot be the whole explanation because it ignores group effects/peer group pressure. At a wider level of focus, therefore, it may be that franchise fees differ not only according to the level of brand capital, technological mix, etc., but because the reference points may differ.

By taking these points into consideration, this chapter seeks to explore five interrelated avenues. Initially, it is to outline how the concept of strategic groups may be applicable to analyses of franchising. Secondly, it seeks to show that not only can the franchise fraternity itself be seen as a strategic group in its own right, but that there are 'sub-groups' in which franchises cohabit clusters with non-franchised concerns. Thirdly, it evaluates levels of potential competition among and between franchised and nonfranchised concerns illustrating similar strategic characteristics. Fourthly, it is to suggest that the degree of rivalry either between or among group member firms influences their decision to franchise; and, finally, to test the assumption that competing franchise firms will also exhibit, via summarizing the terms of their franchise package (initial fees, royalties and assistance) through assigning a binary variable to indicate whether the components fall within a 95% band of error, similar opportunities to investors.

From industry and dyad to strategic groups

In arguing that group level analysis is perhaps more pertinent to analyzing franchises, a move away from the traditional treatment of the collective of the franchise channel of distribution as an industry is made. How appropriate is this move? According to Wilson and Andrews (1951), an 'industry' comprises all businesses which operate processes of a sufficiently similar kind (which implies the possession of substantially similar technical resources) and possess sufficiently similar backgrounds of experience and knowledge. The similarity of backgrounds serves to determine whether each of the incumbents could produce the particular commodity under consideration, and would do so if it were sufficiently attractive to do so. When applied to franchising, a debate arises concerning the extent to which a franchisor is selling a product (the franchise package) or whether the franchise is a strategy to facilitate the distribution of other end-products and/or services. To those propounding that the collective of franchised firms could be construed to be an industry, further circumstantial evidence is provided by the wealth of material indicating that the franchisor is required to have, at least, a number of generic attributes prior to engaging in the activity such as:

1. evidence that the company-owned operation is demonstrably successful;
2. possession and ownership of a distinctive trading image;
3. a managerial culture, structure, and reporting system capable of supporting franchisees;
4. the possession of a system and method capable of being passed on successfully to others within an economically sensible time frame; and
5. the generation of financial returns sufficient to allow the franchisee and franchisor to realize reasonable, if not good, rewards for their efforts (Mendelsohn and Acheson, 1989).

The move to analyzing the collective of franchises in alternative terms than 'industry' is not, however, without precedent. Gerstenhaber (1995), for example, contends that franchising is not an industry or a business but is, in essence, a practical marketing concept employed for the effective distribution of products and/or services. As such, franchising is potentially applicable to many industries rather than being an industry in itself:

> Typically, everyone calls franchising an industry but actually, it is not. It is found in 65 different industries, from fast food to automobiles, after market services to home cleaning and educational and leisure time services. You name it, and probably there is a franchise system that is established in it – or there soon will be. Do not make the mistake that McDonald's and Burger King and Dunkin' Donuts are all there is to franchising. Be sure to add in travel, printing, accounting, home improvement services, etc. (Cherkasky, 1996; p. 6)

Possibly strengthening this position, Huszagh *et al* (1992) posit that when research questions are framed within the context the most 'relevant peer group', theories of competitive strategy and literature can be highly informative in identifying independent variables of enduring significance. From another perspective, it may be argued that if franchising were an industry it would have its own SIC code to reflect its status. It does not. While there may exist a plethora of reasons for the lack of a SIC, including weaknesses in the coding system itself (Clarke, 1989), there is the problem of firms who distribute similar end-products to consumers but who are not franchised. Above all else, franchisors are dependent on the buoyancy of final demand to both attract franchisees and to realize, for example, market share objectives. The differentiation of end-products from the franchise package serves to suggest that a form of diversification has occurred, the extent to which franchisors *per se* possess similar backgrounds and knowledge. Firms may, indeed, illustrate similar experiences in becoming a franchisor, but these are neither necessary nor sufficient criteria for them to be collectively conceptualized as an industry. To do so would be rather like grouping firms illustrating a low cost strategic focus (Porter, 1980) together, without some regard for their position in the value chain and their activities as defined by (for example) SIC codes. At best, describing the franchise fraternity as an industry is little more than an analytic convenience. Strictly, however, the collective noun describing the agglomeration of franchises as an industry is inappropriate.

If the collective noun describing those firms engaging in franchised activity is not an industry, but a group, then what kind of group is it? A potentially instructive approach is the conceptualization of a collective of franchises as a form of 'strategic group', especially as the term emphasizes franchising as a strategy. The term was introduced by Hunt in 1972 to describe the 'symmetry of operations' in an analysis of the home appliance industry. The crux of the theory is that there are different groups of firms within an industry, and that firms are homogeneous within groups, along a set of strategic attributes, and heterogeneous between groups. In this respect, the term 'strategic group' essentially defines 'subindustries' within an industry based on the observed similarity of behaviour along key strategic dimensions. The idea is to group a pre-specified set of firms on the basis of competition so that firms within a group compete more heavily with each other than with firms belonging to different groups (Mitchell, 1991; Cool and Schendel, 1987; McGee and Thomas, 1986; Oster, 1982; Caves and Porter, 1977). Thus, at a broad level of analysis, franchises could comprise one strategic group in a given industry and non-franchised concerns another. In this way, competition within strategic groups is perceived to be similar to that observed within oligopolistic markets, that is, competition amongst the few (Fellner, 1965). Using an analogy from the automobile sector, this idea can be seen more lucidly. Mercedes-Benz and BMW compete together in the luxury car market; in so doing they do not really compete with Honda, Toyota, or Volkswagen, and only to a limited extent with Ford and General Motors. Within the market research field, consumers exhibiting similar cultural, socio-economic, lifestyle and age characteristics have long been evidenced and agglomerated into clusters to establish generalizations and predictions about purchasing behaviour (Miller and Ginter, 1979). In relation to industry, it cannot be so far removed and inconceivable that clusters of firms exhibiting similar strategic characteristics exist.

The concept of strategic groups also has benefits to analysts, corporate planners, and researchers. As firms, within a particular industry, illustrate varying levels of strategic homogeneity (Balakrishnan and Fox, 1993; Nelson, 1991), industry-level analysis may be too broad to explain and/or describe competitive rivalry. At the other extreme, a variety of researchers (see Chapter 7 for a review) have explored the behavioural and relational conditions of the franchise dyad. The recurrent themes of such work are inter-organizational power, conflict, trust, and satisfaction. In being focused on the post-contractual relationship, such work is of significance in providing insight to the facilitating and impeding factors affecting the diffusion of innovations within a dyad but may be of less consequence to explaining the diffusion of franchising within an industry (with the possible exception that the relational aspects may provide a benchmark which others may want to emulate). Additionally, dyad-specific analysis concerning the diffusion of franchising within an industry precludes the use of sophisticated statistical techniques and may be beset with problems of detail, theoretical abstraction and significance. The agglomeration of firms competing on similar strategic dimensions to an intermediate level of aggregation, therefore, permits analysis of how they become more similar or different from each other. In this way, strategic groups provide a practical mechanism for assigning industry participants to groups on the basis of similar strategic dimensions (Saloner, 1991), such as whether they franchise or not. Using this latter approach, Chapter 8 examines the level of attrition within each of the franchise sectors within twenty-five defined industries in Britain and, as such, illustrates levels of strategic group volatility in differing industries. The purpose of this approach is not only to show the level of volatility within the franchise fraternity *per se*, but also to show that the examination of the history of strategic group dynamics produces an insightful view of competitive activity and possible causes of failure (Bognor *et al*, 1996). For example, one rationale for failure may be that the number of incumbents within the strategic group meant that it was inherently unstable which lead to increased competition for franchisees, recruitment costs increased, and some firms were unwilling and/or unable to make such payments (that is, they were unable to surmount effectively the entry barriers to becoming a successful franchisor).

Strategic management texts have long debated the presence of groups of firms illustrating the same strategic configurations (Miles *et al*, 1993), but without examining a firm's strategic posture relative to others one has very little idea against whom it directly competes. In representing the collection of firms a company defines as its primary competitors, this chapter posits that one of the reasons influencing sectoral differences in the diffusion of franchising and contractual terms is organizational reaction within strategic clusters. The underlying contention to this rationale is that members of a strategic group use each other as reference points in the process of strategic choice. Recently, Fiegenbaum and Thomas (1995) showed, by using the context of the insurance industry, that a firm's strategic group membership influences its strategic behaviour; they suggest that a particular firm benchmarks those firms within the same strategic group, as well as targeting positions in competitive space occupied by other strategic groups when making strategy decisions. Similar benchmarking behaviour has also been observed within the automobile sector (Burgers *et al*, 1993; Nohria and Garcia-Pont, 1991; Yoshino and Rangan, 1995), where the nature of rivalry within a strategic group has served to determine whether alliances are formed.

Within this benchmarking activity, the diffusion of franchising within certain sub-sectors is seen as proactiveness by certain strategic group members and oligopolistic reaction by other cluster participants and new entrants. The precedent setting activity by the first movers may have been derived from a comparison between their position at a certain point in time and the actions of others in different industries and markets. Once incorporated within the sector, some companies follow in order to reduce the competitive gap and, thereby, serve to legitimize the use of franchising among certain groups of firms. Yet other companies do not follow. By modelling such behaviour, this chapter presents a different perspective from much of the extant literature concerning strategic groups because it is emphatic of rivalry within and between different strategic groups. Reflecting other benchmarking work and innovation diffusion, there is an underlying rationale that the adoption of franchising, rather than deciding whether a certain site should be franchised, could be partially determined by peer group pressure. Rogers (1995), for example, suggests that a fundamental principle of human communication is that the exchange of ideas occurs most frequently between individuals who are alike, or homophilous, and this can both facilitate and impede the diffusion of innovations. Thus, depending on the values and norms of the incumbent organizations, franchising may or may not occur among groups of homophilous firms (Darr, 1994). Unfortunately, despite its potential importance to examining the diffusion of the organizational form, strategic group rivalry has received scant attention by researchers. Instead, much effort has been orientated towards the identification of strategic groups in order to test a direct, symmetric, and contingent 'strategic group firm → profitability' link (Johnson and Thomas, 1987). Much of the research testing this link has yet to provide any conclusive evidence that such a direct relationship exists (Fiegenbaum and Thomas, 1990; Lawless *et al*, 1989) and has, hence, led to an ever-increasing complexity of statistical methodologies to prove the hypothesis (Lewis and Thomas, 1990). The result has been empirical research which is too data driven, relying on complex statistical methods applied, almost unthinkingly, to available company financial information (Carroll and Wade, 1991). This study does not examine performance issues.

Approaches to strategic group definition

Divergent approaches to the definition of strategic groups indicate a lack of universal acceptance of interpretation and existence (Thomas and Venkatraman, 1987; Kerin *et al*, 1990). At an extreme, Hatten and Hatten (1987) argue that strategic groups do not exist and a strategic group is not an anthropomorphized unified competitive force of many firms. Like the use of 'industry' to describe the collective of firms in franchising, Hatten and Hatten insist that a strategic group is merely an analytical convenience. Such a proposition has led some researchers to employ spatial competition and cognitive taxonomy approaches to provide theoretical explanations of the existence of strategic groups (Reger and Huff, 1993). The identification of strategic groups for this chapter has been based on conversations with industry incumbents and is, therefore, more in the vein of the cognitive taxonomy approach, but the rivalry between and within cluster members is calculated through a spatial competition methodology (described below).

Although simple in theory and a useful way of mapping industry dynamics, the operationalization of the concept of strategic groups has been complex and, often, confusing. Such a situation arises partially as a result of lack of definitional consensus and the general focus by researchers for strategic group identification. Recent debate has been centred on two approaches for establishing the determining characteristics of strategic groups: 'strategies' and 'mobility barrier'.

The 'strategies' approach

The 'strategies' approach to strategic group definition is founded on observing the similarities in firms' behaviours. In contrast to population ecology models and traditional industrial economic models (Hannan and Freeman, 1977; Porter, 1979), strategic management theorists propound that heterogeneity amongst firms varies according to the choices and decisions of management rather than environmental and market share variables alone. Within this perspective, industry participants choose the dimensions of competition and whether to mimic or differentiate themselves from competitors' initiatives. The focus of the 'strategies' approach has been employed to reflect business unit/functional-level strategies (or 'How do we compete in this business?' considerations) as well as corporate strategy decisions (or 'What business should we be in?'). It could specify, therefore, marketing mix considerations and organizational strategies, such as whether or not a firm is franchised.

Beard and Dess (1981), Bourgeois (1980) and Hambrick (1980) have observed that the relevant characteristics of the firm's business-level strategy should be measured relative to the industry range and norms and hence permits the identification of clusters of firms within a particular industry, rather than between industries. Rumelt (1991) and Powell (1996), however, establish that business units differ from one another within industries a great deal more than industries differ from one another, which presents problems for defining the dimensions of firms' business-level strategies for clustering purposes. At a minimum, business-level strategies have been differentiated along two dimensions: business scope commitments, and business resource commitments (Porter, 1980). From these dimensions, Cool and Schendel (1987) define a strategic group as 'a set of firms competing within an industry on the basis of similar combinations of scope and resource commitments' (p. 1103). Companies which pursue franchise-based expansion can be seen to conform to Cool and Schendel's (1987) definition in two respects: their initial motivation to franchise, such as their reliance on franchisee's for capital, low cost growth, and risk-reduction; their use of franchisees to expand the geographic scope of the brand.

Although time-consuming and potentially expensive to enter, one rationale for employing a franchise strategy, rather than engaging in company-owned growth or some other formula, is the expectation that it will yield better financial returns. These returns are viewed to accrue from a variety of different sources and, within the franchising literature, are encompassed in two main research streams: resource constraints and agency theory.

The resource-constraint advocates suggest that small firms become franchisors in order to gain access to three resources that they require in order to realize organizational development: financial capital (via the franchisees' payment of initial fees, lowering wage costs, their payment of their store's fixtures and fittings, payment of rent, and ongoing royalties), human capital (that is, self-motivated managerial talent), and local market knowledge. Some have criticized this school of thought on the basis that franchising is an inefficient method of raising capital (Rubin, 1978) but, when franchisees are considered as representing all three resource requirements as one, the cost of procuring them is possibly lower than when purchased individually (Norton, 1988a). In short, then, franchised growth may be pursued as it reduces the input costs of realizing organizational development and brand dissemination (additionally lowered due to franchisees' contributions of the advertising fund).

According to the agency-perspective proponents, franchising also reduces the continuing costs of development. The costs associated with company-owned units are influenced by:

1. the availability of managerial talent;
2. the importance of local knowledge;
3. geographic distance from headquarters;
4. population density; and
5. the relative proximity of locations to one another (Martin, 1988; Norton, 1988b).

All of these factors affect the cost of travel, co-ordination, communications, and decision-making between headquarters and local managers. As franchisees often risk some proportion of their personal wealth by investing in a particular unit and are motivated by profit, there is a lower propensity to shirk and this reduces (rather than eliminates) the very need for supervision and monitoring. Once released from some of the burdens of monitoring, the franchisor – depending on the demand for the franchise, the level of market growth and nature of competition – can concentrate on expanding the business. In so doing, additional income accrues to the franchisor from the new stock of franchisees and the sale of product (in some cases) to franchisees. By permitting greater brand dissemination and market share through additional capacity and through lower advertising costs, so the franchisor is able to increase profitability and brand value.

Buzzell and Gale (1987) indicate that a positive relationship between profitability (as defined by return on investment) and market share exists. So, the greater and broader the brand dissemination, the greater the rewards. Given that it is the franchisor who owns the trademarks and patents associated with the business, it is he who derives the greatest benefit (Felstead, 1993). Such potential rewards may be a motivating factor for firms to franchise. In becoming a franchisor within a certain sector, however, they are not only increasing the stock of franchises in that market, but also increasing the number of incumbents within that particular strategic group. Of course, one implication of both the agency theory and resource constraints argument is that as the number of firms seeking to improve performance and growth through franchising increases, so the volatility of the strategic group increases. Strategic groups, like industries, can only withstand certain levels of capacity before overcrowding occurs and legitimation falls (Cool and Dierickx, 1993).

The strategies approach may also be applied to examine the degree of similarity among franchisors. The table below provides some circumstantial evidence to support the possible presence of groups among franchisors. Through examining some of the differing franchise categories within the US fast food industry, as set out in the annual *Entrepreneur* magazine survey, it shows that some sectors illustrate more contractual variations (high deviations) than others. It also shows that royalty fees have low levels of variation, unlike the franchise fee where firm-specific variables (such as brand value) may have an influence (Sen, 1993). This situation suggests that firms illustrate pockets of strategic similarity, and that these groups can comprise a relatively small number of businesses as well as rep-

| Sector and number of firms | Franchise fee US$000s | | | | Royalty | |
	Deviation	Mean	Coefficient of variability	Deviation	Mean	Coefficient of variability
Bagels (n = 8)	4.80	21.10	0.23	0.50	4.50	0.11
Bakeries (n = 6)	0.50	21.10	0.02	2.40	5.40	0.44
Fried chicken (n = 8)	7.60	21.50	0.35	0.60	4.10	0.15
Rotisserie chicken (n = 4)	2.20	23.80	0.09	0.40	4.80	0.08
Candy stores (n = 12)	6.30	19.80	0.32	1.80	4.90	0.37
Coffee and tea (n = 12)	4.20	21.30	0.20	0.80	5.80	0.14
Donuts (n = 7)	17.30	18.90	0.92	1.70	4.10	0.41
Hamburgers (n = 13)	11.00	28.70	0.38	2.20	4.90	0.45
Mexican (n = 14)	6.10	19.10	0.32	0.80	4.50	0.18
Pizza (n = 20)	6.20	15.80	0.39	1.10	4.10	0.27
Submarine Sandwiches (n = 20)	5.80	14.20	0.41	1.00	5.20	0.19
Total (N = 124)	8.60	19.80	0.43	1.40	4.80	0.29

Source: *Entrepreneur*, 17th Annual Franchise Survey, January 1996.

Table 4.1: Differences between and within franchises of different sectors of the US fast food industry

resent a larger number of firms. The dynamics of these strategically similar groups may not only account for variations in the penetration of franchising within a particular industry and its component sub-sectors, but also the contractual similarities among certain sets of franchised businesses.

Although widely used, the strategies approach and Cool and Schendel's (1987) definition of strategic groups, in particular, have been found wanting. One of the main weaknesses of the approach has been a tendency to focus on performance differences rather than on the degree and nature of rivalry among units that compete within differing industries. Another has been the tendency to focus on corporate strategy rather than business unit variables, such as marketing mix configurations. Equally, the combined dimensions of scope and resource commitments serve to construe a perception of size; in this sense there is a danger that large firms could be seen to form a different strategic group than small firms. The use of such performance measures as group defining variables is, according to Nayyar (1989) a tautology. Large firms may be large not because they have a different scale of resource commitments and scope of activity to their smaller counterparts, but because they have harnessed their resources and strategies more effectively. As such, small and large firms may reside in the same strategic group, but the extent to which a small firm is able to enter a specific cluster is dependent on the height of the entry barriers and its access to resources.

The 'mobility barrier' approach

From a parallel perspective and concept to the strategic similarity/social closure approaches, McGee (1985) and Mascarenhas and Aaker (1989) argue that strategic groups should be driven by mobility barriers, exit and entry barriers between different strategic clusters since they represent the theoretical core of the concept. Differentiating between mobility barriers, or isolating mechanisms (Rumelt, 1984), such as those which serve to isolate groups of similar firms in a heterogeneous industry and entry barriers such as those which isolate industry participants from potential entrants, they define a strategic group as a grouping of businesses within an industry that is separated from other groupings of businesses by mobility barriers to entry and exit (Peteraf, 1993a). As franchisors – prior to electing to franchise – typically illustrate a history of operating within a particular product/market niche via employing chosen marketing mix configurations, they have already surmounted entry barriers. In becoming a franchisor, they are required to overcome mobility barriers in order to gain access to the resources possessed by franchisees.

According to the mobility barrier approach, each group has its own product substitutes, potential entrants, suppliers and customers as well as rivalry (which may be greater between group members than with firms belonging to other groups). For example, high market share/differentiated supermarkets (such as the major multiples in the UK) wishing to open high street differentiated specialized fast food outlets would be moving into the same competitive arena as McDonald's, Burger King, KFC, etc. In such situations, they would confront mobility barriers which would affect the decision to move. These potential new entrant companies must overcome geographic coverage, brand capital, intangible assets, marketing economies, managerial skill, control systems and experience curve barriers. In order to help overcome such mobility barriers, strategic alliances may be sought. Equally, companies seeking franchised expansion also have to surmount a variety of mobility barriers.

Any small business intending to embark on franchise-based expansion needs to do so from a sound financial and business base. In order to achieve both an ethically run and financially sound business prior to embarking on franchised expansion, the firm must possess the managerial resources and competences as well as possess an appropriate organizational culture. Not all firms possess either and, as such, they represent a mobility barrier. Franchising is not the route to salvation for an ailing company, despite some who propound otherwise, since – if ethically and soundly run – it will not produce an immediate positive cashflow and profits (Mendelsohn and Acheson, 1989). Anyone intending to develop a franchise business needs to spend some time and effort establishing and proving a business idea in terms of its seasonality of sales, the effect of substitute and complementary products, the level of bargaining power over suppliers and nature of customer demand. There is, equally, a necessity to establish and experience the local competitive conditions and compare these to those detailed in an initial business plan. During this stage, the emphasis is very much on adaptation and income growth without organizational development (Greiner, 1972) or, in Porter's (1985) terms, developing the components of the firm's value chain. This distinction between growth and development is an important one. Growth may not entail development since a company could, for example, generate sales growth by broadening its product range – a process which does not require increasing its complexity via the adoption of a new organizational structure nor substantial modification to the manner in which the business is administered (Mount *et al*, 1993). Not all firms survive this formative stage – indeed, about half of all business failures occur within the first two years and a third within the next two to three years (Stewart and Gallagher, 1986).

When seeking growth through organizational development, such as building additional capacity and market presence through franchising, the degree of rigour employed during the transition stage will have implications for the realization of the strategy. Without the development of an organizational infrastructure, culture, and capability designed to manage the growth process, under-performance and failure may ensue. As shown in Chapter 3, this observation is well established by those examining the relationship between strategy, structure and performance, but requires managers to surmount any resistance to change within the organization. Having developed the basic business formula, the owner should then, after a suitable time lapse, seek organizational development through opening an identical outlet in another location. The process of conducting market research to find and establish the potential viability of new premises, contracting builders, architects and other suppliers, generating job descriptions, hiring, training and managing personnel, developing and expanding the management information systems to co-ordinate, control and direct the additional capacity amongst other pre-opening activities entails progressing up a steep learning curve. Nevertheless, it is an essential test of the owner's capability of realizing organizational development.

As part of the necessary infrastructure to manage, co-ordinate and support franchisees, three key documents are needed prior to launching the franchise (Justis *et al*, 1994). Firstly, an operating manual which serves to document the processes and procedures required to manage a unit according to the standards and manner required by the franchisor. Secondly, a franchise contract which stipulates the boundaries of the relationship and the obligations incumbent on both parties is required. Finally, a franchise prospectus is necessary to help advertise and explain the franchise offering, the costs of entry and potential earnings from the business. Depending on the materials and approach taken, the costs of producing these may be expensive since they entail external assistance from consultants, solicitors, accountants, designers and printers.

One vital component of the organizational development stage is the operation of one or more 'pilot' units. These are outlets which are set up by the franchisor in order to test ideas and to develop the offering to the franchisee. Pilot units are undertaken to develop all aspects of the business and to test whether to continue making time and money investments (Boe *et al*, 1987). Since pilots substantially add to the time costs of developing a franchise business, it is not surprising that only a minority of franchisors engage in the process. While research by Silvester (1996) suggests that the majority of franchisors in Britain use pilot operations, when the difference between year of establishment and the year they launched their franchise is compared, not all firms could have operated such units. Instead, there is a reliance on using the existing business as a pilot, but such company-operated units are rarely run under the same conditions as will apply to the proposed franchise system. The result, invariably, is the development of a franchise business based on trial and error, and at the expense and risk of initial franchisees.

In addition to the development of an infrastructure suited to support franchised growth, the franchisor must also develop and nurture a suitable organizational culture and capabilities orientated toward franchisee management. Because it encompasses all aspects of business management, the change from company-owned growth to franchise-based expansion entails a process of radical organizational change, rather than being incremental. Citing the example of Holland & Barrett (a UK-based health food chain which began franchising in the early 1980s), Gourlay (1994) indicates that the reason for stopping franchising in 1987 was that the company had trouble handling independent franchisees within a culture established to manage corporately-owned shops. Culture apart, numerous tried-and-tested businesses have been unsuccessful when following the franchise route because they have been unable to develop or acquire the skills necessary to manage and operate a franchise business. This situation could be symptomatic of a lack of empathy and resource to train and support franchisees, a lack of a suitable management information system to control franchisees, as well as a lack of ability to translate the tacit knowledge of operating a small business into the documentation required to facilitate the necessary transfer of know-how to franchisees. To some extent, high failure rates should be expected as surmounting the mobility barriers to franchising requires new perspectives and managerial behaviour, both of which take time to occur and effort to acquire. Such organizational change is not simply a question of generating (either in-house or otherwise) the three key documents, as some contend.

As shown in Chapters 8 and 9, articles in the popular franchise press and some academic discourses frequently claim, without the necessary benefit of independently-produced corroborating evidence, that franchisors have almost unparalleled levels of success. These perceptions, at best, arise from the belief that franchising confers a variety of benefits on the franchisor that permit them to:

1. realize broader brand dissemination;
2. gain access to capital;
3. improve return on investment; and
4. preclude the development of an expensive organizational structure.

It is axiomatic, however, that the majority of franchisors are small businesses (which, in themselves, are marked by high levels of failure) and only a minority of these ever grow to the extent of employing other people. The trials and costs of developing a small business are problematic enough (Dodge *et al*, 1994) without the additional burden of nurturing a credible franchise operation.

Despite the lower input and ongoing costs of organizational development, the pre-launch financial, managerial, reputation and time costs associated with franchising suggest that it is a growth strategy not to be entered into lightly. It is, logically, going to realize net cash out-flows in the initial stages, rather than being the pot at the end of the rainbow that many may otherwise lead small-firm owners to believe. In fact, the normal problems of small-firm growth are, in all likelihood, going to be magnified and exacerbated rather than reduced and alleviated when pursuing franchised expansion. In short, both agency theorists and resource constraint researchers have argued that firms enter into franchising to overcome the resource limitations and realize growth, but it is because of this effect that they may fail as a franchisor. It may be, therefore, that relatively new franchisor businesses experience relatively high rates of attrition.

The importance of mobility barriers is not only significant to the potential franchisor, but to existing ones too. The nature (that is, the degree to which they are imitable) and height of mobility barriers to differing strategic groups is an important determinant of cluster stability and contestability. Strategic group stability can also alter over time as firms, either via diversification or changing strategic direction, rapidly enter and exit different strategic groups (Caves and Porter, 1977). Competitors in neighbouring customer, product, geographic markets can often enter a strategic group especially when resources, including managerial capabilities, are easily transferable. The failure to raise sufficient mobility barriers in order to help counter potential entry from other strategic groups can lead to increased volatility within a strategic group. For example, the British and US motorcycle industry virtually ignored the entry of Japanese companies into the low powered sector of the market. According to the Boston Consulting Group (1975), UK manufacturers were displaced by the Japanese through poor product reliability accentuated by a reputation for grudging acceptance of warranty claims, and poor availability of spare parts. Furthermore, whereas the Japanese were able to launch numerous new models, no new UK motorcycles had appeared since 1968. The new Japanese models not only emulated the advantages of the British models, but also introduced new product attributes, as well as launched them at prices substantially lower than the British counterparts. In terms of strategic group dynamics, the essentially non-rivalrous behaviour of UK manufacturers and falling mobility barriers meant that the market became contestable.

The same situation is true of some sections of the fast food franchise market where, especially in the USA, Canada, Australia and Britain, foodservice companies have altered their delivery systems in order to enter non-traditional sites and increase brand coverage. By doing so they have been able to compete effectively in the traditional locations occupied by independents and small chain-operated businesses. For example, in Britain, fish and chips shops have been traditionally located in residential areas, not only because they were near to their customers, but to reduce overheads, and away from high street locations where rents are high. During the 1960s, many of KFC franchisees sited their units near to traditional fish and chips shop areas, which served to increase market illiberality for the latter operators. In addition, recent developments in the pizza home delivery sector have meant that fish and chips shop operators have faced additional competitive pressure (Picton and Harrod, 1990; Price, 1993).

While some strategic groups are volatile and unstable, those clusters with high mobility barriers are viewed to have greater stability and lower levels of contestability. Since high cross-elasticities sensitize firms to each other and the perception of mutual dependence, (Caves, 1984), such groups are, in spite of inconclusive evidence (Caves and Ghemawat, 1992), consequently hypothesized to earn persistently greater profits than their rivals in other, more volatile, strategic groups. Although performance may differ between groups, mobility barriers can enable more than one group to survive in the long term. Hallagan and Joerding (1983) have shown that even where mobility barriers are zero, and where a firm's demand may be increased by a rival's advertising investments and efforts (as has been evident in some sectors of the pet food and beer markets), or consumer brand loyalty is present, then multiple strategic groups can coexist in the long term. In other words, there is sufficient space in an industry for innovators and imitators to operate within various market niches.

According to proponents of the mobility barrier approach, differing sub-industries illustrate varying levels of contestability and rivalry depending upon the height and nature of barriers to entry and mobility (Caves and Ghemawat, 1992; Hatten and Hatten, 1987). The barriers raised by the most rivalistic firms, such as those in non-collusive oligopolistic markets, are high and those of smaller firms are virtually contestable in consolidating and fragmented industries. For example, the rapid proliferation of economy/budget hotels in differing national markets by some hotel groups, such as Holiday Inn (see Table 4.2 below), Choice and Accor, suggests that this end of the market is highly fragmented and thus contestable due to low barriers to entry and mobility as well as the localized nature of rivalry. From this situation, a degree of asymmetry is evident since few economy/budget hotels have diversified, as part of retaliatory action, into hotels geared towards a more luxurious provision.

Brand	Americas		Europe/ Middle East		Asia Pacific		Total	
	Hotels	Rooms	Hotels	Rooms	Hotels	Rooms	Hotels	Rooms
Crowne Plaza	48	16,535	30	7,816	16	6,356	94	30,707
Crowne Plaza Resort	5	1,581	0	0	1	750	6	2,331
Sunspree/Resorts	18	3,712	2	209	2	340	22	4,261
Select	1	220	0	0	0	0	1	220
Suites	1	115	0	0	3	416	4	531
Express	274	24,454	0	0	1	56	275	24,510
Garden Court	0	0	60	9,189	0	0	60	9,189
Full Service	1,378	260,621	89	16,862	48	12,259	1,515	289,742
Total System	1,725	307,238	181	34,076	71	20,177	1,977	361,491

Source: Company data

Table 4.2: Regional distribution of Holiday Inn sub-brands

Asymmetrical contestability, as a result of entry through product diversification, has also been observed within the pizza home delivery and sandwiches sectors of the UK fast food industry (Price, 1993). In the former, the market is contestable because restaurant concerns have the ability to enter, and exit the market, at will through augmenting their existing services. As shown in the Case Study at the end of this chapter, asymmetry is evident in the sandwich retail sector through the product diversification efforts of non-specialists. Asymmetry has also been evident within the grocery retail market (Duke, 1991) where the large differentiated players have developed neighbourhood type stores and so are able to compete with discounters, specialist retailers, and convenience stores.[4] Diversification moves such as these suggest that some firms choose to compete in some product-markets if their skills, experiences, and current resources are valuable to serving those markets (Collis, 1991). These firms, therefore, may not have diversified as such, but have sought to increase their specialization along a different axis. Furthermore, those markets which have experienced diversification are those which are typically at the growth stage of their life-cycle. This situation, in turn, implies that all members of strategic groups need not be in the same life-cycle stage and that the industry life-cycle stage of each strategic group could differ (Primeaux, 1985).

Observing strategic groups

In order to gain the benefits of fine-grain analysis and to conform to the original spirit of strategic group research (Harrigan, 1985), the current investigation of strategic groups examines a single industry. To date, only a few empirical studies have operationalized strategic groups by using cross-sectional data (Heggert, 1987; Lawless and Tegarden, 1990; Newman, 1978). Specifically, twenty-one sampled mid-spend and fast food firms were chosen which operated a total of 612 stores (an average of twenty-nine each) in the inner London area at the end of 1994. The foodservice industry was chosen for three reasons:

1. strategic group and market conduct research within fragmented industries is limited;
2. there has been limited application of the strategic group concept to the hospitality sector;
3. foodservice firms have, within the context of a maturing market, sought distributive diversity in order to access non-traditional sites (see Chapter 2). By engaging in this activity, some firms have either entered pre-existing competitive clusters or created other strategic groups. In this sense, it is conceivable on *a priori* grounds, at least, to observe that units of single business organizations can operate within differing strategic groups.

Strategic group and distance proxies

Perhaps reflecting the infancy of theory development and the predominance of fine-grain approaches within strategic group analysis, the number and nature of strategic dimensions utilized by researchers varies according to: the industry under review; whether the research focus is one industry or many; and the rigour employed by the researcher(s). Summarizing and reviewing strategic group research conducted between the period 1972 and 1986, Thomas and Venkatraman (1988) distinguish between those studies that operationalized strategies in narrow terms (focusing on one functional area or one dimension) versus those that conceptualized strategy in broader terms (focusing on multi-functional areas or multi-dimensional areas).

The second dimension of their scheme focuses on the methodologies used to identify strategic groups. Thomas and Venkatraman (1988) establish that some researchers specify the characteristics *a priori* based on theoretical explanation, whereas others use statistical techniques to identify group members. For example, Roper (1992) uses structural features of hotel consortia whilst, within the context of the UK fast food industry, Price (1993) uses geographic reach, store specialization ratio and extent of similarity in operational characteristics to assign *a priori* group members. In contrast, Harrigan (1985) employs the cluster technique to develop simultaneously groupings based on strategic postures involving several strategic variables.

In this study, initially a narrow operationalization of strategy is employed via assigning a binary variable according to whether the firm was engaged in franchising. Secondly, and following Kumar *et al*'s (1990) recommendation, the strategic groups were calculated using a multi-variate approach. This approach is also consistent with the plurality of variables employed in, among others, retail-orientated strategic group analyses (Carrol *et al*, 1992; Hawes and Crittenden, 1984). Within retail businesses, such as fast food and mid-spend restaurants, the strategically relevant differences are variations in the marketing mix attributes they possess (Porac *et al*, 1987), rather than by whether they are part of, for example, a larger vertically-integrated concern. Reed *et al* (1991) observe that many goods and services may be described in terms of their 'characteristics' or attributes; occasionally these descriptions are engineered by the absence of one or more attributes, but are more frequently generated by the relative proportions of each attribute that is present. The various store attributes are an attempt to target and serve differing customer segments; they are the firm's positioning statements because they represent the outcome of marketing programmes for those customer segments targeted for entry. Store attributes are, therefore, an important source of positioning and differentiation and could be useful in the identification of strategic groups (Cowling and Cubbins, 1972).

Perhaps reflective of this logic, Carpenter *et al* (1994) show how differentiation on an 'irrelevant' attribute can create a valued difference between brands and state that meaningless differentiation can be positively valued by buyers. For example, one attribute of fast food restaurants located in city centres which appears to be valued by some customers in Britain is the availability of toilet facilities and, in drive-through formats, parking facilities are seen as important (Price, 1993) because British consumers have a tendency for not eating fast food while they drive. In this sense, even minor differences may be relevant in defining group membership. For this study, twenty-one key proxies are used to determine whether a store belongs to a particular strategic group, and some of these attributes are as listed below. In order to reflect the effects of inflation and various alterations deriving from the imposition of VAT in 1984 and subsequent amendments, the price bands have been altered accordingly. All of the sampled firms have been renamed to maintain anonymity.

Place:
- located on a prime site (that is, high street location with substantial pedestrian traffic);
- has counter/takeaway service;
- offers home delivery; and
- has a drive-through facility.

Product:
- has a licence to sell alcohol;
- breadth of product line, for example hamburgers, pizza, chicken, pasta, ethnic, fish, sandwiches, and dessert items;
- has customer seating facilities;
- has waiting staff; and
- delivers the product on/in crockery.

Price:
- generates an average spend per customer within one of three price bands (as at 1994 prices): 1) <£3.00; 2) >£3.00<£8.00; and 3) >£8.00.

Promotion:
- contributes to below-the-line advertising; and
- contributes to above-the-line advertising.

Although not exhaustive (for example, breakfast items are not included), some of these proxies are derived from interviews with managers of the sampled firms and from a review of the definitional differences between fast food and other foodservice establishments (Price, 1991). This type of research to formulate cluster variables is viewed as superior to other approaches because questioning incumbent managers is seen as encapsulating the key dimensions of competition in an industry, and the variables which are likely to be manipulated and altered to change direction. Thus, the cognitive approach rather than the inductive method to strategic group identification is employed. While the inductive configurations are defined along dimensions that researchers view as important, the cognitive approach relies on perceptions of expert informants to define clustering variables (Ketchen and Shook, 1996), and may be crucial to understanding any given setting. Some of these variables are founded within extant strategic group literature. For example, in accordance market inter-dependency and segmentation discourse, Ball *et al* (1988) observe that the foodservice industry is segmented by product category. As noted in Chapter 2, foodservice companies have sought to broaden their menus in order to diversify risk and maintain/increase customer interest. Such action has served to blur the traditionally defined fast food product sector and alter the market's competitive landscape. This situation affords one of two hypotheses:

1. strategic group participants operating in the same product category may illustrate higher levels of strategic distance; and
2. strategic group participants may illustrate similar store attributes, irrespective of product category (Barnett, 1993).

Within this study, the different foodservice configurations employed by some companies yielded an additional five 'firms' to the sampled twenty-one companies.

Advertising intensity (advertising intensity as a proportion of sales) has been used in a variety of strategic group studies (Oster, 1982; Tremblay, 1985). Many have used the variable to denote the opportunities for product differentiation barriers as an entry to new competition, evaluate brand segmentation in an industry, as well as to evaluate the height of mobility barriers. Empirical research, however, concerning the role of advertising as an entry barrier has shown mixed results. Smith *et al* (1992) found advertising intensity to be a barrier to entry; others found a positive relationship (Oster, 1982). Advertising pools have also been used to differentiate further franchises and non-franchised concerns. Within franchise organizations, advertising contributions are frequently paid into a separate bank account and regarded as an 'advertising pool' which finances the advertising expenditure incurred by the franchisor. In a normal combined franchise and own retail operation, the company units will contribute to the advertising pool on the same basis as the franchisees (Acheson and Paul, 1990).

In order to measure the extent to which business units are similar, the presence of their attributes is considered in binary terms, where the absence of an attribute equates to zero and its existence equals one. This data is then used to compute a matrix, where business units illustrating similar attributes are viewed as competing along similar dimensions and form a strategic group. All binary variables are assumed to be asymmetric and are assigned the same weight to yield a '*Jaccard*-coefficient' or 'affinity' index (Kaufman and Rousseeux, 1990), which is established by finding the similarity between two objects. It is calculated by the function set out below.

$$d(m, n) = (b + c) \div (a + b + c) \tag{1}$$

where, $d(m, n)$ = the difference between two objects m, n; a = the number of variables that equal 1 for both objects; b = the number of variables that equal 1 for object m, but equates to zero for n; and c = the number of variables that equate to zero for object m, but 1 for n. The function where the variables equate to zero for both objects is not calculated because the agreement of two attributes and the presence of a store characteristic is considered more significant than the agreement of two zeros. According to this equation, firms which are exactly strategically similar will record a *Jaccard*-coefficient of one (that is, low strategic distance).

Strategic groups in the London foodservice market

The diagram below (Figure 4.1) summarizes the strategic movements within the sampled business units between 1980 and 1994 through a series of dendrograms; it shows the clusters being combined and values of distance coefficients at each step. In each dendrogram the scaling is conducted by joining the distances of the clusters. Actual distances have been rescaled to a range of one to twenty-five. As there are no satisfactory methods for determining the number of population clusters for any type of cluster analysis (Hartigan, 1975), an artificial line has been drawn at ten. Using this proxy, it is possible to see how the positions of the sampled foodservice companies in London have changed over the period, with a rise in the number of strategic group incumbents and emergence of two new strategic groups. In this respect, the entry of a new incumbent is analogous to the French game of boules because – as in the game – a new entrant to the existing grouping serves to disrupt the existing order and distance between brands. The rise of new strategic groups over the period is due to the emergence of new sub-sectors, such as pizza home delivery, as well as from the entry of new concepts. These allow us to see how some followers to new entrants occupy similar strategic space, but does not illustrate how these like firms interact with one another in certain locations. The relative position of each firm within a particular group and relative to the rest of the sample has been affected by the entry and exit (for example, R_2) of other firms as well as by alterations in the marketing mix configurations of existing incumbents.

From the diagram, it is evident that strategic groups are comprised of firms illustrating similar products and foodservice delivery systems. This tendency serves to confirm Ball *et al*'s (1988) observation concerning the segmentation in the foodservice industry, but there are limits to this generalization. For example, the largest strategic group is composed of firms selling hamburgers and fried chicken and the traditional product boundaries have been blurred as firms have pursued increased product variety rather than just depth within a single product category.

By using the same *Jaccard* coefficient to encapsulate the marketing mix variables, it is possible to make some statements about the differences in strategic distance of the franchised firms and non-franchised firms to suggest that each could be construed to be a different cluster. The hypotheses to be tested are:

Test 1:   the average strategic distance within a cluster of franchised firms is similar to the average strategic distance within a cluster of non-franchised firms (that is, H_0: $\mu_1 - \mu_2 = 0; H_1: \mu_1 - \mu_2 \neq 0$).

Test 2:   the average strategic distance within a cluster of franchised firms is similar to the average strategic distance between that cluster and a group of non-franchised firms.

Test 3:   the average strategic distances within a cluster of non-franchised firms is similar to the average strategic distance between that cluster and a group of franchised firms.

The results of using z-tests to test each null hypothesis, where the critical z ($\alpha = 0.05$) = ± 1.96, indicates that there is no difference in the average strategic distance within a group of franchised firms versus that within a cluster of non-franchised firms (the null hypothesis is accepted at $z = -0.45$). For Tests 2 and 3, as the null hypotheses are rejected ($z = -2.92$ and -2.76 respectively) the average strategic distances in the two latter samples are different. In turn, these results serve to confirm that strategic distances are greater between clusters of firms than within them. Thus, from the sample, it seems that franchises could be construed to be a strategic group within an industry, but one which illustrates similar marketing mix variable to non-franchises.

By comparing the strategic group members to the *Jaccard* coefficients for the year 1994, the initial observation from the data is that there appear to be varying degrees of strategic distances between competing firms within and between each cluster. For example, while firm *A* has a similar marketing mix configuration to that of firm *B*, who, in turn, is closer to firm *C*, it does not follow that *A* is like firm *C* to the same degree that it is like *B*. This means that each firm defines its competitors differently and possibly experiences differing degrees of competitive threat from each competitor: some firms compete with

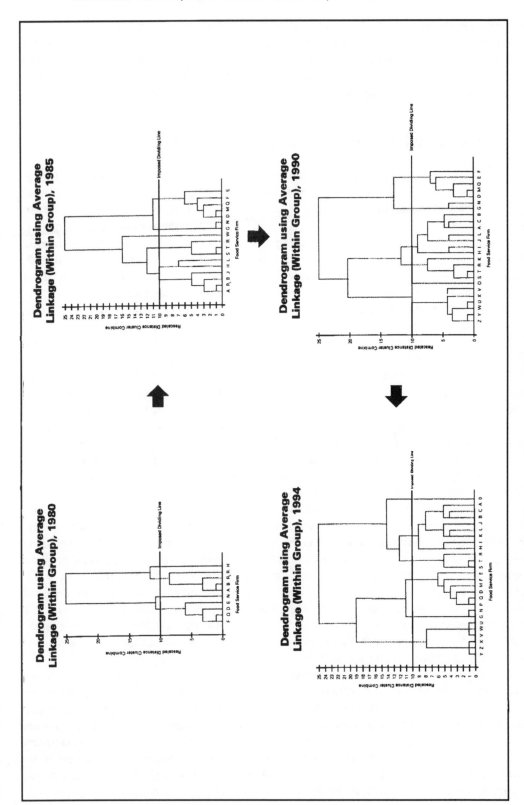

Figure 4.1: Dendograms showing clusters of sampled foodservice companies, 1980–94

and are like their other strategic group members, others do not. Of some note, is the observation that the incumbents of some strategic groups were franchised and, in two, there was a mixture of franchised and non-franchised concerns. This situation seems to suggest that there may indeed be a tit-for-tat reaction within some strategic groups and the decision to franchise. Such an observation is, however, in need of empirical testing.

Rivalry within and between strategic groups

The diffusion of franchising has been shown to differ across and between industries and economies. In spite of the benefits that may accrue from franchising, not all businesses have embraced the strategy nor are they likely to do so. One of the key explanations for this situation is the perception by decision-makers that franchising has differing levels of applicability and legitimacy for their businesses (Jehiel and Molovanu, 1996). A determinant of that legitimacy is the extent to which franchising is already employed by members of a particular strategic group; another is the strategic intent of the decision-makers. For example, a new entrant to a particular strategic group may decide to employ franchising as a method with which to gain rapid market share and reduce exposure to risk. Once used, other cluster participants may quickly follow suit because franchising is perceived to construe such advantages as a lower cost base, higher shareholder returns, increased revenues, and lower risk.

A central tenet to such reactionary behaviour is the notion of comparative advantage. According to Hunt and Morgan (1995), rivalry is focused along one of two dimensions: the relative cost of inputs and the relative value of the output. Using these two proxies, they calculate the matrix presented below (Figure 4.2). Within the matrix, the market-place position of competitive advantage as cell three (for example) results from the firm, relative to its competitors, being able to produce an offering for some market segment or segments that is perceived to be either of superior perceived value by customers, and/or produced at lower costs.

Conversely, a firm is perceived to be at a competitive disadvantage if either the costs of inputs are higher than those realized by a competitor or the value added to the product is seen as inferior in comparison with the same rival. Firms positioned in cell nine need not be at a competitive disadvantage in relation to their rival; such producers may market luxury products whereas the competition sell 'me-too' copies. Equally, firms in cell one may be commodity producers: their products are traded on price alone and are not perceived to be of high added value by customers. Competing in this niche requires the firm to have lower input prices than those of the competition. As shown in the Case Study at the end of this chapter, this is a position in which the majority of sandwich manufacturers in Britain have found themselves.

Significantly, Hunt and Morgan (1995) suggest that competitive advantages accrue through small innovations which, over time, may have a cumulative effect on efficiency and effectiveness. Innovations, whether imitations or not, may serve to reduce input costs and/or differentiate products so much that they are perceived to be superior to rivals' offerings. This matrix is of relevance to the decision to franchise because agency theorists suggest that franchising lowers the firm's ongoing monitoring and administrative costs, as well as costs of labour and advertising. In terms of positioning in the matrix, the lower input costs mean that the franchisor is located in one of the cells labelled one

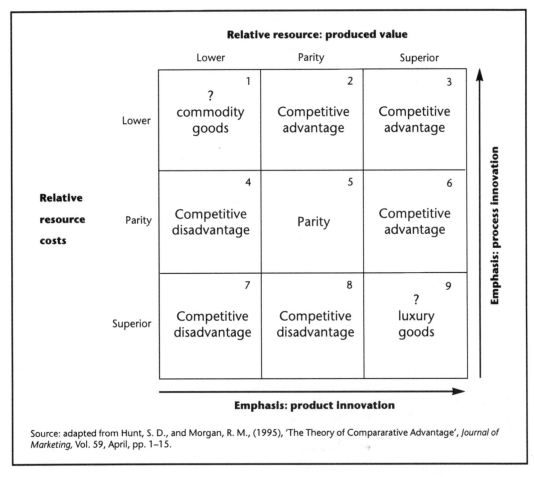

Figure 4.2: Hunt and Morgan's (1995) model of comparative advantage

to three. While the lower input costs may be a sufficient reason for a competitor to follow suit, franchising also has the potential to improve the perceived quality of output through the service provided to the customer. As franchisees are seen to be more motivated than traditional employees because of their investments in buying a franchise and the need to recoup that outlay, franchisees may be willing to open their stores for longer and differentiate themselves from the competition on service (they cannot necessarily modify products as alterations could be in breach of contract). This differentiation and the lower costs of inputs could be, combined, a powerful motivator for a rival to also franchise. Whilst such behaviour may, however, serve to explain partially the diffusion of franchising within a strategic group, it does not necessarily account for the diffusion of franchising between differing clusters. To some degree, we have also tended to simplify the diffusion process by assuming that companies within a strategic group compete with each other more heavily than with firms in other clusters. This subject has been the topic of substantial debate by strategic group researchers, and requires empirical testing.

As seen from the mobility barrier perspective, fundamental similarities and differences in the resources of firms may give rise to patterns of strategic symmetry and asymmetry within an industry. Porter (1979) and Caves and Porter (1977) recognized that there may be important implications of such symmetries for the competitive response patterns amongst firms. Accordingly, they hypothesized that rivalry is greater between participants of different strategic groups than amongst members of the same cluster. They argue that structural similarities among firms predisposes them to react in similar ways to threats from within or outside the group. Similarly, Stigler (1964) posits that the fewer the number of firms in an industry, the easier it is for changes to be detected; their market contact enables them to realize their mutual dependence and counter effect each other's moves with greater accuracy and greater speed. As a result, an interactive kind of corporate behaviour exists by which rival firms in a strategic group counter one another's moves by making similar moves themselves (Knickerbocker, 1973).

Such moves may not only be made according to the alteration of price, but other marketing mix components as well as strategic dimensions (Cool and Schendel, 1987). For example, strategic group members have been shown to make 'tit-for-tat' matching of investments in major product and geographic markets (Li, 1994), resulting in similar dimensions of diversification, verticality, and relatedness. These findings suggest that if a firm within a particular strategic group decides to franchise, then other cluster participants will follow shortly thereafter to negate any first mover advantages. Not only will they follow, but they will also attempt to attract a similar type of franchisee by offering similar contracts to each other. It may be forwarded that for first mover reasons, therefore, the initial and ongoing franchise fees for firms with similar strategic characteristics show little variation. In order for first movers to maintain their lead and for followers to either 'leap-frog' the leader or narrow the competitive gap, firms are required to undertake continuous innovation as well as maintain high levels of franchisee motivation (see Chapters 6 and 7). The maintenance of monopolistic benefits is also dependent on the magnitude of retaliatory action by the follower, the degree of imitation in response, the speed of response, and the timing of the response (Stalk, 1991).

As a result of mutual dependence, implicit collusion should be easier to achieve and sustain than relationships between participants of differing groups, but this collusion is not a simple exercise in any instance. Porter (1979) indicates that the difficulties of oligopolistic co-ordination multiply as the strategic differences between firms increase, meaning that rivalry should increase with the 'strategic distance' between firms. Zajac and Jones (1989) argue, however, that rivalry may be reduced between members of differing groups as their distinct strategic dimensions enable them to signal clearly whether they are staying within the bounds of their strategy. In contradistinction to Porter (1979) and Caves and Porter (1977), they propound that rivalry should decrease as strategic distance increases and competition increases amongst firms within the same group. This intra-group rivalry should result in higher mobility barriers and therefore become less contestable as strategic distance increases (Hatten and Hatten, 1987; Dooley et al, 1996).

Within Zajac and Jones's (1989) perspective, the franchise fees and costs of the later entrants may be below those employed by the first movers. This hypothesis has been tested by Baucus et al (1993), who suggest that the value of a franchise is reflected in its base fees and royalties. The foundation of these fees reflects the franchisor's age, growth, and the market representation of the franchise operation. New franchisors have less recognizable brand names and less representation in markets than their more established counterparts. These new entrants, therefore, charge lower base fees and lower royalties because of their less established reputations. The lower fees, however, may also be focused on attracting franchisees in order to meet growth and market share objectives. In this respect, the franchisors are not necessarily behaving in a collusive manner.

Such a conclusion is supported by Berheim and Whinston (1991) who developed, through mathematical proofs, a model of the effect of firms meeting repeatedly in different markets with their propensity to engage in collusive behaviour. They contend that where firms illustrate similar strategic configurations and operate in similar markets, firms cannot sustain collusive prices. Nonetheless, within the franchise context, a firm may not decide to follow another company which has decided to pursue franchised-based expansion or may decide to price their franchise package without reference to their peer group. This latter type of behaviour has been observed to be widely representative of UK franchisors. Reflecting this sentiment, Mendelsohn (quoted in MacMillan, 1995) notes that most franchisor companies in Britain:

> . . . set their fees by what they can get away with rather than on any meaningful costing system and in light of what the competition are charging.

Such behaviour is not necessarily unique to franchising. As Kerin et al (1992) point out, there is no basis for implicitly assuming that strategic group incumbents will automatically follow a 'me-too' strategy. Some companies may not have the capabilities, resources, or necessary skills to follow; others may have no desire to even if they possessed the prerequisite skills, competences and finances to surmount the mobility barriers to become a successful franchisor. Consequently, according to Zajac and Jones, increasing strategic distance ensues; the further each firm moves along their organizational trajectories the greater the strategic distance between them and the lower the level of rivalry. In this case, lower competitive intensity between franchised and non-franchised firms would be expected.

Additional considerations

The extent to which either the views of Zajac and Jones (1989) or Porter (1979) carry weight needs to be moderated by three factors. Firstly, if firms are competing for customers and other resources in the same market and, in Porter's (1979; 1980) terms, where market interdependence exists, rivalry will be greatest. Secondly, Porter and Caves' (1977) hypothesis of strategic group stability suggests that implicit collusion is evident (Peteraf, 1993a). The problems of co-ordination between members of an oligopoly, however, are well documented. Several authors (such as Gal-Or, 1991) have shown that the relevant parameters for information sharing are:

1. the type of competition;
2. the type of proprietary information, whether strategic or tactical; and
3. the extent to which the products are complements or rivals.

The interdependency between complementary/substitute products has, in some markets, led certain strategic group members to establish more formal inter-organizational relationships, such as alliances (Duysters and Hagedoorn, 1995; Hagedoorn, 1995). Researching information diffusion in particular, Ziv (1993) observes that the communication of private information can increase the profits of all the firms in the market. Consequently, firms will attempt to co-operate and share this information with competitors. The problem for the firms is establishing whether those signals conveyed are truthful or bluffs (Heil and Robertson, 1991). To some degree, the problems of co-ordination and co-operation are captured within the 'prisoners' dilemma' (Koselka, 1993), which is described in the panel on page 215.

Co-ordination problems may also exist within channels of distribution. Shugman (1985), for example, observes that formal agreements can be used to achieve co-ordination among channel members by exerting explicit control over the members who make the agreement. He argues that, as in oligopolistic markets, understandings can be used as a partial substitute for more formal agreements, but channel members obtain greater profits with explicit contracts which provide better co-ordination than implicit understandings. In addition to self-interest and considerations concerning contract type, group size may also create difficulties. As groups increase in size, it becomes increasingly difficult to prevent tacit collusion from dissolving into costly competition. Whilst Green and Porter (1985) indicate that price instability occurs within groups when the number of members exceeds three, Barney and Hoskisson (1990) illustrate that perfect competition dynamics are likely to emerge when there are five or six cluster participants. Such research suggests that when strategic groups attain a certain size, economic performance, knowledge and resources may not vary substantially. In order to enter and survive within strategic groups, incumbents must own and retain key assets, such as brand capital (Mitchell, 1991) and, where possible, property leases and freeholds. Within franchising, the incidences of newcomer franchisor failure may be partially explained by strategic group instability deriving from ine. perience, increased size of the cluster, and difficulties deriving from lack of co-ordination. Strategic group instability may also, therefore, be an additional explanatory factor behind new entrant and new franchisor failure (see Chapters 8 and 9).

The third issue is the measure of rivalry itself. Focusing on the tendency for inconclusive and varying results within the strategic group paradigm, Cool and Diereckx (1993) propound a more elongated relationship through the inclusion of an intervening variable which measures the conditions of strategic group rivalry. By employing changes in industry concentration to evaluate indirect rivalry, Cool and Diereckx indicate that within strategic groups competition is similar to Cournot-type oligopoly. Similar results are also evident from Peteraf's (1993b) study of indirect rivalry amongst and between strategic groups in the airline industry. She utilizes price competition as a measure of rivalrous behaviour, and finds supporting evidence for Caves and Porter's (1977) hypothesis that rivalry is greater between members of strategic groups than among participants of the same cluster; she also observes that in some instances the level of price competition experienced among and between strategic groups differs according to the level of market interdependence.

Although both studies are significant because they do not focus on establishing a direct link between strategic group membership and firm performance, there are weaknesses. The use of concentration measures to evaluate competitive intensity requires the establishment of market boundaries and suitable definitions of a particular industry or market (Brookes, 1995; Curran and Goodfellow, 1989). The typical bases of industry concentration are SIC codes, but Clarke (1989) empirically shows that SIC is only successful at a broad and coarse level. Elsewhere, with regard to the fast food industry, Price (1993) observes that a continuum of supply exists and, at an industry level, incumbents can be grouped according to the business unit's proportion of fast food sales relative to total sales.

The Prisoners' Dilemma

Gulati *et al* (1994) believe that part of the reason why contemporary alliances and oligopolies fail so often is because many partners view them, in game theory terms, as prisoners' dilemma situations. Each partner fears that the other will receive greater pay-offs by acting opportunistically while it co-operates in good faith, the result being lower payoffs than if they had co-operated. The rationale for this is as follows:

In Axelrod's (1984) illustration of co-operation, two prisoners are accused of a crime which, in fact, they did commit. The gaoler's structure the pay-offs to encourage each prisoner to confess: if neither prisoner confesses, both are given light prison sentences. If one prisoner confesses while the other remains silent, the first goes free while the other receives a heavy sentence. If both prisoners confess, both get a heavy sentence but are awarded time off for good behaviour. Neither one knows what the other is going to say. With the maximum payoff lying in self-interest rather than co-operation, each player, clearly, does better by confessing than by remaining silent. Within prisoners' dilemma games, co-operation tends to increase whenever a participant is repeatedly paired with the same partner. Co-operation is evident in the first move, and the players follow suit on each successive move, and defection follows if the partner defects (equally, co-operation if the partner co-operates). Axelrod shows that such 'strategy and counter strategy' behaviour often scored higher than those pursuing non co-operative plays.

Within the context of alliances, a variety of situations exist which are, perhaps, reflective of the prisoners' dilemma.

Scenario I: the firm assumes that whatever it decides to do, its rivals will not react. Under this Cournot duopoly model each firm simply observes what the other does, then attempts to maximize its own profits using alternative strategies. To some extent, these actions could be interpreted as a situation of co-operation since the firms have essentially agreed to differ and allow each to attempt to maximize their pay-offs. Under the paradigm, however, the analogy is one where neither prisoner confesses (or in this case, co-operate to exercise market power) and both are given light prison sentences. That is, the potential returns for adopting such strategies are less than some form of collusion.

Scenario II: the firm assumes that its rivals will react to its own strategies, and uses past experience to assess the manner that this will take. This type of behaviour underlies the kinked demand curve model with firms learning that rivals do not match price increases, but certainly match any price reductions. Here perhaps the application of the prisoners' dilemma framework is more obvious. The firms, who have had prior confrontations, agree to co-operate until one defects through price reductions. Then both defect and a price war emerges. In periods of price stability, non-price competition may intensify. In such situations, the prisoners agree not to attempt to maximize market share through price fluctuations, but defect in other ways, such as improving product packaging and/or increase advertising and promotional activity.

Scenario III: perhaps more of a pure application of the prisoners' dilemma is the final type of non-collusive oligopoly. Instead of using past experience to assess future reactions by rivals, the firm could identify the best possible move the opposition could make to each of its own strategies. This requires the prisoners (or firms) to assess the longevity and nature of their meetings together. This forms the basis of game theory, which is a more explicit assessment of strategy and counter-strategy. Other reasons for failure may be culturally-based, both firm-specific and nationally (Shoenberg *et al*, 1995).

In this way, he shows that the fast food industry's participants transcend the traditional SIC definitions and that inter-industry competition exists. A further point is that concentration ratios are not, in themselves, measures of rivalry but the percentage market sales accounted for by the largest four or eight firms. Kwoka (1981) argues that there is no theoretical basis for supposing that four firms are relevant to industry performance, nor is there any reason to assume that four firms are equally important as implied by the construction of concentration ratios. Changes in industry concentration may alter for a variety of reasons, including rivalrous ones, as well as random fluctuations and diversified mergers (Kumar *et al*, 1990; Buzzell and Gale, 1987). These issues suggest that more specific measures of competition are needed. Peteraf's (1993b) use of price competition is one such specific measure, but within strategic groups any one of several pricing scenarios may be evident at any one time. These pricing issues can provoke differing responses and lead to differing states of cluster equilibrium, presented below. These responses are not mutually exclusive or exhaustive responses. A strategic group participant, for example, could choose a combination of options:

- competitors set the price without reference to each other, and when one alters the price the others refrain from retaliatory action (Hotelling, 1929);
- all firms price identically and if one makes an adjustment, the others match it (Lorsch, 1954);
- pricing is discriminatory and action by one competitor results in an equal and opposite reaction from its rivals (Greenhut and Ohta, 1975); and
- a dominant competitor acts as a price leader and others follow suit. Price wars or instability are viewed as an enforcement device to maintain a co-operative, or tacitly collusive agreement in an uncertain environment (Green and Porter, 1985), such as those experienced in periods of economic recession, market decline, and rapid market growth.

Where price competition is subdued, it is not necessarily indicative of strategic group stability since rivalry on non-price dimensions (such as advertising activity) may be intense. Non-price effects not only blunt the effects of price competition, but broaden the scope of rivalistic action (Oster, 1982; Schultz *et al*, 1984). For example, Chertonay (1988) and Zeithaml *et al* (1988) present a framework of vertical product differentiation where if all goods were offered at the same price, consumers would choose the highest quality good; where prices differed, customers would choose the product with the highest value for money (the price-to-quality ratio). Implicit to such pricing activity is the buyer's perception of value, not the seller's cost. Non-price variables, such as product quality/quantity, have been used extensively in the foodservice market and have served to develop the perception of value by using set prices to capture perceived value. Within the UK foodservice sector, McDonald's, Burger King, and KFC have recently offered value meal selections; Pizza Hut and Deep Pan Pizza have introduced 'buffets' and Pizzaland and Bella Pasta have introduced coupons.

Several researchers observe that the weapons of non-price rivalry often have the characteristic of involving a sunk cost. These sunk costs give weapons, such as price discounts, an additional role to play as commitments that make threats against rivals credible (Thomas, 1996). One of the simplest contexts in which to analyze the role of non-price rivalry in creating credible threats is that of adding capacity – or, within location-bounded organizations, additional business units. It provides a base from which strategic action and reaction can occur and results in the clustering of firms within specific geographic markets. This clustering occurs because when a firm enters a market, or an existing firm relocates, there is a strong tendency for that firm to locate as close as possible to another firm (Brown, 1989). Franchising may be employed by some firms to accelerate the rate of new store openings and by followers to maintain the pace or overtake the leader, but it also increases the probability of competing in and for similar locations. From this location-based rivalry, other components of the marketing mix may be varied in order that the two firms meet on other dimensions (price, for example) in addition to location. Consequently, it is useful to examine strategic group rivalry within fragmented industries as well as the pattern of locational choices employed by franchisors.

Strategic group rivalry in fragmented industries

Strategic groups have been witnessed in a variety of oligopolistic economic settings, including the grocery and retail markets (Lewis and Thomas, 1990; Harrigan, 1985; Hawes and Critten, 1984). For example, reflecting its oligopolistic structure there have been numerous studies into the presence of strategic groups within the brewing industry (Carroll and Wade, 1991; Carroll and Swaminathan, 1992; Hatten and Schendel, 1977; Johnson and Thomas, 1987; McGahan, 1991; Tremblay, 1985). A well-noted characteristic of retail and hospitality texts, however, is the observation that the hotel and catering trade is fragmented. With reference to the hotel sector in Britain, for example, Slattery and Johnson (1992) observe that the four largest operators account for less than 4% of the total hotel stock. At such a level, the sector falls far short of the 40% threshold required for it to conform to definitions of concentrated industries (Porter, 1980). Similar observations of fragmentation have also been made about the restaurant trade and, albeit to a lesser degree, the fast food sector. This fragmentation has, arguably, limited the applicability of strategic group analyses within the hotel sector to multinational studies:

> Oligopolistic practices in the hotel industry can . . . operate internationally. There may be cases where a given chain seeks to offer its standardized product to regular international customers across a whole region at broadly the same tariffs, especially where special features such as executive floors within a standard branded property are concerned. Although such a strategy cannot entirely avoid the realities of local factor markets and the impact of variable exchange rates, the possibilities for such international pricing are still significant. Between chains competing for business in a number of regional centres and operating in broadly the same market segment, the same conditions of oligopoly therefore apply. Within the class level and between brands there have to be broadly similar price/service equations for all direct competitors, and market constraints of trading up or down between classes of hotel also apply. (EIU, 1991; p. 91)

Furthermore, Go (1989) estimates that out of the approximate 11.5 million rooms distributed over hotels and other establishments, the top 200 hotel corporations hold about 2.7 million (over 23%) of these. Such concentration, as well as similarity of international markets served, increases the potential for head-to-head competition in domestic and international markets and, thus, the propensity to seek new locations.

The few studies examining strategic groups in the hospitality industry have tended to employ the strategic similarity approach by using, first, the extent of vertical integration, and, second, geographic scope. For example, Dunning and McQueen's (1982) definition of strategic groups within the international hotel industry is founded on ownership and vertical integration characteristics. They observe the types of groups described in the table below. By comparison, Litteljohn and Beattie (1992) define strategic groups in the European hotel industry according to their geographic reach and compare this feature against the degree to which hotels are the businesses' main interests and firm size (measured in terms of total number of hotels). They find that those companies with hotels as core, tend to internationalize at an early stage of development, that is before the total number of hotels reaches 200. Companies with hotels as one interest in a wider hospitality portfolio, such as Holiday Inn and Accor, have an internationalization ratio (that is, the proportion of foreign-owned rooms to total rooms) of 48%, with some 67% of their sample operating at least 35% of their portfolio outside the home country. Those companies with hotels as one interest in a wider industrial portfolio illustrate the highest levels of internationalization (70%), but this may be partially explained by the fact that nine out of fourteen hotel companies were associated with airlines. Although Dunning and McQueen's (1982) and Litteljohn and Beattie's (1992) strategic groupings lend some insight to the nature and possible role of association in the international hotel industry, they do not allow for functional strategy features, such as the market level of the hotel and its degree of branding. The market level of the hotels may be of some importance as it may dictate whether the firm could pursue a global niche or global high share strategy (Dunning and Norman, 1987; Leontiades, 1991). These latter hotel companies would be those with hotels at differing market levels but with international presence; those pursuing a global niche strategy would be those international hotel companies with a single brand serving a particular market level.

Integration type	No. of trans-national corporations	Foreign hotels (associated)		Number in developed economies	
		No.	%	No.	%
Vertical					
a) Hotel chains with airlines	16	227	27.1	113	21.0
b) Tour operator	6	46	4.5	41	7.8
Horizontal					
a) Independent	56	687	67	384	71.2
b) Hotel consultants & development	3	15	1.5	nil	nil
Total	81	1,025	100.0	539	100.0

Source: Adapted from Dunning, J., and McQueen, M., (1982), 'Multinational Corporations in the International Hotel Industry', *Annals of Tourism Research,* Vol. 9, pp. 69–90.

Table 4.3: Strategic groups in the international hotel industry

It has also been suggested that the use of strategic group analyses, employing fragmented industries as a context, may be a moot exercise because collective strategies have only been recognized as options for firms in concentrated markets (Bresser, 1988). According to Miles *et al* (1993), the use of the term 'fragmented industry' seems to connote substantial industry variety due to loose linked disconnectiveness. The lack of links between the firms in a fragmented industry derives from their small size, location-boundedness and low mobility and entry barriers, which combined, results in diverse and numerous strategic groups.

There is, however, evidence to show that firms in fragmented industries also use similar strategies (Dollinger, 1990). Some firms mimic others' strategies to improve their own strategies by borrowing from others. After the successes enjoyed by McDonald's, Burger King, KFC, and others, this rationale may partially explain how franchising has diffused across the fast food sector among others. Other firms group together to negate the effect of a new or foreign entrant and others may mimic the strategy of a new entrant. This rationale may provide some explanation for the diffusion of franchising and other strategies across industries and economies. For example, within the UK foodservice industry in 1976, Wimpy diversified into counter-service restaurants from its traditional table-service formats, and thereby imitated McDonald's, who entered the market in 1974. In so doing, they also pre-empted the entry of Burger King in 1977 into the same strategic group (see Case Study 2).

The extent to which strategies are diffused in fragmented industries is, in part, dependent on the nature of competition within specific regions. Hatten and Hatten (1987), for example, note that firms within fragmented industries often confront geographically unique markets where the rules of competition and degree of disconnectedness are determined within each market segment. This, according to Dollinger (1990), affords two potential scenarios which are appropriate for the analysis of location-bounded firms, such as those in the retail and hospitality industries: first, firms within a strategic group compete *like* each other but not *with* each other; and secondly, incumbents compete *like* each other and *with* each other. The second scenario is important to the understanding of the dynamics of competition within strategic groups of retailers and diversified concerns, as well as the propensity to franchise. The competitive behaviours captured in the second scenario are consistent with Chamberlain's (1956) view that markets might be thought of as comprising numerous 'chain-linked' sub-markets:

> Retail establishments scattered throughout an urban area are an instance of . . . a 'chain' linking of markets. Gasoline filling stations are another. In either of these cases the market of each seller is most closely linked (having regard only to the spatial factor) to the one nearest him, and the degree of connection lessens quickly with distance until it becomes zero . . . where in this considerations relative to small numbers hold even though the 'group' be large . . . Two new possibilities are suggested by the chain relationship. A cut by one seller may lead to a smaller reduction by the next one to him and dissipate itself without spreading far. Or . . . it might force those nearest him to meet it in full, this in turn forcing others, and so on indefinitely. (pp. 103–104)

In other words, retailers operating in a variety of geographically dispersed markets may respond to a cut in price by:

1. doing nothing;
2. defending by similarly cutting price;
3. engaging in a counter-attack by reducing price in another location;
4. engaging in 'total war' by under-pricing the rival/entrant in every market (Karnani and Wernerfelt, 1985).

In relation to one company's decision to franchise, similar responses may be expected. The non-franchised company could:

1. remain in the current position;
2. defend by launching a franchise of a similar nature;
3. counter-attack by engaging in a joint venture or launch a lower cost franchise;
4. meet the move by instigating a price war to destabilize the market and, thereby, heighten difficulties for the franchisor to recruit franchisees.

There are, of course, other responses; these serve as examples to show that the nature of competitive reaction alters by direction, scale and method.

From a different perspective, Tang and Thomas (1992) suggest that a complete understanding of competition will be possible when the reciprocal links between firm-level strategies and group-level structures are uncovered. This means that additional considerations to pricing issues are needed to investigate the rivalry within and between strategic groups. Here, only one component out of the many combinations comprising a business unit's marketing mix (price, place, promotion, and product) is used in the suggested model to test the notion that strategic group dynamics affect the decision to franchise, that of oligopolistic reaction in locational issues. Specifically, the study forwards measures to examine the tendency for firms to follow each other into differing geographic markets, through adding capacity, and suggests that such imitation also impacts on the decision to franchise. The other aspects of a business unit's marketing mix are employed as variables to distinguish whether a certain store belongs to a particular strategic group. Although oligopolistic reaction, as a form of geographic response, has received growing attention as a determinant of geographic diversification (Dunning and Norman, 1987; Flowers, 1976; Li, 1994; Terpstra and Yu, 1988), it has not been moderated by strategic considerations and has been constrained to studies of internationalization. This study suggests that the concept of oligopolistic reaction is equally applicable to national markets, especially within retailing and other location-bound industries.

A proposed methodology to test intra- and inter-strategic group rivalry

In observing that intra-strategic group rivalry may impact on the decision to franchise, initially, an evaluation of the levels of strategic distance between franchised and non-franchised concerns illustrating similar strategic characteristics is necessary.

Secondly, there is a need to test the degree to which rivalry either between or among group member firms influences their decision to franchise; and, thirdly, to test the assumption that competing franchise firms will also exhibit, via the terms of their franchise package (initial fees, royalties and assistance), similar opportunities to investors. While the initial study may be conducted by calculating, for example, the *Jaccard* coefficient, the latter study entails calculating the degree of multi-market contact within and between strategic group incumbents. Employing such an approach to examine the internationalization choices of advertising agencies, Terpstra and Yu (1988) suggest that formulating invest-ment issues as a decision implies the use of a binary variable representing whether a firm is franchised or not as the measure of investment. They also postulate that the outcomes of the choice can be related to a series of hypothesized factors through a maximum like-lihood logit formulation, as follows:

$$P(F = 1) = 1 / \{1 + \exp[-\beta_0 + \beta_1 MMC + \beta_2 SD + \beta_3 MMC^*SD]\} \tag{2}$$

Where the value of being a franchise (F) is one if the firm is franchised and zero otherwise and where the value of two firms in a dyad being franchised is one and zero otherwise; MMC is a multi-market measure; SD is the strategic distance between members of a par-ticular dyad. Finally, MMC*SD is the interaction between the two variables. One limitation of this study is the failure to account for the impact of market growth. Fran-chise studies by Hoffman and Preble (1991) and Dant (1996) suggest that market growth is a motivating factor concerning the decision to franchise, but they have not tested their contention empirically. This model is wholly external in focus because it does not con-sider the effects of resource constraints, brand equity and managerial factors on the decision to franchise and is, therefore, limited further. Furthermore, all of the indepen-dent variables are calculated as t_{-1}, which represents the year prior to the franchise launch date. By examining the variables a year before the firm became a franchised-business, it is possible to examine the impact of the variables on the decision to franchise. It also allows for the time taken to conduct any feasibility and market research studies.

There is also an implication that the above factors impact on the various com-ponents of the franchise package, which is also testable via [2], where R_i represents the assigned summary value of the vector comprising the firm's franchise package. Lafontaine and Shaw (1996) argue that the high variance of contractual terms among franchise firms in the same industry is due to important firm-level characteristics, such as the quality or level of services provided by the franchisors, which vary significantly across firms and play a significant role in the determination of these fees. The inconclusivity of their results suggests that group, rather than firm or industry effects alone, are relevant to the estab-lishment of franchise fees. One way of operationalizing R_i – denoting base fees, royalties and the nature of assistance given to franchisees in finding a site is via allotting a score (0, or 1, depending on the presence and strength of assistance) to the type of help given. Given that some markets are fragmented, one way of evaluating multi-market contact would be through the consideration of locational aspects (others could be the other com-ponents of the marketing mix as well as certain types of business diversification).

Location and multi-market contact measures

In the USA, the manipulation of the key marketing mix components in the fast food market is based on a highly mobile, car-owning, consumer. Within this context, Claus and Hardwick (1972) estimated that the spatial extent for the trade area of a fast food operation was approximately between two and three miles. Similarly, other US fast food researchers observe that up to 80% of fast food customers live and work within a three-mile radius (Melaniphany, 1992; Zeller *et al*, 1980). Whilst such statistics may have some validity for drive-through operations, visitations to fast food establishments in the UK tend to be more pedestrian-led and thus consideration for cultural differences in consumer behaviour is required.

For simplicity, the geographic spacing between non-like outlets is not measured according to the specifications of extant locational models (see Chapter 9), but rather postal codes are used – in particular, the 119 inner London postal codes. Called 'zip-codes' in the USA, these geographic constructs are one of the bases employed by a variety of research companies to assist client businesses, who subscribe to geo-demographic services, to establish market potential and profiles of potential customers. The necessary locational information for measuring and evaluating multi-market contact for the sampled firms operating within the inner London area between 1980 and 1994 was derived from a combination of menus, property listing from the sampled firms (see the section 'Observing strategic groups'), specialist catering estate agencies, and telephone directories. It should be observed that three of the sampled companies had entered the market and embarked on franchised expansion prior to 1980, but for parsimony, developments between the period 1958 (when several foodservice companies started to expand via franchising) and 1970 are not presented. During the 1980s, the foodservice sector began to consolidate due to buoyant consumer demand and the rapid rise of franchising generally (see Chapter 1). Indicative of this situation, the majority of the sampled franchised firms began operations during this period. Of the sampled firms, eleven used business format franchising, and franchisee-operated restaurants accounted for 62% of the total number of stores. Although this appears to be a small sample, the franchised concerns represent over 80% of the volume of meals served in each of their respective product categories within the Greater London market.

Although illustrating similar strategic characteristics, incumbent firms within a particular cluster may either ignore or react to other group members' behaviour. In the former situation, each firm formulates its strategy unilaterally and, in the latter situation, they explicitly take into account the likely effects of their own strategy on other industry participants. Interdependency is often associated with collusive oligopoly, in which firms may collude or co-operate either tacitly or formally. Despite the existence of such organizations as OPEC within the oil industry and the Association of Coffee Producing Countries within the coffee market, formal collusion is illegal in most countries, including the UK. Measures of tacit behaviour, such as multi-market contact, are therefore indicative of the nature of interdependence between firms and point to the possible existence of an implicit understanding between some organizations concerning one or more components of the marketing mix (such as price).

According to Scott (1982; 1991), multi-market contact in which firms meet can be calculated in two ways: either by tally or by computing probability distributions upon which measurements are calculated. For a specific market, therefore, one computes the probability, $\rho(f)$, that firms will have contact in exactly f of the other markets. Measures of contact that merely tally the markets in which firms meet may be inappropriate because of a lack of a metric or scaling (Heggestad and Rhoades, 1978; Scott, 1982; Becker, 1992). Since contact is a measure of the potential strategic action between firms, it is not enough that the absolute number of contacts is high; it is necessary that the firms perceive the contact as being an important part of their environment. For example, within the London postcode of W1, mid-spend chain G had ten restaurants at the end of 1994, while A operated eight stores. Transposing the expression $EM_{GA,i}$ (where $_i$ is W1), the expected meetings, EM, is eighty. Although high in this market, G's presence in other markets is limited and, consequently, it may be inferred that the two do not actively target one another's markets. An alternative explanation may equally be that, as members of two differing strategic groups, the oligopolistic reaction between A and G is less pronounced than between intra-cluster participants. In short, they do not consider contact with each other as significant because of their differing strategic characteristics and different customer profiles.

The measurement of contact through probability distributions is, therefore, important to differentiate between random and strategic locational choices. This is especially important given that the level of franchisee choice and franchisor assistance in locational issues varies from no assistance to adhering to a strict set of controls. For example, McDonald's selects the location, constructs the building, then leases the package to the franchisee (Boas and Chain, 1976; Felstead, 1993; Love, 1986). Despite such assistance, geographic expansion by franchised fast food chains has been suggested to be a random process because the spatial diffusion of units has not followed conventional rules (Laulajainen, 1987), such as matching specific socio-economic or demographic profiles of target populations. These findings have been corroborated by Jennings (1980), who came to the conclusion that McDonald's expansion across the USA between 1965 and 1978 was random. The chain entered different regions at different times, but did so without an underlying strategic rationale, other than to diffuse the brand. Accordingly, multi-market contact may be random because it is determined by the non-systematic actions of franchisees or by the parent foodservice company. It may also, however, be part of a wider corporate strategy designed at increasing spatial competition against specific rivals. If it is true that location is non-random and has strategic significance, the hypothesis that meetings among and between fast food and mid-spend restaurant cluster members are coincidental may not be credible – implying some strategic action on the part of the firms. Such meetings may not only serve to affect whether franchising is adopted, but the initial costs and ongoing fees associated with franchise-based expansion. It may also be apparent that where multi-market contact is high, the time difference between firm 1 and firm 2 embarking on franchising may be relatively short. Given this null hypothesis, the following text sets out Scott's (1982) methodology to operationalize the probability that firm 1 and firm 2 meet in f other markets.

$$\rho(f) = (C_{s2-1,f})(C_{n-2,s1-1,f})/(C_{n-1,s1-1}) \qquad [3]$$

where $s1$ refers to the number of markets in which firm 1 competes, and $s2$ is the number of markets in which firm 2 competes[5]. In this sense, and given that s is also a function of the number of stores, the measures are indicative of size, or mass. Thus, the motivation to franchise may be a function of a competitor's size at time t. According to Lapin (1993),

$C_{n,r} = n!/r!(n-r)!$; by transposing this function into the components of Scott's (1982) methodology, the following components of the probability model are evident:

$$C_{s2-1,f} \qquad = (s2-1)!/f!(s2-1-f)!; \qquad\qquad\qquad [4]$$

$$C_{n-2,s1-1,f} = (n-2)!/(s1-1-f)! \ (n-s2-s1+1+f)!; \text{ and} \qquad [5]$$

$$C_{n-1,s1-1} \qquad = (n-1)!/(s1-1)! \ (n-s1)! \qquad\qquad\qquad [6]$$

where the factorials are defined by: $0!=1$; $1!=1$; $2!=2*1$; $n!=n*(n-1)*(n-2)\ldots$ etc, and

$$C_{x,y} = 0, \text{ if } x < y \qquad\qquad\qquad\qquad\qquad\qquad [7]$$

By letting A equal the number of markets in which the firms actually meet, it is possible to compute the probability of observing less contact (PMMC) than A by summing the $\rho(f)$s from $f = 0$ to $A - 1$. For a complete analysis, the difference between the observed number of meetings and the mean of the probability distribution measured in standard deviations (ADEV) should be calculated:

$$\text{ADEV} = (A-\mu)/\{[\Sigma(f-\mu)^2]\rho(f)\}^{1/2} \qquad\qquad\qquad [8]$$

where μ signifies the mean number of contacts $\Sigma(f) \rho(f)$.

If the computation results in a high PMMC and a positive ADEV, then a random distribution throughout the firm's markets would imply a smaller number of contacts between firms than the number observed; in other words, a high PMMC indicates substantial strategic opportunities (Mester, 1987). Although not explored here, these variables could then be compared to the year in which the franchisors launched their franchises. The implications of whether multi-market contact is high or low, and the difference between the first mover and the followers entering franchising is presented in the matrix shown as Figure 4.3. It shows that there are three proxies which yield eight positional scenarios within a dyad:

1. multi-market contact;
2. oligopolistic reaction to franchising; and
3. the degree of strategic similarity between the firms.

The scenarios are as follows:

1. the time difference between two firms beginning to franchise is low, multi-market contact is high, and strategic distance between the dyad members is high. When applied to the decision to franchise, this situation suggests that the decision to franchise may have been inspired by inter-group rivalry;
2. the time difference between two firms beginning to franchise is low, multi-market contact is high, and strategic distance between the dyad members is low. This position suggests that the decision to franchise may have been inspired by intra-group rivalry;

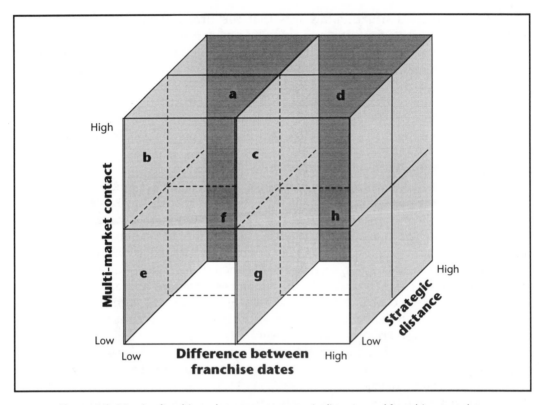

Figure 4.3: Matrix of multi-market contact, strategic distance and franchise start dates

3. where multi-market contact and the time difference is high, and strategic distance is low, the new franchise firm is a 'convert'. According to Carney and Gedajlovic (1991), these 'convert' firms typically begin operations as wholly owned chains, and after many years decide to begin franchising. Historically, these chains have not grown very quickly and franchising appears to be an expedient for growth;

4. the time difference between two firms beginning to franchise is high , multi-market contact is high, and strategic distance between the dyad members is low. This suggests that the franchise firm is a convert which may have been inspired by intra-group rivalry;

5. in the fifth quadrant, multi-market contact is low and the difference between strategically similar adopting franchising and being followed is low. This situation resembles Dollinger's (1990) scenario where a firm competes like, but not with, another cluster member. The new franchisor is likely to be a new entrant to a particular strategic group;

6. the sixth quadrant contains firms which illustrate low levels of multi-market contact and high levels of strategic distance, but little time difference between the dyad members adopting a franchise strategy. This situation suggests that an incumbent of one strategic group uses a firm in another cluster as a benchmark;

7. the time difference between two firms beginning to franchise is high, multi-market contact is low, and strategic distance between the dyad members is

low. This situation suggests that the firm franchise is either a long-established small chain or a single-unit business which has been prompted into expanding via franchising. Via examples of pre-World War II fast food activities, Chapter 1 illustrated that such firms in the USA include Bresler's, Brigham's Inc., KFC, Orange Julius, and The Krystal Co.;

8. the time difference between both dyad members being franchisors is high, multi-market contact is low, and strategic distance between the dyad members is high. This suggests that the two dyad members are non-competitors.

Multi-market contact and franchising

Do the levels of within-group multi-market contact differ? For comparative purposes, a one-way analysis of variance ($ANOVA$) test was used and a Kruskal-Wallis test was used to explore the null hypothesis that there are no multi-market contact differences within the six strategic groups. The difference is that the former method assumes that the sampled multi-market contact measures are normally distributed, whereas the latter is a non-parametric test. Since $F_{crit\alpha = 0.05} = 2.4$, the one-way $ANOVA$ results below illustrate that the computed F ratio of 2.22 is in the region of acceptance of the null hypothesis. Hence, it is possible to conclude, based on these sample results and at the 5% level of significance, there are no differences among the strategic groups in terms of multi-market contact. At a lower level of significance, however, the F ratio is in the region of rejection of the null hypothesis. From the Kruskal-Wallis test (where $df = 5$, $\alpha = 0.05$ and $\alpha = 0.10$), the result ($K = 10.889$), it is evident that the variability of multi-market contact within the strategic groups does not vary where $\alpha = 0.05$ ($\chi^2 = 11.07$), but does so at $\alpha = 0.1$ ($\chi^2 = 9.24$). From this latter result, therefore, it is apparent that rivalry varies more within some strategic groups than others.

Source of variation	df	Sum of squares	Mean square	F-ratio
Among strategic groups	5	1.11	0.222	2.22
Sampling error	49	4.907	0.10	
Total	54	6.017		

Table 4.4: One-way ANOVA results for strategic group membership and multi-market contact

The calculation of the multi-market contact measures also permits insight to the dynamics of the franchised and non-franchised strategic groups and, thereby, help to answer the following question: do franchises illustrate different levels of multi-market contact than non-franchised firms? As in the tests to explore the strategic distances between franchised and non-franchised firms, the null hypotheses are:

Test 1:   the multi-market contact among firms within a cluster of franchises is similar to that among non-franchised firms (that is, H_0: $\mu_1-\mu_2 = 0$; H_1: $\mu_1-\mu_2 \neq 0$).

Test 2:   the multi-market contact among firms within a cluster of franchises is similar to the contact between those firms and a cluster of non-franchised firms.

Test 3: the multi-market contact among firms who are non-franchised firms is similar to the contact between those firms and a cluster of franchised firms.

Using z-tests, where $\alpha = 0.05 = \pm 1.96$, indicates that there is no difference in the average multi-market contact within a group of franchised firms versus that within a cluster of non-franchised firms (the null hypothesis is accepted at $z = -0.778$). For Tests 2 and 3, as the null hypotheses are accepted ($z = -1.136$ and -0.3776 respectively) the average multi-market contact measures in the two latter tests are the same. In turn, these results help to suggest that the multi-market contacts are the same between clusters of firms as within them. From the sample, it seems that firms compete with both franchises and non-franchises. Although not presented here, these conclusions were confirmed by comparing the *ADEV* figures for the within- and between-group measures.

In order to test for the dual effects of strategic distance and multi-market contact on the decision to franchise, the within group effects were separated from the between group measures. As part of the process, two tests were conducted:

1. the role of strategic distance and multi-market contact as individual measures; and
2. the individual roles and the interaction between strategic distance and multi-market contact.

The tests have been calculated for dyads of firms as well as for individual firms. The results for the tests are summarized below. The statistic which examines the partial correlation between the dependent variables and each of the independent variables is the R statistic which can range from -1 to $+1$. A positive value indicates that as either multi-market value or strategic distance decreases (that is, moves closer to one), so does the likelihood of either the individual firm being franchised or both incumbent firms in the dyad are franchised. Small values of R indicate that each of the variables have a small partial contribution to the model. Thus, from Table 4.6, the negative values for the partial correlation results for R indicate that as firms become increasingly similar, the lower the likelihood of franchising occurring. The interaction between strategic and multi-market contact suggests that as the interaction between the variables increases, so does the likelihood of being franchised.

The coefficients within the logistic regression model are interpreted as the log odds associated with a one unit change in the independent variable. For example, the coefficient describing the effect of within group multi-market contact on the likelihood of an individual firm being franchised is 0.0007 (that is, virtually zero). This statistic suggests that when multi-market contact increases by one unit and the value of strategic group distance remains the same, the log odds of the firm being franchised is 0.0007 (or 0.07%). The Exp(β) value is the factor by which the odds changed.

Although there are several ways to test how well the model fits the data, here only two are presented. The first way is to assess how well the model compares with predictions to the observed outcomes through classification tables. The figures below (Tables 4.6 and 4.7) are the classification tables for the individual and dyad measures. From Table 4.6, seven observations between firms which were not franchised were correctly predicted by the model not to be franchised. Similarly, sixty-four observations which were franchised were correctly predicted to be franchised. The off-diagonal entries indicate how many observations were incorrectly classified. A total of thirty-five observations were

Variable	Beta	Standard error	Wald	df	R	Sig	Exp (β)
For indvidual firms							
Without interaction							
MMC	0.0007	0.002	0.1380	1	0.000	0.7103	1.0007
SD	−2.645	1.315	4.0410	1	−0.12	0.0444	0.0710
Constant	2.6321	1.023	6.6176	1		0.0101	
With interaction							
MMC	−16.308	5.6483	8.3363	1	−0.2160	0.0039	0.0000
SD	−17.682	5.8296	9.1999	1	−0.2302	0.0024	0.0000
Interaction	18.121	6.2759	8.3372	1	0.2160	0.0039	74110413
Constant	16.039	5.1696	9.6257	1		0.0019	
For dyads of firms							
Without interaction							
MMC	−2.9269	1.0481	7.7988	1	−0.2758	0.0052	0.0536
SD	−1.6873	1.8277	0.8523	1	0.0000	0.3559	0.1850
Constant	3.2697	1.6541	3.9076	1		0.0481	
With interaction							
MMC	−19.859	8.2720	5.7640	1	−0.2222	0.0164	0.0000
SD	−18.412	8.4430	4.7555	1	−0.1901	0.0292	0.0000
Interaction	21.0898	9.7594	4.6698	1	0.1871	0.0307	1.44E+09
Constant	16.8431	7.1890	5.4891	1		0.0191	

Table 4.5: Within Group Logistic Regression Analysis

Observed		Predicted		% correct
		0	1	
Not franchised	0	7	29	19.44
		(7)	(29)	(19.44)
Franchised	1	6	64	91.43
		(5)	(65)	(92.86)
Overall				66.98
				(67.92)

NB: figures in brackets refer to the interation between MMC and SD.

Table 4.6: Classification table for the 'individual' logistic regression analysis

misclassified in the test, twenty-nine who were classified as franchised and six who were not. Of the non-franchised observations, only 19% were correctly classified and, thus, the model is possibly limited. Of the franchised firms, over 90% were correctly classified. Overall, about two-thirds of the 105 observations were correctly classified.

By comparison, the within-group dyad-level analysis seems to illustrate a better fit. Almost 78% of dyads which contained one or both firms that were non-franchised were correctly classified, and 65% of dyads where both firms are franchised were correctly classified. Overall, about 71% of the fifty-five dyads were correctly classified. When the

Observed		Predicted		% correct
		0	1	
Not franchised	0	21	6	77.78
		(21)	(6)	(77.78)
Franchised	1	10	18	64.29
		(12)	(16)	(57.14)
Overall				70.91
				(67.27)

NB: figures in brackets refer to the interation between MMC and SD.

Table 4.7: Classification table for the 'dyad' logistic regression analysis

interaction between strategic distance and multi-market contact is considered, however, the number which are correctly classified as being franchised falls to about 57%.

The other way of assessing the goodness of fit of the model was to examine how 'likely' the sample results actually are given the parameter estimates. The probability of the observed results is the likelihood. As the likelihood is less than one, the logistic regression uses minus two times the log of the likelihood ($-2LL$) as a measure of how well the estimated model fits the data. A good model is defined as one which results in a high likelihood of the observed results, which computes to a small value for $-2LL$. For the logistic model that contains only the constant in the dyad, $-2LL$ is 76.22 and is 135.84 for the individual equation. Thus, the dyad model is superior than the latter one. When the goodness for fit for the model with all of the independent variables is examined, it is evident that the value of $-2LL$ is yet smaller.

Variable	Dyad only	Interaction	Individual only	Interaction
$-2LL$ for constant only	76.228	76.228	135.846	135.846
$-2LL$ for independent variables	66.211	59.694	130.670	116.629
Goodness for fit	53.978	48.678	105.756	92.496
Model χ^2	10.017	16.534	5.177	19.218
Improvement	10.017	16.534	5.177	19.218
Significance	0.0067	0.0009	0.0751	0.0002

Table 4.8: Goodness for fit statistics for the model

For the test exploring the impact of strategic distance and multi-market contact on the components of the franchise package, initially the degree of similarity of the packages was calculated. Subsequently, an imitation score was created to measure the degree of duplication, where dyads of franchise firms which exhibited similar offerings were classified as one, and zero otherwise. Unlike the above results, the partial correlation coefficient, R, is positive which suggests that as firms become increasingly similar and as they compete with each other, the franchise package increases in similarity. From the classification table, it is evident that about 65% of the observations were correctly classified, but the high $-2LL$ suggests that the model is not as good as some other alternative model.

Variable	Beta	Standard error	Wald	df	R	Sig	Exp (β)
Without interaction							
MMC	1.5804	0.6475	5.9577	1	0.1652	0.0147	4.8567
SD	1.7870	0.9610	3.4578	1	0.1002	0.0630	5.9715
Constant	−1.9099	0.6726	8.0642	1		0.0045	
With interaction							
MMC	3.2569	1.7974	3.2835	1	0.0941	0.0700	25.9697
SD	3.5054	1.9834	3.1238	1	0.0880	0.0772	33.2956
Interaction	−3.1291	3.0733	1.0366	1	0.0000	0.3086	0.0438
Constant	−2.8561	1.1904	5.7563	1		0.0164	

Table 4.9: Logistic regression analysis for components of sampled franchise packages

Observed		Predicted		% correct
		0	1	
Not franchised	0	41 (38)	15 (18)	73.21 (67.86)
Franchised	1	22 (15)	27 (34)	55.10 (69.39)
Overall				64.76 (68.57)

NB: figures in brackets refer to the interation between MMC and SD.

Table 4.10: Classification table for the 'franchise package' logistic regression analysis

Variable	Dyad only	Interaction
−2*LL* for constant only	145.0939	145.0939
−2*LL* for independent variables	135.584	134.524
Goodness for fit	104.966	106.902
Model χ^2	9.510	10.570
Improvement	9.510	10.570
Significance	0.0086	0.0143

Table 4.11: Goodness for fit statistics for the 'franchise package' model

Summary and conclusion

Via a purely exploratory study, this chapter has sought to provide a framework to enrich extant explanations of the decision to franchise through the use of the strategic group concept. To date, research has typically employed the franchise dyad or industry as the prime focus of analysis, rather than the strategic group taxonomy. Indeed, the decision to franchise and the factors behind the establishment of contractual fees in franchising has predominantly relied on the conceptualization of the franchise fraternity as an industry. Within this approach the variability in franchise fees, both between and within industries, has been attributed to differences in technology, extant brand capital, and the quantity and quality of franchisor services (Lafontaine and Shaw, 1996; Michael, 1996; Sen, 1993). Although instructive, the inconclusivity of previous empirical efforts and the failure to account for the effects of both strategic group dynamics and consideration of the role of non-franchised concerns, has undermined such research. By accounting for these variables, this chapter has suggested that the strategic distance between differing members of a cluster and the extent of multi-market contact serves to influence whether a firm may franchise and the associated fees. In so doing, the entry into franchising is seen as an extension of existing rivalry between firms, and it is viewed as having the potential to increase multi-market contact levels between existing group incumbents and new entrants. The group dynamics of franchising within a strategic group and the establishment of contractual fees begins with firm-specific effects but imitators tend to follow soon afterwards to negate potential competitive advantages, and it is this behaviour which may serve to affect the 'stickiness' of franchise fees. The chapter has also illustrated that different strategic groups have differing levels of complexity via the numbers of incumbents and different network relationships within each cluster.

Perhaps one of the main contributions from this chapter is the suggestion that the decision to franchise is not necessarily the result of rational behaviour as propounded by students of franchising with an economics bias. According to Gultman (1996), a rational actor is a player who chooses a best reply to the current population of strategies, but a mechanical actor is one who plays a fixed strategy which will not necessarily be a best reply to the population mix. From some of the data produced in this chapter, it is evident that some firms play a 'me-too' strategy. The degree to which such players are mechanical or rational is subject to debate, but it is evident that not all firms could be said to be rational. In turn, therefore, the research suggests that contributions from strategy discourse are needed to enrich extant explanations of the decision to franchise. In this sense, the decision to franchise is at the heart of much of the debate between economists and strategists concerning models of firm behaviour:

> The only well-worked-out, crisply predictive, and internally consistent theory of firm behaviour is that of rationale maximizing behaviour – the economist's model. Unfortunately, most students of strategy and organization believe it is wrong. The dominant view outside economics is that although organizational actions can usually be individually rationalized by various interested parties, the actions are not consistent, nor can they be expressed, taken as a whole, as the consequences of maximizing choices. It is this split that has generated most of the heat and friction between the perspectives of economics and organization studies. (Rumelt *et al*, 1994; p. 49)

Despite these contributions, the research is not complete. It has not, for example, focused on differing groupings within the franchise fraternity to yield a description of the similarities of franchise packages across industries and the stability of these clusters. In addition, only one measure of rivalry has been used, and other statistical techniques may well have yielded alternative conclusions. Nonetheless, the strategic group is an important concept permitting the modelling of different levels of competition within an industry and the potential for alliances and franchising to occur within certain clusters. For example, some evidence to suggest that fast food and mid-spend restaurants are comprised of differing groups has been provided. The intensity of multi-market competition was particularly acute within clusters (where strategic distance was small) rather than between groups, and especially among franchised concerns.

In spite of its potential use, the strategic group concept has numerous weaknesses. The divergent approaches to strategic group definition and research suggest that the process of theory development is in its infancy (Thomas and Venkatraman, 1988) and is characterized by insufficient theoretic underpinnings, inadequate model specification, the failure to test for a null hypothesis for strategic group membership and haphazard selection of strategic dimensions used to form groups (Reger and Huff, 1993). For example, it is possible to assign firms to differing strategic groups via altering the proxies for membership.

Other weaknesses include a failure to overtly consider the role of environmental factors in determining the number of performance variances amongst strategic groups. Although Primeaux (1985) and Miles *et al* (1993) provide some insight to strategic group dynamics and task environment considerations through reference to industry life-cycle effects, other aspects of the environment may be influential in determining the latitude for strategic choice and industry heterogeneity. In addition, therefore, to Barney and Hoskisson's (1990) call for the development of a theory devised at establishing strategic group existence, some research also is required to establish what environmental conditions lead to differences in strategic groups' population, formation, conduct and performance.

The concept of strategic groups, despite a plethora of limitations, is a useful analytic technique to examine the entry points and subsequent growth patterns of firms. Entry points to an industry are rarely a 'Yes-No' choice (Caves and Porter, 1977; McDougall and Robinson, 1990) rather, entry decisions are made according to the conclusions of an assessment of the market mix configurations and strategic assets of existing incumbents. Once entered, decisions are then made about pursuing a particular growth trajectory, which may lead the firm to exit one strategic and enter another. As part of this entry and exit behaviour, the firm will either be a leader or follower. In turn, these behaviours mean that some firms are constantly shifting and that their strategic groups take different shapes and sizes, rather like shoals of shifting fish as the incumbents act and react to various competitive stimuli and opportunities for increasing status through resource monopolization and the accumulation of capital.

Case Study 6:
Quests for competitive advantages in the UK sandwich sector

There are differing types of suppliers to the retail sandwich market. These range from those which produce the final product to those that supply ingredients, fillings, packaging and the bread itself. The focus of this case study is to outline the contours of three separate but inter-related features of the UK sandwich manufacturing sector and show some of the strategic options currently employed, and those which could be employed to help realize competitive advantages and surmount three structural features of the sector:

1. fragmentation;
2. low profitability;
3. high threat of entry.

Aspects of the UK sandwich market

When researchers examine industries, they typically employ the Standard Industrial Classification (SIC) scheme and have, thereby, possibly constrained their analysis. The fuzzi-ness/blurring of industry boundaries mean that SIC is only successful at a broad and coarse level (Brooks, 1995; Clarke, 1989) suggesting that, as far as retailing is concerned, an alterna-tive approach is necessary. A product-orientated definition of a market, combined with the notion that catering is, in essence, a form of retailing, permits a more fine-grain analysis of the sandwich market and to examine the part played by entrants extending their existing product lines to include sandwiches. Using this approach, a sandwich is any product conforming to the following definition: bread with a cold filling which is served open or wrapped and is purchased from a commercial outlet. Bread in this context refers to rolls, baps, cobs, mini-cottage loaves, french sticks, croissants, ready cut and sliced bread. The fact that the filling is cold differenti-ates it from products such as hamburgers, toasted sandwiches, and hot meat sandwiches.

Within the sandwich market, the inclusion of those employing product extension strategies is particularly important because they account for over three-quarters of the volume of sandwiches sold in Britain and a large proportion of the sector's growth in retail value from £1.1 billion in 1990 to over £2 billion in 1995. It has given rise to the emergence of sandwich manufacturing activities and the dominance of ready-made sandwiches and the decline of tailor-made/customized sandwiches from sandwich bars. Part of the reason for their involve-ment is due to the continuing trend towards snacking and informality at lunchtime, as well as shorter lunch periods. This importance of non-specialist retailers suggests that the nature of competition in the market has changed. As noted in Case Study 3, rivalry within retail markets can be of two forms: intratype (that is, competition among retailers of essentially the same type, for example McDonald's and Burger King) and intertype (that is competition with firms from a variety of retail settings and strategically dissimilar companies). It is evident that com-petition within the sandwich market and, indeed the fast food industry as a whole, has moved from being intratype to intertype with the main thrusts deriving from supermarkets and retail bakeries. The extent to which such retailers have moved into the sandwich market may be quantified. Since a fast food outlet is any retail selling generically defined fast food product[6] (Price, 1993), the extent to which they do this is measured by a specialization ratio and is used to categorize different types of fast food retailer, as defined below:

1. *Specialists:* retail outlets which derive at least 75% of total sales from the sale of fast food products. The sale of fast food is considered to be the business's primary or single aim. Operations in this category include McDonald's, Subway, KFC, and Burger King, among others;

2. *Halfway-houses:* retail outlets which derive between 36% to 74% of total turnover from fast food products. The remainder of sales derives from the sale of other types of products (not fast food). Examples of operations in this category include retail bakeries.

3. *Non-specialists:* retail outlets which derive up to 35% of total sales from fast food products, but at least 65% from other products. Examples of operations in this category include garage forecourts, public houses, and supermarkets.

It is also possible to envisage the sandwich market, as well as other markets (for example, fruiterers and off-licences), as comprising these three distinct categories. This framework suggests that the sandwich market is highly fragmented and that this situation is not just apparent within each category but generally. Within the market, fragmentation is most prominent in the specialist and non-specialist categories. The 'halfway house' category exhibits a degree of concentration and vertical integration which is not necessarily apparent in other sectors of the fast food industry.

Analyzing the structure of the retail sector of the market, Figure 4.4 separates the specialists into two groups, membership of which depends upon the extent of standardization and consistency between the retail concepts. The 'hard brands' are those which illustrate high levels of standardization in decor, corporate identity, service levels, market niche and product quality. The main characteristics of the hard brands include:

1. consistent, precisely specified, and equally portioned food;
2. product not made to order, but part of a pre-set menu;
3. staff have organized routines with precise job specifications;
4. operation planned for large throughput and sales volume;
5. exacting hygiene standards;
6. ongoing product research;
7. products distinctively packaged and easy to handle;
8. high levels of product variety either in one product category, such as sandwiches, or several;
9. defined customer segments; and
10. good locations and promotion.

The 'soft brands' only possess a few of these characteristics, but both types of specialist operation illustrate some degree of product diversity because their product mixes appear to be built around sandwiches, cookies, croissants, soup, bagels, ice-cream, and doughnuts.

Fragmentation

Like the retail end of the market, the sandwich manufacturing segment is highly regionalized, fragmented, and has low barriers to entry. Hence, although the market has illustrated substantial volume and value growth, the top four companies supply no more than 17% of the sandwiches sold in the UK. Below these firms are many producing between 1,000 and

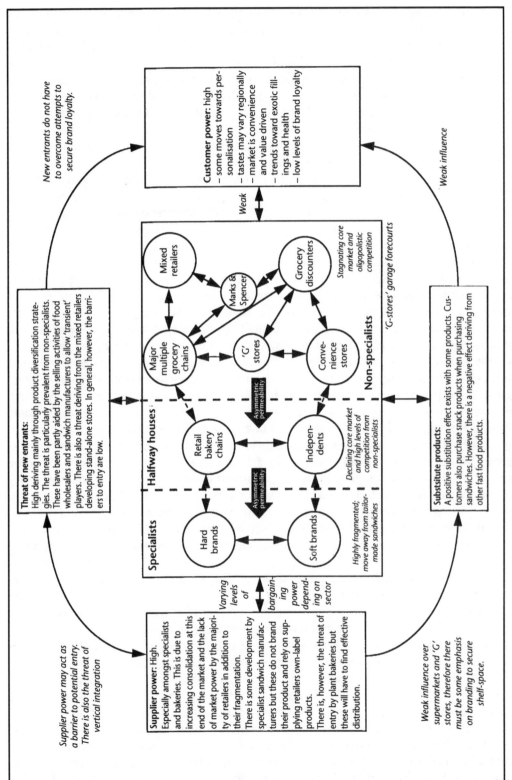

Figure 4.4: Structure of the UK sandwich retail sector

100,000 sandwiches per week, usually distributing them to retailers locally or regionally. Many of the smaller manufacturing companies are under-capitalized and lack the managerial and/or financial resources of the larger manufacturers, and are often forced to supply distribution routes which are often uneconomic – especially as many retailers are demanding sale-or-return guarantees in their contract negotiations. As a result of access to better resources, there is evidence to suggest that the barriers to entry and the levels of bargaining power enjoyed by some producers is increasing and that the sector is becoming polarized. For example, some of the major sandwich manufacturing plants have been instrumental in raising product quality in pre-prepared sandwiches and by generating almost constant demand through a diverse customer base.

One of the key barriers to entry lies in the securing of contracts from large, multi-site clients such as the major grocery retailers, contract caterers, hospitals, universities, and department stores. Secured distribution routes has led to some concentration on improved efficiency through standardized tasks, asking material suppliers to deliver materials to specification (bread manufacturers, for example, have to produce special loaves that will fit into laminated packaging), defined operations, the use of correct equipment, maintenance by anticipation, inspection in line with operations, balanced production lines, and working to quality standards. These standards are increasingly determined by the retailers as well as the necessity to gain competitive advantages. Nonetheless, all of these activities are barriers to entry and have led sandwich manufacturing to being increasingly capital intensive and quality conscious. There has also been increased legislation regarding food safety (for example, the Food Safety Act, 1990) and, because of issues concerning the durability of sandwiches, distribution and chilled storage has become increasingly significant. Of course, some manufacturers are being assisted in this process by equipment manufacturers and designers through machinery which, for example, monitors the efficiency of a whole host of products – which serves to eliminate waste. As sandwiches have been perceived to be highly perishable, this has largely precluded sole supply agreements between manufacturers and multi-site customers operating on a national basis and the development of a national brand of sandwich. As a consequence, some manufacturers have sought joint ventures in order to help maximize their position whereby each participant is responsible for a particular territory and are co-ordinated to produce a branded product. Unfortunately, such activity among the larger concerns has tended not to be overly developed due to lack of trust and uncertainty concerning the potential rewards.

Although the market has seen the emergence of large producers, the majority of sandwich manufacturers, however, are single owner/operator organizations without rigorous production standards and manufacturing know-how to conform to health and safety legislation. Indeed, the Consumer's Association magazine *Which?* found that more than 40% of the sandwiches it tested were unfit for consumption. Furthermore, sandwich production in such units tends to be labour intensive and therefore productive efficiency may not be high. Parts of these quality issues are symptomatic of low levels of profitability and the use of cost-cutting exercises to increase margins. Such manufacturers, therefore, appear to be more interested in gaining short-term advantages rather than necessarily developing their position in the marketplace through the nurturing of competitive advantages based on reputation. Competition, instead, appears to be cost-orientated (especially, like the plant bakery market, as the cost of raw materials is increasing) rather than on differentiating either products and/or service and may have detrimental consequences. Ensuring a low cost base sometimes encourages producers to fail to invest in safety. Part of the focus on the short term is also a result of the low levels of return experienced in the market which, in turn, is symptomatic perhaps of retailer power, industry fragmentation, lack of managerial sophistication, and the lack of differentiated products.

Low profitability

Although low profitability among sandwich producers mirrors the UK food manufacturing sector generally and the private-label producers in particular, the British Sandwich Association (BSA) estimates that the profit realized by sandwich manufacturers is about 3% (that is, lower than the rate of interest), whilst that realized by the retailer is about 30%. Furthermore, the cost of making and selling a sandwich in a sandwich bar/baker's shop is lower than that made from selling ready-made sandwiches at, for example, garage forecourts. As a result of the low margins, rising barriers to entry, increasing levels of competitive rivalry and lack of managerial sophistication within the sandwich manufacturing sector, many of the smaller players will be either shaken out or acquired.

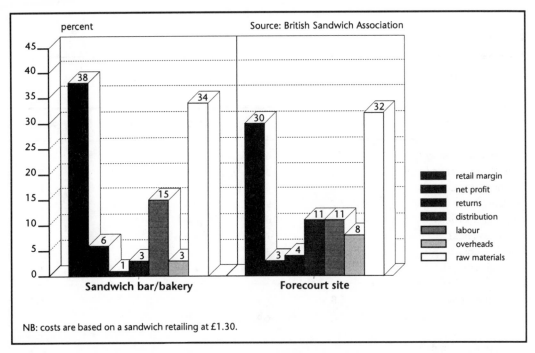

Figure 4.5: Cost breakdowns of sandwiches: sandwich bars/bakers' shop versus garage forecourt

The financial performance of some of the larger sandwich manufacturers confirms the pressure on profitability. Although average sales of the eight sampled firms have more than doubled over the period, trading profit margins are relatively low in comparison to the average margins realized by food manufacturers in Britain. The average trading profit margin in 1993/1994, for example, was only about 7%, and has been in decline for the majority of firms.

High threat of entry

Depending upon the height and nature of entry barriers and market attractiveness, most markets confront possible threats to entry. The UK sandwich manufacturing market confronts competition from a broad spectrum of players ranging from made-to-order retailers to plant bakers, and is exacerbated by the low levels of profitability experienced in the sector. The

Company	94/93	93/92	92/91	91/90	90/89
Britannia Catering	1,582	1,235	593	–	–
Buckingham Foods	43,046	39,134	26,723	22,535	13,781
Consultant Caterers	6,166	5,567	5,267	4,909	3,929
Henry Telfer	23,582	23,895	22,538	20,461	20,527
Smedley's Foods	14,381	12,990	14,200	13,128	11,158
Solway Foods	27,429	20,265	13,285	8,923	4,559
Toft Foods	2,712	1,928	931^	–	389
Wrights of York	15,376	11,978	10,485	9,374	2,878
Total	134,274	116,992	94,022	79,330	57,221
Average	16,784	14,624	11,753	11,333	8,174

Source: Company data
A = 65 weeks.

Table 4.12: Sales (£000's) of some major UK sandwich manufacturers, 1989–94

Company	94/93	93/92	92/91	91/90	90/89
Britannia Catering	5.2	6.7	−5.9	–	–
Buckingham Foods	5.8	5.6	5.9	4.6	5.5
Consultant Caterers	6.2	4.6	5.8	6.6	2.9
Henry Telfer	7.2	9.6	10.0	9.6	10.6
Smedley's Foods	9.4	10.7	18.8	16.6	15.2
Solway Foods	6.4	7.8	7.0	4.5	0.7
Toft Foods	6.3	6.1	2.7^	–	18.8
Wrights of York	8.0	8.1	7.1	−20.3	3.8
Sample average	6.8	7.4	6.4	3.1	8.2
UK food manufacturers' average	8.0	7.8	7.9	8.2	8.2

Source: Company data.
A = 65 weeks.

Table 4.13: Trading margin (%) of some major UK sandwich manufacturers, 1989–94

made-to-order sandwich retailers are typically small businesses – generating, on average, sales of less than £750,000 a year. As such, they are not a substantial threat to sandwich manufacturers. Of more significance are the plant bakeries because they are a threat to both sandwich manufacturers and retailers alike (see Case Study 5). The threat to sandwich manufacturers in particular, derives from, first, the move to value-added products such as morning goods, ethnic breads, and pizza bases; second, their substantial production experience and know-how; and third, their existing relationships with retailers – especially the grocery multiples. The move to value-added products has been instigated by eight inter-connected aspects:

- low retail prices and the rising costs of raw materials;
- low levels of bargaining power with the supermarket multiples;
- over-capacity;
- declining consumption of bread;
- declining efficiency;
- low investment in advertising and marketing;
- lack of brand standardization and marketing economies within their retail units;
- lack of a retail culture and electronic point of sale.

In addition to supplying sandwiches, the bakers are slowly realizing that it is their retail outlets which are also one of the keys to maximizing productive capacity in manufacturing through implementing those features and strategies which drive volume and improve margins through transaction pricing. Ultimately, realizing the potential that may exist within their retail units can be achieved through either the centralization, standardization, and co-ordination of the retail units through specialist retail divisions or divesting the retail outlets to specialist retail management, but maintaining supply agreements between the parties.

Strategic options

The existence and effects of these three inter-related factors suggests that competitive advantages must be sought in order to realize long-term profitability. There are several options which may help to realize such advantages. According to Kay (1993), these value-adding options fall into four categories: architecture, innovation, reputation, and the possession of strategic assets. These involve the following:

1. *Architecture* is a system of relationships within the firm, or between the firm and its divisions, suppliers, and customers. It includes sole supply agreements with retailers, franchising, licensing, strategic alliances, and joint ventures.
2. *Innovation* can be a source of value added, but is often linked to architecture, and is dependent upon the ease of imitation, whether it is continuous, the nature of the organizational climate, and the reward systems to encourage suggestions. The nature of innovation is also partially dependent on the life-cycle stage of the firm and its industry. For example, within the context of the mature UK food market, there was a total of 16,400 new products introduced through the major multiple grocers between 1991 and 1994 (Dixon *et al*, 1995). Over the same period, the number of new products has increased by an average rate of 14% a year;
3. *Reputation* is gained through customer experience of the product and its quality (a particular problem within the sandwich market) and is essentially developed through the brand management process.
4. The ownership of *strategic assets* refers to the distinctive capabilities of the firm and is realized from the possession of economies of scale, the possession of sole supply agreements/large continuous supply contracts, capital investments, through reputation and market/technical knowledge and via strategic action (Amit and Shoemaker, 1993). These strategic assets are influenced by a firm's architecture, innovation, and reputation. Within the sandwich manufacturing sector, some of the larger firms' key strategic assets are the contracts and relationships (some could be construed to be supply partnerships) they possess to supply the major grocery multiples and other large retailers.

As a result of the linkage between strategic assets and the first three sources of competitive advantage, the following paragraphs only explore issues concerned with architecture, reputation, and innovation.

Architecture

It is recognized that there is a variety of potential markets for ready-made sandwiches. There are, however, several key markets as potential/existing buyers for sandwiches: multiple grocers, catering, takeaway units, work places (via contract caterers), CTNs and garage forecourt operations. Placing products within each of these markets requires different methods and organization of sales effort, and impact on the middleman's activities (or how value is added by the middleman). Each of these retail sectors have different structures (ranging from concentrated to fragmented), degrees of competitive rivalry, buyer behaviour and requirements. Companies in fragmented industries typically have little bargaining power with large purchasing chains (Porter, 1980). Buying behaviour, however, throughout an industry is rarely homogenous. The following diagram (Figure 4.6), in recognizing a continuum of supply within the sandwich market, indicates that a range of supplier bargaining positions exist; these range from being minimal amongst the major supermarket multiples to being greater among the small chains and independents. This situation often requires suppliers to identify and respond to the characteristics of each market and adopt contingent supply strategies and structures. The diagram shows the pattern of distribution within the hospitality and retail industry, and indicates that while the national operators may be fewer in number than their more regionalized counter-parts, they have greater bargaining power. For the manufacturer, there is the necessity to be able to consistently supply these retailers according to contractually agreed volumes at the right quality and at the right time and deliver them direct, rather than through warehouses and other distributive nodes in the supply chain. Smaller retail operations require lower levels of volume and this necessitates small drops to be made to a number of sites and often the buyers are owner/operators. This situation means that while supplying retailers with a national geographic scope is an attractive proposition because of the volumes of product passing through such operators may be sufficient to drive economies of scale, it entails higher capabilities and managerial competences but lower latitude for negotiation. In dealing with the major retail grocers, for example, suppliers have responded by:

1. developing national/key accounts which have the responsibility of servicing and selling to small numbers of retail buyers;
2. centralizing their distribution;
3. undertaking product differentiation and above-the-line advertising to jump-over-the-shoulders of retailers and thereby secure market access;
4. supplying own/private-label products; and
5. acquiring other food suppliers.

In turn, this situation means that the smaller manufacturer is left with a paradox: in order to be in the running to supply the nationally-orientated retailer they may have to invest in additional productive capacity, but may be reluctant to make such investments without having contracts to help finance them. Furthermore, the smaller operators are under increasing pressure because the larger manufacturers are seeking to drive volume and economies of scale and higher margins through targeting smaller, regionally-based retail chains.

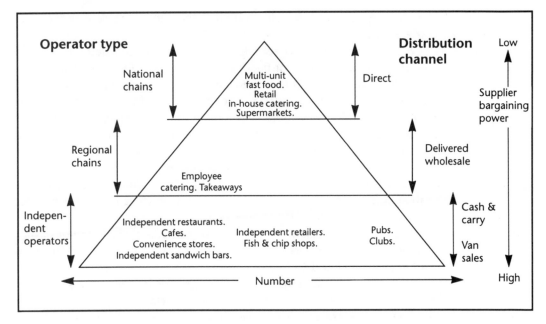

Figure 4.6: *Distribution patterns in the food industry*

Operating in a fragmented market and supplying to largely atomistically structured retail groups has generated a variety of architectural solutions (not all successful) by sandwich manufacturers to increase their size and bargaining power. These solutions have included the development of marketing consortia and franchising. Within both of these, the prime cause of failure has been the pursuit of self-interest over and above the objectives of the entire group. Furthermore, the sandwich manufacturer's franchise offerings have rarely been scrutinized, subjected to feasibility studies, have generally been founded on ill-conceived principles and weak businesses, and none have been members of the BFA (association membership is construed by some to be a symbol of quality). In turn, this situation points to the lack of management cultures orientated towards strategic alliances or franchising. Others have chosen to broaden their brand dissemination through taking an equity stake in selected sandwich manufacturers, who then produce a pre-negotiated proportion of their total output according to the specifications of the equity-holder. The BSA propounds that a potential solution to the industry fragmentation issue, namely networking, may arise from the following series of changes already manifest in the market:

1. The concentration of manufacturing expertise around specialist regional production units with the resources to meet legislative requirements and economics in purchasing, distribution, and marketing. The development of gaining national presence may be achieved through licensing, franchising, and joint venture agreements.
2. The introduction of minimum order values for direct deliveries. As managerial focus is concentrated on increased technological improvements to facilitate product consistency, meet health and safety requirements, productive efficiency and reduced wastage, so the focus on distribution will change from being handled in-house to third parties specializing in distribution. The introduction of

minimum order values should help distributors to establish the viability of certain customer groups;

3. The development of van sales networks. As part of the process described above, there may be an opportunity for the development of van sales and deliveries to increase the level of penetration among individual owner-operator catering and retail businesses, whilst the larger deliveries are handled by larger concerns. The van sales could, subject to favourable feasibility studies, operate on a franchised basis. Out-sourcing distribution in this way should reduce overhead costs and increase profitability. As seen from the cost analysis of sandwiches above, the issue of distribution costs has become an important factor in determining the amount of profit generated per sandwich. It is here that volume and market share are also of importance due to the cost advantages which can accrue. Such cost advantages may derive from the following areas:

    a) Fixed costs: when a distributor's fixed costs (including management salaries and depreciation) are spread over more units as volumes increase, the fixed cost of each unit handled falls.

    b) Delivery costs: increased market share indicates an increase in sales per customer, in which case the fixed cost of a single delivery is spread over more volume, or an increase in customers, in which case the drive time between customers may fall as distances between customers is shorter.

    c) Efficient use of capital: larger facilities such as lorries and warehouse capacity, designed to handle higher volumes, do not generally increase in capital costs in proportion to capacity.

4. The growing role of middlemen and brands. There is a variety of roles for middlemen and these roles are, in part, determined by the structure of the market. The following paragraphs outline these roles.

The independence of middlemen may be preferred over consortia or other third-party agreements, but their position may be also affected by manufacturers developing strongly differentiated products to jump over their shoulders. Within the context of the sandwich market, where many buyers exist as well as many suppliers of 'me-too' (or non-differentiated) products, the role of middlemen is typically the 'independent-specialized' one. This term describes the situation where the middleman is required to perform requested logistics services as well as have good sourcing channels. Critical are:

- the creation of full menus of product type and filling;
- effective use of direct profitability techniques to establish the profitability of products and customer groups;
- the use of sophisticated information technology systems to link the business processes of the different players in the distribution chain and create a quick response service; and
- creative and innovative power to modernize and upgrade the services offered, add new products, and to professionalize the organization on a permanent basis.

To some degree diversified wholesalers (that is, non-specialized sandwich wholesalers/middlemen) are also becoming involved in the supply of sandwiches. They already supply caterers with ingredients for a host of products, including sandwiches, but of late have developed a package of sandwich ingredients which permits a variety of retailers to enter the sandwich retail sector with relative ease. Developments from specialist sandwich wholesalers include the recent introduction of two wholesale sandwich brands. These branded products are designed to appeal to retailers, who can promote and advertise the products, through the use of point-of-sale merchandising activity, more effectively than non-branded items. Others will undoubtedly follow in due course.

Although shelf-life considerations and the pursuit of self-interest have tended to preclude the development of branded sandwiches, the actions of some retailers may serve to reduce industry fragmentation. For example, one national petrol forecourt operator has established a network of sandwich producers to supply its sites and has concentrated some of its managerial resources to co-ordinate and control these manufacturers. Such resources are necessary as there is pressure on retailers to ensure, as part of their due diligence to establish that the products are fit for human consumption, that the sandwiches they distribute are of a sufficiently high standard and conform to legal requirements. The type of networking activity that the forecourt operator has instigated is called a 'constellation'. According to Shepherd (1991), a constellation is a particular type of network characterized by the presence of a leading firm able to co-ordinate a series of smaller operators who work together with the leading firm to produce and sell products of a particular standard and according to specified recipes. This type of growth and method of overcoming industry fragmentation is, therefore, characterized by a leading firm establishing a network of firms, all with a high degree of dependence on the leading organization. Typically, the leading firm will maintain control of certain key matters, such as product quality, image and marketing strategy, to control the group.

Although the development of constellations is at an embryonic stage within the UK sandwich manufacturing sector, the organizational form may eventually be able to realize competitive advantages founded on reputation and innovation. Within the Italian textile sector, for example, similar structures exist but they have been developed to the extent that they have become characterized by a high input of product innovation, as stimulated by a relatively shallow pyramid of power within the constellation. The structure, therefore, permits the constellation to be particularly competitive where an element of innovation and differentiation in the product is beneficial. Finally, constellation growth allows the firm to grow with reduced investment risk.

To some extent, the actions of manufacturers and middlemen alike in seeking potential markets for sandwiches to drive their volume and economies of scale, increases the volatility and instability at the retail end of the market. Research shows that the greater the number of incumbents in a market, the greater the degree of competitive rivalry (Porter, 1985). The effect of this new competition and the convergence of retail supply through the product diversity moves of non-specialists has increased the volatility of the sandwich market. It is clear, by virtue of the number of sandwich retailers, combined with other factors – such as the ease with which machinery replaces labour, stock accumulation, short production times, and customer self-service – means that the sector's degree of responsiveness is also possibly greater than realized hitherto. This means that when demand is high, existing suppliers can quickly satisfy that demand and, equally, when demand falls the barriers to exit are low (and possibly getting lower through the development of 'sale and return' policies by some manufacturers). This flexibility can be observed by the emergence of 'transient' players within the industry. Rather than become fully fledged sandwich retailers, some retail operations have entered the sandwich market through purchasing pre-packaged sandwiches from cash-and-carry organizations and supplying hot snacks in addition to ready-to-eat sandwiches. Most of these operations are only in the retail sandwich market for an average of ten hours per week. This purchasing method is, fundamentally, a low-cost approach to competing in the market because the costs amount to those associated with stock and labour. These can be off-set against the store's other activities.

Innovation and reputation

Despite dealing with a product which is very flexible in terms of the number and types of fillings which can be used, the level of new product activity within the sector appears to be very low. According to Dixon *et al* (1995), there were, on average, 143 new sandwich products a year sold through the major supermarkets between 1991 and 1994. These new sandwich products account for about 3.5% of all new products sold through the multiples during the same period. The lack of product differentiation suggests that on the whole, sandwich manufacturers have become commodity producers. For the large part, the only 'brands' that exist are retailer private label ones and within this the greatest proportion (80%) of the out-of-home sandwiches consumed in Britain are the non-exotic varieties. Indeed, the prawn mayonnaise, chicken, and BLT sandwich are the most popular varieties bought in the UK, and account for over 30% of total retail volumes (Taylor Nelson/AGB, 1995). Yet, selling non-differentiated products is only one option of how to compete in this market. Like othe products, sandwich manufacturers have, fundamentally, four competitive options. These options are based on two dimensions of differentiation: product content and product image (Mathur, 1986). Product content is about what the merchandise will do for the customer, whilst product image is about what it will say about the customer. For example, when a firm manufactures products which have the same content as those of its competitors, differentiation is based on what the firm says about the products. Using these two dimensions, the differing types of sandwiches could be:

1. *Exclusive:* in this instance, the manufacturer produces sandwiches known to be differentiated in content (that is, fillings, quality, bread, etc.) from those offered by other firms. The products are also differentiated on image through branding, advertising, and promotion. These types of product are yet to emerge with any force in the sandwich market.
2. *Special:* attempting to market sandwiches in this way is trying to make customers aware of their innovative and special fillings. The products are not advertised or necessarily branded. This option is one that relates to the made-to-order varieties in sandwich bars, but is also being pursued by some manufacturers (especially the smaller producers);
3. *Augmented:* in this instance, the products are not differentiated in the content or fillings, but on branding and promoting standard products. As mentioned above, there has been some movement to this type of provision; and
4. *Standard:* in this case, the firm does not attempt to differentiate the sandwiches either on the basis of special fillings or image. That is, it is a commodity. This is the position of the majority of sandwich manufacturers.

Conclusion

This Case Study has attempted to show that the structure of the sandwich manufacturing sector is changing. This change derives from the trend towards polarization between large and small players, as well as the potential ease of entry to the market. Of increasing significance are the changes occurring through pressures on profitability, especially by those unable to secure large contracts. It has forced some incumbents to seek as many avenues to market as possible and has, thereby, increased the volatility of the retail sector by virtue of increasing the total number of retail suppliers. As a consequence of such action, it is useful to think of the retail sandwich market as comprising three distinct types of players: specialists, halfway houses, and non-specialists. It is expected that, as a result of increased volatility, there will be increased pressure for differentiation and industry consolidation. Because of these structural aspects, there are several strategic options available to manufacturers which could also have the effect of altering the nature of competition from one based on price to that founded on continuous innovation to permit ongoing differentiation, and competitive advantage.

Notes

1. That is, researchers have described the collective of the franchise channel of distribution as an industry, rather than perhaps being more emphatic of the more strategic issues.

2. Performance issues are also central to industrial economic frameworks, in which variables such as market concentration and entry barriers (Rumelt, 1991; Shepherd, 1972) have long been used as explanations for variances in industry performance. It is suggested that performance and strategy should vary mostly across industries and sectors, rather than within them. In this vein, the franchise industry has lower rates of failure than other economic sectors, and higher rates of return on investment than other industries because all of the incumbent firms have employed the same broadly defined growth strategy, and have used franchising as a method of reducing risk and the capital expenditure associated with company-owned growth. This observation of lower rates of failure has yet to be independently corroborated (Kaufmann, 1996), and there appears to be some concern over the rigour of comparing the performance of the franchise industry with other industries. Strictly, it is illogical to say that the franchise fraternity *per se* illustrates superior performance than other industries because the comparison is not between like incumbents. Rather, the focus of performance comparisons must occur between firms operating within the same SIC defined industry in order to be meaningful (see Chapter 8). When this approach is explored, it is possible to investigate the conditions which may permit franchises to illustrate superior performance than their non-franchised counterparts. In so doing, however, a contribution may be made to an ongoing debate to determine whether strategic homogeneity or strategic heterogeneity yields superior performance. Attempting to resolve this debate, Dooley *et al* (1996) argued that both strategic heterogeneity and strategic homogeneity yield profits and that the position to be avoided is not homogeneity or heterogeneity, but the middle ground between the two extremes. It is conceivable, therefore, that by allocating firms from various industries to groups by the growth vehicle they employ (franchising, tenancies, joint ventures, consortia, etc.), different industries and sub-sectors have differing levels of variety because franchising has varying degrees of legitimation. Within the confines of Dooley *et al*'s (1996) conclusions, heterogeneous industries will yield superior performance and so will those which are homogeneous. Accordingly, where franchising (for example) is either the dominant or

non-dominant growth vehicle, higher performance will ensue. Where industries have moderate levels of strategic variety, or where franchising is just one of several growth options pursued within an industry setting, lower performance will result.

3. As franchises are differentiated from their non-franchised counterparts by these scope and resource commitments, it could be argued that they comprise a strategic group within a particular industry sub-market. When multiplied across an industry, a franchise hierarchy may be conceputalized. One such hierarchy for the hospitality industry is depicted below (Figure 4.7), and shows the differing layers comprising its structure. Within each sub-sector various groups of organizations are presented. From these differing strategic group members, assumed to be franchisors and non-franchised concerns, the degree of diffusion is apparent by the differing sub-sectors and sectors comprising an industry. Where franchising is employed by all incumbent firms of a sub-sector or sector, that particular industry division is a strategic group; where only one firm is franchised that business is a strategic group. At an industry level, therefore, the diffusion of franchising is, simply, the aggregate number of franchisors relative to the population of non-franchisors. At a broad macro-level, the number of franchisors is the total number of firms (operating in differing sub-industries) in an economy.

4. Reflecting this situation, the subsequent diagram (Figure 4.8) shows the UK supermarkets' form of involvement in the fast food/mid-spend restaurants. The diagram shows that the supermarkets do not exist in isolation but are involved in a wide competitive battle. They are able to offer credibility to each of the markets they enter because consumers in Britain have become increasingly discerning, which leads to their receptivity to the better service providers applying their capabilities across product categories.

5. In addition to having an application to two independently run firms, the methodology could also be employed to examine the degree of intra-system competition between franchise-operated outlets and their company-owned counterparts.

6. As noted in Case Study 3, Price (1991; 1993) suggests that fast food retail is defined as the sale of an end, or finished product, which comprises of four basic and generic elements:

a) low relative monetary price;

b) the end product is served quickly, for example two to fifteen minutes for onsite products and about thirty minutes for home delivery;

c) the product is suitable for eating with the fingers, has disposable packaging and, where applicable, disposable cutlery; and

d) finished product durability (such as maintenance of heat, nutritional value, etc.) of minutes and hours, as opposed to longer for snack foods.

Since this definition was formulated, several subsequent publications, such as Ball (1996), have illustrated more elongated and wordy versions, but which retain the essence of the product-orientated approach.

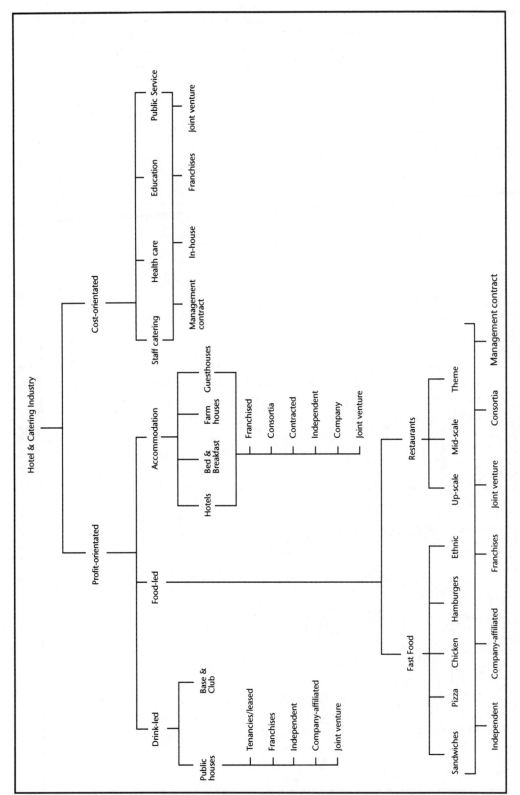

Figure 4.7: *Structure of the hospitality industry*

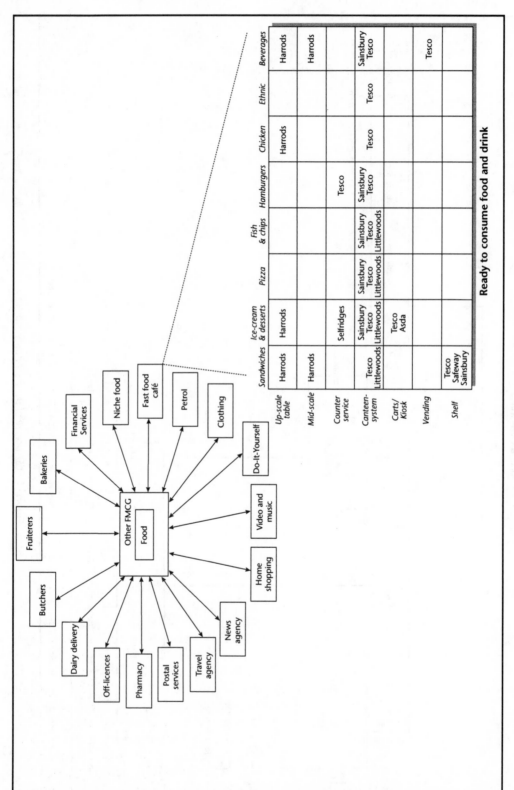

Figure 4.8: Product mix of UK supermarkets and their involvement in catering

	Sandwiches	Ice-cream & desserts	Pizza	Fish & chips	Hamburgers	Chicken	Ethnic	Beverages
Up-scale table	Harrods	Harrods				Harrods		Harrods
Mid-scale	Harrods							Harrods
Counter service		Selfridges			Tesco			
Canteen-system	Tesco Littlewoods	Sainsbury Tesco Littlewoods	Sainsbury Tesco Littlewoods	Sainsbury Tesco Littlewoods	Sainsbury Tesco	Tesco	Tesco	Sainsbury Tesco
Carts/ Kiosk		Tesco Asda						
Vending								Tesco
Shelf	Tesco Safeway Sainsbury							

Ready to consume food and drink

5 | To franchise or not to franchise? A careers approach to franchisee purchase decisions[1]

Opportunities are everywhere. The recession might be drawing to a close, but its continuing legacy is employers' reliance on short-term staff. There may be fewer jobs for life, but there are more jobs in a lifetime.

Lucy Benington, British journalist, *Cosmopolitan*

One can present people with opportunities. One cannot make them equal to them.

Rosamond Lehman, British novelist, *Ballad and the Source*

Introduction

Research attempting to analyze the creation of franchise systems has typically focused on franchisor motivation, with the main arguments of agency theory and resource constraints becoming increasingly well-rehearsed. By contrast, the situations and reasons of individuals (rather than corporate entities) influencing them to become franchisees have received scant attention (Peterson and Dant, 1990; Stanworth and Kaufmann, 1994). In spite of a trend toward the recruitment of corporate franchisees to realize greater brand penetration in non-traditional sites and the selling of units to investor franchisees, individual-operator franchisees are the main focus of franchisor recruitment attention and effort. The costs of attracting and recruiting these individuals may be prohibitive: there are the costs of solicitors, advertising, training, brochures and selection, to name but a few. Some franchisors have sought to reduce these costs through selling additional units to their existing franchisees. Nonetheless, as suggested in Chapter 4, the costs associated with franchisee recruitment and selection may not be recouped by the franchisee's payment of an initial fee. This lack of return on investment arises because that payment may be set according to what the competition is offering, rather than being necessarily based on the franchisor's cost structure, as well as the substantial costs of surmounting the mobility barriers to become a franchisor.

By understanding the broader contextual features influencing the decision to become a franchisee, franchisors may be better able to target suitable candidates. Within personnel functions, a basic task is the generation of profiles of candidates for a particular job by listing ideal and necessary characteristics. This task entails the formulation of a job description followed by a person specification, which defines the candidate's physical make-up, attainments, general intelligence, specialized aptitudes (such as a verbal or numerical facility), interests, disposition (such as self-reliance), and circumstances. In franchising, this recruitment and selection process is *ad hoc*, resulting in a tendency among franchisors to have an imperfect idea of the type and calibre of franchisees they require (MacMillan, 1995, 1996; Wattel, 1969). Part of the reason for this situation is that franchises are often viewed as a product to be sold, and therefore fall under the jurisdiction of sales people and, in the USA, consumer law (Brown, 1969), and outside the scope of the personnel function.[2] Despite the potential importance of alternative interpretations to understanding a franchisee's purchase decision, the sales approach persists. For example, in a review of the recruitment and selection procedures of UK franchisors, Fulop (1996) indicates that:

> For the most part, the Managing Director/Franchise Director is heavily involved in selection procedures. Since these procedures take place over several weeks and sometimes over a few months it is indicative of the importance which the franchisors-interviewees attached to ensuring the selection of appropriate franchisees. (p. 21)

Although insightful, Fulop's (1996) explanation behind the involvement of managing directors and franchise directors in the selection process is not the whole argument. As shown in Chapter 2, Purdy *et al*'s (1996) research shows that 43% of franchisors had fewer than ten outlets in 1995, and a wealth of other literature argues that franchisors are resource-constrained. Therefore, another possible rationale for their involvement is that the franchisor is typically itself a small business, and does not necessarily possess a sophisticated personnel function. Perhaps endorsing this contention, Silvester (1996) shows that the majority of franchisors operate with fewer than ten field support staff, and that franchisors with fewer than ten units have between one and five support staff. Yet another reason is that there appears to be little tradition within franchising to overtly involve specialist recruitment and selection professionals. Perhaps indicative of this orientation, franchise articles predominate in marketing journals and books with few being present in personnel texts. From the practical view point, however, involvement by those in personnel functions and independent research to generate franchisee profiles could permit franchisors to target potential franchisees more closely and efficiently. It could, for example, have four potential beneficial effects:

1. reduce incidences of work-role mismatch;
2. assist people to adapt themselves to the rigours of becoming a franchisee;
3. reduce attempts, by franchisees, to alter the working environment through engaging in innovative/opportunistic behaviours with the potential to be damaging to brand equity; and
4. reduce incidences of franchisee turnover.

These situations are ones which the franchisor may wish to maximize via the use of stringent recruitment and selection procedures, rather than over-reliance on monitoring mechanisms to endure franchisee conformity to contractual clauses (although monitoring systems are of undoubted importance). In addition to fulfilling franchisor needs to improve their recruitment and selection procedures, profiling could have a broader audience. Perhaps importantly, such research may be of potential significance to new business formation and wealth creation within the economy deriving from franchisees. Furthermore, from a theoretical perspective, there is a pressing need to understand the factors influencing the diffusion of franchising, as well as a need to conceptualize the behavioural parameters underlying the franchise concept. After all, not all people want to become franchisees, even if they could afford to do so. Via employing a career decision-making framework, this chapter suggests that the pre-contractual motivators may affect the expectations and subsequent behaviours of franchisees.

Extant approaches

The few studies examining franchisee motivation (such as Felstead, 1991, 1993; Fulop, 1996; Stanworth and Kaufmann, 1994) have all noted that the motivation to become a franchisee is related to the decision to become self-employed. Beyond that consensus, there is some agreement that franchisees pursue this path rather than self-employment proper because they want to be associated with an established business. Although instructive, such rationales do not provide insight as to the underlying influencing factors. One example of work in this vein is Stanworth and Kaufmann's 'action frame of reference' framework. Such an approach rejects positivistic explanations of behaviour as determined by a plethora of external and constraining factors and is concerned with action – not behaviour – and rejects the adoption of a psychological perspective in that it is not limited to specific individuals. By employing such a framework, researchers have attempted to engage potential franchisees' definitions of situations with sufficient degrees of generality as to link subjective meanings with observable outcomes. Hence, Stanworth and Kaufmann (1994) argue, key differences such as prior experiences of self-employment can be investigated as sets of meanings likely to influence future actions and motivational patterns. What is not apparent from such research is why and when people change direction; yet, understanding the motives behind these changes is fundamental to explaining the adoption of franchising by investors.

From another perspective, Hing (1995) applies a consumer decision-making model to the purchase of franchises. She distills the motivation to become a franchisee to a continuum involving five stages – need recognition, information search, alternative evaluation, purchase, and post-purchase outcomes. Only three stages of the model describe activities prior to franchisee start-up or, in Ornstein and Isabella's (1993) marriage analogy, the 'courtship' stage, and these are problematic. For example, at the need recognition stage, she posits that potential franchisees 'desire' some form of entrepreneurial activity. In other words, the franchisee is 'pulled' by this desire, but Hing does not state why they choose franchising as opposed to other forms of self-employment, or other substitutes such as part-time work. She is not necessarily unique in this respect: a similar sentiment has been expressed throughout the popular franchise literature. Expanding on the pull explanations for why some people become franchisees, Housden (1984) observes that they are attracted to the franchise system's brand image and the product itself. She states that franchisees realize the significant savings in time and cost resulting from the use of tested systems, the availability of technical and operational expertise, the benefits of attaining freedom from working for an employer, the perception of low risk and obtaining venture capital that may not otherwise be available.

Hing's (1995) consumer-based approach and some of the more general franchise studies (Housden, 1984) are limited since they assume that the decision-making process is constrained to potential franchisees choosing between differing franchises rather than differing career alternatives. Occupational decision-making research (Osborn, 1990), however, provides at least partial evidence to suggest that career choice is, initially, a comparative process between differing employment forms, meaning that evaluations are not independent. The decision to become a franchisee is not affected only by the attractiveness of other career options, but also by the perceptions of the benefits of franchising. For example, the relative independence of owning a franchise is most attractive to salaried employees, while those features of franchising more associated with its competitive advantage over independent small businesses are attractive to the previously self-employed (Kaufmann and Stanworth, 1995). Whether these motivations are really push factors, however, is open to interpretation.

Pull factors are only partially accurate as some individuals (Boyle, 1994), are 'pushed' into considering franchising for a variety of reasons, including redundancy, career stage and family issues. One of the most common explanations for the rise of new business formation, self-employment and franchising is the effect of recession. Indeed, Hall and Dixon (1989) believe that in periods of high unemployment a substantial amount of capital investment is available for purchasing franchises. Such a perspective is frequently utilized by the extant popular franchise literature to present the franchise option as a magic formula to end the ills of unemployment and the ills attached to working for other people, as well as a promotional tool to sell their products. Although the promotional effort has tended to emphasize the income benefits of becoming a franchisee, the decision to franchise may be more biased towards career progression – especially that deriving from greater independence or to move out of being unemployed. Support for the career progression component is provided by Bevan *et al* (1989) and Vivarelli (1991), who show that the most important motivating factor towards self-employment was a desire for independence combined with 'to earn lots of money'. Such motivations may be equally responsible for the growth in the number of franchisees and licensees. Employees are, arguably, pushed into considering franchising because of a lack of fulfilment and empowered decision-making, while the self-employed may consider franchising because they are pushed by the high degree of risk associated with independence.

Perhaps indicative of these push factors, Boyle (1994) titles her study of the adoption of franchising by milk deliverymen in Britain: *The Rise of the Reluctant Entrepreneurs*; Washer (1994) provides other evidence of push factors by suggesting that about 15% of all franchise applicants are the result of redundancies. As such, the provision of franchise-specific explanations for franchisee motivation without reference to push and antecedent factors is an incomplete rationale. Additionally, it is arguable whether the franchisee is purchasing a 'product' or is 'renting' a trading identity and associated intangible assets since ownership is not transferred. In employing only a customer decision-making framework to franchising, Hing (1995) and others employing a similar sentiment seem to implicitly ignore the substantial work and employment aspects typically associated within the franchise relationship (Felstead, 1993; O'Connell-Davidson, 1994; Stanworth, 1994), and it certainly omits the importance of labour market inequalities and closure theory.

While extant research efforts are significant because they have led to greater insight of the prior employment histories, gender biases (franchising is dominated by men), and perceptions of franchising by franchisees, they do not examine or seek to explain the context in or the process by which the decision to become a franchisee is made. Perhaps one of the reasons for this situation is the use of theoretical models embedded within marketing and consumer decision-making schools of thought to what is, fundamentally, a career decision process, as well as the lack of a holistic approach. For example, the action frame reference framework has played an instructive role in this improvement of the understanding of franchisees' backgrounds, but it has an important limitation: it is overly dependent on only that antecedent variable. Recent research efforts concerning the motivations of individuals to become self-employed, however, indicates that there is a broader array of precursor influences, such as family considerations, career stage, and the individual's social network. Examining these additional factors could help to provide increased explanatory and, perhaps, predictive power to ascertain why certain individuals – and particularly men – to become franchisees and others do not (Nicholson, 1984).

Given the substantial work and employment characteristics of franchising, one alternative approach to help understand why certain individuals become franchisees is to place franchising within the theoretical frameworks describing career choice and development amongst individuals. In particular, as it is axiomatic that few people pursue being a franchisee as an initial career decision, a more applicable analysis is that which places the franchisee decision within the context of a second-career choice. Such a perspective is of wider significance than to franchising alone, since it may also serve to explain, or post-rationalize, why certain individuals pursue part-time and full-time occupational options within an existing organization and others elect to become self-employed. Additionally, with an increase in mergers, acquisitions, decentralization and layoffs, many individuals are unable to depend on a single organization to sustain an entire career. This situation suggests that understanding the processes affecting career choices is of general interest.

What is a 'career'?

Sociological research on occupations and professions employs the term 'career' in different ways and the differences have been the source of some confusion. Summarizing prior research on careers, Evetts (1992) shows that the research tradition on careers in sociology falls into two dimensions:

- *Organizational levels of analysis:* careers as structures and routes, and the process by which organizations renew themselves through descriptions of how employees move through and between positions.
- *Individual levels of analysis:* subjective careers and career strategies. Careers as the series of choices and negotiation of constraints made by people between different opportunities presented to them.

This chapter is focused at the individual level of analysis, but there is an implicit link with organizational careers because the vital processes of employing firms – decentralization, labour flexibility, and growth – have strong effects on the career paths of certain individuals (Haveman and Cohen, 1994). For example, it is generally accepted that there has been increased emphasis on decentralization and labour flexibility since the 1980s as well as an increase in the number of new business foundlings. This period was also marked by a rapid increase in the number of franchisors from 170 in 1984 to 474 in 1995 (NatWest/BFA, 1996). The growth of franchising within the ongoing restructuring of British industry has encouraged between 38% and 68% of franchisees into business who might not otherwise have considered this career option (Felstead, 1993). These trends have, therefore, also broadened the array of career options available to individuals. Many of the areas dominated by new and small businesses and the self-employed, however, have been the recipients of restructuring activities and are the peripheral functions of large corporations with an objective to reduce costs, business risk, as well as withdraw from marginal and unprofitable markets (Keeble *et al*, 1993). Such activity has also affected the quality and nature of jobs and careers available to individuals from one where it was possible to work for an organization for life, to one intermittently marked by unemployment and an underlying and continuing feeling of uncertainty due to the reassertion of management's control over the labour process (Shutt and Whittington, 1986). This situation, in turn, has affected the definition of individual careers to a more holistic interpretation. Perhaps reflecting these changes, it is possible to distinguish between four meanings of the term (Hall, 1976):

1. career as advancement, which sees a career as involving essentially vertical movement between jobs;
2. career advancement as a profession, which associates the idea of career with vertical movement between jobs in certain types of job only (Ashforth and Saks, 1995);
3. career as a life-long sequence of jobs, which regards any individual's set of jobs as constituting a career; and
4. career as a sequence of role-related experiences, so that one may speak of the career of the housewife, the mental patient, or the dying person.

Indicative of the last approach, Epperlein (1987) argues a career as a process that involves the entire life of an individual and, as such, concerns the whole person. An individual's career path can, therefore, be said to comprise the series of job changes that punctuate their entire working life (Greenhaus and Bentall, 1985), or, in short, the 'evolving sequence of a person's work experience over time' (Arthur *et al*, 1989). The term 'career development' is used to explain the dynamics and directions of career change. Whilst there may be an implicit assumption that a career consists of a succession of job moves where advancement is being sought, some early occupational research indicated that career dynamics and overall patterns of work need to be considered. Thus, the traditional interpretation of career as a graded ladder does not account for those people who do not aspire to progress in that manner (satisficers), and it does not accommodate different levels and/or different types of aspirations that people may hold; nor does it reflect the changing nature of career contract between employers and employees from a relational and long-term approach to a more transactional orientation, emphatic of the short term and fundamentally performance-based. By contrast, a theme which runs through occupational choice literature is that a career can be viewed as a set of stages which are moved through with the passing of time, reflecting both an individual's needs and their personality traits and the external forces. Within each career sequence are transition periods which may either involve an objective change in career role or a change in subjective orientation towards the career role. For example, an individual may decide that part-time work is more suited to the realization of meeting an objective to spend more time with their family. Viewed from another perspective, the changes in the employer and employee contractual relationship also signify that there is a general shift from the organizational career to a protean career, a career based on self-direction:

> The protean career is a process which the person, not the organization, is managing. It consists of all the person's varied experiences in education, training, work in organizations, changes in occupational field, etc. The protean career is not what happens to the person in any one organization. The protean person's own personal career choices and search for self-fulfilment are the unifying or integrative elements in his or her life. The criterion of success is internal (psychological success), not external . . . In short, the protean career is shaped more by the individual than by the organization and may be redirected from time to time to meet the needs of the person. (Hall, 1976; p. 201)

Thus, the word 'career' has moved from its traditional noun meaning a series of progressions within a profession or organization to that of its verb interpretation. Franchising certainly comprises one element of a protean career because, for the franchisee, the career does not represent a linear progression of upward moves but an element in a flexible career path. For example, franchisees do not get promoted except perhaps to become a multi-unit and/or multi-brand operator; their contracts typically last five years which, in turn, suggests that after this time the franchisee is once again flexible to decide which path to pursue; and some franchisees elect to become multi-site operators and some are encouraged to do so. This flexibility to choose is of potential significance to understanding the growth in franchising as it represents a dynamic component in career choice theory, which is, for the large part, inherently static due to a reliance on trait factor theory (Katz and Gartner, 1988).

According to Louis (1980) there are five types of career transition:

1. entering or leaving a labour pool;
2. taking on a different role or responsibility within the same organization;
3. moving from one organization to another;
4. changing professions or occupational speciality;
5. leaving a labour pool.

In this way, career changes encompass altering career status and direction. Equally, a change in career may entail one or more of these types. For example, an accountant leaves a practice to become a fast food franchisee would be moving organization, leaving full-time status and altering direction. This chapter is concerned only with broad changes in status, that is the transition from one position on the continuum to another (Figure 5.1), rather than promotions within an organization. In so doing, there is an implicit assumption (in accordance with Kaufmann and Stanworth, 1995) that potential franchisees, for example, are not a homogeneous grouping and that those considering franchising are possibly only a sub-group of one or more larger employment categories (for example, self-employed). Support for this contention is presented below.

Figure 5.1 places franchisees as having less freedom than the self-employed, which is consistent with a plethora of franchise texts and articles. For example, Knight (1984) places the franchisee on a continuum of independence 'exactly mid-way' between 'solo independent entrepreneurs' and 'large corporate managers'. Whilst some

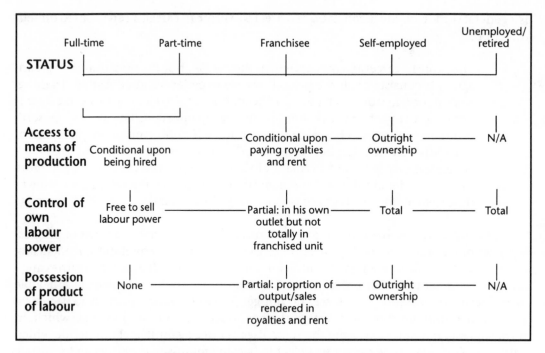

Figure 5.1: Continuum of employment types

franchisees may have different perceptions of their degree of latitude and freedom, a franchisee's status differs from those associated with self-employment because, like the freemen of feudal times, they have to adhere and conform to strict contractual obligations (Arendorff, 1986; Schulz, 1988).

Antecedent factors to choosing franchising

Imagine that two people are at their respective career cross-roads. They are confronted with a variety of choices:

1. go into full-time employment;
2. go into part-time employment;
3. become a franchisee;
4. become self-employed; or
5. retire.

One person decides to go into full-time employment and the other elects to become a franchisee. How and why did they arrive at these choices? According to Parkin (1971), these choices are affected by the type of closure experienced. For example, if an individual is thought to not possess the necessary 'capital' deriving from their biological make-up, this will preclude social mobility as will the lack of the required skills and education, etc.

Chapter 1 illustrated that there were several antecedent factors which were conducive to the rise of franchising in the 1950s in the USA and in the 1980s in Britain, but did not explore individual-level rationales for its adoption. Focusing on the individual specifically, most studies of careers observe that the collectivist and individualist factors, such as education, gender, network, ethnicity, etc., serve to impact on the propensity for an individual to change jobs as well as to become self-employed. According to Baucus and Human (1994), for example, there are three sets of factors which appear to influence the decision to become an entrepreneur:

1. their prior employment experience;
2. the nature of their networks; and
3. individual factors.

These factors are also of some significance to explaining second career choices *per se*. While some career theorists view careers as only pertaining to the work an individual undertakes, a career is also affected by events occurring in the person's personal life, prior experiences, and individual factors such as age, gender, and education levels. Given that occupational aspirations are a subjective interpretation of the opportunity structure, an important omission from numerous career choice studies is the lack of account of the role of values, beliefs and meanings within certain social networks (or 'shibboleths'). Yet others fail to observe that the aforementioned factors are inherent to the closure theory, whereby an individual may only be able to realize a return on their labour in a particular way as a result of being excluded from certain career routes. Figure 5.2, therefore, presents a series, but far from exhaustive, variety of antecedent variable categories including beliefs and values. The variables are examined to present an exploratory level analysis of the motivators to become a franchisee, and each of the factors are perceived to influence or modify the extent to which an individual may follow a particular path. The inter-related variables are derived from a review of entrepreneurship, careers, and some consumer choice literatures, and underlines that decision-making does not occur within a vacuum, but are affect and are affected by an individual's neighbourhood and immediate social network and its level of deprivation and culture. These factors are not only important in their effect on shaping occupational aspirations, but also on educational attainment which, in turn, has a powerful effect on occupational and educational aspirations and horizons (Blustein *et al*, 1994; Furlong *et al*, 1996; Prahalad and Bettis, 1986).

Cultural capital

Choosing to become a franchisee is the result of a complex decision-making process and that exercise is subject to a plethora of influencing and moderating variables. It is not just a question of buying the right franchise at the right price, it requires the individual to have an intention to become a franchisee, which is influenced by three components (Ajzen and Madden (1986), collectively termed 'cultural capital'. Cultural capital refers to the values, beliefs and meanings attached to performing activities. These beliefs can affect choices, such as which restaurant/public house to visit, which hotel/resort to go to (McEwan, 1983; Riley, 1984), perceptions of quality or fitness for use, and possibly which career to pursue, because they affect the knowledge of how to behave in a particular situation. Values represent the idea of what individuals think is desirable or undesirable and these are connected to whether significant others in the individual's network would approve or disapprove (that is, the collective values of the network). Indicative of the role of culture in job choice, some people commit themselves to jobs in

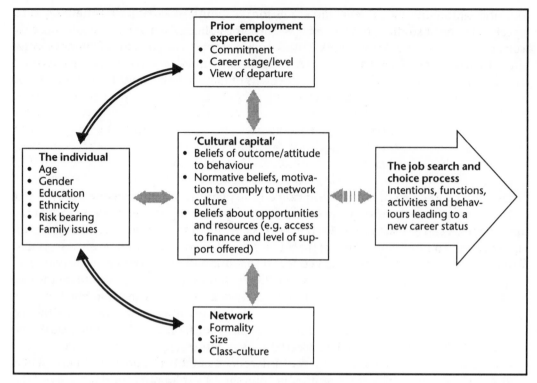

Figure 5.2: Antecedant variables to career choices

which the culture of the workplace and work-mates is more important than the intrinsic qualities of the job (Willis, 1977), such as the operating conditions and degree of latitude. Culture provides people, over time, a broad and consistent view of what sort of people they want to end up working with; they do not necessarily choose careers on the basis of the intrinsic joys of work but according to what kind of work situation is going to be most relevant to the individual.

The decision to pursue a particular career path may also be affected by whether the individual has negative, ambivalent or positive feelings about a certain option and its ability to meet certain objectives. For example, Kaufmann and Stanworth (1995) hypothesize that there exists a positive relationship between an individual's interest in providing employment for family members and an individual's interest in providing an ongoing business to their heirs, and the strength of their expressed likelihood of purchasing a franchise. Their lack of empirical support for these contentions does not mean that they were wrong in their social reproduction assumptions: individuals may indeed believe that franchises can provide employment for their heirs now and in the future, but this belief may not lead them to purchase a franchise.

It is important to observe that beliefs can vary in the strength with which they are held and the degree to which that conviction will lead to action. Possibly indicative of the variance between belief and intentionality, Hatcliffe *et al* (1995) illustrate that the majority of their respondents who did not become a franchisee still held positive beliefs about franchising, and some franchisees held negative beliefs about franchising. One possible rationale for this situation is that some individuals, for instance, may have positive beliefs about franchising but do not act according to those beliefs because of the effects of the antecedent variables. For example, a person may be precluded from certain types of employment because of the prejudices of the employer in areas such as age, ethnicity, and/or gender, among other factors. Equally, a woman may be precluded from becoming a franchisee, even though she has a positive attitude about it, because of the lack of other female franchisees. Yet others may also hold constructive values about franchising but have no intention of becoming one. As much as others may perceive there to be some kudos in becoming a franchisee, the individual may not elect to pursue a certain career track because they perceive that they would not 'fit' into a certain work setting. Lack of the necessary cultural capital for a given situation translates as mis-match, or lack of 'comfort' within a particular setting because the individual finds it difficult to know how to behave and interact with others in situations. Due to lack of experience in being a franchisee, the foundations of these perceptions are based on media representations and what other network members (some of which may be franchisees) tell them. These influences result in a stereotypical representation of, first, the way in which a franchisee operates; second, the manner of franchisor-franchisee interaction; and third, the appropriate behaviour. This perception, which may be wholly inaccurate because of misinformation and the cultural-boundedness of information, then affects choice: some employers will not hire certain ethnic minorities, for example, because of racial stereotypes. In this sense, the intention to become a franchisee requires the individual to have a certain mind-set, held values and motivation, and these differ from those held by people who prefer self-employment, part-time or full-time employment

Arguably, the possession of cultural capital is of more importance to becoming a franchisee than finance and specific human capital (labour and knowledge skills). This said, access to, rather than possession of, a proportion of the obligatory finance requirements is necessary to becoming a franchisee because loans and other financing options are made according to the amount of security the individual can provide, as well as the extent of risk inherent to the venture. This situation requires the franchisee to possess some finance in order to gain funding to cover the cost of becoming a franchisee, but not all of it, as the major clearing banks are generally well-disposed to lending to potential franchisees (the lending institutions perceive the franchise option to be a low-risk venture). Equally, some franchisors have set up 'assistance finding' and other mechanisms to help individuals to become franchisees (Lafontaine, 1992). As will be shown in Chapter 6, possession of specific human capital tends not to be a requirement to being a franchisee and some franchisors only recruit (via exclusion) those without prior self-employment or sector experience.

By summarizing previous research, Katz (1994) indicates that the environmental and individual factors are important influential variables affecting issues of choice, including career choice. The environment carries information cues and signals which might add to, restructure or change knowledge. Such information may be transmitted through a conversation with another person (hence the significance of networks), via the media, visiting a franchise exhibition, or presented in a book, to name but a few information sources. The extent to which such information is employed as part of the decision-making process is dependent on the costs of collecting the information, the perceived status of the information source and the extent to which it concurs with other data. For example, some people tend to not read certain types of newspapers, such as the tabloids, because these individuals believe that the newspapers do not reflect the manner in which they see themselves, or that they convey information which is not written in an accurate, informative and serious manner. The role of information in facilitating awareness of franchising is unquestionable, but it is important to observe that information is conveyed in differing cultural settings (nationally and internationally). For some groups of people, therefore, franchising will mean very little because it is not part of the language employed in their social milieu. Employing an analogy with the urbanization of a peasant boy as a means of illustrating how ways of thinking about the world are mediated by social milieu, we can see how the acquisition of knowledge of new career options, such as franchising, depends upon an irreversible departure of the old world-view:

> For the son of a peasant boy who has grown up within the narrow confines of his village and spends his whole life in the place of his birth, the mode of thinking and speaking characteristic of that village is something that he takes entirely for granted. But for the country lad who goes to the city and adapts himself gradu-ally to city life, the rural mode of living and thinking ceases to be something taken for granted. He has won a certain detachment from it, and he distinguish-es now, perhaps quite consciously, between 'rural' and 'urban' modes of thought and ideas . . . That which within a given group is accepted as absolute appears to be the outsider conditioned by the group situation and recognized as partial (in this case as 'rural'). This type of knowledge presupposes a more detached per-spective. (Mannheim, 1936; quoted in Morgan, 1991; p. 81)

Thus, in some cultures, franchising is an alien concept, but to others it will have greater value. For instance, franchising has been employed as a method of expansion amongst US retailers since the 1950s and so has a higher level of meaning than in other countries; in some cultural settings, becoming a franchisee is not viewed to be a career option. In many countries, including industrial ones, franchising has yet to emerge as a business concept of any significance (see Table 5.1) because franchising activity *per se* may be limited or have a complete lack of presence due to adverse tax, legal, economic development, and educational conditions. In these countries, the lack of franchisor presence possibly miti-gates against legitimation and further development as investors also perceive franchising as an alien concept: for example, there is no Hungarian equivalent of the 'franchise' verb. These cultural differences require franchisors to employ differing tactics in order to real-ize expansion in their desired satellite nation. As a result of the infant state of franchising in China, for example, many pioneering US and French fast food franchisors had to use unorthodox business strategies to enter the market (English and Xau, 1994; Rubin and Allen, 1994). Many of the franchise networks in China are characterized by one or more of the following features:

1. they are founded on a series of joint ventures in major urban areas;
2. they have relied on franchisees from Taiwan, Japan or Hong Kong to open the market; and/or
3. they have sought to balance their foreign exchange through minimizing imported goods.

Cultural and economic differences, therefore, possibly limit the diffusion of information concerning franchising in the cultural and industrial milieu because the press may not perceive it as newsworthy and there are insufficient franchisors to warrant specialist

Country	Franchisors	Franchisees
United States	3,000	250,000
Canada	1,000	65,000
Brazil	932	60,000
Japan	714	139,788
Australia/N.Z.	600	26,000
France	520	30,000
Germany	500	18,000
Britain	414	26,400
Italy	400	18,500
Mexico	375	18,724
Netherlands	341	11,975
Spain	280	18,500
Austria	200	3,000
Hungary	200	10,000
Sweden	200	9,000
Norway	185	3,500
Belgium	150	3,083
Malaysia	125	800
Argentina	100	3,500
Singapore	85	1,600
Finland	70	900
Denmark	68	1,210
Philippines	56	61
Colombia	48	300
Yugoslavia	45	620
Chile	45	25
Czech Republic	35	100
Israel	18	15
Bulgaria	0	7
Total	10,706	720,608

Source: Swartz, L.N., (1995), *Worldwide Franchising Statistics: A Study of Worldwide Franchise Associations,* Arthur Andersen in co-operation with the World Franchising Council, Chicago, Ill.

Table 5.1: Global distribution of franchisors and franchisees

magazines or a trade association. The degree to which individuals' perceive franchising as a valid and viable career alternative is not only a function of their awareness, but also their interpretation of the relative benefits of the option in relation to their personal circumstances (such as life stage factors, prior employment variables and the influence of their network) and its ability to meet objectives compared to other competing alternatives. Franchisees are not completely different from those who establish their own independent businesses but are, in fact, drawn from the population involved in career transitions generally. Consequently, the question arising from this situation is: what is the degree of commonality in the antecedent variables which influence some individuals to become a franchisee whilst others pursue self-employment? Whilst this question has been subject to some investigation in the USA, much has focused on attempting to establish differences between franchisees and entrepreneurs (Brannon, 1986; English and Hoy, 1995; Olm *et al*, 1988) rather than on self-employment. Yet, there is some difference between self-employment and entrepreneurship. Entrepreneurship entails self-employment but self-employment does not entail entrepreneurship (Carland *et al*, 1984).

Prior employment experience

Commitment: Occupational theorists and those investigating attributes of entrepreneurs illustrate that career experiences can affect an individual's choice of subsequent career path, but that there is an intervening variable called commitment (conceptualized as a person's dedication and motivation). In research terms, many other measures of commitment have been generated, but some confusion exists as to what is being evaluated. In an attempt to clarify and resolve the confusion, Morrow (1983) identified five predominant work commitment foci:

1. career commitment, which refers to career identity. For example, some individuals remain as accountants throughout their working life;
2. job commitment or job involvement, whereby an individual, although having a career as an accountant, may decide to specialize within a particular niche such as audit;
3. organizational commitment, which refers to loyalty to a particular company and may either be active or passive (Bar-Hayini and Berman, 1992);
4. individual work values, such as the Protestant work ethic; and
5. union commitment, such as loyalty to a bargaining unit.

Although some empirical validation is required, it appears that the higher the commitment to a particular career, job or organization, the lower the propensity to consider alternatives. Thus, the better an individual's attitude to their vocation, including profession, the lower the tendency to search for another job (Blau, 1988). In this sense, although a person may be dissatisfied with their present job, they could still be sufficiently attracted to it not to move because they feel that it will facilitate the attainment of valued career outcomes more readily than other options. Franchisees seem to illustrate a high level of emphasis on individual work values, as Page (1996) suggests, rather than necessarily being committed to a particular job or career. In a study of attendees at two franchise exhibitions in Britain and people who had converted to franchising, Hatcliffe *et al* (1995) show that the majority of 'converts' had taken a franchise in which they had not gained work experience whilst in employment.

> For most, being a franchisee means rolling up your sleeves and getting down to business. It means setting that alarm for 5 a.m., to get the store ready for the morning rush, making cold calls for five hours straight, and skipping dinner with your family to pull together a last minute proposal for a crucial client. (Page, 1996; p. 185)

Career stage: This research is predicated on the assumption that individuals move through distinct occupational stages in their working life. Each stage is characterized by differences in work attitude and behaviours, types of relationships needed and aspects of work which are valued. Ayree *et al* (1994) suggest that there is some inter-relationship between career-stage and career commitment and indicate that the variables employed to operationalize career stage are: age, organizational and occupational tenure, and positional tenure. Age may not be directly correlated to career stage, however, because a person's career stage may be more influenced by life stage factors. For example, Bailyn's (1977) survey of men in their 30s and 40s investigating the inter-relationship between work and accommodation of family needs, found that some people reduced their emphasis on work to cope with the demands of home life. Issues concerning tenure may be of greater importance because, throughout the differing career stages, an individual is viewed to be at different stages of learning. In the early stages of a career, for instance, the individual experiences their apprenticeship, while in the latter stages the level of learning may be limited and so prompt a decision to look elsewhere. Conversely, however, it is also likely that as the individual has been with the organization for a long period of time, that commitment levels will be higher; Cohen (1991), for example, shows that turnover and turnover intentions are affected by organizational commitment more strongly in the early career stages than the mid- and late-career stages.

View of departure: When something distasteful transpires in the work situation such as redundancy, forced insolvency, contractual termination or conditions/performance falling below a certain acceptable threshold and the individual seeks alternative employment, he is said to have been 'pushed' to seek a new job. If individuals have displayed either high levels of organizational and/or job commitment and are made redundant, they will view their departure as stressful and involuntary. Baucus and Human (1994) argue that these negative perceptions may slow down the new business start-up and the processes employed. As a consequence of these negative feelings, some individuals may decide that they would rather purchase a franchise or own their own business than work for another organization in a full-time post and possibly be betrayed again. Negative feelings may not only derive from the severing of an employer–employee relationship, but also when conditions fall below a certain threshold. The notion of a threshold is consistent with the theory of organizational equilibrium (March and Simon, 1958) which is concerned with the conditions under which an organization can make employees stay in assuring organizational survival. Such theorists refer to employees as 'participants' who receive 'inducements' (such as wages) in return for contributions and they will remain with an organization for as long as the inducement (as measured by the participant) outweighs the contributions. If, on the other hand, the individual becomes aware that the level of satisfaction has fallen below a certain threshold, an active job search is initiated. The model proposes that people are pushed into career choice situations as a result of actual or threatened unemployment and by lack of career progression opportunities and pulled by potentially higher rewards (a combination of pecuniary and non-pecuniary) than their current situation offers.

The individual

Age: The proportion of people changing jobs varies significantly by age, with those in the younger age groups much more likely to change their job than older people. The Labour Force Survey (1991) shows, for example, that almost a quarter of those aged between 16 and 19 who were employees in 1986 had changed employer. By contrast, only 4% of those aged 50 and over had changed employer and just 3% had a new occupation. More than a third of all employees who change occupation were aged under 25, which suggests that those considering becoming a franchisee possibly diminish with age. Like the entry of founder-managers into business ownership, the decision to become a franchisee is typically seen as occurring later in life, at a time when the individual has sufficient capital and experience to enter the activity (Hudson, 1987). In a study of seven franchise systems in Britain, Hough (1986) found that franchisees appear to take up their franchised businesses in their 20s and 30s. About 35% of the franchisees set up in their 30s, compared to 30% in their 20s and 23% in their 40s. According to the NatWest/BFA studies, however, over 40% of franchisees are aged between 40 and 50, and 30% are in their 30s. To some degree an investor's age is significant to the adoption of franchising because it may be indicative of the amount of capital available for investment. Within Hough's (1986) study, for example, only 17% of franchisees started in their 20s in the more expensive franchises.

Education and class: Education has an economic value and it is posited that the education system fosters economic growth and social mobility in five ways:

1. by research and advancement in knowledge;
2. discovering and nurturing human 'potential' talent;
3. increasing the capability of persons to adjust to changes in job opportunities associated with economic growth;
4. it produces people who can then teach;
5. by meeting prospective needs for people with high skills and knowledge.

The franchisor acts as an educator, a provider of human capital to investors, and as a vehicle for social mobility through their training and therefore may foster economic growth in a similar way. As a result of this training and the often repetitive tasks to be performed, the level of educational attainment to become a franchisee need not be high. Perhaps reflecting this situation, the NatWest/BFA surveys report that a quarter of all franchisees had no formal qualifications, and a further quarter had obtained the basic level of state education. These results differ from prior studies of franchisees: Ozanne and Hunt (1971) noted an 'unexpectedly high level of formal education amongst a study of fast food franchisees with only 10% not completing high school at one extreme and a similar proportion obtaining post-graduate qualifications at the other'. Hough's (1986) research showed half of the surveyed franchisees as having either selective state or private education, which renders them different from the population as a whole. There was a distinct pattern linking the buy-in cost of the franchise to the likelihood of having attended a selective state school, had a private education, and left school with some form of qualification. The differing educational backgrounds of franchisees could be argued to be reflective of the differing social status of franchisees compared to the majority of people becoming self-employed.

Despite a wealth of problems in extant approaches to defining social class (Parkin, 1971), some franchisors have argued that social class is of significance to influencing who becomes a franchisee. They contend that certain people within the lower socio-economic groups may be precluded because they cannot gain access to the necessary finance to become a franchisee, and some people within the higher socio-economic groups are attracted to those systems with high levels of brand equity. As their definitions of class, however, are based on the type of employment and income rather than cultural values, so it is not so much income which is important but prior employment experience, education and the individual's network. The utility of such measures as a segmentation tool to analyze who may become a franchisee is limited further because not all members of a particular class want to become a franchisee, even though they may be able to afford to do so. Indeed, Crawford-Welch (1991) contends that:

> Descriptive data, by their very nature, are of little analytical worth in that they are not capable of implying causality and are, in turn, poor indicators of behaviour. They are not actionable . . . Knowing how much an individual earns does not tell us what he or she spends that income on. The fact that a group of individuals fall within the same income category does not mean, by virtue of that fact, that they all possess identical or even similar patterns of consumption and expenditure. Descriptive statistical categories are not capable of inferring individual or group values and patterns of expenditure, and are certainly not capable of inferring the reasons behind those purchase decisions. All descriptive statistics can do is summarize qualities about a data set . . . (pp. 172–73)

A variety of researchers contend that class plays a broad role in affecting career choice, but it is not holistic. Marxists argue that social classes are structured in terms of the conflict between capital and labour and the dominant patterns of capital accumulation which require distinct employment relations (Braverman, 1974; McEwan, 1983): owners versus non-owners, or powerful versus powerless. These sets of relations are supported by social and ideological relations which serve to legitimate the dominance of capital, but require structural continuity to ensure that these positions are reproduced. Thus, social class locates individuals in the division of labour which, in turn, affects their thoughts and values because similar structural positions generate similar conditions of experience and existence, or class-cultures. These experiences affect the world view or mental maps and sense of values and affect the mobility of labour and career choices as they affect perceptions of status:

> We might think of [the] process of reproduction as having two basic 'momments'. In the first place, outside structures and basic class relationships are taken in as symbolic and conceptual relations at the specifically cultural level. The form of this . . . is of cultural penetrations of the conditions of existence of the social group who support the culture . . . In the second 'moment' of the process, structures which have now become sources of meaning, definition and identity provide the basis for decisions and choices in life . . . That is: the factories are filled . . . with workers displaying the necessary apparent gradations between mental and manual capacity and corresponding attitudes to maintain, within broad limits, the present structure of class and production. (Willis, 1977; pp. 173–74)

Many of the claims by the franchise fraternity concerning opportunities to accumulate wealth are more appealing to those with aspirations to move or maintain social class, such as the working class and middle classes. This move is perceived to be upward. In light of much of the manual work undertaken and the lack of ownership of assets, however, whether this move is upward is open to interpretation. It is, perhaps, this openness to interpretation which acts as an inhibitor to becoming a franchisee for some people. It is, however, apparent that classes are not necessarily unified or cohesive social groups: there are divisions both within and between particular classes. The class-cultures represent broad values evident within a social strata; beyond that, a person's values will be affected by their immediate social network and the other antecedent variables. Thus, becoming a franchisee not only requires the individual to possess access to finance, but also the right social and class-cultural capital; they may also do so to overcome exclusion from other social groups within their class.

Gender: Since the 1950s there has been an increasing participation by women in the labour market, with particular bias within the part-time category, which occurred during the de-skilling of the labour process (Braverman, 1974). The economic activity rate for women of working age (over 16) has increased from 30% in 1900 to 71% in 1993, while that of men has fallen from 91% to 86% (Labour Force Survey, 1993). Much of this activity has occurred within the service sectors and particularly within the traditionally female markets (retail and catering), a process which has been labelled by McDowell (1989) as gender segregation and is reflective of a patriarchal society and culture. Arguably, this form of segregation is also indicative of dual closure where females are concentrated into certain occupations, and certain jobs within these.

Research concurs that women occupy a secondary position within the labour market (Stanworth and Stanworth, 1991) and are typically channelled into a narrow band of occupational spheres. Women are particularly prevalent in the hospitality industry, secretarial work, and hairdressing, but within the hotel sector they are functionally segregated into housekeeping management roles (Guerrier, 1986). Within this segregation, the young, women and ethnic minorities are often seen as taking unskilled, low paid, and insecure jobs and are possibly a preferred labour pool in the hospitality industry. Because of their perceived disposability, lack of interest in training, low economism, low solidarism and distinctiveness as a source of labour, employers have greater power and are better able to realize their objectives – the optimization of capital (Barron and Norris, 1976; Byrne, 1986). In some instances, women and ethnic minorities have been drawn into employment in order to deskill the workforce and reduce the bargaining power of a skilled male workforce, in spite of the presence of dual closure.

As an increasing number of businesses adopt flexible working, the proportion of women in the labour market has also risen, but this has not necessarily translated into substantially increased representation in franchising (as franchisees or as franchisors) or self-employment *per se*. Government statistics show that self-employed women account for about 7% of women in the labour market, compared to 16% for men. According to the NatWest/BFA surveys, British women own about a fifth of franchised units and there has also been the emergence of franchised systems specifically targeted at women. Possible reasons for women's lack of involvement in self-employment include perceived lack of support from other family members, ethnic/cultural reasons, as well as perhaps lower risk-bearing tendencies and some women may have different expectations than men concerning lifetime labour force participation, due to expected interruptions to work experience for child rearing. This latter contention reflects the familial ideology approach which asserts that men are the primary breadwinners and women are their dependents; it maintains that woman's primary role is that of housewife and mother. While this sexual division is emphasized to varying degrees within differing cultures, home responsibilities influence the likelihood of women's participation in the labour force, working, hours of work, type of work and career patterns (Melmed, 1996). As women tend not to be self-employed, such observations are also of consequence to establishing some rationale for the low numbers of women franchisors (Dant *et al*, 1996).

Ethnicity: A fourth antecedent variable within the individual grouping is ethnicity. The link between ethnicity and entrepreneurship is widely recognized and has received an increasing amount of research attention. Whilst important, the number of ethnically-owned businesses remains small and the number of ethnically-operated franchises yet smaller (English *et al*, 1988; Murphy, 1995; 1971), but is high when compared to the representation of the relevant ethnic-group. For example, the annual General Household Surveys and Labour Force Surveys show that the proportion of self-employed Indian and Pakistani/Bangladeshi people in Britain is higher than that of whites and the average number of self-employed people in Britain; this situation is true of both genders.

Of the main arguments and perspectives forwarded to explain why ethnic minorities tend to have a higher propensity to become small-business owners, especially within the catering and general retailing sectors, and franchisees, than the rest of the population, one of the most compelling factors is the presence of discriminatory labour market. Jones (1992) argues that this discrimination is particularly acute in service sectors such as retailing, and suggests the presence of racism in the labour market:

> Just as Asian workers have acted as replacement labour in many low wage industries with undesirable working conditions, so in the guise of petty capitalists they now bear the brunt of retailing in various market niches which have been progressively abandoned by the white trader. (p. 11)

As well as the racially discriminatory labour market, many ethnic entrepreneurs confront a further set of constraints that lock them into the least well-rewarded sectors of the economy. According to Jones (1992), some ethnic minorities tend to concentrate on particular sectors such as retailing and catering because they are only low-yielding sectors that offer openings to those with few business resources and low levels of human capital, and labour exploitation:

> Many waiters very understandably found themselves in an 'us and them' situation. Restaurant owners exploited waiters, and clients represented a society which excluded waiters, because of their overseas origins, from better professions. There was dislike, jealousy and resentment, and not without cause. In far too many cases . . . management took harsh disciplinary action . . . staff would be dismissed for the slightest infraction of the rules and on any pretext just to prove how much their livelihood depended on obedience. (Taylor, 1977; p. 87)

In order to play down the issue of race discrimination in the USA some foodservice franchisors have actively started to target minorities (Carlino, 1994) and specialist magazines (for example, *Black Enterprise*) regularly carry features on franchising and the successes of some black franchisees. Despite such targeting activity, McGuire (1971) argues that there are several obstacles to be overcome if franchising activity is to expand among the ethnic communities. These obstacles are not necessarily unique to potential ethnic franchisees, but due to the particular circumstances amongst some of this section of the population, they could achieve critical significance. Among these obstacles, McGuire (1971) argues, are problems of financing initial franchise fees, recruiting motivated franchisees, training the new black entrepreneur, and locating and maintaining the unit. In spite of such obstacles, ethnic franchisees are dominant in the UK in systems such as Perfect Pizza, Wimpy, Starburger, Jenny's Burger, KFC, and Burger King. Within some of these chains, some ethnic minorities are more dominant than others. For example, Perfect Pizza has a high proportion of franchisees of Middle Eastern origin. This situation can be attributed to the spread of information about franchising by members of a particular social networking, rather than the targeting activities of the franchisor. Furthermore, the cultures and values of some ethnic minorities concerning women in the workforce may also affect the degree to which women consider becoming franchisees. Table 5.2, for example, shows that the number of women in employment is low at 24% compared to, for example, the population of West Indian/Guyanese women.

The presence of a racist labour market serves to encourage entrepreneurial activity as a consequence of dual closure. Some ethnic groups may be discriminated against when they seek full-time employment (despite legislation dictating otherwise), and may

Gender/employment status	Ethnic group					
	White	All ethnic	W. Indian, Guyanese	Indian	Pakistani	Other
Men						
In employment	93	87	85	90	79	89
Employee	75	67	72	65	58	70
Full-time	71	62	68	62	53	64
Part-time	4	4	3	3	5	6
Self-employed	16	18	9	23	19	16
On Government training	2	2	3	1	2	2
Unemployed	7	13	16	10	21	11
All economically active	15,095	669	131	229	129	209
All aged 16 and over	20,056	913	165	285	176	286
Women						
In employment	93	88	88	90	77	90
Employee	85	77	83	78	58	77
Full-time	48	54	60	56	37	52
Part-time	38	23	23	22	21	25
Self-employed	7	8	2	10	12	10
On Government training	1	3	2	2	8	2
Unemployed	7	12	12	10	24	10
All economically active	11,505	469	124	149	40	156
All aged 16 and over	21,660	884	176	169	164	274

Source: Labour Force Survey, 1990 and 1991, *Office of Population Censuses and Surveys*, HMSO pg 35.

Table 5.2: *Economically active people aged 16 and over, by sex, employment status and ethnic group, Britain, 1989–91*

compel the individual to seek livelihoods outside established businesses and begin to create their own businesses (Katz, 1994). Confirming this observation, in their examination of initial entry decisions among ethnic proprietors in Britain and France, Phizacklea and Ram (1996) found that unemployment or the inability to find satisfactory work in mainstream employment was the motivating factor for virtually all of the entrepreneurs in their sample. The degree to which such push factors motivate business start-ups, however, varies by denomination. For example, Afro-Caribbeans are more motivated by push factors than Asian and white business people (Wilson, 1984). Nonetheless, while discrimination – or, in some cases, the fear of discrimination – may be responsible for some business start-ups, it is not the sole factor. Another contributing factor may be the degree of insularity of the ethnic group – or, rather, the lack of integration with the broader population in order to help retain and reinforce their cultural identity.

Reflecting the dual aspects of insularity and discrimination, it is generally found in the UK and USA (Hisrich and Brusch, 1986; McGuire, 1971) that most ethnically-owned businesses are mostly marginal operations. The location of the majority of these businesses is within the relevant ethnic population pockets, near to family and social ties. For example, the high ratios of Chinese take-aways to restaurants in Wales, Northern Ireland and the Midland regions of the UK suggest that they have shown a tendency to occupy residential areas abandoned by other players, such as villages and small town communities. In many of these locations, the Chinese take-away is often the sole provider of fast food and this locational aspect may be partially responsible for their survival.

Within such operations there has been a tendency to exploit family labour and make use of their community resources as opposed to integrating within the broader society more fully, via the adoption of franchising. Asian businesses, for example, tend to be financed by family money. Unsurprisingly, therefore, the geographic distribution and density of Chinese restaurants and take-away operations mirrors the spread of the 157,000 resident Chinese population, as shown in the table; this provides a regional illustration of the density of Chinese population to the number of Chinese take-away and restaurant units in 1993. Approximately, 59% of Chinese people in Britain are located in south-east England; in the same area there are 838 (41%) Chinese restaurants, a high proportion of which are located in London's 'China-Town'. A similar situation exists in Manchester as well as internationally (for example, New York and San Francisco). The regions where there are fewer Chinese people per Chinese foodservice operation are the South East and North West, perhaps suggesting a greater propensity to be involved in other economic areas. By comparison, it is also these regions which illustrate the highest density of fast food outlets and restaurants per capita in Britain.

This feature of locating near to family ties and cultural and labour resources is also evident in the Indian market. The West Midlands, for example, accounts for about 19.5% of the resident Indian, Pakistani and Bangladeshi population and about 27% of Britain's 5,800 Indian restaurants. Within these communities, there is also a greater tendency for the businesses to be passed on down the generations, rather than franchised to 'strangers'. The insularity of some ethnic communities, characterized by the use of family labour and neighbourhoods or community resources, serves to insulate people of similar backgrounds and foster a set of cultural attitudes, social contacts and economic opportunities. The embededness of these attitudes serves to isolate different ethnic groups from each other, leading to a lack of trust and a higher propensity for misunderstandings and conflict to occur (Fukuyama, 1995). Some people, therefore, treat franchisor claims that franchising is a safer route into self-employment, with open suspicion. Thus, whilst ethnicity may be an important antecedent variable in affecting career decisions, it may have an external effect on the human-capital accumulation process (Borjas, 1995) and possibly affect the awareness of franchising. People raised in advantageous ethnic environments will be exposed to social and economic factors that increase their productivity, and the larger or more frequent the amount of exposure, the higher the resulting 'quality' of worker (p. 365). Borjas also suggests that skill differentials persist from generation to generation and that the accumulation of human-capital by ethnic children not only depends on their parents' skill, but also the skills of the ethnic group of the parents' generation. In other words, the wealth and cultural setting of the individual's network affects the degree of career mobility and the career options (Snipp, 1985; Willis, 1977). This observation has also been by witnessed by Kelley (1978):

> A high status father is able to give his son an enduring advantage. How he does this is less than clear. Particularly puzzling is the . . . advantage he is able to offer in middle age, long after the son has finished his career. Bernard and Renaud offer the interesting hypothesis that the advantage is from the inheritance of exclusive goods, namely wealth and secondarily offices, professional practices, and the like. The fact that the advantage is larger in less-developed capitalist societies where personal control over businesses, jobs, and capital is more common, supports their theory. But it is not the only possibility; being born into a high status family gives advantages like ambition, diligence, contacts, reputation, and social skills and the like which help at every stage of career. (p. 106)

Region	No. of restaurants	(%)	No. of takeaways	(%)	Total	(%)	Spread (%) of Chinese people
England	1,645	80.8	3,262	79.7	4,907	80.1	94.0
North	95	4.8	253	6.2	348	5.7	2.6
Yorkshire	103	5.1	371	9.0	474	7.7	5.6
East Midlands	115	5.6	386	9.4	501	8.2	5.0
East Anglia	53	2.6	137	3.4	190	3.1	3.9
South East	838	41.0	1,132	27.7	1,970	32.2	59.0
South West	115	5.6	329	8.0	444	7.3	4.4
West Midlands	111	5.5	382	9.3	493	8.0	3.5
North West	215	10.6	272	6.7	487	7.9	10.0
Wales	73	3.5	324	7.9	397	6.5	2.5
Scotland	272	13.5	396	9.8	668	10.9	3.1
N. Ireland	46	2.2	106	2.6	152	2.5	0.4
Total UK	2,036	100.0	4,088	100.0	6,124	100.0	100.0

Table 5.3: Density of Chinese takeaways and restaurant units, 1993

Risk-bearing: Becoming self-employed is thought to construe a high level of risk compared to other employment forms, especially full-time employment. It is, however, misleading to assume that becoming self-employed entails risk *per se*: entrepreneurs believe that they are undertaking calculated risks because of their belief that they have the skills to run their business successfully. Much of the popular franchise press propounds the belief that there may be less risk in taking a franchise than starting an independent business (Baron and Schmidt, 1991; Hough, 1986; Izraeli, 1972; Sklar, 1977). This contention, however, is largely unproven but still persists. Nonetheless, differing people have differing levels of willingness to bear risk, and this affects their career choices. A combination of market imperfections and other factors such as mobility considerations being manifest in family ties, age, local network, and social status (Noe and Barber, 1993) mean that whilst some start their own business, others remain unemployed and some become franchisees, but these classifications are not rigid.

Family issues: Running a business is thought to be a mentally and physically demanding task because the owner is responsible for the success or failure of the enterprise. This situation puts great pressure on the entrepreneur's family because the long hours, commitment, and stresses may cause strains and discontent in the family unit. As a result of the responsibilities of being self-employed, the individual requires informational and emotional support from their social network. Some individuals become self-employed because they inherit their parents' business: Carroll and Mosakawski (1987) indicate that the inheritance process is sequential. In the initial stages, the individual holds 'helping' positions, later followed by ownership and control. The early stage experiences not only climatize the individual to working in a family-owned business but also help them to think of it as a realistic alternative to conventional employment. Research by Hough (1986) shows that about a third of franchisees had fathers who were self-employed at some time, meaning that they had some exposure to self-employment, and this situation was particularly marked in the Wimpy fast food system (which could be attributed to the ethnic background of the franchisees). Katz (1994) argues that family support for the entrepreneurial career, and the decision to be a franchisee, impact on career choice because often family financial resources are used in starting a new venture. One reason, therefore, for not becoming self-employed or a franchisee is the lack of support for the career by the members of the prospective franchisee's/entrepreneur's family.

Network

A key tenet of perfect competition theory is that all market participants are non-differentiable by the information that they hold. The reality of markets, however, is that different quantities and qualities of information are held by differing people, meaning that information has value – or currency – which depreciates over time and must be searched for. In order to gain access to marketplace information, Brush (1992) suggests that job-seekers and potential and existing entrepreneurs employ three different types of activity:

1. business planning;
2. market research;
3. environmental scanning or seeking and collecting information about events in a firm's environment (Ghoshal and Westney, 1991).

Common to each of these activities is networking or using and developing 'connections' in order to get things done and moving ahead in life. A social network comprises a set of nodes (people, organizations), linked by a set of social relationships (friendship, partnerships, market) and may be biased by gender and ethnicity (Kleinman, 1980), an aspect which has the potential to influence the diffusion of particular innovations and job mobility. For example, where there are strong local ties to a particular location, some people will be loathe to move to another town (Brush *et al*, 1976). This variable also has the potential to influence the decision to become a franchisee as some franchisors offer licences in locations which would mean some degree of upheaval in the individual's social ties. Some people may perceive this as a benefit, but others may be willing to forgo the potential benefits of being a franchisee in exchange for maintaining their existing network.

Research concerning networks has received a wealth of attention in the entrepreneurship literature and, within such texts, the entrepreneur is viewed to be embedded in a complex set of social networks (Low and MacMillan, 1988). These networks affect new-idea generation, strategy formulation, uncertainty reduction, time spent during the business start-up process, feasibility studies, and resource collection (Baucus and Human, 1994; Dubini and Aldrich, 1991; Ostagaard and Birley, 1994). They either facilitate or inhibit venture development by enabling or preventing effective linkages between the entrepreneur and the required resources and available economic opportunities. The same situation is, however, equally true of non-entrepreneurial situations, such as searches for a new full-time career (Aldrich and Reese, 1993; Aldrich and Zimmer, 1986; Birley; 1985). For example, individuals who scour the recruitment pages are engaging in market research as well as perhaps environmental scanning activities (they could, for instance, be engaging in a search regarding a competitor's recruitment campaign), but placing their résumé with an employment agency permits them potential access to expertise and participants of a social network with which they are not linked directly. Furthermore, Carroll and Teo (1996) show that non-managerial staff, in particular, benefit financially from various forms of networking activity.

Networks can be categorized in two ways: active and latent; and inner and outer circle networks (Ramachandran and Ramnarayan, 1993). Active networks are those where people are working/conversing with on a regular basis. Conversely, latent networks represent potential networks, such as with friends of close associates. These latent networks may be activated if the individual makes the necessary time investments and may lead to alternative career options, either through direct employment or the provision of information concerning a potential opening within a firm which is yet to advertise. Within the franchise network, some franchisors have sought to develop latent networks to help reduce recruitment costs. The process has entailed the awarding of bonuses to franchisees who introduce individuals (with the potential and capacity to become franchisees themselves) to the franchisor.

Perhaps overlaying the active and latent networks are the supportive nature of the relationships. Individuals have close relationships with members of an inner circle, who provide ongoing emotional support. Such emotional support will not be evident from members of the outer circle, but these do not affect their significance since they could be a valuable source of information. Many researchers concur that entrepreneurs rely extensively on informal networks, comprising mainly inner-circle members such as friends, family, and business people, and less on the formal network of banks, accountants, and lawyers when career and business planning (Curran and Blackburn, 1991). In relation to franchising, The Royal Bank of Scotland (1993) showed that potential franchisees often sought the advice of accountants but they also rely heavily on the views of friends and relations.

Such advice may not, however, be objective. As members of an inner circle are likely to illustrate similar values and cultures, so they may be less able to assess objectively whether a particular route is available to an individual as well as perhaps whether the route, in fact, exists. Because members of the outer circle have a different 'culture', so they could have different perceptions and information which, in turn, could be useful in assessing the viability of a particular career route. For example, in a study of job mobility in the labour market for managers, Granovetter (1974) discovered the central role played by members of outer-circle networks or those with whom one had 'weak ties' in the search for a new job. In order to benefit from alternative opportunities, Burt (1992) notes that it is important that the entrepreneur moves beyond his immediate social network to establish an 'institutional network' of formal links and sources of advice, such as banks, chambers of commerce, and other nodes occupying a point of centrality with particular networks.

At the core of the issues of objectivity and new-idea generation is the subject of network density and diversity. The density of a network refers to the extensiveness of ties between persons or organizations, but diversity is also significant. An entrepreneur needs to be represented in a sufficient number of networks to have some kind of voice in the outside world and to receive new ideas and options for advancement. There is, however, an optimal size to networks because individuals can only spend so much time and energy maintaining network connections before diminishing returns accrue. Of additional importance is the tone of conversation between the members of a network. While social networks play an important role, therefore, in the career decision and planning process by increasing the individual's information and knowledge resources, the level of encouragement and sponsorship by other people also affects career choices and direction (Weenig and Midden, 1991). In a study of the role of outer-circle social networks in new business start-ups, Foss (1993) suggests that constructive criticism tends to be interpreted in a negative way. These negative interpretations reduce the probability to start, but they do not prevent further assembling of information and material resources which could be employed in other ways.

Towards a framework of analysis

A career search is the process by which individuals identify, investigate, and decide among alternative job alternatives. It is a process which is crucial to both individuals seeking employment and the organizations that ultimately hire these individuals, but is affected by a variety of antecedent variables which, either individually or in tandem, act as boundaries to certain career routes. These inhibitors serve to differentiate potential franchisees from those becoming self-employed and those pursuing full-time status or some other employment condition. Moving to a different position on the employment continuum therefore entails overcoming both perceived and actual barriers evident in both the antecedent variables and during the career choice process as well as those present in the labour market. For example, in a review of attitudes to part-time work, a Department of Employment report (1992) indicated that the problems that their respondents had in finding part-time work were: age, lack of awareness of current employment conditions, lack of recent experience, perceived prejudice by employers in employing women with school-age children, the prevalence of 'low-grade' jobs, the lack of availability of part-time work, geographic distance and the perceived lack of flexibility in the jobs. Each of these variables may, therefore, influence the second career search process because these boundaries could direct where and how the individual assesses certain job opportunities. For example, some people may wish to remain in part-time employment because it allows them to realize domestic responsibilities, which means that they would not necessarily consider alternatives, such as franchising or full-time employment that would mitigate against meeting these obligations. These antecedent variables permeate, therefore, each stage of the career search process and may be of some use to help franchisors target potential franchisees more closely:

> ...the majority of franchisors ... confirmed that they have the most difficulty in targeting potential franchisees. A connected problem clearly exists for marketing generally. In essence, it would seem most franchisors are unsure who their potential targets are and how to reach them. Perhaps this is because of insufficient analysis at the outset, or the qualifying criteria for a franchisee being too low. For those at the higher end of the spectrum, the key must be to ascertain a genuine understanding of suitable candidates for the franchise by identifying such factors as age, gender, education, business sophistication, communication skills, personality traits and career objectives, etc. .... Only then can the promotional mix be tailored specifically to the target audience. (MacMillan, 1996; p. 37)

While an understanding each of these variables is of undoubted significance to effective targeting of franchisees, it is also of importance to understanding how the main sets of antecedent variables affect the career choice process. Understanding the process is important because some individuals choose from a variety of employment forms and, by examining the ways in which individuals come to prefer a certain path, so some insight may be gained concerning the impinging factors on the decision to become a franchisee. In order to illustrate how each stage of the career search process is also relevant to the choice of becoming a franchisee, the results of a tracking analysis of attendees to a franchise exhibitions in 1993 are relevant. The research was conducted by the University of Westminster through their association with Blenheim Exhibitions and Conferences Limited, who organize two National Franchise Exhibitions. The first of these is held in the spring in Olympia (London) and the second in the autumn, at the National Exhibition Centre (Birmingham). Each attracts about 10,000 paying visitors, each of whom completes a registration card on entry and some being asked to answer subsequent questions by an interviewer. These respondents to the initial survey were used to define a sample of individuals who had expressed an interest in franchising. Of the research population mailed, a total of 169 (one-third) usable responses were received. Of these replies, eighty-two visited the London exhibition and the remainder attended the one in Birmingham. This chapter only uses the Birmingham study because the initial questionnaire was more suited to answering and illustrating some of the issues inherent to the career decision process. The responses were compared to the original questionnaire, from which it was possible to categorize respondents in the following manner: converts to the new business set-up (those who chose franchising); those who continued in self-employment; those who remained in full-time employment; and 'others'. These categories are based on the career routes chosen after visiting the franchise exhibitions and are limited because the study does not include those people who did not consider franchising at all (if they attended the franchise exhibition, the individual is viewed as considering franchising as a career option). The differing categories in themselves suggest that the initial stages of career choice dynamics, at least, are a comparative process between differing forms of employment (Thomas, 1980). Within each of the career decision stages, the four categories are compared and contrasted to elucidate whether there were any differences between converts and the three other categories.

Many of the varying theories of job search (Blau, 1993; Mihal *et al*, 1984; Osborn, 1990; Soelberg, 1967) suggest that there are distinct stages or phases to job search activity. According to these theories, job search activities follow a logical sequence and that once a job has cleared a particular hurdle with respect to a particular attribute, the individual no longer employs that attribute as a criterion (Osborn, 1990). In order to evaluate the differing career routes and the decisional stages within the career choice stages, a holistic model is required. One of the more comprehensive frameworks which encapsulates the varying stages in which the individuals choose their career is provided by Soelberg (1967). Although possibly dated, it has received only limited criticism (Power and Aldag, 1985), but this may be indicative of its lack of widespread application to job search and choice situations. However, it is of potential use to researchers seeking to describe and compare, for example, the activities that constitute the entrepreneurial process and becoming an employee, rather than factors affecting the process (Katz, 1994; Gartner, 1985). Soelberg's model was developed after conducting detailed interviews with job seekers and a review of decision-making behaviour. The underlying premise of the model is that the individual is always seen 'in motion' in terms of career assessment, decision-making and change (Mihal *et al*, 1984). The model has taken a variety of formats with the number of stages ranging between four and six and illustrates that the job search moves from being extensive, with the individual applying substantial effort to finding a particular job, to being intensive about a particular job. Although the model is essentially sequential, the breadth of the search and the length of time the individual spends exploring possible career avenues, is affected by the amount of information conveyed in their network and from prior learned behaviours which showed that some search actions are more effective than others. Equally, the individual's level of stress and frustration may also be important to affecting the job search behaviours (Barber *et al*, 1994). In accordance with Power and Aldag's (1985) call for simplicity and clarity when employing the model, this chapter presents only four stages of Soelberg's model. These stages are described and related to the franchise context in the following paragraphs.

Phase 1: Identification
The identification stage, illustrated in Figure 5.3, comprises two components. The first constituent is the recognition that a gap exists between the actual state of affairs and the ideal career state. Depending on the individual's tolerance for the discrepancy, after a certain threshold the individual is motivated to seek alternatives to reduce that discrepancy. The discrepancy may be tolerated if the person's commitment to the organization is high; they may feel that the actual state of affairs is only temporary and therefore decide to weather the storm. Alternatively, if the individual feels that the problem is more deep-rooted, they may decide to act. A Department of Employment (1992) study of the motivating factors underlying people's preferences for part-time work showed that commitments and motivations changed not just according to the changing personal circumstances of the individual, but also over time. Respondents to the survey

were separated into three main groups according to their interest in working and the extent to which they are pulled or pushed into such work:

- voluntary part-timers, whose choice to work part-time was primarily associated with child care/domestic responsibilities, although in some instances personal health was also a consideration;
- involuntary part-timers who wanted to work full-time but were unable to do so because of either their domestic responsibilities and/or lack of suitable jobs; and
- involuntary part-timers who did not want to work but needed the income.

Over time these initial motivations changed: some respondents preferred to work on a part-time basis because the perceived benefits of doing so, such as flexibility with coping with domestic responsibilities, outweighed the disadvantages. In other words, they became committed to a particular work pattern which precluded them from considering other forms of work including self-employment and franchising.

The greater the level of satisfaction with the existing state of affairs, therefore, the lower the received desirability of movement will be. March and Simon (1958) suggest that satisfaction is high at work when they meet a variety of antecedent factors:

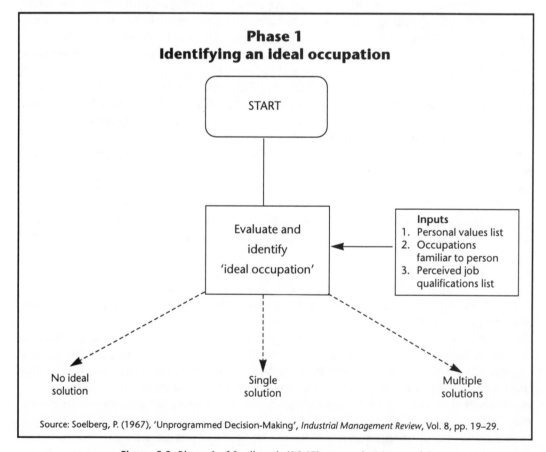

Source: Soelberg, P. (1967), 'Unprogrammed Decision-Making', *Industrial Management Review*, Vol. 8, pp. 19–29.

Figure 5.3: Phase 1 of Soelberg's (1967) career decision model

1. the job characteristics conform to the individual's self-characterization of himself (for example, career stage);
2. instrumental relationships at the workplace are predictable (networks and employer power); and
3. work requirements are compatible with the requirements of other roles that the individual holds (commitment and life stage factors).

The extent to which discrepancies at work may be tolerated is also a function of the state of the labour market and economy at any given time. When jobs are bountiful, voluntary labour movement is high, and is low when jobs are scarce. March and Simon (1958) indicate that the perceived ease of movement for an individual depends on the availability of jobs for which that individual is qualified in organizations visible to him or her. The greater the perceived number of alternatives, the greater the perceived ease of movement. This ease of movement is moderated by factors such as age, ethnicity, networks, cultural capital, education, as well as issues concerning bounded rationality.

Using the language of consumer decision-making models the varying employment choices are affected by the individual's evoked set or, rather, the set of choices which would, in the individual's judgement, serve the same general purpose (Zeithaml, 1988) but is limited by bounded rationality because not all possible alternatives are considered. In other words, the first career solution is selected according to its ability to meet some prior objective; if no solution meets those minimum requirements, aspirations may be lowered and the identification process begins again. An occupational choice is evaluated, therefore, according to its relative attractiveness amongst options that are perceived as substitutes by the individual. The solution may not be the optimal one because it may not be the best career option available (that is, the one which accrues the greatest income flow): it is the one which is 'good enough'. Within bounded rationality, the chosen career is not necessarily based on calculating the opportunity cost – a measurement of the alternatives forgone (Lipsey, 1990). That is, there is no implicit assumption that the process of rational occupational choice between alternative job opportunities is dependent upon the balance of net advantages (MacKay *et al*, 1971; Rottenburg, 1955; Smith, 1976) of independent activity versus working for somebody else, unemployment (Knight, 1921) or becoming a controlled self employed worker – that is, a franchisee (Abell, 1989; Arendorff, 1986; Felstead, 1991; 1993).

Some of the discrepancies affecting movement are apparent from the differing motivations to become self-employed and to cease being self-employed. For example, Bevan *et al*'s (1990) survey of people's differing motivations for entering and leaving self-employment suggests that the most common discrepancy experienced by entrants is the desire for more freedom. Those exiting self-employment do so because of financial problems and because it affected the quality of family life. As noted above, the motivation to become a franchisee can also be observed from the need to reduce a particular discrepancy, such as the need for independence by those in full-time employment and the desire for superior competitive advantages by those currently self-employed. Indicative of this latter situation, Stanworth and Purdy (1994) show that over half of the attendees at franchise exhibitions in Britain are already self-employed, or have been at some time in the past. They also observed that the sharpest levels of interest in buying a franchise emerged amongst those who had previously had their own business but were located back in the wider labour market. These findings corroborate earlier research (Ozanne and Hunt, 1971;

Stanworth, 1991) where it was established that the majority of fast food franchisees had prior experience of self-employment.

The manner by which the discrepancy between the actual state of affairs and the ideal career state is narrowed by reference to certain occupations and careers they are familiar with in terms of their 'personal values list' and 'perceived job qualification list'. These lists are, for the majority of people, tacit (unwritten). Personal values represent desired outcomes and their importance to the individual; job qualifications are the job skills that people believe they have and derive from their prior employment experiences, career stages, socialization, and education. Within these lists, the nature of commitment is of particular importance, and those exploring franchise opportunities seem to be more orientated towards work values rather than loyalty to a particular career, organization, or job.

When the identification phase ends, people can be classified as having: no ideal solution; a single ideal solution; or more than one ideal solution. The extent to which people fall into a particular category can be attributed to self-efficacy, or their belief that they can accomplish specific tasks, and may be as broad as the desire to working for one-self, rather than being as particular as becoming a franchisee. For example, Bevan *et al* (1990) show that the majority of their respondents had the desire to become self-employed rather than necessarily having a specific business idea; Fulop's (1996) research of franchisees' motivations for entering a particular franchise sector indicates that of those franchisees without previous direct employment experience, 'personal interest' proved the most important reason 'or their decision. Bandura (1986) hypothesized that an individual's belief in his/her competence to accomplish specific tasks has four prima-ry sources:

1. vicarious learning (indirect learning from other people's experiences);
2. performance accomplishments;
3. physiological arousal; and
4. verbal persuasion.

For example, a person may be intent on becoming a franchisee because they imagine that they could flourish by running their own business with the assistance of a larger, experi-enced organization. This intention may be based either on the lifestyle of a person that they know or that they have read about (vicarious learning), and a comparison with their personal value list and perceived job qualification list. Those people who remain undecided about their future direction are seen to have lower levels of self-efficacy. This, in turn, suggests that undecided individuals have lower levels of self-esteem, irrational beliefs and anxiety (characteristics which are prevalent among those made redundant) leading to excessive worry and a prolonged career choice process (Blustein *et al*, 1994; Stead *et al*, 1993). Within the career choice process, those in a particular solution class behave similarly during the job search and choice stages; those in different classes behave differently (Power and Aldag, 1985).

Labour does not, therefore, necessarily react in a totally rational manner in response to economic forces. Labour market imperfections (March and Simon, 1958) sug-gest that not all individuals have the means or intent (due, in part, to the time and effort costs of collection) to reach a balance of the 'net advantages', as these workers have lim-ited information and knowledge of the workings of the labour market and job rewards offered by other firms in the local market, or those of being self-employed or being a franchisee (Hunt and Morgan, 1995). Thus, some individuals will only consider, for example, being a full-time employee because they are unaware of or refuse to consider other available employment options. These people direct their efforts and resources to realizing this goal, others may direct their efforts along a variety of directions.

The majority of the surveyed attendees to the Birmingham franchise exhibitions indicated that they were considering employment opportunities other than franchising; within the 'convert' category, however, it appears that some people were intent on becoming a franchisee while others changed their minds later, on finding more about franchising. Of those who did not decide to become a franchisee, the benefits of pursuing employment, setting up on their own, or continuing in their own business were more attractive. When a person is intent on pursuing a particular course, they seek information which is orientated towards achieving their goal, which means that the planning phase is focused towards the marshalling of specific resources. Thus, although the majority of people who later became franchisees were interested in franchising for more than a year, they had an agenda to meet their goal; others were perhaps less focused. Table 5.4 shows that those who later became employees, for example, had been interested in franchising for the least amount of time prior to visiting the exhibition.

Considering areas outside franchising	Converts	Set-up	Continued Employment	Other	Total
Yes	9	6	11	19	6	51
No	7	3	7	14	8	39
Total	16	9	18	33	14	90
Interest in franchising before exhibition					
Last month	2	3	2	10	3	20
1 to 6 months	5	3	3	10	4	25
6 to 12 months	0	2	3	5	4	14
Over 1 year	9	1	10	8	3	31
Total	16	9	18	33	14	90

Table 5.4: Respondents' propensities to search outside franchising

Phase 2: Planning

Figure 5.4 shows that after identifying the necessity to change, a person develops a plan – or an intention – to realize it:

1.　developing measurable criteria to identify and guide the search for a particular job;
2.　allocating attention, time, money and effort to the search;
3.　look for and identify specific alternatives for consideration.

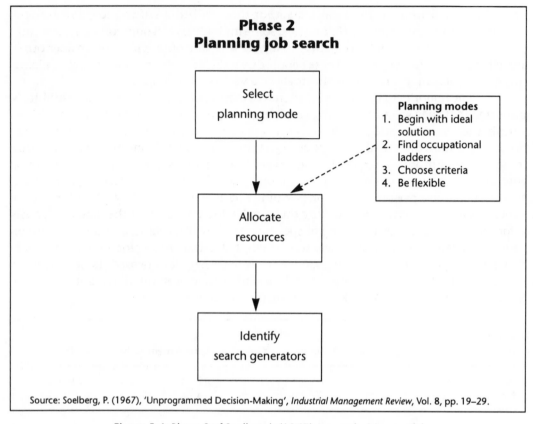

Figure 5.4: *Phase 2 of Soelberg's (1967) career decision model*

According to Mihal *et al* (1984), search generators may be internal or external in focus. Internal search refers to potential career options already known to the individual. Examples of external search generators may range from visiting franchise fairs, networking, talking with colleagues who may be franchisees, career advisers, employment centres, media, franchise directories and sending letters. As noted above, these searches are constrained by the individual's bounded rationality.

When seeking a new post, they engage in one of four planning modes. They:

1. envisage the ideal job and try to think of at least one viable entry level for reaching it;
2. identify the traditional prescribed career paths for aspirants to reach an occupation;
3. define specific qualities that pertain to the job, but not for career development; or
4. decide to be flexible by identifying job alternatives that either close as few doors as possible or are good starting points for later career development (for example, become a franchisee with a view to being wholly self-employed at a later date, or become self-employed as a stop gap).

As noted above, the majority of attendees to the franchise exhibition had decided to be flexible by considering other alternatives to franchising. Perhaps one of the constraining factors to being a franchisee within a particular system is that there appears to be only one option available to the majority of potential investors, but self-employment is more flexible concerning the scale of risk being acquired. Carroll and Mosakowski (1987) indicate that there are at least four common routes by which an individual can become self-employed:

1. an individual goes into business for him- or herself by initiating a sole proprietorship to sell his or her services or other products;
2. an individual starts a new firm with at least one employee and operates it from the owner-manager position;
3. an individual assumes or inherits the owner-manager position of an existing firm he or she previously worked for or was associated with in some other way;
4. an individual purchases outright and begins to manage an existing firm for which he or she did not previously work.

Phase 3: Search and choice

This stage begins when the first search generator is activated and is complete when the individual announces that they are no longer interested in seeking alternatives. In this stage, potential careers can pass through a variety stages of investigation, from information collection and decisions, to whether the option should be accepted or rejected according to whether it meets certain criteria. During the search stage, individuals may change their aspirations and the evaluation criteria are subject to alteration. For example, the attendees to the Birmingham franchise exhibition were asked to assess their likelihood of becoming a franchisee, and it is apparent that although converts were generally disposed to becoming a franchisee some people changed their minds from being undecided/likely to converting. It is also apparent that the self-assessments of likelihood to buy a franchise at the time of attending an exhibition appear to have some predictive value. Of those who were later to become franchisees, it is evident that they planned to take action in the immediate future, which suggests intentionality.

The factors affecting the screening procedure include the number of jobs passing the initial screening process, the amount of research resource available, number of rejections, and the identification of a suitable job. Of the converts, about 40% only considered two franchises seriously; a quarter considered only one and another quarter considered three. This situation is mirrored in Soelberg's (1967) career choice process: people stop searching after making an implicit choice and they are quite certain of receiving an offer from the companies, when resources are running out or when two or more acceptable alternatives have been identified. When an implicit choice has not been made, Soelberg (1967) argues that people undertake an elaborate job selection process to decide which option to take. The implicit cost of acquiring information to direct the decision-making process affects the extensiveness of the search. Such costs not only refer to potential monetary outlay, but to time, convenience, decision-delay and the costs of acquiring the knowledge to find the information and, once found, to interpret it. Typically, therefore, searches are often superficial. The search stage is further complicated since people screen jobs concurrently and may identify a variety of acceptable posts during the search stage and activate various search processes throughout the search process.

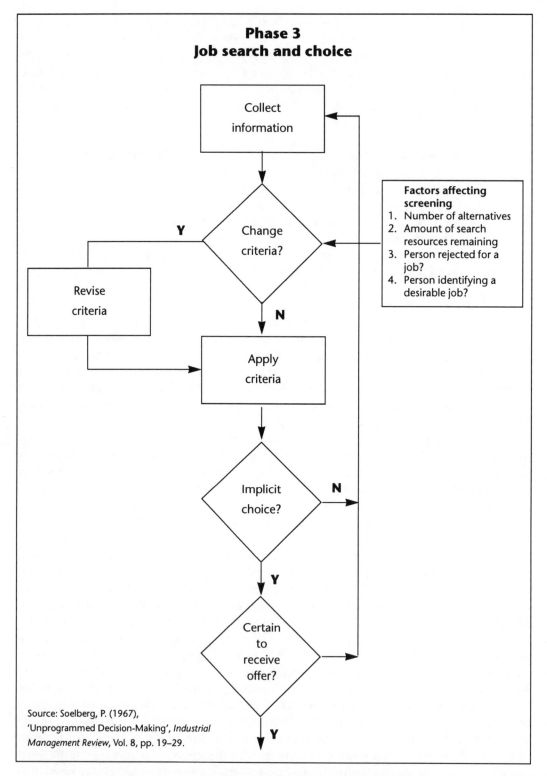

Figure 5.5: Phase 3 of Soelberg's (1967) career decision model

Likelihood	Converts	Set-up	Continued	Employment	Other	Total
Definitely	2	1	0	2	0	5
Very likely	4	2	1	5	3	15
Likely	8	3	9	7	3	30
Undecided	2	3	8	17	7	37
Unlikely	0	0	0	2	1	3
Total	16	9	18	33	14	90
Planning next action						
Next month	5	1	0	4	1	11
1 to 2 months	5	2	2	2	3	14
Next 6 months	3	3	4	13	4	27
Next year	1	2	6	10	0	19
Some time	2	1	6	4	6	19
Not planning	0	0	0	0	0	0
Total	16	9	18	33	14	90

Table 5.5: Self-assessed likelihood of buying a franchise at time of visiting the exhibition

During the search, an implicit job choice is made. Jobs are evaluated against absolute standards (that is, against primary and secondary goals); people implicitly select the first job they judge to more than adequately meet their goals. Of some importance to the career choice is the individual's level of uncertainty of the length of time that they will be unemployed (arising from the perceptions, albeit founded on incomplete knowledge, of the number and type of actual employment opportunities available). The perception that those people who have been unemployed for a prolonged period are unsaleable commodities within the labour market, and are perceived to be unsuitable for work by employers and unlikely to be recruited, is influential in affecting the movement towards self-employment or becoming a franchisee. It could be affective at two stages: within the initial period of unemployment or at the latter stages. Evidence seems to suggest, however, that the long-term unemployed, as a result of disillusionment, do not tend to job-search as intensively as those who have been out of work for shorter time periods and may not have access to the necessary financial or network resources required (Layard *et al*, 1991). This said, it has yet to be ascertained whether the long-term unemployed also exhibit relatively low levels of search for self-employment opportunities.

Phase 4: Decision confirmation and commitment

Illustrated in the diagram below (Figure 5.6), Phase 4 is characterized by people's decision confirmation, which serves to verify information about the implicit job choice, to provide a post-rationalization for accepting a particular route, to provide time to ensure other, better, offers are not forthcoming, and to allow the opportunity to back out. During this comfort zone building stage (Baucus and Human, 1994), people emphasize the good points of the job and collect only biased information and bargain only with representatives of the selected organizations. Reflecting this situation, exhibitors at franchise trade shows indicate that they often meet and discuss their offering with those people

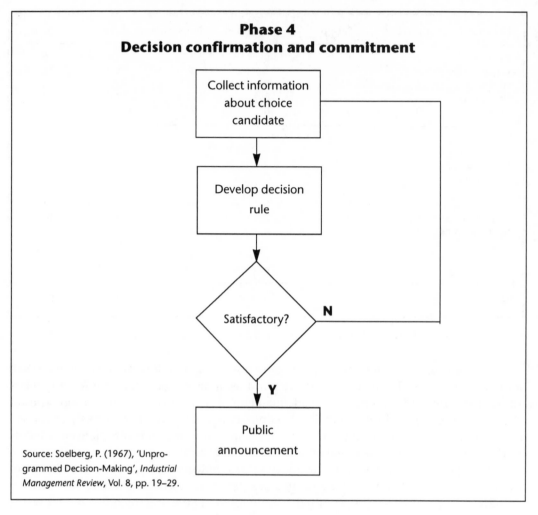

Phase 4
Decision confirmation and commitment

Source: Soelberg, P. (1967), 'Unprogrammed Decision-Making', *Industrial Management Review*, Vol. 8, pp. 19–29.

Figure 5.6: Phase 4 of Soelberg's (1967) career decision model

Reason for not becoming a franchisee	Set-up	Continued	Employment	Other	Total
Lack of bank support	3	2	2	1	8
Lack of response from franchisor	1	1	0	0	2
Perceive franchising to be high risk	1	3	7	7	18
Lack of family support	0	0	1	0	1
Too much control by franchisor	2	9	6	2	19
Employment is more secure	0	1	18	2	21
Was given an offer of a job	1	0	9	0	10
Other	4	6	5	8	23
Total	12	22	48	20	102

NB: *respondents provided multiple answers.*

Table 5.6: Reasons for not becoming a franchisee

who have already applied and are about to become franchisees (Hatcliffe *et al*, 1995). Once the individual is prepared to make a commitment to the confirmed choice candidate, they are anxious to make a public announcement explaining and garnering support for their decision. According to the survey, those people who did not convert tended to perceive that the franchisor had too much control in the franchise relationship, and that becoming a franchisee was an employment option characterized by high levels of risk. Other disadvantages and benefits of franchising are listed below.

The relative merits of franchising

The advantages and disadvantages of franchising depend to some extent on the nature and content of the agreement, but there are several core balancing factors which commonly relate to the kinds of activities that franchising involves. From the following lists, it is evident that franchising tends to favour the franchisor more than the franchisee, partially reflecting the inherent imbalance of power between the two parties.

Franchisee advantages

Of the most popular franchise myths, franchising is seen to construe competitive advantages to both the franchisor and franchisee, such as reduced probability of failure (Ayling, 1988). Whilst the presence and nature of competitive advantages by simply being a member of a franchise system are questionable (see Chapter 8), the common perception of franchising is that the level of risk incurred by the franchisee is reduced, especially in mature franchises. In these more established franchise operations, the franchisee is required to use tested operating procedures and internal controls to mitigate the effects of his inexperience and ineptitude. The franchisee is provided with an established brand name, enforced quality maintenance through quality control, locational analysis on setting up operations, initial training and continued field supervision. It from this perception of lower risk that many of the other advantages accruing to the franchisee are seen to derive:

- Access to a period of training and the acquisition of technical expertise and other skills and intangible cultural assets which serve to enhance reputation, such as a commitment to quality.
- As the business format or product should have been market tested (some franchisors have more pre-franchise experience than others), the franchisee has access to a tried and tested format.
- No need to purchase goodwill. This said, some franchisees include the initial franchise costs as goodwill and depreciate it over the duration of the franchise contract.
- The opportunity to acquire a high turnover and branded business – but this does not necessarily equate with ongoing success. High sales do not mean high profit.
- Access and benefit from the franchisor's investment in new product development and marketing effort.
- Easier entry into business with more available support to assist with site selection, and negotiating with planning officers and developers.

- Although this is very much related to the type and franchisor's brand equity, there may be a lower capital requirement than starting business independently.
- There are improved opportunities of obtaining low cost loan facilities from banks due to the perception of low risk.
- Being part of a group, there may be opportunities to lower the cost of inputs and raw materials.
- Due to operating manuals and the contractual positioning of the franchisee within the network, the franchisee may feel lower levels of role ambiguity than independent start-ups.
- Access to potential mentors in either other franchisees and/or regional franchise manager.
- Despite contractual obligations, franchisees are at least likely to feel to have operational freedom and decision-making authority.

Against these advantages, however, are the following disadvantages to the franchisee:

Franchisee disadvantages

- Franchising is not 'self-employment' as many, especially the popular press and franchise exhibition organizers, contest. It is a halfway house between self-employment and being an employee (Knight, 1984; Kessler, 1957).
- The franchisee is dependent upon the franchisor to maintain brand equity and value. Brand mismanagement by the franchisor, or resulting from adverse publicity concerning franchisor-franchisee relationships, can be detrimental to the whole system.
- The franchisee lives off profit whereas the franchisor is motivated by sales. As such the franchisor may instigate policies designed to improve sales volumes, such as price discounts, which may be detrimental to store profitability.
- Contrary to popular myth, franchisor failure rates vary with their relevant economic sector and competitive peer group. They are not static and some franchise 'sectors' illustrate greater risk than others (see Chapter 8). The failure of a franchisor may leave the franchisee with a business which is not viable in isolation.
- A common provision found in business format agreements is that the franchisee will pay the franchise fees 'without deduction and set-off'. But, in some instances, the franchisor's financial position has deteriorated such that it has ceased to provide any management or advertising services to its franchisees (Adams, 1994). Consequently, franchisees feel that they are paying for nothing and fail to pay their dues. This then leads to the perception that both parties are in breach of contract and, in turn, could lead to litigation.
- The franchise contract is non-negotiable. The franchisor has tight control over the product and business supported by a legal contract weighted in favour of the franchisor, and the contract can be modified unilaterally by the franchisor (Hunt, 1972).
- There is no franchise-specific legislation in the UK, unlike the USA. As such, some people – typically those with redundancy payments – have become

(and, regrettably, will be) the target of less scrupulous operators (Brown, 1969; Baillieu, 1988).

- The franchisee cannot exit at will and is not at liberty to sell the franchise even though the business is legally separate from the franchisor. The sale is subject to franchisor approval.
- Not all franchisors have been subject to feasibility studies to test whether their business is able to be franchised. Indeed, MacMillan (1995) and Farrell (1984) suggest that prior to franchising, the firm typically has insufficient business experience in terms of company-owned outlets and an insufficient regard for pilot operations, with too many companies being attracted by the prospect of realizing first mover advantages. Relatedly, not all franchisors enter into franchising using a systematic approach and there is some reliance on 'muddling through' (such practices may increase franchisee risk) as shown by MacMillan. He observes that franchisor expansion, at least in the UK, has tended to follow a general four-stage pattern, as follows:
  - Initially shooting in the dark (influenced by competition and perceived wisdom in industry).
  - Getting a little arrogant (feeling of having got things under control and a belief that franchising is relatively easy).
  - A period of re-examination and loss of confidence (as mature franchisees get more powerful and flex their muscles and cause disruption in the network).
  - Uncertainty over future recruitment policies and, indeed, recruitment candidates.
- The franchisee is unlikely to meet self-actualization and security needs (Ozanne and Hunt, 1971).
- The majority of franchisors are, in themselves, small businesses and confront many of the issues and problems inherent to such concerns. For example, reviewing the qualitative causes and symptoms of business failure, Argenti (1976) indicates that failing firms are characterized by one-man rule, lack of depth of management skill, weak finance function, unbalanced skills and knowledge at board-level, as well as high gearing levels. Although Argenti does not make this point, these symptoms tend to be more prevalent within small businesses rather than their larger counterparts. Some such weak companies then take on a 'big project' – such as franchising – which, while not excessively large when launched, can become a burden when something goes wrong – a not infrequent occurrence with projects.
- Fast food franchisees, in particular, work long hours with the franchisor sometimes contractually determining the hours of work.
- Franchisees may be 'positioned' by the franchisor in volatile or uncertain environments, whilst company-owned operations are placed in more munificent and less dynamic environments.
- Territory agreements may be difficult to enforce in practice and it is often in the franchisor's interest to build additional units within a region. Typically, it is then left to the franchisee to prove (through, for example, commissioning market research) that cannibalization of sales is occurring.
- With tie-in franchises, the franchisee may not gain advantages accruing

from transfer pricing opportunities due to the franchisor attempting to realize monopoly powers (Hewitt, 1964).

- The franchise may not meet the franchisee's expectations since the franchisor's sales pitch is likely to be misleadingly favourable to the franchise (the franchisor typically also attempts to control information dissemination about the franchise due to fears of imitation). This may lead to false expectations and dissatisfaction to occur, otherwise called work-role transition mismatch (West and Rushton, 1989). Since the consequences of this state of affairs are surprise and some difficulty, franchisees may either adapt themselves to the environment, change the environment to suit them, or seek to leave (Nicholson, 1984).

- After the relationship has been terminated, the ex-franchisee is still subject to abide by some of the franchise contract's clauses (Nicholl, 1995). For example, a franchisee may feel at the end of the contract term that the knowledge they have acquired and the goodwill they have built up, is sufficient for them to succeed in providing the goods or services under another trading identity. Most franchise contracts help to preclude this opportunity for varying lengths of time by protecting the franchisor through:
  1. provisions in the covenants of restraint of trade which prevent the franchisee trading from the same site;
  2. preventing the ex-franchisee setting up a competing business from another site within such proximity to the former business that it will damage the surviving goodwill of the former franchise outlet (Adams, 1994);
  3. preventing the franchisee from damaging other franchised outlets by establishing a competing business in close proximity to them; and
  4. preventing the former franchisee from soliciting customers of the former business and employing his/her former employees or franchisor's employees.

Summary and conclusion

While a plethora of research has been devoted towards the examination of the motivations to franchise from the franchisor's perspective, the same cannot be said of franchisees. What little research exists in the public domain is characterized by the use of action frame of reference and consumer decision-making approaches. Although of significance because they at least provide some insight to the individual's decision to franchise, the frameworks are inherently limited. The limitations exist because the frameworks do not encompass a sufficiently broad array of antecedent variables which, either collectively or individually, have the power to influence employment choice as well as be able to help franchisors increase the sophistication of their generally blunt targeting tools. Whereas the consumer-decision models place consideration to the choice between different franchises rather than between different forms of employment (Baucus *et al*, 1993), the action frame of reference focuses only on prior employment experience, which is too narrow.

This chapter has argued that the decision to become a franchisee is embedded within career choices rather than being necessarily orientated towards product purchase decisions. Following Parkin (1971) and by drawing on prior research the chapter has argued that the nature, and possibly the frequency, of transitions among labour force states (employment, unemployment, self-employment, franchising) differ significantly among ethnic and gender groups and therefore have significant consequences for who becomes a franchisee. As a result of the intertwining of personal and organizational careers (Gunz, 1989), such variables may also have implications for who becomes a franchisor. Employment instability is more pervasive among minority and female workers (Barber *et al*, 1994) and, as such, analysis along closure theory lines may generate potentially new insights to who becomes a franchisee or a franchisor. It is perhaps no coincidence that franchising is dominated by men. In this vein of closure/labour inequality theory, the chapter posits that the decision to become a franchisee is dependent on three sets of inter-related antecedent variables, including social network, life stage, and prior employment experiences. Within these sets, the question of what motivates a person to become a franchisee versus some other form of self-employment is a function of a variety of factors, including ethnicity, gender, commitment, career stage, age, and education. These variables permeate the individual's career choice procedure, which itself is not a rationale process, and are culturally embedded. Therefore, it is culture, in particular class-culture, which is the ultimate differentiator in determining who becomes a franchisee and who does not:

> . . . it cannot be assumed that cultural forms are *determined* in some way as an automatic reflex by macro determinations such as class location, region, educational background. Certainly these variables are important and cannot be overlooked but *how* do they impinge on behaviour? . . . We need to understand how structures become sources of meaning and determinants on behaviour in the cultural milieu *at its own level* . . . In the case of job choice among the unqualified working class, for instance, we can *predict* final employment quite well from class background, geographic location, local opportunity structure, and educational attainment. Certainly these factors will give us a better guide than expressed intention from individuals say during vocational guidance counselling. But what is it to say in any sense that these variables *determinate* job choice? We are still left with the problem of the forms of decision taking and of the apparent willing acceptance of restricted opportunities . . . For a proper treatment . . . we must go to the cultural milieu. (Willis, 1977; pp. 17–72 – emphasis in the original)

Against the antecedent variables, the chapter has presented a model of the career choice process. Rather than applying it, however, to understanding how people choose specific job types, such as a chef, the model is applied to the legal form decision. Using Soelberg's (1967) career choice model and information from the University of Westminster's survey of attendees to franchise exhibitions, the chapter has sought to illustrate that there are varying degrees of intentionality in the decision to become a franchisee, and that the choice process comprises four different phases. The length of time within each phase is a function of intentionality and self-efficacy. Those individuals who are intent on becoming a franchisee spend less time than those who do so from unconscious and unintended antecedents, a finding which is consistent with the literature concerning the desire to become self-employed. Katz and Gartner (1988) and Bird (1988), for example, show that entrepreneurs' intentions guide goal setting, communication, organization, and other types of work.

While the chapter has argued for a more holistic approach to understanding the motivations and inhibitors to becoming a franchisee, there remains an important weakness which can only be resolved with additional research. The chapter has presented a model with two sets of variables influencing the propensity to become a franchisee: the antecedent variables and the career choice process. It has, however, only hypothesized that there is a link between the two components – the antecedent variables affect the career choice process – rather than empirically showing that a link between the two exists. Nonetheless, it possibly represents an initial step in the right direction. The prevalence of blunt targeting tools by franchisors means that there is at least some potential for more sophisticated approaches, but the development of such approaches would benefit from the input of researchers and practitioners with a bias in human resources, rather than remaining in the domain of those with marketing and selling foci.

Notes

1. I am grateful to Professor John Stanworth and his research team at the University of Westminster for allowing the use of some of their replies of their survey of attendees of the Birmingham franchise exhibitions. I am also grateful to Monica Briggs. Without their input, this chapter could not have been written.

2. In the UK, there is no specific franchise legislation and, when coming to the contract, the franchisee is viewed, not as a consumer but as a 'business person'. If the individual was legally defined as a consumer, then some pre-contractual negotiation may be required to occur and the franchisor may be required to divulge the operations manual.

Innovation:
the route to sustainable
competitive advantage and survival?

6 | Types and sources of innovation in franchising[1]

We keep moving forward, opening new doors, and doing new things, because we're curious and curiosity keeps leading us down new paths.

Walt Disney, Film-maker and animator, *The Man Behind the Magic*

The ability to learn faster than your competitors may be the only sustainable competitive advantage.

Arie De Geus, Business Strategist at Royal Dutch/Shell, quoted in Peter M. Senge, *The Fifth Discipline: The Art & Practice of the Learning Organization*

Introduction

The growth of franchising in the USA and Britain since the 1950s has led to this business form assuming an increasing importance in a number of academic debates, including the fields of law, marketing, organization theory, and service growth. Its diffusion and application to differing economic settings suggest that franchising is, in itself, a form of innovation with its origins in feudalism. The last few chapters have illustrated that the rate of diffusion is determined by the combined elements of legitimacy, rivalry, strategic and career choices, and barriers to its adoption, such as resistance to change. The rate and extent of adoption not only alters the structure of the industry sector in which the activity is occurring, but also has the potential to change the balance of the collective of franchises in an economy *per se* from being biased towards, for example, the fast food sector to non-food retailers. Arguably, however, the diffusion of franchising is also affected by the degree of success of the adopters and their ability to manage their franchisees. It is also dependent on the franchisors' ability to nurture innovation within the system.

Despite the franchisor's initial innovative effort in adopting franchising as an organizational form, corporate survival at different stages of an industry's evolution requires differing levels of innovation and efficiency (Strebel, 1987). As the competitive environment changes, therefore, there is a requirement for innovation to occur in order to adapt to the rigours of the market and maintain competitive advantage. Given the position of the franchisee in terms of nearness to customers, and the franchisor's emphasis on continued sales growth (Housden, 1984), factors influencing franchisee innovativeness are potentially crucial.

Traditional and 'strategic alliance' views of franchising

A recurrent theme within definitions of franchising and subsequent academic debate is the notion of an organization established to conduct channel functions. English (1993), for example, has attempted to position franchising as a form of wholesaling activity, as do Winsor and Dant (1993) in recommending the use of 'backward franchising' to revitalize the US manufacturing sector. Although acknowledging that product name franchises are vertical, other researchers have questioned the extent to which business format franchisees can be viewed as middlemen. They argue that franchising is more a form of horizontal integration since it is conducted by retail marketers of goods and services which sell rights to other organizations at the same distribution level. Those examining the motivations to franchise have attempted to address the possibility of using various mechanisms for improving channel co-ordination and lowering the monitoring costs of distribution systems (Grossman and Hart, 1986; Shugman, 1985). Integral to such perspectives is the tenet that the franchisee is little more than a function to realize low-cost distribution and broader brand dissemination, rather than having a more self-actualizing role, such as assistance in the sustainability of the business, to offer the franchise relationship. In this vein, franchisees are perceived to have little decision-making authority over the tasks, workflow and procedures that encompass their function (Ford and Fottler, 1995).

Of late, the traditional perspective, dominant in marketing and economic texts, concerning the franchisee's role has been challenged. After all, whilst not independent in the sense of the conventional small-business person, franchisees do not see themselves as mere functionaries or as conventional employees either, and have certain expectations of participation in the processes of which they are an integral part. Specifically, Hoffman and Preble (1991) and McIntyre *et al* (1994) propose a more comprehensive view of franchising, not as vertical or horizontal, retail or wholesale, but as a form of strategic alliance that may encompass all of these. Under this interpretation, franchising is viewed as an organizational form whereby franchisor and franchisee, as distinct entities, 'band together' over a period of time in order to gain competitive advantages over other firms in their respective markets (Lewis, 1990). They posit that franchises are a type of strategic alliance since there appears to be substantial definitional conformance between the two organizational forms.

In particular, McIntyre *et al* (1994) support their argument by comparing and contrasting the four features of strategic alliances propounded by Collins and Doorley (1991), namely:

1. joint dependency of alliance members;
2. collaboration between alliance members;
3. an impact on the competitive position of alliance members (presumed to be positive); and
4. relationship longevity.

To some, arguing whether a franchise is a strategic alliance is a somewhat academic and pedantic exercise. Nonetheless, it raises fundamental questions concerning the franchise relationship and its sustainability, as well as providing a methodology to address some of the weaknesses of previous work on intra-channel conflict (Schul and Little, 1985). This said, McIntyre *et al*'s challenge is incomplete, a flaw which has the potential to undermine its significance. It is incomplete as it fails to take explicit consideration of technological transfers.

Perhaps reflecting its increasing international business bias, however, strategic alliance literature is replete with the notion of technological transfer. Indeed, some argue that the core element of a strategic alliance is a trading partnership of information, knowledge, technologies, skills or products (or 'technological transfers') that enhances the effectiveness of the competitive strategies of the participating firms. Such enhancement is achieved through mutually beneficial trade and may result in the realization of competitive advantages, sustainability and Ricardian[2] rents (Atuahene-Gima, 1993; Friar and Horwitch, 1985; Teece, 1986) through the development of new working practices, processes and products. In their omission, then, McIntyre *et al* may have inadvertently added some weight to Yoshino and Rangan's (1995) contention that business format franchise operations, whilst recognized as a hybrid form of economic organization (Norton, 1988; Powell, 1990; Williamson, 1975), cannot be perceived to be strategic alliances because they do not illustrate definitional conformity.

In their argument, Yoshino and Rangan (1995) adopt a specific definition of strategic alliances, which is in sharp contrast to those who claim that strategic alliances encompass all forms of hybrid organizations. An example from this latter school is succinctly propounded by the European Commission's statistical office, Eurostat, who state that: 'Alliances are any form of company co-operation, involving equity investment or not, regardless of the duration and objectives of the partnership' (p. 23). Such a broad perspective is also propounded by Goold *et al* (1994):

> The term 'alliance' suggests a relationship that is based on more than short-term arm's length dealings. There is an intention to co-operate in some way, with a view to mutual benefits that would not be achieved by a string of purely 'spot market' transactions ... Alliances therefore occupy the middle ground on a spectrum between purely arm's length markets at one extreme, and full ownership by the same parent at the other. This middle ground covers a broad range of relationship, and the term 'alliance' can be used to cover quite different subsets of these relationships. (pp. 430–31)

Unlike those employing broader interpretations, like that of Eurostat and others (such as Collins and Doorley, 1991; Jarillo, 1993), Yoshino and Rangan view strategic alliances as possessing simultaneously the following three *necessary* and *sufficient* characteristics:

1. The two or more firms that unite to pursue a set of agreed-upon goals remain independent subsequent to the formation of the alliance.
2. The partners share the benefits of the alliance and control over the performance of assigned tasks – perhaps the most distinctive characteristic of alliances and one that makes them so difficult to manage.
3. The partner firms contribute on a continuing basis in one or more key strategic areas, for example, technology, products, and so forth. (p. 5)

The sentiment that franchises are not strategic alliances has been expressed elsewhere (for example, Hergert and Morris, 1988; Mody, 1993; Yuan and Wang, 1995), and is in danger of becoming an accepted point of view. The basis of this argument is that franchises cannot be viewed as organizational forms emphatic of innovation and symmetric technological transfers, unlike joint research and development agreements, research consortia and joint ventures.

Perhaps underlining this aspect, Richard Freeman (1990), Corporate Chief Economist at ICI, differentiates companies into 'developer' and 'franchiser' categories. The developers are the providers of technical progress and are characterized by four features. They sustain long-term research and development outlays to innovate products; they train staff to generate their innovation capability; they cross-subsidize innovation between businesses; and, finally, they tend to be technology intensive organizations being engaged in basic research as well as developmental research. They are in the minority of firms in the UK. By contrast, 'franchisers' are dominant in British industry and are marked by the following: they have a short-term outlook and shorter time frame than innovators; they do no basic research and undertake very little developmental research; most of them rely on developers or innovators for product development; and they are the main conduit through which the benefits of innovation flow through to society. Strategic alliances are seen to occur between developers and, albeit less commonly, between developers and franchisers seeking to nurture comparative advantages rather than just between franchisers.

Equally, McIntyre *et al*'s omission may also leave unaddressed the frequent claims that:

> Franchisors do not want creativity . . . they want conformity. (English and Hoy, 1995; p. 5)

> Franchisors do not want innovation . . . they want replication! Innovation in a structured organization is inherently illegitimate as it unavoidably disrupts the status quo. (Kirzner, 1973; quoted in English and Hoy, 1995)

> The franchisor will not allow the business format to be changed. (Stern, 1995; p. 30)

> Most franchisors are ruthless with franchisees who attempt to bend the rules to suit their own particular circumstances because the whole basis of franchising is uniformity. (Horne, 1995; p. 45)

These claims are based on the popular tenet that franchises are based on a 'proven' and 'tried-and-tested recipe' for business success. Such contentions and claims may, however, not be generally accurate or appropriate given the relational and operational aspects of franchise arrangements. They also appear to contradict the general advice given to both potential franchisees and franchisors that, when assessing whether to enter the activity, the product/service has a long-term future and that the franchise should have a strong brand image. Terms such as 'proven' and 'tried-and-tested' suggest that the franchisor's business has, at least, survived over time and surmounted some of the initial hurdles of building a brand – a process which, in itself, requires and entails both adaptation and innovation.

According to von Braun (1990), competition today is increasingly about product quality and novelty rather than price. The result, he argues, has been the rapid shortening of average product life-cycles over the last fifty years – from twenty to five years in food products, from fifteen years to less than five in toys. In retailing and foodservice the pace of change occurs at an equally rapid rate. Some of the architectural and restaurant design press (Jones, 1988) suggests that the average customer appeal of particular fixtures, fittings and facia is less than five years. For some products it is less than two years.

As the pace of product alterations and changes continues to accelerate, the capacity to manage successful innovation becomes a critical source of competitive advantage, sustainability and brand valuation. In this environment the importance of replication and standardization would appear to offer only short-term benefits to brand valuation (Kay, 1993; Pennings and Harianto, 1992) and are only minimal conditions of good brand husbandry. Most of the successful brands which have lasted the decades have shifted to incorporate new technology, ingredients and packaging developments to circumvent the product life-cycle (Doyle, 1989). McDonald's, for example, has over 25% more basic menu items than it did in 1980. What appears to matter for survival is not the single successful product, but the continuous development of new products and services. Such action may not be employed to adapt and react to prevailing market conditions. By responding to market opportunities in novel ways, firms also shape and create new opportunities; by producing new values, firms create new customers and new markets.

It is also a truism that at least some franchise organizations do survive in fast-changing marketplaces and this, in itself, suggests testament to an institutionalized ability to innovate. Unfortunately, this ability has yet to receive the research attention it deserves. Commonsense seems to tell us that the franchise relationship must be dynamic and adaptive to changing conditions because no contract can cover all contingencies (Williamson, 1991). It also tells that 'franchisers', whilst inactive in product innovation, may be more active in other areas. Nonetheless, despite the emergence of new forms of distribution and new products within retailing and fast food, fundamental questions remain: What prompts franchisor and franchisee to innovate? Are there any similarities and commonalities in these? What prompts the franchisee to share innovations with both the franchisor and other franchisees? And, in sharing innovations, does this mean that franchises are, indeed, a form of strategic alliance?

In order to (ideally) initiate future debate and research by beginning to answer these questions and, in the process, seek to corroborate either McIntyre *et al* or Yoshino and Rangan, this chapter begins by examining the differing types of innovation and how franchising relates to these. It then provides examples of innovations within franchise systems, followed by an outline of the conditions that prompt innovative activity by franchisors and franchisees. The questions concerning the sharing of innovations in franchising are explored in Chapter 7. Arguably, however, the degree to which franchisees and franchisors innovate and share those innovations cannot be understood without careful attention to the personal, organizational, technological, and environmental contexts in which it occurs. As prior research (Damanpour, 1991; Meyer and Goes, 1988; Moch and Morse, 1977) have shown that the type of innovation serves as a moderating factor in affecting the diffusion of innovations, even very modest innovations are of relevance since the culmulative effects of continuous small-scale innovation, multiplied across many business units, can bestow significant competitive advantages (Gold, 1981; Sahal, 1984). Rowe and Boise (1974) suggest that distinguishing types of innovation is necessary for understanding their determinants. Despite limitations in providing a holistic analysis of the innovation process (Wolfe, 1994), the categorizations of innovation that have received the most attention are: product and process; radical and incremental; and administrative and technical. The following paragraphs apply each type to the franchise context.

'Product' and 'process' innovations

Classifying innovations according to product and process serves to differentiate the focus of the innovation. According to Utterback and Abernathy (1975), product innovations are new products or services to meet an external user need. By contrast, process innovations are new elements to the manner by which the products and services are made and sold. Although product and services are, for convenience, grouped together there is evidence to indicate that the correlates of service and product innovation are dissimilar. Martin and Horner (1993) indicate that successful service innovations require more time from idea to launch than do successful products, and successful service innovations have more participation by senior management than do successful product innovations. This approach to innovation is partly supported by, for example, Booz, Allen and Hamilton (1982), who report a greater degree of formality and bureaucratization in the processes for successful versus unsuccessful firms. Maidique and Zirger (1984) also conclude that new product success is likely to be greater when the process is well planned and co-ordinated. By summarizing a wealth of corroborating research findings, Perry (1995) finds that a more organically structured organization is more suited to product innovation.

In addition to differences between products and services, process and product innovations occur at differing stages of the organizational life-cycle. As a technology evolves, product innovation gives way to process innovation, making it difficult for the innovating entity to revert to new product innovations (Abernathy and Utterback, 1978). Each type of innovation is adopted at differing stages of the life-cycle and, as such, differing structures are necessary at each stage. For example, during maturity and illiberal economic conditions there is greater emphasis on price competition and cost control requiring a mechanistically-orientated organization, whereas the early stages necessitate a more organic approach to encourage incremental product alterations (Donaldson, 1985; Strebel, 1987). As part of such process innovation, some firms may seek to reduce costs and gain market share in maturity via the adoption of franchised expansion and sub-contracting (Bresnen and Fowler, 1994; Sanghavi, 1990; Tarbutton, 1986). Within the mature US fast food industry, some (such as Pizza Hut, Taco Bell, KFC and Little Caesar's Pizza) have formulated new service formats, such as home delivery and kiosks (Hume, 1992; Waldsmith, 1988), whilst also developing new products. Such new formats are also evident in the grocery market in the form of stores with smaller sales space and fewer product lines and have brought grocery multiples into closer competition with convenience stores. Like the foodservice market, such innovations have emerged in response to segment saturation (Carrol *et al*, 1992; Duke, 1991; Gripsrud and Gronhaug, 1985). Unlike the foodservice and grocery sectors, product innovation has tended to predominate within the hotel industry, through product-market segmentation and multiple brands, with some hotel groups (such as Accor, Holiday Inn, and Marriott) developing a portfolio of brands (Pizam and Calantone, 1987).

The innovation type and structure adopted for the decline stage is dependent upon the end-game strategy pursued. In such scenarios, Harrigan (1980) suggests that where firms are not already offering substitute products, or know little of the alternative's economics, firms should innovate in this manner so as to 'monitor the rate of commercialization of the new technology' – inferring both process and product innovation. Alternatively, if in end-game scenarios, products become more 'commodity-like' then it is probable that all but the lowest cost producer will lose market share. This situation suggests that process innovation ought to be pursued to facilitate the lower cost base, a strategy for which small firms have illustrated some preference (Parker, 1989). Some products in declining markets could be differentiable and may well justify further investment, or in other words, require an emphasis on product innovation (Gold, 1981).

'Radical' and 'incremental' innovations

Innovations can also be classified according to the extent of change, or their degree of 'disruptiveness' (Zaltman *et al*, 1973), they make in the existing social systems of an adopting organization. Incremental innovation introduces relatively minor changes to the existing product and exploits the potential of the existing design (Nelson and Winter, 1982; Sahal, 1984). Radical innovation is based on a different set of engineering and scientific principles and opens up new markets and potential applications (Dewar and Dutton, 1986; Freeman and Perez 1988).

Within the context of the biotechnology industries, alliances have been sought with small companies to benefit from radical innovations (Shan *et al*, 1994). Consistent with findings showing that incremental product innovativeness increases with firm size, but that radical product innovations are more prevalent among small firms (Fritz, 1989), franchisees and franchisors could be a potential source of radical innovation because they are, predominantly, small businesses. To some degree, the small size aspect of the franchisees is underlined by the number they employ. A survey of a sample of twenty-two limited liability UK pizza home delivery franchisees showed that the companies failed to record employee data (Price, 1995). Of those that did, however, the average number per unit was one manager and six staff. This equates to about the industry norm. The restaurant and fast food industry represents about a quarter of all employees in the hotel and catering market, which is slightly lower than the number working in hotels and pubs. In 1993, there were about 300,000 employees in the UK restaurant and fast food sector. Given that there were about 46,000 restaurant and fast food businesses operating in 1993, there are about seven employees per business (with a large standard deviation). This underlines the polarized nature of the sector.

Unfortunately, generalizations concerning the radicality of innovation and firm size cannot be made; prior empirical research examining the relationship between firm size and innovation activity is not conclusive (Raffa and Zollo, 1994). For example, Mansfield (1981) shows that a positive relationship between large firms and innovativeness is apparent, whereas Ettlie (1983) observes that smaller firms are more innovative. A plethora of reasons may exist for the inconclusivity of size → innovativeness results. These may be attributed to definitional and methodological differences, as well as the heterogeneity of the small-firm sector (Birley and Westhead, 1990). As small firms are characterized by differing 'internal' variables of ownership, management and product structure, these may have implications for innovativeness.

Unlike other firm size → innovativeness analysis, correlates of innovation amongst some franchises may alter according to two size variables: the size of the franchise system and the size of franchisees. Small franchise systems and franchisees may illustrate similar facilitators of innovativeness as other small businesses (Stanworth, 1994), such as narrow managerial focus, motivated management, little bureaucracy, short communication lines but offset against lack of time and technical myopia (Nooteboom, 1994). They may also be more orientated towards radical product innovations, but unlike non-affiliated concerns, the franchisee may be constrained by the franchisor. Such potentially similar innovation foci may become blurred as the franchise system becomes larger, with some degree of divergence becoming apparent between the franchisor and franchisee.

Radical innovation is more likely to be of significance at the beginning and decline stages of a life-cycle, but incremental innovation gains primacy during the adolescent and mature stages. For example, Pickworth (1989) observes that since the adoption of scientific management principles by the fast food industry, a series of incremental innovations at the technical core has occurred which has served to differentiate one service operation from another. Whereas McDonald's system offers little room for competing on product personalization, Burger King invites the customer to 'have it your way'™, and Wendy's has 256 versions of their hamburgers.

The radicalness of an innovation could serve to moderate the adoption/implementation process within an organization due to their risk and cost. The extent to which technological transfers are likely to be burdened by high costs is determined by:

1. the newness of the technology;
2. the extent to which the technology is a departure from the state of art;
3. the proximity and number of substitutes; and
4. the amount of previous technological transfer experience of the parties involved (Davidson and McFetridge, 1984).

In being risk-averse and resource-constrained, franchisors may, therefore, have an in-built resistance to such radical innovations. Leavitt (1965) conceptualizes the organization as a diamond, in which task, technology, people and structure are inter-related and mutually adjusting, indicating the complexity of social systems. According to the scale and impact of the innovation, when technology is changed the other components typically adjust to dampen out its impact, thereby potentially creating conflict (Stern, 1971). Chapter 3 indicated that this form of behaviour can affect whether franchising is adopted by certain firms.

Another component of technology that influences risk is its source. By deriving from the administrative core, there may be an inherent barrier to its adoption by the technical core (Zmud, 1982). This, in turn, may infer that there is some linkage between innovativeness and the pre-existing channel climate. The following paragraphs outline some of the implications that source of innovation may have on innovativeness.

'Administrative' and 'technical' innovations

Whilst the product, process, radical and incremental attributes of innovation are concerned with its scale and scope, innovation can also be differentiated by its source, either internally or externally (Hauschildt, 1992). There is a variety intra-corporate sources from which knowledge for innovations may be derived, such as patents, universities, competitors, suppliers, customers, affiliated companies, social networks, inter-locking directorates (Zajac, 1988), partners of co-operation as well as other industries (Von Hippel, 1982). Innovations may also derive from within the organization through, for example, in-house research and development teams, quality circles (Shea, 1986), suggestion boxes, in-house news-sheets and as a result of strategic reviews. These endogeneous sources may otherwise be redefined as 'administrative' and 'technical' innovations.

Organizations comprise technical and administrative cores (Weick; 1976). Perhaps reflecting the orientation and key skills embedded within each core, Evan (1966) distinguishes between technical and administrative innovation to facilitate differentiation between social structure and technology. A technical innovation is, essentially, related to basic work-related activities and may be an idea for a new product, production process or service. Within foodservice operations, the technical core comprises a production core, or non-customer-contact workers, and a service core, comprising customer contact personnel.

Difficulties may also arise due to the prevalence of Tayloristic practices and the separation of conception from execution that such norms have produced (Braverman, 1974), which is also a feature of franchises (franchisees only 'rent' the brand name and technical know-how). The fragmentation of labour and the lack of ownership, therefore, may serve to constrain innovative activity, enforce franchisor power, and maintain the *status quo*. This competence may also affect innovativeness of the franchise. For example, new franchisors may be less innovative than those who have been able quickly to assimilate the administrative innovation that franchised expansion entails and sell their offering to a queue of potential investors. Another source of potential conflict is the orientation of each core.

Each core has its own sphere of expertise and that technical innovations will tend to derive from the technical core, whilst administrative ones will derive from the administrative core (Evan, 1966). In small businesses, especially owner-operator concerns, the two cores may be hard to distinguish (Shailer, 1993) and the situation may become blurred within multi-divisional enterprises where there may be an element of overlap in administrative activities. Although a possible over-simplification, within the context of franchise businesses, franchisors may be equated to the administrative core of the organization since they are orientated to governance issues such as planning (Barney and Ouchi, 1986) and monitoring the system (Rubin, 1990), whilst some franchisees comprise the technical core (multi-unit and multi-brand franchisees should have their own administrative cores). Given the operational and functional focus of the franchisee, they may be a source of both technical and administrative (albeit possibly limited) innovation.

Perhaps reflecting the social differentiation between the two, technical ideas proposed by people outside the technical core will be less likely to be adopted and thus require a consultative approach to implementation (Zmud, 1982). Hence, the determinants of innovation within each core may differ. For example, the correlates of innovation at the administrative core are low professionalism, high formalization and high centralization, whilst the inverse of these conditions is true of innovation within the technical core (Daft, 1978). Where there are dual distribution systems, the franchisor has access to a technical core other than franchisees. Potentially, therefore, dual-system franchises may be more innovative than wholly-owned or wholly-franchised systems. Harrigan (1985) and Bradach and Eccles (1989) incorporate the concept of tapered integration from economics to argue that firms often 'strategically employ plural forms' of organization. They infer that franchise systems employ dual distribution not only because some individual outlets are best suited for one form and some for another, but because the existence of each form positively impacts on the management of the other side of the business. Company-owned operations permit the franchisor to gain operational insights, credibility, maintain and monitor standards (thereby maintaining brand consistency) on a day-to-day basis, help resolve any problems encountered by franchisees, facilitate more thorough market testing of new products/services/systems, the ability to monitor market trends more accurately and increase the strength of the franchise.

As implied by Zmud (1982), the source of innovation may have implications for its adoption. For example, some administrative cores may not be receptive to innovations deriving from external sources because of a 'not made here' tendency; even though such an attitude could be detrimental to performance (Brown, 1991). Whilst such technological xenophobia may preclude innovativeness, the source of innovation may also affect the extent to which a particular innovation is perceived to be radical or incremental within a particular industry context (Gold, 1981). Afuah and Bahram (1995) posit that innovation which may be incremental to, for example, a manufacturer, may turn out to be radical to customers, and something else to suppliers of components.

Within the franchise context, Chapter 2 shows that the use of franchising may be a norm in some economic sectors, but in other markets alternative forms of affiliation have primacy, such as tenancies in the public house sector and company-owership in retail bakeries. This, in turn, suggests that organizational capabilities to change to franchised-based expansion and perceptions of the opportunities that franchising, as an administrative innovation, may have to offer within differing sub-sectors are, in practice highly sticky, and organizations may become fixed in particular tracks and trajectories of growth (Greenwood and Hinings, 1988). For example, although franchising had been employed as a distribution system since the late nineteenth century, Benetton was the first firm in Italy, and possibly the world, to introduce a system of franchising in the textile and clothing industry (Bruce, 1987; Belussi, 1989).

Such adaptation from one economic sector to another is also evident at the technical core. The McDonald brothers, for instance, sought technical innovations designed to save labour and waste as well as speed up the process of delivery to the customer (Kroc, 1977; Love, 1986). But, each innovation made the service more uniform; each refinement served the cause of standardization, volume and profit. In this process, they recruited the help of a local mechanical engineer without any previous experience of the food industry, Ed Toman. Some of Toman's designs were very ordinary but others were 'ingenious' (Love, 1986: p. 17), such as the hand-held stainless steel pump dispenser which required just a single squeeze to dispense the required amount of ketchup and mustard onto a bun. A variation of this device is still in use in McDonald's restaurants today.

Although to be proved empirically, these examples suggest that there may be some linkage between innovation source → radicalness →innovativeness. Yet, there could be other linkages between innovation source, innovation type and innovativeness. By using the sources and types of innovation as proxies and orthogonal, rather than being separate, innovations can be seen to be multi-dimensional. They can, for example, be radical – in comparison to either the industry norms and/or the existing products/services and processes already in place – and derive from outside the firm as well as more orientated toward one core than another.

Incidences of innovative activity

All organizations learn. Some firms make a deliberate attempt to learn in order to enhance their capabilities and their chances of survival; others make less of a focused effort to learn. Research suggests that this latter category may comprise small businesses, such as franchises. Given that the majority of franchisor concerns are small businesses, to some it follows that they do not engage in the formation of collaborative agreement designed to enhance learning because the potential additions to market power, asset complementarity, and cost reductions are perceived to be lower, even though such co-joint activity may be conducive to sustainability.

Whilst technological collaboration has been observed as a rationale of singular importance among the various motivations for strategic alliances (Bidault and Cummings, 1994; Tyler and Steensma, 1995), including obtaining access to a competitor's technology (Vonortas, 1994), the same cannot be said of franchising. Although Justis and Judd (1989), for example, indicate that collaboration between franchisor and franchisee reduces the costs and risks associated with a number of activities, including product testing and development, entering into franchising is rarely pursued to enhance innovativeness *per se*. Companies enter into franchising for a plethora of reasons, including market share (Churchill, 1991), capital raising, risk management, to reduce the costs of monitoring (Klein, 1980; Minkler, 1990) and increase the control of actors within looser forms of affiliation, such as tenancies. Franchisees innovate by linking employees, customers, suppliers, and investors in an entrepreneurial event, namely the creation of a new local organization (Carland *et al*, 1984; Gassenheimer *et al*, 1996). Whilst this is, in itself, an initial process of innovation, the question is whether franchisors and franchisees are innovative after they have signed the contract with each other.

Arguably, if franchisors were concerned to incorporate innovative capability and competitive advantages based on innovation, franchisors would possibly contract franchisees with entrepreneurial characteristics in addition to those with desirable net worth, business skills, ambition and personal commitment (Meloan, 1988; Weinrauch, 1986). If they illustrate such behaviour, it may, in turn, suggest that franchises are strategic alliances. Despite definitional conflicts, entrepreneurship, in essence, involves the process of creating value by bringing together a unique package of resources to exploit an opportunity (Stevenson *et al*, 1989). Under this guise, the entrepreneurship construct has three implicit dimensions: innovativeness, risk-taking and proactiveness, with the first two perceived as important to the successful operation of a franchise (Withane, 1991) and the other as being significant to the early exploitation of opportunities. The last construct is dependent on the ownership of innovative capacity and recognizing an opportunity to deploy that capacity. Several studies establish that franchisees often complain about the controls to facilities provided by the franchisors and the lack of autonomy in decision-making (Ayling, 1987; Knight, 1984). According to this research, some franchisees feel that they were not manifesting their desired level of entrepreneurial spirit as they were provided with little opportunity to participate in strategy formulation for their businesses and this may be a recipe for overt conflict. Dandridge and Falbe (1994), for example, suggest that some hostile actions by franchisees are related to them seeking opportunities for more entrepreneurial initiative.

These hostile actions infer the presence of opportunism. It also suggests that some form of innovative activity and ability is present amongst franchisees, despite emphasis by franchisors on standardization. If undirected and not given a forum to communicate and express this innovative capacity, undoubtedly some franchisees may be motivated to engage in opportunistic behaviour. This said, not all actions can be described in a negative sense. There are two divergent forms of 'opportunism': managerial and strategic. According to Brill (1994), managerial opportunism refers to instances where:

> . . . managers distort or conceal information, or refrain from acting as promised, expected, or obliged in hope or anticipation of realizing a benefit for themselves or their firm at the expense of another . . . Managerial opportunism is undesirable, then, because it involves the consumption of slack resources that might have been used to further the objectives of the channel network or particular dyadic relationship within it. (p. 211)

Managerial opportunism is unlaterally-orientated behaviour deriving from the strategic manipulation of information and the self-believed threats and promises regarding future conduct. Unlike the overt managerial opportunism present in the second scenario, strategic opportunism is generally regarded in a positive light. It describes a manager's 'ability to remain focused on the long-term objectives while staying flexible enough to solve day-to-day problems and recognize new opportunities' (Isenberg, 1987: p. 92). Strategic opportunism is thus perceived to be desirable because it does not involve the consumption of slack resources that might have been employed to further the objectives of the channel network or particular dyadic relationship within it. Rather, it uses these slack resources to further the objectives and could be instrumental to brand improvements. However, the extent to which strategic opportunism may be interpreted as managerial opportunism is dependent on the degree to which duplicity plays a central role in shaping the behaviour (John, 1984) and reliant upon the specific nature of the franchisor-franchisee relationship (a point which is explained more fully below). For example, in restrictive franchise systems emphatic of maintaining the *status quo*, any innovation may be perceived as illegitimate and managerially opportunistic – even though this very activity may be necessary to the survival of the franchise relationship; in looser forms, such action may be expected and, indeed, be in-built.

Interestingly, Flack (1992) provides a trio of simplistic and perhaps hypothesized scenarios, illustrating how franchisee-initiated innovation can either be managerially or strategically opportunistic. The innovations are a response to illiberal market conditions (such as highly competitive markets) that has led to the presence of spare capacity. In each scenario the franchisor's use of power to the innovation is pivotal in affecting the extent to which it is implemented system-wide. In two of the scenarios, innovation occurs within the context of hidden actions. These franchisees are motivated by self-interest, which is translated as an attempt to realize superior performance, and the franchisor operates under conditions of incomplete information (Bergen *et al*, 1992).

In Flack's first scenario ('scenario 1'), because of intensifying competition, a midspend pizza franchisee initiates and markets a new pasta buffet service without reference to the franchisor. It is accepted by the franchisor, albeit provisional on test results, because there are positive outcomes (namely incremental sales and profit growth). In the second scenario ('scenario 2'), a printer/copier franchisee engages in selling small table-top copiers, also without reference to the franchisor (despite other service and product innovations being fully tested at his/her expense). Here the benevolent franchisor pursues a policy of strict enforcement of the contract since the innovation is seen as detrimental to the business of the franchise system. Finally, the third franchisee formulates a proposal describing the innovation which is then submitted to the franchisor for approval ('scenario 3'). The franchisor then passes the plan over to a standards committee for review and recommendation. After testing, the innovation is adopted system-wide. These scenarios suggest that the perceived threat to brand equity and the existence of mechanisms to permit effective problem-solving may be conducive to franchise system innovativeness.

Flack recommends that the franchisor ought to be consistent in managing franchisee-initiated innovation rather than being rigid about system uniformity. Managing with the constraints of increasingly illiberal market conditions means that the franchisor must also adapt and accept that, if they are to remain in the system, franchisees require some flexibility to conform to contextual conditions.

Whilst rigidity concerning system uniformity may be impractical, the advice concerning managerial consistency possibly runs counter to the findings of intra-corporate strategic fit research and the management of strategic business units (SBU). A SBU refers to a division, product line, or other profit centre within a company that produces and markets a well-defined set of customers, and competes with a distinct set of competitors and, ideally, should be able to stand alone from the rest of the company. Bartlett and Ghoshal (1991) linked the differing strategic roles exhibited by SBUs to distinct intra-corporate structural arrangements. These arrangements were defined along three dimensions: formalization, centralization, and socialization. Those businesses realizing superior economic rents were those that illustrated a greater degree of corporate level structure–SBU strategy alignment. Intra-corporate relationships between corporate headquarters and more innovative SBUs (or those which are of more importance to the firm) should be managed with more decentralization, openness, socialization and less formalization. By comparison, contributor SBUs require high centralization in order to facilitate the redirection of competences and resources to other, more strategically important SBUs (Ghoshal and Nohria, 1989). This suggests that the franchisor requires managerial complexity in order to manage innovation successfully.

In addition to the hypothesized scenarios (such as 1 and 3 above), strategic opportunism has been witnessed in a variety of hospitality settings. Perhaps the most celebrated are those observed in the McDonald's chain. Cited by both Love (1986) and Shook and Shook (1993), is the example of franchisee Lou Groen, who owned a franchise in a predominantly Catholic neighbourhood. He found, on Fridays, that his restaurant was not as busy as at other times of the week. On that particular day his customers tended to eat fish from competing chains, such as Big Boy. In order to maintain sales volumes, Groen developed a fish-sandwich. After some negotiations with the franchisor and a year later, the 'Filet-of-Fish' was introduced system-wide.

Further evidence of franchisee-initiated innovation is suggested by Cohen, McDonald's vice president of licensing (quoted in Shook and Shook, 1993), who explains:

> Experimentation has been very healthy for the system, and we encourage it from our franchisees. Most of the major break-throughs in our menu line were made by franchisees and, in most cases, they did it while working in conjunction with us. In some cases, particularly in the early days, we told them not to do something, but because the franchisees were aggressive entrepreneurs, they did it anyway and convinced us that it was a great idea. (p. 151)

More recently, Ed Rensi, President and CEO of McDonald's USA, has said:

> Most of our new product ideas come from franchisees. Jim Delligatti, an owner/operator in Pittsburgh, came up with the idea for the Big Mac. Initially, he was rejected because we weren't interested in expanding the menu. Subsequently, an employee encouraged him to try it, and Pittsburgh had tremendous sales results. Our Egg Muffin came from an owner/operator in California. (*Success* magazine, November 1995; pp. 91–93)

Opportunism is not just peculiar to franchisees: it is also apparent among franchisors and can serve to generate mistrust and lower channel satisfaction levels (McAfee and Schwartz, 1994). For example, in the mature US fast food market, franchisors such as Blimpie, Burger King, Carvel, KFC, Taco Bell and Little Caesar's have all experienced threatened litigation by franchisees who have seen their territories encroached on by the use of process innovations, such as the use of kiosk-type stores and carts in non-traditional sites. Other developments include the opportunity of offering their product lines – once exclusive to franchisees – to supermarkets and convenience store retailers; and the use of telemarketing (including the use of the Internet). This allows customers to mail or telephone orders directly for merchandise products (amongst others) to a warehouse and so by-pass franchisees.

Such actions are perceived as opportunistic by franchisees since the franchisor realizes net gains from royalties and revenues even when franchisees' sales decline following their chains' increased market penetration. Via the example of opportunism, therefore, it appears that franchisees and franchisors may illustrate innovative capability through new ideas concerning new products, working practices and processes. These may also be asymmetric or, more specifically, concealed or pursued to benefit one party more than another. Such asymmetry may also be apparent at differing times within strategic alliances. Doz (1988), for example, observes that:

> The relative values of the respective contributions of the partners vary over time and may be very asymmetrical at almost any given point in time. There is a need, then, to keep in perspective the contributions over the life (potential) of the partnership and not to be swayed by what currently looks like a serious imbalance. (p. 324)

Given this situation, it may be that in the assessment of whether franchises are strategic alliances, franchises were omitted. This omission may exist because the franchisor provides the franchisee with training and the brand specifications (as discussed below) and on the speculation that franchises are not characterized by bilateral technological transfers. In the process, the 'assessors' (for example, Yoshino and Rangan) possibly did not take a longer-term perspective. The above has suggested that both franchisors and franchisees do express innovative behaviour. This behaviour may be construed to be positive or negative depending on the impact (actual or not) on existing vested interests. Nonetheless, it is apparent from conversations with franchisees that not all franchisees and franchisors exhibit innovative behaviour. One explanation for the difference is that some franchise members have a lower capacity for innovation, which serves not only to differentiate them from other franchises but also strategic alliances. As inferred above, this capacity is an important hygiene factor for the realization of opportunities through innovative behaviour. If an individual's innovative capacity is an important hygiene factor for organizational innovative behaviour, what is it?

Aspects of innovative capacity in franchises

As one of the initial features that serve to define strategic alliances, Yoshino and Rangan observe that two or more firms unite to pursue a set of agreed-upon goals. The firms also remain independent subsequent to the formation of the alliance. To argue that franchises may differ from strategic alliances, as the latter are marked by linkages between 'firms', may be misleading since there is, perhaps, an assumption that franchises form agreements with individuals. Firms encompass a continuum of forms ranging from public limited companies, limited liability concerns and partnerships to sole traders, to name but a few. Whilst franchisees, especially in the foodservice industry, have also illustrated a variety of other firm-types, the NatWest/BFA surveys indicate that the majority of franchisees operate as sole traders and partnerships (see Figure 6.1). Equally, the 1990s has seen the emergence of corporate franchisees, such as contract catering concerns (for example, Compass and Gardner Merchant), thereby blurring this distinction further between strategic alliances and franchises. Although this counter-argument may consitute an initial step in establishing whether franchises are strategic alliances, it may have little more than superficial importance. Of greater importance is the notion that franchisees are 'firms' since they possess complementary competences. These not only give them the capacity to fulfil their role as a franchisee, but also the capacity to be innovative.

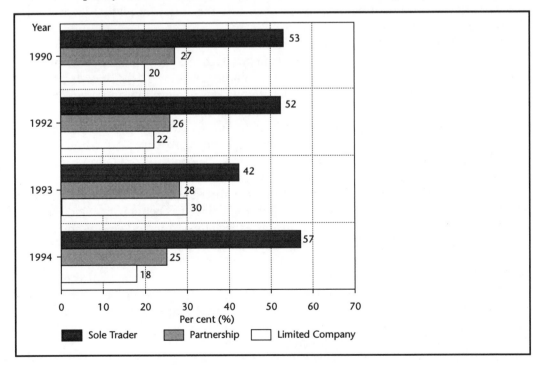

Figure 6.1: Company status of UK franchisees

Competences

Reve (1990) argues that the 'firm' is a nexus of internal and external contracts, where each contract is differentiated by the required skills and incentives to develop and protect core skills. Internal contracts facilitate hierarchical governance and entail organizational incentives (for example, wage systems); bilateral governance (exemplified by 'joint ventures, licensing, franchising or other types of coalitions': p. 137) is defined by a set of external contracts and entails interorganizational incentives. In order for a firm to achieve strategic goals, Reve posits that core skills need to be supplemented by complementary skills (often controlled by other organizations) which, in turn, provides incentives to enter into co-operative agreements.

Central to this perspective is the notion that the firm is a collection of assets on which core skills are built. Such assets include those required to manufacture and distribute products, or physical capital and human capital (within service organizations), as well as intangible assets, such as knowledge capital and organizational capital (defined as tacit). At an organizational level, the up-grading of these assets to maintain or increase competitive advantage ultimately depends on individual learning and the sharing of newly acquired concepts with others in the organization (Kim, 1993). As much of this individual learning occurs via the assessment of new situations with prior experiences and lessons learnt from those experiences, a person's tacit knowledge is significant in the innovation process. This process also serves to add to the stock of tacit knowledge. Innovations occur when new situations require a solution that may have either been appropriate to an alternative situation but not apparent in the current context, or when a new situation requires a totally novel solution but where the individual's education and/or social network can be brought to bear. In either case, individual learning has occurred and the stock of tacit knowledge added to.

In this sense, intangible assets are alternatively labelled 'tacit knowledge', and are the foundation of skills and capability. Tacit knowledge is person-embodied, informal and non-tangible in nature and is the sum of the nature and diversity of prior experiences (career and personal), socialization, age, education, social networking, and previous training. In being embodied in both the franchisor and franchisee, it is these factors which are possibly of great importance in affecting the franchise's capacity for innovation. By contrast, explicit or objective knowledge is information or instructions which can be formulated in words and symbols and can, therefore, be copied, stored, and transferred by impersonal means such as written documents or computer files. Such knowledge serves to summarize some aspects and, once transmitted as information, can facilitate adding to the stock of tacit knowledge and has been viewed as being particularly important in the context of innovation and diffusion, especially within and among small firms (Nonaka, 1994; Nooteboom, 1994), and in the generation of non-imitable advantages. Being the result of a cumulative process based on learning through experience, prior career, social network, the restructuring and addition of information, as well as from previous problem-solving activities, tacit knowledge is the legacy of the firm's (and franchisee's) own history. Accordingly, the 'firm' is conceptualized as:

Firm = *f*(core skills, organizational incentives, complementary skills, inter-organizational incentives)

(Reve, T. (1990), 'The Firm as a Nexus of Internal and External Contracts' in Aoki, M. Gustafsson, B., and Williamson, O.E. (Eds) *The Firm as a Nexus of Treaties*, Sage Publications, London.)

This formulation is then summarized as:

Firm = *f*(strategic capabilities, strategic alliances)

Franchise systems are perceived to possess complementary skills since the franchisor provides training, operating manuals etc., and the franchisee supplies their labour, finance and royalty payments. McIntyre *et al*, along with some of the popular franchise press, propose that franchises are collaborative since, for example, an often cited rationale for franchising is for the franchisor to gain access to local market knowledge. The franchisor gains such knowledge in exchange for the provision of business know-how. A wealth of research has argued that gaining access to such knowledge has also been observed in the motivations to form joint ventures (Harrigan, 1988; Konieczny and Petrick, 1994). Undoubtedly, whilst the provision of such proprietary knowledge by the franchisee may be construed, in itself, as a form of bilateral technological transfer (Seurat, 1979), and bring closer the comparison between strategic alliances and franchises, such informational exchanges are not innovative in themselves, but may lead to innovation and added brand value.

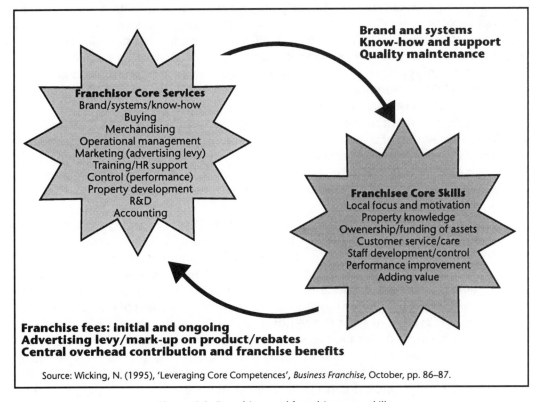

Source: Wicking, N. (1995), 'Leveraging Core Competences', *Business Franchise*, October, pp. 86–87.

Figure 6.2: Franchisor and franchisee core skills

Adopting a broader perspective, Wicking (1995), possibly reflecting the hierarchical differences between the franchisor and franchisee, indicates that main franchisor skills are managerial in nature, whereas those of the franchisee are more operationally-orientated (see Figure 6.2). In so doing, he also provides additional support for the notion that franchisors are administrative in focus, whilst franchisees are more technically-orientated.

In this sense, franchisees are firms because they, at least, have their own core skills and organizational incentives, such as staff wages and profit. They also provide and receive complementary skills and are involved in interorganizational incentives via the royalty process. Such attributes suggest that the franchisee is a distinct entity complementing the franchisor's activities in building brand equity, rather than just being a distributive mechanism. In their very complementarity, franchises may, therefore, be perceived to be a form of strategic alliance. Teece (1986), for example, indicates that asset complementarity is an important factor for the formation of strategic alliances in order to realize an efficient and effective value chain. Similarly, Prahalad and Hamel (1990) note that in many industries it is unlikely that an organization can master all the key competencies required for survival. In such circumstances, it becomes essential that organizations form collaborations to gain access to such competencies (or assets). The identification and rent of complementary assets, which are not necessarily owned by one firm via integration may lead to a more competitive and flexible configuration, than an attempt to acquire them all under direct ownership and control (Stuckey and White, 1993).

Strategic capabilities are not static but, rather, change over time, are subject to imitation, able to be superceded and need to be continuously developed and renewed as environments change. Business and strategic alliance success is, then, partially dependent on the partners' ability to develop competences in the light of changing conditions (Doz, 1988). It therefore appears that the notion of shared innovative capabilities is significant as it is these which have implications for the propensity to create and sustain competitive advantage via the development of an efficient and effective value chain.

Perhaps importantly, however, Wicking (1995) suggests that a core franchisor service is the provision of research and development. This sentiment is also expressed by Acheson (1995), who observes that the franchisee will expect the franchisor to provide product or concept innovation, including their investigation of their marketability and compatibility with the existing business. A similar sentiment is expressed by Khan (1992):

> Franchising is fundamentally based on innovation and uniqueness in products and services provided. In order to be competitive, a franchisor should always be involved in innovative addition to the products and services offered by the system. This can be in the form of additions to the menu, refinement of equipment, new methods of preparation, or a revised method of service. Successful franchises are continuously upgrading almost every constituent of the business. The need is evidenced from the trends in franchise restaurants. Franchises which started strictly as fast food operations selling hamburgers are now selling chicken, fish, and steak and have drive-thru's, salad-bars, and delivery services. Innovation should be applicable to the franchise system, which demands simplicity and duplication on a large scale. (p. 95)

According to their argument, the franchisor is seen to possess the necessary competences for innovation; it is only a question of when the innovative ought to be employed. In this sense, perhaps, these arguments may be construed to be similar to Yoshino and Rangan's (1995) perspective: they appear to assume inherently that franchises are rarely characterized by bilateral technological transfers, since the majority of informational exchanges are unilateral. This suggestion gains additional meaning when compared to Pine's (1991) adaptation of Dahlman and Westphal's (1983) technology transfer model to the hospitality industry, where three levels of technological transfer are evident:

Level 1: The *capability to operate* a technology; for example, to run a fast food restaurant.
Level 2: *Investment capability* required to create new productive capacity; such as new restaurants.
Level 3: *Innovation capability/capacity;* to modify and improve methods, products, and services in fast food restaurants.

Each level of technology transfer requires different types of skills and support from the franchisor. Level 1 is relatively apparent via the obligation to provide numerous services to franchisees, such as job training, site location advice, operating manuals etc. In this sense, the technological flow is essentially asymmetric. This may exist, in part, due to recruitment and selection biases by the franchisor (illustrated below) in order to realize power, lower costs of technological transfer and operational standardization. Level 2 may also be taught by the franchisor, but is also partially dependent on the franchisee's managerial capability. Some franchisees are more capable than others in being multi-unit and/or multi-branded operators. Kaufmann (1992), for example, argues that there may be some decay in managerial performance within multi-unit franchisees. This decay is associated with similar problems that beset small companies when they expand beyond a size-threshold, namely those associated with delegation and increased span of control. In strategic alliances, Level 1 and 2 transfers are perceived as given, whilst Level 3 is often the objective. In this sense, Level 3 capability is not simply a form of technological transfer in itself, but is determined by the nature of previously acquired tacit knowledge and social capital, and augmented by the provision of Level 1 and 2 capabilities. Level 3 is often the most difficult to achieve, since it requires imagination rather than just technical ability (Pine, 1991). As innovative capability is, in part, the sum of the stock of tacit knowledge, Level 3 is also susceptible to forgetfulness and loss from lack of practice of acquired skills.

At a general level and within franchising, realizing Level 3 may be additionally difficult for three reasons:

1. not all franchisees (and franchisors) possess the same learning abilities, education, socialization levels and histories, i.e. they do not possess the same intangible assets;
2. at an organizational level, innovative capability may also be affected by the departure of a key member of staff and/or franchisee;
3. not all franchisors provide the same standard of training and do not necessarily customize their training packages according to the franchisee's learning capability (LaVan *et al*, 1986).

One possible explanation for this latter case may be resource constraints concerning training budgets as well as a lack of prior experience in training personnel or franchisees. As a result of these factors, either individually or combined, some franchises will be more innovative than others. Differences among franchises and lack of customization of training suggests that there are questions as to whether the degree of training is sufficient to overcome the limited work experience and managerial deficiencies that many franchisees possess (McGuire, 1971). Although the relatively meagre initial training may be compensated for if franchisor field support programmes provided extensive follow-up and assistance, these visits cannot always overcome the obstacles of insufficient experience and non-entrepreneurial outlook. Franchise training executives point out that their principal difficulty is not providing the technical or managerial skills requisite to their operations, but in changing the would-be franchisee's outlook from that of an hourly or salaried employee to that of an independent entrepreneur (despite the fact that they are really neither). Such infrequent visits, even when the franchisor and franchisee are committed to information sharing, can be a poor mechanism of transferring tacit knowledge when the individuals from inside the organization are unfamiliar with each other and are, as a consequence, reluctant to share information (Howells, 1995).

Despite these differences, in Wicking's (1995) diagram franchisees' innovative skills/innovation contributions are not detailed (although they may be included in the 'catch-all' titles of 'performance improvement' and 'adding-value'), and could be interpreted as missing. There may be little justification for this situation when one considers opportunistic behaviour and that an important component of core capabilities and realizing innovative capability is education. British franchisees appear to be educated to a similar level as UK managers who are, in turn, only marginally better qualified than the population at large (Davis and Caves, 1987; NatWest/BFA, 1993; 1994). As such, the lack of franchisee innovation contributions may not be solely attributed to educational differences between the franchisee and franchisor.

Perhaps of most significance behind the omission is the argument that the franchisor is more concerned with developing brand standardization, maintaining it via power differences, rather than innovation (English and Hoy, 1995). Arguably, if franchisors were orientated toward Level 3 transfers, like strategic alliance members, then they would recruit those with career histories and knowledge capital as well as those with entrepreneurial characteristics which would serve this need. Cohen and Levinthal (1990), for instance, argue that the ability to recognize the value of new ideas and apply them to commercial ends, partially depends on the base of prior knowledge. By illustrating recruitment biases, there is evidence that franchisors do not necessarily exhibit an overt orientation towards incorporating innovative capability, but it is perhaps apparent in more subtle ways.

Recruitment biases

As noted in the introduction to this book, recruitment biases are a form of insidious control and power. Within the 'industrial economic' perspective of franchising (Hough, 1986), power in the franchise (as well as perhaps the employer-employee) relationship is evident *ex-ante* due to recruitment biases away from experiential (tacit) knowledge and asymmetric possession of objective (taught) knowledge. Unlike strategic alliances where complementary of resources are sought, it is suggested that franchisors normally prefer new entrants without prior experience, because they are more amenable to training and operational compliance with the franchisor's instructions, thereby possibly lowering technological transfer costs and, at least, maintaining operating standardization (Stanworth, 1995). Other stated reasons for such a preference are that 'outsiders' are less likely to introduce preconceived ideas or 'bad ideas' which might interfere with the franchisor's training programme, or 'contaminate' other franchisees and be detrimental to brand equity. In other words, knowledge is power and the possession of experiential knowledge by certain franchisees may serve to undermine the franchisor's reputation/image with other franchisees through the exercising of usurpationary power.

Recruitment biases away from experiential knowledge (only acquired via actual operational experience) have been explored along two dimensions: previous self-employed experience and prior operational line experience of potential franchisees. With regard to the former, Stanworth and Purdy (1993) show that about half of those seeking to become a franchisee at franchise exhibitions are, or have been, in self-employment. In spite of the size of this pool of potential franchisees, many franchisors discriminate against self-employed people. Such actions perhaps reflects some concern about franchisors' ability to retain control over previously self-employed franchisees rather than, perhaps, to view them as a potential source of innovation. Such biases, however, are not universal (MacMillan, 1995). The tendency to prefer candidates without self-employment experience is more marked with the more experienced franchisor (that is, about 41% of responses among franchisors with less than five years involvement in franchising, through to 75% in franchises more than ten years old). Such biases are also most pronounced in retail franchises, but are less so in distribution and business service franchises.

The lower levels of recruitment bias exhibited by the smaller franchisees may be due to the necessity of overcoming tight resource constraints, as well to reduce the burden on them. That is, they cannot afford to discriminate against those with prior operational and/or self-employment experience. Another possible explanation behind these recruitment biases is that the smaller, younger franchisors are using those franchisees with prior experience to develop their own knowledge capital. This, in turn, would make such franchise systems closer to strategic alliances.

By expressing such biases franchisors may be encouraging *ex-post* homophily or, rather, promoting a single organizational mind-set (i.e., the franchisor's) among the franchisees. The degree of homophily between people is a persuasive factor which encourages people to adopt the same innovations (Dearing, 1993), and serve to reduce conflict and monitoring costs. Yet, by pursuing *ex-ante* heterophily – or diverse mind-sets – in recruitment and selection, they may have inherent innovative capacity. Accordingly, the argument concerning recruitment biases is not clear-cut, but it does have an effect.

In addition to biases away from experiential knowledge possessed by the self-employed, fast food franchisors discriminate against people who had experience in their field of operation (Ozanne and Hunt, 1971). Such discrimination was revealed both by the experience of franchisee respondents and franchisors' expressed preferences. They also showed, however, that franchisees with direct experience within restaurants or fast food outlets ranked second or third highest of thirteen franchisee financial performance groups. Such biased practices have little changed: 77% of young franchisors and 92% of experienced franchisors discriminate against potential franchisees with prior operating line experience (MacMillan, 1995). The implication of this form of bias against experiential knowledge is that franchisors might be concerned primarily to establish a power difference (there is also an additional issue concerning trust which is explained below) over their franchisees from the outset via their recruitment policies and, thereby, possibly curtail innovativeness. It may also be argued, conversely, that the franchisor's recruitment biases away from those with prior specific work experience may actually serve to promote innovation. In this vein, anthropological studies seem to suggest that people illustrate an innate diversity and are naturally curious (Gedo, 1990). As such, biases away from the self-employed and those with prior operating experience may be insufficient to promote the innovative capacity of the franchise system.

Developing from the knowledge capital arguments, Hofer and Schendel (1978) indicate that there is some consensus that the greater the diversity of socialization and experience the more there exists a reservoir of potential innovation. Cohen and Levinthal (1990) contend that a diversity of knowledge is important for innovation because it increases the prospect that incoming insights will relate to what is already known. People's learning ability permits them constantly to improve services, to transfer their knowledge from one domain to another and to combine resources in innovative ways, and makes them a valuable resource in the innovation process (Farjoun, 1994). This observation is supported by other research streams. Wolf *et al* (1990), for instance, expound that people actively select appropriate skills or transfer knowledge for a given occasion from their own individual sources. This, they argue, involves defining or recognizing a problem as belonging to a certain category; the wider the range of situations the more likely they are to build up a repertoire of very general problem types and schemata for dealing with these. The more general the schemata, the more varied the particular situations for which they have a response.

Accordingly, it may be expected that older franchise companies may be less innovative than their counterparts, despite the latter having a lower knowledge capital base in the short-run. Such a hypothesis has some support. For example, Chapter 3 showed that some managers may be unwilling to change the *status quo* because of their length of tenure. In contrast to the arguments concerning tenure, Hambrick and Mason (1984) posit that a manager's age, education and experience are indicators of an individual's flexibility, capability and risk-taking propensities. They contend that if managers have spent their careers in the industry or organization, they will have a limited knowledge base from which to analyze and understand competitors and environmental change. Since some franchisors are biased against prior operating experience, under Hambrick and Mason's rationale, such systems may illustrate greater innovativeness than their counterparts or wholly-owned chains where previous experience is a hygiene factor for entry. Similarly, they argue that the educational level is positively related to organizational innovation or the organization's openness to change. Whilst formal education is important, also of significance to the individual's capacity for innovation is the degree of non-formal education received. Non-formal education refers to the combination of the franchisee's socialization, diversity of experience, age, prior career path, and prior training (that is, their tacit knowledge).

Nonetheless, the contention is possibly contradicted by knowledge capital arguments. As knowledge is accumulated within the organization, so there is potentially greater innovative capability. Under this latter argument, mature franchises could be construed to be more innovative than their younger counterparts. The extent to which either is true depends on the nature of the situation and the similarity/convergence of thought concerning new situations. For example, some organizations have been shown to try to maintain the *status quo* through recruiting, selecting and developing individuals who are perceived to have the same mind-set as the incumbent management, a policy that also serves to reinforce the existing culture (Hambrick *et al*, 1993). As some situations have the potential to make at least some knowledge capital redundant, so the organization's ability to adapt may be moderated by franchisor recruitment biases. In some instances, franchisees with prior self-employment and specific work experience may be able to help overcome such redundancies (these redundancies could be more prevalent in small franchise systems), because they may have experience of coping under crisis.

In addition to the effects of franchisee diversity, innovativeness is also being affected by the possession of objective knowledge by the franchisee. This is reflective of market imperfections for the technology; the seller (the franchisor) and the buyer (the franchisee) do not possess equal information about the technology or its application. Yet, the potential franchisee requires information about the franchise and the franchisor to make a rational decision whether to apply to become a system member. Under asymmetric information conditions, a potential franchisee might be reluctant to undertake specific investment without some assurance of its profitability, but as the less informed party the agent may be aware of the franchisor's incentive to convey misinformation (thereby affecting the possibility of imitation). A regular complaint about franchise brochures and popular franchise press is the tendency to be overly optimistic about the potential returns of the system (Ozanne and Hunt, 1971).[5] Such optimism may lead the franchisee to have inflated and unrealistic expectations of the wealth he will accrue by joining a particular system. When these expectations are unrealized, dissatisfaction and conflict may ensue. Nonetheless, the possession of objective knowledge will also affect the franchisee's position on the learning curve and, if too much information is conveyed, may persuade the potential franchisee to imitate the franchisor's concept. This situation requires the franchisor to tread a careful line in promoting the franchise.

Social capital

A further aspect with the potential to affect both franchisors' and franchisees' level of tacit knowledge is the degree and nature of their social capital. In spite of the attempts by some franchisors to control the level and nature of innovative behaviour within the franchise system via recruitment biases and the dispersion of objective knowledge, there is one area that is beyond his control: social capital. According to Burt (1992), social capital is different from financial capital and knowledge capital in two ways: it is owned jointly by the parties to a relationship and it concerns rate of return in the market production equation. In other words, social capital cannot be owned more by one member of a relationship than the other. As noted in Chapter 5, personal networks can play a significant role in affecting career choices and exist prior to franchisees joining a particular system. Through relations with colleagues, friends, family members and customers, come the opportunities to transform financial and human capital into profit (Burt, 1992: p. 9). Reflecting on this capability, Lipparini and Sobero (1994) conclude:

> In a competitive environment where the actors are not atomistic, but exist within a system of actors, the relational capability could represent for entrepreneurial firms the way to gain a sustainable competitive advantage. The notion of an entrepreneur who focuses on a specific business idea as an expert in a limited area of activity is obsolete. Rather, we found entrepreneurs who, exploiting basic

experiences seek new combinations among the various inter-firm ties, relying on such linkages as a vehicle for transferring and combining their organizationally embedded learning capabilities. Recognizing the entrepreneur's ability to generate new knowledge by combining internal and external learning could be a critical variable in understanding SME's innovative capabilities. (p. 136)

In this way, a franchisee's discussion within his social network concerning a particular issue may result in realizing an innovative solution. This is especially true if the discussion occurs between members of the network with weak ties (network members who are not as tightly affiliated to other members of the same network), as these are more likely to possess different information and differing viewpoints than people with whom the franchisee has strong relationships (Burt, 1992). Nonetheless, in filling the gap between the individuals that comprise his immediate social network and the members of the franchise organization, the franchisee occupies a point of centrality from which he may or may not decide to share the innovation with other franchisees and the franchisor (of course, this depends on the nature of the innovation and relationship between the social network members). As they have their own social capital, the same situation is equally true of franchisors.

Social networks do not only encompass friends, work colleagues, associates, and family members, but also refer to members of trade associations, government agencies, interest organizations and *ad hoc* groups. Examples of trade organizations include the BFA, the Pizza and Pasta Association as well as the British Institute of Innkeeping amongst others. These bodies may serve to increase innovativeness via their collection and dissemination of news and new product launches by suppliers. The extent to which such bodies may be initiators of ideas to both sides of the franchise relationship is, in part, affected by their membership. In the UK, for example, the degree of outside contact with franchisees from other franchised businesses is low, suggesting there may be little dissemination of best practices and innovation across franchises.

There may be a danger to infer from these examples that innovations deriving from the possession of social capital are wholly based on *ad hoc* discussion, but they may also derive from more formal ties, such as interlocking directorates. Although research concerning interlocking directorates dates back to the early 1900s (Borch and Huse, 1993), it has only been since the 1970s that researchers have studied such interlocks from two compatible, but not mutually exclusive perspectives, called here 'intraclass' and 'interorganizational co-ordination' (Burt, 1980). Within the 'intraclass' vein, directors form part of a business elite or capital class who are actors possessing some common interests. In pursuit of their interests and the maintenance of class solidarity, capitalists establish relationships with other capitalists to formulate and co-ordinate general interests, which may be a catalyst for innovation. Whilst a plethora of anti-trust research has been conducted to elucidate the potential for abuses of power among organizations with interlocking directorates, the issue of co-ordination has remained problematic. In other words, it still remains relatively unclear how interlocks manipulate resources and are structured in order to express and maintain class solidarity (Ornstein, 1984; Palmer, 1983; Stearns and Mizrurchi, 1986). The inconclusivity of such research suggests that interlocks are only indicators of potential power relationships between companies at the highest level. It is not possible to infer that directors generally exploit networks of board memberships for political gain merely because such potential exists (Roy *et al*, 1994). Possibly reflective of status divisions within the capitalist class and the overt exercising of exclusionary power, the characterization of the corporate elite as relatively cohesive, organized and advancing its joint interests in the political arena is on the mark when applied to a select segment, but off the mark when taken to describe the entire elite (Useem, 1982).

Within the interorganizational co-ordination framework, organizations are entities which possess interests and require resources in order to function. Although true of all organizations, it is particularly so of small firms. According to Butler *et al* (1992), interorganizational networks are important in providing information and assistance during the start-up stage, and help to establish legitimacy through connecting the entrepreneur to vested interest constituencies and industry players. These linkages form the basis of networks that help to ensure the transfer of knowledge and facilitate the survival of new start-ups and the continuance of existing firms. An implicit feature of small firms is the shallowness of knowledge concerning particular issues due to the lack of functional specialists; knowledge also tends to be narrow which is a potentially dangerous scenario as know-how needed for some aspect of running the business may not be taken into account (Nooteboom, 1994). In pursuit of these interests and resources, directors establish relationships. Interlocking directorates may provide the opportunity to exchange specific information about their operations or market information about the sectors in which they are based. This information may allow them to formulate strategies and policies that are more sensitive to their environments and could provide the basis for tacit forms of interorganizational co-ordination, such as anti-competitive price setting as well as innovation. Within the context of interdependence, interlocking directorates may have functions resembling those of strategic alliances and may lead to their formation (Larson, 1991; Pennings, 1980).

Table 6.1 below shows the results of an examination of the director details of 118 limited liability accounts from the McDonald's, Burger King, Wimpy, KFC, Perfect Pizza, Domino's Pizza, Harry Ramsden's and Pizza Express systems. The focus of analysis is the direct interlock. A direct interlock exists when one individual is a director of two different organizations (other than subsidiaries) and there is a direct path between the two organizations (Pennings, 1980). By contrast, an indirect interlock exists when two organizations are connected by a path through one or more third organizations. Unlike direct interlocks, the indirect form may have little relevance for inter-organizational relationships. Pennings proffers two explanations for this situation. In the first instance, information which is transmitted through two or more intermediaries is likely to lose richness and any derived benefits become marginally decreased. In the second instance, these interlocks are only one form of indirect access between firms because information may reach an organization through a variety of other routes. The results show that franchisors and franchisees do not form interlocking directorates amongst themselves, which is potentially significant to innovativeness, but they may individually become involved in them.

Interlocking directorates have been observed and researched in numerous large organizations to establish their impact on other, usually external, stakeholders to the buisnesses. A key aspect of small businesses (and hence the majority of franchisees) is the inability to separate ownership and control. As in most small concerns the franchisee was also manager, director and owner of the business. The table below presents the sizes of the boards of directors and the total number of directors involved. On the whole, it appears that the majority are not involved in interlocking directorates through the use of

Size of franchisee firm by no. of directors	All directors		Non-executive directors within the firm		Directors' links (no. of other firms)	
	No.	%	No.	%	No.	%
1	14	12	12	67	7	19
2	52	44	4	22	19	50
3	37	32	2	11	7	19
4	12	10	–	–	3	8
5	3	2	–	–	2	4
Total firms	118	100	18	100	38	100

NB. Figures in main table refer to number of firms.

Table 6.1: *Interlocking directorates among UK fast food franchisee firms*

non-executive directors which, in turn, suggests greater reliance on less formal relation-ships as a source of innovation (for example, from trade associations, friends, suppliers, banks and accountants).

As the number of directors increases, so it appears that the number of direc-torates rises. These tend to occur with the franchisees becoming directors of other firms. This pattern seems to suggest that as franchisee firms grow, they have the potential to become better informed and more innovative. We can only be speculative about this because the extent to which interlocking directorates (for example) are able to affect the introduction of new ideas depends on their stock of tacit knowledge and their ability to influence the directors of the benefits of adopting an innovation. Additionally, the table shows that the majority of fast food franchisee organizations have two or three directors, which also has implications for franchise system learning. It suggests that although innovations may be fragmented because they are retained by one person, they can also be retained among small, close-knit groups but not transmitted beyond those collectives.

Given the benefits of weak ties, innovative potential may be enhanced if non-executive directors originate from outside the industry setting of the franchisee. The study suggests that fast food franchisees are involved in this form of interlock in less than 10% of instances, a situation which appears consistent with larger hotel and catering con-cerns. For comparative purposes, a review of the details of 326 directors of hotel, catering and tourism concerns in *The Directors Directory, 1995* (a publication that details directors of organizations generating annual sales of at least £10 million and share capital in excess of £50,000) was conducted. This publication revealed that only 17% had interlocking directorates, but the majority of these were with firms outside the sector.

Despite the potential for innovation, not all small-business owners and fran-chisees perceive the benefits of interlocking directorates in a positive manner, rather they may have a distrust of both their subordinates and others outside their domain (for exam-ple, consultants and bankers). Reflective of such behaviour, they are unwilling to seek and respond to expert sources of help and are insulated from the perceived threat of new ideas, which may serve to undermine their power, authority and belief that they are 'always right' (Osborne, 1991). These sentiments prevail even though they are misconceptions which are potentially detrimental to performance (see Chapter 9 for an empirical test of interlocking directorates' influence on franchisee performance). When such sentiments prevail among independent entrepreneurs, it may preclude them from realizing franchised expansion, because they cannot trust 'outsiders' from divulging business secrets or to do the job correctly. Such situations are not so much an inability to learn, as unwillingness, and may derive from not only a fear of change but also because of past experiences of success or failure in the management of innovation.

One possible suggestion of this behaviour may be apparent from the lack of evidence pointing to a marked divorce between ownership and control amongst the sampled companies. Most franchisee companies had two directors and two shareholders and, of those that differed, the added shareholder was typically the company secretary. Such research mirrors other work concerning the structure and control of small businesses in general and within the hotel industry (Borsch and Huse, 1993). These attitudes of distrust may also prevail within certain cultures. For example, in a study of the restaurant ownership patterns in Hong Kong, Lan and Khan (1995) show that international companies tend to use franchising in order to moderate their risk and gain local market knowledge, whilst the indigenous companies tend toward family ownership.

Implications for franchises

This chapter has so far suggested that franchisees are firms, due to the presence of core competences and that they, at least, possess the capacity for innovation as a result of their tacit knowledge. As this is the sum of prior and ongoing socialization, they typically come to the relationship with at least some level of knowledge and social capital, despite or because of franchisor recruitment biases. Put differently, franchisees come to the arrangement with at least some conceptual learning capability – they are capable of thinking about why things are done in the first place, sometimes challenging the very existence of prevailing conditions and procedures (Kim, 1993). Additionally, franchisors, via the provision of Level 1 and Level 2 capabilities, provide franchisees with at least some of the competences required to operate a unit. Specifically, the franchisor provides operational learning or the steps to do a particular task, such as filling out forms or operating a piece of machinery, but this may vary according to the quality of their input.

Some franchise organizations have become increasingly sophisticated in how they develop franchisees' operating ability through the combined use of classroom and hands-on techniques, whilst others, typically the small franchisors, rely on the franchisee's prior experience to help them muddle through. Since tacit knowledge acquisition often involves 'learning by doing' and 'learning by using' associated with direct on-the-job contact with new equipment, work practice or operation, so the provision of Level 1 and 2 capabilities may serve not only to provide the franchisees with their skills, but also serve to increase innovative capability within the franchise system (see Figure 6.3). Additionally, franchisees' tacit knowledge and their capacity for innovation are also increased during the relationship via the franchisee's social network.

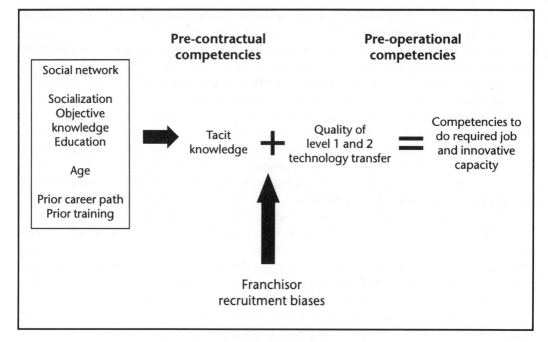

Figure 6.3: *Components of innovative capacity*

As there is substantial variability in both the factors which comprise tacit knowledge, the capacity to be innovative is also variable. Such variance can be employed to generate taxonomies of franchisor and franchisee types, which in turn have implications for franchise system innovativeness. Prior research has differentiated franchisors along a variety of univariate dimensions, including format, geographic reach (Bush *et al*, 1976), power (Hough, 1986; Manaseri, 1993) and initial franchise fee (Sen, 1993). Employing a more robust multi-variate approach, Carney and Gedajlovic (1991) propound that franchisors can be categorized along the variables suggested by resource scarcity and administrative efficiency arguments; their franchisor types are listed as:

1. rapid growers;
2. expensive conservatives;
3. converters;
4. mature franchisors; and
5. unsuccessful.

Specifically, 'rapid growers' are those that have been franchising for the shortest time and have larger retail networks than all but the 'mature franchisors'; 'conservative expensive' price their units higher than any other group and franchisees are given contracts of long duration; 'franchise converts' are the oldest retail systems and begin as wholly-owned chains and, after many years decide to begin franchising; 'mature franchisors' have been franchising for a relatively long time, longer than organizations following any other dominant strategy; and 'unsuccessful' have not developed a successful market formula, that is, their business concept is not robust and the low prices charged for franchise opportunities reflects a poor competitive position.

Although this taxonomy has yet to be accepted via empirical research (Castro-giovanni *et al*, 1995), it nevertheless may offer some insight into the innovativeness of one franchisor type *vis-à-vis* another, but restricts comparisons between franchised and non-franchise based organizational forms. For example, it may be that one of the features that differentiates mature franchisors and conservatives from unsuccessful is the innovation-content and volume of the business. This might arise because the franchisees have developed an intimate knowledge of the tasks and a long-standing relationship with the franchisor and, as a consequence, could be better placed to contribute to the business.

In addition to franchisor differences, are dissimilarities among different types of franchisee. By thinking of franchising as a decentralized profit-centre approach to portfolio management, it is possible to see some of the similarities apparent between franchisees and SBUs more lucidly. This, in turn, suggests that intra-corporate aspects could impinge on franchisee innovativeness. There has been considerable research examining how multi-business concerns should manage relationships between corporate level and their SBUs (Goold *et al*, 1994), with companies such as the Boston Consulting Group developing a growth-share matrix and GE/McKinsey employing business screen portfolio matrices (McKiernan, 1992) to map the process. Recent research within SBU management stream has focused on whether differing degrees of decentralization should be employed contingent on the strategy of the SBU or, in short, intra-corporate strategic fit (Gupta and Govindarajan, 1991). Studies such as these are concerned with explaining how the link between an SBU's strategy and its performance is moderated by the SBU's relationship with corporate management (Golden, 1992).

Such research may well have implications for the explanatory variables of bilateral technological transfers in franchise businesses. Bartlett and Ghoshal (1991) suggest that corporations confront varied environmental conditions and competitiveness that require flexible strategic responses and attention to 'custom-managing' each SBU. The variability of this behaviour is, however, constrained by the necessity to maintain role integrity and reduce the potential for conflict. Role integrity is a pattern of behaviour expected of a person which is based on a given social position or context. A function of the exchange partners' capacity is to be consistent over time, to manage conflicting roles, and achieve the required level of task complexity for a role (Spriggs and Nevin, 1994). Complexity exists in franchising, because there is some degree of interdependence required to maintain, at least, brand equity which means that franchise members don a variety of roles; for example, the franchisor's role ranges from trainer to policeman. Bartlett and Ghoshal identified four strategic roles for SBUs, based on a two-dimensional matrix (see Figure 6.4). One dimension is the level of local resources and capabilities within the SBU; the other dimension is the strategic importance of the SBU to the entire firm, measured by the significance of a particular environment to the company's overall strategy. From both these dimensions, four strategic roles result: strategic leader, contributor, implementer and 'black-hole'.[6] These strategic roles are, in turn, moderating variables in that they affect the diffusion and adoption of certain innovations; for example, contributors may illustrate a bias toward process innovations.

It is conceivable (although yet to be empirically investigated) that franchisee firms, whilst conforming to the general brand specifications set by the franchisor, exhibit differing strategic characteristics (Dickson, 1983). Within the context of the fast food industry, for example, some franchisees have illustrated defensive strategies via seeking to improve the efficiency of their existing operations (Barreye, 1988). Such franchisees

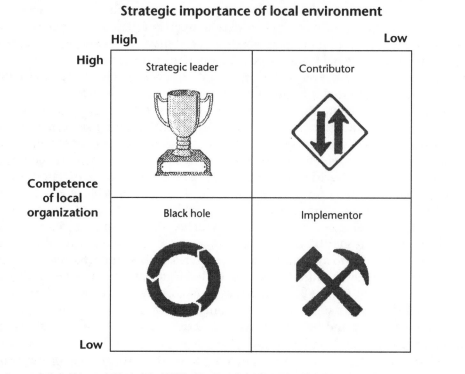

Strategic importance of local environment

Figure 6.4: Matrix of SBU-types

illustrate comparatively (to other SBUs) high levels of competence, but may be strategically unimportant. Some other franchisees have sought to diversify their risk and lower their dependency becoming multi-unit and multi-branded concerns within a particular geographic niche, thereby possibly increasing their significance to the franchisor by being a source of new products and services. The main benefit of multi-concept franchising is that a franchisee may operate more units in a specific geographic area than remaining with a single franchise (Bradach, 1994). By operating a number of differing concepts and outlets, the franchisees are able to improve their competence in operating such businesses and bargaining power with the franchisor over a period of time (Lowell, 1991).

English and Hoy (1995) have examined the notion of franchisees as innovating entrepreneurs and suggest that multi-unit franchisees may well be particularly fruitful territory in which to concentrate the search for franchisee entrepreneurs/innovators, because they have broad terms of reference. By being closely involved with a number of concepts, the multi-concept franchisee may embody a source of both product and process innovation, but may be compromised by contractual obligations to its franchisors, potentially confounding attempts to gain access to some innovations via the back door. Multi-unit/brand operators may be located, depending on the strategic significance of their market, in either the 'strategic leader' or 'contributor' quadrants of Ghoshal and Barlett's SBU-matrix. Due to differences in investment capability others may be classified as either 'black holes' or 'implementers'. Unlike their more competent counter-parts, such franchisees may be less of a potential source of innovation.

Given that the Australian, Canadian, UK and US fast food industries have developed a second tier via franchisee acquisitions and multi-concept franchising, the potential innovation is a broad one. Whilst some of this activity has occurred as a reaction to franchisees exhausting their own territories, slowing growth and intense competition, it has also occurred as a result of franchisees pursuing such policies from the outset (Luxenberg, 1985). Multi-unit franchising has also arisen out of franchisees, especially fast food, taking on additional stores, because the initial ones were money-losers (Lanthier, 1995). Multi-unit franchisees have also emerged as a result of franchisor push. Some franchisors actively encourage those who are believed to possess managerial expertise to own and/or supervise several franchise units (Robicheaux et al, 1994). Such proactive expansionism is hypothesized to be a positive correlate of innovativeness (Gort and Singamsetti, 1987).

Summarizing the above argument, it is evident that franchises, like strategic alliances, are perceived to possess complementary assets. These assets derive from the franchisees' prior career and educational histories as well as being taught to them by the franchisor. As such, franchisees may be considered to be 'firms' in their own right rather than being simple distributive mechanisms. The possession of such assets increases the likelihood that franchisees may be able to contribute to brand value even though franchisors may attempt to discourage innovative behaviour via their recruitment biases. These practices appear to persist in spite of the realization that, in order to maintain competitive position via an efficient and effective value chain, it is necessary for organizational members to up-grade their competences. This said, the possession of innovative capacity, whilst a necessary condition for innovative behaviour, is not in itself a sufficient one. In addition to capacity, are triggers which, upon their recognition, serve to deploy the innovative capability. Where that capability does not exist or the triggers are not recognized, so the firm is thus perceived to illustrate a lack of 'fit' with its environment which, in turn, has the potential to adversely affect performance (Hrebiniak and Joyce, 1985).

Triggers of innovation in franchise systems

The triggers, or determinants, of innovation have attracted a wealth of research effort, which has been attributed to both organizational factors as well as exogenous ones, such as the product life-cycle (see 'Product and Process Innovations', p. 298). For example, Chapter 1 argued that there were a number of environmental and technological facilitators (for example, a pool of potential investors and system standardization) to realize franchised expansion; it also argued that some individuals were eager to franchise in order to take advantage of buoyant levels of growth in consumer expenditure and partially to negate first mover advantages via the monopolization of resources. In this sense, the franchisors' objectives played a key role in triggering the adoption of franchised growth. Developing from this, an important tenet of Yoshino and Rangan's (1995) strategic alliance definition is that the presence of shared goals between the member firms is an important trigger of innovation. These shared goals may take a variety of forms, such as to increase efficiency through shared initiatives or to fill a market gap via the manufacture of a new type of product. Given their significance, goals may also serve as triggers of innovation within franchise systems.

Franchisor goals

As inferred by Flack's (1992) scenarios, the extent to which opportunism may be present within a franchise system is partially dependent upon the degree of goal divergence between the franchisee and franchisor. Unlike some strategic alliances, goal congruity in franchises may not be readily apparent. It has also been suggested that franchises comprise groups of actors (like most organizations at large), who often have conflicting priorities, objectives and values (Stern and El-Ansary, 1982). Management discourse and some franchise literature generally assumes that organizational members have a commonality of purpose, such as profit maximization, but this has not been reflected empirically (Eliashberg and Michie, 1984; McAlister *et al*, 1986). There is a basic flaw built into the structure of franchising (Cohen, 1971), that of the continuing and potentially destructive conflict between franchisor and franchisee. For the most part, such conflict tends to be latent which means that there is the potential for conflict to erupt into observable forms, but may never be actualized.

Latent conflict exists in the discrepancy between the interests of the powerful and the unarticulated preferences of those they exclude from decision-making (Lukes, 1974). The crystallization of different preferences is not up to the franchisor, but the franchisee exercising choice under conditions of relatively limited autonomy and independently of the franchisor. In other words, franchising is marked by an implicit divergence of sub-unit goals; when one franchise member engages in behaviour that serves to stress this goal divergence, latent conflict becomes more pronounced and becomes observable. Although apparent prior to formation because of the differences between capital and labour as well as within social classes, goal divergence within the franchise relationship exists because of the differing cost structures inherent to the franchisor's organization, versus those of the franchisees and this may be a catalyst for opportunistic behaviour.

Depending on the proportion of company-owned to franchisee-operated units, franchisor revenue is generally seen to derive through franchise fees, royalties and the sale of goods and services to franchisees rather than end-consumers (O'Hara and Thomas, 1986). Given that the franchisor should have the necessary infrastructure and overhead to service the franchisee from the outset of the relationship, initial fees are rarely related to output and in this sense are neither a marginal cost nor marginal revenue to the franchisor. In theory at least the initial fee should make some contribution to meeting the franchisor's fixed costs (which may, in fact, be tiered as a result of increased overhead requirement to support additional franchisees). By arising from continuing operations, the provision of goods and sales to franchisees is a function of the number of franchisees and volume of their sales, and is marginal both in terms of cost and revenue. As a result, the franchisor's average revenue curve is related to the franchisees' average revenue curve, both of which are downward sloping to the right (Mittelstaedt and Stassen, 1990). Despite incurring marginal servicing costs, the franchisor does not, generally, assume the marginal costs attributable to the sale of goods and services to consumers, unlike the franchisee.

As a result of the downward sloping demand curve, a reduction in the franchisee's end price realizes an increase in the quantity of product sold. Because the franchisor does not incur the marginal costs of production, all of marginal revenue from the additional quantity sold is additional profit. Since marginal costs equal zero the franchisor is able to increase his profits through the efforts of the franchisee, rather than solely through the success of his own operation. His basic goal may be to make his profit as an organizer, a seller of expertise, or the seller of a product to franchisees as opposed to end-consumers, which conditions the franchisor's orientation towards innovation. Where the franchisor controls and operates his own stores, the objective could still be manifest through his pricing policies.

Reflecting this possibility, Lafontaine (1995), in a study of price differences between franchisee- and franchisor-operated stores in the US fast food market, shows that the franchisor's revenue growth orientation can be potentially damaging to franchisees' businesses in three ways:

1. *Franchisor opportunism:* as company-owned units are profit centres for franchisors, prices at such units may be higher than in franchisee-operated stores.
2. *Double-marginalization:* an up-stream monopolist sells an input to a downstream firm at a set a price above marginal cost. If the downstream firm also has market power, it will choose a price that is higher, and a quantity that is lower than the price that would maximize joint profits. Since royalties, in effect, represent a tax on output it can be thought of as a downward shift on the franchisee's demand curve. This shift creates pressures for the franchisee to raise price, possibly above that of the franchisor's company-owned units.
3. *Horizontal externalities* or *'within-system competition'*: where franchisees prices are higher than those of the franchisor, the demand elasticity arguments suggest that the franchisor may benefit possibly to the detriment of the franchisee.

Whilst prevalent in the US fast food sector, such predatory pricing behaviour may be less overt in international markets. The *Economist* publication conducts an annual survey of the price of McDonald's 'Big Mac' hamburger to examine exchange rate purchasing parity. They observe that the chain's US outlets illustrate a far greater degree of price variability than is evident internationally. Within Europe and the UK, it should be observed that, on the issue of price, franchisors may only suggest/recommend them, meaning that franchisees have some latitude in the area. This can be seen, for example, from the 'only at participating stores' slogan in Burger King and KFC television advertisements emphasizing price discounts. To dictate prices would be in possible breach of Office of Fair Trading precedents, the Fair Trading Act 1973, Competition Act 1980 and Commission Regulation (EEC) No. 4087/88. Despite such legislation, some franchisors have effectively circumvented such legislation through providing franchisees with menus with the prices already set. The franchisee then has to incur the costs and inconvenience of altering the menu prices – in short, the franchisor generates a disincentive to change.

Further evidence of latent conflict within franchising has been provided by Wadsmith (1996), whose survey of American franchisees suggests that 40% of them have poor relationships with their franchisor. The franchisees' experiences of franchisors' orientation toward pursuing self-interest indicated that there was potential for the latent conflict to be aggravated into a more observable form and affect brand equity. Wadsmith's results indicate that 55% of franchisees would not advise others to join their franchise systems because of the following sentiments:

- over 46% of surveyed franchisees felt discounting and promotional activities that hurt their profits were forced on them by the franchisor;
- 57% said that the goods and services they purchased from their franchisor were over-priced;
- 68% of franchisees said that they were not getting their money's worth from advertising fees;
- over 61% said that their franchisors gave inadequate support;
- 40% said that the franchisor had encroached on their territory in some way.

Although not placed within an over-arching theory indicative of the exercising of the differing types of power (exclusionary, usurpationary, and dual closure), a special edition of the *Journal of Business Venturing* (1996, Vol. 11, No. 4) examined the dynamics of the franchise relationship. Most appear to provide empirical support for the presence of conflict (latent and otherwise) between the franchisor and franchisee and point to the presence of innovation and opportunism as being the source of exacerbating that conflict:

> Franchisees foster dissension by ignoring franchisors' goals in pursuit of their entrepreneurial interests, possibly misrepresenting costs and revenues, or by withholding royalties. They may disagree about competitive methods, refuse to participate in innovative marketing strategies, deviate from the franchisor's formula, resist changes needed to keep the system competitive, or 'buy franchise units expecting to get rich and not work' ... Franchisors provoke dissension with partners by encroaching on franchisees' markets, unfairly terminating franchisees, failing to disclose information, misrepresenting costs or revenues, fabricating successes, or waffling on premises for services. (Baucus *et al*, 1996; p. 362)

> The fact that franchise agreements are framed to emphasize sales growth, that opportunities are discussed in the context of growth, and that perceived franchisor suasion emphasized sales growth may be responsible for the entrepreneur-franchisee's almost uniform response in spite of declining market opportunities. Franchisees may consider buying market share through lower margins as the only option, because they have not been sensitized to other strategy options ... In sum, the evidence seems to suggest that franchisors' attempts at direct strategy may contribute to lower franchisee profitability but generally increases the level of sales. (Phan *et al*, 1996; p. 396)

In addition to affecting franchisor-franchisee relations, goal differences and the marginal cost aspects may focus the franchisor towards product line extensions. These extensions have the benefits of helping to keep the brand contemporary and interesting, they exploit the latent equity in a brand and permit new product introduction, at a much lower cost and greatly reduced risk than through the launch of totally new products. Product line extensions also serve to increase the volume of product sold to the franchisee, but may be inconsistent with realizing the franchisor's objectives. New products serve to maintain or increase revenues from the existing network, rather than necessarily facilitating additional organizational development via new capacity. As a result, cost structures serve to bias the franchisor more towards opening new stores since the volume of products sold to new franchisees may be greater than just product line additions; franchisors receive increased contributions to fixed costs from initial fees; and the impact on brand dissemination is greater as a result of additional market presence and increased contributions to the advertising fund, thereby affecting brand value.

The orientation towards product innovation may differ by economic and industry contexts, suggesting some stickiness in technological transfers between different franchise firms resulting from traditional practices. For example, within the context of the US franchise market, Lafontaine (1992) shows that the amount of inputs sold by franchisors to franchisees is generally quite small. In the restaurant and fast food industry, the value of inputs sold by franchisors averages only 4.5% of franchisees' sales; in the auto-rental industry it was 0.1% and about 30% in non-food retailing. The volume of inputs has also received negative treatment by US anti-trust legislation, especially under the Sherman Act (see: Siegal v. Chicken Delight 1971; Sasser v. Carvel 1962; Kentucky Fried Chicken v. Diversified Packaging 1977 and Strasser, 1986 and Joseph, 1989 for a review of other relevant cases). In the UK similar restrictions apply via, for example, the monopoly provisions of the Fair Trading Act 1973. Franchisees tend to be unrestricted in their purchasing activity, but quality and standards are preserved by specification.

In order to benefit from both new product developments and increased brand penetration through opening new stores, it may prove more advantageous for franchisors to form partnership agreements with 'developer' manufacturers to generate new product ideas. Freeman (1990) contends that such organizations already have core competences in innovation and are likely to be already involved in in-house research and development activity (Pavitt et al, 1989) as well as research consortia (Mowery, 1983; Olleros and Mac-Donald, 1988; Werner, 1993). Such relationships may serve to strengthen franchisor brand value by allowing the franchisor to concentrate on selling franchises, whilst the creation of joint purchaser-supplier fusion teams with specific improvement objectives allows him access to a continuous stream of new product ideas and profit maximization. Although such agreements may occur between vertically differentiated firms, they may also occur horizontally. For example, in the US hotel industry, some companies have acquired and continued to run different hotel brands in order to increase revenue growth and diversify risk by offering a number of brands. One of the main thrusts by franchisors within the foodservice industry has been the formation of dual-brand outlets among firms with complementary/substitute product ranges. Such action has culminated in two main results from which the franchisor benefits: initially, it permits the franchisor to sell a new package to potential franchisees – for example, a combined Pizza Hut and Choice Hotel; secondly, it increases the franchisee's total sales volume from which both franchisors may benefit. The franchisee, by contrast, has to incur the additional costs of altering their site, but may be willing to do so in order to improve performance. As shall be seen below, some franchisees have actually initiated such dual-branding approaches.

Franchisee goals

Whilst the franchisor's objective may be biased toward sales growth, the franchisee is more orientated towards profits. Unlike some franchisors, the franchisee incurs both the fixed and marginal costs of production, where the latter increases as the quantity sold rises. As additional revenue from a lower price realizes lower contributions to fixed costs, the franchisee will only be motivated to increase sales until the marginal revenue derived from additional units sold equates to marginal costs. Whilst such objective differences may also exist inside divisions and departments of non-franchised organizations, within franchise firms it is perhaps more overt and exists for the duration of the contract. As a goal for wholly-owned divisions sales growth may be a part of a broader objective to gain market share and only be sustained as long as profits do not fall below a certain threshold; in franchising, the pursuit of sales growth may be pursued to realize the franchisor's accumulation of capital irrespective of franchisee profitability. The franchisor, in effect, may have the ability to realize superior financial performance by causing the franchisee to make decisions and follow policies which do not help to optimize franchisee profits (Kaufmann and Rangan, 1990), leading to the potential for overt conflict to arise. This difference, in itself, may be a source of non-co-operation since an increase in a franchisee's turnover is neither a necessary nor sufficient condition for an increase in franchisee profits (Felstead, 1993) and may adversely affect the latter's earnings (which are derived from profits) and standard of living.

But some strategic alliances are also 'Trojan Horses' (James, 1989) due to lack of goal congruity. Some firms, especially Japanese-owned, view alliances as an opportunity to leapfrog learning curves. In short, they perceive strategic alliances as learning races, where the key is to learn fastest in order to renege later at an advantage. This rationale has been attributed as being the primary cause of the high number of strategic alliance failures: about one-third of strategic alliances are outright failures (Gulati *et al*, 1994). Although there is a variety of perspectives concerning the causes of strategic alliance failures (Lorange and Roos, 1991) there is some agreement that, in the long run, the competitive advantages of many Western firms were more often eroded than strengthened by alliances (Hamel, 1991). This erosion has been caused, in part, because of the strategic intent behind their formation. A misinterpretation of one alliance member's strategic intent may lead to an under-estimation of their ability and/or desire to move upon the learning curve (Bailetti and Callahan, 1993) by leveraging core competencies to enhance existing capabilities. In this way, latent conflict may co-exist, at least temporarily, with co-operative actions.

Despite having some commonality in the trade mark identity, the differing orientations toward brand valuation by the franchisee and franchisor may lead them to illustrate divergent innovative behaviours. Since franchisees benefit from unit profit while franchisors benefit from network sales, franchisees may be more biased toward process innovations to reduce operating costs. This is especially true of hotel franchisees, where franchise fees represent the second largest operating expense. Such emphasis on process innovations may be the outcome of the franchise royalties being, in effect, a tax on output which serves to move the franchisee's average revenue curve downward to the left. Triggers for innovation may also arise from the franchisees' own conflict with their own labour and rivalry with other firms, which in itself is the economic driving force of capitalist accumulation and is a condition of survival (Pitelis, 1991). This conflict arises since the franchisee has to incur the costs of production and live off profits; if the firm has to pay more for any factor of prduction than it uses, the cost of producing each level of output will rise and so erode profits.

Conflict with labour necessitates the ability to substitute factors of production via technological and organizational improvements, which, ideally, realizes the simultaneous enhancement of control over labour and the degree of exploitation, work intensity and productivity (or 'process optimization'). For example, fast food franchisee units are seen as more efficient than their company-owned counterparts since they illustrate lower wages-to-turnover ratios as a result of franchisees' adoption of labour flexibility practices, such as job rotation, job enrichment and use of part-timers (Card and Krueger, 1994; Krueger, 1991). Within the UK fast food franchise sector, the emphasis on trying to lower labour costs has been evidenced from the use of zero-hours contracting among some Burger King franchisees. This practice only reached public notice when Burger King was condemned for paying a student employee only £1 for a five-hour shift when the usual rate was £3.10 per hour. In addition to affecting the monetary aspects of the franchisee-labour relationship, it has also affected non-monetary aspects (for example, some franchisees require their staff to purchase their uniforms).

The focus by franchisees on costs of production has also led some to form consortia and thereby increase their bargaining power with their franchisor and facilitate the lowering of input costs. For example, in the USA, Domino's Pizza, Burger King, Taco Bell and Dairy Queen franchisees have sought alternative supply routes rather than routinely relying on those of their franchisor. This, in turn, suggests that whilst process innovations by franchisees derive, in part, from conflict with their labour it may also derive from rivalry with the franchisor.

An additional factor affecting franchisees' propensity to be orientated toward process innovations is the issue of time management. For the smaller franchisee, the emphasis on process innovations may derive from a desire to increase their own efficiency and time to do other things (Norton, 1988). For example, Love and Hoey (1990) cite multi-unit McDonald's franchisee owner, Al Boxely, who spent a disproportionate amount of time preparing employee work schedules. He found that by developing and using computer software he was not only able to improve his time management, but also lower costs by reducing manning levels. Equally, several Florida and California-based Burger King franchisees have up-graded their security systems in order to deter burglary as well as increase the effectiveness of employee monitoring – the savings on food, for example, by each of these franchisees has amounted to over US$1,200 a month (Baum, 1995).

Despite some focus on process innovations, it is evident from the Lou Groen and Flack (1992) scenarios cited earlier that some franchisees are also able to develop new products. These illustrations appear to suggest that franchisees may only be product-orientated when there is some threat which has a potentially adverse affect on their the propensity to generate profit (the source of the franchisee's livelihood) since it has a negative impact on franchisee sales levels. As such, there are lower contributions towards meeting fixed costs of running the operation and repaying the costs of joining the system. Within the scenarios, the focus of the threat was external.

Porter (1980) has argued that the characteristics of an organization's environment, specifically the task or contextual environment (Thompson, 1967), has a significant role in creating pressure for innovation. Certain aspects of the environment have been operationalized via a multitude of variables (see for example, Jurkovich, 1974). An important dimension of the task environment affecting organizational strategy is perceived to be munificence (Dess and Beard, 1984), which is an expression of surplus (or scarcity) of resources. This external dimension has also been employed, albeit slightly modified, by numerous marketing channels scholars (for example, Achrol *et al*, 1983; Achrol and Stern, 1988; Dwyer and Welsh, 1985) in their examination of the interplay between local environmental conditions and relational aspects of the focal dyad. In this respect, it has implications for both franchisor and franchisee innovativeness.

Resource dependency theory proposes that the need for external resources and information determines the degree of dependence on the environment (Boyd, 1990; Collis, 1991). Firms of all types confront differing levels of dependence on an environment which is perceived as a pool of resources with the degree of scarcity called munificence (Castrogiovanni, 1991). The availability of these slack resources helps to decide whether management must conform or adapt to the prevailing environmental conditions within specific constraints or, alternatively, exercise some degree of flexibility and choice. The extent of conformance to the environmental conditions is, in part, also dependent upon management's abilities and competence (recall the Carney and Gedajlovic, and Bartlett and Ghoshal typologies). Specht (1993) propounds that environmental munificence may interact with the carrying capacity of an industry and affect new organization formation rates. She argues that as resources are made available for new-firm foundlings, carrying capacity for new organizations may increase followed by a formation rate increase.

Within the context of the franchise sector, Specht's (1993) arguments are relevant since, as observed in Chapter 1, the level of support (or absence of support) by government and financial institutions can affect the growth of franchising (Garceau, 1989; Walker and Greenstreet, 1991). As resources are used, their availability decreases, causing a decrease in carrying capacity and, subsequently, in the formation rate, but an increase in the pressure to be innovative. For instance, as franchisors experience growing difficulties in recruiting franchisees from traditional channels, they are likely to spawn innovational initiatives in other areas of the labour market, for example, women and poorly capitalized but otherwise suitable individuals. In Britain, for example, Domino's Pizza has recently developed a scheme to attract franchisees that do not necessarily have access to the initial capital to join the system, but who have the necessary personal attributes. Under the scheme, the franchisee pays a bond of £5,000 and is self-employed, but leases all of the store's fixtures and fittings etc. from the franchisor (and is, consequently, positioned between being an employee and franchisee). This temporal analysis suggests that an inverse relationship between innovativeness and munificence exists.

Consistent with Abernathy and Utterback's (1978) product life-cycle findings, as an industry matures munificence falls and there is increased pressure on the firm to adopt process innovations to increase efficiency. Given that franchisees and franchisors operate in differing environments, however, varying levels of environmental munificence may be apparent (see Chapter 9). These differences may require that whilst product innovations are appropriate for one market, they are less so for another and require that, in some areas, radical innovations are necessary. These differences are a potential source of conflict since the franchisor may be inherently opposed to local market differentiation as it affects brand value and the *status quo*. In the mid-1980s, some US multi-brand fast food franchisees responded to intense competition within their local markets by combining the concepts so that whilst the brands remained distinct in their own right, customers were able, for example, to purchase their main course from one concept and their dessert from another. Such actions had the net effect of transforming latent conflict into a more overt form.

From an operational perspective, the degree of munificence within the local task environment may also affect the extent of slack resources, which in itself affects innovativeness. For example, in the Lou Groen case slack resources existed because a competitor had a product which attracted custom on Fridays whilst he had unused capacity. As a result of this capacity he had both an opportunity and a necessity (the need to make contributions to fixed costs) to innovate. A variety of definitions of slack exist, but Bourgeois' (1981) interpretation encapsulates most attempts. He defines slack as:

> that cushion of actual or potential resources which allows an organization to adapt successfully to internal . . . or . . . external pressures for change in strategy . . . as well as to initiate changes in strategy with respect to the external environment. (p. 30)

Unlike environmental munificence, therefore, increasing slack, or surplus, resources in an organization raises the probability of innovation and adaptability to task environments (Cyert and March, 1963). Slack resources may also affect the type of innovative activity. Damanpour (1991), for example, indicates that organizational slack has a stronger effect on technical, rather than administrative, innovations. Equally, the relationship between innovativeness and organizational slack may also alter by type of slack.

Singh (1986) differentiates between two types of slack, absorbed and unabsorbed. Whereas absorbed slack indicates the slack absorbed within the costs of organization, unabsorbed slack refers to uncommitted liquid resources. He observes that unabsorbed slack may buffer the organization from 'downside' risks and makes experimentation acceptable, whereas absorbed slack means that there is pressure to innovate in order to reduce costs and raise income.[7] UK fast food franchisees generally illustrate lower levels of unabsorbed slack than franchisors (Price, 1993), which echoes similar conclusions to those expressed by Bucklin (1971) in his 'Russian Roulette' interpretation of franchising:

> To devotees of the sport of gambling, Russian roulette is the supreme game . . . Franchising may be just this kind of game, except that five of the bullet chambers are loaded instead of just one. Fortunately, the cartridges are packed with only such niceties as seventy-two hour work weeks and a minimum-wage-busting pay scale, rather than with gun-powder. The empty chamber consists of that long awaited pile of riches at the end of the rainbow. (p. 39)

Given the arguments concerning franchisees' conflict with their labour, time management and rivalry, there is, therefore, an implication that franchisees are more concerned with absorbed slack, rather than unabsorbed slack. Due to these conditions, some franchisees may not be flexible enough to engage in ongoing experimentation, despite some having the competences to do so, and are consequently more orientated toward overcoming situations which are potentially threatening to their income and survival. For some this means developing new products, whilst maintaining a focus on production costs, a process which brings them into potential conflict with the franchisor as product development is in their domain (recall the social differentiation arguments).

The above paragraphs have argued that franchisors may be more orientated toward product innovations. Conversely, franchisees tend to be biased toward process innovations, but may engage in product development as a result of organizational slack deriving from low munificence. The main implication deriving from these divergent orientations toward innovation is that franchisors may be tolerant of franchisee incremental process improvements designed to realize increased profits and may, indeed, expect them as long as they are not detrimental to brand image. Indeed, successful foodservice organizations tend to be those that nurture a good reputation through service and utilize innovation in facilities, layout and equipment in order to reduce labour costs and increase manager and crew productivity (West and Olsen, 1989). Such successes may be instrumental in attracting additional franchisees because of the existing profitable ones. Within these parameters such innovative activity may remain hidden and not expected to be shared (although they may be beneficial to realizing profit improvements within the franchisor's own stores as well as other franchisees). Franchisors, however, may be less tolerant of hidden franchisee-initiated product improvements or radically innovative process innovations because these are potentially detrimental to brand value.

From an empowerment perspective, the bias towards process innovation suggests that franchisees are able to make some decisions concerning job content (Ford and Fottler, 1995) without reference to the franchisor. They may, once an opportunity for improvement is recognized, develop alternatives concerning the redesign of their own and their employees' tasks and develop a variety of new skills. Once implemented their developments and redesigns may, in turn, lead to greater franchisee satisfaction as a result of feelings of accomplishment and growth. The likely continued success of this form of empowerment is dependent on the nature and quality of franchisor support for their activities and whether the innovations impact on the value of the franchisee's business through improved profitability and cash flow. Franchisees are seen to have less power to initiate more radical innovations, such as those concerning job context issues, because these aspects are the domain of the franchisor [see Wicking's (1995) diagram earlier].

Recognizing the need for innovation

The most important moderating factor in affecting innovative behaviour is the recognition or realization that the opportunity or necessity for innovation exists. Indeed, one has to achieve awareness of how one is currently performing before an alternative can be considered rationally (Nooteboom, 1994). Hambrick and Mason (1984) observed that management teams, like all groups of decision-makers, operate under conditions of bounded rationality. The teams' perceptions, assumptions and interpretations of environmental events will determine how their companies respond to these events and how well they perform (Prahalad and Bettis, 1986). These perceptions, assumptions and interpretations are processed through their 'world view' or schemas which, in turn, represent beliefs, theories and propositions based on prior career histories. Careers vary in their content and length and, as such, are not fallible guides to interpreting changing environmental conditions or opportunities for performance improvement. In this vein, studies of one of the most basic diagnostic techniques, SWOT (strengths, weaknesses, opportunities and threats) analysis, have shown that perceptions of events are biased by hierarchical position, language and culture (Ireland *et al*, 1987). To use an analogy: climbing to the top of an organization is similar to climbing a series of hills with each subsequent hill being higher than the previous one: the individual's world view of the organization is dependent on the height of the current hill. Furthermore, information-seeking or data-gathering techniques that require formal planning or significant time and money costs are not popular environmental-scanning techniques for small-business owners (Callahan and Cassar, 1995). These findings suggest that, although environments are information-rich with clues to guide action, interpretation-poor systems preclude the transformation of that data to knowledge and, ultimately, strategic direction. In some cases, a certain issue, such as a new market entrant, will be assumed to be of little relevance to performance. Due to misdiagnosis and lack of understanding of the magnitude of the threat, that new entrant adversely affects the business. A situation similar to this was responsible for the demise of the British motorcycle industry after the entry of the Japanese. In other business situations, immediate action is taken and yet others will see complete denial prevail.

Here, some comparison with the slow-boiled frog example is appropriate. According to scientists, when a frog is placed in cold water which is then slowly heated, the frog does not react and can be boiled to death. However, when placed in water which is heated rapidly, the frog reacts by leaping out of the water. The analogy offers direct comparisons to the firm in need of innovation or a turnaround strategy (see Chapter 9). If that need is under-stated and goes unrecognized, it may have dire consequences for the health of the firm. In order to avoid being boiled, awareness of the environment and operational aspects are necessary through continual monitoring and scanning. Of course, management style is also influential because even though a decision-maker may have been pre-warned, he may not trust the reliability of the source or possess an unshaken belief that only he is right. That is, the world view has become a core rigidity impeding change.

Once the potential threat or opportunity has been recognized a set of actions is initiated to either negate the threat or realize the opportunity. Lawson (1980) has identifies and describes the creative process as comprising a common five-stage set (see Figure 6.5 on page 334). These stages are: first insight, preparation, incubation, illumination and verification. Given that at least some of the stages rely on perception and understanding, the illumination stage may be constrained by the nature of the individual's tacit knowledge.

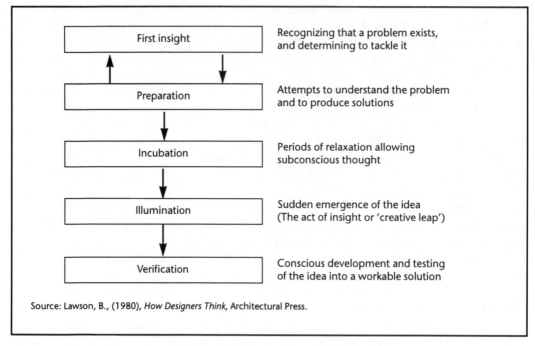

First insight	Recognizing that a problem exists, and determining to tackle it
Preparation	Attempts to understand the problem and to produce solutions
Incubation	Periods of relaxation allowing subconscious thought
Illumination	Sudden emergence of the idea (The act of insight or 'creative leap')
Verification	Conscious development and testing of the idea into a workable solution

Source: Lawson, B., (1980), *How Designers Think*, Architectural Press.

Figure 6.5: *Five-stage model of the creative process*

Summary and conclusion

Extant franchise literature has consistently and, some would argue, persistently propounded that innovation derives from the franchisor and suggested that the contributions made by franchisees are limited. Yet, franchisors that do not encourage the franchisee involvement in the innovation process are possibly not optimizing their competitive advantages, and the propensity for improved performance and survival (especially given the ever-shortening product life-cycles). Indeed, some of the innovations deriving from the franchisee community have proved to be the most enduring and successful: the Big Mac in McDonald's, Blizzards in Dairy Queen, and the introduction of value meals are testament to the efforts of franchisees. In this respect, the franchise literature illustrates a degree of similarity with the assumptions made of peasants in the discourse on feudalism:

> The debate on technical innovations is . . . vitiated by the bizarre idea that the lord was the entrepreneur and the large estate the context. The peasantry on the other hand, and no doubt not deliberately, is depicted as a weak and anaemic class without resources or initiative. The peasant is too rarely credited with any sophisticated technical knowledge. If tenants have vines, they must have learned to cultivate them on the demesne, and in the tenth century the planting contracts

are a clear demonstration of the confidence of the great landowners in the ability of peasants. If they pay their dues in honey and wax, these historians presume that they must have found a little in the woods. And yet the barbarian laws speak of apiculture and the polyptiques and inventories mention dues paid in hives; and it is well known what skill and attention to detail is required for beekeeping. Much could be said also about the origin of techniques of clothmaking. Did the Frisians, who wove brightly colored and precious cloth, learn how do it in the networks of the estate? But there were no large estates in Frisia! The southern peasants brought to the judges leather dyed red in imitation of Cordoba leather; in the twelfth century they were forced to hand over their store of vermillion to the town tradesman. In many things the towns learned from the countryside, and perhaps the men learned from the women. (Poly and Bournazel, 1991: p. 255)

This chapter has suggested that some franchisors and franchisees are involved in innovative activity and that there may be in-built innovative potential in franchises. This is due to the presence of franchisee-based competences, which derived from prior career histories, experiences, social capital and those acquired from the franchisor. The deployment of these capabilities may also derive from goal incongruity, the presence of organizational slack, the munificence of local competitive conditions and length of tenure. These determinants are common to both franchisors and franchisees and may, however, be moderated by the recognition that innovation is needed (see Figure 6.6), as well as by relational issues. Together, the degree of innovative capability and the triggers serve to determine whether innovation occurs and the nature of that innovation, but any room for non-incremental innovations is given at the franchisor's behest. In addition to possessing innovation potential, there are also some initial parallels between

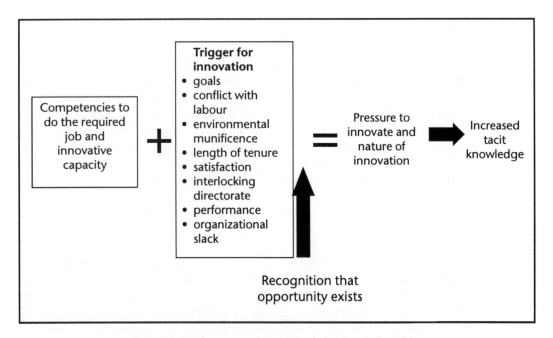

Figure 6.6: Influences on innovative behaviour in franchises

franchises and strategic alliances, but they cannot be said to be strategic alliances in a pure sense.

Reve (1990) argues that in order to understand how strategic capabilities are created and up-graded, we need to go into theories of entrepreneurship or innovation. Some prior research suggests that franchisees are often frustrated from expressing entrepreneurial behaviour, but this is nevertheless apparent through opportunism. Whilst opportunism may be detrimental to the franchise relationship, such a research focus is insufficient because it does not tell why the franchisee expressed opportunistic behaviour. Of greater importance to the franchise relationship and business survival is the process of individual learning and the recognition of the need for innovation. By only tentatively touching upon this notion of opportunism and the cited examples, it is apparent that franchisees are involved in fragmented learning. That is, they learn from their past experiences and interaction with their own social network, but the franchise organization as a whole does not learn because the infrequent visits by franchisor managerial staff and executives may be insufficient in themselves in guiding franchisees to share their innovations. As seen from the scenarios, in some franchises innovative activity may be hidden and in others be shared with the franchisor. Of greater significance, perhaps, to franchise system innovativeness are the relational conditions deriving from the franchise contract (encompassing, for example, the degree of goal divergence, dependence and overt imbalance in shared benefits) and nature of relational exchanges (linked to nature of communication, power and trust) within these contractual boundaries which induce some franchisees to behave in a managerially opportunistic manner, whilst others are more strategic. Some of these are considered in Chapter 7.

Notes

1. This chapter is a version of papers presented at the Institute of Small Business Affairs Conference, Paisley, Scotland, 15–17 November 1995 and the Tenth Annual Conference of the Society of Franchising, Honolulu, Hawaii, 17–18 February 1996, where it was awarded 1st place by the Society of Franchising for the 1996 Best International Paper and MCB University Press's Outstanding Paper Award. It is also a version of the arguments presented in Stanworth *et al* (1995), 'Correlates of Innovation in Franchise Systems', *Research Working Paper*, Series 2: No. 8 (May), Faculty of Business, Management & Social Studies, University of Westminster Press, London. It is reproduced with permission.

2. Ricardian rents are the earnings derived from firm-specific, non-imitable advantages.

3. Sharma *et al* (1981) observe 'a moderator variable has been defined as one which systematically modifies either the form and/or strength of relationship between a predictor and criterion variable' (p. 291). They illustrate that there are different types of moderating variables depending upon whether it interacts with the predictor variable and whether it related to either the criterion and/or predictor. Accordingly, different moderator categories may influence the

strength and/or form of relationship between the criterion and predictor variables.

4. Amit and Shoemaker (1993) observe that capabilities 'refer to a firm's capacity to deploy resources, usually in combination, using organizational processes, that are firm-specific and are developed over time through complex interactions among the firm's resources' (p. 35). Hall (1993) differentiates capabilities based on competencies as 'functional capability' and 'cultural capability'. Functional capability relates to the ability to do specific things; it results from the knowledge, skill and experience of employees and other input forces, for example, suppliers. By contrast, cultural capability applies to the organization as a whole. It incorporates people's habits, attitudes, beliefs and values. Competencies are considered strategic if they differentiate a company strategically. Quinn (1980) has argued that effective competition is not so much founded on 'strategic leaps' but small-scale innovations that exploit existing capabilities. Whilst there are some (e.g. agency theorists) who perceive that franchising seeks to help leverage resources, it also entails competence leveraging to enhance functional capabilities, via the franchisee gaining access to information and operational experience.

5. In this way, such information may not provide the potential franchisee with a realistic job preview (RJP), despite the benefits that such realism may convey to the franchisor (such as more closely matching *ex-ante* and *ex-post* franchisee expectations) in order to affect positive satisfaction. Breaugh and Billings (1988) posit that an RJP 'must convey accurate information . . . it must be specific and broad in scope . . . it must be credible . . . [and] . . . contain important information about the job and the organization being considered by the applicant' (p. 294).

6. According to the taxonomy, a 'strategic leader' has a high degree of local resources and competence, is located in a strategically significant market, and is a barometer of market conditions and potential opportunities and threats. The 'contributor' operates in a strategically unimportant market but has distinctive capability. By comparison, an 'implementor' reflects limited strategic significance of the SBU and has 'just enough competence to maintain its local position' (p. 179). The final category, a 'black hole', indicates low strategic importance and low competence. Unlike earlier conceptions of SBU strategies, which were founded on more generic strategic typologies (Porter, 1985; Miles and Snow, 1978), the roles that Barlett and Ghoshal (1991) assigned to SBUs are related to other SBUs within a corporate portfolio and, thus, uniquely intra-corporate (Galunic and Eisenhardt, 1994).

7. Although a simple measure, operationalizing organizational slack requires some degree of care. Singh (1986) quantifies absorbed slack by the amount of overhead divided by total income. Unabsorbed slack is measured by the quick, or current, ratio. Such measures, however, should be viewed with caution. Fleming (1986) argues that the current ratio can change rapidly during a short time

and this phenomenon makes the current ratio subject to manipulation when management wishes to window-dress financial statements to make them appear more favourable than they really are.

7 | Influences on sharing innovations in the franchise dyad: the roles of power and culture

True freedom is not the absence of structure – letting the employees go off and do whatever they want – but rather a clear structure that enables people to work within established boundaries in an autonomous and creative way.

Eric Fromm, US psychologist, *Escape from Freedom*

One of the vices or the virtue of decentralization is that people don't share ideas.

Antony J. F. O'Reilly, US academic, *New York Times*, 1988

Introduction

The rising costs of new product and process developments, rapid technological diffusion, shorter product life-cycles, and increasing competitive turbulence have meant that innovation is increasingly important as a source of competitive advantage. It has also become significant in reducing the tendency of 'strategic drift', or the extent to which the organization is out of line with the environment in which it operates (Johnson, 1992). In order to facilitate such advantages and survival, many companies are finding collaborative relationships a beneficial method to generate new ideas, processes, and products. These technological collaborations are defined as any activity where two or more partners contribute differential resources and technological know-how to agreed complementary aims (Shan *et al*, 1994). In representing ongoing arrangements where partners mutually share their expertise and output, these technological collaborations are viewed as strategic alliances (Yoshino and Rangan, 1995). As a result of the perceived lack of such mutual sharing activity, franchises are not construed to be strategic alliances. This belief exists because the flow of technology is viewed as being a one-way transfer, from the franchisor to the franchisee. It also exists, however, in spite of anecdotal evidence to the contrary, because of the presence of innovative capability among franchisees, differing objectives, and varying levels of environmental munificence. This situation suggests that franchises are not all they could be because of the exercising of exclusionary power. If there is evidence to show that franchisees are involved in innovative activity, then the lack of technological collaboration infers that much of the potential of this effort is possibly wasted; it also suggests that there are relational impediments to sharing innovations in franchises.

In order to explore the nature of these impediments, the focus of this chapter is on the individual franchisee-franchisor relationship. This focus also limits the chapter's comprehensiveness. As observed by Van de Ven *et al* (1975) and Provan (1983), inter-organizational relationships can be studied at three distinct levels. The first approach is to examine the relations between individual channel dyads in order to gain understanding of linkage evolution and bargaining power issues that may otherwise be missed when examining more complex arrangements involving numerous players. A second approach has been to focus one particular organization and the cluster of dyads maintained by it. Such work has attempted to establish why and when organizations become involved in alliances and the structural and strategic implications of their involvement. This is, essentially, the approach encompassed by Achrol *et al* (1983), who examine relationships between suppliers, government bodies and the environment and a core organizational body. The third method relates to focusing on an entire network or web among linked organizations. As part of the information sharing process, the focus of this chapter provides an analysis of the transactions between dyad actors, rather than the individual firm or the channel as a whole, to complete a model of the potential determinants of franchise system innovativeness.

While focusing on the individual dyad, it is important to observe that not all franchises are equally innovative and some franchise participants are more innovative than others. These differences possibly point to different levels of innovative resource among franchises, as well as different status; after all, is not the success of companies such as McDonald's not only due to their tolerance for innovations, but also the access to franchisees who are able to recognize that innovation is fundamental to survival and profits? The last chapter suggested that there are several situational and relational factors which may serve to impact on the extent of the variable rate of innovative activity:

- the franchisor-franchisee relationship may be more complex than that between a corporate entity and its own units (Boyle *et al*, 1992; Hennart, 1993);
- franchisees adapt by choice to the rigours of local market conditions within the constraints imposed on them (Hrebiniak and Joyce, 1985; Marlin *et al*, 1994; Usher, 1989);
- even those governed by restrictive contracts have been responsible for new product developments (Shook and Shook, 1993); and
- franchisees differ in their attitudes towards risk and effort which may, in turn, affect their innovativeness (Katz and Owen, 1992).

Misconceptions about the nature of the franchisee-franchisor relationships, as well as the failure to account for agent heterogeneity, franchisee price-setting activity and promotional investments (Gal-Or, 1991; Nault and Dexter, 1994) may have led some researchers to generalize that technological transfer may be asymmetric. The observation of integrative issue-resolving mechanisms, such as problem-solving, within some market channels (for example, fast food franchises) has, however, cast further doubt on the generalist premise that such apparatus is rare in unilateral systems (Dant and Schul, 1992). While the factors listed above may serve to affect innovativeness, it is not complete. Arguably, another factor influencing the variability of issue-resolving and innovative activity is partly a function of the importance which each party attaches to innovation. In this sense, although franchises are not a form of technological collaboration in its true form, sharing innovations may occur anyway because both the franchisor and franchisee believe in the potential benefits of the activity: competitive advantage, sustained demand, and added motivation deriving from a sense of increased participation. By both parties showing a belief that innovation is important, they could be said to illustrate similar cultures and have a relationship to exchange new ideas and innovations. In all probability, such relationships will be more pronounced in the older franchise systems.

What is culture?

Culture is ubiquitous, and this book has made numerous references to it as being central to franchising because it affects the way in which franchisees are managed and the diffusion of franchising. As shown in Figure 7.1 below, culture exists at differing levels and in varying contexts of life. For example, countries and geographic regions are distinguished by differing beliefs, values, rituals, and attitudes to risk and collective behaviour; social classes and industries are seen to reflect different cultures, and in recent years there has been a great deal of interest in the concepts of organizational culture and sub-culture. Deal and Kennedy (1988) argue that culture has a powerful influence throughout an organization; it affects practically everything in corporate life and otherwise, including who gets promoted and what decisions are made, to how employees dress and the success of a business. Drawn from anthropology and in spite of its pervasiveness, definitions of culture vary according to not only what should be included in the term, but also where the emphasis should lie (Alvesson and Berg, 1992). In some instances, a few authors tend to refer to culture in broad terminology. These researchers interpret culture as the symbols, beliefs and patterns of behaviours learned, produced and created by people, and who express their values in the artefacts and buildings they use and inhabit (Strati, 1992). While such a broad approach may be employed fruitfully to examine the differences between franchises, it has limitations when exploring for the presence of cultural differences within a franchise. Franchisees typically do not have the freedom to choose their store's architecture, livery, or corporate symbols because they are stipulated by the franchisor. A potential conclusion deriving from the application of this definition is that

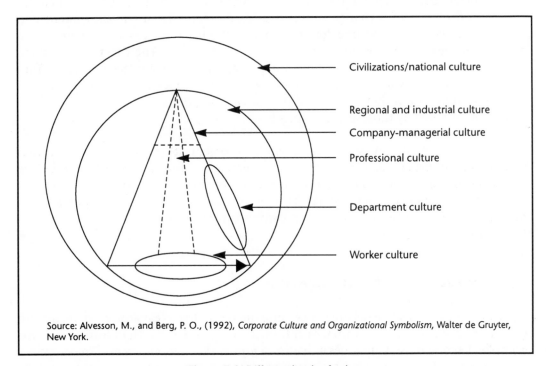

Source: Alvesson, M., and Berg, P. O., (1992), *Corporate Culture and Organizational Symbolism*, Walter de Gruyter, New York.

Figure 7.1: Different levels of culture

franchisees do not have their own culture, but mirror that of their franchisors. In this respect, therefore, their culture is a direct imitation of that exposed by the dominant capitalist class. Differing objectives, and latent conflict, however, possibly mitigates against a common culture and points to the presence of a more 'negotiated version' of the dominant value system.

Other researchers view culture within a narrower focus, viewing it as a common system of values, beliefs, system of values, beliefs and norms (Pettigrew, 1979). According to Strati (1992), shared assumptions, beliefs and norms define behavioural norms and expectations; it is the 'glue' that holds communities together and represents their social energy and personalities, as well as desirable practices. As this definition allows us to see different sub-sets of shared values within an organization, it is this latter approach which is adopted in this chapter, and is employed to generate a framework with which to explore how differing levels of culture can affect the flow and sharing of innovations within franchises. Reflective of their respective positions in the organizational hierarchy, it is assumed that franchisees illustrate a worker culture and franchisors exhibit the traits of company-managerial cultures.

The contention that there are differing types of culture within the same organizational form is, in part, supported by a large body of research which illustrates the inertia of some departments to the introduction of new technology. Pine (1987) summarizes the sentiment encapsulated in such inertia:

> Whatever the reasons for introducing any change, people will tend to resist, indeed it is possible to regard man's normal state as a change resisting one. People are expected to deploy a stable personality and adhere to the norms of behaviour accepted in their own social system. Therefore, to become a positive contributor to a change situation at work people need encouragement and reward. Fear of machine domination, loss of skills, even loss of employment do not create an atmosphere which is receptive to change. These factors will add to normal resistance of change of any sort and may prevent the workforce from adopting new technology willingly. Whether these factors are real or imaginary is irrelevant: if they are perceived as threatening then a defensive position will be adopted by those affected. (p. 30)

The observation of differing sub-cultures within an organization also derives from studies of worker cultures on factory floors, which suggests that the cultural patterns achieve their form and character as the result of the tension implicit in the worker-management relationship (Alvesson and Berg, 1992). This tension arises from labour's lack of bargaining power with capitalists, due to the non-ownership of factors of production other than their willingness and ability to work.

Structuring for innovation

There is still some debate concerning the most effective manner for organizing for innovation: should it be formal or informal? Booz, Allen and Hamilton (1982), for example, describe most companies as having a formal innovation process. They report a greater degree of formality and bureaucratization in the process for successful versus unsuccessful firms. Furthermore, Maidique and Zirger (1984) conclude that new product success is likely to be greater when the process is well planned and co-ordinated. Others disagree: writers such as Mintzberg (1979), Burns and Stalker (1961), and Kanter (1985) have offered fairly solid evidence to suggest that organically structured organizations are best equipped to cope with innovation and change. Mintzberg sees 'adhocracy' as the most creative and innovative organizational form. In a review of how organizations structure themselves for innovation, Mezias and Glynn (1993) suggest that the varying methods of organizing for innovation can be distilled to three approaches:

1. *Institutional approach*, which emphasizes the theme of rational, functional, planned innovation. According to this approach, successful innovation is seen as the outcome of an organized, purposeful and systematic process. While there is a wealth of research advocating this approach, such as that within the quality circle literature, most concur that the institutionalized approach is conducive to incremental innovation rather than radical 'breakthrough' forms.

2. *Revolutional approach*, which involves conscious efforts to move away from the current organizational paradigm and entails developing mechanisms, such as *ad hoc* teams or autonomous work teams operating outside the existing organizational structure. One such approach is 'intrapreneuring', which is entrepreneurship and innovation within mechanistic structures. What Pinchot (1986) terms 'intrapreneurs' (entrepreneurs within corporations) manage to innovate in structured environments, often by creating a pool of adhocratically organized space within a broader mechanistic whole and supported by the presence of powerful sponsors/protectors or mentors.

3. *Evolutionary approaches* are less intentional than either the institutional or revolutionary approaches to innovation. They represent more experimental attempts at innovation and, as Mezias and Glynn (1993) observe, this approach embodies an important idea that innovation is a chaotic, probabilistic process.

Reflecting the recourse to deliberate learning via co-operative behaviour by international organizations, a wealth of research examining the differing attributes of strategic alliances has emerged. For example, Tidd (1993) observes that there has been a significant increase in collaborative activity between manufacturing firms of late, with the most common cited reason for entering into such arrangements being the access to complementary technology and the access to new markets. Such activity has spawned a wealth of analysis concerning the co-ordination and managerial aspects of collaborative technology arrangements (Bailetti and Callahan, 1993; Berry and Taggart, 1994; Hagedoorn, 1993; 1995; Kogut *et al*, 1995) and joint ventures (Hamel, 1991; Harrigan, 1985). Much of this research has been orientated towards the explanation for the formation of operative agreements between large concerns and also between large firms and small businesses. Such research infers that whilst innovation and knowledge acquisition is a major rationale for formation, firm size may affect the propensity to co-operation. In short, oligopolistic industry leader businesses, given their diversity and size, may have more to gain in terms of market power, cost reductions and asset complementarity than small firms (Colombo, 1995) from such administrative innovation. For example, pharmaceutical giant Glaxo has ten strategic research alliances with biotechnology firms which have knowledge of specific disease areas that are complementary to Glaxo's core expertise.

The previous chapters have shown that the decision to franchise represents the revolutional form of innovation which may either occur through the intentions of the business managers, of through a more evolutional approach. Chapter 6 suggested further that, despite the franchisor's initial innovative effort in adopting franchising as an organizational form, researchers do not perceive franchise realtionships as strategic alliances; they are not organizational forms orientated towards continuous innovation and do not have cultures which are designed intentionally to nurture and develop innovation. This sentiment is partially reflected in the observation that franchisors desire conformity rather than innovation, even though the franchise contract and franchise operating manuals are written within bounded rationality which, in turn, suggests that they are subject to change. They are, therefore, inherent adjustment mechanisms to changing environmental conditions (Heide, 1994).

Franchises, especially within the context of foodservice, tend to be portrayed as 'machine bureaucracies' (Mintzberg, 1979) where the subunits are tightly coupled, their goals are subordinated to those of the organization, and their autonomy is minimized. In Ford and Fottler's (1995) empowerment model, franchisees are perceived to have little power in affecting either their job context or job content (Chapter 2). Consistent with this view are frequent claims that 'franchisors seek replication not innovation and conformity not creativity' from their franchisees (English and Hoy, 1995). While structure is important to the realization of innovation, arguably it is more a reflection of the culture of the organization. For example, Pheysey (1993) suggests that culture affects organizational design through a preference for centralized or decentralized forms as well as through preferences for work simplification or job enlargement. Organizational cultures also reflect how organizations learn: some make a conscious effort to develop new ideas through encouraging organizational members to participate via suggestion schemes, quality circles, etc.; others do not make such explicit overtures but employ informal methods; and some only learn by their mistakes. The differing approaches employed are reflective of the degree of commitment to developing superior competitive advantages based on innovation, and are susceptible to alteration according to the differing motives of management.

Within franchising the differing emphasis, whether formal or evolutionary, franchisors place on innovation may be ascertained according to the presence of collective and participative bodies. Due to the presence of innovative capability and exogenous conditions, among other factors, conducive to innovation there is at least some other circumstantial evidence to point to a more evolutionary approach, but may equally point to a lack of shared innovation *per se*. Perhaps reflecting the existence of *ex-ante* adjustment methods, franchisees and franchisors have reported that informal contact between them and their franchisor tends to occur on a weekly or monthly basis, but a significant proportion occurs on a quarterly basis. Importantly for innovation sharing, franchisees said that they generally initiated these contacts in the majority of instances, in order to seek solutions to technical and other operating problems (Stanworth, 1991). In some franchise chains, an institutional approach is evident since the communication of new ideas has been facilitated by the formation of collective and participative bodies, such as franchise advisory councils and consultative committees, but these are not widespread.

A franchise advisory council (FAC) is a group of franchisees who meet regularly with company executives to discuss important policy and operational issues. Its franchisee members present their ideas and concerns to the executives, and the executives present their plans for changes or future marketing or operating programmes to franchisees (Perry, 1992). Despite their potential benefits, to date the presence of such bodies has been limited because, at least, in Europe such bodies within the hospitality industry are relatively rare; in the UK, for example, only an eighth of hospitality franchises have formal representative organizations (one of the lowest levels of formal representation in the British franchise sectors). The dearth of FACs in Britain may, in itself, warrant further research effort since there may be parallels between the level of formal representation in hospitality franchises and the level of labour collectivization in catering generally. As FACs are not trade unions, there may be some danger that comparisons with trade unions may be limited. Nonetheless, in terms of the level of collectivization generally with the catering industry, there appear to be some similarities between FACs and trade unions. According to the Department of Employment, union representation amongst catering employees stands at about 8% – the lowest in British industry (see Table 7.1).

Sector/year	1989	1990	1991	1992
Hotel and catering	11	11	10	8
All UK industries	39	38	33	30

Source: *Labour Force Survey.*

Table 7.1: UK trade union density (%): hotel and catering versus all industries

Various rationales have been forwarded to explain this situation including:

1. employees in catering do not seem to illustrate the typical employer-employee relationship since tipping means that they are working for themselves (Cobble, 1991; Paules, 1991);
2. lack of union selling points to catering employees;
3. small average size of units and industry fragmentation;
4. autocratic and paternalistic management;
5. overt anti-union sentiments by some caterers;
6. predominance of family-owned concerns;
7. deskilling, leading to relatively low replaceability costs;
8. high labour turnover;
9. prevalence of part-time and marginal workers;
10. the high proportion of women in the catering industry (unionism has been perceived a male-dominated domain); and
11. 'mine-host' mentality of employees.

In franchises, FACs may not be present due to:

1. the perception by franchisees that they are trade unions – in the fast food industry in the USA, franchisees have collectivized to help fight unionization amongst their employees (Luxenburg, 1985);
2. the geographic dispersement of franchisees;
3. paternalistic management by franchisor;
4. the lack of time – the 'Russian Roulette' argument (Chapter 6);
5. that they cut across feelings of independence (Felstead, 1993);
6. the active discouragement by franchisors;
7. the perception that they are a franchisor 'spying' mechanism to identify troublemakers; and
8. the small size of many franchises.

In the USA and Australia, franchise advisory bodies are more commonplace (McCosker *et al*, 1995; Perry, 1992), and may affect the propensity for bilateral technological transfers. Shared learning may occur because FACs serve to permit franchisees to maintain a positive focus which may, in turn, help to increase profits; reinforce social and structural trust components; encourage co-operation and communication (providing the franchisor with 'reality checks'); gather and communicate divergent points of view and act as a forum for idea exchange. In this way, such bodies may be a source of competitive advantage rather than unit growth (Dandrige and Falbe, 1994). Such advantages may accrue in three ways. Firstly, the franchisee is often the closest to consumers and most aware of their needs, and can therefore direct innovative effort. Secondly, franchisee participation may increase the acceptance of decisions, as they will be more aware of the factors that led to the decision. Thirdly, if franchisees are made to feel part of the decision-making structure, system co-ordination is more likely to be achieved (Guiltinan *et al*, 1980; Mockler and Easop, 1968).

While these benefits are important to the survival of the franchise, the lack of such bodies in European franchises does not necessarily mean that the propensity for shared innovation is lower. Ideally, a franchise is the synergistic combination of a franchisee and franchisor working together to serve customers better, and the success of the franchise system is a function of how well the franchisee and franchisor perform, together and separately (Spriggs and Nevin, 1994). The extent to which franchise relationships are synergistic and are able to build brand value jointly is, in part, a function of the compatibility of the franchisee and franchisor cultures concerning innovation and communicating those ideas to others, as well as the nature of the relationship between the franchise participants. For example, franchisors may illustrate a culture emphatic of new product developments, while franchisees may exhibit a culture emphatic of innovations to realize process improvements. While both stress innovation, the extent to which the franchisor can persuade the franchisee to adopt a new product may have its limitations. The franchisee could, for instance, be concerned that the new product may increase the costs of production. In order for the innovation to be diffused, the franchisor could either resolve the franchisees concerns, or force them to adopt it.

The lack of bargaining power by franchisees deriving from a lack of collectivization, suggests that these *ex-ante* adjustment mechanisms are likely to be *ad hoc*, not shared and may not be mutually beneficial. The absence of mutuality may be due to differing tacit knowledge levels, varying quality levels of training, differing innovation triggers, and recognition capability. Given that some innovative behaviour may be counter to franchisor interests, the franchisee may be coerced to return the relationship to equilibrium by amending his ways (via imbalanced power relations).

After examining how innovation is stressed within differing organizational cultures, Kono (1990) formulates a continuum (illustrated below) to show that there are seven factors which facilitate the classification of cultures according to the decision-making process and overt behaviour patterns:

1. values that the member believes;
2. information collection;
3. idea generation;
4. evaluation of ideas and risk-taking;
5. co-operation;
6. loyalty to the organization; and
7. the value of the task to the employee, or morale of the member.

Using these variables, he suggests the following five organizational forms:

1. *Vitalized type:* in the vitalized culture type, members put emphasis on innovation, have a sense of one family or one community, and share common values. The goal of organization is clearly understood, and the members understand the meaning of jobs clearly. Information is actively collected from the outside, and is customer-oriented. The organization has good communication both vertically and horizontally. Ideas for improvement are presented voluntarily, and members perform duties in anticipation of the expectations of others. Opposing ideas towards seniors and colleagues are presented. Members take risks and feel that there is little social distance between them and their seniors.
2. *Follow-the-leader and vitalized type:* the feature of this type of culture is that its members follow a strong leader who is often the founder of the company. They trust the ability of their leader, and important information and ideas come from the top management. As long as management makes good decisions, this type of culture works well, but once top management gets older and begins to make the wrong decisions, this type shifts to stagnant with strong leader type described below.
3. *Bureaucratic type:* Kono (1990) observes that in companies with this culture, rules and standards increase, the behaviour of employees is bound by these rules, and they do not try to take risks.
4. *Stagnant type:* members of this type of culture repeat old patterns of behaviour, and their information collection is internally-oriented and insensitive to changes in the environment. Members, on the whole, do not generate new ideas. This type appears in companies with monopolistic market shares and in public organizations.
5. *Stagnant with strong leader type:* here top management is autocratic, but their decisions are wrong and the employees who have to obey orders lose their initiative. A company with a Type 2 culture might develop into this type, when the top management stays in position for too long.

Elements	Type 1 Vitalized	Type 2 Follow the leader and vitalized	Type 3 Bureaucratic	Type 4.1 Stagnant	Type 4.2 Stagnant and follow the leader
General characteristics	Value in innovation. Many ideas presented.	Follow the leader.	Procedures and rules are respected.	Tradition orientated.	Follow the leader.
1. Value	Innovation.	Following the leader is value.	Procedure-orientated. Safety first.	Safety first.	Safety of self. Safety first.
2. Information	Information collection is orientated to outside the environment.	Information comes from the higher ranks.	Orientated to technical knowledge.	Internally orientated.	Top down.
3. Idea presentation	Many spontaneous ideas presented. Many opposing ideas.	Do only as directed. No opposing ideas.	Perfect and completed plan is necessary. High level of specialization.	Habitual few new ideas. No opposing ideas.	Few new ideas presented. Do as directed.
4. Risk taking	Not afraid of failure.	Failure is the responsibility of the leader.	Afraid of failure.	Afraid of failure.	Afraid of failure.
5. Co-operation	Little social distance between the leader and the follower. Good teamwork.	Follow the leader. Mutually competitive.	Hierarchy is necessary. Responsibility and authority are clear.	Do not trust the higher ranks. Mutually separated.	Large vertical social distance. Mutually separated.
6. Loyalty to the organization	Two extremes.	Work for lifetime.	Work for lifetime.	Quit the company if better opportunities are available.	Quit the company if better opportunities are available.

Table 7.2: Cultures and structures for innovation

In the vitalized types, innovative capability is permitted to be expressed where-as in the bureaucratic and stagnant types, the capability is repressed. Due to a lack of expression, innovative capability is not practised and the *status quo* becomes embedded and ingrained. As the environment changes, so the strategy of the organization will grad-ually, perhaps imperceptibly, become less and less in line with its environment (Johnson, 1992). Change in these organizations will be problematic and treated with suspicion because it entails the enshrined culture to be changed. By ranking these differing cultures towards the emphasis innovation into high, medium and low, and suggesting that the members of the franchise dyad have the potential to illustrate different levels of impor-tance concerning innovation, the following matrix is presented. It shows that franchisors and franchisees can either have similar cultures regarding innovation or dissimilar ones; where they are dissimilar the sharing of innovations may be problematic and give rise to conflict. Conversely, where both parties are vitalized towards innovation this could be construed to be a technological collaboration, and where both are stagnant there may be a high probability of failure. Although there has been a tendency for some researchers, when speaking about organizational culture, to assume that management culture is com-mon to all personnel throughout the firm, to do so implicitly suggests a unitary perspective.

Under the unitary approach, all interested parties are assumed to be bound together by a common goal. As the organization is a team, rational analysis can conse-quently be encouraged to predominate in decision-making. This perspective, however, finds it difficult to deal with the idea of competing interests and either latent and/or explicit conflict. If opposition occurs, it is perceived as some form of aberration, instigat-ed by troublemakers and people who do not share the same culture (Fox, 1973). As shown in Chapter 6, there seems to be little evidence to support this perspective in relation to franchising. Franchises are marketed by latent conflict deriving from the participant's dif-fering sources of revenue and the franchisees illustrating higher levels of dependency on the relationship than franchisors. When conditions adversely affect the realization of such objectives, latent conflict becomes more pronounced and expressed (Andaleeb, 1996).

The issues deriving from goal divergence from the franchisor focuses franchisees on the fine-tuning of the service-delivery system, rather than necessarily affecting the degree of standardization among units – which could mean that they have breached the franchise contract. In this fine-tuning activity, franchisees are seen to be empowered to the extent that they have the capability and motivation to alter their job content in a similar way to semi-autonomous teams, but is limited to those aspects of the business that do not affect brand capital. Freedom for franchisees to alter job context is less encompassing, except in such areas as their organizational structure and tier staff reward systems. Within Ford and Fottler's (1995) empowerment taxonomy, franchisees are seen as having deci-sion-making authority over all aspects of their job content (problem identification, alternative development and evaluation stages), but may be excluded from issues con-cerning choice and implementation. Given this latitude, some franchises are marked more by 'participatory empowerment' rather than the self-management that much of the pop-ular franchise press propound and have more to contribute than distributive mechanisms.

The differing objectives and dependencies in franchising suggest that pluralism is a more appropriate framework to analyze the potential impediments and facilitators to sharing innovation. Pluralism means that there is a plurality of groups, which have different world views. These groups are, potentially at least, in conflict with each other because they perceive problems and solutions differently. Unlike the unitary perspective, such conflict is normal and legitimate, and decision-making may be more politically motivated rather than rationally-based. Chapter 3 illustrated that the development of strategy and the modification of organizational structure, to permit the realization of objectives, is founded in cultural, political, and cognitive terms. Such variables are also significant in the organization of innovation; for example, some managers have a vested interest in maintaining the *status quo* because their very reason for existence often rests on preserving stable relationships and behavioural patterns. Consequently, if a franchise is to be effective, these tensions differing cultures must be managed through collaboration and consensus.

Being positioned between hierarchical and market governance forums, franchises may experience difficulties in unilaterally adapting to market conditions in an overt manner (Williamson, 1991), because the adaptation and ensuing administrative control must be agreed upon and shared: it must be a function of the degree of consensus and compromise between the cultures of the franchisee and franchisor. Where innovation does not occur, either both parties illustrate the same cultures (that is, stagnant cultures) or one party has been unable to alter the attitudes to innovation held by the dominant party. For example, some of the franchisor's managerial staff may be reluctant to allow quality circles or suggestion schemes because they fear that some suggestions will reflect badly on them. They fear that if franchisees make suggestions which lead to genuine improvements, senior management will blame them for not having come up with the ideas.

While the preferred types for innovation are 1 and 2 (see Table 7.2), researchers suggest that franchisors appear to be reflective of the bureaucratic type because the contracts frequently contain unilateral specifications of standard operating procedures, incentive systems and termination clauses. The essentials of the franchise relationship appear to be: first, how to ensure that an agent acts in the interest of the principal; and second, that principals have incomplete information, in that it may be difficult for the principal *ex-ante* to identify the most suitable agent to engage (pre-contractual) and *ex-post* to monitor the activities of agents (moral hazard). When moral hazard exists at the technical core, it is to the principal's benefit to hire managers to supervise the workers on behalf of the principal, and more workers should be hired. The degree of supervision is higher with managers and supervisors. Profits from both production and the other economic activities are also increased when managers are hired. *Ex-ante* issues may lead franchisors to recruitment biases and seek to reduce *ex-post* moral hazard by increasing the level of comparability of agents, achieved by uniformity of agreement (contractual standardization) to realize a standardized offering. Franchisees may exhibit a bureaucratic culture too because they may fear losing their investment if found to be engaging in opportunistic behaviour. Alternatively, the necessity to generate profit may mean that franchisees' cultures are more orientated towards innovation.

Although the diagram has suggested that franchisees and franchisors can exhibit similar or different cultures regarding innovation, these cultures do not affect whether the innovations are shared *per se*; compatible cultures only means that there is an increased likelihood of shared activity. The extent to which innovations are shared is not only a function of the compatibility between the two cultures but, according to some texts, also the climate of relations between the two parties during specific exchange

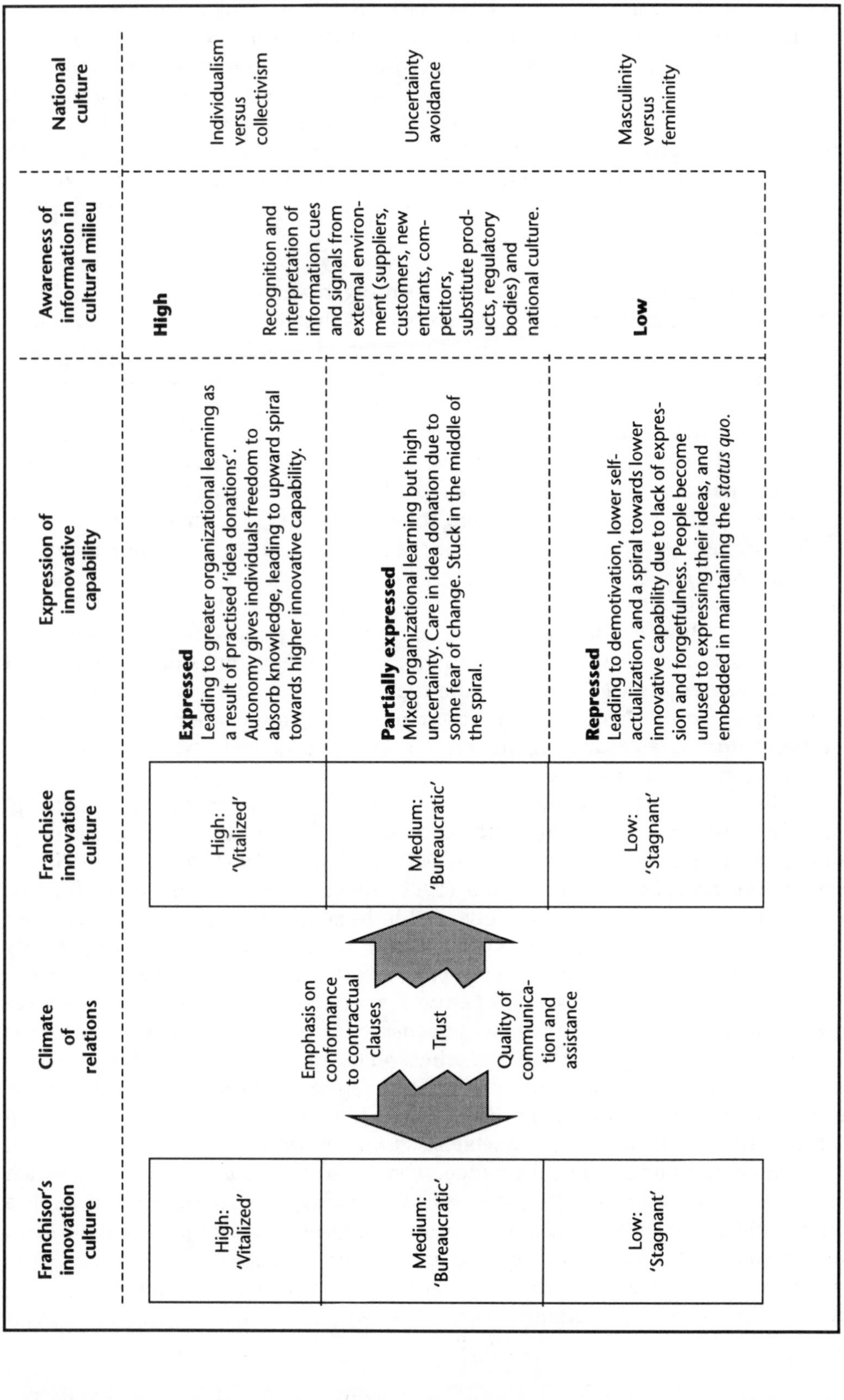

Franchisor's innovation culture	Climate of relations	Franchisee innovation culture	Expression of innovative capability	Awareness of information in cultural milieu	National culture
				High	Individualism versus collectivism
High: 'Vitalized'		High: 'Vitalized'	**Expressed** Leading to greater organizational learning as a result of practised 'idea donations'. Autonomy gives individuals freedom to absorb knowledge, leading to upward spiral towards higher innovative capability.	Recognition and interpretation of information cues and signals from external environment (suppliers, customers, new entrants, competitors, substitute products, regulatory bodies) and national culture.	Uncertainty avoidance
Medium: 'Bureaucratic'	Emphasis on conformance to contractual clauses / Trust / Quality of communication and assistance	Medium: 'Bureaucratic'	**Partially expressed** Mixed organizational learning but high uncertainty. Care in idea donation due to some fear of change. Stuck in the middle of the spiral.		Masculinity versus femininity
Low: 'Stagnant'		Low: 'Stagnant'	**Repressed** Leading to demotivation, lower self-actualization, and a spiral towards lower innovative capability due to lack of expression and forgetfulness. People become unused to expressing their ideas, and embedded in maintaining the *status quo*.	**Low**	

Figure 7.2: Franchisee and franchisor cultures for innovation

episodes. Climate is defined in terms of the perceptions, expectations, and feelings that individuals have of how their department or work unit is managed (Hellneigal and Slocum, 1974). Climate is seen to differ from culture because it is much more in the fore-ground of the organizational members' perceptions, whereas culture is more in the background: climate concerns attitudes rather than deeper values. Climate, however, is affected by culture, and people's perceptions define both, but it is indicative of culture (Boyle and Dwyer, 1995; Burke and Litwin, 1992). Recently, Denison (1996) suggested that the differences between culture and climate may be superficial, and therefore only culture is apt:

> On the surface, the distinction between organizational climate and organiza-
> tional culture may appear to be quite clear: Climate refers to a situation and its
> link to thoughts, feelings, and the behaviours of organizational members. Thus,
> it is a temporal subjective, and often subject to direct manipulation by people
> with power and influence. Culture, by contrast, refers to an evolved context
> (within which the situation maybe embedded). Thus, it is rooted in history, col-
> lectively held, and sufficiently complex to resist many attempts at direct
> manipulation . . . However, at a deeper level . . . these seemingly clear distinc-
> tions begin to disappear . . . [and these differences] . . . should be viewed as
> differences in interpretation rather than the differences in the phenomenon.
> (pp. 644–45)

Thus, without a culture conducive to sharing innovations, the individual members of the dyad may pursue their own interests; some franchisors, for example, may seek product innovations without consideration for the franchisee's production costs. Some fran-chisees may be able to adjust to environmental conditions by employing process innovations – for example, altering the ergonomics of the kitchen – which do not affect the brand specifications in an overt manner.

This means that some social dynamics are significant as they may serve to damp-en out the implementation and perceived benefits of innovation, as well as joint innovation development (Bessant and Grunt, 1985; Lamming, 1993; Rothwell, 1985; Von Hippel, 1988). Although McIntyre *et al* (1994) suggest that franchises are strategic alliances because the participants are involved in building brand equity through their investments in advertising, the relationship also has to illustrate some degree of affinity and trust or disgruntled franchisees could act in ways which could prove detrimental to brand value. Given the interdependent nature of the relationship (albeit, the franchisee is typically more dependent on the franchisor than vice versa), there is a necessity for the franchise participants to understand each other and the motivations behind their respec-tive businesses in order to realize competitive advantages. The last chapter suggested that franchises, like organizations at large, have varying levels of implicit innovative capabil-ity, which derives from the differing schemas, social networks, careers, objectives and competitive environments which the franchise participants inhabit. The degree to which this resource can be used to develop competitive advantages based on innovation, is a function of the emphasis that the franchisor and franchisee place on innovation which, in turn, is reflected in their respective cultures.

Relational aspects and innovation

A key tenet of McIntyre *et al*'s (1994) proposition is that franchising is a relationship between two independent parties. Whilst a variety of definitions of franchising also highlight this feature, questions have arisen concerning the reality of legal independence of franchisees (Felstead, 1993; Knight, 1984; Sklar, 1977), especially when there is also a tendency to conceptualize them as shirk-proof channel mechanisms. The level of independence is important as, when compromised, it may serve to curtail innovative behaviour – despite the necessity for action. The following paragraphs describe the relative dependency of both the franchisee and franchisor; they suggest that due to an inherent imbalance in the relationship benefits are not 'shared', but are relative to the power positions of each member.

Whilst founded contractually, the real basis of behaviour in the franchise dyad is social exchange. Of particular importance within this social exchange are the notions of power (the inverse of dependency) and trust which permeate the franchise relationship. Despite power permeating both *ex-ante* and *ex-post* aspects of the franchise relationship, the existence of innovative capacity and the presence of certain triggers indicate that *ex-post* conditions are particularly important to determining whether actions are taken bilaterally or independently. Unlike *ex-ante* considerations, the role of power in lowering moral hazard within the focal dyad relationship illustrates a long research history. In this vein, power has been viewed as the independent variable in most empirical studies of the relationship between power, conflict and satisfaction (Gaski, 1984; Robicheaux and Coleman, 1994; Stern and Reve, 1980) and will be significant in affecting franchise system innovation levels.

In focal dyad research, power has always been seen as an important driving force influencing the action of the members (French and Raven, 1959; Pfeffer and Salanicik, 1978). Power within the context of marketing channels is viewed as '. . . the ability of one individual or group to prompt another unit to do what it would not have otherwise done' (El-Ansary and Stern, 1972). The power of a channel member is founded on the ownership of resources which permits the 'control [over] the decision variables in the marketing strategy of another member in a given channel at a different level of distribution' (El-Ansary and Stern, 1972). Recent research has dichotomized power into coercive and non-coercive forms (for example, Gaski and Nevin, 1985). Whereas the former is operationalized as punishment that the franchisor may exercise, non-coercive power is characterized as the assistance that a franchisor may offer (such as expertise, brand, market knowledge) and is perhaps more reflective of aspects of trust (discussed below).

Franchisee dependency

One method of evaluating dependency is to measure the number of clients/customers on which the firm is reliant. The self-employed in the book publishing industry, for example, are essentially casualized employees, rather than independent self-employed because they are reliant upon a small number of 'clients' – in the majority of cases, just one (Stanworth and Stanworth; 1995). Business format franchisees have many clients, but they are dependent on the franchisor for the business idea/format/trademark (over which the franchisor retains control) to service them. The notion of shared control, therefore, may not be evident in franchises because the franchisor controls the relationship through the ownership of the factors of production and intangible assets. Such control is evident and exercised within three key aspects of the franchise relationship:

> First, despite operating without close and direct supervision, franchisees are required to operate within procedures and often subject to unilateral change. Moreover, franchisees are sometimes committed to adhere to franchisor-set per-formance targets, and, in any case, to give the aim of the franchisor (turnover maximization) primacy in the running of the business. Secondly, while they appropriate the profits (and losses) of the business, they do so only after they have made turnover payments to the franchisor. Thirdly, although franchisees buy or lease much of the physical business apparatus, some parts remain in the hands of the franchisor, and some have franchisor-imposed restrictions on their use both during and after the currency of the agreement. Furthermore, fran-chisees have no ownership rights in the intangible assets – they simply 'borrow' the business idea, trading name and/or format. (Felstead, 1993; p. 116)

Like the employment contract, therefore, the franchise contract is a source of power since it serves to establish the boundaries of behaviour and tolerance zones. Within this, con-tractual uniformity has been viewed as an important source of protection from the opportunistic behaviour of franchisees (Fudenberg and Tirole, 1990) and the potentially adverse effects of non-standardization amongst units. Indeed, it has been observed that the bedrock of the franchise operation is the preservation of strict uniformity between outlets in order to realize brand equity (Adams and Pritchard-Jones, 1990; Norton, 1988). Maintaining operating standardization entails that the terms of individual agreements should not be negotiable. Proponents of this view argue that offers to change terms ought to be treated with suspicion, since it suggests that the franchisor may be prepared to enter into different agreements with different franchisees. They also posit that contractual vari-ation may jeopardize the success of the operation and that it suggests market weakness on the part of the franchisor. Yet opportunism in franchising persists, suggesting an inabili-ty of non-discrimination clauses to curb it (McAfee and Schwartz, 1994), and in the process inferring that some franchisees have a culture orientated towards innovation. Since not all franchisors and franchisees are equally opportunistic, however, it may be conceivable that contractual variability permits greater system innovativeness (since it is in-built) than contractual uniformity. Although bounded rationality may also be con-strued to be a form of flexibility, it may in fact act as a barrier to change due to vested interests in maintaining the *status quo*.

Whilst the variability of franchise contracts among different franchisors may be considerable, alone it has been argued that substantial uniformity and rigidity is evident, despite the dynamic nature of markets and franchisee learning ability. For example, Lafontaine (1992) observes that all franchisors offer the same contract which, in the majority, is non-negotiable except perhaps on non-monetary aspects. In an attempt to gauge the degree of contractual uniformity, the initial fees and royalty levies of sixty-nine fast food franchisors included in the 1990 and 1995 *Entrepreneur* magazine's survey of US and Canadian franchises were assessed. The results (below) show that over half altered their initial fee and less than a third changed their royalty levy; twelve franchisors changed both aspects. Some companies decreased their levies, possibly reflecting market maturity and economic conditions. This situation infers that variability is pronounced, but does not say that they are optimal or vary according to the local environmental conditions confronted by the franchisee.

Contractual uniformity may permit policing economies via the provision of a benchmark of acceptable behaviour. Deviance and/or behaviour not in the franchisor's interest can then be gauged with relative ease and acted upon. Since franchisee income depends strongly on unit profitability, and franchise contracts include provisions that tend to make the franchisee comply with the franchisor's objectives, the franchisee will lose substantially more wealth from detected shirking than a company-employed manager. This fear may, in turn, affect the franchisee's culture concerning the emphasis on innovation from being one, for example, which is vitalized to being stagnant. Despite the threat of loss of wealth, the marketing mix elements may have to alter in response to exogenous and internal pressures and opportunities and, as a consequence, contractual uniformity appears inefficient given the likely heterogeneity of franchisees and local market conditions. No matter how rigid the balance of power may have been at the beginning of the agreement, environmental conditions and changes in the franchisee's problem-solving skills may serve to shift the nature of the relationship through the necessity for adaptation and innovation.

As a reflection of these aspects, perhaps, various agency theories predict that the franchisor should offer a menu of contracts featuring differing royalty rates (Lafontaine, 1992; 1993), which may permit greater adaptability to environmental conditions and potential franchisee characteristics. Katz and Owen (1992), for example, observe that the optimal contract can be found from the franchisor by establishing the average willingness to take risks, and the average willingness to expend effort. In the adaptability vein, Taco John has one of the few franchise contracts that has been developed co-operatively with its franchisees. The contract contains explicit accountability (for example, how advertising contributions are spent), flexibility (multiple suppliers) and territorial exclusivity.

Initial fee band (US$)	Variable	Initial fees		Management levy		No. changing	
		1990	1995	1990	1995	Fees	Levy
≥25K	Mean	28.7	26.6	4.5	4.4		
n = 21	σ	4.4	7.3	1.7	1.1	8	4
	Variability	0.15	0.27	0.38	0.25		
≥15K≥24K	Mean	18.2	20	4.5	5.0		
n = 31	σ	2.5	6.9	1.2	0.9	17	11
	Variability	0.14	0.35	0.27	0.18		
≥14K	Mean	8.4	13	3.9	4.2		
n = 17	σ	3.5	4.9	1.8	1.6	12	5
	Variability	0.42	0.38	0.46	0.38		
Sample n - 69	Mean	19	20.3	4.3	4.6		
	σ	8.2	8.3	1.5	1.2	37	20

Table 7.3: Contractual variability among US fast food franchises

Overt rigidity on maintaining uniformity, despite pressures for variation, may be detrimental to the realization of franchisee satisfaction, competitive advantages, and may point to an embeddedness of X-inefficiency. According to Lebenstein and Maital (1994), X-inefficiency is the failure of a productive unit to utilize fully the resources it commands and hence attain its efficiency frontier the maximum level of output possible under the prevailing resources and circumstances. It is the gap between the output actually *attained* by the unit and the output which is potentially *attainable* with existing resources and technology. As in businesses generally, franchises exhibit X-inefficiency, because of:

1. differing levels of individual motivation;
2. differing levels of managerial knowledge, financial capital and trustworthiness;
3. varying management styles among franchisees (that is, intra-plant differences); and
4. the extent to which trading partners work together – for example, under 'partnership-type' supply agreements, efficiency may increase due to the supplier and buyers having a better understanding of each other's requirements.

Using these differing types, increased X-inefficiency could occur as a result of low levels of motivation deriving from an uncompromising management style.

Increases in X-inefficiency within some franchises may also derive, in part, from organizational defensive routines or an unwillingness to admit to error by the franchisor via the implementation of any policy, practice, or action preventing the people involved from embarrassment or threat, and at the same time, preventing them from learning how to reduce the causes of embarrassment or threat (Argyris, 1988). Such rigidity, whilst serving some of the bureaucratic needs such as demands for reliability and non-discrimination (March and Simon, 1958), increases the amount of difficulty dealing with franchisees and customers. *Inter alia,* overt adherence to contractual uniformity by the franchisor, whilst permitting consistency in dealing with franchisees, may be negatively correlated with bilateral technological transfers, but positively correlated with managerial opportunism. Such systems are conflictual and likely to be an 'unsuccessful' type of franchise and are consistent with the view that incongruent attitudes promote conflict and the withholding of information. In this sense, franchisees may be acting as employees typically do, when expressing their dissatisfaction in a disorganized, non-collective manner:

> . . . in unorganized conflict the worker typically responds to the oppressive situation in the only way open to him, as an individual: by withdrawal from the source of discontent, or in the case of certain forms of individual sabotage or indiscipline, by reacting against the immediate manifestations of his oppression. (Hyam, 1977: p. 53)

> . . . lack of power (the capacity to mobilize resources and people to get things done) tends to create managers who are more concerned about guarding their territories than collaborating with others to benefit the organization. (Kanter, 1985)

Reflecting such individual action, Brill (1994), for example, illustrates that the greater the degree of relational restrictiveness, the lower the level of compliance and morale among franchise managers, increasing the potential for deviant behaviour and hidden actions. As noted above, however, such action may be moderated by the degree of franchisee dependency. Provan and Skinner (1989), like Brill, establish that dealer opportunism is positively correlated to supplier control over dealer decisions, but the more dependent a dealer (or franchisee) is on his supplier (or franchisor), the less the dealer will be opportunistic. This said, a variety of research illustrates that power is not a pervasive concept and a channel member's use of power is situation-specific (Etgar, 1979; Anderson and Narus, 1990).

Possibly reflecting this situation, Stanworth (1984) observes that whereas strategic limitations are enforced at an everyday level, operational autonomy is much more evenly spread between franchisors and franchisees than is suggested by consideration of the formal level alone. There are clear limits to the control franchisors can exercise physically or normatively at the operational level. In some instances, such as personnel issues in the individual franchised outlet, the franchisor would not wish to be greatly involved in any case, but in others, such as hours of opening, the franchisor often finds it convenient not to be restrictive since over-supervision may produce negative results. Nonetheless, even where franchisees have discretion over certain marketing variables, such as price-based promotions, franchisees have been found to relinquish control to franchisors (Anand and Stern, 1985; Anand, 1987). For example, profitable decisions initiated by the franchisor were attributed to internal characteristics of the franchisor, such as ability and effort; unprofitable decisions initiated by the franchisor were attributed to factors external to the franchisor, such as store location and luck; their own profitable decisions were attributed to external factors; and their own unprofitable decisions were attributed to internal causes, such as lack of ability or effort (this is not unusual: indeed, it appears commonplace within franchising to attribute personal reasons for under-performance and failure – see Chapters 8 and 9).

Two other points also serve to question the notion of franchisee independence: learning capability and financial independence. Firstly, in the initial stages of the relationship, franchisees are dependent on the franchisor for sources of information and how to apply the acquired knowledge, but as the franchisee gains experience they may become less dependent. The lower dependency on the franchisor's cumulative experience may be acute as the franchisee acquires additional units, but only up to the point where managerial decay is apparent. The development of franchisee experience and resultant lower dependency has caused Hall and Dixon (1989) to argue, albeit not empirically, that franchise systems are characterized by franchisee life-cycles in which franchisee's dependency and satisfaction are the main variables.

In the initial stage of the relationship, Hall and Dixon (1989) observe that there is heavy reliance on the franchisor for training and assistance; the franchisee has a high degree of satisfaction compared to employee status. As the franchisee becomes more familiar with the system and methods, satisfaction begins to fall – the franchisor has less apparent day-to-day involvement but continues to exert control. The franchisee resents continuing franchisor control and service fees and may consider selling and opening his own independent business. Satisfaction continues to fall until, at its lowest level, resentment is high since the franchisee feels that he has done it all on his own – he may seek early termination of the contract. If the franchisee stays with the system, he may begin to recognize the importance of the franchisor's role in their success and reconciles their feelings. He then settles down to a constant and acceptable level of satisfaction. The franchisee-franchisor relationship is now perceived to be stable.

This franchise life-cycle indicates that technological transfer may indeed be asymmetric in the early stages of the franchise relationship, but in the later stages it may become more bilateral. As the business develops, success could be attributed to local initiative which possibly creates some degree of overlap on issues such as product development, marketing activities and marketing development. This overlap may, in turn, be a source of conflict (Brown *et al*, 1986; Pettitt, 1988), which may serve to end a franchise relationship, as well as strategic alliances. In this sense, the length of tenure may be influential to bilateral flows.

Whilst joint ventures and other types of strategic alliance illustrate high failure rates (Beamish, 1988; Tomlinson, 1970), most definitions stress their longevity. For example, Porter and Fuller (1985) suggest that the average length of tenure for joint ventures is over twenty years. A study of joint venture failure by Kogut (1988) shows that 60% are terminated within a life-cycle of six years. By contrast, most franchise contracts have a five- to ten-year operating period before the parties renew their obligations or decide to separate (Adams and Pritchard-Jones, 1990; Kaufmann and Lafontaine, 1994). Prior research (Kimberly and Evanisko, 1981) suggests that a positive relationship exists between the longevity of managers in their jobs and innovativeness. Long tenure provides legitimacy, intimate knowledge of tasks and insight of managing the socio-political processes to help overcome obstacles. McIntyre *et al* (1994) observe that franchises are strategic alliances because of the length of tenure. Given the relatively short tenure within franchise organizations compared to joint ventures, franchises may be hypothesized to show lower levels of innovativeness than joint ventures and, *inter alia,* may not be construed to be an alliance. This said, there may be evidence of collinearity since product innovations during a business's tenure as an industry incumbent influences its survival (Banbury and Mitchell, 1995; Mathur, 1986). As a result of this tenure issue there may be an additional case for franchisors to form partnership agreements with suppliers rather than with franchisees.

There may, however, be an argument which develops McIntyre *et al*'s point further. Since the majority of franchise agreements are of short tenure, there may be an increased incentive for the franchisee to innovate: the valuation of his business at the end of the term of the franchise contract. A plethora of models of valuation for brands and companies exist, but the question of value is ultimately settled when the franchisee and buyer agree a price. As franchisors are not willing to quantify their buy-out practices due to fears of dulling franchisees' incentives (Dnes, 1989), innovative activity may serve to improve the seller's bargaining power. In being orientated toward profits and net cash flows, so franchisee innovative activity may be more biased toward process innovations to lower operating costs. These process innovations serve to realize a continuing income flow during the course of the contract term to provide revenue for living expenses, repaying the initial costs of entering the franchise, and increasing the value of the business at its end.

The second question about franchisee independence concerns financial status. Given the relatively high cost of entry compared to some franchises, fast food franchisees also illustrate high financial dependence. Lambert and Lewis (1991) indicate that financial dependence is based on the percentage of assets invested in, and the income derived from the business. Using McDonald's as a case study, Kaufmann and Lafontaine (1994) argue that the company's desire for a particular type of individual to operate its franchises, namely owner-operators whose livelihood will be tied to the success of their outlet(s), increases the likelihood that franchisees will face liquidity constraints and, thereby, increases the dependence on the franchisor. This situation suggests that they depend on the partnership for their very survival in the early stages of the relationship. Such dependency may also affect innovativeness. Typically, these changes cost money and time, which a franchisee may not have. As such, some franchisees may decide to leave their shops as they cannot afford to incur additional expenditure and the company-owned units adapt to the changes. This situation, in turn, diminishes the corporate image (a situation experienced by both KFC and Wimpy) and can be detrimental to franchisee performance. As a result of this financial dependency and the possible threat of losing their livelihood or having sanctions imposed, especially in high brand equity systems, there will be a greater incentive not to deviate from the franchisor's blue-print. This situation could also explain why some franchisees are motivated to share their product innovations with the franchisor.

Franchisor dependency

Some researchers, for example Combs and Castrogiovanni (1994), Dnes (1992), and Thompson (1994), argue that franchisors are dependent on franchisees to realize monitoring economies, risk spreading, local knowledge and growth objectives deriving from resource constraints (or they would be wholly-owned chains). Due to their customer interface, franchisees and their staff are an integral component of brand personality; as such, franchisors are also dependent on franchisees to at least maintain brand value via their focus on the servicing of customers. This dependency may be moderated by the franchisees' financial dependency and by monitoring measures which serve to determine the level of predictability in the service encounter (Suprenant and Soloman, 1987; Zeithaml *et al*, 1988). For example, some fast food franchisors have embraced point-of-sale technology to ensure consistent customer service via recording the style, accuracy, and efficiency of processing orders, by their employees and franchisees.

Such dependency may moderate the manner in which the franchisor copes with franchisee-initiated innovations. For example, in markets seen as strategically important, environmental munificence impacts on the key relational processes since franchisors may be dependent on their franchisees for market access and growth. As such, franchisors cannot blatantly seek control over decision variables and they must be more participative and less conflict-orientated (Dwyer *et al*, 1986) – in other words, there is an incentive to undertake bilateral technological transfers. The franchisor may, however, also seek to reduce dependency by opening company-owned units in the market, possibly adversely affecting trust, or via buying the units once the franchise contract has elapsed. Less strategically important environments may not justify the franchisor's resources to enable conflict management and franchisee participation in joint problem-solving (Baye *et al*, 1996). This means that the degree of dependence on the franchisor will vary across franchisees and franchises; but, despite these differences, franchisees' dependence on the franchisor, generally, will be substantially higher than the franchisor's dependence on the franchisee. This is not to say that, as a result of such a dependency, franchisees have power; there is an implicit imbalance in dependency between the franchisor and franchisee. The devolution of responsibility that franchising involves is not accompanied by a decentralization in managerial power and authority; whilst the franchisor certainly reaps benefits from its 'partnership' with franchisees, the same cannot be said for franchisees (O'Connell-Davidson, 1994). Indeed, it is reasonable to assume that the franchise agreement has been written so as to provide maximum benefit to the franchisor (Olson, 1971). Chapter 3 shows, for example, that franchising tends to benefit the franchisor more than the franchisee; certain franchise contracts contain clauses which enable the franchisor to terminate the arrangement because of a franchisee's non-conformance with obligations, or financial insolvency. Such franchise contracts do not have reciprocal measures should the franchisor fail to provide their requirements. The franchisee can initiate legal proceedings against the franchisor should certain contractually-specified clause remain unmet. Franchisees, on the whole, cannot unilaterally terminate the agreement. In alliances, power relations between the incumbents are perceived to be perhaps more equitable.

As opposed to strategic alliances, which are perceived to be between lateral firms (despite some being between firms at differing stages of production), franchising is an asymmetric bureaucratic network (Feuer, 1989; Grandori and Soda, 1995; Trutko *et al*, 1993). Franchising entails a contractually-based transfer of technology from the franchisor to the franchisees and among the franchisees. Unlike some strategic alliances, franchising also requires the restriction of franchisee autonomy (requiring hierarchical supervision) to varying degrees as a result of the contractual nature of the agreement (Felstead, 1993; Manaresi, 1993) to ensure brand conformity. Business format franchising, then, may be construed to be akin to the multi-divisional (M-) form of organization, characterized by the decentralization of operational decision-making to profit-centred quasi-firms and the provision of monitoring systems at head office. Despite such decentralization, the M-form of organization serves to increase franchisor flexibility and power and reduce risk. In essence, it increases the ability to divest under-performing units and such action, in appropriate circumstances, can help the M-form function more effectively. In being hierarchical, franchises may be viewed as similar to vertically integrated systems since they offer a significant amount of control to the franchisor (Felstead, 1993; Lal, 1990) through the provisions to monitor franchisees. Due to the differences in power and dependency, there are structural differences between franchises and strategic alliances.

The dependency differences suggest that, although innovativeness may not be asymmetric, the latitude to innovate and its dissemination throughout a franchise system may be controlled by the franchisor. Within strategic alliances, depending on the partners, such control by one partner may not be so overt. One way in which strategic alliance partners may retain their independence is through controlling what is traded: the technology transferred through internalization may differ from that more willingly transferred through alliances (Hagedoorn, 1993). According to this argument, the technology transfer in strategic alliances may be non-core or be in areas where commonality exits. In franchises, this is not true. Suitably qualified franchisees gain access to the core technology after they have signed the contract.

Socio-political process considerations

So far it has been contended that the franchisor is the main beneficiary of the franchise relationship and that franchisee dependency may not only serve to dampen the expression of innovative capability, but also determine the franchisee's culture regarding innovation. Furthermore, it has been suggested that overt adherence to the contract may be a recipe for conflict because the governance form becomes more market-orientated and uni-dimensional. As a result, there is a need for the franchisor to be more bilateral, which requires the development of a softer approach to the relationship. Power and rigidity are important influencing factors of channel member satisfaction, co-operative behaviour, and by inference, franchise system innovation. Nonetheless, as Schul *et al* (1983) posit and empirically show, channel member satisfaction is not affected by power alone, but by internal socio-political processes.

By referring to the dominant sentiments and behaviours which characterize the interactions between channel members, the internal socio-political processes encompass relational variables, such as channel member satisfaction and trust. These aspects occur within the parameters of the contract and derive from behaviour conforming to contractual conditions; if the franchisor's service levels fall below a certain level then the behaviour is seen as not fulfilling contractual obligations, creating dissatisfaction. If the franchisee fails to conform to pre-set standards, termination of the relationship may ensue. For example, one of KFC's new Indian units was closed for allegedly breaching hygiene regulations.

The dimensions of the internal socio-political processes may be affected by financial performance expectations and also determine the success of the relationship. When the franchisee comes to the agreement he will have certain performance expectations (deriving from franchisor-produced data). Should actual performance fail to meet these expectations, conflict and opportunism could ensue deriving from lack of trust and disconfirmation. Although franchisee performance levels are, undoubtedly, an important trigger of innovation, it is not considered here but in Chapters 8 and 9 as part of a review of franchisor and franchisee failure. Nonetheless, it is important to observe that when under-performance ensues, franchisor assistance may serve to reduce conflict and opportunistic behaviour.

Recently, there have been a number of questions concerning the role of internal socio-political processes (non-coercive power) as a source of influence over franchisees (Brown *et al*, 1986). Some researchers have indicated that there is a general lack of empirical evidence to show that non-coercive power serves to influence franchisee behaviour. Despite these concerns, the researchers have not necessarily proved that non-coercive power does not influence behaviour, consequently we cannot say conclusively that it is of less importance in affecting the franchisees' propensity to share their innovations. Common logic suggests that non-coercive power is probably more important. This form of power has been employed to maintain store uniformity, via building functional capability (Narus and Anderson, 1988). It has been recognized as an effective way to achieve control and probably more economic than breaking the relationship if contractual conformance is not maintained; some empirical evidence suggests that the presence and exercise of coercive power tends to increase the propensity for channel conflict, while the opposite is true of non-coercive power (Lusch, 1977). Other research indicates that, in contrast to non-coercive power, coercive power has a negative relationship with channel member satisfaction and has beneficial effects on channel performance, morale and co-operation (Lusch, 1977; Schul and Little, 1985; Sibley and Michie, 1982). Indeed, in a study of the US fast food industry, Hunt and Nevin (1974) show that the avoidance of coercive power by franchisors is likely to yield the following:

1. Franchisees are likely to have a higher morale.
2. Franchisees are more likely to co-operate with the franchisor.
3. Franchisees are less likely to terminate their contracts.
4. Franchisees are less likely to file individual suits against the franchisor.
5. Franchisees are less likely to file class action suits.
6. Franchisees are less likely to seek protective legislation.

A key aspect of non-coercive power is the role of trust and, being an inherent feature of the franchisor's degree of consideration of their franchisees, deserves further examination. To date, this variable has received limited attention in franchise research as well as other hybrid organizational forms. Indeed, economic models and some strategic alliance literature assume that partners are implicitly untrustworthy. Agency theorists also advocate prudence (through the form of legal and contractual protection) since it is difficult to ascertain which franchisees are trustworthy due to information asymmetries. While some form of safeguard is necessary, trust may not only have implications for ownership arrangements, whether wholly-owned, franchised, joint venture etc., but also co-operation, managerial opportunism, competitive advantage and communication, amongst other behavioural aspects of the focal dyad (Young and Wilkinson, 1989). For example, Lewis and Lambert (1991) show that fast food franchisee performance and satisfaction are related but moderated by the amount of credit or blame a franchisee attributes to the franchisor – or rather the degree to which the franchisee perceives the franchisor to be acting in his/her interest. So, what do we mean by 'trust'?

According to Barney and Hansen (1994), trust is the reliance by one person, group, or firm upon an accepted duty on the part of another person, group, or firm to recognize and protect the rights and interests of all others engaged in a joint endeavour or economic exchange (p. 393). In other words, trust is the antithesis of managerial opportunism. Dahlstrom and Nygaard (1995) indicate that trust is an integral part of the franchisee relationship and to innovation:

> Franchisees entrust the franchisor to develop new market venues (e.g., food courts), products, promotional campaigns, and administrative methods. By contrast, franchisors trust retail managers to maintain product service and quality. When the level of trust dwindles, customer satisfaction diminishes and the franchise system is prone to failure. Franchisees that cannot trust the franchisor to enhance the business system risk losing customers to innovative competitors. (p. 339)

Trust has two components – the structural and the social – each of which supplement and reinforce each other, rather than substitute one another (Madhok, 1995). The social dimension of trust refers to mutually-orientated behaviour, which serves to enhance understanding between the two parties and the motivation to co-operate. The structural component refers to the complementarity of the resources contributed, such as the franchisee's local knowledge, financial resources and motivation and the franchisor's brand equity, business system, assistance and image. The level of trust in franchises is assumed to be semi-strong, rather than being weak or strong, due to the presence of governance devices used to impose costs of various kinds on parties behaving opportunistically (Barney and Hansen, 1994). In this sense, franchises may be seen to characterize strategic alliances. Weak forms of trust exist where there are limited opportunities for opportunistic behaviour, such as commodity markets, and strong forms are evident in culturally-bound environments where engaging in opportunistic behaviour violates values, standards and principles.

Such differences in trust may have implications for satisfaction and innovativeness. Strong trust is hypothesized to exist amongst children and their parents (Barney and Hansen, 1994; Clark and Payne, 1995). Within the context of *ex-post* franchise conditions, franchisees in the initial stages have been similarly paralleled to children due to their high dependence and satisfaction. As mentioned earlier, channel member satisfaction illustrates a life-cycle effect, affected in part by the perceived quality of assistance given to the franchisee (Hing, 1995; Morrison, 1996). Within the context of trust, there may be a high perception of franchisee trust in the early stages leading to high levels of satisfaction (which may be a result of the franchisor's recruitment biases). If satisfaction wanes over time, so may levels of trust unless assistance levels remain high (Mayer *et al*, 1995). If, however, the assistance is perceived to be of poor quality, then the franchisee may feel that the franchisor is working against him and seeking goals incompatible with his.

A refinement on Madhok's (1995) work in the trust trichotomy is propounded by Sako (1992), who posits that there are three types of trust: contractual, competence and goodwill. The first is based on both partners keeping promises and consistently adhering to the moral norms of honesty. Arguably, one of the reasons that managerial opportunism is damaging to franchise relationships is that one party has contravened the business norms. The second type of trust, competence trust, refers to the expectation of a partner performing its role competently. In the franchise relationship, the parties entrust a franchisee to perform a task which the franchisor has the ability to perform, or it may entrust the franchisee to perform functions that are outside his capability. This competence trust may serve to increase franchisee dissatisfaction where the level of assistance is poor, but – because of recruitment biases – may also serve to endear franchisee trust in the initial stages. It also provides an additional rationale (to those explored earlier) for franchisor recruitment biases, since those with prior operational experience cannot be trusted to perform tasks according to the franchisor's specifications. The final type of trust is goodwill trust. In this case, there is the expectation that franchisors and franchisees (for example) are committed to take initiatives to exploit new opportunities over and above that which was explicitly promised. Where goodwill trust is low, franchisors may be overtly committed to maintaining contractual and competence trust through the provision of training and regular site visits.

The extent and nature to which contractual and competence trust are emphasized may serve to dictate, in part, the channel climate and the extent to which goodwill trust is apparent. For example, where goodwill trust is low, franchisees may only perform those tasks that are inspected of them rather than expected of them. Since innovation is rarely a contractual obligation in franchises but is within some strategic alliances, so some franchisees might be – depending on their perceptions of the relationship – more orientated to sharing their innovations than others. Equally, others may not decide to share their process innovations from which other franchise members could benefit. As long as the innovation is not detrimental to brand image (that is, it breaches contractual trust), such behaviour could not be construed to be opportunistic because it breached goodwill trust.

Trust, however, does not work alone; it is intertwined with power and communication. In some instances, trust may be an alternative to power because it can serve to deliver results without coercion (Young and Wilkinson, 1989). In other situations, force may be the only solution to realizing the desired results. A major precursor of trust and bilateral technological transfer, is communication (Morgan and Hunt, 1994), which may either be formal or informal and the identification of particular individual roles within each group (the franchisor and franchisee), and which can improve the level of inter-group trust. Communications and role identification play an important role in realizing benefits in quasi-integrated channels. Channel members achieve co-ordination through frequent two-way interchanges, but these interchanges may vary according to quality, content, and tone. Mohr and Spekman (1994) observe that communication quality is a key aspect of information transmission, and includes accuracy, timeliness, adequacy, and credibility of the information exchanged. Importantly for information exchanges, communication quality is associated with communication frequency: if exchange partners perceive that their communication fulfils their requirements, they will communicate more frequently (Mohr and Sohi, 1995). Such behaviour has implications for the sharing of innovations because as the dialogue between a franchisor and franchisee increases, there is a greater opportunity for idea-swapping based on trust. Where the quality of communication is poor, inaccurate, and based on reinforcing the contract, trust is low and the propensity for information exchanges is also low.

Typical of some group dynamics, in franchise systems are two types of relationship: complementary or reciprocal (Bateson, 1973). Parenthesizing, Bateson indicates a third type called the symmetrical form, in which the group members of two groups have the same aspirations, behaviours, and engage in responses of the same type. For example, if group A boasts to a member of group B, the latter will also respond with a boast. In short, they engage in tit-for-tat exchanges. This form of relationship may not be representative of the franchise relationship, since the two members differ in their aspirations. In the complementary form, the aspirations and behaviour of the groups are fundamentally different and may be evident in the franchise context where the franchisor treats members of company-owned units ('Group A') with one set pattern (say, A, B, C) and exhibit a different set of patterns (say D, E, F) in dealings with the franchisees ('Group B'). In reply to D, E, F, the members of Group B exhibit the patterns G, H, I, but among themselves adopt patterns J, K, L. Thus, the response to D, E, F is G, H, I and vice versa.

According to Bateson (1973), the differentiation between the two groups may become progressive. If pattern D, E, F includes patterns regarded as assertive while G, H, I includes submissiveness, it is probable that this situation will lead to further assertiveness, which will promote further submissiveness. In this relationship, contractual trust between the two groups may be limited since, for example, should some form of reproach follow a franchisor's visit, it could be construed to be a form of supervision rather than perhaps assistance. In turn, such visits could serve to reduce franchisee trust since the franchisor may be perceived to have an ulterior motive.

By contrast, a reciprocal relationship between the two groups may be evident where, for example, the behaviour patterns E and H are adopted by each group in their dealings with the other group. Instead of Group B consistently replying to E with H, sometimes it replies with pattern E. For example, some franchisees may reciprocate the franchisor's transference of knowledge with his own rather than, perhaps, accepting the usual franchisor-franchisee relationship. Bateson (1973) argues that this latter form of relationship is superior to the complementary form as behaviour patterns are compensated and balanced within, and do not tend toward breakdown. The franchisee's trust of the franchisor increases when the franchisee perceives communication to be an open, two-way exchange. *Inter alia*, as trust increases so do information exchanges and opportunism falls, as Gassenheimer *et al* (1996) infer from their empirical study of co-operative behaviour in franchises:

> Participative communication represents one means for minimizing disputes. It directly increases franchisees' satisfaction and assessments of performance, offsetting the opportunism's negative impact. This finding conflicts with franchisors' efforts to conceal information from franchisees, fearing information could occasion acts of opportunism . . . Franchisees may recognize the legitimacy of franchisors' actions, feel more satisfied with relations and positively contribute if franchisors communicate the need for strategic changes. (p. 77)

An important aspect of communication is influence strategies (Anderson and Weitz, 1992; Frazier and Summers, 1984). Influence can be regarded as the efforts on a firm's decision-making and/or overt behaviour which result from the application or use (intentional or not) of another firm's power (Wilkinson, 1974). The more a franchise organization is viewed as a set of coupled units, where joint actions rest on negotiations, the greater the need for encouragement and implementation of innovations. This means that diffusion strategies must emphasize the need to influence and mobilize coalitions in order to provide the necessary support for an innovation and its diffusion (Sadanand, 1989; Weick, 1976).

A variety of researchers (Gold, 1981; Mahajan *et al*, 1990) have drawn attention to the problems of implementation that result in innovations being technical successes but organizational failures. Their analyses are emphatic of the organizational complexity and the social inertia (an expression of usurpationary power) that dampen out the effects of radical innovation, as a result of political agendas and lack of prior experience in managing innovation and smothering the process. Depending on the nature of the innovation, its diffusion throughout a system may thus require the franchisor and franchisee to adopt differing influence methods and differing influence intensities (Maute and Locander, 1994). For example, the 'Filet-of-Fish' appeared to be a minor development to the franchisee as it represented an extension of the existing product selection to an adjacent product space to attract incremental business (Rao and McLaughlin, 1989). To the franchisor, however, it was perceived to be somewhat radical, as seen by Ray Kroc's reaction when first broached about the idea:

> Hell no! I don't care if the Pope himself comes to Cincinnati. He can eat hamburgers like everybody else. We are not going to stink up our restaurants with any of your damned old fish! (Kroc, 1977: p. 145)

The adoption of the product was due, in part, to the efforts to exert influence and, perhaps, the choice of influence method employed by the franchisee on the one hand and the willingness of the franchisor to at least consider change rather than dismissing the notion out-of-hand. Consistent with Damanpour (1991) and Hage (1980), this situation, in turn, may suggest that organizational culture/franchisor disposition to change is positively correlated or is, at least, a hygiene factor in affecting radical change. In Powell's

(1990) trichotomy, presented in Chapter 2, this form of adjustment is located within the bilateral column and, due to mutual adjustment arising from negotiation, may be construed to be more of a strategic alliance.

Frazier and Summers (1984) employ a compelling taxonomy of influence strategies where promises, threats, legalistic pleas and requests are 'direct' strategies, and information exchanges and recommendations are 'indirect' and are relevant to the negotiation process:

- *Promise:* Source certifies to extend specific reward contingent on the target's compliance;
- *Threat:* Source informs the target that failure to comply will result in negative sanctions;
- *Legalistic plea:* Source contends that target compliance is required by formal agreement;
- *Request:* Source asks target to comply; no mention of subsequent sanctions;
- *Information exchange:* Source supplies information with no specific action requested or otherwise indicated; and
- *Recommendation:* Source stresses that specific target action is needed for the latter to achieve desired outcomes.

Boyle *et al* (1992) show that corporate-owned channels and franchisors employ recommendations, requests, legalistic pleas and threat influence strategies more than promises or information exchanges. Given the potential for social inertia in innovation diffusion, during the diffusion process of a particular innovation, strategic alliances and franchisors tend to rely most heavily on information exchange. Requests, recommendations, and promises will be moderately relied upon, and threats and legalistic pleas will be used least frequently (coercive power). Information exchange and request strategies are positively correlated with innovation adoption, but negatively associated with threats, promises and legalistic pleas. Anecdotal support exists from a variety of fast food illustrations. Using the context of the Burger King franchise system, Swart and Donno (1981) observe that the franchisor develops new products, systems, and procedures, but must, in turn, persuade franchisees to adopt them on a cost-to-benefit basis. Any change or new procedure developed for the system must demonstrate its validity to franchisees on the basis of increased sales and profits, and to provide more than an adequate return on investment.

This 'sell, not tell' approach helped Pizza Hut to overcome franchisee resistance to the introduction of delivery services on a system-wide, as opposed to the regional basis it had been operating on, as well as Dunkin' Donuts to implement new distribution strategies (Kaufmann, 1987). By contrast, the UK home delivery concern Perfect Pizza adopted a top-down path to the implementation of its new central telephone system, the 'Pizza Hotline', rather than the more consultative approach as advocated by Swart and Donno (amongst others). Conflict between some franchisees and the franchisor resulted from the coercive implementation method (Darling and Taylor, 1989; Frazier *et al*, 1989) and the franchisor's determination that the system be implemented (Staw, 1981). Despite the benefits that such a system could accrue (Cummings, 1987), some franchisees were reluctant to adopt it because they viewed it as a method of increasing the franchisor's control and to weed out those that had been fraudulent. As the system could be used to check turnover levels per unit (and then to royalty payments), some franchisees claimed that the central telephone system was a form of 'spying'. Others claimed that the franchisor could not be trusted and was behaving in an opportunistic manner because:

- they feared that the system meant that franchisees lost their local telephone line due to calls being routed centrally which, in turn, led to the demise of their goodwill in local communities and reduced the value of their business;
- they perceived that the franchisor's charge of £0.30 per order for using the system was excessive and worried that there would be further increases. In a price-sensitive market, they were concerned that they could not pass on the levy to consumers and would, as a result, become less competitive and lose personal wealth; and
- they were concerned that the system had not been properly tested and feared that the system would 'crash' on busy nights, thereby resulting in lost sales.

This said, other franchisors within the fast food industry have shown a more problem-solving approach to resolve low risk issues that entail low precedent-setting. But, when the issue has high precedent-setting potential, third-party intervention may help to reconcile the differences (Dant and Schul, 1992) and, thus, the influence strategy by the franchisor may vary with the radicalness of the proposed innovation. For example, the adoption of incremental innovations will tend to rely on a problem-solving approach – utilizing information exchanges between the franchisee and franchisor. By contrast, the diffusion and adoption of more radical innovation is reliant on more direct approaches. Differences are also apparent by franchisee dependency, whereby those who were highly dependent on the franchisor were the recipients of more direct influence strategies. Consistent with Dahlstrom *et al*'s (1986) findings, those who were less dependent were the recipient of more indirect approaches.

To some degree, the above arguments have posited that bilateral transfers may occur as a result of franchisee interaction with the franchisor and then dissemination to other franchisees. Such individual interaction may be either formal, such as the franchisee formulating a proposal, or informally. Bilateral transfers may also arise from formal collective action, such as from FACs and membership of trade associations. Finally, innovation may derive from informal collective bodies, such as 'clans' (Ouchi, 1980). A clan is a small group with common cultures and high trust levels exchanging information, but fall into three basic types: economic–co-operative, social–integrative and blood-kinship (Alvesson and Lindkvist, 1993). The economic–co-operative clan members believe that in the long run their economic interests will be best served by co-operative behaviour within the clan. The process here is more 'collegial' between individuals with lateral relationships and might be evident due to some franchisees within the same system communicating informally on an irregular basis to discuss particular issues and operational methods. In the social–integrative clan, members make judgements about their involvement in the organization based on non-economic factors such as enjoying the work, the feeling of belonging and identifying with the aims of the group; in the blood-kinship clan is made up of blood relations.

The social–integrative clan is usually witnessed in a formal sense as trade associations, but is perhaps apparent informally through the way in which some groups of hotel staff meet to socialize in their workplace (Shamir, 1981). These social groupings may affect the level of tolerance of more economic conditions of their workplace. The blood-kinship form is apparent as a practice within some franchise systems is to only offer the franchise to family members. The economic–co-operative collective has also recently been witnessed operating in the UK franchise sector. An interview with the British licence-holder of a printing operation revealed that new franchisees often relied upon advice from other franchisees, rather than the franchisor, in order to safeguard themselves against deficiencies and inaccuracies in the franchise manual, which if adhered to would prove costly. When this situation eventually came to the notice of the franchisor, he instigated a competition urging franchisees to notify head office of such technical innovations. Though many franchisees made such innovations, and often shared them with other franchisees, only three have subsequently co-operated in the franchisor's attempt to 'gain ownership' of them and institutionalize them in the manual. It may be possible that such behaviour may be close to the norm, rather than being an exception, and indicates the scale of the potential for the release of local innovative flair in a collaborative environment. In Sako's (1992) terms the franchisor had lost some degree of competence trust with the franchisees due to errors in the operations manual, leading to non-co-operation. By doing so, they were not in breach of contractual trust but goodwill trust. Arguably, another rationale for non-co-operation is that the franchisor requested that the franchisees formalize tacit knowledge, and they may not have had either the motivation or necessarily the capability to achieve this.

Much of the above discourse has been emphatic of franchisor-individual franchisee relationships and the implications for sharing innovations. The extent to which individual learning is translated into franchise system innovation is dependent upon on the relationship, in particular the nature and degree of trust and communication, between the franchisee and franchisor as well as that between the franchisees themselves. These differing scenarios suggest that there are three forms of information exchange which may occur: fragmented learning (where the innovation remains informal and undiffused); among clans (where the innovation remains informal, but diffused); or bureaucratized (where the innovation is typically codified – operations manuals, etc. – and diffused among organizational members). With regard to the latter, FACs are seen as bureaucratic because they are formal forums with their own rules and rituals, for information exchange.

The extent to which the innovation is diffused is dependent upon the conditions governing the relationship between the differing parties. The diagram below (Figure 7.3) illustrates the differing scenarios by which innovation occurs and is diffused. The x-axis shows the extent of 'diffusion' of information, that is, the size of the 'audience' reached by the information. 'Diffused' information is information that is readily shared whereas 'undiffused' information is not readily shared. The y-axis shows another aspect of communication: the 'codification' of the information. Codification is the process of replacing direct experience with symbols. This enables the recording of experiences and their communication to a wider audience (for example, in a written letter). The process of codification, however, also results in a loss of some of the richness of detail of the original experience; one can no longer get the 'whole picture'. By contrast, uncodified communication involves all the subtleties of face-to-face or non-verbal communication; in certain contexts, a shrug or a wink can convey meaning that would be difficult or even impossible to convey indirectly in writing. But uncodified information can also require more effort from the recipient:

> A . . . complication with uncodified information is that its lack of structure leaves much room for personal motivation, attitude, and belief to fill the gap in interpretation. Quite often a prior sharing of context or experience will not of itself suffice to get a fuzzy message across. There must also be some sharing of values to ensure that the communicating parties are on the same wavelength . . . Shared values are the cement that binds together our partial and fragmented experiences, setting them into a coherent pattern . . . The sharing of uncodified information, in sum, requires a level of familiarity and trust between communicating parties that can usually only be built up in or around a face-to-face situation. (Boisot, 1987, pp. 50–51)

Codified information has been converted into words or formulae in order to reach a greater audience. But the process of codification always involves some simplification of the message, and less can be assumed about the prior knowledge or experience of the audience. There may be little opportunity for testing of understanding or feedback. To illustrate the difference between codified and uncodified communication, the purchase of shares by computer on the internal stock exchange can be achieved by 'codified' means. In contrast companies collaborating in a joint product development project may need to exchange a large amount of 'uncodified' information, as well as some 'codified' information. In summary, 'codified information is information that can easily be set out on paper, whilst uncodified can not' (Boisot, 1987; Price, 1996). It should be observed that while 'market' refers to widely dispersed and codified information, it is not costless to acquire. Going to libraries, for example, is not a mass culture exercise; libraries tend to be 'free-goods' because there is typically no entry fee, but the proportion of users is not as high as other sources of codified information (such as newspaper readers).

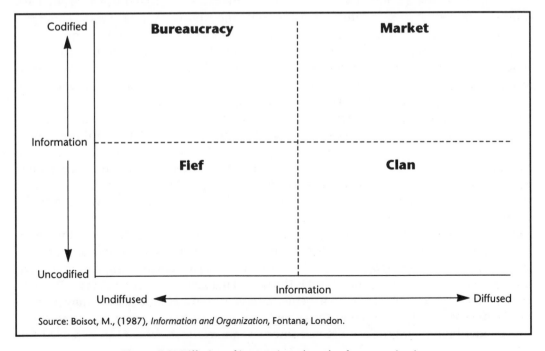

Source: Boisot, M., (1987), *Information and Organization*, Fontana, London.

Figure 7.3: Diffusion of innovation: the role of communication

Reflecting that some differentiation of the term 'fragmented learning' is necessary, it suggests that innovation can be dispersed among immediate members of a franchisee concern or can remain the proprietorship of one person. The former are labelled a 'fief' (not to be confused with the feudalistic form), which, according to Boisot (1987), is a social organization comprised of a very small number of people with a certain culture, such as family-owned and franchisee owner-operated concerns. Perceived to be a sub-set of a clan, much of the information exchange is uncodified, necessitating face-to-face communication. Surrounding the focal dyad are market conditions; as noted elsewhere, these conditions may act as a trigger for individual learning to occur.

The emphasis of the diagram is to suggest that the setting of innovation moves from fragmented learning to clans and then is bureaucratized by being written up in operating manuals, but could in some circumstances move directly from fragmented learning to formalization. The 'fief' may either be the franchisor or a franchisee. The case of the franchisee has already been discussed, but the franchisor may exhibit some degree of favouritism with strategic leader/contributor franchisees and initially diffuse the innovation informally with them. Of course, the clan may, in some instances, be the franchisor, as the innovation is diffused among company-owned stores on a trial basis prior to being detailed in any documentation for system-wide dissemination and use.

Sharing of benefits

Another factor which may mitigate against sharing innovations is the extent to which the franchisor and franchisee share the benefits of such activity. Much of the popular franchise press and McIntyre *et al* (1994) tend to portray the franchise relationship as a 'partnership' with both parties benefiting. As a result of some of the aspects concerning the power imbalance described above, there are some concerns as to whether franchisors and franchisees share the relative benefits of the agreement (another of Yoshino and Rangan's strategic alliance descriptors) as well as any innovations. In spite of these concerns, however, equality in the distribution of benefits is not a necessary condition of contractual exchanges (Macneil, 1980) and imbalances could also be evident in strategic alliances (Faulkner, 1995). Of more importance is an 'even' distribution of the benefits of the relationship, such as adequate returns accruing to both parties rather than either one trying to maximize their position over the other via opportunistic behaviour.

Within strategic alliances, the notion of even distribution may be more appropriate than terms which infer equality amongst partners, such as 'shared'. Killing (1982), for example, differentiates between three types of joint venture according to the degree of parental involvement and control forms. He identifies these types as: dominant parent strategy, the shared management strategy and the independent strategy. The dominant parent strategy (Type 1) may be equated to the wholly-owned subsidiary with the dominant partner instrumental in the selection of most of the enterprise operational managers. This strategy is viewed as most appropriate when it is forced to form a joint venture in order to comply with host government's requirements or when one partner perceives its involvement as a financial investment. Such a strategy is not commonplace (Datta, 1988). The most common form is the shared management venture (Type 2) where both parents are responsible for management. In such ventures, one partner may provide the technological know-how and the other knowledge of the local market. Type 3, the independent joint venture, is quite rare since few are relatively free of interference from either parent.

McIntyre *et al* (1994) indicate that franchising permits competitive advantages to accrue to both the franchisor and franchisee. It enhances franchisor advantages over independent concerns since it should (theoretically at least) permit access to three resources which they require in order to realize organizational development: financial capital (via the franchisee's payment of initial fees, reduced wage bill, the franchisee's payment of their store's fixtures and fittings, payment of rent, and ongoing royalties); human capital (that is, self-motivated managerial talent); and local market knowledge. Some have criticized this school of thought on the basis that franchising is an inefficient method of raising capital but, when franchisees are considered as representing all three resource requirements as one, the cost of procuring these resources is possibly lower than when purchased individually (Norton, 1988). In short, then, franchised growth may be pursued as it reduces the input costs of realizing organizational development and brand dissemination, additionally lowered due to franchisees' contributions of the advertising fund.

According to those researchers advocating the agency-perspective, franchising also reduces the ongoing costs of development. This is because franchisees are motivated by profit which, in turn, lowers their propensity to shirk and thus reduces (not eliminate) the very need for supervision and monitoring. Once released from some of the burdens of monitoring, the franchisor – depending on the saleability of the franchise, the level of market growth and nature of competition – can concentrate on expanding the business. In so doing, additional income accrues to the franchisor from the new stock of franchisees and the sale of product (in some cases) to franchisees.

By permitting greater brand dissemination and market share through additional capacity and through lower advertising costs, the franchisor is able to increase profitability and brand value with minimum capital investment (Hoffman and Preble, 1991; Pratt, 1993). In achieving rapid proliferation, it is argued that both the franchisor and franchisee realize the benefits of greater brand dissemination and market share. For example, Buzzell and Gale (1987) indicate that a positive relationship between profitability and market share exists. As a consequence, the greater the brand dissemination, the greater the rewards. Given that it is the franchisor who owns the intangible assets, it is he who derives the greatest benefit via greater brand equity achieved through additional unit openings as well as through joint advertising funds and effort (Buccola, 1991). The franchisor also benefits since franchising reduces monitoring costs and may be construed to be a hybrid capital market (Jenson, 1989) since it is an alternative (albeit inefficient) method of raising finance (Rubin, 1978).

As well as construing benefits on the franchisor, franchising, according to McIntyre *et al* (1994), is also perceived to enhance franchisees' competitive advantages. These advantages are particularly seen to accrue via the franchisee gaining access to a 'proven system', the use of trade names, marketing expertise, managerial experience and advertising support (Dant and Berger, 1994; Khan, 1992). Whilst the popular franchise press and some academic texts spread these advantages as being generally evident in most franchise systems, there are compelling arguments to the contrary. Bracker and Pearson (1986), for instance, found no improvement in performance of a group of small businesses differentiated by whether they were franchise operated or not. More recently, Pilling (1991) found it questionable whether franchisees' competitive advantages in areas such as purchasing benefits, brand recognition and managerial assistance were enhanced by the franchise arrangement.

From a differing perspective, research has established that different franchise sectors illustrate varying levels of risk. Where risk, as measured by the number of business discontinuances, increases, franchisors' involvement and investment decreases (Lafontaine, 1993, 1994; Martin, 1988; Norton, 1988). In the context of the US hotel industry, chain-managed hotels were found to be more prevalent in stable and moderately stable environments than they were in volatile ones (Dev and Brown, 1991). Franchised units, however, were more prevalent in moderate and volatile environments. Whilst such differences have implications for the nature of innovative activity, there appears to be some debate, generally and in the fast food sector, as to whether franchisees have lower rates of attrition as a result of such risk transfer compared to wholly-owned concerns (see Chapters 8 and 9 for a review). Equally, there is also some concern over the rate of franchisor attrition which, in turn, suggests that only a minority of franchises are 'proven'. Such concern only serves to question further the supposed mutuality of competitive advantages and possible sharing of innovations that many propound are evident with franchise systems.

The role of national culture

The above paragraphs have focused specifically on the individual franchise member's capacity for innovation and how innovative behaviour is affected by relational aspects. These issues, however, do not occur within a vacuum. Prior research (for example, Porter, 1990) has established that economic, educational, political and legal variables have a clear role in affecting innovative behaviour since they represent the infrastructure which may serve to enhance certain types of innovation. These infrastructure variables may pertain to either a country or to a particular region. Feldman (1993), for example, illustrates that there is a tendency for product innovations to cluster in territories which contain concentrations of innovative inputs, such as university research and development, industrial research and development, the presence of related industry and the presence of specialized business services. But cultural setting is also instrumental. As noted above, the cultural differences in trust (Fukuyama, 1995) may be instrumental in determining whether franchising is employed as a method to expand local small businesses. Kale and McIntyre (1991) observe that cultural differences have considerable impact on marketing channels along three dimensions:

1. initiation processes, why and how firms begin channel relationships;
2. implementation processes, how personnel of firms attempt to manage and co-ordinate ongoing channel relationships; and
3. review processes, how personnel of firms evaluate the rewards or losses achieved from channel relationships.

Operationalizing culture consists of:

1. individualism;
2. power distance;
3. uncertainty avoidance;
4. masculinity.

Each variable is orthogonal and exhibits implications for innovativeness.

Morris *et al* (1994) compare the role of individuals (predominant in Western economies) versus groups or collectives (prevalent in Japan) in facilitating entrepreneurship and innovation in organization. The researchers establish that entrepreneurship declines as collectivism is emphasized, but innovation rises. Shane (1993) also establishes a positive correlation between rates of innovation and culture, and he argues that if countries wish to increase their rates of innovation, public policies that increase the amount of money spent on research and development or industrial infrastructure may not be enough. Power distance refers to the extent of inequality in society, attitudes towards superiors and subordinates and attitudes towards conflict and co-operation. Subordinates in societies where power distance is large view managers as autocratic decision-makers; where it is small, more participative methods are apparent.

Uncertainty avoidance is measured by the extent of conservatism within the society. For example, where conservatism is high people feel a need to avoid risk and create security. Within the context of the franchise relationship, strong conservatism would be apparent through the low tolerance of variability, and the low levels of role ambiguity. Although Kale and McIntyre (1991) do not refer to information exchanges explicitly, it may be that firms in strongly conservative cultures would stress formal exchange practices in the flow of information and goods. They would also be governed by clear and unambiguous policies and procedures for each channel member. Firms in low conservative countries are more flexible.

Kale and McIntyre's (1991) final cultural variable, the degree of masculinity in society (evident from attitudes towards work, achievement and confrontation) may also affect the degree to which information exchange occurs. Whereas masculine-orientated societies are inherently conflictual, the converse is apparent in more feminine cultures. It may be, for instance, that the channel climate in feminine cultures displays greater trust, more use of non-coercive power and higher satisfaction levels than masculine ones.

Summary and conclusion

There is some anecdotal evidence of bilateral technological transfers in franchises. Such anecdotes infer that some franchises and franchisees are more innovative than others, but fail to suggest possible explanations for the differences. Chapter 6 suggested that these differences are partially explained by the differing levels of tacit knowledge possessed by the franchisee, the differing triggers of innovation and the recognition of the need for innovation. This chapter developed these themes further by suggesting that the variability of innovative effort may be due to differences in culture. This is not so say, however, that the innovation process is ongoing because the franchisor can have an impact on the franchisee's culture for innovation; the franchisor is instrumental in determining the extent of dissemination of an innovation in a franchise system and for providing the inter-organizational culture for innovative activity. Such a culture may include actively encouraging innovation (Benetton is widely cited as having encouraged 'learning races' amongst its network partners, where financial rewards are given to those who contribute value-creating ideas to the network) or it may be more passive.

This chapter has also argued that franchisees communicate amongst each other and the basis of that communication could derive from commonality of problems. Thus, although the franchisor may not want innovation but replication, standardization may, paradoxically, assist innovation diffusion because uniform services share more common problems and opportunities for improvement with incremental innovations (Johnston and Leenders, 1990). The sharing process is moderated by relational issues, but when communicated innovations are shown to diffuse via a variety of forums which may vary by their formality.

As a result of some autonomy over some aspects of job content and job context, perhaps a more appropriate model for understanding future fast food franchise organizations is Astley and Zajac's (1991) notion of an 'adaptively rational' model of organization in which 'flexible coupling' is the dominant paradigm. The difference between mechanistic and flexibly coupled organizations lies in the extent to which activities are programmed in advance. Flexibility to respond to environmental aspects is therefore inbuilt. Organizational structure, in this case, is not simply a blueprint for the programming of tasks but, instead, represents patterns of interaction and communication between personnel engaged in decision-making. Increasing the amount of communication across sub-unit boundaries through cross-functional teams and other lateral co-ordinating devices facilitates learning and innovation.

Together Chapters 6 and 7 have attempted only to identify some of the key correlates of innovation in franchising and develop them into a general model from which empirical research may follow. It is not asserted that the analysis is comprehensive by any imagination but rather a step towards a better understanding of franchising at a general level and, hopefully, a catalyst and platform for much-needed further research effort and debate to assess the extent to which franchises are strategic alliances. Such research is necessary because of the following issues:

1. a lack of understanding of the causes and barriers to innovation within business format franchises and, indeed, retailing in general (Julien and Raymond, 1994);
2. the increasing significance of franchising (especially within the hospitality industries);
3. the pervasiveness of non-price competition;
4. the apparent criticality of innovation to the development and maintenance of competitive advantages (Schnaars, 1994);
5. the need for comparative research concerning the innovation process in various types of organizations (Evan and Black, 1967; Wolfe, 1994); and
6. the tendency by food and drink manufacturers to view the retailer – rather than the branded manufacturer – as the principal innovator.

The chapters have posited that business format franchises cannot be construed to be strategic alliances according to Yoshino and Rangan's (1995) interpretation since they do not illustrate the three necessary and sufficient conditions, but they do illustrate some of them. This said, they do not necessarily adhere to the strategic alliance conditions employed by McIntyre *et al* (1994) either. In one sense franchises are like strategic alliances since there is innovative capacity, compatibility of resources and goal ambiguity (but areas of commonality) and semi-strong trust. In another sense, there is little independence *per se*, but only varying degrees of dependence and the mutual benefits are not necessarily shared. As a consequence, some business format franchises may be thought of as hybrid forms of strategic alliance.

As mentioned earlier, Kay (1993) observes that competitive advantages derive from the manner in which an organization is structured (its 'architecture'), the possession of strategic assets (non-tradeable, firm-specific resources), its reputation and innovative activity. Some marketing channel research has been devoted to estimating the structural benefits and the environmental determinants of differing organizational forms, but perhaps the area with the potential to construe competitive advantages and possibly superior economic rents is the development of innovative capability within the franchise system. This requires using franchisees as strategic assets rather than just distributive mechanisms, and necessitates franchisors to harness and up-grade their innovative capability to the mutual benefit of both parties. Such action may serve to enhance the franchisor's reputation in the marketplace as well as to enhance the probability of survival. As in similar research concerning corporate ventures, understanding the benefits and determinants of innovation may permit the firm to discover alternative ways of combining its resources and incorporate difficult-to-imitate routines (McGrath *et al*, 1994).

Despite a plethora of limitations, the last two chapters have attempted to illustrate that the correlates of innovation are manifold. Some of these are distilled and outlined in the 'general propositions' below. These may be empirically tested by other researchers in order to provide concrete evidence for and against the 'creativity versus conformity debate':

H_1 Levels of franchise system innovativeness will correlate with the negative expression of environmental munificence.

H_2 Levels of franchise system innovativeness will correlate positively with levels of environmental complexity.

H_3 Levels of franchise system innovativeness will correlate positively with levels of environmental dynamism.

H_4 Levels of franchise system innovativeness will correlate positively with levels of organizational slack.

H_5 Levels of franchise system innovativeness will correlate positively with levels of organizational autonomy.

H_6 Levels of current franchise system innovativeness will correlate positively with past experiences of success or failure in the management of innovation.

H_7 A positive relationship will exist between franchisor training investment and franchisee innovativeness.

H_8 A positive relationship will exist between levels of variety and achievement in a franchisee's previous career and membership of interlocking networks and innovativeness as a franchisee.

H_9 Franchisors will adjust their franchisee recruitment priorities over time in line with their perceived needs for franchisee innovation.

H_{10} Franchisees will generally experience sufficient functional autonomy to facilitate their meaningful participation in the process of franchise innovation to the extent that 'ownership' of innovations may be withheld from franchisors.

H_{11} Franchisors will devise a range of administrative procedures over time to gain access to the fruits of franchisee ideas and innovations.

H_{12} Franchisee innovativeness will tend to be more orientated towards process innovations than being product-biased.

Although there has been some theoretical development examining franchising as an innovation, a dearth of analysis and research still exists for the analysis of how franchisees may be a source of Ricardian rents via their ideas for new products and process improvements. As an initial stepping-stone to filling this gap, comparative analysis concerning innovativeness in franchise organizations may be conducted by comparing and contrasting the correlates between franchisors and/or franchisees operating in the same industry/market sector. Equally, research effort may be directed to ascertaining the similarities and differences in relationships between innovativeness determinants concerning franchisors and/or franchisees in differing industry/market sectors. Furthermore, it is conceivable that, like businesses at large, some franchisees are more innovative than others. This may also warrant specific research concerning intra-system correlates of innovation. Unlike some organizations, however, major distinguishing factors influencing franchisee learning capability may not be primarily organizational and individual in nature (Zajac *et al*, 1991), but also environmental, as a result of operating in differing local/micro-level competitive conditions.

Issues concerning franchise withdrawal rates and death

8 | Behind the veneer of success: propensities for franchisor failure[1]

Ignore all the statistics that tell you 95% of all new businesses fail in the first eight years. Not only are these 'statistics' riddled with widely wrong assumptions, and false failure rates, but they don't apply to you. Dwelling on the statistics is like staying up to study divorce rates on your wedding night.

Paul Dickson, writer, *International Management*, 1986

A little-known fact is that the Apollo moon missions were on course less than 1% of the time. The mission was composed of almost constant mid-course corrections. That's also true of most business situations. Yet few people have the guts to own up to that reality.

James A. Belasco, US academic, *Teaching the Elephant to Dance*

Introduction

In spite of a long history, the development of franchising as a popular strategy for growth in the UK business sector is more recent. Chapter 1 illustrated that the late 1970s, and particularly the 1980s, saw increased emphasis on government assistance to small firms via the removal of discriminatory legislation and providing an environment where small firms could thrive. It was during this period that small firms began to proliferate as a result of the combined effects of government support, large-business decentralization, unemployment, the rise of services, privatization, and increased economic uncertainty (Storey, 1994). Indeed, according to the National Westminster Bank ('NatWest'), there were an estimated four million business start-ups between June 1984 and December 1994.

As part of this proliferation, franchised-based expansion also flourished, with the number of franchisors increasing, according to NatWest/BFA statistics, from 170 in 1984 to 414 in 1994, and 474 in 1995 (see Figure 8.1). During that same period, the value of the UK franchise market increased from £0.9 billion to £5.5 billion in 1994 (£5.9 billion in 1995), but the majority of this growth occurred during the 1980s. Being subject to the same economic forces as other businesses, as well as perhaps falling legitimation, the franchise market has remained relatively static during the 1990s and its value has declined in real terms from £5.24 billion in 1990 to £4.4 billion in 1994. Given the rise in the number of franchisors, it appears that there are more fish in a smaller pond. When the number of franchise systems and the market values of franchising activity in the UK are divided by one another to yield average system sales, it is evident that the rate of decline is more acute than is suggested by a simple adjustment for inflation. Rather than there necessarily being an up-turn in 1995, Figure 8.2 illustrates that there is, instead, a sharp decline. Indeed, average system sales, when adjusted for inflation, have been in decline since 1988. This situation may point to the probability that many of the newer entrants are

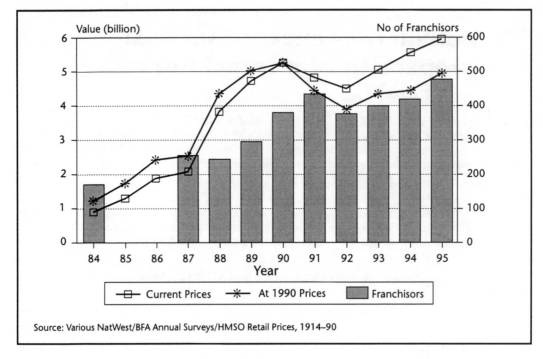

Figure 8.1: *Growth of UK franchising, 1984–95*

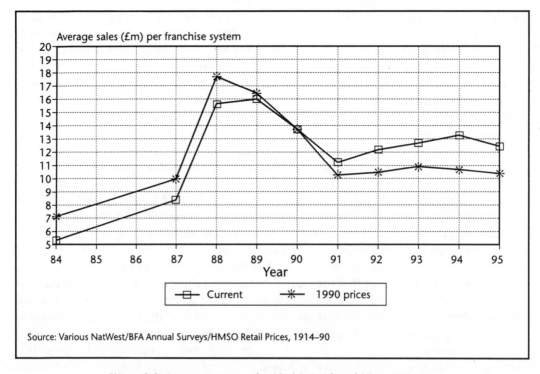

Figure 8.2: *Average system sales (£m) in UK franchising, 1984–95*

small companies which, collectively, would have the effect of reducing the average contribution to the market value. If true, the implied polarity between the market incumbents does not auger well for the survival of the smaller firms, unless they occupy a defensible niche. Of course, the decline in the average sales figures could also be attributed to the withdrawal of a few large franchise systems, but there appears to be little *a priori* corroborating evidence for this hypothesis.

A similar situation is also apparent in the USA. Here, numerous academics and franchise advisers have observed that the value of franchising expanded by around 300% between 1975 and 1990. Once such claims are adjusted for inflation, however, the absolute growth rate falls to 58.5%, and the average annual rate from 9.4% to 3.1% (see Figure 8.3). In six years of this period, franchise growth in the US was either zero or negative (Trutko *et al*, 1993). Some of this fall is undoubtedly attributable to the decline in product-name franchises since the oil crisis of 1974/1975. Nonetheless, while the growth in business format franchising has been faster than that of its product-name counterpart, the latter part of the 1980s has been relatively flat. As in Britain, the expansion and contraction of franchising in the USA seems to have closely followed general economic trends. Between 1975 and 1989, Gross National Product in the USA grew by 53% in real terms against a comparable growth in franchise sales of about 59%. The decline in franchise sales (in real terms) between 1979 and 1982 again closely reflected the wider economic situation. As the US economy recovered during the mid-1980s, franchise sales reflected the upturn, as they did during the subsequent economic downturn towards the end of the 1980s.

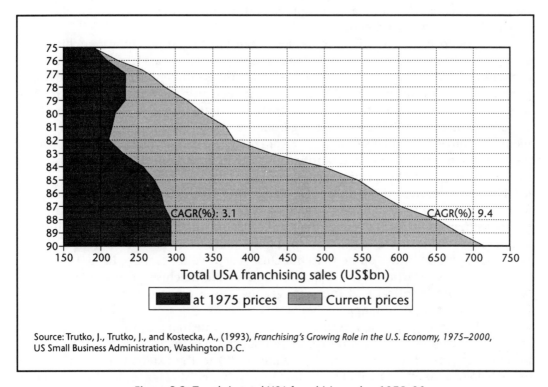

Source: Trutko, J., Trutko, J., and Kostecka, A., (1993), *Franchising's Growing Role in the U.S. Economy, 1975–2000*, US Small Business Administration, Washington D.C.

Figure 8.3: Trends in total USA franchising sales, 1975–90

Although a variety of definitions and data sources of failure exist, most researchers concur that the same period also witnessed a high rate of small-business attrition. According to the Insolvency Service, for example, there were a total number of 177,000 liquidations in Britain between 1984 and 1994, of which the majority were accounted for by small concerns. This tendency toward failure by small firms has been widely documented and appears to be a recurrent theme throughout small-business discourse, as well as the literature concerning the adoption and generation of innovations (Rogers, 1995). For example, according to Dixon *et al* (1995) and Harrison (1996), there are over 5,100 new food and drink products in development at any one time in Europe, but only about 2% of these achieve success by generating sales of over £5 million within two years. A key tenet, however, in the popular franchise press, is that the foundations of franchise businesses are made of sterner stuff than small businesses and innovations. The 'How-to' literature, franchisor brochures/newsletters, recruitment pamphlets, etc., and some academic research (for example, Castrogiovanni *et al*, 1993) indicate on a regular basis that franchising experiences rates of failure wholly atypical of those expected in the field of small business (of which franchises are a sub-set) or strategic alliances. This sentiment has continued throughout the 1990s, in spite of static market conditions and despite at least some evidence (Figure 8.1) that franchisor withdrawals have occurred relatively frequently during the 1990s. The focus of the success rhetoric is especially targeted upon potential franchisees who are encouraged to invest in a 'proven system' which permits them to gain access to marketing expertise, managerial experience and advertising support (Thompson, 1971). Often employing uncorroborated franchisor-reported data numerous researchers and marketeers propound, in ever-increasing bullish terms, that franchising is a magic formula for people to end the ills of unemployment and the ills attached to working for other people.

The focus of such rhetoric has also been targeted at potential franchisors. In short, it is argued, franchising should lower the risks normally associated with entering business and expanding an existing one. Reflecting this sentiment, Dickinson (1981) suggests that franchising is a suitable strategy for reducing small-business failure. The message to potential franchisors is that entry into franchising requires low levels of investment and net cash inflows deriving from the royalty process, lower labour requirements and broader brand dissemination. Nonetheless, the level of risk associated within franchise press articles is rarely quantified and illustrations from the USA are applied to the UK situation thereby making such comparisons, at best, dubious and, at worst, misleading. Furthermore, although the target audience is potential investors, the propensity for such texts to mislead (whether intentionally or otherwise) is exacerbated by the failure to distinguish between whether their subject is the franchisee or franchisor. Indeed, some sources claim that 'franchises are five times more likely to succeed than independent start-ups' and others opine that 'franchisees are five times more likely to succeed than independent start-ups'. The suggestion here is that franchise system and franchisee failure rates are identical and interchangeable. The examples quoted in the panel opposite typify the populist approaches.

Whilst the popular press simply tends to replicate franchisor-produced data, the sentiment and possible myth has also been reproduced in both the 'How-to' literature and in more academic texts (for example, Ayling, 1988) to the extent that it has almost become dogma. As an element of marketing theory, franchising is a topic which has been well documented. Much of this literature – in spite of the significance of mobility barriers

The populist approaches to franchise failure

1. 'Relatively few franchises fail because most receive a comprehensive training package as part of the agreement'. (*Marketing Week*, 27 October 1989)

2. 'Putting success into the context of small business, commercial failures in franchising are considerably lower than the 42% defaults in the Government Loan Guarantee Scheme; and considerably less than the 43% closures within three years under the Enterprise Allowance Scheme or the general small business closure rate of 34% in the same time. The position in the UK is fast approaching that recorded in the US where nearly 38% of individual start-ups go out of business after the first year of operation, 57% after the second year; 67% after the third year; and 73% after the fourth year . . . By stark contrast . . . only 3% of franchises are discontinued in the US after one year; 6% after the second year; and 7% after the third and fourth years. After five years, 92% of franchises are still in operation . . .' (Brandenberg, 1989, p. 143)

3. 'The knowledge and proven track record of the franchisor makes you around five times more likely to succeed with a franchise than with a conventional small business start-up.' (*Independent on Sunday*, 21 February 1993)

4. '80% of Franchises Succeed.' (Advertisement, *Franchise World*, May–June 1993)

5. 'As a route for entrepreneurs to launch into business, franchising has one big plus: there are usually far fewer failures than other business start-ups.' (*The Times*, 20 April 1994)

6. 'Franchises are five times more likely to succeed than independent business start-ups.' (Advertisement, *Sunday Express*, 1 October 1995)

7. 'Whilst an increasing number of other countries also have thriving franchise industries, we remain the envy of many, because of the overall performance achieved here. I don't want to dwell on statistical data, which is available from reliable sources such as the British Franchise Association and the banks. Suffice to say, however, that the UK franchise industry has a record of continuing healthy growth with few failures.' (Williams, 1995, p. 36)

8. 'The success rate for franchise-owned businesses is very high. According to studies conducted by the US/Department of Commerce from 1971 to 1987, less than 5% of franchised businesses failed or were discontinued in each of those years.' (*Small Business Administration*, 1996)

9. 'Reputable franchising of the kind represented by the British Franchise Association has a nearly 95% success rate in establishing franchisees in business. This is not surprising. Surveys show that the vast majority (85%) of people becoming franchisees want to be in business on their own account. They also show that most of them find the reassurance they expect from their franchisor.' (Sir Bernard Ingham, President of the British Franchise Association, *Franchise World Directory*, 1997)

– extols the virtues without substantial empirical testing of this method of growth and diversification, as offering substantial benefits to both the franchisor and franchisee (despite the inherent imbalance in the relationship between the two). Nowhere is this seen as being more apparent than in the fast food industry where large companies, such as McDonald's, KFC, Burger King and Domino's Pizza, etc., serve as examples of the success that companies could achieve if they use franchising as a vehicle to growth.

Indeed, to some (for example, Acheson and Wicking, 1992; Acheson, 1993; Cross and Walker, 1987; Shook and Shook, 1993) fast food and franchising represents a particularly formidable marriage, when coping with difficult economic conditions. Franchising has been cited by others as a critical success factor for success in the foodservice market (for example, Felenstein, 1988; Lee, 1987). Within this perspective, fast food franchises are generally seen as being relatively low risk as they are cash rich and require low levels of stock and other current assets although they do require a higher level of investment than many other types of franchise. For example, Felstead (1993) illustrates that the average franchise investment costs (set-up costs, franchise fees and working capital) in the UK catering sector was £260,609 whereas the overall average in franchising *per se* was £69,125. Perhaps underlining the high entry costs, are the burdens of site acquisition which varying according to the specifications of the brand involved. Focusing on this variance, the *Caterer & Hotelkeeper* magazine conducted a survey of the unit developments in the UK fast food and restaurant sector between 1984 and 1985. Table 8.1 provides some examples from that research and shows that there is substantial variability in the development costs.

It is generally acknowledged that these costs reached a peak in the property boom of the late 1980s, but have since fallen and, as such, these figures are approximately representative of the contemporary market. The high level of initial investment in fast food franchises is, in part, reflective of the costs of equipment and property as well as an element of brand equity: 'failed' restaurants and independent restaurants often have very low levels of initial investment and promotion (English and Willems, 1994).

Perhaps emphasizing and exacerbating the perceived low rates of attrition in franchising, the major UK clearing banks are generally favourable towards lending to both prospective franchisees and franchisors (Stern and Stanworth, 1994). In general,

Brand name	Status	Service type	Average cost (£000)
Happy Eater (n = 10)	Co-owned	Table	247
Wimpy (n = 7)	Franchise	Counter	379
Spud-U-Like (n = 6)	Franchise	Counter	53
McDonald's (n = 22)	Co-owned	Counter	500
Average			365
Standard deviation			165

Source: *Caterer & Hotelkeeper,* various issues 1984–85.

Table 8.1: Average set-up costs in the fast food market

depending on the individual, banks provide approximately 60% of the finance required to open a franchise. Sometimes they provide a higher level of loan funding and lower rates of interest than a conventional business person could usually expect to receive. Indeed, a survey by Price (1993) showed that a recurring interest rate within fast food franchisees' accounts in the early 1990s was about 2.5% above the base rate. These results echo comments by Perkins (1988), who indicates that, for well-established franchise operations, the major clearing banks have custom-tailored finance packages for new franchisees consisting of the following terms:

- term loans of five to ten years, financing up to two-thirds of the setting-up costs;
- an overdraft facility to assist with working capital;
- a low-cost interest rate usually in the range of 2.5% to 4% over the bank's base rate, depending on the quality of the security offered; and
- capital repayment holiday of up to two years, if appropriate.

Additional clearing bank interests and commitment to franchising, especially within the UK, is also evidenced from the fact that most of the large high-street banks have developed specialist franchise service departments and in this respect, at least, are unique in Europe. The banks' franchise departments have, essentially, three main objectives: to establish close links with franchisors, in order that they are able to assist branches when they are approached for loans by existing or potential franchisees of the franchise in question; the production of detailed information packages for branch managers, customers and the general public interested in franchising; to develop their small-business portfolio.

Whilst there is little suggestion that the banks' role is more than just information dissemination and 'facilitators', their interest in franchising serves to give some degree of credibility to the perception, especially by potential franchisees, of low rates of risk and failure. Whilst some of this endorsement may be unwitting, in other instances it could be perceived to be intentional. The main clearing banks have entered the franchise 'advice' market mainly because it offers them a new route to broaden their business loan services. *Inter alia*, just because a bank agrees to provide a loan to a franchisee does not mean that they have conducted an exhaustive check by reviewing the financial stability, business history, track record of directors, calculating the credit scores of existing franchisees or even speaking to existing franchisees of a particular system. Unfortunately, the same criticism is potentially applicable to solicitors.

In summary, then, franchises have been promoted and possibly sanctioned by the clearing banks, within the popular and academic press alike, as a relatively risk-free entry method to potential entrants of business management. Given the arguments concerning the legitimation process by population ecologists, such sentiments are perhaps to be expected as incumbents defend their chosen organizational form from competing alternatives. There are, however, problems with such a message. In view of the lack of non-corroborated franchise failure data, there appears to be a suggestion that the link between franchising and low levels of failure is a highly speculative one, but also one that illustrates a popular line of thought. Indeed, the very thought of the 'tried and tested' business format being vulnerable to failure is an anathema to many in the franchise fraternity. Nonetheless, there is some evidence from Britain and the United States that franchisors not only fail but do so on a regular basis (Lafontaine and Shaw, 1996b; Price, 1996;

Stanworth, 1995; Shane, 1996). Accordingly, there appears to be some question concerning the accuracy and appropriateness of views propounding low rates of failure.

The purpose of this chapter is, via a purely exploratory study, to examine just how troubled franchising's 'troubled dream world' (Burck, 1970) really is. Prior to this, some background on attrition rates in the franchise sector is provided in order to gain a better understanding of its magnitude, nature and the problems associated with its measurement. As seen from above, the popular franchise press and some academics frequently claim that franchisors experience almost unparalleled levels of success. As shown in Chapter 3, these perceptions, at best, arise from the belief that franchising confers a variety of benefits on franchisors that permit them to:

1. realize broader brand dissemination;
2. gain access to capital;
3. negate competitors' first mover advantages;
4. realize personal ambitions of controlling a large network;
5. lower risk and improve return on investment; and
6. preclude the development of an expensive organizational structure.

The foundations of these expectations, however, may be ill-founded. It is axiomatic that the majority of franchisors are small businesses (which, in themselves, are marked by high levels of failure) and only a minority of these ever grow to the extent of employing other people. As noted in Chapter 4, the trials and costs of developing a small business are problematic enough (Dodge *et al*, 1994; Storey, 1994) without the additional burden of nurturing a credible franchise operation. The financial, managerial, reputation and time costs (among other mobility barriers) associated with franchising suggest that it is a growth strategy not to be entered into lightly. It is, logically, going to realize net cash out-flows in the initial stages, rather than being the pot at the end of the rainbow that may otherwise lead small firm owners to believe. In fact, the normal problems of small-firm growth are, in all likelihood, going to be magnified and exacerbated rather than reduced and alleviated when pursuing franchised expansion. In short, Thompson (1994) argues that firms enter into franchising to overcome the Penrose effect (a shortage of managerial and financial resources) and realize growth, but it is precisely because of this effect that they may fail as a franchisor. It may be, therefore, that relatively new franchisor businesses experience relatively high rates of attrition. Once the magnitude of franchisor failure is measured, some explanation for the reasons behind the attrition rates can be made.

For comparative purposes and to provide some illustration of volatility, this chapter summarizes, as an end-note, some government-produced attrition statistics. The potential dangers of franchised expansion are also enhanced by comparing the differing sets of government data of business demise to NatWest/BFA data concerning franchisee failures. The rationale for its inclusion is to illustrate that when, as part of the career choice process, a potential franchisee or budding franchisor evaluates the degree of risk within (for example) a particular hospitality venture, they do so with particularly blunt tools. Their bluntness derives from the differing definitions of failure and the lack of sector-specific data concerning franchise failure rates. As an adjunct, a review of over forty UK hotel and catering text books and numerous journals, suggests that the topic of failure, as a scholarly subject, is woefully under-reported and under-researched (despite being a prominent feature of the hospitality industry and the availability of statistical data detailing failures within it).

Problems of quantification

It is commonly believed that the number of firms going out of business in the UK reached record levels between 1990 and 1993 and this view is, in part, supported by the government-produced insolvency figures. It is equally well established that small-business failure rates are quite high, especially in the first five years of operations (Cochran, 1981; Dickinson, 1981). Ganguly (1985) and Stewart and Gallagher (1986), for example, show that, of those companies which fail within ten years of starting business, about half of failures occur within the first two-and-a-half years and a third within the next two-and-a-half years. According to Timmons (1986), between 20% and 30% of new starters fail during their first year of existence, and after six years fewer than half survive. This said, there is still much about the mechanics and processes of business development and failure that remains unknown because of definitional and methodological problems and, in franchising, this situation is particularly acute.

The knowledge gap is exacerbated by the variety of sources of failure data employing different proxies. As each definition affects the reported statistics regarding the rate of failure, the available information on attrition in the hospitality industry (and generally) is potentially confusing, conflicting and may represent different economic phenomena. Indeed, Cochran (1981), in a review of small-business mortality rates concludes:

> . . . although much is written about small-business failure, reliable information about who fails, why, and at what rate is hampered by differences in definitions, data sources and methodologies. The myriad studies of business mortality, with their various conceptions of failure and different purposes and research designs speak to the subject with a babble of tongues. (p. 59)

This is a sentiment echoed by Bruno and Leidecker (1988):

> No two experts agree on a definition of business failure. Some conclude that failure only occurs when a firm files for some form of bankruptcy. Others contend that there are numerous forms of organizational death, including bankcruptcy, merger, or acquisition. Still others argue that failure occurs if the firm fails to meet its responsibilities to the stakeholders of the organization, including employees, suppliers, the community as a whole, and customers, as well as the owners. (p. 51)

Yet, there are a variety of uses for dependable data. For example, Cochran (1981) suggests that:

1. The lack of reliable measure of failure precludes understanding failure. This is especially true when examining incidences of franchisee attrition. In arguing for the importance of a suitable yardstick of failure, Cross (1994) observes:

Advocates of franchising often point to low failure rates as an advantage of this method of doing business, and low failure rates are widely quoted in various publications and franchisor's promotional materials. This is fine as long as readers are aware of what the failure rate actually measures. (p. 8)

2. Without a yardstick of failure, the accurate evaluation of policies and programmes designed to help small businesses is precluded.
3. Without information on the rate and extent of failure, the ability to predict and the knowledge of business cycles are deficient.
4. Alternative forms of enterprise, such as co-operatives, and community development projects, as well as, perhaps, franchises, might be judged more fairly and realistically if a suitable measure of small-business mortality existed.

Additionally, by establishing levels or rates of failure, the degree of risk in pursuing a particular course of action may be assessed at the planning stage. It thus provides the business planner with the opportunity, via the use of simple statistical scenario (for example, Monte-Carlo simulation) and probability methods, to generate alternative courses of action. This requires the data to be quantified, a process often beset with emotional problems let alone definitional ones.

One of the root causes of problems in quantifying failure is the defensive stance of many when broached about the subject of failure – its unpalatability, its pejorative connotations (Scott and Lewis, 1984) – as well as, perhaps, an effort to reduce the effects of potentially adverse publicity. As franchisors typically base royalties on sales as well as receive monies from the sale of raw materials to franchisees, under-performing franchisees are in danger of becoming disgruntled and leaving the system. When publicized, such grievances and evidence of failure could have a negative effect on the franchise's brand equity, franchisee morale and the queue of potential franchisees (Caves and Murphy, 1976; Kaufmann and Lafontaine, 1994; Norton, 1988b; Sen, 1993) which may, in turn, preclude the realization of economies of scale. Clearly, therefore, promoting low rates of failure and sustaining franchisee motivation levels may be of singular importance to realizing competitive advantage (Lillis *et al*, 1976).

Not all businesses and potential franchisees lend themselves to franchising and some franchises are more secure than others (as will be shown). Partially inspired by the early successes of KFC, McDonald's and Pizza Hut, however, and the dream of getting rich and/or the need for security, many people have turned to it. Any talk of failure, therefore, has been interpreted by such advocates of franchising as being negative rather than being, perhaps, objective. Arguably, the lack of attention to attrition by the popular franchise press and purveyors of franchise advice, for example lawyers, accountants, consultants, is partially reflective of vested interests (for example, advertising revenues, legal fees) which only contributes to the general perception that franchise failures are relatively rare occurrences when, in fact, such observations may be no more than conjecture and franchisees often have more than their life-savings to lose. To a large extent, the dearth of research effort concerning franchise attrition exists because franchisors have some degree of vested interest in not contributing to the debate. Favourable and uncorroborated attrition statistics may, for example, prove useful to franchisors when attracting new franchisees. The vested interest in and the necessity of presenting franchising in 'success' terms, is aptly summarized by Kursch (1968), who insists that:

Franchising cannot afford a truly high rate of 'financial' failures (i.e., those resulting from non-personal reasons, such as disenchantment, disillusionment). If that were the case, it would be the end of franchising. The fact that the successful franchise is 'packaged success' lies at the very heart of the franchise boom. (p. 51)

Concurrent to company-specific concerns, therefore, is also an element of 'industry' reputation. Franchising in Britain developed a rather bad name in the late 1960s and 1970s because, after the initial successes of fast food companies such as KFC and Wimpy, unscrupulous operators were attracted by the potential gains on offer (note that the coefficient of imitation for the early period of UK franchising suggests increasing word-of-mouth and influence). These operators found it relatively easy to lure the gullible with their promises of doubling their investment in the first few weeks of operation. The initial fee was often banked and the franchisors disappeared. Simultaneous to such activity was the rise of pyramid selling schemes (see the panel on page 390 for a definition) some of which were involved in fraudulent and illegal activities. One such company was the cosmetics distribution company and Swiss-registered Koscot Interplanetary (UK). It was subject to a liquidation order by the government in 1972 after it generated £500,000 in two years by selling virtually worthless franchises. These practices led to the formation of the BFA in 1977, and since then effort and resources have been devoted to portraying franchising in a better and more positive light.

Researching the level of attrition in franchising has proved problematic because of the degree of self-interest within the franchise fraternity, as a whole, to promote low failure rates (Stanworth, 1994). It has, however, also been beset by research methodological issues such as the lack of response by failed or failing franchise systems to respond to research surveys; discontinuance figures may not be included as 'failures' by some (Hoy, 1994; Knight, 1986); and reliance by researchers (for example, Castrogiovanni *et al*, 1993) to utilize members of the BFA or International Franchise Association for sampling frames when, typically, disreputable franchise companies and a large number of franchisors are not members. There is, therefore, a need for greater objectivity, entailing non-reliance on franchisors to self-report attrition rates, as well as a different, more scientific, methodology to evaluate the magnitude of franchisee and franchisor failures. Cross (1994), for example, suggests that in order to measure the success of franchising objectively, researchers must overcome an 'information void':

> The only systematically compiled statistics on franchise failure rates have been provided in the 'Franchising in the Economy' reports and periodic membership of the International Franchise Association. While these efforts are commendable and undoubtedly well-intentioned, both are based on potentially incomplete and inaccurate data submitted by franchisors. (p. 1)

Perhaps of greatest significance to potential investors is the tendency by some to quote a franchise 'industry' attrition figure (often produced by trade bodies) which is potentially misleading, since it infers that all franchises, irrespective of economic context and status of the franchise itself, are potentially equally safe. But the franchise fraternity comprises of disparate activities ranging from milk distribution, printing services to fast food retail etc., and thus providing an 'industry' figure serves to disguise potentially significant

Approaches to pyramid selling schemes

For the purposes of clarity, it is useful to distinguish between pyramid selling schemes and multi-level franchises. According to Stockstill (1985), the latter combines both traditional product distribution and direct selling techniques. Consequences stem from promotional marketing plans which allow distributors to enlist other participants to sell the product. Typically, the product travels through the chain of distribution at a wholesale cost to the lower level of distributors, who sell it at a retail price to the consumer. Intermediate distributors profit not only through their retail sales, but also through a series of bonuses or override commissions from the sales volumes of their underlings. As a distributor acquires more down-line sales people, he ascends within the distribution system and his bonus increases. Most multi-level franchises have three or four levels.

Stockstill observes that 'pyramid schemes likewise involve three or four levels through which products are channelled to the ultimate customer. A participant can normally enter at any level. He (and, typically, she) is required to purchase a predetermined amount of the company's product at a percentage of its retail cost. The higher levels of the distribution resell their products to the next level below at a percentage of cost, and so on. One or two lower levels of the pyramid sell their goods to consumers at the full retail price. The top levels are entitled to earn fees by recruiting others into the distribution plan. A higher-level participant is entitled to a fee when a lower-level participant is elevated. Often, however, a salesperson will not be elevated at all unless he or she finds a replacement to fill the position to be vacated'(p. 55).

By contrast others, such as the Department of Trade & Industry (DTI), perceive little difference between pyramid selling and multi-level selling. The DTI observes that 'pyramid selling is now more often called multi-level selling or network marketing. It is a way of selling goods or services through a trading scheme which operates on more than one level. People who join such a scheme (called 'participants') buy goods or services from the company running the scheme or from other participants and then sell them to the general public usually in their homes'.

Unlike some areas, pyramid selling is legal in the UK but must comply with a host of legal requirements. It must comply with Part XI of the Fair Trading Act 1973, The Pyramid Selling Schemes Regulations 1989 and the Pyramid Selling Schemes (Amendment) 1989. Additionally, advertising for recruits and the products must conform to the standards set by the Advertising Standards Authority, the Trade Descriptions Act 1968 and the Misleading Advertising Regulations 1988.

sector variations. Some economic sectors and strategic groups are more competitive, volatile, have lower barriers to entry and exit, and have lower levels of consumer loyalty than others. In turn, these features suggest that the degree of risk between different franchise 'sectors' is substantially different (Lafontaine, 1994). Indeed, in a paper testing whether franchised businesses operating between 1971 and 1981 were less risky than non-franchised businesses, Padmanabhan (1986) found that the degree of risk (the proportion of discontinued businesses to the total number of businesses) was higher for independently-owned businesses compared to franchises. Importantly, some individual franchise sectors (such as business aids and services, automotive services and fast food) illustrated higher levels of risk compared to others.

There is, perhaps, also a danger that fast food franchise attrition statistics are not evaluated by researchers and potential franchisees against the norms of the catering industry or sector norms but, rather, the norms of the franchising community overall. Competitive strategy research suggests, however, that while particular variables of the franchise environment may influence performance, greater insight flows generally from studies that explicitly recognize that the most relevant 'peer population' of the franchisor is not other franchisors, but all contemporary product competitors and enterprises marketing potential substitutes (Huszagh et al, 1992; Miller and Ginter, 1979). As a result of comparing franchise attrition statistics with those of a particular industry, potential franchisees are therefore comparing oranges and lemons.

By providing figures for the 'franchise industry' when, arguably, there is no such thing, there is a suggestion that franchise trade bodies and press are, perhaps, attempting to generate positive network externalities. Put alternatively, the aim is to increase the legitimation of franchising. The main motivation behind these externalities is to increase awareness of franchising as a career option, and thereby the number of potential adopters, as well as the number of franchisors. According to Bental and Speigal (1995),

> network externalities in consumption are present when the number of consumers who purchase a particular good is an important quality characteristic of that good, which affects the utility derived by consumers either directly or indirectly. (p. 197)

For franchisors, the benefits of increased consumption of their 'goods' take the form of increased revenues and market share. For the trade bodies, consultants, solicitors, and accountants, the benefits derive from the revenues spent on feasibility studies, contracts, and increased economic significance of franchising. In particular, the franchise trade bodies have been attempting to generate positive adoption and investment externalities. The adoption externality has two sources. Firstly, growing numbers of franchisees increases the size and growth of the 'industry', as does its economic significance (and the kudos that goes with such status), and revenues to franchisors. Direct evidence of this form of externality to gain possible institutional support and further legitimation is apparent from the BFA's own literature to potential franchisors in their 'Questions and Answers' pack, where franchising is presented as having the potential to solve the unemployment problem:

> The BFA has a strong message for Parliament – one not yet fully understood by Government, or indeed the Opposition parties. It is simply that within the

disciplines of a franchise operation new businesses can be more readily and quickly created without the same degree of risk attending other such ventures. With the pressing problem of high unemployment, particularly amongst the young, the franchise principle offers a very real, if not complete solution.

The BFA is not unique in this respect:

> Overall . . . what the economy needs is a boost of enthusiasm and common sense – and franchising seems to provide all the right ingredients for a proliferating small-business based regeneration – which is in turn strategically important to economic regeneration. And we must encourage the Government to acknowledge the fact that franchising delivers the economic goods they are so desperately seeking. (Quoted in *Franchise Confidential*, part of the *Franchise Magazine*, autumn edition, 1996; p. 3)

There is also, perhaps, some indirect evidence of researchers attempting to generate this first type of externality through their projections concerning the growth of franchising:

> The industry total in 1995, to judge from shifts at present in the underlying trend, is likely to be £12.5 billion. (Power, 1990; p. 12)

> Rapidly changing business conditions and the dissolution of EC trade barriers by January 1993 will have a marked effect on plans of existing UK franchisors for 1995. Last year's estimate of £11bn by 1994 has now been increased to £12.5bn by 1995. The underlying trend shows an average year-on-year increase of 12% in Systems, 15% in Units, 11% in average Unit turnover and 11% in Employment. (NatWest/BFA press release for the Seventh National Survey of Franchising in Britain, 1990)

> Projecting to 1997 . . . the business format franchising industry will be worth £10.5 billion. (NatWest/BFA Franchise Survey, 1992; pp.7–8)

By comparing Figure 8.1 with the Power (1990) projection, as well as with the added benefit of hindsight, we can see that these forecasted values of over £12 billion are clearly inaccurate. The 'industry' in 1994 was valued, by the NatWest/BFA, at £5.5 billion. So, is the NatWest/BFA forecast correct? Without adjusting for inflation, it is apparent, by using NatWest/BFA 'industry' size data for the period 1984–92 to generate a simple linear trend equation by the least squares method (where 1984 equals zero), that such 'crystal-ball gazing' is, in probability, inaccurate too. By extrapolating the trend line to the year 2000, it is only then that the UK franchise sector reaches £10 billion. When the size data for 1993 and 1994 are also used, the date moves to the year 2003. The figure of £12.5 billion is, using the latter method, reached in the year 2009! It should, however, be observed that the linear trend equation is a less than accurate forecasting tool. It only serves to show the general direction of growth.

Nonetheless, in spite of the decline in the market value of franchising in real terms, and the inaccuracies of forecasts made by the franchise fraternity (which are evident even by using simplistic forecasting methods), there appears to be a persistent belief about the buoyancy of future growth levels. Indeed, the Director General of the Confederation of British Industry, Howard Davies, in a speech opening an exhibition for franchises commented that:

> . . . I am convinced that franchising is a big growth area. There is some survey evidence to suggest that it may well double in the UK in the next four to five years. That expansion could be a major source of new employment in the economy. (Quoted in *Franchise World*, March–April 1994; p. 9)

The second, and perhaps more important, adoption externality is related to the first in that a larger franchise network makes the activity possibly more attractive to potential franchisors and franchisees. The 'investment' externality occurs as a given franchisor's investment in marketing effort to recruit franchisees benefits other franchises through greater dissemination of franchising as a career option as well as through increased investments generated by those additional franchisees (Kogut *et al*, 1995; Nault and Dexter, 1994). The disadvantage of an approach which fails to distinguish between different types of franchise is that potential investors may perceive all franchises to be more-or-less of equal risk. In a price sensitive investor market, therefore, potential franchisees may trade down to cheaper, newer and less proven franchises and, in the process, possibly acquire greater levels of risk. For example, a UK study succeeded in tracking 169 potential franchisees after attending a franchise exposition/exhibition (Hatcliffe *et al*, 1995). Of these, thirty-four (20%) took up a franchise within two years and the majority (73%) had bought franchises with a maximum cost of £20,000. Nearly a quarter of their sample quickly failed. These were concentrated amongst franchise systems at the very lowest end of the price spectrum. Interestingly, these respondents had not borrowed money from their bank to assist with the purchase/setting-up of the franchised operation, and thereby lowering the risk of jeopardizing other capital assets such as their homes.

Another root cause of the difficulties in measuring failure is not only its pejorative associations, but also the orientation of the definitions employed. One research strand measures the number of business deaths, whilst another evaluates decline. In being a strategy that results in an organizational form (as organizational structures tend to follow strategy), and thus susceptible to alteration under certain conditions, it is not necessarily appropriate to equate the withdrawal from franchised-based expansion with the death of the franchisor. In some cases, this conclusion is undoubtedly true and in other situations the entry into franchising may serve to exacerbate decline and tendency toward failure. It is, however, important to observe that the conclusion is not generally true: a franchisor may decide to withdraw from the activity since it may not be conducive, for example, to realizing the new strategic direction and growth trajectory of the firm. When Mansfield Breweries withdrew from franchising its Berni Inn brand and involvement with two other franchise businesses (Rainbow International and Bonanza Restaurants, which were realizing low returns on investment), for instance, the management claimed that the divestment was due to a desire to concentrate on core competencies. In this sense, we are perhaps dealing with strategic group volatility rather than franchise industry attrition. To do this, however, the strategic group is defined according to the strategies approach (Cool and Schendel, 1987); firms are categorized by whether they are involved in franchising or not. Thus, the evaluation of franchisor failures is to measure intra-strategic group volatility: it is to quantify the level of franchisor failure within an industry; it is not to measure franchise versus non-franchise attrition rates – this is an inter-strategic group analysis and is beset by problems of comparability and definitions of failure.

Prior studies of franchisor failure

Anecdotal evidence suggests that there is an abundance of franchisor failures. Within the hospitality industry, for example, US concepts such as Little Caesar's Pizza, Popeye's Famous Fried Chicken, Subway, and Arby's which, although successful in the USA, Middle East, and the Pacific Rim, withdrew from Britain after a relatively short period of time. The statistics produced by trade associations and government bodies, however, do not support such anecdotal evidence. The NatWest/BFA annual surveys, for example, indicate that the average annual franchisor withdrawal rate between 1986 and 1989 was about 7% and 9% for the period 1990–94 (see Table 8.2). In the USA, the Department of Commerce (1988) reported an average of 140 franchisors withdrew from franchising each year between the period 1980–86. These researchers do not reveal further information, such as the size of the franchise network when failure occurs, tenure in franchising, age prior to becoming a franchisor, or sectoral differences. In addition, Stanworth (1995) is concerned that such data is not independent and corroborated by those in the academic fraternity and elsewhere.

With most academic discussions of franchising targeting issues such as the franchisor's decision to franchise, patterns of franchisee motivation, and franchisor-franchisee relations, the subject of franchisor attrition has been described as a 'very quiet debate' because of the dearth of research exploring this topic (Stanworth, 1995). Yet the very quietness of the debate seems to contrast against the privately-held beliefs of some franchise researchers, and an abundance of anecdotal evidence which potentially points to the possibility of a rate of franchisor attrition which is higher than the proclamations of those seeking further legitimation would have the public believe. These researchers may have their own reasons for not contributing to the debate, but their silence in the public domain could be (mis)construed to mean that they support the success rhetoric propounded within the popular franchise press and trade associations when, in fact, the opposite may be true (in some quarters, silence is taken to mean consent). Within the populist vein, franchisor failure is assumed to be minimal due to the franchisor's access to resources (for example, franchisees' capital) which should, at least, facilitate survival. This

Year	87	88	89	90	91	92	93	94	Growth/year
Systems	253	244	295	379	432	373	396	414	7.3
Withdrawals	20	20	21	21	33	35	21	55	15.5
Rate	*7.9*	*8.2*	*7.1*	*5.5*	*7.6*	*14.7*	*5.3*	*13.2*	*7.6*

Source: Annual BFA/Nat West Reports (various years).

Table 8.2: BFA/NatWest rate of franchisor withdrawals, 1987–94

said, however, the subject of franchisor failure gains a certain degree of popularity at times within the press, and this is especially so when the failed franchisor is well known. As an academic study, however, the topic of franchisor failure is an important area of study particularly as there may be a heightened level of risk imbued on the franchisee brought about by the withdrawal of the franchisor. Reflecting on this aspect, Lafontaine and Shaw (1996b) comment:

> ... business-format franchising in the US has not been growing at the formidable rate that the press often suggests. Rather, while many firms keep entering into franchising, giving this impression of tremendous growth, many are also exiting, leading to an overall growth at best commensurate with that of the economy ... Given the impact that franchisor exit must have on franchisee success, it is disconcerting to find so much of it, and have so little capacity to predict it. (p. 1)

One of the reasons for the heightened level of risk imbued on the franchisee by franchisor withdrawal is the former's high level of dependency on the latter. Franchisees are viewed within the more traditional franchise texts as being dependent on the franchisor for the:

1. business idea;
2. product;
3. brand investments, such as advertising;
4. knowledge; and, in some instances,
5. innovations.

This dependency serves to possibly increase the level of risk because, as in strategic alliances, when one party shuts down, or alters strategic direction, businesses that collaborated with that partner usually lose access – or suffer reduced access – to the capabilities that were the purpose of that collaboration. Exploring the issues of survival in hybrid organizational forms after one partner fails, albeit not in the franchise context, Singh and Mitchell (1996) observe that the survivors

> ... may be able to internalize the partner's capabilities after a partner fails either by internal development or by purchasing the assets of the failed business. However, firms usually form inter-organizational relationships because they lack the ability, time, or money needed to internalize the necessary capabilities. (p. 101)

Possibly spurred by the significance of the debate, as well as ethical considerations, four studies (Lafontaine and Shaw, 1996b; Price, 1996; Shane, 1996; Stanworth, 1994; 1995) have done much to contest the success rhetoric, to increase the volume of the franchisor attrition argument, and to bring a new sense of realism to the franchise fraternity and its literature. Some of these studies have focused on quantifying and exploring the descriptive attributes, such as age, franchise fees, number of outlets, etc., of failed franchisors. With titles such as *Dispelling the Myths Surrounding Franchise Failure Rates* (Stanworth, 1995), *Franchising Growth in the U.S. Market: Myth and Reality* (Lafontaine and Shaw, 1996b), and *Behind the Veneer of Success* (Price, 1996), the focus of this research has been to question the popular belief perpetuated by franchisors, franchise exposition organizers, and trade associations, that franchisors illustrate low rates of withdrawal. As significant as these studies are to alerting potential investors to the propensity of withdrawal, some of the results of the few extant studies has been the emergence of several questions concerning the broader descriptive variables of failed franchisors, such as:

1. Do withdrawal rates differ by strategic group?
2. How long do firms franchise?
3. Do failed franchisors live fast and die young?
4. Do the patterns and rate of growth differ for failures?
5. Are the levels of franchise fees different for failed franchisors?
6. Why do franchisors fail?
7. What happens post-withdrawal from franchising?

While exploring whether differences in withdrawal rates are statistically significant according to the various strategic groups in the franchise fraternity has numerous practi-

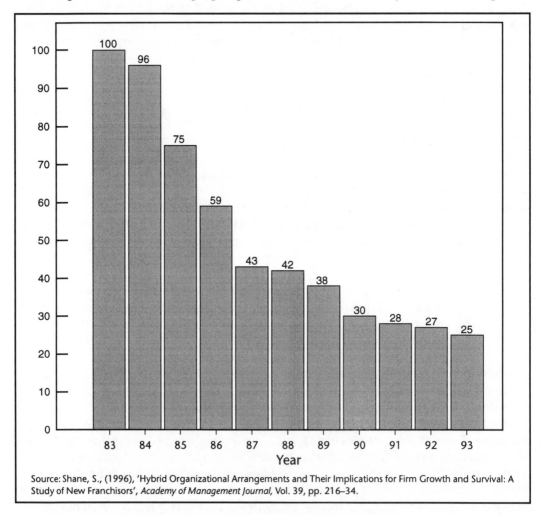

Source: Shane, S., (1996), 'Hybrid Organizational Arrangements and Their Implications for Firm Growth and Survival: A Study of New Franchisors', *Academy of Management Journal*, Vol. 39, pp. 216–34.

Figure 8.4: Franchisor failures in the USA, 1983–93

cal applications, extant studies of franchisor failure illustrate some polarization in resolving question 3. One set of researchers has noted that the presence of an inverse relationship between success as a franchisor and the amount of time devoted to developing the business prior to franchising: those with shorter periods of pre-franchising experience are more prone to withdrawal. Another group disagrees with this observation and finds, instead, that young and old businesses are equally prone to withdrawal. Resolving this issue is not only important for the provision of advice to potential franchisees, but also to the possible broader acceptance that franchisors illustrate high rates of attrition. Specifically, Shane (1996) shows, using a sample of 138 new US-based franchisors, that about three-quarters failed over a ten-year period. Younger franchise systems appeared especially prone to failure, with years two, three and four illustrating the fastest rates of decline. Such findings are consistent with Hudson (1986), who suggests that there is an initial 'honeymoon' period immediately following the formation of the firm. Following this, is a period of high risk during which the firm is particularly susceptible to insolvency. Hudson shows that the time differential between formation and death is likely to be between two to three years. In predominantly small firms, a similar honeymoon period may be evident for franchisors. In recently reported research, Lafontaine and Shaw's (1996b) study of 2,545 US franchisors between 1980 and 1992 corroborated the high overall failure rates in the USA reported by Shane. Somewhat surprisingly, Lafontaine and Shaw did not corroborate the claim that there is a much higher attrition rate in the earlier, developmental, years in franchising. Rather, they find strong continuous attrition over the whole period covered by their data, and indicate that less than 30% of franchisors who embarked on franchised expansion in 1980/81 were still engaged in the activity in 1992.

Year	N	1980	1981	1982	1983	1984	1985	1986	1987	1988	1989	1990	1991	1992
1980	294	100	88.4	84.0	76.5	65.6	59.2	53.1	49.3	42.2	41.5	37.8	32.7	28.6
1981	233		100	95.3	87.6	76.0	68.7	58.8	52.8	45.5	44.6	42.9	32.2	29.2
1982	242			100	93.8	86.8	79.3	72.3	67.4	59.5	57.9	53.3	46.3	41.7
1983	208				100	91.3	85.6	81.7	73.1	63.0	61.1	57.7	45.7	39.4
1984	217					100	95.4	91.2	87.1	81.1	80.6	76.0	64.5	55.3
1985	207						100	94.2	92.8	86.5	85.0	80.7	66.2	53.6
1986	243							100	97.5	94.7	91.8	83.5	70.4	61.7
1987	223								100	93.7	89.7	83.9	69.1	62.3
1988	186									100	96.8	91.9	81.7	67.7
1989	180										100	96.1	88.3	77.7
1990	139											100	91.4	81.3
1991	120												100	86.7
1992	53													100
Total	2545													

Source: Lafontaine, F., and Shaw, K.L., (1996b), 'Franchising Growth in the U.S. Market: Myth and Reality'

Table 8.3: *Number of franchises in Lafontaine and Shaw's (1996b) sample starting to franchise in a given year (N) and percentage still franchising in subsequent years*

Although Shane's rate of withdrawal is faster, the implications of the Lafontaine and Shaw study is of more concern to both franchisors and franchisees alike. This is because the latter researchers suggest that mature franchises are almost as prone to withdrawal as their younger counterparts. Arguably, one of the reasons behind the differences in Shane's and Lafontaine and Shaw's findings is partially attributable to the structure of their respective samples. Shane's inclusion of a high proportion of fast food and restaurant concerns may have biased his findings because of the short life-cycles evident in that market. But this divergence between Lafontaine and Shaw and Shane is further complicated by the suggestion of a middle ground between these polarized positions. In a survey of franchisors operating in Britain during the decade 1984–94, but without the benefit of substantial statistical testing, Price (1996) found that the failures illustrated high levels of variability in their age prior to franchising. This situation seemed to suggest that withdrawing firms tended either to be established firms or young firms.

The implication of such research is that it illustrates that the rate of franchisor withdrawal is higher than has perhaps been appreciated hitherto by trade associations, etc., and is higher for franchisors than franchisees (Kursch, 1968). While there are undoubted ethical and moral dimensions to these findings, the divergence of the results in these few, but significant, studies of franchisor failure is of concern because it could undermine the significance of this vein of enquiry. Importantly, the divergence possibly raises questions about the research itself by implying that the studies may have suffered from sample heterogeneity concerns or generalizability limitations. As the findings of such research could have substantial applications and implications for studies on franchisee performance and theoretical work concerning (for example) the motivation to franchise, the disparate results cannot be permitted to remain unaddressed. Therefore, in addition to answering the list of questions shown above, the purpose of this chapter is also to provide an empirical test to generate evidence which either corroborates the contention that young businesses are more prone to failure as a franchisor, or finds more validity in the counter-argument.

Study one: initial scale

Stanworth (1994), in an attempt to generate some data fairly quickly for illustrative purposes for a Government report, decided to assess survival levels amongst a sample of seventy-four franchises known to be in existence a decade earlier, but also to expand the survivor/non-survivor dichotomy along a five-category continuum. In order to provide some initial indication of the scale of franchisor failure within the UK fast food/restaurant trade, a re-examination of Stanworth's (1994; 1995) data was conducted. These seventy-four companies were featured in the franchise listings section of the January–April 1984 edition of *Franchise World*, the first (and in 1984) the only regular franchise magazine in Britain. The seventy-four firms are judged to have represented between one-third and one-half of all of the systems in existence in Britain at that time, and included many of the better-known systems, thought to be least prone to failure. For instance, the list of seventy-four systems contained five of the original eight founder members of the BFA. Nonetheless, it also contained a failrly strong representation of 'young' franchises. The latter, due to their relative youth had little by way of a known brand name and were strongly dependent upon advertising alone when seeking franchisees. When the survey was first done, the exercise of categorizing these companies on the survival continuum was undertaken by eight separate authorities drawn from the franchise industry, and was undertaken on the basis of their current knowledge or best judgement. Of these eight, three bankers and two journalists worked in concert to produce five responses overall. Each of the panel of experts was asked to classify each franchise company on a scale ranging A–E, correlating to the following:

A. The company is still in existence. The company is generally considered a franchise success story and is still achieving healthy growth rates.

B. The company is still in existence. The company is generally considered a franchise success story, but appears to have reached something near market saturation now.

C. The company is still in existence. The company is not generally considered a franchise success story and appears to have experienced generally turbulent trading conditions and failed to achieve its earlier goals.

D. The company is still in existence in some form at least – possibly now as a company-owned operation. The company is generally considered to have failed as a franchise.

E. The company failed as a franchise and has since disappeared from view.

The results illustrate that about half of the restaurant/fast food franchises evident in 1984 have since failed. This is slightly lower than the franchisors classified as 'other'. Restaurants and fast food franchisors represented about 31% of all failed franchisors in the period. More specifically, within the context of the restaurant and fast food market, the rate of franchisor failures amounted to about 47% which compares to about two-thirds in the 'other' category. One of the main conclusions to emerge from the test was one of a relatively high rate of franchisor attrition. At best, it appears that only about one in four franchisors could be described as a success story over a ten-year period (categories A and B). Such statistics may serve to help potential franchisees provide some measure against the general advice that, when evaluating franchise options, they should establish the ability to sustain the business. It should, however, also be observed that there have been numerous other companies entering into franchising since 1984 and who have

| Category | Response type | | | | | |
	A	B	C	D	E	Total
Restaurants & fast food	14	5	14	7	25	65
Other	30	39	35	33	168	305
Total	*44*	*44*	*49*	*40*	*193*	*370*
% of responses	21.5	7.8	21.5	10.8	38.4	100.0
Restaurants as % of total	32	11	29	18	13	17.6

Data derived from Stanworth (1994; 1995).

Table 8.4: *Proportion of restaurant and fast food franchisor failures, 1984–94*

subsequently failed before 1994. Furthermore, those companies who have been categorized as 'C' may not, in fact, be construed to have failed as such. Some of these companies may have elected to remain a small franchise system and/or only expand within a specific geographic niche.

Study two: temporal differences

In order to evaluate the temporal differences in the proportion of failures during the 1986–94 period (data prior to 1986 was not available) and furnish further corroborating evidence, information provided by Franchise Development Services Ltd detailing 554 UK and US franchisors advertising for UK franchisees in their publication *The Franchise Magazine* was analyzed. The time period was divided into two, 1986–89 and 1990–94 (the recessionary period), and the sample compared against Franchise Development Service's entries in their sister (but annual) publication, *The United Kingdom Franchise Directory* for January 1990 and January 1995. Where a company had advertised in the magazine but was not listed in the directories, it was assumed that the firm had withdrawn from the UK franchise scene (that is, franchisor failure does not necessarily equate with the demise of the company). The directory has been recognized as one of the most comprehensive surveys (but not complete) of the UK franchise fraternity (Stanworth, 1994) since directory entrants are not required to pay advertising fees in order to qualify for inclusion, and is the British equivalent of the *Entrepreneur* magazine's survey of US franchises. Given the ownership links of the magazine and directories, advertisers (if still a franchisor) are almost certain to be included.

Although not entirely representative since some franchisors have a greater propensity to use this advertising medium than others, the results suggest that there has been a substantial rise in the number of franchisor failures. Nonetheless, the proportion of discontinuances increased from about 47% to almost two-thirds. That is, of the 296 franchisors who advertised between 1986 and 1989, about half had withdrawn from the activity by January, 1990. With regard to fast food/catering franchisors, the rate of discontinuance declined to around 40%. Fast food/catering franchisors accounted for, on average, 16% of total franchisor discontinuances. Of those franchisors (all types) present in 1989, eighty – or about a third of the 1989 sample – had left UK franchising by the end of 1994. The figures, therefore, seem to imply that the majority of failures were new entrants to the franchise market.

Over the entire period, approximately 56% of franchisor advertisers left franchising. Such results compare to those presented above, but cannot be compared to the NatWest/BFA generated data due to sampling and definitional differences. The results also clearly suggest that the franchise market can be dichotomized into core and periphery brands, where the latter are most at risk. Perhaps reflecting this division, Brian Smart, Director of the British Franchise Association, suggests that, at most, only about 46% of franchisors may survive:

> The fact of the matter is that out of 373 franchisors (the number identified by the NatWest/BFA surveys in 1992) in the UK, those with any significant growth potential are probably something under 200. The remainder may, or may not survive. (1994; p. 50)

Sector	1986–89	1990–94	No. present in 1989 but not 1994
No. of fast food/catering franchisors	24	22	
No. of discontinuances	11	9	9
Ratio (%)	45.8	40.9	
No. of non-food franchisors	272	236	
No. of discontinuances	127	161	
Ratio (%)	46.7	62.4	
Total franchisors	296	258	
Total discontinuances	138	170	80
Ratio (%)	46.6	65.9	11.3

Table 8.5: Temporal analysis of UK franchisor discontinuances

The tendency for franchisor failures to be high within young businesses is consistent with a plethora of international research findings (for example, Franchise Task Force, 1991; Hough, 1986; Ozanne and Hunt, 1971; Shane, 1996). To some, the tendency of failures toward the smaller end of the size continuum may be 'fortunate' or 'a relief', because only relatively few franchisees may be affected. It is, however, important to note that the regularity of these failures means that their cumulative effect possibly outweighs that of large franchisor failures. Given that franchisors with fewer than ten units represent about half of all UK franchises, such results are, perhaps, of some concern. In short, even small failures are failures nonetheless and cannot be simply brushed aside by the franchise fraternity, who generally consider the notion of franchisor failure an oxymoron or an anathema.

Study three: characteristics of franchisor failures

Given the perceived increasing importance and utility of establishing sectoral differences on franchisor attrition rates, a third method was employed to evaluate these dimensions. The research was conducted by evaluating all of the entries contained in two sets of franchise directories: *The United Kingdom Franchise Directory* (UKFD) and, as an initial estimate of the rate of franchisor withdrawal from directories, *The Franchise World Directory* (FWD). Between the first edition of *UKFD* in 1984 and the eleventh in 1995, there were a total of 4,384 entries in the directories, yielding 1,658 different companies (edition six was not published). Of the latter 1,121 (two-thirds) were usable as they were business format franchises and because their entry contained the required necessary and sufficient data. By contrast, *FWD* contained a total of 3,722 entries between the first edition in 1984 and the eleventh in 1995, of which only the 2,429 (65%) recorded between 1989 and 1995 were used. Because of their use as a yardstick, the data extracted from the *FWD* directories were not required to contain the same richness of detail as the usable *UKFD* entries. These latter entries were required to contain the following information:

1. the year of formation and year of starting to franchise;
2. the number of company-operated units and the number of franchisee-operated units;
3. the cost of the franchise and a description of the product/service on offer.

Where components of the above data mix were missing, some attempt to complete them was made by referring to entries contained within two competing directories and in rival trade magazines, namely *Franchise World*, *Business Franchise* and *Dalton's Weekly*. These latter sources were not employed as the primary data sources due to their lack of comprehensiveness, but were used to confirm details about the number of stores and whether the franchises were on offer for sale in Britain or not:

> The listings in this directory include companies operating in the UK who do not sell franchises, but who are associated with companies which franchise in other countries. These are primarily companies, which are either wholly-owned by the foreign franchisor, or operating in the UK under some form of direct franchise, or joint venture scheme, with the foreign franchisor.
>
> They have been included in the interests of completeness, and to endorse their legal rights by recording the fact that their systems and business marks are established and operative in the UK.
>
> Also listed are UK franchisors, which franchise abroad, but not in Britain, and a number of U.S. franchisors we believe to be interested in entering the UK. (*Franchise World, Directory of Franchising*, 1984; p. 22)

The rationale for the data mix is as follows. Given the time requirements necessary to establish a business format and then develop a method to franchise it, those franchisors that have not made the necessarily investments of time, effort, and money may be more likely to fail because both their business and its franchise is untested. That is, managerial competences to co-ordinate, control, and direct the business and the franchise concept are undeveloped. As such, the time difference between formation and launching the franchise may prove a significant variable between survivors and non-survivors. This variable has been operationalized by a plethora of franchise research, and much of the 'How-to' literature suggests a time lag of up to four years between business inception and launching the franchise. This, however, undoubtedly varies according to the nature of the business and the number of adaptations required to transform the business into a franchise concept. When operationalizing the variable for this study, it became apparent that at least one-third of the usable entries referred to the year of inception of the franchise company, not the franchisor (some franchisors seek to moderate their risk by establishing a legally separate entity for the franchise). In order to overcome this issue, the inception dates of the usable sample were subject to checks with information released to Companies House, resulting in amendments to 37% of entries in *UKFD*. As Companies House, via a database listing all dissolved limited liability concerns over the last twenty years, also details those businesses which have gone into liquidation and receivership, the names of a random sample of franchisors from a plethora of industries were compared against this list. This comparison allowed the differentiation of those businesses who had withdrawn from franchising against those who had also failed as a business. Withdrawal from franchising was evaluated according to whether the franchise was entered in the directories.

Before the analysis is presented, it is important to make an observation about the measure of withdrawal employed in this study. Some readers may rightly question the legitimacy of categorizing a franchise as a non-surivivor simply because it is listed in a directory one year, and not the following year, nor any year thereafter. Yet other readers may be of the opinion that the firm is still in operation but not seeking further franchise expansion in order to concentrate on company-owned operations or to stabilize the system during a period of reorganization. In this case, a firm may choose not to include a listing in a directory. Equally, perhaps the firm is still in operation but is in the process of expanding outside the UK, and chooses not to include a listing for this reason. Clearly, there are different scenarios under which a franchise might not be listed in a directory, yet not correctly identified as non-survivor. As eloquent as some of the hypotheses for a franchise not being listed in a directory may become, they all miss the point of conducting the substantial checks and rechecks on the sample frame. The apparent truth of the situation is that franchise firms are listed in directories in the UK, irrespective of whether the firms want to be included or not, and are therefore seen by potential franchisees as candidates for further research. What the firms are able to influence is the level of detail contained within their entry in the respective directories. It is for this reason that some entries had data missing and some entries were no more than a company name and address; it is for this reason that substantial checks with other data sources were conducted. Franchisors, like any organization, are able to determine where and how they advertise their offering in the UK: they may not wish to publicize their offering in a directory but elect to employ other vehicles. Thus, if anything, the companies who are (for example) advertising their offering elsewhere are most likely to be included in the miscellaneous category.

With regard to the ownership patterns of the units, two sets of information were sought: the total number of outlets opened between inception and failure and the number of company-owned units opened during the same time period. One possible reason for the decision for withdrawal may be the total rate of growth and the lack of necessary resource to manage, support, control and direct that growth. An alternative rationale for withdrawal, however, may be the lack of ongoing commitment to the activity. This subset of failed franchisors may have concentrated their resource on developing company-owned stores. Such data needs to be moderated by the total entry costs of the franchise. If these were too high (in comparison to the rest of the franchisor's peer group) for the perceived brand value being purchased, then, rather than lowering price because it falls below pre-established opportunity costs, exit from franchising ensues. The launch date of the franchise was further employed to calculate the length of survival post-launch.

Although both sets of directories are sub-divided into differing products and services, analysis revealed that the entries contained within each category were typically inconsistent with the stated definition at the beginning of each directory and often changed quite arbitrarily. Whilst not detracting from the directories' undoubted use to potential franchisees and researchers as a reference source, this situation required that all entries were re-categorized according to new sectoral definitions, as defined by the 1992 SIC schema. The rationale for assigning franchisors to strategic groups based on this schema is that strategic clusters are oftened defined as 'sub-industries'. Based on the fact that assigning firms to SIC codes serves to differentiate the kinds of goods and services produced by those firms (irrespective of whether they are franchised), it appears reasonable, therefore, to assume that franchised concerns within a particular SIC could be construed to be a sub-industry because they are distinguished from non-franchised firms within the same overall industry classification.

Those entries which did not contain the required data, even after searching else-where, were redefined as 'miscellaneous' to give a total sample of 1,658 from the *UKFD* sources, but were only used to help estimate the total rate of failure by year. It should be noted that the samples include both domestic and foreign entrants. The rationale for the latter's inclusion is to do not only with the fact that franchises are on offer to potential franchisees within Britain, but also with the dominance of foreign franchises in the country. According to Stanworth (1994), for example, US franchises represent about 11% of all franchise systems in the UK. Unlike many of the domestic franchises, however, these foreign-owned systems have substantial presence in the country and are, for the large part, household names (for example, McDonald's and KFC). The effects of such presence

SIC sector description	Industry sub-sector	UKFD No.	%
Manufacture of pulp and paper products; publishing and printing	Print and publishing	49	3
Construction	Constructon	147	9
Wholesale and retail trade; repair of motor vehicles, motorcycles and personal and household goods	Car maintenance Wholesale Retail Non-store retail }	357	21
Hotels and restaurants	Hotel and catering	88	5
Transport, storage and communication	Taxi/cabs Travel agency Courier }	43	3
Financial intermediation	Financial services	21	1
Real estate, renting and business activities	Real estate Rental Consultancy Accounting Employment agency Legal Advertising Comm. cleaning General business }	299	18
Health and social work	Health care	12	1
Other community, social and personal service activities	Drainage Personal services Domestic services Driving school }	105	6
	'Miscellaneous'	537	32
	Total	1,658	100

Table 8.6: Composition of the sample for study

may have a negative effect on the survival rates of new foreign-owned franchisors as well as new domestic systems.

By collectivizing the sample in the manner shown below (Table 8.6), some comparisons with the government-produced failure statistics could then be made. This comparative study was facilitated by comparing the description of the franchise with the 1992-SIC definitions (Central Statistical Office, 1992) and then sampling (with 120 companies or one-fifth of the *UKFD* 'survivor' category) for errors via acceptance sampling techniques. The sub-sample of franchisors' SIC details was derived from a combination of Extel Workstation, Dun & Bradstreet and the ICC companies' databases, which do not detail failed companies. The rationale behind this safety check is that businesses can be deceptively difficult to define, despite the strategic importance of the activity (Abell, 1978; Bucklin, 1963; Murphy and Enis, 1986).

Question 1: Do withdrawal rates differ by strategic group?

The test from the *FWD* directories yielded an average withdrawal rate between 1989 and 1994 of just 18%. Assuming that the population of withdrawn franchises is normally distributed, inferences from these statistics can be made about the population of franchises at large. By employing inductive reasoning to make statements about the average level of withdrawal within the total population of franchises in Britain, it would appear that this would fall somewhere in the range of about 8% to 28% (at 95% confidence). The realized average figure of 18% was problematic because it seemed to contradict all hypotheses concerning the susceptibility of small businesses to failure as well as the comparable franchise studies from the USA. Nonetheless, the exercise suggests that the rate of franchisor withdrawal should be in excess of 18% and possibly greater than 28% given the longer time frame employed in the *UKFD* sample.

The following table (Table 8.7) illustrates the number of entries by broad SIC and relevant sub-categories. Of the total companies (that is, usable sample and 'miscellaneous' category) in the *UKFD* sample, 601 or 36% belonged to surviving franchisor companies, whilst the remainder represented those who had withdrawn. The failure figures indicate substantial variability of survival rates by sector and sub-sector. In turn, this potentially confirms the proposition that the provision of non-sectoral statistics severely limits the extent to which new entrants are able to gauge risk levels. Perhaps unsurprisingly, the sectors with the highest propensities for franchisor failure are those hit hardest by the recession, namely construction, hotels and catering, and retail. In the *UKFD* sample, these sectors collectively accounted for over 40% of franchisor withdrawals during the period. The sector with the highest withdrawal rate, at almost 80%, was the general business category. But are these sectoral variations statistically different?

From the table, and within the constraints of an exploratory study, only two null hypotheses are tested:

1. that there is no relationship between strategic group affiliation and withdrawal rates; and
2. there is no difference among strategic groups illustrating 'low', 'intermediate', and 'high' levels of withdrawals.

Industry	Sub-sector	Survivors	'Failures'	% of failures	Failure rate (%)
Print & publishing	Print & publishing	29	20	3.6	41
Construction	Construction	66	81	14.5	55
Wholesale & retail	Car maintenance	49	34	6.3	42
	Wholesale	13	19	3.4	59
	Retail	67	94	16.8	58
	Non-store retail	40	41	7.3	51
	Sub-total	*169*	*188*	*33.8*	*53*
Hotel & catering	Hotel & catering	39	49	8.8	57
Transport, storage,	Taxi/cabs	5	2	0.2	29
communication	Travel agency	8	6	1.4	50
	Courier	15	7	1.4	35
	Sub-total	*28*	*15*	*3.0*	*39*
Financial intermediation	Financial services	11	10	1.8	48
Real estate, renting,	Real estate	29	25	4.5	46
business	Rental	22	29	5.2	54
	Consultancy	17	7	1.1	27
	Accounting	19	13	2.3	41
	Employment agency	11	14	2.5	56
	Legal	5	2	0.2	29
	Advertising	24	10	1.8	29
	Commercial cleaning	9	5	1.1	36
	General business	12	46	8.2	79
	Sub-total	*148*	*151*	*26.8*	*50*
Health & social work	Health care	9	3	0.5	25
Other services &	Drainage	5	5	1.1	50
community	Personal services	41	22	4.1	37
	Domestic services	15	12	2.1	44
	Driving school	4	1	0.1	20
	Sub-total	*65*	*40*	*7.3*	*39*
'Miscellaneous'	'Miscellaneous'	37	500	40.0	93
Totals:					
With 'Miscellaneous'	All franchisors	601	1,057	100.0	64
No 'Miscellaneous'	Modified franchiors	564	557		50

Table 8.7: Sectoral differences in franchisor withdrawal rates within the UKFD sample

Although possibly simplistic, a Pearson chi-square test was used to prove these hypotheses, where:

Test 1:

H_0:   strategic group affiliation and the number of withdrawals and survivors are independent and unrelated (that is, the probability that a franchisor falls into a given category is the product of the marginal probabilities of the two defining categories, strategic group type and survivor/failure).

H_1:   strategic group affiliation and the number of withdrawals and survivors are dependent variables (that is, there is a relationship between the strategic group and withdrawal variables).

Test 2:

H_0:   the overall number of withdrawal rates is equal, that is: H_0: $\pi_1 = \pi_2 = \pi_3$.
H_1:   not all withdrawal rates are equal, that is: not all H_1: $\pi_1 = \pi_2 = \pi_3$.

Where: π_1 = proportion of strategic groups with lower withdrawal rates.
         π_2 = proportion of strategic groups with intermediate withdrawal rates.
         π_3 = proportion of strategic groups with high withdrawal rates.

Each of the null hypotheses is tested at the 1% and 5% levels of significance. Therefore, by following the general formula for the degrees of freedom: $df = (r - 1)(k - 1)$, where r denotes rows and k = columns, the degrees of freedom for Test 1 is 24. In turn, this means that critical $\chi^2 = 42.98$ when $df = 24$, $\alpha = 0.01$, and critical $\chi^2 = 36.42$, when $df = 24$, $\alpha = 0.05$. For Test 1, the calculated test statistic of 32.94 is not greater than the critical $\alpha = 0.05$ let alone the critical $\alpha = 0.01$ value. Thus, within the limits of the chi-square test, the null hypothesis cannot be rejected, and the hypothesis that the two variables are independent is accepted. To help substantiate this result, a Kruskal-Wallis test was conducted, where the franchise fraternity was divided into its broad SIC codes and the sub-industries were ranked according to their withdrawal rates and according to the number of failures. From the parameters of $df = 8$, $\alpha = 0.01$, $\chi^2 = 15.5$ and where $df = 8$, $\alpha = 0.05$, critical $\chi^2 = 20.09$ the computed K value for the withdrawal rates of 9.18 means that the null hypothesis must be accepted. In order to reject the null hypothesis, α must equal 0.5, which suggests that withdrawal rates may vary by chance. Since the number of failures yielded $K = 7.78$, a similar conclusion is apparent. There is, it seems, no discernible difference in the withdrawal rate between the strategic groups. This situation, however, does not, in itself, provide support for those propounding the use of a single failure statistic. One of the reasons for this situation is that there were no intervening or moderating variables, such as the nature of intra- and inter-strategic group rivalry or a measure accounting for the role of mobility barriers. Without the inclusion of moderating variables, such as rivalry and the product life-cycle stage of franchising in the sampled industries, the answer to the question of whether attrition rates by strategic group is no. In this respect, the test can be compared to those studies which have failed to prove a direct strategic group → performance relationship.

For Test 2, there appear to be three points of interest:

1. Do the various strategic groups experience different withdrawal levels and rates?
2. Are there differences between clusters of sectors showing high, intermediate, and low rates of withdrawal rates?
3. If the answer to the second question is yes, then where does the bias lie?

By finding the percentage share that each strategic group contributes to the total number of franchise withdrawals, the null hypothesis for Test 2a is that all strategic groups have the same level of failures. Since the calculated chi-statistic equals 112.5 the null hypothesis is rejected, but when the withdrawal rates are used as the basis for testing the null hypothesis is accepted. For Test 2b, withdrawal rates were divided into three class intervals of low, intermediate and high by using the following formula to calculate the intervals: [highest rate of failure less lowest rate of failure]/3, to yield intervals of 20%, and critical $\chi^2 = 5.99$ (where $df = 2$, $\alpha = 0.05$), and critical $\chi^2 = 9.21$ (where $df = 2$, $\alpha = 0.01$). Since the calculated statistic of $\chi^2 = 11.9$ exceeds the critical values, the null hypothesis is rejected because the majority of strategic groups appear to have a withdrawal rate of between 40% and 59%. Indeed, a test (Test 2c) to prove the null hypothesis that the intermediate category had double the number of strategic groups was accepted at the 1% level of significance, but was rejected at the 5% level. Given the implication that most franchise strategic groups have realized a withdrawal rate in excess of 40%, it is of concern that the generation of network externalities appears to continue irrespective of the extant rate of withdrawal within strategic groups and whether the clusters can hold the capacity of new franchise businesses.

Question 2: How long do firms franchise?

Of some significance to potential franchisees is the franchisor's survival rate post-launch. Table 8.8 suggests that the average length of time between launch and withdrawal is less than five years and in some instances is less than three years, but requires substantiation through more sophisticated techniques.

From a differing viewpoint, the length of time firms pursue particular strategies is quantifiable and may provide insight concerning the length of the legitimation process in differing industries. The techniques permitting the quantification of such legitimation have parallels in other spheres of life. For example, insurance firms and others assessing risk typically employ actuarial tables to analyze the time interval between two events, such as that between the diagnosis of a disease and death. Within UK franchising, such tables do not necessarily exist and, as such, there is a fundamental question: how long do firms franchise? The solution to this question is complicated by the fact that the withdrawal from franchising does not occur for all franchisors during the time period under observation, and that the actual period may not be the same for all of the sampled firms. That is, not all franchisors withdraw and not every one embarks on franchised expansion at the same time. One statistical technique for analyzing the time interval between launch and withdrawal when the second event does not necessarily happen to all of the sample is a follow-up life table.

In order to devise follow-up life tables for Britain's franchising fraternity, the period of observation (1984–95) is sub-divided into single years and, for each interval, all

Industry/sub-sector	Average no. of years between franchise launch and failure
Print & publishing	4.1
Construction	4.1
Car maintenance	5.5
Wholesale	4.1
Retail	5.1
Non-store retail	4.6
Hotel & catering	5.2
Taxi/cabs	5.0
Travel agency	3.7
Courier	2.5
Financial services	2.6
Real estate	4.8
Rental	3.9
Consultancy	3.8
Accounting	3.5
Employment agency	2.2
Legal	2.5
Advertising	3.5
Commercial cleaning	6.0
General business	4.0
Health care	2.5
Drainage	3.5
Personal services	6.0
Domestic services	3.5
Driving school	4.0

Table 8.8: Survival time for non-survivors

franchisors who have been observed at least that long are used to calculate the probability of withdrawal. For example, assume that information concerning one hundred franchisors was collected, of which thirty withdrew and seventy are still franchising. Two withdrew in 1984 and there were two new entrants. As four franchisors have been observed for one year or less, the remainder have been involved in franchising for one year or more. The probabilities estimated from each of the intervals are then used to estimate the overall probability of withdrawal occurring at different time points, where the population sample for each subsequent time interval (for example, 1989–95) is defined by the function:

$$\Sigma F(t) = [F(t-1) - X(t-1)] \qquad\qquad [1]$$

where $F(t)$ is the number of franchisors in period t; and $X(t-1)$ is the number of franchisor exits from the previous time interval. The life tables were computed for the UK franchise fraternity as a whole as well as for each sub-sector. It should be observed that, for parsimony, only the *UKFD* sample is presented, and the results of these tests are presented in the series of tables below representing the total sample, and those sub-sectors where $n >$ 30. The contents of the life tables are as follows:

Interval start time: the table measures the amount of experience of the franchisors. Thus all firms have less than one year's experience and, as franchisors withdraw, so the level of experience gets progressively lower. Each interval extends from its start time up to the start time of the next interval. Hence, experience is measured in the following time frames: $0 < 1$ years; $1 < 2$ years; $2 < 3$ years, etc.

Number entering this interval: see the formula described above.

Number withdrawn during this interval: the number of franchisors withdrawing from the activity after x years of experience.

Number exposed to risk: this is the number of franchisors with x years experience minus one-half of those withdrawing during year x.

Number of terminal events: the number of franchisor withdrawals.

Proportion of terminal events: an estimate of the probability of franchisor withdrawal occurring in a time interval for a franchisor that has survived to the beginning of that interval. It is calculated as the number of terminal events divided by the number exposed to risk.

Proportion surviving: the number surviving is one minus the proportion of terminal events.

Cumulative proportion surviving at end: an estimate of the probability of surviving to the end of a time period. It is calculated as the result of the proportion surviving this interval and the proportion surviving all previous time periods.

Probability density: is an estimate of the probability per period of time of experiencing a franchisor withdrawal in the time interval.

Hazard rate: is an estimate of the probability per unit of time that a franchisor has survived to the beginning of a time period will experience withdrawal in that interval.

Standard error of the cumulative proportion surviving: an estimate of the variability of the estimate of the cumulative proportion surviving.

Standard error of the probability density: is an estimate of the variability of the estimated probability density.

Median survival time: is the time point at which the value of the cumulative survival function is 0.5 or, rather, the time point by which half of all franchisors are expected to withdraw.

Interval start time	No. entering this interval	No. withd. during interval	No. exposed to risk	No. of terminal events	Propn terminating	Propn surviving	Cumul. propn surviving at end	Prob. density	Hazard rate	SE of cumul. surv.	SE of prob. density	SE of hazard rate
.0	49.0	8.0	45.0	.0	.0000	1.0000	1.0000	.0000	.0000	.0000	.0000	.0000
1.0	41.0	3.0	39.5	4.0	.1013	.8987	.8987	.1013	.1067	.0480	.0480	.0533
2.0	34.0	5.0	31.5	6.0	.1905	.8095	.7275	.1712	.2105	.0739	.0635	.0855
3.0	23.0	2.0	22.0	2.0	.0909	.9091	.6614	.0661	.0952	.0806	.0451	.0673
4.0	19.0	1.0	18.5	2.0	.1081	.8919	.5899	.0715	.1143	.0863	.0485	.0807
5.0	16.0	2.0	15.0	3.0	.2000	.8000	.4719	.1180	.2222	.0921	.0633	.1275
6.0	11.0	1.0	10.5	.0	.0000	1.0000	.4719	.0000	.0000	.0921	.0000	.0000
7.0	10.0	1.0	9.5	.0	.0000	1.0000	.4719	.0000	.0000	.0921	.0000	.0000
8.0	9.0	1.0	8.5	1.0	.1176	.8824	.4164	.0555	.1250	.0966	.0533	.1248
9.0	7.0	.0	7.0	.0	.0000	1.0000	.4164	.0000	.0000	.0966	.0000	.0000
10.0+	7.0	5.0	4.5	2.0	.4444	.5556	.2313	**	**	.1113	**	**

The median survival time for these data is 5.76

Table 8.9: Life table for print and publishing franchisors (UKFD sample)

Interval start time	No. entering this interval	No. withd. during interval	No. exposed to risk	No. of terminal events	Propn terminating	Propn surviving	Cumul. propn surviving at end	Prob. density	Hazard rate	SE of cumul. surv.	SE of prob. density	SE of hazard rate
.0	147.0	12.0	141.0	.0	.0000	1.0000	1.0000	.0000	.0000	.0000	.0000	.0000
1.0	135.0	7.0	131.5	12.0	.0913	.9087	.9087	.0913	.0956	.0251	.0251	.0276
2.0	116.0	5.0	113.5	14.0	.1233	.8767	.7967	.1121	.1315	.0357	.0282	.0351
3.0	97.0	8.0	93.0	10.0	.1075	.8925	.7110	.0857	.1136	.0408	.0259	.0359
4.0	79.0	7.0	75.5	14.0	.1854	.8146	.5792	.1318	.2044	.0460	.0327	.0543
5.0	58.0	5.0	55.5	11.0	.1982	.8018	.4644	.1148	.2200	.0482	.0323	.0659
6.0	42.0	1.0	41.5	9.0	.2169	.7831	.3637	.1007	.2432	.0480	.0315	.0805
7.0	32.0	4.0	30.0	5.0	.1667	.8333	.3030	.0606	.1818	.0471	.0260	.0810
8.0	23.0	1.0	22.5	2.0	.0889	.9111	.2761	.0269	.0930	.0466	.0187	.0657
9.0	20.0	2.0	19.0	1.0	.0526	.9474	.2616	.0145	.0541	.0463	.0144	.0540
10.0+	17.0	14.0	10.0	3.0	.3000	.7000	.1831	**	**	.0499	**	**

The median survival time for these data is 5.69

Table 8.10: Life table for construction franchisors (UKFD sample)

Interval start time	No. entering this interval	No. withd. during interval	No. exposed to risk	No. of terminal events	Propn terminating	Propn surviving	Cumul. propn surviving at end	Prob. density	Hazard rate	SE of cumul. surv.	SE of prob. density	SE of hazard rate
.0	83.0	8.0	79.0	.0	.0000	1.0000	1.0000	.0000	.0000	.0000	.0000	.0000
1.0	75.0	2.0	74.0	6.0	.0811	.9189	.9189	.0811	.0845	.0317	.0317	.0345
2.0	67.0	7.0	63.5	6.0	.0945	.9055	.8321	.0868	.0992	.0443	.0339	.0404
3.0	54.0	3.0	52.5	3.0	.0571	.9429	.7845	.0475	.0588	.0496	.0268	.0339
4.0	48.0	2.0	47.0	5.0	.1064	.8936	.7011	.0835	.1124	.0566	.0357	.0502
5.0	41.0	3.0	39.5	3.0	.0759	.9241	.6478	.0532	.0789	.0601	.0299	.0455
6.0	35.0	4.0	33.0	2.0	.0606	.9394	.6086	.0393	.0625	.0625	.0272	.0442
7.0	29.0	4.0	27.0	.0	.0000	1.0000	.6086	.0000	.0000	.0625	.0000	.0000
8.0	25.0	5.0	22.5	.0	.0000	1.0000	.6086	.0000	.0000	.0625	.0000	.0000
9.0	20.0	4.0	18.0	1.0	.0556	.9444	.5748	.0338	.0571	.0676	.0330	.0571
10.0+	15.0	7.0	11.5	8.0	.6957	.3043	.1749	**	**	.0807	**	**

The median survival time for these data is 10.00+

Table 8.11: Life table for car maintenance franchisors (UKFD sample)

Interval start time	No. entering this interval	No. withd. during interval	No. exposed to risk	No. of terminal events	Propn terminating	Propn surviving	Cumul. propn surviving at end	Prob. density	Hazard rate	SE of cumul. surv.	SE of prob. density	SE of hazard rate
.0	161.0	14.0	154.0	.0	.0000	1.0000	1.0000	.0000	.0000	.0000	.0000	.0000
1.0	147.0	8.0	143.0	4.0	.0280	.9720	.9720	.0280	.0284	.0138	.0138	.0142
2.0	135.0	4.0	133.0	14.0	.1053	.8947	.8697	.1023	.1111	.0287	.0259	.0296
3.0	117.0	5.0	114.5	14.0	.1223	.8777	.7634	.1063	.1302	.0366	.0269	.0347
4.0	98.0	7.0	94.5	16.0	.1693	.8307	.6341	.1292	.1850	.0423	.0301	.0460
5.0	75.0	5.0	72.5	17.0	.2345	.7655	.4854	.1487	.2656	.0452	.0331	.0639
6.0	53.0	2.0	52.0	7.0	.1346	.8654	.4201	.0653	.1443	.0454	.0238	.0544
7.0	44.0	2.0	43.0	4.0	.0930	.9070	.3810	.0391	.0976	.0452	.0191	.0487
8.0	38.0	2.0	37.0	9.0	.2432	.7568	.2883	.0927	.2769	.0435	.0290	.0914
9.0	27.0	3.0	25.5	2.0	.0784	.9216	.2657	.0226	.0816	.0429	.0157	.0577
10.0+	22.0	15.0	14.5	7.0	.4828	.5172	.1374	**	**	.0413	**	**

The median survival time for these data is 5.90

Table 8.12: Life table for retail franchisors (UKFD sample)

Interval start time	No. entering this interval	No. withd. during interval	No. exposed to risk	No. of terminal events	Propn terminating	Propn surviving	Cumul. propn surviving at end	Prob. density	Hazard rate	SE of cumul. surv.	SE of prob. density	SE of hazard rate
.0	81.0	2.0	80.0	.0	.0000	1.0000	1.0000	.0000	.0000	.0000	.0000	.0000
1.0	79.0	11.0	73.5	6.0	.0816	.9184	.9184	.0816	.0851	.0319	.0319	.0347
2.0	62.0	4.0	60.0	8.0	.1333	.8667	.7959	.1224	.1429	.0489	.0405	.0504
3.0	50.0	4.0	48.0	7.0	.1458	.8542	.6798	.1161	.1573	.0582	.0412	.0593
4.0	39.0	2.0	38.0	5.0	.1316	.8684	.5904	.0895	.1408	.0628	.0381	.0628
5.0	32.0	4.0	30.0	8.0	.2667	.7333	.4330	.1574	.3077	.0663	.0505	.1075
6.0	20.0	3.0	18.5	2.0	.1081	.8919	.3861	.0468	.1143	.0669	.0321	.0807
7.0	15.0	2.0	14.0	1.0	.0714	.9286	.3586	.0276	.0741	.0675	.0270	.0740
8.0	12.0	1.0	11.5	.0	.0000	1.0000	.3856	.0000	.0000	.0675	.0000	.0000
9.0	11.0	1.0	10.5	.0	.0000	1.0000	.3586	.0000	.0000	.0675	.0000	.0000
10.0+	10.0	6.0	7.0	4.0	.5714	.4286	.1537	**	**	.0730	**	**

The median survival time for these data is 5.57

Table 8.13: Life table for non-store retail franchisors (UKFD sample)

Interval start time	No. entering this interval	No. withd. during interval	No. exposed to risk	No. of terminal events	Propn terminating	Propn surviving	Cumul. propn surviving at end	Prob. density	Hazard rate	SE of cumul. surv.	SE of prob. density	SE of hazard rate
.0	88.0	3.0	86.5	.0	.0000	1.0000	1.0000	.0000	.0000	.0000	.0000	.0000
1.0	85.0	.0	85.0	7.0	.0824	.9176	.9176	.0824	.0859	.0298	.0298	.0324
2.0	78.0	2.0	77.0	7.0	.0909	.9091	.8342	.0834	.0952	.0405	.0302	.0360
3.0	69.0	6.0	66.0	9.0	.1364	.8636	.7205	.1138	.1463	.0496	.0357	.0486
4.0	54.0	7.0	50.5	3.0	.0594	.9406	.6777	.0428	.0612	.0525	.0241	.0353
5.0	44.0	1.0	43.5	5.0	.1149	.8851	.5998	.0779	.1220	.0568	.0333	.0544
6.0	38.0	2.0	37.0	5.0	.1351	.8649	.5187	.0811	.1449	.0596	.0346	.0646
7.0	31.0	1.0	30.5	2.0	.0656	.9344	.4847	.0340	.0678	.0604	.0236	.0479
8.0	28.0	2.0	27.0	2.0	.0741	.9259	.4488	.0359	.0769	.0610	.0248	.0544
9.0	24.0	3.0	22.5	3.0	.1333	.8667	.3890	.0598	.1429	.0619	.0332	.0823
10.0+	18.0	12.0	12.0	6.0	.5000	.5000	.1945	**	**	.0641	**	**

The median survival time for these data is 7.55

Table 8.14: Life table for hotel and catering franchisors (UKFD sample)

Interval start time	No. entering this interval	No. withd. during interval	No. exposed to risk	No. of terminal events	Propn termin-ating	Propn surviving	Cumul. propn surviving at end	Prob. density	Hazard rate	SE of cumul. surv.	SE of prob. density	SE of hazard rate
.0	54.0	9.0	49.5	.0	.0000	1.0000	1.0000	.0000	.0000	.0000	.0000	.0000
1.0	45.0	3.0	43.5	.0	.0000	1.0000	1.0000	.0000	.0000	.0000	.0000	.0000
2.0	42.0	5.0	39.5	8.0	.2025	.7975	.7975	.2025	.2254	.0639	.0639	.0792
3.0	29.0	1.0	28.5	5.0	.1754	.8246	.6576	.1399	.1923	.0775	.0579	.0856
4.0	23.0	2.0	22.0	3.0	.1364	.8636	.5679	.0897	.1463	.0824	.0493	.0843
5.0	18.0	.0	18.0	2.0	.1111	.8889	.5048	.0631	.1176	.0845	.0431	.0830
6.0	16.0	1.0	15.5	1.0	.0645	.9355	.4722	.0326	.0667	.0851	.0320	.0666
7.0	14.0	.0	14.0	2.0	.1429	.8571	.4048	.0675	.1538	.0853	.0458	.1085
8.0	12.0	3.0	10.5	.0	.0000	1.0000	.4048	.0000	.0000	.0853	.0000	.0000
9.0	9.0	.0	9.0	1.0	.1111	.8889	.3598	.0450	.1176	.0868	.0434	.1174
10.0+	8.0	5.0	5.5	3.0	.5455	.4545	.1635	**	**	.0860	**	**

The median survival time for these data is 6.15

Table 8.15: Life table for real estate franchisors (UKFD sample)

Interval start time	No. entering this interval	No. withd. during interval	No. exposed to risk	No. of terminal events	Propn termin-ating	Propn surviving	Cumul. propn surviving at end	Prob. density	Hazard rate	SE of cumul. surv.	SE of prob. density	SE of hazard rate
.0	51.0	4.0	49.0	.0	.0000	1.0000	1.0000	.0000	.0000	.0000	.0000	.0000
1.0	47.0	4.0	45.0	4.0	.0889	.9111	.9111	.0889	.0930	.0424	.0424	.0465
2.0	39.0	2.0	38.0	6.0	.1579	.8421	.7673	.1439	.1714	.0647	.0543	.0697
3.0	31.0	3.0	29.5	2.0	.0678	.9322	.7152	.0520	.0702	.0700	.0358	.0496
4.0	26.0	2.0	25.0	7.0	.2800	.7200	.5150	.2003	.3256	.0816	.0671	.1214
5.0	17.0	.0	17.0	3.0	.1765	.8235	.4241	.0909	.1935	.0824	.0497	.1112
6.0	14.0	.0	14.0	4.0	.2857	.7143	.3029	.1212	.3333	.0780	.0564	.1643
7.0	10.0	.0	10.0	1.0	.1000	.9000	.2726	.0303	.1053	.0759	.0298	.1051
8.0	9.0	2.0	8.0	1.0	.1250	.8750	.2386	.0341	.1333	.0736	.0333	.1330
9.0	6.0	2.0	5.0	.0	.0000	1.0000	.2386	.0000	.0000	.0736	.0000	.0000
10.0+	4.0	3.0	2.5	1.0	.4000	.6000	.1431	**	**	.0861	**	**

The median survival time for these data is 5.16

Table 8.16: Life table for rental franchisors (UKFD sample)

Interval start time	No. entering this interval	No. withd. during interval	No. exposed to risk	No. of terminal events	Propn termin-ating	Propn surviving	Cumul. propn surviving at end	Prob. density	Hazard rate	SE of cumul. surv.	SE of prob. density	SE of hazard rate
.0	34.0	7.0	30.5	.0	.0000	1.0000	1.0000	.0000	.0000	.0000	.0000	.0000
1.0	27.0	7.0	23.5	3.0	.1277	.8723	.8723	.1277	.1364	.0688	.0688	.0785
2.0	17.0	1.0	16.5	1.0	.0606	.9394	.8195	.0529	.0625	.0825	.0514	.0625
3.0	15.0	2.0	14.0	3.0	.2143	.7857	.6439	.1756	.2400	.1108	.0916	.1376
4.0	10.0	1.0	9.5	.0	.0000	1.0000	.6439	.0000	.0000	.1108	.0000	.0000
5.0	9.0	1.0	8.5	1.0	.1176	.8824	.5681	.0757	.1250	.1209	.0723	.1248
6.0	7.0	.0	7.0	.0	.0000	1.0000	.5681	.0000	.0000	.1209	.0000	.0000
7.0	7.0	1.0	6.5	1.0	.1538	.8462	.4807	.0874	.1667	.1301	.0825	.1661
8.0	5.0	1.0	4.5	.0	.0000	1.0000	.4807	.0000	.0000	.1301	.0000	.0000
9.0	4.0	2.0	3.0	1.0	.3333	.6667	.3205	.1602	.4000	.1570	.1378	.3919
10.0+	1.0	1.0	.5	.0	.0000	1.0000	.3205	**	**	.1570	**	**

The median survival time for these data is 7.78

Table 8.17: Life table for advertising franchisors (UKFD sample)

Interval start time	No. entering this interval	No. withd. during interval	No. exposed to risk	No. of terminal events	Propn termin-ating	Propn surviving	Cumul. propn surviving at end	Prob. density	Hazard rate	SE of cumul. surv.	SE of prob. density	SE of hazard rate
.0	58.0	2.0	57.0	.0	.0000	1.0000	1.0000	.0000	.0000	.0000	.0000	.0000
1.0	56.0	.0	56.0	5.0	.0893	.9107	.9107	.0893	.0935	.0381	.0381	.0418
2.0	51.0	1.0	50.5	9.0	.1782	.8218	.7484	.1623	.1957	.0582	.0495	.0649
3.0	41.0	5.0	38.5	9.0	.2338	.7662	.5735	.1750	.2647	.0678	.0528	.0875
4.0	27.0	1.0	26.5	11.0	.4151	.5849	.3354	.2380	.5238	.0677	.0617	.1524
5.0	15.0	1.0	14.5	4.0	.2759	.7241	.2429	.0925	.3200	.0629	.0436	.1579
6.0	10.0	.0	10.0	5.0	.5000	.5000	.1214	.1214	.6667	.0496	.0496	.2811
7.0	5.0	1.0	4.5	1.0	.2222	.7778	.0945	.0270	.2500	.0454	.0262	.2480
8.0	3.0	.0	3.0	.0	.0000	1.0000	.0945	.0000	.0000	.0454	.0000	.0000
9.0	3.0	1.0	2.5	.0	.0000	1.0000	.0945	.0000	.0000	.0454	.0000	.0000
10.0+	2.0	.0	2.0	2.0	1.0000	.0000	.0000	**	**	.0000	**	**

The median survival time for these data is 4.31

Table 8.18: Life table for general business franchisors (UKFD sample)

Interval start time	No. entering this interval	No. withd. during interval	No. exposed to risk	No. of terminal events	Propn termin-ating	Propn surviving	Cumul. propn surviving at end	Prob. density	Hazard rate	SE of cumul. surv.	SE of prob. density	SE of hazard rate
.0	63.0	4.0	61.0	.0	.0000	1.0000	1.0000	.0000	.0000	.0000	.0000	.0000
1.0	59.0	8.0	55.0	1.0	.0182	.9818	.9818	.0182	.0183	.0180	.0180	.0183
2.0	50.0	7.0	46.5	4.0	.0860	.9140	.8974	.0845	.0899	.0436	.0404	.0449
3.0	39.0	2.0	38.0	3.0	.0789	.9211	.8265	.0708	.0822	.0562	.0394	.0474
4.0	34.0	1.0	33.5	2.0	.0597	.9403	.7772	.0493	.0615	.0627	.0340	.0435
5.0	31.0	2.0	30.0	1.0	.0333	.9667	.7513	.0259	.0339	.0658	.0256	.0339
6.0	28.0	1.0	27.5	5.0	.1818	.8182	.6147	.1366	.2000	.0771	.0565	.0890
7.0	22.0	3.0	20.5	2.0	.0976	.9024	.5547	.0600	.1026	.0804	.0410	.0724
8.0	17.0	4.0	15.0	1.0	.0667	.9333	.5177	.0370	.0690	.0831	.0361	.0689
9.0	12.0	.0	12.0	1.0	.0833	.9167	.4746	.0431	.0870	.0867	.0419	.0869
10.0+	11.0	9.0	6.5	2.0	.3077	.6923	.3286	**	**	.1048	**	**

The median survival time for these data is 9.41

Table 8.19: Life table for personal services franchisors (UKFD sample)

Interval start time	No. entering this interval	No. withd. during interval	No. exposed to risk	No. of terminal events	Propn termin-ating	Propn surviving	Cumul. propn surviving at end	Prob. density	Hazard rate	SE of cumul. surv.	SE of prob. density	SE of hazard rate
.0	1121.0	95.0	1073.5	.0	.0000	1.0000	1.0000	.0000	.0000	.0000	.0000	.0000
1.0	1026.0	79.0	986.5	74.0	.0750	.9250	.9250	.0750	.0779	.0084	.0084	.0091
2.0	873.0	57.0	844.5	107.0	.1267	.8733	.8078	.1172	.1353	.0129	.0106	.0130
3.0	709.0	55.0	681.5	81.0	.1189	.8811	.7118	.0960	.1264	.0151	.0101	.0140
4.0	573.0	44.0	551.0	84.0	.1525	.8475	.6033	.1085	.1650	.0168	.0111	.0179
5.0	445.0	32.0	429.0	71.0	.1655	.8345	.5034	.0998	.1804	.0177	.0112	.0213
6.0	342.0	21.0	331.5	45.0	.1357	.8643	.4351	.0683	.1456	.0180	.0098	.0217
7.0	276.0	25.0	263.5	26.0	.0987	.9013	.3922	.0429	.1038	.0181	.0082	.0203
8.0	225.0	30.0	210.0	17.0	.0810	.9190	.3604	.0317	.0844	.0182	.0075	.0204
9.0	178.0	22.0	167.0	11.0	.0659	.9341	.3367	.0237	.0681	.0184	.0070	.0205
10.0+	145.0	104.0	93.0	41.0	.4409	.5591	.1882	**	**	.0201	**	**

The median survival time for these data is 6.05

Table 8.20: Life table for all franchisors in Britain (UKFD sample) : version 1.

Interval start time	No. entering this interval	No. withd. during interval	No. exposed to risk	No. of terminal events	Propn termin- ating	Propn surviving	Cumul. propn surviving at end	Prob. density	Hazard rate		SE of cumul. surv.	SE of prob. density	SE of hazard rate
.0	1121.0	95.0	1073.5	.0	.0000	1.0000	1.0000	.0000	.0000		.0000	.0000	.0000
1.0	1026.0	79.0	986.5	74.0	.0750	.9250	.9250	.0750	.0779		.0084	.0084	.0091
2.0	873.0	57.0	844.5	107.0	.1267	.8733	.8078	.1172	.1353		.0129	.0106	.0130
3.0	709.0	55.0	681.5	81.0	.1189	.8811	.7118	.0960	.1264		.0151	.0101	.0140
4.0	573.0	44.0	551.0	84.0	.1525	.8475	.6033	.1085	.1650		.0168	.0111	.0179
5.0	445.0	32.0	429.0	71.0	.1655	.8345	.5034	.0998	.1804		.0177	.0112	.0213
6.0	342.0	21.0	331.5	45.0	.1357	.8643	.4351	.0683	.1456		.0180	.0098	.0217
7.0	276.0	25.0	263.5	26.0	.0987	.9013	.3922	.0429	.1038		.0181	.0082	.0203
8.0	225.0	30.0	210.0	17.0	.0810	.9190	.3604	.0317	.0844		.0182	.0075	.0204
9.0	178.0	22.0	167.0	11.0	.0659	.9341	.3367	.0237	.0681		.0184	.0070	.0205
10.0	145.0	24.0	133.0	12.0	.0902	.9098	.3063	.0304	.0945		.0187	.0085	.0272
11.0	109.0	21.0	98.5	4.0	.0406	.9594	.2939	.0124	.0415		.0189	.0061	.0207
12.0	84.0	12.0	78.0	2.0	.0256	.9744	.2863	.0075	.0260		.0192	.0053	.0184
13.0	70.0	4.0	68.0	5.0	.0735	.9265	.2653	.0211	.0763		.0199	.0092	.0341
14.0	61.0	9.0	56.5	4.0	.0708	.9292	.2465	.0188	.0734		.0206	.0092	.0367
15.0	48.0	3.0	46.5	3.0	.0645	.9355	.2306	.0159	.0667		.0212	.0090	.0385
16.0	42.0	5.0	39.5	1.0	.0253	.9747	.2247	.0058	.0256		.0215	.0058	.0256
17.0	36.0	2.0	35.0	1.0	.0286	.9714	.2183	.0064	.0290		.0218	.0064	.0290
18.0	33.0	3.0	31.5	.0	.0000	1.0000	.2183	.0000	.0000		.0218	.0000	.0000
19.0	30.0	2.0	29.0	2.0	.0690	.9310	.2033	.0151	.0714		.0228	.0104	.0505
20.0+	26.0	19.0	16.5	7.0	.4242	.5758	.1170	**	**		.0280	**	**

The median survival time for these data is 6.05

Table 8.21: Life table for all franchisors in Britain (UKFD sample) : version 2.

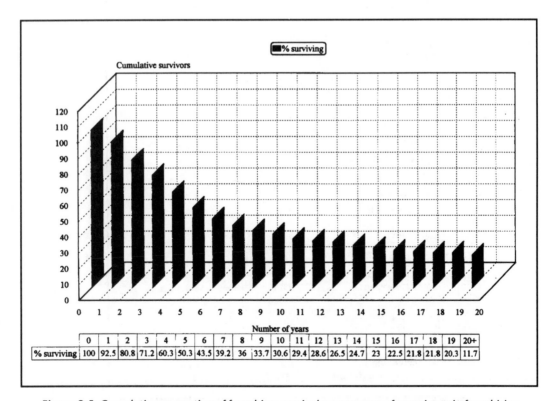

Figure 8.5: Cumulative proportion of franchisor survival versus years of experience in franchising

By only referring to the two tables depicting the entire franchise fraternity for ten and less than twenty years of experience, it is apparent that the majority of terminal events occur within the first four years of experience. These figures are consistent with those produced by Shane (1996b):

> Because over half of new franchisors cease to franchise during the first four years, potential franchisees should be very wary of buying into systems that have not yet reached their fourth anniversary.

Indicative of this situation is that the median survival time is only six years. It is significant that, in Britain, only about 31% of franchisors have up to ten years experience and

Industry/sub-sector	Median years	Cumulative experience (%)
Print & publishing	5.76	41.64
Construction	5.69	26.16
Car maintenance	10.00+	57.48
Wholesale	4.58	15.47
Retail	5.9	26.57
Non-store retail	5.57	35.86
Hotel & catering	7.55	38.90
Taxi/cabs	10.00+	50.00
Travel agency	6.79	22.62
Courier	10.00+	60.99
Financial services	4.54	33.33
Real estate	6.15	35.98
Rental	5.16	23.86
Consultancy	10.00+	56.26
Accounting	4.98	31.00
Employment agency	3.28	32.95
Legal	3.75	40.00
Advertising	7.78	32.05
Commercial cleaning	10.00+	55.79
General business	4.31	9.45
Health care	6.64	36.67
Drainage	7.63	44.44
Personal services	9.41	47.46
Domestic services	9.04	33.8
Driving school	10.00+	75.00
All franchisors	6.05	33.67
Mean	6.98	38.54
Standard deviation	2.22	14.70
Coefficient of variation	0.32	0.38

Table 8.22: Summary of median values and cumulative experience (≥9 years)

about 20% have up to nineteen years of experience in the activity. Such a finding is potentially at odds with conventional franchise wisdom: a recurrent theme throughout most of the franchise press is that franchisees should, when evaluating which system (if any) to join, establish whether the product or service has a long-term future. These statistics infer that some differentiation is perhaps necessary. Whilst the product/service may have a long-term future, the franchisor may not.

Table 8.22 summarizes the results for the median and cumulative proportion with more than nine years experience in franchising by industry. It is evident that there are some sectoral differences in the rate at which franchisors withdraw from the activity. The time point by which half of all franchisors are expected to withdraw is about seven years which, when one considers that the average franchisee contract is five years, suggests that some franchisors appear not to franchise after one contract duration. The table also shows that, on average, only about 39% of franchisors have at least nine years experience, with the wholesaler, 'general' business, travel agency, construction, and retailers showing that less than 30% have the same degree of experience in franchising. Some of these differences need to be treated with some care because not all of the industries sampled are at the same stage of development in terms of the extent of franchise penetration. This apparent anomaly, of course, raises another question, which is a subject for additional research: at what stage does the franchise fraternity within a particular industry setting reach its carrying capacity?

Additional care is required in interpreting the life tables because there is an underlying assumption in the implicit calculations that survival experience does not change during the course of the study. This is an assumption which is not necessarily valid. For example, if the economic conditions and the level of market illiberality changes during the observation period, there may be little logic in presenting all of the cases in a single life table. In using a life table, it is assumed that a franchisor who launches a franchise in year t will behave in the same way as a firm embarking on franchised expansion in year $t - 1$. It is also necessary to assume that franchisors which do not withdraw during the period of observation ('censored' cases) do not differ from those that are not censored. These could, however, be critical issues. For example, the differences between censored and uncensored cases in the franchising industry may be a function of the following variables:

1. experience prior to franchising;
2. ownership pattern;
3. growth pattern;
4. franchise fee.

Each of these variables needs to be accounted for separately in order to moderate the inferences made from the life tables.

Question 3: Do failed franchisors live fast and die young?

A key point of difference between the franchisor attrition analysis conducted by Lafontaine and Shaw (1996b) and that by Shane (1996) is the issue of age. Whereas Shane found that newer companies, that is those less than four years old, were more subject to withdrawing from franchising, Lafontaine and Shaw contend that attrition rates are not markedly different. Which conclusion is more appropriate for the UK franchise fraternity? From the *UKFD* sample, it appears that there is more support for Shane's findings, rather than those of Lafontaine and Shaw, but this requires some statistical verification. Table 8.23 displays the average (or $\bar{x}$) length of time between franchisor inception and the launch of their franchise for the *UKFD* sample. It is interesting to observe that those sectors with high (that is, over 50%) attrition rates are also those with generally short time periods between inception and franchise launch. Although there are exceptions, such as accountancy and wholesaling, such a finding must be moderated by the lack of a variable representing the quality of business experience prior to franchising and the high variability (that is, high standard deviations – or σ) within each sample. This variability seems to suggest that some of the failing firms within those categories with high standard deviations tend to be either established firms (who are unable to adapt to franchised based expansion or, at least, not committed to it) or young businesses. *Primae facie*, by comparing the industry/sector average with the standard deviation for each variable, it appears that those franchisors prone to withdrawal tend to be those with limited experience prior to launching their franchise. In some instances, however, this difference is marginal and, in others, it is reversed. This latter finding suggests that some franchisors are perhaps unable to negate the first mover advantages of the sectoral pioneers. Are these findings statistically valid?

Statistically, there are two ways of helping to establish the relationship between age and propensity to survive: the survival function, and the hazard function. Both of these are derived from the Cox regression model. From the survival function – or the proportion of franchisors 'surviving' at a particular point in time – it is possible to calculate the cumulative survival function for franchises of different ages. To examine the effects of age upon survival, a Cox regression is calculated whereby survival time is the dependent variable and the age of the firm when the franchise is launched as the covariate:

$$S_t = [S_{0(t)}]^{e\,(\beta x)} \qquad\qquad [2]$$

where, $S_{0(t)}$ is the baseline survival function calculated in the life tables; e is the exponent for the regression beta (β) multiplied by the age of the franchisor (x). Table 8.24 contains the statistic for the age variable when it is entered into the Cox regression model. It shows that the coefficient for age is -0.0156, with an observed significance level of 0.0006, which means that it is possible to reject the null hypothesis that population value of the coefficient is zero. Given that the exponent to which the baseline survival curve is raised is less than one, the resulting survival times are greater than those of the baseline. This situation is also apparent from the column labelled 'Exp.(β)', which indicates the percentage change in the survival rate for a unit increase in the age covariate. From the table, Exp.(β) is 0.98, and this means that the probability of survival is greater for older firms than younger ones. The 95% confidence intervals for e^β are presented in the final two columns. Since the interval does not include the value of one, it is possible to reject the null hypothesis that experience prior to franchising is not related to survival. Thus, the longer the experience of the firm prior to franchising, the better the prospects for survival. As a consequence, the results of the Cox regression test find support for Shane's (1996) contention rather than those made by Lafontaine and Shaw (1996b).

The corollary of the survival rate is the hazard rate – or death rate at time *t*, which tells us how likely the experience of withdrawal is given that it survived to that time. The hazard function, via the Cox regression model, is not a probability but a death rate per unit of time, so it need not be less than one and is factored into two component pieces.

| Industry/sub-sector | Inception versus franchising | | | | | |
| | All sample | | | Non-survivors | | |
	$\bar{x}$	σ	Coefficient of variation	$\bar{x}$	σ	Coefficient of variation
Print & publishing	2.9	5.2	1.79	1.3	1.6	1.23
Construction	4.2	8.9	2.12	3.2	7.0	2.19
Car maintenance	5.5	15.4	2.80	2.7	4.9	1.81
Wholesale	5.4	17.6	3.26	7.0	22.1	3.16
Retail	8.1	22.2	2.74	5.9	13.9	2.36
Non-store retail	6.7	18.1	2.70	5.6	12.5	2.23
Hotel & catering	11.1	34	3.06	5.1	12.7	2.49
Taxi/cabs	6.6	4.8	0.73	2.6	2.0	1.30
Travel agency	10.5	17.0	1.62	10.9	12.6	1.16
Courier	3.5	5.4	1.54	3.6	5.8	1.61
Financial services	10.9	31.8	2.92	4.4	4.8	1.09
Real estate	5.2	8.2	1.58	2.1	3.6	1.71
Rental	3.8	7.5	1.97	2.0	3.2	1.60
Consultancy	10.5	31.9	3.04	2.3	3.3	1.43
Accounting	3.7	5.5	1.49	4.2	6.6	1.57
Employment agency	5.7	12.6	2.21	2.2	1.7	0.77
Legal	1.1	0.8	0.73	1.0	0.0	0.00
Advertising	2.1	3.3	1.57	0.7	0.6	0.86
Commercial cleaning	3.4	5.5	1.62	3.0	2.1	0.70
General business	2.9	5.6	1.93	3.0	6.0	2.00
Health care	2.2	2.3	1.05	2.0	1.4	0.70
Drainage	2.2	4.0	1.82	4.4	4.8	1.09
Personal services	5.1	8.2	1.61	4.1	4.7	1.15
Domestic services	1.8	1.6	0.89	1.4	1.5	1.07
Driving school	15.4	28.8	1.87	2.0	0.0	0.00

Table 8.23: Characteristics of non-surviving franchisors

| Variables in the equation | | | | | | | | 95% CI for Exp. (ß) | |
Variable	ß	S.E.	Wald	df	Sig.	R	Exp.(ß)	Lower	Upper
AGE	−0.0156	0.0045	11.8824	1	0.0006	−0.0378	0.9845	0.9758	0.9933
Overall Chi-square:		12.277		1	0.0005				

Table 8.24: Cox regression statistics for age prior to franchising

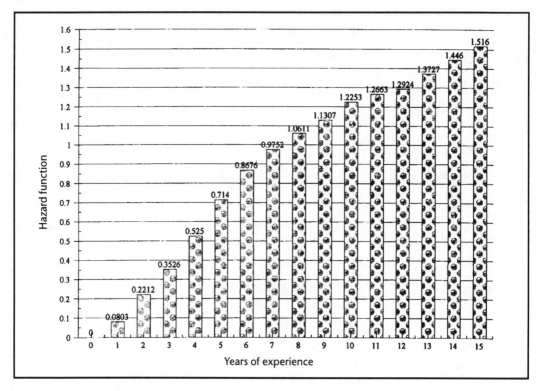

Figure 8.6: The baseline cumulative hazard function for franchisors

The base line hazard $H_{O(t)}$ (the baseline cumulative hazard function, without modifying for age, for the sampled franchisors is illustrated in the schematic below) depends on time, while the dependent variable p (or $e^{[\beta^*age]}$) depends only on the values of the covariates and the regression coefficients. Rather than raising the baseline function to the power of beta multiplied by age, the baseline hazard is multiplied by $e^{[\beta^*age]}$. That is,

$$H_t = [H_{O(t)}]e^{(\beta x)} \qquad [3]$$

Thus, it appears that the older the firm prior to franchising, the lower the hazard. This result, however, requires further substantiation because one of the assumptions within the Cox regression model, is that for any two observations, the ratio of the estimated hazard across time is constant. This assumption can be misleading because there are situations in which such an assumption is not realistic (that is, the hazard may not be proportional). Indeed, Shane's (1996b) observation that young franchisor companies are more prone to withdrawal means that there is an experience effect: the hazards of franchising may be less pronounced for older businesses. It is, therefore, quite possible that the hazard functions of young and older firms embarking on franchised expansion are not related by a constant multiplier. In testing for the appropriateness of a constant multiplier, two inter-related approaches were adopted: a log-linear analysis and the inclusion of a time dependent variable. Initially, the sample was dichotomized by assigning a binary variable to indicate the level of experience prior to embarking on franchising. In accordance with prior research (such as Mendelsohn and Acheson, 1989; Sherman, 1993), zero referred to more than four years experience and one otherwise. This variable was then matched against whether the franchisor was a survivor or not (where one equated to the presence of the withdrawal event and zero otherwise) to test whether the levels of pre-franchising activity and survival independent from one another. A Pearson chi-square statistic of 12.8 and a very small (less than 0.0005) observed significance level associated with that chi-square of 0.0003 serves to reject the independence model. As the goodness-of-fit test served to reject the hypothesis that the variables are independent, a log-linear model was used to explore the type of relationship between experience prior to franchising and survival, via functions such as the following:

$$\ln{(n)} = \mu + \lambda \left(\begin{array}{c} survival \\ yes \end{array} \right) + \lambda \left(\begin{array}{c} experience \\ yes \end{array} \right) + \lambda \left(\begin{array}{c} survival \\ yes \end{array} \right) \left(\begin{array}{c} experience \\ yes \end{array} \right)$$

in which μ is the average of the logs of the frequencies in the matrix, and the λ parameters represent the increments/decrements from μ for particular values of the rows and columns variables. Thus, the term

$$\lambda \left(\begin{array}{c} survival \\ yes \end{array} \right)$$

indicates the effect of being in the survivor category, and the term

$$\lambda \left(\begin{array}{c} survival \\ yes \end{array} \right) \left(\begin{array}{c} experience \\ yes \end{array} \right)$$

represents the interaction of being a survivor and having experience of four years or more prior to franchising. These interaction parameters indicate the amount of difference between the sums of the effects taken individually or collectively. They represent the interference associated with combinations of the variables. Hence, if less than four years of experience prior to franchising results in low levels of survival, the number of cases in the non-survivor and less than four years experience cell would be higher than the number expected only on the frequency of non-survivors and the frequency of inexperienced businesses alone. This excess is represented by a positive value for

$$\lambda \left(\begin{array}{c} survival \\ no \end{array} \right) \left(\begin{array}{c} experience \\ no \end{array} \right)$$

If experience of less than four years increases the propensity for survival, the value will be negative. If experience neither increases nor decreases the survival, the interaction parameter is zero (thus, the null hypothesis is $\lambda = 0$). The results, presented below, show that there is a positive interaction parameter between inexperience and non-survival. In this instance, therefore, there appears to be some support for Shane's (1996b) contention in the context of the British franchise fraternity because if experience decreased survival rates, the parameter would be negative. The test of the null hypothesis is based on the z-value, in which those values greater than 1.96 in absolute value are significant at the 0.05 level; the 95% confidence interval for

$$\lambda \begin{pmatrix} survival \\ no \end{pmatrix} \begin{pmatrix} experience \\ no \end{pmatrix}$$

is within the lower limit of 0.532 and the upper limit of 0.184.

Estimates for λ	Coefficient	Standard error	Z-Value	Lower 95% CI	Upper 95% CI
Experience*Survival	0.119	0.033	3.55	0.532	0.184
Experience	−0.464	0.033	−13.91	−0.530	−0.399
Survival	0.575	0.033	1.72	−0.008	0.123

Table 8.25: Estimates for λ for survival and experience prior to franchising

As the level of hazard appears to be non-proportional, a further test was conducted in which a cumulative hazard plot for the two sub-sets of experience was constructed to see if the baseline hazard functions for the two sub-samples were parallel: if they are, then the proportional hazard assumption is valid. Figure 8.7 illustrates that the hazard for firms with less than four years of experience is higher than that for more experienced concerns. In turn, this situation suggests that the proportional hazard function may not be appropriate.

As the main question of interest is whether survival differs according to the time prior to embarking on franchising, a model was developed that incorporated non-proportional hazards over time through a time dependent covariate:

$$H_t = [H_{0(t)}]e^{(\beta 1 * \text{experience}) + (\beta 2 * \text{experience} * \text{t\_cov}\_)} \qquad [4]$$

Where, the hazard function was calculated for the non-surviving franchisors by using a categorical experience variable (where zero signified a pre-franchise age of more than four years, and one otherwise) and then for experience with different sub-sets with differing levels of years of franchising activity. Table 8.27 shows the result of fitting the model with the age prior to franchising variable against age with a series of time dependent variables (in which t_cov_>4 years; >5 years; >6 years; and >7 years). From the indicator variable coefficients and their significance levels, it is evident that there is an experience effect and that it is not constant over time. As the beta coefficient for experience by time is positive in some instances, it suggests that embarking on franchising with

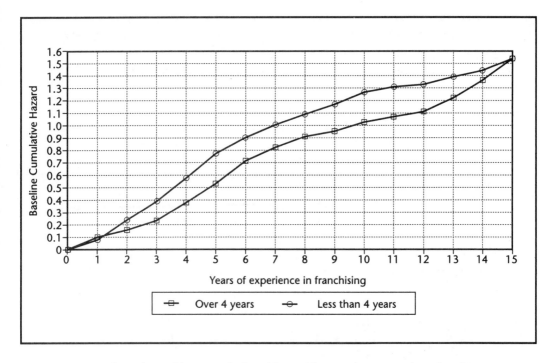

Figure 8.7: *Cumulative hazard functions for franchisors with ≥4 and >4 years of pre-franchise experience*

more than four years experience is better during the early years but its superiority decreases over time. For example, failed franchisors with more than four years of experience and over four years activity have a beta coefficient of 0.19 whereas it is –0.27 otherwise. Comparing the values in column labelled Exp.(β) with the positive beta variable suggests that the estimated risk of failure after four years of franchising is 1.2 times greater for inexperienced franchisors, compared to a franchisor with more experience. Not surprisingly, the risk of failure for inexperienced franchisors relative to their more experienced counterparts increases to a threshold of five years in franchising, and then falls. In this sense, in finding the middle ground, these results corroborate both Shane and Lafontaine and Shaw and yet support neither of them.

The above paragraphs have sought to provide corroborating evidence for either side of the 'age prior to franchising → survival' debate, and thereby help to address the gap left by extant researchers in the franchisor attrition vein. The results suggest that franchisors of less than four years old are more prone to failure than those over that threshold, but there also appears to be a learning effect. Accordingly, some support has been generated for both sides of the debate and, yet, neither one. By moderating for the effects of the quantity of experience (not quality), the test has illustrated that relatively inexperienced firms are more prone to failure in the early period and that this level fell to be in parallel with more mature concerns. This situation possibly points to the ability of younger firms to learn and adopt policies which prolong their survival, as well as perhaps a willingness to recruit and sign even poorly qualified franchisees. It also perhaps points to the failure of older companies which embark on franchising to realize administrative inefficiencies, possibly deriving from not being able to recruit sufficient franchisees to make the

Variable	β	S.E.	Wald	df	Sig.	R	Exp.(β)	Overall χ^2
Experience	−0.2714	0.0669	16.4325	1	0.0001	−0.456	0.7623	18.038
t_cov_>4	0.1886	0.1011	3.4813	1	0.0621	0.0146	1.2075	(Sig. = 0.0001)
Experience	−0.2511	0.0598	17.6274	1	0.000	−0.0475	0.7780	18.209
t_cov_>5	0.2091	0.1096	3.6380	1	0.565	0.0154	1.2325	(Sig. = 0.0001)
Experience	−0.2162	0.0555	15.1453	1	0.0001	−0.0436	0.8056	15.988
t_cov_>6	0.1274	0.1270	1.0072	1	0.3156	0.0000	1.1359	(Sig. = 0.0003)
Experience	−0.2067	0.0537	14.8226	1	0.0001	−0.0430	0.8132	15.588
t_cov_>6	0.106	0.1457	0.5297	1	0.4667	0.0000	1.1119	(Sig. = 0.0004)

Table 8.26: Hazard statistics for time dependent covariates by age prior to franchising

strategy viable or because their recruitment policies may have been too stringent. Such firms may have decided to maintain the few franchisees they had, but also to nullify the detrimental effects of net cash-outflows via withdrawal.

As with prior studies, there are limitations to the findings. The main one is that differing time thresholds have not been tested to provide a sensitivity analysis, or to suggest an optimal relationship between age prior to franchising and the tendency for franchisor survival. The second is that the research pertains to the British franchise fraternity which, therefore, limits its possible generalizability to other countries where franchising is in a lesser or greater state of maturation. Furthermore, the research lacks measures for the quality of business experience, the managerial competencies, and the financial performance prior to embarking on franchising. Given the importance of understanding the rationale behind franchisor withdrawal and sustaining the momentum of the sense of realism permeating franchising's troubled dream world (Burck, 1970), these issues must be accounted for in subsequent research.

Question 4: Do the patterns and rate of growth differ for failures?

The above analysis indicates that it is the younger franchisors which are more subject to withdrawal than those with more experience. Is this tendency just a function of a lack of business experience or are there other factors? Arguably, of some importance is the rate of expansion because this affects the degree of support and cohesion within the organizational structure. In franchising, the growth rate is influenced by the attractiveness of the franchise offer to potential franchisees, and the maintenance of franchisee motivation in the longer term. Survival, therefore, requires the strategic management of expansion. Steinberg (1995), for example, shows (anecdotally) that franchisor bankruptcy occurs via acquiring or selling units rapidly rather than more cautiously. The franchisors force expansion before they have the experience, managerial resource, expertise, time, culture and are ready to cope with franchisees and so a form of managerial decay quickly sets in (which may contribute to franchisee failure). For those expanding too quickly, a vicious downward spiral is apparent whereby the franchisors become dependent on the sale of new franchises to generate cash flow, but do not have the resources to control, monitor and co-ordinate the units. Standards begin to slip and opportunism is widespread, brand credibility is lost and, unless redressed, under-performance ensues. Sherman (1993) summarizes this position by noting that franchisors who develop strategic plans that focus on the quantity of franchisees and expansion, rather than on the quality of franchisees and training, are surely headed for disaster.

The extent to which this latter behaviour is evident in Britain appears, *primae facie*, to be limited (see Table 8.27). For example, between the date of inception and

Industry/Sub-sector	No. of franchisee-operated				No. of company-owned stores			
	All sample		Non-survivors		All sample		Non-survivors	
	$\bar{x}$	σ	$\bar{x}$	σ	$\bar{x}$	σ	$\bar{x}$	σ
Print & publishing	29.3	48.3	19.4	24.3	2.3	4.4	2.1	2.1
Construction	11.6	13.0	11.7	12.4	1.3	1.3	1.3	0.9
Car maintenance	34.9	55.3	11.9	13.5	22.2	133	4.6	12.3
Wholesale	31.4	106	37.2	132.8	2.7	4.0	2.4	3.5
Retail	25.8	69.4	17.6	44.2	22.0	57.7	19.7	50.1
Non-store retail	90.1	307	24.3	47.0	40.7	174	9.6	26.3
Hotel & catering	69.3	288	7.4	13.0	83.9	389	8.6	12.7
Taxi-cabs	67.7	32.0	15.6	1.5	32.9	2.7	4.7	2.0
Travel agency	30.6	27.4	21.3	26.0	16.6	43.9	7.4	14.6
Courier	60.8	71.1	27.4	25.9	12.7	5.4	11.0	17.6
Financial services	53.5	121	5.3	5.3	25.0	99.6	2.3	1.6
Real estate	18.4	27.4	19.0	23.1	14.5	54.6	16.4	66.2
Rental	33.1	62.4	17.2	36.5	10.3	27.6	5.7	12.7
Consultancy	22.6	28.8	8.5	8.3	1.3	1.3	1.3	0.9
Accounting	20.5	19.4	17.1	11.9	2.1	3.2	1.9	2.7
Employment agency	12.9	20.3	6.7	12.6	10.7	21.0	8.6	19.0
Legal	64.3	34.2	44.0	43.0	0.4	0.5	0.5	0.5
Advertising	14.7	16.2	13.4	11.1	6.5	25.0	5.4	11.6
Comm. cleaning	47.0	82.3	20.8	9.2	1.8	2.2	1.0	0.0
General business	12.2	18.6	10.6	17.3	2.8	6.6	3.1	7.3
Health care	30.1	43.0	1.5	0.9	3.7	6.1	2.0	4.3
Drainage	38.4	35.9	19.8	26.2	1.5	2.0	1.4	2.3
Personal services	29.9	43.8	21.7	27.4	10.0	30.2	8.5	15.6
Domestic services	55.4	91.5	13.8	11.8	2.3	3.4	3.3	4.5
Driving school	411	795	15.0	0.0	42.8	53.2	1.0	0.0

Table 8.27: Store ownership patterns by all sample and non-survivors

withdrawal from franchising, the majority of failed franchisors opened fewer than three units a year. Despite such low rates of expansion, however, Steinberg's process may still have been present since the failed franchisors may not have had the culture and/or capability in the first instance to cope with franchise-based expansion. On the other hand, the decision to withdraw from the activity may have derived from the apparent lack of interest by potential franchisees on what was on offer. Such a situation is perhaps indicative of the lack of ability to cope with organizational development, the lack of brand power, and package of benefits compared to their larger counterparts and higher-priced franchise-package.

The high standard deviations evident within some markets (such as driving schools and hotel and catering) point to a concentrated/ing franchise market. These companies have reached critical mass and have substantial experience in franchise-based expansion. Given this situation, the larger franchisors seem to have a steady queue of potential investors from which they can pick and choose, and would require new entrants to surmount substantial mobility barriers. By contrast, the smaller franchisors tend not to have such liberty, and possibly price their franchise packages in order to realize the highest contributions to meeting the fixed costs of franchised-expansion; it is these firms that are most likely to suffer from growing pains. Indicative of such pains, the confidence intervals suggest that non-surviving franchisors had at least 12 units ($\alpha = 0.01$). In addition Table 8.28 shows that the non-surviving franchisors had, on the whole, a lower ratio of company-owned outlets to franchisee-operated ones. The all-industry average was a total of eighty-eight outlets. Non-surviving franchisors operated, on average, twenty-three outlets. Given that non-surviving franchisors had, on average, a lower number of outlets, it points to a lower rate of expansion. This slow rate of growth may, in itself, partially explain the decision to withdraw. Given the expectations of growth compared to its reality, some franchisors may have become disillusioned and withdrawn. Nonetheless, it is equally evident that many franchisors did not seek to replace the slow pace of franchised expansion with their own units. On average, there was a dearth of company-owned units as is evident from the table.

The different characteristics of franchisor attrition also provide some *a priori* support for Carney and Gedajlovic's (1991) typology of franchisors (see Chapter 6). Possibly due to the managerial requirements to support a rapidly expanding network, Gerney and Gedajlovic hypothesize that the survival rate of rapid growers may be quite low. As such systems expand, however, they receive the benefits of increased cash flows and broader brand dissemination. Unsuccessful franchisors illustrate the highest rate of failure due to inherent weaknesses in their business concepts. These results suggest some support for Carney and Gedajlovic's untested and uncorroborated assertion that the unsuccessful group contains firms which will probably fail. Mature franchisors and conservative expensive categories exhibit the lowest rate of failure. Franchise converts, typically represented by large firms, entering into franchising to improve responsiveness, flexibility and to lower labour costs, also illustrate comparatively high rates of failure. Failure at franchising their businesses within this latter category may be because of a lack of organizational culture and support orientated toward franchising, and one which leans more toward controlled company-owned expansion.

Are the points made describing the differences between the entire sample and the failed franchisors statistically valid? Table 8.29 presents the results of a two-way analysis of variance (*ANOVA*) procedure to test the null hypotheses that:

Industry/Sub-sector	All franchisors		Non-survivors	
	Outlets	Ratio	Outlets	Ratio
Print & publishing	31.6	12.7	21.5	9.2
Construction	12.9	8.9	13.0	9.0
Car maintenance	57.1	1.6	16.5	2.6
Wholesale	34.1	11.6	39.5	15.5
Retail	47.8	1.2	37.3	0.9
Non-store retail	130.8	2.2	33.9	2.5
Hotel & catering	153.2	0.8	16.0	0.9
Taxi-cabs	100.6	2.1	20.3	3.3
Travel agency	47.2	1.8	28.7	2.9
Courier	73.5	4.8	38.4	2.5
Financial services	78.5	2.1	7.6	2.3
Real estate	32.9	1.3	35.4	1.2
Rental	43.4	3.2	22.9	3.0
Consultancy	23.9	17.4	9.8	6.5
Accounting	22.6	9.8	19.0	9.0
Employment agency	23.6	1.2	15.3	0.8
Legal	64.7	160.8	44.5	88.0
Advertising	21.2	2.3	18.8	2.5
Comm. cleaning	48.8	26.1	21.8	20.8
General business	15.0	4.4	13.7	3.4
Health care	33.8	8.3	3.5	0.8
Drainage	39.9	25.6	21.2	14.1
Personal services	39.9	3.0	30.2	2.6
Domestic services	57.7	24.1	17.1	4.2
Driving schools	453.8	9.6	16.0	15.0
All industry average	67.5	13.8	22.5	8.9
Standard deviation	87.5	31.6	10.8	17.4
Lower level confidence int. ($\alpha = 0.05$)	31.5	0.84	18.0	1.8
Upper level confidence int. ($\alpha = 0.05$)	103.6	26.9	26.9	16.1
Lower level confidence int. ($\alpha = 0.01$)	18.6	–3.8	16.4	–0.8
Upper level confidence int. ($\alpha = 0.01$)	116.5	31.5	28.5	18.6

'Outlets' refers to average total (i.e. franchised and company-owned) units.
'Ratio' refers to the ratio of franchised outlets to company-owned outlets.

Table 8.28: System growth rates of non-survivors

1. there is no difference between the average number of franchisee-operated stores between the total sample and the failed group, and there are no differences by industry (if there are differences, these will be due to the impact of the non-survivors);

2) there is no difference between the average number of company-operated stores between the total sample and the failed group, and there are no differences by industry.

Source of variation	Sum of squares	Degree of freedom	Mean square	P-value	F-ratio
Among samples					
(N and failed grouping)	15,746.0	1	15,746	0.0316	1.017
Among industries	73,778.2	24	3,074	0.0483	5.21
Sampling error	72,509.6	24	3,021.2		
Total	162,033.8	49			

Table 8.29: Two-way ANOVA table for analysis of franchisee-owned stores by industry sector

Using the 5% level of significance (that is, $\alpha = 0.05$), the required F-ratio for the rejection of the first hypothesis (that there is no difference in the average number of franchisee-operated stores and the total sample) is $F_{crit} = 4.26$; for the second hypothesis, that there are no differences in the average number of franchisee-operated stores by industry, $F_{crit} = 1.98$. Thus, the calculated F-ratio for the differences between the failed grouping and the total sample, in the above table, is in the region of rejection of the null hypothesis. There are significant differences in the average franchisee-operated stores for the failed grouping and the total sample. By contrast, the F-ratio for the industry effects falls within the region of acceptance, which suggests that there are no significant differences in the number of franchisee-operated stores by industry. When the level of significance is relaxed to let $\alpha = 0.10$, these results were supported. The first hypothesis falls into the region of rejection ($F = 5.20$; $F_{crit} = 2.92$); and the second hypothesis is in the region of acceptance ($F_{crit} = 1.70$; $F = 1.01$).

The same methodology was also used to test whether there are any differences in the average number of company-owned and operated stores. The results (shown in Table 8.30) indicate that, by using the 5% level of significance parameter, that there are significant differences ($F_{crit} = 4.25$; $F = 7.00$) between the failed grouping and the total sample. As in the test for franchisee-operated stores, the F-ratio for the industry effects falls within the region of acceptance, which points to no significant differences in the number of company-operated stores by industry. When the level of significance is eased to let $\alpha = 0.10$, these results were supported. The first hypothesis falls in the region of rejection ($F = 7.00$; $F_{crit} = 2.92$), and the second hypothesis is in the region of acceptance ($F_{crit} = 1.70$; $F = 1.36$).

Source of variation	Sum of squares	Degrees of freedom	Mean square	P-value	F-ratio
Among samples					
(N and failed grouping)	1,144.3	1	1,144.3	0.014	7.00
Among industries	5,371.3	24	223.8	0.223	1.37
Sampling error	3,923.2	24	163.5		
Total	10,438.8	49			

Table 8.30: Two-way ANOVA table for analysis of co-owned stores by industry sector

Question 5: Are the levels of franchise fees different for failed franchisors?

Extant franchise research seems to suggest that franchise fees reflect the brand capital of the franchisor and the technological components comprising the business (Lafontaine and Shaw, 1996). Some argue that the fees are also a method of signalling the franchise's quality, and as such it may be expected that not only are there statistically significant differences between non-surviving franchisors but there are substantial variations by industry setting. Using the two-way *ANOVA* method, the table below indicates that where $\alpha = 0.05$, there are substantial difference by franchise fees by industry but there are less statistically different franchise fees between the total sample and those franchisors which withdrew.

	Franchise fee (£)			
Industry/Sub-sector	**All samples**		**Non-survivors**	
	$\overline{\times}$	$\mho$	$\overline{\times}$	$\mho$
Print & publishing	31,564	42,894	23,645	31,337
Construction	15,867	19,156	18,292	23,900
Car maintenance	24,122	43,186	17,722	13,354
Wholesale	29,698	46,517	16,403	12,958
Retail	56,126	66,868	59,963	75,215
Non-store retail	13,467	19,601	17,713	26,299
Hotel & catering	98,758	171,729	108,320	209,388
Taxi-cabs	16,656	8,643	18,929	12,000
Travel agency	18,539	28,508	21,143	33,029
Courier	40,128	58,659	26,494	10,826
Financial services	21,010	28,003	11,875	7,332
Real estate	18,363	17,568	24,240	20,839
Rental	24,373	27,773	22,295	24,173
Consultancy	21,506	23,819	17,000	5,598
Accounting	10,446	4,719	10,411	5,535
Employment agency	17,794	15,115	16,960	11,491
Legal	10,606	5,938	11,248	3,753
Advertising	12,922	15,514	9,875	7,554
Comm. cleaning	27,776	30,814	29,232	35,486
General business	16,254	18,948	15,299	15,030
Health care	13,866	14,366	6,374	4,546
Drainage	20,080	13,900	20,260	14,378
Personal services	24,053	34,241	31,995	50,566
Domestic services	19,665	22,245	28,500	29,681
Driving school	16,000	73,448	25,000	N/A

Table 8.31: Fee characteristics of non-surviving franchisors

Source of variation	Sum of squares	Degrees of freedom	Mean square	F-ratio	F-critical
Among samples					
(*N* and failed grouping)	2184468	1	2184468	0.0100	4.26
Among industries	17460991743	24	727541323	33.6	1.98
Sampling error	519142573	24	21630941		
Total	17982318784	49			

Table 8.32: Two-way ANOVA table for analysis of franchise fees according to industry sector

Question 6: Why do franchisors fail?

As noted earlier, it seems that there is a recurring message within the popular franchise press which contends that franchising should lower the risks normally associated with entering business and expanding an existing one. The advantages accruing to the firm from this form expansion is broadly encapsulated in the agency and resource explanations of franchising. According to the advocates of these theories, franchising permits the firm to lower the input and ongoing costs of organizational development. Within the resource-constraint explanations, franchising is employed to gain access to:

1. financial capital (via the franchisees' payment of initial fees, lowering wage costs, their payment of their store's fixtures and fittings, payment of rent, and ongoing royalties);
2. human capital (that is, self-motivated managerial talent);
3. local market knowledge.

Although this school of thought has attracted some criticism on the basis that franchising is an inefficient method of raising capital, when franchisees are considered as representing all three resource requirements as one, the costs of procuring them as 'a package' is possibly lower than when purchased individually.

In contradistinction to those propounding resource-constraint explanations, advocates of the agency-perspective (such as Brickley and Dark, 1987) argue that franchising reduces the continuing costs of development and allows the realization of administrative efficiency. In this sense, the agency-theory explanation could be construed to apply more to the more established concerns, whereas the orientation of the resource-constraint perspective could be seen to be more applicable to describing younger firms' entry to franchising. The costs associated with company-owned units are influenced by:

1. the availability of managerial talent;
2. the importance of local knowledge;
3. geographic distance from headquarters;
4. population density;
5. the relative proximity of locations to one another.

All of these factors affect the cost of travel, co-ordination, communications, and decision-making between headquarters and local managers. As franchisees risk some proportion of their personal wealth by investing in a particular unit and are motivated by profit, there is a lower propensity to 'shirk' and this reduces (rather than eliminates) the need for supervision and monitoring. Once released from some of the burdens of monitoring, the franchisor can concentrate on expanding the business. In so doing, additional income accrues to the franchisor from the new stock of franchisees and the sale of product (in some cases) to franchisees. By permitting greater brand dissemination and market share through additional capacity and lower advertising costs, so the franchisor is able to increase profitability and brand value.

Both of these explanations of franchising seem to be emphatic of what is potentially attainable from franchising. Not all franchisors, however, will necessarily achieve the objectives because of a plethora of reasons: their expectations may not be realistic, or they may have misjudged the resource requirements of recruiting, selecting, training, motivating, and advising franchisees. Within the confines of the resource-constraint explanation, franchising may indeed permit firms to surmount managerial and financial limitations to thereby realize low-cost growth, but it is because of the characteristics implicit to many small and weak firms that they may be unable to surmount the mobility barriers necessary to becoming a franchisor. Possibly reflecting this situation, the three strands of research examining company decline, turnaround, and failure have been emphatic of managerial and financial issues rather than rationales which are exogenous to the firm. This emphasis is also evident from numerous studies of organizational design, which has explored management's role in shaping a company's strategic direction through employing cognitive taxonomy and contingency methodologies (see Chapter 3). Thus, the role of management and managerial choice is central (Hudson, 1989), and as such it is only this aspect which is considered in the following paragraphs.

Some decisions to close a business or change strategic direction may be initiated by the death of the owner and motivational reasons (such as the owner wishing to retire or move on because returns have not risen above a certain threshold), where there is latitude for choice or death has been initiated by risk-averse creditors (where choice is restricted). Despite inconclusive evidence, there appears to be increasing evidence of the former occurring through the ownership direction thesis, which points to the premise that franchising and franchisees may simply be a short-term, early stage, development feature in the growth pattern of certain businesses. It is contended that once the franchisee's financial, human capital and local market intelligence resources have been effectively utilized and are no longer considered as premium (that is, the legitimation of franchising by the franchisor falls), the franchisor will convert to other growth strategies. There are, however, other explanations for such behaviour, which is founded not so much within the apparent alleviation of resource constraints by franchising, but on their exacerbation. Rather than continue to incur further losses, the franchisor withdraws from the activity (Cross and Walker, 1988) because he does not have the resources to surmount effectively the mobility barriers to entry to become a successful franchisor.

In a critical review of the generic reasons behind small-firm failure, Hall (1992) observes that the causes of failure are multi-dimensional[2] and supports other research which argues that the most common reasons for the success, or failure, of a small business appear to be:

1. management competence (or incompetence);
2. lack of delegation;
3. lack of management depth;
4. poor or no planning;
5. the ability (or inability) to secure adequate financial resources (Cochran, 1981; Dun and Bradstreet, 1981; Fredland and Morris, 1976; Hambrick and Crozier, 1985; Peterson *et al*, 1983).

Differentiating between symptoms and causes of failure, Argenti (1976) suggests that these reasons are causes of death and that decline and eventual death may be triggered by undertaking, for example, a 'big project'. In this sense big projects, such as franchised expansion, within weak firms carry an implicit threat of organizational death.

Weak firms are, however, not alone in experiencing failure. Whilst large firms also decline and die, they also experience strategy failures such as internationalization through franchising. As mentioned above, the UK franchise sector has witnessed numerous failed market entries by, in the main, US franchisors. Their failure in the UK can be attributed to the following explanations:

- they tend to gravitate to London as an initial entry point. Few franchisor companies who have used this strategy since the 1980s have shown success. The high property rents mean that companies' break-even points are high. Furthermore, some entrants do not have, or are unable to gain access to knowledge of the complex property legislation in the UK;
- they are unknown to UK customers and advertising is expensive since, typically, the companies tend to only open between one and five outlets, few of which are company-owned;
- they tend to use either franchising or branches as an entry strategy rather than acquisition to build company presence. To some extent, however, acquisition opportunities are few and far between due to the structure of the industry;
- they typically recruit master franchisees, via the use of brokers, without one or more of the following:
  1. sufficient knowledge of the UK market;
  2. the difficulties of recruiting franchisees;
  3. sufficient resources and infrastructure to sustain the franchise and its development. That is, they tend to opt for an individual franchisee rather than a corporate one as their bargaining power is lower;
- sometimes the franchisor does not have sufficient resources to manage, control or co-ordinate an international division. Yet they internationalize because they are convinced that there is an unexploited opportunity. In other cases, the franchisor has little intention of supporting the franchisee but sells the territory in order to benefit financially;
- there is a tendency for the franchisors to be ethnocentric. That is, foreign expansion is viewed as an appendix to domestic operations rather than adapting to the prevailing market conditions. For example, Walker (1989), in a comparative study of US franchise domestic and internationalization strategies, showed that over two-thirds of his respondents did not modify

their marketing strategies when they expanded into other countries. Among those systems that adapted, they typically made adaptations in only two or three of seven major strategic areas. Such findings are corroborated by similar research (for example, Eroglu, 1992; Hopkins, 1996; Huszagh *et al*, 1992) which suggests that the majority of franchisors feel that success depends more on standardization rather than making culturally-appropriate modifications;

- they choose to compete on a head-to-head basis with the established industry players. The fact that these firms belong to a highly competitive industry group appears to be ignored. In addition to overcoming political, legal, cultural and industry barriers to market entry, foreign companies must also surmount the barriers of a specific market in order to compete in the desired niche.

In addition to these reasons, Ashman (1987) identifies that one of the other main problems encountered by US franchisors establishing market presence in foreign countries is the difficulties associated with recruiting enough qualified franchisees. By far the greatest problem, however, identified by Ashman (see Table 8.33) is governmental and legal restrictions. The applicability of this finding may be limited as the UK franchise sector is not as legalistic as that of the USA.

In short, then, failure by small and larger franchisors alike ensues as a result of under-estimating the financial and managerial costs of the project as well as lack of ability. Such features are not peculiar to foreign entrants, but are also evident in domestic franchisors. Recent studies have provided evidence that strategic factors and management and financial resource deficiencies are important determinants of small-business failures. The importance of such factors to franchisors has been perceived by agency theorists and others, such as Brickley and Dark (1987) and Hoy (1994) as limited, since franchising increases the probability of a new firm's survival rate by permitting the rapid development of economies of scale as well as those deriving from cash inflows from franchisees.

These observations presuppose, however, that the firm has developed the basic business idea in terms of over-coming any seasonality of demand, marketing, product-service pricing, staffing requirements, has well-documented processes and procedures to formulate an operations manual and developed an organizational culture orientated

Issue	Proportion (%)
Government or legal restrictions	59.6
Difficulties in recruiting enough qualified franchisees	44.2
Lack of sufficient local funding	36.5
Difficulty of controlling franchisees	36.5
Difficulty of redesigning the franchise package so to make it saleable to franchisees in foreign markets	28.8
Trademark and/or copyright obstacles	28.8

Table 8.33: Problems encountered by US firms establishing franchises in foreign countries

towards franchisee management. It also assumes that the franchisor has additionally drawn up a franchise contract and franchise prospectus. These two documents and the operations manual require a great deal of time, administration, attention to detail and, usually expensive external help from consultants, solicitors and accountants. In short, the observation assumes that the franchisor has acquired the necessary infrastructure to support franchisees. In addition to the time and resource costs that such modifications entail, the observation also assumes that the firm can withstand the economic costs of establishing a franchise concept and recruiting franchisees.

The reality of high expenses in realizing the objective of becoming a franchisor is in stark contrast to those attempting to generate positive network externalities. These seem to suggest that the costs of entering franchising are low. Indeed, a promotional letter by a government body aptly reflects this sentiment:

> Franchising is just one of many ways in which you can develop your business. It requires total commitment, but is extremely rewarding, *needing minimal capital investment* (my emphasis). (Department of Trade and Industry, Business Link)

On a similar note, *Entrepreneur* magazine in its publication *Franchising and Expanding Your Business*, claimed that franchising facilitates:

> Expansion of your business idea with minimal capital. You have no contingent liability as you would if you found the capital yourself and took the loans necessary to expand. You don't have to take long-term equipment payouts. The franchisee does all of this because he or she is investing in the capital.

To some extent, the above optimism is perhaps justified in the sense that expansion via franchising will cost a franchisor less than it would a corporate entity, due to the fact that franchisees carry some of the investment burden. The promise of low-cost expansion, however, can serve to blind would-be franchisors to the typically high costs of franchise system piloting and the even more expensive task of franchise system development through to 'break-even' point. Contrary to the promise of low-cost expansion, owners intent on launching a franchise may find themselves involved in a number of years' hard work before it recruits its first franchisee. The owners will find that they are not simply involved in testing one business idea but two – a conventional business configuration plus an allied franchise format. The costs associated with entry, recruitment and managing a franchised network are often understated and much higher than originally forecast by many franchisors. In a review of US franchising activity, for example, Trutko *et al* (1993) indicate that the direct costs of franchisee recruitment (printing franchise brochures, producing video tapes and salesperson's compensation) post-entry amounted to, on average, US$8,000 and estimate that the initial franchise development costs can exceed US$500,000. Thus, they state that:

> The development of a business from a proven concept to the sale of its first franchise is typically a long, expensive, and risky process for the franchisor. Even excluding the costs of direct management involvement, the franchisor bears sizeable 'upfront' costs for developing a programme before it can be marketed to franchisees. (pp. 7–1)

In the UK, Ellingham (1995), via a series of worked cash-flow illustrations – although not discounted cash-flows – suggests that the total entry costs (consisting of professional fees, the development of training manuals, design and printing of prospectus material, and advertising, but not managerial time, a pilot operation or trade exhibitions) amount to about £50,000 and indicates that such costs will vary widely according to:

1. the type of business;
2. the degree of conversion required from the existing concept;
3. the availability of time, resources and skills within the company which is franchising;
4. the proposed approach to franchising.

Once the franchise has been launched, Ellingham further suggests that the salaries and general overheads required to manage the franchise amounts to an additional £40,000. He assumes that the firm requires few adaptations to become a franchisor. Initial costs would, undoubtedly, be higher in firms which require large-scale adaptations. Nonetheless, even after allowing for adaptation costs, the costs of advertising the franchise offering (and building a public relations profile for it) are omitted – a situation which suggests some degree of conservatism by Ellingham. For example, franchisors typically pay between £8,000 and £10,000 for the privilege of exhibiting their franchise offering to trade fair visitors and there may also be the additional burden of:

1. local/regional advertising;
2. the time costs of maintaining the momentum of the application; and
3. the organizational costs associated with exhibitions.

Given that the average sales turnover per small business is less than £250,000 (Fuller, 1994), even Ellingham's calculated entry costs could not only be prohibitive, but are also undoubtedly understated and could force those intent on franchising to seek risk-prone short cuts to realize their ambition. Nonetheless, such estimates could be viewed as conservative when compared against the welter of more bullish opinion from either poorly-informed journalists or those with vested interests to protect.

Even the above-mentioned *Entrepreneur* Magazine Group publication, as part of a franchise feasibility questionnaire poses the question to would-be franchisors: 'Do you have more than US$250,000 to invest in the development of your franchise concept?' (1995; p. 6). Furthermore, in a series of worked examples within the context of the US marketplace, Seltz (1982) indicates that the precise quantification of capital requirements in an industry is highly dependent upon the specifics of the franchisor's capabilities, strengths and weaknesses. Subject to these qualifications, he estimated that the franchisor's initial capital requirements will fall into the range of US$150,000 to US$1 million *prior* to a properly capitalized, functioning prototype. It should be noted that Seltz's calculations were made in 1982 and that, due to the effects of inflation since then, these costs have undoubtedly risen. The same is true of Ellingham's scenarios: an article written by Orrin in the 1988 *Franchise World Directory* employs exactly the same figures as those shown by Ellingham. The effects of inflation, however, between 1988 and 1995 have not been accounted for, which by default possibly fuels the perception that franchising is a low-cost route of expansion. Indicative of the costs incurred, Pierre Levicky (the founder of a UK-based French-style bistro chain called Pierre Victoire) estimated that his initial costs of pursuing franchised expansion amounted to £1 million, with an operations manual costing £15,000, an initial franchise agreement costing £9,000 and an annual salary of £25,000 for a training manager. He indicated that the early economies of scale were poor and that he only broke even after opening twenty-five stores. In Ellingham's (1995) scenarios, even after making favourable allowances, the franchise does not break even until year four. In year five the position is such that there is a five-fold increase in revenues compared to year four. But the realization of this position is dependent on fifteen units being opened during the period and is achieved without incurring the costs of prior borrowed money, the existence of any contingency funding, the capital cost and overhead requirement of a pilot operation (which is assumed to be operating profitably at the time of launch), depreciation or tax! Similar conclusions are evident from the BFA's Franchisor's Manual[3] in which a new franchisor incurs debt of almost £90,000 in the third year post-launch, but realizes net inflows over the following two years to achieve credit of about £140,000 in year five (see Table 8.34). The franchisor starts up with £100,000 longer-term loan capital plus £70,000 of owner's funds. In addition to this, the system needs a bank borrowing facility which peaks at £89,000 in year 3, and finally moves into credit in year 5. The important point to make, is that such projections have been made without the benefit of being subject to sensitivity testing and that some small companies may not be able to withstand debts of the magnitude illustrated in the table. Yet, events may not go as planned. For example, by allowing for a 5% reduction in the value of receipts and a 5% increase in the level of payments, the table shows that the bank account amounts to £54,000 – or about 40% of the expected value – in year 5. There is also the need for a borrowing requirement of £111,000 which, if a 10% reduction in the value of receipts and a 10% increase in the level of payment was incurred, would rise to £164,000 – nearly twice the original borrowing requirement.

Given the lack of sensitivity analyses and the implicit failings in Ellingham's and Orrin's calculations, and those presented by the BFA, the expected earnings may be overly optimistic. In support of this contention, Silvester's (1996) survey of 146 franchisors in Britain shows that the majority (65%) of franchise systems of less than five years old believe that they require twenty units to break even; as the franchises mature, 42% believe that the answer is between twenty and fifty units, and some franchisors thought that the break-even point was somewhere in excess of fifty units. Given that most UK franchise systems only comprise ten or fewer units and survive less than five years post-franchise launch, there is at least a suggestion that the costs of entry may have, through under-estimating the true costs of franchising a business, contributed to the franchisor's demise. Indicative of the significance of under-funding, Silvester (1996) shows that the majority (69%) of her study of young franchisors invested less than £100,000 in setting up their franchise offering; her respondents also indicated that a shortage of funds, within the first five years of operating, for financing growth was a major contributing factor to the survival of their franchise systems. Indeed, Ellingham goes on to illustrate some of the financial consequences should franchised expansion be slower than planned. In these situations, borrowing reaches about £130,000 and the system fails to reach its break-even point in year five of post-pilot trading.

The initial costs of franchising will also place a burden on the franchisor because of the costs associated with franchisee recruitment. In a survey of UK franchisors, MacMillan (1995) shows that 72% of his sample estimated recruitment costs were between

Expected scenario	Set-up period	Year 1		Year 2		Year 3		Year 4		Year 5	
		1st half	2nd half	1st half	2nd half	1st half	2nd half	1st half	2nd half	1st half	2nd half
Franchisees recruited	–	–	–	2	3	4	4	6	7	7	8
Total number of franchisees	–	–	–	2	5	9	13	19	26	33	41
Receipts											
Franchise fees (recurring)				£12	£31	£58	£86	£128	£178	£231	£294
Franchise fees (initial)				£7	£11	£14	£14	£21	£25	£25	£28
Share capital	£70										
Loan capital (5-year term)	£100										
Total receipts (A)	**£170**			**£19**	**£42**	**£72**	**£100**	**£149**	**£203**	**£256**	**£322**
Payments											
Capital expenditure	£29										
Development expenditure	£107										
Loan repayments	*	*	*	*	*	*	£20	£20	£20	£20	£20
Direct costs				£5	£12	£24	£37	£56	£78	£102	£128
Staff costs		£20	£20	£21	£22	£30	£31	£32	£32	£33	£34
Overheads		£9	£9	£10	£10	£14	£14	£14	£15	£15	£16
Corporation tax											
ACT											
Value Added Tax		(£12)	(£1)		£1	£3	£5	£8	£12	£16	£20
Loan stock interest		£6	£6	£6	£6	£6	£6	£4	£3	£2	£1
Dividends											
Interest on bank balance			£1	£2	£4	£4	£5	£5	£2	(£1)	(£5)
Total payments (B)	**£136**	**£23**	**£35**	**£44**	**£55**	**£81**	**£118**	**£139**	**£162**	**£187**	**£214**
Net cash flow (A–B)	£34	(£23)	(£35)	(£25)	(£13)	(£9)	(£18)	£10	£41	£69	£108
Opening balance		£34	£11	(£24)	(£49)	(£62)	(£71)	(£89)	(£79)	(£38)	£31
Bank a/c credit/overdraft	**£34**	**£11**	**(£24)**	**(£49)**	**(£62)**	**(£71)**	**(£89)**	**(£79)**	**(£38)**	**£31**	**£139**
Quick sensitivity											
Assume receipts lower by 5%	£170	£24	£37	£18	£40	£68	£95	£142	£193	£243	£306
Assume receipts up by 5%	£136	(£24)	(£37)	£46	£58	£85	£112	£146	£156	£196	£225
Net cash flow	£34	£34	£10	(£28)	(£18)	(£17)	(£17)	(£4)	£37	£47	£81
Opening balance	£34	£10		(£27)	(£55)	(£73)	(£90)	(£107)	(£111)	(£74)	(£27)
Bank a/c credit/overdraft		(£27)	(£27)	(£55)	(£73)	(£90)	(£107)	(£111)	(£74)	(£27)	£54

Source: BFA Franchisor's Manual (1987)

* = 3-year capital repayment holiday; all figures = 000s

Table 8.34: New franchise system: expected and modelled cash-flow scenarios

£5,000–£10,000 per franchisee. Notably, some 9% indicate recruitment costs to be in excess of £20,000 and over a quarter of those with up to two years franchising experience did not know what they spent on recruitment. Given the rather *ad hoc* manner by which franchisors set their initial fees and that the majority of franchisors only recruit 5% or less of their initial leads – an expensive process in itself – it is reasonable to assume that many franchisors do not realize a profit out of the recruitment process (Sen, 1993).

The problems of franchisee recruitment have also been examined by Silvester (1996) as part of her research asking franchisors to identify the greatest challenges to their growth and survival at three stages in their development: inception to two years; three to five years; and six to ten years. Summarizing her results, the diagrams below (Figures 8.8, 8.9 and 8.10) display some clear patterns. For example, in the first two years of existence, her respondents felt that 'shortage of funds' was the single most important challenge to a new franchise system, followed by 'franchisee recruitment', 'building a franchisee support network', 'franchisee management', 'getting the brand-name known' and, finally, the issues of competition from other franchise systems and non-franchised systems. It is, however, noticeable that firms in the oldest age bracket, when recalling the early stages of development, suggested that 'shortage of funds' was a more important factor than the younger systems seem to realize and that 'franchisee recruitment' was a lesser problem. This difference of opinion may be attributable to the possibility of the younger franchisors having unrealistic expectations of the rate of development, as well as perhaps issues of timing. The older firms were in their development stages when franchising *per se* was experiencing real growth, whereas the newer firms have developed during a period of consolidation. There is also a question of priority; the older franchise systems feel that the first two years are a period requiring strong net investment rather than being an opportunity to accumulate wealth from franchisee investments.

Franchisors in all three age groups were then asked to identify the major problems and challenges arising at the three- to five-year stage. Here, much the same observation emerges with franchisors in the first age bracket still stressing issues of franchisee recruitment and those in the older age ranges balancing this perspective with a continued emphasis also on 'shortage of funds'. The final graph shows the overall responses for the threats within the final age bracket, and because of the small number of responses from the younger franchisors, just those for the most experienced firms are included. Even after all of their experience, however, these older franchise systems reported that 'difficulties with franchisee recruitment' still prevailed as a major problem.

Exploring the issue of franchisee recruitment further, and using the three franchisor age frames of 0–2, 3–5, and 6–10 years, Silvester's respondents were asked their perceptions of the number of operational franchised outlets required to match the overhead costs of the franchisor's management support network. Of the firms in the 0–2 years grouping, 51% perceived that the break-even point was relatively low in terms of number of outlets (that is between 1–10). By comparison, the more experienced firms in the 3–5 year age group were less likely to show that it was as low as this (only 40% thought so) and were more likely than their less experienced counterparts to suggest 11–20 or more than twenty outlets. Finally, the most experienced group of all, those in the 6–10 years age group, were more likely to opt for the 21–50 age range as their perception of break-even. Only a quarter of respondents in this group felt that the break-even point lay in the 1–10 outlet size band, compared to about half who thought that the break-even point was 21–50 outlets or more. It seems, therefore, that optimism

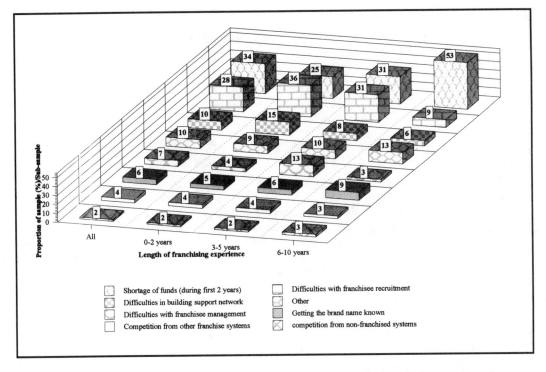

Figure 8.8: *Greatest threats to survival during first two years (by franchising experience)*

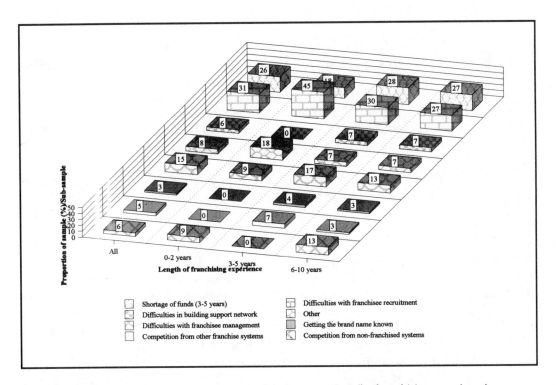

Figure 8.9: *Greatest threats to survival during years 3–5 (by franchising experience)*

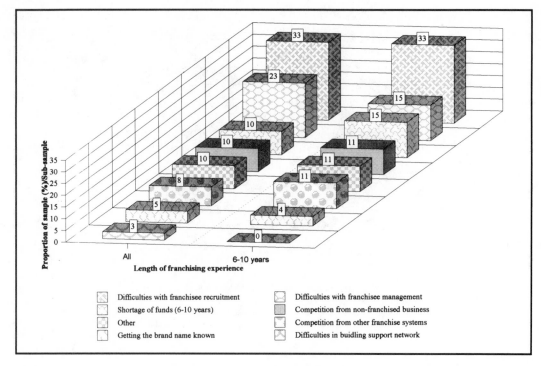

Figure 8.10: Greatest threats to survival during years 6–10 (by franchising experience)

becomes tempered by experience as earlier estimates of the break-even point come to be viewed as optimistic.

It is apparent, therefore, that overly optimistic messages from authoritative sources sometimes imply that franchising is a low-cost growth option for small business-es and an effective method of realizing cost rationalization and improved service levels for larger concerns. Silvester's (1996) results, however, show that insufficient finance poses a greater threat to survival than many younger franchisors possibly realize. Delays in reaching the break-even size of an operation may well stretch the system to breaking-point if there are no contingency plans and if the business is under-resourced from the outset.

The network externality argument, therefore, appears only to serve to generate expectations of positive cash in-flows via franchising when, in the short term at least, the net effects of entering the activity are cash-outflows (it is, however, acknowledged that there is a need for further research examining the financial perfomance of franchisors pre- and post-launch of their franchise offering). Given that the marketing costs for fran-chisees are the heaviest burden for smaller franchisors who have fewer franchisees over which to spread the costs, disconfirmation of these expectations may lead some new incumbents to leave franchised-based expansion for alternative cheaper forms and others to possibly shelve organizational development altogether, and opt for business development instead. From these examples concerning the capital requirements of fran-chising, the transaction costs of realizing franchised expansion appear to be expensive in the short run, but could be cheaper in the longer term (Langlois, 1992).

Such costs and managerial requirements infer that there appears to be little evidence to suggest that franchising can either reduce the probability of small-firm failure or increase their chances of survival *per se*. Resources within small businesses are often constrained by cost and quality considerations as well as the reliance on short-term debt for survival. Both agency theorists and proponents of the resource-constrained approach to organizational growth have argued that franchising may be pursued because it is a cheaper form of expansion than the company-owned route. The initial resource requirements for franchising, however, may well stretch the firm beyond what can be otherwise managed. In this sense, the entry into franchising by some small firms may, in fact, be the catalyst which leads to their demise because it then impacts on the franchisor's ability to develop an organizational structure designed to control and develop their franchise network and reduce the latitude to eliminate any weaknesses that may have been present in the early stages of franchising. According to Sherman (1993), some of the 'structural' reasons for franchisor failure include:

- a lack of proper disclosure documents and/or compliance system;
- a failure to provide adequate support;
- the lack of an effective franchise communications system;
- a complex and inadequate operations manual;
- having inadequate site selection criteria and procedures;
- the lack of a proper screening system for prospective franchisees;
- having an unworkable economic relationship with franchisees; and
- the lack of effective financial controls.

In addition to these factors, failure may occur due to the lack of initial investment in a feasibility study to ascertain whether the business is suitable for franchised-based expansion (Mendelsohn and Acheson, 1989). Echoing this sentiment, Justis *et al* (1994) indicate that the successful entry into franchising is, in part, dependent on the potential franchisor's understanding of their customer market, the development of proper financial controls, the recruitment of well-qualified individuals to manage the franchise, the existence of an operating manual, and sound legal documentation. To reiterate the point made in Chapter 3, however, the results of such feasibility studies are open to abuse and tend to be employed to provide support for a belief in a particular strategic option. Thus, to some extent, franchisor failure may be symptomatic of having overly optimistic expectations of the true financial costs of franchise-based expansion and of the failure to nurture an organizational culture, structure and systems to cope with the requirements of franchising (Cross and Walker, 1988). These characteristics, in turn, may provide additional explanations why those new to franchising are less successful in the activity than the more mature franchisors. Small firms, the majority of franchisors, do not tend to be systematized via documenting their administrative procedures, do not have business plans or necessarily have the expertise, time or resources to conduct such work or have such work done for them. Rather, there appears to be a strong task-orientation and focus on survival with a potentially dangerous belief that franchising will provide them with a tremendous opportunity for success. This belief is reinforced by the plethora of of 'How-to' books, which also seem to suggest that small firms are able to launch and operate their franchise business on a 'Do-it-yourself' basis – a potentially damaging proposition.

Yet, not only is it evident that franchise failure can be attributed to a number of interacting causes, but that the high proportion of withdrawing companies suggests that the generation of network externalities can be damaging. Such an observation is in line with the key findings of the Population Ecology framework: environments illustrate only limited levels of capacity. Thus when industries exceed a certain capacity, the rate of exit increases. Studies of organizational populations in the US and Bavarian brewing industries (for example) as well as the franchise market have provided strong empirical support for the density-dependent model (Carroll and Wade, 1991; Pilling *et al*, 1995; Swathinathan and Weidenmayer, 1991). Therefore, it appears that the emphasis by suppliers of franchise advice on generating network externalities may no longer be generally appropriate. After all, there are only so many people who are willing to become franchisees (see Chapter 5) and there are only so many companies which can become franchisors. There is therefore a need for researchers to establish the carrying capacities of the franchise strategic groups.

So far, this chapter has sought to explore some of the organizational characteristics of those franchisors withdrawing from the activity *vis-à-vis* those surviving, but an important question remains: how many of those withdrawals also go on to fail as a business?

Question 7: What happens post-withdrawal from franchising?

Within the ownership redirection thesis there appears to be an implicit assumption that once a company has withdrawn from franchising, it goes on to pursue its growth trajectory via alternative means. One implication of such an assumption is a perception that the business goes on to enjoy some business success because it is enriched by the acquired resources possessed by its (former) franchisees. In this way, franchising is seen as having made some contribution to the business's on-going success. From this hypothesis, it would be reasonable to expect the hypothesis (to test but one) to be supported, that only a low proportion of former franchisors subsequently fail as a business.

In order to test the hypothesis, life tables were generated for the former franchisors by comparing the year of franchise withdrawal with the year of registering as dissolved. To reiterate, the details of all dissolved limited liability concerns in Britain are stored at Companies House. In order to capture those firms which had ceased to franchise in 1994, the period of observation was defined as 1984–96. The sample of one hundred ex-franchisors was randomly chosen. From the life table (Table 8.35), it is evident that 40% of dissolutions occurred within four years after withdrawing from franchising. Thus, from this sample, it appears that death ensues relatively quickly after franchise withdrawal. It would therefore appear that franchising may have been employed as a mechanism by inherently weak and under-resourced companies seeking to raise finance in order to try to prolong survival rather than, perhaps, being more orientated towards building their organization. Such businesses may have been inherently weak because of insufficient start-up capital, poor management accounting procedures and debt, poor business forecasting, high gearing levels, and having insufficient working capital. Although the results serve to help qualify some of the beliefs that ex-franchisors may go on to enjoy growth, the degree to which the results of this test are generalizable is open to some speculation. For the large part, the ex-franchisors tended to fail as a business during the recessionary period.

Policy implications

The study indicates that franchise operations are quite vulnerable to failure in the early years of their development. Some researchers have argued that this situation may war-

Interval start time	No. entering this interval	No. withd. during interval	No. exposed to risk	No. of terminal events	Propn termin- ating	Propn surviving	Cumul. propn surviving at end	Prob. density	Hazard rate	SE of cumul. surv.	SE of prob. density	SE of hazard rate
.0	100.0	.0	100.0	.0	.0000	1.0000	1.0000	.0000	.0000	.0000	.0000	.0000
1.0	100.0	1.0	99.5	17.0	.1709	.8291	.8291	.1709	.1868	.0377	.0377	.0451
2.0	82.0	10.0	77.0	13.0	.1688	.8312	.6892	.1400	.1844	.0473	.0360	.0509
3.0	59.0	6.0	56.0	10.0	.1786	.8214	.5661	.1231	.1961	.0525	.0363	.0617
4.0	43.0	9.0	38.5	5.0	.1299	.8701	.4926	.0735	.1389	.0550	.0314	.0620
5.0	29.0	11.0	23.5	4.0	.1702	.8298	.4087	.0838	.1860	.0595	.0393	.0926
6.0	14.0	4.0	12.0	.0	.0000	1.0000	.4087	.0000	.0000	.0595	.0000	.0000
7.0	10.0	6.0	7.0	2.0	.2857	.7143	.2920	.1168	.3333	.0817	.0718	.2324
8.0	2.0	1.0	1.5	1.0	.6667	.3333	.0973	.1946	1.0000	.1156	.1249	.8660

The median survival time for these data is 4.90

Table 8.35: Life table measuring time between franchise withdrawal and death

rant a special government forum and assistance that would be targeted at franchise opera-tions in the early stages of their development. This perspective gains added validity when one considers that franchising has encouraged between 38% and 68% of franchisees into business who might not otherwise have considered this career option (Felstead, 1993). Arguably, however, small firms already have access to such a forum and support. It is mani-fest through government initiatives, such as the Training and Enterprise Councils (TECs) as well as the newly formed Diagnostic and Consultancy Service. But these bodies typically have a broader array of advisory functions, rather than being franchise-specific. As such, they may need greater sensitivities to firms seeking to expand through franchising and provide implementational support rather than the opportunity to gain access to advisers just cover-ing the feasibility of franchising or the legal contours of the activity. Equally, these services need to be effectively communicated to budding franchisors – not by employing the sales hype typically associated with the franchise fraternity, but by detailing the requirements and risks associated with franchised expansion and then how the services are able to help sur-mount these issues. After all, informed decision-making requires a sound basis in fact.

Although the TECs have the responsibility for enterprise training in small firms, they also offer small firms the opportunity to gain access to credited consultants who typ-ically only spend up to three days with the client to identify and diagnose areas of weaknesses. Whilst such a service may be invaluable since they serve to crystallize the magnitude and nature of problem areas, the standard and extent of this service through-out the UK is highly variable (due to an overt orientation toward local businesses) as is the subsequent support to resolve the problem. Furthermore, some TECs only use consultants and other such advisers as a form of independent recommendation in order to sell their own advisory services, often non-tailored to client-specific requirements (Beaton, 1995). Given the TECs' focus, within franchises their role may be limited to training the fran-chisor how to be a franchisor and assisting the writing of operations manuals and other documentation required to train franchisees.

The Diagnostic and Consultancy Service, on the other hand, provides subsidised management consultancy to help small firms and comprises two services: the provision of holistic diagnosis of business strengths and weaknesses and a full strategic consultan-cy. It is this forum that, potentially, has the most to offer budding franchisors since it is able to benchmark a small business's existing systems and structure against the best prac-tice criteria required for franchised-based expansion.

Although such services may help improve the franchisor's knowledge and alleviate some of the resource constraints of franchising, they may only have a marginal influence of improving the quality of franchises on offer. There will be, undoubtedly, some franchisors who will want to circumvent these services and those who enter franchising who shouldn't. These practices only serve to maintain or increase the level of franchisor withdrawals as well as put franchisees at risk. In order to reduce both franchisor withdrawal rates and franchisee risk, some form of regulation of franchisors should be encouraged whereby they have to submit all documentation regarding the franchise offering, full history details of directors, and the trading history of the firm. MacMillan (1995) suggests that the BFA should insist that all franchisors complete a voluntary disclosure document like that employed in Canada. Such a document is up-dated on an annual basis and contains the following information:

- a brief history of the franchised business, including audited financial statements;
- disclosure of the names of each shareholder having more than 10% of voting shares and a brief history of their business experience;
- a list of all existing locations and the date that they joined the system with details of any franchisee association or advisory council;
- a list of all corporate outlets owned by the franchisor and their opening dates;
- details of the required investment divided among various categories, such as franchise fee, initial capital expenditure, initial inventory, etc.;
- a statement with respect to any previous bankruptcy over the preceding ten-year period;
- details of any convictions by the directors or contracting shareholders for fraud and embezzlement, etc.

Although trade bodies, such as the BFA, should have taken the lead in this process, membership is voluntary, there are many more ex-members than members and the membership itself is dominated by solicitors, consultants and accountants rather than franchisors. Indeed, Silvester's (1996) study of franchisors showed that over two-thirds of her sample were not members of the BFA; their reasons for non-membership ranged from a belief that the BFA suffered from a lack of credibility to the lack of value for money deriving from high costs of membership combined with unclear benefits of membership. As such, its impact on improving the quality of franchising in the UK has been possibly limited. Such comments are not meant as criticisms for their own sake. Indeed, the state of UK franchising may have been worse without it. But it is clear that the BFA needs greater powers and legitimate authority to monitor the franchise sector.

Summary and conclusion

Through a purely exploratory study, this chapter has sought to challenge a key tenet of the franchise fraternity: that franchisors experience low levels of failure. The purpose of the chapter is to highlight that there has been, to date, a significant lack of debate by practitioners and researchers alike of the magnitude and rationale for franchisor failure and how these relate to the franchisor's relevant industry grouping. Strategic groups have also been shown to illustrate differing levels of permeability and volatility (Lewis and Thomas, 1990; Mascarenhas, 1989) depending on the height and nature of the mobility barriers. Becoming a franchisor (especially a successful one) requires the firm to surmount mobility barriers, such as having an organizational culture and structure suitable for controlling and co-ordinating franchisees. Not all franchisors possess the financial and managerial capabilities and resources to surmount these mobility barriers and sustain their position beside these other strategic group members selling franchises. Viewed from this perspective, there appears to be an abundance of anecdotal evidence that suggests that the level of franchisor failure is higher than 'official' statistics suggest and that there are differing status groups of franchises. This research has revealed that the franchise fraternity is segmented into what might be seen as the mature, well-established stable 'core' of franchises comprising the household names we all know so well, and then the more vulnerable 'periphery' made up of smaller and younger names. In fact, approaching half of all franchise systems currently operating in Britain were established post-1990 and have fewer than ten outlets. As such, they are on a steep learning curve and face considerable challenges. Academics must, therefore, be wary of uncritically accepting ideas which have as yet insufficient grounding due to a lack of independent corroboration.

The key to understanding why franchisor failure occurs appears to be a better understanding of the motivations to become a franchisor. Strategic group analysis may enrich extant understandings of such motivations. Chapter 4 suggests, for example, that the competitive dynamics within and between strategic groups not only affects the decision to franchise, but the contractual terms and whether to franchise particular units. Discussion of failure and success will be shallow without a comparison of the volatility of the franchisor's industry group and expected gains from franchised growth, which can only be achieved by yet more research. A prerequisite for such a comparison is a means of adequately describing failure; it seems that this is a research priority. Without a solid framework, fragmentary data accumulated by differing agencies will be difficult to interpret and compare in order to facilitate informed decision-making. This chapter represents a cautious move in that direction, but there are numerous opportunities for additional and complementary research.

Although the research in this chapter may be construed to be academic, it has significant practical implications. The messages for potential franchisees appear to be that they should, in the preliminary choice process, ensure that the franchisor should be:

- an experienced manager before starting to franchise;
- established more than five years;
- have costs and fees no higher than comparable franchises in the same economic sector; and
- have the resources to survive the initial years and sustain growth.

Managers and small-businessmen, keen to realize the potential benefits that franchising may offer, cannot be blamed for seizing on attractive ideas. Trade associations, researchers, bankers, accountants, consultants and solicitors, however, have a duty to be more cautious, and to move beyond folklore. The magnitude of failures suggests it is essential that potential franchisors realistically evaluate all that is involved in franchising, and be committed to the success of their franchisees and the strengthening of their franchising programme. Indeed, because there is a high rate of franchisor failure, especially in the early years, Sherman (1993) argues that there is a need for 'responsible franchising', in which some of the key components include:

- a proven prototype location that serves as the basis of the franchising programme because the stores have been tested, refined, and operated successfully and are consistently profitable;
- a strong management team who understand the particular industry in which the company operates as well as the legal and business aspects of franchising as a vehicle to growth;
- sufficient capitalization to launch and sustain the franchising programme to ensure that capital is available to the franchisor to provide both initial and ongoing support and assistance to franchisees;
- a distinctive and protected trade identity via the necessary trademark registration procedure;
- effective financial controls and an effective compliance and proper disclosure system;
- a proper screening system for prospective franchisees;
- effective site selection techniques, the provision of adequate franchisee support, and mechanisms for resolving conflicts with franchisees;
- research and development capabilities for the introduction of new products and services on an ongoing basis to consumers through the franchised network;
- a communication system that facilitates a continuing and open dialogue with the franchisees; and
- effective advertising, marketing, and public relations programmes designed to recruit prospective franchisees as well as consumers to the sites operated by franchisees.

The extent of failure also clearly means that franchising is not a panacea for every low-performing business. A situation may arise where an independent manager, whose business is suffering lower-than-average performance, could have unrealistic expectations of what franchise agreements have to offer (Weinrauch, 1986). Indeed, in a review of the financial performance of over one hundred UK franchisors, Chater and Fernique (1990) observe that almost one-third of franchisors were losing money and one in ten was insolvent and trading illegally. Perhaps realizing some of the risks involved in franchising, some franchisors have created a legally separate limited liability company to manage their franchise.

The above discourse has argued that potential entrants need to compare like with like when assessing the degree of risk inherent to franchising. After all, franchisors are a strategic group within a particular economic setting, rather than being an 'industry'. The ease with which this may be successfully achieved, however, is limited due to problems of vested interest, the pejorative associations, and research and quantification differences. With regard to the latter point, the chapter suggests that there is a variety of differing methods to quantify firm deaths which serve to compound problems of comparability between franchise and general death rates. This said, some of the available statistics underline the volatility of those UK industries where franchises prevail. They also infer that its franchise sector is also characterized by higher levels of failure than perhaps experienced in other industries' franchise market (even though it is lower than the average).

As in any study, there are limitations. The main one here is that, in spite of their comprehensiveness, the franchise directories are far from complete or consistent. The lack of consensus between the different franchise directories and their entries means that this study can be no more than exploratory. In spite of statistically significant samples, therefore, this study suffers from similar drawbacks as those evident in the analyses conducted by the BFA/NatWest studies, among others. Every year, some franchise directories contain entries not evident in others, thereby leading to some conflict when attempting to assess the size of the franchise fraternity and its volatility (Purdy et al, 1996). Furthermore, a few new franchisors are found that have been franchising for some time. But as these are only the survivors, so there may be numerous others who have entered the franchise market only to fail shortly thereafter and whose presence remains unrecorded. Thus, if anything, the above studies are potentially understating both the true level of activity in the market and its volatility. Nevertheless, in his foreword to the 1996 edition of the *Franchise World Directory*, Sir Bernard Ingham (President of the BFA and former Press Secretary to Lady Margaret Thatcher) observes that:

> Every time I pick up a new brief about the British franchise industry the numbers change – upwards. This is a major growth industry, advancing at about 10% a year and now turning over some £5.5 billion. This is not surprising because it is a relatively secure way into business and has great potential. (p. 7)

Clearly, given that the UK franchise fraternity has declined in real value terms since 1990 and in average sales per system since 1988, such sentiments are not wholly accurate. Nonetheless, there may, indeed, be some hope that the value of the franchise market and number of franchisors will grow in the future, but this is dependent on the ability to be continually innovative in the face of increasingly mature markets. It is also evident that so will the number of franchisor failures unless advisory resources are effectively mobilized. Recently, a government organization called Business Link launched a programme which assesses potential franchisors' business plans and suitability of their existing systems, structures, etc., to manage franchisees. Unfortunately, such services are still at the evolutionary stage of development and, until this situation is remedied, the proportion of franchisees at risk from franchisor failures will also continue to rise. But there exists an important proviso: these advisory bodies can only assist those who want help in establishing their franchise. There are plenty of potential franchisors who will not want help because they feel that they can do it more efficiently and effectively themselves. This situation can only be remedied by legislation; not surprisingly, however, any legislative threshold to becoming a franchisor has been strongly resisted by both franchisors and the BFA. Meanwhile, as even some of those who have been helped seem to have built their franchise offering on foundations on sand we are, in turn, left with a conundrum: how can franchising be safe for franchisees if so many franchisors fail?

> In general . . . the current state of [the] franchise nation can be summed up in two words – deeply troubled. For all their past successes, precious few systems are

minting money for franchisees today. Most markets are crowded, and expenses are rising. Even worse, new evidence suggests that the whole franchising model, far from being a consummate business paradigm for the late 20th century, as its advocates claim, is so riddled with problems and ill will that opening a franchise can often be riskier and less desirable than simply starting your own business. (Serwer, 1995; p. 58)

An end-note on failure in the UK hospitality industry

In order to provide a sense of scale of franchisor deaths and withdrawals, the following paragraphs compare the data with the average number of VAT deregistrations, bankruptcies/deeds of arrangement, and liquidations in the hospitality industry. It should, however, be observed that franchisor withdrawal and death figures are strictly non-comparable: franchising is a strategy, VAT deregistrations, bankruptcies/deeds of arrangement, and liquidations are deaths. What is being established by this comparison is some indication of the magnitude of franchisor withdrawals relative to the volatility of the hospitality industry.

Comparisons with VAT deregistrations

In Britain, all trading businesses with turnover in excess of a specified turnover threshold are required to register for VAT. This data can then be used as a building block to establish the population of firms within a certain economic sector as well as in the economy generally. It also distinguishes between different types of legal form (whether sole trader, partnership or limited liability) and provides data on numbers of firms according to turnover which, in turn, can be used to evaluate polarization in the economy and by economic sub-sector. This said, such data is also unreliable as the VAT threshold changes and the manner in which the information is collected is also susceptible to alteration. For example, as a result of changes in the VAT threshold, some companies have been excluded from the population of units which has served to lower the number of VAT registrations and deregistrations in absolute terms. Hence, not all of the deregistrations can be attributed to 'failing' firms. Daly (1987) shows that a business may be deregistered for a variety of reasons, including:

1. trader goes out of business;
2. trader goes out of business, buyer already registered;
3. trader changes legal identity;
4. trader falls below exemption rate;
5. trader no longer a taxable person;
6. trader makes only zero-rated products; and
7. trader accepts invitation to deregister.

He shows, by using the data for 1987, that in the catering market (for instance) 34% deregistered because the trader went out of business and 52% because of acquisition. By contrast, 58% of all UK deregistrations were a result of the trader going out of business; 21% were because of acquisition. Arguably, the bias toward acquisition in the catering sector – and the store-based retail market – reflects its property base and potential value to a purchaser. Further, registration and deregistration may not coincide with the beginning and ending of trading. For example, a firm may well trade for some time before its turnover warrants registration for VAT. Equally, a firm can register before starting to trade and may not deregister until after ceasing to trade. Indeed, the NatWest *Review of Small Business Trends* (1994) observes:

> VAT registrations and deregistrations are not synonymous for business births and deaths . . . because of the threshold increase, they will cover fewer firms. (p. 36)

Their data shows that, on average, twenty-three months elapse before a quarter of catering firms deregister (the all-industry average is two years); fifty-one months go by before half of catering concerns deregister (versus sixty months otherwise). Only 26% are still registered after ten years. It appears that the highest rates of deregistration are during the second and third years.

Table 8.36 illustrates VAT registrations and deregistrations in the hotel and catering sector between 1980 and 1993. It shows that the catering industry represented, between 1980 and 1993 about 10% of all registrations and 11% of total deregistrations. In terms of deregistration ranking, the catering industry came fourth, superseded by 'other services', retailing, and wholesaling. Further, during the five-year period 1988–93, there were 118,510 VAT registrations in the catering sector compared to 120,390 deregistrations, which suggests that for every deregistration there was a registration. These figures suggest that the catering industry is highly volatile and as a sub-set, *inter alia,* some may expect that its franchise sector may also be high. Unfortunately, there is currently little evidence with which to directly compare franchise and catering deregistrations and this is, perhaps, a subject for further research – especially as some franchisors contractually oblige their franchisees to register for VAT (Adams and Pritchard-Jones, 1991), even though their sales levels may be below the VAT threshold. The reasons why some franchisors stipulate that their franchisees do this is for administrative purposes, especially if there is a requirement to purchase product from the franchisor, and as a way of reducing opportunistic behaviour. Franchisors feel that franchisees may be less inclined to defraud the tax authorities than them. Importantly for measuring failure through VAT deregistrations, however, some franchisees deregister sometimes only a year later if they are still under the exemption rate. Thus, evaluating franchisee failure through VAT deregistrations may not be wholly appropriate.

From a different perspective, Ganguly (1985) shows that small VAT-registered firms have a higher probability of failure than larger concerns. According to this data, about 13% of all business failures have sales of less than £100,000. In the hospitality market, the element of risk is such that 49% of catering firms and 71% of fast food businesses were in this sales band in 1992.

Comparisons with bankruptcies/liquidations/insolvencies

Unlike the USA, the term 'bankruptcy' in the UK only refers to an individual in a court of law. Such an individual is discharged from paying debts which he/she is unable to pay by the Court. As a consequence, they cannot obtain new credit or undertake new business activities. Insolvencies, by contrast, refer to an individual and/or a firm that has

	Hotel & catering		UK industry		Proportion (%)	
Year	VAT Registration	VAT Deregistration	VAT Registration	VAT Deregistration	Registrations	Deregistrations
1980	15,426	15,102	158,300	142,300	9.6	10.6
1981	14,994	13,725	152,100	120,000	12.5	11.4
1982	16,402	16,190	166,000	145,400	9.9	11.3
1983	17,806	16,420	180,000	145,000	9.9	11.3
1984	19,776	17,591	182,000	152,000	10.9	11.6
1985	18,138	17,902	183,000	163,000	9.9	11.0
1986	19,323	18,782	192,000	165,000	10.1	11.4
1987	22,087	20,015	210,000	169,000	10.5	11.8
1988	22,268	20,549	240,000	172,000	9.3	11.9
1989	21,539	19,914	256,000	176,000	8.4	11.3
1990	19,819	18,789	239,000	184,000	8.3	10.2
1991	17,863	19,013	206,000	203,000	8.7	9.4
1992	18,695	21,688	188,000	230,000	9.9	9.4
1993	18,326	20,437	190,000	218,000	9.6	9.4

Source: NatWest *Review of Small Business Trends* (1994), No. 2, December, pp. 38–39.

Table 8.36: VAT registrations and deregistrations: UK hospitality sector versus all industries

insufficient assets to meet debts or liabilities.[4] A firm is only termed insolvent if the creditors call in their debts and they cannot be met. Regular figures are published on insolvencies and they include liquidations, where these are 'compulsory' or 'creditors voluntary' liquidations, and bankruptcies. The table indicates that the rate of franchisor withdrawals is, in general, higher than this measure of failure.

Liquidation refers to the process by which a company's existence as a legal entity ceases by 'winding-up'. Such a process can be initiated at the behest of the creditors where the company is insolvent ('compulsory'), or by the company directors or shareholders ('voluntary') illustrating 'Samson-like' behaviour. Data concerning compulsory and creditor voluntary liquidations in England, Wales and Scotland shows that the hotel and catering industry represents about 4% of the compulsory set and about 2.5% of the voluntary set (see Table 8.37). Using a different measure, the catering sector has, according to government statistics, accounted for an average of 7.4% of all bankruptcies and about 4% of all insolvencies in England and Wales between 1989 and 1993. Whilst such statistics suggest a relatively high level of attrition within the hotel and catering industry, they differ by sub-sector. Touche Ross (1995), for example, infer that failure[5] rates are higher amongst restaurants than hotels and public houses. Such statistics lend some weight to anecdotes that estimate that approximately 80% to 90% of restaurants fail in their first three years of life (Russell-Cobb, 1990) and to the perception that the catering market is a 'Cinderella' industry, that is one to dabble in but not take too seriously.

Year	UK hotel & catering		All UK industry		Proportion (%)	
	Compulsory	Voluntary	Compulsory	Voluntary	Compulsory	Voluntary
1983	198	235	5,070	8,857	3.9	2.7
1984	156	241	5,532	8,712	2.8	2.8
1985	177	214	6,067	9,368	2.9	2.3
1986	156	233	5,503	9,413	2.8	2.4
1986–87	149	229	4,882	9,412	3.1	2.4
1987–88	220	169	3,911	7,064	5.6	2.4
1988–89	209	159	3,789	6,011	5.5	2.6
1989–90	221	179	4,511	6,981	4.9	2.7
1990–91	293	260	7,043	10,378	4.2	2.5
1991–92	419	434	9,210	14,127	4.5	3.1
1992–93	561	473	9,861	15,164	5.8	3.1
1993–94	497	408	7,905	11,964	6.3	3.4
1994–95	371	343	6,479	9,627	5.7	3.6

Source: The Insolvency Service (various years).

Table 8.37: *Number of 'compulsory' and 'voluntary' liquidations: the hospitality sector versus all industries*

Category	Receiverships			Liquidations			Total		
Year	92	93	94	92	93	94	92	93	94
Hotels	154	111	58	97	90	74	251	201	132
Pubs	116	77	50	133	156	99	249	233	149
Restaurants	36	18	28	199	209	160	235	227	188
Other	14	5	15	82	45	51	96	50	66
Total	*320*	*211*	*151*	*511*	*500*	*384*	*831*	*711*	*535*

Source: Touche Ross quoted by *Caterer & Hotelkeeper*, January 1995.

Table 8.38: *Failures in the UK catering market by sub-sector, 1992–94*

Comparisons with exits from self-employment

The Labour Force Survey has monitored the number of entrants and exits from self-employment by broad SIC sector since 1984. It is evident that the determinants of self-employment inflows are not the same as its outflows; for example, changes in business cycles are not necessarily reflective of all motivations to enter and leave direct employment (Bevan *et al*, 1989; Vivarelli, 1991). Indeed, Granger *et al* (1995) differentiate between four self-employment career types (which may also be applicable to understanding franchisees' career paths and attrition): 'refugees', 'missionaries', 'trade-offs', and 'converts'. Refugees takes a direct employment job on first entering the labour market and develop a strong attachment to their job; when made redundant the self-employment option is taken up but the refugee would return to a job as an employee if and when one became available. The missionary leaves employment because of the perceived attractions that self-employment may offer. The trade-off category includes those who have become self-employed in order to take a break from direct employment to accommodate the constraints of some non-work activity. The final category, converts, represent those who have become self-employed as a stop-gap strategy but later show little interest in returning to direct employment. Those people exiting self-employment, the 'refugees' and 'trade-offs', could be deemed to be owners of businesses which have ceased to trade and, consequently, add to the rate of attrition.

Although not divided by self-employment type, data from Table 8.39 suggests that the self-employed account for about 16% of those employed in retail and distributive trade activities and, whilst not illustrating entrants and exits with a particular year, shows that there has been an increase in the number of self-employed since 1984. However, there has been a fall in their number since 1989. Such a trend is perhaps at odds with research which suggests that the number of self-employed is influenced by the nature of the business cycle (Storey, 1994), where declining economic conditions are paralleled with increases in the number of self-employed.

Hotel & catering/distribution/repairs (000s)				Hotel & catering	Proportion
Year	Employees	Self-employed	All	(000's)	(%)
1984	3,980	784	4,764	960	20.2
1985	3,989	786	4,775	994	20.2
1986	4,028	781	4,809	995	20.7
1987	4,173	811	4,964	1,000	20.1
1988	4,342	831	5,173	1,078	20.8
1989	4,475	833	5,308	1,169	22.0
1990	4,476	814	5,290	1,225	23.2
1991	4,417	762	5,179	1,198	23.1
1992	4,356	728	5,084	1,180	23.2

Source: Department of Employment (various years).

Table 8.39: Number of employees in the UK hotel and catering sector

As a result of these issues, the statistics concerning the number of exits from self-employment are perhaps only loosely indicate the volatility of businesses registered under retailing. Furthermore, comparability with other statistics concerning attrition is limited as the level of aggregation is higher than the VAT data. For example, the table illustrates that the number of employees in the hospitality sector is about a fifth of those engaged in retailing and the distributive trades. From the differing definitions of death it appears that business failure within the hospitality industry is a regular occurrence, representing between 3% and 6% of all failures in the UK economy. When the data is modified to compare the rate of franchisor withdrawals and deaths in the hospitality industry, it is evident that those people attempting to generate positive externalities are not necessarily representing the franchise sector according to specific contexts and dynamics.

Notes

1. Some of my work examining franchisor failures in the UK has been reprinted from a study conducted for the Small Business Research Trust. It is reproduced and amended with permission. The analysis contained in this chapter would not have been possible without the kind help of Franchise Development Services Ltd, Castle House, Castle Meadow, Norwich, NR2 1PJ, who made copies of their annually produced *United Kingdom Franchise Directory* available for research purposes and analysis. I am equally grateful to *Franchise World Magazine*, James House, Nottingham Road, London, SE17 7EA.

2. According to Hall (1992), the following seven generic reasons are responsible for small-firm deaths:

1. *Operational management aspects:* under-capitalization; failure to generate a business plan; poor management of debt; constrained flexibility in decision-making; inaccurate costing and estimating; poor management accounting; poor supervision of staff; overstocking; late delivery of materials; loss of experienced personnel; skill shortage of staff.
2. *Strategic aspects:* lack of demand for products; funding associated companies; reliance on a few customers; competitor behaviour; reliance on a few suppliers; new entrants into market.
3. *Environmental aspects:* high interest rates; fire, theft.
4. *Personal aspects:* disagreement with partners; ill health; excessive remuneration.
5. *Technological aspects:* inferior product; no previous experience or knowledge; use of inferior materials.
6. *Marketing:* poor forecasting; under-pricing; adverse publicity; over-pricing.
7. *Rises in:* overhead costs; operating costs; fixed costs; labour costs; material costs.

3. I am grateful to David Purdy of the International Franchise Research Centre for alerting me to this model.

4. Balthory (1984) observes that there are different degrees of severity of insolvency: acute, chronic and terminal. Acute insolvency is characterized by:

1. Insufficient cash in the present or short term (under one accounting year) to meet financial obligations as they fall due.
2. Inadequate powers over collection of receivables.
3. Inadequate or non-existent present/short-term financing mechanisms.
4. Cash flows inadequate to support total credit in the present or short term.
5. Business may be carried on because the firm's debts are so large that the lives of the supplier companies depend on the debts being carried.
6. Business may be carried on because the company's debts are so comparatively small that creditors realize the cost-efficiency of collection.

Chronic insolvency is marked by the following features:

1. Inability to meet financial obligations as they fall due over two or more accounting periods.
2. Increasingly deeper degree of total indebtedness.
3. Gradual extinction of internal financing methods.
4. Encumbrance of assets with charges.
5. Preponderance of trade creditor financing.

Finally, terminal insolvency is distinguished by:

1. The inability to fund more or less permanent changes in the balance sheet.
2. Misalignment of cash-flows over five accounting periods or more.
3. Significantly adverse external factors of a recurrent nature.
4. Business may be carried on in national interest (pp. 7–8).

5. They differentiate between liquidations and receiverships in quantifying failure. Whilst the former have been described above, receiverships are different. Under this process, an administrative receiver can be appointed by the court, but a preferred method is for the company to issue a secured credit, referred to as a debenture with a floating charge. This gives the creditor security over an identifiable pool of assets, but not over the specific assets in that pool. The role of the administrative receiver is to realize the security and, after deducting his expenses and paying prior ranking interests, to pay the debenture holder up to the amount of secured interest. The balance is paid to the company, its liquidator or any subsequent ranking security holder. Although appointed by a creditor, the administrative receiver acts as an agent for the company and has broad powers including the ability to manage the company's business and to sell assets.

9 | Franchisee financial performance: comparisons with non-franchised firms and the role of the environment

We are always buying nostrums of some kind, those patent medicines sold with exaggerated claims, even in business, where we call them concepts, because we're always looking for simple formulas that will solve our complex problems.

Harold Geneen, chairman of ITT, *Managing*

The tendency to hide unfavourable information often occurs in companies that are quick to reward success and equally quick to punish failure.

Robert M. Tomasako, Principal of Temple, Barker & Sloan, *Downsizing*

Introduction

Every business and marketplace has its own myths, sagas, fables, tales, and legends; the franchise fraternity is no exception. Among such myths as franchisees are free men, a recurrent tale propounded by the popular franchise literature is that franchisees illustrate superior performance and survival rates compared to non-franchised concerns. Possibly reflecting this message, one of the most common recommendations at a career crossroads is to become a franchisee and/or open a fast food restaurant. Such advice is regularly employed as a promotional tool to advertise franchise expositions and exhibitions, as well as to sell magazines on franchising. The popular press tends to present the franchise option as a magic formula to end the ills of unemployment and the ills attached to working for other people. The following quotes are typical examples of such a sentiment, which seems to appear with almost monotonous regularity:

> Could you run a sandwich bar? How about a photographic studio, pizza parlour, petrol station or recruitment agency? You may think you could, but how much do you know, for example, about buying stock or chasing debtors? One way of minimizing the risk of starting a small business is by buying a franchise. (Riding, 1996; p. 21)

> Franchising, one of the most successful business systems created by the mind of man and woman, is still relatively unknown throughout the world. That is because it is transparent, i.e. you cannot tell whether that shop on the main street or the vendor who provides a certain service is a franchisee or an independent business person. But, generally, speaking, the firm you do business with will reveal itself as a franchised business because it will be around a lot longer. That is the key to franchising – it is far and away more successful almost all of the time . . . The old franchise axiom that 'you're in business for yourself but not by yourself' works more than 95% of the time. And that number

generally represents the non-closure rate for franchising . . . only 3–5% close each year (and most of these are really transferred to other owners or to the franchisor), and after five years 85% of those opened are still doing business under the original ownerships. (Cherkasky, 1996; p. 5)

The success rate for franchise operations is far higher than that of other small businesses mainly due to the support offered by the franchisor, the shared knowledge available, the economies of scale to be gained from the relationship with the franchisor, the established image and identity of the franchisor and the benefits from the franchisor's marketing efforts. (Promotional literature for an academic journal: *Franchising Research: An International Journal*)

This latter quote is of particular concern because, in deriving from academia, it suggests that its authors appear to have employed the accepted orthodoxy for promotional purposes without first verifying whether such dogma is, in fact, accurate. As Chapter 8 illustrated, not all franchisors are successful, have economies of scale, or even proven experience. How can franchisees be safe if, to use a proverb, the foundations of the franchisor's house are built on sand? Perhaps more blatant than these quotes are the claims made by Blenheim Expositions Inc., a company that produces a variety of franchise trade shows and expositions who, in promoting the International Franchise Exposition in 1992, claimed the following in their advertisements:

1. 'According to a recent Gallup Poll, 94% of franchise owners are successful, averaging $124,290 in pre-tax profits';
2. 'A recent independent survey showed that franchise owners enjoy an incredible 94% success rate and average income of more than 124,000 dollars';
3. 'If you buy a franchise business, your chances of success are 94%. THAT'S A FACT, according to a recent Gallup Poll. Conversely, it's estimated that only 35% of independent business start-ups survive five years.'

These last claims received severe criticism by the US Federal Trade Commission for being misrepresentative and methodologically incorrect. No former franchise owners were contacted and the survey included a disproportionate number of multiple franchisees. Although of concern in their own right, unfortunately such claims and practices are not restricted to just the popular franchise press and exhibition organizers in the USA, but academics and the major banks seeking to improve their small-business portfolio internationally.

The result of such propaganda has been the perception, by potential franchisees and franchisors alike, that franchising offers a fast lane into a business otherwise wrought with risk and uncertainty. Perhaps reflective of this sentiment of low risk of failure, albeit within the context of the US market, are the rather static reported levels of franchisee failure over the last few decades. For example, Kursch (1968) quotes a 'failure' rate of 4%, so does Thompson (1971), Vaughn (1979), the varying 'Franchising in the Economy' reports, Kosetecka (1987) and, more recently, Castrogiovanni *et al* (1993). No doubt there are numerous others and plenty more to come as legal protection for franchisees becomes widespread and franchisors argue that such legislation is unnecessary due to the low attrition rates. The usual rationale behind this assertion is that the franchisee benefits from franchisor training, pooled advertising activity and the availability of continuing managerial support. Perhaps indicative of such a belief, Kaufmann and Stanworth (1995) hypothesize that the greater an individual's interest in providing an ongoing business to his heirs, the stronger will be his expressed likelihood of purchasing a franchise – even though the reality of the situation is that franchises tend to fall more towards the individualist spectrum of exclusionary power (see the Introduction to the book). As few non-franchised concerns are perceived to have access to pooled resources, it is purported that they consequently record lower rates of performance and have a higher propensity for failure. In other words, an independent business would be perceived to be an inferior choice to those seeking to bequeath an ongoing business to their heirs. Chapter 8, however, shows that the quantification of failure, especially in franchising, is highly problematic, meaning that we are unable to ascertain, with any high degree of certainty, whether becoming a franchisee is a safer route into business than the independent start-up method. In turn, this uncertainty suggests that there needs to be closer scrutiny by regularity bodies of the advertisements franchisors and exhibition organizers, in particular, place in the public domain and, thus, to people who may be susceptible to being misled. Given the investments required to become a franchisee and the often untested claims of success by those with vested interests, there is a need for franchisors and exhibition organizers to adopt a more ethical and mature stance.

Perhaps indicative of the start of a backlash against the rhetoric of those with vested interests, the issues concerning franchisee attrition have begun to develop into its own literature (Bates, 1995; Cross, 1994; Emerson, 1991). Such efforts have been directed towards to an estimation of the safety of franchising *vis-à-vis* non-franchised routes. Unfortunately, however, researchers exploring this avenue have often been dismissed vitriolically by the franchise fraternity as critics or mavericks seeking to tarnish the 'good name of franchising', rather than being perceived as good researchers and analysts who do not accept franchising's apparent success at face value and/or want to quantify or qualify that success. Such dismissal is particularly prevalent in the USA, where there are substantial vested interests at stake, but it is also evident in Britain, Australia, and Canada.

> Critics of franchising will list a dozen reasons why you should be fearful of investing in a franchise. They can tell you numerous horror stories about failed franchises . . . It's true that some of the nearly 3,000 franchise companies in America deliver less than they promise. It's true that some of the nearly 600,000 franchised outlets in the USA fail. But if the majority of these businesses prosper (whereas most non-franchised businesses fail) there must be more that's right with franchising than wrong with it. (Hayes, 1994).

In light of the lack of non-corroborated franchise failure data, however, and the lack of accurate quantification, as well as the use of examples from the USA, there appears to be a suggestion that the link between franchising and low levels of failure is a highly speculative one, but one that illustrates a popular line of thought. Significantly, the contention that franchisees illustrate superior financial performance compared to their non-franchised counterparts has rarely been tested empirically. Nonetheless, reflecting the possibility of a spurious link, a number of researchers have aggressively criticized the findings of US-based research company Frandata, which suggested that franchise loans are a safe risk for bank lending as the closure rate, amongst those it surveyed, was less than 2%

(Nichols, 1995). Equally, the Federal Trade Commission argues that there is no accurate data available to prove that franchises have a lower failure rate than new businesses. This observation is particularly reflective of the UK where franchise research is still in its infancy *per se*. There is, therefore, a need for some independently generated data to help establish whether franchisees illustrate superior financial performance than non-franchised businesses and to examine the performance differences among franchises.

Unlike the orientation of Chapter 8, realizing these objectives necessitates an examination of franchisee performance rather than death. Failure does not just refer to death, but also under-performance and decline (Miller, 1977). Such a focus is necessary since evaluating franchisee attrition is fraught with vested interests and has proved highly problematic in the past. As part of this second investigation, and by expanding on previous research analyzing the credit scores of fast food franchisees (Price, 1993), some effort is devoted to examining the variation of franchisee economic rents. This examination is conducted through the multiple test of the null hypothesis that the proportion of fast food franchisees with above average performance does not vary according to the favourability of certain exogenous conditions. Instead, by focusing on decline, an outline of the options that franchisors may pursue in assisting floundering franchisees is presented.

Prior studies of franchisee performance

Much of the research concerning performance differences between franchised and non-franchised concerns derives from the franchise fraternity itself, rather than being independently generated. There also exist differences in definitions of performance and failure. Nonetheless, methodological issues aside for the moment, by using uncorroborated franchisor data the conclusion that franchises illustrate lower rates of failure than non-franchised firms may not be entirely appropriate. Table 9.1 compares failure rates within the catering industry versus those experienced by franchisees. In absolute terms, there appear to be more failures in the hospitality industry than in franchising. The figure for franchising may, however, be lower since the data presented below includes franchise failures in Scotland. Whilst of some general interest, such information is of limited use as the two industries differ in their composition. The franchise 'market' contains businesses from a variety of SIC codes, not just hotel and catering concerns.

In terms of rate of attrition, the NatWest/BFA surveys indicate an average total failure rate of 10.5% (11% in 1993) within the franchise sector, of which about 35% are for commercial reasons. That is, they have failed as a result of being bought back, closure, sold off or changing the franchisee. These represent about 2% to 3% of all insolvencies and bankruptcies in England and Wales. By comparison, the proportion of insolvencies and bankruptcies in the English and Welsh hospitality markets appears to have risen to represent approximately 3% of VAT-registered caterers in those markets and also represents over 6% of all insolvencies and bankruptcies in England and Wales. *Primae facie*, using commercial failures as a proxy for franchisee attrition rates, the death rate in the hospitality market exceeds that of the franchise 'industry'. But when the total figure is employed, the franchisee attrition rate is the same as, if not slightly higher than, the hospitality industry. It is also notable that the franchisee failure statistics appear to have fallen when others have increased. For the reasons stated in 'Problems of quantification' in Chapter 8, however, the degree of comparability here is limited.

Whilst VAT deregistration, bankruptcy and insolvency data has provided at least some insight to the level of business deaths in the hospitality industry, only a limited view of the exit rate in its franchisee sub-sector has emerged. As mentioned in Chapter 8, the establishment of franchisee failure rates is problematic for a variety of reasons. Emerson (1990) and Cross (1994), however, suggest that a turnover rate (or rate of discontinuance) may be a more meaningful statistic, since it defines the difficulty of opening a successful franchise. Watson and Everett (1986) suggest that discontinuance is suitable proxy for failure as it suggests that resources have been shifted to more profitable opportunities and may be of more use in comparing industries. Discontinuance is defined as either change of ownership or closure (McEvoy and Aldrich, 1984). However, in franchising there may be built-in discontinuance since most franchises operate for a fixed term, for example five years, after which the franchisee may decide to resign or move on. The decision to stay or leave a particular system may be reflective of the life-stage of the franchisee and degree of satisfaction between the franchisee and franchisor. Referring to discontinuance indirectly, Parker (1973), for example, observes that:

As he acquires managerial skills and grows to resent the constraining, inflexible influence placed upon him by the franchisor, he may look for ways out of the relationship. As his personal success grows so do his opportunities for investments elsewhere. (pp. 227–28)

Industry	1988	1989	1990	1991	1992	1993
Hotel & catering bankruptcies	625	719	867	1,481	2,366	2,437
Hotel & catering insolvencies	359	371	489	748	1,010	912
Hotels & catering total[1]	984	1,090	1,356	2,229	3,376	3,349
No. of Hotel & catering units[1]	n/a	111,405	112,829	111,916	107,413[2]	104,702
Rate of attrition (%)	n/a	1.0	1.2	2.0	3.1	3.2
UK bankruptcies	7,728	8,141	12,060	22,632	32,106	31,016
UK insolvencies	9,427	10,456	15,051	21,827	24,425	20,708
Total UK industry[1]	17,155	18,597	27,111	44,459	56,531	51,724
Hotels & catering %[1]	5.7	5.9	5.0	5.0	6.0	6.5
Total no. of franchise failures	1,546	1,577	1,419	1,800	1,765	1,760
% failure[3] rate amongst franchises (all types)	9.7	9.5	10.4	11.9	10.5	11.0
Franchisee failure for commercial reasons	325	310	316	545	630	360
% franchise commercial failure as a % total industry insolvencies	3.5	3.3	3.0	3.6	2.6	1.7

Source: Department of Trade/Business Monitor PA1003/BFA/National Westminster Bank (various years)
[1] = refers to England & Wales only and population of units refers to no. of VAT registered units;
[2] = expanded to include business registered for VAT with turnover below VAT threshold;
[3] = refers to 'forced' and 'voluntary' changes.

Table 9.1: UK bankruptcies and insolvencies

For such measure to be of use, however, the rates of discontinuance in franchising need to reflect the changes of ownership within the term of the franchise. This proviso further exacerbates the degree of comparability to other sectors and industries. Nevertheless, of late, the low rates of franchisee failure propounded by many franchisors have been open to question. In a study examining various owner traits and operational characteristics of a sample of US-based franchise and non-franchise young firms, Bates (1995) empirically shows that franchisees have a higher rate of discontinuance than the cohort of independent firms. He argues, therefore, that it appears that franchise 'industry' claims of higher survival rates among young franchisee businesses, relative to independent start-ups, may be untenable. This contention is also partially supported by the National Restaurant Association who observe that the discontinuance level in the US fast food franchises was about 29% (see Table 9.2) in the 1980s, which is twice the level for all service firms and nearly triple the rate for all businesses. There is only circumstantial evidence to suggest that the UK discontinuance rate may also be high. Examining UK franchisee attrition between 1987/88 and 1992, Power (1993) illustrates a discontinuance rate of 28% over the five years under review. Comparing 'closers' and 'continuers', he shows that the prospects for survival of catering, health and beauty and leisure franchisees were lower than that for other business format franchisees.

Data problems, such as the US-bias and inconclusive nature of British research, suggests that an alternative measure of failure is required rather than to necessarily rely on franchisor/franchisee responses and trade bodies with their vested interests. One such approach is the measurement of decline and the tendency for under-performance. This necessitates access to franchisee data, some of which is in the public domain through the registration of company accounts. It is, however, also an approach where a dearth of empirical research and statistics exist but one which may be of greater significance to managers and franchisors. It permits them to readily identify weak players and deploy resources to facilitate turnarounds. So, what do we mean by the term 'failure as decline'?

Year	Company-owned			Franchisee-owned		
	Discontinued	Total	(%)	Discontinued	Total	(%)
1980	392	17,826	2.3	1,408	42,133	3.4
1981	401	19,355	2.3	1,454	42,491	3.5
1982	354	19,857	1.8	1,084	43,700	2.6
1983	445	21,785	2.2	1,085	45,743	2.5
1984	306	22,951	1.4	1,024	47,544	2.2
1985	537	23,574	2.3	1,622	50,318	3.4
1986	601	24,364	2.6	1,435	53,839	2.9

Source: National Restaurant Association, 1989.

Table 9.2: Discontinuance of franchised restaurants in the USA

Failure as 'decline'

Starting from the premise that failure is predictable due to the existence of observable symptoms, a substantial body of literature shows that statistical methods utilizing financial ratios can predict company failures with a reasonable, but varying, degree of success (Balthory, 1985). Others, for example Argenti (1976), have employed more qualitative approaches to evaluating decline where the financial ratios are symptomatic of underlying causes, such as weak management, autocracy and the inability to adapt to prevailing circumstances. Under both research streams, failure is not defined as death, but rather characterized by protracted periods of poor profits and eroding market share (Miller, 1977; Slatter, 1984). Thus trouble, taking the form of declining or lower than average performance, manifests itself before failure. Bankruptcy and insolvency is the final stage in a company's inability or lack of consideration to anticipate, recognize, avoid, neutralize, or adapt to external or internal pressures that threaten the organization's long-term survival (Weitzel and Jonsson, 1989; Hambrick and D'Aveni, 1988).

Perhaps reflective of the economic conditions between 1989 and 1995, some fast food franchisors, like the major grocery chains, have long been discounting their prices and advertising heavily to generate sales. Whilst volumes of meals served may have improved, it has also resulted in pressure on and decreased profitability on their operations and those of their franchisees. Symptomatic of such conditions and other company-specific problems, Haynes (1995) reported, after analyzing 1,978 restaurant and catering companies, that over half of all companies surveyed experienced financial problems in 1994 in Britain, but also established that the market was now growing with average sales increasing. Employing a credit score methodology to categorize the companies' financial health into one of five rankings (strong, good, mediocre, caution and danger), the report indicated that (in 1994) 57% (1993: 67%) of UK restaurant and catering firms were rated 'caution' or 'danger'. In such companies, failure may not be imminent but reflects the urgent need for change in the structure and/or finances of a company. Only 30% of UK restaurant and catering companies were rated 'strong' or 'good' performers in 1994, compared to 23% in 1993. These results may help to confirm arguments positing that the sharp increase in the number of bankruptcies and insolvencies within the hotel and catering industry over the last four years meant that there must have been numerous companies in difficulties before the recession reached its low point.

One exception to the general dearth of research on the subject of failure as decline in franchises is Price (1993), who employs a solvency-score measure (Taffler's z-score) to evaluate performance differences between three different categories:

1. fast food franchisees;
2. franchisors from a variety of differing economic settings;
3. non-franchised fast food concerns.

His results suggest that fast food franchisee companies illustrated a greater tendency to good performance than franchisors between 1987 and 1990. Both franchisors and fast food franchisees illustrated superior performance to non-franchised fast food companies. In spite of this effort, the study only employed a small sample (eighteen in each category), only used one performance variable, and did not investigate whether the differences between and among the firms in each category were statistically significant. The current study seeks to build on those tentative foundations by employing a multi-variate analysis to empirically test the popular tenet that franchisees illustrate superior financial performance. Using the UK fast food industry as a context, we seek to elucidate financial performance differences between franchisees and non-franchised businesses in particular. Although the study is conducted with a larger sample size (described below), the latitude to generalize the results into other economic settings and cultures is strictly limited. The limitation is a result of the differing competitive conditions, norms of behaviour, and economic growth levels.

Why do franchisees fail?

The rationale for franchisee failure are manifold, but according to Cross and Walker (1988), fall into five main categories:

1. Business fraud, such as the use of celebrities to attract investors to ill-founded franchise schemes (not necessarily evident in Britain).
2. Intra-system competition, involving franchise outlets being located too close together and cannibalizing sales but maximizing the franchisor's sales-based royalties (Hadfield, 1991; Kaufmann and Rangan, 1990).
3. Insufficient ongoing support of franchisees, encompassing advertising support, pre-opening programmes and management assistance. Such a situation may arise from constraints on the franchisor's resources and/or the franchisor having too much focus on new store openings. This latter cause has been observed in a number of fast food chains (Lanthier, 1995).
4. Poor franchisee screening resulting in a mis-match between franchisee's attributes and success criteria.
5. Persistent franchisor-franchisee conflict.

Of all of the rationale for franchisee failure, point 4 is the main reason cited by many franchisors. Reflecting the overlap between generic and franchise-specific reasons and the inherent and expedient bias toward 'personal failure' explanations of franchisee attrition (Kursch, 1968), when acknowledgement of franchisee failure is made by the 'industry', the emphasis is typically put on franchisee incompetence – for example, 'They did not do their homework' or 'did not realize just how hard the work was'. Indeed, it has been observed, by some, that prospective franchisees sometimes bring failure on themselves as they fail to write a business plan and are often reluctant to employ professional advisers to evaluate franchise offerings because of cost considerations and difficulties in identifying specialist franchise solicitors. Yet, the franchisor typically prefers franchisees without prior direct or self-employment experience and constrains the amount of information concerning the franchise due to fears of imitation! Other researchers, such as (Ozanne and Hunt, 1971), argue that some of the franchisor literature concerning projected earnings is over-inflated and over-optimistic. This situation reduces the possibility of objective assessment in the first instance.

Equally, failure may ensue because the franchisee takes on a store which is inherently weak – a fact that may not have been communicated to the franchisee – and is unable to realize a turnaround. Seltz (1982), for example, illustrates that some franchisors may be implicitly biased toward such action. He suggests that where a store has shown a history of break-even or close to break-even, the decision may not be between maintaining the unit as a company-owned operation or transferring it to franchisee ownership. Rather, the choice may be between transferring it to franchisee ownership or 'writing-off' the company's investment in it.

Confirming the findings of Chapters 6 and 7, this observation suggests that some franchisees appear to fail because franchisors do not share the relative risks and benefits of their relationship with each other. Rather, some franchisors differentiate their vertical structure according to the level of environmental risk and volatility (Desai and Srinivasan, 1993; Gallini and Lutz, 1992; Hanson, 1995). Whilst such practices have been researched within the context of the US franchise sector, Amin *et al* (1986) and Mason (1989) suggest that such policies are also evident in the UK. Specifically, they infer that large firms have encouraged management buy-outs and franchising as a means of withdrawing from marginal and unprofitable markets and, thereby, shift the burden of risk away from the parent body to the newly formed independent company or franchisee.

Although instructive, these research streams have not considered, explicitly, the relationship between franchisee financial performance and environmental instability. Yet, there may be important implications for the franchise relationship deriving from such work. For example, by shifting the burden of risk in this way, some franchisors may be jeopardizing their reputations and continuity of income flow from franchisees in certain markets. Conversely, however, the franchisee may, in fact, be able to derive a livelihood from a volatile, risk-laden market due to advertising investments (Desai, 1994), their profit orientation and the franchisee's vested interest in making the unit/s work (Agrawal and Lal, 1995). Profitability may be affected as a result of the franchisee's implicit conflict with labour and competitors as well as from the sheer effort devoted to their business to recoup their initial investments. Such inter-organizational incentives, therefore, may have implications for the performance of franchisee-operated units:

> Running a McDonald's is a three-hundred-sixty-three days-a-year business [the restaurants are closed only on Thanksgiving and Christmas], and an owner-operator, with his personal interests and incentives can inherently do a better job than a chain manager. (Love, 1986: pp. 292–93)

Being located at the point of sale, the franchisee ought to be able to respond much more quickly to changes in market conditions, although the nature of this response is partially restricted by the parameters of the franchise agreement. Some franchisees are, however, better able to alter their cost structures than others in response to exogenous conditions and survive in areas of low population density (Dahlstrom and Nygaard, 1994). As such, where intra-brand performance variances are not explained by environmental factors, alternative explanations – for example, franchisee behavioural variables and franchisee-franchisor relational issues – may be significant. This said, competence is, in part, dependent on the quality of training that the franchisee receives and their learning capability (Pettit, 1988). Thus, where environmental factors play little part, inter-brand performance differences may be due to brand-specific aspects, which would be consistent with other franchise research. For example, Baucus *et al* (1993) and Sen (1993) illustrate that franchisors vary their royalties and initial fees according to the perceived quality of the franchise, where the higher the fees the higher the quality of the brand, training and potential returns. Chapter 4 suggests that these fees may also be determined by the strategic group dynamics in which franchisors operate.

Some franchisors provide their franchisees with good training, ongoing support, and both above-the-line and below-the-line advertising which can result in high levels of motivation and partially explain inter-brand performance differences. Whilst the quality of such support may alter by the nature of the franchisor, franchisees in 'good' systems are perceived as illustrating 'better' and 'wider' management skills than the owners/managers of non-franchised small firms (Ibrahim, 1985; Pashigan, 1961). Such managerial superiority is seen to derive from the training the franchisee receives once accepted into the system. Franchisee failures tend to be perceived as those who experienced difficulty in conforming to the franchisor's plan either as a result of being previously self-employed, under-capitalization, overtly high franchisee renumeration or because of ineffective implementation ability (Power, 1993) in areas such as delegation, marketing strategy, staff training, strategic planning, management of cash flow and accounting system. Yet, there are a variety of interpretations of 'training', the processes it encompasses and the outcomes of those processes (Campanelli *et al*, 1994), suggesting that blaming the franchisee for failure is not always apt – although probably convenient.

In this sense, perhaps, the arguments supporting low rates of franchisee attrition are indicative of studies comparing the characteristics of exiting subsidiaries with those of exiting independents. According to this research (Kamshad, 1994; Phillips and Kirchhoff, 1989), single plant firms are far more prone to exit than subsidiary plants. This may reflect the latter benefiting from experience existing elsewhere in the business as well as, perhaps, a tolerance towards sub-optimal performance. Consistent with the conceptualization of business format franchises as a form of M-type organization, franchisees may be viewed as a 'subsidiaries' as, in spite of being legally independent from the franchisor, they are contractually obliged to adhere to the franchisor's strategy. Although the tolerance argument – or franchisee satisificing behaviour – has not been subject to research effort, circumstantial evidence points to its presence.

As franchisors gain their revenue from sales volumes, they may have little interest in franchisee profitability; the banks may be tolerant as long as the debt is being serviced; and the franchisees, with their lack of experience and high levels of satisfaction in the initial stages, may not be motivated toward self-actualization and have lower levels of achievement and initiative than entrepreneurs (Anderson and Weitz, 1992). In a study examining franchisee satisfaction, Hing (1995) observed that 70% of her respondents thought that their business was more successful because it was franchised. But, given that few franchisees generally have had experience in the same business setting and of self-employment, their basis for comparison is questionable. Nevertheless, it suggests that this belief may permit franchisees to be tolerant to low levels of performance since they believe that independent concerns are comparatively worse off than they are – even though it may, in fact, not be true – and the perceived exit and switching costs of other employment options are high and are, in part, governed by the franchise contract. Furthermore, as franchisees are not entrepreneurial and more risk averse (English and Hoy, 1995), so they are perhaps more likely to have different opportunity cost thresholds, concentrate on survival rather than growth, and thus have a greater propensity to live with lower returns in the short term (Cooper *et al*, 1992; Dodge *et al*, 1994).

Additional 'personal failure' reasons include:

- went ahead despite family opposition;
- spent money on good things of life before they had earned it;
- could not stomach selling demands of the job;
- did not have the self-discipline to cope with the loneliness of a small business;
- under-funded and misled the franchisor on the amount of funds available.

Although not examined here specifically due to the lack of widespread practice, another potential risk factor to the franchisee is whether the franchisor is a 'habitual' owner. Hall (1995) suggests that habitual owners tend to fall into two categories: 'serial' and 'portfolio' owners. The former are those who own one business after another but effectively only one business at a time. The previous businesses may have been either voluntarily or involuntarily sold or closed. The latter are those who own more than one business simultaneously. The franchisee is possibly at greater risk by joining a habitual franchisor than single-business operators who have a longer track record. For example, if the business is voluntarily sold – either because of being acquired or performance falling below a certain pre-defined threshold – the acquirer may not wish to expand via franchising or have an organization orientated toward franchisee management. Equally, if the previous companies have been closed involuntarily the implications of becoming a franchisee are perhaps more obvious. With portfolio franchisors, the franchisee should question the franchisor's degree of commitment to the concept as well as their ability to manage two or more different businesses.

Failure has also been attributed to the franchisee's initial motivation for joining a system. The franchisee may be motivated, in part, to purchase a franchise to escape from either unemployment or poor job prospects but may not have the skills to manage his or her own business (Ashman, 1987; Justis et al, 1993). But the notion that unemployed founders of firms and franchisees are likely to be inferior is largely conjecture rather than based on empirical evidence. This conjecture assumes that individuals pushed into pursuing their career either through franchising or self-employment will be less able and have less time and fewer resources, to identify market niches and competitive conditions, and to develop new skills. Whilst there are undoubtedly some who have limited adaptability to being a franchisee or wholly self-employed, others are more successful (Kitson, 1995). Thus, franchisors who rely on such 'personal failure' explanations may not be addressing the true cause of some franchisees' demise. For example, it may be argued that financial problems may lead to franchisee disillusionment and failure. Equally, franchisors' claims in the recruitment process may lead the franchisee to have high expectations which bear little correlation to the reality of the situation, leading to work transition mis-match.

Conversely, when a franchisee is financially successful, the causal factors are typically attributed to the benefits of the franchise system without acknowledgement of the environmental conditions under which the franchisee is trading, especially as some franchisees operate in volatile environments. Indeed, franchisee survival has often been attributed, by franchisors and researchers alike, to the nature of the franchise system which places the majority of owner-operators at the point of sale. This reflects a possible bias toward process innovations, and franchisees' costs tend to be lower than those experienced at company-owned outlets. This said, there is often more of a tendency for franchisees to pass wage increases on to the customer, but this may be less evident amongst franchisors as a result of being more sensitive to their competitors (Card and Krueger, 1994; Sheldon, 1967).

Such observations in themselves, however, may derive from promotional material distributed by franchisors. Clapham and Schwenk (1991), for example, show that there is a tendency for managers to take credit for good outcomes and lay blame on the environment for poor outcomes. This, they argue, may result from a kind of cognitive bias which affects the way in which managers recall events prior to positive and negative outcomes. When planning for the future, they focus on those actions which their companies can take to achieve these outcomes; good results 'prove' their rationale often lies in the action they took. If the outcomes are negative, it is not possible to explain them through management actions. In franchise systems, therefore, franchisee failure is almost automatically attributed to personal reasons or the environment. So, are franchisors right in their diagnosis? In order to test this the effect of environmental munificence on franchisee performance is examined.

'Location, location, location'

It has often been noted that the three most important properties of a retail store, hotel and small business are 'location, location, location' (Cortjsens and Cortjsens, 1995). Indeed, Mason and Harrison (1985) and, latterly, Keeble *et al* (1993) conclude that the local environment may be an important influence upon the prospects of small-firm performance and survival (O'Farrell and Hitchins, 1988; Feldman, 1995; Sheppard, 1995). Traditionally, resource-based theorists have differentiated between favourable and unfavourable environments with the former being abundantly equipped with labour, managerial expertise, potential customers, material supplies and infrastructure (Christensen and Montgomery, 1981; Porter, 1979). According to this perspective, unfavourable environmental (or resource deficient) conditions have a potentially negative effect on performance and survival, but may be a prompt for innovation.

Reflecting a tendency toward resource explanations, a prodigious amount of academic research has analyzed the rationale behind retail location. For example, locational attributes have been viewed as one of the most important determinants of hospitality business and franchisee performance (Baum and Mezias, 1992; Dunning, 1989; Seltz, 1982), with price and promotion being of secondary significance (Kimes and Fitzsimmons, 1990). These locational attributes may encompass a wide variety of variables and will differ according to the business under review. For example, hotel location may be determined, in part, by the projected number of tourists, proximity to shopping, restaurants, businesses, cultural activities and other outside activities (Fish and Rudolph, 1986; Troy and Beals, 1982). By contrast, fast food operations are more orientated toward density of traffic – be they pedestrian (especially in Britain) or in an automobile – and their proximity to shopping, leisure, banking facilities, etc. (Ball *et al*, 1988; West, 1992).

Within the context of retail and foodservice establishments, researchers have distinguished between the selection of a trading area and the selection of a particular site (Melaniphy, 1992; Stefanelli, 1990), where each potentially affects performance. The trading area decision depends not only on its population density *per se*, but also its distribution of income, competition, working patterns of the local population, propensity to eat out and the economic growth of the area (Min, 1987; Sim and Gleeson, 1994) and is a hygiene factor for survival.

Thus, the trading area characteristics potentially affecting performance of fast food units appear to be dichotomized into poor performers being located near to infrequent users and stronger performers being in areas with customers illustrating more frequent use. In the UK, people who never or very rarely frequent fast food/takeaway establishments are those over 55, lower income groups and those not working or those without dependent children. Infrequent users are more likely to be housewives, the AB and E socio-economic groups and those aged over 34. High frequency customers are likely to be the young (Yavas and Vardiabasis, 1987), those living in south-east England, one-person households, in socio-economic groups C1C2 and D, and men and women in employment. Soberon-Ferrer and Dardis (1991), however, establish that there are differences between full-time and part-time working wife households for meals purchased out-of-the-home, with part-timers spending less than full-timers. However, there are differences by product category. For example, adults who frequent fast food hamburger bars tend to be in low-income groups with an average household income of about £125 per week; those eating fish and chips tend to be more affluent (CACI, 1994). But regions with sufficient hygiene factors also tend to be those with the highest concentration of competing businesses. Inter alia, the greater the density of customers with such characteristics, the more munificent the environment but the greater the propensity for competition.

In relation to franchises, much of the literature has concerned the extent to which the franchisor will add units within a particular location (either their own and/or other franchisees) and the impact of such decisions on franchisee market share and unit sales (Ghosh and Craig, 1991; Mathewson and Winter, 1994; Zeller *et al*, 1980). In being sales orientated, the franchisor has two options to increase revenue: increase sales from existing stores (through, for example, new products and advertising); or expand the number of outlets. The latter option is viewed as preferable to the franchisor since the incremental income from new stores will be greater than from new products, it permits the potential for economies of scale to be attained, strengthens the network *vis-à-vis* the competition and has a more immediate impact than the first option. The addition of new units in close proximity to existing units (whilst facilitating monitoring economies), however, may serve to cannibalize sales, lower performance and cause discontent within the franchise system (Anderson and Naurus, 1984; Bernstein, 1994; Kaufmann and Rangan, 1990; Lovell, 1971). From a theoretical perspective, the potential for cannibalization, discontent and failings in traditional methods of site selection, such as analogue, checklist and gravity or spatial models (Current and Storbeck, 1994; Kaufmann *et al*, 1995), has prompted researchers to develop a location allocation model to systematically evaluate multi-store locations. This latter approach helps to determine the best locations for new retail outlets based on corporate objectives and allocations of consumers to those locations, but has tended to remain theoretical and, although instructive, has not been tested on 'live examples'. The traditional methods of site selection employed by franchisors vary greatly – some employ the checklist option – and others use a multiple regression model (Melaniphy, 1992).

In general, therefore, the resource-based vein indicates that the agglomeration of certain types of retailer to certain trading areas is motivated by the accessibility of customers, oligopolistic reaction (Julian and Castrogiovanni, 1995; Knickerbocker, 1973), the reduction in travel and search costs of imperfectly informed customers and the possibility of increased profitability deriving from clustering (Brown, 1989). Within franchising, the clustering of units derives from the economics of monitoring franchisee units, increases the barriers to entry in a territory and the desire to generate brand equity within a particular locale prior to diversifying more widely. When resource explanations are applied to the UK, it could be argued that Greater London and the rest of the south east provide the most favourable environments for fast food and other retailer firm performance (Vaessen and Keeble, 1995). Using a simple product-portfolio matrix to illustrate the regional bias (Perlitz, 1991) of the catering industry, it is evident that London and the south-east of England are the cash cows of the UK hospitality industries. Other government defined standard regions, such as the south west, Wales and the East Midlands, appear to be 'stars' and the 'problems' (*P*) being the West Midlands and Yorkshire. The diagonal divides the regions into those which have lost market share against those which have gained.

The dominance and position of south-east England as a cash cow is also apparent from the average relative market shares of the differing regions between 1990 and 1993. The rest of the south east region has a market share almost one and a half times that of Greater London. The other markets have markets less than half the size of the rest of the south east.

Whilst cash cows have an entrenched superior market position (Day, 1977; Hedley, 1977), portfolio analysts suggest that such markets are unattractive since there is little

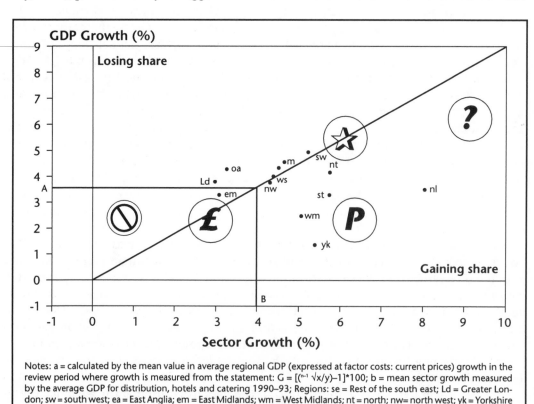

Notes: a = calculated by the mean value in average regional GDP (expressed at factor costs: current prices) growth in the review period where growth is measured from the statement: $G = [(^{n-1}\sqrt{x/y})-1]*100$; b = mean sector growth measured by the average GDP for distribution, hotels and catering 1990–93; Regions: se = Rest of the south east; Ld = Greater London; sw = south west; ea = East Anglia; em = East Midlands; wm = West Midlands; nt = north; nw= north west; yk = Yorkshire & Humberside; st = Scotland; ws = Wales; and ni = Northern Ireland.

Figure 9.1: Matrix for the UK catering industry, 1990–93

additional growth and 'crowded market conditions'. Indeed, Greater London and the south east illustrate the highest concentration of catering establishments per capita in the UK. It is these local environment conditions which may be of greater significance in affecting firm survival rates (Roure and Maidique, 1986) and, hence, a possible explanation for why the regions have the highest proportion of franchised restaurants in Britain (Horwath International, 1991). Thus, although regions outside south east England may be less resource abundant, they may be more conducive to realizing short-term superior performance as competitive intensity is lower.

However, others contend that the retailing and hospitality industries' aphorism is not entirely accurate. For example, Rumelt (1991) empirically observes that the most important sources of corporate performance in US manufacturing businesses derive from the resources or market positions that are specific to particular business units rather than to corporate resources or to membership in an industry. Further, recent literature on the population ecology of organizations (Aldrich, 1979; Hannan and Freeman, 1977; McKelvey, 1981) propound a Darwinistic process to be evident in that the environment plays an important role in affecting the fates of firms via creating pressure to adapt in a particular manner.

As a result of these managerial aspects, exogenous variables may not be addressing the true causes of a franchisor/franchisee's demise. There is growing evidence that managerial problems constitute a major reason for small-firm failure (Larson and Clute, 1979). A study of common causes in organizational decline (Bilbeault, 1982) concludes that 67% of them are due to managerial reasons or structural defects; only the remainder are the result of external factors. This said, there is little evidence illustrating the extent of impact which exogenous factors have on franchisees' performance. In support of Bilbeault's (1982) conclusions, are the dominance of operational, strategic and marketing influences in small-business failures. For example, Wada (1977), Renaghan (1976) and Keyt *et al* (1994) establish that locational aspects are of little importance to customers' purchasing behaviour and the success of fast food establishments. They argue that the cleanliness of the restaurant and speed of service are important purchasing determinants of fast food.

Methodology

In order to explore the performance of fast food franchisees relative to each other and non-franchised concerns, three empirical tests are conducted. These are detailed in the panel below. The sample of study for the first two tests is a selection of UK corporate/limited liability franchisees from differing fast food product categories, operating between 1989 and 1993. From a possible sample of 250 limited liability franchisees under eight franchisors, fifty-nine[2] were analyzed: eighteen from firm A, twenty-three from firm B, and eighteen from firm C (the chains have been kept anonymous for reasons of confidentiality). The reasons for omission of certain franchisors and franchisees include the companies being formed post-1989 (such as the majority of McDonald's, Perfect Pizza and Domino's Pizza franchisees), acquisition of the franchisee, differing foodservice operations (delivery versus counter and table service) and the fact that the franchises were subsidiaries of a larger concern (which, due to consolidated accounts, proved difficult to analyze for the franchise business alone).

Approaches of study

Study One: Franchisee performance and environmental munificence:
Sample size: Non-modified accounts: 25; Modified accounts sample: 59. All firms are franchisees.
Financial measures: Non-modified accounts: liquidity; net assets, Taffler's z-score; free cash flow to equity. Modified accounts: liquidity; net assets.
Environmental variables: Growth in GDP; regional average and marginal propensity to consume meals away from home; income distribution; proportion of women in employment; proportion of population under 15 years of age; ratio of one-person households; number of people per catering establishment.
Null hypothesis: The proportion of fast food franchisees with above-average performance does not vary according to the favourableness of certain exogeneous variables.

Study Two: Interlocking directorates and franchisee performance
Sample size: Modified accounts sample: 59. All firms are franchisees.
Financial measures: Modified accounts: return on shareholder's funds to total liabilities.
Null hypothesis: Franchisees with interlocking directorates do not illustrate superior performance to those without such inter-firm linkages.

Study Three: Performance differences between franchisees and non-franchised firms
Sample: Modified accounts sample: 134 (67 franchisees and 67 non-franchised firms).
Financial measures: Modified accounts: liquidity; quick ratio; shareholder's funds to total liabilities.
Null hypothesis: Differences in performance between franchisees and non-franchised concerns are not statistically significant.

Their financial details were collected and analyzed from Companies House[3] to monitor the sampled companies' level of performance as the UK economy slipped from growth into recession. Some limited liability franchisees had registered as dissolved or in receivership, but comparison of financial data with going concerns proved unfeasible since the former – typically – had only submitted accounts for one year. Of the usable accounts, twenty-five (42.4%) provided unabbreviated accounts to Companies House. These, therefore, have been evaluated from a broader array of perspectives than the approaches employed to analyze those with abbreviated accounts. Furthermore, the current study, because it concentrates on franchisee limited liability concerns, provides an incomplete coverage of the performance of fast food franchisee businesses. Restrictions on data availability, however, mean that the inclusion and comparison of non-limited liability concerns are unlikely to be overcome in the near future. The samples, in operating 253 units between them, are predominantly multi-unit franchisees, reflecting their increasing pervasiveness in the UK fast food industry (Bradach, 1994; Lowell, 1991). In being multi-unit franchisees, the sample represents, on average, about a quarter of the stores in the respective systems.

It should be observed that the proportion of limited liability franchisees in the fast food industry is relatively high compared to other franchise sectors.[4] To some extent, this may infer some degree of risk within the market. Most directors regard limited liability as the biggest advantage accruing from company status since, in the event of failure, a director may lose the business and his home (Page, 1984). In non-limited liability scenarios, the director may be made personally bankrupt. Indeed, given the uncertain economic climate of the early 1990s, risk-reduction may provide a partial explanation for the fall in the proportion of sole trader franchisees and the small increase in partnerships but rapid rise of limited liability franchisees.

In addition to elucidating differences between and among franchisees according to environmental criteria, a test is also conducted to establish whether performance differences accrue according to the presence of interlocking directorates. As noted in Chapter 6, some fast food franchisees are marked by their involvement with other businesses and this form of social capital may have implications for performance depending on the nature and volume of communication between the network actors. Chapter 8 has shown that, depending on the definition of failure, the catering industry is relatively volatile and comprises primarily small businesses. Perhaps indicative of the size issue, Chapter 6 also suggested that there are relatively few fast food franchisee firms with interlocking directorates. This finding appears to be consistent with UK retailing as a whole (Berkley-Thomas, 1978). Whilst there is a plethora of reasons for this situation, including lack of new incumbent experience, by examining the adage that 'two heads are better than one', a wealth of research has analyzed the propensity and benefits of entrepreneurial networking among new ventures and small businesses (Aldrich and Zimmer, 1986; Aldrich and Reese, 1993; Birley, 1985) and the subsequent implications for survival.

The high failure rate for new firms suggests a 'liability of newness' during their legimation process. Singh *et al* (1986) argue that this liability occurs because younger organizations have to learn new roles as social actors, co-ordinate new roles for employees and deal with problems of operating in a new marketplace. In order to overcome this liability, entrepreneurs must establish external legitimacy because it carries the possibility of increasing the likelihood of survival. The network of vested interests and constituencies of resources this process entails could also be important in the continuing operations of a business, especially in the reduction of uncertainty, mitigation of conflicts, be a source of competitive advantage, innovation and harmonization of interests and economize on environmental monitoring (Dollinger and Golden, 1992; Low and MacMillan, 1988; Ostgaard and Birley, 1994). In this sense, such networks may be interpreted as conjugate (Astley and Fombrun, 1982) since they represent the efforts of organizations to share resources or information in order to improve their organizational outputs and chances of survival. Possibly reflecting the benefit of information sharing and legitimation, Sheppard (1994; 1995) finds that interlocks between boards of directors have a statistically significant relationship to a corporation's likelihood of survival. Accordingly, franchisee businesses with interlocks may illustrate superior performance to those without such inter-firm linkages.

Environmental variables

In order to assess how the variablity of differing performance measures by regional environmental conditions, two levels of analysis were conducted: through individual measures and holistically. In the holistic analysis, the exogenous variables were placed into clusters to differentiate between differing levels of regional favourability.[5] Harrigan (1985) employs this methodology to evaluate strategic groups and indicates that the pupose of cluster analysis is to place objects, or clusters, suggested by the data, not defined *a priori*, such that objects in a given cluster tend to be similar in some sense, and objects in different clusters tend to be dissimilar. By using *ANOVA*, the differing clusters are then used as treatment groups to test the null hypothesis that exogeneous conditions do not affect performance. The *ANOVA* methodology is used to test the hyothesis that franchisee performance achieved does not differ by brand at a 5% level of significance. Sample size considerations preclude the use of *ANOVA* to analyze both inter- and intra-brand differences. As such, intra-brand performance differences are examined using the hypothesis test for comparing proportions to examine the null hypotheses that franchisee performance differs according to some of the following trading area environmental criteria perceived as critical success factors in franchising and fast food (as discussed above).

Growth in regional gross domestic product (GDPG). Due to the wide variation in the sizes of regions (defined according to government boundaries), comparisons of regional accounts are usually made in terms of per capita measures. In regions where the population has increased or fallen significantly, the growth in regional income may also be affected. Data concerning regional GDP is readily available from government sources and in order to differentiate between low and high regional economies, the mean value was calculated for each year. Under the environmental munificance hypotheses, franchisees in high-growth regional economies should illustrate superior performance compared to franchisees of the same brand in low-growth economies. It should be observed that, unlike the USA, regional inflation indices do not exist. As such, the UK figures are expressed in current prices.

Combined with measures of unemployment, low levels of GDP growth have been blamed for low levels of performance and failure (Altman, 1983; Desai and Montes, 1990; DiPietro and Sawhney, 1977; Simmons, 1989; Stewart and Gallagher, 1986). Whilst unemployment (measured here as the proportion of the civilian population *registering as unemployed* or *UNEM*) has illustrated an inverse relationship with performance in some countries, in the context of the UK market it is unclear what the hypothesized effect might be. The unemployment statistic, in particular, has been subject to numerous re-definitions by the government.

Regional average propensity (APC) and marginal propensity (MPC) to consume meals away from home. In accordance with economic studies, the average propensity to consume meals away from home is calculated by the simple function of total expenditure as a proportion of total disposable income. By contrast, the MPC is the proportion of each new increment of disposable income that is spent on consumption. Data concerning the average weekly household expenditure on meals consumed outside the home and average weekly disposable incomes is available from the annual *Family Expenditure Surveys*. Again, in order to differentiate between high- and low-growth consumption propensities, the mean is calculated. It is expected that those franchisees operating in regional economies with high average and marginal propensities to consume will illustrate superior performance to those operating in low-growth regional economies.

Income distribution (Y^d). It is axiomatic that wealth is unevenly distributed throughout economies. However, as income is the main determinant of socio-economic definition, statistics concerning the regional distribution of income should be indicative of the socio-economic bias of the territory. With regard to fast food consumption, infrequent customers tend to be those at the extremes of the socio-economic continuum, especially the lower end. As such, undue bias toward these extremities suggests that it will have a negative impact on performance. The variable was calculated from regional data produced in the *Family Expenditure Surveys* and divided into the categories employed by the geodemographic organization, CACI Ltd. As mentioned above, those households earning less than £125 per week were perceived as constituting the lower end of the socio-economic continuum but had one of the highest propensities to consume hamburgers and 'other' (including chicken) fast food products.

Other variables include: *proportion of women in employment (FEM)* as a ratio of the civilian workforce; proportion of *population under 15 years of age (YTH)*; ratio of *one-person households (SING)*; and *number of people per catering establishments (POP^n)*.

Performance variables

Measuring franchisee performance, like most aspects of the franchise literature, is under-researched. The few texts examining the subject have tended to adopt the franchisor's perspective, which in itself is indicative of some vested interest. For example, Chambers (1996) defines an under-performing franchisee as 'the franchisee who is not achieving the sales levels that the franchisor thinks he should' (p. 6). He then goes on to suggest that sales differences are the root of many serious disputes between the franchisee and franchisor; he also suggests different causes of the low levels of sales and some possible remedies. Yet, as Chapter 6 shows, the franchisee does not live off sales, but profit. To reiterate sales increases is neither a necessary nor sufficient condition for an increase in franchisee profits. Sales levels are a hygiene factor for the realization of profits and, according to portfolio theory (McKiernan, 1992), managers pursue sales growth even at the expense of profit. For the franchisee, such a policy would mean a negative impact on his ability to accumulate capital and, therefore, likely to be a trigger for conflict.

Rather than reflecting the franchisor's interests, although it should be of interest to franchisors whether a franchisee is financially buoyant, we do not measure performance in sales terms and evaluate performance differences within a single franchisor brand and between brands. Due to the submission of summarized accounts, inter-brand comparisons are based on univariate measures. For those submitting non-summarized accounts, multivariate measures are used. Although failure is, arguably, a multi-dimensional concept and is unlikely to be encapsulated in a single ratio, the univariate approach is the most popular method employed by analysts to provide a picture of a company's comparative health. For parsimony, only three such measures are calculated.

Liquidity (C^u). As noted earlier, solvency is important to survival and although long-term insolvency is equivalent to failure, it is precipitated by short-term insolvency. This latter condition is defined as an excess of current liabilities over current assets. It is this situation which also prompts many auditors to qualify their client's accounts.[6] There are two short-term solvency ratios in common use (the current ratio and the quick ratio) and, via time series analysis are potentially important symptoms of decline. In this study, only the current ratio is employed as the low levels of stock (as indicated by an average stock to sales ratio of about 2%) held by many fast food businesses mean that, often, the degree of difference between the two ratios is negligible. Although to some (Davies, 1991; Morley, 1984), the current ratio should be not less than two, the average and median current ratio for the UK restaurant and fast food sector between 1989 and 1993 was 0.5:1 (Dun & Bradstreet, 1995; ICC Reports, 1995). Such a low level of liquidity may be indicative of the tendency to borrow in the short term, but should be of little concern to the main brands. In the case of the smaller brands (such as new franchisors and their franchisees), it suggests that they may not be in a position to meet their debts as they fall due. The current ratio has also been employed as a measure of unabsorbed organizational slack (Singh, 1988). Such slack may help the firm to cushion the effects of an illiberal environment and, therefore, the higher the degree of slack the healthier the firm.

Free Cash Flow to Equity (FCFE). The free cash flow to equity ratio is the residual cash flow after meeting the firm's financial needs.[7] It can be negative, in which case the firm has to raise new equity, by raising finance. If it is positive, it could be (but is not always) paid out as dividend to equity investors. Although net income is more commonly employed to measure the return to equity investors, free cash flow represents the cash flow after operating expenses, interest, principal payments, and capital expenditure. As such, it is of significance to the franchisee since it, in effect, represents all of their earnings. Additionally, Welsch and White (1981), concentrating on financial problems and financial analysis models particular to small businesses, pinpointed the principal concern as cashflow. Derived from the sample of twenty-five limited liability fast food franchisee firms with non-modified accounts used in Study One, Table 9.3 (which may be of interest to potential franchisees) illustrates that cash flow was more of an issue in years one and two (being less than 2% of sales). In later years, there is an improvement in free cash flow, and this is achieved against increasing operating costs.

Net Assets (NA). Due to the prevalence of companies providing abbreviated accounts, the net assets are calculated, where net assets are equated with total assets (fixed assets + intangible assets + current assets) less total liabilities. This measure (typically presented by the natural logarithm) has been employed by a variety of researchers (for example, Shepherd, 1971) to measure firm size. The measure represents the capital cost aspect of entry barriers and that effect alters with relative, not absolute, size. Given that franchisee firm size (in addition to environmental and brand affiliation considerations) may impact on performance, net assets is used as a variable in a two-factor randomized *ANOVA* test. Other researchers and practitioners have employed net assets as a valuation technique for unquoted concerns. In this capacity, net assets differences by brand affiliation may be indicative of supporting evidence for the contention that some franchises create greater value and ex-post economic rents than others (Kaufmann and Lafontaine, 1994).

Multi-Discriminant Factors (Z^{Tfr}). Whilst univariate performance measures have received some criticism for their inability to reflect the multidimensional nature of decline, some researchers (for example, Keasey and Watson, 1985; 1986) have urged caution in the application of multidiscriminant analysis to small enterprises, such as franchises. They argue that many of the models are based on large publicly quoted concerns (where failures are relatively rare) and that small firms have low levels of diversity (Brooksbank, 1991), and differing financial and managerial structures. These aspects mean that small businesses are a very different animal from those encapsulated in traditional multi-discriminant methods. Others (for example, Robertson and Mills, 1988; Zmijewski, 1984) urge caution as reseachers typically estimate financial distress prediction models employ-

Profit & loss aspects		Year 1	Year 2	Year 3	Year 4	Year 5
Sales		100.0	100.0	100.0	100.0	100.0
Less:	Cost of sales	53.81	52.93	47.74	47.56	57.87
Gross profit		46.19	47.07	52.26	52.44	42.13
Operating costs	Staff costs	22.66	22.24	23.82	23.47	22.12
	Others (inc. rent)	12.58	13.97	18.91	17.21	20.01
	Total	35.24	36.22	42.72	40.68	42.13
Plus:	Other revenues	0.87	−0.31	0.75	3.09	0.64
Net costs		34.27	36.53	41.98	37.59	41.50
EBITDA		11.82	10.53	10.28	14.85	12.42
Less:	Depreciation	5.02	5.01	5.25	5.61	4.92
EBIT		6.79	5.52	5.04	9.24	7.50
Less:	Interest	3.64	4.04	4.51	4.04	2.68
EBT		3.16	1.48	0.53	5.21	4.81
Less:	Tax	1.65	0.74	0.75	1.28	1.72
Earnings		1.50	0.74	−0.22	3.92	3.09
Plus:	Depreciation	5.02	5.01	5.25	5.61	4.92
Operating cash		6.52	5.75	5.03	9.53	8.01
Balance sheet aspects		Year 1	Year 2	Year 3	Year 4	Year 5
Current assets		13.22	11.03	16.57	16.24	13.38
Less	Current liabilities	33.17	29.17	33.55	30.33	27.36
Working capital		−19.95	−18.68	−16.98	−14.09	−13.98
Annual change in working capital		−7.53	−1.59	2.30	2.82	−1.65
Net capital expenditure		12.8	5.4	−2.2	2.8	5.1
Free cash flow to equity		1.24	1.95	4.94	3.87	4.56
Ratios		Year 1	Year 2	Year 3	Year 4	Year 5
	Current ratio	0.40	0.37	0.49	0.54	0.49
	Quick ratio	0.37	0.34	0.46	0.51	0.45
	Stock ratio	0.13	0.13	0.12	0.10	0.12

Note: Except ratios, all figures are a percent of sales.

Table 9.3: Operating ratios for fast food franchisees

ing non-random samples, comparing the characteristics of failed and non-failed concerns. More recently, Aziz *et al* (1988) have criticized multidiscriminant analysis on the basis that the ratios included in such prediction models are based on 'a type of *ad hoc* pragmatism rather than a sound theoretical work' and, without the development of a theory of symptoms, there is little reason to expect a sustainable correlation between independent variables and the event to be predicted (Blum, 1974).

Much of the criticism of corporate failure models, however, is based on their ability to predict failure rather than simply present a snapshot of the comparative health of a firm. Although some researchers (Adams, 1992; Bruno *et al*, 1987; Edminster, 1972; Laitinen, 1992; Ohlson, 1980; Zavgren and Freidman, 1988), provide some vindication of the predictive power of multi-discriminant analysis, here it is used in a descriptive sense to quantify the degree of corporate risk. Unlike univariate analyses, the measures evaluate differing aspects of economic information in a set of accounts. As such, the many cases of low performance and possible franchisor/franchisee demise may have been observed earlier if this, more holistic, method was employed. *Inter alia,* if franchisees and franchisors alike measured their own and each other's company health, then this could prevent some of the less than effective crisis management, or firefighting, which has been adopted in the past.

Although there is a variety of widely recognized models to measure company health and performance, following Price (1993), Taffler's model is employed. According to Taffler (1984; 1995), a 'z' score – that is, the result of adding up different weighted ratios[8] – in excess of 0.2 and certainly 0.3 is characteristic of companies with good long-term survival prospects. Below 0.2 and certainly 0.0 is strongly indicative of symptoms of low performance and failure. Whilst companies can and do survive with scores in this 'danger zone' of 0.0 to 0.2, it is also clear that companies that consistently exceed 0.2 are likely to remain solvent and be successful for some time to come. The others, with scores in the danger zone, have some illnesses or defects, perhaps of a managerial/structural nature, which require attention before outright failure ensues. Just as potential franchisees should be wary of franchisors with low scores, however, so they should be equally guarded against those illustrating scores far in excess of the sector average.

Taffler's model is used in preference to other models here since it is not dependent upon the sampled firms being quoted on the stock exchange and is, therefore, more readily applicable to the hotel and catering/foodservice industry, especially given the density of small companies within its population. Furthermore, given the general structure of small companies' balance sheets and use of short-term loans, the 'no credit interval' in Taffler's model is of some importance when analyzing such companies' degree of health. The fact that the model was originally devised to analyze UK companies, unlike the methodology employed by Haynes (1995), only increases its applicability to the UK fast food sector.

Methodology for Study Three

One of the keys to evaluating performance differences is an understanding of what is meant by 'performance', especially as the term is dependent on the stand-point of the researcher. As a result of being branded (the strength of which is dependent on the franchisor's prior experience and investments in advertising and promotion) and advertising investments, franchisees may realize, on average, superior sales levels compared to their non-franchised counterparts. As the franchisor benefits from high levels of sales, it is in his interest to promote sales volumes because of the link to royalties. For the franchisor, franchisees are seen to illustrate superior performance compared to non-franchised businesses because they illustrate higher sales levels. As a result of their training, franchisees may be able to translate these higher sales into higher profits by modifications to their production processes (see Chapter 6). Whilst franchisees may benefit in this manner, they are contractually required, irrespective of profitability, to submit a proportion (typically 10%) of their net sales to the franchisor as rent for the brand name and to contribute to an advertising pool (Acheson and Paul, 1990). This is the equivalent to a tax on output which independent businesses do not have to bear; consequently it may be that independent businesses illustrate superior profitability to franchisees. As the focus of attention of the main text is the issues surrounding the individual's decision to become a franchisee, it is issues concerning profitability and solvency that are most pertinent. Like the independent businessman, the viability of a franchisee's business is reflected in its solvency.

The financial performance of 134 companies, comprising sixty-seven limited liability franchisee and sixty-seven non-franchised fast food businesses, for the years 1990–94 was calculated. The franchisees belong to the following systems: Wimpy, Burger King, KFC, Perfect Pizza, Domino's Pizza, Snappy Tomato Pizza and McDonald's. The independent concerns were selected in a semi-structured manner in that they were in a similar size classification bracket to the franchisees and were not involved in franchising activity of any manner. Since some of the sample submitted modified accounts to Companies House, the study only evaluates the performance differences between franchisees and non-franchised concerns using credit and gearing ratios (namely, the liquidity ratio, quick ratio and shareholder's funds to total liabilities). As franchisees typically incorporate the initial franchise fees into intangible assets (Lal, 1990; Sen, 1993), they may be expected to generate lower returns on assets and activity ratios. Independent start-ups, by contrast, do not usually acquire substantial brand capital at the outset of business activities and, therefore, may have a lower asset base than franchisees. This additional cost of entry could also mean that franchisees have higher borrowing ratios (shareholder's funds to total liabilities) than independent concerns. One-way *ANOVA* and an *F*-test are used to establish the statistical differences between the two groups. An *F*-test is closely associated to *ANOVA* and yields an *F* statistic. This is the ratio of the variance between groups (explained variance) to the variance within groups (unexplained variance).

Results of Studies One and Two

The tables below report the results of this research. Table 9.4 summarizes the different performance variables for each of the brands reviewed. It indicates that, on average, all franchisees increased in size and value over the period and saw decline in 1993. Firm C's franchisees illustrated the greatest increases in net assets, compared to the two other chains. In terms of liquidity, the sample illustrated slightly higher current ratios than the UK fast food and restaurant average, perhaps reflecting their brand strength. This said, there is an important proviso. When a franchisee applies to take on another unit from the franchisor, a financial assessment is conducted as part of a broader review of their capability (such as their conformance to the franchisor's operating standards, their organizational structure, sales growth, etc.) to manage the additional capacity (Lowell, 1991). The financial review typically includes establishing the franchisee's net cash flow, gearing, outstanding indebtedness to the franchisor, and liquidity, with parameters of the current ratio being set at between 0.7:1 to 0.85:1 (depending on the franchise system). The table shows that the current ratio for the sampled franchisees falls below these thresholds, which could affect the franchisee's ability to take on additional units and the franchisor's ability to expand the system through the existing stable of franchisees. This capability appeared to be constrained further in 1990, since the average liquidity, free cash flow and z-score fell. Average FCFE, however, has illustrated a return to buoyancy. This said, the standard deviations of the liquidity, z-score, and FCFE performance variables indicate that the sample is somewhat polarized. Indeed, the t-test range for FCFE is broad implying, through inductive reasoning, that some franchisees generate more cash than others. This polarity is, perhaps, more evident in the z-scores with the high standard deviations and over half of the sample generating a score of less than 0.2. On a related note, agency theorists predict that the franchisor will pay rents to the franchisee, an amount greater than the franchisee's best alternative employment. This means that franchisees are 'overpaid' relative to their outside opportunities such as managing a similar business (Michael, 1996). The average FCFE figures below appear to be substantially in excess of the average salary, of between £15,700 to £19,000, paid to a fast food manager in company-owned outlets in Britain, and therefore seems to provide some support for the 'overpaid' thesis. It should, however, be remembered that the universal applicability of this statement is strictly limited. The sample of franchisee firms includes multi-unit operators and derives from well-established brands, and even some of these realized negative FCFE. In addition, it is also appropriate to compare franchisees with independently-owned and operated concerns with franchisees rather than with employee salaries alone. The location of the units may also have a role to play. So, franchisee characteristics aside, what role do conditions within the franchisee's trading region play in affecting performance?

Brand and ratio	1989	1990	1991	1992	1993
B					
Net assets (£)	568,689	713,093	762,320	880,492	821,682
Current ratio (:1)	0.65	0.43	0.74	0.57	0.56
C					
Net assets (£)	436,247	606,544	798,600	810,715	800,543
Current ratio (:1)	0.55	0.61	0.61	0.64	0.55
A					
Net assets (£)	64,571	79,223	101,587	106,117	97,855
Current ratio (:1)	0.57	0.64	0.71	0.73	0.54
All (n = 59)					
Net assets (£)	374,484	487,202	571,809	619,056	594,404
Current ratio (:1)	0.60	0.55	0.69	0.64	0.55
FCFE (n = 25)					
$\bar{\times}$	68,573	–13,239	86,806	115,967	127,609
σ	367,282	302,827	244,940	303,834	320,681
t-test (α = 0.5):					
Upper range	220,187	111,768	187,917	241,389	259,982
Lower range	–83,041	–138,246	–14,305	–9,456	–4,764
Z^{Tfr} (n = 25)					
$\bar{\times}$	0.257	0.106	0.245	0.249	0.254
σ	0.222	0.624	0.591	0.270	0.274
% Z^{Tfr} ≤0.0	12	16	24	8	12
% Z^{Tfr} ≥0.0≤0.2	36	44	48	48	44

Table 9.4: Average annual performance measures for sampled fast food franchisees, 1989–93

Table 9.5 shows results of the brand affiliation-univariate performance *ANOVA* tests. The null hypothesis of interest is that brand affiliation does not yield average performance differences, that is:

$$H_0: \alpha_k = 0 \text{ and } H_1: \alpha_k \neq 0$$

The performance measures for each franchisee were summarized by calculating the mean, standard deviation and, to reduce the effects of outliers, the absolute deviation (Hartigan, 1975). Since the computed value of the F statistics are not greater than $F_{crit} = 3.136$, the hypothesis of no brand effect cannot be rejected at the 5% level of significance. The table provides support for the null hypothesis in that brand affiliation does not yield statistically different levels of net assets and liquidity. What differences exist are perhaps reflective of the differing economic costs of becoming a franchisee with the brands under review; they also suggest that, by using net assets as measure of value, some brands have greater value than others, but not overly so. These figures may be of some significance to potential franchisees seeking to realize potentially high returns and provides partial

Source of variation	SS	MS	F-ratio	P-value
Brand v. net assets				
Absolute deviation				
Between group	1.6E + 11	7.8E + 10	1.323	0.273
Within group	3.9E + 12	5.9E + 10		
Total	4.0E + 12			
Mean				
Between group	7.25E + 11	3.62E + 11	0.228	0.796
Within group	1.05E + 11	1.58E + 12		
Total	1.05E + 11			
Standard deviation				
Between group	2.36E + 11	1.18E + 11	1.463	0.239
Within group	5.32E + 11	8.06E + 10		
Total	5.56E + 12			
Brand v. current ratio				
Absolute deviation				
Between group	0.29	0.145	1.486	0.234
Within group	6.42	0.097		
Total	6.71			
Mean				
Between group	0.2	0.098	0.298	0.743
Within group	21.63	0.328		
Total	21.83			
Standard deviation				
Between group	0.38	0.192	1.526	0.225
Within group	8.30	0.125		
Total	8.69			

NB: df within group = 2; between group = 66; Critical F = 3.136

Table 9.5: One-way ANOVA results: brand affiliation versus performance

evidence to negate the network externality approach to promoting franchises. Despite perceived inter-brand differences, brand name does not, in itself, equate with franchisee success. Albeit with reference to McDonald's, Kroc (1977) summarizes this point:

> McDonald's does not confer success on anyone. It takes guts and staying power to make it with one of our restaurants. At the same time, it doesn't require any unusual appitude or intellect. Any man with common sense, dedication to principles, and a love of hard work can do it . . . There are hazards and pitfalls, of course, just as there are in any small business. And some locations go along for years with a very modest volume. (p. 111)

Table 9.6 shows the results of the some of environment-univariate performance intra- and inter-brand tests. The null hypothesis is that the proportion of fast food franchisees with current ratios and net assets above the relevant average is as high in unfavourable environments ($H_{\pi a}$) as in high growth areas ($H_{\pi b}$). If accepted, the results suggest that performance does not necessarily alter by trading area favourability. From the table, it is evident that, for the large part, the proportion of high-performing franchisees in unfavourable regions is as high – if not higher – as those in more munificent areas. The few rejections of the null hypothesis suggest, within the B and C systems, that franchisees with above average net assets in low-growth areas are not as populous as they are in high-growth regions; within A, those franchisees with above average liquidity/unabsorbed slack are not as prevalent in regions with a high propensity to consume meals outside the home. The B and C results suggest that those franchisees in low-growth areas tend to be smaller/of lower value than their counterparts in high-growth regions. Unlike C's franchisees, however, B's results would also be rejected where $\alpha = 0.01$. The intra-brand test also suggests that franchisees in trading areas with low densities of catering establishments/capita are smaller/of lower value than those in higher density regions. Further

Brand	Measure	GDPG	APC	POPn	SING	AGE	Y^d
B	Current ratio	0.861	−0.109	−0.571	0.126	0.595	0.054
	Net assets	−3.203	−0.134	−0.571	0.126	0.668	0.054
C	Current ratio	0.485	0.941	−0.983	0.983	1.290	0.983
	Net assets	1.692	0.521	−0.521	0.521	1.503	−0.516
A	Current ratio	−1.056	−1.714	−0.943	−1.718	−0.517	−0.531
	Net assets	1.370	0.716	0.000	0.108	1.033	1.333
All	Current ratio	0.290	−0.140	−1.976	−0.551	0.665	0.230
(n = 59)	Net assets	1.292	−0.240	−0.850	−0.017	1.444	−0.059
All	FCFE	0.459	0.510	0.661	−0.134	0.429	−0.574
(n = 25)	Z^{tr} where:						
	$Z^{tr} \geq X$	0.814	−0.493	0.033	0.226	−1.108	0.167
	$Z^{tr} \geq 0.0 \leq 0.2$	−1.206	0.652	0.301	−0.190	1.108	−1.051

NB: all figures = z-statistic for $H_0 : H_{\pi a} \geq H_{\pi b}$; $\alpha = 0.05$, one-tail = +1.645 or −1.645

Table 9.6: Hypothesis test results: GDPG, APC, POP^n, SING, AGE and Y^d

investigation of this aspect revealed that the sampled franchisees in high-density regions operated, typically, two or more units and the trading areas were characterized by an above-average population. The A results suggest that those franchisees in regions with low APCs illustrate lower levels of liquidity/unabsorbed slack than those in trading areas with higher APCs. Employing Singh's (1986) arguments (see Chapter 6), these franchisees have less of a buffer to the downside risks of experimentation, even when innovation may serve to improve performance and the franchisee has greater latitude for adaptations than others (A's franchise contract is not as 'hard' as those of B or C).

The final table concerning individual environmental variables on franchisee performance (Table 9.7) presents the remainder of the results for the unemployment, MPC, and proportion of women in civilian employment. Of these tests, almost all accept the null hypothesis where $\alpha = 0.05$. Of the few rejections, are that A's franchisees with above-average slack/liquidity in regions with lower than average one-person households are not as populous as in areas where singles are more prevalent. Furthermore, C's franchisees with above-average value/size are not as prevalent in areas with below-average marginal propensities to consume. Equally, whilst the majority of tests provide support for the null hypothesis, when $\alpha = 0.10$, A's franchisees with above-average liquidity in regions with below-average MPC and FEM are not as prevalent as in their counterparts and C's franchisees with above-average net assets and liquidity are not as populous in regions where the proportion of young persons are below the national average. Similar conclusions can also be drawn about the distribution of FCFE when environments are graded as either illustrating high or low MPCs and levels of women in employment as well as the distribution of z-scores between zero and 0.2.

In accordance with Castrogiovanni (1991), munificence was established by calculating the growth of each of the nine exogenous variables for each territory. The growth rates of each variable were then ranked, where one represented the highest level of growth and twelve the lowest. The only exception to this scheme was the unemployment vari-

Brand	Measure	UNEM	MPC	FEM
A	Current ratio	0.682	1.294	1.512
	Net assets	0.861	−0.831	−1.340
B	Current ratio	0.984	−0.373	−1.107
	Net assets	−0.295	0.584	0.296
C	Curent ratio	0.983	−1.190	0.253
	Net assets	0.521	−2.347	−0.142
All	Current ratio	0.940	−0.094	−0.171
(n = 59)	Net assets	−0.265	−0.203	−0.171
All	FCFE	−0.064	−1.314	1.250
(n = 25)	Z^{th} where:			
	$Z^{\text{th}} \geq X$	0.396	−0.700	−0.202
	$Z^{\text{th}} \geq 0.0 \leq 0.2$	−0.825	1.388	0.600

NB: all figures = z-statistic for $H_0:H_{\pi a} \geq H_{\pi b}$; $\alpha = 0.05$, one–tail = +1.645 or −1.645

Table 9.7: Hypothesis test results: UNEM, MPC, and FEM

Source of variation	SS	MS	F-ratio	P-value	Critical F
Region v. net assets					
Between group	8.91E + 11	4.5E + 11	0.976	0.382	3.123
Within group	3.3E + 11	4.6E + 11			
Total	3.4E + 13				
Region v. current ratio					
Between group	1.36E + 00	0.681	2.234	0.114	3.123
Within group	2.20E + 01	0.305			
Total	2.33E + 01				
Two-way ANOVA: region and size v. liquidity					
Sample	2.502	0.417	2.02	0.068	2.170
Column	0.839	0.419	2.03	0.130	3.070
Interaction	2.770	0.231	1.12	0.352	1.829
Within group	26.00	0.206			
Total	32.13				

NB: df for one-way: within group = 2; within group = 72; total = 74.

Table 9.8: One-way and two-way ANOVA results:
region v. performance and region and firm size v. liquidity

able since high levels of growth in this variable represents lower environmental munificence. The sum of the ranks then provided a single score of environmental munificence, where twenty-one represented high levels of munificence and ninety-seven the converse. The three clusters were then calculated by estimating the class intervals in the frequency distribution of ranks. At this more holistic level, one-way *ANOVA* tests were used to test the null hyothesis that different regions are not associated with differing average liquidity/slack and value. As the computed value of the *F* statistics were not greater than the critical values, the contention that liquidity/slack alters by firm size and region cannot be supported statistically.

Taken individually, these results suggest that some franchisees are better able to illustrate superior performance despite the environmental conditions. They also imply that whilst certain environmental criteria are important for attracting fast food players to certain regions, they do not appear to influence performance significantly. Holistically, however, they imply that there are, perhaps, differences in the criteria which initially attract a fast food business to locate in a certain trading area and that which enables the business to realize above-average performance. The results also have implications for how under-performing franchisees ought to be assisted. These implications are reviewed below.

Results of Study Two

The return on shareholder's fund to total liabilities measure evaluates the degree of borrowing, or gearing, incurred by a company. An *F*-test was used to establish where the difference between franchisees with interlocks illustrated superior performance to those without. The results, in Table 9.9, show that the *F*-ratio falls in the region of rejection. As such, there appear to be significant differences between those franchisees involved in interlocking directorates and those who are not. Thus, firms with interlocks and those without illustrate differing levels of variability in their gearing levels. Perhaps importantly, the variability of gearing among firms with interlocks is lower than those without.

Source of Variation	Mean	Variance	F-ratio	Critical F (one-tail)
(Return on shareholder funds to total liabilities)				
Interlocks	19.4	849	11.0	2.08
Non-interlocks	52.4	9409		

Table 9.9: F-test two sample for variances: interlocking versus non-interlocking firms

Results from Study Three

The table below shows the one-way *ANOVA* results for the test of the null hypothesis that franchisees and non-franchised concerns do not illustrate statistically different performance differences. That null hypothesis is rejected because the critical *F* statistic is greater than the critical *F* figure (where $\alpha = 0.05$). In turn, since the computed values of *F* fall in the rejection region, the results suggest that independent businesses and franchised businesses do not yield the same average performance levels. This situation also appears true if a smaller significance level, such as $\alpha = 0.01$, is used, but could be different if an alternative methodology was to be employed.

Source of variation	SS	MS	F-ratio	P-value	Critical F
Franchise v. non-franchise (return on shareholder funds)					
Between group	50.2	50.2	0.006	0.94	3.913
Within group	1057723	80.3			
Total	1057773				
Franchise v. non-franchise (quick ratio)					
Between group	7.76	7.76	7.62	0.007	3.913
Within group	132.3	1.01			
Total	140.0				
Franchise v. non-franchise (liquidity ratio)					
Between group	6.67	6.67	8.81	0.003	3.913
Within group	98.5	0.76			
Total	105.2				

Table 9.10: One-way ANOVA results: franchisees v. non-franchisees' performance differences

These results suggest that there are performance differences between franchised and non-franchised concerns, but these differences need not be in favour of franchising. Results concerning the differences between the return on shareholder funds to total liabilities, for example, were affected by the number of franchisees and independent concerns which recorded negative funds. Significantly, however, the number of franchisees with negative shareholder funds exceeded the number of independent businesses, suggesting that some franchisees have been drawing funds against their company rather than living off its proceeds. In general, the return achieved for shareholders should always exceed the return on total capital employed. This is because the purpose of borrowing should be to obtain capital at a lower cost than it could be provided by shareholders, thereby enhancing their earnings. If the return achieved for shareholders is less than that obtained on total capital, this objective is not being achieved. Upon closer inspection of the two samples, it became evident that more franchisees than independent businesses were increasing their degree of funding in their firms. This situation may suggest that the franchisees were possibly under-funded in the first instance or that they have expanded their portfolio, and have yet to see the returns accrue.

The table below provides *ANOVA* tests to establish the annual differences between franchisee-operated concerns and non-franchised businesses. The null hypothesis that there are *no* statistically significant differences in the shareholders funds to total liabilities measure of franchisees and independent businesses. A comparison of the descriptive statistics for each of the financial measures for franchisees and non-franchised businesses shows that the level of shareholders' funds to total liabilities was lower for franchisees than for independent businesses, and that the latter illustrated a broader range of values than their franchisee counterparts. From the minimum and maximum figures for this measure, it is clear that both sets have seen the shareholder funds value increase but for the franchisees the upper values have been in decline.

With regard to the liquidity and quick ratios, it is evident that the franchisee performance was, on average, lower than the independent businesses. Such a finding helps to corroborate earlier research (Price, 1993) which suggests that franchisees illustrate lower levels of unabsorbed organizational slack than independents. This situation, in turn, infers that franchisees may be less inclined to participate in experimental innovative activity. The low level of the current ratio could also have implications for the franchisees' success in convincing their franchisors to award them additional outlets, but this is also dependent on the buoyancy of other financial ratios and non-financial criteria apart from liquidity. With the exception of Year 3, the computed F-ratio is in the region of rejection (where $F_{crit} = 3.91$, $\alpha = 0.05$), and therefore it is possible to conclude that based on these sample results there are statistically significant differences in the liquidity of franchisees versus independent concerns. As the quick ratio is derived from the liquidity ratio, a similar situation is apparent.

Year	Source of variance in shareholder funds	SS	MS	F-ratio	P-value
1	Within Group	226430	226430	5.63	0.019
	Between Group	5300482	40155		
	Total	5526912			
2	Within Group	38474051	38474051	1.15	0.286
	Between Group	4420664086	33489879		
	Total	4459138137			
3	Within Group	43262.7	43262.7	2.371	0.126
	Between Group	2408150	18243		
	Total	2451412.7			
4	Within Group	32187	32187	2.31	0.131
	Between Group	1842762	13960		
	Total	1874949			

Year	Source of variance in quick ratios	SS	MS	F-ratio	P-value
1	Within Group	23.01	23.01	5.86	0.017
	Between Group	514.22	3.93		
	Total	537.23			
2	Within Group	4.55	4.55	7.50	0.007
	Between Group	79.44	0.610		
	Total	83.99			
3	Within Group	3.38	3.38	3.21	0.076
	Between Group	139.04	1.05		
	Total	143.42			
4	Within Group	3.54	3.54	4.40	0.038
	Between Group	84.43	0.804		
	Total	87.97			

Year	Source of variance in liquidity	SS	MS	F-ratio	P-value
1	Within Group	11.14	11.14	10.7	0.001
	Between Group	137.49	1.04		
	Total	148.63			
2	Within Group	5.46	5.46	8.60	0.004
	Between Group	83.30	0.63		
	Total	88.76			
3	Within Group	4.11	4.11	3.73	0.060
	Between Group	145.55	1.10		
	Total	149.66			
4	Within Group	6.39	6.39	5.73	0.018
	Between Group	147.36	1.12		
	Total	153.75			

Table 9.11: ANOVA tests for performance variances: franchised versus non-franchised firms

Implications for turnaround strategies

The above levels of performance suggest (albeit not specifically), within certain environmental conditions, that some franchisees are more adept than others in realizing superior performance. Such performance differences could be a source of franchise discontent and, if left unchecked, trigger a sequence of events which ultimately ends with franchisee termination, default to lenders, and unit turnover or closure. Holmberg and Morgan (1996) conceptualize this process as a continuum comprising the stages shown in Figure 9.2.

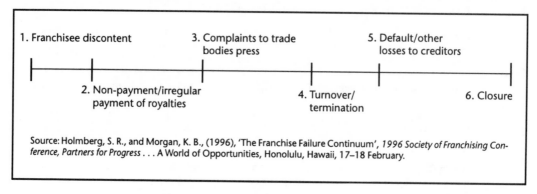

Source: Holmberg, S. R., and Morgan, K. B., (1996), 'The Franchise Failure Continuum', *1996 Society of Franchising Conference, Partners for Progress . . . A World of Opportunities*, Honolulu, Hawaii, 17–18 February.

Figure 9.2: The franchise failure continuum

The researchers suggest that not every franchise failure will touch upon every point on the continuum. Nonetheless, franchisee discontent is an important precursor to failure. The main sources of this discontent may, as shown in Chapter 7, be relational (the quality of advice by the franchisor to its franchisee is flawed), and be the result of intra-brand competition, or be personal (being a franchisee has not proved to be a suitable career decision). As shown from the studies in this chapter, franchisee discontent could also derive from sub-optimal financial performance. Given its significance as a precursor to eventual failure, finding a cure to this discontent is potentially significant to maintaining brand equity and the queue of new franchisees to the system. Whilst performance differences seem to suggest that franchisors and some franchisees are tolerant of low levels of performance, given the critical importance of franchisee motivation and possible link between financial problems leading to personal failure, it is important that franchisor companies develop well-defined strategies to facilitate the turnaround of under-performing franchisees. Unfortunately, it is in this area that the theoretical literature on turnaround strategies seems to offer little to the practitioner operating within a constrained internal environment (Gruca and Nath, 1994; Jennings and Seaman, 1994). There are, however, options which may serve to improve performance. The following briefly outlines the differing turnaround options and how they relate to the context of franchises.

Background

In a review of corporate turnaround literature, Hoffman (1989) defines turnaround strategies as the set of activities employed to halt and stimulate an improvement of performance. Most studies, however, distinguish between operating and strategic turnarounds (Robbins and Pearce, 1992). The strategic turnaround process typically consists of manipulating the strategic components, such as repositioning the entire business to appeal to a new set of customers. It also requires retraining and, ultimately, a change of alliance (Khandwalla, 1992; Zimmerman, 1989; Hambrick and Schecter, 1983). By contrast, the operating turnaround entails helping a company to pursue its current strategy more efficiently and consists of efforts to control costs, make more efficient use of assets and possible changes in the management processes (Boyle and Desai, 1991; Hofer, 1980). Although various authors attach differing breadths of interpretation to 'strategic' in reference to such turnarounds, here it refers to the manipulation of the marketing mix and the transfer of knowledge that improves organizational effectiveness. Such manipulation and transfer of knowedge assists franchisees to become congruent with their environment and, thereby, improve performance. The extent to which strategic adaptation may be pursued by the franchisee is seen as dependent on three factors: the extent of the decline; franchisee diagnostic competence; and the environment. But, as argued in Chapter 6, whilst the franchisee is relatively free to pursue certain cost-based adaptations, the strategic option may be mitigated by franchisor-franchisee dyadic conditions.

Due to the centralized, branded and standardized nature of some retail franchise organizations, the traditional strategic turnaround option may be often unfeasible for franchisee companies, since they have to adhere to the specifications of the franchise agreement. The only time that a franchisee may be involved in a strategic repositioning policy is if the franchisor chooses, or is required, to alter their focus (or if the franchisee needs to move its own branded units). Such a policy may be implemented even if the franchisees are profitable and successful. In such cases franchisees have been known to leave the franchise system and set up in direct competition to the ex-franchisor (as happened with KFC in 1986). Such limitations suggest some degree of bureaucratic dysfunctionality and suggests that, in this case, bureaucracy is not the best form of administration. As these factors have already received attention (Chapter 3), the following paragraphs outline some of the diagnostic aspects and environmental issues impinging on the strategic turnaround option.

Franchisee diagnosis

Within both streams of the business turnaround literature and wherever the blame for the causes of company decline is placed, an implicit feature of both turnaround options appears to be that upon management's recognition that a problem exists, policies and strategies will be put into place to remedy the situation – that is, strategy follows from environmental analysis. The criticality of the financial situation, measured in terms of the immediacy of the threat to a firm's survival, is reflected in the financial scores and financial ratios. In short, the ratios help determine whether the management of the financially troubled firm should pursue an operating turnaround or a strategic turnaround to return to growth, should they have the latitude and capability to do so. This hypothesis assumes, however, that managers not only recognize that the firm is in need of altering course but are also able to equate the cause of their decline with its effects. Yet, such an assumption may not hold (Prahalad and Bettis, 1986).

Lorange and Vancil (1986) suggest that it is often difficult for management to recognize gradual performance decline, rather they must be sensitized to the fact that decline is almost unavoidable unless they possess a coherent plan to overcome the causes of the situation. But the necessary sensitization process may be affected by managerial incompetence (that is, lack the necessary competences), a strong belief in their own infallibility (that is, management with a successful performance history begin to believe in its own world-view), inefficient information filters (for example, second tier management only giving the top tier information that they think is necessary), and inertia deriving from different interpretations of a common cause of decline; some may interpret a decline in demand as a temporary matter whilst others may perceive it to be of greater significance. Thus, these differing interpretations trigger different decision processes and different behaviours (Nutt, 1993) and possibly result in different outcomes. For some, inappropriate diagnosis will exacerbate the situation and others may realize some room for maneouvre through correct alignment of cause and effect. Nevertheless, the longer it takes the incumbent management to recognize and admit that they have a performance issue and initiate remedial action, the greater are the chances that the control over its turnaround strategy is passed to others who may have goals that are incompatible with those of the firm.

All of these rigidities may be evident amongst fast food franchisees who, on the whole, tend not to be professional managers and, as such, most of them illustrate low levels of strategic choice for two basic reasons: they are legally constrained by the franchisor's broad strategy (rather than the cost focus) and most franchisees tend to have very little experience of industry or business (Chapter 6). Their immediate environments also tend to be constrained by the franchisor specifying the suppliers and thus reducing the number and variety of input organizations with which the franchisees may interact (English, 1993; Klien and Saft, 1985). There may additionally be low levels of latitude for adaptation since resources and technology are determined by the franchisor. As seen from Chapter 6, these factors reduce the franchisee's ability to cope with periods of trouble, but this lower flexibility has to be partially offset against the franchisee's prior career history and the nature of his social capital and whether the franchisee firm is characterized by interlocking directorates. The situation is, however, compounded by increasing dynamism (that is, change which is difficult to predict) due to the number and variety of new entrants to the fast food market.

Environmental aspects

A recurring debate throughout strategic management discourse is the degree of determinism of 'strategic fit' between the firm's internal resources, structure and its environment. It is posited by one school of thought that managers have some degree of choice in the manner by which they adapt to environmental conditions; the other (the population ecologists) propound that managers have minimal latitude in determining strategic fit. Within the latter perspective firms are seen to fail, primarily, because they have chosen inappropriate strategies or have implemented them ineffectively or inconsistently (Thompson, 1967). That is, they have failed to adapt to their environments through choice or incompetence.

Recent literature on the population ecology of organizations (Hannan and Freeman, 1977; Aldrich, 1979; McKelvey, 1981) propound a Darwinistic process, in that the environment selects out various common organizational forms. Management choice is therefore assumed to be minimalized. Hence, there is only a rather limited number of possible strategies and structures feasible in any type of environment and a few favoured strategies and structures cause the organizations pursuing them to thrive at the expense of competitors. Within this vein, the emphasis of much of the turnaround literature has been on providing management with recipes (O'Neill, 1986; Muller, 1985; Spencer, 1979) for dealing with problems of under-performance according to the severity of the situation at hand. Arguably, however, under illiberal conditions, a cost-based approach – or retrenchment – should be expected. Firms under 'threat' typically tighten control, restrict the flow of information and reduce participation in decision-making, and focus more effort on internal adaptation rather than external change. As such, in regard to franchisees, the manner of adaptation may be restricted to altering the cost base to improve performance since strategic considerations are either perceived as contrained or not considered in the first instance (Pilling *et al*, 1995). But such a focus may not have been equally applicable to each franchisee. For some, perhaps a more strategic approach may have been more appropriate.

The intra-brand performance differences suggest that, in some areas, the franchisor's marketing mix may be sufficient but, in others, the franchisees need to alter their cost structures. This, in turn, suggests that, whilst there may be an inherent conflict with labour and competitive rivalry, the orientation towards profit by some franchisees is better developed than others. In this way, there may also be intra-system differences in the level of adaptation, which are additional to inter-system adaptation levels. Thus, rather than a Darwinistic effect, different states of adaptation are perhaps evident. In the construction of his adaptation framework, Chakravarthy (1982) argued that several niches are available to an organization for surviving the conditions of its environment, and that these niches can be further arranged in a hierarchy based on the extent of an organization's level of adaptation. Chakravarthy proposed three levels or niches which he called 'adaptive states' and consisted, respectively, of organizations with a high level of adaptation, a medium level of adaptation, and a low level of adaptation. As a consequence of illustrating differing levels of strategic fit, Chakravarthy conceptualized that each level of adaptation would yield certain performances, with the high level of adaptation (or optimal strategy-structure match) yielding superior performances. Hence, implicit to Chakravarthy's framework, the role of the environment is less deterministic and some degree of managerial choice can be exercised (Child, 1972; Hrebiniak and Joyce, 1985; Marlin et al, 1994; Miles and Snow, 1994).

Synthesis

From the different states of adaptation and cluster analysis of the differing environment types, the following matrix can be used to position the sampled companies. From the matrix, it may be inferred that those in the bottom right-hand squares are those in need of the greatest assistance from their franchisors. In Bartlett and Ghoshal's (1991) terminology, such players are, perhaps, 'implementors' whilst those in the bottom left-hand squares are 'black holes'. Equally, those in the top right-hand corner may be 'contributors' and those positioned top-left are 'strategic leaders'. It is these which may be used as possible teachers to the weaker players to change their cost structures to the rigours of their environments. Indeed, of the sampled franchisees, the under-performers illustrated, on average, higher stock ratios, higher levels of stock to other current assets, higher levels of current liabilities and lower net assets than others.

Contingent with the necessity for internal differentiation in dealing with franchisees, the diagram suggests that there is a need to tailor training to a franchisee's learning ability and alter cost structures according to the rigours of the local environment. Such differentiation in training does not appear to be the norm in franchising and is a

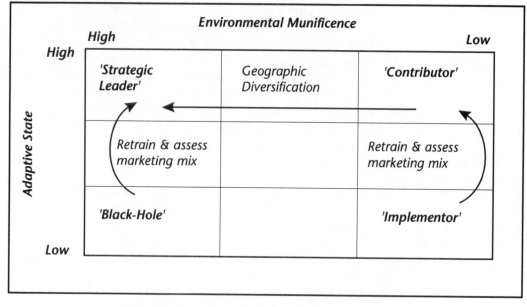

Figure 9.3: Adaptation-environmental munificence matrix

potential source of frustration, opportunistic behaviour, as well as lessened productivity for the franchisee (LaVan *et al*, 1986). Altering the level of franchisee support and latitude of discretion according to their ability and environment could also take other, additional, forms. After all, there is no evidence to show that training, in itself, improves business performance (Storey, 1994). Arguably, given the increasing maturity and competitiveness of the foodservice sector, there are lessons to be learnt from the car dealer network (see the panel on page 490).

If low performance levels persist they will adversely affect the franchisees' motivation and possibly create conflict. The diagram shows only three potential remedies to franchisee under-performance, and although situation-specific, the emphasis on improving efficiency favoured by many franchisees may be only one component of the turnaround process. According to Arogyaswamy *et al* (1995), successful turnarounds encompass three stages:

1. emphasis on efficiency improvements;
2. involving stakeholders;
3. the stabilization of the internal climate and decision processes.

The permeations of each stage change according to whether the turnaround is strategic or more incremental. Applying their framework to the franchise context, Table 9.12 provides examples of how the franchisor may help stem franchisee under-performance and performance decline from both a strategic and cost-based perspective. In so doing, it suggests that whilst franchisor involvement in the strategic turnaround option is implicit, there are areas in cost-based turnarounds where the franchisor may take an advisory and active role.

The dynamics of UK car dealerships

New cars are distributed and sold in Britain primarily through networks of dealers but, according to research by the Department of Trade & Industry (DTI) and the Retail Motor Industry Federation (1995) there are too many car dealers, many of them too small, with levels of profitability too low to be sustainable in the long term. Dealers have expressed some disenchantment with their prime franchise role in selling new cars, especially as there is very weak new car sales profitability and there is evidence of a decline in new car ownership while there is growth in the used car sector. Furthermore, some manufacturers have illustrated some unwillingness to allow dealers to innovate and exploit economies of scale, and some dealer groups have been unwilling to develop strategic opportunities with manufacturers. Not only does this position suggest that some of the contractual restraints require review, but also that assistance be given to facilitate improved performance. Under the traditional dealership contract the manufacturer sought to encourage the dealer to concentrate their efforts on promoting the sale and subsequent servicing of individual brands of cars, or 'marques', to the exclusion of other manufacturers' marques. These efforts were to be concentrated in a particular locality where, it was thought, a small business could develop and maintain contacts in which it was located (MMC, 1992). The dealership contract was characterized by combined exclusivity and selectivity, where exclusivity referred to the territory limitations and selectivity to a system whereby the supplier appoints any number of dealers it likes, wherever it likes, and the dealer remains free to handle products from competing marques. In 1992, the Monopolies and Mergers Commission found a number of restrictions imposed by suppliers in their agreements with dealers which were not in the public interest and recommended the change of these. The commission recommended the removal of five restrictions on franchised dealers which:

1. limited the dealer's freedom to advertise outside his designated territory;
2. limited the dealer's freedom to hold or acquire dealerships outside that designated territory;
3. prevented a dealer holding or acquiring competing dealerships within his designated territory;
4. restricted the extent to which a dealer could sell car-related goods or provide services; and
5. limited the total number of supplier's cars that any dealer or dealer group could sell in any given period.

Since this time, the car dealership network has begun to consolidate and increase its bargaining position *vis-à-vis* the manufacturers via the acquisition of some of the smaller concerns and dealers moving into multiple ownership. By itself, however, increased bargaining power may be insufficient to ensure the long-term health and strength of the UK retail motor industry. Accordingly, the DTI survey recommends what is essentially a change in the manufacturers' culture through advocating ideas such as the following:

- placing the financial and organizational health of dealers at the forefront of marketing policies;
- taking a total view of the supply chain and using realistic forecasts to plan production that better matches market demand;
- avoiding advertising and marketing campaigns that publicly undermine the integrity of franchised dealers;
- for dealers to be prepared to become involved in joint strategic and decision-making forums with manufacturers, and to support jointly agreed policies;
- for dealers, and especially dealer groups, to consider the skills and abilities of their workforce and develop plans to harness a growing pool of better qualified people. They should be prepared to change employment and reward policies if necessary.

Prior research (Achrol and Etzel, 1992) suggests that franchisors do not seem to alter their goals and services to franchisees by the degree of munificence in the environment, only by the degree of dynamism. This chapter suggests that such policies may be in need of some revision. During the course of undertaking research for this chapter, some franchisors (from a variety of economic sectors), albeit informally, admitted that very few – if any – of them monitored their franchisees' financial performance (some did not even request to look at final year statements). Although this is perhaps understandable given the lean management structures, the small nature of most franchisors' businesses, and 'soft' contracts of some franchisors, such an attitude serves to reduce the up-grading of performance to fire-fighting as opposed to being more proactive and, possibly, strategic in their dealings with franchisees. In another sense, the lack of financial monitoring may be a casualty of the continuing use of franchising as a method of decentralization, as well as perhaps the lack of an overt interest in the franchisee's profit performance. Thus, the emphasis within these companies appears to be on maintaining a low-cost form of distribution relationship where the franchisee performance issues suggest that a more differentiated approach may be required. According to Lassar and Kerr (1996), the source of competitive advantage for brand owners offering differentiated support is based on product performance (perceived quality and consistency), associated services, and brand image; the brand owners of differentiated support companies are likely to expend considerable effort in controlling channel activities, whereas those following a more low-cost option are characterized by fewer support efforts because management perceives that such behaviour increases efficiency.

Arguably, one of the problems is basis of royalty payments being founded on sales rather than profit; many franchisors argue, however, that the establishment of royalties in any other way is precluded by a suitable profit measure because the franchisee may be motivated to 'hide' certain costs and, thereby, lower the payments to the franchisor. Clearly, given the competitive significance of franchisee performance and motivation, this attitude is in need of some review. Furthermore, a recurrent rationale employed by franchisors to explain franchisee failure is the dysfunctionality of their site selection and/or recruitment and selection procedures rather than their monitoring systems, perhaps reflecting an in-built bias towards personal failure explanations. But all are important. While some franchisors have increased the sophistication of their selection procedures through the use of psychometric profiling tests, on the whole the use of these techniques is not widespread (Fulop, 1996). In addition, fewer franchisors seek to correlate the psychometric profiles of their franchisees with key financial performance ratios and/or the tendency for certain individuals to become multi-unit operators. Such an exercise could allow them to increase the probability of increasing brand dissemination and performance through focusing their recruitment/selection activities on individuals who are likely to realize superior results. Thus, extant turnaround strategies are often limited to changing the franchisee either through changing the profile and/or replacing a failed franchisee with another. This option appears to be pursued rather than, perhaps, altering marketing mix issues (there are a number of exceptions to this generalization). Given the rise of multi-unit operators, however, the potential damage caused by a loss of tacit knowledge stock, and the strategic significance of franchisees' motivation levels, there must be a change in franchisor culture to nurture franchisee loyalty. It requires the development of a suitable structure and a package of solutions and products to help floundering

	Turnaround stage	
Turnaround type/option		**Turnaround type/option**
Strategic reorientation		*Incremental/Cost bias*
1) *Emphasis on work redesign: Process innovations/multi-skilling; Improve forecasting techniques; Modernize plant and equipment; Become member of purchasing consortia. *Seek revenue increases: Targeted local promotional activity; Local price discounting/off peak demand promotions; Improved training and personal selling techniques through suggestive selling; New product development/broaden customer base; Allowing franchisees to expand into unrelated areas; Geographic expansion/internationalization; Permitting franchisees to acquire other franchisee organizations; Permitting franchisees to become multi-branded.	EFFICIENCY IMPROVEMENTS	*Asset sell-offs & cost focus: If multi-unit operator: – Sell unit to a 'contributor'; – Sell unit to 'strategic leader'; – Convert unit to co-owned status; Redundancies/part-timers; Lower product variety; Change supplier; Benchmark competitors' costs
2) *Garner franchisees' senior staff support Fresh induction of managers Initiation of staff participation	STAKEHOLDER RELATIONSHIPS	*Recommitting banks & creditors to organization *Bargain with suppliers *Alter contract: Reduce royalty payments for a period; Base royalty payments on profits as opposed to turnover. *Bargain with landlord *Involve other franchisees
3) *Change management[1] *Change reward systems *Encourage new thinking	STABILIZATION OF INTERNAL CLIMATE & DECISION PROCESSES	*Management continuity *Tighter controls *Remotivate franchisee

[1] = refers to multi-unit operators and change franchisee and/or territory management not franchisee

Table 9.12: Turnaround options for franchisees

franchisees. This is something which McDonald's has adopted through its 'task forces' which tackle the problems of under-performing stores. Here the franchisor has adopted a consulting role to maintaining franchisee motivation and survival.

In order for the franchisor to identify and assist under-performing franchisees the franchisor must have the capability and mechanisms for recognizing that franchisee decline is occurring. Specifically, a management information system which integrates and compares their sales and profit performance is required; this could entail some loss of control by franchisees. Although Galbraith (1973) has argued that decentralization facilitates information processing at the source of an event that required decision-making, the ability to make informed decisions at this level may be limited by ability and recognition, and the power to rectify the problem in an appropriate manner. By providing accounting information, therefore, to the franchisor, franchisees could expect, by way of return, assistance when required, but this is a double-edged sword. The propensity for such information sharing is dependent on the nature of the relationship between the franchisee and franchisor. Mohr and Sohi (1995) show that closer ties result in more frequent and more relevant information exchanges between partners and are instrumental in partnership success. If one partner is not performing according to expectations, however, there may be recriminations and a lack of trust may develop if left unresolved; information deriving from the other partner regarding potential improvements could be treated with suspicion and take longer to engineer a turnaround of the business. Being proactive to issue resolution is, therefore, important to partnership success. Smoothing over or ignoring/avoiding the issue is at odds with the cultures of successful partnerships; such techniques do not 'fit' with the proactive tone of a partnership in which the problems of one party become the problems affecting both parties (Mohr and Spekman, 1994). In some instances, taking a proactive role could also entail changing the franchisor's role from one of monitoring to adding-value. From a conventional viewpoint, the tasks of the corporate centre are to optimize the corporate portfolio, co-ordinate critical resources and decision-making process, positively influence the general external environment and thus ensure the growth and development of the company (Hungenberg, 1993; Goold *et al* 1994). As a result of intensifying competition and pressures on cost, this role has been challenged because not only do centres have to ensure the future growth and development of the company, but they have to prove their right to exist by contributing value.

There is substantial evidence (Orpen, 1985; Robinson, 1982; Robinson and Pearce; 1984; Pearce and Robbins, 1993) to suggest that small firms benefit most when they conduct strategic planning with the help of outsiders. Furthermore, irrespective of source, Chrisman and Leslie (1989) indicate that there is a positive relationship between improved performance and the type of assistance given, especially where industry-specific knowledge exists. Such knowledge is implicit, in some form, to most franchisors as well as other franchisees and, as indicated earlier with regard to subsidiaries, it is this which may serve to reduce attrition rates and increase performance (Kumar *et al*, 1995). As mentioned above, some of the more successful franchisees may also be used to retrain their under-performing counterparts. One of the benefits of this approach is that there is less of a political barrier in the retraining process.

The suggested options infer that the franchisee should, in order to garner stakeholder support, be proactive in approaching creditors, such as the banks. However, given that small firms, in particular (Dodge *et al*, 1994), may experience difficulties in identifying decline, there may be a case for the banks taking a more proactive stance. Although Stern and Stanworth (1993; 1994) show that banks are generally supportive of franchising, they do not tend to be proactive in the identification of potential problems. Yet, there are several areas where banks may help to facilitate an effective operating turnaround:

- communicate more effectively with franchisors and franchisees through regular reviews of the businesses (Royal Bank of Scotland, 1993);
- alter their image. They should be seen as more than a vehicle to get capital; they need to develop packages which help franchisees on an ongoing basis;
- they need to be actively involved in the turnaround process;
- defer interest payments or lower interest payments for a set period;

- refer to independent experts to get an independent overview of the market and company performance when the franchisee first approaches the bank; and
- tie in any loans to finance the franchisor's growth plans to the success of its franchisees. Thus, should the franchisor allow franchisee under-performance to persist and failure to occur, the franchisor incurs a penalty by paying a higher rate of interest.

Although these are only suggestions, the emphasis is to permit horizontal linkages or the development of management systems that reinforce co-ordination and linkages between the units. The traditional perspectives of organizations are becoming obsolete through the use of networks and the use of information technology (Beaumont and Sutherland, 1992). Typically, in most UK and US organizations, information and communication technologies have been used to reinforce centralized decision-making which has, in turn, developed a culture within which head office is seen as the focal point. However, with some fast food franchisees showing sub-optimal performance, there is a need for the franchisors to develop systems which empower unit managers. This would permit action at individual local branch level while maintaining head office control – for example, the development of specific local market offers, as implemented by the major retail banks, by using local management input to introduce a specific local differentiation. To some extent, this empowering only deals with tactical elements and could be unsuitable where strategic solutions are required.

The need to find solutions for floundering franchisees should be emphasized given the dangers of adverse publicity on the queue of potential investors and the amount of time and investment employed by some to train franchisees. In the USA, for example, Popeye's Famous Fried Chicken franchisees and other management personnel are trained at the Popeye's Institute of Polytechnic (other fast food companies have their own 'colleges' and 'universities'). Its training programme is divided into two parts. The first part consists of a one-week 'investor training program'. The investor curriculum includes seminars in real estate, finance, purchasing, operations, management, marketing and advertising. Following this, the participant enters into a nine-week management course which is designed to educate the participant in all parts of restaurant operation. Whilst such training is more than most independent and 'mom-and-pop' operators receive, it does not guarantee financial success. Other chains, such as McDonald's, operate training 'universities' and 'colleges'.

Whilst the above has stressed the need to focus on under-performing franchisees, there is also a requirement to assist 'strategic leaders' and 'contributors'. The diagram (Figure 9.4) suggests that one way by which contributors may be helped is via permitting them to diversify into more munificent trading areas. This permission should, however, only occur depending upon an assessment of the franchisee's ability to manage additional units, else managerial decay may occur. Strategic leaders should also be encouraged to acquire additional units in order to help maximize their positions.

This said, some franchisors may wish to reduce their reliance on a few, large franchisees due to power considerations. Bygrave (1992), for example, shows that the greater the size of franchisees, the higher the propensity for conflicts to occur. Such a situation, however, may be more indicative of the climate of relations between the two

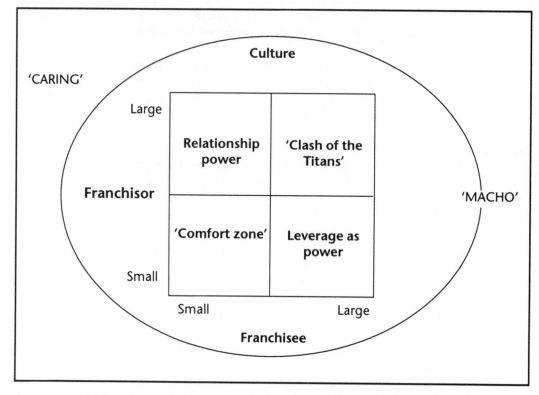

Figure 9.4: *Culture and bargaining relations between franchisors and franchisees*

parties and their respeective cultures concerning innovation. As noted in Chapter 7, the climate of relations in franchising is determined by the nature and quality of communication between the two parties and the extent on emphasis on maintaining the *status quo*. The differing cultures and climates of the relations between the franchisor and franchisee and their respective bargaining power (determined by size) is depicted as a matrix. It shows that the higher propensity of conflicts which Bygrave refers to is only one state of affairs operating under 'macho' climate conditions: a 'clash of the titans'. This situation is where both parties are intent on winning over the other and subjugating them to their way of thinking; it has been witnessed within the context of the UK grocery market where large retail operations and large manufacturers argue over delivery times, pricing, and other components of the marketing mix. The alternative position would be to adopt a more 'caring' culture and be more relational – a more feminine culture perhaps (Gheradi, 1995). Similar situations are evident with small companies. If franchisors are to prevent possible damage to brand equity deriving from under-performing franchisees and nurture competitive advantages based on innovation, the climate of relations needs to be changed.

Summary and conclusion

The popular franchise press and academic literature is replete with the observation that franchisees illustrate superior performance to non-franchised concerns. This observation often derives from uncorroborated franchisor sources and is beset with problems of not being able to be compared with sectoral statistics. As noted in Chapter 8, there are three main concerns with extant franchise failure statistics:

1. presenting an 'industry' figure when franchising consists of disparate activities;
2. there are high levels of vested interest by those associated with franchises;
3. quantifying failure illustrates definitional and methodological inconsistencies.

Assessing the level of company deaths within a particular market, such as the hospitality industry, is also problematic due to differing approaches to the subject. These range from VAT deregistrations, bankruptcies and deeds of arrangements, receiverships, discontinuances and changes in the number of self-employed. The differences in approach only serve to compound the problems of comparability.

The relative financial strength of franchisors may also affect the performance of franchisees. Weak franchisors possibly compound the propensity to fail due to their inability, arising from resource constraints, to help franchisees either efficiently or effectively. Furthermore, some franchise consultants suggest that the minimum time that should elapse before a company can consider franchising is one trading year and a survey of 400 US fast food franchisors (Price, 1993) showed that 71% offer franchises within five years of being established. Some 27% of these offer franchises in the same year that they were established. The failure data (especially Shane, 1996) suggests that this minimum incubation, or 'gestation' period is possibly too short. In Hudson's (1987) terms, such companies are possibly still in their honeymoon period. Perhaps a more prudent approach would be to advise at least five years trading for some businesses. Even here, however, there may be some potential for failure without rigorous assessment of the extent to which the business is suitable for franchised expansion.

Whilst the evaluation of the number of deaths is beset with problems, perhaps a more useful methodology for existing franchisors and franchisees would be to define failure as decline and/or low levels of performance. Using this approach, an investigation into the variation of fast food franchisee performance according to certain exogenous criteria was conducted. In the majority of instances, the null hypotheses were supported. One possible explanation for this situation is that some franchisees are better able to alter their cost structures, sustain high levels of organizational slack and maintain value according to the rigours of their environment than others. By using the results of the cluster analysis to differentiate between differing environmental types and Chakravathy's (1982) continuum of adaptation, a matrix is presented to compare franchisees. This matrix suggests, using Bartlett and Ghoshal's (1991) framework, that differing cost structures exist according to environmental munificence and franchisee ability. While this inference is, however, in need of further theoretic and empirical testing, it underlines the need for franchise researchers to account for how contextual differences affect controls in intra-franchisor-franchisee relationships (Dwyer *et al*, 1986; Nohria and Ghoshal, 1994).

As with any study, the extent to which generalizations may be made is limited in several respects. Other than sample size considerations, the first limitation of this study is the reliance on franchisees who have submitted abbreviated accounts. This has limited the ability of the study to assess return on investment, sales, profit and loss sheet structures and a broader array of performance measures. Equally, there are alternative measures of liquidity, such as current liabilities as a proportion of net worth (shareholders funds less intangible assets), which could yield a greater number of incidences where the null hypotheses are rejected. This observation is also true of the environmental aspects. For example Williams (1995) shows, within the context of the US market, that franchise businesses in states with franchise termination legislation have a higher discontinuance rate than those without. The analysis is further limited by the use of broad definitions of trading areas when, perhaps, narrower boundaries are more appropriate (Min, 1987), as is the use of an inflation-adjusted measure of environmental favourability. Another limitation is the underlying assumption that Taffler's model can be applied to this sector of the food-service market. This has not yet been statistically proved, and, until it has been, implies that other interpretations of the inter-brand results could exist. However, until such a time that a sector-specific multi-discriminant model is developed, Taffler's equation has potentially greater application to non-quoted and new companies in the UK fast food industry than other, non-domestic, models.

After the development of a suitable sector-specific model, Taffler's equation will be a useful yardstick for comparative studies. Nevertheless, in spite of these obvious limitations, given that there are over 20,000 companies in the UK involved in franchising, the results of this study suggest that performance levels in the sector are under-monitored, especially as average performance of some franchisees declined during the reviewed period. Although there are difficulties in evaluating the level of failure within the franchise sector, uncorroborated franchisor data suggests that the level of failure is possibly above that which is comfortable or acceptable. By employing measures of decline, arguably a better assessment of the financial health of the franchise fraternity may be gauged. After all, not all of the failures could have been unforeseen.

As both the fast food and franchise 'industries' become increasingly diverse and competitive, it is clear that the application and extension of research concerning company health, failure prediction and turnaround strategies in this area and other firms confronting constrained environments require further emphasis. The chapter has also posited that there is a necessity for greater objectivity in assessing franchisee attrition rates, and to compare like with like – especially as some sectors are more volatile than others and franchisees are, typically, exposed to greater risk than franchisors (Mason, 1993). However, whilst objective data concerning failure may be of interest in its own right, there may also be a necessity for franchisors to employ methods that provide evidence of franchisee under-performance in order that a proactive stance may be taken.

There are also limitations deriving from the use of financial measures *per se*. Argenti (1976), for example, suggests that financial performance is only one characteristic of a failing organization and called for a more multi-dimensional approach to performance measurement. One such approach is the 'balanced score-card' method (Kaplan and Norton, 1996), which measures performance from three additional perspectives: those of customers, internal business process, and learning and growth. It therefore enables companies to monitor financial results while simultaneously monitoring progress in building the capabilities and acquiring the intangible assets they need.

As such, it represents a more robust method to examine under-performing companies and provides some insight as to the appropriate remedial action.

As in most failures, franchise failures are observable. To reiterate, trouble manifests itself before failure taking the form of declining or lower than average performance. Bankruptcy or insolvency is only the final stage in a company's inability to anticipate, recognize, avoid, neutralize or adapt to internal or external pressures that threaten the organization's long-term survival. Thus, financial failures may be symptomatic of franchisee disillusionment and disenchantment with the business (that is, the franchisee may feel that they are not realizing self-actualization, which leads to a desire to move on and neglect of the business). Alternatively, the franchisee's feelings of disconfirmation may be symptomatic of the lack of financial success of the business. Either way, resolving these feelings may be cheaper than recruiting a new franchisee and endear the franchisor to other franchisees, if successful. This orientation suggests that franchisors and franchisees alike must monitor their own and each other's performance and munificence of the general business climate to help facilitate the realization of the low failure rates that many in the franchise fraternity propound. Of course, there will be some instances where the franchisee's personal circumstances are so acute that all possible efforts fail to achieve the desired result of a turnaround. Nevertheless, at least some satisfaction and enhanced reputation may be derived from the fact that at least something was done.

This chapter also suggests that franchisors need to be more realistic of the potential returns that a franchisee may realize (Hayes, 1994) and some need to be more cautious in awarding franchises (Wattel, 1969). The point is this: although there has been a tendency to rely on personal explanations of franchisee failure rather than financial ones, the reputation and development costs associated with franchised-based expansion suggest that franchising cannot afford a truly high rate of failure *per se* – let alone just financial ones. But, rather than trying to disguise failure rates, franchisor effort and commitment are necessary to alter the position by being more selective and effective in recruiting franchisees and being more proactive in assisting them. After all, as most franchisors are inherently biased away from potential franchisees with prior self-employment and sector experience, to then blame franchisee failure predominantly on personal reasons (such as lack of ability) is self-defeating and, in all probability, a self-fulfilled prophecy.

Notes

1. Government-produced inflation indices for the UK catering industry, and its various sub-sectors, suggest that the market witnessed rapid increases in prices in the latter half of the 1980s and early 1990s. The rate of increase, reflecting the UK trends in inflation generally, have levelled off. Much of the increases in the catering market were in excess of the retail price index – especially in contract catering. Whilst some of this may be due to lower subsidies, it also reflects the tendency in the catering industry as a whole to pass cost increases on to the customer. In more concentrated markets, such as the supermarket sector and certain strategic groupings in the foodservice market, there has been less of a tendency to engage in such action for fear that it may make some less price-competitive.

2. Although a sample size of fifty-nine appears small, statistically it is large. Statistically speaking, large samples mean more than thirty. However, it is impossible to be precise, as a sample does not remain 'small' until it gets to twenty-nine, and then suddenly becomes large. The sampling distribution on samples from a non-normal population gradually becomes more and more normal. By the time the sample reaches thirty, the errors introduced by assuming the sampling distribution to be exactly normal are negligible (Lapin, 1993).

3. In the UK it is possible to obtain financial and other information on those franchisees which trade as limited companies. Such companies, like other limited liability concerns, are legally required to submit annual accounts to Companies House in a pre-specified format, at which time it becomes public information upon payment of a fee. In the event of a business choosing, or being required to, trade either as a sole proprietorship or partnership, (that is, without the benefit of limited liability), then the accounts remain a private matter between the owner and the Inland Revenue.

4. The proportion of limited liability franchisees also varies by company in the fast food industry. For example, in 1994, McDonald's (UK) only had nine of its eighty franchisees as limited liability concerns – in some pizza home delivery concerns, they account for over 40%.

5. This is a slight modification of some of the approaches employed by international business researchers to identify the export market potential for a variety of different products. Several studies (Green and Kohli, 1991; Terpstra and Yu, 1988; Thakur and Das, 1991) discuss the importance of using multiple indicators of market potential and describe data extrapolation methods that can be used in conjunction with these indicators to obtain estimates of environmental munificence. The indicators suggested for use and extrapolation in these papers include economic, geographic, cultural, political and infrastructure variables associated with individual countries. Some (Harrell and Kiefer, 1981) have assigned subjective weights to the variables in order to generate a figure for country attractiveness. A more statistically robust method of evaluating the similarities and differences is the use of cluster analysis (Sethi, 1971). In contrast, perhaps, to such scientific methods, McDonald's employs a highly simplistic approach (and one which may be indicative of ethnocentrism), via employing density and market size variables, to 'guesstimate' the carrying capacity of a particular country:

[Population of *Country X* / # of people per McDonald's in U.S.] * [Per capita income of *Country X* / Per Capita income of U.S.] = Potential Penetration of McDonald's in *Country X*.

Source: Serwer, A.E. (1994), 'McDonald's Conquers the World', *Fortune,* 17 October, pp. 59–69.

6. If the auditor doubts the figures presented in the accounts, then the report to shareholders must be 'qualified' and the nature of these doubts stated. Indeed, the Auditing Standard on 'Qualifications in Audit Reports' (APG 1980) states that the auditor should:

qualify his report by referring to all material matters about which he has reservations. All reasons for the qualifications, together with a quantification of its effect on the financial statements if this is both relevant and practicable . . . A qualified audit report should leave the reader in no doubt as to its meaning and its implications for an understanding of the financial statements.

However, the UK Auditing Standards explicitly recognize the problems associated with auditing the accounts of small companies, notably having to rely on the assurances of the directors that all transactions are entered in the books – this may be difficult in cash concerns such as fast food businesses and where the shareholders are also directors, owners and the day-to-day management (indeed, the catering trade has often acknowledged – albeit 'off-the-record' – the presence of 'little black books'). In such cases, provided that the directors are able to provide the necessary assurances and that there is no evidence that these assurances are inaccurate, the Auditing Guidelines recommend the issue of a small company qualified report. None of the sampled franchisee companies had any audit qualifications that indicated that the auditor had disagreed with the directors and the figures presented in the financial statements. This is not surprising given the general level of reliance amongst small firms on their auditors to present the annual accounts for them.

Probably one of the most serious types of audit qualification is the 'going concern' qualification. The financial accounts of companies are drawn up on the assumption that the business will continue to operate as an ongoing concern in the foreseeable future. Hence, the accounts will not show any provisions for losses caused by winding up or the forced sale of part of the business to raise finance. The 'going concern' qualification means that the auditors are unsure as to whether the business may be a going concern since (for the most part) the firms are generating pre-tax losses and have current liabilities in excess of current assets. For the majority of such firms the ability for them to be a going concern is, in part, dependent upon the willingness of directors and financiers to maintain their investment. This said, there may be some circumstantial evidence to suggest that the under-performance issue – and the probability of failure – may be higher than the going concern statistics suggest. Kelly (1995), for example, shows that only one in seven companies which failed between 1987 and 1994 carried a warning from auditors in its last set of accounts about its status as a going concern. An earlier survey found that among 107 listed industrial and distribution companies which failed from 1977 to 1986, 26% had carried an auditor's qualification about their status. This compares to 17 % among 62 comparable companies between 1987 and 1994. Further, the going concern principle must not be applied if the auditor believes that the company is in serious financial difficulties which render this assumption unrealistic. Hence, some of the sampled firms where the going concern qualification is missing may be those either in serious financial difficulties or those who have yet to register their accounts with Companies House.

Further, whilst a going concern qualification may hasten a failing company's demise, *there is no evidence that an otherwise healthy company has been forced into liquidation by the issue of a going concern qualification.* Thus for suppliers of companies (franchised or otherwise), there may be an incentive to adopt a cash-on- delivery approach rather than refuse to renew credit facilities. It is important that the credit policy concerning organizations with going concern qualifications should be derived from an analysis of the company's financial performance. The relatively high proportion of going concern qualifications may also be indicative of the comparative youth of the firms. Combined with a reliance on banks as a source of finance and the costs of starting a new business, it should perhaps be expected that current liabilities exceed current assets. However, it is also apparent that as the sampled firms have been in business longer than five years – the critical period for a new business – the same argument cannot apply.

7. According to Damodaran (1994), the free flow to equity ratio for a geared concern (and therefore applicable to the majority of fast food franchisee businesses) is calculated as follows:

1. Revenues less operating expenses = *EBITDA*
2. *EBITDA* less depreciation and amortization = *EBIT*
3. *EBIT* less interest and taxes = *Net Income*
4. *Net Income* plus depreciation and amortization = *Operating Cash Flows*
5. *Operating Cash Flows* less (Net Capital Expenditure and Working Capital requirements) = *Free Cash Flows to Equity*.

8. Taffler's Z-score takes the following form: $Z = c_0 + c_1 x_1 + c_2 x_2 + c_3 x_3 + c_4 x_4$

Where:

x_1 = profit before tax / current liabilities (53%)
x_2 = current assets / total liabilities (13%)
x_3 = current liabilities / total assets (18%)
x_4 = no credit interval (16%)

$c_0 \ldots c_4$ are the coefficients and percentages in brackets represent the Mosteller-Wallace contributions of the ratios to the power of the working model (Taffler, 1995; pp. 4–5).

Final comments

10 | Towards an anthropology of the franchise relationship: the role of fiefs, clans, witch doctors and professors

Co-authored with Howard Price and Brian Kenny

Organizations in the West have learned the importance of organizing their businesses into cross-functional teams, focused on key business processes. In the future, even this will not be enough. Successful businesses will create value by implementing innovations across organizational boundaries: 'cross-functional' teams will become 'cross-organizational' teams. Franchises will only be able to demonstrate lower rates of failure than other business forms through the use of such cross-organizational teams. The fundamental challenges to the nurturing of cross-functional and cross-organizational teams are social rather than technical, involving issues of trust, co-operation, power and politics. As a result of these demands, the roles and relationships required for best practice franchise management are changing. This final chapter, by drawing on the key observations of previous chapters, introduces new models that have been developed in order to understand the cultural context of franchise relationships, and the roles and relationships needed for the realization of competitive advantages through continuous innovation.

Introduction

Imagine a piece of land twenty miles long and twenty miles wide. Picture it wild, inhabited by animals small and large. Now visualize a compact group of sixty human beings, camping in the middle of this territory. Try to see yourself sitting there, as a member of this tiny tribe, with the landscape, your landscape, spreading out around you, farther than you can see. No one apart from your tribe uses this vast space. It is your exclusive home-range, your tribal hunting ground. Every so often the men in your group set off in pursuit of prey. The women gather fruits and berries. The children play noisily around the camp site, imitating the hunting techniques of their fathers. If the tribe is successful and swells in size, a splinter group will set off to colonize a new territory. Little by little the species will spread.

Now imagine a piece of land twenty miles long and twenty miles wide. Picture it civilized, inhabited by machines and buildings. Now visualize a compact group of six million human beings camping in the middle of this territory. See yourself sitting there, with the complexity of the huge city spreading out all around you, farther than you can see.

Now compare these two pictures. In the second scene there are a hundred-thousand individuals for every one in the first scene. The space has remained the same. Speaking in evolutionary terms, this dramatic change has been almost instantaneous; it has taken a mere few thousand years to convert scene one into scene two. The human animal appears to have adapted brilliantly to his extra-ordinary new condition, but he has not had time to change biologically, to evolve into a new, genetically civilized species. The civilizing process has been accomplished entirely be learning and conditioning. Biologically he is still the simple tribal animal depicted in scene one. He lived like that, not for a few centuries, but for a million hard years.

So much has happened in the past few thousand years, the urban years, the crowded years of civilized man, that we find it hard to grasp the idea that this is no more than a minute part of the human story. It is so familiar to us that we vaguely imagine that we grew into it gradually and that, as a result, we are biologically fully equipped to deal with all the new social hazards. If we force ourselves to be coolly objective about it, we are bound to admit that this is not so. It is only our incredible plasticity, our ingenious adaptability, that makes it seem so. The simple tribal hunter is doing his best to wear his new trappings lightly and proudly; but they are complex, cumbersome garments and he keeps tripping over them. (Morris, 1969; pp. 13–14)

Franchise management and the tribal hunter

A paradox is a statement or proposition, despite sound reasoning from an accept-able premise, that is actually self-contradictory. Anyone browsing the bookshelves of any business bookshop may wonder if every aspect of organizational life is beset by paradoxes. After all, especially over the last few years, a plethora of books and pamphlets has been written with the 'paradox' word somewhere in the title: *The Age of Paradox* by Handy, *Paradox: The Next Strategic Dimension* by McKenzie, *The Corporate Paradox* by Felstead, and *The Paradox of Success* by O'Neil are examples of such work. Whether the subject matter contained in these books and this book may be construed to be paradoxes is open to substantial variation, depending on the soundness of reasoning and the acceptability of the premise. To some, the propositions are not so much paradoxes as conundrums. This book has sought to explore a paradox within the world of franchising from a multi-disciplinary perspective, rather than relying on the traditional franchise literature alone. The paradox is: how can franchisors stress conformity, rather than innovation, and also simultaneously expect fewer failures than independent businesses? In examining this paradox it is evident that franchising is, in itself, an innovation and the ability to realize further continuous innovation is important to survival.

The evolution of economies, societies and technology as well as the rapid rate of change required to sustain consumer interest has led to increasing complexity and uncertainty for many organizations. This uncertainty limits their ability to develop long-term plans, and increases their need to be able to adapt to their environment and respond to the surprises that will arise:

> A few years ago we were saying that the 'Management of Change' is the biggest challenge organizational leaders face. Today we hear that the problem is no longer the management of change but the management of 'surprise', and we academics are asked more and more frequently to explain not just how organizations can make major transformations, but how organizations can do these activities faster and faster. (Schien, 1993; p. 85)

For many organizations, the idea of an end-user 'product' as a piece of hardware has changed to encompass software (smart products), fashion and lifestyle, information, service and consultancy (Peters, 1992). The same is also true in industrial markets, where buyers expect to develop value-added relationships with their suppliers, encompassing much more than simply the supply of a product at a particular price. The increasing importance of the 'soft' elements of products, in combination with the development of technology and systems that enable the production of small batch sizes at relatively low cost, has led to increased product differentiation and customization. Technology has reduced the cost of manufacturing products, particularly labour cost as a proportion of total cost, enabling much more attention to be paid to 'value-added' activities. Franchising is perceived by some authors (especially proponents of agency theory) to be an example of such value-adding activity. Franchisees are motivated to provide superior service in order to help recoup their investment, and thereby realize greater access to the factors of production and status, through repeat patronage by customers. In this sense, franchising can help firms to fill holes in networks of similar service products.

The emphasis on adding value, however, requires firms to augment and differentiate both their existing products and services. Mathur (1986) indicates that the dynamic nature of consumer markets and ever-increasing buying sophistication means that products must be differentiated. As the degree to which an innovation is perceived as being better than the idea it supersedes has a direct impact on the likelihood of adoption (Rogers, 1995), the original model loses market share as competitor models surpass it (Schnaars, 1994). This situation, in turn, is leading to the increasing importance of knowledge and ideas as major sources of value and wealth in developed societies. Some writers have interpreted this as the emergence of 'knowledge as capital', leading to the need for a redefinition of business economics (Hall, 1992; Handy, 1993, 1994). In this paradigm the function of an organization is to make knowledge productive, and people with knowledge will have to gain new knowledge every three or four years or become obsolete. Some organizations, such as Benetton and McDonald's are already espousing these values, and recognize that knowledge is a key strategic asset which possesses some non-imitable qualities.

From this viewpoint, Nelson and Winter's (1983) evolutionary approach to innovation seems particularly cogent: they state that the trajectory (direction) of technical developments by firms in an industry would be affected by their 'selection environments' or targeted customer base, these environments being made up of economic, cultural and political/legislative factors, which also constitute antecedent variables and affect how a firm may compete. Despite comments concerning the emphasis on standardization and conformance to the business blueprint, franchises require ongoing innovation in order to survive and, because of the role of social networks, there may exist a need to alter the manner in which franchising, as an innovation in itself, is diffused within potential investor markets. Chapters 1 and 3, for example, suggest that firms which might benefit from adopting franchising must be aware of its trajectory and decide whether to follow it as well as surmount mobility barriers and internal politics (the exercising of usurpationary power); those who do not, may be aware of other innovations which are perceived to permit the realization of their objectives more closely or are unable to overcome the mobility barriers necessary to being a franchisor. Such an evolutionary process suggest that organizations are experimental learning systems which respond to threats and opportunities in the external environment: These responses are translated as changes to strategy and structure, and derive from the reading and interpretation of competitors' actions, intentions, goals, motives, or the internal situation (see Chapters 3 and 4).

But what has franchise management and the discourse about innovation got to do with tribal hunters? Franchising is a method (an innovative one) of colonizing different territories, and many practitioners refer to the success required of a business prior to embarking on franchised expansion. In this sense, a franchise firm may be compared to a tribe which has swelled in size and then dispersed. While the satellite tribe (the franchisee) will have acquired knowledge of running a business from the franchisor (imitating the hunting techniques), the subsequent survival of both the franchisor and franchisee is dependent on their ability to learn and adapt to prevailing environmental conditions, a process which entails change. Of course, this situation assumes that franchisees, like the tribal hunters, have the autonomy, flexibility and capability to initiate innovations:

> Each extended family was autonomous and self-sufficient, and the individuals who comprised it had each learned the variety of skills necessary to survive . . . It was this autonomy of the small groups composed of multi-skilled individuals that allowed the society to spread itself out in its search for the dispersed resources. Effectively, this gave the . . . [tribal hunter] . . . the ability to cover large areas of territory without losing the flexibility to capitalize on success wherever it was found . . . using modern business concepts, one would describe their 'strategy' as opportunistic and emergent rather than deliberate and planned. (Hurst, 1995; pp. 16–17)

Franchisees have varying levels of autonomy depending on the 'hardness' of the contract and the franchisor's tolerance for new ideas, and some are involved in process innovations to improve cash flows and profitability. This book has suggested that franchisors cannot, in fact, survive without innovation and the rate of failure in franchising is higher than has been suggested hitherto; it has also argued that innovative behaviour is natural and emergent, rather than being wholly intentional. Such an argument may represent a departure from past approaches because although researchers have developed rational, scientific explanations of the need for change, unfortunately the tone has a tendency to be too prescriptive: these are the new realities of operating in a world where innovation and organizational architecture are important sources of competitive advantage, and managers need to implement them. In being prescriptive, there is often too much emphasis on the rationality and intentionality of strategy and not on the emergence and subsequent adoption of certain innovations as being constrained by cognitive limits on rational action and the micro-politics of organizations (the exclusionary and usurpationary power dynamics of intra-organizational networks). Yet, intentionality is typically little more than the post-rationalization of actions which were initiated by incomplete knowledge and differing world-views. This book, especially Chapters 1 and 2, has noted the often *ad hoc* manner in which innovations, such as the M-form of organization, evolve and are diffused and has suggested that the spread of franchising has been equally unplanned. By considering the implications of the evolutionary perspective and the necessity for innovation, we have argued that there appears to be a need for franchise researchers to re-examine some of their assumptions, as well as a necessity to explore how their subject for study interacts with their environments.

Unfortunately, such research activity has so far been limited. It is unhelpful to suggest that franchisors are overtly concerned with standardization and conformance to standards, without considering the effects of such comments and conclusions: without effective communication and joint efforts for innovation, the latent conflict within franchises can move to widespread, internecine struggles. In short, therefore, the paradox may arise because of the inconsistent conclusions which have been recorded by researchers rather than being necessarily founded in reality. In turn, the fact that some franchises are involved in the nurturing of innovation and that the rate of attrition is high suggests that perhaps other researchers' reasoning behind the component parts of the paradox has not been sound. After all, franchisors and franchise advisers have a vested interest in showing that franchises have low rates of failure and innovative behaviour. This is not only natural but also necessary for survival, and has been witnessed in systems with 'hard' franchise contracts. Also, some 'opportunism' is a form of, and is dependent on, innovation and is a natural consequence of the power and status imbalances of the franchise capitalist system.

So, where does this situation leave us? It seems apparent that the level of failure in franchising is higher than has been publicly admitted previously and that some franchises are more involved in ongoing innovative activity than others. Thus, franchising appears to suffer from many of the structural and behavioural problems which are evident in other organizations and networks (Achrol, 1996), such as the Japanese keiretsu system. Concurrent with exploring the topics of failure and the determinants of innovation within franchising specifically, there are recurrent themes throughout this book: innovation, networks (intra- and inter-organizational), and culture. All of these exist within a societal form based on imbalances of access to the factors of production and on the exclusion of some sections of the population from these factors. Summarized in Figure 10.1, each of these variables may provide additional explanations for the performance of franchises and the spread of innovations. For example, new franchises may fail not only because of the competitive dynamics, but also because of the following cultural reasons:

1. the franchisor dampens innovative effort (he does not have a culture orientated towards innovation) within his own organization;
2. the franchisor does not have a culture orientated towards the management of relationships between and continued support of franchisees;
3. the franchise exists within a network inhabited by other firms which are not innovative.

Networks are the weave in the fabric of society and are fundamental in facilitating and inhibiting the diffusion of information and innovations. This book has proposed that, as with the diffusion of other innovations, social networks are a critical influence on the spread of franchising. Although much effort is exerted and expended in advertising franchising to both potential franchisees and franchisors, we have not witnessed a hypodermic needle effect in subsequent adoption rates in either franchise systems, industries, or economies. Under this metaphor, there would be a direct, immediate and powerful effect on the diffusion of franchising after the use of advertising and other mass communication techniques to broaden awareness. The media has not proved omnipotent in influencing people or businesses to adopt franchising in a direct, immediate, and powerful manner (Rogers, 1995). Rather, as shown in Chapters 4 and 5, the decision to become a franchisor or franchisee – and hence the legitimation of franchising – is dependent upon franchising's diffusion along interpersonal communication channels. After all, people tend to listen and read only that matter in which they have an interest. From this awareness and knowledge of franchising (albeit incomplete), individuals pass to persuasion (assessment of the relative benefits), to a decision to adopt or reject, and then to implementation. While awareness is the result of the cacophony of noise generated by the media, personal networks are important in persuading the individual to adopt or reject innovations (Chisholm, 1996).

Reflecting the significance of networks to superior performance and the generation of competitive advantages, Burt (1992) argues that competitive behaviour and its results can be observed in terms of player access to 'holes' in the social structure of the marketplace. Within networks, as a whole, players are connected to certain others through systems of trust, obligations and dependencies. Burt proposes that, by dint of who is connected to whom, holes or disconnections exist in the social structure of the competitive arena. These holes, or niches, are entrepreneurial opportunities for information access, innovation, timing, referrals, and control. Where holes exist, opportunities are present which may be exploited. For example, holes in product networks are oppor-

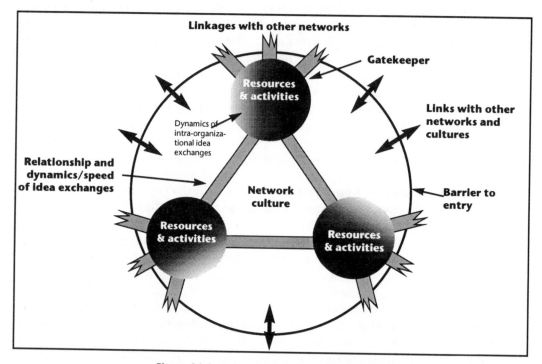

Figure 10.1: Culture, networks and innovation

tunities for differentiation and the realization of increased revenue streams. In this way, when firms elect to franchise they, either intentionally or otherwise, may be seeking to fill certain financial, management, product and geographic holes. When recruiting franchisees with certain levels and types of resources, motivation, and tacit knowledge they may be behaving as tribal gatherers; these franchisees may, for example, be able to recognize that gaps are present in the franchisor's existing array of products and offer ideas which, once implemented, serve to sustain and feed the other system members.

Issues concerning culture are also viewed to be of central importance to the dynamics of innovation dissemination because the spread of ideas is affected by the values, implications, and meanings network members attach to them. For example, some members of a network may not embrace change with the same enthusiasm that others do, which affects the speed of diffusion. To some extent, the diffusion process is impeded because of a natural tendency to make evaluations, which is common in almost all interchange of language but is particularly heightened where emotions (such as feelings of threat) are involved. These evaluations are based on the tone and clarity of the communication, the understanding or misunderstanding of the subject matter, and how it fits with prior learning and cultural values. In this vein, Chapter 7 illustrated that some franchisees developed their own innovations because they had learnt that the franchisor's operating manual was not wholly accurate. Reflecting its importance, each of the chapters has made at least one reference to culture: franchising exists in our social history because of feudalism; franchisors must have an organizational culture orientated towards the management of franchisees; franchising must exist within cultures in order to be considered as a career option by potential franchises and as a development option for certain firms; the diffusion of franchising may be impeded or facilitated by the extent to which organizational cultures and sub-cultures within intra-organizational networks embrace change; and franchisors and franchisees may have different cultures regarding innovation. The dual significance of social networks and culture within a society stratified by access to the factors of prodcution as well as gender, religon, and ethnicity, etc., means that the fundamental challenges to the spread of franchising and the development of competitive advantages based on innovation are, therefore, social rather than technical. The challenges take the following forms: how can groups of people work collaboratively together, as teams, when they have some shared interests and some differences? How can trust be developed in order that collaboration might flourish and, thereby, offer some support for McIntyre *et al*'s (1994) contention that franchises are a form of strategic alliance? How can the unavoidable realities of power and politics be addressed?

When we see the fundamental challenges of relationships inherent to franchising – power, trust, conflict, satisfaction, and reliability – and innovation management in this light, it becomes clear that these are the same social challenges that have faced humankind for several thousand years. Humans deal with the challenges of communication, co-operation and competition within networks by developing cultures. Within these cultures, *roles, rituals and relationships* emerge, in order to maintain and reinforce the structure and function of different intra- and inter-organizational network members. Looking at the innovative organizations of the 1990s in this way provides an insight into how franchise businesses might be managed. In summarizing this book, the following discourse, therefore, starts with a brief review of our existing knowledge about creativity and learning in intra-organizational webs because it is this which affects the spread of ideas, through imitation and relationships, within inter-organizational networks. For example, if a company has a relationship with another innovative company, it may have positive effects upon other relationships.

The chapter then examines some of the issues concerning innovation and learning between organizations. In both sections, culture is viewed as the 'glue' which holds the network together and is significant as a facilitating mechanism to the permeation of new knowledge within a network via the roles and rituals performed by the incumbent actors. By providing understanding of the rise and success of franchising in this way, it is hoped that the issues of networks, cultures, and innovation may become foci for subsequent debate, and may, in the process, alter the nature and conceptualization of future franchising theory, research, and management (Achrol, 1996). Clearly, not all franchises have an emphasis on standardization which precludes innovation. The more successful franchisees are able to harness the innovative capabilities possessed by their franchisees in a positive way and such relationships are, therefore, more akin to strategic alliances (see Chapter 6). Others do not have such cultures or relationships and are, therefore, possibly more prone to failure because of the competitive dynamics of markets. What is different about the innovative franchises is not only the culture inherent to the network, but also the roles of the franchisor and franchisee. But what are these roles? Drawing on the reviews of the literature and the book, this chapter adapts and extends a theoretical framework proposed by Price (1996) to better understand the *cultural context* of franchise relationships, and the roles that need to be developed in order to achieve successful diffusion of innovation in franchises and other networks. By understanding the roles required for successful innovation in franchises, some insight may be provided to help franchisors nurture the flow of new ideas and assist in the turnaround of under-performing franchisees.

Creativity within organizations: from manufacturing to mento-facturing

There seems to be general consensus that knowledge is a form of capital which, together with the rise of information technology, has resulted in a change from manual labour to mental labour. As such, it is the ownership of such intangible resources which is one of the bases of capital accumulation. These 'mento-facturing' skills, together with heightened uncertainty within task environments, suggest that a key feature of survival for an enterprise will be the ability of its members to generate new ideas, identify potential problems and solutions and share them. Unfortunately, while these problem are latent human instincts, they have tended not to be fully utilized in business because of an emphasis on the separation of capital and labour:

> The exploratory drive is now recognized to be a basic, primarily biological instinct, as basic as the instincts of hunger and sex; it can on occasions be even more powerful than these. Countless experiments – starting with Darwin himself – have shown that curiosity, and the 'seeking out of thrills', is an instinctual urge in rats, birds, dolphins, chimpanzees and man; and so is what behaviourists call 'Ludic Behaviour' – playfulness. (Keostler, 1967; p. 153)

> I am tempted to define *creativity* . . . as the healthy enjoyment of the search for novelty. The neurophysiologists tell us that the propensity for such exploration is actually wired into the brain. (Gedo, 1990; p. 35: emphasis in the original)

The term most often used in management terminology for this 'search for thrills' is innovation, but in franchising texts it is often referred to as opportunism (which is seen in negative terms). It is not necessary that these ideas are new *per se*, but new to the adopting organization. Thus, while franchising may not be a new concept and have its origins in feudal society, in itself it is an innovation to many because it represents a method of surmounting resource constraints. As an innovation representing changes in strategy and organization structure, the decision to franchise and its subsequent implementation is typically a response to changing environmental and/or organizational conditions as well as the adoption of franchising by competitors. But this is a process which requires the firm to overcome mobility barriers. For any type of innovation to be implemented, management must be able to recognize and support opportunities for change to existing practices, routines and structures. Chapter 4, for example, illustrated that the dynamics of the adoption of franchising appears to be determined more by reference to other peer group members operating within a particular product/market niche in order to preclude the monopolization of resources and access to capital embodied by the franchisee. The diffusion of franchising is, hence, partially affected by the range of alternatives and the decision-maker's awareness of them, willingness to change, and overcoming any resistance to change within the organization. As inferred in Chapters 6 and 9, it is this issue of recognition which may preclude the need for innovation and the presence of sub-optimal financial performance but is of critical importance to initiating responses and the remedial process.

Recognizing that a particular process/product may be applicable to a certain context means that people must learn from their environment and reconcile new information with their existing stock of tacit knowledge. Indeed, many researchers propose that organizational renewal hinges on individual learning – a process that necessarily requires additions to or changes in mental models (Barr *et al*, 1992). In this sense, learning and creativity are inter-connected; new information and learning may lead to new insights, opportunities, and deeper levels of understanding about a particular subject. Learning has been defined as 'a relatively persistent change in an individual's possible behaviour, due to experience factors which influence it' (Fontana, 1984; p. 118). The use of the term 'possible behaviour' is of note, since the individual does not have to demonstrate that a new behaviour has been added to the 'repertoire'. The process of experiential learning involves a cycle of reflecting on experience, deriving some abstractions or generalizations from this reflection, and then experimenting with these new concepts in the outside world (Kolb, 1974). Experimentation leads to further experience and further reflection, and then experimenting with these new concepts in the outside world. This leads to further experience and further reflection, and generalization. Revans (1984) also views learning from an experiential perspective, but in his description of action learning, he summarizes learning with the 'learning equation': learning = P + Q, where P is 'programmed knowledge' and Q is 'questioning insight', Q can never be taught and comes from experience and 'trial and error'. P learning adds to the sum of knowledge, and Q learning reorganizes it (Brooks, 1992). As Chapter 3 shows, there are, however, certain blockages to learning which can also inhibit the decision to franchise, namely the idolization of past experience, functional fixedness, hidden assumptions, satisficing behaviour, confirmation bias, the charismatic influence of other managers, and managers' impulse to spontaneous action (Kaufmann, 1991; Revans, 1985). Argyris (1982) focuses on the problem of managers whose learning is blocked by either emotions or past experience. He later identifies difficult situations as requiring 'double loop' learning, where the manager needs to break out of inappropriate habits of thought:

> One type of organizational learning involves the production of matches, or the detection and correction of mismatches, without change in the underlying governing policies or values. This is called single loop learning. A second type, double loop learning, does require re·examination and change of governing values. Single loop learning is actually related to the routine, immediate task. Double loop learning is related to the non-routine, the long range outcome. (Argyris, 1983; p. 116)

Single loop learning in franchising has been shown to be present both in contract negotiation situations (Chapter 7), and during the relationship by Lukas *et al* (1996):

> The marketing manager of a franchise system observes a shortfall in franchisee monthly sales. The marketing manager's sales expectation is determined by the criteria of effective performance adopted by the franchise system. The marketing manager inquires into the gap between achieved sales level and expected sales level to determine a new marketing strategy (i.e., learning by adaption) that will bring sales back on target for the franchise system. The criteria of effective performance remain unquestioned in this single-loop learning process. (p. 237)

Single loop learning is present during the contract negotiation stage of the franchise relationship because the franchisor typically offers a contract which does not vary by the environmental munificence of the region a franchisee operates in, by the franchisee's willingness to take risk, and expend effort. Overt rigidity on maintaining uniformity, as stipulated in the contract, may be detrimental to the realization of franchisee satisfaction, competitive advantages, and may point to an embeddedness of X-inefficiency.

The notion that there are various 'levels' of learning is common in the technological transfer discourse and in the literature concerning knowledge. One such framework is from Bateson (1972): *Zero learning* occurs where there is minimal change in responses over time. There is an absence of correction through 'trial and error'. *Level One learning* is learning that results in the acquisition of *specific facts*, knowledge or responses, such as those passed on from the franchisor to the franchisee in order to operate their stores. This is typical of many learning situations and of some basic problem-solving situations. The results of such learning are difficult to apply, outside the specific situation. *Level Two learning* requires an understanding of the *context* of specific facts and responses. Bateson coined the term 'deutero-learning' to describe learning at this level which results in an appreciation of how specific facts and responses may be organized and how they relate to the outside world. Such an understanding allows the development of strategies for learning, or 'learning to learn'. Finally, *Level Three learning* requires a critical review of the assumptions that were made in the development of learning strategies at Level Two. This awareness would enable the learner to develop and refine his or her own learning strategies, but this tends to be a rare occurrence since it requires an individual to critically examine his own values and assumptions. In the complex business environment, the quality of learning taking place at these 'higher' levels will be critical for business survival. Such learning is not possible without overcoming such barriers as an awareness of the self, of the environment, and of a range of possible approaches and outcomes.

Common sense might suggest that learning and problem-solving are closely related, but some of the ideas already considered illustrate that prior learning can inhibit problem-solving. Asher's Neo-Field Theory says that whilst learning is forming concepts in a cognitive system, problem-solving is the inverse of this, in that problem-solving involves disrupting established concepts (Davis, 1966). Distinctions can also be drawn between the process of problem-finding and the process of problem-solving. In regard to management development, Revans (1984) differentiates between 'puzzles' and 'problems'. Puzzles have only one possible solution; how to do it and when the puzzle is complete is clear to everyone (such as a crossword or jigsaw puzzle). Thus a person can be assured that, if he or she is clever enough, the puzzle can be solved. Most management problems do not fall into this category. According to the traditional franchise literature, the decision to grow through franchising, for example, is an attempt to surmount the problems caused by resource constraints, employee shirking, uncertainty and limited market knowledge. Chapter 2, however, illustrated that there is a variety of alternatives to franchising which can resolve these problems in a similar way, but their diffusion illustrates varying degrees of concentration by industry sub-sector. As such, there appears to be a greater reliance on existing mental maps rather than tapping into other world-views contained within an alternative social network. Some managers and administrators often confront situations in which their mental maps are vague or may need to be reconstituted (McCaskey, 1991) and therefore seek to employ techniques which have precedents elsewhere within their industry grouping. But the use of a particular strategy, despite precedents, may not be wholly appropriate for the new adopter because the competitive dynamics of the marketplace and resource mix of the firm are different from when the idea was first used. Moreover, managing 'surprise' involves political and social issues of considerable uncertainty. Discovered problems do not have a clearly formulated task, instead there is vague unease and dimly felt emotional or intellectual tension. Because the problem itself has yet to be defined, there cannot be an agreed method for resolving the tension. For the same reason, one cannot even imagine in advance what a solution might be or how sustainable that solution may be (Barr *et al*, 1992; Csikszentmihalyi, 1990).

In addition to the uncertainty of whether a particular solution is the correct one, it is clear that innovation implementation involves change in organizations and in their environments. Such change can be either incremental or radical (Kanter, 1985; Clark and Staunton, 1989). An incremental innovation will involve what Smith and Tranfield (1991) have described as Morphostatic change – adjustment to the environment. Chapter 6 suggested that this may be the dominant form of innovative activity because of the implicit and latent conflict between franchisees and their franchisor, as well as between franchisees and their labour, and differing levels of environmental munificence. These issues mean franchisees are motivated to make incremental improvements/innovations to increase their wealth both during the course of the franchise contract and at its termination. This type of innovation is very close to the idea of continuous improvement. A radical innovation will be Morphogenic – it will involve 'breaking the mould' (Schumpeter's 'Creative Destruction', 1911). Surmounting the mobility barriers necessary to become a franchisor often entails radical – or fundamental (Strebel, 1987) – innovation and breaking the orientation of the existing approach. As shown in Chapter 6, however, once a firm has become a franchisor there is a tendency and emphasis by some to dampen further innovative activity for the sake of maintaining the *status quo* (by ensuring that the business blueprint is not altered) and stressing conformance to standards.

As also illustrated in Chapter 6, Lawson (1980) has identified a common set of five stages described in the literature of the creative process. These stages are: first insight, preparation, incubation, illumination and verification. Lawson was writing about individuals, but Gordon (1961) observed that 'the individual process in the creative enterprise enjoys a direct analogy in the group process' and is therefore pertinent to how innovations are diffused and how innovations may evolve from group dynamics. Pursuing a career as either a franchisee or franchisor is also a creative process. By using Lawson's (1980) five-stage model as a framework, the diagram (Figure 10.2) illustrates these processes and the relevant supporting chapters. It shows that social milieu plays an important part in affecting the awareness and subsequent diffusion of franchising. Here some comparison with Mannheim's (1936) analogy of the urbanization of a peasant boy can be made. In some industries and economies, franchising does not prevail because other organizational forms have become the accepted norm. When a person is exposed to alternatives, they are able to distinguish between the advantages and disadvantages – albeit within the confines of bounded rationality – of differing solutions to their problem. Despite its importance and relevance to becoming a franchisee and a franchisor, as well as the clarity which Lawson brings, the creative process is still largely a mystery. Jung (1933) said that 'the creative act will forever elude understanding', and that creativity 'plumbs the depths of primordial vision'. Such vision is seen 'as in a glass darkly'. Whatever the mysteries of the process, creativity is born out of the juxtaposition of different, conflicting ideas. As shown in Chapter 6, writers and researches have identified the importance of groups of people with different experiences and intellectual backgrounds to the development of creative solutions. For this reason, franchisors' recruitment biases are potentially significant to the innovative process and continuous learning in franchises.

Imai *et al* (1985), observed that such juxtaposition of ideas was necessary for 'variety amplification' in the product development process. At a more theoretical level, Koestler (1967) and de Bono (1973) stress the importance of introducing concepts that have no obvious relevance via introducing 'discontinuities' and 're-patterning', as well as the 'bisociation' of differing ideas. Gerstenfeld (1970) and, latterly, Lessard and Zaheer (1996) note the importance of cross-fertilization of ideas resulting from a mixture of specialisms to strategic decision-making. One of the most important changes in business organizations in recent decades has been the increased use of cross-functional teams, or cross-departmental/intra-organizational networks, in order to yield effective, co-ordinated and more robust strategic responses to increasingly volatile and uncertain task environments (Cohen and Levinthal, 1990; Schwenk, 1988). These teams initially emerged as cross-functional product development groups set up to support 'concurrent engineering', first in the Far East and later in the West (Imai *et al*, 1985; Coxhead and Davis, 1992). Such teams typically include representatives from purchasing, design, development, manufacturing, quality and marketing. They may either be self-managing (Ouchi, 1982; Imai *et al*, 1985) or have some form of leader or project champion (Coxhead and Davis, 1992). More recently, the same cross-functional approach has been applied to other business processes, including supply chain management, but its use in franchising

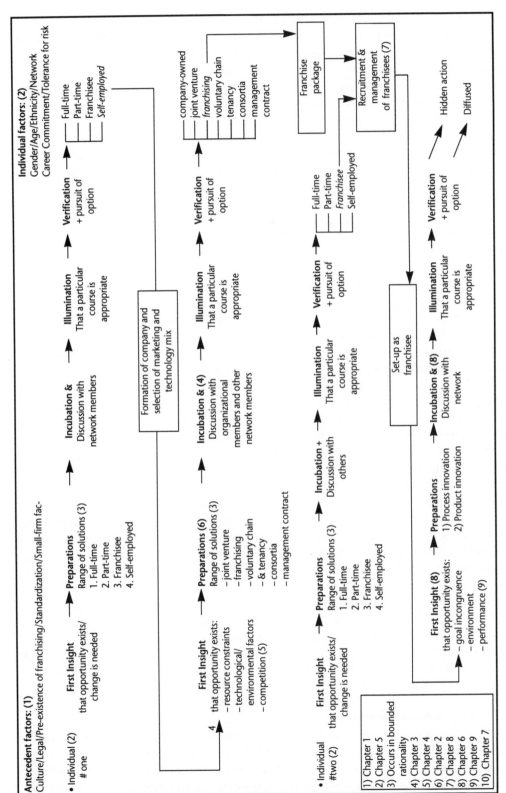

Figure 10.2: *Five-stage model of the creative process and its application to franchising*

has been limited. For example, Silvester (1996) suggests that franchisee recruitment is an ongoing problem for many franchisees subsequent to their launch. Yet, there appears to be little overt use of personnel specialists to help facilitate some form of solution to this problem, which possibly points to the lack of an organizational culture orientated towards the use of cross-functional teams for problem-solving purposes and the resource-constrained nature of many franchisors (Thompson, 1994).

Whilst such frameworks have done much to further our understanding about the individual learning process, extant understanding of the phenomenon in inter-organizational networks is under-developed (Hamel, 1991). As Huber (1991) concludes after an extensive review of organizational learning discourse, 'there is little in the way of substantiated theory concerning organizational learning, and there is considerable need and opportunity to fill many gaps'. This said, there appears to be some consensus regarding the role of culture in organizational learning.

In a review of the literature on learning organizations, Price (1996) reveals that there are a few recurrent themes some of which are applicable to franchising. Firstly, the authors suggest that learning organizations have a holistic/integrative emphasis by employing such terminology as 'whole picture, holistic, vision, framework, awareness'. This relates to the overall level of 'awareness' that exists in the organization, not only the awareness of the 'leaders' but also of the followers. Both 'self-awareness' and an awareness of the environment are required. Secondly, the authors indicate that there is a strong orientation towards change, via the use of words such as: 'forward looking, experimentation encouraged, change/transformation, fluid roles'. In franchises, experimentation with the basic business formula is not encouraged, but there appears to be some acceptance that franchisees will engage in process innovations to improve profitability, and that franchisees may not have the organizational slack to be involved in trials of new ideas. Thirdly, there is an emphasis on teams and team rewards: 'collegiality, team rewards, shared responsibility'. Although franchises have been described as teams and as strategic alliances by McIntyre et al (1994) because of the mutuality of interests, this has not necessarily been extended to the innovation process. Fourthly, organizational cultures emphatic of learning stress the importance of creativity and risk-sharing: 'encourages innovation, entrepreneur, risk-taking, creative'. Finally, texts describing learning organizations refer to the presence of open and mutually supportive cultures: 'open work environment, trust, shared responsibility, norms, values, lateral communication and "clan culture"' (explained later in this chapter). There is wide agreement that an open and supportive culture is required if the learning is to be 'transformational'. Some writers (McGill et al, 1992; O'Hare, 1988) draw a distinction between organizational learning at what could be described as Bateson's Level One, which is seen as necessary but not sufficient, and the more 'transforming' learning necessary to ensure continuing survival in turbulent times (that is, Level Two learning in an organizational context). Huber (1991) analyzes organizational learning under four constructs: knowledge acquisition, information distribution, information interpretation, and organizational memory, as follows.

Knowledge acquisition

Organizations have some knowledge 'at birth' inherited from the parents or founders; franchisee businesses have both the knowledge of the franchisee and that which they have purchased from the franchisor. They then gain more knowledge from experience, which can be a source of innovation to the franchise system if diffused.

Knowledge within organizations is also affected by the mobility of labour: firms are able to 'purchase' expert and experiential knowledge by recruiting suitable individuals, which in turn means that another firm has possibly had its stock reduced. As some franchisors are biased away from recruiting people with self-employment and/or sector-specific experience, but recruit those embarking on a second career, so they have people with a broad spread of new ideas in their systems. Organizations can also carry out 'self-appraisal', which means monitoring the effectiveness of teams and the psychological health of the members of the organization (Huber, 1991). In franchising, this appraisal process is typically conducted by the franchisor, who is seeking to ensure brand conformity, maintenance of high standards, and sales growth, as well as by the franchisee who is motivated to seek ways to improve cash-flow. 'Searching' is described as the process of sensing and monitoring the organization's internal and external environments. This would cover activities ranging from strategic marketing research at the 'macro' level, to the activities of information gatekeepers at the business unit and functional level. This category also includes performance monitoring, but appears to be a process which is conducted to varying degrees within franchising (Chapter 9).

Information distribution

This relates to the way in which information is shared around the organization. By having an effective information distribution system, the organization increases the likelihood of ideas being combined in new and potentially creative ways. The construct relates to 'soft' as well as 'hard' data, but the extent to which this information is a function of the climate of franchisor-franchisee relations, and their individual emphasis on innovation. Some franchise organizations do survive in fast-changing market places and this in itself is testament to an institutionalized ability to innovate and adapt. Despite a stress upon predictable bureaucratic structures, detailed manuals and prescribed methods of operation, franchise organizations tend to operate in tandem with informal networks, in-house news-sheets, and normal everyday contacts and communications, all of which act as filters for ideas.

Information interpretation and organizational memory

Organizational knowledge refers to the stock of information within a network. Meanings are attributed to information received by the organization. Shared value systems play a significant part in this aspect of learning. 'Unlearning' of existing methods is also of importance to innovation because habits can preclude the realization of new ideas and behaviours. Although much of the management of change literature argues that such unlearning should occur through a conscious unmoulding and breaking of habits to facilitate the generation of new ideas, innovation may also occur through default. Stocks of knowledge capital and the flow of new ideas is altered by the lack of practice and use of certain types of knowledge because they are not appropriate at a particular time, and become forgotten. This forgotten knowledge may lead to the adoption of new behaviours, which may either be beneficial or opportunistic. Organizational memory is also affected by the amount of hard information stored on computers and hard-copy and remembered by individuals. Equally important is 'soft' or cultural information – such as remembering how certain individuals reacted in particular situations.

Any consideration of organizational learning needs to recognize that learning is taking place at different places within the organization hierarchy or structure. Imai *et al* (1985) refer to this as 'multi-learning', that is, learning at the level of the individual, the work group and the organization. At the work group level, Kolb's (1974) analysis of learning styles identifies a potential benefit from cross-functional team working. Kolb identified that different functions tended to display different preferred learning styles; a team that combined a balanced mix of learning styles could be particularly effective. Additionally, the cross-functional team provides the opportunity to bring together different views, experiences and approaches. A further and important advantage of the cross-functional team in relation to learning is that it provides the opportunity for individuals in the team to use each other to develop their own learning. An outline of the potential ways of 'using others to learn' is given in Table 10.1. This shows that an important proviso for learning is clearing the way for knowledge acquisition to occur. Some franchisors, as a result of their fear of changes to the business blueprint, do not encourage the cross-fertilization of ideas for new ways of doing things. As a consequence, any learning activity and subsequent action conducted by franchisees is translated as opportunism; if suppression of expressions of new ideas results, a 'black-market' in knowledge transference is created. That is, it occurs in an *ad hoc* fashion among networks of franchisees without necessarily being sanctioned by the franchisor. Such a situation means that the learning is not diffused to the potential benefit of all members within a network. Of course, this situation suggests that it is the franchisees, alone, which are involved in learning. But franchisors innovate too. Chapter 7 suggests that franchisors and franchisees can differ in their respective cultures towards innovation, and that conflict may occur as a result of these differences because one party is not receptive to further learning. Thus, franchisees may be opposed to franchisor-initiated innovations as they do not perceive the value of such activity in a positive way.

Stressing the importance of organizational culture, Lessard and Zaheer (1996) argue that while the strategic decision-making process requires the integration of such distributed knowledge through inter-functional co-operation, this integration may be difficult to achieve because of, firstly, a lack of mechanisms; secondly, lack of incentives to foster co-operation across intra- and inter-organizational boundaries; and thirdly, the presence of subcultures with differing emphasis on innovation (see Chapter 7); and of non-overlapping 'thought-worlds' (silo-based thinking) within organizations because problems are framed in different ways (the franchisor may frame solutions on the basis of improving sales growth and the franchisee on how to improve cash-flow).

Surmounting these barriers is of fundamental importance; the extent to which an enterprise can create conditions that maximize the productive creativity of its members will become a key success factor to the realization of competitive advantages based on innovation. The organizational culture will affect the level and quality of creativity, since there is evidence that environmental conditions are at least as important as individual potential for creativity (this is another version of the nature/nurture debate). Research by Amabile (1990) on scientists, for example, found that:

> The environment was a much more salient factor than the individual for these R&D scientists in their experience of specific creative . . . events. Certainly, at a macroscopic level, personal factors such as general intelligence, experience in the field, and ability to think creatively are the major influences on the output

Category	Using others as	Example
Clearing the way for learning		
Accepting	Means of releasing, dispelling, catharting allowing the expressing of one's negative feelings, thoughts.	Sharing negative feelings, father confessor.
Stimulating	Source of energy, enthusiasm.	Energizing, others provide enthusiasm.
Confirming	Source of confirmation, reinforcement, confidence, support, encouragement.	Seeking confidence, assurance.
Sanctioning	Means of permitting, legitimizing, authorizing.	Makes allowance for failure, permits risk-taking, seek permission to try things out.
Structuring	Shaping, organizing one's learning opportunities.	Exposes me to new situations, sets up opportunities to observe.
Tooling up for learning		
Equipping	Source of understanding of methods of learning.	Provides techniques for learning.
Direct learning interventions		
Advising	Source of recommendations, suggestions, guidance.	Provides ideas about what to do.
Exposing	Means of drawing out, clarifying one's ideas, feelings, assumptions.	Looking for a listener, clarify what I think.
Building	Developing ideas, progressing, extending ideas.	Seek out others on the same wavelength.
Testing	Sounding out, anticipating snags, identifying faults, trial opinion.	Seek objective criticism from others, use them as guinea pigs.
Confronting	Alternative viewpoints and perspectives, challenging, disconfirming.	Get them to be devil's advocate, expose one's self to thoughts from other cultures.
Feeding back	Means of reviewing, source of observations and feedback on one's actions and their consequences.	Asking feedback from someone who knows you, ask others to observe you.
Explaining	Source of help in clarifying, making sense of what's been happening.	Help identify underlying causes, using consultant to interpret/make sense of things.
Modelling	Sources of examples of behaviour; a focus of imitation, demonstrations.	Watching positive and negative models.
Sharing	Source of second-hand, vicarious experience, assessing others, experiencing and learning through listening and questioning.	Others sharing their experiences, reading others' writing.

Source: Stuart, R., (1984), 'Using others to learn' in *Handbook of Management Development*, pp. 125–43.

Table 10.1: Strategies for using others to learn

of creative ideas by R&D scientists. But, assuming that hiring practices at major corporations select individuals who exhibit relatively high levels of these personal qualities, the variance above this baseline may well be accounted for primarily by factors in the work environment. (p. 72)

Similar findings have been found within non-scientific environments by Oldham and Cummings (1996):

> These results . . . suggest that managements should consider both personal and contextual factors to increase creativity in work organizations. Specifically, our results suggest that if creativity at work is to be enhanced, an individualized or selective approach to management may be warranted. For example, individuals with levels of creativity-relevant personal characteristics might be identified through the use of assessment instruments . . . Individuals demonstrating high creative potential relative to these norms might then be surrounded with contextual conditions that support intrinsic motivation. (p. 626)

Thus, while some franchisors may be biased towards recruiting those people with the potential to add knowledge and generate innovations within the system, the extent to which new ideas are diffused within a system is dependent on the culture for innovation within the firm and the climate of relations between the organizational members. Chapter 7 illustrated that differing organizations have varying cultures orientated towards innovation; some companies actively encourage learning and the generation of new knowledge, while others illustrate an emphasis on maintaining the *status quo*. The degree to which ideas are communicated within either a franchisor or a franchisee company is dependent on the climate of relations between the management and its staff. The culture is affected by the relative power positions of each organizational member as well as the nature and degree of trust and the ability for each party to influence or persuade the other of the relative benefits of adopting a particular innovation.

So far, we have focused our comment on the creative process within organizations, and have suggested that:

1. creativity is a natural instinct, linked to tacit knowledge, socialization, and prior career experiences. Thus, the contention that franchisors override these natural instincts in favour of maintaining the *status quo* suggests that they are not employing or harnessing the level of knowledge capital to the benefit of their organization. This situation results in franchisee opportunism, a sense of a lack of fulfilment by franchisees, and tension and overt conflict in the franchise system;

2. like the creative process of becoming a franchisee or franchisor, the creative process at individual and group levels is inter-related and includes similar stages and occurs within a social milieu (see Chapter 5);

3. organizational creativity is often a social process involving teams – whether formal (quality circles) or otherwise – working in collaboration, rather than exceptional individuals working alone. If team members have different backgrounds, then this can stimulate creativity. If the team is built up from members of different, collaborating organizations, then the potential for

innovation is particularly high. Franchisees have this potential because of the recruitment biases of the franchisor and the differing task environments in which franchisees operate;

4. the level and quality of creative output will be significantly affected by the environment and social networks within that environment.

Our brief review has also suggested that the nurturing of innovation is problematic. There exist numerous inhibitors to creativity in intra-organizational networks which, in broad terms, are attributable to individual and cultural factors. The inherent difficulties of developing and maintaining an organizational culture which is emphatic of innovation, the necessities of competitive effectiveness and efficiency mean that focusing internally, alone, is insufficient. All organizations and individuals are involved in networks and relationships with others: in franchising, these are between the franchisor and franchisee, suppliers, those offering substitute/complementary products, etc. (Achrol *et al*, 1983). As a consequence of such connections, there exists the potential for firms to form collaborative agreements, which may serve to generate competitive advantages. Several studies, especially within the strategic alliance literature, have suggested the importance of interactions between member firms for successful innovation and new idea generation. For example, Rothwell (1985) stresses the importance of networking in product development; Von Hippel (1988) describes the process of 'informal know-how trading' between individuals in different firms and refers to 'the distributed innovation process as a system'; Bessant and Grunt (1985) report a similar process in German engineering companies; Blois (1972), Teece (1986), Contractor and Lorange (1988) explain the need for collaboration in terms of access to complementary assets, resulting in vertical quasi-integration; and Reve (1990) emphasizes the importance of such alliances at the strategic level. Recognizing this potential, some firms have sought to develop new products and processes through cross-organizational teams, that is project teams with members nominated from different collaborating organizations. Some of these teams are also cross-functional in nature.

Inter-organizational networks and the emergence of cross-organizational teams

Networks prevail at all levels of everyday life and have been used to describe the different connections in transport systems, communities, communications, information technology, etc. Chapter 2 illustrates that the term has also been employed to describe the array of organizational forms between hierarchies and markets, such as joint ventures, franchises, tenancies, symbol groups, constellations, and consortia (Baden-Fuller and Lorenzoni, 1993; Contractor and Lorange, 1988; Jarillo, 1988; Macbeth and Ferguson, 1994; Miles and Snow, 1992; Thorelli, 1986). The increasing commonality of inter-organizational networks is reflected elsewhere. Although there is a dearth of research of such mechanisms in the context of the hospitality industry, there is strong consensus about the emergence of new organizational forms, porous organizational boundaries and networks (Nohria and Eccles, 1992) and their use in a variety of economic settings such as grocery retailing (see Table 10.2), and as methods for realizing future organizational growth:

Groups	Members	Country
European Retail Alliance	Kroninklijke Ahold	Netherlands
	Argyll	UK
	Groupe Casino	France
Associated Marketing Services	Kroninklijke Ahold	Netherlands
	Argyll	UK
	Groupe Casino	France
	Allkauf	Germany
	Edeka	Germany
	ICA	Sweden
	K-Group	Finland
	Grouppo Rinascente	Italy
	Mercadona	Spain
	Hakon Gruppen	Norway
	Superquinn	Ireland
	Jeronimo Martins Retail	Portugal
European Marketing Distribution	Markant Handels AG	Germany
	Markant Foodmarketing bv	Netherlands
	Selex Gruppo Commerciale	Italy
	Selex Iberica	Spain
	Uniarme	Portugal
	ZEV	Austria
	Superkob	Denmark
	Nisa Today's	UK
	Unil	Norway
	Musgrave	Ireland
	Dagreb	Sweden
Buying International Group	Spar Osterreich	Austria
	Dagrofa A/S	Denmark
	Tuko	Finland
	Hellaspar	Greece
	Bernag Ovag	Switzerland
	Despar Italia	Italy
	Unigro NV	Netherlands
	Undis	Belgium
	Spar (UK)	UK
	BWD Foods/Spar	Ireland
Eurogroup	GIB Group	Belgium
	Rewe-Zentrale AG	Germany
	Vendex	Netherlands
	Co-op Schweiz	Switzerland
Deuro Buying Group	Carrefour	France
	Metro Gruppe	Germany
	Makro	Netherlands
Viking Retail Alliance	K-Group	Finland
	ICA	Sweden
	Hakon	Norway and Sweden

Table 10.2: Examples of international alliances and buying groups in grocery retail

The plant of 1999 will be a 'flotilla', consisting of modules centered either around a stage in the production process or around a number of closely related operations. (Drucker, 1990; pp. 98–9)

With increasing environmental uncertainty and competitive pressure, more attention is being paid to the advantages of network relationships, rather than vertical integration or simple arm's length contracting (Grossmann and Hart, 1986, Powell, 1990). Each of these differing forms, however, mean that the participants have to trade off the advantages of such relationships (lower risk, for example) with lower levels of control. For some, the fear of loss of control will preclude them from entering into certain types of agreements. As franchises occupy the middle ground between hierarchies and markets, and behavioural considerations affect their adoption and use, further research concerning the behavioural and cultural dynamics of franchising is a *sine qua non*. Given the rise of the spread of such organizational forms and the efficacy of developing competitive advantages on innovation, special attention needs to be given to the role of social networks within these organizational webs (Higgins, 1996; Kay, 1993).

As noted earlier, social networks and their dynamics play an important role in facilitating learning, the diffusion of innovations (such as franchises); they have also been shown to influence the subsequent adoption of new practices within a franchise system, gaining access to resources, and can affect performance. For example, Chapter 9 suggested that a particular type of social network, interlocking directorates, may have influence on the borrowing levels within franchisee-owned businesses, and their very presence provides some evidence (albeit circumstantial) that the diffusion of innovation occurs within franchising. Of particular importance to these webs is the nature of interaction between their various members and the mobility of those actors because it is these exchanges which affect the diffusion of innovations within and between networks and cultures.

By using an historical example, we can see the diffusion process between differing networks in action. The world's earliest known copper objects and trinkets were fabricated in tribes located in Turkey and Iran around 8000 BC. There is archaeological evidence of the know-how of copper mining reaching the Balkans by 5000 BC, and middle Europe a thousand years later. Of course, the knowledge was not generally diffused among all members of a village, but possessed by specialists who fulfilled a specific role and performed particular tasks. Initially, these trinkets may have assumed religious and ritualistic importance, which served to heighten the importance and power of the smelters. The diffusion of the copper mining and smelting technology was achieved by the spread of prospectors and smelters with the necessary know-how from one tribe to another and the development of trade between villages. It was also facilitated by the willingness of the tribal gatekeepers to allow the strangers into their village and the communication – whether via verbal or 'show-how' means – of that technology through exchanging ideas and toolmaking skills. Whilst in the neighbouring villages, therefore, it is likely that the strangers were exposed to other ideas either via trade or by observation, and so acquired additional knowledge capital. Drawn together by trade and technology, and the sharing of common rituals, the network of interacting tribes developed similar cultures.

Reflecting the importance of exchange, an international grouping of researchers, the International Marketing and Purchasing Group (IMP), has developed an interaction model that describes the influences on social exchanges within industrial

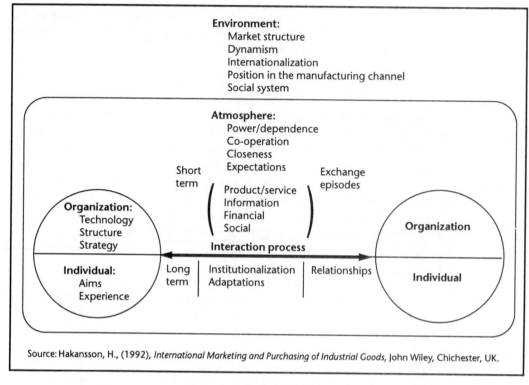

Source: Hakansson, H., (1992), *International Marketing and Purchasing of Industrial Goods*, John Wiley, Chichester, UK.

Figure 10.3: The IMP interaction model

markets – such as franchises. The assumptions for their network model, shown in Figure 10.3, are that:

1. both buyers and sellers are viewed to be active participants in a market;
2. that the relationship is typically longer than those occurring in market transactions (such as sending a letter or buying groceries);
3. the links between the two parties involved in the interaction becomes institutionalized into a set of roles that each party expects the other to perform; and
4. close relationships are based on previous interactions and mutual evaluation.

The model includes four groups of variables at various levels of analysis. The highest is the environmental level, which includes overall industry characteristics such as the structure of the market (fragmented or concentrated, munificence, volatility, height and nature of entry and mobility barriers, threats from substitute products, and customer segmentation and dynamics). A key theme throughout this book has been that the dynamics of the environment places stress on the necessity for innovation in order to develop and maintain competitive advantages, and that these dynamics occur within a social milieu. This social milieu may preclude the use of certain types of relationship either because there is no precedent for it within that culture, or because of legislative/taxation restrictions (recall that the governments of some LDCs prefer joint ventures to acquisitions and that cartels tend to be illegal in most countries). The second level is the atmosphere, which includes variables that are directly affected by the relationship between the dyad members. These variables are of a political nature and encompass power, dependence, trust and influence, and serve to affect the manner and degree to which a particular innovation is diffused.

Relationships between intra-organizational network members (or actors) exist at varying levels of a micro–macro continuum: between individuals, between departments, and between business units/divisions. They also occur at varying levels within inter-organizational networks: between organizations involved in a particular strategic group, between networks of firms from different strategic groups – otherwise labelled pooling and complementary respectively (Nohria and Garcia-Pont, 1991) – and also occur between towns, cities and between countries which are cemented by military treaties, international trade agreements, royal and state visits, and joint common foreign policies. Reflecting the differing levels of analysis, the IMP model distinguishes between organizational and individual networks. The interaction process is described in terms of both short-term episodes (markets) and, in the longer term, bilateral relationships and by adaptations to environmental forces and to realize certain goals.

In order to realize opportunities and gain access to resources and competencies needed for survival, the individual will search for and evaluate actual or potential changes in the environment when engaging in relationships and attempt to source those actors which control specific resources (such as information, finance, know-how and experience). There is considerable theoretical and research support for the importance of collaborative learning across organizational boundaries. For example, in relation to innovation, Twiss (1992) asserts that the greatest advances in an industry setting have been made across industrial boundaries; Gerstenfield's (1970) list of characteristics of the creative organization cites the cross-fertilization of ideas resulting from a mixture of specialisms and porous organizational boundaries; Allen (1977) identifies the importance of technological gatekeepers in accessing technology from outside the organization; and Crane (1972) uses the term 'invisible college' to describe the exchange of information between different technical specialists in an industry. Extant research in franchising suggests that the use of such multi-functional project teams is limited because the flow of knowledge is seen to be asymmetric, from the franchisor to the franchisees, rather than being reciprocal, and the use of FACs is limited. Within the process of technological transfer, the franchisor's emphasis is on levels one and two, not three. In this sense, the extent to which franchises can be construed to be a form of strategic alliance as McIntyre *et al* (1994) contend, is limited.

Actors

Figure 10.4 illustrates the varying levels at which network members, or actors, operate. Actors perform and control activities and, through exchange processes, develop relationships with each other. Franchisees, for example, operate business units and control the operating standards of those units; in exchange for using the franchisor's brand and know-how, they pay royalties. In networks, the relationship developing process is based on adaptation and mutuality. Mutuality concerns the parties' preparedness and interest to interact, and is affected by the level of trust between actors. Adaptations are the results of continuous interactions of mutual interest and may not, because of the climate of relations between the network partners, be viewed in a positive light. For example, in the UK, Perfect Pizza attempted to introduce a centralized telephone ordering system

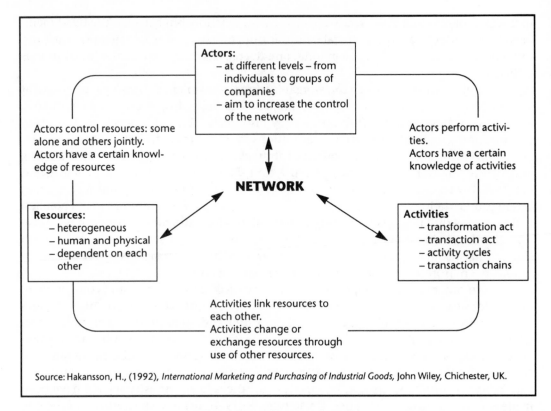

Actors:
– at different levels – from individuals to groups of companies
– aim to increase the control of the network

Actors control resources: some alone and others jointly. Actors have a certain knowledge of resources

Actors perform activities.
Actors have a certain knowledge of activities

NETWORK

Resources:
– heterogeneous
– human and physical
– dependent on each other

Activities
– transformation act
– transaction act
– activity cycles
– transaction chains

Activities link resources to each other.
Activities change or exchange resources through use of other resources.

Source: Hakansson, H., (1992), *International Marketing and Purchasing of Industrial Goods*, John Wiley, Chichester, UK.

Figure 10.4: The network model

which was designed to improve the speed of response and permit the company to use database marketing. Unfortunately, it tried to implement the system by fiat and the programme failed. Arguably, there may have been a different result if there had been consultation and better relationships between the franchisor and its franchisees in the first instance. Actors base their activities on control, which can be direct or indirect, over resources. Direct control is established through ownership and indirect control is based on relationships to other actors and the dependence on those actors. In the franchise relationship, the franchisor controls all aspects of the business, except the franchisee's own labour force. Actors can be seen to be goal orientated and the general goal of actors is to increase their control over the network. Franchisors already control their network in a variety of ways (for example, they nominate suppliers and they determine brand standards), and are orientated towards sales growth. Franchisees, on the other hand, are motivated by profit and seek to exercise control over the labour they employ. Each of these goals provide the actors to innovate in different ways. Control of activities can be attained through control over resources and of knowledge. Actors in a network have heterogeneous knowledge about activities, resources and other actors in the network (see Chapter 6), and this knowledge is developed through experience with activities.

The combined resources and skills of the actors serve to reduce the level of risk. For example, it is axiomatic in texts concerned with the internationalization of businesses that firms which seek entry to regions which are culturally dissimilar will form joint ventures or employ franchising rather than direct investments. The moderating factors to such a search process are the internal structure of the organization, its culture, its bundle of resources, and trust of others. These variables affect how individuals and the organization will engage in activities that lead to relationships between different actors in either a positive or negative manner. As a result of the differing resources and ability to fulfil certain motivational factors (physiological, security, social, ego, self-actualization, etc.) by the various actors, individuals and firms will engage in interactions of different types. Hence, the interaction process can become quite complex and there are varying levels of interdependency between actors. For example, an organization may employ certain out-sourced organizations and teleworkers more than others because of trust, even though the other actors possess matching capabilities. Similarly, customers may frequent certain types of stores more than others because they believe that the array of goods and service better meets their needs and image than others.

Focusing on the relational issues between network actors specifically, Hakansson (1992) develops further the interaction model contained within the IMP conceptualization of buyer-seller relationships. Whereas the IMP model only illustrates the relationship between two actors, Hakansson shows that, in networks, there are many actors involved with other actors – a situation which can become quite complex not only because of the number of actors but also the varying relationships between them. Reflecting this situation, Chapter 4 showed, by illustrating a multi-market contact model to help to establish whether rivalry serves to increase the probability of franchised expansion, that market incumbents meet each other to varying degrees within differing geographic configurations. The patterns and nature of relationships between actors and the resources they possess (see below) determine the network structure. Examining the different sources of power and control within networks, Provan (1983), for example, suggests that control is the principal way of distinguishing between federated and non-federated networks. In a federated network, the affiliated organizations agree to relinquish control over certain activities to the federation's management organization, or FMO (consortia, cartels, and trade associations are examples of such networks); non-federated networks such as interlocking directorates, joint ventures, joint purchase decisions, and general resource exchange agreements are controlled and managed by the organizations involved in the linkage.

Of course, the complexity of networks increases over time because of stability and change, and these dynamics affect the flow of new ideas and concepts into the network and may also affect the inherent culture. During the natural course of everyday life, the parameters or boundaries to networks are subject to shift due to introductions to new individuals and organizations in formal and informal settings, changing environments, or serendipitous meetings. In this way, networks are almost scyphozoan (or a type of holonic network) because their shape/structure is not rigid (tropic), the different actors fulfil different functions in response to different stimuli, and the searching activity of actors can be likened to the probing of tentacles. As all of these differing interactions lead to the forging of differing relationships with people of differing world-views, they may be sources of innovation. Therefore, the holonic organization evolves continually owing to its interaction with the environment and is self-learning. Despite this propensity for change, the structure of networks is affected by history: as we have mentioned, some organizations are reluctant to forge close relationships with others, for instance, because of past experiences. Equally, the market share and returns generated by a company today may be influenced by its previous investments in new product/process development.

Furthermore, some ethnic minority/religious networks become isolated because of the actors' wish to remain culturally different from the society around them, and/or because the society around them is biased against them (see Chapter 5) and barriers (expressed in behaviour, attitude, and socialization); in such closed networks, innovation may be stymied or progress along a particular trajectory. Thus, when seeking answers to problems of strategic direction, managers and job-seekers do not survey an intellectual universe of possibilities, but are hemmed in by their existing resources, assumptions and world-views.

Some of the cultural aspects within inter-organizational relationship between network actors have been observed in clans. Introduced in Chapter 7, the theoretical background for the clan derives from Durkheim, who criticized contracts as a means of regulating behaviour:

> It will be said that there are contracts. But, first of all, social relations are not capable of assuming this juridical form . . . A contract is not self-sufficient, but supposes a regulation which is as extensive and complicated as life itself . . . A contract is only a truce, and very precarious, it suspends hostilities only for a time. (Durkheim, 1933; p. 365)

Although there are different types of clan (Alvesson and Lindkvist, 1993), such as the social integrative and economic co-operative clans, Durkheim defined a clan as an intimate association of individuals who are connected to each other through a variety of ties and provides great regularity of relations and may in fact be more directive than the other, more explicit mechanisms. This leads to the concept of 'soft contracting':

> Under hard contracting, the parties remain relatively autonomous, each is expected to press his or her interests vigorously, and contracting is relatively complete. Soft contracting, by contrast, presumes much closer identity of interests between the parties, and formal contracts are much less complete. This is the clan-type management style. (Williamson and Ouchi, 1980; p. 361)

For instance:

> In a clan, equity is achieved serially rather than on the spot. That is, one clan member may be unfairly underpaid for three years before his true contribution is known, but everyone knows that his contribution will ultimately be recognized, that he will still be there, and that equity will be achieved in the end. That is what is meant by serial equity. It is asking quite a lot of someone to continue to work hard for three years of underpayment, especially assuming universal self-interest. For that reason, a clan will emerge only if there is a strong social memory. (Ouchi, 1982; pp. 27–28)

Alvesson and Lindkvist (1993) give research examples of business organizations where the 'social integrative' clan mode predominates. This evidence supports the view that successful businesses may be driven by clans in which social considerations (at least sometimes) outweigh economic ones. Ouchi (1982) highlights the importance of trust in the clan. He quotes the French anthropologist Marcel Mauss, who noted 'the willingness to be in someone else's debt is an important signal of trust'. Thorelli (1986) offers an interesting view:

trust is 'an assumption or reliance on the part of A that if either A or B encounters a problem in the fulfilment of his implicit or explicit transactional obligations, B may be counted on to do what A would do if B's resources were at A's disposal' (p. 37).

Activities

Activities occur when one or more actors in a network combine, develop, exchange or create resources by using other resources. There are two types of activities: transformation and transfer (Hakansson, 1992). Transformation activities change resources in some way and transfer activities transfer the direct control of one resource from one actor to another. As with any supply chain, transfer activities in franchises link transformation activities of different actors. Figure 10.5 illustrates the links between a franchised fast food outlet, a franchisor and supplier and examples of the various activities undertaken by each. In line with the lack of vertical integration among foodservice franchises, it shows that there is a direct relationship between the franchisor and the supplier and an indirect relationship between the supplier and the franchisee. An indirect relationship is classified as the relationship between two firms which are not directly related but which is mediated by a third firm with which they both have a relationship. A direct relationship, by contrast, exists when an activity is tightly coupled (Weick, 1976). In franchises, some suppliers are nominated by the franchisor and the manufacturers provide the franchisee with goods which are authorized and also produce goods which are specified by the franchisor. Despite some attempts through vertical integration, a single actor cannot control all of the activities within a supply chain or franchise network. Furthermore, as the different components of the supply chain are interlinked and usually co-ordinated and adapted to fit the other actors' activities, a change in one activity can affect other activities and force them to change (Hakansson, 1992)

Resources

In order to be able to perform any activities, actors must have resources. These resources may be tangible – fixed assets, financial resources and other working capital – or intangible, such as know-how or reputation. Resources are combined, developed, exchanged or created in order to deliver a product or service. Thus, in franchising, the franchisee exchanges financial resources, labour, knowledge of local market conditions, royalties and undertakes to conform to contractual specifications in exchange for the franchisor's business know-how, experience, and competencies and access to brand capital. To perform transformation activities, transformation resources are required and for transfer activities, transfer resources are needed. There exists an inter-dependency between transformation and transfer resources: in order to transform materials into an end product, the raw materials, labour, knowledge, and capital equipment have to be transferred from other parts of the supply chain to the production area; to transform an individual into a franchisee, the franchisor must transfer know-how through training and the franchisee must transfer monies to the franchisor.

When resources are exchanged, relationships emerge which may develop and be cemented as learning and the number and quality of episodes increases over time. For example, in international markets, entrants may elect to surmount mental-map distance barriers (the factors preventing the or disturbing the flow of information between the firm and target nations, including linguistic, institutional, cultural, and political factors) by forging joint ventures, but as the firm becomes more familiar with the operation factors

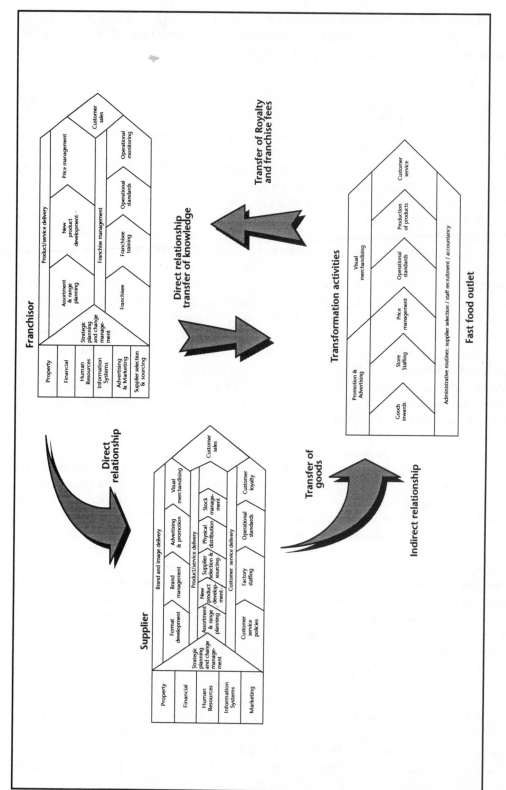

Figure 10.5: Activities in a franchise dyad

and conditions of the satellite country so they change to direct investment (Barkema *et al*, 1996). Resources can be controlled through ownership and through relationships and exchange, and where a resource is scarce actors will seek to control it directly. This ownership serves to help position the actor in the network *vis-à-vis* other actors. Within the biotechnology sector, for example, large pharmaceutical companies have forged links with small research-driven organizations because of the specialist know-how they possess. Given the criticality of innovation in the sector, the ownership of research and development competencies by these small firms and the relationship they have with the larger concerns means that they possibly occupy a position of centrality. It is a feature of this market, however, that the ownership of the new product lies in the hands of the pharmaceutical organization rather than the research firm. The research firm is able to survive because exclusivity is enforced only within each drug category and the firms are permitted to have competing relations in different drug categories (Nohria and Garcia-Pont, 1991). A key observation about resources is that they are heterogeneous and, when combined, new knowledge emerges which creates opportunities for innovation (Hakansson, 1992). When people come to exchange situations, such as franchises, they come with their prior experiences and know-how, and these are enhanced by the input of know-how from the franchisor and experiences of operating a particular outlet in a particular environment. The use and value of a specific resource is dependent, therefore, on how it is combined with other resources, and while a franchise may represent the combination of heterogeneous resources, the addition of inputs from franchisees creates a new level of heterogeneity.

Womack and Jones (1994) use the term 'lean enterprise' to describe a collection of firms working collaboratively to serve a specific end-user market whilst optimizing the use of resources throughout the entire 'value stream'. Jarillo (1988) uses the term 'strategic network' to describe the same phenomenon. Collaboration between firms in a network can generate value for the whole network, but in order for this value to be realized the network must share some common goals. Some contracts will be needed, but as Durkheim (1933) says, a contract is only a truce. Long-term success based on continuous innovation requires the development of relationships and trust throughout the network. Again, however, the degree to which this occurs is affected by the network culture.

Summarizing the above, franchises, like other networks, are characterized by actors who engage in activities and possess resources. These activities and resources form the basis for positioning actors within a network and for the relationships between other network members, and are susceptible to change by the dynamics of the network and its culture. As the network changes, however, its culture also changes. In this sense resources are depreciable and are imitable, and this situation may cause actors to reassess their relationships with each other. As a result of the differing resources possessed by different actors, the relationships are of differing types and forms. Some relationships will result in new levels of resource heterogeneity while others will not. Not all of the variances in inter-organizational networks, however, can be attributed to the ownership of different resources or culture alone. It also requires the actors to fulfil roles and perform rituals.

Cultures and roles in inter-organizational networks

As mentioned in Chapter 7, Boisot (1987) introduced a framework for categorizing organizational types, which was based on the communication and processing of information within an anthropological context. Jarillo (1988, 1993) also categorized organizational types, but using a different framework: the 'legal form' (that is, single entity versus a number of legally separate firms) and the 'nature of the relationships'. The following paragraphs introduce a matrix that integrates these two perspectives – the strategic (Jarillo) and the anthropological (Boisot). The matrix is shown in Figure 10.6. The framework is based on the following premises, which are consistent with the IMP network model: first, that business interactions involve the exchange of information in various forms (both 'hard' and 'soft'): second, that over time such transactions can develop into relationships; and finally, that business enterprises can take various forms, some of which can be made up of several legal entities rather than a single firm. The elements of analysis are therefore 'information communication', 'type of relationship' and 'legal form'.

In the diagram, the x-axis shows two separate but related dimensions of any communication. One dimension is the extent of 'diffusion' of information, that is, the size of the 'audience' reached by the information. The second dimension is the legal form of the firm. At one extreme of the axis would be a small single firm without a developed network. Here, the amount of information diffusion will be a relatively low ('undiffused'). At the other extreme, a large network of firms involving a large number of people will enable wide diffusion.

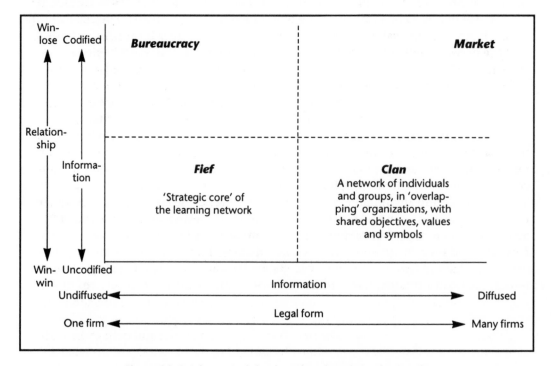

Figure 10.6: A framework for the cultural analysis of networks

The *y*-axis shows two more aspects of communication. The first dimension is the extent of 'codification' of the information. Codification is the process of replacing direct experience with symbols and enables the recording of experiences and their communication to a wider audience. The second dimension on the *y*-axis is the 'relationship' between communicating parties. The continuum used here is between 'win-win' and 'win-lose'. Price (1996) aligns 'win-win' with uncodified information and 'win-lose' with codified information. The reason for this hypothesis is as follows. Most business communications will involve a mix of both codified and uncodified information. Business experiences, however suggest that it is the presence of relatively uncodified information that 'makes the difference' when trying to reach a 'win-win' relationship. The observation that the protagonists are around the table and talking is universally seen as better news than if they are communicating only by formal business letters, press releases or, even worse, via lawyers. Indeed, this is a key message of Chapter 9: it is better for a franchisor to develop systems which facilitate the identification of under-performing franchisees rather than allowing them to continue along a trajectory of failure and, thereby, assist in their turnaround. After all, franchisee insolvency is damaging to brand equity, the queue of potential investors, and diminishes any competitive advantages based on reputation. Managing and dealing with feelings, impressions and motivations requires the full breadth of interpersonal skills – uncodified 'art' supplementing codified 'science'. When attempting to reach agreement in business, 'facts' and 'feelings' are equally important.

Within this analytical framework, four *cultural styles* can be identified. A *bureaucracy* is an impersonal form of social network. Codified information is communicated within a single legal entity – Williamson's 'hierarchy'. The lack of shared values and the limited richness of the information makes 'win-lose' relationships the norm. A *market* is represented by many firms exchanging codified information. The opportunity for creative solutions to be developed from open exchanges of personal information is limited. 'Hard contracting' and 'win-lose' relationships prevail. A *fief* is a social organization made up of a very small number of people, with shared values and beliefs. Much of the information exchanged is uncodified, necessitating face-to-face communication. Typically, there is an informal power relationship involving a charismatic leader. Price (1996) positions this toward the 'single firm' end of the matrix or, within franchising, the individual franchisee and his staff. An example of such a group would be a senior management team within the 'strategic core' of a network. The personal relationships between a small number of individuals present the opportunity for 'win-win' relationships (we are not claiming that all fiefs are 'win-win' relationships, merely that they present the opportunity for such relationships).

As previously mentioned in this chapter, the clan group is of interest for several reasons in relation to economic effectiveness, learning and innovation. The socialization process, the development of shared values, soft contracting and trust provide the opportunity for powerful 'win-win' relationships. Comparing the characteristics of a clan with those of an innovative organization (supportive culture, holistic emphasis on creativity and risk-sharing) leads to an interesting conclusion. An innovative organization can be seen as a clan organizational type with one important additional element: high levels of 'exploratory drive'. An innovative organization is, in essence, a clan in search of thrills. The framework of fiefs, clans, bureaucracies and markets provides a vehicle for the analysis of organizations. In particular, we have focused on what this framework tell us about innovative organizations, and a consideration of the cultural setting of a specific node in the network, some of which will be suppliers and other franchisees and/or the franchisor. Figure 10.7,from Price (1996) shows the relationship between a buyer and a supplier (for example, a franchisor and a manufacturer).

At the centre of the innovative organization is the strategic core. The model recognizes the need for leadership, even (or particularly) in a learning organization. But this is a 'lean' core team of perhaps half a dozen visionaries and strategists, probably with a charismatic leader. The role of this team includes what Snow *et al* (1992) call the 'network architect'. Recognizing that some key competencies can only be obtained by vertical collaboration, and that the source of value creation is their interface with other organizations, these visionaries set about creating and recreating their network. Designing an element of the network and launching the network-building process are essentially entrepreneurial, involving a mixture of creative, financial and political skills. The architect role

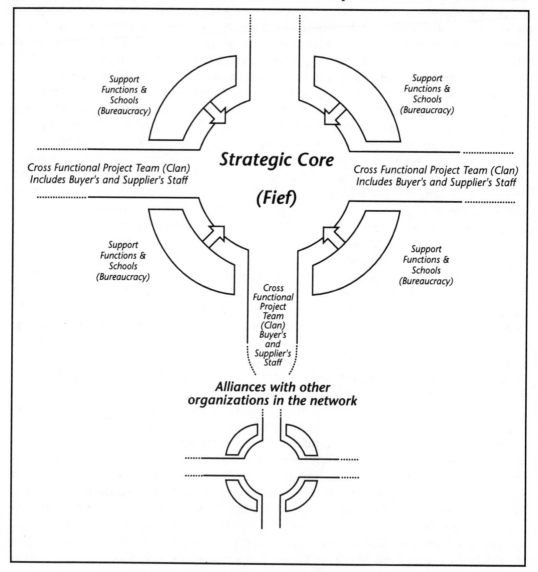

Figure 10.7: *A cultural model of an innovative network organization*

also involves developing the organization's self-awareness, including its overall social-psychological health. The strategic core will interact with other stakeholders, both directly and through the clans. The cultural setting of the strategic core is the fief.

Growing directly from the strategic core are the tentacles of many cross-functional project teams. Team members carry out the lead operator role proposed by Snow *et al* (1992), which involves building the network. In addition, some members also need to carry out the caretaker role, nurturing a sense of belonging amongst the team. Team members therefore need not only functional/operational skills as supplied by the franchisor, but also team working and social-integrative skills developed through regular communication and joint problem-solving activities. The sense of belonging felt by members is a mixture of social integrative and economic co-operative. The project team activities reach outside the borders of the organization, searching for interactions with compatible firms. Once network links are formed, the relationship-building process begins. Potential partners may either be nominated by the strategic core or discovered by the project team. Eventually, the team will include the buyer's and supplier's staff working together as a single, cosmopolitan clan. Drawing on the 'bisociation' derived from their different careers, socialization, network contacts, task environments in a context of developing trust, a high level of profitable innovation becomes possible.

Supporting both the fief and its clans are the technical specialists. Their roles are important, since they constantly seek out best practice and extend the body of knowledge in the organization's key competencies. They may donate specialists to the clan teams as and when needed. They represent the 'functions as schools' approach suggested by Womack and Jones (1994). Ideally, staff will regularly rotate between project team and functional specialist roles in order to broaden individual development. The support spe-

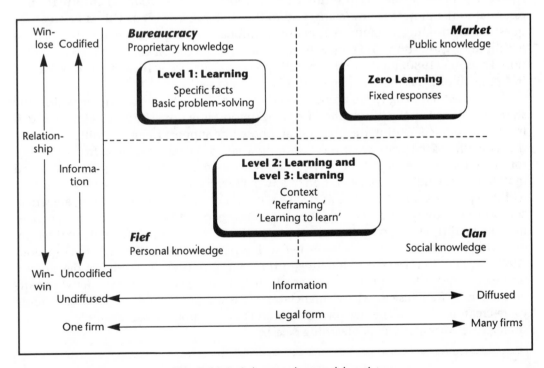

Figure 10.8: Culture and network learning

cialists may develop the rules of discipline used in the clans, supporting the caretaker role. The cultural setting of the specialists is bureaucracy. A contribution of this cultural model of an innovative organization is that it recognizes the need for different organizational sub-cultures in different parts of the organization and of the network. It also allows the development of various research questions regarding the processes that organizations use to form vertical collaborations.

Intra-organizational network learning

Previous sections of this chapter and book have emphasized the strategic importance of facilitating learning not only within the organization but between organizations, and particularly in the 'quasi-firm' where the firm's borders overlap. As the framework in the cultural model of an innovative network organization includes some hypotheses regarding the acquisition of information, can it tell us anything about innovative learning within networks? Learning of different types takes place within the different cultural setting as below and as contended in Chapter 7. Day-to-day problem-solving can be supported by the bureaucracy, but the transformational learning required for innovation takes place in the fief and its associated clans. Relating Huber's (1991) constructs or organizational learning to the cultural framework reveals that all the organizational grouping and cultural styles have a role to play in organizational learning (Figures 10.8 and 10.9).

Vital 'hard' information is acquired from the external environment and the franchisor through manuals and internal press, which becomes Revans' 'programmed' knowledge: such information is essential in running the business, and unless project-specific, it is processed via the functions/schools. The less codified information is essential to the project teams (clans) and to the strategic core (fief). This is Revans' 'Q': questioning insight. Out of this type of organizational learning comes new self-awareness within the organization, and hence the motivation for technical and managerial innovation. Lawson's (1980) model of the creative process, described earlier, can also be viewed from this cultural perspective (Figure 10.10).

The 'first insight' that a business opportunity exists might emerge within the strategic core assisted by information from the support functions. Insight is almost by definition uncodified. During the preparation phase, the support functions will investigate the feasibility of the proposed project, gaining what hard data is available from the environment. During the incubation phase, the strategists/fief will 'kick around' the idea and mull it over, including a consideration of any political aspects. (This stage may be shared with the project team/clan.) The next stages, of illumination and verification, are where additional creativity is needed, and the clan will carry out this role, sending its tentacles into the market, testing both the technical and the 'soft and fuzzy' elements of the idea, involving partner organizations in the network as necessary. Baden-Fuller and Lorenzoni (1993) and Jarillo (1993) have identified firms that have been successful in developing 'strategic networks'. Such firms have encouraged 'learning races' amongst network partners, such as franchisees, where financial rewards are given to those who contribute value-creating ideas to the network (Benetton is often quoted as an example of such a strategic network carrying out learning races).

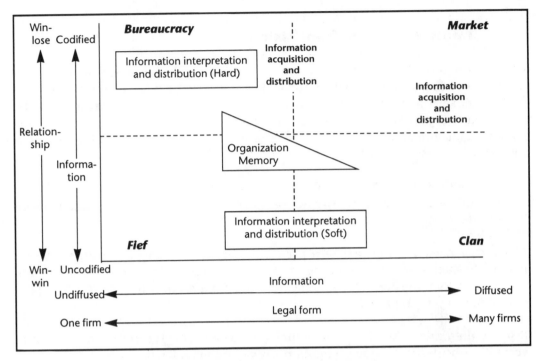

Figure 10.9: Network learning: a cultural perspective

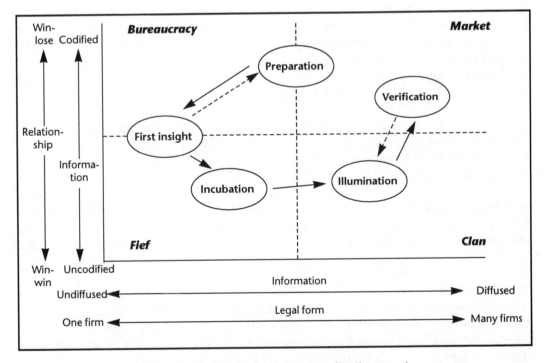

Figure 10.10: The creative process: a cultural perspective

Implications for franchising

The preceding sections have considered issues in the business environment in outline. Emerging organizational forms have been identified, along with the implications for strategic and operational management. But what are the implications of these changes for franchise organizations? As the franchise literature is replete with references to the contractual nature of the relationship, an outline of the franchisor's traditional contractual is provided as a benchmark.

Contractual franchising roles

In the more contractually-based paradigm of franchising, franchisors and members of their functional departments carried out the following roles.

Commercial gatekeeper: (informational role). In this role, the franchisor controlled how much information was divulged to suppliers and franchisees. In its most extreme form, other members of the organization were prevented from having discussions with suppliers unless a buyer was present.

Resource investigator: This is not strictly similar to Belbin's (1981) description of an extroverted, enthusiastic, curious, communicative individual who has a capacity for contacting people and exploring anything new. Rather, within the franchise context, the individual is involved researching technical and commercial aspects of the franchise markets. In this role, for example, the franchisor decides to franchise because of lack of local market knowledge. As the store's potential becomes apparent through trading, so the franchisor may decide to convert the unit to company-owned status. This role also encompasses establishing the knowledge required to become a franchisor and setting out the parameters of the supplier and franchisee activities. Given the resource constraint arguments concerning the motivation to franchise (Chapter 3), the resource investigator title could also be used as a descriptor of the recruitment process of franchisees.

Legal bureaucrat (contract administration role). This role involved drafting agreements designed to protect the company from sharp practice by suppliers or unforeseen events. This is a position adopted by many franchisors to ensure conformance to standards and contractual obligations.

Poker player: (bargaining role). Keeping information a closely guarded secret, the franchising manager tried to bluff and bargain towards a 'good' (zero-sum) deal through reducing the amount of information in the public domain and, thereby, reduce the chances of imitation.

The cultural perspective of these roles is shown in Figure 10.11. It can be seen that all the roles are based at the bureaucracy/market interface, exchanging codified data in a 'win-lose' relationship. The potential for the generation of value, the emergence of innovative ideas, or the development of strategy is therefore low In this contractual mode, it becomes difficult or even impossible for the franchisee to contribute to competitive advantage.

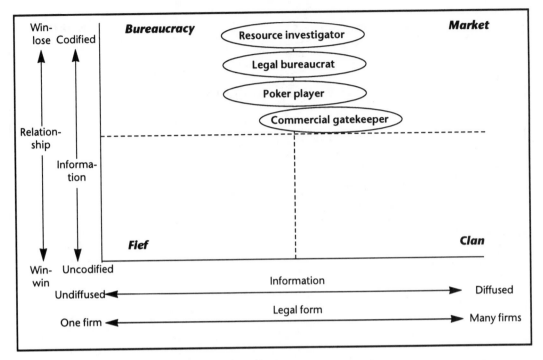

Figure 10.11: Contractual franchising roles

Emerging franchising roles

Spekman *et al* (1994) have proposed an alternative range of strategic roles for those in the transfer activities in networks. These are based on removing the tension between firms through partnering and the breaking down of functional barriers in order to permit learning and innovation to be diffused.

Many franchise problems transcend the simple distributive function mentality encompassed by economists. It becomes necessary to think of franchising as a process rather than as a distribution mechanism – a process involving staff from throughout the organization. Referring back to the 'innovative organization' model in the previous section, some franchise 'specialists' will be located within the support functions and 'schools', whilst others will be located in cross-functional and 'cross-organizational' project teams. Significant supply chain thinking will be necessary within the strategic core.

Although important to the realization of brand equity, under the new paradigm, the traditional roles would be de-emphasized, and new roles would appear. The commercial gatekeeper role becomes less necessary because communication is more open and team-based. Resource investigator remains an important role, but there is more cross-functional team involvement and more emphasis on the strategic resource issues. The legal bureaucrat role will become de-emphasized to allow development of 'goodwill trust' (Sako, 1992). The 'win-lose' *poker player* would be replaced by negotiation. In addition, some new roles will emerge, as shown in Figure 10.12.

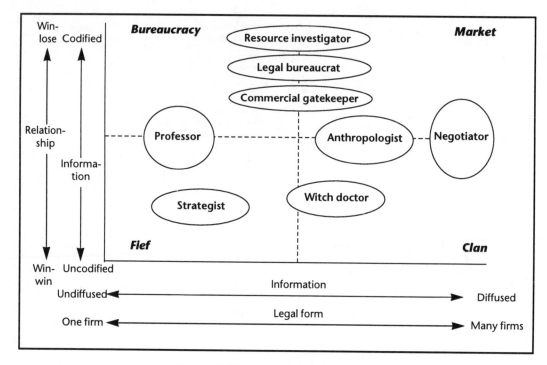

Figure 10.12: Emerging franchising roles

Industrial anthropologist. A key role within the strategic franchise management process will be understanding the norms, values, attitudes and beliefs of franchisees and suppliers in the network and those of potential new franchisees. It will be necessary to make judgements about how these elements of culture will interact in the 'quasi-firm'. The task may be to find 'compatible' cultures, rather than 'similar' cultures.

Witch doctor/priest. The franchisee management process will need to extend to managing certain symbolic activities, in order to support emerging relationships. This idea is not as fanciful as it may sound; franchisee awards days are an existing example. The role may include a 'pastoral' aspect of reinforcing certain beliefs and values, and perhaps taking some confessions. Within existing franchise networks, this position tends to be occupied by solicitors and lawyers who, like witch doctors in small-scale societies, act as interlocutors or go-betweens in order to facilitate a mutually acceptable solution (Midelfort, 1982).

Professor. In a genuine learning organization, one of the roles of the franchise manager is 'professor of supply management': how to increase sales volumes and maintain franchisee profitability. But this should not be interpreted in a pedagogic way. The aim, in conjunction with other members of the managerial team, is to facilitate higher levels of learning within cross-functional teams. Only if such learning is successfully facilitated will the organization maintain its awareness and be prepared for the innovations and transformations that will be necessary.

Strategist. The final 'new franchise role' is that of strategist – the 'network architect'. Organizations will wish to attempt to design their network at the strategic level. The strategic franchise management role will contribute to decisions regarding:

1. to what extent the organization can position itself as a strategic hub or core within certain networks of innovative suppliers;
2. what strategies to use in order to interface with franchisees with strategically important competencies;
3. understanding what the effects might be of changes in one link in the network on the rest of the network (coping with interconnectedness).

Conclusion

Networks, culture and innovations permeate all aspects of society: some networks illustrate conservative cultures and are emphatic of maintaining the *status quo* and traditional values, and dampen the velocity of the flow of new ideas. Other networks take this behaviour to extremes and exhibit isolationist cultures and yet others are more open to new ideas. At a macro-level, some of the Pacific Rim countries have encouraged the formation of alliances between domestic organizations and foreign firms in order to acquire new knowledge and skills. These variations are also evident in franchising: franchises are networks of interlocking organizations and individuals. These individuals, in turn, are involved in other networks, possess resources, are engaged in value-adding activities and information interchanges. Some of these franchise networks are not as innovative as others because of the power of one or more network member, and their efforts in emphasizing conformance standards and standardization. Others are more dynamic and exhibit a culture which is open to the exchange of ideas and are characterized by one or more sponsors of innovation. Given the rapid dynamism of the marketplace and increasing consumer sophistication, it is the latter networks which are likely to survive. Together with a growing tendency for governments to regulate franchise agreements, it is evident that there may be a need to change the way franchising works. There is, perhaps, a need for greater fairness in the franchise contract and a need to harness the implicit innovative capability that many franchisees possess, especially given a growing trend for franchisees to be multi-unit and multi-brand operators, if franchising is to be a dominant organizational paradigm in the 21st-century marketplace. As part of this process of change, franchisors could do worse than using the strategic alliance model as their benchmark.

As part of this change process, it is important to observe that individuals, through fulfilling specific roles and engaging in particular rituals to reinforce the network's culture, facilitate or impede the flow of new ideas. This chapter has attempted to briefly outline these roles and has, in the process, explored a neglected question in the emerging theory of franchise management – how can the evolving relationships needed for continuous innovation be developed and managed? In order to explore this question, we have had to travel a considerable distance away from the notion of humans as rational, scientific and economically motivated. 'Soft contracting' refers to the process of reaching agreements, based on trust and mutual understanding. The parties realize that they do not have enough information to make a perfect agreement and operate within the confines of bounded rationality. They rely, to some extent, on 'gut feel' about each other, built up over a period of close working relationships. The agreement may turn out to be unbalanced in the short term, but it is necessary to take the 'long view'. Within the context of inter-organizational networks, a social affiliate clan works together because the people involved like to work with each other and gain some satisfaction from the quality of work that they produce together. Innovation and creativity are mysterious processes that do not respond predictably to purely rational economic circumstances. Innovations are part of an evolutionary process by which a particular idea and/or mechanism is adapted to the required situation rather than necessarily being suitable for all purposes. Furthermore, culture and the process of 'condition setting' across organizational boundaries encourages innovation.

It has been demonstrated that the cultural setting on these new relationships is the domain of fiefs and clans rather than the traditional setting of bureaucracies, franchisees and markets. Within this new cultural setting, a number of new roles have been identified, which will be necessary to create and sustain relationships. The scope of these roles is so wide that it is clear that the franchise process will become cross-functional and distributed throughout the organization. The management of these roles will be a strategic issue, since it will be the key to competitive advantage for many organizations. It is now necessary for the franchise literature to reflect the multi-disciplinary skills required to manage franchisees by becoming diverse in scope and in the theoretical frameworks employed.

Extant franchise research, with its roots in legal, marketing and economics texts has shown a preoccupation with agency theory, transaction cost analysis, ownership redirection, and risk reduction theory. These theories are, in and of themselves, incomplete rationales for explaining why firms decide to franchise, for example, and other activities to do with the dynamics of franchising. Of particular concern is the lack of consideration of alternative explanations of activities in franchise businesses which, although not founded within the franchise research literature, has a rich history in other academic discourse. Such a situation requires franchise researchers to cross the cultural boundaries inherent to other academic disciplines, and to create cross-functional/disciplinary research teams. After all, franchising is, in itself, a multi-functional activity because it encompasses marketing, legal, personnel, geographic and finance concerns.

> Artists get very interested in each other's work and learn a great deal from how other artists have solved problems. Here, too, we could learn by spending more time with colleagues from related but different disciplines. It is comforting for the social psychologist trained in questionnaire or laboratory methods to spend time with colleagues who have the same training, but it might be more productive for that psychologist to go into the field with an ethnographer or become a participant observer in a real organization. We can only see that to which we expose ourselves and, I fear, we have limited our exposure too much to the artificial. We will not learn about the power of culture unless we cross real cultural boundaries. This is an uncomfortable process, as every traveller in a foreign country knows, but I believe it is essential if we are to develop organization studies as a viable and practical field. (Shein, 1996; p. 239)

The necessity for considering alternative schools of thought within franchise research does not only arise out of a need for enriching extant arguments, but also for the potential impact of small pieces of information on businesses and the way we conceptualize the franchise world. By being open to very different, even juxtaposing, perspectives franchise research may be transformed. Given the potential impact of new information and the fact that this book has been written within the confines of the author's bounded rationality, it is conceivable that the key themes are open to different interpretations and substantial modification as time and knowledge advance.

Reflecting a recurrent theme throughout this book, we expressed the view in the introduction to this chapter that the development of collaborative relationships has been a challenge for mankind throughout history. Not all have been successful in realizing this process. The same is undoubtedly true of franchising. Chapter 8 illustrates, for example, that some franchisors do not have the managerial or financial resources to surmount the mobility barriers necessary to become a successful franchisor, and Chapter 9 suggested that there is a need for franchisors to upgrade their extant monitoring systems in order to add value to their services to franchisees by identifying under-performing operations and take a proactive stance in engineering a turnaround. In one sense, it could be argued that failure in franchising occurs, in part, due to the lack of available skills and culture to manage the array of relationships within continually changing networks. After all, the majority of franchisors are, in themselves, small organizations with comparatively small networks and operate without many of the cultural skills to ensure survival through innovation. It is clear that we live in an increasingly complex and dynamic world where innovation, culture, structural stratification, and networks play significant roles in affecting the success and future trajectory of franchising. In order to survive, cultures and networks emphatic of flexibility and malleability are the foundations of success, rather than overt emphasis on conformance to standards and replication.

> It is the miracle of civilized survival that the human co-operative urge reasserts itself so strongly and so repeatedly. There is so much working against it, and yet it keeps on coming back. We like to think of this as the conquest of bestial weaknesses by the powers of intellectual altruism, as if ethics and morality were some kind of modern invention. If this were true, it is doubtful if we would be here today to proclaim it. If we did not carry in us the basic biological urge to co-operate with our fellow men, we would never have survived as a species. If our hunting ancestors had really been ruthless, greedy tyrants loaded with 'original sin', the human success story would have petered out long ago. (Morris, 1969; pp. 25–26).

Notes

1. Of KPMG Management Consulting and Centre for Research in Strategic Purchasing and Supply, School of Management, University of Bath, UK.

2. Of School of Business, University of Huddersfield, UK.

References

Foreword: Nature of the paradox

Banbury, C. M., and Mitchell, W., (1995), 'The Effects of Introducing Important Incremental Innovations on Market Share and Survival', *Strategic Management Journal*, Vol. 16, pp. 161–182.

Clarke, R. N., (1989), 'SICs as Delineators of Economic Markets', *Journal of Business*, Vol. 62, pp. 17–31.

Dant, R. P., Brush, C. G., and Iniesta, F. I., (1996), 'Participation Patterns of Women in Franchising', *Journal of Small Business Management*, Vol. 34, No. 2, pp. 14–28.

Economist, (1996), 'MacWorld', *The Economist*, 29 June, pp. 77–78.

Gunz, H., (1989), 'The Dual Meaning of Managerial Careers: Organizational and Individual Levels of Analysis', *Journal of Management Studies*, Vol. 26, No 3, pp. 225–250.

Hartman, E., (1988), *Foundations of Organization Theory*, Ballinger Publishing Company, Cambridge, Massachusetts.

Hunt, S. D., and Morgan, R. M., (1995), 'The Theory of Comparative Advantage', *Journal of Marketing*, Vol. 59, April, pp. 1–15.

Justis, R., and Judd, R., (1989), *Franchising*, South-Western Publishing Co, Cincinnati, Ohio.

Kay, J. A., (1993), *Foundations of Corporate Success: How Business Strategies Add Value*, Oxford University Press, Oxford.

Kotabe, M., and Swan, K. S., (1995), 'The Role of Strategic Alliances in High-Technology New Product Development', *Strategic Management Journal*, Vol. 16, pp. 621–636.

MacMillan, A., (1996), quoted in 'Hype and Hoorays for Franchising', The Enterprise Page, *The Guardian*, March, p. 20.

McIntyre, F. S., Young, J. A., Gilbert, F. W., (1994), 'Franchising: A Strategic Alliance Perspective', Society of Franchising Conference: Understanding And Accepting Different Perspectives . . . Empowering Relationships In 1994 And Beyond, Las Vegas, Nevada, 13–14 February.

National Westminster Bank/British Franchise Association, (1993), *Survey 1993*, British Franchise Association, London.

National Westminster Bank/British Franchise Association, (1994), *Survey 1994*, British Franchise Association, London.

National Westminster Bank/British Franchise Association, (1995), *Survey 1995*, British Franchise Association, London.

National Westminster Bank/British Franchise Association, (1996), *Survey 1996*, British Franchise Association, London.

Porter, M. E., (1980), *Competitive Strategy: Techniques for Analysing Industries and Competitors*, Free Press, New York.

Rosenbloom, B., (1995), *Marketing Channels: A Management View*, Fifth Edition, The Dryden Press, Fort Worth Texas.

Shan, W., Walker, G., and Kogut, B., (1994), 'Interfirm Cooperation and Startup Innovation in the Biotechnology Industry', *Strategic Management Journal*, Vol. 15, pp. 387–394.

Tannenbaum, J. A., (1996), 'The Best Franchisors Rely On A Bottom-up Approach for New Ideas', *Wall Street Journal*, 23 May.

Yoshino, M. Y., and Rangan, U. S., (1995), *Strategic Alliances: An Entrepreneurial Approach to Globalization*, Harvard Business School Press, Boston, Massachusetts.

Introduction: Interpretations of franchising

Adams, J. N., and Pritchard-Jones, K. V., (1990), *Franchising: Practice and Precedents in Business Format Franchising*, Butterworths, London.

Anand, P., (1987), 'Inducing Franchisees to Relinquish Control: An Attribution Analysis', *Journal of Marketing Research*, Vol. XXIV, May, pp. 215–221.

Baillieu, D., (1988), *Streetwise Franchising*, Hutchinson Business, London.

Berkley-Thomas, A., (1978), 'The British Business Elite: the Case of the Retail Sector', *Sociological Review*, Vol. 26, pp. 305–324.

Black, J. A., and Boal, K. B., (1994), 'Strategic Resources, Traits, Configurations and Paths to Sustainable Competitive Advantage', *Strategic Management Journal*, Vol. 15, pp. 131–148.

Blau, P. M., and Schoenherr, R. A., (1971), *The Structure of Organizations*, Basic Books, New York.

Braudel, F., (1982), *The Wheels of Commerce: Civilization and Capitalism 15th-18th Century*, Volume II, translation from the French by Sian Reynolds, Collins, London.

Brown, H., (1969), *Franchising: Trap for the Trusting*, Little Brown & Company, Boston, Massachusetts.

Burt, R. S., (1992), *Structural Holes: The Social Structure of Competition*, Harvard University Press, Cambridge, Massachusetts.

Cohen, J. S., (1971), 'Conflict and its Resolution in a Franchise System', pp. 175–183 in Thompson, D. N., (ed.), *Contractual Marketing Systems*, Heath Lexington Books, Lexington, Massachusetts.

Conway, M., Pizzamiglio, M. T., and Mount, L., (1996), 'Status, Communality, and Agency: Implications for Stereotypes of Gender and Other Groups', *Journal of Personality and Social Psychology*, Vol. 71, pp. 25–38.

Curran, J., and Stanworth, J., (1983), 'Franchising in the Modern Economy – Towards a Theoretical Understanding', *International Small Business Journal*, Vol. 2, No. 1, Autumn, pp. 8–26.

Dant, R. P., Brush, C. G., and Iniesta, F. I., (1996), 'Participation Patterns of Women in Franchising', *Journal of Small Business Management*, Vol. 34, No. 2, pp. 14–28.

Domberger, S., and Middleton, J., (1985), 'Franchising in Practice: The Case of Independent Television in the UK', *Fiscal Studies*, Vol. 6, No. 1, pp. 17–32.

Felstead, A., (1993), *The Corporate Paradox Power and Control in the Business Franchise*, Routledge, London.

Feuer, D., (1989), 'Franchising the Training Game', *Training*, Vol. 26, February, pp. 40–45.

Franchise Development Services (1995), *United Kingdom Franchise Directory*: Edition Eleven, FDS, Norfolk, UK.

Fulop, C., (1996), *Overview of the Franchise Marketplace*, Centre for Franchise Research, City University Business School, London.

Gerstenhaber, M., (1988), 'Franchising Redefined as System Leasing', *Franchise World*, March/May, p. 14.

Hackett, D. W., (1977), *Franchising: The State of the Art*, Monograph Series, No. 9, American Marketing Association.

Hall, P., and Dixon, R., (1989), *Franchising*, NatWest Small Business Bookshelf, Pitman Publishing, London.

Hamel, G., and Prahalad, C. K., (1990), 'The Core Competence of the Corporation', *Harvard Business Review*, March–April, pp. 75–84.

Hatcliffe, M., Mills, V., Purdy, D., and Stanworth, J., (1995), *Prospective Franchisees*, Lloyds Bank, IFRC Franchising in Britain Report, Vol. 1, No. 1, University of Westminster, London.

Hergert, M., and Morris, D., (1988), 'Trends in International Collaborative Agreements', pp. 99–109 in Contractor, F. K., and Lorange, P., (eds), *Cooperative Strategies in International Business*, Lexington Books, Lexington, Massachusetts.

Holson, L. M., (1996), 'Have We Got A Deal For You', *SmartMoney*, April, pp. 110–119.

Honig-Haftel, S., and Jones, W. P., (1996), 'Franchisee Associations: A Description of their Partnering Role and Importance Within the US Franchise Industry', *Franchise Research: An International Journal*, Vol. 1, No. 2, pp. 40–44.

Hough, J., (1986), *Power and Authority and their consequences in franchise organizations: a study of the relationship between franchisors and franchisees*, Unpublished PhD thesis, Faculty of Management Studies, Polytechnic of Central London.

Houghton, P., and Timperley, N., (1992), *Charity Franchising*, Directory of Social Change, London.

Howard, J. A., (1994), 'A Social Cognitive Conception of Social Structure', *Social Psychology Quarterly*, Vol. 57, No. 3, pp. 210–227.

Hunt, S. D., (1973), 'The Trend Toward Company-Operated Units in Franchise Chains', *Journal of Retailing*, Summer, pp. 3–12.

Izraeli, D., (1971), *Franchising and the Total Distribution System*, Longman, London.

Jaffe, A. B., and Kanter, D. M., (1990), 'Market Power of Local Cable Television Franchises: Evidence from the Effects of Deregulation', *RAND Journal of Economics*, Vol. 21, No. 2, pp. 226–234.

Kaufmann, P. J., and Stanworth, J., (1995), 'The Decision to Purchase a Franchise: A Study of Prospective Franchisees', *Journal of Small Business Management*, Vol. 33, No. 4, pp. 22–33.

Kay, J. A., (1993), *Foundations of Corporate Success: How Business Strategies Add Value*, Oxford University Press, Oxford.

Khan, M. A., (1992), *Restaurant Franchising*, Van Nostrand Reinhold, New York.

Knight, R. M., (1984), 'The Independence of the Franchise Entrepreneurs,' *Journal of Small Business Management*, Vol. 23, April, pp. 53–61.

Konopa, L. J., (1963), 'What is Meant By Franchise Selling?', *Journal of Marketing*, April, pp. 35–37.

Krueger, A., (1991), 'Ownership, Agency and Wages: An Examination of Franchising in the Fast Food Industry', *Quarterly Journal of Economics*, Vol. 56, Issue 1, February, pp. 75–101.

Lafontaine, F., (1992), 'Agency Theory and Franchising: Some Empirical Results', *RAND Journal of Economics*, Vol. 23, No. 2, pp. 263–283.

Langdon, P., (1986), *Orange Roofs, Golden Arches: The Architecture of American Chain Restaurants*, Knopf, New York.

Lewis, M. C., and Lambert, D. M., (1991), 'A Model of Channel Member Performance, Dependence, and Satisfaction', *Journal of Retailing*, Vol. 67, pp. 205–225.

MacMillan, A., (1995), *Aspects of Franchise Recruitment*, Unpublished MBA Dissertation, University of Edinburgh.

Mallan, B., (1978), 'Channel Power: A form of Economic Exploitation', *European Journal of Marketing*, Vol. 12, No. 2, pp. 194–202.

Martin, R. E., (1996), 'The Market for Franchise Opportunities', *Bulletin of Economic Research*, Vol. 48, pp. 97–114.

Marx, K., and Engels, F., (1967), *The Communist Manifesto*, Penguin Books, Harmondsworth.

McKiernan, P., (1992), *Strategies of Growth*, Routledge, London.

Mendelsohn, M., (1992), *The Guide to Franchising*, Cassell, London.

Micheal, S. C., (1996), 'To Franchise or Not to Franchise: An Analysis of Decision Rights and Organizational Share Forms', *Journal of Business Venturing*, Vol. 11, pp. 57–71.

Miller, J., (1996), 'Grazing Notes', *Sunday Express Magazine*, 15 September, pp. 4–5.

MMC, (1994), *Monopolies and Mergers Commission: Icecream*, A report on the supply in the UK of ice cream for immediate consumption, HMSO, London.

National Westminster Bank/British Franchise Association, (1995), *Survey 1995*, British Franchise Association, London.

Parker, S. R., Brown, R. K., Child, J., Smith, M. A., (1972), *The Sociology of Industry*, Allen & Unwin, London.

Parkin, F., (1971), *Class Inequality and Political Order: Social Stratification in Capitalist and Communist Societies*, Granada Publishing, London.

Parkin, F., (1974), *Social Analysis of Class Structure*, Tavistock, London.

Peterson, A., and Dant, R., (1990), 'Perceived Advantages of the Franchise Option From the Franchisee Perspective: Empirical Insights from a Service Franchise', *Journal of Small Business Management*, Vol. 28, No. 3, pp. 46–61.

Pintel, G., and Diamond, J., (1991), *Retailing*, Fifth Edition, Prentice Hall, Englewood Cliffs, New Jersey.

Porter, M. E., (1985), *Competitive Advantage: Creating and Sustaining Superior Performance*, Free Press, New York.

Prager, R. A., (1990), 'Firm Behaviour in Franchise Monopoly Markets', *RAND Journal of Economics*, Vol. 21, No. 2, pp. 211–225.

Raab, S. S., and Matusky, G., (1987), *The Blueprint for Franchising a Business*, John Wiley & Sons, New York.

Ridley, S., (1995), 'Seeing the Forest from the Trees: Emergence of the Competitive Franchise', *Electricity Journal*, Vol. 8, No. 4, pp. 39–44.

Riley, M., (1984), 'Hotels and Group Identity', *Tourism Management*, June, pp. 102–109.

Robertson, R. L., and Aston, L. J., (1992), 'Technological Choice and the Organization of Work in Capitalist Firms', *Economic History Review*, Vol. XLV, pp. 330–349.

Rosenberg, R., and Bedell, M., (1969), *Profits From Franchising*, McGraw-Hill, New York.

Rubin, P. H., (1978), 'The Theory of the Firm and the Structure of the Franchise Contract', *Journal of Law and Economics*, Vol. 21, pp. 223–233.

Salaman, G., (1981), *Class and the Corporation*, Fontana, London.

Sanghavi, N., (1990), *Retail Franchising in the 1990's*, Longman Group, Harlow, Essex.

Seltz, D. S., (1982), *The Complete Handbook of Franchising*, AddisonWesley Publishing Company, Reading, Massachusetts.

Sen, K. C., (1993), 'The Use of Initial Fees and Royalties in Business Format Franchising', *Managerial and Decision Economics*, Vol. 14, pp. 175–190.

Shepard, A., (1993), 'Contractual Form, Retail Price and Asset Characteristics in Gasoline Retailing', *RAND Journal of Economics*, Vol. 24, No. 1, pp. 58–77.

Sherman, A. J., (1993), 'Building a Foundation for the Responsible Development of a Franchising Program', Excellence '93: A Bridge to Success, Proceedings of the 1993 Society of Franchising Conference, San Francisco, California, 7–8 February..

Shook, C., and Shook, R. L., (1993), *Franchising: The Business Strategy that Changed the World*, Prentice Hall, Englewood Cliffs, New Jersey.

Shropshire, K. L., (1995), *The Sports Franchise Game: Cities in Pursuit of Sports Franchises, Events, Stadiums, and Arenas*, University of Pennsylvania, Philadelphia.

Stanworth, J., and Kaufmann, P., (1996), 'Similarities and Differences in UK and US Franchise Research Data: Towards a Dynamic Model of Franchisee Motivation', *International Small Business Journal*, Vol. 14, No. 3, pp. 57–70.

Stern, P., and Stanworth, J., (1988), 'The Development of Franchising in Britain', *NatWest Quarterly Review*, May, pp. 34–38.

Stern, P., and Stanworth, J., (1994), 'Improving Small Business Rates Via Franchising – the Role of Banks in Europe,' *International Small Business Journal*, Vol. 12, No. 2, pp. 15–25.

Stokowski, P. A., (1994), *Leisure In Society: A Network Structural Perspective*, Mansell, London.

Tauber, E. M., (1981), 'Brand Franchise Extension: New Product Benefits from Existing Brand Names', *Business Horizons*, Vol. 47, pp. 36–41.

Vaughn, C., (1979), *Franchising: Its Nature, Scope, Advantages, and Development*, Lexington Books, Lexington, Massachusetts.

Veljanovski, C., (1987), 'British Cable and Satellite Television Policies', *National Westminster Bank Quarterly Review*, November, pp. 28–40.

Vickers, J., and Yarrow, G., (1988), *Privatization: An Economic Analysis*, MIT Press, Cambridge Massachusetts.

Willis, P., (1977), *Learning to Labour: Why working class kids get working class jobs*, Gower, Aldershot.

Winsor, R. D., and Quinones, R. L., (1994), 'The Nature and Scope of Franchising: A review of Functional and Legal Definitions', Society of Franchising Conference: Understanding And Accepting Different Perspectives … Empowering Relationships In 1994 And Beyond, Las Vegas, Nevada, 13–14 February.

Zupan, M. A., (1989), 'Cable Franchise Renewals: Do Incumbent Firms Behave Opportunistically?', *RAND Journal of Economics*, Vol. 20, pp. 473–482.

Chapter 1: Franchising: the commercialization of 'bastard' feudalism?

Abell, M., (1989), *The Franchise Option – A Legal Guide*, Waterlow Publishers, London.

Adams, J. N., and Pritchard-Jones, K. V., (1990), *Franchising: Practice and Precedents in Business Format Franchising*, Butterworths, London.

Aiken, M. and Hage, J., (1971), 'The Organic Organization and Innovation', *Sociology*, Vol. 5, pp. 63–82

Armour, R. A., and Teece, D. J., (1978), 'Organizational Structure and Economic Performance: A Test of the Multi-Divisional Hypothesis', *Bell Journal of Economics*, Vol. 9, pp. 106–122.

Astley, W. G., and Fombrun, C. J., (1983), 'Collective Strategy: Social Ecology of Organizational Environments', *Academy of Management Review*, Vol. 8, No. 4, pp. 576–587.

Ayling, D., (1988), 'Franchising in the UK', *The Quarterly Review of Marketing*, Vol. 13, Summer, pp. 19–24.

Balasubramanian, S. K., and Ghosh, A. K., (1992), 'Classifying Early Product Life Cycle Forms via a Diffusion Model: Problems and Prospects', *International Journal of Research in Marketing*, Vol. 9, pp. 345–352.

Balasubramanian, S. K., and Ghosh, A. K., (1992b), 'Reliability Criteria Bolster Classification Decisions: A Reply to Jones', *International Journal of Research in Marketing*, Vol. 9, pp. 355–357.

Barker, T. C., McKenzie, J. C., and Yudkin, J., (1966), *Our Changing Fare: Two Hundred Years of British Food Habits*, MacGibbon & Kee, London.

Bass, F. M., (1969), 'A New Product Growth Model for Consumer Durables', *Management Science*, January, pp. 215–277.

Batchelor, C., (1991), 'Pressure on New Recruits', Survey, *Financial Times*, 4–5 May.

Baucus, D. A., Baucus, M. S., and Human, S. E., (1993), 'Choosing A Franchise: How Base Fees and Royalties Relate to the Value of the Franchise', *Journal of Small Business Management*, Vol. 31, No. 2, pp. 91–104.

Beaston, M., (1993), 'Trends in Pay Flexibility', *Employment Gazette*, September, pp. 405–415.

Beesley, M., and Wilson, P., (1982), 'Government Aid to the Small Firm since Bolton', pp. 181–199, in Stanworth, J., Westrip, A., Watkins, D., and Lewis, J., (eds), *Perspectives on a Decade of Small Business Research: Bolton Ten Years On*, Gower, Aldershot.

Bellamy, J. G., (1989), *Bastard Feudalism and the Law*, Routledge, London.

Bernstein, L. M., (1969), 'Does Franchising Create A Secure Outlet for the Small Aspiring Entrepreneur?', *Journal of Retailing*, Vol. 44, No. 4, pp. 21–38.

Bevan, J., Clark, G., Banerji, N., and Hakim, C., (1989), *Barriers to Business Startups: A Study of the Flow Into and Out of Self Employment, Research Paper 71*, Department of Employment, London.

Bloch, M., (1962), *Feudal Society, Volume 1, The Growth of Ties of Dependence*, Routledge and Kegan Paul Ltd, London.

Bloch, M., (1962), *Feudal Society, Volume 2, Social Classes and Political Organization*, Routledge and Kegan Paul Ltd, London.

Blois, K. J., (1983), 'The Structure of Service Firms and Their Marketing Policies', *Strategic Management Journal*, Vol. 4, pp. 251–261.

Boe, K. L., Ginalski, W., and Henward III, D. M., (1987), *The Franchise Option: How to Expand Your Business Through Franchising*, International Franchise Association, Washington.

Boorstin, D. J., (1964), *The Image: A Guide to Pseudo- Events in America*, Harper, New York.

Boyle, E., (1994), 'The Rise of the Reluctant Entrepreneurs', *International Small Business Journal*, Vol. 12, No. 2, pp. 63–69.

Braverman, H., (1974), *Labor and Monopoly Capital: The Degradation of Work in the Twentieth Century*, Monthly Review Press, New York.

Bresnen, M., and Fowler, C., (1994), 'The Organizational Correlates and Consequences of Sub-contracting: Evidence From a Survey of South Wales Businesses', *Journal of Management Studies*, Vol. 31, pp. 847–864.

Brickley, J. A., and Dark, F. H., (1987), 'The Choice of Organizational Form: The Case of Franchising', *Journal of Financial Economics*, Vol. 18, pp. 401–421.

Brown, R., (1991), 'Managing the 'S' Curves of Innovation', *Journal of Marketing Management*, Vol. 7, No. 2, pp. 189–202.

Bryson, B., (1994), *Made in America*, Minerva, London.

Burck, C. G., (1970), 'Franchising's Troubled Dream World', *Fortune*, March, pp. 116–121, 148, 150 & 152.

Burnett, J., (1963), 'The Baking Industry in the Nineteenth Century', *Business History*, Volume V, No. 2, pp. 98–108.

Buzzell, R. D., and Gale, B. T., (1987), *The PIMS Principles: Linking Strategy to Performance*, FreePress, New York.

Carney, M., and Gedajlovic, E., (1991), 'Vertical Integration in Franchise Systems: Agency Theory and Resource Explanations', *Strategic Management Journal*, Vol. 12, No. 8, November, pp. 607–629.

Carnes, R. B., and Brand, H., (1977), 'Productivity and New Technology in Eating and Drinking Places', *Monthly Labor Review*, September, pp. 10–14.

Carter, O., (1990), *An Illustrated History of British Railway Hotels, 1838–1983*, Silver Link Publishing, St Micheal's, Lancashire, UK.

Carroll, G. R., and Swaminathan, A., (1992), 'The Organizational Ecology of Strategic Groups in the American Brewing Industry from 1975–1990', *Industrial and Corporate Change*, Vol. 1, No. 1, pp. 65–97.

Carroll, G. R., and Wade, J., (1991), 'Density Dependence in the Organizational Evolution of the American Brewing Industry Across Different Levels of Analysis', *Social Science Research*, Vol. 20, pp. 271–302.

Central Statistical Office, (1996), *Annual Abstract of Statistics*, London, HMSO.

Chandler, A. D., Jr., (1962), *Strategy and Structure*, MIT Press, Cambridge, Massachusetts.

Chase, R. B., (1978), 'Where Does the Customer Fit in a Service Operation?', *Harvard Business Review*, November/December, pp. 137–142.

Clipson, C., (1991), 'Innovation by Design', pp. 97–105 in Henry, J., and Walker, D., (eds), *Managing Innovation*, Sage Publications, London.

Dant, R. P., (1996), 'Motivations for Franchising: Rhetoric versus Reality', *International Small Business Journal*, Vol. 14, No. 1, pp. 10–32.

Davis, H. W. S., (1922), *Medieval Europe*, Williams and Norgate, London.

Davis, W., (1991), 'The Innovators', pp. 142–149, in Henry, J., and Walker, D., (eds), *Managing Innovation*, Sage Publications, London.

Davidson, A. B., (1995), 'The Medieval Monastery As Franchise Monopolist', *Journal of Economic Behaviour and Organisation*, Vol. 27, pp. 119–128.

Day, G. S., (1984), *Strategic Market Planning*, West Publishing Co., St. Paul.

Dicke, T. S., (1992), *Franchising in America: The development of a business method, 1840–1980*, University of North Carolina Press, Chapel Hill.

Dingle, A. E., (1972), 'Drink and Working-Class Living Standards in Britain, 1870–1914', *Economic History Review*, Vol. XXV, pp. 608–622.

Dixon, D. F., (1962), 'The Development of the Solus System of Petrol Distribution in the United Kingdom, 1950–1960', *Economica*, February, pp. 40–52.

Dixon, D. F., (1963), 'Petrol Distribution in the United Kingdom, 1900–1950', *Business History*, Vol. VI, No. 1, pp. 1–19.

Dixon, D. F., (1967), 'The Growth of Competition Among the Standard Oil Companies in the U. S., 1911–1961', *Business History*, Vol. X, No. 1, pp. 1–29.

Donaldson, L., (1987), 'Strategy, Structural Adjustment to Regain Fit: in Defence of Contingency Theory', *Journal of Management Studies*, Vol. 24, pp. 1–24.

Donnachie, I., (1977), 'Sources of Capital and Capitalization in the Scottish Brewing Industry, c. 1750–1830', *Economic History Review*, Vol. XXX, pp. 269–283.

Easingwood, C. J., (1987), 'Early Product Life Cycle Forms for Infrequently Purchased Major Products', *International Journal of Research in Marketing*, Vol. 4, pp. 3–9.

Easingwood, C. J., and Lunn, S. O., (1992), 'Diffusion Paths in a High-tech Environment: Clusters and Commonalities', *R&D Management*, Vol. 22, No. 1, pp. 69–80.

Easingwood, C. J., Mahajan, V., and Muller, E., (1981), 'A Nonsymmetric Responding Logistic Model for Forecasting Technological Substitution', *Technological Forecasting and Social Change*, Vol. 20, No. 9, pp. 199–213.

Easingwood, C. J., Mahajan, V., and Muller, E., (1983), 'A Non-uniform Influence Innovation Diffusion Model of New Product Acceptance', *Marketing Science*, Vol. 2, No. 3, pp. 273–295.

Ellis, J., (1996), 'A Perspective to Collaborative Supplier Relationships from Economic and Historical Theory', Fifth International Annual IPSERA Conference, Eindhoven University of Technology, Eindhoven, The Netherlands, 1–3 April.

Emerson, R. L., (1980), 'Expansion Abroad: A Solution to Fast Food's Slow Growth?', *Cornell Hotel and Restaurant Association Quarterly*, Vol. 21, No. 4, pp. 24–30.

Emerson, R. L., (1990), *The New Economics of Fast Food*, Van Nostrand Reinhold, New York.

English, W., (1993), 'Franchising, By Its Proper Name, is Wholesaling!', *Journal of Marketing Channels*, Vol. 2, No. 3, pp. 24–30.

Evans, D. S., and Leighton, L. S., (1990), 'Small Business Formation by Unemployed and Employed Workers', *Small Business Economics*, Vol. 12, No. 4, pp. 319–330.

Felstead, A. (1993), *The Corporate Paradox Power and Control in the Business Franchise*, Routledge, London.

Fitzsimmons, J. A., (1985), 'Consumer Participation and Productivity in Service Operations', *Interfaces*, Vol. 15, No. 3, pp. 60–67.

Forward, J., and Fulop, C., (1993a), *Large Firms Entry in Franchising: Strategic and Operational Issues*, City University Business School, London.

Forward, J., and Fulop, C., (1993b), 'Elements of a Franchise: The Experiences of Established Firms', *Service Industries Journal*, Vol. 13, No. 4, pp. 159–178.

Fuller, T., (1994), *Small Business Trends 1994/1998*, Durham University Business School.

Fulop, C., (1996), *Overview of the Franchise Marketplace*, Centre for Franchise Research, City University Business School, London.

Gansof, F. L., (1966), *Feudalism*, Longmans, Green & Co. Ltd, London.

Gatignon, H., and Robertson, T. S., (1989), 'Technology Diffusion: An Empirical Test of Competitive Effects', *Journal of Marketing*, January, Vol. 53, pp. 35–49.

Gold, B., (1981), 'Technological Diffusions in Industry: Research Needs and Shortcomings', *Journal of Industrial Economics*, Vol. 24, No. 3, pp. 247–269.

Gourvish, T. R., and Wilson, R. G., (1985), 'Profitability in the Brewing Industry, 1885–1914', *Business History*, Vol. XXVII, No. 2, July, pp. 146–165.

Grant, C., (1985), *Business Format Franchising: A System For Growth*, Economist Intelligence Unit, London.

Hackett, D. W., (1977), *Franchising: The State of the Art*, Monograph Series, No. 9, American Marketing Association.

Hall, W. P., (1964), 'Franchising – New Scope for an Old Technique', *Harvard Business Review*, January–February, Vol. 42, pp. 60–72.

Hall, P., and Dixon, R., (1989), *Franchising*, NatWest Small Business Bookshelf, Pitman Publishing, London.

Hannan, M. T., and Carroll, G. R., (1992), *Dynamics of Organizational Populations: Density, Legitimation, and Competition*, Oxford University Press, Oxford.

Hannan, M. T., Carroll, G. R., Dundon, E. A., and Torres, J. C., (1995), 'Organizational Evolution in a Multinational Context: Entries of Automobile Manufacturers in Belgium, Britain, France, Germany, and Italy', *American Sociological Review*, Vol. 60, pp. 509–528.

Hatcliffe, M., Mills, V., Purdy, D., and Stanworth, J., (1995), 'Prospective Franchisees', Lloyds Bank, *IFRC Franchising in Britain Report*, Vol. 1, No. 1, University of Westminster.

Haverson, P., (1991), 'Every Walk of Life Covered by a Franchise', Survey, *Financial Times*, 4–5 May.

Hawkins, K. H., and Pass, C. L., (1979), *The Brewing Industry: A Study of Industrial Organization and Public Policy*, London.

Haydon, P., (1995), *The English Pub: A History*, Robert Hale, London.

Henderson, R. M., and Clark, K. B., (1989), 'Architectural Innovation: The Reconfiguration of Existing Product Technologies and the Failure of Established Firms', *Administrative Science Quarterly*, Vol. 35, pp. 9–30.

Hicks, M., (1995), *Bastard Feudalism*, Longman, London.

Hill, C. W. L., and Pickering, J. F., (1986), 'Divisionalization, Decentralization, and Performance of Large United Kingdom Companies', *Journal of Management Studies*, Vol. 23, No. 1, pp. 26–50.

Horwath International, (1991), *Franchising in the Economy*, International Edition, Evan City, Pennsylvannia.

Housden, J., (1984), *Franchising and Other Business Relations in Hotel and Catering Industry Services*, Heinemann, London.

Huberman, M., (1995), 'Some Early Evidence of Worksharing: Lancashire Before 1850', *Business History*, Vol. 37, pp. 1–26.

Jack, A., (1957), 'The Channels of Distribution for an Innovation: The Sewing Machine Industry in America 1860–1865', pp. 113–141 in *Explorations in Entrepreneurial History*, Harvard University Research Center in Entrepreneurial History, Cambridge, Massachusetts.

Jeffreys, J. B., (1954), *Retail Trading in Britain, 1985–1950*, Cambridge University Press, Cambridge.

Jones, P., (1988), 'The Impact of Trends in Service Operations on Food Delivery Systems', *International Journal of Operational Production Manufacturing*, Vol. 8, No. 7 pp 23–30.

Justis, R., and Judd, R., (1986), 'Master Franchising: A New Look', *Journal of Small Business Management*, July, pp. 16–21.

Kanter, R. M., (1985), *The Change Masters*, Unwin Hyman. London.

Karpik, P., and Roahi-Belkaoui, A., (1994), 'The Effect of the Implementation of the Multi-Divisional Structure on Shareholder Wealth: The Contingency of Diversification', *Journal of Business Finance & Accountancy*, Vol. 21, No. 3, pp. 349–366.

Kaufmann, P. J., and Dant, R., (1996), 'Multi-unit Franchising: Growth and Management Issues', *Journal of Business Venturing*, Vol. 11, pp. 343–358.

Kaufmann, P. J., and Lafontaine, F., (1994), 'Costs of Control: The Source of Economic Rents For McDonald's Franchisees', *Journal of Law & Economics*, Vol. XXXVII, pp. 417–453.

Keeble, D., and Wever E., (eds) (1986), *New Firms and Regional Development in Europe*, Croom Helm, London.

Keeble, D., Walker, S., and Robson, M., (1993), *New Firm Formation and Small Business Growth: Spatial and Temporal Variations and Determinants in the United Kingdom*, Research Paper 15, Department of Employment, London.

Khan, M. A., (1992), *Restaurant Franchising*, Van Nostrand Reinhold, New York.

Kikulis, L. M., Slack, T., and Hinings, C. R., (1995), 'Sector-Specific Patterns of Organizational Design Change', *Journal of Management Studies*, Vol. 32, No. 1, January, pp. 67–100.

Klein, B., and Saft, L. F., (1985), 'The Law of Economics of Franchise Tying Contracts', *Journal of Law and Economics*, Vol. XXVIII, May, pp. 345–361.

Knox, D. M., (1958), 'The Development of the Tied House System in London', *Oxford Economic Papers*, Vol. X, pp. 66–83.

Kochen, M., and Deutsch, K. W., (1980), *Decentralization Sketches Towards a Rational Theory*, Oelgeschlager, Gunn & Hain, Cambridge, Massachusetts.

Kottak, C. P., (1983), 'Rituals at McDonald's', *Natural History*, Vol. 87, January, pp. 75–82.

Kursch, H., (1968), *The Franchise Boom: How You Can Profit In It*, Prentice Hall, Englewood Cliffs, New Jersey.

Langdon, P., (1986), *Orange Roofs, Golden Arches: The Architecture of American Chain Restaurants*, Knopf, New York.

Leidner, R., (1993), *Fast Food, Fast Talk, Service Work and the Routinization of Everyday Life*, University of California Press, Berkeley, California.

Levitt, T., (1976), 'The Industrialization of Service', *Harvard Business Review*, September–October, pp. 63–74.

Litteljohn, D., (1993), 'Hospitality Research: Philosophies and Progress', pp. 209–232 in Teare, R., Moutinho, L., and Morgan, L., (eds), *Managing and Marketing Services in the 1990s*, Cassell, London.

Love, J. F., (1986), *McDonald's – Behind the Arches*, Bantam Books Inc., New York.

Luxenberg, S., (1985), *Roadside Empires – How the Chains Franchised America*, Viking Penguin Inc., New York.

MacMillan, K., and Farmer, D., (1979), 'Redefining the Boundaries of the Firm', *Journal of Industrial Economics*, Vol. XXVII, No. 3, pp. 277–285.

Marquardt, R. A., and Murdock, G. W., (1986), 'An Evaluation of Franchising Trends and Their Implications for the Retailing Industry', Society of Franchising, First Annual Conference, Omaha, Nebraska, 28–30 September.

Martin, R. E., (1988), 'Franchising and Risk Management', *American Economic Review*, Vol. 78, No. 5, pp. 954–968.

Martin, R. E., (1996), 'The Market for Franchise Opportunities', *Bulletin of Economic Research*, Vol. 48, pp. 97–114.

Marvel, H., (1982), 'Exclusive Dealing', *Journal of Law & Economics*, Vol. Vol. XXV, pp. 1–26.

Mathers, C. J., (1988), 'Family Partnerships and International Trade in Early Modern Europe: Merchants from Burgos in England and France, 1470–1570', *Business History Review*, Vol. 62, pp. 367–397.

Mayhew, H., (1851), *London Labour and the London Poor*, Spring Books, London.

Mayhew, N., (1995), 'Modelling Medieval Monetarism', pp. 55–77 in Britnell, R. H., and Campbell, B. M. S., (eds), *A Commercialising Economy: England 1086–c. 1300*, Manchester University Press, Manchester, UK.

McKiernan, P., (1992), *Strategies of Growth*, Routledge, London.

McMahon, P. S., and Schmelzer, C. D., (1989), 'The Role of the Customer in the Food Service Encounter', *Hospitality Education and Research Journal*, Special Issue, Annual CHRIE Conference Proceedings, pp. 427–434.

Meager, N., (1992), 'Does Unemployment Lead to Self-Employment?', *Small Business Economics*, Vol. 4, No. 2, pp. 87–104.

Mendelsohn, M., (1992), *The Guide to Franchising*, Cassell, London.

Miles, R. E., and Snow, C. C., (1986), 'Organizations: New Concepts for New Forms', *California Management Review*, Vol. XXVIII, No. 3, pp. 62–73.

Milsom, S. F. C., (1976), *The Legal Framework of English Feudalism*, Cambridge University Press, Cambridge.

Mintzberg, H., Waters, J., Pettigrew, A. M., and Butler, R., (1990), 'Studying Deciding: An Exchange of Views Between Mintzberg and Waters, Pettigrew, and Butler', *Organization Studies*, Vol. 11, No. 1, pp. 1–16.

Mockler, R. J., and Easop, H., (1968), 'Guidelines for More Effective Planning and Management of Franchise Systems', *Research Monograph*, College of Business Administration, Georgia State University.

Monckton, H. A., (1966), *A History of English Ale & Beer*, The Bodley Head, London.

Monckton, H. A., (1969), *A History of the English Public House*, The Bodley Head, London.

Morison, J., and Leith, P., (1992), *The Barrister's World and the Nature of the Law*, Open University Press, Milton Keynes, UK.

Mowery, D. C., (1983), 'The Relationship Between Intra-Firm and Contractual Forms of Industrial Research in American Manufacturing, 1900–1940', *Explorations in Economic Thought*, Vol. 20, pp. 351–374.

Myers, A. R., (1974), *England in the Late Middle Ages*, Eighth Edition, Penguin Books, London.

National Westminster Bank/British Franchise Association, (1984), *Franchising in Great Britain: The Industry and the Market*, Power Research Associates, London.

National Westminster Bank/Bristish Franchise Association, (1990), *Survey 1990*, Bristish Franchise Association, London.

Nelson, R., and Winter, S., (1983), *An Evolutionary Theory of Economic Change*, Harvard University Press, Massachusetts.

Nichols, D., (1988), 'The Fast Food Dilemma', *Incentive Marketing*, March, pp. 46–49.

Norton, S. W., (1988), 'An Empirical Look at Franchising as an Organizational Form', *Journal of Business*, Vol. 61, No. 2, pp. 197–219.

Nowlis, M., (1988), *Food Service Personnel of Tomorrow: Robots and Computers*, Autumn Symposium Papers, International Association of Hotel Management Schools, Leeds Polytechnic.

O'Connell-Davidson, J., (1994), 'What Do Franchisors Do? Control and Commercialization in Milk Distribution', *Work, Employment & Society*, Vol. 8, No. 1, pp. 23–44.

Ozanne, U. B., and Hunt, S. D., (1971), *The Economic Effects of Franchising*, Report Prepared for the Small Business Administration and Select Committee on Small Business, US Senate, September, Graduate School of Business, Wisconsin.

Palmer, J., (1983), 'Automatic Food Service: The Meal of the Future?', *Cornell Hotel and Restaurant Administration Quarterly*, Vol. 23, No. 2.

Pendergast, M., (1993), *For God, Country and Coca-Cola*, Weidenfield and Nicolson, London.

Pickworth, J. R., (1989), 'Service Delivery Systems in the Food Service Industry', *International Journal of Hospitality Management*, Vol. 7, pp. 43–62.

Pillsbury, R., (1990), *From Boarding House to Bistro*, Unwin Hyam Inc., London.

Pinch, T. J., and Bijker, W. E., (1984), 'The Social Construction of Artefacts: or How the Sociology of Science and the Science of Technology Might Benefit Each Other', *Social Studies of Science*, Vol. 16, No. 3.

Pollert, A., (1988), 'Dismantling Flexibility', *Capital and Class*, No. 34, Spring, pp. 42–75.

Poly, J. P., and Bournazel, E., (1991), *The Feudal Transformation 900–1200*, Holmes and Meier, London.

Porter, M. E., (1980), *Competitive Strategy: Techniques for Analysing Industries and Competitors*, Free Press, New York.

Postan, M. M., (1962), 'Foreword', in Bloch, M., (1962), *Feudal Society, Volume 1, The Growth of Ties of Dependence*, Routledge and Kegan Paul Ltd, London.

Postan, M. M., (1986), *The Medieval Economy and Society: An Economic History of Britain in the Middle Ages*, Penguin Books, London.

Priestland, G., (1972), *Frying Tonight: The Saga of Fish & Chips*, Gentry Books, London.

Reiter, E., (1991), *Making Fast Food: From the Frying Pan Into the Fryer*, McGill-Queen's University Press, Montreal.

Rogers, E. M., (1995), *Diffusion of Innovations*, Free Press, New York.

Sass, T. R., and Gisser, M., (1989), 'Agency Costs, Firm Size, and Exclusive Dealing', *Journal of Law & Economics*, Vol. XXXII, pp. 381–390.

Scarborough, H., and Lannon, R., (1994), 'The Successful Exploitation of New Technology in Banking', pp. 248–259, in Weild, D., and Rhodes, E., (eds), *Implementing New Technologies: Innovation and the Management of Technology*, 2nd Edition, NCC Blackwell Ltd, London.

Scase, R., and Goffee, R., (1987), *The Real World of the Small Business Owner*, Croom Helm, London.

Schmookler, J., (1966), *Invention and Economic Growth*, Harvard University Press, Cambridge, Massachusetts.

Scott, P., (1994), 'Property Markets and Growth of Multiple Retailing in Britian, 1919–1939', *Business History*, Vol. 36, No. 3, pp. 1–28.

Sen, K. C., (1993), 'The Use of Initial Fees and Royalties in Business Format Franchising', *Managerial and Decision Economics*, Vol. 14, pp. 175–190.

Shook, C., and Shook, R. L., (1993), *Franchising: The Business Strategy that Changed the World*, Prentice Hall, Englewood Cliffs, New Jersey.

Shutt, J., and Whittington, R., (1986), 'Large Firm Strategies and the Rise of Small Units', in Faulkner, T., Beaver, G., Lewis, J., and Gobb, A., (eds), *Readings in Small Business*, Gower, Aldershot.

Smith, B. A., (1990), *Franchising in the 1990s*, Notes for Ernst & Young Lecture.

Stanworth, J., (1984), *A Study of Power Relationships amd Their Consequences in Franchise Organizations*, Report to the Economic and Social Research Council, Polytechnic of Central London, London.

Stanworth, J., (1994), *The impact of franchising on the development prospects of small and medium-sized enterprises (SMEs) in the United Kingdom*, Report prepared for the Department of Trade and Industry, London.

Stanworth, J., (1995), 'Research Note: Penetrating the Mists Surrounding Franchisor Failure Rates – Some Old Lessons For New Businesses,' *International Small Business Journal*, Vol. 13, No. 2, pp. 59–63.

Stanworth, J., Curran, J., and Hough, J., (1984), 'The Franchised Small Business: Formal and Operational Dimensions of Independence', in Lewis, J., Stanworth, J., and Gibb, A., (eds), *Success and Failure in Small Business*, Gower, Aldershot, UK.

Stanworth, J., and Smith, B., (1991), *The Barclays Guide to Franchising for the Small Business*, Basil Blackwell, Oxford.

Stern, P., and Stanworth, J., (1988) 'The Development of Franchising in Britain', *NatWest Quarterly Review*, May, pp. 34–38.

Storey, D. J., (1994), *Understanding the Small Business Sector*, Routledge, London.

Storey, D. J., and Johnson, S., (1987), *Job Generation and Labour Market Change*, MacMillan, Basingstoke.

Storey, D. J., and Strange, A., (1992), *Entrepreneurship in Cleveland 1979–1989: A Study of the Effects of the Enterprise Culture*, Research Series No. 3, June, Department of Employment, London.

Strebel, P., (1987), 'Organizing for Innovation over an Industry Cycle', *Strategic Management Journal*, pp. 117–124.

Stuckey, J., and White, D., (1993), 'When and When Not to Vertically Integrate', *Sloan Management Review*, Spring, pp. 71–85.

Tarbutton, L. T., (1986), *Franchising: the How-to Book*, Prentice Hall, New Jersey.

Taylor, D., (1977), *Fortune, Fame & Folly: British Hotels and Catering from 1878 to 1978*, Chapel River Press, Andover, Hants, UK.

Teece, D. J., (1980), 'The Diffusion of an Administrative Innovation', *Management Science*, Vol. 26, pp. 446–470.

Thompson, E. P., (1991), *The Making of the English Working Class*, Penguin Books, London.

Thompson, R. S., (1983), 'Diffusion of the M-form Structure in the UK: Rate of Imitation and Inter-Industry Differences', *International Journal of Industrial Organization*, Vol. 1, No. 3, pp. 297–315.

Trutko, J., Trutko, J., and Kostecka, A., (1993), *Franchising's Role in the US Economy, 1975–2000*, US Business Administration, Washington, DC.

US Department of Commerce (various years), *Franchising in the Economy*, prepared by Andrew Kostecka, Washington DC.

US Department of Commerce (various years), *Statistical Abstracts of the United States*, Bureau of Census, Annual Editions, Washington DC.

Vaizey, J., (1960), *The Brewing Industry, 1886–1951: An Economic Study*, Pitman & Sons, London.

Vaughn, C., (1979), *Franchising: Its Nature, Scope, Advantages, and Development*, Lexington Books, Lexington, Massachusetts.

Walton, J. K., (1992), *Fish and Chips and the Working Class, 1870–1940*, Leicester University Press, London.

Watson, K., (1996), 'Banks and Industrial Finance: The Experience of Brewers, 1880–1913', *Economic History Review*, Vol. XLIX, No. 1, pp. 58–81.

Weinrauch, D. J., (1986), 'Franchising an Established Business', *Journal of Small Business Management*, Vol. 24, No. 3, pp. 1–7.

Williamson, O. E., (1975), *Markets and Hierarchies*, Free-Press, New York.

Winner, L., (1977), *Autonomous Technology: Technics-Out-of-Control as a Theme in Political Thought*, MIT Press, Cambridge, Massachusetts.

Woods, R. H., (1991), 'Hospitality's Industry: Who Wrote What About When', *Cornell Hotel and Restaurant Administration Quarterly*, Vol. 3, pp. 89–95.

Yavas, B. F., (1988), Macroeconomic Influences on Restaurant Franchising in the United States,' *Society of Franchising Proceedings: Forging Partnerships for Competitive Advantage*, San Francisco, California, 31 January–2 February.

Case Study 1: The Development of KFC (GB) Ltd

Angeline, J. F., and Hale, W. C., (1970), *Fast Food Franchising: 1970–1975*, Arthur D. Little Inc, Cambridge, Massachusetts.

Apte, U. E., and Reynolds, C. C., (1995), 'Quality Management at Kentucky Fried Chicken', *Interfaces*, Vol. 25, No. 3, May–June, pp. 6–21.

Bartlett, C. A., and Ghoshal, S., (1992), 'Kentucky Fried Chicken (Japan) Ltd'; pp. 662–678 in *Transactional Management: Text, Cases, and Readings in Cross-Border Management*, Irwin, Boston, Massachusetts.

Khan, M. A., (1992), *Restaurant Franchising*, Van Nostrand Reinhold, New York.

Klein, G. A. C., (1979), *The Expansion of Franchise Systems in a New Country: Kentucky Fried Chicken and Wimpy in South Africa*, PH. D Dissertation, University of Washington.

Case Study 2: The intertwined histories of Burger King and Wimpy

Love, J. F., (1986), *McDonald's – Behind the Arches*, Bantam Books Inc., New York.

Price, S., (1992), 'Fast Food Provision in the UK', pp. 39–61, in Ball, S. D., (ed.), *Fast Food Operations and Their Management*, Stanely Thornes, Cheltenham, UK.

Smith, L.,(1980), 'Burger King Puts Down Its Dukes', *Fortune*, 16 June, pp. 90–98.

Chapter 2: To franchise or not to franchise?
The role of strategic choice

Alpander, G. G., (1991), 'Developing Managers' Ability to Empower Employees', *Journal of Management Development*, Vol. 10, No. 3, pp. 13–24.

Bailey, J., Clarke-Hill, C. M., and Robinson, T. M., (1995), 'Towards a Taxonomy of International Retail Alliances', *The Service Industries Journal*, Vol. 15, No. 4, pp. 25–41.

Barley, S. R., Freeman, J., and Hybels, R. C., (1992) 'Strategic Alliances in Commercial Biotechnology', pp. 311–346 in Nohria, N., and Eccles, R. G., (eds), *Networks and Organizations: Structure, Form, and Action*, Harvard Business School Press, Boston, Massachusetts.

Baron, S. R., and Schmidt, R. A., (1991), 'Operational Aspects of Retail Franchises', *International Journal of Retail & Distribution*, Vol. 19, No. 2, pp. 13–19.

Belasco, J. A., and Stayer, R. C., (1994), 'Why Empowerment Doesn't Empower: The Bankruptcy of Current Paradigms', *Business Horizons*, March–April, pp. 29–41.

Bowen, D. E., and Lawler III, E. E., (1992), 'The Empowerment of Service Workers: What, Why, How, and When', *Sloan Management Review*, Spring, pp. 31–40.

Bowen, D. E., and Lawler III, E. E., (1995), 'Empowing Service Employees', *Sloan Management Review*, Summer, pp. 79–84.

Boyd, H. W. Jnr., and Piercy, I., (1963), 'Retailing in Great Britain', *Journal of Marketing*, January, pp. 29–35.

Brass, D. J., and Burkhardt, M. E., (1992), 'Centrality and Power in Organizations', in Nohria, N., and Eccles, R. G., (eds), *Networks and Organizations: Structure, Form, and Action*, Harvard Business School Press, Boston, Massachusetts.

Brickley, J. A., and Dark, F. H., (1987), 'The Choice of Organizational Form: The Case of Franchising', *Journal of Financial Economics*, Vol. 18, June, pp. 401–421.

Brown, D., (1992), 'Why Participative Management Won't Work Here', *Management Review*, June, pp. 42–46.

Bygrave, W. D., (1992), 'Partnership Franchising: Maximizing Entrepreneurial and Financial Leverage in Franchising', pp. 575–586, in Churchill, N. C., et al, (eds), *Frontiers of Entrepreneurship Research*, Babson College Entrepreneurship Research Conference, Babson Park, Massachusetts.

Byrne, A., (1993), 'International Hotel Consortia', pp. 126–132 in Jones, P., and Pizam, A., (eds), *The International Hospitality Industry: Organizational and Operational Issues*, Pitman Publishing, London.

Byrne, D., (1986), *Waiting For Change? Working Hotel and Catering*, Low Pay Pamphlet No. 42, Low Pay Unit, London.

Caves, P. E., and Murphy, W. F., (1976), 'Franchising: Firms, Markets and Intangible Assets', *Southern Economic Journal*, Vol. 42, April, pp. 572–586.

Child, J., (1972), 'Organizational Structure, Environment and Performance: The Role of Strategic Choice', *Sociology*, Vol. 6, pp. 2–21.

Connell, J. M., (1992), 'Branding Hotel Portfolios', *International Journal of Contemporary Hospitality Management*, Vol. 4, No. 1., pp. 26–32.

Cool, K., and Dierickx, I., (1993), 'Rivalry, Strategic Groups, and Firm Profitability', *Strategic Management Journal*, Vol. 14, pp. 47–60.

Cyert, R. M., and March, J. G., (1963), *A Behavioural Theory of the Firm*, Prentice Hall, Englewood Cliffs, New Jersey.

Davé, U., (1984), 'US Multinational Involvement in the International Hotel Sector', *The Service Industries Journal*, Vol. 4, pp. 48–63.

Dollinger, M. J., (1990), 'The Evolution of Collective Strategies in Fragmented Industries', *Academy of Management Review*, Vol. 15, No. 2, pp. 266–285.

Dunning, J. H., and Khundu, S. K., (1995), 'The Internationalization of the Hotel Industry – Some New Findings From a New Field Study', *Management International Review*, Vol. 35, 2nd Quarter, pp. 101–133.

Dunning, J. F., and McQueen, M., (1982), 'Multinational Corporations in the Hotel Industry', *Anals of Tourism Research*, Vol. 9, pp. 69–90.

Eyster, J., (1977), 'Administering the Hotel Management Contract: An Analysis of Owner and Operator Concerns', *Cornell Hotel Restaurant Administration Quarterly*, August, pp. 12–20.

Felstead, A. (1993), *The Corporate Paradox Power and Control in the Business Franchise*, Routledge, London.

Ford, R. C., and Fottler, M. D., (1995), 'Empowerment: A Matter of Degree', *Academy of Management Executive*, Vol. 9, No. 3, pp. 21–29.

Forward, J., and Fulop, C., (1993), 'Elements of a Franchise: The Experiences of Established Firms', *The Service Industries Journal*, Vol. 13, No. 4, pp. 159–178.

Freeman, L. C., (1979), 'Centrality in Social Networks: Conceptual Clarification', *Social Networks*, Vol. 2, pp. 22–41.

Gatignon, H., and Robertson, T. S., (1989), 'Technology Diffusion: An Empirical Test of Competitive Effects', *Journal of Marketing*, Vol. 53, January, pp. 35–49.

Greenwood, R., and Hinings, C. R., (1988), 'Organizational Design Types, Tracks and the Dynamics of Strategic Change', *Organization Studies*, Vol. 9, pp. 293–316.

Hall, R. H., (1987), *Organizations: Structures, Processes and Outcomes*, 4th Edition, Prentice Hall International, Englewood Cliffs, New Jersey.

Hamel, G., (1991), 'Competition for Competence and Inter-Partner Learning within International Strategic Alliances', *Strategic Management Journal*, Vol. 12, Special Issue, pp. 69–82.

Hamilton, W., (1996), 'Brands Must Change Channels', *Marketing Week*, 16 February, p. 28.

Harrigan, K. R., (1986), *Managing For Joint Venture Success*, Lexington Books, Lexington, Massachusetts.

Harrigan, K. R., (1988), 'Joint Ventures and Competitive Strategy', *Strategic Management Journal*, Vol. 6, pp. 55–73.

Harrison, L., and Johnson, K., (1992), *International Hotel Groups Directory*, Hotel Portfolio Research, London.

Heskett, J. L., Jones, T. O., Loveman, G. W., Sasser, W. E., and Schlesinger, L. A., (1994), 'Putting the Service Chain to Work', *Harvard Business Review*, March–April, pp. 164–174.

Hitt, M. A., and Tyler, B. B., (1991), 'Strategic Decision Models: Integrating Different Perspectives', *Strategic Management Journal*, Vol. 12, pp. 327–351.

Housden, J., (1984), *Franchising and Other Business Relations in Hotel and Catering Industry Services*, Heinemann, London.

Horwath International, (1992), *The Case for Management Contracts*, Horwath International, London.

Howe, W. S., (1992), *Retailing Management*, MacMillan, London.

Jones, P., and Davies, A., (1991), 'Empowerment: A Study of General Managers of Four Star Hotel Properties in the UK', *International Journal of Hospitality Management*, Vol. 10, No. 3, pp. 211–217.

Johnson, K., and Harrison, L., (1993), *The UK Hotels Directory*, Cassell, London.

Justis, R. T., Taylor, L., and Nielsen, W., (1986), 'The Franchising Economy', Society of Franchising, First Annual Conference, Omaha, Nebraska, 28–30 September.

Kaufmann, G., (1991), 'Problem-solving and Creativity', pp. 103–134, in Henry, J., (ed.), *Creative Management*, Sage Publications, London.

Kaufmann, P. J., (1992) 'The Impact of Managerial Performance Decay on Franchisors' Store Allocation Strategies', *Journal of Marketing Channels*, Vol. 1, No. 4, pp. 51–79.

Kay, J. A., (1993), *Foundations of Corporate Success: How Business Strategies Add Value*, Oxford University Press, Oxford.

Keegan, B. M., (1983), 'Leadership in the Hospitality Industry', in Casee, E., and Reuland, R., (eds), *The Management of Hospitality*, Hogere Hotelschool, The Hague, Pergamon Press, Oxford.

Kent, D. H., (1991), 'Joint Ventures vs. Non Joint Ventures: An Empirical Investigation', *Strategic Management Journal*, Vol. 12, pp. 387–394.

Killing, J. P., (1982), 'How to Make A Joint Venture Work', *Harvard Business Review*, May–June, pp. 120–127.

Knox, D. M., (1958), 'The Development of the Tied House System in London', *Oxford Economic Papers*, Vol. X, pp. 66–83.

Koss-Feder, L., (1994), 'Alliances Strengthen Marketing Efforts', *Hotel & Motel Management*, 15 August, p. 16.

Krueger, A., (1991), 'Ownership, Agency, and Wages: An Examination of Franchising in the Fast Food Industry', *Quarterly Journal of Economics*, Vol. 56, Issue 1, pp. 621–636.

Koss-Feder, L., (1994), 'Alliances Strengthen Marketing Efforts', *Hotel & Motel Management*, 15 August, p. 16.

Lamb, H., and Piercy, S., (1987), 'Big Mac is Watching You', *New Society*, 9 October, pp. 17–20.

Lashley, C., (1994), 'Empowerment: Meanings and Myths', *Hospitality*, August/September, No. 145, pg. 19.

Leal, A. R., (1974), *Retailing*, Edward Arnold Ltd, London.

Litteljohn, D., (1982), 'The Role of Consortia in Great Britain', *Service Industries Journal*, Vol. 2, No. 1, pp. 79–91.

Litteljohn, D., (1985), 'Towards an Economic Analysis of Trans/Multinational Hotel Companies', *International Journal of Hospitality Journal*, Vol. 4, pp. 157–165.

Lorange, P., and Roos, J., (1993), *Strategic Alliances – Formation, Implementation and Evolution*, Blackwell Publishers, Cambridge, Massachusetts.

Mahajan, V., Muller, E., and Bass, F., (1990), 'New Product Diffusion Models in Marketing: A Review and Direction for Research', *Journal of Marketing*, Vol. 54, No. 1, pp. 1–26.

Marlin, D., Lamont, B. T., Hoffman, J. J., (1994), 'Choice Situation, Strategy and Performance: Re-examination', *Strategic Management Journal*, Vol. 15, pp. 229–239.

McKiernan, P., (1992), *Strategies of Growth*, Routledge, London.

Miles, G., Snow, C. C., and Sharfman, M. P., (1993), 'Industry Variety and Performance', *Strategic Management Journal*, Vol. 14, pp. 163–178.

Miller, D., (1981), 'Toward a New Contingency Approach: The Search for Organizational Gestalts', *Journal of Management Studies*, Vol. 18, pp. 1–26.

Mintzberg, H., and Waters, J., (1985), 'Of Strategies, Deliberate and Emergent', *Strategic Management Journal*, Vol. 6, pp. 257–272.

Mintzberg, H., Waters, J., Pettigrew, A. M., and Butler, R., (1990), 'Studying Deciding: An Exchange of Views Between Mintzberg and Waters, Pettigrew, and Butler', *Organization Studies*, Vol. 11, No. 1, pp. 1–16.

Morrison, A. J., and Roth, K., (1992), 'A Taxonomy of Business-level Strategies in Global Industries', *Strategic Management Journal*, Vol. 13, pp. 399–418.

Nation's Restaurant News, (1995), 'Top 100 Chains Ranked by U. S. Systemwide Food Service Sales', *Nation's Restaurant News*, 7 August.

Nohria, N., and Eccles, R. G., (1992), 'Face-to-Face: Making Network Organizations Work', pp. 288–308 in Nohria, N., and Eccles, R. G., (eds), *Networks and Organizations: Structure, Form, and Action*, Harvard Business School Press, Boston, Massachusetts.

Pannell Kerr Forster, (1993), *Trends in the Hotel Industry*, International Edition, Pannell Kerr Forster Associates, London.

Peterson, A., and Dant, R., (1990), 'Perceived Advantages of the Franchise Option From the Franchisee Perspective: Empirical Insights from a Service Franchise', *Journal of Small Business Management*, Vol. 28, No. 3, pp. 46–61.

Poorani, A. A., and Smith, D. R., (1994), 'Applicability of Hotel Franchising to Bed and Breakfast Industry', Society of Franchising Conference: Understanding And Accepting Different Perspectives . . . Empowering Relationships In 1994 And Beyond, Las Vegas, Nevada, 13–14 February.

Powell, W. W., (1990), 'Neither Market nor Hierarchy: Network Forms of Organization', *Research in Organizational Behaviour*, Vol. 12, pp. 295–356.

Primeaux, W. J., Jnr., (1985), 'A Method for Determining Strategic Groups and Life Cycles in an Industry', pp. 315–327 in Thomas, H., and Gardner, D. M., (eds), *Strategic Marketing and Management*, John Wiley and Sons, Chichester.

Publican, (1996), 'Market Report', *The Publican*, 7 January.

Publican, (1996), 'Survey', *The Publican*, 12 August.

Purdy, D., Stanworth, J., and Hatcliffe, M., (1996), *Franchising in Figures, Franchising in Britain*, Lloyds Banks, & International Franchise Research Centre, Vol. 1, No. 2, University of Westminster.

Rainnie, A., (1989), *Employee Relations in Small Firms – Small Isn't Beautiful*, Routledge, London.

Ring, P. S., and Ven de Ven, A. H. L., (1992), 'Structuring Co-operative Relationships Between Organizations', *Strategic Management Journal*, Vol. 13, pp. 483–498.

Ritzer, G., (1983), 'The 'McDonaldization' of Society', *Journal of American Culture*, Vol. 6, No. 1, Spring, pp. 100–107.

Rogers, E. M, (1983), *The Diffusion of Innovations*, Free Press, New York.

Roper, A., (1992), *Hotel Consortia Strategies and Structure: An Analysis of the Emergence of Hotel Consortia as Transorganizational Forms*, Unpublished PhD dissertation, University of Huddersfield, UK.

Roper, A., (1995), 'The Emergence of Hotel Consortia as Transorganizational Forms', *International Journal of Contemporary Hospitality Management*, Vol. 7, No. 1, pp 4–9.

Rumelt, R. P., (1974), *Strategy, Structure, and Financial Performance*, Division of Research, Graduate School of Business Administration, Harvard University, Boston.

Schultz, C., (1994), 'Hotels and Travel Agents: The New Partnership', *Cornell Hotel Restaurant Administration Quarterly*, Vol. 35, No. 2, pp. 45–50.

Schlesinger, L. A., and Hallowell, R., (1991), 'Taco Bell Corp.', *Teaching Note* (5–692–058), Harvard Business School, Boston, Massachusetts

Scott, M., Roberts, I., Holroyd, G., and Sawbridge, D., (1989), *Management and Industrial Relations in Small Firms*, Department of Employment Research, Paper No. 70, London.

Selin, S., and Beason, K., (1991), 'Interorganizational Relations in Tourism', *Anals of Tourism Research*, Vol. 18, pp. 639–652.

Slattery, P., (1991), 'Hotel Branding in the 1990s', *EIU Travel and Tourism Analyst*, No. 1, pp. 23–35.

Slattery, P., and Johnson, S. M., (1992), *Quoted hotel companies: The European Markets*, Klienwort Benson Research, 6th Annual Review, Klienwort Benson Ltd, London.

Slattery, P., and Litteljohn, D., (1991), 'The Structure of Europe's Economies and Demand for Hotel Accommodation', *EIU Travel and Tourism Analyst*.

Slattery, P., Roper, A., and Boer, A., (1985), 'Hotel Consortia: Their Acivities, Structure, and Growth,' *The Service Industries Journal*, Vol. 5, No. 2, pp. 192–199.

Stanworth, C., and Stanworth, J., (1995), 'The Self-Employed Without Employees – Autonomous or Atypical?', *Industrial Relations Journal*, Vol. 26, pp. 221–229.

Teare, R., and Olsen, M., (1992), *International Hospitality Corporate Strategy in Practice*, Pitman, London.

Trutko, J., Trutko, J., and Kostecka, A., (1993), *Franchising's Role in the US Economy, 1975–2000*, US Business Administration, Washington, DC.

Unwin, L., Johnson, K., (1990), *The UK Hotels Directory*, Cassell, London.

Vandermerwe, S., Lovelock, C., and Taishoff, M., (1994), *Competing Through Services: Strategy and Implementation*, Prentice Hall, London.

White, M., (1973), 'Management Styles in Hotels', *HCIMA Journal*, October.

Wicking, N., (1995), 'Franchising Versus Other Third Parties', *Business Franchise*, July/August, pp. 45 & 47.

Williamson, O. E., (1975), *Market and Hierarchies: Analysis and Antitrust Implications*, Free Press, New York.

Williamson, O. E., (1991), 'Strategizing, Economizing, and Economic Organization', *Strategic Management Journal*, Vol. 12, pp. 75–94.

Wrigley, L., (1970), *Divisional Autonomy and Diversification*, Doctoral Dissertation, Harvard Business School, Boston.

Case Study 3: The new fasces of the fast food market?

The Emergence for Consortia in Pizza Home Delivery

Anon, (1996), 'Retail trade up by 30.1% in five years', *The Grocer*, March 23, p. 10.

Ball, S. D., (1996), 'Whither the Small Independent Take-away?', *International Journal of Contemporary Hospitality Management*, Vol. 8, No. 5, pp. 25–29.

Caves, R. E., and Ghemawat, P., (1992), 'Identifying Mobility Barriers', *Strategic Management Journal*, Vol. 13, pp. 1–12.

Central Statistical Office, (1996), *Annual Abstract of Statistics*, HSMO, London.

Cummings, L. E., (1987), 'Information Technology Supporting Fast Food Phone-In Responsiveness', *International Journal of Hospitality Management*, Vol. 6, No. 4, pp. 225–228.

Dixon, J., Harrison, M., Arthurs, J., (1995), *1994 UK New Product Activity Report*, Campden & Chorleywood Research Association, Chorleywood, Hampshire.

Dixon, R., (1983), 'The Speed of Price Adjustment', *Journal of Industrial Economics*, Vol. XXXII, No. 1, pp. 25–37.

Duke, R., (1991), 'Post-saturation Competition in UK Grocery Retailing', *Journal of Marketing Management*, Vol. 7, pp. 63–75.

Emerson, R. L., (1990), *The New Economics of Fast Food*, Van Nostrand Reinhold, New York.

Hatten and Hatten, (1987), 'Strategic Groups, asymmetrical mobility barriers and contestability', *Strategic Management Journal*, Vol. 8, pp. 329–342.

Howe, W. S., (1992), *Retailing Management*, MacMillan, London.

Ingene, C. A., (1983), 'Intertype Competition: Restaurants versus Grocery Stores', *Journal of Retailing*, Vol. 53, pp. 50–75.

Jones, P., (1993), 'Book Reviews', *International Journal of Hospitality Management*, Vol. 12, No. 2, pp. 215–217.

Marshall, D. W., and Warren, R. M., (1987), 'Does the Independent Butcher Have a Unique Selling Point', *Food Marketing*, Vol. 3, No. 1, pp. 107–117.

Osborne, R. L., (1991), 'The Dark Side of the Entrepreneur', *Long Range Planning*, Vol. 19, No. 2, pp. 26–31.

Pickworth, J. R., (1988), 'Service Delivery Systems in the Food Service Industry', *International Journal of Hospitality Management*, Vol. 7, No. 1, pp. 43–62.

Porter, M. E., (1980), *Competitive Strategy: Techniques for Analysing Industries and Competitors*, Free Press, New York.

Poorani, A. A., and Smith, D. R., (1994), 'Applicability of Hotel Franchising to Bed and Breakfast Industry', Society of Franchising Conference: Understanding And Accepting Different Perspectives . . . Empowering Relationships In 1994 And Beyond, Las Vegas, Nevada, 13–14 February.

Price, S., (1991), *An Analysis of the UK Fast Food Market Structure*, Hotel & Catering Research Centre, Huddersfield Polytechnic, UK.

Price, S., (1992), 'Fast Food Provision in the UK', pp. 39–61, in Ball, S. D., (ed.), *Fast Food Operations and Their Management*, Stanely Thornes, Cheltenham, UK.

Price, S., (1993a), *The UK Fast Food Industry 1993*, Cassell, London.

Price, S., (1993b), 'Branded A Success', *Caterer & Hotelkeeper*, 11 November, pp. 37–40.

Price, S., (1995a), *A Strategic Review of the UK Pizza & Pasta Market*, The Pizza & Pasta Association, Wantage, Oxon.

Price, S., (1995b), 'The UK Pizza Market: The Twilight of Adolescence?', The Pizza & Pasta Association Open Day, Lancaster Hotel, 29 June.

Scholl-Poensgen, A., (1983), 'Management of Fast Food Chains', pp. 203–219 in Casee, E., and Reuland, R., (eds), *The Management of Hospitality*, Pergamon Press, Oxford.

Case Study 4: The changing face of hotel restaurants

BDO Hospitality Consulting, (1994), *The United Kingdom Hotel Industry*, BDO Hospitality Consulting, London.
Carper, J., (1994), 'Food Choices: Outsource or do it yourself', *Hotels*, September, pp. 19–20.
Crawford-Welch, S., (1991), 'International marketing in the hospitality industry', chapter 11, pp. 166-193, in Teare, R., and Boer, A., (eds), *Strategic Hospitality Management*, Cassell, London.
Ford, R. C., and Fottler, M. D., (1995), 'Empowerment: A Matter of Degree', *Academy of Management Executive*, Vol. 9, No. 3, pp. 21–29.
Hensdill, C., (1996), 'Partnerships in Dining', *Hotels*, pp. 57–60.
Langston, J., and Price, S., (1994), 'Reviewing the Performance of Corporate Food and Beverage', pp. 39–47, in Davis, B., and Lockwood, A., (eds), *Food and Beverage Management: A Selection of Readings*, Butterworth Heinemann, Oxford.
Lichtenstien, D. R., and Burton, S., (1989), 'The Relationship Between Perceived and Objective Price-Quality', *Journal of Marketing Research*, Vol. XXVI, pp. 429–443.
Parasuraman, A., Zeithaml, V. A., Berry, L. L., (1988), 'SERVQUAL: A Multiple-Item Scale for Measuring Consumer Perceptions of Service Quality', *Journal of Retailing*, Vol. 64, pp. 12–37.
Schneider-Wexler, M., (1992), 'Lease Your Restaurant to an Independent Operator', *Hotels*, May, pp. 79–80.
Schneider-Wexler, M., (1994), 'Name Chefs, Food Chains Team Up with Hotels', *Hotels*, May, pp. 67–70.
Solomon, K. I., and Katz, N., (1981), *Profitable Restaurant Management*, 2nd edition, Prentice-Hall, Englewood-Cliffs, NJ.
Wheatley, J. J., Chiu, J. S., Goldman, A., (1981), 'Physical Quality, Price and Perceptions of Product Quality: Implications for Retailers', *Journal of Retailing*, Vol. 57, pp. 100–116.
Zeithaml, V. A., Berry, L. L., and Parasuraman, A., (1988), 'Communication and Control Processes in the Delivery of Service Quality', *Journal of Marketing*, Vol. 52, April, pp. 35–48.

Chapter 3: Evaluating the decision to franchise

Argenti, J., (1976), *Corporate Collapse: The Causes and Symptoms*, McGraw-Hill, London.
Ashdown Group, (1994), *Taking the Pulse of the Hotel Market*, Ashdown Group, London.
Ashman, R. T., (1987), 'The Way Ahead for Franchising and Licencing', First European Franchising and Licencing Conference, Glasgow, 15–16 June.
Astley, W. G., and Fombrun, C. J., (1983), 'Collective Strategy: Social Ecology of Organizational Environments', *Academy of Management Review*, Vol. 8, No. 4, pp. 576–587.
Barley, S. R., (1990), 'The Alignment of Technology and Structure through Roles and Networks', *Administrative Science Quarterly*, Vol. 35, pp. 61–103.
Barr, P. S., Stimpert, J. L., and Huff, A. S., (1992), 'Cognitive Change, Strategic Action, and Organizational Renewal', *Strategic Management Journal*, Vol. 13, Special Issue, Summer, pp. 15–36.
Beamish, P. W., (1985), 'The Characteristics of Joint Ventures in Developed and Developing Countries', *Colombia Journal of World Business*, Vol. 20, Autumn, pp. 13–19.
Berg, S., and Friedman, P., (1980), 'Causes and Effects of Joint Venture Activity: Knowledge Acquisition versus Parent Horizontality', *Antitrust Bulletin*, Spring, pp. 143–168.
Blau, P. M., (1973), *The Organization of Academic Work*, John Wiley and Sons Inc., New York.
Braverman, H., (1974), *Labor and Monopoly Capital: The Degradation of Work in the Twentieth Century*, Monthly Review Press, New York.
Brickley, J. A., and Dark, F. H., (1987), 'The Choice of Organizational Form: The Case of Franchising,' *Journal of Financial Economics*, Vol. 18, June, pp. 401–421.
Butler, S., and Skipper, J. K., (1981), 'Working for Tips: an Examination of Trust and Reciprocity in a Secondary Relationship of the Restaurant Organization', *The Sociological Quarterly*, Vol. 22, Winter, pp. 15–27.
Burns, T., and Stalker, G. M., (1961), *The Management of Innovation*, Tavistock Publications, London.
Callahan and Cassar, (1995) 'Small Business Owners' Assessments of Their Abilities to Perform and Interpret Formal Market Studies', *Journal of Small Business Management*, Vol. 33, No. 4, pp. 1–9.
Carney, M., and Gedajlovic, E., (1991), 'Vertical Integration in Franchise Systems: Agency Theory and Resource Explanations', *Strategic Management Journal*, Vol. 12, No. 8, November, pp. 607–629.
Caves, P. E., and Murphy, W. F., (1976), 'Franchising: Firms, Markets and Intangible Assets', *Southern Economic Journal*, Vol. 42, April, pp. 572–586.
Chan, P. S., and Justis, R. T., (1995), 'Franchising in Indonesia', 1995 Society of Franchising Conference, The International Challenge . . . Towards New Franchising Relationships, San Juan, Puerto Rico, February.
Chandler, A. D., Jr., (1962), *Strategy and Structure*, MIT Press, Cambridge, Massachusetts.
Child, J., (1972), 'Organizational Structure, Environment and Performance: The Role of Strategic Choice', *Sociology*, Vol. 6, pp. 2–21.
Churchill, D., (1991), 'Expansion Routes', Survey, *Financial Times*, 4/5 May.

Combs, J. G., and Castrogiovanni, G. J., (1994), 'Franchisor Strategy; A Proposed Model and Empirical Test of Franchisee versus Company-ownership', *Journal of Small Business Management*, Vol. 32, No. 2, pp. 37–48.

Contractor, F. J., and Lorange, P., (1988), *Co-operative Strategies in International Business*, Lexington Books, Lexington, Massachusetts

Cuba, R. C., and Milbourn, G., (1982), 'Delegating for Small Business Success', *American Journal of Small Business*, Vol. VII, No. 2, October–December, pp. 33–42.

Damanpour, F., (1991), 'Organizational Innovation: A Meta-Analysis of Effects of Determinants and Moderators', *Academy of Management Journal*, Vol. 34, pp. 555–590.

Dant, R. P., (1996), 'Motivations for Franchising: Rhetoric versus Reality', *International Small Business Journal*, Vol. 14, No. 1, pp. 10–32.

Dant, R. P., Kaufmann, P. J., and Robicheaux, R. A., (1996), 'The Restructuring of Franchise Systems: An Empirical Assessment of Ownership Redirection Patterns', *Journal of Marketing*, forthcoming.

Dant, R. P., and Schul, P. L., (1992), 'Conflict Resolution Processes in Contractual Channels of Distribution', *Journal of Marketing*, Vol. 56, January, pp. 38–54.

Dev, C., and Brown, J. R., (1990), 'Marketing Strategy, Vertical Structure, and Performance in the Lodging Industry: A Contingency Approach', *International Journal of Hospitality Management*, Vol. 9, No. 3, pp. 269–280.

Dollinger, M. J., and Golden, P. A., (1992), 'Interorganizational and Collective Strategies in Small Firms: Environmental Effects and Performance', *Journal of Management*, Vol. 18, No. 4, pp. 695–715.

Donaldson, L., (1982), 'Divisionalization and Size: a Theoretical and Empirical Critique', *Organization Studies*, Vol. 3, No. 4, pp. 321–337

Donaldson, L., (1985), 'Organization Design and the Lifecycles of Products', *Journal of Management Studies*, Vol. 22, No. 1, pp. 25–37.

Donaldson, L., (1986), 'Research Note: The Interaction of Size and Diversification as a Determinant of Divisionalization Grinyer Revisited', *Organization Studies*, Vol. 7, No. 4, pp. 367–379.

Donaldson, L., (1987), 'Strategy, Structural Adjustment to Regain Fit: in Defence of Contingency Theory', *Journal of Management Studies*, Vol. 24, pp. 1–24.

DTI, (1995), *Small Firms in Britain 1995*, HSMO, London.

Duncker, K., (1945), 'On Problem Solving', *Psychological Monographs*, Vol. 58, No. 5.

Dunning, J. H., (1989), 'Multinational Enterprises and the Growth of Services: Some Conceptual and Theoretical Issues', *The Service Industries Journal*, pp. 539.

Dutton, J. E., (1993), 'Interpretations on Automatic: A Different View of Strategic Issue Diagnosis', *Journal of Management Studies*, Vol. 30, pp. 339–357.

Economist Intelligence Unit, (1995), 'Retail Franchising in Italy', *Marketing in Europe, Group 3: Chemists' Goods, Household Goods, Domestic Appliances*, September, pp. 87–98.

Ellingham, T., (1995), 'Financial Aspects of Launching a Franchise', pp. 79–84 in *Franchise World Directory, 1996*, Franchise World Publications, London.

Felstead, A., (1991), 'The Social Organization of the Franchise: A Case of 'Controlled Self-Employment', *Work, Employment and Society*, Vol. 110, No. 5, May, pp. 17–23.

Felstead, A. (1993), *The Corporate Paradox Power and Control in the Business Franchise*, Routledge, London.

Forward, J., and Fulop, C., (1993), *Large Firms Entry in Franchising: Strategic and Operational Issues*, City University Business School, London.

Fox, A., (1973), 'Industrial Relations: A Social Critique of Pluralist Ideology', pp. 185–233, in Child, J., (ed.), *Man and Organization*, Allen & Unwin, London.

Galaskiewicz, J., (1979), 'The Structure of Community Organizational Networks', *Social Forces*, Vol. 57, No. 4, pp. 1346–1364.

Galaskiewicz, J., (1985), 'Interorganizational Relations', *Annual Review of Sociology*, Vol. 11, Annual Reviews Inc., Palo Alto, C. A.

Gomes-Casseres, B., (1996), *The Alliance Revolution: The New Shape of Business Rivalry*, Harvard University Press, Cambridge, Massachusetts.

Gourlay, R., (1994), 'Bring On The Clones', *Financial Times*, 12 April, p. 13

Gray, B., (1985), 'Conditions Facilitating Interorganizational Colloaboration', *Human Relations*, Vol. 38, pp. 911–936.

Greenhaus, J. H., and Bentall, N. J., (1985), 'Sources of Conflict between Work and Family Roles', *Academy of Management Review*, Vol. 10, No. 1, pp. 76–88.

Greenwood, R., and Hinings, C. R., (1988a), 'Organizational Design Types, Tracks and the Dynamics of Strategic Change', *Organization Studies*, Vol. 9, pp. 293–316.

Greenwood, R., and Hinings, C. R., (1988b), 'Organization Adaptation: Strategic Choice and Environment Determinism', *Administrative Science Quarterly*, Vol. 30, No. 3, pp. 336–349.

Greiner, L. E., (1972), 'Evolution and Revolution as Organizations Grow', *Harvard Business Review*, Vol. 50, pp. 37–46.

Gretton, J., and Harrison, A., (1983), 'Franchising in the Public Sector', Public Money Seminar, Wolfson College, Oxford, 15 April.

Hakim, C., (1987), 'Trends in the Flexible Workforce', *Employment Gazette*, Vol. 95, November, pp. 549–560.

Hall, D., and Saias, M., (1980), 'Strategy follows structure!', *Strategic Management Journal*, Vol. 1, pp. 149–164.

Hall, P., and Dixon, R., (1989), *Franchising*, NatWest Small Business Bookshelf, Pitman Publishing, London.

Hamel, G., (1991), 'Competition for Competence and Inter-Partner Learning within International Strategic Alliances', *Strategic Management Journal*, Vol. 12, Special Issue, pp. 69–82

Hill, C. W., Hwang, P., and Kim, W. C., (1990), 'An Eclectic Theory of the Choice of International Entry Mode', *Strategic Management Journal*, Vol. 11, pp. 117–128.

Hitt, M. A., and Tyler, B. B., (1991), 'Strategic Decision Models: Integrating Different Perspectives', *Strategic Management Journal*, Vol. 12, pp. 327–352.

Hoffman, R. C., and Preble, J. F., (1991), 'Franchising: Selecting a Strategy for Rapid Growth,' *Long Range Planning*, Vol. 24, No. 4, pp. 74–85.

Hoffman, S. R., and Preble, J. F., (1995), 'Franchising Systems Around the Globe: A Status Report', *Journal of Small Business Management*, Vol. 33, April, pp. 80–88.

Hornsey, T., and Dann, D., (1984), *Manpower Management in the Hotel and Catering Industry*, Batsford, London.

Housden, J., (1984), *Franchising and Other Business Relations in Hotel and Catering Industry Services*, Heinemann, London.

Howard, J. A., (1994), 'A Social Cognitive Conception of Social Structure', *Social Psychology Quarterly*, Vol. 57, No. 3, pp. 210–227.

Hrebiniak, L. G., and Joyce, W. F., (1985), 'Organizational Adaptation: Strategic Choice and Environmental Determinism', *Administrative Science Quarterly*, Vol. 30, pp. 336–349.

Huff, J. O., Huff, A. S., and Thomas, H., (1992), 'Strategic Renewal and the Interaction of Cumulative Stress and Inertia', *Strategic Management Journal*, Vol. 13, Special Issue, Summer, pp. 55–76.

Hunt, S. D., (1973), 'The Trend Toward Company-Operated Units in Franchise Chains', *Journal of Retailing*, Summer, pp. 3–12.

Hutt, M. D., Walker, B. A., and Frankwick, G. L., (1995), 'Hurdle the Cross-Functional Barriers to Strategic Change', *Sloan Management Review*, No. 2, pp. 22–30.

Isenberg, (1987), 'The Tactics of Strategic Opportunism', *Harvard Business Review*, Vol. 65, March–April, pp. 92–97.

Johnson, G., (1992), 'Managing Strategic Change – Strategy, Culture and Action', *Long Range Planning*, Vol. 25, No. 1, pp. 28–36.

Jordans, (1988), *Britain's Franchising Industry*, Jordans & Sons, Bristol, UK.

Josias, A., and McIntyre, F. S., (1995), 'Franchising in Brazil', 1995 Society of Franchising Conference, The International Challenge . . . Towards New Franchising Relationships, San Juan, Puerto Rico, February.

Julian, S. D., and Castrogiovanni, G. J, (1995), 'Franchisor Geographic Expansion', *Journal of Small Business Management*, Vol. 33, April, pp. 1–11.

Kaufmann, G., (1991), 'Problem-solving and Creativity', pp. 103–134, in Henry, J., (ed.), *Creative Management*, Sage Publications, London.

Kaufmann, P., and Dant., R., (1996), 'Multi-unit Franchising: Growth and Management Issues', *Journal of Business Venturing*, Vol. 11, pp. 343–358.

Kaufmann, P. J, and Lebenstein, H., (1988), 'International Business Format Franchising and Retail Entrepreneurship: A Possible Source of Retail Know-How for Developing Countries', *Journal of Development Planning*, Vol. 18, pp. 165–179.

Kaufmann, P. J., and Stanworth, J., (1995), 'The Decision to Purchase a Franchise: A Study of Prospective Franchisees', *Journal of Small Business Management*, Vol. 33, No. 4, pp. 22–33.

Kerin, R. A., Varadarajan, P. R., Peterson, R. A. (1992) 'First Mover Advantage: A Synthesis, Conceptual Framework, and Research Propositions,' *Journal of Marketing*, Vol. 56, October, pp. 33–52.

Kikulis, L. M., Slack, T., and Hinings, C. R., (1995), 'Sector-Specific Patterns of Organizational Design Change', *Journal of Management Studies*, Vol. 32, No. 1, January, pp. 67–100.

Klein, B., (1980), 'Transaction Costs of 'Unfair' Contractual Arrangements', *American Economic Review*, Vol. 70, pp. 356–362.

Lafontaine, F., (1992), 'Agency Theory and Franchising: Some Empirical Results', *RAND Journal of Economics*, Vol. 23, No. 2, pp. 263–283.

Langley, A., (1990), 'Patterns in the Use of Formal Analysis in Strategic Decisions', *Organization Studies*, Vol. 11, No. 1, pp. 17–45.

Leiberman, M. B., and Montgomery, D. B., (1988), 'First Mover Advantages', *Strategic Management Journal*, Vol. 9, pp. 41–58.

Leonard-Barton, D., (1992), 'Core Capabilities and Core Rigidities: A Paradox in New Product Development', *Strategic Management Journal*, Vol. 13, Special Issue, Summer, pp. 111–126.

Lessard, D. R., and Zaheer, S., (1996), 'Breaking the Silos: Distributed Knowledge and Strategic Responses to Volatile Exchange Rates', *Strategic Management Review*, Vol. 17, pp. 513–533.

Lewis, M. C., and Lambert, D. M., (1991), 'A Model of Channel Member Performance, Dependence, and Satisfaction', *Journal of Retailing*, Vol. 67, pp. 205–225.

Lillis, C. M., Narayana, and Gillman, J. C., (1976), 'Competitive Advantage Variation over the Life Cycle of a Franchise', *Journal of Marketing*, pp. 77–80.

Lowe, A., (1988), 'Small Hotel Survival – An Inductive Approach', *International Journal of Hospitality Management*, Vol. 7, No. 3, pp. 197–223.

Luffman, G., Sanderson, S., Lea, E., and Kenny, B., (1991), *Business Policy: An Analytical Introduction*, Basil Blackwell, Oxford.

Lusch, R., (1977), 'Franchisee Satisfaction: Causes and Consequences', *International Journal of Physical Distribution*, Vol. 7, pp. 128–140.

Lyles, M. A., Baird, I. S., Orris, J. B., and Kuratko, D. F., (1993), 'Formalized Planning in Small Businesses: Increasing Strategic Choices', *Journal of Small Business Management*, Vol. 31, No. 2, pp. 38–50.

MacCaskey, M. B., (1991), 'Mapping: Creating, Maintaining, and Relinquishing Conceptual Frameworks', pp. 135–152 in J., Henry, (ed.), *Creative Management*, Sage Publications, London.

MacDonald, M., (1992), *Strategic Marketing Planning*, Kogan Page, London.

Mahoney, J. T., and Pandian, J. R., (1992), 'The Resource-based View Within the Conversation of Strategic Management', *Strategic Management Journal*, Vol. 13, pp. 363–380.

Manolis, C., Dahlstrom, R., and Nygaard, A., (1995), 'A Preliminary Investigation of Ownership Conversions in Francllised Distribution Systems', *Journal of Applied Business Research*, Vol. 11, No. 2, pp. 1–8.

Marlin, D., Lamont, B. T., and Hoffman, J. J., (1994), 'Choice Situation, Strategy and Performance: A Reexamination', *Strategic Management Journal*, Vol. 15, pp. 229–239.

Mars, G., and Mitchell, P., (1979), *Room for Reform*, Open University Press, Milton Keynes

Mars, G., and Nicod, M., (1984), *The World of Waiters*, Allen & Unwin, London.

Martin, R. E., (1988), 'Franchising and Risk Management', *American Economic Review*, Vol. 78, No. 5, pp. 954–968.

Mathewson, G. F., and Winter, R. A., (1985), 'The Economics of Franchise Contracts', *Journal of Law and Economics*, Vol. 28, pp. 503–526.

McGee, M. B., Hogstrom, N., Kronstrom, C., (1995), *Franchising in Sweden*, American Emassy, Stockholm.

McKiernan, P., (1992), *Strategies of Growth*, Routledge, London.

Meloan, T. W., (1988), 'The Pros and Cons of Franchising: Two Views, Opportunity and Risk', *Business Forum*, Summer, pp. 14–18.

Mendelsohn, M., and Acheson, D., (1989), *How to Franchise Your Business*, Franchise World Publications, London.

Merrill, R. S., (1968), 'Technology', in Sills, D. E., (ed.), *International Encyclopedia of the Social Sciences*, MacMillan and Free Press, New York, NY.

Meyer, A. D., and Goes, J. B., (1988), 'Organizational Assimilation of Innovations: A Multi-level Contextual Analysis', *Academy of Management Journal*, Vol. 31, pp. 897–923.

Micheal, S. C., (1996), 'To Franchise or Not to Franchise: An Analysis of Decision Rights and Organizational Share Forms', *Journal of Business Venturing*, Vol. 11, pp. 57–71.

Miller, D., (1977), 'Common Syndromes of Business Failure', *Business Horizons*, November, pp. 43–53.

Minkler, A. P., (1990), 'Empirical Analysis of a Firm's Decision to Franchise', *Economica*, Vol. 34, pp. 77–82.

Mintzberg, H., (1973), *The Nature of Managerial Work*, Harper and Row, New York.

Mintzberg, H., (1979), *The Structuring of Organizations*, Prentice-Hall Inc., Englewood Cliffs, New Jersey.

Moch, M. K., and Morse, E. V., (1977), 'Size, Centralization and Organizational Adoption of Innovations', *American Sociological Review*, Vol. 42, pp. 716–725.

Mount, J., Zinger, T., and Forsyth, G. R., (1993), 'Organizing for Development in the Small Business', *Long Range Planning*, Vol. 26, No. 5, pp. 111–120.

Mouzelis, N., (1975), *Organization & Bureaucracy*, 2nd edition, Heinmann, London.

Nailon, P., (1978), 'Tipping A Behavioural Review', *HCIMA Review*, Vol. 2, pp. 231–241.

Neisser, U., (1976), *Cognition and Reality: Principles and Implications of Cognitive Psychology*, Freeman, San Francisco.

Nelson, R. R., (1991), 'Why Do Firms Differ, and How Does it Matter?', *Strategic Management Journal*, Vol. 12, Special Issue, Winter, pp. 61–74.

Norton, S. W., (1988a), 'An Empirical Look at Franchising as an Organizational Form', *Journal of Business*, Vol. 61, No. 2, pp. 197–219.

Norton, S. W., (1988b), 'Franchising, Brand Name, and the Entrepreneurial Capacity Problem', *Strategic Management Journal*, Vol. 9, pp. 105–114.

Nutt, P. C., (1993), 'Flexible Decision Styles and the Choices of Top Executives', *Journal of Management Studies*, Vol. 30, pp. 695–721.

Oliver, C., (1990), 'Determinants of Interorganizational Relationships: Integration and Future Directions', *Academy of Management Review*, Vol. 15, pp. 241–265.

Oxenfeldt, A. R., and Kelly, A. O., (1969), 'Will Successful Franchise Chains Ultimately Become Wholly-Owned Chains?', *Journal of Retailing*, Vol. 44, pp. 69–87.

Porter, M. E., (1980), *Competitive Strategy: Techniques for Analysing Industries and Competitors*, Free Press, New York.

Porter, M. E., (1985), *Competitive Advantage: Creating and Sustaining Superior Performance*, Free Press, New York.

Prahalad, C. K., and Bettis, R. A., (1986), 'The Dominant Logic: a New Linkage between Diversity and Performance', *Strategic Management Journal*, Vol. 7, pp. 485–501.

Ranson, S., Hinings, R., Greenwood, R., (1980), 'The Structuring of Organizational Structures', *Administrative Science Quarterly*, Vol. 25, No. 2, March, pp. 1–17.

Robinson, W. T., Fornell, C., and Sullivan, M., (1992), 'Are Market Pioneers Intrinsically Stronger than Later Entrants?', *Strategic Management Journal*, Vol. 13, pp. 609–624.

Rock, M. L., and Rock, R. H., (1990), *Corporate Restructuring – A Guide to Creating the Premium-Valued Company*, McGraw-Hill, Inc., New York.

Rubin, P. H., (1978), 'The Theory of the Firm and the Structure of the Franchise Contract', *Journal of Law and Economics*, Vol. 21, pp. 223–233.

Rumelt, R. P, (1974), *Strategy, Structure, and Financial Performance*, Division of Research, Graduate School of Business Administration, Harvard University, Boston.

Rumelt, R. P, (1991), 'How Much Does Industry Matter?', *Strategic Management Journal*, Vol. 12, No. 3, pp. 167–186.

Sanghavi, N., (1990), *Retail Franchising in the 1990's*, Longman Group, Harlow, Essex.

Schoonhoven, C. B., (1980), 'Problems with Contingency Theory: Testing Assumptions Hidden Within the Language of Contingency Theory,' *Administrative Science Quarterly*, Vol. 25, pp. 1–17.

Schreyögg, G., (1980), 'Contingency and Choice in Organization Theory', *Organization Studies*, Vol. 1, No. 4, pp. 305–326.

Schwenk, C., (1985), 'Cognitive Simplification Processes in Strategic Decision-Making', *Strategic Management Journal*, Vol. 5, pp. 111–128.

Seltz, D. S., (1982), *The Complete Handbook of Franchising*, Addison-Wesley Publishing Company, Reading, Massachusetts.

Shamir, B., (1978), 'Between Bureaucracy and Hospitality: Some Organizational Characteristics of Hotels', *Journal of Management Studies*, Vol. 15, pp. 285–307.

Shamir, B., (1981), 'The Workplace as a Community: The Case of British Hotels', *Industrial Relations Journal*, Vol. 12, No. 6, pp. 4555.

Shane, S. A., (1996), 'Why Franchise Companies Expand Overseas', *Journal of Business Venturing*, Vol. 11, pp. 73–88.

Slattery, P., (1976), *The Hotel as an Organization*, Msc Dissertation, University of Strathclyde.

Slattery, P., and Clark, A., (1988), 'Major Variables in the Corporate Structure of Hotel Groups', *International Journal of Hospitality Management*, Vol. 7, No. 2., pp. 117–130.

Stanislao, J., and Stanislao, B. C., (1983), 'Dealing with Resistance to Change', *Business Horizons*, July–August, pp. 74–78.

Stern, P., and Stanworth, J., (1994), 'Improving Small Business Rates Via Franchising – the Role of Banks in Europe,' *International Small Business Journal*, Vol. 12, No. 2, pp. 15–25.

Storholm, G., and Kavil, S., (1992), 'Impediments to International Franchising in the Business Format Sector', *Journal of Marketing Channels*, Vol. 1, No. 4, pp. 81–95.

Surprenant, C. F., and Solomon, M. R., (1987), 'Predictability and Personalization in the Service Encounter', *Journal of Marketing*, Vol. 51, April, pp. 86–96.

Thompson, R. S., (1994), 'The Franchise Life-cycle and the Penrose Effect', *Journal of Economic Behavior and Organization*, Vol. 24, No. 2, pp. 207–218.

Tuncalp, S., (1991), 'The Problems & Prospects for Franchising in the Arabian Peninsula: The Case of Saudi Arabia', *International Journal of Retail & Distribution Management*, Vol. 19, No. 4, pp. 28–37.

Tyler, B. B., and Steensma, H. K., (1995), 'Evaluating Technological Collaborative Opportunities: A Cognitive Modelling Perspective', *Strategic Management Journal*, Vol. 16, pp. 43–70.

Utterback, J. M., and Abernathy, W. J., (1975), 'A Dynamic Model of Process and Product Innovation', *Omega*, Vol. 6, No. 3, pp. 639–656.

Waldinger, R., Ward, R., and Aldrich, H., (1985), 'Ethnic Business and Occupational Mobility in Advanced Societies', *Sociology*, Vol. 19, No. 4, pp 586–597.

Walker, D., (1989), *A Comparison of International Versus Domestic Expansion by U. S. Franchise Systems*, International Franchise Association, Washington DC.

Walsh, J. P., and Dewar, R. D., (1987), 'Formalization and the Organizational Life Cycle', *Journal of Management Studies*, Vol. 24, No. 3 (May), pp. 215–232.

Weber, M. (1947), *The Theory of Social and Economic Organization*, (translated by A. M. Henderson and Talcott Parsons, ed. Talcott Parsons), Oxford University Press, Oxford.

White, M., (1973), 'Management Styles in Hotels', *HCIMA Journal*, October.

Whitehead, M., (1991), 'International Franchising – Marks & Spencer: A Case Study', *International Journal of Retail & Distribution Management*, Vol. 19, No. 2, pp. 10–12.

Whyte, W. F., (1948), *Human Relations in the Restaurant Industry*, McGraw-Hill, New York.

Williamson, O. E., (1975), *Market and Hierarchies: Analysis and Antitrust Implications*. Free Press, New York.

Williamson, O. E., (1985), *The Economic Institutions of Capitalism*, Free Press, New York.

Williamson, O. E., (1991), 'Strategizing, Economizing, and Economic Organization', *Strategic Management Journal*, Vol. 12, pp. 75–94.

Whittington, R., (1993), *What is Strategy – And Does It Matter?*, Routledge, London.

Woodward, J., (1965), *Industrial Organization: Theory & Practice*, Oxford University Press, London.

Wrigley, L., (1970), *Divisional Autonomy and Diversification*, Doctoral Dissertation, Harvard Business School, Boston.

Yavas, B. F., and Vardiabasis, D., (1987), 'The Determinants of US International Fast Food Franchising: An Application to the Pacific Rim', pp. 27–30, in *Developments in Marketing Science, Vol. X: Proceedings from the 11th Annual Conference of the Academy of Marketing Science*, Florida: Bar Harbor, May.

Zanzi, A., (1987), 'Determinants of Organic/Mechanistic Tendencies in a Public Accounting Firm,' *Journal of Management Studies*, Vol. 24, No. 2 (March), pp. 125–132.

Case Study 5: Efficiency in the UK bakery market

Burnett, J., (1963), 'The Baking Industry in the Nineteenth Century', *Business History*, Volume V, No. 2, pp. 98–108.
Central Statistical Office, (1994), *Retail Inquiry*, HSMO, London.
Cowling, K., Stoneman, P., Cubbin, J., Cable, J., Hall, G., Domberger, S., and Dutton, P., (1980), *Mergers and Economic Performance*, Cambridge University Press, Cambridge.
Dixon, R., (1983), 'The Speed of Price Adjustment', *Journal of Industrial Economics*, Vol. XXXII, No. 1, pp. 25–37.
Messinger, P. R., and Narasimhan, C., (1995), 'Has Power Shifted in the Grocery Channel?', *Marketing Science*, Vol. 14, No. 2, pp. 189–223.
Misterek, S. D. A., Dooley, K. J., and Anderson, J. C., (1991), 'Productivity as a Performance Measure', *International Journal of Operations & Production Management*, Vol. 12, No. 1, pp. 29–45.
Scherer, F. M., (1980), *Industrial Market Structure and Economic Performance*, Rand McNally, Chicago, Second Edition.
Sigsworth, E. M., (1965), 'Science and the Brewing Industry, 1850–1900', *Economic History Review*, Vol. XVII, pp. 536–550.
Terpstra, V., and Yu, C. J., (1988), 'Piggybacking: A Quick Road to Internationalization', *International Marketing Review*, Vol. 7, No. 4, pp. 52–63.

Chapter 4: Strategic groups, multi-market contact, and the decision to franchise

Acheson, D., and Paul, R., (1990), *Franchising, Business Briefing*, Institute of Chartered Accountants in England & Wales, London.
Achrol, R. S., (1996), 'The Franchise as a Network Organization', Proceedings of the 10th Society of Franchising, Partners for Progress . . . A World of Opportunities, Honolulu, Hawaii, 17–18 February.
Axelrod, R., (1984), *The Evolution of Cooperation*, Basic Books, New York
Balakrishnan, S., and Fox, I., (1993), 'Asset Specificity, Firm Heterogeneity and Capital Structure', *Strategic Management Journal*, Vol. 14. No. 1, pp. 3–16.
Ball, S., Black, A. D., and West, A., (1988), *Britain's Fast Food Industry*, Jordans & Sons Ltd, Bristol, UK.
Baucus, D. A., Baucus, M. S., and Human, S. E., (1993), 'Choosing A Franchise: How Base Fees and Royalties Relate to the Value of the Franchise', *Journal of Small Business Management*, Vol. 31, April, No. 2, pp. 91–104.
Barnett, W. P., (1993), 'Strategic Deterence Among Multipoint Competitors', *Industrial and Corporate Change*, Vol. 2, No. 1, pp. 249–278.
Barney, J. B., and Hoskisson, R. E., (1990), 'Strategic Groups: Unntested Assertions and Research Proposals', *Managerial and Decision Economics*, Vol. 11, pp. 187–198.
Beard, D. W., and Dess, G. G., (1981), 'Corporate Level Strategy, Business and Level Strategy, and Firm Performance', *Academy of Management Journal*, December, pp. 663–688.
Becker, B., (1992), 'Philadephia's Luxury Hotels: Boom or Bust?' *Cornell Hotel and Restaurant Association Quarterly*, April, pp. 33–42.
Bernheim, B., and Whinston, M. D., (1991), 'Multimarket Contact and Collusive Behaviour', *RAND Journal of Economics*, Vol. 21, No. 1, pp. 1–26.
Boas, M., and Chain, S., (1976), *Big Mac: The Unauthorized Story of McDonald's*, E. P. Dutton & Co., Inc., New York.
Boe, K. L., Ginalski, W., and Henward III, D. M., (1987), *The Franchise Option: How to Expand Your Business Through Franchising*, International Franchise Association, Washington.
Bognor, W. C., Thomas, H., and McGee, J., (1996), 'A Longitudinal Study of the Competitive Positions and Entry Paths of European Firms in the U. S. Pharmaceutical Market', *Strategic Management Journal*, Vol. 17, pp. 85–108.
Boston Consulting Group, (1975), *The British Motorcycle Industry*, Boston Consulting Group, Boston.
Bourgeois, L. J., (1980), 'Performance and Consensus', *Strategic Management Journal*, Vol. 1, pp. 227–248.
Bresser, R. K., (1988), 'Matching Collective and Competitive Strategies', *Strategic Management Journal*, Vol. 9, pp. 375–385.
Brooks, G. R., (1995), 'Defining Market Boundaries', *Strategic Management Journal*, Vol. 16, pp. 535–549.
Brown, S., (1989), 'Retail Location Theory: The Legacy of Harold Hotelling', *Journal of Retailing*, Vol. 65, pp. 450–469.
Burgers, W. P., Hill, C. W. L., and Kim, C. K., (1993), 'A Theory of Global Strategic Alliances: The Case of the Global Auto Industry', *Strategic Management Journal*, Vol. 14, pp. 416–432.
Buzzell, R. D., and Gale, B. T., (1987), *The PIMS Principles: Linking Strategy to Performance*, Free Press, New York.
Carney, M., and Gedajlovic, E., (1991), 'Vertical Integration in Franchise Systems: Agency Theory and Resource Explanations', *Strategic Management Journal*, Vol. 12, No. 8, November pp. 607–629.
Carpenter, G. S., Glazer, R., and Nakamoto, K., (1994), 'Meaningful Brands from Meaningless Differentiation: The Dependence of Irrelevant Attributes', *Journal of Marketing Research*, Vol. XXXI, pp. 339–351.
Carrol, C., Lewis, P. M., and Thomas, H., (1992), 'Developing Competitive Strategies in Retailing', *Long Range Planning*, Vol. 25, April, pp. 81–88.

Carroll, G. R., and Swaminathan, A., (1992), 'The Organizational Ecology of Strategic Groups in the American Brewing Industry from 1975–1990', *Industrial and Corporate Change*, Vol. 1, No. 1, pp. 65–97.

Carroll, G. R., and Wade, J., (1991), 'Density Dependence in the Organizational Evolution of the American Brewing Industry across Different Levels of Analysis', *Social Science Research*, Vol. 20, pp. 271–302.

Caves, R. E., and Porter, M. E., (1977), 'From Entry Barriers to Mobility Barriers: Conjectural Decisions and Contrieved Deterence to New Entrants', *Quarterly Journal of Economics*, Vol., 91, pp. 241–261.

Caves, R. E., (1984), 'Economic Analysis and the Quest for Competitive Advantage', *American Economic Review*, pp. 127–132.

Caves, R. E., and Ghemawat, P., (1992), 'Identifying Mobility Barriers', *Strategic Management Journal*, Vol. 13, No. 1, pp. 1–12.

Chamberlain, E. H., (1956), *The Theory of Monopolistic Competition*, Harvard University Press, Cambridge, Massachusetts.

Cherkasky, W. B., (1996), 'Franchising: a key to business success', *Franchising Research: An International Journal*, Vol. 1, No. 3, pp. 5–8.

Clarke, R. N., (1989), 'SICs as Delineators of Economic Markets', *Journal of Business*, Vol. 62, pp. 17–31.

Claus, R. J., and Hardwick, W. G., (1972), *The Mobile Consumer: Automobile-Orientated Retailing and Site Selection*, Collier-MacMillan Canada Ltd., Don Mills, Ontario.

Collis, D. J., (1991), 'A Resource-based Analysis of Global Competition: The Case of the Bearings Industry', *Strategic Management Journal*, Vol. 12, Special Issue, Summer, pp. 37–68.

Combs, J. G., and Castrogiovanni, G. J., (1994), 'Franchisor Strategy: A Proposed Model and Empirical Test of Franchisee versus Company-ownership', *Journal of Small Business Management*, Vol. 32, No. 2, pp. 37–48.

Cool, K., and Schendel, D., (1987), 'Strategic Group Formation and Performance: US Pharmaceutical Industry, 1963–1982', *Management Science*, Vol. 33, pp. 1102–24.

Cool, K., and Dierickx, I., (1993), 'Rivalry, Strategic Groups and Firm Profitability', *Strategic Management Journal*, Vol. 14, pp. 47–59.

Cowling, K., and Cubbin, J., (1972) 'Hedonic Price Indexes for UK Cars', *Economic Journal*, Vol. 82, pp. 963–978

Crawford-Welch, S., (1991), 'International Marketing in the Hospitality Industry', pp. 166–193, in Teare, R., and Boer, A., (eds), chapter 11, *Strategic Hospitality Management*, Cassell, London.

Curran, J. G. M., and Goodfellow, J. H., (1989), 'Theoretical and Practical Issues in the Determination of Market Boundaries', *European Journal of Marketing*, Vol. 24, pp. 16–28.

Dant, R. P., (1996), 'Motivations for Franchising: Rhetoric versus Reality', *International Small Business Journal*, Vol. 14, No. 1, pp. 10–32.

Darr, E. D., (1994), *Partner Similarity and Knowledge Transfer in English Franchise Organizations*, Ph.D. dissertation, Carnegie-Mellon University, USA

Desai, P., and Srinivasan, K., (1993), 'Demand Signalling Under Observable Effort in Franchising Linear and Non-Linear Price Contracts', *Working Paper #1058*, March, Krannert Graduate School of Management, Purdue University.

Dodge, H. R., Fullerton, S., and Robbins, J. E., (1994), 'Stage of the Organizational Life Cycle and Competition as Mediators of Problem Perception for Small Businesses', *Strategic Management Journal*, Vol. 15, pp. 121–134.

Dollinger, M. J., (1990), 'The Evolution of Collective Strategies in Fragmented Industries', *Academy of Management Review*, Vol. 15, No. 2, pp. 266–285.

Dooley, R. S., Fowler, D. M., and Miller, A., (1996), 'The Benefits of Strategic Homogeniety and Strategic Heterogeniety: Theoretical and Empirical Evidence Resolving Past Differences', *Strategic Management Journal*, Vol. 17, No. 4, pp. 293–306.

Dow, D., (1993), 'Strategic Group Theory – 20 Years Later: What Do We Know and Where Are We Heading?', University of Melbourne Graduate School of Management, *Working Paper No. 2*, March.

Duke, R., (1991), 'Post-saturation Competition in UK Grocery Retailing', *Journal of Marketing Management*, Vol. 7, pp. 63–75.

Dunning, J. H., and McQueen, M., (1982), 'Multinational Corporations in the International Hotel Industry', *Annals of Tourism Research*, Vol. 9, pp. 69–90.

Dunning, J., and Norman, G., (1987), 'The Location Choices of Offices of International Companies', *Environment and Planning*, Vol. 19, pp. 613–637.

Duysters, G., and Hagedoorn, J. (1995) 'Strategic Groups and Inter-Firm Networks in International High-tech Industries', *Journal of Management Studies*, Vol. 32, No. 3, pp. 359–381.

Eaton, B. C., Lipsey, R. G., (1975), 'The Principle of Minimum Differentiation Reconsidered: Some New Developments in Theory of Spatial Competition', *Review of Economic Studies*, Vol. 42, pp. 27–49.

EIU, (1991), *Competitive Strategies Within the Hotel Industry*, Economist Intelligence Unit, London.

Fellner, W., (1965), *Competition Among the Few; Oligopoly and Similar Market Structures*, Augustus M. Kelly, New York.

Felstead, A. (1993), *The Corporate Paradox – Power and Control in the Business Franchise*, Routledge, London.

Fiegenbaum, A., and Thomas, H., (1990), 'Strategic Groups and Performance: The U. S. Insurance Industry, 1970–84', *Strategic Management Journal*, Vol. 11, pp. 197–215.

Fiegenbaum, A., and Thomas, H., (1995), 'Strategic Groups: Theory, Modeling and Empirical Examination of Industry and Competitive Strategy', *Strategic Management Journal*, Vol. 16, pp. 461–476.

Flowers, E. B., (1976), 'Oligopolistic Reactions in European and Canadian Direct Investment in the US', *Journal of International Business Studies*, Autumn/Winter, pp. 43–55.

Galbraith, C., and Schendel, D., (1983), 'An Empirical Analysis of Strategy Types', *Strategic Management Journal*, Vol. 4, pp. 153–173.

Gal-Or, E., (1991) 'Optimal Franchising in Oligopolistic Markets with Uncertain Demand', *International Journal of Industrial Organization*, Vol. 9, No. 3, pp. 343–364.

Gannon, C. A., (1985), 'Product Differentiation and Locational Competition in Spatial Markets', *International Economic Review*, Vol. 18, No. 2, pp. 293–322.

Gerstenhaber, M., (1995), 'Franchising Calls for the Best of Relations', pp. 32–34 in *Franchise World Directory*, Eleventh Edition, Franchise World Publications, London.

Go, F., (1989) 'International Hotel Industry – Capitalising on Change', *Tourism Management*, September, pp. 195–220.

Gourlay, R., (1994), 'Bring On The Clones', *Financial Times*, 12 April, p. 13.

Green, E. J., and Porter, R. H., (1985), 'Non-Cooperative Collusion under Imperfect Price Information', *Econometrica*, Vol. 52, No. 1, January, pp. 87–100.

Greenhut, M. L., and Ohta, H., (1975), *Theory of Spatial Pricing and Market Areas*, Duke University Press, Durham, North Carolina.

Greiner, L. E., (1972), 'Evolution and Revolution as Organizations Grow', *Harvard Business Review*, Vol. 50, pp. 37–46.

Gulati,R., Khanna, T., and Nohria, N., (1994), 'Unilateral Commitments and the Importance of Process in Alliances', *Sloan Management Review*, Spring, pp. 61–69.

Gultman, J. M., (1996), 'Rational Actors, Tit-for-Tat Types, and the Evolution of Co-operation', *Journal of Economic Behaviour & Organization*, Vol. 29, pp. 27–56.

Hagedoorn, J., (1995), 'A Note on International Market Leaders and Networks of Strategic Technology Partnering', *Strategic Management Journal*, Vol. 16, pp. 241–250.

Hallagan, W., and Joerding, W., (1983), 'Polymorphic Equilibrium in Advertising', *Bell Journal of Economics*, Vol. 14, No. 1, Spring, pp. 191–201.

Hambrick, D. C., (1980), 'Operationalizing the Concept of Business-level Strategy in Research, *Academy of Management Review*, Vol. 5, pp. 567–576.

Hannan, M., and Freeman, J., (1977), 'The Population Ecology of Organizations', *American Journal of Sociology*, Vol. 83, pp. 929–964.

Harrigan, K. R., (1985), 'An Application of Clustering for Strategic Group Analysis', *Strategic Management Journal*, Vol. 6, pp. 55–73.

Hartigan, J., (1975), *Clustering Algorithms*, Wiley-Interscience, New York.

Hatten, K. J., and Hatten, M. L., (1987), 'Strategic Groups, Asymmetrical Mobility Barriers and Contestability', *Strategic Management Journal*, 8, pp. 329–342.

Hatten, K. J., and Schendel, D. E., (1977), 'Hetrogeniety Within an Industry: Firm Conduct in the U. S. Brewing Industry', *Journal of Industrial Economics*, Vol. XXVI, No. 2, pp. 97–113.

Hawes, J. M., and Crittenden, W. F., (1984), 'A Taxonomy of Competitive Retailing Strategies', *Strategic Management Journal*, Vol. 5, pp. 257–287.

Heggestad, A. A., and Rhoades, S. A., (1987), 'Multi-market Interdependence and Local Market Competition in Banking', *Review of Economics and Statistics*, Vol. 60, pp. 523–532.

Heggert, M., (1987), 'Causes and Consequences of Strategic Grouping in U. S. Manufacturing Industries', *International Studies of Management and Organization*, No. 1, pp. 26–49.

Heil, O., and Robertson, T. S., (1991), 'Towards a Theory of Competitive Market Signaling: A Research Agenda', *Strategic Management Journal*, Vol. 12, pp. 403–418.

Higson, C., and Orhnial, A., (1985), 'Towards an Economic Analysis of Franchising', *Discussion Paper in Political Economy*, Kingston Polytechnic, UK.

Hoffman, R. C., and Preble, J. F., (1991), 'Franchising: Selecting a Strategy for Rapid Growth', *Long Range Planning*, Vol. 24, No. 4, pp 74–85.

Hotelling, H., (1929), 'Stability in Competition', *The Economic Journal*, Vol. 39, March, pp. 41–57.

Hunt, M. S., (1972), *Competition in the Major Home Appliance Industry, 1960–1970*, Ph. D. Dissertation, Harvard University.

Hunt, S. D., and Morgan, R. M., (1995), 'The Theory of Comparative Advantage', *Journal of Marketing*, Vol. 59, April, pp. 1–15.

Huszagh, S. M., Huszagh, F., and Franwick, G. L., (1992), 'International Franchising in the Context of Competitive Strategy and the Theory of the Firm', *International Marketing Review*, Vol. 9, No. 5, pp. 5–18.

Jehiel, P., and Moldovanu, B., (1996), 'Strategic Participation', *RAND Journal of Economics*, Vol. 27, No. 1, pp. 84–98.

Jennings, J. J., (1980), 'The Burger Kingdom: Growth and Diffusion of McDonald's in the US, 1965–1978', *Abstracts of the 35th Annual Meeting, Southeastern Division, Association of American Geographics*, Blacksburg, V. A. November 23–25.

Johnson, G., and Thomas, H., (1987), 'The Industry Context of Strategy, Structure and Performance: The UK Brewing Industry', *Strategic Management Journal*, Vol. 8, pp. 343–361.

Justis, R. T., Castrogiovanni, G. J., and Chan, P. S., (1994), 'Franchisor Quick-Start', 1994 Society of Franchising Conference Understanding And Accepting Different Perspectives . . . Empowering Relationships in 1994 And Beyond, Las Vegas, Nevada, 13–14 February.

Kaufman, L., and Rousseuw, P. J., (1990), *Finding Groups in Data: An Introduction to Cluster Analysis*, John Wiley & Sons, New York.

Kaufmann, P. J., (1996), 'The State of Research in Franchising', *Franchising Research: An International Journal*, Vol. 1, No. 1, pp. 4–7.

Kaufmann, P. J., and Stanworth, J., (1995), 'The Decision to Purchase a Franchise: A Study of Prospective Franchisees', *Journal of Small Business Management*, Vol. 33, No. 4. pp. 22–33.

Karnai, A., and Wernerfelt, B., (1985), 'Multiple Joint Competition', *Strategic Management Journal*, Vol. 6, pp. 87–96.

Kerin, R. A., Mahajan, V., and Varadarajan, P. R., (1990), *Contemporary Perspectives on Strategic Market Planning*, Allyn and Bacon, London.

Kerin, R. A., Varadarajan, P. R., and Peterson, R. A., (1992), 'First Mover Advantage: A Synthesis, Conceptual Framework, and Research Propositions', *Journal of Marketing*, Vol. 56, No. 5, pp. 441–458.

Ketchen, D. J., and Shook, C. L., (1996), 'The Application of Cluster Analysis in Strategic Management Research: An Analysis and Critique', *Strategic Management Journal*, Vol. 17, pp. 441–458.

Knickerbocker, F., (1973), *Oligopolistic Reaction and the Multinational Enterprise*, Harvard University Press, Boston, Massachusetts.

Kumar, K. R., Thomas, H., and Fiegenbaum. A., (1990), 'Strategic Groupings as Competitive Benchmarks for Formulating Future Competitive Strategy: A Modelling Approach', *Managerial and Decision Economics*, Vol. 11, pp. 99–109.

Kwoka, Jnr., J. E., (1981), 'Does the Choice of Concentration Really Matter?', *Journal of Industrial Economics*, Vol. XXIX, June, pp. 445–53.

Lafontaine, F., and Shaw, (1996), 'Firm-Specific Effects in Franchise Contracting: Sources and Implications', 1996 Society of Franchising Conference Partners for Progress . . . A World of Opportunities, Honolulu, 17 February.

Lapin, L. L., (1993), *Statistics for Modern Business Decisions*, The Dryden Press, Fort Worth, Texas.

Laulajainen, R., (1987), *Spatial Strategies in Retailing*, D. Reidel Publishing Company, Dorecht, Netherlands.

Lawless, M., Bergh, D., and Wilsted, W., (1989), 'Performance Differences Among Strategic Group Members; An Examination of Individual Firm Capability', *Journal of Management*, pp. 649–661.

Lawless, M. W., and Tegarden, L. K. F., (1990), 'Choice and Determinism: A Reply', *Strategic Management Journal*, Vol. 11, pp. 575–577.

Leontiades, J., (1991), 'Going Global – Global Strategies Versus National Strategies', pp. 67–75, in Freeman, N. J., (ed.), *Strategic Management in Major Multinational Companies; The Best of Long Range Planning*, No. 8, Pergamon Press, London.

Lewis, P., and Thomas, H., (1990), 'The Linkage Between Strategy, Strategic Groups and Performance in the U. K. Retail Grocery Industry', *Strategic Management Journal*, Vol. 1, pp. 385–397.

Li, J., (1994), 'International Expansion Strategy of Service MNCs', *Management International Review*, Vol. 34, No. 3, pp. 217–234.

Litteljohn, D., and Beattie, R., (1991), 'The European Hotel Industry; Corporate Structures and Expansion Strategies', *Tourism Management*, March, pp. 27–33.

Losch, A., (1954), *The Economics of Location*, Yale University Press, New Haven, Connecticut.

Love, J. F., (1986), *McDonald's Behind the Arches*, Bantam Books Inc., New York.

MacMillan, A., (1995), *Aspects of Franchise Recruitment*, Unpublished MBA Dissertation, University of Edinburgh.

Martin, R. E., (1988), 'Franchising and Risk Management', *American Economic Review*, Vol. 78, No. 5, pp. 954–968.

Martin, R. E., (1996), 'The Market for Franchise Opportunities', *Bulletin of Economic Research*, Vol. 48, pp. 97–114.

Mascarenhas, B., and Aaker, D. A., (1989), 'Mobility Barriers and Strategic Groups', *Strategic Management Journal*, Vol. 10, pp. 475–485.

McGahan, A. M., (1991), 'The Emergence of the National Brewing Oligopoly: Competition in the American Market, 1933–1985', *Business History Review*, Vol. 65, pp. 229–284.

McGee, J., (1985), 'Strategic Groups: Review and Prospects', pp. 293–314 in Thomas, H., and Gardner, D. M., (eds), *Strategic Marketing and Management*, John Wiley and Sons, Chichester.

McGhee, J., and Thomas, H., (1986), 'Strategic Groups, Industry Structure and Strategic Management,' *Strategic Management Journal*, Vol. 7, pp. 141–60.

Melaniphy. J., (1992), *Restaurant and Fast Food Site Selection*, Wiley, New York.

Mendelsohn, M., and Acheson, D., (1989), *How to Franchise Your Business*, Franchise World Publications, London.

Mester, L. J., (1987), 'Multiple Market Contact between Savings and Loans', *Journal of Money, Credit and Banking*, Vol. 19, pp. 538–549.

Micheal, S. C., (1996), 'To Franchise or Not to Franchise: An Analysis of Decision Rights and Organizational Share Forms', *Journal of Business Venturing*, Vol. 11, pp. 57–71.

Miles, G., Snow, C. C., and Sharfman, M. P., (1993), 'Industry Variety and Performance', *Strategic Management Journal*, Vol. 14, pp. 163–177.

Miller, K. E., and Ginter, J. L., (1979), 'An Investigation of Situational Variation in Brand Choice Behaviour and Attitude', *Journal of Marketing Research*, Vol. XVI, February, pp. 111–123.

Mitchell, W., (1991), 'Dual Clocks: Entry Order Influences on Incumbent and New Comer Market Share and Survival When Specialized Assets Retain Their Value', *Strategic Management Journal*, 12, pp. 85–100.

Mount, J., Zinger, T., and Forsyth, G. R., (1993), 'Organizing for Development in the Small Business', *Long Range Planning*, Vol. 26, No. 5, pp. 111–120.

Nayyar, P., (1989), 'Research Notes and Communications, Strategic Groups: A Comment', *Strategic Management Journal*, Vol. 10, pp. 101–103.

Nelson, R. R., (1991), 'Why Do Firms Differ, and How Does it Matter?', *Strategic Management Journal*, Vol. 12, Special Issue, Winter, pp. 61–74.

Newman, H. H., (1978), 'Strategic Groups and the Structure/Performance Relationships', *Review of Economics and Statistics*, Vol. 60, pp. 417–427.

Nohria, N., and Garcia-Point, C., (1991), 'Global Strategic Linkages and Industry Structure', *Strategic Management Journal*, Special Issue, Summer, Vol. 12, pp. 105–124.

Norton, S. W., (1988a), 'An Empirical Look at Franchising as an Organizational Form', *Journal of Business*, Vol. 61, No. 2, pp. 197–219.

Norton, S. W., (1988b), 'Franchising, Brand Name, and the Entrepreneurial Capacity Problem', *Strategic Management Journal*, Vol. 9, pp. 105–114.

Oster, S., (1982), 'Intra-industry Structure and the Ease of the Strategic Change', *Review of Economics and Statistics*, August, 376–383.

Peteraf, M. A., (1993a), 'The Cornerstones of Competitive Advantage: A Resource-based View', *Strategic Management Journal*, Vol. 14, No. 3, pp. 179–192.

Perteraf, M. A., (1993b), 'Intra-Industry Structure and the Response Towards Rivals', *Managerial and Decision Economics*, Vol. 14, No. 6, pp. 519–528.

Picton, P., and Harrod, R., (1990), *The Gourmet's Guide to Fish & Chips*, Alan Sutton Publishing Ltd, Stroud, Gloucestershire.

Porac, J. F., Thomas, H., and Emme, B., (1987), 'Knowing the Competition the Mental Models of Retailing Strategists', pp. 59–89 in Johnson, G., (ed.) *Business Strategy and Retailing*, John Wiley & Sons, Chichester.

Porter, M. E., (1979), 'The Structure Within Industries and Companies' Performance', *Review of Economics and Statistics*, Vol. 61, pp. 214–228.

Porter, M. E., (1980), *Competitive Strategy: Techniques for Analysing Industries and Competitors*, Free Press, New York.

Porter, M. E., (1985), *Competitive Advantage: Creating and Sustaining Superior Performance*, Free Press, New York.

Powell, T. C., (1996), 'How Much Does Industry Matter? An Alternative Empirical Test', *Strategic Management Journal*, Vol. 17, pp. 323–334.

Price, S., (1991), *An Analysis of the UK Fast Food market Structure*, Hotel & Catering Research Centre, Huddersfield Polytechnic, UK.

Price, S., (1993), *The UK Fast Food Industry: A Market Analysis*, Cassell, London.

Primeaux, W. J. Jnr., (1985), 'A Method for Determining Strategic Groups and Life Cycles of an Industry', pp. 315–327 in Thomas, H., and Gardner, D. M., (eds), *Strategic Marketing and Management*, John Wiley and Sons, Chichester.

Reed, G. V., Binks, M. R., and Ennew, C. T., (1991), 'Matching the Characteristics of a Service to the Preferences of Customers', *Managerial and Decision Economics*, Vol. 12, No. 3, pp. 231–240.

Reger, R. K., and Huff, A. S., (1993), 'Strategic Groups: A Cognitive Perspective', *Strategic Management Journal*, Vol. 14, pp. 103–124.

Rogers, E., (1995), *Diffusion of Innovations*, Free Press, New York.

Roper, A., (1992), *Hotel Consortia Strategies and Structure: An Analysis of the Emergence of Hotel Consortia as Transorganizational Forms*, Unpublished PhD dissertation, University of Huddersfield, UK.

Rubin, P. H., (1978), 'The Theory of the Firm and the Structure of the Franchise Contract', *Journal of Law and Economics*, Vol. 21, pp. 223–233.

Rumelt, R. P., (1984), 'Towards a Strategic Theory of the Firm', pp. 556–571 in Lamb, R. B., (ed.), *Competitive Strategic Management*, Prentice-Hall, Englewood-Cliffs, New Jersey.

Rumelt, R. P., (1991), 'How Much Does Industry Matter?', *Strategic Management Journal*, Vol. 12, No. 3, pp. 167–186.

Rumelt, R. P., Schendel, D. E., and Teece, D. J., (1994), *Fundamental Issues in Strategy*, Harvard Business School Press, Boston, Massachusetts.

Saloner, G., (1991), 'Modeling, Game Theory, and Strategic Management', *Strategic Management Journal*, Special Issue, Winter, pp. 119–136.

Schulz, D. E., Martin, D., and Brown, W. P., (1984), *Strategic Advertising Campaigns*, National Textbook Company, Chicago.

Scott, J. T., (1982), 'Multi-Market Contact and Economic Performance', *Review of Economics and Statistics*, Vol. 64, pp. 368–375.

Scott, J. T., (1991), 'Multimarket Contact Among Diversified Oligopolists', *International Journal of Industrial Organization*, Vol. 9, pp. 225–228.

Sen, K. C., (1993), 'The Use of Initial Fees and Royalties in Business Format Franchising', *Managerial and Decision Economics*, Vol. 14, pp. 175–190.

Sheperd, W. G., (1972), 'The Elements of Market Structure', *The Review of Economics and Statistics*, pp. 25–35.

Shoenberg, R., Denuelle, N., and Norburn, D., (1995), 'The Minimization of Cultural Differences Within Cross-border Partnerships', *European Business Journal*, Vol. 7, No. 1, pp. 8–16.

Shugman, S. M., (1985), 'Implicit Understandings in Channels of Distribution', *Marketing Science*, Vol. 31, No. 4, pp. 435–460.

Silvester, T., (1996), *Growth Constraints on Young British Franchise Systems*, MBA dissertation, University of Greenwich, London.

Slattery, P., and Johnson, S. M., (1992), *Quoted Hotel Companies: The European markets*, Kleinwort Benson Research, 6th Annual Review, Kleinwort Benson Ltd, London.

Smith, K. G., Grimm, C. M., and Gannon, M. J., (1992), *Dynamics of Competitive Strategy*, Sage Publications, Newbury Park, California.

Spinelli, S., (1996), 'The Pitfalls and Potential of Franchising', Mastering Enterprise, *Financial Times*, December, pp. 8–9.

Stalk, G., (1991), 'Time – The Next Source of Competitive Advantage', pp. 39–60 in Montgomery, C. A., and Porter, M. E., Strategy, *Harvard Business Review*, Boston.

Stewart, H., and Gallagher, C. C., (1986), 'Business Death and Firm Size in the UK', *International Small Business Journal*, Vol. 4, No. 1, pp. 42–57.

Stigler, G. J., (1964), 'A Theory of Oligopoly', *Journal of Political Economy*, February, pp. 44–61.

Tang, M., and Thomas, H., (1992), 'The Concept of Strategic Groups: Theoretical Construct and Analytical Convenience', *Managerial and Decision Economics*, Vol. 13, pp. 323–329.

Terpstra, V., and Yu, C. M., (1988), 'Determinants of Foreign Direct Investment of US Advertising Agencies, *Journal of International Business Studies*, Spring, pp. 33–47.

Thomas, H., and Venkatraman, N., (1988), 'Research on Strategic Groups: Progress and Prognosis', *Journal of Management Studies*, November, pp. 537–555.

Thomas, L. A., (1996), 'Advertising Sunk Costs and Credible Spatial Preemption', *Strategic Management Journal*, Vol. 17, pp. 481–498.

Tremblay, V. J., (1985), 'Strategic Groups and the Demand for Beer', *Journal of Industrial Economics*, December, Vol. XXXIV, No. 2, pp. 183–198.

Wilson, T., and Andrews, P. W. S., (1951), *Oxford Studies in the Price Mechanism*, Oxford University Press, London.

Yoshino, M. Y., and Rangan, U. S., (1995), *Strategic Alliances: An Entrepreneurial Approach to Globalization*, Harvard Business School Press, Boston, Massachusetts.

Zajac, E. J., and Jones, G. R., (1989), *Strategic Groups and Intra-Industry Co-ordination*, Unpublished Paper, Kellogg Graduate School of Management, North-western University, Evanston, Illinois.

Zeithaml, V. A., Berry, L. L., and Parasuraman, A., (1988), 'Communication and Control Processes in the Delivery of Service Quality', *Journal of Marketing*, Vol. 52, April, pp. 35–48.

Zeller, R. E., Achabal, D. D., and Brown, L. A., (1980), 'Market Penetration and Locational Conflict in Franchise Systems', *Decision Sciences*, Vol. 80, pp. 58–80.

Ziv, A., (1993), 'Information Sharing in Oligopoly: The Truth-Telling Problem', *RAND Journal of Economics*, Vol. 24, pp. 455–465.

Case Study 6: Quests for competitive advantages in the UK sandwich sector

Amit, R., and Shoemaker, P. J. H., (1993), 'Strategic Assets and Organizational Rent', *Strategic Management Journal*, Vol. 14, pp. 33–46.

Ball, S. D., (1996), 'Fast Food', pp. 172–189, in Jones, P., (ed.), *Introduction to Hospitality Operations*, Cassell, London.

Brooks, G. R., (1995), 'Defining Market Boundaries', *Strategic Management Journal*, Vol. 16, pp. 535–549.

Clarke, R. N., (1989), 'SICs as Delineators of Economic Markets', *Journal of Business*, Vol. 62, pp. 17–31.

Dixon, J., Harrison, M., Arthurs, J., (1995), *1994 UK New Product Activity Report*, Campden & Chorleywood Research Association, Chorleywood, Hampshire.

Kay, J. A., (1993), *Foundations of Corporate Success: How Business Strategies Add Value*, Oxford University Press, Oxford.

Mathur, S. S., (1986), 'How Firms Compete: A New Classification of Generic Strategies', The City University Business School, *Working Paper, No. 81*.

Porter, M. E., (1980), *Competitive Strategy: Techniques for Analysing Industries and Competitors*, Free Press, New York.

Porter, M. E., (1985), *Competitive Advantage: Creating and Sustaining Superior Performance*, Free Press, New York.

Price, S., (1993), *The UK Fast Food Industry: A Market Analysis*, Cassell, London.

Shepherd, J., (1991), 'Entrepreneurial Growth Through Constellations', *Journal of Business Venturing*, Vol. 6, pp. 363–373.

Taylor Nelson/AGB, (1995), *Special Report: Sandwiches Purchased out of Home*, Taylor Nelson, Epsom, UK.

Chapter 5: To franchise or not to franchise?
A careers approach to franchisee purchase decisions

Abell, M., (1989), *The Franchise Option – A Legal Guide*, Waterlow Publishers, London.

Adams, J. N., (1994), 'Franchise Agreements: Avoiding Pitfalls', *Journal of Business Law*, November, pp. 566–573.

Ajzen, I., and Madden, T. J., (1996), 'Prediction of Goal Directed Behaviour, Attitudes, Intentions and Perceived Behavioural Control', *Journal of Experimental Social Psychology*, Vol. 22, pp. 453–474.

Aldrich, H. E., and Zimmer, C., (1986), 'Entrepreneurship Through Social Networks', pp. 3–24 in Sexton, D., and Smiler, R., (eds), *The Art & Science of Entrepreneurship*, Ballinger, New York.

Aldrich, H. E., and Reese, P. R., (1993), 'Does Networking Pay-Off? A Panel Study of Entrepreneurs in the Research Triangle', pp. 325–339 in Churchill N. C., et al (eds), *Frontiers of Entrepreneurial Research*, Babson Entrepreneurship Research Conference, Babson Park, Massachusetts.

Arendorff, P. A., (1986), 'Denmark: Franchising and Employment Contracts', *Journal of International and Distribution Law*, Vol. 1, No. 2, December.

Argenti, J., (1976), *Corporate Collapse: The Causes and Symptoms*, McGraw-Hill, London.

Arthur, M. B., Hall, D. T., and Lawrence, B. S., (eds), (1989), *Handbook of Career Theory*, Cambridge University Press, Cambridge, Massachusetts.

Ashforth, B. E., and Saks, A. M., (1995), 'Work-role transitions: A Longitudinal Examination of the Nicholson model', *Journal of Occupational and Organizational Psychology*, Vol. 68, pp. 157–175.

Ayling, D., (1988), 'Franchising in the UK', *The Quarterly Review of Marketing*, Vol. 13, Summer, pp. 19–24.

Ayree, S., Chay, Y. W., and Chew, J., (1994), 'An Investigation of the Predictors and Outcomes of Career Commitment in Three Career Stages', Vol. 44, *Journal of Vocational Behaviour*, pp. 1–16.

Baillieu, D., (1988), *Streetwise Franchising*, Hutchison Business, London.

Bailyn, L., (1977), 'Involvement and Accomodation in Technical Careers: An Enquiry in Relation to Work and Mid-Career'. In Van Meanen, J., (ed.), *Organizational Careers: Some New Perspectives*, John Wiley & Sons, Chichester.

Bandura, A., (1986), *Social Foundations of Thought and Action: A Social Cognitive Theory*, Prentice Hall, Englewood Cliffs, New Jersey.

Barber, A. E., Daly, C. L., Giannantonio, C. M., and Philips, J. M., (1994), 'Job Search Activities: An Examination of Changes over Time', *Personnel Psychology*, Vol. 47, pp. 739–765.

Bar-Hayini, A., and Berman, G., (1992), 'The Dimensions of Organizational Commitment', *Journal of Organizational Behaviour*, Vol. 13, pp. 379–387.

Baron, S. R., and Schmidt, R. A., (1991), 'Operational Aspects of Retail Franchises', *International Journal of Retail & Distribution*, Vol. 19, No. 2, pp. 13–19.

Barron, R. D., and Norris, G. M., (1977), 'Sexual Divisions in the Labour Market', pp. 47–69 in Barker, D. L., and Allen, S., (eds), *Dependence and Exploration in Work and Marriage*, Longman, London.

Baucus, D. A., Baucus, M. S., and Human, S. E., (1993), 'Choosing A Franchise: How Base Fees and Royalties Relate to the Value of the Franchise', *Journal of Small Business Management*, Vol. 31, April, No. 2, pp. 91–104.

Baucus, D. A., and Human, S. E., (1994), 'Second-Career Entrepreneurs: A Multiple Case Study of Entrepreneurial Processes and Antecedent Variables', *Entrepreneurship, Theory & Practice*, Winter, pp. 41–53.

Bevan, J., Clark, G., Ganerji, N., and Hakim, C., (1989), *Barriers to Business Start-ups: A Study of the Flow Into and Out of Self-employment*, Research Paper 71, Department of Employment, London.

Bird, B., (1988), 'Implementing Entrepreneurial Ideas: The Case for Intention', *Academy of Management Review*, Vol. 13, No. 3, pp. 442–453.

Blau, G. J., (1985), 'The Measurement and Prediction of Career Commitment', *Journal of Occupational Psychology*, Vol. 58, pp. 277–288.

Blau, G. J., (1988), 'Further Exploring the Meaning and the Measurement of Career Commitment', *Journal of Vocational Behaviour*, Vol. 32, pp. 284–297.

Blau, G. J., (1993), 'Work Adjustment Theory: A Critique and Suggestions for Future Research and Applications', *Journal of Vocational Behaviour*, Vol. 42, pp. 105–122.

Blau, G. J., Paul, A., and St. John, N., (1993), 'On Developing a General Index of Work Commitment', *Journal of Vocational Behaviour*, Vol. 42, pp. 298–314.

Blustein, D. L., Pauling, M. L., De Mania, M. E., and Faye, M., (1994), 'Relation Between Exploratory and Choice Factors and Decisional Progress', *Journal of Vocational Behaviour*, Vol. 44, pp. 75–90.

Borjas, G. J., (1995), 'Ethnicity, Neighborhoods, and Human-Capital Externalities', *American Economic Review*, Vol. 85, No. 3, pp. 365–390.

Boyle, E., (1994), 'The Rise of the Reluctant Entrepreneurs', *International Small Business Journal*, Vol. 12, No. 2, pp. 63–69.

Braverman, H., (1974), *Labor and Monopoly Capital: The Degradation of Work in the Twentieth Century*, Monthly Review Press, New York.

Brown, H., (1969), *Franchising: Trap for the Trusting*, Little Brown & Company, Boston, Massachusetts.

Brush, C., (1992), 'Marketplace Information Scanning Activities of New Manufacturing Ventures', *Journal of Small Business Management*, Vol. 30, pp. 41–51.

Burt, R. S., (1992), *Structural Holes: The Social Structure of Competition*, Harvard University Press, Cambridge, Massachusetts.

Bush, R. R., Tatham, R. L., and Hair, J. F., (1976), 'Community Location Decisions by Franchisors, a Comparative Analysis', *Journal of Retailing*, Vol. 52, pp. 33–42.

Byrne, D., (1986), *Waiting for Change? Working in Hotel and Catering*, Low Pay Pamphlet No. 42, Low Pay Unit, London.

Carland, J. W., Hoy, F., Boulton, W. R., and Carland, J. C., (1984), 'Differentiating Entrepeneurs from Small Business Owners: A Conceptualization', *Academy of Management Review*, Vol. 9, No. 2, pp. 354–359.

Carlino, W., (1994), 'Denny's NDI Sign Minority Franchising Agreement', *Nations's Restaurant News*, Vol. 28, No. 46, 21 November, p. 7.

Carroll, G. R., and Mosakowski, E., (1987), 'The Career Dynamics of Self-Employment', *Administrative Science Quarterly*, Vol. 32, pp. 570–589.

Carroll, G. R., and Teo, A. C., (1996), 'On the Social Networks of Managers', *Academy of Management Journal*, Vol. 39, pp. 271–302.

Cohen, A., (1991), 'Career Stage as a Moderator of Relationships between Organizational Commitment and its Outcomes: A Meta-Analysis', *Journal of Occupational Psychology*, Vol. 64, pp. 253–268.

Chay, Y. W., (1993), 'Social Support, Individual Differences and Well-being: A Study of Small Business Entrepreneurs and Employees', *Journal of Occupational Psychology*, Vol. 66, pp. 285–303.

Crawford-Welch, S., (1991), 'International Marketing in theHospitality Industry', in chapter 11, pp. 166–193, Teare, R., and Boer, A., (eds,) *Strategic Hospitality Management*, Cassell, London.

Dant, R. P., Brush, C. G., and Iniesta, F. I., (1996), 'Participation Patterns of Women in Franchising', *Journal of Small Business Management*, Vol. 34, No. 2, pp. 14–28.

Department of Employment (1992), *Attitudes to Part-time Employment: A Report on Qualitative Research*, Department of Employment, London.

Dubini, P., and Aldrich, H., (1991), 'Personal and Extended Networks are Central to the Entrepreneurial Process', *Journal of Business Venturing*, Vol. 6, pp. 305–313.

English, W., and Hoy, F., (1995), 'Are Franchisees Actually Entrepreneurs?', 1995 Society of Franchising Conference,Partners for Progress . . . A World of Opportunities, Honolulu, Hawaii, 17–18 February.

English, W., and Xau, C., (1994), 'Franchising in China: A Look at KFC and McDonald's', 1994 Society of Franchising Conference, Understanding And Accepting Different Perspectives . . . Empowering Relationships in 1994 And Beyond, Las Vegas, Nevada, 13–14 February.

Epperlein, P. M., (1987), *The Career Development and Career Aspirations of Hotel and Catering Students at The University of Surrey*, Department of Management Studies, University of Surrey.

Evetts, J., (1992), 'Dimensions of Careers: Avoiding Reification in the Analysis of Change', *Sociology*, Vol. 26, pp. 1–21.

Farrell, K., (1984), 'Franchise Prototypes', *Venture*, January, pp. 38–43.

Felstead, A., (1991), 'The Social Organization of the Franchise: A Case of 'Controlled Self-Employment', *Work, Employment and Society*, Vol. 110, No. 5, May, pp. 17–23.

Felstead, A. (1993), *The Corporate Paradox – Power and Control in the Business Franchise*, Routledge, London.

Foss, L., (1993), 'Resources, Networks, and Entrepreneurship: A survey of 153 starters and 84 non-starters in the Cod Farming industry in Norway', pp. 355–367, in Churchill N. C., et al, (eds), *Frontiers of Entrepreneurial Research*, Babson Entrepreneurship Research Conference.

Fulop, J. C., (1996), *An Investigation of the Needs and Attitudes of the Franchise Marketplace*, Centre for Franchise Research, City University Business School, London.

Fukuyama, F., (1995), *Trust: The Social Virtues and the Creation of Prosperity*, Hamish Hamilton, London.

Furlong, A., Biggart, C., and Cartmel, F., (1996), 'Neighbourhoods, Opportunity Structures, and Occupational Aspirations', *Sociology*, Vol. 30, pp. 551–565.

Ghoshal, S., and Westney, D. E., (1991), 'Organizing Competitor Analysis Systems,' *Strategic Management Journal*, Vol. 12, pp. 17–32.

Granovetter, M. S., (1974), *Getting A Job*, Harvard University Press, Cambridge, Massachussets.

Greenhaus, J. H., and Bentall, N. J., (1985), 'Sources of Conflict between Work an Family Roles', *Academy of Management Review*, Vol. 10, No. 1, pp. 76–88.

Guerrier, Y., (1986), 'Hotel Manager – An Unsuitable Job for a Woman?', *The Service Industries Journal*, Vol. 6, No. 2, pp. 227–240.

Gunz, H., (1989), 'The Dual Meaning of Managerial Careers: Organizational and Individual Levels of Analysis', *Journal of Management Studies*, Vol. 26, No. 3, pp. 225– 250.

Hall, D. T., (1976), *Careers in Organizations*, Goodyear, New York.

Hall, P., and Dixon, R., (1989), *Franchising*, NatWest Small Business Bookshelf, Pitman Publishing, London.

Hatcliffe, M., Mills, V., Purdy, D., and Stanworth, J., (1995), 'Prospective Franchisees', Lloyds Bank, IFRC Franchising in Britain Report, Vol. 1, No. 1, University of Westminster.

Haveman, H. A., and Cohen, L. E., (1994), 'The Ecological Dynamics of Careers: The Impact of Organizational Founding, Dissolution, and Merger on Job Mobility', *American Journal of Sociology*, Vol. 100, No. 1, pp. 104–152.

Hewitt, C. M., (1964), 'The Furore Over Dealer Franchises', pp. 274–270, in Hollander, S. C., (ed.), *Exploration in Retailing*, Michigan State University, East Lansing, Michigan.

Hing, N., (1995), 'Franchisee Satisfaction: Contributors and Consequences', *Journal of Small Business Management*, Vol. 33, No. 2, April, pp. 12–25.

Hisrich, R. D., and Peters, M. P., (1989), *Entrepreneurship: Starting, Developing, and Managing a New Enterprise*, Irwin, Homewood, Illinois.

Hough, J., (1986), *Power and Authority and their Consequences in Franchise Organizations: A Study of the Relationships between Franchisors and Franchisees*, Unpublished PhD thesis, Faculty of Management Studies, Polytechnic of Central London, London.

Housden, J., (1984), *Franchising and Other Business Relationships in Hotel and Catering Industry Services*, Heinemann, London.

Hudson, J., (1987), 'Company Births in Great Britain and Institutional Environment', *International Small Business Journal*, Vol. 6, pp. 57–69.

Hunt, S. D., (1972), The Socio-economic Consequences of the Franchise System of Distribution', *Journal of Marketing*, Vol. 36, pp. 32–38.

Hunt, S. D., and Morgan, R. M., (1995), 'The Theory of Comparative Advantage', *Journal of Marketing*, Vol. 59, April, pp. 1–15.

Izraeli, D., (1972), *Franchising and the Total Distribution System*, Longman, London.

Jones, R. T., (1992), 'Ethnic Business and the Post-Fordist Entrepreneurial Renaissance' in Gillingwater, D., and Totterdill, P., (eds), *Prospects for Industrial Policy in the 1990's: the Case of the British Clothing Industry*, Gower, Aldershot.

Katz, J., and Gartner, W. B., (1988), 'Properties of Emerging Organizations', *Academy of Management Review*, Vol. 13, No. 3, pp. 429–441.

Katz, J. A, (1994), 'Modelling Entrepreneurial Career Progressions: Concepts and Considerations', *Entrepreneurship, Theory & Practice*, Winter, Vol. 19, pp. 23–40.

Kaufmann, P. J., and Stanworth, J., (1995), 'The Decision to Purchase a Franchise: A Study of Prospective Franchisees', *Journal of Small Business Management*, Vol. 33, No. 4, pp. 22–23.

Keeble, D., Walker, S., and Robson, M., (1993), *New Firm Foundation and Small Business Growth: Spatial and Temporal Variations and Determinants in the United Kingdom*, Employment and Department Research Series, No. 15, September.

Kelley, J., (1978), 'Wealth and Family Background in the Occupational Career: Theory and Cross-Cultural Data', *British Journal of Sociology*, Vol. 29, pp. 94–109.

Kessler, F., (1957), 'Automobile Dealer Franchises: Vertical Integration by Contract', *Yale Law Journal*, Vol. 66, No. 8, pp. 345–361.

Kleiman, C., (1980), *Women's Networks*, Lippencott & Crowell, New York.

Knight, F. H., (1921), *Risk, Uncertainty and Profit*, Houghton Miffin, New York.

Knight, R. M., (1984), 'The Independence of the Franchise Entrepreneurs', *Journal of Small Business Management*, April, pp. 53–61.

Lafontaine, F., (1992), 'Agency Theory and Franchising: Some Empirical Results', *RAND Journal of Economics*, Vol. 23, No. 2, pp. 263–283.

Layard, R., Nickell, S., and Jackman, R., (1991), *Unemployment: Macroeconomic Performance and the Labour Market*, Oxford University Press, Oxford.

Lipsey, R. G., (1990), *An Introduction to Positive Economics*, Seventh Edition, Weidenfeld and Nicolson, London.

Louis, M. R., (1980), 'Surprise and Sense Making: What Newcomers Experience in Entering Unfamiliar Organizational Settings', *Administrative Science Quarterly*, Vol. 25, pp. 226–251.

Lowe, M. B., and MacMillan, L. C., (1988), 'Entrepreneurship: Past and Future Challenges', *Journal of Management*, Vol. 14, pp. 139–161.

MacKay, D. I., Boddy, D., Brack, J., Diack, J. A., and Jones, N., (1971), *Labour Markets Under Different Employment Conditions*, University of Glasgow Social and Economic Studies, No. 22, George Allen and Unwin, London.

MacMillan, A., (1995), *Aspects of Franchise Recruitment*, Unpublished MBA Dissertation, University of Edinburgh.

MacMillan, A., (1996), *Aspects of Franchise Recruitment*, International Franchise Research Centre, Special Studies Series No. 8, February.

Mannheim, K., (1936), *Ideology and Utopia*, Harcourt, Brace and World, New York, quoted in Morgan, G., 'Paradigms, Metaphors, and Puzzle Solving in Organization Theory', pp. 81–99 in Henry, J., (ed.), *Creative Management*, Sage Publications Ltd, London.

March, J. G., and Simon, H. A., (1958), *Organizations*, John Wiley and Sons Inc., London.

McDowell, L., (1989), 'Gender Divisions', pp. 159–198 in Hamnett, C., McDowell, L., and Sarre, P., (eds), *The Changing Social Structure*, Sage Publications Ltd, London.

McEwan, J., (1983), 'Cultural Forms and Social Processes: the pub as a Social and Cultural institution', in Tomlinson, A., (ed.), *Leisure and Popular Cultural Forms*, Brighton Polytechnic, Eastbourne, UK.

McGuire, E. P., (1971), 'The Feasibility of Minority-Group Capitalism Through Franchising,' pp. 81–96 in Thompson, D. N., (ed.), *Contractual Marketing Systems*, Heath Lexington Books, Lexington, Massachusetts.

Melmed, T., (1996), 'Career Success: An Assessment of a Gender Specific Model', *Journal of Occupational and Organizational Psychology*, Vol. 69, pp. 217–242.

Mihal, W. L., Sorce, P. A., and Comte, T. E., (1984), 'A Process Model of Individual Career Decision-Making', *Academy of Management Review*, Vol. 19, No. 1, pp. 95–103.

Morrow, P., (1983), 'Concept Redundancy in Organizational Research: The Case of Work Commitment', *Academy of Management Review*, Vol. 8, pp. 486–500.

Murphy, C. J., (1995), 'A Comparison Between African-American Franchise and Non-Franchise Entrepreneurs in Terms of Enhancement and Support Strategies', The International Challenge . . . Towards New Franchising Relationships, Proceedings of the 9th Conference of The Society of Franchising, Puerto Rico, 21–22 January.

National Westminster Bank/British Franchise Association, (1996), *Survey 1996*, British Franchise Association, London.

Neumark, D., Bank, R. J., and Van Nort, K. D., (1996), 'Sex Discrimination in Restaurant Hiring: An Audit Study', *Quarterly Journal of Economics*, Vol. CXI, pp. 915–942.

Nicholl, C. C., (1995), 'Does Termination of a Franchise of Indefinite Duration Require 'Judicial Legislation'?', *Journal of Business Law*, September, pp. 472–489.

Nicholson, N., (1984), 'A Theory of Work Role Transitions', *Administrative Science Quarterly*, Vol. 14, No. 2, pp. 172–191.

Noe, R. A., and Barber, A. E., (1993), 'Willingness to Accept Mobility Opportunities: Destination Makes A Difference', *Journal of Organizational Behaviour*, Vol. 14, pp. 159–175.

O'Connell-Davidson, J., (1994), 'What Do Franchisors Do? Control and Commercialization in Milk Distribution', *Work Employment & Society*, Vol. 8, No. 1, pp. 23–44.

Office of Population Censuses and Surveys (1991), *Labour Force Survey*, HSMO, London.

Olm, K. W., Eddy, G. G., and Adamaya, A. R., (1988), 'Selecting Franchisee Prospects', 1988 Society of Franchising Conference, Forging Partnerships for Competitive Advantage, San Francisco, California, 31 January–2 February.

Orstein, S., and Isabella, L. A., (1993), 'Making Sense of Careers: A Review 1989–1992', *Journal of Management*, Vol. 19, No. 2, pp. 243–267.

Osborn, D., (1990), 'A Re-examination of the Organizational Choice Process', *Journal of Vocational Behaviour*, Vol. 36, pp. 328–333.

Osborne, R. L., (1991), 'The Dark Side of the Entrepreneur', *Long Range Planning*, Vol. 24, No. 3, pp. 26–31.

Ostagaard, T. A., and Birley, S., (1994), 'Personal Networks and Firm Competitive Strategy – a Strategic or Coincidental Match?', *Journal of Business Venturing*, Vol. 9, pp. 281–305.

Ozanne, U. B., and Hunt, S. D., (1971), *The Economic Effects of Franchising*, Report Prepared for the Small Business Administration and Select Committee on Small Business, US Senate, September, Graduate School of Business, University of Wisconsin.

Page, H., (1996), 'What it's Really like to be a Franchisee', *Entrepreneur*, pp. 185–186.

Parkin, F., (1971), *Class Inequality and Political Order: Social Stratification in Capitalist and Communist Societies*, Granada Publishing, London.

Peterson, A., and Dant, R., (1990), 'Perceived advantages of the Franchise Option from the Franchise Perspective: Empirical Insights from a Service Franchise', *Journal of Small Business Management*, Vol. 28, No. 3, pp. 46–61.

Prahalad, C. K., and Bettis, R. A., (1986), 'The Dominant Logic: a New Linkage between Diversity and Performance', *Strategic Management Journal*, Vol. 7, pp. 485–501.

Phizacklea, A., and Ram, M., (1996), 'Being Your own Boss: Ethnic Minority Entrepreneurs in Comparative Perspective', *Work, Employment & Society*, Vol. 10, pp. 319–339.

Power, D. J., and Aldag, R. J., (1985), 'Soelberg's Job Search and Choice Model: A Clarification, Review, and Critique', *Academy of Management Review*, Vol. 10, pp. 48–58.

Purdy, D., Stanworth, J., and Hatcliffe, M., (1996), *Franchising in Figures, Franchising in Britain*, Lloyds Banks, & International Franchise Research Centre, Vol. 1, No. 2, University of Westminster.

Ramachandran, K., and Ramnarayanm, S., (1993), 'Entrepreneurial Orientation and Networking: Some Indian Evidence', *Journal of Business Venturing*, Vol. 8, pp. 513–524.

Riley, M., (1984), 'Hotels and Group Identity', *Tourism Management*, June, pp. 102–109.

Royal Bank of Scotland, (1993), *Survey of Franchise Marketplace*, Royal Bank of Scotland, London.

Rubin, E., and Allen, G., (1994), *The Franchisng Market in China*, American Embassy, Beijing, China.

Schulz, A., (1988), 'Germany: Are Franchisees Salaried Employees?', *Journal of International and Distribution Law*, Vol. 2, No. 3, March.

Shutt, J., and Whittington, R., (1986), 'Large Firm Strategies and the Rise of Small Units', in Faulker, T., Beaver, G., Lewis, J., and Gobb, A., (eds), *Readings in Small Business*, Gover, Aldershot.

Silvester, T., (1996), *Growth Constraints on Young British Franchise Systems*, MBA dissertation, University of Greenwich, London.

Sklar, F., (1977), 'Franchises and Independence: Interorganizational Power Relations in a Contractual Context', *Urban Studies*, Vol. 6, No. 1.

Snipp, C. M., (1985), 'Working-class Differentiation and Men's Career Mobility', *British Journal of Sociology*, Vol. 34, pp. 354–382.

Soelberg, P., (1967), 'Unprogrammed Decision Making', *Industrial Management Review*, Vol. 8, pp. 19–29.

Stanworth, J., (1991), 'Franchising and the Franchise Relationships in the European Community', in chapter 5, Abell, M., (ed.), *European Franchising: Law and Practice in the European Community*, Vol. 1, Waterlow Publishers, London.

Stanworth, J., (1994), *The Impact of Franchising on the Development Prospects of Small and Medium-sized Enterprises (SMEs) in the United Kingdom*, Report prepared for the Department of Trade and Industry, London.

Stanworth, J. and Kanfmann, P. J., (1994), 'Towards a Dynamic Model of Franchise Motivational', Society of Franchising Conference, Understanding and Accepting different perspectives . . . Experiencing Relationships in 1994 and Beyond, Las Vegas, 13 February.

Stanworth, J., and Purdy, D., (1993), *The Blenheim/University of Westminster Franchise Guide: Spring 1993*, International Franchise Research Centre, Special Studies Series, No. 1, September, University of Westminster.

Stead, G. B., Watson, M. B., and Foxcroft, C. D., (1993), 'The Relation Between Career Indecision and Irrational Beliefs Among University Students', *Journal of Business Behaviour*, Vol. 42, pp. 155–169.

Swartz, L. N., (1995), *Worldwide Franchising Statistics: A Study of Worldwide Franchise Associations*, Arthur Andersen in cooperation with the World Franchising Council, Chicago, Illinios.

Taylor, D., (1977), *Fortune, Fame & Folly: British Hotels and Catering from 1878 to 1978*, Chapel River Press, Andover, Hants, UK.

Vivarelli, M., (1991), 'The Birth of New Enterprises', *Small Business Economics*, Vol. 3, pp. 215–223.

Washer, L., (1994), 'The Best Business-to-Business Franchises', *Business Franchise*, Vol. 19, No. 11, pp. 48–52.

Waldinger, R., Ward, R., and Aldrich, H., (1985), 'Ethnic Business and Occupational Mobility in Advanced Societies', *Sociology*, Vol. 19, No. 4, pp 586–597.

Wattel, H., (1969), 'Are Franchisors Realistic and Successful in their Selection of Franchisees?', *Journal of Retailing*, Vol. 44, No. 4, pp. 54–68.

Weening, M. W. H., and Midden, C. J. H., (1991), 'Communication Network Influences on Information Diffusion and Persuasion', *Journal of Personality and Social Psychology*, Vol. 61, pp. 734–742.

West, M., and Rushton, R., (1989), 'Mismatches in Work-Role Transition', *Journal of Occupational Psychology*, Vol. 62, pp. 271–286.

Willis, P., (1977), *Learning to Labour: Why working class kids get working class jobs*, Gower, Aldershot.

Wilson, P., (1984), 'Black Business in Britain: a survey of Afro-Caribbean businesses in Brent', pp. 125–156 in Lewis, J., Stanworth, J., and Gibb, A., (eds) *Success and Failure in Small Business*, Gower, Aldershot.

Van Maanen, J., Schein, E. H., (1979), 'Toward A Theory of Organizational Socialization', pp. 209–264 in Staw, B., (ed.), *Research in Organizational Behaviour*, JAI Press, Greenwich Connecticut.

Zeithamal, V. A., Berry, L. L., and Parasurman, A., (1988), 'Communication and Control Processes in the Delivery of Service Quality', *Journal of Marketing*, Vol. 52, April, pp. 35–48.

Chapter 6: Types and sources of innovation in franchising

Abernathy, W. J., and Utterback, J. L., (1978), 'Patterns of Industrial Innovation', *Technology Review*, June/July, pp. 41–47.

Acheson, D., (1995), 'The Big Balancing Act – Fixing the Initial and On-going Fees', pp. 81–84 in *Franchise World Directory*, Eleventh Edition, Franchise World Publications, London.

Achrol, R. S., Reve, T., and Stern, L. W., (1983), 'The Environment of Marketing Channel Dyads: A Framework for Comparative Analysis', *Journal of Marketing*, Vol. 47, Autumn, pp. 55–67.

Achrol, R. S., and Stern, L. W., (1988), 'Environmental Determinants of Decision-Making Uncertainty in Marketing Channels', *Journal of Marketing Research*, Vol. XXV, February, pp. 36–50.

Afuah, A. N., and Bahram, N., (1995), 'The Hypercube of Innovation', *Research Policy*, Vol. 24, pp. 51–76.

Amit, R., and Shoemaker, P. J. H., (1993), 'Strategic Assets and Organizational Rent', *Strategic Management Journal*, Vol. 14, pp. 33–46.

Anand, P., (1987), 'Inducing Franchisees to Relinquish Control: An Attribution Analysis', *Journal of Marketing Research*, Vol. XXIV, May, pp. 215–221.

Anand, P., and Stern, L. W., (1985), 'A Sociopsychological Explanation for Why Marketing Channel Members Relinquish Control', *Journal of Marketing Research*, Vol. XXII, November, pp. 365–376.

Atuahene-Gima, K., (1993), 'Relative Importance of Firm and Managerial Influences on International Technology Licensing Behaviour', *International Marketing Review*, Vol. 10, No. 2., pp 4–21.

Ayling, D., (1987), 'Franchising has its Dark side', *Accountancy*, February, pp. 113.

Bailetti, A. J., and Callahan, J. R., (1993), 'The Co-ordination Structure of International Collaborative Technology Agreements', *R&D Management*, Vol. 23, No. 2, pp. 129–146.

Barney, J. B., and Ouchi, W. G., (1986), *Organizational Economics*, Jossey-Bass, San Francisco, California.

Bartlett, C. A., and Ghoshal, B., (1991), 'Tap Your Subsidiaries for Global Reach', pp. 171–188 in Montgomery, C. A., and Porter, M. E., (eds), *Strategy: Seeking and Securing Competitive Advantage*, Harvard Business School Publishing, Boston, Massachusetts.

Bateson, G., (1973), *Steps To An Ecology of Mind*, Paladin, St Albans, UK.

Baucus, D. A., Baucus, M. S., and Human, S. E., (1996), 'Consensus in Franchise Organizations: A Co-operative Arrangement Among Entrepreneurs', *Journal of Business Venturing*, Vol. 11, pp. 359–378.

Baum, C., (1995), 'Beefing Up Security', *Security*, Vol. 32, No. 9, September, pp. 18–19.

Barreye P. Y., (1988), 'The Concept of 'Impartition' Policies: A Different Approach to Vertical Integration', *Strategic Management Journal*, Vol. 9, pp. 507–520.

Belussi, F. (1989), 'Benetton: A Case of Corporate Strategy for Innovation in Traditional Sectors', pp. 116–133, in Dodgson, M., (ed.), *Technology Strategy and the Firm: Management and Public Policy*, Longman, Harlow, England.

Bergen, M., Dutta, S., and Wlaker, O. C. Jr., (1992), 'Agency Relationships in Marketing: A Review of the Implications and Applications of Agency and Related Theories', *Journal of Marketing*, Vol. 56, July, pp. 1–24.

Bidault, F., and Cummings, T., (1994), 'Innovating Through Alliances: Expectations and Limitations', *R&D Management*, Vol. 24, No. 1, pp. 33–45.

Birley, S., and Westhead, P., (1990), 'Growth and Performance Contrasts between 'Types' of Small Firms', *Strategic Management Journal*, Vol. 11, pp 535–557.

Booz, Allen and Hamilton, (1982), *New Products Management for the 1980s – Phase II*, Chicago, Illinois.

Borch, O. J., and Huse, M., (1993), 'Informal Strategic Networks and the Board of Directors', *Entrepreneurship, Theory and Practice*, Vol. 18, No. 1, Autumn, pp. 23–35.

Bourgeois, L. J., (1981), 'On the Measurement of Organizational Slack', *Academy of Management Review*, Vol. 6, pp. 29–39.

Boyd, B. K., (1990), 'Corporate Linkages and Organizational Environment: A Test of the Resource Dependence Model', *Strategic Management Journal*, Vol. 11, pp. 419–430.

Bradach, J. L., (1994), 'Chains within Chains: The Role of Multi-unit Franchisees', 1994 Society of Franchising Conference, Understanding And Accepting Different Perspectives . . . Empowering Relationships in 1994 And Beyond, Las Vegas, Nevada, 13–14 February.

Bradach, J. L., and Eccles, R. G., (1989), 'Price, Authority and Trust: From Ideal Types to Plural Forms', *Annual Review of Sociology*, Vol. 15, pp. 97–118.

Braverman, H., (1974), *Labor and Monopoly Capital: The Degradation of Work in the Twentieth Century*, Monthly Review Press, New York.

Breaugh, J. A., and Billings, R. S., (1988), 'The Realistic Job Preview: Five Key Elements and their Importance for Research and Practice', *Journal of Business and Psychology*, Vol. 2, No. 4, Summer, pp. 291–305.

Brill, J. E., (1994), 'Beyond Managerial Opportunism: Supplier Power and Managerial Compliance in a Franchised Marketing Channel', *Journal of Business Research*, Vol. 30, pp. 211–223.

Brown, R., (1991), 'Managing the 'S' curves of Innovation', *Journal of Marketing Management*, Vol. 7, No. 2, pp. 189–202.

Brown, W. B., (1984), 'Firm-Like Behaviour in Markets: The Administered Channel', *International Journal of Industrial Organization*, Vol. 2, pp. 263–276.

Bucklin (1971), 'The Economic Base of Franchising', pp. 33–62 in Thompson, D. N., (ed.), *Contractual Marketing Systems*, Heath Lexington Books, Lexington, Massachusetts.

Burt, R. S., (1980), 'Autonomy in a Social Topology', *American Journal of Sociology*, Vol. 85, pp. 892–925.

Burt, R. S., (1992), *Structural Holes: The Social Structure of Competition*, Harvard University Press, Cambridge, Massachusetts.

Bush, R. R., Tatham, R. L., and Hair, J. F., (1976), 'Community Location Decisions by Franchisors, a Comparative Analysis', *Journal of Retailing*, Vol. 52, pp. 33–42.

Butler, J. E., Phan, P., and Hansen, G. S., (1992), 'Strategic Alliances Through Interorganizational Networks: A Path to Entrepreneurial Success', pp. 525–537 in in Churchill, N. C. et al (eds), *Frontiers of Entrepreneurship Research*, Babson College Entrepreneurship Research Conference, Babson Park, Massachusetts.

Callahan and Cassar, (1995), 'Small Business Owners' Assessments of Their Abilities to Perform and Interpret Formal Market Studies', *Journal of Small Business Management*, Vol. 33, No. 4, pp. 1–9.

Card, D., and Krueger, A. B., (1994), 'Minimum Wages and Employment: A Case Study of the Fast Food in New Jersey and Pennsylvannia', *American Economic Review*, Vol. 84, No. 4, pp. 772–793.

Carland, J. W., Hoy, F., Boulton, W. R., and Carland, J. C., (1984), 'Differentiating Entrepreneurs from Small Business Owners: A Conceptualization', *Academy of Management Review*, Vol. 9, No. 2, pp. 354–359.

Carney, M., and Gedajlovic, E., (1991), 'Vertical Integration in Franchise Systems: Agency Theory and Resource Explanations', *Strategic Management Journal*, Vol. 12, No. 8, November, pp. 607–629.

Carrol, C., Lewis, P. M., and Thomas, H., (1992), 'Developing Competitive Strategies in Retailing', *Long Range Planning*, Vol. 25, April, pp. 81–88.

Castrogiovanni, G. J., (1991), 'Environmental Munificence: A Theoretical Assessment', *Academy of Management Review*, Vol. 16, No. 3, pp. 542–565.

Castrogiovanni, G. J., Bennett, N., and Combs, J. G. (1995), 'Franchisor Types: Reexamination and Clarification', *Journal of Small Business Management*, Vol. 35, No. 1, pp. 45–55.

Churchill, D., (1991), 'Expansion Routes', Survey, *Financial Times*, 4/5 May.

Cohen, J. S., (1971), 'Conflict and its Resolution in a Franchise System', pp. 175–184 in Thompson, D. N., (ed.), *Contractual Marketing Systems*, Heath Lexington Books, Lexington, Massachusetts.

Cohen, W., and Levinthal, D., (1990), 'Absorptive Capacity: A New Perspective on Learning and Innovation', *Administrative Science Quarterly*, Vol. 35, pp. 128–152.

Collins, T. M., and Doorley III, T. L., (1991), *Teaming Up for the 90s: A Guide to International Joint Ventures and Strategic Alliances*, Business One Irwin, Homewood, Illinois.

Collis, D. J., (1991), 'A Resource-based Analysis of Global Competition: The Case of the Bearing Industry', *Strategic Management Journal*, Vol. 12, Special Issue, Summer, pp. 49–68.

Cyert, R. M., and March, J. G., (1963), *A Behavioural theory of the Firm*, Prentice Hall, Englewood Cliffs, New Jersey.

Daft, R. L., (1978), 'A Dual-Core Model of Organizational Innovation', *Academy of Management Journal*, Vol. 21, No. 2, pp. 193–210.

Dahlman, C., and Westphal, L., (1983), 'The Transfer of Technology-Issues in the Acquisition of Technological Capability by Developing Countries', *Finance & Development*, December.

Damanpour, F., (1991), 'Organizational Innovation: A Meta-Analysis of Effects of Determinants and Moderators', *Academy of Management Journal*, Vol. 34, pp. 555–590.

Dandridge, T., and Falbe, C., (1994), 'The Influence of Franchisees Beyond Their Local Domains', *International Small Business Journal*, Vol. 12, No. 2, pp. 39–49.

Davidson, W. H., and McFetridge, D. G., (1984), 'International Technology Transactions and the Theory of the Firm', *Journal of Industrial Economics*, Vol. XXXII, pp. 253–264.

Davis, S., and Caves, R. E., (1987), *Britain's Productivity Gap*, Cambridge University Press, Cambridge.

Dearing, J. W., (1993), 'Rethinking Technology Transfer', *International Journal of Technology Management*, Special Issues on Industry-University-Government Cooperation, Vol. 8, Nos 6/7/8, pp. 478–485.

Dess, G. G., and Beard, D. W., (1984), 'Dimensions of Organizational Task Environments', *Administrative Science Quarterly*, March, pp. 52–73.

Dewar, R. D., and Dutton, F. T., (1986), 'The Adoption of Radical and Incremental Innovations: An Empirical Analysis', *Management Science*, Vol. 32, pp. 1422–1433.

Dickson, P. R., (1983), 'Channel Dependence Matrix: New Techniques for Understanding and Managing the Channel', *Journal of Marketing*, Vol. 47, Summer, pp. 35–44.

Donaldson, L., (1985), 'Organization Design and the Life-cycles of Products', *Journal of Management Studies*, Vol. 22, No. 1, pp. 25–37.

Doyle, P., (1989), 'Building Successful Brands: The Strategic Options', *Journal of Marketing Management*, Vol. 5, No. 1, pp. 77–95.

Doz, Y., (1988), 'Technology Partnerships between Larger and Smaller Firms: Some Critical Issues,' pp. 317–338 in Contractor, F., and Lorange, P., (eds), *Cooperative Strategies in International Business*, Lexington Books, Massachusetts.

Duke, R., (1991), 'Post-saturation Competition in UK Grocery Retailing', *Journal of Marketing Management*, Vol. 7, pp. 63–75.

Dwyer, F. R., and Welsh, M. A., (1985), 'Environmental Relationships and the Internal Political Economy of Marketing Channels', *Journal of Marketing Research*, Vol. 22, November, pp. 397–414.

Eliashberg, J., and Mitchie, D. A. (1989), 'Multiple Goal Sets as Determinants of Marketing Channel Conflict: An Empirical Study', *Journal of Marketing Research*, Vol. 31, February, pp 75–88.

English, W., (1993), 'Franchising, by Its Proper Name, is Wholesaling!', *Journal of Marketing Channels*, Vol. 2, No. 3, pp. 1–25.

English, W., and Hoy, F., (1995), 'Are Franchisees Actually Entrepreneurs?', 1995 Society of Franchising Conference, Partners for Progress . . . A World of Opportunities, Honolulu, Hawaii, 17–18 February.

Ettlie, J. E., (1983), 'Organizational Policy and Innovation among Suppliers to the Food Processing Sector', *Academy of Management Journal*, Vol. 26, March, pp. 27–44.

Evan, W. M., (1966), 'Organizational Lag', *Human Organization*, Vol. 25, pp. 51–53.

Farjoun, M., (1994), 'Beyond Industry Boundaries: Human Expertise, Diversification and Resource-Related Industry Groups', *Organization Science*, Vol. 5, No. 2, May, pp. 185–199.

Felstead, A. (1993), *The Corporate Paradox – Power and Control in the Business Franchise*, Routledge, London.

Flack, R., (1992), 'Franchisee-Initiated Innovation', pp. 51–52 in Murphy, C. S., and Matusky, G., (eds), *Franchise Relations Handbook*, International Franchise Association, Washington D. C.

Fleming, M. M. K., (1986), 'The Current Ratio Revisited' *Business Horizons*, May–June. pp. 74–77.

Ford, R. C., and Fottler, M. D., (1995), 'Empowerment: A Matter of Degree', *Academy of Management Executive*, Vol. 9, No. 3, pp. 21–29.

Freeman, C. and Perz, C., (1988), 'Structural Crises of Adjustment, Business Cycles and Investment', in Dosi, G., Freeman, C., Nelson, R., Silverberg, G., and Soete, L., (eds), *Technical Change and Economic Theory*, Pinter London.

Freeman, R., (1990), 'Innovation and Growth: Does UK and the City Recognize that Innovation is Essential for Profitable and Sustainable Growth?', Innovation and Short-termism Conference, DTI Innovation and Advisory Board and the Financial Timers, 25 June, London.

Friar, J., and Horwitch, M., (1985), 'The Emergence of Technology Strategy: A New Dimension of Strategic Management', *Technology in Society*, Vol. 7, No. 2/3, pp. 143–78.

Fritz, W., (1989), 'Determinants of Product Innovation Activities', *European Journal of Marketing*, Vol. 23, No. 10, pp. 32–43.

Galunic, C. D., and Eisenhardt, K. M., (1994), 'Renewing the Strategy-Structure-Performance Paradigm', *Research in Organizational Behaviour*, Vol. 16, pp. 215–255.

Garceau, P., (1989), 'Financing a Franchise', *Canadian Banker*, Vol. 96, Vol. 2, Mar/April, pp. 24–29.

Gassenheimer, J. B., Baucus, D. B., and Baucus, M. S., (1996), 'Cooperative Arrangement Among Entrepreneurs: An Analysis of Opportunism and Communication in Franchise Structures', *Journal of Business Research*, Vol. 36, pp. 67–79.

Gedo, J. E., (1990), 'More on Creativity and its Vicissitudes', pp. 35–45, in Runco, M., and Albert, R. M., (eds), *Theories of Creativity*, Sage, Newbury Park, California.

Ghoshal, S., and Nohria, N., (1989), 'Internal Differentiation within Multinational Corporations', *Strategic Management Journal*, Vol. 10, pp. 323–337.

Gold, B., (1981), 'Technological Diffusions in Industry: Research Needs and Shortcomings', *Journal of Industrial Economics*, Vol. 24, No. 3, pp. 247–269.

Goolds, M., Campbell, A., and Alexander, A., (1994), *Corporate-Level Strategy – Creating Value in the Multi-Business Company*, John Wiley & Sons, New York.

Gort, M., and Singamsetti, R., (1987), 'Innovation and the Personality Profiles of Firms', *International Journal of Industrial Organization*, Vol. 5, pp. 115–126.

Greenwood, R., and Hinings, C. R., (1988), 'Organizational Design Types, Tracks and the Dynamics of Strategic Change', *Organization Studies*, Vol. 9, pp. 293–316.

Gripsud, G., and Gronhaug, K., (1985), 'Structure and Strategy in Grocery Retailing: A Sociometric Approach', *Journal of Industrial Economics*, Vol. 33, No. 3, March, pp. 339–347.

Golden, B. R., (1992), 'SBU Strategy and Performance: The Moderating Effects of the Corporate-SBU Relationship', *Strategic Management Journal*, Vol. 13, pp. 145–158.

Grossmann, S. J., and Hart, O. D., (1986), 'The Costs and Benefits of Ownership: A Theory of Vertical and Lateral Integration', *Journal of Political Economy*, Vol. 94, No. 4, pp. 691–719.

Gulati, R., Kharma, T., and Nohria, N., (1994), 'Unilateral Comitments and the Importance of Process in Alliances', *Sloan Management Review*, Spring, pp. 61–70.

Gupta, A. K., and Govindrajan, V., (1991), 'Knowledge Flows and the Structure of Control within Multi-national Corporations', *Academy of Management Review*, Vol. 16, No. 4, pp. 768–792.

Hall, R., (1993), 'A Framework Linking Intangible Resources and Capabilities to Sustainable Competitive Advantage', *Strategic Management Journal*, Vol. 14, pp. 607–618.

Hambrick, D. C., and Geletkanycz, M. C., and Frederickson, J. W., (1993), 'Top Executive Commitments to the Status Quo: Some Tests of its Determinants', *Strategic Management Journal*, Vol. 14, No. 6, pp. 401–418.

Hambrick, D. C., and Mason, D. A., (1984), 'Upper Echelons: The Organization as a Reflection of its Top Managers', *Academy of Management Review*, Vol. 9, No. 2, pp. 687–707.

Hamel, G., (1991), 'Competition for Competence and Inter-Partner Learning within International Strategic Alliances', *Strategic Management Journal*, Vol. 12, Special Issue, pp. 69–82.

Harrigan, K. R., (1980), *Strategies for Declining Businesses*, D. C. Heath, Lexington, Massachussets.

Harrigan, K. R., (1985), *Strategic Flexibility: A Management Guide for Changing Times*, Lexington Books, Lexington, Massachusetts.

Harrigan, K. R., (1988), 'Joint Ventures and Competitive Strategy', *Strategic Management Journal*, Vol. 9, pp. 141–158.

Hauschildt, J., (1992), 'External Acquisition of Knowledge for Innovations – A Research Agenda', *R&D Management*, Vol. 22, No. 2, pp. 105–109.

Hergert, M., and Morris, D., (1988), 'Trends in International Collaborative Agreements', pp. 99–109, in Contractor, F. K., and Lorange, P., (eds), *Co-operative Strategies in International Business*, Lexington Books, Lexington, Massachusetts.

Hofer, C. W., and Schendel, D., (1978), *Strategy Formulation: Analytical Concepts*, West Publishing Co, St Paul, Minnesota.

Horne, J., (1995), 'The Elements of the Franchise Package', pp. 32–35 in *Franchise World Directory*, Eleventh Edition, Franchise World Publications, London.

Hough, J., (1986), *Power and Authority and Their Consequences in Franchise Organizations: A Study of the Relationship between Franchisors and Franchisees*, Unpublished PhD thesis, Faculty of Management Studies, Polytechnic of Central London, London.

Housden, J., (1984), *Franchising and Other Business Relations in Hotel and Catering Industry Services*, Heinemann, London.

Howells, J., (1995), *Tacit Knowledge and Technology Transfer*, ESRC Centre for Business Research, University of Cambridge, Working Paper No. 16, September.

Hrebiniak, L. G., and Joyce, W. F., (1985), 'Organizational Adaptation: Strategic Choice and Environmental Determinism', *Administrative Science Quarterly*, Vol. 30, pp. 336–349.

Hume, S., (1992), 'Fast-Food Chains Cook Up Ways to Improve Service', *Advertising Age*, 8 June, Vol. 63, pp. 3 & 46.

Ireland, R. D., Hitt, M. A., Bettis, R. A., and De Porras, D. A., (1987), 'Strategy Formulation Processes: Differences in Perceptions of Strengths and Weaknesses and Environmental Uncertainty by Managerial Level', *Strategic Management Journal*, Vol. 8, pp. 469–485.

Isenberg, (1987), 'The Tactics of Strategic Opportunism', *Harvard Business Review*, Vol. 65, March–April, pp. 92–97.

James, B. G., (1989), 'Alliances: The New Strategic Focus,' in Lloyd, B., (ed.), 'Entrepreneurship Creating and Managing New Ventures', *The Best of Long Range Planning*, No. 2, Pergamon Press, Oxford.

James, B. G., (1989), *Trojan Horse: The Ultimate Challenge to Western Industry*, Mercury Books, W. H. Allens & Co., London.

Jarillo, J. C., (1993), *Strategic Networks – Creating the Borderless Organization*, Butterworth-Heinemann Ltd, Oxford.

John, G., (1984), 'An Empirical Investigation of Some Antecedents of Opportunism in a Marketing Channel', *Journal of Marketing Research*, Vol. XXI, August, pp. 278–289.

Jones, P., (1988), 'The Impact of Trends in Service Operations on Food Delivery Systems', *International Journal of Operational Production Manufacturing*, Vol. 8, No. 7, pp. 23–30.

Justis, R., and Judd, R., (1989), *Franchising*, South-Western Publishing Co., Cincinnati, Ohio.

Kaufmann, P. J., (1992), 'The Impact of Managerial Performance Decay on Franchisors' Store Allocation Strategies', *Journal of Marketing Channels*, Vol. 1, No. 4, pp. 51–79.

Kaufmann, P. J., and Rangan, V. K., (1990), 'A Model for Managing System Conflict During Franchise Expansion', *Journal of Retailing*, Vol. 66, pp. 155–173.

Kay, J. A., (1993), *Foundations of Corporate Success: How Business Strategies Add Value*, Oxford University Press, Oxford.

Khan, M. A., (1992). *Restaurant Franchising*, Van Nostrand Reinhold, New York.

Kim, D. H., (1993), 'The Link between Individual and Organizational Learning', *Sloan Management Review*, Vol. 35, No. 1, pp. 37–49.

Kirzner, I. M., (1973), *Competition and Entrepreneurship*, University of Chicago Press, Chicago, Illinois.

Klein, B., (1980), 'Transaction Costs of 'Unfair' Contractual Arrangements', *American Economic Review*, Vol. 70, pp. 356–362.

Knight, R. M. (1984), 'The Independence of the Franchise Entrepreneurs', *Journal of Small Business Management*, April, pp. 53–61.

Kroc, R., (1977), *Grinding It Out: The Making of McDonald's*, Contemporary Books, Chicago, Illinois.

Krueger, A., (1991), 'Ownership, Agency and Wages: An Examination of Franchising in the Fast Food Industry', *Quarterly Journal of Economics*, Vol. 56, Issue 1, February, pp. 75–101.

Lafontaine, F., (1992), 'Agency Theory and Franchising: Some Empirical Results', *RAND Journal of Economics*, Vol. 23, No. 2, pp. 263–283.

Lafontaine, F., (1995), 'Within Market Price Dispersion in Franchise Chains', The International Challenge. . . Towards News Franchising Relationships, Proceedings of the 9th Conference of The Society of Franchising, Puerto Rico, 21– 22 January.

Lanthier, C., (1995), 'Subway Bites', *Financial Post*, 25 November, p. 6.

LaVan, H., Latona, J. C., Coye, R. W., (1986), 'Training and Development in the Franchisor-Franchisee Relationship', 1986 Society of Franchising, First Annual Conference, Omaha, Nebraska, 29–30 September.

Lawson, B., (1980), *How Designers Think*, Architectural Press, London.

Leavitt, H. J., (1965), 'Applying Organizational Change in Industry: Structural, Technological and Humanistic Approaches', in March, J. G., (ed.), *Handbook of Organizations*, Rand McNally, Chicago, Illinois.

Lewis, J. D., (1990), *Partnerships for Profit: Structuring and Managing Strategic Alliances*, Free Press, New York.

Lipparini, A., and Sobero, M., (1994), 'The Glue and the Pieces: Entrepreneurship and Innovation in Small Firm Networks', *Journal of Business Venturing*, Vol. 9, No. 2, pp. 125–140.

Lorange, P., and Roos, J., (1991), 'Why Some Strategic Alliances Succeed and Others Fail', *Journal of Business Strategy*, January/ February, pp. 25–30.

Love, J. F., (1986), *McDonald's – Behind the Arches*, Bantam Books Inc., New York.

Love, R. R., and Hoey, J. M., (1990), 'Management Science Improves Fast-Food Operations', *Interfaces*, Vol. 20, No. 2, March–April, pp. 21–29.

Lowell, H. B., (1991), *Multiple-Unit Franchising: The Key to Rapid System Growth*, Brownstein Zeidman and Schomer, Washington D. C.

Lukes, S., (1974), *Power: A Radical View*, The MacMillan Press for the British Sociological Association, London.

Luxenberg, S., (1985), *Roadside Empires – How the Chains Franchised America*, Viking Penguin Inc., New York.

MacMillan, A., (1995), *Aspects of Franchise Recruitment*, Unpublished MBA Dissertation, University of Edinburgh.

Maidique, M. A., and Zirger, B. J., (1984), 'A Study of Success and Failure in Product Innovation: The Case of the US Electronic Industry', *I. E. E. E. Transactions in Engineering Management*, E. M., 31 November, pp. 192–203.

Manaseri, A., (1993), *Franchise Channel Relationships: A Cross-Country Comaprison*, Unpublished PH. D Thesis, London Business School, London.

Mansfield, E., (1981), 'Composition of R&D Expenditure: Relationship to Size of Firm, Concentration, and Innovative Output', *Review of Economics and Statistics*, Vol. 63, November, pp. 610–14.

Martin, C. R., and Horner, D. A., (1993), 'Services Innovation: Successfil versus Unsuccessful Firms', *International Journal of Service Industry Management*, Vol. 14, pp. 49–65.

McAfee, R. P., and Schwarz, M., (1994), 'Opportunism in Multilateral Vertical Contracting: Non-discrimination, Exclusivity, and Uniformity', *American Economic Review*, No. 84, No. 1, pp. 210–230.

McAlister, L., Bazerman, M. H., and Fader, P., (1986), 'Power and Goal Setting in Channel Negotiations', *Journal of Marketing Research*, Vol. 33, August, pp. 228–236.

McGuire, E. P., (1971), 'The Feasibility of Minority-Group Capitalism Through Franchising', pp. 81–96 in Thompson, D. N., (ed.), *Contractual Marketing Systems*, Heath Lexington Books, Lexington, Massachusetts.

McIntyre, F. S., Young, J. A., Gilbert, F. W., (1994), 'Franchising: A Strategic Alliance Perspective', Society of Franchising Conference: Understanding And Accepting Different Perspectives . . . Empowering Relationships In 1994 And Beyond, Las Vegas, Nevada, 13–14 February.

McKiernan, P., (1992), *Strategies of Growth*, Routledge, London.

Meloan, T. W., (1988), 'The Pros and Cons of Franchising – Two Views: Opportunity and Risk', *Business Forum*, Vol. 13, No. 3, Summer, pp. 14–18.

Meyer, A. D., and Goes, J. B., (1988), 'Organizational Assimilation of Innovations: A Multi-level Contextual Analysis', *Academy of Management Journal*, Vol. 31, pp. 897–923.

Miles, R. E., and Snow, C. C., (1986), 'Organizations: New Concepts for New Forms', *California Management Review*, Vol. XXVIII, No. 3, pp. 62–73.

Minkler, A. P., (1990), 'Empirical Analysis of a Firm's Decision to Franchise', *Economica*, Vol. 34, pp. 77–82.

Mittelstaedt, R. A., and Stassen, R. E., (1990), 'Economic Sources of Conflict in Franchising Organizations', 1990 Society of Franchising, Franchising: Evolution in the Midst of Change, Scottsdale, Arizona, 22–24 February.

Moch, M. K., and Morse, E. V., (1977), 'Size, Centralization and Organizational Adoption of Innovations', *American Sociological Review*, Vol. 42, pp. 716–725.

Mody, A., (1993), 'Learning through Alliances', *Journal of Economic Behaviour & Organization*, Vol. 20, No. 2, pp. 151–170.

Mowery, D. C., (1983), 'The Relationship Between Intrafirm and Contractual Forms of Industrial Research in American Manufacturing, 1900–1940', *Explorations in Economic Thought*, Vol. 20, pp. 351–374.

National Westminster Bank/British Franchise Association, (1993), *Survey 1993*, British Franchise Association, London.

National Westminster Bank/British Franchise Association, (1994), *Survey 1994*, British Franchise Association, London.

Nelson, R., and Winter, S., (1983), *An Evolutionary Theory of Economic Change*, Harvard University Press, Cambridge, MA.

Nonaka, I., (1994), 'A Dynamic Theory of Organizational Knowledge Creation', *Organization Science*, Vol. 5, No. 1, pp. 14–37.

Nooteboom, B., (1994), 'Innovation and Diffusion in Small Firms: Theory and Evidence', *Small Business Economics*, Vol. 6, pp. 327–347.

Norton, S. W., (1988), 'An Empirical Look at Franchising as an Organizational Form', *Journal of Business*, Vol. 61, No. 2, pp. 197–219.

O'Hara and Thomas (1986), 'Franchise Systems: The Internal Dynamics of Sales Growth and Dual Distribution', 1986 Society of Franchising Conference, First Annual Conference, Omaha, Nebraska, 28–30 September.

Olleros, F. J., and MacDonald, R. J., (1988), 'Strategic Alliances: Managing Complementarity to Capitalize on Emerging Technology', *Technovation*, Vol. 7, pp. 155–176.

Ornstein, M., (1984), 'Interlocking Directorates in Canada: Intercorporate or Class Alliance?', *Administrative Science Quarterly*, Vol. 29, pp. 210–231.

Osborne, R. L., (1991), 'The Dark Side of the Entrepreneur', *Long Range Planning*, Vol. 24, No. 3, pp. 26–31.

Ozanne, U. B., and Hunt, S. D., (1971), *The Economic Effects of Franchising*, Select Committee on Small Business, US Senate, September, Washington DC.

Palmer, D., (1983), 'Broken Ties: Interlocking Directorates and Inter-corporate Coordination', *Administrative Science Quarterly*, Vol. 28, pp. 40–55.

Palmer, D., Frieland, R., and Frieland, J. V., (1986), 'The Ties that Bind: Determinants of Stability in a Corporate Interlock Network', *American Sociological Review*, Vol. 51.

Parker, B., (1989), 'Strategies for Small Domestic Firms in Decline Industries', *International Small Business Journal*, Vol. 8, pp. 3–26.

Pavitt, K., Robson, M. and Townsend, J., (1989), 'Technological Accumulation, Diversification and Organization in UK Companies 1945–1983', *Management Science*, Vol. 35, No. 1, pp. 3–26.

Pennings, J., (1980), *Interlocking Directorates*, Jossey-Bass, San Francisco, California.

Pennings, J. M., and Harianto, F., (1992), 'The Diffusion of Technological Innovation in the Commercial Banking Industry', *Strategic Management Journal*, Vol. 13, pp. 29–49.

Perry, T. S., (1995), 'Designing a Culture for Creativity', *Research Technology Management*, March–April, Vol. 38, No. 2, pp. 14–17.

Phan, P. H., Butler, J. E., and Lee, S. H., (1996), 'Crossing Mother: Entrepreneur-Franchisees' Attempts to Reduce Franchisor Influence', *Journal of Business Venturing*, Vol. 11, pp. 379–402.

Pickworth, J. R., (1989), 'Service Delivery Systems in the Food Service Industry', *International Journal of Hospitality Management*, Vol. 7, pp. 43–62.

Pine, R. J, (1991), *Technology Transfer in the Hotel Industry*, PH. D. Thesis, University of Bradford, UK.

Pitelis, C., (1991), *Market and Non-market Hierarchies: Theory of Institutional Failure*, Basil Blackwell, Oxford.

Pizam, A., and Calantone, R., (1987), 'Beyond Psychographics: Values as Determinants of Tourist Behaviour', *International Journal of Hospitality Management*, Vol. 6, No. 3, pp. 203–220.

Poly, J. P., and Bournazel, E., (1991), *The Feudal Transformation 900–1200*, Holmes and Meier, London.

Porter, M. E., (1980), *Competitive strategy: Techniques for Analysing Industries and Competitors*, Free Press, New York.

Potter, D. V., (1989), 'The Customer's Eye of Innovation', *Journal of Product Innovation Management*, Vol. 6, pp. 35–42.

Powell, W. W., (1990), 'Neither Market nor Hierarchy: Network Forms of Organization', *Research in Organizational Behaviour*, Vol. 12, pp. 295–356.

Prahalad, C. K., and Bettis, R. A., (1986), 'The Dominant Logic: a New Linkage between Diversity and Performance', *Strategic Management Journal*, Vol. 7, pp. 485–501.

Prahalad, C. K., and Hamel, G., (1990), 'The Core Competence of the Organization', pp. 277–299 in Montgomery, C. A., and Porter, M. E., (eds), *Strategy: Seeking and Securing Competitive Advantage*, Harvard Business School Publishing, Boston, Massachusetts.

Price, S., (1993), *The UK Fast Food Industry: A Market Analysis*, Cassell, London.

Price, S., (1995), *A Strategic Review of the UK Pizza & Pasta Market*, The Pizza & Pasta Association, Wantage, Oxon.

Quinn, J. B., (1980), *Strategies for Change: Logical Incrementalism*, Irwin, Homewood, Illinois.

Raffa, M., and Zollo, G., (1994), 'Sources of Innovation and Professionals in Small Innovative Firms', *International Journal of Technology Management*, Vol. 9, Nos 3/4, pp. 481–496.

Reve, T., (1990), 'The Firm as a Nexus of Internal and External Contracts', in Aoki, M., Gustafsson, B., and Williamson, O. E., (eds), *The Firm as a Nexus of Treaties*, Sage Publications, London.

Robicheaux, R. A., Dant, R., and Kaufmann, P. J., (1994), 'Multiple Unit Franchising in the Fast Food Industry in the United States: Incidence and Operating Characteristics', 1994 Society of Franchising Conference, Understanding And Accepting Different Perspectives . . . Empowering Relationships in 1994 And Beyond, Las Vegas, Nevada, 13–14 February.

Rowe, L. A., and Boise, W. B., (1974), 'Organizational Innovation: Current Research and Evolving Concepts', *Public Administration Review*, Vol. 34, pp. 284–293.

Roy, M. R., Fox, M. A., and Hamilton, R. T., (1994), 'Board Size and Potential Corporate Interlocks in Australasia, 1984–1993', *Australian Journal of Management*, Vol. 19, pp. 201–217.

Rubin, P. H., (1990), *Managing Business Transactions*, Free Press, New York.

Sanghavi, N., (1990), *Retail Franchising in the 1990's*, Longman Group, Harlow, Essex.

Sahal, D., (1984), 'The Innovation Dynamics and Technological Cycles in the Computer Industry', *Omega*, Vol. 12, No. 2, pp. 153–163.

Schul, P. L., Pride, W., and Little, T. L., (1985), 'Channel Climate: Its Impact on Channel Members' Satisfaction', *Journal of Retailing*, Vol. 52, pp. 13–30.

Sen, K. C., (1993), 'The Use of Initial Fees and Royalties in Business Format Franchising', *Managerial and Decision Economics*, Vol. 14, pp. 175–190.

Seurat, S., (1979), *Technology Transfer: A Realistic Approach*, Gulf Publishing, Houston, Texas.

Shailer, G. E. P., (1993), 'The Irrelevance of Organizational Boundaries of Owner-Managed Firms', *Small Business Economics*, Vol. 5, pp. 229–237.

Shan, W., Walker, G., and Kogut, B., (1994), 'Interfirm Cooperation and Startup Innovation in the Biotechnology Industry', *Strategic Management Journal*, Vol. 15, pp. 387–394.

Sharma, S. Durand, R. M, and Gur-Arie, O., (1981), 'Identification and Analysis of Moderator Variables', *Journal of Marketing Research*, Vol. 28, pp. 291–300.

Shea, G., (1986), 'Quality Circles: The Danger of Bottled Change', *Sloan Management Review*, Spring, pp. 33–46.

Shook, C., and Shook, R. L., (1993), *Franchising: The Business Strategy that Changed the World*, Prentice Hall, Englewood Cliffs, New Jersey.

Shugman, S. M., (1985), 'Implicit Understandings in Channels of Distribution', *Marketing Science*, Vol. 31, No. 4, pp. 435–460.

Singh, J. V., (1986), 'Performance, Slack and Risk Taking in Organizational Decision Making', *Academy of Management Journal*, Vol. 29, pp. 562–585.

Specht, P. H., (1993), 'Munificence and Carrying Capacity of the Environment and Organization Formation', *Entrepreneurship, Theory and Practice*, Vol. 17, Winter, pp. 77–85.

Spriggs, M., and Nevin J. R., (1995), 'Understanding the Nature of the Franchise Relationship: A Key to Model and Theory Development', 1994 Society of Franchising Conference, Understanding And Accepting Different Perspectives . . . Empowering Realtionships in 1994 And Beyond, Las Vegas, Nevada, 13–14 February.

Stanworth, J., (1984), *A Study of Power Relationships and Their Consequences in Franchise Organizations*, Report to the Economic and Social research Council, Polytechnic of Central London, London.

Stanworth, J., and Purdy, D., (1993), *The Blenheim/University of Westminster Franchise Guide: Spring 1993*, International Franchise Research Centre, Special Studies Series, No. 1, September, University of Westminster.

Stearns, L. B., and Mizruchi, M. S., (1986), 'Broken-tie Reconstitution and the Functions of Interorganizational Interlocks: A Re-examination', *Administrative Science Quarterly*, Vol. 31, pp. 522–538.

Stern, L. W., (1971), 'Potential Conflict Management Mechanisms in Distribution Channels: in Interorganizational Analysis', pp. 111–146 in Thompson, D. N., (ed.), *Contractual Marketing Systems*, Heath Lexington Books, Lexington, Massachusetts.

Stern, L. W., and El-Ansary, A. I., (1982), *Marketing Channels*, 2nd Edition, Prentice Hall, Englewood Cliffs, New Jersey.

Stern, P., (1995), 'The Two Partners of Franchising', pp. 23–27 in *Franchise World Directory*, Eleventh Edition, Franchise World Publications, London.

Stuckey, J., and White, D., (1993), 'When and When Not to Vertically Integrate', *Sloan Management Review*, Spring, pp. 71–85.

Strebel, P., (1987), 'Organizing for Innovation Over an Industry Cycle,' *Strategic Management Journal*, Vol. 8, pp. 117–124.

Stevenson, J., Roberts, M., and Grousebeck, H., (1989), *New Business Ventures and the Entrepreneur*, Irwin, Homewood, Illinios.

Tarbutton, L. T., (1986), *Franchising: the How-to Book*, Prentice Hall, New Jersey.

Teece, D. J., (1986), 'Profiting from Technological Innovation: Implications for Integration, Collaboration, Licensing and Public Policy', *Research Policy*, Vol. 15, pp. 285–305.

Thompson, J. D., (1967), *Organizations in Action*, McGraw-Hill, New York.

Tyler, B. B., and Steensma, H. K., (1995), 'Evaluating Technological Collaborative Opportunities: A Cognitive Modelling Perspective', *Strategic Management Journal*, Vol. 16, pp. 43–70.

Useem, M., (1982), 'Classwide Rationality in the Politics of Managers and Directors of Large Corporations in the United States and Great Britain', *Administrative Science Quarterly*, Vol. 27, pp. 199–226.

Utterback, J. M., and Abernathy, W. J., (1975), 'A Dynamic Model of Process and Product Innovation', *Omega*, Vol. 6, No. 3, pp. 639–656.

Von Braun, C. F., (1990) 'The Acceleration Trap', *Sloan Management Review*, Autumn, pp. 49–55.

Von Hippel, E., (1982), 'Approbiability of Innovation Benefit as a Predictor of the Source of Innovation', *Research Policy*, Vol. 11, No. 2, pp. 95–115.

Vonortas, N. S., (1994), 'Inter-Firm Co-operation with Perfectly Appropriable Research', *International Journal of Industrial Organization*, Vol. 12, No. 3, pp. 413–435.

Wadsmith, F. H., (1996), 'Many Franchisees not Happy with Parent Companies', *Entrepreneur* Magazine's Daily Biz Insider, Friday's Business News for 8 March.

Waldsmith, L., (1988), 'How to Succeed in a Saturated Market', *American Demographics*, Vol. 10, November, pp. 42–43.

Walker, R., and Greenstreet, D., (1990), 'The Effect of Government Incentives and Assistance on Location and Job Growth in Manufacturing', *Regional Studies*, Vol. 25, No. 1, pp. 13–30.

Weick, K. E., (1976), 'Educational Organizations As Loosely Coupled Systems', *Administrative Science Quarterly*, Vol. 21, No. 1, March, pp. 1–19.

Weinrauch, D. J., (1986), 'Franchising an Established Business', *Journal of Small Business Management*, Vol. 24, July, pp. 1–7.

Werner, J., (1993), 'Towards Second Generation R&D Consortia', *International Journal of Technology Management*, Vol. 8, Nos. 6/7/8, pp. 587–595.

West, J. J., and Olsen, M. D., (1989), 'Competitive Tactics in Food Service: Are High Performers Different?', *Cornell Hotel and Restaurant Association Quarterly*, May, Vol. 30, No. 1, pp. 68–71.

Wicking, N., (1995), 'Leveraging Core Competencies', *Business Franchise*, October, pp. 86–87.

Williamson, O. E., (1975), *Market and Hierarchies: Analysis and Antitrust Implications*, Free Press, New York.

Williamson, O. E., (1991), 'Strategizing, Economising, and Economic Organization', *Strategic Management Journal*, Vol. 12, pp. 75–94.

Withane, S., (1991), 'Franchising and Franchisee Behaviour: An examination of Opinions, personal Characteristics, and Motives of Canadian Franchisee Entrepreneurs', *Journal of Small Business Management*, No. 1, pp. 22–29.

Wolf, A., Fortheringhame, J., and Grey, A., (1990), *Learning in Context: Patterns of Skills Transfer and Training Implications*, Research Development Series, No. 58, Department of Employment.

Wolfe, R. A., (1994), 'Organizational Innovation: Review, Critique and Suggested Research Directions', *Journal of Management Studies*, Vol. 31, No. 3, pp. 405–431.

Yoshino, M. Y., and Rangan, U. S., (1995), *Strategic Alliances: An Entrepreneurial Approach to Globalization*, Harvard Business School Press, Boston, Massachusetts.

Yuan, B., and Wang, M. Y., (1995), 'The Influential Factors for the Effectiveness of International Strategic Alliances of High-tech Industry in Taiwan', *International Journal of Technology Management*, Vol. 10, No. 7/8, pp. 777–787.

Zaltman, G., Duncan, R., and Holbeck, J., (1973), *Innovations and Organizations*, Wiley, New York.

Zmud, R. M., (1982), 'Diffusion of Modern Software Practices; Influence of Centralization and Formalization', *Management Science*, Vol. 28, pp. 1421–1431.

Chapter 7: Influences on sharing innovations in the franchise dyad: the roles of power and culture

Achrol, R. S., Reve, T., and Stern, L. W., (1983), 'The Environment of Marketing Channel Dyads: A Framework for Comparative Analysis', *Journal of Marketing*, Vol. 47, Autumn, pp. 55–67.

Adams, J. N., and Pritchard-Jones, K. V., (1990), *Franchising: Practice and Precedents in Business Format Franchising*, Butterworths, London.

Agyris, C., (1983), 'Action Science and Intervention', *Journal of Applied Science*, Vol. 19, pp. 115–140.

Alvesson, M., and Berg, P. O., (1992), *Corporate Culture and Organizational Symbolism*, Walter de Gruyter, New York.

Alvesson, M., and Lindkvist, L., (1993), 'Transaction Costs, Clans and Corporate Culture', *Journal of Management Studies*, Vol. 30 pp. 427–457

Anand, P., (1987), 'Including Franchisees to Relinquish Control: An Attribution Analysis', *Journal of Marketing Research*, Vol. XXIV, May, pp. 215–221.

Anand, P., and Stern, L. W., (1985), 'A Sociopsychological Explanation for Why Marketing Channel Members Relinquish Control', *Journal of Marketing Research*, Vol. XXII, November, pp. 365–376.

Andaleeb, S. S., (1996), 'An Experimental Investigation of Satisfaction and Commitment in Marketing Channels: The Roles of Trust and Dependence', *Journal of Retailing*, Vol. 72, pp. 77–93.

Anderson, E., and Weitz, B., (1992), 'The Uses of Pledges to Build and Sustain Commitment in Distribution Channels', *Journal of Marketing Research*, Vol. XXIV, February, pp. 18–34.

Anderson, J. C., and Narus, J. A., (1990), 'A Model of Distributor Firm and Manufacturing Firm Working Partnerships', *Journal of Marketing*, Vol. 54, January, pp. 42–58.

Antony, P., (1994), *Managing Culture*, Open University Press, Buckingham, Buckingham.

Astley, W. G., and Zajac, E. J., (1991), 'Intraorganizational Power and Organizational Design: Reconciling Rational and Coalition Models of Organization', *Organization Science*, Vol. 2, No. 4, November, pp. 399–411.

Bailetti, A. J., and Callahan, J. R., (1993), 'The Co-ordination Structure of International Collaborative Technology Agreements', *R&D Management*, Vol. 23, No. 2, pp. 129–146.

Banbury, C. M., and Mitchell, W., (1995), 'The Effects of Introducing Important Incremental Innovations on Market Share and Survival' *Strategic Management Journal*, Vol. 16, pp. 161–182.

Barney, J. B., and Hansen, M. H., (1994), 'Trustworthiness as a Source of Competitive Advantage', *Strategic Management Journal*, Vol. 15, Special Issue, pp. 175–190.

Bateson, G., (1973), *Steps To An Ecology of Mind*, Paladin, St Albans, UK.

Baye, M. R., Crocker, K. J., and Ju, J., (1996), 'Divisionalization, Franchising and Divesture Incentives in Oligopoly', *American Economic Review*, Vol. 86, No. 1, pp. 225–243.

Beamish, P. W., (1988), *Multinational Joint Ventures in Developing Countries*, Routledge, New York.

Berry, M. M. J., and Taggart, J. H., (1994), 'Managing Technology and Innovation: A Review', *R&D Management*, Vol. 24, No. 4, pp. 341–353.

Bessant, J. R., and Grunt M., (1985), *Management of Manufacturing Innovation in the United Kingdom and West Germany*, Gower, Aldershot, UK.

Boisot, M., (1987), *Information and Organization*, Fontana, London.

Booz, Allen and Hamilton, (1982), *New Products Management for the 1980s – Phase II*, Chicago, Illinois.

Boyle, B., Dwyer, R., Robicheaux, R. A., and Simpson, J. T., (1992), 'Influence Strategies in Marketing Channels: Measures and Use in Different Relationship Structures', *Journal of Marketing Research*, Vol. XXIV, November, pp. 462–473.

Boyle, B., and Dwyer, R. F., (1995), 'Power, Bureaucracy, Influence, and Performance: Their Relationships in Industrial Distribution Channels', *Journal of Business Research*, Vol. 32, pp. 189–200.

Bracker, J. S., and Pearson, J. N., (1986), 'The Impact of Franchising on the Financial Performance of Small firms', *Journal of the Academy of Marketing Science*, Vol. 14, Winter, pp. 10–17.

Brill, J. E., (1994), 'Beyond Managerial Opportunism: Supplier Power and Managerial Compliance in a Franchised Marketing Channel', *Journal of Business Research*, Vol. 30, pp. 211–223.

Brown, J. R., Johnson, J. L., and Lim, Y. K., (1986), 'Behavioral Relations in Marketing Channels: A Review of Cross-Cultural Comparison', 1986 Society of Franchising Conference, First Annual Conference, Omaha, Nebraska, 28–30 September.

Buccola, S. T., (1991), 'Entitlements and Distributive Equity in Cooperative Marketing Pools', *Journal of Economic Behaviour and Organization*, Vol. 15, pp. 257–268.

Burke, W. W., and Litwin, G. H., (1992), 'A Causal Model of Organizational Performance and Change', *Journal of Management*, Vol. 18, No. 3, pp. 523–545.

Burns, T., and Stalker, G. M., (1961), *The Management of Innovation*, Tavistock Publications, London.

Buzzell, R. D., and Gale, B. T., (1987), *The PIMS Principles: Linking Strategy to Performance*, Free Press, New York.

Clark, M. C., and Payne, R. L., (1995), *Interpersonal Trust: A Review and Reconceptualization*, Business Studies Discussion Paper, No. 95. 6, Sheffield University Management School, Sheffield, UK.

Cobble, D. S., (1991), *Dishing It Out: Waitresses and Their Unions in the Twentieth Century*, University of Illinois, Urbana, Illinois.

Colombo, M. G., (1995), 'Firm Size and Cooperation: The Determinants of Cooperative Agreements in Infrmation Technology Industries', *Industrial Journal of the Economics of Business*, Vol. 2, No. 1, pp. 3–27.

Combs, J. G., and Castrogiovanni, G. J., (1994), 'Franchisor Strategy: A Proposed Model and Empirical Test of Franchisee versus Company-Ownership', *Journal of Small Business Management*, Vol. 32, No. 2, pp. 37–48.

Cummings, L. E., (1987), 'Information Technology Supporting Fast Food Phone-In Responsiveness', *International Journal of Hospitality Management*, Vol. 6, No. 4, pp. 225–228.

Dahlstorm, R., Dwyer, R., and Oh, S. (1986), 'Interfirm Influence Strategies in Franchise Channels of Distribution', 1986 Society of Franchising Conference, First Annual Conference, Omaha, Nebraska, 28–30 September.

Dahlstorm, R., and Nygaard, A., (1995), 'An Exploratory Investigation of Interpersonal Trust in New and Mature Market Economies', *Journal of Retailing*, Vol. 71, No. 4, pp. 339–361.

Damanpour, F., (1991), 'Organizational Innovation: A Meta-Analysis of Effects of Determinants and Moderators', *Academy of Management Journal*, Vol. 34, pp. 555–590.

Dandridge, T., and Falbe, C., (1994), 'The Influence of Franchisees Beyond Their Local Domains', *International Small Business Journal*, January–March, Vol. 12, No. 2, pp. 39–49.

Dant, R. P., and Berger, P. D., (1994), 'Modelling Cooperative Advertising Decisions in Franchising', *Working Paper #94–11*, School of Management, Boston University, Boston, Massachussets.

Dant, R. P., and Schul, P. L., (1992), 'Conflict Resolution Processes in Contractual Channels of Distribution', *Journal of Marketing*, Vol. 56, January, pp. 38–54.

Darling, J. R., and Taylor, R. E., (1989), ' A Model for Reducing Internal Resistance to Change in a Firm's International Marketing Strategy', *European Journal of Marketing*, Vol. 23, No. 7, pp. 34–41.

Datta, D. K., (1988), 'International Joint Ventures: A Framework for Analysis', *Journal of General Management*, Vol. 14, No. 2, Winter, pp. 78–90.

Deal, T., and Kennedy A., (1988), *Corporate Cultures*, Penguin, London.

Denis, D. R., (1996), 'What is the Difference Between Organizational Culture and Organizational Climate? A Native's Point of View on a Decade of Paradigm Wars', *Academy of Management Review*, Vol., pp. 619–645.

Dev, C. S., and Brown, J. R., (1991), 'Franchising and Other Operating Arrangements in the Lodging Industry: A Strategic Comparison', *Hospitality Research Journal*, Vol. 14, No. 3, pp. 23–42.

Dnes, A. W., (1988), *An Economic Analysis of Contractual Relationships in Franchising Systems with Case Studies*, Unpublished Ph.D. dissertation, University of Edinburgh.

Dwyer, R., Oh, S., and Lagrace, R., (1986), 'Exploring the Environmental and Behavioural Antecedents of Franchisee Trust and Satisfaction', 1986 Society of Franchising Conference, First Annual Conference, Omaha, Nebraska, 28–30 September.

El-Ansary, A., and Stern, L. W., (1972), 'Power Measurement in the Distribution Channel', *Journal of Marketing Research*, Vol. IX, February, pp. 47–52.

English, W., and Hoy, F., (1995), 'Are Franchisees Actually Entrepreneurs?', 1995 Society of Franchising Conference, Partners for Progress . . . A World of Opportunities, Honolulu, Hawaii, 17–18 February.

Etgar, M., (1979), 'Sources and Types of Interchannel Conflict', *Journal of Retailing*, Vol. 55, No. 1, pp. 61–68.

Evan, W. M., and Black., G., (1967), 'Innovation in Business Organizations: Some Factors Associated with Success of Failure of Staff Proposals, *Journal of Business*, Vol. 40, pp. 519–530.

Faulkner, D., (1995), *International Strategic Alliances*, McGraw-Hill, London.

Feldman, M. P., (1993), 'An Examination of the Geography of Innovation', *Industrial and Corporate Change*, Vol. 2, No. 3, pp. 451–470.

Felstead, A., (1993), *The Corporate Paradox – Power and Control in the Business Franchise*, Routledge, London.

Feuer, D., (1989), 'Franchising the Training Game', *Training*, Vol. 26, February, pp. 40–45.

Ford, R. C., and Fottler, M. D., (1995), 'Empowerment: A Matter of Degree', *Academy of Management Executive*, Vol. 9, No. 3, pp. 21–29.

Frazier, G. L., and Summers, J. O., (1984), 'Interfirm Influence Strategies and Their Application within Distribution Channels', *Journal of Marketing*, Vol. 48, January, pp. 52–69.

French, J. R. P., and Raven, B., (1959), 'The Bases of Social Power', pp. 156–163, in Cartwright, D., (ed.), *Studies in Social Power*, University of Michigan Press, Ann Arbor, Michigan.

Fudenberg, G., and Tirole, J., (1990), 'Moral Hazard and Renegotiation in Agency Contracts', *Econometrica*, November, Vol. 56, No. 6, pp. 1279–1320.

Fukuyama, F., (1995), *Trust: The Social Virtues and the Creation of Prosperity*, Hamish Hamilton, London.

Gal-Or, E., (1991), 'Optimal Franchising in Oligopolistic Markets with Uncertain Demand', *International Journal of Industrial Organization*, Vol. 9, No. 3, pp. 343–364.

Gaski, J. F., (1984), 'The Theory of Power and Conflict in Channels of Distribution', *Journal of Marketing*, Vol, 48, pp. 9–29.

Gaski, J. F., and Nevin, J. R., (1985), 'The Differential Effects of Exercised and Unexercised Power Sources in a Marketing Channel', *Journal of Marketing Research*, Vol. XXII, May, pp. 130–142.

Gassenheimer, J. B., Baucus, D. B., and Baucus, M. S., (1996), 'Cooperative Arrangements Among Entrepreneurs: An Analysis of Opportunism and Communication in Franchise Structures', *Journal of Business Research*, Vol. 36, pp. 67–79.

Gold, B., (1981), 'Technological Diffusions in Industry: Research Needs and Shortcomings', *Journal of Industrial Economics*, Vol. 24, No. 3, pp. 247–269.

Grandori, A., and Soda, G., (1995), 'Inter-firm Networks: Antecedents, Mechanisms, and Forms', *Organization Studies*, Vol. 16, No. 2, pp. 183–214.

Guiltinan, J. P., Rejab, I. B., and Rogers, W. C., (1980), 'Factors Influencing Coordination in a Franchise Channel', *Journal of Retailing*, Vol. 56, No. 3, Autumn, pp. 41–58.

Hage, J., (1980), *Theories of Organizations*, Wiley, New York.

Hagedoorn, J., (1993), 'Understanding the Rationale of Strategic Technology Partnering: Inter-organizational Modes of Co-operation and Sectoral Differences,' *Strategic Management Journal*, Vol. 14, pp. 371–376.

Hagedoorn, J., (1995), 'A Note on International Market Leaders and Networks of Strategic Technology Partnering', *Strategic Management Journal*, Vol. 16., pp. 241–250.

Hall, P., and Dixon, R., (1989), *Franchising*, NatWest Small Business Bookshelf, Pitman Publishing, London.

Hamel, G., (1991), 'Competition for Competence and Inter-Partner Learning within International Strategic Alliances', *Strategic Management Journal*, Vol. 12, Special Issue, pp. 69–82.

Harrigan, K. R., (1985), *Strategic Flexibility: A Management Guide for Changing Times*, Lexington Books, Lexington, Massachusetts.

Heide, J. B., (1994), 'Interorganizational Governance in Marketing Channels,' *Journal of Marketing*, Vol. 58, January, pp. 71–85.

Hellneigel, D., and Slocum. J., (1974), 'Organizational Climate: Measures, Research, and Contingencies,' *Academy of Management Journal*, Vol. 17, No. 2, pp. 255–280.

Hennart, J. F., (1993), 'Explaining the Swollen Middle: Why Most Transactions are a Mix of 'Market' and 'Hierarchy', *Organization Science*, Vol. 4, No. 4, pp. 529–547.

Hing, N., (1995), 'Franchise Satisfaction: Contributors and Consequences', *Journal of Small Business Management*, Vol. 33, No. 2, April, pp. 12–25.

Hoffman, R. C., and Preble, J. F., (1991), 'Franchising: Selecting a Strategy for Rapid Growth,' *Long Range Planning*, Vol. 24, No. 4, pp. 74–85.

Hrebiniak, L. G., and Joyce, W. F., (1985), 'Organizational Adaption: Strategic Choice and Environmental Determinism', *Administrative Science Quarterly*, Vol. 30, pp. 336–349.

Hunt, S. D., and Nevin, J. R., (1974), 'Power in Channels of Distribution: Sources and Consequences', *Journal of Marketing Research*, Vol. 11, pp. 186–193.

Jenson, M. C., (1989), 'Eclipse of the Public Corporation', *Harvard Business Review*, September–October, pp. 61–74.

Johnson, G., (1992), 'Managing Strategic Change – Strategy, Culture and Action', *Long Range Planning*, Vol. 25, No. 1, pp. 28–36.

Johnston, D. A., and Leenders, M. R., (1990), 'The Diffusion of Innovation Within Multi-Unit Firms', *International Journal of Operational Management*, Vol. 10, No. 5, pp. 15–25.

Julien, P. A., and Raymond, L., (1994), 'Factors of New Technology Adoption', *Entrepreneurship Theory and Practice*, Vol. 18, No. 4, Summer, pp. 79–90.

Kale, S. H., and McIntyre, R. P., (1991), 'Distribution Channel Relationships in Diverse Cultures', *International Marketing Review*, Vol. 8, No. 3, pp. 31–45.

Kanter R. M. (1985), *The Change Masters*, Counterpoint, London.

Katz, B. G., and Owen, J., (1992), 'On the Existence of Franchise Contracts and Some of their Implications', *International Journal of Industrial Organisation*, Vol. 10, No. 4, pp. 567–593.

Kaufmann, P. J., (1987), 'Pizza Hut: Home Delivery', *Harvard Case Services*, Boston, Massachusetts.

Kaufmann, P. J., and Lafontaine, F. F., (1994), 'Costs of Control: The Source of Economics Rents for McDonald's Franchisees, *Journal of Law and Economics*, Vol. XXXVIII, pp. 417–453.

Kay, J. A., (1993), *Foundations of Corporate Success: How Business Strategies Add Value*, Oxford University Press, Oxford.

Khan, M. A., (1992), *Restaurant Franchising*, Van Nostrand Reinhold, New York.

Killing, J. P., (1982), 'How to Make a Global Joint Venture Work', *Harvard Business Review*, May–June, pp. 120–127.

Kimberly, J. R., and Evanisko, M. J., (1981), 'Organiation innovation: the Influence of Individual, Organizational and Contextual Factors on Hospital Adoption of Technological and Administrative Innovations', *Academy of Management Journal*, Vol. 24, pp. 684–713.

Knight, R. M., (1984), 'The Independence of the Franchise Entrepreneurs', *Journal of Small Business Management*, April, pp. 53–61.

Kogut, B., Walker, G., and Kim, D. J., (1995), 'Cooperation and Entry Induction as an an Exension of Technological Rivalry', *Research Policy*, pp. 77–95.

Kogut, B., (1988), 'Joint Ventures: Theoretical and Empirical Perspectives', *Strategic Management Journal*, Vol. 9, pp. 319–332.

Kono, T., (1990), 'Corporate Culture and Long Range Planning', *Long Range Planning*, Vol. 23, No. 4, pp. 9–19.

Kroc, R., (1977), *Grinding It Out: The Making of McDonald's*, Contemporary Books, Chicago, Illinois.

Lafontaine, F., (1992), 'Agency Theory and Franchising: Some Empirical Results', *RAND Journal of Economics*, Vol. 23, No. 2, pp. 263–283.

Lafontaine, F., (1993), 'Contractual Arrangements as Signalling Devices: Evidence from Franchising', *Journal of Law, Economics and Organization*, Autumn, Vol. 9, No. 2, pp. 256–289.

Lafontaine, F., (1994), 'Risk in Franchising: A Look at Some Measurement Issues', Understanding and Accepting Different Perspectives . . . Empowering Relationships in 1994 and Beyond, Society of Franchising, Las Vegas, Nevada, 13–14 February.

Lal, R., (1990), 'Improving Channel Coordination through Franchising', *Marketing Science*, Vol. 9, No. 4, pp. 299–318.

Lamming, R. C., (1993), *Beyond Partnership: Strategies for Innovation and Lean Supply*, Prentice Hall, London.

Leibenstein, H., and Maital, S., (1994), 'The Foundations of X-inefficiency', *Journal of Economic Behaviour and Organization*, Vol. 23, No. 3, pp. 251–268.

Lewis, M. C., and Lambert, D. M., (1991), 'A Model of Channel Member Performance', *Journal of Retailing*, Vol. 67, No. 2, pp. 205–225.

Lusch, R., (1977), 'Franchisee Satisfaction: Causes and Consequences', *International Journal of Physical Distribution*, Vol. 7, pp. 128–140.

Luxenberg, S., (1985), *Roadside Empires – How the Chains Franchised America*, Viking Penguin, Inc., New York.

Macneil, I. R., (1980), *The New Social Contract: An Inquiry into Modern Contractual Relations*, Yale University Press, New Haven, Connecticut.

Madhok, A., (1995), 'Revisiting Multinational Firms' Tolerance for Joint Ventures: A Trust-based Approach', *Journal of International Business Studies*, Vol. 26, First Quarter, pp. 117–137.

Mahajan, V., Muller, E., and Bass, F., (1990), 'New Product Diffusion Models in Marketing: A Review and Direction for Research', *Journal of Marketing*, Vol. 54, No. 1, pp. 1–26.

Maidique, M. A., and Zirger, B. J., (1984), 'A Study of Success and Failure in Product Innovation: The Case of the US Electronic Industry', *I. E. E. E. Transactions in Engineering Management*, E. M., 31 November, pp. 192–203.

Manaseri, A., (1993), *Franchise Channel Relationships: A Cross-Country Comaprison*, Unpblished PH. D Thesis, London Business School, London.

March, J. G., and Simon, H. A., (1958), *Organizations*, John Wiley and Sons, Inc., London.

Marlin, D., Lamont, B. T., and Hoffman, J. J., (1994), 'Choice Situation, Strategy and Performance: A Re-examination', *Strategic Management Journal*, Vol. 15, pp. 229–239.

Mathur, S. S., (1986), How Firms Compete: A New Classification of Generic Strategies, The City University Business School, *Working Paper, No. 81*.

Maute, M. F., and Locander, W. B., (1994), 'Innovation as a Socio-political process: An Empirical Analysis of Influence Behaviour among New Product Managers', *Journal of Business Research*, Vol. 30, pp. 161–174.

Mayer, R. C., Davis, J. H., and Schoorman, F. D., (1995), 'An Incentive Model of Organizational Trust', *Academy of Management Review*, Vol. 20, No. 3, pp. 709–734.

McAfee, R. P., and Schwarz, M., (1994), 'Opportunism in Mutilateral Vertical Contracting: Non-discrimination, Exclusivity, and Uniformity', *American Economic Review*, No. 84, No. 1, pp. 210–230.

McCosker, C. F., Frazer, L., and Peniero, D., (1995), 'An Exploration of Franchise Advisory Councils: Expectations and Relationships', 1995 Society of Franchising Conference The International Challenge . . . Towards New Franchising Relationships, San Juan, Puerto Rico.

McGrath, R. G., Venkatraman, S., and MacMillan, I., (1994), 'The Advantage Chain: Antecedents to Rents from Internal Corporate Ventures', *Journal of Business Venturing*, Vol. 9, pp. 351–369.

McIntyre, F. S., Young, J. A., Gilbert, F. W., (1994), 'Franchising: A Strategic Alliance Perspective', Society of Franchising Conference: Understanding And Accepting Different Perspectives . . . Empowering Relationships In 1994 And Beyond, Las Vegas, Nevada, 13–14 February.

McNally, K., (1995), *External Equity Finance for Technology-based Firms in the UK: The Role of Corporate Venture Capital*, Working Paper, University of Southampton, UK.

Mezias, S. J., and Glynn, M. A., (1993), 'The Three Faces OF Corporate Renewal: Institution, Revolution, and Evolution', *Strategic Management Journal*, Vol. 14, pp. 77–101.

Mintzberg, H., (1979), *The Structuring of Organizations*, Prentice-Hall Inc., Englewood Cliffs, New Jersey.

Mockler, R. J., and Easop, H., (1968), *Guidelines for More Effective Planning and Management of Franchise Systems*, Research Monograph, College of Business Administration, Georgia State University.

Mohr, J. J., and Sohi, R. S., (1995), 'Communication Flows in Distribution Channels: Impact on Assessments of Communication Quality and Satisfaction', *Journal of Retailing*, Vol. 71, No. 4, pp. 393–416.

Mohr, J. J., and Spekman, R., (1994), 'Characteristics of Partnership Success: Partnership Attributes, Communication Behaviour, and Conflict Resolution Techniques', *Strategic Management Journal*, Vol. 15, pp. 135–152.

Morgan, R. M., and Hunt, S. D., (1994), 'The Commitment-Trust Theory of Relationship Marketing', *Journal of Marketing*, Vol. 58, July, pp. 20–38.

Morris, M. H., Davis, D. L., and Allen, J. W., (1994), 'Fostering Corporate Entrepreneurship: Cross Cultural Comparisons of the Importance of Individualism versus Collectivism', *Journal of International Business Studies*, First Quarter, pp. 65–89.

Morrison, K. A., (1996), 'An Empirical Test of a Model of Franchisee Job Satisfaction', *Journal of Small Business Management*, Vol. 34, No. 3, pp. 27–42.

Nault, B. R. and Dexter, A. S., (1994), 'Adoption, Transfers and Incentives in a Franchise Network with Positive Externalities', *Marketing Science*, Vol. 13, No. 4, Autumn, pp. 412–423.

Norton, S. W., (1988a), 'An Empirical Look at Franchising as an Organizational Form', *Journal of Business*, Vol. 61, No. 2, pp. 197–219.

Norton, S. W., (1988b), 'Franchising, Brand Name, and the Entrepreneurial Capacity Problem', *Strategic Management Journal*, Vol. 9, pp. 105–114.

Olson, R. S., (1971), 'The Franchise Agreement: Head I Win – Tails Your Lose!', *Management Accountant*, June, pp. 37–41.

O'Connell-Davidson, J., (1994), 'What Do Franchisors Do? Control and Commercialization in Milk Distribution', *Work, Employment & Society*, Vol. 8, No. 1, pp. 23–44.

Ouchi, W. G., (1980), 'Markets, Bureaucracies and Clans', *Administrative Science Quarterly*, Vol. 25, pp. 129–141

Paules, G. F., (1991), *Dishing It Out: Power Resistance: Power and Resistance Among Waitresses in a New Jersey Restaurant*, Temple University, Philadelphia, Pennsylvannia.

Perry, R. L, (1992), 'Franchisee-Initiated Innovation', pp. 56–59 in Murphy, C. S., and Matusky, G., (eds), *Franchise Relations Handbook*, International Franchise Association, Washington D. C.

Perry, T. S., (1995), 'Designing a Culture for Creativity', *Research Technology Management*, March–April, Vol. 38, No. 2, pp. 14–17.

Pettigrew, A. M., (1979), 'On Studying Organizational Cultures', *Administrative Science Quarterly*, Vol. 24, pp. 570–581.

Pettit, S. J., (1988), 'Marketing Decision Making Within Franchised Systems', 1988 Society of Franchising, Forging Partnerships for Competitive Advantage, San Francisco, California, 31 January–2 February.

Pfeffer, J., and Salanicik, G. R., (1978), *The External Control of Organizations*, Harper and Row, New York.

Pheysey, D. C., (1993), *Organizational Cultures*, Routledge, London and New York.

Pilling, B. K., (1991), 'Assessing Competitive Advantage in Small Businesses: An Application to Franchising', *Journal of Small Business Management*, Vol. 29, October, pp. 55–63.

Pinchot III, G., (1986), *Intrapreneuring*, Harper and Row, London and New York.

Pine, R., (187), *Management of Technological Change in the Catering Industry*, Avebury, Aldershot.

Porter, M. E., and Fuller, M. B., (1985), 'Coalitions and Global Strategy', pp. 315–343 in Porter, M. E, (ed.) *Competition in Global Industries*, Harvard Business School Press, Boston, Massachusetts.

Porter, M. E., (1990), *The Competitive Advantage of Nations*, Free Press, New York.

Powell, W. W., (1990), 'Neither Market nor Hierarchy: Network Forms of Organization', *Research in Organizational Behaviour*, Vol. 12, pp. 295–356.

Price, H., (1996), 'The Anthropology of the Supply Chain: Fiefs, Clans, Witch-doctors and Professors', *European Journal of Purchasing and Supply Chain Management*, Vol. 2, pp. 87–105.

Provan, K. G., (1983), 'The Federation as an Interorganizational Linkage Network', *Academy of Management Review*, Vol. 8, No. 1, pp. 79–89.

Provan, K. G., and Skinner, S. J, (1989), 'Interorganizational Dependence and Control as Pedictors of Opportunism in Dealer-Supplier Relations', *Academy of Management Journal*, Vol. 32, No. 1, pp. 202–212.

Rao, V. R., and McLaughlin, E. W., (1989), 'Modelling the Decision to Add New Products by Channel Intermediaries', *Journal of Marketing*, Vol. 53, January, pp. 80–88.

Robicheaux, R. A., and Coleman, J. E., (1990), 'The Structure of Marketing Channel Relationships', *Journal of the Academy of Marketing Science*, Vol. 22, No. 1, pp. 38–51.

Rothwell, R., (1985), 'Project Sappho: A Comparative Study of Success and Failure in Industrial Innovation', in Rothwell R and Zegveld W *Reindustrialisation and Technology*, Longman, London.

Rubin, P. H., (1978), 'The Theory of the Firm and the Structure of the Franchise Contract', *Journal of Law and Economics*, Vol. 21, pp. 223–233.

Sadanand, V., (1992), 'Endogenous Diffusion of Technology', *International Journal of Industrial Organizations*, Vol. 7, No. 4, pp. 471–488.

Sako, M., (1992), *Prices, Quality and Trust: Inter-firm Relations in Britain and Japan*, Cambridge University Press, London.

Schul, P. L., Pride, W., and Little, T. L., (1983), 'Channel Climate: Its Impact on Channel Members' Satisfaction', *Journal of Retailing*, Vol. 52, Winter, pp. 13–30.

Schul, P. L., and Little, T. L., (1985), 'The Impact of Channel Leadership Behaviour on Intrachannel Conflict', *Journal of Marketing*, Vol. 47, Summer, pp. 21–34.

Schnaars, S. P., (1994), *Managing Imitation Strategies*, Free Press, New York.

Shamir, B., (1981), 'The Workplace as a Community: The Case of British Hotels', *Industrial Relations Journal*, Vol. 12, No. 6, pp. 45–55.

Shan, W., Walker, G., and Kogut, B., (1994), 'Interfirm Cooperation and Startup Innovation in the Biotechnology Industry', *Strategic Management Journal*, Vol. 15, pp. 387–394.

Shane, S., (1993), 'Cultural Influences on National Rates of Innovation', *Journal of Business Venturing*, Vol. 8, pp. 59–74.

Shook, C., and Shook, R. L., (1993), *Franchising: The Business Strategy that Changed the World*, Prentice Hall, Englewood Cliffs, New Jersey.

Sibley, S. D., and Michie, D. A., (1982), 'An Exploratory Investigation of Cooperation in a Franchise Channel', *Journal of Retailing*, Vol. 58, Winter, pp. 23–38.

Skinner, S. J., and Guiltinan, J. P., (1985), 'Perceptions of Channel Control', *Journal of Retailing*, Vol. 61, pp. 65–88.

Sklar, F., (1977), 'Franchises and Independence: Interorganizational Power Relations in a Contractual Context', *Urban Studies*, Vol. 6, No. 1.

Spriggs, M., and Nevin J. R., (1995), 'Understanding the Nature of the Franchise Relationship: A Key to Model and Theory Development', 1994 Society of Franchising Conference, Understanding And Accepting Different Perspectives . . . Empowering Realtionships in 1994 And Beyond, Las Vegas, Nevada, 13–14 February.

Stanworth, C., and Stanworth, J., (1995), 'The Self-Employed Without Employees – Autonomous or Atypical?', *Industrial Relations Journal*, Vol. 26, No. 3, pp. 221–229.

Stanworth, J., (1984), *A Study of Power Relationships and their Consequences in Franchise Organizations*, Report to the Economic and Social Research Council, Polytechnic of Central London, London.

Stanworth, J., (1991), 'Franchising and the Franchise Relationship in the European Community', in chapter 5, Abell, M., (ed.), *European Franchising: Law and Practice in the European Community*, Vol. 1, Waterlow Publishers, London.

Staw, B., (1981), 'The Escalation of Commitment to a Course of Action', *Academy of Management Review*, Vol. 4, pp. 577–587.

Strati, A., (1992), 'Aesthetic Understanding of Organizational Life', *Academy of Management Review*, Vol. 3, pp. 568–581.

Stern, L. W., and Reeve, T., (1980), 'Distribution Channels as Political Economies: A Framework for Comparative Analysis', *Journal of Marketing*, Vol. 44, pp. 52–64.

Surprenant, C. F., and Soloman, M. R., (1987), 'Predictability and Personalization in the Service Encounter', *Journal of Marketing*, Vol. 51, April, pp. 86–96.

Swart, W., and Donno, L., (1981), 'Simulation Modelling Improves Operations, Planning, and Productivity of Fast Food Restaurants', *Interfaces*, Vol. 11, No. 6, pp. 35–47.

Thompson, R. S., (1994), 'The Franchise Life-cycle and the Penrose Effect', *Journal of Economic Behaviour and Organization*, Vol. 24, No. 2, pp. 207–218.

Tidd, J., (1993), 'Technological Innovation, Organizational Linkages, and Strategic Degrees of Freedom', *Technology Analysis & Strategic Management*, Vol. 5, No. 3, pp. 273–284.

Tomlinson, J. W. C., (1970), *The Joint Venture Process in International Business: India and Pakistan*, MIT Press, Cambridge, Massachussets.

Trutko, J., Trutko, J., and Kostecka, A., (1993), *Franchising's Role in the US Economy, 1975–2000*, US Business Administration, Washington, DC.

Usher, J., (1989), 'Adaptive Change in Franchise Organizations: An Evolutionary Process Model', in *Proceedings of the Administrative Sciences Association of Canada*, pp. 39–48.

Van de Ven, A. H., Emmett, D. C. and Koenig, R, Jr., (1975), 'Frameworks of Interorganizational Analysis', pp. 19–38 in Negandhi, A. R. (ed.), *Interorganization Theory*, Center for Business and Economic Research Kent State University, Ohio.

Von Hippel, E., (1988), *The Sources of Innovation*, Oxford University Press, Oxford.

Weick, K. E., (1976), 'Educational Organizations As Loosely Coupled Systems', *Administrative Science Quarterly*, Vol. 21, No. 1, March, pp. 1–19.

Wilkinson, I., (1974), *Power in Distribution Channels*, Cranfield Research Papers in Marketing & Logistics Session 1973–1974, Cranfield School of Management, Cranfield, UK.

Wolfe, R. A., (1994), 'Organizational Innovation: Review, Critique and Suggested Research Directions', *Journal of Management Studies*, Vol. 31, No. 3, pp. 405–431.

Williamson, O. E., (1991), 'Strategizing, Economizing, and Economic Organizations,' *Strategic Management Journal*, Vol. 12, pp. 75–94.

Yoshino, M. Y., and Rangan, U. S., (1995), *Strategic Alliances: An Entrepreneurial Approach to Globalization*, Harvard Business School Press, Boston, Massachusetts.

Young, L. C., and Wilkinson, I. F., (1989), 'The Role of Trust and Co-operation in Marketing Channels', *European Journal of Marketing*, Vol. 23, No. 2, pp. 109–124.

Zajac, E., Golden, B. R., and Shortell, S. M., (1991), 'New Organizational Forms for Enhancing Innovation: The Case of Internal Joint Ventures', *Management Science*, Vol. 17, No. 2, pp. 170–184.

Zeithaml, V. A., Berry, L. L., and Parasuraman, A., (1988) 'Communication and Control Processes in the Delivery of Service Quality', *Journal of Marketing*, Vol. 52, April, pp. 35–48.

Chapter 8: Behind the veneer of success: propensities for franchisor failure

Abell, D. F., (1978), 'Strategic Windows', *Journal of Marketing*, July, pp. 21–26.

Acheson, D., and Wicking, N., (1992), 'Fast Food Franchising and Finance', pp. 147–168 in Ball, S. (ed.) *Fast Food Operations and their Management*, Stanley Thornes (Publishers) Ltd, Cheltenham, Gloucestershire, UK.

Acheson, D., (1993), 'Fast Food Franchising: Perfect Partners', *Business Franchise*, July/August, pp. 16–17.

Argenti, J., (1976), *Corporate Collapse: The Causes and Symptoms*, McGraw-Hill, London.

Ashman, R. T., (1987), 'The Way Ahead for Franchising and Licencing', First European Franchising and Licencing Conference, Glasgow, 15–16 June.

Ayling, D., (1988), 'Franchising in the UK', *The Quarterly Review of Marketing*, Vol. 13, Summer, pp. 19–24.

Balthory, A., (1984), *Predicting Corporate Collapse: Credit Analysis in the Determination and Forecasting of Insolvent Companies*, Financial Times Business Information Ltd, London.

Beaton, D., (1995), *The Cost-effectiveness of Open and Flexible Learning for TECs*, Research Series No. 53, Department of Employment.

Bental, B., and Speigal, M., (1995), 'Network Competition, Product Quality, And Market Coverage in the Presence of Network Externalities', *Industrial Journal of Economics*, Vol. XLIII, June, pp. 197–208.

Bernstien, C., (1994), 'Franchising: Explosive Issues Fuel Debate', *Restaurant Business*, Vol. 104, No. 24, 15 October, pp. 61–67.

Boe, K. L., Ginalski, W., and Henward III, D. M., (1987), *The Franchise Option: How to Expand Your Business Through Franchising*, International Franchise Association, Washington. DC.

Brandenberg, M., (1989), 'Franchising into the Nineties', *Accountancy*, February, pp. 142–145.

Brickley, J. A., and Dark, F. H., (1987), 'The Choice of Organizational Form: The Case of Franchising,' *Journal of Financial Economics*, Vol. 18, June, pp. 401–421.

Bruno, A. V., and Leidecker, J. K., (1988), 'Causes of New Venture Failure, 1960s vs. 1980s', *Business Horizons*, Vol. 31, No. 6, pp. 51–56.

Burck, C. G., (1970), 'Franchising's Troubled Dream World', *Fortune*, pp. 116–121, 148, 150, &152.

Buzzell, R. D., and Gale, B. T., (1987), *The PIMS Principles: Linking Strategy to Performance*, Free Press, New York.

Carroll, G. R., and Swaminathan, A., (1992), 'The Organizational Ecology of Strategic Groups in the American Brewing Industry from 1975–1990', *Industrial and Corporate Change*, Vol. 1, No. 1, pp. 65–97.

Carroll, G. R., and Wade, J., (1991), 'Density Dependence in the Organizational Evolution of the American Brewing Industry across Different Levels of Analysis', *Social Science Research*, Vol. 20, pp. 271–302.

Castrogiovanni, G. L., Justis, R. T., and Julian, S. T., (1993), 'Franchise Failure Rates: An Assessment of Magnitude', *Journal of Small Business Management*, Vol. 31, April, pp. 105–115.

Caves, P. E., and Murphy, W. F., (1976), 'Franchising: Firms, Markets and Intangible Assets', *Southern Economic Journal*, Vol. 42, April, pp. 572–586.

Chater, R. E. J., and Fernique, F., (1990), *The Financial Performance of Top 100 UK Business Format Franchising Companies*, CAMC Publications, Wantage, UK.

Cochran, A. B., (1981), Small Business Mortality Rate: A Review of the Literature,' *Journal of Small Business Management*, Vol. 19, No. 4, pp. 50–59.

Cool, K., and Schendel, D., (1987), 'Strategic Group Formation and Performance: US Pharmaceutical Industry, 1963–1982', *Management Science*, Vol. 33, pp. 1102–24.

Cross, J., (1994), 'Franchising Failures: Definitional and Measurement Issues', 1994 Society of Franchising Conference, Understanding And Accepting Different Perspectives . . . Empowering Relationships in 1994 And Beyond, Las Vegas, Nevada, 13–14 February.

Cross, J., and Walker, B., (1988), 'Franchise Failures: More Questions than Answers', 1988 Society of Franchising Conference, Forging Partnerships for Competitive Advantage, San Francisco, California, 31 January/1 February.

Central Statistical Office, (1992), *Standard Industrial Classification of Economic Activities 1992*, HMSO.

Daly, M., (1987), 'Lifespan of Businesses Registered for VAT', *British Business*, 3 April, pp. 28–9.

Davidson, A. B., (1995), 'The Medieval Monastry As Franchise Monopolist', *Journal of Economic Behaviour and Organisation*, Vol. 27, pp. 119–128.

Davies, H., (1994), quoted in 'Franchisor's Role: One Stop Shop For Business Advice', *Franchise World*, March–April, pp. 8–9.

Dickinson, R., (1981), 'Business Failure Rate,' American Journal of Small Business, Vol. 6, No. 2, pp. 17–25.

Directory of Directors (1995), *Directors and Their Board Appointments* 116th Edition, Reed Information Services, East Grinwood, West Sussex.

Dixon, J., Harrison, M., Arthurs, J., (1995), *1994 UK New Product Activity Report*, Campden & Chorleywood Research Association, Chorleywood, Hampshire.

Dodge, H. R., Fullerton, S., and Robbins, J. E., (1994), 'Stage of the Organisational Life Cycle and Competition as Mediators of Problem Perception for Small Businesses', *Strategic Management Journal*, Vol. 15, pp. 121–134.

Dun & Bradstreet, (1981), *The Failure Record*, New York.

Easingwood, C. J., (1987), 'Early Product Life Cycle Forms for Infrequently Purchased Major Products', *International Journal of Research in Marketing*, Vol. 4, pp. 3–9.

Easingwood, C. J., and Lunn, S. O., (1992), 'Diffusion Paths in a High-tech Environment: Clusters and Commonalities', *R&D Management*, Vol. 22, No. 1, pp. 69–80.

Easingwood, C. J., Mahajan, V., and Muller, E., (1981), 'A Nonsymmetric Responding Logistic Model for Forecasting Technological Substitution', *Technological Forecasting and Social Change*, Vol. 20, No. 9, pp. 199–213.

Easingwood, C. J., Mahajan, V., and Muller, E., (1983), 'A Non Uniform Influence Innovation Diffusion Model of New Product Acceptance', *Marketing Science*, Vol. 2, No. 3, pp. 273–295.

Ellingham, T., (1995), 'Financial Aspects of Launching a Franchise', in *Franchise World Directory*, 1996, Franchise World Publications, London.

English, W., and Willems, J., (1994), 'Franchise vs. Non-Franchise Restaurant Attrition: Year-Four of a Yellow Pages Longitudinal Analysis', 1994 Society of Franchising Conference, Understanding And Accepting Different Perspectives . . . Empowering Relationships in 1994 And Beyond, Las Vegas, Nevada, 13–14 February.

Eroglu, S., (1991), The Internationalisation of US Franchisees: Organizational and Environmental Determinants', Society of Franchising: Embracing the Future, Miami Beach, Florida, 9–10 February.

Felenstein, T. (1988) 'Restaurant Franchising – Is There Still Room for Survival?', *Cornell Hotel and Restaurant Association Quarterly*, May, pp. 5–18.

Felstead, A., (1993), *The Corporate Paradox Power and Control in the Business Franchise*, Routledge, London.

Franchise Task Force, (1991), *Final Report of the Franchising Task Force*, Queanbeyan, Better Printing Service, Australia.

Fredland, J. E., and Morris, C. E., (1976), 'A Cross Section Analysis of Small Business Failure', *American Journal of Small Business*, Vol. 1, pp. 7–18.

Fuller, T., (1994), *Small Business Trends 1994/1998*, Durham University Business School.

Ganguly, P., (1985), *UK Small Business Statistics and International Comparisons*, Harper and Row, London.

Gerstenhaber, M., (1988), 'Franchising Redefined as System Leasing', *Franchise World*, March/May, p. 14.

Gourlay, R., (1994), 'Bring On The Clones', *Financial Times*, 12 April, p. 13.

Hall, G., (1992), 'Reasons for Insolvency Amongst Small Firms – A Review and Fresh Evidence', *Small Business Economics*, Vol. 4, pp. 237–250.

Hambrick, D. C., and Crozier, L. M., (1985), 'Stumblers and Stars in the Management of Rapid Growth', *Journal of Business Venturing*, Vol. 1, pp. 31–45.

Hannan, M. T., and Carroll, G. R., (1992), *Dynamics of Organizational Populations: Density, Legitimation, and Competition*, Oxford University Press, Oxford.

Harrison, K., (1996), 'A Winning Formula', *Supermarketing*, 12 April, No. 1218, pp. 18–21.

Hatcliffe, M., Mills, V., Purdy, D., and Stanworth, J., (1995), *Prospective Franchisees*, Lloyds Bank, IFRC Franchising in Britain Report, Vol. 1, No. 1, University of Westminster, London.

Hopkins, D. M., (1996), 'International Differences: Standardization versus Adaptation to Cultural Differences', *Franchising Research: An International Journal*, Vol. 1, pp. 15–24.

Hough, J., (1986), *Power and Authority and their Consequences in Franchise Organizations: A Study of the Relationships between Franchisors and Franchisees*, Unpublished PhD thesis, Faculty of Management Studies, Polytechnic of Central London, London.

Hoy, F., (1994), 'The Dark Side of Franchising or Appreciating Flaws in an Imperfect World', *International Small Business Journal*, Vol. 12, pp. 26–38.

Hudson, J., (1989), 'The Birth and Death of Firms', *Quarterly Review of Economics and Business*, Vol. 29, No. 2, pp. 68–86.

Huszagh, S. M., Huszagh, F., and McIntyre, F. S., (1992), 'International Franchising in the Context of Competitive Strategy and the Theory of the Firm', *International Marketing Review*, Vol. 9, No. 5, pp. 5–18.

Ingham, B., (1995), 'Foreword', *Franchise World Directory 1996*, Franchise World Publications, London.

International Franchise Association, (1996), *Study of Franchised Unit Turnover as Defined by Item 20 of the 'New Format' Uniform Franchise Offering Circular*, International Franchise Association, Washington DC.

Kaufmann P. J., and Lafontaine, F., (1994), 'Costs of Control: The Sources of Economic Rents for McDonald's Franchisees', *Journal of Law and Economics*, Vol. 37, pp. 417–453.

Knight, R. M., (1986), 'Franchising From the Franchisor and Franchisee Points of View', *Journal of Small Business Management*, July, pp. 9–15.

Kursch, H., (1968), *The Franchise Boom: How You Can Profit In It*, Prentice Hall, Englewood Cliffs, New Jersey.

Lafontaine, F., (1994), 'Risk in Franchising: A Look at Some Measurement Issues', 1994 Society of Franchising Conference, Understanding And Accepting Different Perspectives . . . Empowering Relationships in 1994 And Beyond, Las Vegas, Nevada, 13–14 February.

Lafontaine, F., and Shaw, K., (1996), *The Dynamics of Franchise Contracting: Evidence from Panel Data, Working Paper Series*, Working Paper 5585, National Bureau of Economic Research Inc.

Lafontaine, F., and Shaw, K., (1996b), *Franchising Growth and Reality in the U. S. Market: Myth and Reality*, University of Michigan/Carnegie Mellon University

Lee, D. R., (1987), 'Why Some Succeed Where Others Fail', *Cornell Hotel and Restaurant Association Quarterly*, November, pp. 33–37.

Lillis, C., Narayana, C. L., and Gilman, J. L., (1976), 'Competitive Advantage Variation Over the Life Cycle of a Franchise', *Journal of Marketing*, Vol. 40, No. 4, pp. 77–80.

MacMillan, A., (1995), *Aspects of Franchise Recruitment*, Unpublished MBA Dissertation, University of Edinburgh.

Mendelsohn, M., and Acheson, D., (1989), *How to Franchise Your Business*, Franchise World Publications, London.

Miller, K. E., and Ginter, J. L., (1979), 'An Investigation of Situational Variation in Brand Choice Behaviour and Attitude', *Journal of Marketing Research*, Vol. XVI, February, pp. 111–123.

NatWest Review of Small Business Trends (1994), Vol. 4, December.

National Westminster Bank/British Franchise Association, (1991), *Survey 1991*, British Franchise Association, London.

National Westminster Bank/British Franchise Association, (1992), *Survey 1992*, British Franchise Association, London.

National Westminster Bank/British Franchise Association, (1993), *Survey 1993*, British Franchise Association, London.

National Westminster Bank/British Franchise Association, (1994), *Survey 1994*, British Franchise Association, London.

National Westminster Bank/British Franchise Association, (1995), *Survey 1995*, British Franchise Association, London.

National Westminster Bank/British Franchise Association, (1996), *Survey 1996*, British Franchise Association, London.

Nault, B. R. and Dexter, A. S., (1994), 'Adoption, Transfers and Incentives in a Franchise Network with Positive Externalities', *Marketing Science*, Vol. 13, No. 4, Autumn, pp. 412–423.

Norton, S. W., (1988a), 'An Empirical Look at Franchising as an Organizational Form', *Journal of Business*, Vol. 61, No. 2, pp. 197–219.

Norton, S. W., (1988b), 'Franchising, Brand Name, and the Entrepreneurial Capacity Problem', *Strategic Management Journal*, Vol. 9, pp. 105–114.

Orrin, P., (1988), 'The Financial Path of the Franchisor', *Franchise World Directory*, Franchise World Publications, London.

Ozanne, U. B., and Hunt, S. D., (1971), The Economic Effects of Franchising, Report Prepared for the Small Business Administration and Select Committee on Small Business, US Senate, September, Graduate School of Business, University of Wisconsin.

Padmanabhan, K. H., (1986), 'Are Franchised Businesses Less Risky than the Non-Franchised Business?', Society of Franchising, First Annual Conference, Omaha, Nebraska, 28–30 September.

Perkins, J., (1988), 'Arranging Finance Through the Banks', *Franchise World Directory 1988*, Franchise World Publications, London.

Peterson, R., Rozmetsky, G., and Ridgway, N. M., (1983), 'Perceived Causes of Small Business Failures', *American Journal of Small Businesses*, Vol. VIII, No. 1, July/September, pp. 15–19.

Price, S., (1993), 'The Performance of Fast Food Franchises in Britain', *International Journal of Hospitality Management*, Vol. 5, No. 3, pp 10–15.

Price, S., (1996), *Behind the Veneer of Success: Propensities for UK Franchisor Failure*, Small Business Research Trust, The Open University, Milton Keynes.

Power, M. C., (1990), *NatWest/BFA Survey, 1990*, Power Associates, London

Rogers, E., (1995), *The Diffusion of Innovations*, Free Press, New York.

Rosenberg, R., and Bedell, M., (1969), *Profits From Franchising*, McGraw-Hill, New York.

Sen, K. C., (1993), 'The Use of Initial Fees and Royalties in Business Format Franchising', *Managerial and Decision Economics*, Vol. 14, pp. 175–190.

Serwer, A. E., (1995), 'Trouble in Franchise Nation', *Fortune*, 16 March, pp. 57–62.

Scott, M., and Lewis, J., (1984), 'Rethinking Entrepreneurial Failure', in Lewis, J., Stanworth, J., and Gibb, A., (eds) *Success and Failure in Small Business*, pp. 29–56, Gower Publishing Co Ltd, Aldershot.

Shane, S., (1996), 'Hybrid Organizational Arrangements and their Implications for Firm Growth and Survival: A Study of New Franchisors', *Academy of Management Journal*, Vol. 39, pp. 216–234.

Sherman, A. J., (1993), 'Preface: The Management of Franchising in the Twenty-First Century', pp. xi–xv in Sherman, A. J., (ed.), *The Franchising Handbook*, American Management Association, New York.

Silvester, T., (1996), *Growth Constraints on Young British Franchise Systems*, MBA dissertation, University of Greenwich, London.

Singh, K., and Mitchell, W., (1996), 'Precarious Collaboration: Business Survival After Partners Shut Down of Form New Partnerships', *Strategic Management Journal*, Special Issue, Vol. 17, pp. 99–116.

Smart, B., (1994), Cross-Talk, *Franchise World*, May–June, pp. 45–48.

Stanworth, J., (1994), *The impact of franchising on the development prospects of small and mediumsized enterprises (SMEs) in the United Kingdom*, Report prepared for the Department of Trade and Industry.

Stanworth, J., (1995), 'Research Note: Penetrating the Mists Surrounding Franchisor Failure Rates – Some Old Lessons For New Businesses,' *International Small Business Journal*, Vol. 13, No. 2, pp. 59–63.

Steinberg, C., (1995), 'Turnarounds!', *Success*, Vol. 42, No. 1, pp. 71–77.

Stewart, H., and Gallagher, C. C., (1986), 'Business Death and Firm Size in the UK', *International Small Business Journal*, Vol. 4, No. 1, pp. 42–57.

Stern, P., and Stanworth J., (1994), 'Improving Small Business Survival Rates via Franchising The Role of Banks in Europe', *International Small Business Journal*, Volume 12, No. 2, January/March, pp. 15–25.

Stockstill, L. E., (1985), 'Multilevel Franchise or Pyramid Scheme?', *Journal of Small Business Management*, Vol. 23, No. 4, pp. 54–58.

Storey, D., (1994), *Understanding the Small Business Sector*, Routledge, London and New York.

Thompson, D. N., (1971), 'Contractual Marketing Systems: An Overview', pp. 3–30 in Thompson, D. N., (ed.), *Contractual Marketing Systems*, Heath Lexington Books, Lexington, Massachusetts.

Thompson, R. S., (1994), 'The Franchise Life-cycle and the Penrose Effect', *Journal of Economic Behavior and Organization*, Vol. 24, No. 2, pp. 207–218.

Timmons, J. A., (1988), 'Grow up big', in Sexton, D. L., and Smilor, R. W., (eds), *The Art of Entrepreneurship*, Ballinger, Cambridge, Massachusetts.

Trutko, J., Trutko, J., and Kostecka, A., (1993), *Franchising's Role in the US Economy, 1975–2000*, US Business Administration, Washington, DC.

Walker, D., (1989), *A Comparison of International Versus Domestic Expansion by U. S. Franchise Systems*, International Franchise Association, Washington DC.

Weinrauch, D. J., (1986), 'Franchising an Established Business,' *Journal of Small Business Management*, Vol. 24, July, pp. 1–7.

Williams, P., (1995), 'British is Best', *Business Franchise*, November, pp. 36–37.

Chapter 9: Franchisee financial performance: comparisons with non-franchised firms and the role of the environment

Acheson, D., and Paul, R., (1990), *Franchising*, Business Briefing, Institute of Chartered Accountants in England & Wales, London.

Achrol, R. S., and Etzel, M. J., (1992), 'The Effect of Market Environment on Franchise Goals and Franchisor Services', Summary, pp. 585–586, in Churchill, N. C., et al, (eds), *Frontiers of Entrepreneurship Research*, Babson College Entrepreneurship Research Conference, Babson Park, Massachusetts.

Adams, D. J., (1992), 'Do Corporate Failure Prediction Models Work?', *International Journal of Contemporary Hospitality Management*, Vol. 3, No. 4, pp. 25–29.

Agrawal, D., and Lal, R., (1995), 'Contractual Agreements in Franchising', *Journal of Marketing Research*, Vol. 32, May, pp. 213–221.

Aldrich, H. E., (1979), *Organizations and Environments*, Prentice Hall, Englewood Cliffs, New Jersey.

Aldrich, H. E., and Zimmer, C., (1986), 'Entrepreneurship through Social Network', pp. 3–24, in Sexton, D., and Smiler, R., (eds), *The Art & Science of Entrepreneurship*, Ballinger, New York.

Aldrich, H. E., and Reese, P. R., (1993), 'Does Networking Pay-Off? A Panel Study of Entrepreneurs in the Research Triangle', pp. 325–339 in Churchill, N. C., et al, (eds), *Frontiers of Entrepreneurship Research*, Babson College Entrepreneurship Research Conference, Babson Park, Massachusetts.

Altman, E. I., (1983), *Corporate Financial Distress. A Complete Guide to Predicting, Avoiding, and Dealing with Bankruptcy*, John Wiley & Sons Inc., New York.

Anderson, J. C., and Narus, J. A., (1990), 'A Model of the Distributor's Perspective of Distributor-Manufacturer Working Relationships', *Journal of Marketing*, Vol. 48, January, pp. 62–74.

Anderson, E., and Weitz, B., (1992), 'The Uses of Pledges to Build and Sustain Commitment in Distribution Channels', *Journal of Marketing Research*, Vol. XXIV, February, pp. 18–34.

Argenti, J., (1976), *Corporate Collapse: The Causes and Symptoms*, McGraw-Hill, London.

Arogyswamy, K., Barker III, V. L., and Yasai-Ardekani, M., (1995), 'Firm Turnarounds: An Integrative Two-Stage Model', *Journal of Management Studies*, Vol. 32, No. 4, pp. 493–525.

Ashman, R. T., (1987), The Way Ahead for Franchising and Licencing, First European Franchising and Licencing Conference, Glasgow, 15–16 June.

Astley, W. G., and Fombrun, C. J., (1983), 'Collective Strategy: Social Ecology of Organizational Environments', Academy of Management Review, Vol. 8, No. 4, pp. 576–587.

Aziz, A., Emanuel, D. C., and Lawson, G., (1988), 'Bankruptcy Prediction – An Investigation of Cash-Flow Based Models', *Journal of Management Studies*, Vol. 25, No. 5, pp. 419, 437.

Ball, S., Black, A. D., and West, A., (1988), *Britain's Fast Food Industry*, Jordans & Sons Ltd, Bristol, UK.

Balthory, A., (1985), *Predicting Corporate Collapse: Credit analysis in the Determination and Forecasting of Insolvent Companies*, Financial Times Business Information Ltd., London.

Bartlett, C. A., and Ghoshal, S., (1991), 'Global Strategic Management: Impact on the New Frontiers of Strategy Research', *Strategic Management Journal*, Vol. 12, Special Issue, pp. 5–16.

Bates, T., (1995), 'Analysis of Survival Rates Among Franchisee and Independent Small Business Set-ups', *Journal of Small Business Management*, Vol. 33, April, No. 2, pp. 26–36.

Baucus, D. A., Baucus, M. S., and Human, S. E., (1993), 'Choosing A Franchise: How Base Fees and Royalties Relate to the Value of the Franchise', *Journal of Small Business Management*, Vol. 31, April, No. 2, pp. 91–104.

Baum, J. A. C., and Mezias, S. J., (1992), 'Localized Competition and Organizational Failure in the Manhattan Hotel Industry, 1888–1990', *Administrative Science Quarterly*, Vol. 37, pp. 580–604.

Beaumont, J. R., and Sutherland, E., (1992), *Information Resources Management*, Butterworth Heinemann, London.

Bernstien, C., (1994), 'Franchising Explosive Issues Fuel Debate', *Restaurant Business*, Vol. 104, No. 24, 15 October, pp. 61–67.

Bilbeault, D. G., (1982), *Corporate Turnaround: How Managers Turn Losers Into Winners*, McGraw-Hill, New York, New York.

Birley, S., (1985), 'The Role of Networks in the Entrepreneurial Process', *Journal of Business Venturing*, Vol. 1, No. 1, pp. 107–117.

Blum, M., (1974), 'Failing Company Discriminant Analysis', *Journal of Accounting Research*, Spring, pp. 1–25.

Boyle, R. D., and Desai, H. B., (1991), 'Turnaround Strategies for Small Firms', *Journal of Small Business Management*, Vol. 29, No. 3, pp. 33–42.

Bradach, J. L., (1994), 'Chains within Chains: The Role of Multi-unit Franchisees', 1994 Society of Franchising Conference, Understanding And Accepting Different Perspectives . . . Empowering Relationships In 1994 And Beyond, Las Vegas, 13–14 February.

Brooksbank, R., (1991), 'Defining the Small Business: A New Classification of Company Size', *Entrepreneurship and Regional Development*, Vol. 3, pp. 17–31.

Brown, S., (1989), 'Retail Location Theory: The Legacy of Harold Hotelling', *Journal of Retailing*, Vol. 65, pp. 450–469.

Bruno, A. V., Leidecker, J. K., and Harder, J. W., (1987), 'Why Firms Fail, ' *Business Horizons*, March–April, pp. 50–58.

Bygrave, W. D., (1993), 'Partnership Franchising: Maximizing Entrepreneurial and Financial Leverage in Franchising', pp. 575–586, in Churchill, N. C., et al (eds), *Frontiers of Entrepreneurship Research*, Babson College Entrepreneurship Research Conference, Babson Park, Massachusetts.

CACI Ltd, (1994), *The Geodemographic Pocket Book: A Portrait of Britain's Products, Towns, Counties, and Marketplaces*, CACI Ltd in association with NTC Publications Ltd.

Campanelli, P., Channell, J., McAulay, E., Renouf, A., and Thomas, R., (1994), *Training: An Exploration of the Word and the Concept with an Analysis of the Implications for Survey Design*, Department of Employment, Research Series No. 30, London.

Card, D., and Krueger, A. B., (1994), 'Minimum Wages and Employment: A Case Study of the Fast Food in New Jersey and Pennsylvannia', *American Economic Review*, Vol. 84, No. 4, pp. 772–793.

Castrogiovanni, G. J., (1991), 'Environment Munificence: A Theoretical Assessment', *Academy of Management Review*, Vol. 16, No. 3, pp. 542–565.

Castrogiovanni, G. L., Justis, R. T., and Julian, S. T., (1993), 'Franchise Failure Rates: An Assessment of Magnitude', *Journal of Small Business Management*, Vol. 31, No. 2, pp. 105–115.

Chambers, J., (1996), 'Under-performing Franchisees: Prevention & Cure', *Franchise Link*, The British Franchise Association Magazine, March, pp. 6–7.

Chakravathy, B. S., (1982), 'Adaptation: A Promising Metaphor for Strategic Management', *Academy of Management Review*, Vol. 7, pp. 35–44.

Cherkasky, W. B., (1996), 'Franchising: a key to business success', *Franchising Research: An International Journal*, Vol. 1, No. 3, pp. 5–8.

Child, J., (1972), 'Organizational Structure, Environment and Performance: The Role of Strategic Choice', *Sociology*, Vol. 6, pp. 2–21.

Chisman, J. L., and Leslie, J., (1989), 'Strategic, Administrative, and Operating Problems: The Impact of Outsiders on Small Firm Performance', *Entrepreneurship, Theory and Practice*, Vol. 4, pp. 37–51.

Christensen, H. K., and Montgomery, C. A., (1981), 'Corporate Economic Performance: Diversification Strategy Versus Market Structure', *Strategic Management Journal*, Vol. 2, pp. 327–343.

Clapham, S. E., and Schwenk, C. R., (1991), 'Self-Serving Attributions, Managerial Cognition, and Company Performance', *Strategic Management Journal*, Vol. 12, pp. 219–229.

Cooper, A., Folta, T., Gimeno-Gascon, J., and Woo, C. Y., (1992), 'Entrepreneurs' Exit Decisions: The Role of Threshold Expectations', *Working Paper # 1018*, Krannert Graduate School of Management, Purdue University.

Cross, J., (1994), 'Franchising Failures: Definitional and Measurement Issues', 1994 Society of Franchising Conference, Understanding And Accepting Different Perspectives . . . Empowering Relationships In 1994 And Beyond, Las Vegas, 13–14 February.

Cross, J., and Walker, B., (1988), 'Franchise Failures: More Questions and Answers', 1986 Society of Franchising, First Annual Conference, Omaha, Nebraska, 29–30 September.

Curran, J. R., and Storbeck, J. E., (1994), 'A Multi-Objective Approach to Design Franchise Network Outlets', *Journal of the Operational Research Society*, Vol. 45, No. 1, pp. 71–81.

Dahlstorm, R., and Nygaard, A., (1994), 'A Preliminary Investigation of Franchised Oil Distribution in Norway', *Journal of Retailing*, Vol. 70, No. 2, pp. 179–191.

Damodaran, A., (1994), *Damodaran on Valuation: Security Analysis for Investment and Corporate Finance*, John Wiley, New York.

Desai, M., and Montes, A., (1982), ' Macro-economic Model of Bankruptcies in the British Economy 1945–1980', *British Review of Economic Issues*, Vol. 4, pp. 1–14.

Desai, P., and Srinivasan, K., (1993), 'Demand Signalling under Observable Effort in Franchising Linear and Non-Linear Price Contracts', *Working Paper # 1058*, March, Krannert Graduate School of Management, Purdue University.

Desai, P., (1994), 'Advertising Fee in Business Format Franchising', *Working Paper # 1059*, April, Krannert Graduate School of Management, Purdue University.

Davies, D., (1991), *The Art of Managing Finance*, McGraw-Hill, London.

Day, G. S., (1977), 'Diagnosing the Product Portfolio', *Journal of Marketing*, Vol. 41, April, pp. 29–38.

DiPietro, W., and Sawhney, B., (1977), 'Business Failure, Managerial Competence, and Macro-Economic Variables', *American Journal of Small Business*, Vol. 2, No. 2, pp. 4–15.

Dodge, H. R., Fullerton, S., and Robbins, J. E., (1994), 'Stage of the Organizational Life Cycle and Competition as Mediators of Problem Perception for Small Businesses', *Strategic Management Journal*, Vol. 15, pp. 121–134.

Dollinger, M. J., and Golden, P. A., (1992), 'Interorganizational and Collective Strategies in Small Firms: Environmental Effects and Performance', *Journal of Management*, Vol. 18, No. 4, pp. 695–715.

Dun & Bradstreet, (1995), *Key Business Ratios*, Dun & Bradstreet Ltd, UK.

Dunning, J. H., (1989), 'Multinational Enterprises and the Growth of Services: Some Conceptual and Theoretical Issues', *The Services Industries Journal*, pp. 5–39.

Dwyer, F. R., Schurr, P. H., and Oh, S., (1987), 'Developing Buyer-Seller Relationships', *Journal of Marketing*, Vol. 51, April, pp. 11–27.

Edminister, R. O., (1972), 'An Empirical Test for Financial Ratio Analysis for Small Business Failure Prediction', *Journal of Financial and Quantitative Analysis*, March, pp. 1477–1493.

Emerson, R. L., (1990), *The New Economics of Fast Food*, Van Nostrand Reinhold, New York.

English, W., (1993), 'Franchising, by Its Proper Name, is Wholesaling!', *Journal of Marketing Channels*, Vol. 2, No. 3, pp. 1–25.

English, W. and Hoy, F., (1995), 'Are Franchisees Actually Entrepreneurs?' Society of Franchising Conference Proceedings, The International Challenge – Towards New Franchising Relationships, Honolulu, Hawaii, 17 –18 February.

Fish, M., and Rudolph, P., (1986), 'The Impact of Changing Conditions on International Resort Returns: A Case Study in a Developing Country', *International Journal of Hospitality Management*, Vol. 5, pp. 63–69.

Fulop, C., (1996), *An investigation of the needs and attitudes of the franchise marketplace*, Centre for Franchise Research, City University Business School, London.

Galbraith, J. R., (1973), *Designing Complex Organizations*, Addison-Wesley, Reading, Massachusetts.

Gallini, N. T., and Lutz, N. A., (1992), 'Dual Distribution and Royalty Fees in Franchising', *Journal of Law, Economics and Organization*, Vol. 8, October, pp. 471–501.

Gheradi, S., (1995), *Gender, Symbolism and Organizational Cultures*, Sage Publications, London.

Ghosh, A., and Craig, C. S., (1991), 'FRANSYS: A Franchise Distribution System Location Model', *Journal of Retailing*, Vol. 67, pp. 466–495.

Goold, M., Campbell, A., and Alexander, A., (1994), *Corporate-Level Strategy – Creating Value in the Multi-Business Company*, John-Wiley & Sons, New York.

Gopinath, C., (1991), 'Turnaround: Recognizing Decline and Initiating Intervention', *Long Range Planning*, Vol. 24, No. 6, pp. 96–101.

Green, R. T., and Kohli, A. K., (1991), 'Export Market Identification; The Role of Economics Size and Socio-Economic Development', *Management International Review*, Vol. 31, No. 1, pp. 37–50.

Gruca, T. S., and Nath, D., (1994), 'Regulatory Change, Constraints on Adaptation and Organizational Failure; An Empirical Analysis of Acute Care Hospitals', *Strategic Management Journal*, Vol. 15, pp. 345–363.

Hadfield, G. K., (1991), 'Credible spatial preemption through franchising', *RAND Journal of Economics*, Vol. 22, No. 4, pp. 531–543.

Hall, P. J., (1995), 'Habitual Owners of Small Business', Chapter 15, pp. 217–230, in Chiltern, F., Robertson, M., and Marshall, I., (eds), *Small Firms, Partnerships for Growth*, Paul Chapman Publishing.

Hambrick, D. C., and D'Aveni, R. A., (1988), 'Large Cooperate Failures as Downward Spirals', *Administrative Science Quarterly*, Vol. 33, pp. 1–23.

Hambrick, D. C., and Schecter. S., (1983), 'Turnaround Strategies for Mature Industrial-Product Business Units', *Academy of Managment Journal*, Vol. 26, No. 2, pp. 231–248.

Hannan, M., and Freeman, J., (1977), 'The Population Ecology of Organizations', *International Economic Review*, May, Vol. 83, pp. 929–964.

Hanson, G. T., (1985), 'Incomplete Contracts, Risk and Ownership', *International Economic Review*, May, Vol. 36, No. 2, pp. 341–364.

Harrell, G. D., and Kiefer, R. O., (1981), 'Multinational Strategic Portfolios', *Business Topics*, Winter, pp. 5–15, Michigan State Unversity, East Lausing, Michigan.

Harrigan, K. R., (1985), *Strategic Flexibility: A Management Guide for Changing Times*, Lexington Books, Lexington, Massachusetts.

Hartigan, J., (1975), *Clustering Algorithms*, Wiley-Interscience, New York.

Hayes, J. P., (1994), *Taking the Fear out of Franchising*, The Internet Presence & Publishing Corporation: 'http://www. ip. net/legal. html.'

Haynes, M., (1995), *Plimsoll Portfolio Analysis: Restaurant & Catering*, 1st Edition, Plimsoll Publishing, Middlesbrough, UK.

Hedley, B., (1977), 'Strategy and the 'Business Portfolio', *Long Range Planning*, Vol. 10, February, pp. 9–15.

Hing, N., (1995), 'Franchise Satisfaction; Contributors and Consequences', *Journal of Small Business Management*, Vol. 33, No. 2, April, pp. 12–25.

Hofer, C. H., (1980), 'Turnaround Strategies', *The Journal of Business Strategy*, Vol. 1, No. 1, pp. 19–31.

Hoffman, R. C., (1989), 'Strategies for Corporate Turnarounds: What do We Know About Them?', *Journal of General Management*, Vol. 14, No. 3, pp. 46–67.

Holmberg, S. R., and Morgan, K. B., (1996), 'The Franchise Failure Continuum', 1996 Society of Franchising Conference, Partners for Progress . . . A World of Opportunities, Honolulu, Hawaii, 17–18 February.

Horwath International (1991), *Franchising in the Economy*, International Edition, IFA Publications, Evans City, Pennsylvannia.

Hrebiniak, L. G., and Joyce, W. F., (1985), 'Organizational Adaptation: Strategic Choice and Environmental Determinism', *Administrative Science Quarterly*, Vol. 30, pp. 336–349.

Hudson, J., (1987), 'Company Births in Great Britain and Institutional Environment', *International Small Business Journal*, Vol. 6, pp. 57–69.

Hudson, J., (1989), 'The Birth and Death of Firms', Quarterly Review of Economics and Business, Vol. 29, No. 2, pp. 68–86.

Hungenberg, H., (1993), 'How to Ensure that Headquarters Add Value', *Long Range Planning*, Vol. 26, No. 6, pp. 62–73.

Ibrahim, A. B., (1985), 'Is Franchising the Answer to Small Business Failure Rate? An Empirical Investigation', 30th Annual World Conference of the International Council for Small Business, Small Business in the Entrepreneurial Era, Montreal, Canada, 16–19 June.

ICC, (1994), *Restaurant and Contract Catering Industry*, Fourth Edition, ICC Information Group Ltd, London.

Jennings, D. F., and Seaman, S,L., (1994), 'High and Low Levels of Organizational Adaptation: An Empircal Analysis of Strategy, Structure, and Performance', *Strategic Management Journal*, Vol. 15, pp. 459–475.

Julian, S. D., and Castrogiovanni, G. J, (1995), 'Franchisor Geographic Expansion', *Journal of Small Business Management*, Vol. 33, April, pp. 1–11.

Justis, R. T., Castrogiovanni, G. J., and Chan, P. S., (1994), 'Franchisor Quick-start', 1994 Society of Franchising Conference, Understanding And Accepting Different Perspectives . . . Empowering Relationships In 1994 And Beyond, Las Vegas, 13–14 February.

Kamshad, K. M., (1994), 'Firm Growth and Survival: Does Ownership Structure Matter?', *Journal of Economics and Management Strategy*', Vol. 3, No. 3, pp. 521–544.

Kaplan, R. S., and Norton, D. P., (1996), 'Using the Balanced Scorecard as Strategic Management System', *Harvard Business Review*, January–February, pp. 75–85.

Kaufmann, P. J., Donthu, N., and Brooks, C., (1995), 'Sequential or Global Site Selection: A Simulation and Comparison', 1995 Society of Franchising Conference, The International Challenge . . . Towards New Franchising Relationships, San Juan, Puerto Rico.

Kaufmann, P. J., and Lafontaine, F. F., (1994), 'Costs of Control: The Source of Economics Rents for McDonald's Franchisees, *Journal of Law and Economics*, Vol. XXXVIII, pp. 417–453.

Kaufmann, P. J., and Rangan, V. K., (1990), 'A Model for Managing System Conflict During Franchise Expansion', *Journal of Retailing*, Vol. 66, pp. 155–173.

Kaufmann, P. J., and Stanworth, J., (1995), 'The Decision to Purchase a Franchise: A Study of Prospective Franchisees', *Journal of Small Business Management*, Vol. 33, No. 4, pp. 22–23.

Keasey, K., and Watson, R., (1985), 'The Uses and Abuses of Small Firm Failure Prediction Models', *Business Graduate*, January, pp. 30–32.

Keasey, K., and Watson, R., (1986), 'The Prediction of Small Company Failure: Some Behavioural Evidence from the UK,' *Journal of Accounting Research*, Winter, pp. 49–57.

Kelly, J., (1995), 'Study of Failed Companies Questions Auditors Role', *Financial Times*, 10 April.

Keyt, J. C., Yavas, V., and Reicken, G., (1994), 'Importance-Performance Analysis: A Case Study in Restaurant Positioning', *International Journal of Retail & Distribution Management*, Vol. 22, No. 5, pp. 35–40.

Khandwalla, P. N., (1992), *Innovative Corporate Turnarounds*, Sage Publications, London.

Kimes, S. E., and Fitzsimmons, J. A., (1990), 'Selecting Profitable Hotel Sites at La Quinta Motor Inns', *Interfaces*, Vol. 20, No. 2, March, pp. 12–20.

Kitson, M., (1995), Seed corn or chaff? Unemployment & small firm performance, ESRC Centre for Business Research, University of Cambridge, *Working Paper No. 2*, February.

Klein, B., and Saft, L. F., (1985), 'The Law and Economics of Franchise Tying Contracts', *Journal of Law and Economics*, Vol. XXVIII, May, pp. 345–361.

Knickerbocker, F., (1973), *Oligopolistic Reaction and the Multinational Enterprise*, Harvard University Press, Boston, Massachusetts.

Kroc, R., (1977), *Grinding It Out: The Making of McDonald's*, Contemporary Books, Chicago, Illinois.

Kumar, N., Scheer, L. K., and Steenkamp, J. E. M., (1985), 'The Effects of Perceived Interdependence on Dealer Performance', *Journal of Marketing Research*, Vol. XXXII, August, pp. 348–356.

Laitinen, E. K., (1992), 'Prediction of Failure of a Newly Founded Firm', *Journal of Business Venturing*, Vol. 7, No. 4, September, pp. 323–340.

Lal, R., (1990), 'Improving Channel Coordination Through Franchising', *Marketing Science*, Vol. 9, No. 4, pp. 299–318.

Lanthier, C., (1995), 'Subway Bites', *Financial Post*, 25 November, p. 6.

Lapin, L. L., (1993), *Statistics for Modern Business Decisions*, The Dryden Press, Fort Worth, Texas.

Larson, C. M., and Clute, R. C., (1979), 'The Failure Syndrome', *American Journal of Small Business*, Vol. 4, No. 2, pp. 35–43.

Lassar, W. M., and Kerr, J. L., (1996), 'Strategy and Control in Supplier-Distributor Relationships: An Agency Perspective', *Strategic Management Journal*, Vol. 17, pp. 613–632.

LaVan, H., Latona, J. C., Coye, R. W., (1986), 'Training and Development in the Franchisor-Franchisee Relationship', 1986 Society of Franchising, First Annual Conference, Omaha, Nebraska, 29–30 September.

Lorange, P., and Vancil, R. F., (1987), 'How to Design a Strategic Plan', *Harvard Business Review*, Vol. 54, pp. 75–81.

Love, J. F., (1986), *McDonald's – Behind the Arches*, Bantam Books Inc., New York.

Lovell, M. C., (1971), 'Optimal Franchising in Theory', pp. 63–78 in Thompson, D. N., (ed.), *Contractual Marketing Systems*, D. C. Heath, Lexington, Massachusetts.

Lowe, M. B., and Macmillan, L. C., (1988), 'Entrepreneurship: Past and Future Challenges', *Journal of Management*, Vol. 14, pp. 139–161.

Lowell, H. B., (1991), *Multiple-Unit Franchising: The Key to Rapid System Growth*, Brownstein Zeidman and Schomer, Washington D. C.

Marlin, D., Lamont, B. T., and Hoffman, J. J., (1994), 'Choice Situation, Strategy and Performance: A Reexamination', *Strategic Management Journal*, Vol. 15, pp. 229–239.

Mason, C. M., and Harrison, R. T., (1995), 'Why Franchising Works: An Analysis of Property Rights and Organizational Share Forms', pp. 676–687, in Churchill, N. C. et al (eds), *Frontiers of Entrepreneurship Research*, Babson College Entrepreneurship Research Conference, Babson Park, Massachusetts.

Mathewson, G. F., and Winter, R. A., (1985), 'The Economics of Franchise Contracts', *Journal of Law and Economics*, Vol. 28, pp. 503–526.

McKiernan, P., (1992), *Strategies of Growth*, Routledge, London.

McKelvey, W., (1981), *Organizational Systematics*, University of California Press, Los Angeles, California.

McKenzie, J., (1996), *Paradox: The Next Strategic Dimension – Using Conflict to Re-energize Your Business*, McGraw-Hill, New York.

Melaniphy, J., (1992), *Restaurant and Fast Food Site Selection*, Wiley, New York.

Michael, S. C., (1996), 'Rents and Competitive Advantage in Franchising', *Franchising Research: An International Journal*, Vol. 1, No. 3, pp. 38–43.

Miles, R. E., and Snow, C. C., (1994), *Fit, Failure & the Hall of Fame*, Free Press, New York.

Miller, D., (1977), 'Common Syndromes of Business Failure', *Business Horizons*, November, pp. 43–53.

Min, H., (1987), 'A Location Model for Fast Food Restaurants', *Omega*, Vol. 15, No. 5.

Mohr, J. J., and Sohi, R. S., (1995), 'Communication Flows in Distribution Channels: Impact on Assessments of Communication Quality and Satisfaction', *Journal of Retailing*, Vol. 71, No. 4, pp. 393–416.

Mohr, J. J., and Spekman, R., (1994), 'Charactristics of Partnership Success: Partnership Attributes, Communication Behaviour, and Conflict Resolution Techniques', *Strategic Management Journal*, Vol. 15, pp. 135–152.

Morley, M. F., (1984), *Ratio Analysis, Institute of Chartered Accountants of Scotland*, Monograph, Gee & Co. (Publishers) Ltd.

Muller, R., (1985), 'Corporate Crisis Management ', *Long Range Planning*, Vol. 18, pp. 38–48.

Nichols, D., (1995), 'Critics Take Potshots at Franchise Study', *Restaurant Business*, Vol. 94, No. 10, July, p. 24.

Nohria, N., and GarciaPont, C., (1991), 'Global Strategic Linkages and Industry Structure', *Strategic Management Journal*, Special Issue, Summer, Vol. 12, pp. 105–124.

Nutt, P. C., (1993), 'Flexible Decision Styles and the Choices of Top Executives', *Journal of Management Studies*, Vol. 30, pp. 695–721.

O'Farrell, P. N., and Hitchins, D. W. N., (1988), 'Alternative Theories of Small Firm Growth: A Critical Review', *Environment and Planning*, Vol. 20, p. 1382.

Ohlson, J. A., (1980), 'Financial Ratios and the Probablistic Prediction of Bankruptcy', *Journal of Accounting Research*, Vol. 18, No. 1, pp. 109–132.

O'Neill, H. O., (1986), 'Turnaround and Recovery: What Strategy Do You Need?', *Long Range Planning*, Vol. 19, No. 1, pp. 80–88.

Orpen, C., (1985), 'The Effects of Long Range Planning on Small Business Performance', *Journal of Small Business Management*, Vol. 23, No. 1, pp. 35–45.

Ostagaard, T. A., and Birley, S., (1994), 'Personal Networks and Firm Competitive Strategy – A Strategic or Coincidental Match?', *Journal of Business Venturing*, Vol. 9, pp. 281–305.

Ozanne, U. B., and Hunt, S. D., (1971), *The Economic Effects of Franchising, Report Prepared for the Small Business Administration and Select Committee on Small Business*, US Senate, September, Graduate School of Business, University of Wisconsin.

Page, M. J., (1984), 'Corporate Financial Reporting and the Small Independent Company', *Accounting and Business Research*, Vol. 15, Summer, pp. 271–282.

Parker, L. L., (1973), 'Contractual Market Expansion – A Short Run Phenomenon?', *International Journal of Physical Distribution*, Vol. 3, Spring, 1973.

Pashigan, B. P., (1961), *The Distribution of Automobiles: An Economic Analysis of the Franchise System*, Prentice Hall, Englewood Cliffs, New Jersey.

Pearce, J. A., and Robbins, D. K., (1993), 'Toward Improved Theory & Research on Business Turnaround', *Journal of Management*, Vol. 19, pp. 613–636.

Perlitz, M., (1991), 'Country-Portfolio Analysis – Assessing Country Risk and Opportunity', pp. 101–118 in Freedman, N. J., (ed.), *Strategic Management in Major Multinational Companies: The Best of Long Range Planning*, No. 8, Pergamon Press, London.

Pettit, S. J., (1988), 'Marketing Decision Making Within Franchised Systems', 1988 Society of Franchising, Forging Partnerships for Competitive Advantage, San Francisco, California, 31 January–2 February.

Phillips, B. D., and Kirchhoff, B. A., (1989), 'Formation, Growth and Survival; Small Firm Dynamics in the US Economy', *Small Business Economics*, Vol. 1, pp. 65–74.

Pilling, B. K., Henson, S. W., and Yoo, B., (1995), 'Competition Among Franchises, Company-Owned Units and Independent Operators: A Population Ecology Application', *Journal of Marketing Channels*, Vol. 4, No. 1/2, pp. 175–195.

Porter, M. E., (1979), 'The Structure within Industries and Companies' Performance', *Review of Economics and Statistics*, Vol. 61, pp. 214–228.

Prahalad, C. K., and Bettis, R. A., (1986), 'The Dominant Logic: A New Linkage between Diversity and Performance', *Strategic Management Journal*, Vol. 7, pp. 485–501.

Price, S., (1993), 'The Performance of Fast Food Franchises in Britain', *International Journal of Hospitality Management*, Vol. 5, No. 3, pp. 10–15.

Power, M., (1993), *Business Format Franchisees Closing or Continuing 1987–1992*, Power Research Associates, London.

Riding, R., (1996), 'In the Name of the Franchise', *The Times*, 12 March, p. 21.

Robbins, D. K., and Pearce II, J. A., (1992), 'Turnaround: Retrenchment and Recovery', *Strategic Management Journal*, Vol. 13, pp. 287–309.

Robertson, J., and Mills, R. W. (1988), 'Company Failure or Company Health? – Techniques for Measuring Company Health', *Long Range Planning*, Vol. 21, No. 2, pp. 70–77.

Robinson, R. B., (1982), 'The Importance of 'Outsiders' in Small Firm Strategic Planning', *Academy of Management Journal*, Vol. 10, pp. 17–23.

Robinson, R. B., and Pearce, II, J. A., (1984), 'Research Thrusts in Small Firm Planning', *Academy of Management Review*, Vol. 9, pp. 128–137.

Roure, J. B., and Maidique, M. A., (1986), 'Linking Pre-funding Factors and High-technology Venture Success: An Exploratory Study', *Journal of Business Venturing*, pp. 295–306.

Royal Bank of Scotland, (1993), *Survey of Franchise Marketplace*, Royal Bank of Scotland, London.

Rumelt, R., (1991), 'How Much Does Industry Matter?', *Strategic Management Journal*, Vol. 12, No. 3, pp. 167–186.

Seltz, D. S., (1982), *The Complete Handbook of Franchising*, Addison-Wesley Publishing Company, Reading, Massachusetts.

Sen, K. C., (1993), 'The Use of Initial Fees and Royalties in Business Format Franchising', *Managerial and Decision Economics*, Vol. 14, pp. 175–190.

Serwer, A. E., (1994), 'McDonald's Conquers the World', *Fortune*, 17 October, pp. 59–69.

Sethi, S. P., (1971), 'Comparative Cluster Analysis for World Markets', *Journal of Marketing Research*, Vol. VIII, August, pp. 348–354.

Shane, S. A., (1996), 'Hybrid Organizational Arrangements and their Implications for Firm Growth and Survival: A Study of New Franchisors', *Academy of Management Journal*, Vol. 39, pp. 216–234.

Shelton, J. P., (1967), 'Allocative Efficiency vs. X-Efficiency: Comment', *American Economic Review*, Vol. 57, October, pp. 1252–1258.

Sheppard, J. P., (1994), 'Strategy and Bankruptcy: An Exploration into Organizational Death', *Journal of Management*, Vol. 20, Winter, pp. 795–834.

Sheppard, J. P., (1995), 'A Resource Dependence Approach to Organizational Failure', *Social Science Research*, pp. 28–62.

Sim, B., and Gleeson, W., (1994), *'How to Run Your Own Restaurant'*, Kogan Page, London.

Simmons, P., (1989), 'Bad Luck and Fixed Costs in Personal Bankruptcies', *Economic Journal*, Vol. 99, pp. 92–107.

Singh, J. V., (1986), 'Performance, Slack and Risk Taking in Organizational Decision Making', *Academy of Management Journal*, Vol. 29, pp. 562–585.

Singh, J. V., Tucker, D. J., and House, R. J., (1986), 'Organizational Legitimacy and the Liability of Newness', *Administrative Science Quarterly*, Vol. 31, pp. 171–193.

Soberon-Ferrer, H., and Dardis, R., (1991), 'Determinants of Household Expenditures for Services', *Journal of Consumer Research*, Vol. 17, March, pp. 385–397.

Spender, J. D., (1979), *Strategy Making in Business*, Unpublished Ph. D. Disseration, Manchester Business School, Manchester.

Staw, B., (1981), 'The Escalation of Commitment to a Course of Action', *Academy of Management Review*, Vol. 4, pp. 577–587.

Stefanelli, J., (1990), *The Sale and Purchase of Restaurants*, John Wiley & Sons Inc, New York.

Stern, P., and Stanworth, J., (1988), 'The Development of Franchising in Britain', *NatWest Quarterly Review*, May, pp. 34–38

Stern, P., and Stanworth, J., (1988), 'Improving Small Business Rates Via Franchising – The Role of Banks in Europe', *International Small Business Journal*, Vol. 12, No. 2, pp. 15–25.

Stewart, H., and Gallagher, C. C., (1986), 'Business Death and Firm Size in the UK', *International Small Business Journal*, Vol. 4, No. 1, pp. 42–57.

Storey, D. J., (1994), *Understanding the Small Business Sector*, Routledge, London.

Taffler, R. J., (1982), 'Forecasting Company Failure in the UK Using Discriminant Analysis and Financial Ratio', *Journal of the Royal Statistical Society (A)*, Vol. 145, Part 3, pp. 342–358.

Taffler, R. J., (1995), *The Use of the Z-score Approach in Practice*, Working Paper 95/1, Centre for Empirical Research in Finance and Accounting, City University Business School, London.

Terpstra, V., and Yu, C. M., (1988), 'Determinants of Foreign Direct Investment of US Advertising Agencies', *Journal of International Business Studies*, Spring, pp. 33–47.

Thakur, M., and Das, T. K., (1991), 'Managing the Growth-Share Matrix: A Four-Nation Study in Two Industries', *Management International Review*, Vol. 31, No. 2, pp. 139–159.

Thompson, D. N., (1971), 'Contractual Marketing Systems: An Overview', pp. 3–32 in Thompson, D. N., (ed.), *Contractual Marketing Systems*, Heath Lexington, Massachusetts.

Thompson, J. D., (1967), *Organizations in Action*, McGraw-Hill, New York.

Troy, D. A., and Beals, P., (1982), 'Hotel Feasibility Analysis, Parts I & II', *Cornell Hotel and Restaurant Administration Quarterly*, Vol. 23, pp. 10–17.

Vaessen, P., and Keeble, D., (1995), *Growth-Orientated SMEs in Unfavourable Regional Environments*, ESRC Centre for Business Research, University of Cambridge Working Paper Series.

Vaughn, C., (1979), *Franchising: Its Nature, Scope, Advantages, and Development*, Lexington Books, Lexington, Massachusetts.

Venkatraman, S., Van de Ven, A. H., Buckeye, J., and Hudson, J., (1990), 'Start-up in a Turbulent Environment: A Process Model of Failure Among Firms with High Customer Dependence', *Journal of Business Venturing*, Vol. 5, No. 5, pp. 277–296.

Wada, M., (1977), *An Experimental Study Between Lifestyle, Product Attributes, and Brand Choice*, PH. D Dissertation, Department of marketing, The Graduate School, The Pennsylvannia State University.

Watson, J., and Everett, J., (1986), 'Defining Small Business Failure', *International and Small Business Journal*, Vol. 11, No. 3, pp. 35–43.

Wattel, H., (1969), 'Are Franchisors Realistic and Successful in their Selection of Franchisees?', *Journal of Retailing*, Vol. 44, No. 4, pp. 54–68.

Weitzel, W., and Jonsson, E., (1989), 'Decline in Organizations: A Literature Integration and Extension', *Administrative Science Quarterly*, Vol. 34, No. 1, pp. 91–109.

Welsch, J. A., and White, J. F., (1981), 'A Small Business Is Not A Little Big Business', *Harvard Business Review*, Vol. 59, No. 4, pp. 18–32.

West, A., (1992), 'Fast Food Marketing', pp. 98–126 in Ball, S. D., (ed.), *Fast Food Operations and Their Management*, Stanley Thornes (Publishers) Ltd, Cheltenham, Gloustershire.

Williams, D., (1995), 'A Comparison of Business Discontinuations in States With and Without Franchise Termination Laws', 1995 Society of Franchising Conference, The International Challenge . . . Towards New Franchising Relationships, San Juan, Puerto Rico.

Yavas, B. F., and Vardiabasis, D., (1987), 'The Determinants of US International Fast Food Franchising: An Application to the Pacific Rim', in *Developments in Marketing Science*, Vol. X: Proceedings from the 11th Annual Conference of the Academy of Marketing Science, Florida: Bar Harbor, May, pp. 27–30.

Zavgren, C. V., and Friedman, G. E., (1988), 'Are Bankruptcy Models Worthwhile? An Application in Securities Analysis', *Management International Review*, Vol. 28, No. 1, pp. 34–44.

Zeller, R. E., Achabal, D. D., and Brown, L. A., (1980), 'Market Penetration and Locational Conflict in Franchise Systems', *Decision Sciences*, Vol. 80, pp. 58–80.

Zimmerman, F. M., (1989), 'Managing A Successful Turnaround', *Long Range Planning*, Vol. 22, No. 3, pp. 105–124.

Zmijewski, M. E., (1984), 'Methodological Issues Related to the Estimation of Financial Distress Prediction Models', *Journal of Accounting Research*, Vol. 22, Supplement, pp. 59–82.

Chapter 10: Towards an anthropology of the franchise relationship: the roles of fiefs, clans, witch doctors and professors

Achrol, R. S., (1996), *The Franchise as a Network Organization*, Proceedings of the 10th Society of Franchising, Partners for Progress . . . A World of Opportunities, Honolulu, Hawaii, 17–18 February.

Achrol, R. S., Reve, T. and Stern, L. W. (1983), 'The Environment of Marketing Channel Dyads: A Framework for Comparative Analysis', *Journal of Marketing*, Vol. 47, Autumn, pp. 55–67.

Allen, T. J., (1977), *Managing of Flow and Technology*, MIT Press, Cambridge Massachusetts.

Alvesson, M., and Lindkvist, L., (1993), 'Transaction Costs, Clans and Corporate Culture', *Journal of Management Studies*, Vol. 30, pp. 427–457

Amabile, T., (1990), 'The Social Psychology of Creativity and Beyond' pp. 61–91 in Runco, M ., and Albert, R. S., (eds), *Theories of Creativity*, Sage Publications, London

Argyris, C., (1982), *Reasoning, Learning and Action*, Jossey-Bass, London.

Argyris, C., (1983), 'Action Science and Intervention', *Journal of Applied Behavioural Science*, Vol. 19, pp. 115–140.

Barkema, H. G., Bell, J. H. J., and Pennings, J. M., (1996), 'Foreign Entry, Cultural Barriers, and Learning', *Strategic Management Journal*, Vol. 17, pp. 151–166.

Barr, P. S., Stimpert, J. L., and Huff, A. S., (1992), 'Cognitive Change, Strategic Action, and Organizational Renewal', *Strategic Management Journal*, Vol. 13, Special Issue, Summer, pp. 15–36.

Baden-Fuller, C., and Lorenzoni, G., (1993), 'Creating a strategic centre to manage a web or partners', Proceedings of 9th IMP Conference, September.

Bateson, G., (1972), *Steps to an Ecology of Mind*, Intertext, London.

Belbin, R. M., (1981), *Management Teams: Why they Succeed or Fail*, Heinemann, London.

Bessant, J. R., and Grunt, M., (1985), *Management of Manufacturing Innovation in the United Kingdom and West Germany*, Gower, Aldershot.

Blois, K. J., (1972), 'Vertical Quasi-integration', *Journal of Industrial Economics*, Vol. 20, No. 3.

Boisot, M., (1987), *Information and Organization*, Fontana, London.

Brooks, A. K., (1992), 'Building Learning Organizations: The Individual-culture Interaction', *Human Resource Development Quarterly* Vol. 3, No. 4.

Burt, R. S., (1992), *Structural Holes: The Social Structure of Competition*, Harvard University Press, Cambridge, Massachusetts.

Chisholm, R. F., (1996), 'On the Meaning of Networks', *Group & Organization Management*, Vol. 21, pp. 216–235.

Clark, P., and Staunton, N., (1989), *Innovation and Technology in Organisation*, Routledge, London.

Cohen, W., and Levinthal, D., (1990), 'Absorptive Capacity: A New Perspective on Learning and Innovation', *Administrative Science Quarterly*, Vol. 35, pp. 128–152.

Contractor, F. J., and Lorange, P., (1988), 'Why Should Firms Cooperate? The Strategy and Economies Basis for Cooperative Ventures', in Contractor, F. J., and Lorange, P., (eds), *Cooperative Strategies in Business Markets*, Lexington Books, Lexington, Massachusetts.

Coxhead, H., and Davis, J., (1992), *New Product Development – A Review of the Literature*, Working Paper HWP 6/92, Henley Management College.

Crane, D., (1972), *Invisible Colleges: Diffusion of Knowledge in Scientific Communities*, University of Chicago Press, Chicago.

Csikszentmihalyi, M., (1990), 'The Domain of Creativity', pp. 190–212 in Runco, M., and Albert, R. S., (eds), *Theories of Creativity*, Sage Publications, London.

Davis, (1966), cited in Radford, J., and Burton, A., (1974) *Thinking: Its Nature and Development*, Wiley, London.

De Bono, E., (1973), *Lateral Thinking for Management*, McGraw-Hill, London.

Drucker, P. F., (1990), 'The Emerging Theory of Manufacturing', *Harvard Business Review*, Vol. 68, May–June, pp. 94–102.

Durkheim, E., (1933), *The Division of Labour in Society*, (translated by G Simpson), Free Press, New York.

Felstead, A., (1993), *The Corporate Paradox – Power and Control in the Business Franchise*, Routledge, London.

Fontana, D., (1984), 'Learning and Teaching', pp. 118–132 in *Psychology for Managers*, Macmillan, London.

Gedo, J. E., (1990), 'More on Creativity and its Vicissitudes', pp. 35–45 in Runco, M., and Albert, R. S., (ed.), *Theories of Creativity Sage Publications*, Newbury Park. pp 35–45.

Gerstenfeld, A., (1970), *Effective Management of Research and Development*, Addison-Wesley, Reading, Massachusetts.

Gordon, W. J. J., (1961), *Synectics*, Harper and Row, New York.

Grossmann, S. J., and Hart, O. D., (1986), 'The Costs and Benefits of Ownership: A Theory of Vertical and Lateral Integration', *Journal of Political Economy*, Vol. 94, No. 4, pp. 691–719.

Hakansson, H., (ed.), (1992), *International Marketing and Purchasing of Industrial Goods*, John Wiley, Chichester, UK

Hamel, G., (1991), 'Competition for Competence and Inter-Partner Learning within International Strategic Alliances', *Strategic Management Journal*, Vol. 12, Special Issue, pp. 69–82.

Handy, C., (1993), *The Age of Unreason* London: Hutchinson.

Handy, C., (1994), *The Empty Raincoat* London: Hutchinson.

Handy, C., (1995), *The Age of Paradox*, Harvard Business School Press, Boston, Massachusetts.

Higgins, J. M., (1996), 'Innovate or Evaporate: Creative Techniques for Strategists', *Long Range Planning*, Vol. 29, No. 3, pp. 370–380.

Huber, G. H., (1991), 'Organizational Learning: The Contributing Processes and their Literatures', *Organisational Science* Vol. 2, No. 1, pp. 88–115.

Hurst, D., (1995), *Crisis and Renewal*, Harvard Business School Press, Boston, Massachusetts.

Imai, K., Nonaka, T., and Takeuchi, H., (1985), 'Managing the New Product Development Process: How Japanese Companies Learn and Unlearn', in Clark K., Hayes, R., and Lorenz, C., (eds), *The Uneasy Alliance Managing the Productivity-Technology Dilemma*, Harvard University Press, Boston, Massachusetts.

Jarillo, J. C., (1988), 'On Strategic Networks' *Strategic Management Journal*, Vol. 9, pp. 31–41.

Jarillo, J. C., (1993) *Strategic Networks: Creating the Borderless Organisation*, Butterworth Heinemann, Oxford.

Jung, C. G., (1933), 'Psychology and literature' *Modern Man in Search of a Soul* (translated by Dell W. S., and Baynes, C. F), Routledge, London.

Kanter, R. M., (1985), *The Change Masters*, Counterpoint, London.

Kaufmann, G., (1991), 'Problem-solving and Creativity', pp. 103–134, in Henry, J., (ed.), *Creative Management*, Sage Publications, London.

Kay, J. A., (1993), *Foundations of Corporate Success: How Business Strategies Add Value*, Oxford University Press, Oxford.

Koestler, A., (1967), *The Ghosts in the Machine*, Hutchinson, London.

Kolb, D. A., (1974), *Organizational Psychology: A Book of Reading*, Prentice Hall, London.

Lawson, B., (1980), *How Designers Think*, Architectural Press, London.

Lessard, D. R., and Zaheer, S., (1996), 'Breaking the Silos: Distributed Knowledge and Strategic Responses to Volatile Exchange Rates', *Strategic Management Review*, Vol. 17, pp. 513–533.

Lukas, B. A., Hult, G. T. M., and Ferrell, O. C., (1996), 'A Theoretical Perspective of the Antecedents and Consequences of Organizational Learning in Marketing Channels', *Journal of Business Research*, Vol. 36, pp. 233–244.

Macbeth, D. K., and Ferguson, N., (1994), *Partnership Sourcing; An Integrated Supply chain Approach*, FT/Pitman, London.

Mannheim, K., (1936), *Ideology and Utopia*, Harcourt, Brace and World, New York, quoted in Morgan, G., 'Paradigms, Metaphors, and Puzzle Solving in Organization Theory', pp. 81–99 in Henry, J., (ed.), *Creative Management*, Sage Publications Ltd, London.

Mathur, S. S., (1986), How Firms Compete: A New Classification of Generic Strategies, The City University Business School, *Working Paper, No. 81*.

McCaskey, M. B., (1991), 'Mapping, Creating, Maintaining, and Relinquishing Conceptual Frameworks', pp. 135–152 in Henry, J., (ed.), *Creative Management*, Sage Publications, London.

McGill, M. E., Slocum, J. W., and Lei, D., (1992), 'Management practices in Learning Organizations', *Organisational Dynamics*, pp. 5–16.

McIntyre, F. S., Young, J. A., Gilbert, F. W., (1994), 'Franchising: A Strategic Alliance Perspective', Society of Franchising Conference: Understanding And Accepting Different Perspectives . . . Empowering Relationships In 1994 And Beyond, Las Vegas, Nevada, 13–14 February.

McKenzie, J., (1996), *Paradox: The Next Strategic Dimension – Using Conflict to Re-energize Your Business*, McGraw-Hill, New York.

Midelfort, H. C. E., (1982), 'The Social Position of the Witch in Southwestern Germany', pp. 174–189 in Marwick, M., (ed.) *Witchcraft and Sorcery*, Penguin, London.

Miles, R. E., and Snow, C. C., (1992), 'Causes of Failure in Network Organizations', *California Management Review* Summer.

Morris, D., (1969), *The Human Zoo*, Jonathan Cape, London.

Nelson, R., and Winter, S., (1983), *An Evolutionary Theory of Economic Change*, Harvard University Press, Boston, Massachusetts.

Nohria, N., and Eccles, R. G., (1992), 'Face-to-Face: Making Network Organizations Work', pp. 288–308 in Nohria, N., and Eccles, R. G., (eds), *Networks and Organizations: Structure, Form, and Action*, Harvard Business School Press, Boston, Massachusetts.

Nohria, N., and GarciaPont, C., (1991), 'Global Strategic Linkages and Industry Structure', *Strategic Management Journal*, Special Issue, Summer, Vol. 12, pp. 105124.

O'Hare, M., (1988), *Innovative: How to Gain and Sustain Competitive Advantage,*Blackwell, Oxford.

O'Neil, J. R., (1996), *The Paradox of Success*, McGraw-Hill, New York

Oldham, G., and Cummings, A., (1996), 'Employee Creativity: Personal and Contextual Factors at Work', *Academy of Management Journal*, Vol. 39, pp. 607–634.

Ouchi, W. G., (1982), *Theory Z*, Avon Books, New York.

Peters, T., (1992), *Liberation Management*, Macmillan, New York.

Powell, W. W., (1990), 'Neither Market nor Hierarchy: Network Forms of Organization', *Research in Organizational Behaviour*, Vol. 12, pp. 295–356.

Price, H., (1996), 'The Anthropology of the Supply Chain: Fiefs, Clans, Witch-doctors and Professors', *European Journal of Purchasing and Supply Chain Management*, Vol. 2, pp. 87–105.

Provan, K. G., (1983), 'The Federation as Interorganizational Linkage Network', *Academy of Management Review*, Vol. 8, pp. 79–89.

Revans, R. W., (1984), *Action Learning* (Video), Bradford: MCB University Press.

Revans, R. W., (1985), *Action Learning*, London: Blond and Briggs, London.

Reve, T., (1990), 'The Firm as Nexus of Internal and External Contracts' pp. 133–161 in Aoki, M., Gustafsson, B., and Williamson, O. E., (eds), *The Firm as a Nexus of Treaties* London: Sage Publications, London.

Rogers, E., (1995), *Diffusion of Innovations*, Free Press, New York.

Rothwell R., (1985), 'Project Sappho: A Comparative Study of Success and Failure in Industrial Innovation' in Rothwell R., and Zegveld, W., (eds), *Reindustrialisation and Technology*, Longman, London.

Sako, M., (1992), *Prices Quality and Trust*, Cambridge University Press, New York.

Schien E. H., (1993), ''How Can Organizations Learn Faster? The Challenge of Entering the Green Room' *Sloan Management Review*, Vol., Winter, pp. 85–92.

Schein, E. H., (1996), 'Culture: The Missing Concept in Organization Studies', *Administrative Science Quarterly*, Vol. 41, pp. 229–240.

Schnaars, S. P., (1994), *Managing Imitation Strategies*, Free Press, New York.

Schumpeter, J., (1911), *The Theory of Economic Development*, Oxford University Press, New York.

Schwenk, C. R., (1988), 'The Cognitive Perspective on Strategic Decision Making', *Journal of Management Studies*, Vol. 25, No. 1, pp. 41–55.

Silvester, T., (1996), *Growth Constraints on Young British Franchise Systems*, MBA dissertation, University of Greenwich, London.

Smith, S., and Tranfield, D., (1991), *Managing Change: Creating Competitive Advantage*, IFS Publications, London.

Snow, C. C., Miles, R. E., Coleman, H. J., (1992), 'Managing 21st Century Network Organizations', *Organisational Dynamics*, Vol. 20, pp. 5–20.

Spekman, R., Kamauff, J. W., and Salmond, D. J., (1994), 'At Last Purchasing is Becoming Strategic', *Long Range Planning*, Vol. 27, pp. 76–84.

Strebel, P., (1987), 'Organizing for Innovation Over an Industry Cycle,' *Strategic Management Journal*, Vol. 8, pp. 117–124.

Stuart, R., (1984), 'Using Others to Learn', pp. 125–143, i.

Teece, D. J., (1986), 'Profiting from Technological Innovation: Implications for Integration, Collaboration, Licensing and Public Policy', *Research Policy*, Vol. 15, pp. 285–305.

Thompson, R. S., (1994), 'The Franchise Life-cycle and the Penrose Effect', *Journal of Economic Behaviour and Organization*, Vol. 24, No. 2, pp. 207–218.

Thorelli, H. B., (1986), 'Networks: Between Hierarchies and Markets', *Strategic Management Journal*, Vol. 7, pp. 37–51.

Twiss, B., (1992), *Managing Technology Innovation*, Pitman, London.

Von Hippel, E., (1988), *The Sources of Innovation*, Oxford University Press, Oxford.

Weick, K. E., (1976), 'Educational Organizations As Loosely Coupled Systems', *Administrative Science Quarterly*, Vol. 21, No. 1, March, pp. 1–19.

Williamson, O. E., and Ouchi, W. G., (1981), 'The Markets and Hierarchies Program and Research: Origins, Implications, Prospects', pp. 347–370 in Van de Ven, A. H., and Joyce, W. F, (eds), *Perspectives on Organisational Design and Behaviour*, John Wiley, New York.

Womack, J. P., and Jones, D. T., (1994), 'From Lean Production to the Lean Enterprise', *Harvard Business Review* March–April.

Associations and institutions

Alliance of Independent Retailers & Businesses
Alliance House, 14 Pierpoint St, Worcester,
Worcestershire WR1 1TA
☎ 01905-612-733; fax: 01905-21501

American Association of Franchisees and Dealers
PO Box 81887, San Diego, CA, 92138-1887
☎ (800) 733-9858

Argentine Franchise Association
Sante Fe 995, piso 4, Buenos Aires, 1059
☎ 54-1-393-263; fax: 54-1-393-5263

Asociacion Colombiana De Franquicias
Apartado Aereo 25200, Cali
☎ 57-23-311-086; fax: 57-23-317-138

Austrian Franchise Association
Nonntaler Haupstrasse 48, Salzburg, 5020
☎ 43-662-82-56-70; fax: 43-662-82-56-71

Automatic Vending Association of Britain
Bassett House, High Street, Banstead, Surrey, SM7 2LZ
☎ 01737-357-211; fax: 01737-370-501

Belgian Franchising Association
1840 Londerzeel
☎ 32-52-30-56-25

Brazil Franchise Association
Travessa Meriupe, 18, Vila Mariana, Sau Paulo,
SP04012
☎ 55-11-571-1303; fax: 55-11-575-5590

Brewers Association of Scotland
6 Colme St, Edinburgh, Midlothian, EH3 6AD
☎ 0131-225-4681; fax: 0131-220-1132

British Bottler's Institute
PO Box 16, Alton, Hampshire GU34 4NZ
☎ 01420-23632

British Chicken Information Service
Bury House, 126-128 Cromwell Rd, Kensington,
London SW7 4ET
☎ 0171-373-7757; fax: 0171-373-3926

British Contract Furnishing Ltd
Suite 116, The Business Design Centre, 52 Upper St,
Islington, London N1 0QH
☎ 0171-226-6641; fax: 0171-288-6190

British Disposable Products Association
Papermakers House, Rivenhall Rd, Westlea, Swindon,
Wiltshire SN5 7BE
☎ 0793-886-086; fax: 01793-886-182

British Federation of Hotel, Guest House & Self-
Catering Associations
5 Sandcroft Rd, Blackpool, Lancashire FY1 2RY
☎ 01253-352683

British Franchise Association
Franchise Chambers, Thames View, Newtown Rd,
Henley on Thames, Oxfordshire RG19 1HG
☎ 01491-578-049

British Hospitality Association
40 Duke St, London W1M 6HR
☎ 0171-499-6641; fax: 0171-355-4596

British Independent Grocers Association
Federation House, 17 Farnborough St, Farnborough,
Hampshire GU14 8AG
☎ 01252-515-001; fax: 01252-515-002

British Institute of Innkeeping
51/53 High St, Camberley Surrey, GU15 3RG
☎ 01276-684-449; fax: 01276-23045

British Meat Manufacturers Association
19 Cornwall Terrace London NW1 4QP
☎ 0171-935-7980; fax: 0171-487-4734

British Sandwich Association
29 Market Place, Wantage, Oxfordshire OX12 8BG
☎ 01235-772-207; fax: 01235-769-044

British Soft Drinks Association
22 Stukeley St, London WC2B 5LR
☎ 0171-430-0356; 0171-831-6014

Bulgarian Franchise Association
25A Orchid Street, 9000 Varna
☎ 359-256-891; fax: 359-256-891

Canadian Franchise Association
5045 Orbitor Drive, Suite 201, Bldg 12, Mississuaga, Ontario, L4W 4Y4
☎ 905-625-2896; fax: 905-625-9076

Catering Equipment Distributors Association of Great Britain
7 Stafford Place, Weston Super Mare, Avon BS23 2QZ
☎ 01934-628-600; fax: 01934-641-175

Catering Equipment Importers Association
7 Hamilton Way, Wallington, Surrey SM6 9NJ
☎ 0181-669-8121; fax: 0181-647-1128

Catering Equipment Manufacturers Association
Carlyle House, 235 Vauxhall Bridge Rd, London SW1V 1EJ
☎ 0171-233-7724; fax: 0171-828-0667

Catering Managers Association
Mount Pleasant, Egton, Whitby, N. Yorkshire YO21 1UE
☎ 01947-85514; fax: 01642-816250

Civic Catering Association
275 Wigan Lane, Wigan, Lancashire WN1 2NT
☎ 01942-47992

Cookery & Food Association
1 Victoria Parade, 331 Sandycombe Rd, Richmond, Surrey TW9 3NB
☎ 0181-948-3870; fax: 0181-332-6326

Danish Franchise Association
Amaliegade 31A, Copenhagen, 1256
☎ 45-33-15-60-11; fax: 45-33-91-03-46

Direct Tea Supplies Ltd
4-8 Victoria St, Brentwood, Essex CM14 5EE
☎ 012277-225-792; fax: 01277-224-761

European Catering Association (Great Britain)
United House, North Rd, London N7 9DP
☎ 0171-700-0098; fax: 0171-700-7599

Finnish Franchise Association
PI 39, Helsinki, SF-08501
☎ 358-12-334-584; fax: 358-12-334-542

Flour Advisory Association
21 Arlington St, London SW1A 1RN
☎ 0171-493 2521; 0171-493-6785

Flour Milling & Baking Research Association
Rickmansworth Rd, Chorleywood, Rickmansworth, Hertsfordshire WD3 5SH
☎ 01923-284-111; fax: 01923-284-539

Food & Drink Federation
6 Catherine St, London WC2B 5JJ
☎ 0171-836-2460; fax: 0171-836-0580

Food Services Association
56 Ring Rd, Leicester, Leicestershire LE2 3RR
☎ 0116-270-5760

Franchisors Association of Australia and New Zealand
Unit 9, 2-6 Hunter Street, Parramatta, New South Wales, 2150
☎ 61-2-891-4933; fax: 61-2-891-4474

French Franchise Association
9 Boulevard des Italiens, Paris, F-75002
☎ 33-1-42-60-0022; fax: 33-1-42-60-0311

German Franchise Association
Paul Heyse Str., 33-35, Munchen, 0336
☎ 49-89-53-50-27; fax: 49-89-53-13-23

Hong Kong Franchise Association
22/F United Centre, 95 Queensway
☎ 852-2529-9229; fax: 852-2527-9843

Hotel Catering & Institutional Management Association
191 Trinity Rd, London SW17 7HN
☎ 0181-672-4251

Hungarian Franchise Association
POB 446, Budapest, H-1537
☎ 361-212-4124; fax: 361-212-5712

Ice Cream Federation
1 Green St, London W1Y 3RG
☎ 0171-629-0738

Indonesian Franchise Association
Jl. Pembanguan I/7, Jakarta, 10130
☎ 62-21-3800-233; fax: 62-21-3802-448

Institute of British Bakers
☎ 50 Sandygate R, Sheffield, S. Yorkshire S10 5RY

International Coffee Organisation
22 Berners St, London W1P 4DO
☎ 0171-580-8591; fax: 0171-580-6129

International Franchise Association
1350 New York Avenue, NW Suite 900, Washington DC, 20005-4709
☎ 202-628-8000; fax: 202-628-0812

Irish Franchise Association
13 Frankfield Terrace, Summerhill South, Cork
☎ 353-21-270-859; fax: 353-21-270-850

Italian Franchise Association
Corso Di Porta Nuova. 3, Milano, 20121
☎ 39-2-2290-3779; fax: 39-2-6555-919

Japan Franchise Association
Elsa Building, Roppongi 3-13-12, Minatoku, Tokyo, 106
☎ 81-3-3401-0421-; fax: 81-3-3423-2019

Leatherhead Food Research Association
Randalls Rd, Leatherhead, Surrey KT22 7RY
☎ 01372-376-761; fax: 01372-386-228

London Chamber of Commerce & Industry
69 Cannon St, London EC4N 5AB
☎ 0171-248-4444; fax: 0171-489-0391

Malaysian Franchise Association
Implementation Coordination Unit, Jalan Dato'Onn,
Fran. Dev. Div., PM's Dept., Kuala Lumpur, 50502
☎ 60-3-232-1957; fax: 60-3-230-1951

Mexican Franchise Association
Insurgentes Sur 1783, #303, Colonia Guadalupe Inn,
Mexico, DF-01020
☎ 525-661-0655; fax: 525-661-0655

Milk Marketing Board
Marketing Development Division, Thames Ditton
Surrey KT7 0EL
☎ 0181-398-4101; fax: 0181-398-8485

Mobile & Outside Caterers Association of Great Britain
MOCA House, 180 Lincoln Road North, Olton,
Birmingham B27 6RP
☎ 021-693-7000

National Association of Master Bakers
21 Baldock St, Ware, Hertfordshire SG12 9DH
☎ 01920-468-061; fax: 01920-461-632

National Dairy Council
5-7 John Princes St, London W1M 0AP
☎ 0171-499-7822; fax: 0171-408-1353

Netherlands Franchise Association
Boomberglaan 12, Hilversum, 1217 RR
☎ 31-35-243-444

Norwegian Franchise Association
Handelen Hovedorganisisjon, Postboks 2483 Solli,
Oslo, 20202
☎ 47-2-55-82-20; fax: 47-2-55-82-25

Packaging Distributors Association
Rivenhall Rd, Westlea, Swindon, Wiltshire SN5 7BO
☎ 01793-886-086; fax: 01793-886-182

Pizza & Pasta Association
29 Market Place, Wantage, Oxfordshire OX12 8BG
☎ 01235-772-207; fax: 01235-769-044

Pre-Packed Flour Association
6 Catherine St, London WC2B 5JJ
☎ 0171-836-2460; fax: 0171-836-0580

Sea Fish Authority
18 Logie Mill, Logie Green Rd, Edinburgh, Midlothian
EH3 7LA
☎ 0131-558-3331; fax: 0131-558-1442

Shellfish Association of Great Britain
Fishmonger's Hall, London Bridge, London EC4R 9EL
☎ 0171-283-8305; fax: 0171-929-1389

South African Franchise Association
Kenlaw House, 27 De Beer Street, Po Box 31708,
Braamfontein, 2017
☎ 27-11-403-3468; fax: 27-11-403-1279

Swedish Franchise Association
Box 5512-S., Greugatan 34, Stockholm, 11485
☎ 46-8-660-8610; fax: 46-8-662-7457

Swiss Franchise Association
Pilatusstrasse 55, Luzern, 6003
☎ 41-41-222-001; fax: 41-41-222-004

Tea Council
Sir John Lyon House, 5 High Timber St, London EC4 3NJ
☎ 0171-248-1024; fax: 0171-329-4568

Vegetarian Society of the United Kingdom
Parkdale, Durham Rd, Altrinham, Cheshire WA14 4OG
☎ 0161-928-0793; fax: 0161-926-9182

Name index

Subject index